P9-DZA-033

BRITISH WRITERS

BRITISH WRITERS

Edited under the auspices of the British Council

IAN SCOTT-KILVERT
General Editor

SUPPLEMENT I

GRAHAM GREENE
TO
TOM STOPPARD

CHARLES SCRIBNER'S SONS / NEW YORK

British writers. Supplement.

CONTENTS: 1. Graham Greene to Tom Stoppard.—
Bibliography: p.
Includes index.
1. English literature—20th century—History and criticism.
2. English literature—20th century—Bio-bibliography.
3. Authors, English—20th century—Biography.
I. Scott-Kilvert, Ian. II. British Council. III. Title.
PR85.B688 Suppl. 820'.9 87-16648
ISBN 0–684–18612–8 (v. 1)

ISBN 0–684–15798–5 (v. 1)
ISBN 0–684–16407–8 (v. 2)
ISBN 0–684–16408–6 (v. 3)
ISBN 0–684–16635–6 (v. 4)
ISBN 0–684–16636–4 (v. 5)
ISBN 0–684–16637–2 (v. 6)
ISBN 0–684–16638–0 (v. 7)
ISBN 0–684–17417–0 (v. 8)
ISBN 0–684–18612–8 (Supp. I)

Published simultaneously in Canada
by Collier Macmillan Canada, Inc.

1 3 5 7 9 11 13 15 17 19 V/C 20 18 16 14 12 10 8 6 4 2

PRINTED IN THE UNITED STATES OF AMERICA

The paper in this book meets the guidelines for
permanence and durability of the Committee on
Production Guidelines for Book Longevity of the
Council on Library Resources.

Acknowledgment is gratefully made to those publishers and individuals who permitted the use of the following materials in copyright.

"Samuel Beckett"

From "Whoroscope," "Echo's Bones," "Sanies 1," and "Cascando" from *Collected Poems in English and French* by Samuel Beckett. Copyright © 1977 by Samu Beckett. Published by Grove Press, Inc. From *Collec Poems 1930–1978,* by Samuel Beckett, copyright 1930, 1932, 1934, 1935, 1938, 1959, 1961, 1962, 19 1976, 1977, 1984, 1986 by Samuel Beckett. Courte John Calder (Publishers) Ltd, London. From *Cascando* Samuel Beckett. Copyright © 1963 by Samuel Becke *Waiting for Godot* by Samuel Beckett. Copyright © 19 by Grove Press, Inc. Renewed 1982 by Samuel Becke

Endgame: A Play in One Act, Followed by Act Without Words: A Mime for One Player by Samuel Beckett. Copyright © 1958 by Grove Press, Inc. Renewed 1986 by Grove Press, Inc. *Happy Days: A Play in Two Acts* by Samuel Beckett. Copyright © 1961 by Grove Press, Inc. *Eh Joe* by Samuel Beckett. Copyright © 1967 by Samuel Beckett. *Krapp's Last Tape* by Samuel Beckett. Copyright © 1957 by Samuel Beckett. Copyright © 1958, 1959, 1960 by Grove Press, Inc. Reprinted by permission of Faber & Faber, Ltd.

"William Golding"

Excerpts from "The Ladder and the Tree," "Egypt from My Inside," and "Fable" from *The Hot Gates* by William Golding. Copyright © 1965 by William Golding. *The Spire* by William Golding. Copyright © 1964 by William Golding. *The Inheritors* by William Golding. Copyright © 1955 by William Golding. *Pincher Martin* by William Golding. Copyright © 1956 by William Golding. *Free Fall* by William Golding. Copyright © 1959 by William Golding. Published by Harcourt Brace Jovanovich Inc. Reprinted by permission of Faber & Faber, Ltd. Excerpts reprinted by permission of The Putnam Publishing Group from *Lord of the Flies* by William Golding. Copyright © 1954 by William Golding. Reprinted by permission of Faber & Faber, Ltd. Excerpts from *Darkness Visible* by William Golding. Copyright © 1979 by William Golding. *Rites of Passage* by William Golding. Copyright © 1980 by William Golding. *The Paper Men* by William Golding. Copyright © 1984 by William Golding. Reprinted by permission of Farrar, Straus and Giroux, Inc. Selections from *Poems* by William Golding. Copyright © 1934 by William Golding. Reprinted by permission of William Golding and Faber & Faber, Ltd.

"Lawrence Durrell"

From "Carol on Corfu," "Politics," "Journals of Progress," "Eternal Contemporaries," "Conon in Alexandria," "Delos," "Father Nicholas His Death: Corfu," "Chanel," and "Patmos" from *Collected Poems, 1931–1974* by Lawrence Durrell. Copyright © 1980 by Lawrence Durrell. Reprinted by permission of Viking Penguin, Inc. Reprinted by permission of Faber & Faber, Ltd.

"Dylan Thomas"

Excerpts from Dylan Thomas, *The Poems of Dylan Thomas.* Copyright 1938, 1939, by New Directions Publishing Corporation. Copyright 1945, by the Trustees for the Copyrights of Dylan Thomas. Copyright 1952, 1953 by Dylan Thomas. "Poem in October" was first published in *Poetry.* Reprinted by permission of New Directions Publishing Corporation. Also with kind permission of David Higham Associates. Published by J. M. Dent.

"Philip Larkin"

Excerpts from *High Windows* by Philip Larkin. Copyright © 1974 by Philip Larkin. Reprinted by permission of Farrar, Straus and Giroux, Inc. Excerpts from *The North Ship* by Philip Larkin. Copyright © 1974 by Philip Larkin. *The Whitsun Weddings* by Philip Larkin. Copyright © 1964 by Philip Larkin. *High Windows* by Philip Larkin. Copyright © 1974 by Philip Larkin. Selections of uncollected verse by Philip Larkin. Reprinted by permission of Faber & Faber, Ltd. Quotations from "I Remember, I Remember," "Deceptions," "Places, Loved Ones," "Next, Please," "Toads," "Poetry of Departures," "Triple Time," and "Church Going" are reprinted from *The Less Deceived* by Philip Larkin by permission of the Marvell Press, England.

"Ted Hughes"

Selected lines of poetry from the following: *New Selected Poems* by Ted Hughes. Copyright © 1982 by Ted Hughes. *Crow: The Life and Songs of the Crow* by Ted Hughes. Copyright © 1971 by Ted Hughes. *Moortown* by Ted Hughes. Copyright © 1979 by Ted Hughes. *Gaudete* by Ted Hughes. Copyright © 1977 by Ted Hughes. *The Hawk in the Rain* by Ted Hughes. Copyright © 1956, 1957 by Ted Hughes. *River: New Poems* by Ted Hughes. Copyright © 1983 by Ted Hughes. All selections reprinted by permission of Harper and Row, Publishers, Inc. Reprinted by permission of Faber & Faber, Ltd. Selections from *The Tiger's Bones and Other Plays for Children* by Ted Hughes. Copyright © 1973 by Ted Hughes. From "Bride and Groom" from *Cave Birds: An Alchemical Cave Drama* by Ted Hughes. Copyright © 1978 by Ted Hughes. Reprinted by permission of Viking Penguin, Inc. *The Tiger's Bones and Other Plays for Children* published originally in the U.K. as *The Coming of the Kings* by Ted Hughes. Copyright © 1970 by Ted Hughes. Selections reprinted by permission of Faber & Faber, Ltd. Selections from *Season Songs* by Ted Hughes. Copyright © 1976 by Ted Hughes. Reprinted by permission of Viking Penguin, Inc. *All Around the Year* (Published by John Murray) by Ted Hughes. Copyright © 1979 by Ted Hughes. *Remains of Elmet* by Ted Hughes. Copyright © 1979 by Ted Hughes. *Wodwo* by Ted Hughes. Copyright © 1967 by Ted Hughes. *Lupercal* by Ted Hughes. Copyright © 1960 by Ted Hughes. Reprinted by permission of Faber & Faber, Ltd.

Editorial Staff

List of Subjects in Supplement I

Introduction

British Writers is designed as a work of reference to complement *American Writers,* the eight-volume set of literary biographies of authors past and present, which was first published in 1974. In the same way as its American counterpart, which first appeared in the form of individual pamphlets published by the University of Minnesota Press, the British collection originates from a series of separate articles entitled *Writers and Their Work.* This series was initiated by the British Council in 1950 as a part of its worldwide program to support the teaching of English language and literature, an activity carried on both in the English-speaking world and in many countries in which English is not the mother tongue.

The articles are intended to appeal to a wide readership, including students in secondary and advanced education, teachers, librarians, scholars, editors, and critics, as well as the general public. Their purpose is to provide an introduction to the work of writers who have made a significant contribution to English literature, to stimulate the reader's enjoyment of the text, and to give students the means to pursue the subject further. The series begins in the fourteenth century and extends to the present day, and is printed in chronological order according to the date of the subject's birth. The articles are far from conforming to a fixed pattern, but speaking generally each begins with a short biographical section, the main body of the text being devoted to a survey of the subject's principal writings and an assessment of the work as a whole. Each article is equipped with a selected bibliography that records the subject's writings in chronological order, in the form both of collected editions and of separate works, including modern and paperback editions. The bibliography concludes with a list of biographical and critical publications, including both books and articles, to guide the reader who is interested in further research. In the case of authors such as Chaucer or Shakespeare, whose writings have inspired extensive criticism and commentary, the critical section is further subdivided and provides a useful record of the new fields of research that have developed over the past hundred years.

British Writers is not conceived as an encyclopedia of literature, nor is it a series of articles planned so comprehensively as to include every writer of historical importance. Its character is rather that of a critical anthology possessing both the virtues and the limitations of such a grouping. It offers neither the schematized form of the encyclopedia nor the completeness of design of the literary history. On the other hand it is limited neither by the impersonality of the one nor the uniformity of the other. Since each contributor speaks with only one voice out of many, he is principally concerned with explaining his subject as fully as possible rather than with establishing an order of merit or making "placing" comparisons (since each contributor might well "place" differently). The prime task is one of presentation and exposition rather than of assigning critical praise or censure. The contributors to the first volume consist of distinguished literary scholars and critics—later volumes include contributions by poets, novelists, historians, and biographers. Each writes as an enthusiast for his subject, and each sets out to explain what are the qualities that make an author worth reading.

As with its immediate predecessors in the main set, Supplement I contains some inevitable overlapping. Thus, the later novels of E. M. Forster and Ford Madox Ford, which are dealt with in Volume VI, are often considered by critics to belong to the "modern movement," that phrase being applied internationally and to all the arts in respect of work of a radically experimental nature produced during the first four decades of the century (see Volume VII, p. xii). Conversely Volume VII also includes the work of Ivy Compton-Burnett, who, although she continued to write until the 1960's, declared, "I do not feel I have any real organic knowledge of life later than about 1910." Again, while it is convenient to consider World War II as a watershed between Volume VII and its successor, several writers such as Robert Graves, Evelyn Waugh, Anthony Powell, and F. R. Leavis, all of whom produced some of their best writing after 1945, have been assigned to the earlier volume. Graham Greene is a year older than Anthony Powell, but as will be seen in the present essay, there is a good case for assessing the greater part of his work in the context of the postwar era.

In order to produce a series of volumes all bounded by significant dates and of approximately equal size, an upper limit of twenty-five essays was set for each. The "placing" of contemporary reputations is a notoriously difficult task, and there were many more than twenty-five candidates, especially among novelists and dramatists, for admission to Supplement I. Time and the preferences of the common reader generally award such ratings more decisively than the labors of the critics, but often only after the lapse of many years. For the present, the quality of critical attention that a given writer has attracted has played an important part in the final selection. This said, the further task of introducing such a selection might be compared to an attempt to tack down a flying carpet.

The novel has grown up over the last three centuries as a peculiarly intimate form of verbal artifice enacted between author and reader, providing entertainment, enlightenment, or both. D. H. Lawrence described it as "the one bright book of life," capable of enlarging our consciousness and intensifying our existence; he claimed that "the novel is the highest example of subtle interrelatedness that man has discovered . . . the novel can help us to live as nothing else can." With rare exceptions, novel-reading is not a performance art, as poetry and drama may be, but rather a solitary, silent, and lengthy input, made possible by printing technology and leisure. This makes it a form that exalts the significance of the individual, and it is no coincidence that the novel originated and developed in an era when an educated middle class and its ideal of individualism flourished in economic, cultural, and social terms. In the eighteenth century the novelist often assumed a tentative attitude to his fiction, disguising it as travel writing, autobiography, or exchanges of letters; or, as in *Tristram Shandy,* blurring the line between author and narrator. These devices have many parallels at the present time, but are now practiced for quite different reasons.

In the nineteenth century a new synthesis was developed between fiction and fact. Fictional events were presented more objectively and realistically so as to resemble history; the author withdrew to the position of observer or recorder; and noticeably few novels were written about writing novels. H. G. Wells acutely summed up this period and its sequel:

> Throughout the nineteenth century the art of fiction floated upon the same assumptions [as did social life] of social fixity. The Novel in English was produced in an atmosphere of security for the entertainment of secure people, who liked to feel established and safe for good. The criticism of it began to be irritated and perplexed when, through a new instability, the splintered frame began to get into the picture.

This last metaphor is not only singularly ap with regard to the new kind of relation betwee author and protagonist that was introduced b James Joyce into *A Portrait of the Artist* (1916), but i also epitomizes the kind of innovations that wer the work of the leading writers of the moder movement (discussed in the introduction to Vo ume VII). These were not brought forward simpl for the sake of "making it new." Rather, they wer required because the new generation had becom convinced that, as Virginia Woolf expressed i "whether we call it the life of the spirit, truth, c reality, this, the essential thing, has moved off, an refuses to be contained any longer in such ill-fittir vestments" (for example, the kind of minutely re alistic descriptive technique employed by Arno Bennett).

By the end of the 1930's the modern moveme might be said to have run its course, and thereaft the outbreak of World War II temporarily inte rupted the creative lives of most British novelis But this period also coincided with a new phase literary and aesthetic history. It was now not on the writer's approach to his material but also t nature of reality and the novel's capacity to repr sent it that were called into question. The novel h traditionally earned its credibility and its li enhancing reputation by reporting individual experience of a world of phenomena, human and material, that are common to author and reader. In it we expect the contingencies of life to be ordered and assessed. This requirement was now questioned by the apostles of the *nouveau roman,* or nonfiction novel, such as Alain Robbe-Grillet; a similar tendency appears in the fiction of Samuel Beckett. They claim that the belief in a meaningful link between man and his surroundings (originally a religious conception) is a fallacy. There is no solidarity between humans and objects; they are mutually indifferent. Hence, the very language of fiction should be refashioned so that it describes data in exclusively material terms without attributing any human significance to them. Similarly, the writer's traditional and much prized function of creating character in the hitherto accepted sense was challenged by developments in science. Just as Einsteinian physics deconstructed traditional conceptions of matter, so the evolution of psychological theory has challenged assumptions concerning individuality. Thus, the idea of the multiplicity of consciousness, the presence within the psyche of all that it has ever experienced, and the proposition that our deepest and truest motives for behavior are concealed from us have tended to dissolve the concept of the unique and integral personality. Other theorists have come to dispute the power of the printed word to communicate truth or represent reality, compared with the resources of cinema or television. A television news program may appear to us to present life already fictionalized; fact may appear more bizarre than the imagination could make it, thus depriving the author of another province of authority. In his book *The Fabulators* (1967) Robert Scholes contends that "when it comes to representing *things,* one picture is worth a thousand words and one motion picture a million. In face of competition from the cinema, fiction must abandon its attempt to represent reality, and rely more upon the power of words to stimulate the imagination." The novelist, of course, might counter that unless the cinema is being discussed as a completely separate art form (and one devoid of narrative content), the last sentence contains a non sequitur, since it is a common experience that a film adapted from a novel debases rather than enhances the reality of the original; or, going on to the attack, he might claim that the novel possesses techniques, such as the flash-forward—employed, for example, by Muriel Spark—that the cinema has never attempted. Scholes's proposition implies in its context a distinction between empirical and fictional modes of narration, which are discussed later.

For ten years or more after the end of World War II, the attention of British novelists was occupied by the common problems of absorbing the experiences of war and of adjusting their lives to peace, to a moderate though far-reaching social revolution, and to the loss of empire and of major-power status. Britain had been spared the humiliations and violent upheavals wrought elsewhere by defeat, occupation, and liberation; and in many spheres of life deep-rooted preferences and continuities had survived almost undisturbed. In the intellectual sphere, British literary life is often criticized for lacking the ferment and turbulence of ideas that are customary in Europe and in the United States. Thus, in the immediate postwar period the challenge noted above to the realist tradition as providing an intellectually acceptable foundation for the novel found little response. The pioneers of the modern movement were dead, and their immediate successors, who had established themselves in the 1930's, authors such as C. P. Snow, Evelyn Waugh, and Anthony Powell, were in no sense disciples; all three were engaged by the 1950's in composing lengthy novel cycles—*Strangers and Brothers, Sword of Honour,* and *A Dance to the Music of Time*—which were firmly based upon a technique of realist narrative and characterization.

It is worth noting here that British novelists display an exceptional and consistent attachment to the realist tradition. Perhaps this preference corresponds to the empirical, nonanalytical strain that runs through British philosophical writing. Certainly the influence of the Old Masters—Jane Austen, Charles Dickens, George Eliot—appears more pervasive and irremovable than that of the the great French forebears of the French novel upon French novelists of the present day. Thus, in the early 1950's Snow explicitly maintained that the modern movement represented only a short-lived diversion and that, after the Edwardians, the mainstream of British fiction had resumed its course in the realist current through the novels of Greene, Orwell, Waugh, and Snow himself. This judgment was echoed by the young writers of the Movement (notably Kingsley Amis), although this group's view of fiction differed considerably from its view of poetry. In poetry the Movement attacked the inflated diction and bogus romanticism that were alleged to have been inspired by the writings and life-style of Dylan Thomas and also by the New Apocalypse poets of the 1940's. In fiction its support for the realist tradition was linked to its dislike for another variety of the "phony," as they saw it. This was the elderly Bloomsbury intelligentsia and its allies in the cultural establishment, in particular Cyril Connolly and his journal, *Horizon,* which had championed the modern movement and some of its postwar followers in Europe and America. In this case the attack was directed against pretentiousness, obscurity, and metropolitan sophistication, which were contrasted with the provincial and English virtues of plain speaking and common sense.

Amis first established himself as a satirical writer and his novel *I Like It Here* (1958) caught a mood of the moment. Written in the aftermath of Suez, it expressed a spirit of withdrawal into an insular and xenophobic perimeter; and in such a climate, cosmopolitan and experimental writing in other parts of the West presented easy targets for attack. The 1950's also witnessed the appearance of many novels and plays based on working-class life, although in many instances the author was describing the adventure of escaping or dropping out rather than involvement. Such writing represented something of a new wave in English literature; but here too it was generally grounded in a realist technique, and the themes were of local rather than universal interest.

At about the same time a surprising but prophetic view of the situation of the novel was expressed in Waugh's *The Ordeal of Gilbert Pinfold* (1957). He wrote: "It may happen in the next hundred years that the English novelists of the present day will come to be valued, as we now value the artists and craftsmen of the late eighteenth century. The originators, the exuberant men, are extinct, and in their place subsists and modestly flourishes a generation notable for elegance and variety of contrivance."

The "exuberant men" are those who possess the irresistible creative vigor to change the form and the potentialities of the novel, and since the death of Joyce no novelist of this stature has appeared. Instead we have a remarkably wide-ranging "variety of contrivance," a sophisticated understanding of the novelist's craft and a capacity for experiment within the existing genres. This brings us back to the distinction noted earlier by Scholes between the empirical and fictional modes of narration. According to his definition, the writer in the empirical mode aims to tell his tale as history shaped by the imagination and strives after verisimilitude. There are variations within this approach, such as the "faction" novel, based on documentary records, such as Truman Capote's *In Cold Blood* (1966) or Thomas Kenneally's *Schindler's Ark* (1982). The fictional mode, on the other hand, includes romance, allegory, fable, parody, and pastiche, and many of the authors discussed in Supplement I have experimented with one or several of these categories.

In this connection it is worth remembering that the novel—defined earlier as a peculiarly intimate form of verbal artifice enacted between author and reader—has scarcely changed at all in terms of the author's technology (except for the substitution of typewriter or word processor for pen) since the days of Daniel Defoe. The other arts—painting, sculpture, and music—are far more open to technological innovation, as are the associated literary media of poetry, drama, cinema, television, and radio. The novelist of the late twentieth century has had to take account of all these changes in contrast to the relative immobility of his own methods.

On the other hand, while critical studies between the two world wars were largely devoted to poetry, ever since the end of World War II they have been mainly focused upon fiction. In the words of Frank Kermode, "In our phase of civility the novel is the central form of literary art"—in other words, the one best equipped to express the complexities and paradoxes of modern experience. Of course, even if theories of fiction have become the staple diet of literary critics, novelists do not shape their creations according to academic doctrines or critical abstractions. Nevertheless, the nature of the novelist's gift requires him to keep in touch with the changing currents of sensibility and taste, and this will be demonstrated by the comments of contemporary writers, either in critical essays or debates or in personal statement.

Graham Greene published his first novel, *The Man Within,* in 1929; therefore his literary career spans the entire period covered by the present volume. He may be regarded as a contemporary rather than a modern writer, in the sense discussed in the introduction to Volume VII (p. xii):

> the modern writer is one who re-examines the foundations of his art. He is especially concerned with innovations in form, technique, modes of sensibility, vocabulary, linguistic structure . . . by comparison with the contemporary writer his imaginative world is timeless. . . . The contemporary writer pays less attention to formal or linguistic experiment. His fiction draws its vitality from the world he lives in, from its historical, political, economic, and social character; and he feels himself well qualified to interpret the changing circumstances of his age.

Greene's early work was clearly influenced by the writing of Joseph Conrad, who might be described as a grandfather of the modern movement. The prophetically cinematic quality of Conrad's plots, especially prominent in *The Secret Agent* (1907), is developed even more strikingly by Greene in, for example, *It's a Battlefield* (1934). As in the case of *The Secret Agent,* the novel deals with social action; yet it does not present a vision of society as a whole, but rather a succession of dramatic scenes that stand out from the surrounding darkness. There are two other resemblances to Conrad, both coincidental. It is the Far East, Africa, and Latin America that have supplied both men with some of their richest themes. And Conrad's experience of the sea, like Greene's of journalism, imparted to each a quality common to both professions—a flair for storytelling that holds the reader almost against his will.

The problem that confronts the present-day novelist concerning the nature of reality is not only a matter of aesthetics or fictional technique. Greene became convinced, as Bernard Bergonzi's essay makes clear, that modern Western civilization had become a hollow shell and that "authentic existence was more likely to be found in supposedly savage places" than in the tedium of modern urban life. In this respect he has proved himself to be (again like Conrad) a prophetic writer. Patrick White arrived at a similar conclusion early in his career. The problem has many facets, but it is noteworthy that of the fifteen novelists discussed in this volume, ten have spent an important part of their writing careers abroad and chosen foreign settings for much of their work. And of the other five, William Golding has set most of his novels elsewhere in either time or place.

The variety of Greene's fiction is so wide that Bergonzi aptly describes him as having led a succession of careers. He examines at length the part played by religious themes in the early novels and political themes in the later. The essay concludes with a survey of the new turn that Greene's writing career has taken since 1980—the series of short novels composed as fables or fantasies in a satirical vein.

This volume also includes an Irishman often writing in French, an Australian, a West Indian, and two naturalized Central Europeans. Arthur Koestler, the senior of these, belongs to a species of writer that has always flourished on the Continent, though rarely in Britain—the novelist who is also an intellectual possessing an encyclopedic breadth of interests and who, in this instance, combined the life of reflection with the life of action. André Malraux was a comparable figure. As a journalist and editor, Koestler witnessed on the spot many of the formative historical events of the interwar years—inflation in Central Europe, early Zionism, the rise of the Nazis, the Moscow purges, and the Spanish Civil War. But he was no mere newsman, overwhelmed by the ephemera of journalism. He could hold his own in any intellectual company; was equally at home in Berlin, Vienna, Paris, and London; and acquired a scientific education that far outran the range of the majority of men of letters. At the same time, in his inclination to live and move outside the study, he could claim in Robert Browning's words (often associated with Graham Greene), "our interest's on the dangerous edge of things."

John Atkins pays due tribute to *Darkness at Noon* (1941), Koestler's classic political novel on which his reputation rests secure. It is believable that a British writer might have conceived the historical, and the prison setting, but only a Central or Eastern European could have created the terminology of the political dialogue, which gives the book its enduring significance. He also singles out for praise the two volumes of memoirs, *Arrow in the Blue* (1952) and *The Invisible Writing* (1954), which will surely take their place among the great European autobiographies of the century. Elsewhere he discusses not only the novels but also Koestler's other writings on political and historical topics and on the philosophy of science, which require notice so as to compose a balanced portrait of a writer of such diverse and unconventional gifts.

Of all the authors included in this volume, Samuel Beckett has the closest associations with the modern movement. He knew and worked with Joyce, and one of his earliest critical studies was devoted to Proust. An earlier influence, however, was that of Descartes, whose famous dictum *Cogito ergo sum* evidently reinforced Beckett's conviction that all existence takes place in the head and all external contact is an illusion. Or to quote one of Beckett's characters, "Murphy's mind pictured itself as a large, hollow sphere hermetically closed to the universe without. He neither thought a kick because he felt one, nor felt one because he thought one." From Proust, Jean-Jacques Mayoux tells us, Beckett absorbed the concept that the alien world begins with one's body. In his critique of Proust, Beckett discusses the condition of sleep and of madness as privileged states purified from illusory external connections. "We are then back," he claims, "in the only world that has reality and significance, the world of our latent consciousness." He is emphasizing here Proust's perception that man's only conquest of reality depends upon his use of the involuntary memory; this belief runs through the whole of Beckett's creative writing.

Beckett's novels and plays have a predominantly philosophical bent; his purpose is a search for the nature of reality rather than the construction of plausible fictions. In each of the novels, Mayoux suggests, the title character represents an embodiment, an avatar of the author, who knows that he exists and signifies only to himself. The speakers, Watt, Malone, and others, have no reality apart from their creator. "They are names on whom Beckett confers the responsibility for passing his time." Thus, everything in *Watt* deals with aspects of Watt. But he "of himself, knew nothing. And so he needed to be witnessed." *Esse est percipi* is another key concept in Beckett's oeuvre. He is deeply preoccupied with the difficulties of human communication and with man's sentence, as he sees it, to solitude. He expresses this preoccupation through a symbolism of blindness and immobility, which is especially pervasive in his later plays, and of an existence stripped down to the bare essentials of nutrition and excretion.

Waiting for Godot (1952) became by far the best known of Beckett's works, because here the author hit upon two themes that are broadly based in their appeal—the passive bewilderment of the individual in an age of doubt and the existence of a spiritually derelict condition in the midst of the contemporary world of material ease and plenty. Moreover, he succeeded in creating a theatrical impact with a play that offers neither plot nor momentum—it is a tour de force of inactivity—and in enlivening this desolate vision with a ubiquitous presence of wit. The technique that combines and animates these elements may be described as philosophical clowning, speculative dialogue being interwoven with vaudeville patter. The clown debunks his betters and destroys all values, because values, once formalized, are false. The ridiculous formal clothes he wears, bowler hat and tattered tailcoat, are not meant to fit, but rather to be revealed as a disguise. Mayoux's essay traces Beckett's literary development from the early poems, through the novels, and the plays for theater and radio, and finally to the short, rigorously compressed fables or visions of the last few years. He notes Beckett's adoption of the French language for many of his writings, a choice that seems designed to emphasize his antipathy to the foreignness or externality of all language. In effect, Beckett has never become a French writer, but rather remains an Irishman writing in French.

At the end of his essay on Beckett, Mayoux remarks that among the prose writers of our time only William Golding gives some approximation to the power of language that Beckett possesses. By a curious coincidence both writers achieved an international eminence and something of a revolution in taste at the same time—the mid 1950's—by means of a difficult and thoroughly original work (for *Godot* was not seen in London until 1955). Golding's first novel, *Lord of the Flies* (1954), had been refused by many publishers and was at first received with incomprehension by many critics and readers. Yet within a very few years it became a contemporary classic and a prescribed book in English studies all over the world. The initial mystification was probably due to the fact that Golding was the first of the postwar writers to cast a novel in the form of a fable. This particular fable, a reminder of man's innate propensity for evil, struck a note somewha consonant with that of the brooding suspense of *Waiting for Godot;* both partook of the anguish of the time, the fears of a world newly overshadowed by the nuclear threat.

The theme that pervades much of Golding's fictional oeuvre is that of the fall of man. Human consciousness gives mankind a biological advantage, at a price: the knowledge of evil. To be innocent, as the humanoid predecessors of *Homo sapiens* in Golding's second novel, *The Inheritors* (1955), is to know nothing. Yet it is difficult to trace any single line of development in Golding's work. His technical resource is such as to enable him, as has often been remarked, to begin each book as if it were his first; thus, the approach may be anthropological, as in *Lord of the Flies* and *The Inheritors,* or psychological, as in *The Pyramid* (1967). Harold Watts has noted two sentences from *Free Fall* (1959): "I have hung all systems on the wall like a row of useless hats. They do not fit. . . . But I have lived enough of my life to require a pattern that fits over everything I know, and where can I find that?" "The mind cannot hold more than so much: but understanding requires a sweep that takes in the whole of remembered time, and then can pause." He suggests that Golding tries on a succession of hats, all expressive of different ranges of human aspiration, and that each novel signals a deliberate pause.

Stephen Medcalf's essay surveys the whole range of Golding's writing—novels, plays, poetry, and essays—and calls attention to an unexpected vein of comedy manifested in Golding's late work. He stresses the peculiar effect of reading the novels, that you ought not to be the same person at the end of the book as at the beginning and that the process of reinterpreting the book begins as soon as the first picture of what is happening has been established. Thus, it is unwise to read about one of the novels before reading it.

Lawrence Durrell first became known as a poet and travel writer who excelled at evoking the essence of Greece and the Near East in terms of both the landscape and its peoples. His first ambitious venture into fiction, *The Black Book,* published in Paris in 1938, did not become available in Britain until the 1970's, and it is still little known. It was not until the appearance of *The Alexandria Quartet* (1957–1960) that he became internationally famous. It is rare for a single work to transform not only the stature of an author but the nature of his reputation. The *Quartet* both secured for Durrell a European acclaim, such as had been earned by Byron and Wilde as writers undervalued by their compatriots, and also focused attention upon his fiction as the work of a pioneer who had unmistakably parted company from the postwar realist approach.

In his *Key to Modern Poetry* (1952) Durrell had outlined some of his ideas concerning personality and the cyclical, rather than linear, movement of time. In the *Quartet* he embodied these to a degree that revealed him as the most innovative British novelist of the 1950's. Keith Brown's analysis of the *Quartet* pays especial attention to the well-known prefatory note to *Balthazar* (1958), which likens the time sense employed in the *Quartet* to Einsteinian theory, and he considers how far this analogy is illuminating. The closing pages of this section are particularly valuable for their discussion of the various levels at which the *Quartet* can be read.

Keith Brown's essay differs from most critiques of Durrell's writing in rating *The Black Book* as his most lasting, and *Tunc* (1968) and *Nunquam* (1970) as his greatest intellectual achievement. The *Quartet* is generally agreed to display a number of the characteristics of ancient Greek romance fiction: Brown places *Tunc* and *Nunquam* in the genre of Menippean satire; that is to say, the author here employs erudite allusion and parody, exploits the fantastic and the grotesque, draws upon the tradition of philosophical debate and shows himself less interested in people than in mental attitudes.

Martin Dodsworth's study of Durrell's verse surveys his lyric poetry and his plays and makes the cardinal point that Durrell does not recognize a meaningful distinction between poetry and prose. Much of his own prose resembles his poetry in that it is concerned with the path to illumination: it is about being or becoming an artist. Accordingly, the essay also provides a view, which is complementary to Brown's, of certain aspects of *The Black Book* and of the *Quartet.*

At the outset of his career Patrick White was strongly conscious of the influences of James Joyce and Virginia Woolf. But inheriting as he did a sparsely, not a densely, populated literary culture, he was spared many of the problems of the British novelist described earlier, among them the misgiving that "it had all been done before, and better" or that, in Virginia Woolf's words, "reality has moved off, and refuses to be contained any longer in such ill-fitting vestments." On the contrary, the twentieth-century writer in Australia was confronted, as D. H. Lawrence had perceived, with a challenge and an opportunity unique in the English-speaking world, in the form of two sharply antithetical terrains and ways of life—the life of the populous cities and suburbs of the coastal fringe and the life of the other Australia, the empty interior of infinite distances and unimaginable age.

In "The Prodigal Son," White describes how after his English public-school and university education, literary beginnings in London, and wartime service in the Royal Air Force, he returned to Australia in 1946. His aim was "to reach the state of humility and simplicity which is the only desirable one for an artist or for a man. . . . Writing, which had meant the practice of an art by a polished mind in civilised surroundings, became a struggle to create completely fresh forms out of the rocks and sticks of words. . . . I began to see things for the first time." The eventual result of this second apprenticeship was a fictional oeuvre that comprehends both a supra-European and a supra-Australian dimension. In terms of style, White created a prose that recalls the descriptive exuberance and satirical vehemence of Dickens. In terms of observation, the figures he sees, as James remarked of Balzac, "immediately begin to bristle with all their characteristics . . . every mark and sign, inward and outward, that they possess," and this minute scrutiny was applied to all walks of society—the business élite of the great cities, the small suburban householder, the poor immigrant, and the isolated farmer of the Outback. In terms of form, White's imagination has embraced the chronicle of family life, counterpointed by an ever-present awareness of solitude (*The Tree of Man,* 1955), the historical epic of exploration (*Voss,* 1957), the study of suburban life with visionary dimensions (*Riders in the Chariot,* 1961)—to name only three examples of his range, apart from his own favorites, *The Aunt's Story* (1948), *The Solid Mandala* (1966), and *The Twyborn Affair* (1979). R. F. Brissenden's essay aptly sums up White's achievement by quoting, from *Voss,* Laura Trevelyan's verdict on the principal character: "The country is his by right of vision." Of all the authors discussed in this volume, White approaches most closely to Waugh's category of "the originators, the exuberant men."

Angus Wilson was among the first new writers to establish a reputation immediately after World War II. He did this through two collections of stories that described with keen observation and mordant wit the transition experienced by the British middle class from a position of privilege between the wars to the era of austerity and the welfare state. In these early years of peace he found British fiction excessively dominated by nostalgia. He considered at first that he had learned all he could from the experiments of the modern movement and favored a return to the realist treatment of experience. Ten years later he had come to believe that this approach had hardened into a new orthodoxy and that in restoring social breadth to the novel the realist writers of the 1950's had sacrificed depth of perception. The novel, he maintains, depends upon a personal vision, and the novelist makes as much or as little use of the real world as he needs to project that vision. For this purpose fantasy may be more serviceable than realism: novelists take what they will, when and where they will. Throughout his career he has shown himself an acute critic of fiction past and present, and his own development bears witness to a strenuous search for fresh approaches. After publishing three novels cast in the realist mold, he turned to a completely different form in *The Old Men at the Zoo* (1961), a fable that is set in the future and describes England at war against a European alliance. In *No Laughing Matter* (1967) he again explored fresh territory, in this instance offering a panorama of British society over half a century presented through a domestic chronicle. Here the medium is literary parody. Successive generations of the Matthews family are characterized through charades or fantasies in which the author exploits his power of mimicry, which he has rightly always regarded as one of his strongest gifts. K. W. Gransden's essay traces the complex course of Wilson's development as a novelist and storywriter; he gives a full account of the breadth of Wilson's range, and of his resourcefulness, especially in his later years in adapting his gifts to different fictional genres.

Anthony Burgess is arguably the most prolific, versatile, and inventive novelist of the postwar period. He has experimented in virtually every fictional genre, beginning with realist novels based on personal experience in the Far East and in Britain; political satire (*Honey for the Bears,* 1963), anti-Utopian fable (*A Clockwork Orange* and *The Wanting Seed,* both 1962); espionage thriller (*Tremor of Intent,* 1966); historical fiction (*Nothing Like the Sun,* 1964) anthropological fantasy (*MF,* 1971); and historical fiction tailored for television (*A.D.,* 1986; and *The Kingdom of the Wicked,* 1985). A brilliant reviewer of fellow novelists, he does not appear to be encumbered by preconceived ideas concerning the nature of fiction. The characteristics that persist throughout these many experiments with form are the loose, episodic nature of his storytelling and a prodigious linguistic energy that expresses itself in puns, word games, and the coinage of new words: Shakespeare and Joyce are his most revered masters. Despite his love for a now-vanished England, he is the last person who could be accused of an outlook dominated by nostalgia.

Carol Dix observes that in Burgess' early fiction, written in a comparatively realist vein, he excels at describing the discords that afflict a society (first Malaysia, later Britain) at a time of rapid historical transition. Noting the prevalence of black comedy in his writing, she stresses the Augustinian pessimism, which finds echoes in the novels of Greene, Golding, and Spark (Burgess is a Catholic) and which has led him to the conclusion that the depravity of man far outweighs the evidence of transcendent goodness in his nature. The essay divides Burgess' novels into three main groups: those concerned with social realism and satire; those with a philosophical outlook; and those primarily inspired by his fascination with the use of language. Certainly his most imaginative—for example, *A Clockwork Orange*—and probably his most durable writing is to be found in the second group.

Ruth Whittaker remarks that Muriel Spark, who began her writing career as a poet and critic, resisted writing a novel until after her conversion to Roman Catholicism in her late thirties—"From that time I began to see life as a whole rather than as a series of disconnected happenings." This view of the world has been crucial in determining her approach to many of the aesthetic problems that face the contemporary novelist. Thus, the question of the nature of reality assumes quite a different form when the author believes that reality lies not in familiar material phenomena, but rather in the realm of God. In this light, "contingency"—the random, unexpected turn of events—forms part of a supernatural plan, and the normal linear time sequence, and with it the effects of suspense, are transformed when the outcome is preordained.

Again, in her characterization, Muriel Spark proceeds from a starting point that differs sharply from that of a secular novelist, such as Iris Murdoch. The latter's presentation of character is in sympathy with the view put forward in John Bayley's *Characters of Love.* "What I understand by an author's love for his characters is a delight in their independent existence as *other people* . . . an intense interest in their personality . . . combined with a respect for their freedom." Spark has created strikingly individual characters; but their qualities and actions are shown as subordinate to the overriding plan. She does not stress the paradoxes or inconsistencies of personality for their own sake, nor dwell on the interior psychological motivation of her creations: she admits to a "lack of expectancy" concerning them.

All the above factors place Spark's fiction in strong contrast to that of other practitioners of the postwar novel. She rejects the solipsistic approach of Beckett, which denies a link between man and the rest of creation; and she differs radically from the liberal conception of personality, which informs in various ways the fiction of Angus Wilson, Iris Murdoch, and Doris Lessing. She has returned to the convention of the omniscience of the author, but in a fashion different from that of the nineteenth-century novelists, who loaded their texts with minutely realistic detail. Her novels show an exceptional economy of plot and her methods of description and characterization are intensely selective. But she has also shown an unceasing interest in the theory of fiction and has repeatedly experimented with fresh forms.

Ruth Whittaker calls attention to the remarkable aptness of tone that Spark brings to novels of completely different content and emotional key. "I am intent upon getting a tone of writing suitable for a theme," she has said. Her success in achieving this is especially notable in two contrasting novels, *Memento Mori* (1959) and *The Prime of Miss Jean Brodie* (1961).

In recent years her work has taken the form of short satirical novels in which plot and characterization have been compressed and the action accelerated to the point of melodrama, and a casual, worldly style of narration and dialogue adopted so as to sharpen the impact of the parablelike nature of these tales. *The Takeover* (1976), which is set in Italy and deals with terrorism, sophisticated crime, the manipulation of the law, and the illusory nature of wealth is perhaps her most successful achievement in this genre. But she has never written to a formula, and the present essay justly stresses the diversity of her fictional range, and her capacity for imaginative renewal.

Iris Murdoch is a professional teacher of philosophy. Her novels are by no means limited to a simplification or demonstration of ideas put forward in another medium, but some of her nonfictional writings throw a useful light upon her practice in fiction. Her first novel, *Under the Net* (1954), provides some valuable clues to its successors. "All theorising is flight. We must be ruled by the situation itself and this is unutterably particular. Indeed, it is something to which we can never get close enough, however hard we try, as it were, to crawl under the net." This proposition refers to the writer's duty to get under the net of theoretical description and approach as nearly as possible to the truth. The truth, however, requires some further explanation. The phrase implies a rejection of the Sartrean existential and solipsistic view of life, and an insistence upon respect for "contingency," a key word in Murdoch's writings that refers to what is random, accidental, and particular about people. Contingency, the argument runs, destroys fantasy and leads us to the real, and "literature must always be a battle between real people and images." "Truth" also includes the author's desire to restore a richer and deeper awareness of human personality which is linked to her concept of love, defined as "the extremely difficult realisation that something other than oneself is real." This train of thought has an important bearing on Murdoch's view of characterization.

Murdoch's fictional oeuvre is now so large that there are good grounds for a selective approach such as A. S. Byatt has adopted in this study. She devotes the first third of her essay to discussing the relation between the critical and philosophical writings and the novels, paying especial attention to such crucial essays as "Against Dryness" (1961) and "The Sublime and the Beautiful Revisited" (1959). In discussing the novels she does not follow a chronological order, but rather divides them into groups, examines recurrent themes, and interrelates novels as widely separated as *Under the Net* and *The Black Prince* (1973).

The postscript to the essay, which reviews the novels and essays that have appeared since 1980, leaves the impression that despite Murdoch's observance of some of the conventions of the realist tradition, her fiction of recent years has been increasingly employed as a vehicle for ideas, in particular religious ideas. She regards the nineteenth-century novel "as a major product of religion"—for its creators "the religious background went without saying." She also considers that the modern demythologizing of religion "could bring religion back into the realm of the believable." One of her novels, *The Philosopher's Pupil* (1983), attempts both to embody ancient pagan myth in a credible modern setting and to present believable epiphanies of Christian mythology in a similar light.

Of all the work by women authors discussed in this volume, the writing of Doris Lessing covers the widest range. This is not surprising in view of the independence and mobility of her career. She grew up in Rhodesia, established herself as a writer in London in the 1950's, and has since traveled widely in Europe and the United States. Her first five novels and her early stories all have African settings.

With her second book, *Martha Quest* (1952), she embarked upon the five-volume novel cycle *The Children of Violence,* which is in one aspect a bildungsroman; however, her heroine does not confine herself to the customary search for her own individuality but explores wider issues, such as class or racial conflict. This series represents, in fact, the only sustained attempt by a British author to record the "ideological feel" of the midcentury. The early novels were written in the realist tradition, and the first, in particular, *The Grass Is Singing* (1950), made its appeal through the originality and the clarity of its vision of the white presence in Africa. But long before the cycle was complete—in the final volume the scene shifts to London—she had come to share the dissatisfaction of many of her contemporaries with the realist mode of narration, and in 1962 she published *The Golden Notebook,* still probably the most famous of her novels. "I keep trying to write the truth, and it's not true," her heroine Anna Wulf declares. Anna's dilemma, however, is not only a matter of writer's block or simply an artistic problem; it includes the difficulties of being a free woman, of "attempting to live the kind of life women have never lived before." The solution adopted was to keep four separate notebooks so as to impose a superficial order on the raw material of experience: interspersed with these is Anna's genuine novel, *Free Women,* printed in a different typeface. "I wanted to write a short formal novel to enclose the rest . . . to suggest what

INTRODUCTION

I think a great many writers feel about the formal novel—that it's not doing its work any more."

Broadly speaking, Lessing's fiction has passed through three phases. In the first—*The Children of Violence* cycle—the individual is studied in the context of collective conflicts and loyalties. In the second—beginning with *The Golden Notebook,* and most notably in three novels of the 1970's, *Briefing for a Descent into Hell, The Summer Before the Dark,* and *Memoirs of a Survivor*—the angle of vision turns inward: the author enters the realm of the subconscious in search of the meaning of experience after the normal marks of identification and compass bearings of the individual personality have disappeared. In the third, which begins in 1979, she embarks upon the space fiction cycle, the *Canopus in Argos Archives.* In these books social and psychological problems are still examined, but in a cosmological context, which distances the author alike from the ideological conflicts of the present day and from the ordeals of the individual psyche. But concurrently with this immense enterprise, she has continued her excursions into realist territory with *The Diaries of Jane Somers* (1984) and *The Good Terrorist* (1986).

Evelyn Waugh's phrase "a variety of elegant contrivance" seems especially appropriate in describing the novels of John Fowles. Fowles has achieved the rare feat of sustaining a mass readership while consistently engaging the attention of the critics. In his early novels he showed himself a master of suspense and of ingenuity in shaping intricate plots. These assets were supplemented by a sophisticated narrative technique and an increasingly complex texture of literary allusion.

Of the two categories distinguished earlier by Robert Scholes, Fowles has followed the fictional rather than the empirical, each of his first two novels being cast in the form of the romance. Superficially, both *The Collector* (1963) and *The Magus* (1966), which were quickly adapted to the cinema, offer startling varieties of sexual encounter. Read at a deeper level, the literary ancestry that Michael Thorpe discerns is traceable in *The Collector* to the imprisoned and persecuted heroine of Samuel Richardson's *Clarissa Harlowe,* and in *The Magus* to *The Tempest.* Fowles has himself also acknowledged the influence of Alain Fournier's *Le Grand Meaulnes,* and has quoted the French writer's saying, "I like the marvellous only inside the real." Literary artifice is carried much further in *The French Lieutenant's Woman* (1969). Here the narrative deliberately imitates the Victorian mode of fiction of the 1860's and is carefully documented with historical and literary references to, and quotations from, the period. Nevertheless, the author bases the novel's final effect on a juxtaposition of Victorian and modern attitudes, and the principal characters gradually emerge as post–nineteenth-century figures.

Discussing Fowles's later work, Thorpe sees *Daniel Martin,* which as "a writer's novel" has affinities with *The Golden Notebook,* as possibly marking a transitional stage in Fowles's development. Whether he will proceed to the writer's task, as defined by George Lukacs, of "living through and thinking out the great contemporary problems" remains an open question.

David Storey is the only postwar writer besides Beckett who has achieved success both in the novel and in the drama. In both forms his writing revolves around certain recurrent topics. These include personal experiences as a rugby player, teacher, and employee in many nonliterary occupations, and—in a wider perspective—the breakdown of marriage, mental and emotional collapse, and the conflict between the generations. He can be seen as a contemporary writer, in the sense discussed earlier, rather than a modern one. But as John Russell Taylor notes in his essay, Storey's practice of beginning a project and then laying it aside, sometimes for years, makes it difficult to chart his development. His first novel, the much acclaimed *This Sporting Life* (1960), which presented a gladiatorial type of hero, was classed mistakenly as one of the then-fashionable studies of working-class life. It was not until his third novel, *Radcliffe* (1963), that a fictional enterprise of greater scope was revealed. *This Sporting Life* was intended to express the physical element in the author's makeup and its successor, *Flight into Camden* (1960), the spiritual interior. The opposing halves were brought face to face in *Radcliffe,* with a hint that a fourth work that would reconcile the two lay ahead. *Radcliffe* is by far Storey's most ambitious venture to date—indeed, the centerpiece of his career. His gift for vivid reporting, demonstrated in the first two books, developed into a denser, more elaborate mode of observation and a deeper power of characterization. The split between soul and body is represented in the characters of Radcliffe, the passive upper-class intellectual, and Tolson, the aggressive working man, and symbolized in their homosexual attachment, which culminates in Radcliffe's murder of his lover and subsequent mental collapse. The conflict is also identified with "the split in the whole of Western society." Storey has not resorted here to a deliberate imitation or parody of earlier literary models, such as has been noted in the later work of Wilson or Fowles. Nevertheless, the book abounds with echoes of D. H. Lawrence (notably of the relationship between Crich and Birkin in *Women in Love*) and of Dostoevsky.

Storey has shown himself to be an extremely accomplished dramatist, though less of an originator than others of the playwrights discussed here. His plays deal with a range of topics similar to those we find in his novels. In pieces such as *The Changing Room* (1972) and *The Contractor* (1969) he shows a Kiplingesque skill in making real to his audience the nature of the work or play that dominates the lives of his characters, and yet these works are no mere documentaries: they are peopled with living individuals, the web that connects their lives is subtly traced, and their dialogue is as spontaneous as it is revealing. In *The Restoration of Arnold Middleton* (1967) and *Home* (1970), both of which deal with mental disturbance, he treads this difficult path with unerring delicacy and control. Commenting on the difference between creating a novel and a play, he has written: "Writing a novel is like launching an unmanned ship. You may direct it in a certain direction, but thereafter you have no further control . . . it's out of your hands. A play is like a properly crewed ship. You can modify from moment to moment, take account of the climate of feeling at any particular performance, test out ideas, and if they don't work as you want them to, change them."

Of the ten novelists discussed here who have lived or traveled for long periods outside Britain, V. S. Naipaul occupies a singular position. He was born into a Brahmin family in Trinidad, and educated there in English; but he does not feel himself rooted in the West Indies, in his ancestral India, or in Britain, where he has spent most of his life: he has taken up a stance of detached and equitable criticism alike of the African, the Indian, and the British heritages. Yet among the ten novelists, only he and Patrick White obtained an Oxbridge degree, and he has won all the most sought after British literary awards. He is a contemporary of the talented group of West Indian novelists who began to publish in the 1950's; in the breadth of his appeal and the consistent excellence of his work he has surpassed them all. Because of the unfamiliarity to the British public of his material, the writer in a newly developing literature (as too in the case of Patrick White) is comparatively untroubled by the fear that reality is eluding him. And for similar reasons the link between the novel and its social setting is not called into question.

The first phase of Naipaul's novel writing based on a West Indian background culminated in his masterly Trinidadian family chronicle, *A House for Mr Biswas* (1961). But Naipaul has always been sensitive to contemporary developments in the art of fiction; and when in the 1960's his writing began to embrace a political dimension, its form and technique passed through significant changes. In turning his attention to a wider, more complex scene, he began to deal with public topics through the medium of travel writing and personal reporting—*The Middle Passage* (1962) and *An Area of Darkness* (1964)—or historical survey—*The Loss of El Dorado* (1969). In *The Mimic Men* (1967) he again shifted his authorial stance and wrote a confessional novel that has affinities with *Darkness At Noon;* as a study of a failed revolutionary, it offers a remarkable analysis of the role of a political challenger in the Third World. *A Bend in the River* (1979), which describes the contemporary ebb and flow of human tides across the continent of Africa, epitomizes the dominant preoccupation of Naipaul's whole literary career: that is, an imaginative charting of the process of which he first became aware in his London bed-sitter in 1950—the great postwar movement of peoples, accompanied by a great shaking-up of old cultures and old ideas.

In his summing-up, Thorpe quotes a tribute to Naipaul for having discovered "the novel of the new synthetic world"—that is, a world in which nationality is blurred or displaced, the unity of society is fragmented, and the impulse toward independence and social justice fails to produce a viable new order. He has succeeded in combining a command of West Indian dialect English with an impressive mastery of a formal English prose style. And in his portrayal of the Third World he has gone beyond isolated instances of the colonial experience so as to present more successfully than any other novelist a comprehensive vision of the world's half-made societies.

Paul Scott began to write novels at the same time as his contemporaries—that is, in the early 1950's. But it was not until ten years later, with the beginning of publication of *The Raj Quartet* (1966–1975), that his books came to be as widely read as theirs. He spent most of his life in England, except for the crucial three years of active service in India in the 1940's on which not only the *Quartet* but most of his other novels are based. Like White and Naipaul, Scott set out to describe a scene that was largely unknown to British readers but also embodied a historical process. In consequence he too was comparatively unaffected by the problem of the nature of reality, which has beset so many of his British contemporaries in the effort to create an original and yet credible vision of an overfamiliar scene.

Nevertheless, it is clear from his earlier books that he had devoted much thought and experiment to the technique of the novelist's craft, and in the *Quartet* he perfected these refinements. Its dominant Eurasian theme—the relations between men and women, or men and men, of different races—runs through all his earlier writing. Patrick Swinden examines the gradual development of the art with which Scott handles the factors of place and time, and the movement of his narrative. Thus, in *The Chinese Love Pavilion* he creates a symbolic location, a place in which past happenings exercise a mysterious influence over present events, precisely the role that is played by the Bibighar Gardens in the *Quartet.* And in *The Birds of Paradise* he anticipates the narrative technique of the *Quartet,* in which related themes are kept before the reader through the slow unfolding of several narratives in parallel; and with the same method, different or conflicting aspects of the truth are gradually unveiled. The *Quartet* needs to be read in conjunction with *Staying On,* because the latter book provides not only a brilliant tragicomic picture of postindependence India from the point of view of the British who chose to remain but also an indispensable coda to the design of the *Quartet.* Finally, Swinden pays tribute to the remarkable diversity of Scott's prose—taut and vivid in the scenes of action, lyrical, comic, or judicially grave as the context requires.

Poets generally begin to write earlier and make their names sooner than novelists or dramatists. Of the poets discussed in this volume, Dylan Thomas and Philip Larkin are dead, Lawrence Durrell is seventy-five, and Ted Hughes is nearing sixty. It might appear surprising, therefore, that no poets of a later generation appear on the list. The fact is that no younger British poet commands an international reputation or would meet the criterion mentioned earlier of having attracted a significant measure of critical attention. Surveying the scene nearly twenty years ago in the critical anthology *The Survival of Poetry* (1970), Martin Dodsworth noted that "a new kind of poetry has created a new kind of audience." In the growth of this audience the public reading given by Allen Ginsberg and others that filled the Albert Hall in 1965 was a historical landmark. Since then, the new public and its writers have both remained distinct from their predecessors. "The new audience," Dodsworth continued, "is young and frankly uncritical in any academic sense: it expects its poets to speak boldly, to be unafraid of emotion and to be unsympathetic towards conventional middle-class sentiments. . . . The link between jazz and poetry is important: both music and reading [aloud] are expected to induce a sense of community between audience and performers. Its recurrent plea is for the extension of individual freedom . . . it is expressive of a total reaction against the conventional organisation of society."

When Dylan Thomas died in 1953, his name had been known for twenty years; his earliest poems had in fact begun to appear only a little after Auden's. It might be argued that much of his best verse was written by 1945 and, hence, his work could properly have been included in Volume VII. On the other hand Thomas was to become a kind of living legend or image of the romantic poet—only his fellow Celt William Butler Yeats has created a comparable, though rather more dignified, aura in modern times—but this public persona did not develop fully until near the end of Thomas's life. The Thomas legend depended partly upon the bardic and declamatory nature of his verse; partly upon his bohemian life-style; and partly upon his extraordinary vocal powers, which enabled him to communicate—despite the obscurity of some of his writing—with mass audiences through the radio and public readings.

Thomas's verse originated in the romantic culture that provided a countercurrent in the mid 1930's to the writings of the Auden-Spender group. The latter, with their middle-class origins and university education, displayed a sense of guilt at their comparative security and a social and political puritanism directed against the smug and regressive outlook of their class. This puritanism was expressed in a choice of topical themes and a politically conscious treatment of them. "The poet is in some sense a leader," declared Michael Roberts, editor of the *New Signatures* anthology (1932), which published the verse of Auden and several of his associates. Although Thomas, who was brought up in a teacher's, not a factory worker's, family, did not go to university, he shared none of the sense of guilt just mentioned; and when he gravitated to London at the age of twenty, he instinctively associated with poets such as George Barker, who did live a Villonesque, hand-to-mouth existence. Indeed Thomas's penchant for the bohemian life-style may well have risen from a reaction against the austerity of Welsh middle-class life. Both Barker's and Thomas's verse was far more directly lyrical in nature than that of the Auden group. Thomas's inspiration fed, in particular, from his deep and potent recollections of childhood, the intense frustrations of adolescent sexuality, a sacramental feeling for nature, and an intoxication with words comparable to that of the young John Keats. Both Thomas and Barker were influenced by surrealism. They accepted the idea that the poet should use images suggested by other images; but in contrast to the French surrealists, unduly discordant images were rejected, and the poem was shaped with due regard to rhyme and metrical form. The late G. S. Fraser, one of Thomas's most acute critics, remarked that despite the power of his public personality, Thomas did not dramatize his personal life in his poetry, nor build himself up as a character. Neither did he handle the fashionable contemporary themes of doubt or division within the self. "His is a poetry of unitary response"; the world he creates is at one with itself.

In his summing-up, Leslie Norris considers how much of Thomas's work has survived the passage of time and finds that the *Collected Poems* shows us a continuous development and refining of Thomas's technical skills. Tracing the pattern of his career, he notes that Thomas was never so poetically fertile after 1937; that *Deaths and Entrances* marked his arrival as a mature poet; but that thereafter only six poems were judged worthy of inclusion in *Collected Poems.* He believes that the enduring quality of Thomas's verse depends partly upon the extraordinary power of its appeal to the senses, partly upon the capacity of the words to make an effect that goes beyond meaning.

Twenty years after the romantic reaction against the Audenesque poetic idiom, the pendulum moved again. This time the swing was not in favor of a poetry of political awareness. But in other respects the critical precepts of the Movement of the late 1950's would have been familiar to Geoffrey Grigson, editor of *New Verse,* which had contained some of the best writing of Auden and his associates. Grigson underlined the desirability of clear statements, objective description and an easy and colloquial diction, and stressed the part played in composition by the conscious mind.

Philip Larkin was to prove by far the outstanding poet of the group, which was journalistically and somewhat incongruously labeled "the Movement" in 1954. He shared with his Oxford contemporary and friend Kingsley Amis a cheerful irreverence and philistinism that was directed, as noted earlier, against the excessive piety of the cultural establishment in respect of the classical and European tradition. "Nobody," declared the latter, "wants any more poems about philosophers or paintings or novelists or art galleries or mythology or foreign cities or other poems. At least I hope nobody wants them." The Movement could more easily be identified by shared antagonisms than by shared aims. It reacted strongly against experimentalism in poetic forms; against the "Thomas legend"—partly at least on the ground that the false glamour of a bohemian life-style had helped to destroy an important talent—against inflated language and ambitious emotional gestures. It took a reductive view of human expectations: "Come off it!" was its implied exhortation to its readers, in the name of common sense. Larkin himself took pains to debunk any hint that his childhood or adolescence contained a treasure store of visionary recollections: the guiding light that he seems to have followed throughout his writing was "not to be taken in."

Larkin greatly admired Thomas Hardy's poetry, and his own work displays much of that writer's fatalism, wry humor, perception of the disparity between desire and reality, and consequent stoicism, and, likewise, a terse and pithy diction. Alan Brownjohn's essay skillfully avoids the danger of describing Larkin's work too much in terms of defensive attitudes and negative virtues. He indicates the poet's continually developing mastery of rhyme, rhythm and metrical structure, and the studied yet often inspired choice of imagery and language, now formal, now vigorously colloquial, as well as his rare command—again reminiscent of Hardy—of a frequently monosyllabic diction:

> Being brave
> Lets no one off the grave.

He shows that in spite of Larkin's opposition to the modern movement, he succeeded in creating a poetry that is indisputably modern in both its content and its cadences.

The Hawk in the Rain, Ted Hughes's first volume of poems, was published in 1957, when the author was living in the United States. It appeared in the year after *New Lines,* the anthology that contained much of the early work of the Movement group, thus marking the emergence of two sharply distinct currents of postwar poetry. In the verse of the Movement writers, rationality, common sense, and skepticism played an important part: opponents of its antiromantic stance criticized such writing as confined by the typically English limitations of primness and reticence. In Larkin's poem "Wires" the cattle are taught the lesson of life's limits by means of electrified fences. The teachability of these domesticated creatures may be set against the predatory character of Hughes's symbols of nature—the hawk, the wolf, and the pike. Keith Sagar quotes a review of *New Lines* in which the poet Charles Tomlinson remarks of its contributors, "They showed a singular want of vital awareness of the continuum outside themselves, of the mystery embodied over against them of the created universe," and suggests that this vital awareness is the outstanding characteristic of Hughes's work.

This awareness first expressed itself in a confident assertion of biological forces, cast in the form of lyrics inspired by the animal world. All his life Hughes has envisaged animals as living representatives of the true world, "the world under the world." Hughes has composed much verse and prose for children, and in a talk on the writing of poetry entitled "Capturing Animals" (figuratively speaking), he remarked, "This is hunting, and the poem is a new species of creature, a new specimen of life outside your own." "The Thought-Fox" exemplifies this kind of lyric. It might be termed the Platonic idea of a fox. In Hughes's words, "It will live for ever. It will never suffer from hunger or hounds. I have it with me wherever I go." The fox is realized, as are Hughes's other creatures, partly by his gifts of onomatopoeia and his vigorous use of consonants directed at making words felt through all the five senses.

It was an important advantage to Hughes, Keith Sagar believes, to have been brought up on the border between town and country; in his native north the contrast between the rural and the industrial scene is far more sudden and arresting than in the south. This early experience of the split in our civilization between the creative and the destructive forces in the world impressed upon him a dualistic view of life, which has only gradually been harmonized in his writing. He has expressed this conception especially powerfully in the *Crow* sequence of poems, beginning in 1970. In Eskimo folklore the crow was the first creature in the world, and in this cycle, a ubiquitous agent in primitive cosmology—not exactly an alternative Creator, but a force intermediate between God and man. Hughes is capable of the visionary grandeur and eloquence of a prophet; his verse stands in the line of descent between Blake and Lawrence, but he is a writer of uneven execution. *Crow* is a key work in his oeuvre, and in quoting passages that demonstrate the understatement and even the comedy of which Hughes is capable, Keith Sagar calls attention to qualities in the cycle to which few critics have done justice. In general, he defends Hughes from the familiar charge that his stock-in-trade is violence; he points out that Hughes deals with aspects of violence precisely because he lacks the insulation or complacency that enable most of us to ignore the subject. Hughes's work is a living proof, as Dodsworth has remarked, that English poetry in the 1980's is still a romantic poetry.

During the first half of the century British drama was scarcely touched by the influence of the modern movement, apart from some of the late work of Sean O'Casey. Serious plays and comedies alike were constructed within a realistic framework of events, dialogue, and setting. Conventional revelations, catastrophes, and intruders entered the action; and in the end a conventional resolution of conflicts emerged. The theater was sustained by a middle-class public: its expectations could equally well be summed up by Wells's remarks quoted earlier concerning the nineteenth-century novel: "produced in an atmosphere of security for the entertainment of people who liked to feel established and safe for good." This situation continued until the mid 1950's. The theatrical repertory was controlled by commercial management and the star system of artists and directors. Imports were of a scarcely less conventional kind, consisting mainly of the plays of Jean Giraudoux and Jean Anouilh. This system could easily accommodate the plays of the only surviving modernist, T. S. Eliot, which scarcely dented the mold.

In the mid 1950's many forces of change began to appear. The most far-reaching were the influences of the rival media—the cinema, television, and radio, all of which served to transform the dramatist's approach to his material. The dramatist began to compose with the freedom of a screenplay writer. As with the novel, by whose development the drama has seldom remained for long unaffected, a different view of reality evolved. A playwright might cut rapidly from scene to scene, introduce flashbacks and changes in time, speed, and focus, thus liberating himself from the fixed sets and constricted imaginative range of the proscenium stage. Characters might be transformed in fantasy into historical personages and back again. Responding to the individual's sense of alienation from society, the writer, hitherto bound by the conception of drama as a literature of relationships, now commanded the resources to create a theater of the individual in which speech and plot might express the character's sheer isolation from his fellows.

At the same time, radical changes took place in theatrical organization. The founding of the National Theatre was followed by the creation of the Royal Shakespeare Company and an expansion of its repertory to include modern and international drama and by the growth of repertory theaters in the provinces, which replaced the old-fashioned commercial circuits. Commercial management largely withdrew from the staging of serious drama, which was henceforth sustained by the national companies, the provincial repertories, and the fringe theaters and the theater workshops in the larger cities; these last, often situated in basements, attics, or warehouses, further stimulated the break with the proscenium stage.

Equally important were the changes in the dramatic profession. Shakespeare was a player, Marlowe a venturesome graduate and man of letters; and the theater in Britain has generally been kept supplied by these categories of writers down to the era of Shaw, Priestley, Coward, and Rattigan. But for the past thirty years it has been the theater and the film, the television and radio studios, rather than the study, in which the writer has shaped his theories and visions of drama and learned its techniques. The result has been to transform the action into a series of powerfully realized moments or images, not necessarily causally connected, and the text from a literary composition, replete with generalizations or epigrams, to a script in which physical movements or silences may be as significant as words: a play might, for example, be constructed on documentary lines, as in Arnold Wesker's *The Kitchen* (1961).

Three of the historical landmarks of this period were the productions of Beckett's *Waiting for Godot* (1952), Osborne's *Look Back in Anger* (1956), and Pinter's *The Birthday Party* (1959). The first introduced British audiences to the dramatic potentialities of nonillusionist writing and production. The second was not only a highly topical play in its view of postwar Britain, but it also ushered in a new style of acting and, through the Royal Court Theatre, provided a new base for the rising generation of playwrights. The third presented another original mode of writing, in which dialogue is tautened by repetitions, failures of communication, and significant silences. These two plays by Beckett and Osborne and Pinter's later *The Caretaker* (1960) quickly attained the status of modern classics.

During and after the late 1950's the output of new drama rapidly increased and no less rapidly divided in many different directions. These categories will be touched on in relation to the individual dramatists discussed below. One reason for this sudden and wide diversification was that the acting profession—in Britain always oversupplied—now included a number of working-class or lower-middle-class students who had won subsidized places at schools of acting. They could master the vocal training required for the classics but rightly felt that their natural or regional accent and vocabulary found little or no scope in traditional theater productions. Their talents demanded a theater that was only at this date being born.

INTRODUCTION

The expression "performance theater" may throw some light on the nature of John Osborne's writing. To one looking at his work as a whole it becomes clear that the instant success of *Look Back in Anger* did not arise from any revolutionary innovation in dramatic construction. Nor from an ideological message, although the play was intensely topical and unerringly touched the nerve of contemporary discontents. Its appeal rested above all upon the author's command of language. He had devised a phraseology that expressed "the very age and body of the time, its form and pressure." More than any other contemporary dramatist, Osborne composes elaborate vocal solos to establish his characters; in *Look Back in Anger,* at least, the display of temperament becomes a substitute for action. It is noteworthy that most of Osborne's plays contain a leading character with something of the virtuoso in his makeup. In *The Entertainer* (1957) it is a vaudeville comedian; in *Luther* (1961), a preacher; in *Inadmissible Evidence* (1965), an attorney; in *A Patriot for Me* (1966), a "role-player" at once a senior army officer, spy, and concealed homosexual. Trussler's essay makes the point that Osborne's interest in words sometimes blinds him to the technical requirements of his craft. He concludes that when his style emerges naturally from his theme, his work is as satisfying in its shape as it is rhetorically effective.

Opening an exhibition on the work of Samuel Beckett, Harold Pinter recalled that years before Beckett had become famous, Pinter had borrowed one of his novels from a public library. Noticing that it had only been taken out once in ten years, he decided that he would be paying a suitable tribute by keeping it. "I admire Beckett's work so much," he has said, "that something of its texture may appear in mine."

The influence, if any, is most apparent in Pinter's early plays, such as *The Birthday Party* (1959) or *The Room* (1960), which might be described as theater of the interior. Here the action is limited to the meeting of two or three characters to talk to themselves or, marginally, to one another. Like Beckett, Pinter perceived the dramatic importance of the individual's bewilderment in the face of modern society and his consequent effort to isolate some small area of personal experience or private myth so as to defend his identity. Both dramatists also exploited the theatrical potential of vaudeville comic patter as an ingredient in ostensibly serious dialogue. However, Pinter did not adopt this approach from a position of philosophical solipsism such as Beckett's but, rather, through pragmatic observation of how his contemporaries attempt or fail to communicate; he has created as many cinema or television screenplays as works for the theater. Thus while Beckett's characters in his later plays become increasingly detached from any social context, or even from the human body, Pinter's are increasingly carefully "placed" in their relationships. By contrast with the lunar landscape of *Waiting for Godot,* Pinter's early plays are located in "the room," a center of security and sanctuary for the individual psyche.

"There are no hard distinctions between what is real and what is unreal, what is true and what is false." This assumption of the impossibility of verification is a prominent feature of Pinter's dramatic idiom. Another is noncommunication, the employment in dialogue of an evasive response or one disjoined from what has just been said; or, alternatively, communication through the unsaid. The first play in which these devices were employed with masterly effect was *The Caretaker,* in which much of the dramatic tension depends on mutually exclusive fantasies that are eloquently voiced by the three characters. A third is domination asserted by verbal means; this process often shows the intruder attempting to gain possession of "the room," the psychological integrity of its owner.

Between his earliest short pieces and his full-length mature plays such as *The Homecoming,* Pinter has created a thoroughly original modern dramaturgy. Through his technique of alternating dialogue, soliloquy, thinking aloud, interrogation, confession, fabrication, and silence, he has recast the convention of the sequential plot, while retaining the resources of suspense, mystery, and revelation, and also giving full play to the performer's gifts. John Russell Taylor notes the close links between Pinter's successive plays, each of which often takes up themes or devices from its predecessor, and describes the connections between his prolific output for the cinema, television, and radio and his stage plays. He pays especial tribute to Pinter's command of speech and of specialized vocabulary, formal or slangy, intimate or abusive, and ranks him as the contemporary writer most likely to survive permanently in our dramatic literature.

INTRODUCTION

Peter Shaffer scored an immediate success with his first play, which appeared when the new movement in the British theater was in full flow. The piece, however, *Five Finger Exercise* (1958) was a domestic drama cast in the mold of the "well-made play." Shaffer stands closer than most of his contemporaries to the line of descent of literary playwrights, writing to be read as well as performed. And while his art has developed slowly, his reputation was quickly established; his plays have always been sought after in the West End and at the National Theatre, and presented by the most gifted directors in the profession, beginning with John Gielgud.

Shaffer has never reverted to the conventional technique of his first success, but has continued to experiment with a remarkable variety of dramatic forms. His next major enterprise, *The Royal Hunt of the Sun* (1964), was a brilliantly staged chronicle play concerning Pizarro's conquest of the Inca empire. This was followed by *Black Comedy* (1968), a farce based on the Chinese theatrical device of reversing light and darkness so that the audience has vision when the players do not, and vice versa. In *Equus* (1973) he dramatized a psychiatric case history; here, while the material is thoroughly contemporary, the plot is unfolded, as in Greek tragedy, through a series of revelations that involve both psychiatrist and patient. Shaffer gives exceptional attention to the revision of his texts, and nowhere more so than in *Amadeus* (1980), which was revised three times for the theater, and still more drastically for the cinema. Classical music has been a lifelong interest of his, and in this study of the relation between musical genius and the divine will he has created a strikingly original fusion of musical and dramatic elements.

Taylor traces the gradual evolution of Shaffer's powers. He has been a man of the theater from the outset, and he has succeeded in mastering the resources of the modern stage to a degree that places him in the front rank of living dramatists.

Edward Bond's plays may be described as belonging to the theater of challenge. The drama, in his view, provides a way of judging society and helping to change it. Thus, its true aim is political and social rather than aesthetic: "to hold the mirror up to Nature," as Hamlet expressed it, is to encourage narcissism. Acting in the Aristotelian sense *(mimesis)* is a false simulation of feeling, even a betrayal of political activism. We cannot, according to this line of thought, discover a character's motives by analyzing his soul, and Bond is said to direct his actors not to attempt an understanding of a character in terms of individual psychology.

Bond attracted notice with his first play, *Saved* (1966), because of the public revulsion caused by a scene in which a baby was stoned to death by a group of layabouts. This understandable reaction missed the point of the episode. Bond's purpose was partly to depict a state of deprivation and mindless violence in which such an event could take place. But at a deeper level his aim was to return to the ancient roots of drama, evoking the atavistic fury that accompanies a sacrificial killing. Still further removed from the audience was an unstated rationalization on the author's part, which he later revealed in print. "Clearly the stoning of a baby to death in a London park is a typical English understatement; compared to the strategic bombing of German towns, it is a negligible atrocity; compared to the cultural and emotional deprivation of most of our children, its consequences are insignificant." This pronouncement may be set alongside Blake's "Better to kill an infant in its cradle than to nurse unacted desires."

Bond's first two plays were concerned with what he would describe as the oppressed classes in Britain. In his third, *Early Morning* (1968), he turns to the oppressors. Here his caricatures of Queen Victoria, Gladstone, Florence Nightingale, and others are intended to counter the idealized images of the history books. Four of Bond's plays have been devoted to historical or mythical subjects—in other words, topics distanced from present-day Britain—and in these he seeks to create a more politically "usable" past. In *Bingo* (1974) Shakespeare is judged in respect of his alleged collaboration with local landowners to enclose a piece of common land, thereby evicting some hereditary small-holders. In *Lear* (1972) Bond remodels the character of the king because he considered that Shakespeare's ruler offered us an anatomy of human values, thus counseling us as to how to survive in a corrupt society, instead of showing us how to change it.

Bond is unique among modern British dramatists in writing prefaces or manifestos to a number of his plays. Although he styles his theater "rational," "rationalist" might be a more accurate description

Unlike Shaw, he does not seek to win over readers or audiences by appeals to the intelligence; his prefaces are, broadly speaking, sermons to the converted. Still he cannot be classified as an agitprop dramatist. Simon Trussler's essay justly points out that the sparks of hope that emerge from his tragedies or near-tragedies are found in small actions, which are the product of the individual, unpredictable human will.

In some aspects the plays of Tom Stoppard might be classed with those of Osborne as "performance drama." He takes a similar pleasure in exploiting the vocal virtuosity of the actor, while his ingenuity in devising comic stage business and zany spectacle adds a rich extra dimension to the text. At the same time, he writes, like Shaffer with a strong awareness of literary tradition. His plays abound in literary allusions, and he is the most dazzling parodist and pasticheur of his time, witness the sendups of philosophical discourse in *Jumpers* (1972) and the debate on art and the state in *Travesties* (1975); his writings would be outstanding for their intellectual energy alone. He possesses a Joycean nose for ambiguities and double meanings and a gift for punning that would surely have delighted Shakespeare; thus, his plays require being read as well as seen.

Early in his career he declared that he wrote primarily out of a love of language and without any social objective. Also that "if you are angered by a particular piece of injustice, you can hardly do worse than write a play about it." Beneath the guise of Shakespearean verbal clowning and quibbling, his most substantial early plays, *Rosencrantz and Guildenstern Are Dead* (1966) and *Jumpers,* are concerned with the perennial philosophical enigmas—the nature of reality, the meaning of life, the existence of God. Stripped down to their basic structures, these plays alternate thesis and antithesis without proceeding to synthesis, while *Travesties* is cast in the form of a brilliant literary charade rather than a plotted play. However, in the course of time, as Christopher Bigsby points out, Stoppard began to seek space for his moral convictions to operate, the result being pieces such as *Professional Foul* and *Night and Day* (both 1978), in which he declares his allegiance to a plural political order and an open, not a closed, system of ideas. At the same time, his zest for having work in performance has found another outlet in his prolific output of translations and adaptations of foreign plays; while he has always been a rapid worker, his serious creations are few and carefully executed. Bigsby finds that Stoppard's consistent dramatic aim has been to exploit the processes whereby we create the worlds we inhabit through the language that we choose to describe them. He is the youngest of the writers discussed in these pages, and a particularly innovative one, and there seems every likelihood that he will continue to surprise and entertain his public with fresh inventions.

The *Writers and Their Work* series was founded by Laurence Brander, then director of publications at the British Council. The first editor was T. O. Beachcroft, himself a distinguished writer of short stories. His successors were the late Bonamy Dobrée, formerly Professor of English Literature at the University of Leeds; Geoffrey Bullough, Professor Emeritus of English Literature, King's College, London, and author of *The Narrative and Dramatic Sources of Shakespeare;* and since 1970 the present writer. To these founders and predecessors *British Writers* is deeply indebted for the design of the series, the planning of its scope, and the distinction of their editorship, and I personally for many years of friendship and advice, and invaluable experience generously shared.

—Ian Scott-Kilvert

Chronological Table

1904 Russo-Japanese war (1904–1905)
Construction of the Panama Canal begins
The ultraviolet lamp invented
The engineering firm of Rolls Royce founded
Chekhov's *The Cherry Orchard*
Conrad's *Nostromo*
Henry James's *The Golden Bowl*
Kipling's *Traffics and Discoveries*
Georges Rouault's *Head of a Tragic Clown*
G. M. Trevelyan's *England Under the Stuarts*
Puccini's *Madame Butterfly*
First Shaw-Granville Barker season at the Royal Court Theatre
The Abbey Theatre founded in Dublin
Deaths of Anton Chekhov, Leslie Stephen, and Antonín Dvořák
Salvador Dali born
Graham Greene born
Christopher Isherwood born

1905 Russian sailors on the battleship *Potemkin* mutiny
After riots and a general strike the czar concedes demands by the Duma for legislative powers, a wider franchise, and civil liberties
Albert Einstein publishes his first theory of relativity
The Austin Motor Company founded
Bennett's *Tales of the Five Towns*
Claude Debussy's *La mer*
E. M. Forster's *Where Angels Fear to Tread*
Richard Strauss's *Salome*
H. G. Wells's *Kipps*
Oscar Wilde's *De Profundis*
Norman Cameron born
Arthur Koestler born
Anthony Powell born
Charles Percy (C. P.) Snow born

1906 Liberals win a landslide victory in the British general election
The Trades Disputes Act legitimizes peaceful picketing in Britain
Captain Dreyfus rehabilitated in France
J. J. Thomson begins research on gamma rays
The U.S. Pure Food and Drug Act passed
Churchill's *Lord Randolph Churchill*
Galsworthy's *The Man of Property*
Kipling's *Puck of Pook's Hill*
Shaw's *The Doctor's Dilemma*
Yeats's *Poems 1899–1905*
Deaths of Pierre Curie, Paul Cézanne, Henrik Ibsen
Samuel Beckett born
John Betjeman born

1907 Exhibition of cubist paintings in Paris
Henry Adams' *The Education of Henry Adams*
Henri Bergson's *Creative Evolution*
Conrad's *The Secret Agent*
Forster's *The Longest Journey*
André Gide's *La porte étroite*
Shaw's *John Bull's Other Island* and *Major Barbara*
Synge's *The Playboy of the Western World*
Trevelyan's *Garibaldi's Defence of the Roman Republic*
Death of Edvard Grieg
Death of Francis Thompson
Wystan Hugh (W. H.) Auden born
Louis MacNeice born

CHRONOLOGICAL TABLE

1908 Herbert Asquith becomes prime minister
David Lloyd George becomes chancellor of the exchequer
William Howard Taft elected president
The Young Turks seize power in Istanbul
Henry Ford's Model T car produced
Bennett's *The Old Wives' Tale*
Pierre Bonnard's *Nude Against the Light*
Georges Braque's *House at L'Estaque*
Chesterton's *The Man Who Was Thursday*
Jacob Epstein's *Figures* erected in London
Forster's *A Room with a View*
Anatole France's *L'Ile des pingouins*
Henri Matisse's *Bonheur de Vivre*
Edward Elgar's *First Symphony*
Ford Madox Ford founds the *English Review*

1909 The Young Turks depose Sultan Abdul Hamid
The Anglo-Persian Oil Company formed
Louis Bleriot crosses the English Channel from France by monoplane
Admiral Robert Peary reaches the North Pole
Sigmund Freud lectures at Clark University (Worcester, Mass.) on psychoanalysis
Sergei Diaghilev's Ballets Russes opens in Paris
Galsworthy's *Strife*
Hardy's *Time's Laughingstocks*
Claude Monet's *Water Lilies*
Trevelyan's *Garibaldi and the Thousand*
Wells's *Tono-Bungay* first published (book form, 1909)
Deaths of George Meredith, John Millington Synge, and Algernon Charles Swinburne

910–1936 Reign of King George V

1910 The Liberals win the British general election
Marie Curie's *Treatise on Radiography*
Arthur Evans excavates Cnossus
Edouard Manet and the first post-impressionist exhibition in London
Filippo Marinetti publishes "Manifesto of the Futurist Painters"
Norman Angell's *The Great Illusion*
Bennett's *Clayhanger*
Forster's *Howards End*
Galsworthy's *Justice* and *The Silver Box*
Kipling's *Rewards and Fairies*
Rimsky-Korsakov's *Le coq d'or*
Stravinsky's *The Fire-Bird*
Vaughan Williams' *A Sea Symphony*
Wells's *The History of Mr. Polly*
Wells's *The New Machiavelli* first published (in book form, 1911)
Deaths of William James, Leo Tolstoy, Henri (Le Douanier) Rousseau, and Mark Twain

1911 Lloyd George introduces National Health Insurance Bill
Suffragette riots in Whitehall
Roald Amundsen reaches the South Pole
Bennett's *The Card*
Chagall's *Self Portrait with Seven Fingers*
Conrad's *Under Western Eyes*
D. H. Lawrence's *The White Peacock*
Katherine Mansfield's *In a German Pension*
Edward Marsh edits *Georgian Poetry*
George Moore's *Hail and Farewell* (1911–1914)
Strauss's *Der Rosenkavalier*
Stravinsky's *Petrouchka*
Trevelyan's *Garibaldi and the Making of Italy*
Mahler's *Das Lied van der Erde*
William Golding born

1912 Woodrow Wilson elected president
SS *Titanic* sinks on its maiden voyage
Five million Americans go to the movies daily; London has 400 movie theaters
Second post-impressionist exhibition in London
Bennett's and Edward Knoblock's *Milestones*
Constantin Brancusi's *Maiastra*
Wassily Kandinsky's *Black Lines*
D. H. Lawrence's *The Trespasser*
Lawrence Durrell born

	Roy Fuller born
	F. T. Prince born
	Patrick White born
1913	Second Balkan War begins
	Henry Ford pioneers factory assembly technique through conveyor belts
	Epstein's *Tomb of Oscar Wilde*
	New York Armory Show introduces modern art to the world
	Alain-Fournier's *Le Grand Meaulnes*
	Freud's *Totem and Taboo*
	D. H. Lawrence's *Sons and Lovers*
	Mann's *Death in Venice*
	Proust's *Du côté de chez Swann* (first volume of *À la recherche du temps perdu,* 1913–1922)
	Ravel's *Daphnis and Chloe*
	Edward Lowbury born
	Angus Wilson born
1914	The Panama Canal opens (formal dedication on 12 July 1920)
	Irish Home Rule Bill passed in the House of Commons
	Archduke Franz Ferdinand assassinated at Sarajevo
	World War I begins
	Battles of the Marne, Masurian Lakes, and Falkland Islands
	Joyce's *Dubliners*
	Shaw's *Pygmalion* and *Androcles and the Lion*
	Yeats's *Responsibilities*
	Wyndham Lewis publishes *Blast* magazine and *The Vorticist Manifesto*
	Henry Reed born
	Dylan Thomas born
1915	The Dardanelles campaign begins
	Britain and Germany begin naval and submarine blockades
	The *Lusitania* is sunk
	Hugo Junkers manufactures the first fighter aircraft
	Poison gas used for the first time
	First Zeppelin raid in London
	Rupert Brooke's *1914: Five Sonnets*
	Norman Douglas' *Old Calabria*
	D. W. Griffith's *The Birth of a Nation*
	Gustav Holst's *The Planets*
	D. H. Lawrence's *The Rainbow*
	Wyndham Lewis' *The Crowd*
	Somerset Maugham's *Of Human Bondage*
	Pablo Picasso's *Harlequin*
	Jean Sibelius' *Fifth Symphony*
	Deaths of Rupert Brooke, Julian Grenfell, and Charles Sorley
	George Fraser born
	Alun Lewis born
1916	Evacuation of Gallipoli and the Dardanelles
	Battles of the Somme, Jutland, and Verdun
	Britain introduces conscription
	The Easter Rebellion in Dublin
	Asquith resigns and David Lloyd George becomes prime minister
	The Sykes-Picot agreement on the partition of Turkey
	First military tanks used
	Woodrow Wilson reelected president
	Henri Barbusse's *Le feu*
	Griffith's *Intolerance*
	Joyce's *Portrait of the Artist as a Young Man*
	Jung's *Psychology of the Unconscious*
	George Moore's *The Brook Kerith*
	Edith Sitwell edits *Wheels* (1916–1921)
	Wells's *Mr. Britling Sees It Through*
	Death of Henry James
	Death of Lord Kitchener
	Gavin Ewart born
	Bernard Gutteridge born
	John Manifold born
1917	U.S. enters World War I
	Czar Nicholas II abdicates
	The Balfour Declaration on a Jewis national home in Palestine
	The Bolshevik Revolution
	Georges Clemenceau elected prim minister of France
	Lenin appointed chief commissa Trotsky appointed minister of fo eign affairs
	Conrad's *The Shadow-Line*
	Douglas' *South Wind*
	Eliot's *Prufrock and Other Observations*
	Modigliani's *Nude with Necklace*
	Sassoon's *The Old Huntsman*
	Prokofiev's *Classical Symphony*
	Yeats's *The Wild Swans at Coole*

	Death of Edward Thomas
	Death of Edgar Degas
	Anthony Burgess born
	Charles Causley born
	John Fitzgerald Kennedy born
1918	Wilson puts forward Fourteen Points for World Peace
	Central Powers and Russia sign the Treaty of Brest-Litovsk
	Execution of Czar Nicholas II and his family
	Kaiser Wilhelm II abdicates
	The Armistice signed
	Women granted the vote at age thirty in Britain
	Rupert Brooke's *Collected Poems*
	Gerard Manley Hopkins' *Poems*
	Joyce's *Exiles*
	Lewis' *Tarr*
	Sassoon's *Counter-Attack*
	Oswald Spengler's *The Decline of the West*
	Lytton Strachey's *Eminent Victorians*
	Béla Bartók's *Bluebeard's Castle*
	Elgar's *Cello Concerto*
	Charlie Chaplin's *Shoulder Arms*
	Deaths of Claude Debussy, Wilfred Owen, and Isaac Rosenberg
	Muriel Spark born
1919	The Versailles Peace Treaty signed
	J. W. Alcock and A. W. Brown make first transatlantic flight
	Ross Smith flies from London to Australia
	National Socialist party founded in Germany
	Benito Mussolini founds the Fascist party in Italy
	Sinn Fein Congress adopts declaration of independence in Dublin
	Eamon De Valera elected president of Sinn Fein party
	Communist Third International founded
	Lady Astor elected first woman Member of Parliament
	Prohibition in the U.S.
	John Maynard Keynes's *The Economic Consequences of the Peace*
	Eliot's *Poems*
	Maugham's *The Moon and Sixpence*
	Shaw's *Heartbreak House*
	The Bauhaus school of design, building, and crafts founded by Walter Gropius
	Amedeo Modigliani's *Self-Portrait*
	Death of Theodore Roosevelt
	Death of Pierre Renoir
	John Bayliss born
	Margot Fonteyn born
	Hamish Henderson born
	Edmund Hillary born
	Doris (Tayler) Lessing born
	Iris Murdoch born
	Michael Riviere born
1920	The League of Nations established
	Warren G. Harding elected president
	Senate votes against joining the League and rejects the Treaty of Versailles
	The Nineteenth Amendment gives women the right to vote
	White Russian forces of Denikin and Kolchak defeated by the Bolsheviks
	Karel Čapek's *R.U.R.*
	Galsworthy's *In Chancery* and *The Skin Game*
	Sinclair Lewis' *Main Street*
	Katherine Mansfield's *Bliss*
	Matisse's *Odalisques* (1920–1925)
	Ezra Pound's *Hugh Selwyn Mauberly*
	Paul Valéry's *Le Cimetière Marin*
	Yeats's *Michael Robartes and the Dancer*
	Keith Douglas born
	Paul Scott born
1921	Britain signs peace with Ireland
	First medium-wave radio broadcast in U.S.
	The British Broadcasting Corporation founded
	Braque's *Still Life with Guitar*
	Chaplin's *The Kid*
	Aldous Huxley's *Crome Yellow*
	Paul Klee's *The Fish*
	D. H. Lawrence's *Women in Love*
	John McTaggart's *The Nature of Existence*, vol. I (vol. II, 1927)
	George Moore's *Héloïse and Abélard*
	Eugene O'Neill's *The Emperor Jones*
	Luigi Pirandello's *Six Characters in Search of an Author*

	Shaw's *Back to Methuselah*
	Strachey's *Queen Victoria*
1922	Lloyd George's Coalition government succeeded by Bonar Law's Conservative government
	Benito Mussolini marches on Rome and forms a government
	William Cosgrave elected president of the Irish Free State
	The BBC begins broadcasting in London
	Lord Carnarvon and Howard Carter discover Tutankhamen's tomb
	The PEN club founded in London
	The *Criterion* founded with T. S. Eliot as editor
	Eliot's *The Waste Land*
	A. E. Housman's *Last Poems*
	Joyce's *Ulysses*
	D. H. Lawrence's *Aaron's Rod* and *England, My England*
	Sinclair Lewis's *Babbitt*
	O'Neill's *Anna Christie*
	Pirandello's *Henry IV*
	Edith Sitwell's *Façade*
	Virginia Woolf's *Jacob's Room*
	Yeats's *The Trembling of the Veil*
	Death of Marcel Proust
	Kingsley Amis born
	Sidney Keyes born
	Philip Larkin born
	Alan Ross born
	Vernon Scannell born
1923	The Union of Soviet Socialist Republics established
	French and Belgian troops occupy the Ruhr in consequence of Germany's failure to pay reparations
	Mustafa Kemal (Ataturk) proclaims Turkey a republic and is elected president
	Warren G. Harding dies; Calvin Coolidge becomes president
	Stanley Baldwin succeeds Bonar Law as prime minister
	Adolf Hitler's attempted coup in Munich fails
	Time magazine begins publishing
	E. N. da Costa Andrade's *The Structure of the Atom*
	Bennett's *Riceyman Steps*
	Churchill's *The World Crisis* (1923–1927)
	J. E. Flecker's *Hassan* produced
	Paul Klee's *Magic Theatre*
	Lawrence's *Kangaroo*
	Rainer Maria Rilke's *Duino Elegies* and *Sonnets to Orpheus*
	Sibelius' *Sixth Symphony*
	Picasso's *Seated Woman*
	William Walton's *Façade*
	Death of Katherine Mansfield
1924	Ramsay Macdonald forms first Labour government, loses general election, and is succeeded by Stanley Baldwin
	Calvin Coolidge elected president
	Noël Coward's *The Vortex*
	Forster's *A Passage to India*
	Mann's *The Magic Mountain*
	Shaw's *St. Joan*
	Sibelius' *Seventh Symphony*
	Deaths of Joseph Conrad, Anatole France, Franz Kafka, Giacomo Puccini, Woodrow Wilson, and Lenin
1925	Reza Khan becomes shah of Iran
	First surrealist exhibition held in Paris
	Alban Berg's *Wozzeck*
	Chaplin's *The Gold Rush*
	John Dos Passos' *Manhattan Transfer*
	Theodore Dreiser's *An American Tragedy*
	Sergei Eisenstein's *Battleship Potemkin*
	F. Scott Fitzgerald's *The Great Gatsby*
	André Gide's *Les faux monnayeurs*
	Hardy's *Human Shows and Far Phantasie*
	Huxley's *Those Barren Leaves*
	Kafka's *The Trial*
	O'Casey's *Juno and the Paycock*
	Virginia Woolf's *Mrs. Dalloway* an *The Common Reader*
	Brancusi's *Bird in Space*
	Shostakovich's *First Symphony*
	Sibelius' *Tapiola*
1926	Ford's *A Man Could Stand Up*
	Gide's *Si le grain ne meurt*
	Hemingway's *The Sun Also Rises*
	Kafka's *The Castle*
	D. H. Lawrence's *The Plumed Serpent*
	T. E. Lawrence's *Seven Pillars of Wisdo* privately circulated

Maugham's *The Casuarina Tree*
O'Casey's *The Plough and the Stars*
Puccini's *Turandot*
Death of Claude Monet
Death of Rainer Maria Rilke
John Fowles born
Peter Shaffer born

1927 General Chiang Kai-shek becomes prime minister in China
Trotsky expelled by the Communist party as a deviationist; Stalin becomes leader of the party and dictator of the USSR
Charles Lindbergh flies from New York to Paris
J. W. Dunne's *An Experiment with Time*
Freud's *Autobiography* translated into English
Alberto Giacometti's *Observing Head*
Ernest Hemingway's *Men Without Women*
Fritz Lang's *Metropolis*
Wyndham Lewis' *Time and Western Man*
F. W. Murnau's *Sunrise*
Proust's *Le temps retrouvé* posthumously published
Stravinsky's *Oedipus Rex*
Virginia Woolf's *To the Lighthouse*

1928 The Kellogg-Briand Pact, outlawing war and providing for peaceful settlement of disputes, signed in Paris by sixty-two nations, including the USSR
Herbert Hoover elected president
Women's suffrage granted at age twenty-one in Britain
Alexander Fleming discovers penicillin
Bertolt Brecht and Kurt Weill's *The Threepenny Opera*
Eisenstein's *October*
Huxley's *Point Counter Point*
Christopher Isherwood's *All the Conspirators*
D. H. Lawrence's *Lady Chatterley's Lover*
Wyndham Lewis' *The Childermass*
Matisse's *Seated Odalisque*
Munch's *Girl on a Sofa*
Shaw's *Intelligent Woman's Guide to Socialism*
Virginia Woolf's *Orlando*
Yeats's *The Tower*
Death of Thomas Hardy

1929 The Labour party wins British general election
Trotsky expelled from USSR
Museum of Modern Art opens in New York
Collapse of U.S. stock exchange begins world economic crisis
Robert Bridges's *The Testament of Beauty*
William Faulkner's *The Sound and the Fury*
Robert Graves's *Goodbye to All That*
Hemingway's *A Farewell to Arms*
Ernst Junger's *The Storm of Steel*
Hugo von Hoffmansthal's *Poems*
Henry Moore's *Reclining Figure*
J. B. Priestley's *The Good Companions*
Erich Maria Remarque's *All Quiet on the Western Front*
Shaw's *The Applecart*
R. C. Sheriff's *Journey's End*
Edith Sitwell's *Gold Coast Customs*
Thomas Wolfe's *Look Homeward, Angel*
Virginia Woolf's *A Room of One's Own*
Yeats's *The Winding Stair*
Second surrealist manifesto; Salvador Dali joins the surrealists
Epstein's *Night and Day*
Mondrian's *Composition with Yellow Blue*
Walton's *Viola Concerto*
John Osborne born

1930 Allied occupation of the Rhineland ends
Mohandas Gandhi opens civil disobedience campaign in India
The *Daily Worker,* journal of the British Communist party, begins publishing
J. W. Reppe makes artificial fabrics from an acetylene base
Auden's *Poems*
Noël Coward's *Private Lives*
Eliot's *Ash Wednesday*
Wyndham Lewis's *The Apes of God*
Maugham's *Cakes and Ale*
Ezra Pound's *XXX Cantos*
Evelyn Waugh's *Vile Bodies*
Von Sternberg's *The Blue Angel* and

Milestone's *All Quiet on the Western Front*

Deaths of Robert Bridges, Arthur Conan Doyle, and D. H. Lawrence

Ted Hughes born

Harold Pinter born

1931 The failure of the Credit Anstalt in Austria starts a financial collapse in Central Europe

Britain abandons the gold standard; the pound falls by twenty-five percent

Mutiny in the Royal Navy at Invergordon over pay cuts

Ramsay Macdonald resigns, splits the Cabinet, and is expelled by the Labour party; in the general election the National Government wins by a majority of 500 seats

The statute of Westminster defines dominion status

Ninette de Valois founds the Vic-Wells Ballet (eventually the Royal Ballet)

Chaplin's *City Lights,* René Clair's *Le Million,* and Leontine Sagan's *Mädchen in Uniform*

Coward's *Cavalcade*

Dali's *The Persistence of Memory*

O'Neill's *Mourning Becomes Electra*

Anthony Powell's *Afternoon Men*

Antoine de Saint Exupéry's *Vol de nuit*

Walton's *Belshazzar's Feast*

Virginia Woolf's *The Waves*

Death of Arnold Bennett

1932 Franklin D. Roosevelt elected president

Paul von Hindenburg elected president of Germany; Franz von Papen elected chancellor

Sir Oswald Mosley founds British Union of Fascists

The BBC takes over development of television from J. L. Baird's company

Basic English of 850 words designed as a prospective international language

The Folger Library opens in Washington, D.C.

The Shakespeare Memorial Theatre opens in Stratford upon Avon

Faulkner's *Light in August*

Huxley's *Brave New World*

F. R. Leavis' *New Bearings in English Poetry*

Boris Pasternak's *Second Birth*

Ravel's *Concerto for Left Hand*

Rouault's *Christ Mocked by Soldiers*

Waugh's *Black Mischief*

Yeats's *Words for Music Perhaps*

Death of Lady Augusta Gregory

Death of Lytton Strachey

V. S. Naipaul born

1933 Roosevelt inaugurates the New Dea

Hitler becomes chancellor of Germany

The Reichstag set on fire

Hitler suspends civil liberties an freedom of the press; German trad unions suppressed

George Balanchine and Lincoln Kirstein found the School of America Ballet

André Malraux's *La condition humaine*

Orwell's *Down and Out in Paris and Lon-don*

Gertrude Stein's *The Autobiography* *Alice B. Toklas*

Death of John Galsworthy

Death of George Moore

David Storey born

1934 The League Disarmament Conferenc ends in failure

USSR admitted to the League

Hitler becomes Führer

Civil war in Austria; Engelbert Dol fuss assassinated in attempted Na coup

Frédéric Joliot and Irene Joliot-Cur discover artificial (induced) radi activity

Beckett's *More Pricks than Kicks*

Einstein's *My Philosophy*

Fitzgerald's *Tender Is the Night*

Graves's *I, Claudius* and *Claudius the G*

Toynbee's *A Study of History* begi publication (1934–1954)

Waugh's *A Handful of Dust*

Deaths of Marie Curie, Frederi

	Delius, Edward Elgar, and Gustav Holst
	Edward Bond born
1935	Grigori Zinoviev and other Soviet leaders convicted of treason
	Stanley Baldwin becomes prime minister in National Government; National Government wins general election in Britain
	Italy invades Abyssinia
	Germany repudiates disarmament clauses of Treaty of Versailles
	Germany reintroduces compulsory military service and outlaws the Jews
	Robert Watson-Watt builds first practical radar equipment
	Karl Jaspers' *Suffering and Existence*
	Ivy Compton-Burnett's *A House and Its Head*
	Eliot's *Murder in the Cathedral*
	Barbara Hepworth's *Three Forms*
	George Gershwin's *Porgy and Bess*
	Greene's *England Made Me*
	Isherwood's *Mr. Norris Changes Trains*
	Malraux's *Le temps du mépris*
	Yeats's *Dramatis Personae*
	Klee's *Child Consecrated to Suffering*
	Benedict Nicholson's *White Relief*
	Death of T. E. Lawrence
1936	**Edward VIII accedes to the throne in January; abdicates in December**
36–1952	**Reign of George VI**
1936	German troops occupy the Rhineland
	Ninety-nine percent of German electorate vote for Nazi candidates
	The Popular Front wins general election in France; Léon Blum becomes prime minister
	The Popular Front wins general election in Spain
	Spanish Civil War begins
	Italian troops occupy Addis Ababa; Abyssinia annexed by Italy
	BBC begins television service from Alexandra Palace
	Auden's *Look, Stranger!*
	Auden and Isherwood's *The Ascent of F-6*
	A. J. Ayer's *Language, Truth and Logic*
	Chaplin's *Modern Times*
	Greene's *A Gun for Sale*
	Huxley's *Eyeless in Gaza*
	Keynes's *General Theory of Employment*
	F. R. Leavis' *Revaluation*
	Mondrian's *Composition in Red and Blue*
	Dylan Thomas' *Twenty-five Poems*
	Wells's *The Shape of Things to Come* filmed
	Deaths of A. E. Housman, Rudyard Kipling, G. K. Chesterton, Maxim Gorky, and Luigi Pirandello
1937	Trial of Karl Radek and other Soviet leaders
	Neville Chamberlain succeeds Stanley Baldwin as prime minister
	China and Japan at war
	Frank Whittle designs jet engine
	Picasso's *Guernica*
	Shostakovich's *Fifth Symphony*
	Magritte's *La reproduction interdite*
	Hemingway's *To Have and Have Not*
	Malraux's *L'Espoir*
	Orwell's *The Road to Wigan Pier*
	Priestley's *Time and the Conways*
	Woolf's *The Years*
	Deaths of J. M. Barrie, Ivor Gurney, Ramsay Macdonald, Ernest Rutherford, and Maurice Ravel
	Tom Stoppard born
1938	Trial of Nikolai Bukharin and other Soviet political leaders
	Austria occupied by German troops and declared part of the Reich
	Hitler states his determination to annex Sudetenland from Czechoslovakia
	Britain, France, Germany, and Italy sign the Munich agreement
	German troops occupy Sudetenland
	Edward Hulton founds *Picture Post*
	Beckett's *Murphy*
	Cyril Connolly's *Enemies of Promise*
	Durrell's *The Black Book*
	Faulkner's *The Unvanquished*
	Graham Greene's *Brighton Rock*
	Hindemith's *Mathis der Maler*
	Jean Renoir's *La grande illusion*
	Jean-Paul Sartre's *La nausée*
	Yeats's *New Poems*

Anthony Asquith's *Pygmalion* and Walt Disney's *Snow White*
Death of Karel Čapek
Death of Mustafa Kemal (Ataturk)

1939 German troops occupy Bohemia and Moravia; Czechoslovakia incorporated into Third Reich
Madrid surrenders to General Franco; the Spanish Civil War ends
Italy invades Albania
Spain joins Germany, Italy, and Japan in anti-Comintern Pact
Britain and France pledge support to Poland, Romania, and Greece
USSR proposes defensive alliance with Britain; British military mission visits Moscow
USSR and Germany sign nonaggression treaty, secretly providing for partition of Poland between them
Germany invades Poland; Britain, France, and Germany at war
USSR invades Finland
New York World's Fair opens
Eliot's *The Family Reunion*
Isherwood's *Good-bye to Berlin*
Joyce's *Finnegan's Wake* (1922–1939)
Koestler's *The Gladiators*
MacNeice's *Autumn Journal*
Powell's *What's Become of Waring?*
Deaths of Ford Madox Ford, Sigmund Freud, and William Butler Yeats

1940 Churchill becomes prime minister
Italy declares war on France, Britain, and Greece
General De Gaulle founds Free French Movement
The Battle of Britain and the bombing of London
Roosevelt re-elected for third term
Betjeman's *Old Lights for New Chancels*
Chaplin's *The Great Dictator*
Disney's *Fantasia*
Greene's *The Power and the Glory*
Hemingway's *For Whom the Bell Tolls*
C. P. Snow's *Strangers and Brothers* (retitled *George Passant* in 1970, when entire sequence of ten novels, published 1940–1970, was entitled *Strangers and Brothers*)

1941 German forces occupy Yugoslavia, Greece, and Crete, and invade USSR
Lend-Lease agreement between U.S. and Britain
President Roosevelt and Winston Churchill sign the Atlantic Charter
Japanese forces attack Pearl Harbor, U.S. declares war on Japan, Germany, Italy; Britain on Japan
Auden's *New Year Letter*
James Burnham's *The Managerial Revolution*
F. Scott Fitzgerald's *The Last Tycoon*
Huxley's *Grey Eminence*
Koestler's *Darkness at Noon*
Shostakovich's Seventh Symphony
Tippett's *A Child of Our Time*
Orson Welles's *Citizen Kane*
Virginia Woolf's *Between the Acts*
Deaths of Henri Bergson, James Joyce, Virginia Woolf

1942 Japanese forces capture Singapore, Hong Kong, Bataan, Manila
German forces capture Tobruk
U.S. fleet defeats the Japanese in the Coral Sea, captures Guadalcanal
Battle of El Alamein
Allied forces land in French North Africa
Atom first split at University of Chicago
William Beveridge's *Social Insurance and Allied Services*
Albert Camus's *L'Étranger*
Joyce Cary's *To Be a Pilgrim*
Edith Sitwell's *Street Songs*
Waugh's *Put Out More Flags*

1943 German forces surrender at Stalingrad
German and Italian forces surrender in North Africa
Italy surrenders to Allies and declares war on Germany
Cairo conference between Roosevelt, Churchill, Chiang Kai-shek
Teheran conference between Roosevelt, Churchill, Stalin
Durrell's *A Private Country*
Eliot's *Four Quartets*
Koestler's *Arrival and Departure*

Henry Moore's *Madonna and Child*
Sartre's *Les mouches*
Vaughan Williams' Fifth Symphony

1944 Allied forces land in Normandy and southern France
Allied forces enter Rome
Attempted assassination of Hitler fails
Liberation of Paris
U.S. forces land in Philippines
German offensive in the Ardennes halted
President Roosevelt reelected for fourth term
Education Act passed in Britain
Pay-As-You-Earn income tax introduced
Beveridge's *Full Employment in a Free Society*
Cary's *The Horse's Mouth*
Huxley's *Time Must Have a Stop*
Maugham's *The Razor's Edge*
Sartre's *Huis Clos*
Edith Sitwell's *Green Song and Other Poems*
Graham Sutherland's *Christ on the Cross*
Trevelyan's *English Social History*

1945 British and Indian forces open offensive in Burma
Yalta conference between Roosevelt, Churchill, Stalin
Mussolini executed by Italian partisans
President Roosevelt dies; succeeded by Harry S. Truman
Hitler commits suicide; German forces surrender
The Potsdam Peace Conference
The United Nations Charter ratified in San Francisco
The Labour Party wins British General Election
Atomic bombs dropped on Hiroshima and Nagasaki
Surrender of Japanese forces ends World War II
Trial of Nazi war criminals opens at Nuremberg
All-India Congress demands British withdrawal from India
De Gaulle elected president of French Provisional Government; resigns the next year
Civil war between Chiang Kai-shek and Mao-Tse-Tung begins in China
Betjeman's *New Bats in Old Belfries*
Britten's *Peter Grimes*
Koestler's *The Yogi and the Commissar*
Orwell's *Animal Farm*
Russell's *History of Western Philosophy*
Sartre's *The Age of Reason*
Edith Sitwell's *The Song of the Cold*
Waugh's *Brideshead Revisited*
Deaths of Béla Bartók, Lloyd George, Paul Valéry

1946 Bills to nationalize railways, coal mines, and the Bank of England passed in Britain
Nuremberg Trials concluded
United Nations General Assembly meets in New York as its permanent headquarters
The Arab Council inaugurated in Britain
Frederick Ashton's *Symphonic Variations*
Britten's *The Rape of Lucretia*
David Lean's *Great Expectations*
O'Neill's *The Iceman Cometh*
Roberto Rosselini's *Paisà*
Thomas' *Deaths and Entrances*
Death of H. G. Wells

1947 President Truman announces program of aid to Greece and Turkey and outlines the "Truman Doctrine"
Independence of India proclaimed; partition between India and Pakistan, and communal strife between Hindus and Muslims follows
General Marshall calls for a European recovery program
First supersonic air flight
Britain's first atomic pile at Harwell comes into operation
Edinburgh festival established
Discovery of the Dead Sea Scrolls in Palestine
Princess Elizabeth marries Philip Mountbatten, duke of Edinburgh
Auden's *Age of Anxiety*
Camus's *La peste*

Chaplin's *Monsieur Verdoux*
Priestley's *An Inspector Calls*
Sitwell's *The Shadow of Cain*
Waugh's *Scott-King's Modern Europe*

1948 Gandhi assassinated
Czech Communist Party seizes power
Pan-European movement (1948–1958) begins with the formation of the permanent Organization for European Economic Cooperation (OEEC)
Berlin airlift begins as USSR halts road and rail traffic to the city
British mandate in Palestine ends; Israeli provisional government formed
Yugoslavia expelled from Soviet bloc
Columbia Records introduces the long-playing record
Truman re-elected for second term
Greene's *The Heart of the Matter*
Huxley's *Ape and Essence*
F. R. Leavis' *The Great Tradition*
Pound's *Cantos*
Priestley's *The Linden Tree*
Waugh's *The Loved One*
White's *The Aunt's Story*
Prince Charles born

1949 North Atlantic Treaty Organization established with headquarters in Brussels
Berlin blockade lifted
German Federal Republic recognized; capital established at Bonn
Konrad Adenauer becomes German chancellor
Simone de Beauvoir's *The Second Sex*
Cary's *A Fearful Joy*
Arthur Miller's *Death of a Salesman*
Orwell's *Nineteen Eighty-four*

1950 Korean War breaks out
Nobel Prize for literature awarded to Bertrand Russell
R. H. S. Crossman's *The God That Failed*
T. S. Eliot's *The Cocktail Party*
Doris Lessing's *The Grass Is Singing*
Wyndham Lewis' *Rude Assignment*
George Orwell's *Shooting an Elephant*
Carol Reed's *The Third Man*
Dylan Thomas' *Twenty-six Poems*
Deaths of George Bernard Shaw and Jan Christiaan Smuts

1951 Guy Burgess and Donald Maclean defect from Britain to USSR
The Conservative party under Winston Churchill wins British genera
election
The Festival of Britain celebates bot the centenary of the Crystal Palac Exhibition and British postwar re covery
Electric power is produced by atomi energy at Arcon, Idaho
W. H. Auden's *Nones*
Samuel Beckett's *Molloy* and *Malon Dies*
Benjamin Britten's *Billy Budd*
Greene's *The End of the Affair*
Akira Kurosawa's *Rashomon*
Lewis' *Rotting Hill*
Anthony Powell's *A Question of U bringing* (first volume of *A Dance the Music of Time,* 1951–1975)
J. D. Salinger's *The Catcher in the Ry*
C. P. Snow's *The Masters*
Igor Stravinsky's *The Rake's Progress*
Deaths of Ernest Bevin, Herma Broch, André Gide, Constant Lar bert, and Henri Philippe Pétain

1952– Reign of Queen Elizabeth II

1952 At Eniwetok Atoll the U.S. detona the first hydrogen bomb
The European Coal and Steel Co munity comes into being
Radiocarbon dating introduced to chaeology
Michael Ventris deciphers Linear script
Dwight D. Eisenhower elected U president
Beckett's *Waiting for Godot*
Charles Chaplin's *Limelight*
Ernest Hemingway's *The Old Man the Sea*
Arthur Koestler's *Arrow in the Blue*
F. R. Leavis' *The Common Pursuit*
Lessing's *Martha Quest* (first volum *The Children of Violence,* 1952–19
Thomas' *Collected Poems*
Evelyn Waugh's *Men at Arms* (volume of *Sword of Honour,* 19 1961)
Angus Wilson's *Hemlock and After*
Deaths of Stafford Cripps, Bened

Croce, George VI, Eva Perón, and Chaim Weizmann

1953 Constitution for a European political community drafted
Georgy Malenkov succeeds Stalin
Julius and Ethel Rosenberg executed for passing U.S. secrets to the USSR
Cease-fire declared in Korea
Edmund Hillary and his Sherpa guide, Tenzing Norkay, scale Mt. Everest
Nobel Prize for literature awarded to Winston Churchill
General Mohammed Naguib proclaims Egypt a republic
Beckett's *Watt*
Joyce Cary's *Except the Lord*
Robert Graves's *Poems 1953*
Deaths of Sergey Prokofiev, Joseph Stalin, and Dylan Thomas

1954 First atomic submarine, *Nautilus*, is launched by the U.S.
Dien Bien Phu captured by the Vietminh
Geneva Conference ends French dominion over Indochina
U.S. Supreme Court declares racial segregation in schools unconstitutional
Nasser becomes president of Egypt
Nobel Prize for literature awarded to Ernest Hemingway
Kingsley Amis' *Lucky Jim*
John Betjeman's *A Few Late Chrysanthemums*
William Golding's *Lord of the Flies*
Christopher Isherwood's *The World in the Evening*
Koestler's *The Invisible Writing*
Iris Murdoch's *Under the Net*
C. P. Snow's *The New Men*
Thomas' *Under Milk Wood*
Deaths of Wilhelm Furtwängler and Henri Matisse

1955 Warsaw Pact signed
West Germany enters NATO as Allied occupation ends
The Conservative party under Anthony Eden wins British general election
Cary's *Not Honour More*
Greene's *The Quiet American*
Philip Larkin's *The Less Deceived*
F. R. Leavis' *D. H. Lawrence, Novelist*
Vladimir Nabokov's *Lolita*
Patrick White's *The Tree of Man*
Deaths of Albert Einstein, Alexander Fleming, Cordell Hull, and Thomas Mann

1956 Nasser's nationalization of the Suez Canal leads to Israeli, British, and French armed intervention
Uprising in Hungary suppressed by Soviet troops
Krushchev denounces Stalin at Twentieth Communist Party Congress
Eisenhower reelected U.S. president
Anthony Burgess' *Time for a Tiger*
Golding's *Pincher Martin*
Murdoch's *Flight from the Enchanter*
John Osborne's *Look Back in Anger*
Snow's *Homecomings*
Edmund Wilson's *Anglo-Saxon Attitudes*
Death of Alexander Korda

1957 The USSR launches the first artificial earth satellite, *Sputnik I*
Eden succeeded by Harold Macmillan
Suez Canal reopened
Eisenhower Doctrine formulated
Parliament receives the Wolfenden Report on Homosexuality and Prostitution
Nobel Prize for literature awarded to Albert Camus
Beckett's *Endgame* and *All That Fall*
Lawrence Durrell's *Justine* (first volume of *The Alexandria Quartet*, 1957–1960)
Ted Hughes's *The Hawk in the Rain*
Murdoch's *The Sandcastle*
V. S. Naipaul's *The Mystic Masseur*
Eugene O'Neill's *Long Day's Journey into Night*
Osborne's *The Entertainer*
Muriel Spark's *The Comforters*
White's *Voss*
Deaths of Joyce Cary, Wyndham Lewis, Jean Sibelius, and Arturo Toscanini

1958 European Economic Community established
Krushchev succeeds Bulganin as Soviet premier

Charles de Gaulle becomes head of France's newly constituted Fifth Republic
The United Arab Republic formed by Egypt and Syria
The U.S. sends troops into Lebanon
First U.S. satellite, *Explorer 1*, launched
Alaska becomes forty-ninth state
Nobel Prize for literature awarded to Boris Pasternak
Beckett's *Krapp's Last Tape*
John Kenneth Galbraith's *The Affluent Society*
Greene's *Our Man in Havana*
Murdoch's *The Bell*
Pasternak's *Dr. Zhivago*
Snow's *The Conscience of the Rich*
Death of Ralph Vaughan Williams

1959 Fidel Castro assumes power in Cuba
St. Lawrence Seaway opens
The European Free Trade Association founded
Hawaii becomes the fiftieth state
The Conservative party under Harold Macmillan wins British general election
Brendan Behan's *The Hostage*
Golding's *Free Fall*
Graves's *Collected Poems*
Koestler's *The Sleepwalkers*
Harold Pinter's *The Birthday Party*
Snow's *The Two Cultures and the Scientific Revolution*
Spark's *Memento Mori*
Deaths of Jacob Epstein, George Marshall, and Stanley Spencer

1960 South Africa bans the African National Congress and Pan-African Congress
The Congo achieves independence
John F. Kennedy elected U.S. president
The U.S. bathyscaphe *Trieste* descends to 35,800 feet
Publication of the unexpurgated *Lady Chatterley's Lover* permitted by court
Auden's *Hommage to Clio*
Betjeman's *Summoned by Bells*
Pinter's *The Caretaker*
Snow's *The Affair*
David Storey's *This Sporting Life*
Deaths of Aneurin Bevan, Albert Camus, Lewis Namier, and Boris Pasternak

1961 South Africa leaves the British Commonwealth
Sierra Leone and Tanganyika achieve independence
The Berlin Wall erected
The New English Bible published
Beckett's *How It Is*
Greene's *A Burnt-Out Case*
Koestler's *The Lotus and the Robot*
Murdoch's *A Severed Head*
Naipaul's *A House for Mr Biswas*
Osborne's *Luther*
Spark's *The Prime of Miss Jean Brodie*
White's *Riders in the Chariot*
Deaths of Thomas Beecham, Da Hammarskjold, and Ernest Hemingway

1962 John Glenn becomes first U.S. astro naut to orbit earth
The U.S. launches the spacecraft *Ma iner* to explore Venus
Algeria achieves independence
Cuban missile crisis ends in with drawal of Soviet missiles fro Cuba
Adolf Eichmann executed in Israel f Nazi war crimes
Second Vatican Council convened b Pope John XXIII
Nobel Prize for literature awarded John Steinbeck
Edward Albee's *Who's Afraid of Virgi Woolf?*
Beckett's *Happy Days*
Anthony Burgess' *A Clockwork Ora* and *The Wanting Seed*
Aldous Huxley's *Island*
Isherwood's *Down There on a Visit*
Lessing's *The Golden Notebook*
Nabokov's *Pale Fire*
Aleksandr Solzhenitsyn's *One Day the Life of Ivan Denisovich*
Deaths of Fritz Kreisler, Kirsten Fl stad, Eleanor Roosevelt, and Bru Walter

1963 Britain, the U.S., and the USSR sig test-ban treaty
Britain refused entry to the Europ Economic Community
The USSR puts into orbit

	first woman astronaut, Valentina Tereshkova
	Paul VI becomes pope
	President Kennedy assassinated and Lyndon Johnson assumes office
	Nobel Prize for literature awarded to George Seferis
	Britten's *War Requiem*
	John Fowles's *The Collector*
	Murdoch's *The Unicorn*
	Spark's *The Girls of Slender Means*
	Storey's *Radcliffe*
	John Updike's *The Centaur*
	Deaths of William Beveridge, Georges Braque, Jean Cocteau, Robert Frost, Aldous Huxley, and Pope John XXIII
1964	Tonkin Gulf incident leads to retaliatory strikes by U.S. aircraft against North Vietnam
	Greece and Turkey contend for control of Cyprus
	Britain grants licenses to drill for oil in the North Sea
	The Shakespeare Quatercentenary celebrated
	Lyndon Johnson elected U.S. president
	The Labour party under Harold Wilson wins British general election
	Nobel Prize for literature awarded to Jean-Paul Sartre
	Saul Bellow's *Herzog*
	Burgess' *Nothing Like the Sun*
	Golding's *The Spire*
	Isherwood's *A Single Man*
	Stanley Kubrick's *Dr. Strangelove*
	Larkin's *The Whitsun Weddings*
	Naipaul's *An Area of Darkness*
	Peter Shaffer's *The Royal Hunt of the Sun*
	Snow's *Corridors of Power*
	Deaths of Douglas MacArthur, Jawaharlal Nehru, Sean O'Casey, Cole Porter, and Edith Sitwell
1965	The first U.S. combat forces land in Vietnam
	The U.S. spacecraft *Mariner* transmits photographs of Mars
	British Petroleum Company finds oil in the North Sea
	War breaks out between India and Pakistan
	Rhodesia declares its independence
	Ontario power failure blacks out the Canadian and U.S. east coasts
	Nobel Prize for literature awarded to Mikhail Sholokhov
	Robert Lowell's *For the Union Dead*
	Norman Mailer's *An American Dream*
	Osborne's *Inadmissible Evidence*
	Pinter's *The Homecoming*
	Spark's *The Mandelbaum Gate*
	Deaths of Winston Churchill, T. S. Eliot, Somerset Maugham, Albert Schweitzer, and Adlai Stevenson
1966	The Labour party under Harold Wilson wins British general election
	The Archbishop of Canterbury visits Pope Paul VI
	Florence, Italy, severely damaged by floods
	Paris exhibition celebrates Picasso's eighty-fifth birthday
	Fowles's *The Magus*
	Greene's *The Comedians*
	Osborne's *A Patriot for Me*
	Paul Scott's *The Jewel in the Crown* (first volume of *The Raj Quartet,* 1966–1975)
	White's *The Solid Mandala*
	Deaths of Anna Akhmatova, Walt Disney, Alberto Giacometti, Wieland Wagner, and Evelyn Waugh
1967	Thurgood Marshall becomes first black U.S. Supreme Court justice
	Six-Day War pits Israel against Egypt and Syria
	Biafra's secession from Nigeria leads to civil war
	Francis Chichester completes solo circumnavigation of the globe
	Dr. Christiaan Barnard performs first heart transplant operation, in South Africa
	China explodes its first hydrogen bomb
	Golding's *The Pyramid*
	Hughes's *Wodwo*
	Isherwood's *A Meeting by the River*
	Naipaul's *The Mimic Men*
	Tom Stoppard's *Rosencrantz and Guildenstern Are Dead*
	Orson Welles's *Chimes at Midnight*
	Angus Wilson's *No Laughing Matter*

Deaths of Konrad Adenauer, Clement Attlee, Zoltán Kodály, René Magritte, André Maurois, and Siegfried Sassoon

1968 Violent student protests erupt in France and West Germany
Warsaw Pact troops occupy Czechoslovakia
Violence in Northern Ireland causes Britain to send in troops
Tet offensive by Communist forces launched against South Vietnam's cities
Theater censorship ended in Britain
Robert Kennedy and Martin Luther King, Jr., assassinated
Richard Nixon elected U.S. president
Booker Prize for fiction established
Durrell's *Tunc*
Graves's *Poems 1965–1968*
Osborne's *The Hotel in Amsterdam*
Snow's *The Sleep of Reason*
Solzhenitsyn's *The First Circle* and *Cancer Ward*
Spark's *The Public Image*
Deaths of Yury Gagarin, Upton Sinclair, and John Steinbeck

1969 Humans set foot on the moon for the first time when astronauts descend to its surface in a landing vehicle from the U.S. spacecraft *Apollo 11*
The Soviet unmanned spacecraft *Venus V* lands on Venus
Capital punishment abolished in Britain
Colonel Muammar Qaddafi seizes power in Libya
Solzhenitsyn expelled from the USSR
Nobel Prize for literature awarded to Samuel Beckett
Fowles's *The French Lieutenant's Woman*
Storey's *The Contractor*
Deaths of Ivy Compton-Burnett, Dwight D. Eisenhower, Ho Chi Minh, and Osbert Sitwell

1970 Civil war in Nigeria ends with Biafra's surrender
U.S. planes bomb Cambodia
The Conservative party under Edward Heath wins British general election
Nobel Prize for literature awarded to Aleksandr Solzhenitsyn
Durrell's *Nunquam*
Hughes's *Crow*
F. R. Leavis and Q. D. Leavis' *Dickens the Novelist*
Snow's *Last Things*
Spark's *The Driver's Seat*
Deaths of Charles de Gaulle, E. M. Forster, François Mauriac, Bertrand Russell, Antonio Salazar, and Giuseppe Ungaretti

1971 Communist China given Nationalis China's UN seat
Decimal currency introduced to Britain
Indira Gandhi becomes India's prim minister
Nobel Prize for literature awarded t Heinrich Böll
Bond's *The Pope's Wedding*
Naipaul's *In a Free State*
Pinter's *Old Times*
Spark's *Not to Disturb*
Deaths of Louis Armstrong, Nikit Krushchev, Harold Lloyd, Georg Seferis, Igor Stravinsky, and Lu chino Visconti

1972 The civil strife of "Bloody Sunda causes Northern Ireland to con under the direct rule of Westmi ster
Nixon becomes the first U.S. pres dent to visit Moscow and Beijin
The Watergate break-in precipita scandal in U.S.
Eleven Israeli athletes killed by te rorists at Munich Olympics
Nixon reelected U.S. president
Bond's *Lear*
Snow's *The Malcontents*
Stoppard's *Jumpers*
Deaths of Maurice Chevalier, Fran Chichester, Ezra Pound, Harry T man, and Edmund Wilson

1973 Britain, Ireland, and Denmark er European Economic Communit
Egypt and Syria attack Israel in Yom Kippur War

	Energy crisis in Britain reduces production to a three-day week
	Nobel Prize for literature awarded to Patrick White
	Bond's *The Sea*
	Greene's *The Honorary Consul*
	Lessing's *The Summer Before the Dark*
	Murdoch's *The Black Prince*
	Shaffer's *Equus*
	White's *The Eye of the Storm*
	Deaths of W. H. Auden, Pablo Casals, Noël Coward, Lyndon Johnson, Otto Klemperer, Pablo Neruda, and Pablo Picasso
1974	Miners strike in Britain
	Greece's military junta overthrown
	Emperor Haile Selassie of Ethiopia deposed
	President Makarios of Cyprus replaced by military coup
	Nixon resigns as U.S president and is succeeded by Gerald Ford
	Betjeman's *A Nip in the Air*
	Bond's *Bingo*
	Durrell's *Monsieur* (first volume of *The Avignon Quintet,* 1974–1985)
	Larkin's *The High Windows*
	Solzhenitsyn's *The Gulag Archipelago*
	Spark's *The Abbess of Crewe*
	Deaths of Duke Ellington, Samuel Goldwyn, Charles Lindbergh, Juan Perón, Georges Pompidou, and Vittorio de Sica
1975	The U.S. *Apollo* and Soviet *Soyuz* spacecrafts rendezvous in space
	The Helsinki Accords on human rights signed
	U.S. forces leave Vietnam
	King Juan Carlos succeeds Franco as Spain's head of state
	Nobel Prize for literature awarded to Eugenio Montale
	Deaths of Nikolay Bulganin, Chiang Kai-shek, Eamon de Valera, Francisco Franco, Haile Selassie, Dmitry Shostakovich, and P. G. Wodehouse
1976	New U.S. copyright law goes into effect
	Israeli commandos free hostages from hijacked plane at Entebbe, Uganda
	British and French SST Concordes make first regularly scheduled commercial flights
	The U.S. celebrates its bicentennial
	Jimmy Carter elected U.S. president
	Byron and Shelley manuscripts discovered in Barclay's Bank, Pall Mall
	Hughes's *Seasons' Songs*
	Koestler's *The Thirteenth Tribe*
	Scott's *Staying On*
	Spark's *The Take-over*
	White's *A Fringe of Leaves*
	Deaths of Benjamin Britten, Chou En-lai, Max Ernst, André Malraux, Mao Tse-tung, Viscount Montgomery of Alamein, and Paul Robeson
1977	Silver jubilee of Queen Elizabeth II celebrated
	Egyptian president Anwar el-Sadat visits Israel
	"Gang of Four" expelled from Chinese Communist party
	First woman ordained in the U.S. Episcopal church
	After twenty-nine years in power, Israel's Labour party is defeated by the Likud party
	Fowles's *Daniel Martin*
	Hughes's *Gaudete*
	Deaths of Anthony Eden, Maria Callas, Charles Chaplin, Robert Lowell, Vladimir Nabokov, and Leopold Stokowski
1978	Treaty between Israel and Egypt negotiated at Camp David
	Pope John Paul I dies a month after his coronation and is succeeded by Karol Cardinal Wojtyła, who takes the name John Paul II
	Former Italian premier Aldo Moro murdered by left-wing terrorists
	Nobel Prize for literature awarded to Isaac Bashevis Singer
	Greene's *The Human Factor*
	Hughes's *Cave Birds*
	Murdoch's *The Sea, The Sea*
	Deaths of Giorgio De Chirico, Aram Khachaturian, Jomo Kenyatta, F. R.

Leavis, Pope Paul VI, and Ignazio Silone

1979 The U.S. and China establish diplomatic relations
Ayatollah Khomeini takes power in Iran and his supporters hold U.S. embassy staff hostage in Teheran
Rhodesia becomes Zimbabwe
Earl Mountbatten assassinated
The U.S. hands over Canal Zone to Panama
The USSR invades Afghanistan
The Conservative party under Margaret Thatcher wins British general election
Nobel Prize for literature awarded to Odysseus Elytis
Golding's *Darkness Visible*
Hughes's *Moortown*
Lessing's *Shikasta* (first volume of *Canopus in Argos, Archives,* 1979–)
Naipaul's *A Bend in the River*
Spark's *Territorial Rights*
White's *The Twyborn Affair*

1980 Iran-Iraq war begins
Strikes in Gdansk give rise to the Solidarity movement
Mt. St. Helen's erupts in Washington State
British steelworkers strike for the first time since 1926
More than fifty nations boycott Moscow Olympics
Ronald Reagan elected U.S. president
Burgess's *Earthly Powers*
Golding's *Rites of Passage*
Shaffer's *Amadeus*
Storey's *A Prodigal Child*
Angus Wilson's *Setting the World on Fire*
Deaths of Alfred Hitchcock, Oskar Kokoschka, Henry Miller, Jean-Paul Sartre, Peter Sellers, C. P. Snow, Shah of Iran, Graham Sutherland, Marshal Tito, and Mae West

1981 Greece admitted to the European Economic Community
Iran hostage crisis ends with release of U.S. embassy staff
Twelve Labour MPs and nine peers found British Social Democratic party
Socialist party under François Mitterand wins French general election
Rupert Murdoch buys *The Times* of London
Turkish gunman wounds Pope John Paul II in assassination attempt
U.S. gunman wounds President Reagan in assassination attempt
President Sadat of Egypt assassinated
Nobel Prize for literature awarded to Elias Canetti
Spark's *Loitering with Intent*
Deaths of Samuel Barber, Pamela Hansford Johnson (Lady Snow), Q. D. Leavis, and Lote Lenya

1982 Britain drives Argentina's invasion force out of the Falkland Islands
U.S. space shuttle makes first successful trip
Yuri Andropov becomes general secretary of the Central Committee of the Soviet Communist party
Israel invades Lebanon
First artificial heart implanted at Salt Lake City hospital
Bellow's *The Dean's December*
Greene's *Monsignor Quixote*
Deaths of Louis Aragon, Leonid Brezhnev, Princess Grace of Monaco, and Arthur Rubinstein

1983 South Korean airliner with 269 aboard shot down after straying into Soviet airspace
U.S. forces invade Grenada following left-wing coup
Widespread protests erupt over placement of nuclear missiles in Europe
The £1 coin comes into circulation in Britain
Australia wins the America's Cup
Nobel Prize for literature awarded to William Golding
Hughes's *River*
Murdoch's *The Philosopher's Pupil*
Deaths of George Balanchine, Luis Buñuel, Kenneth Clark, Arthur Koestler, Joan Miró, Nikolaus

Pevsner, Ralph Richardson, William Walton, and Tennessee Williams

1984 Konstantin Chernenko becomes general secretary of the Central Committee of the Soviet Communist party
Prime Minister Indira Gandhi of India assassinated by Sikh bodyguards
Toxic gas leak at Bhopal, India, plant kills 2,000
British miners go on strike
Irish Republican Army attempts to kill Prime Minister Thatcher with bomb detonated at a Brighton hotel
World Court holds against U.S. mining of Nicaraguan harbors
Golding's *The Paper Men*
Lessing's *The Diary of Jane Somers*
Spark's *The Only Problem*
Deaths of Yuri Andropov, John Betjeman, Truman Capote, William Empson, J. B. Priestley, and Mikhail Sholokhov

List of Contributors

JOHN ATKINS. Lecturer in English Literature, University of Lodz (1970–1976). Has contributed stories, poems, and essays to a wide variety of periodicals and collections. Publications include full-length critical studies of George Orwell, Ernest Hemingway, Arthur Koestler, Aldous Huxley, Graham Greene, and J. B. Priestley; *Tomorrow Revealed*; *Six Novelists Look at Society*; *Sex in Literature* (series): *The Erotic Impulse in Literature* (vol. I), *The Classical Experience of the Sexual Impulse* (vol. II), *The Medieval Experience* (vol. III), *High Noon: The Seventeenth and Eighteenth Centuries* (vol. IV); and *British Spy Fiction.* **Arthur Koestler**.

BERNARD BERGONZI. Professor of English (1971–), Pro-Vice-Chancellor (1979–1982), University of Warwick; Visiting Professor, Stanford University (1982). Has written extensively on late-nineteenth- and twentieth-century literature, including studies of H. G. Wells, Gerard Manley Hopkins, T. S. Eliot, and the literature of World War I. Publications include *Reading the Thirties*; *The Situation of the Novel*; *The Roman Persuasion* (fiction); and *The Myth of Modernism and Twentieth Century Literature.* **Graham Greene**.

CHRISTOPHER BIGSBY. Writer and broadcaster. Professor of American History and Literature, University of East Anglia. Has published books on English and American drama, popular culture, black literature, and dada and surrealism. Publications include *Contemporary English Drama* (editor); *The Second Black Renaissance; A Critical Introduction to Twentieth Century American Drama* (3 vols.); and monographs on Edward Albee, Joe Orton, and David Mamet. **Tom Stoppard**.

ROBERT BRISSENDEN. Former Reader in English at the Australian National University, Canberra. Fellow of the Australian Academy of Humanities. Has published numerous articles on Australian, American, and English literature. Publications include *Virtue in Distress: Studies in the Novel of Sentiment from Richardson to Sade* and four volumes of poetry. **Patrick White**.

KEITH BROWN. Førsteamanuensis, University of Oslo (1965–). Has published many articles on literary topics, particularly the Elizabethan theater, the writings of Thomas Hobbes, and British fiction since World War I; and edited Hobbes Studies. **Lawrence Durrell**.

ALAN BROWNJOHN. Poet and critic. Senior Lecturer in English, Battersea College of Education and Polytechnic of the South Bank, London (1965–1979). Has published seven volumes of poetry, including *Collected Poems,* and edited three anthologies of verse. Translated (with Sandy Brownjohn) Goethe's play *Torquato Tasso.* Cholmondeley Award for Poetry (1979). **Philip Larkin**.

A. S. BYATT. Novelist, critic, and broadcaster. Lecturer (1972–1981) and Senior Lecturer (1981–1983) in English, University College, London. Associate of Newnham College, Cambridge (1977–). Member of Social Effects of Television Advisory Group—the BBC (1974–1977); Board of the Creative and Performing Arts (1985–); Committee on English (1986–). Judge for the Booker, Hawthornden, and David Higham Literary prizes. Publications include *Degrees of Freedom: The Novels of Iris Murdoch*; *Wordsworth and Coleridge in Their Time*; *Iris Murdoch*; *The Game*; *The Virgin in the Garden*; *Still Life*; *Sugar and Other Stories*; and an edition of George Eliot's *The Mill on the Floss.* **Iris Murdoch**.

CAROL DIX. Contributor to the *Guardian* and the *Sunday Times* (London) (1970–1978). Has written extensively on the arts and on women's topics fo journals in London and New York. Publications include *The Camargue*; *D. H. Lawrence and Women*; *The New Mother Syndrome*; and (as Carol Maxwell Eady) *Her Royal Destiny*. **Anthony Burgess**.

MARTIN DODSWORTH. Senior Lecturer in English, Royal Holloway and Bedford New College, University of London. Poetry critic for the *Guardian* (1970–) and editor of *English,* the journal of the English Association (1975–). Publications include *Hamlet Closely Observed* and the symposium *The Survival of Poetry: A Contemporary Survey* (editor). **Lawrence Durrell**.

KARL WATTS GRANSDEN. Reader in English and Comparative Literature, University of Warwick (1970–). Publications include *John Donne*; *Virgil's Iliad: A Study in Epic Narrative*; *The Last Picnic* (poems); and works on E. M. Forster, Graham Greene, and classical and Renaissance literary topics. **Angus Wilson**.

JEAN-JACQUES MAYOUX. Lecturer and Senior Lecturer, in French Literature, University of Liverpool (1925–1936). Professor of English Literature, University of Nancy (1936). Taught at the universities of Lyon and Nancy (1941–1943). Professor of English Literature, the Sorbonne (1951–1973). Publications include critical monographs on Herman Melville, James Joyce, and William Shakespeare; "Vivants piliers" and "Sous de vastes" (critical essays). Has contributed to many collective works of criticism, including the Beckett Colloquium in Berlin. Wrote introductions to three bilingual texts of Beckett's works. Translated Shakespeare's *The Tempest* and *As You Like It; The Poems of D. H. Lawrence;* Joseph Conrad's *Heart of Darkness, The Secret Sharer,* and *Amy Foster;* and two books on English painting. **Samuel Beckett**.

STEPHEN MEDCALF. Reader in English, School of European Studies, University of Sussex (1979–). Has written on ancient, medieval, and modern literature, especially on Vergil, G. K. Chesterton, P. G. Wodehouse, and Charles Williams. Publications include *The Later Middle Ages* (editor and contributor); a study of T. S. Eliot, *An Anatomy of Conciousness,* and a literary study of the Bible, *To All True Tastes Excelling* (both forthcoming). Contributed to the commemorative work *William Golding: The Man and His Books.* **William Golding**.

LESLIE NORRIS. Poet, critic, and short-story writer. Professor of English, Brigham Young University (1985–). Contributor to the *New Yorker* and *New Criterion.* Publications include *Walking the White Fields* (selected poems); *Sliding and Other Stories*; studies of the work of Anglo-Welsh writers, particularly Edward Thomas, Glyn Jones, Vernon Watkins, and Dylan Thomas. Winner of the David Higham Memorial Award for Fiction (1978); the Katherine Mansfield Triennial Short Story Award (1981); and the Cholmondeley Poetry Prize (1978). **Dylan Thomas**.

KEITH SAGAR. Reader in English Literature, Extramural Department, University of Manchester. Publications include *The Art of Ted Hughes*; *Ted Hughes: A Bibliography* (with Stephen Tabor); *The Art of D. H. Lawrence*; *The Life of D. H. Lawrence*; *D. H. Lawrence: Life into Art.* Editor of *The Achievement of Ted Hughes,* of several Lawrence texts, and of the final volume of the Cambridge edition of Lawrence's *Letters.* **Ted Hughes**.

PATRICK SWINDEN. Senior Lecturer in English, University of Manchester (1978–). Author of books on Shakespeare and on Victorian and modern fiction. Publications include *Unofficial Selves: Character in the Novel from Dickens to the Present Day* and *The English Novel of History and Society 1940–1980.* His most recent book is *Copleston's Rose: Some Reflections on Intention and Purpose in Literature.* **Paul Scott**.

JOHN RUSSELL TAYLOR. Former film critic (1962–1972) and now art critic, the *Times* (London) (1978–). Editor of Films and Filming (1983–). Professor, Division of Cinema, University of Southern California (1972–1978). Author of thirty-five books on the theater, cinema, and art, including bibliographies of Alfred Hitchcock, Alec Guiness, and Orson Welles, and studies of the art-nouveau book in Britain, the well-made play tradition, and the Hollywood musical. Publications also include *The Angry Theatre: A Guide to the New British Drama*; *The Second Wave: British Dramatists for the Seventies*; and *Strangers in Paradise: The Hollywood Emigres 1933–1950.* **Harold Pinter**; **Peter Shaffer**; **David Storey**.

MICHAEL THORPE. Professor of English, Mount Allison University, New Brunswick, Canada. Previously held posts at the universities of Calgary, Leiden, and Nanyang (Singapore). Visiting Professor, University of Mysore. Visiting Research Fellow, the Centre for American and Commonwealth Arts, University of Exeter. Publications include *Siegfried Sassoon: A Critical Study; Clough: The Critical Heritage; The Poetry of Edmund Blunden; Doris Lessing's Africa;* and two volumes of poetry, *By the Niger* and *Out of the Storm.* **John Fowles; Doris Lessing; V. S. Naipaul**.

SIMON TRUSSLER. Editor of *New Theatre Quarterly* (1985–). Senior Lecturer in Drama, Goldsmiths' College, University of London (1981–); Visiting Professor, University of California at Santa Barbara (1983). Theater critic of the *Tribune* (1966–1972); London theater critic for the *Drama Review* (New York) (1965–1970). Has written extensively on contemporary British theater and drama, including studies of Arden, Bond, Osborne, Pinter, Wesker, and Whiting. Editor of the Royal Shakespeare Company's *Annual Record* (1978–1985), of the series *Swan Theatre Plays* (1986–), and of the Methuen *Writers on File* series (1985–). Has also published widely in the field of theater bibliography and taxonomy and edited collections and individual texts of Jacobean and eighteenth-century plays. **Edward Bond; John Osborne**.

RUTH WHITTAKER. Tutor (part-time), University of East Anglia and the Open University. Publications include *The Faith and Fiction of Muriel Spark* and critical studies in progress on Laurence Sterne and Doris Lessing. **Muriel Spark**.

BRITISH WRITERS

GRAHAM GREENE

(1904–   )

Bernard Bergonzi

I

GRAHAM GREENE has had an exceptionally long literary career, extending over sixty years. In 1925 he published a volume of undergraduate verse. It was succeeded by more than twenty novels as well as collections of short stories, several plays, and miscellaneous books of travel writing, biography, essays, and film criticism. In 1984, when he reached his eightieth birthday, he published *Getting to Know the General,* an autobiographical work about his friendship with Omar Torrijos, sometime president of Panama. It was followed in 1985 by a literary curiosity in the shape of a short novel, *The Tenth Man,* which had been written forty years earlier as the basis for a film and then forgotten. Greene's long life as man and writer makes it more appropriate to refer to his successive careers rather than a single unified one. In Greene's and the century's eighties he looks a different kind of writer from the figure he presented in the 1950's, when critics first began to take him seriously.

Despite his work in other genres, it is as a novelist that Greene is primarily known and admired. And as a novelist he has passed through several stages: as a writer of quasi-thrillers that are cinematic in technique and melodramatic in story and atmosphere; as an explorer of tormenting religious dilemmas and extreme situations in the so-called Catholic novels that made him internationally famous after World War II; as a cool observer of political violence and ideological dramas in the Third World; and, most recently, as a fictional joker, sometimes sinister, sometimes genial. Greene's appeal is unusually wide, since he commands a large popular readership as well as being increasingly a focus of academic critical attention.

Despite the many phases of Greene's work, the task of discussing it as a totality is made easier by the persistence of an unmistakable literary personality. There are certain qualities—of sensibility, style, narrative device, forms of characterization—that mark out a Greene novel, early or late. Critics attempt to sum them up by using the shorthand term "Greeneland"; it has become a cliché, and one that Greene understandably finds irritating, though there is some evidence that he colluded with it in the past; but it is so convenient that it is hard to avoid.

Greene has always been very reticent about himself. He has produced a number of autobiographical writings that say quite a lot about his childhood and adolescence and very little about his personal life as an adult. They continually loop back to his novels, their genesis and circumstances of composition; the man is in a sense created by the writings rather than the other way around. There are certain characteristics that Greene shares with other British writers of his generation. He came from the English professional classes, his father being headmaster of a minor "public" (that is, private) school at Berkhamsted, a few miles to the north of London. Born on 2 October 1904, he was old enough to be aware of World War I but too young to fight in it; it was remembered as a shadow over his later childhood, as it was for other writers of what Samuel Hynes has called the "Auden generation." The salient personal facts about Greene that have affected his entire career as a writer can be reduced to three: he had a happy childhood followed by a bored, unhappy adolescence, when he underwent psychoanalysis; in 1926 he entered the Catholic Church on the occasion of his marriage to a Catholic; and he has lived out of England for much of his life.

Two important aspects of Greene the writer, opposed but covertly related, are the melodramatist and the joker. They combine in a bizarre form in a very late novel, *Doctor Fischer of Geneva or the Bomb Party,* but they recur throughout his work, early and late. Certain themes continually appear, like a pattern in a carpet: betrayal, duplicity, pursuit. For Greene, betrayal and childhood are closely related. His volume of essays, *The Lost Childhood* (1951), carries an epigraph from the Irish poet George Russell, who wrote as "A.E.": "In the lost boyhood of Judas/Christ was betrayed." The idea that childhood is betrayed as the shades of the adult prison-house close round is a romantic literary theme, and in *Brighton Rock* it is said of Pinkie, the teenage gangster, "hell lay around him in his infancy," in a deliberate distortion of Wordsworth's "Immortality Ode." In Greene's fiction, and particularly in his short stories, children are often betrayed—by other children, by adults, by life itself. "The Basement Room" (1935) is a poignant study of a child who unwittingly betrays his adult friend. Throughout his life Greene has been fascinated by the figure of the betrayer and of the traitor, as is apparent in his sympathetic presentation of the spy Maurice Castle in *The Human Factor,* and, in real life, in his admiration for the British spy Kim Philby, whom he had known in World War II and whom he continued to regard as a friend after his exposure and defection to the Soviet Union.

Greene's first novel, *The Man Within* (1929), is untypical of his later work insofar as it is a historical costume drama, set among Sussex smugglers at the beginning of the nineteenth century. But his major themes or obsessions are already in evidence. The central figure, Andrews, is a smuggler who is reluctantly following the trade of his swaggering, bullying father. Andrews is on the run from his comrades, whom he has betrayed to the law. He is given sanctuary by a beautiful, pure, remote young woman called Elizabeth, who persuades him to give evidence against the other smugglers in court. She is the first of the madonna types who recur in Greene's fiction; the other woman in the novel is Lucy, the mistress of the prosecuting counsel, Sir Henry Merriman. She embodies the opposed type of the whore, who also recurs, if less frequently. The contrast between madonna and whore recalls a familiar Catholic typological opposition: that of the Virgin Mary and Mary Magdalene. In Greene's case its roots are probably temperamental, reinforced by the masters of fictional romance, such as Robert Louis Stevenson and Joseph Conrad, who heavily influenced *The Man Within* and his other early novels. *The Man Within* is a little too carefully written, and its literary effects are overcalculated. As an adventure story it moves forward vigorously and the suspense is well sustained; in these ways it points to Greene's later novels of betrayal and pursuit. Its epigraph, from Sir Thomas Browne, reflects his abiding fascination with doubleness or duplicity: "There's another man within me that's angry with me." There were to be a succession of such double men in Greene's fiction: the Third Man, Our Man in Havana, the Tenth Man.

In this early novel the melodramatist is dominant, but the joker makes what looks in hindsight like a small appearance. Sir Henry Merriman bears Greene's own name—he was christened Henry Graham—and is the first of a succession of male characters called "Henry"; later ones include Henry Scobie, the tragic hero of *The Heart of the Matter,* the cuckolded civil servant Henry Miles in *The End of the Affair,* and Henry Pulling, the retired bank manager who is the narrator of *Travels with My Aunt.* Most recently, Greene's one-act play *Yes and No* invokes a dramatist called "Henry Privet." Greene has been an active practical joker in life, and he is fond of jokey self-reference in his fiction, notwithstanding his reticence about direct autobiographical revelation. Philip Stratford has written of Greene's long preoccupation with things that are green or colored green (like "Privet" in the instance just referred to) and with the proper names "Greene" or "Green"; he is also, it seems, drawn to the chromatic opposite of green, shown in the recurrence of the girls' names "Rose" and "Coral" (reinforced in *Brighton Rock* by the union of Rose and Pinkie). There is a revealing small instance of this sly playing with names in Greene's novel of 1934, *It's a Battlefield,* where a character of working-class London origins is doubly burdened in life by the possession of "brains" and the outlandish Christian name of "Conrad." When he asks his parents why he was christened so oddly, they can only say that he was called after a merchant seaman of that name who once lodged in the house and of whom they can remember nothing remarkable. As Greene himself acknowledged, *It's a Battlefield* is a novel in which the influence of Joseph Conrad, who was once a merchant seaman, is excessively strong. Other echoes and repetitions of names in Greene's fiction may be significant but remain inexplicable; why, for instance, should the principal male and female characters in both *The End of the Affair* and *The Human Factor* be called Maurice and Sarah?

Greene followed *The Man Within* with two more romantic novels, *The Name of Action* (1930) and *Rumour at Nightfall* (1931), set, respectively, in modern Germany and nineteenth-century Spain. Greene has suppressed them both and never allowed them to be reprinted. In his second volume of autobiography, *Ways of Escape* (1980), he has written: "Both books are of a badness beyond the power of criticism properly to evoke—the prose flat and stilted and in the case of *Rumour at Nightfall* pretentious (the young writer had obviously been reading again and alas! admiring Conrad's worst novel, *The Arrow of Gold*), the characterisation non-existent." *Rumour at Nightfall* is of some interest for the pattern of Greene's entire career because it provides an early example of his interest in the Hispanic world, which shows in many of his later novels.

In 1932 Greene published *Stamboul Train* (U.S. title, *Orient Express*), in which he finally hit on a subject matter and treatment that he was able successfully to develop for the rest of the 1930's. Although Greene himself has tended to dismiss his prewar novels and they are sometimes regarded by critics as no more than apprentice work, I believe them to be an important part of his literary achievement. In these books Greene wrote about the contemporary world in a striking combination of public and personal idioms. In their public dimensions they are representative of their period. Greene continually focuses on significant images of the age, particularly those of the British urban scene; as a writer of observant fictional documentary he has something in common with other novelists of his generation who emerged in the early 1930's, such as George Orwell and Christopher Isherwood. Greene was, at this stage, an intensely cinematic writer; many passages in his early novels, such as the opening paragraph of *Stamboul Train,* recall the films of the time:

> The purser took the last landing-card in his hand and watched the passengers cross the grey wet quay, over a wilderness of rails and points, round the corners of abandoned trucks. They went with coat-collars turned up and hunched shoulders; on the tables in the long coaches lamps were lit and glowed through the rain like a chain of blue beads. A giant crane swept and descended, and the clatter of the winch drowned for a moment the pervading sounds of water, water falling from the overcast sky, water washing against the sides of channel steamer and quay. It was half-past four in the afternoon.

It is worth noting that Greene was a professional film critic between 1935 and 1940, and his collected film reviews, *The Pleasure Dome* (1974), is a volume of considerable and many-faceted interest. It has much to say about the films of the 1930's and is very revealing of the myths and images of the age; it also conveys, obliquely, quite a lot about Greene's state of mind. In his distaste for the products and culture of Hollywood, we see the origins of Greene's anti-Americanism. The film reviews illuminate the novels he was writing at the time by showing his familiarity with cinematic techniques; there are places where the fiction seems to echo the film criticism, and vice versa. (I have said more about this in my book *Reading the Thirties*.) A curious incidental point about Greene's film reviews is that some of them were ghost-written by his friend, the late Kenneth Allott—poet, critic, and subsequently co-author of one of the first critical books on Greene. He had evidently absorbed Greene's style very effectively, and there is no surviving evidence to show which reviews Allott in fact wrote.

The extent to which Greene's fiction of the 1930's was directly influenced by the cinema is complicated by other factors, particularly the literary influence of Conrad, who was a strongly cinematic writer virtually before the cinema existed (passages in *The Secret Agent* are as filmlike as anything in Greene). In their "public" dimensions these novels are immersed in the popular culture of the 1930's, not only the cinema but also the thriller and the detective novel. The thriller was a natural vehicle for Greene's perennial theme of the hunted man. He was also conscious of the radio and gramophone and the resultant dissemination of dance music and popular songs. Nearly all his prewar novels contain snatches of song lyrics composed by Greene in a skillful pastiche of the sophisticated or sentimental productions of Cole Porter or Ira Gershwin (again, a topic discussed at some length in *Reading the Thirties*). Aspects of these novels anticipate what was later formulated, with reference to painting and sculpture, as "pop art," where a serious artist makes deliberate use of the artifacts of mass culture for his own aesthetic ends. It is significant that *Stamboul Train* was first published not as a novel but as an "entertainment," as were *A Gun for Sale* and *The Confidential Agent.* Greene originally made the distinction because he regarded his novels as artistically serious and his entertainments as mere pot-boilers written for money. It was, from the beginning, a rather factitious distinction; although the entertainments may be a little closer to the genres of popular fiction, they are not less well written than the novels and are just as pervaded by Greene's personal vision of life. *Brighton Rock,* which I take to be Greene's most substantial novel of the 1930's, was originally described in the first American edition as an entertainment; Greene has dropped the distinction in the collected edition of his work. During the 1970's and 1980's the generic distinctions among kinds of fiction, which may have seemed clear-cut in the 1930's, have become blurred.

In their "public" aspects Greene's prewar novels are very much of their time in their concern with social documentary, thrillers, films, and popular music. But in their "personal" aspects they are uniquely and unmistakably by Greene. This is most evident in their style, which is elaborately, sometimes extravagantly, metaphorical in a way that immediately distinguishes it from the flat, laconic, descriptive manner of contemporaries such as Orwell, Isherwood, and the early Anthony Powell. Greene's impulse toward figurative language shows itself in startling similes, in which the abstract is seen in minutely concrete terms: "Camaraderie, good nature, cheeriness fell like shutters before a plate glass window"; or, "his sympathy didn't belong, it could be peeled off his eyes like an auction ticket from an ancient flint instrument." Occasionally Greene reverses the process, presenting the concrete in terms of the abstract: "He drank the brandy down like damnation." In his autobiography Greene has deplored these rhetorical devices, blaming them on his early taste for the Metaphysical poets of the seventeenth century and their elaborate conceits. A contemporary influence may have been the fanciful similes in the poetry of W. H. Auden, whom Greene greatly admired. Sometimes, it is true, Greene's similes are too bizarre to be effective, but when they work they import a poetic dimension into the urban realism of the fiction, as K. W. Gransden has shown. In *Brighton Rock,* in particular, the similes rise to a strange surrealistic intensity that goes beyond the registration of unexpected resemblances. Consider, for instance, the description of the face of the young girl Rose when she is in a stubborn mood: "The bony and determined face stared back at her: all the fight there was in the world lay there—warships cleared for action and bombing fleets took flight between the set eyes and the stubborn mouth. It was like the map of a campaign marked with flags." The girl's features are transformed into a montage of 1930's newsreel shots. These images are both public and private and evidently had an obsessional significance for Greene, for he repeats some of them in his next novel, *The Confidential Agent:* "bombing planes took flight from between his eyes, and in his brain the mountains shook with shell-bursts." Another stylistic device to which Greene was much addicted is the tripartite list of items in apposition without conjunctions (known in classical rhetoric, as Gransden points out, as "tricolon in asyndeton"): " 'I've seen you with him,' she lied: a courtyard, a sewing wench beside the fire, the cock crowing"; "He preferred the distrust, the barbarity, the betrayals"; "the broken bridge, the torn-up track, the horror of seventy years ahead"; and "It had the furtiveness of lust, the sombreness of religion, the gaiety of stolen cigarettes."

Such things make Greene's style, in his novels of the 1930's and early 1940's, instantly recognizable and easily parodyable. Yet more is involved than a personal manner that can be idiosyncratic to the point of affectation, though there is some point to that charge. If the style is the man, then Greene's rhetorical devices may arise from something in the depths of his temperament. The essence of metaphor is to compare one thing with another; a further term is always involved, a pointing beyond the immediate fact or experience, which is why figurative devices are unusual in the fiction of realistic description. Greene's extensive use of simile seems to reflect his desire for significance, a word that includes the idea of the "sign" and denotes a pointing beyond the immediately given. Greene explores this need for significance in his essays of the 1930's and 1940's; it can, of course, be related to his Catholic beliefs, but its roots seem deeply temperamental, recalling his lifelong struggle against boredom and his need for "ways of escape," to quote the title of his second volume of autobiography.

Although *Stamboul Train* is a minor novel, it shows Greene coming to terms with the contemporary world and turning from the romance model to a fictional formula popular in the early 1930's. It is the kind of novel that brings together a cosmopolitan and heterogeneous collection of people in the arbitrary confines of a luxury hotel or international express train. (Agatha Christie's *Murder in the Calais Coach,* published a year after *Stamboul Train,* is a classically famous detective story that also uses the formula.) *Stamboul Train* was filmed, though the film version was rather overshadowed by other "train" films such as *Shanghai Express, Rome Express,* and the Russian *Turksib.* In Greene's novel a variegated group of passengers, mainly English, travel across Europe on the Orient Express to Istanbul. They include a young Jewish businessman, Carleton Myatt, who is a complex neurotic character, and a young chorus girl, Coral Musker, with whom he is briefly involved; she is one of Greene's recurring female types, innocent, waiflike, vulnerable. Others on the journey and in the story are Dr. Czinner, a Yugoslav political refugee returning to participate in a revolution in his native country, and Mabel Warren, a lesbian journalist. With the possible exception of Myatt, they are types rather than characters, and though this might suggest a deficiency in Greene's art, if one assumes him to be aspiring toward total fictional realism, it is worth recalling that he has more than once gone on record as favoring the "type" over the "fully rounded" fictional character. This may have been making a virtue of necessity, but it had some basis in his world view.

Aspects of *Stamboul Train* faintly look forward to scenes and episodes of Greene's later fiction. Dr. Czinner and his revolutionary aspirations represent a sketchy gesture toward the political contexts of the 1930's, an interest much more fully developed in Greene's fictional explorations of repression and resistance in the Third World from the 1950's onward. In *Stamboul Train* Dr. Czinner is captured at the Yugoslav frontier, and the ideological exchanges between him and his captor, the chief of police, Colonel Hartrep, anticipate later debates, notably those between the priest and the lieutenant in *The Power and the Glory.*

In his next novel, *It's a Battlefield* (1934), Greene turned to contemporary London. It is a technically complex work, and I agree with Roger Sharrock's judgment that it is Greene's most accomplished novel before *Brighton Rock* and one of the best novels of its period. The central situation of the plot is simple. A London bus driver, Jim Drover (who never appears in the action), has killed a policeman at a political demonstration and is under sentence of death for murder. There is widespread agitation for a reprieve, and suspense is generated throughout the novel by uncertainty if it will be granted. The central characters are Jim's wife, Milly; his brother, Conrad, an embittered white-collar worker (the one burdened with "brains" and an outlandish Christian name); and Milly's sister, Kay, an extrovert factory girl with a cheerfully amoral attitude toward sex. Set apart from the other characters is the Assistant Commissioner of the police, a lonely, unnamed figure who moves across the scenes of the action and whose reflections embody much of Greene's view of the world. His origin in Conrad's *The Secret Agent* is unmistakable, and the influence of this novel on Greene's is uncomfortably strong. Nevertheless, what Greene writes is more than pastiche, and he is able to adapt Conrad to his own purposes. Other influences may be the panoramic urban visions of James Joyce's *Ulysses* and Virginia Woolf's *Mrs. Dalloway.*

The strength of *It's a Battlefield* is not so much in its rather commonplace story nor in its characterization, which is still strongly typological, but in what Sharrock has called its urban poetry, with which Greene fuses the public and the personal. The camera eye moves continually over London in cinematic ranging shots and occasional close-ups. The language and presentation are pervaded by Greene's obsessional perceptions. His vision of London, and by extension of life itself, is of a battlefield, and a battlefield like that of Inkerman in the Crimean War, which was fought in mist so that groups of soldiers were isolated from each other, ignorant of the general progress of the battle. Greene's urban poetry emerges from what looks like the extremity of realism; the images of the modern city succeed each other like shots in a film, or are juxtaposed in the random fashion of a newspaper:

> The man who tears paper patterns and the male soprano were performing before the pit queues, the shutters of the shops had all gone up, the prostitutes were moving west. The feature pictures had come on the second time at the super-cinemas, and the taxi ranks were melting and re-forming. In the Café Français in Little Compton Street a man at the counter served two coffees and sold a packet of "Weights." The match factory in Battersea pounded out the last ten thousand boxes, working overtime. The cars in the Oxford Street fun-fair rattled and bounced, and the evening papers went to press for the last edition—"The Streatham Rape and Murder. Latest Developments," "Mr. MacDonald Flies to Lossiemouth," "Disarmament Conference Adjourns," "Special Service for Footballers," "Family of Insured Couple Draw £10,000. Insure Today." At each station on the Outer Circle a train stopped every two minutes.
>
> (ch. 1)

At the end of this seemingly objective survey Greene the joker reveals himself. There never has been a section of the London underground railway system called the "Outer Circle"; what is now the "Circle Line" would have been known in the 1930's as the "Inner Circle." But Dante refers to the outer circle of Hell in the *Inferno,* and this forms a recurring motif in Greene's novel. In the preceding paragraph the Assistant Commissioner, visiting a prison, thinks: "He had a dim memory that someone had once mapped hell in circles, and as the searchlight swooped and touched and passed, and the bell ceased clanging for Block C to go to their cells, he thought, 'this is only the outer circle.' "

In *It's a Battlefield* Greeneland is put on the map for the first time. It is a dismal urban wasteland, stalked by evil and betrayal; but it is also the modern world, lit up, literally or figuratively, by the glittering images of mass culture, whose fascination the author reluctantly acknowledges. The inescapable, recurring adjective for Greeneland is seedy. It has been used to excess by Greene's critics, but he employed it frequently himself in his fiction and film reviews of the 1930's. Greeneland has two aspects: if one is the modern city, the other is the jungle, the desert, the so-called savage places in remote parts of the globe. In *It's a Battlefield* the Assistant Commissioner frequently compares London with the African jungle, where he had previously served, preferring the natural to the urban jungle. Greene's own quest for significance made him feel increasingly that modern English civilization was a hollow shell and that authentic existence was more likely to be discovered in the real jungle, or some other lawless topography. Within a few years this quest was to take him to West Africa and Mexico; much further ahead lay many more visits to Africa, Indochina, and Latin America.

Greene's next novel, *England Made Me* (1935; U.S. title, *The Shipwrecked*), is one of which he has said, in *Ways of Escape,* he has "a soft spot in [his] heart for," although, as he acknowledges, this taste has not been shared by the public at large. It represents a move toward the mainstream realistic novel, involving a theme of some psychological depth and complexity, with characters rather than types at the center of the action. It is set in Stockholm, a city that Greene confesses he knew very little of at the time. The central characters are a sister and brother, Kate and Anthony Farrant. Anthony is a charming but feckless man in his thirties, an ex-public-school ne'er-do-well, a type Greene has often portrayed in fiction; Kate is the secretary and mistress of Krogh, a shady Swedish tycoon. The central human interest is the incestuous affection between Kate and Anthony, of which they themselves are not fully aware. Greene tends to be distracted from this weighty and sensitive topic by other concerns, such as his presentation of Krogh as an evil, scheming financial genius, another recurring type in the demonology of the 1930's; as Greene later acknowledged, Krogh refused to come alive as a character. This may have been because Greene had no opportunity really to get to know someone like Krogh or his milieu. On the other hand, an originally very minor figure, Minty, the inevitably seedy expatriate Anglo-Catholic journalist, became (as Greene has described) altogether too alive and commanding for the balance of the book. The most memorable things in *England Made Me* are, on the whole, marginal to the main theme, such as the character of Minty and the description of a flight made by Krogh's henchman, Fred Hall, from Amsterdam to Stockholm, which gives a vivid sense of what civil flying was like in the Europe of over fifty years ago. But in its major themes and treatment *England Made Me* sags, and Greene's attempt at a Joycean stream of consciousness is half-hearted. The Stockholm setting, too, is thin compared with the rich evocation of London in Anthony's consciousness. Notwithstanding the novel's aspiration toward straightforward realism, it reveals Greene the melodramatist. Below the realistic surface there are hints of Jacobean tragedy in the incest theme and in the surrounding gallery of villains and grotesques. In his book *British Dramatists* Greene wrote about John Webster's *Duchess of Malfi* in terms of high praise, suggesting a temperamental affinity. But the long-term effect of *England Made Me* may have been to spoil Greene's chances of receiving the Nobel Prize for Literature. Some members of the Swedish Academy may well have disliked his treatment of Sweden in this early novel.

With *A Gun for Sale* (U.S. title, *This Gun for Hire*), published in 1936 as an entertainment, Greene returned to the subject with which he was most at home. It embodies his central theme of the hunted man, drawing on the conventions of the thriller and the gangster movie. The settings are entirely English and urban, moving from London to the Midland city of Nottwich (based on Nottingham, where Greene lived as a young man). The central figure, Raven, is like a malcontent from Jacobean drama. He is a professional killer, his life has been warped by a wretched childhood, and he is physically disfigured by a harelip. At the beginning of the novel he murders a prominent European statesman who is working for peace. He is then cheated by his paymasters, who pay him in forged notes, and he has to flee from the police. Raven is a depraved creature, but he attracts the reader's reluctant sympathy. *A Gun for Sale* is pervaded by Greene's urban poetry and shows the world in cinematic gray or black. It is very conscious of its historical moment; war threatens, and a mock air raid plays a part in the plot. The sinister figure of the arms magnate, Sir Marcus Stein, who is very old and sick but still powerful—it is he who wanted the statesman murdered—is a familiar type from the demonology of the 1930's; a caricature, perhaps, but done with more conviction than Krogh in *England Made Me.*

Greene's other entertainment of the 1930's, *The Confidential Agent* (1939), has the generic qualities that its title suggests and also reflects contemporary history. The hero is another man on the run, and like some other Greene characters he has no name, being known only as D. (There may have been some influence here of Franz Kafka, who was beginning to be read in England at the time.) D. comes from an unnamed foreign country where a civil war is raging; the Spanish Civil War is clearly intended though not identified as such. D. is a scholar in normal life, now working for his government on a special mission to purchase coal. Once in England he is ruthlessly pursued by enemy agents, and his life is in danger. *The Confidential Agent* is, of course, more than just a thriller, for it raises Greene's perennial themes of trust, loyalty, and betrayal; in *Ways of Escape* he refers to the way the book enacts "the predicament of the agent with scruples, who is not trusted by his own party and who realises that his party is right not to trust him." In further reflections in *Ways of Escape,* Greene remarks on the way in which *The Confidential Agent* anticipated features of English life, such as holiday camps, which did not become familiar until much later. Closer both to history and to Greene's own art is the moment when D. listens to a radio talk on the Problem of Indochina. In 1938 there was no visible unrest in that region, but it was to preoccupy the postwar world for decades and to provide the subject of one of Greene's major novels of the 1950's, *The Quiet American.* Indeed, there is an uncanny quality of anticipation in Greene, which made him write *Our Man in Havana* before the Cuban missile crisis, *A Burnt-Out Case* before the Congo civil war, and *The Honorary Consul* before a British ambassador was kidnapped by Uruguayan revolutionaries.

Between *A Gun for Sale* and *The Confidential Agent* Greene published *Brighton Rock* (1938), which was originally conceived as an entertainment, but is, in my judgment, his most substantial and rewarding novel of the decade. It is not, indeed, a work of conventional realism, for it is a novel of multiple genres. As a thriller it is superbly tense and fast-moving. It is indeed realistic in the cinematic accuracy with which it presents Brighton low and high life, though the realism is mediated by Greene's idiosyncratic, metaphorical prose, whose stylistic devices here run to a considerable degree of baroque or surrealistic elaboration. It is also the first of his novels in which Catholic themes play any part, and so has elements of the moral or religious fable. The theme of the hunted man is announced in the arresting opening sentence: "Hale knew, before he had been in Brighton three hours, that they meant to murder him." Hale is indeed murdered, or at least dies in a way that looks like murder, and the focus shifts to his murderer, the seventeen-year-old gangster, Pinkie. Pinkie is one of Greene's most memorable figures, though he cannot be described as a conventionally realistic fictional character. He is a fuller version of the doomed and damned Raven. Pinkie is undoubtedly a creation of Greene the melodramatist; he possesses a strange combination of purity and wickedness. There is some division in Greene's implied attitude toward his character: does Pinkie's depravity arise from the wretched conditions of a slum childhood, when the sight of his parents' sexual activity made him loathe the idea of sex, or is Pinkie essentially evil—a dark angel whose nature has nothing to do with his social origins? This division or indecision in Greene is apparent in his writings of this period. He sometimes seems to adopt the left-wing political attitudes common in the Auden generation, and in some respects they have remained constant in his fiction, notably in the postwar books set in Latin America. At other times he expresses a conviction in the realities of evil and hell, and a skepticism about progress and reform, which spring from a Catholic-conservative pessimism about human nature.

Brighton Rock is a transitional work. It is the best of Greene's novels of the decade, exploring the

English urban dimension of Greeneland in a characteristic combination of the cinematic and the poetic. It can also be seen as the first of a "Catholic" sequence continued in *The Power and the Glory, The Heart of the Matter,* and *The End of the Affair.* It is worth recalling that Greene had been a Catholic for twelve years before he published *Brighton Rock,* and there had been no previous hint of his religious convictions in his fiction. However, in an essay called "Henry James: The Religious Aspect," first published in 1933, we find him praising James for a sense of supernatural evil that had affinities with Catholic beliefs and for being at least a religious novelist manqué. Greene quoted from T. S. Eliot's well-known essay on Charles Baudelaire in which Eliot asserts that man's glory can be seen in his capacity for damnation as well as his capacity for salvation; the dire thing about the modern world is that many of its inhabitants are not men enough to be damned. Greene sees James as possessing a much stronger sense of damnation than of salvation, having this much in common with Baudelaire; his own character, Pinkie, is in the same situation. Pinkie is indelibly marked by his Catholic origins, though for him Hell is a much stronger possibility than Heaven.

This early essay by Greene is more illuminating about its author than about James, and it provides clues for understanding how Catholicism works in his novels. There was much discussion in the 1940's, particularly among Catholics, of the theological implications of Greene's fiction, and to what extent his Catholicism was Augustinian or Jansenistic or actually heretical. Catholic readers tended to take sides about it; the difficulty arose from not understanding the dangers of trying to extract coherent doctrine from works of fiction. It is now evident, in the light of his later work, that Catholicism in Greene's fiction, like his picture of modern England, was mediated by a temperament that enjoyed melodramatic extremes and oppositions, and for whom the realities of hell and damnation were a way of alleviating the boredom generated by a secular bourgeois world. Greene's interest in Catholicism was dramatic rather than doctrinal; life seemed more real when people were poised between salvation and damnation. It is relevant to recall the line from Robert Browning's "Bishop Blougram's Apology," which Greene has quoted more than once and which could serve as an epigraph to all his fiction, Catholic or secular: "Our interest's on the dangerous edge of things" (1.395). Greene is a very literary writer and a very well-read one, and it was natural that he looked to literary models for his newfound sense of religious melodrama. Henry James provided one, as did Eliot's version of Baudelaire; and from Baudelaire, Greene moved on to a number of French Catholic writers, not all entirely orthodox, of the late nineteenth and twentieth centuries, whom he wrote about or alluded to or drew on for the epigraphs of his novels: Léon Bloy, Charles Péguy, Georges Bernanos, François Mauriac. Here Greene found reinforcement for his sense of life as an intense and dangerous spiritual drama. What looked to English readers like dangerous religious dilemmas and speculations arose not from theology but from a particular, exotic literary tradition.

Pinkie, it has to be repeated, is not a realistic fictional character. As I have suggested, it is easy to point to his disparate aspects: he is a psychopathically disturbed, underprivileged youth, a victim of social deprivation; he is also an embodiment of pure diabolic will and energy, harking back beyond the French Catholic literary tradition to Fyodor Dostoevsky. At the same time, he also belongs in a native tradition; like Raven, he recalls the villains of Jacobean drama, beyond whom lay the more remote figure of the Vice in the old morality plays, about which Greene has written with informed admiration. In his presentation of Pinkie, Greene reflects something of the modernist dismissal of stable, consistent literary characters. Pinkie's vitality is unmistakable, while his plausibility is more arguable; many readers will sympathize with Orwell's complaint that *Brighton Rock*

> presupposes that the most brutishly stupid person can, merely by having been brought up a Catholic, be capable of great intellectual subtlety. Pinkie, the race course gangster, is a species of satanist, while his still more limited girl friend understands and even states the difference between the categories "right and wrong" and "good and evil."
>
> (*Collected Essays, Journalism and Letters,* vol. 4, p. 500

There are times, certainly, when Pinkie loses a credibility, as when he distorts the Latin words o the Creed to "Credo in unum Satanum." The dif ference between "good and evil" and "right an wrong" to which Orwell refers is central to th literary-theological frame of reference withi which Greene was working. It presupposes an absolute opposition between the divine and the human, or between grace and nature. Good and evil are God-given absolutes, whereas right and wrong are merely humanistic substitutes for these transcendental values. In *Brighton Rock* Rose and Pinkie understand the former because of the superior knowledge that their Catholic upbringing has given them, whereas the cheerful, promiscuous Ida Arnold, full of sentimental decencies and with a heart of gold, understands only the latter. Ida's values seem to be dismissed in the novel, yet it is she who triumphs in the end, when she pursues Pinkie to a horrible death, "doubled up in appalling agony: it was as if the flames had literally got him." In terms of later, more humanistic developments in Catholic theology, the opposition between the two sets of values has no real foundation; "right and wrong" represent a real if imperfect apprehension of "good and evil." *Brighton Rock* cannot be satisfactorily read for its doctrine or as a realistic novel; if it works—and this author thinks it does—it is as a kind of poem.

II

THE 1930's were a busy decade for Greene. As well as the nine novels he published between 1929 and 1939, he wrote a collection of short stories, along with critical essays, book reviews, and film reviews, many of them preserved in his *Collected Essays* (1969) and *The Pleasure Dome.* A curiosity, showing the breadth of his interests, is a biography of the Restoration poet Lord Rochester, which was written in 1934 but remained unpublished until 1974. More significantly, there are Greene's travel books *Journey Without Maps* (1936) and *The Lawless Roads* (1939; U.S. title, *Another Mexico*) about his visits to, respectively, Liberia and Mexico. The travel book was a popular form of the period, when authors would obtain publishers' advances to write accounts of faraway places. Greene, however, was more than a detached recorder of the exotic splendors of nature or the oddities of native life. He believed, like the Assistant Commissioner in *It's a Battlefield,* that authentic existence was more likely to be found in supposedly savage places than in the medium of modern civilization. These travel books contain some of his most deeply personal writing. In West Africa Greene experienced much discomfort and some danger, which he conveys vividly, though whatever he saw and felt is colored by his obsessive consciousness. Greene claimed that he loathed West Africa, but there is an undercurrent of affection, renewed during World War II when he was an intelligence officer in Sierra Leone. In *Journey Without Maps* Greene presents himself as though he were a solitary traveler, apart from his African servants and bearers. In fact, he was accompanied by his cousin Barbara Greene, who later published her own account of the journey. When he visited Mexico, Greene was concerned with spiritual as well as physical extremity, for the immediate purpose of his journey was to investigate the fierce persecution of the Catholic Church by an antireligious government. Greene was fascinated as well as repelled by the harshness of the landscape and the intensities of human deprivation and suffering that he found in Mexico. The immediate result of this visit was the novel that many readers regard as his best, *The Power and the Glory* (1940; U.S. title, *The Labyrinthine Ways*). By the end of the 1930's Greeneland was moving away from urban England to new locations in Africa and Latin America.

The Power and the Glory is the most Catholic of Greene's novels and the most accessible of his so-called Catholic novels. The abiding themes of his fiction are very apparent: pursuit, suffering, betrayal, the clash of innocence and experience. *The Power and the Glory* is also a study of sanctity and failure, seeing the two as intimately related. Its central figure, the "whiskey priest," is a more psychologically complex character than anyone in Greene's earlier novels; to this extent *The Power and the Glory* is closer to traditional realistic fiction. But it still has elements of the morality play, that early dramatic form so admired by Greene, particularly in the typological opposition of the priest and the atheistic police lieutenant. The priest has depth and arouses sympathy, but he is never named, like the duchess in Greene's favorite Jacobean play, *The Duchess of Malfi.* In the eyes of the world and the conventionally pious, he seems unworthy, an almost complete failure. He is an alcoholic who has abandoned much of his priestly practice, and he has fathered a child. Nevertheless, in a part of Mexico where the persecution of religion is fiercest and where the penalty for being a priest is death, he persists in trying, in secret, to say mass and bring the sacraments to the people. He is the archetypal man on the run, partly inspired by the Jesuit missionaries in Elizabethan England who were also trying to carry out their priestly functions while being hunted by the agents of the state, with a price on their heads. The broad appeal of such a situation has made the book popular among those who do not share Greene's religious world view. As John Spurling has written: "For non-Catholic readers it is precisely the personal, dogged, earthbound nature of the priest's faith, the fact that the religious sense is not objectified in anything so out-of-the way as even 'a presence above a croquet lawn' [the reference is to an account, in *The Lawless Roads,* of a religious experience in childhood], which makes the book credible and sympathetic" (*Graham Greene,* p. 36).

The Power and the Glory has much in common with Greene's earlier novels, particularly the restless, ranging cinematic eye and the metaphorical prose. But the Mexican setting is new and strange, though it seems as much a projection from within the author's consciousness as the impact of an objective, alien reality. The priest and the lieutenant, the hunted and the hunter, are the central figures, though there are many lesser ones, some of them significant Greenian types. There is the young girl, Coral, innocent but clear-sighted, the child of an English expatriate family, who shelters the priest when he is on the run; in contrast to her is the priest's daughter, Brigitta, prematurely corrupted by the world. There are the upright German-American couple, the Lehrs, whose Protestant innocence or ignorance is contrasted with Catholic understanding; they are an early embodiment in Greene's fiction of his conviction that Americans do not know enough about life and that this ignorance can be harmful. The most vicious character in the book is another man on the run, the American gangster Calver. At the end of the novel the priest, having crossed the border to safety in a state where Catholicism is tolerated and not actively persecuted, deliberately goes back to the dying Calver, who he has been told is a Catholic and wants a priest. Calver dies impenitent and the priest is finally captured by his pursuer, the lieutenant of police, to face a death sentence.

The "border" (Browning's "the dangerous edge of things") is a central concept in Greene's literary imagination. He reflects on it at some length in *The Lawless Roads* as he describes crossing the frontier, metaphorical as well as literal, between the United States and Mexico. As a boy Greene had been in the unsettling and anomalous position of attending as a weekly boarder the school where his father was headmaster, but returning to the family home in the same building for weekends; this meant passing through a green baize door from the cold institutionalized severity and minor cruelties of the school to the warm and happy environment of home. Such divisions in experience continued to fascinate him, and they ramify in his fiction.

The Power and the Glory deserves its high reputation, and there are some memorable scenes in it, one of the finest occurring when the priest, arrested on the minor charge of possessing liquor and not yet identified as a priest, spends a night in a crowded prison cell full of assorted human types. Yet there is a certain weakness in the novel in that it is too diagrammatic, notably in the opposition between lieutenant and priest, atheist and believer, dedicated respectively to progress and salvation. Greene tries to be fair to the lieutenant, who is a good man in humanistic terms but altogether too schematic and two-dimensional. *The Power and the Glory* is an implicitly conservative book ideologically, in that it accepts the poverty of the Mexican Indians as a fact of nature and even a positive aid to their ultimate salvation; in later novels with a Latin American setting, such as *The Comedians* and *The Honorary Consul,* Greene implies that revolutionary struggle for human betterment is right and unavoidable. In *The Power and the Glory* the drama remains wholly individual. It is a moving demonstration of how a sinner can be a saint and how spiritual strength can arise from physical weakness, but it is still a little too much of a demonstration.

The Ministry of Fear (1943) is the last of Greene's entertainments, and it is a more obscure and confusing book than its predecessors, partly, perhaps because its central character's mind is supposed t be out of focus. Arthur Rowe has been acquitted o the mercy killing of his sick wife, but he lives wit the guilt of this action. It is wartime and his memory has been affected by the explosion of a bom He gets inadvertently caught up with a Nazi sp ring and is accused of a murder he did not commi In *A Gun for Sale* and *The Confidential Agent* war ha been a threat in the background; in *The Ministry Fear* it is a present reality. A strong element of th novel is its vivid evocation of the bombing of Lon don. (Greene set down his experience of that tim in the brief journal "London 1940–41" in *Ways of Escape.*) In a more subjective way the novel reflects Greene's perennial interest in dreams and the importance of childhood experience; a green baize door appears as a physical entity. *The Ministry of Fear* remains a minor part of Greene's oeuvre, written during his period in West Africa on secret-service work. He went there late in 1941 and during the voyage wrote a short book, *British Dramatists* (1942) —in fact an illustrated, bound pamphlet for a series called Britain in Pictures. It is of some interest in obliquely illustrating Greene's attitudes of the early 1940's to life as well as to literature. He writes of his admiration for *Everyman* and *The Duchess of Malfi.* He says that William Shakespeare's great tragic figures are as much the embodiment of qualities and passions in the Morality tradition as satisfying "characters": "Here is the watershed between the morality and the play of character: the tension between the two is perfectly kept: there is dialectical perfection. After Shakespeare, character —which was to have its dramatic triumphs—won a too-costly victory." It is perhaps worth noting that when Pinkie, toward the end of his desperate career in *Brighton Rock,* says, "It's no good stopping now. We got to go on . . . ," he is in effect paraphrasing Macbeth's words: "I am in blood/Stepp'd in so far that, should I wade no more,/Returning were as tedious as go o'er" (*Macbeth,* III.4). Greene continued to be suspicious of character as an end in itself, mainly, it seems, because it lacks the transcendental significance given by a religious view of life; a few years later he applied a similar argument to fiction, saying that with the death of Henry James the religious sense was lost to the English novel and that "the characters of such distinguished writers as Mrs. Virginia Woolf and Mr. E. M. Forster wandered like cardboard symbols through a world that was paper-thin" ("François Mauriac," *Collected Essays*). This was the aesthetic that sustained Greene in his "Catholic" phase.

In West Africa he found himself, if not at home, at least in familiar territory, where the wild inner landscape of his imagination acquired a tangible form. Greene has written of it in *Ways of Escape*: "Greeneland perhaps: I can only say it is the land in which I have passed much of my life." In Sierra Leone Greene absorbed the experience of place and atmosphere that was to appear, several years later, in his next novel, *The Heart of the Matter.* His work for the secret service also gave him an understanding of the stratagems and techniques of intelligence work that he was to treat farcically in *Our Man in Havana* and seriously in *The Human Factor.*

Greene returned to England in 1944 with the pattern of his life radically changed. For many years he had been a busy, London-based man of letters working as a novelist, critic, and reviewer. Picking up the threads of life again, he found himself working for the cinema as a scriptwriter; curiously, when Greene began writing for the films his prose became less cinematic. One of the first products of this new phase of Greene's life had a strange history. In 1944 he wrote, in the form of a novella, the outline for a film set in France under the German occupation. This material was never used, and for forty years it lay forgotten in the archives of a film company. In 1985, after its discovery, it was published as *The Tenth Man,* with an introduction by Greene. *The Tenth Man* is a good vintage Greene narrative with the familiar themes of betrayal and pursuit and deception. A number of hostages in a prison are ordered to be shot by the Nazis. One of them, a wealthy lawyer, persuades another prisoner to take his place, in exchange for his country house and all his wealth. This man agrees, and before he is shot makes a will leaving everything to his mother and sister. After his release from prison the lawyer, now penniless, makes his way to what was once his ancestral home and meets the dead man's sister. *The Tenth Man* is a taut and powerful tale, with the qualities of a legend or fable; it makes good use of the traditional folklore motif of the doppelgänger, when a stranger turns up claiming to be the real survivor. In his introduction Greene records his reaction to the rediscovered story: "What surprised and aggravated me most of all was that I found this forgotten story very readable—indeed I prefer it in many ways to *The Third Man.*" I am inclined to agree with Greene: *The Tenth Man* is more substantial than *The Third Man,* though that is his most famous work of fiction written for the cinema. Inevitably one's reading of *The Third Man* is affected by the stark images of Carol Reed's famous film set in the ruins of postwar Vienna, and by Orson Welles's memorable performance as Harry Lime, the last of Greene's quasi-Jacobean melodramatic villains.

After the war Greene's literary production proceeded at a slower pace than in the 1930's, and *The Heart of the Matter* did not appear until 1948. This is the most notorious of his Catholic novels; it is at the same time far more of a conventional novel than *Brighton Rock* or *The Power and the Glory.* Its central figure, Major Scobie, is more of a traditional fictional character, less of a type than the whiskey priest or Pinkie. Major Scobie is a good but flawed man, like a traditional tragic hero, and *The Heart of the Matter* has something of the largeness of scope and forward drive of a classical tragedy. Its story is too complicated to be easily summarized; what one most remembers about the book is not the plot or Scobie's torturing dilemmas but its setting and atmosphere. It is set in West Africa during World War II, and Greene achieves a fine distillation of his memories of that time and place, mixed with elements taken from his visit to Liberia in 1934. It is the familiarly exotic Greeneland but more richly rendered, in the intensities of heat, the rats and cockroaches, and the prevailing sense of physical and moral corruption. Scobie is a middle-aged Catholic police officer, a man of celebrated rectitude who is a fuller version of the Assistant Commissioner in *It's a Battlefield.* Yet Scobie's life is a mess; he no longer loves his ailing, neurotic, intellectually pretentious wife; but he pities her, and pity, the novel implies, is a dangerous virtue. Greene's mistrust of pity was first apparent in *The Ministry of Fear;* it is contrasted with the more profound virtue of compassion, though the difference is not altogether easy to grasp. But pity undoubtedly leads to Scobie's undoing, as he moves on to adultery and compliance in corruption—even, perhaps, in murder—and then to receiving Communion in a state of mortal sin, and on to the ultimate and technically unforgivable sin of suicide. If *The Heart of the Matter* is a tragedy, it is also a Christian tragedy, a form that some critics have said cannot exist; Scobie moves inexorably on, not merely to temporal death or disaster, but to damnation. Whether Scobie is actually damned is a topic that has attracted much discussion among Catholic readers. Among non-Catholics the argument has tended to be about the contradictions within Scobie: is he a self-deceiving neurotic, or is he a genuinely good man for whom everything goes wrong, and who is tragically trapped in a course of action from which in human terms there is no escape? It is not surprising that critics have interpreted him in quite different ways. He is a remarkably humble man, almost to the point of lacking any sense of self-worth; but he also, and perhaps for the same reason, can seem strangely arrogant, particularly at the end of his sad life, when, from pitying his wife and his mistress, he goes on to pity God.

The Heart of the Matter lacks the broad human appeal of *The Power and the Glory* despite its greater psychological depth. In the perspective of Greene's later work the novel has a new emphasis. It still reflects the French literary Catholic tradition, as in its invocation in an epigraph of Péguy's claim that the sinner himself is at the heart of Christianity, and in placing the possibility of damnation as the climax of the story. Yet in its presentation of Scobie it shows that Greene was more sympathetic to the humanistic ideal of character than he had once been. And though a theological frame of reference is still explicit, there is also a sense that it is being tested to destruction.

Greene's next novel, *The End of the Affair* (1951), still looked very Catholic, with a paradoxical epigraph from the melodramatic French Catholic novelist Léon Bloy: "Man has places in his heart which do not yet exist, and into them enters suffering, in order that they may have existence." God is more overtly a character than in *The Heart of the Matter,* even to the point of intervening in the action; there are suggestions of actual miracles, which Greene had never approached in his earlier Catholi fiction. At the same time, it is a different kind o novel from anything he had previously written formally and thematically. It is a first-person narrative told by Maurice Bendrix, who is a novelist an an unbeliever, and the essence of his story is ho he lost his lover, Sarah Miles, the wife of a civ servant, to God, whom he ultimately acknowl edges as a rival and a more powerful maker plots. Bendrix is in the fullest sense a comple character, revealing himself as his narrative un folds as a real and understandable if not very lik able man. In the skillful development of Bendrix account of himself, Greene is evidently indebted Ford Madox Ford's *The Good Soldier,* a novel greatly admires. *The End of the Affair* treats tim fluidly, but most of it takes place toward the e of the war when London was under attack fro flying bombs, and in the early months of pea The presentation of London is more direct a prosaic than in Greene's fiction of the 1930's; t metaphorical urban poetry and the cinema effects have now gone. Henceforth, as Roger Sh rock has shown, Greene's prose is soberly aphor tic rather than poetic. Bendrix is a new type in Greene's fiction, though one that is to become familiar. He is an isolated figure like Pinkie and the whiskey priest and Scobie, but he is not a Catholic, and he does not exist in their spiritually problematic dimension. Rather, he looks forward to the lonely, cynical, sometimes embittered observers of the human scene who are to provide the central consciousness of Greene's novels from the 1950's onward: Fowler in *The Quiet American,* Query in *A Burnt-Out Case,* Brown in *The Comedians.* Bendrix is a man of stronger passions than them, however, and his narrative is full of intensities of feeling; David Lodge has remarked on the frequency with which the words "love" and "hate" recur in the book.

Sexual love is at the heart of the action in a way that is new in Greene's fiction, and his central female character, Sarah, is a Magdalene-like figure who moves from sin to sanctity, from human love to divine love. It is her capacity for the former, it is implied, that impels her to seek the latter. She dies of pneumonia, and after her death strange things happen to people she had been involved with: a small boy instantly recovers from a grave illness, and an atheist preacher who had been in love with her is suddenly and inexplicably cured of a disfiguring birthmark. These events may, of course, be medical improbabilities, not impossibilities; or they may be what the faithful regard as miracles, works wrought by the intercession of Sarah, now a saint in heaven. Such things still mark *The End of the Affair* as a Catholic novel, disconcertingly so for some humanist readers, just as the emphasis on sex disturbs some of Greene's devout Catholic readers. Yet the emphasis on salvation rather than damnation is a new note, and there is no longer an absolute opposition between belief and unbelief. Maurice Bendrix ends the novel still an unbeliever, but his last words form a kind of bleak prayer: "O God, You've done enough, You've robbed me of enough, I'm too tired and old to learn to love, leave me alone for ever." For several years Greene's fictional practice and his personal aesthetic had been predicated on an absolute opposition between the religious and the human orders. In *The End of the Affair* the two orders have become inextricably mixed, with the love of man leading potentially to the love of God. This short, austere work remains one of Greene's most impressive achievements in fiction.

III

WITH *The End of the Affair* Greene's Catholic fiction came to an end, though he pursued some of its characteristic themes—adultery, loss of faith, suicide—in his first two plays, *The Living Room* (1953) and *The Potting Shed* (1957). Ten years after *The End of the Affair* Greene did indeed publish another novel concerned with Catholic questions, *A Burnt-Out Case,* though its treatment of them is very different from the earlier novels that had made him famous as a Catholic novelist, a description he always rejected, preferring to call himself a Catholic who wrote novels. The heavily Catholic phase of his fiction lasted no more than thirteen years, from 1938 to 1951. *The Quiet American,* which came out in 1955, opened a new phase that has, in effect, lasted for thirty years. Henceforth, Greene appeared as a writer more concerned with politics than with religion, setting his fiction in what we conventionally call the Third World: Indochina at a time when the French were still the imperial power, in *The Quiet American;* and different parts of Latin America in *Our Man in Havana, The Comedians, Travels with My Aunt, The Honorary Consul,* and *Getting to Know the General,* which emerged as a memoir instead of the novel that Greene wanted to write but was unable to. These parts of the world are still recognizably Greeneland, but the picture of them is significantly different from its earlier manifestations, whether the London of the 1930's or the Mexico of *The Power and the Glory* and the West Africa of *The Heart of the Matter.* Greene's vision of those places was obsessional and haunted, rendered with elaborate rhetoric and metaphor. In his postwar books he observes the world with the sharp but weary eye of the practiced traveler or the cynical reporter, like the journalist Fowler in *The Quiet American.* And the prose is correspondingly cooler and flatter. Greene himself took on a number of assignments as a foreign correspondent during the 1950's, in Indochina, where he gathered the material for *The Quiet American,* and in Kenya, during the Mau-Mau insurrection. The political sympathies implied in these novels are on the side of popular movements of liberation and against imperialism, usually American. To some extent they show a continuity with one aspect of Greene's writing of the 1930's: the intermittently left-wing sympathies that made Orwell think that Greene might be the first Catholic fellow traveler of the Communists. On the other hand the spiritual quietism with which Greene regards the poverty and deprivation of the Mexican Indians in *The Power and the Glory* has been replaced by an activist spirit of social justice (in some measure paralleling developments in official Catholic attitudes).

The Quiet American and Greene's next novel, *Our Man in Havana,* both have memorable titles that have generated a variety of journalistic clichés ("the something American" or "our man in . . ."). *The Quiet American* has things in common with *The End of the Affair;* like the earlier novel it is formally tight and carefully planned, sober in tone and language; and its central consciousness, Harry Fowler, has something of Maurice Bendrix's sour view of life. But he lacks Bendrix's passionate intensities; indeed, for much of the novel he shows little capacity for real feelings of any kind, and God is absent from the action. As a historical text, *The Quiet American* vividly documents the desperate attempt by the French in the 1950's to maintain their colonial rule in Indochina, and it anticipates the many bitter years that lay ahead when the Americans replaced the French and Indochina became known as Vietnam. The English journalist Harry Fowler is, at first, cynically indifferent to the fortunes of either side. In some respects, he recalls a stock Hollywood type, the tough journalist—a Bogart figure, perhaps—who is concerned only about doing a good professional job without sentiment getting in the way. But Harry Fowler's life is complicated by the young American secret agent, Alden Pyle. He is for Greene an embodiment of a kind of American innocence that he believes to be dangerous and ultimately destructive. In the novel Pyle is working to set up a third force between the French and Communists, and his endeavors end in death and destruction. Fowler is shaken from his detachment and is instrumental in helping to eliminate Pyle.

Schematically, the novel is polarized in a Jamesian way between the European experience of Fowler and the American innocence of Pyle, and there is no doubt that Greene favors the former. However much of a realist and reporter he appears to be, he remains a very literary writer whose early immersion in Henry James has colored his later apprehensions of America. In *The Quiet American* Greene's anti-Americanism becomes explicit, although it had been anticipated by his presentation of the Lehrs in *The Power and the Glory,* the kindly but stupid couple who are too innocent or too ignorant to have any real understanding of Mexico or Catholicism. This attitude is an understandable irritant and stumbling block for American readers of Greene, but it is worth unraveling its causes and constituents. Politically, Greene's anti-Americanism is directed against American imperialism, particularly in Latin America. But in Greene's case this position is the product of more than political radicalism. His attitudes originated in the 1930's and were apparent in his days as a film critic, when he continually expressed scorn and derision for the products of Hollywood and the cultural attitudes that underlay them. One aspect, at least, of Greene's anti-Americanism is rooted in the European conservative's distaste for American mass culture. There is also a purely personal consideration. Because Greene was for a very short time a member of the Communist party as an undergraduate, he was for several years refused entry to the United States or was permitted only a restricted entry visa. This petty restriction was eventually revoked, but Greene has never forgiven it, and the joker in him loses no opportunity to embarrass official America, as he shows in *Getting to Know the General.*

However critical Greene is of official American attitudes, he can be equally scathing and satirical about the British establishment. This is very evident in his next novel, *Our Man in Havana* (1958) which represented a move by Greene into sardoni comedy. Mr. Wormold, the humble representativ in Havana of a vacuum-cleaner company, is casually recruited into the British secret service. Havin nothing in particular to report, he invents fictiona stories of ever-increasing ingenuity, culminating i the discovery of alleged rocket installations in th mountains of the Cuban interior. The supposedl authenticating photographs are in fact of parts o a vacuum cleaner. Greene is here interestingly anticipating the Cuban missile crisis of 1962, albeit i a farcical way. *Our Man in Havana* is set in the las days of the Batista regime, and although the Cuba revolution looms vaguely in the background, the is no hint of the advent of Fidel Castro, which too place a few months after the book was publishe and of his transforming effect on the Western hem isphere. Still, Greene was not trying to write a ser ous political novel of the kind he later produced i *The Comedians* and *The Honorary Consul.* What he d produce is a highly entertaining and readable farce that mocks the kind of secret-service operations with which he had become familiar in West Africa during World War II.

Catholic themes treated in a quite new way reappear in *A Burnt-Out Case* (1961). It was foreshadowed by a short story called "A Visit to Morin," published in 1957, in which a young Englishman on holiday in France visits a distinguished elderly French Catholic writer whose books he knows and admires. He discovers that this man, Morin, is no longer a Catholic; at least he has lost his overt belief in Catholicism, though in some unexplained, paradoxical way faith remains. This story might be seen as indicating a crisis in Greene's own relationship to the Catholic Church and as marking a farewell to the French Catholic tradition of Bloy, Bernanos, and Mauriac that had inspired his own earlier Catholic novels. Morin is a fictional character, of course, not a persona for Greene; but it is worth noting that the distinction between belief, seen as a matter of conscious adherence to doctrine, and faith, as a deeper stratum of commitment, is acknowledged by Greene in his conversations with Marie-Françoise Allain, in the latter's book *The Other Man.* The central figure of *A Burnt-Out Case,* Querry, is another of Greene's new-style weary, cynical protagonists; he is an eminent Catholic architect, famous for his churches and cathedrals, who has lost his faith and retreated to a leper colony, in the depths of what was then still the Belgian Congo, in order to get away from his admirers and recover his peace of mind. It would be too simple to assume that the famous Catholic architect necessarily equals the famous Catholic novelist, but there are elements in Querry's rather thin and schematic story that point in that direction; both the character and author have received similar acclamations, even to the point of having their pictures on the cover of *Time.*

On the face of it, *A Burnt-Out Case* repudiates the values of Greene's earlier Catholic novels, and some Catholic readers were disconcerted by it, such as his friend Evelyn Waugh, who took it as indicating an actual loss of faith on Greene's part. In a subsequent interview Greene briskly disposed of Waugh's objection to the book in a slightly disingenuous fashion: "I hadn't lost faith, my character Querry lost *his* faith. Nothing to do with me." It is certainly true that *A Burnt-Out Case* is pervaded by a much more humanistic kind of Catholicism than one finds in Greene's previous novels or their French antecedents, which are so conscious of the division between nature and grace. Querry argues with the Father Superior of the leper settlement—Greene's taste for debates in fiction is one thing carried over from the earlier phase—about the separation between religious and human virtues. Querry, though no longer a believing Catholic, still thinks in the old categories, though he sees them from outside: "You try to draw everything into the net of your faith, father, but you can't steal all the virtues. Gentleness isn't Christian, self-sacrifice isn't Christian, charity isn't, remorse isn't." But the Father Superior asserts the exact opposite; preaching to his flock he tells them that when they love or are merciful, it is Jesus who does these things in them. This reflects later developments in Catholic theology, which stress that all good things come from God, that nature and grace are interdependent, and that there is a virtual and implicit Christianity as well as a doctrinally informed and committed Christianity. As ideas these are interesting and congenial, but they do not make *A Burnt-Out Case* a particularly convincing work of fiction; it seems a much thinner work than the antihumanistic *Brighton Rock.*

Five years later Greene published what is undoubtedly one of his finest novels, *The Comedians* (1966), set in the francophone black republic of Haiti under the odious dictatorship of François "Papa Doc" Duvalier. Haiti as Greene describes it is appallingly cruel and corrupt, an extreme and peculiar region of Greeneland. At the same time, the novel is good-humored in a way new in Greene's fiction; Greene as joker is present in the way the three main characters are given the most common surnames in English: Brown, Smith, and Jones. Brown is the central consciousness, a world-weary, cynical observer in the mold of Fowler and Querry, but he has more of a sense of humor, and he shares the action with other protagonists of a different temperament. Roger Sharrock has written well of the fresh direction Greene took in *The Comedians,* and his words are worth quoting at some length:

> Yet there is a difference in *The Comedians,* and the difference marks a decisive change in tone and emphasis which is felt in all of Greene's subsequent novels. The scene is open, not oppressively enclosed, and laughter is possible even in the dark night of Haiti; sometimes it is

> critical laughter, sometimes a quite disinterested sympathetic humour. The comedy that Greene had demonstrated in asides, and in ancillary characters and episodes, and to which he had given fuller rein in some of the entertainments (*Loser Takes All* and *Our Man in Havana* are cases in point), now moves nearer to the centre of the stage in a major novel. . . . The strength of *The Comedians, The Honorary Consul,* and their successors, resides in the broad, tolerant range of a vision that is at once comic and intensely serious. To quote Brown again, invoking the absent God in whom he no longer believes, "all are driven by an authoritative practical joker towards the extreme point of comedy."
>
> (*Saints, Sinners and Comedians,* pp. 222–223)

There are unambiguously admirable characters in *The Comedians,* like the Marxist doctor, Dr. Magiot, engaged in resistance against Duvalier's dictatorship, and a visiting American couple, the Smiths. They are crusading vegetarians and upholders of a wide assortment of good causes—Mr. Smith has the hazy distinction of once having stood as a candidate for the United States presidency on the ticket of the Vegetarian party. They have the naiveté that we expect of Greene's Americans, and to some extent they are more developed versions of the Lehrs in *The Power and the Glory.* There is a peculiar innocence about their efforts to advance the vegetarian cause amid the poverty and violence of Haiti. But their innocence lacks the destructive quality to be found in Greene's earlier fictional Americans, Alden Pyle in particular. They are basically good people, with the quality of being able to learn from their experience. The Smiths stand as a reminder that Greene can portray Americans sympathetically; so does the elderly, unsuccessful American expatriate on a Caribbean island who appears in one of his best short stories, "Cheap in August."

Greene's next novel, *Travels with My Aunt* (1969), culminates in another grim part of Latin America, the Paraguay of General Stroessner, but the treatment is determinedly comic. Henry Pulling, a retired bank manager of quiet habits, reluctantly agrees to set out on picaresque travels with his fun-loving, bohemian, septuagenarian Aunt Augusta and her black lover, Wordsworth. Greene has said that this novel reflects the manic side of a manic-depressive writer—the depressive side was represented eight years earlier by *A Burnt-Out Case*—and called it, in *Ways of Escape,* the only book he has written for the fun of it. There are some good comic moments in *Travels with My Aunt,* but much of the comedy strikes me as forced or merely facetious; Greene without doubt has a sense of humor, but he is not enough of a purely comic writer to sustain that spirit through a whole novel without the contrasting presence of different qualities. The literary joker is much in evidence as he engages in self-allusions, invoking earlier novels such as *Stamboul Train* and *Brighton Rock.*

In Greene's next novel, *The Honorary Consul* (1973), we are once more in South America, this time in a remote province of northern Argentina. This is a "serious" political novel, though there are elements of comedy, particularly in the presentation of the eponymous honorary consul, Charley Fortnum. He is a British businessman, a dim and rather absurd figure who is the local honorary consul for Britain (though he has, strictly, no longer any legal right to the title). He is kidnapped by some inept revolutionaries in mistake for the American ambassador. Much of the novel focuses on Eduardo Plarr, a local doctor of partly British origins who is one of Greene's familiar later types lonely, cynical, and wary of much human engagement. However, he is a decent man and a dedicate doctor, illustrating the tendency of people i Greene's later novels to be rather better as peopl than are the characters in his early books. After th kidnapping of his friend Charley, Plarr gets tangle up with the revolutionaries; their leader, Leon, is a old acquaintance, a former priest who is now guerrilla fighter. In the latter part of the novel ther is a long debate between Plarr and Leon. It goes o throughout the night in a village hut, while the lives are in danger from the police. Both are ex Catholics but the idea of God is still real to ther and they argue at length about religion and ideo ogy and revolution, in a more elaborate version earlier debates in Greene's fiction: between t priest and the lieutenant in *The Power and the Glor* between Querry and the Father Superior and D Collin in *A Burnt-Out Case.* This debate goes too long, but *The Honorary Consul* is a generally su cessful work, among the best of Greene's postw novels.

Its successor, *The Human Factor* (1978), is, I thir one of his weakest. In more than one sense it rep sents a return to Greene's origins. As a novel abo spies and secret agents it goes back to the mod of his earliest fiction, as well as drawing on his o experience in World War II. Its central figure, Ma rice Castle, lives in Berkhamsted, the small Hertfordshire town just outside London where Greene grew up and which was the scene of the formative childhood experiences described in his autobiographical writings. And it is the first of Greene's novels to be set wholly in England since *The End of the Affair.* Maurice Castle works for British intelligence; he is also, in a small way, a Soviet agent. He does this not out of great ideological commitment to communism or the Soviet Union—like most of Greene's major characters he is a skeptic about ideologies—but out of gratitude to the Communists who had helped his black wife escape from South Africa as a political refugee. *The Human Factor* is a tired book, lacking conviction, and it suggests that the vein of the secret-agent story that had served Greene well for many years was finally running out. The fictional texture is thin, and the rendering of London is perfunctory, in contrast to the intimate sense of the city that Greene had conveyed so well in the 1930's. Indeed, there is much about *The Human Factor* that reminds us that Greene, who lives in the south of France, has been physically cut off from day-to-day English life for many years. It is full of missed opportunities, like the conversation between two of its characters, Hargreaves and the richly sinister Dr. Percival, after lunch at the Reform Club, which ought, somehow, to be more blackly comic than it is.

The Human Factor raises the larger question of Greene's apparent sympathy for communism. This undoubtedly exists, though it takes an idiosyncratic form; Greene has never shown any great regard for the Soviet Union and has protested against the Soviet persecution of writers, but he is on the side of the Marxist revolutionaries of Latin America. Such people are sympathetically portrayed in his novels (Dr. Magiot in *The Comedians* and Luis in *The Honorary Consul*); and in *Getting to Know the General* Greene writes warmly of the Sandinista government in Nicaragua. There are a number of related attitudes involved: a compassionate and idealistic identification with the poor and oppressed; a conviction that Marxist-led revolution is the only likely way to improve their lot; and a degree of Greene's perennial anti-Americanism. Nevertheless, Greene's political vision remains extremely individualistic, in some respects naive. He has more than once expressed his conviction that "disloyalty" is a necessary human quality, particularly for the writer. This attitude leads to paradoxes and, ultimately, contradictions. Greene has expressed admiration for his old friend and colleague, the British spy and traitor Kim Philby, saying that Philby was a man who remained loyal throughout his life to his belief in Soviet communism. For Greene this kind of loyalty is somehow preferable to Philby's disloyalty to his country. The issue is raised in *The Human Factor,* where Castle's personally motivated disloyalty is sympathetically regarded. Roger Sharrock remarks in his discussion of this book on Greene's "peculiar belief in the entirely personal valuation of action, as if decisions were taken quite apart from group codes or inherited standards." Again, Greene's long physical absence from British life may be a factor. Sharrock's insight suggests both the strengths and weaknesses of Greene's fictional treatment of the human condition. Greene is undoubtedly liable to political confusions. In his conversations with Marie-Françoise Allain he admits that present-day Soviet realities are far removed from the ideal of "communism with a human face" to which he has aspired, and he confesses to being of two minds about Castro: "I admire his courage and his efficiency, but I question his authoritarianism" (*The Other Man,* p. 111). Greene does, however, assert an admirable principle when he invokes Tom Paine's maxim: "We must guard even our enemies against injustice."

IV

In 1980 Greene made one of his surprising fresh starts when he published *Doctor Fischer of Geneva or the Bomb Party.* This short novel is a moral fable and a fantasy; it has some of the qualities of a dream, recalling how often Greene has described dreams in his fiction and drawn on them for literary effect. Doctor Fischer is one of his most magnificently horrible creations; he is a Swiss millionaire with a totally negative view of human nature. He is surrounded by a circle of greedy, sycophantic disciples—one could hardly call them "friends"—who are willing to endure any amount of humiliation at the hands of Fischer so as to acquire the riches he cynically bestows upon them. Fischer manipulates the world in a kind of monstrous parody of divine providence. He also embodies the idea of the novelist-as-joker, which has always fascinated Greene.

The narrator is Jones, a hard-up, middle-aged Englishman who works as a translator of business correspondence in a Geneva chocolate factory, and who lost his right hand in the bombing of London —a disability that leads us back to the air raids that form the background of *The Ministry of Fear* and Greene's wartime journal. There is Fischer's beautiful and gentle daughter, Anna-Louise, who is the opposite of her father in all possible ways. She falls in love with Jones and braves her father's anger by marrying him; they are idyllically happy for a short time, before she is killed in a skiing accident. And there is the elderly clerk, Steiner, who had been innocently in love with Fischer's wife and was ruined by him in revenge. At the end of the story Fischer too is dead, by his own hand, in an ultimate triumph of pure negation. It is a sad and sometimes shocking novel, but it is also a comedy, in the grim robust vein of Ben Jonson's dramatic exposures of human greed and folly. And the stuff of folklore lies not far below the surface. After the weariness of *The Human Factor,* Greene triumphantly renewed his art in an unpredictable way.

Doctor Fischer was followed by another, more genial comedy, *Monsignor Quixote* (1982). This is a serene, playful book, where Greene the joker is in a gentler mood. He plays with the idea of fiction, with the opposed systems of Catholicism and Marxism, even with his own reputation. It is a reflective and self-reflective story that looks back over more than fifty years of fiction making. The book is presented as a latter-day *Don Quixote* about the picaresque adventures of a humble Spanish priest, Monsignor Quixote, who is a direct descendant of Cervantes' character, or so we are told. From the beginning Greene raises questions about the relation of fact to fiction, and a few pages into the novel a sophisticated Italian bishop remarks, "perhaps we are all fictions, Father, in the mind of God." *Monsignor Quixote* is Greene's culminating treatment of the Hispanic world with which he has been concerned for so long, and it is a return to Spain itself after the many fictional explorations of Latin America. In *Ways of Escape* Greene refers to the debt his religious thinking owes to the great Spanish philosopher Miguel de Unamuno. He remarks that as a young man he read Unamuno's *Life and Death of Don Quixote* and then appeared to have forgotten about the book. But it had a long-term hidden effect, working in what Greene calls "the cellars of the unconscious." He concludes, "At the end of a long journey, without myself knowing the course which I had been taking, I found myself in 'A Visit to Morin' and *A Burnt-Out Case* in that tragi-comic region of La Mancha where I expect to stay." Monsignor Quixote is Greene's conscious tribute to Catholic quixotry in a work deliberately imitative of Cervantes' great original, not only in reproducing some of the same adventures but even in the style and chapter headings.

When the story opens Father Quixote behaves with simple Christian charity to a visiting Italian bishop whose car has broken down in his village. The grateful bishop proves to be an influential Vatican dignitary, and before long word comes from Rome that Father Quixote is to be promoted to the rank of monsignor. This does not please his own bishop, who has little time for him and believes that the pope must have taken leave of his senses to bestow such an honor. The newly elevated monsignor decides to take a little holiday and sets out in his battered old Seat 600 car, nicknamed Rocinante, accompanied by his friend and adversary, Sancho, the Communist ex-mayor of the village, who has just lost his post in an election and feels the need for a holiday himself. Their shared adventures in the footsteps of Cervantes' archetypal couple provide the action, but much of the interest comes from their arguments. Quixote and Sancho are doughty upholders of the causes of Catholicism and communism, respectively, eager to score points off each other. But when they are really at ease, after a little wine, each is prepared to admit that his conviction is not quite absolute, and that belief is sometimes mingled with doubt. These debates echo the many previous ones in Greene's fiction, particularly those in *The Power and the Glory,* to which novel Greene inserts some clues. At one point Monsignor Quixote refuses another glass of wine, saying, "I fear if I'm not careful I shall become what I've heard called a whiskey priest," and later he says he has no relatives except a second cousin in Mexico. But the world of Monsignor Quixote is not divided between opposed absolutes. Greene's priest and Communist are presented as good men, united by more than what divides them, struggling to live decently and help humanity as best they can without the comfort of absolute and unreflecting convictions. At the end, an undogmatic love triumphs. *Monsignor Quixote* is a serenely good-humored book—the fruit of a long life of experience and reflection—and it contains some of Greene's best comic writing.

In his excellent discussion of this novel Roger Sharrock shows how it brings together and reconciles some of the major themes of the earlier fiction: the remoteness of man from God without the dynamic of love; the debate between Catholicism and humanism, leading on to a shared commitment; and the effect of the experience of a fallen world on an innocent mind. In *Monsignor Quixote* we see Greene taking what appears to be a Prospero-like farewell to his life and art; to say this is not to rule out the possibility of Greene's writing another novel, just as Shakespeare continued to write plays after the apparent valediction in *The Tempest.*

The sheer length of Greene's career continues to be one of the most important things about it. Looked at in one way, it has been marked by remarkable variety; although primarily a novelist, he has written in many literary and journalistic forms. Even in the primary form of the novel, he has shown great variety of subject and treatment, from the early romances and the urban poetry of the thrillerlike entertainments to the spiritual dilemmas of the Catholic novels. After these came the shift of direction when Greene appeared primarily as a novelist of political interests writing about revolution and struggle in the Third World, particularly Latin America. After seeming for many years to be a writer without much sense of humor (apart from the "grim grin" that appears in one distorted version of his name), he then emerged as something of a comic novelist. And in the latest phase of his career, he has turned to fable and fantasy. Greene has not wholly escaped the dangers of self-imitation that attend the popular writer with an extensive career. But they have been more than compensated for by his capacity for self-renewal and the trying of fresh options; and his self-imitations, or perhaps one should say self-allusions, are increasingly deliberate and conscious, in the spirit of the intertextual joker. Greene has been a Catholic all his adult life, and his conversations with Marie-Françoise Allain make it clear that he still regards himself as one, though his relationship with the institutional church is not what it once was. But the distance between the bleak Augustinian absolutes that polarized *Brighton Rock,* his first overtly Catholic novel, and the humanistic, self-doubting, undogmatic Catholicism that is sympathetically presented in *Monsignor Quixote,* is immense.

Yet underlying the variety there is continuity. His preoccupation with solitude, pursuit, betrayal, and deception recurs in different forms from the early novels to the late. Roger Sharrock has even referred to "a fresh disguise for the single novel he is writing all the time." Greene is the most private of writers and has always discouraged speculation about his personality; but it is evident that the conflict between innocence and experience goes very deep in him. It is a theme often present in Henry James, who was one of Greene's earliest literary admirations, though in existential and personal terms it is evidently rooted in his own childhood experience, about which he has written much more explicitly than about his later life, and to which his psychoanalysis in adolescence is clearly relevant. Related to this conflict is a sense of guilt and complicity in guilt, considerations that dominate the Catholic fiction. When in the 1950's he moved from religious to political themes he engaged in what Sharrock calls "a reshuffling of the cards, not the introduction of a new pack. . . . Greene has changed the field of interest of his fiction without departing from its essential concern with the agony of moral decision" (pp. 130, 197). The personality may be elusive, but its obsessions are unmistakable.

Greene's favorite Browning line, "Our interest's on the dangerous edge of things," frequently comes to mind when one contemplates his career. Within the novels there is a recurring fascination with things that are drawn to their apparent opposites: the sinner who becomes, or may become, a saint; the atheist who is conscious of God; the revolutionary who was once a priest; the Catholic and the Communist who have a mutual dependence. Similar paradoxical oppositions occur when we try to get a sense of the kind of novelist Greene is. It is evident he is not a modernist; he has not followed in the aesthetic tracks of Joyce or William Faulkner or Samuel Beckett, and he has a wide readership among those who look for the traditional satisfactions of narrative rather than artistic innovation. Greene is a practitioner of what Roland Barthes has called the "classic realist text"; he works in a tradition of nineteenth-century realism, using the novel form to provide information about remote parts of the globe; he has not hesitated to bring a reportorial dimension into his fiction; there are places that Greene has, in several senses, put on the map for his readers: Brighton or West Africa or Haiti, for instance. Yet Greene's realism is not solid or unreflecting, and it is continually on the edge of other literary or dramatic forms: the adventure story, the thriller, the morality play, the gangster film, the dream-fantasy, the fable. He is not so easily categorized as some of his contemporaries. He is, indeed, like a realist of an earlier generation in being popular; whatever else Greene is, he is an outstanding storyteller, and his general reputation seems assured. With academic critics his reputation is less certain; for some, at least, his popularity puts him on a dangerous edge of things. Greene remains sufficiently individual to resist canonization; he is a survival from a time when literary culture was less divided. He may not be a great writer, ready for insertion into an academic canon; but he is an extraordinarily good one.

SELECTED BIBLIOGRAPHY

I. Bibliography. R.A. Wobbe, *Graham Greene: A Bibliography and Guide to Research* (New York and London, 1979).

II. Collected Works. *Collected Essays* (London, 1969); *Triple Pursuit* (New York, 1971); J. R. Taylor, ed., *Graham Greene on Film: Collected Film Criticism* (New York, 1972); *Collected Stories* (London, 1972); P. Stratford, ed., *The Portable Graham Greene* (New York, 1973; rev. ed., 1977); *Shades of Greene* (London, 1975); *Collected Plays* (Harmondsworth, 1985).

III. Selected Works. *Babbling April* (Oxford, 1925), poems; *The Man Within* (London, 1929); *The Name of Action* (London, 1930); *Rumour at Nightfall* (London, 1931); *Stamboul Train* (London, 1932), U.S. title, *Orient Express; It's a Battlefield* (London, 1934); *The Bear Fell Free* (London, 1935); *England Made Me* (London, 1935), U.S. title, *The Shipwrecked; A Gun for Sale* (London, 1936), U.S. title, *This Gun for Hire; Journey Without Maps* (London, 1936), travel; *Brighton Rock* (London, 1938); *The Lawless Roads* (London, 1939), U.S. title, *Another Mexico,* travel; *The Confidential Agent* (London, 1939).

The Power and the Glory (London, 1940), U.S. title originally *The Labyrinthine Ways; British Dramatists* (London, 1942), criticism; *The Ministry of Fear* (London, 1943); *The Heart of the Matter* (London, 1948); *The Third Man and the Fallen Idol* (London, 1950); *The Lost Childhood* (London, 1951); *The End of the Affair* (London, 1951); *The Living Room* (London, 1953), play; *The Quiet American* (London, 1955); *Loser Takes All* (London, 1955); *The Potting Shed* (London, 1957), play; *Our Man in Havana* (London, 1958); *A Burnt-Out Case* (London, 1961); *In Search of a Character: Two African Journals* (London, 1961), travel; *The Comedians* (London, 1966); *Travels with My Aunt* (London, 1969); *A Sort of Life* (London, 1971), autobiography; *The Honorary Consul* (London, 1973); *Lord Rochester's Monkey* (London, 1974), biography; *The Human Factor* (London, 1978); *Ways of Escape* (London, 1980), autobiography; *Doctor Fischer of Geneva or the Bomb Party* (London, 1980); *J'Accuse, the Dark Side of Nice* (London, 1982), polemic; *Monsignor Quixote* (London, 1982); *Getting to Know the General* (London, 1984), memoir; *The Tenth Man* (London, 1985).

IV. Biographical and Critical Studies. K. Allott and M. Farris, *The Art of Graham Greene* (London, 1951); D. O'Donnell (C. C. O'Brien), *Maria Cross; Imaginative Patterns in a Group of Catholic Writers* (London, 1953); S. O'Faoláin, *The Vanishing Hero* (London, 1956); J. Atkins, *Graham Greene* (London, 1952; rev. ed., 1966); R. W. B. Lewis, *The Picaresque Saint* (Philadelphia, 1959); P. Stratford, "Unlocking the Potting Shed," in the *Kenyon Review* (Winter 1962); F. Kermode, *Puzzles and Epiphanies* (London, 1962); D. Pryce-Jones, *Graham Greene* (Edinburgh, 1963; rev. ed., 1973); W. Allen, *Tradition and Dream: The English and American Novel from the Twenties to Our Time* (London, 1964); P. Stratford, *Faith and Fiction: Creative Process in Greene and Mauriac* (Notre Dame, Ind., 1964); J. M. Ross, *Memoirs of the Forties* (London, 1965); R. O. Evans, ed., *Graham Greene: Some Critical Considerations* (Lexington, Ky., 1967); G. Orwell, *Collected Essays, Journalism and Letters* (Harmondsworth, 1968), ed. by S. Orwell and I. Angus; D. Lodge, *The Novelist at the Crossroads* (Ithaca, N.Y., and London, 1971); S. Hynes, ed., *Graham Greene: A Collection of Critical Essays* (Englewood Cliffs, N.J., and London, 1973); G. D. Phillips, *Graham Greene: The Films of His Fiction* (New York and London, 1974); S. Hynes, *The Auden Generation* (New York and London, 1976); J. P. Kulshrestha, *Graham Greene: The Novelist* (Delhi, India, 1977); B. Bergonzi, *Reading the Thirties: Texts and Contexts* (London, 1978); K. W. Gransden, "Graham Greene's Rhetoric," in *Essays in Criticism* (January 1981); M.-F. Allain, *The Other Man: Conversations with Graham Greene* (New York, 1983); D. Gallagher, ed., *The Essays, Articles and Reviews of Evelyn Waugh* (Boston and London, 1983); J. Spurling, *Graham Greene* (New York and London, 1983); R. Sharrock, *Saints, Sinners and Comedians: The Novels of Graham Greene* (Notre Dame, Ind., and Tunbridge Wells, England, 1984); P. French, "Greene on the Screen," in *Encounter* (July–August 1985).

ARTHUR KOESTLER

(1905–1983)

John Atkins

THE remarkable career of Arthur Koestler falls into two virtually independent parts. In the first part he was feeling his way through the political jungle, particularly through the areas of communism and Zionism. In the second part he retired in frustration from the jungle and devoted himself to a study of the philosophy of science. But let us take him chronologically and first consider the youthful Koestler.

He was born in Budapest on 5 September 1905 of Jewish parents. (His father's family came from Russia, and later Koestler was to advance a theory that most of the people we call Jews originated in an area near the Caspian Sea.) In 1919 the family moved to Vienna. From 1922 to 1926 he studied engineering at the Polytechnical University of Vienna. It was then that Koestler made a critical and characteristic decision: instead of embarking on a career as an engineer he decided to throw in his lot with the Zionists, and off he went to Palestine. His talents did not lie, however, in the kibbutz. A year later he was in Berlin, working at the headquarters of the Revisionist group, which opposed orthodox Zionist policy. When he returned to Jerusalem it was as Middle East correspondent for the Ullstein Press. This was an important step for him, as he was a brilliant journalist and remained one for the rest of his life.

In 1929 Koestler was in Paris for the Ullstein News Service, another section of the huge Ullstein Trust. In the following year he was back in Berlin as science editor and then as foreign editor for the *Berliner Zeitung am Mittag.* The year 1932 was a critical one in Koestler's career. He had joined the Communist party, and he went to Russia to write pro-Soviet articles for the liberal European press. From Russia he went back to Paris after a short break in his native city, Budapest, working on the World Committee for the Relief of Victims of German Fascism, the first of a long series of Comintern "fronts." In 1935, he made an excursion to the Saar to witness the plebiscite; in 1936, three visits to Spain, where the civil war was being fought, ended in his capture by the Franco forces, imprisonment, and sentence of death. Koestler, one of the great survivors, survived, but when war broke out in 1939 he was interned in France. In 1940 he joined the Foreign Legion and escaped to England, where he added another prison to his collection: Pentonville. (During World War II it was common practice for the British government to intern all foreigners until they had been vetted, that is, declared politically acceptable.) And then, at last, he was allowed to join the Pioneer Corps and take part in the struggle against Hitler.

This is a whirlwind tour because Koestler led a whirlwind life. It is time to stop for breath and examine this initial period in more detail.

THE YOUNG POLITICIAN

LIKE so many of the younger generation in the early years of this century, Koestler was attracted by the socialist ideal. Also like so many he made the mistake of identifying communism, as practiced in the Soviet Union, with socialism. He was led astray by the use of that attractive word, "scientific," which had been annexed by the Marxists. When he came to write his autobiography, he said: "Marxian dialectics is a method which enables an idiot to sound extremely clever." Koestler became progressively disillusioned, although it took a long time for the truth to sink in. When at last he broke off relations with his old Communist colleagues, he was able to fall back on his early enthusiasm for science, which in fact had never died but had simply remained dormant. Without this alternative Koestler would almost certainly have disappeared into some kind of journalistic limbo, as did so many others who went through the same damaging experience.

Koestler gave an account of these early years in two superb volumes of autobiography, *Arrow in the Blue* (1952) and *The Invisible Writing* (1954). Apart from the quality of the writing, which is remarkable (like Conrad, he became a master of literary English, though he spoke with a strong Middle European accent), these books can be regarded as a pilgrimage that became symbolic for a whole generation of people who were appalled by the injustice of capitalist and imperialist society—who flocked to join Communist parties, especially when fascism established itself over half of Europe, and then discovered, to their dismay, that their chosen salvation was riddled with its own forms of corruption. "The sun was setting on the Age of Reason," Koestler wrote. And out of the turmoil came one of the finest political novels of our time: *Darkness at Noon* (1941).

The two books of autobiography are among the most important in the whole of Koestler's oeuvre. This may sound surprising—autobiographies usually come late in an author's career and usually have an air of adventitiousness about them: "I am now a public figure, and some account of my life experience is expected of me." But this is absolutely untrue of Koestler. These books not only come midway in his career—and at a highly significant moment, when he is deliberately preparing to change course—but they are the best account we have of a sensitive and sincere mind battling with the dangers and despairs that characterized the period between the two great wars, with its horrifying inflation, the brutal rise of fascism, and the betrayal of socialism in Russia, culminating with the collapse of political hope that appeared to be the consequence of the Spanish Civil War. Koestler had to write these books: in no other way could he describe the period in all its fullness. In *Arrow* he asks why he is writing an autobiography. His reply is that he was moved by a desire to share his experiences with others, but that two processes were at work. One he calls the "Chronicler's Urge," which is concerned with external events, and the other the "*Ecce Homo* motive," which concerns internal events. In this way he combined his own experience with that of his generation.

In a Spanish prison he decided that, if he ever got out, he would write a completely frank autobiography. This is easier to promise than to carry out, as many other authors have also discovered. (To the unthinking, "frankness" means sex; in reality it involves a tremendous range of shame.) One of the franknesses that his earlier self might have ridiculed was the conviction that a higher order of reality than the mundane existed. "It was a text written in invisible ink. . . . And although one could not read it, the knowledge that it existed was sufficient to alter the texture of one's own existence." This gives the clue to the title of the second volume of autobiography, *The Invisible Writing.* Koestler had by then gone beyond definite, simplistic philosophies; in their stead he offered no more than an unformulated humanism, but it was backed by absolute conviction. An earlier generation might have spoken of "divine grace."

One of the outstanding qualities of these autobiographies is their candor. Koestler never posed as a hero. He is extremely self-critical, but his is not the mock humility of the comfortable essayist who expects the reader to contradict him. He was keenly aware of his short stature, which he characteristically and brutally termed "undersized." He always looked less mature than his real age, which meant that others were not always prepared to treat him as an adult. As a result, he tended to act aggressively. His strong inferiority complex produced the usual degree of compensation. One of his Communist coworkers in Paris, Otto Katz, once remarked: "We all have inferiority complexes of various sizes, but yours isn't a complex—it's a cathedral"—a remark that appears to have impressed Koestler, for he repeats it more than once. Koestler admits that he was disliked by most of his colleagues, both at school and at work. On the other hand, when he relaxed he could be quite charming (this has been attested to by several witnesses), to the extent that the shift in his moods was so marked that he was sometimes suspected of a mild form of schizophrenia. But somewhere amidst this hotchpotch lay genius of a kind. At the age of twenty-five, he was already something of a journalistic wunderkind. And twenty years later one of his colleagues of that period told him, "When you first came to my office you were not human—you were a machine-gun."

Something was driving him, some kind of obsession. For him dedication to a cause was a psychological necessity. (Koestler called it a "physical" necessity, but this is difficult to follow.) At the age of thirty he was disillusioned but still pursuing the "arrow in the blue," the perfect cause, the ideal Helen, the infallible leader. He was fully aware of this strand in his makeup:

> It gradually dawned on me that my only happy periods were the periods when I was chasing after the arrow in one shape or another. It was the only form of life which gave me peace of mind—not the prim feeling of virtue of do-gooders and hospital sisters, but the creative joy, the happy furore of building and shaping, of adding a brick to the edifice of that more humane future in which I still believed. It was at the same time an outlet for the chronic indignation which was gnawing at one's guts during the seven years of darkness.
>
> (*The Invisible Writing,* ch. 22)

There were many aspects of the Communist movement that worried Koestler. One of them was the remoteness of so many comrades from the mundane lives of ordinary people. Some of the young intellectuals, or eternal adolescents as he called them, whom he met in the party had never done any serious work in their lives. They were therefore "professional revolutionaries." They thought that to be a true revolutionary one should be utterly cold and merciless; a conscience rendered one unfit for the revolution, which required complete ruthlessness for the sake of the larger aim.

Koestler's first experience of the comrades and their methods was in Berlin. It was only when he went to Russia, specifically to write books about the new heaven on earth, that he slowly discovered how their dogmatic attitudes could poison the mind. He traveled through the Ukraine and wrote a book called *Red Days and White Nights* (1933). It was written unashamedly for the party and consists largely of rhapsodic accounts of tractor factories and the Dnieper Dam project. Koestler quoted sections of this book in *The Invisible Writing.* It was meant to be published in several languages but appeared only in German "in a mutilated version." Writing it, he said, acted on him like a sorting machine. He called it an occupational therapy that helped him to overcome his doubts and to rearrange his impressions in the desired form. Thus things that shocked him were classified as the "heritage of the past," and what he liked became the "seeds of the future." He soon discovered that if the party was to approve, one didn't write about individuals but about groups. The tendency of any book, fiction included, had to be "operative," that is, didactic. As it is impossible to write a book without mentioning individuals, they had to be representatives of a group (a class, party, or political attitude). At first Koestler went along with this. In the early stages after conversion one accepts that anything that helps the party is permissible; doubts seep in later. Koestler was clear-sighted enough to recognize that the impression made on his mind in those days was not easily eradicated. "The effects of years of indoctrination reached deeper than the conscious mind, and are easily traceable in my novels even ten years after the break."

When the Spanish Civil War broke out Koestler was already in partial revolt against Marxist methods. (He never at any time attacked the ideals that had attracted him in his youth.) His period in Franco's prison completed a psychological change that would probably have occurred in any case, for his prison experiences added a new dimension to his dissatisfaction with the materialism and apparent rationalism of his Marxist training. He became convinced that there were other forces (mysterious, not understood, "out there"—no one has yet invented the language to describe these feelings satisfactorily) that should not be denied in a full and proper understanding of the human condition. Koestler related these semiconscious promptings to a phrase of Ernst Juenger's that had struck him forcibly: "the anti-materialistic nostalgia of the masses."

Writers have often written about the condemned cell. Here, the writer was actually in it. In a short introduction to *Dialogue with Death* (1941) Koestler wrote, "The experimenter became identical with the rabbit." It is a vivid account of the months he spent as Franco's prisoner, knowing he had been condemned to death and expecting the sentence to be carried out any day without notice. At the end, the reprieve having been granted (through an exchange with a prisoner held by the government), he listed some of the familiar misconceptions the rest of us make about prison life. Chief among these is the belief that it is unbelievably monotonous. This is not so, writes Koestler: "life in a cell is one long chain of excitements." Every sound is pregnant with possibilities.

It is a curious thing that Koestler says very little in this book about his slightly paranormal experiences (for nothing sensational happened) in prison. He left this to *The Invisible Writing,* where he referred to them as "hours by the window." "Window" certainly has a double meaning. Perhaps it took time for him fully to realize the significance of what he had gone through. Or perhaps he felt that 1937, while the civil war was still being fought, was not the best time for him to publicize such unexpected possibilities, which might be regarded as an unjustifiable diversion from the war against fascism. Whatever the reason, *Dialogue with Death* is largely, though not entirely, on the level of conscious narration. It was certainly an excellent preparation for his masterpiece, *Darkness at Noon,* which is set almost entirely in a prison for political offenders. Koestler discovered, for example, that the self-respect of the prisoner is one of the first casualties. He kept a diary, and the following is from the entry for 15 March 1937:

> Despite all my feelings of self-respect I cannot help looking on the warders as superior beings. The consciousness of being confined acts like a slow poison, transforming the entire character. This is more than a mere psychological change, it is not an inferiority complex—it is, rather, an inevitable natural process. When I was writing my novel about the gladiators I always wondered why the Roman slaves, who were twice, three times as numerous as the freemen, did not turn the tables on their masters. Now it is beginning gradually to dawn on me what the slave mentality really is. I could wish that everyone who talks of mass psychology should experience a year of prison.

He also discovered, surprisingly considering the passions roused by this war, that there could be a humane side to prison life. Physically, the Spanish prison was a very superior one, far superior to Pentonville, which came later on his itinerary. There were rules that had to be obeyed—sometimes ridiculously. For example, there were occasions when a prisoner would have a medical examination twenty-four hours before his execution and then be put on a milk diet through fear of appendicitis. "The inertia of routine showed itself to be more powerful than the forces of the present; tradition contemptuously outlived death. It was an extremely humane, positively comfortable prison—picnics were held by the open gravesides." When Koestler first arrived he was bullied and shouted at and subjected to various humiliations. But as the weeks passed he became accepted as one of the regulars, and at times his warders would even call in for a chat and a smoke.

Koestler dedicated the book to Nicolas, an unknown victim of fascism. He was a militiaman of peasant stock who one day simply ceased to appear on the patio for exercise. Presumably he was shot. Koestler wrote a touching tribute to this man; in it he combined the compassion for the weak and unfortunate with the contempt for the exploiter that had been the basis of his early socialist idealism, but which his Communist comrades had set aside as ineffective weapons in a power struggle.

> Little you were, a little Andalusian peasant, with soft, slightly prominent eyes, one of the poor and humble. This book is dedicated to you. What good does it do you? You could not read it even if you were still alive. That is why they shot you, because you had the impudence to wish to learn to read. You and a few million like you, who seized your old firearms to defend the new order which might perhaps some day have taught you to read.
>
> They call it armed rebellion, Nicolas. They call it the hand of Moscow, Nicolas. They call it the instinct of the rabble, Nicolas.
>
> That a man should want to learn to read.
>
> My God, they should really have sent you to Geneva in a cage, with the inscription: "Ecce Homo, Anno Domini, 1937."

Koestler owed his reprieve to the activities of individuals and organizations in England who bombarded Franco with telegrams and letters of protest. Most of them did not know him. He was particularly impressed because among fifty-eight M.P.s who wrote, twenty-two were Conservatives.

THE COMMUNIST BETRAYAL

THE Marxist corruption of a noble ideal was the most painful experience Koestler went through during the first half of his life. He began *The Invisible Writing* with a quotation from Pablo Picasso: "I went to communism as one goes to a spring of fresh water." To this he added, "and I left communism as one clambers out of a poisoned river strewn with the wreckage of flooded cities and the corpses of the drowned."

The major criticism that could be made of Marxism, and the one that spotlighted its ultimate lack of reality, was that it was a closed system. A Communist could prove everything he believed and believe everything he could prove. A closed system sharpens the mind; within its narrow confines there is little room for discussion and none for disagreement. It is a cleverness that affords no protection against the crudest imbecilities. Communism satisfies the thirst for the absolute, a disease that Koestler called "Absolutitis—the All or Nothing Mentality." Koestler was fair game for this in his youth. He followed his arrow into the blue, convinced that it would score a bull's-eye in truth. He bypassed God and chose first of all the Promised Land and then the Communist party. Although these objects of faith occurred in that order, the second made a comparatively much greater impression on him. He was wise enough to know that character does not change. Even after rejecting communism, he knew that he still thirsted for the absolute. In his later phase he sought a metaphysical absolute, but being more mature he realized that quick and final answers were not to be had.

The essence of the Communist betrayal, in practical terms, lay in the movement's substitution of power for Utopia. The satisfied party member was the one who discovered power, even if in a minor capacity, and found it good. When you have power you give orders that have to be obeyed; the idea of justifying the order slowly drops out of view. In Koestler's one and only play, *Twilight Bar* (1945), a character says of her subjects (or victims), "If I want them to be happy, they've got to be happy, whether they like it or not." If anyone complained that he was not happy, the closed system would prove that he ought to be happy; if he still complained, sterner measures could be taken.

In 1950 Koestler contributed an important essay to a volume with the significant and provocative title *The God That Failed.* The god is communism. The list of contributors is imposing, for they are all writers whose integrity can hardly be questioned: Ignazio Silone, André Gide, Richard Wright, Louis Fischer, and Stephen Spender, in addition to Koestler. In his essay Koestler affirmed certain perennial commonplaces that lie at the basis of European civilization:

> . . that man is a reality, mankind an abstraction; that men cannot be treated as units in operations of political arithmetic because they behave like the symbols for zero and the infinite, which dislocate all mathematical operations; that the end justifies the means only within very narrow limits; that ethics is not a function of social utility, and charity not a petty-bourgeois sentiment but the gravitational force which keeps civilisation in its orbit.

This sounds trite, but none of these statements was compatible with Communist faith, Koestler wrote. During the early days of his party membership he managed to disregard the world of fact that surrounded him. Everything could be perceived through a veil of dialectic interpretation. It was a blissful state: the party was infallible, the irritating business of thinking and making choices and coming to decisions no longer bothered him. And he learned to speak loftily of history with a capital H. The proletariat embodied the active principle in history.

In 1931 the threat of fascism loomed over Europe; it had triumphed in Italy and was about to triumph in Germany. Russia provided an inspiring alternative. Twenty years later the situation was desperate. The threat to democracy and to European culture came from Russia. This time there was no inspiring alternative. One either had to abandon hope altogether or fall back on the traditional, even despised, values of the past. "In the 'thirties there existed a specious hope," he wrote in *Arrow in the Blue;* "in the 'fifties, only an uneasy resignation. Not I alone—the whole century has grown middle-aged." It wasn't until the war was over that the true significance of the political situation struck him with full force. There had been that terrible moment when the swastika was hoisted on Moscow airport in honor of Ribbentrop's arrival, and the Red Army band broke into the *Horst Wessel* song. That had meant the end for Koestler so far as any Communist affiliation was concerned. If the comrades still wanted to call him a counter-revolutionary, this was a matter of indifference to Koestler.

Meanwhile the war still had to be fought and won. It was possible that the Western democracies, which had behaved so perfidiously in their attitude to fascist totalitarianism in the past, might even yet recover their nerve when faced by the Stalinist version that had replaced it. But the signs were not promising. Koestler's last political novel, *The Age of Longing* (1951), reflects his despair. It is filled with an overwhelming sense of inevitable defeat.

But this is rushing ahead. Why, Koestler wondered, had socialism (the true version, that is, not its Communist counterpart) been such an abject failure? Social democrats had been in power in Germany, Austria, France, and Britain, yet they could not even produce a first-class daily paper with a mass circulation. The *Daily Herald* and its continental equivalents had never been more than "dreary provincial Party rags." The reason, Koestler felt, lay in lack of imagination, lack of a human approach to ordinary people.[1] Socialists could not resist viewing people as targets for propaganda, not as living realities whose interests, tastes, and foibles had to be understood and shared if the face of the world was to be changed. The party bosses came from the people but were not of the people. Communism, which Koestler had originally equated with socialism, had appeared to be the logical extension of liberalism, the progressive humanistic trend. But it was so tempting, especially for the professional revolutionary, to omit the humanism as a kind of useless sentimentality.

Throughout his career Koestler clung to his belief in European culture. It represents a magnificent tradition that is shared by the numerous and different races that make up the whole. But as a young man he felt it was being challenged so severely that it might be broken and destroyed for ever. The injustices of capitalism were becoming more marked, despite the efforts of reformers and philanthropists. It was this fear that impelled him and many of his contemporaries into the Communist movement: "It was a mass migration of the sons and daughters of the European bourgeoisie trying to escape from the collapsing world of their parents." Inflation and economic depression accelerated the sense of despair and the need for positive action. It was natural that the beneficiaries of capitalism might well seek another way out—the fascist way out, for this, according to the received wisdom of the time, was monopoly capitalism defending itself. Europe became polarized. The pauperized elements of the bourgeoisie became rebels of the right or the left. "Fascists and Communists shared about equally the benefits of the social migration," Koestler wrote in *Arrow in the Blue.*

A clear-cut picture, appealing to the simple mind. What Koestler did not understand at the time, and what many sincere left-wingers still do not understand, is that the new grouping was not basically a confrontation between fascism (right) and communism (left) but between totalitarianism and democracy. Koestler eventually came to this conclusion, perhaps a little later than George Orwell, with whom he became friendly when he settled in England after the war. Orwell's point (which infuriated so many on the left) was that the extreme wings were closer to each other than they were to any other groupings. This challenged the Marxist assumption that fascism was merely the capitalist sector with its back to the wall.

There are two important points to be made at this stage. One is a matter of terminology. In 1950 Koestler made a speech at the Congress for Cultural Freedom, proposed and supported by Ernst Reuben, burgomaster of West Berlin, where it was held, in which he attacked the use of the terms "left" and "right," as bearing no relation to political realities. His speech attracted a tremendous amount of attention and became the focal point of the entire congress. The other matter is far more important and deserves the term "insight," which is used so freely in the discussion of ideas. It is that psychology had been restored to its position as an important factor in political analysis. The Communists, with their faith in economic determinism and materialism, had banned psychology along with metaphysics. Koestler realized that much of recent European history can be understood only in psychological terms. (Later, in his second phase, he made a similar concession to metaphysics, which many Marxists had virtually identified with superstition.) The millions of Germans who flocked to Hitler's standard should never have done so, according to Communist theory. But Koestler went further than this, penetrating the Soviet heartland. What had been the main stumbling block to economic development and an improved standard of living in the Soviet Union?—the peasantry. If the peasantry are simply regarded as economic units differing in no way from the urban proletariat, they will remain, Koestler argued, an intractable problem. The peasantry present a psychological problem, but Marxism does not allow for psychology in its closed system. (The same can be said of sociology: there is no need for sociology when al the answers are known.)

From 1939 to 1943 Koestler published three political novels (which will be discussed later) and a third volume of autobiography, *Scum of the Earth* (1941). This gives an account of his experiences in France after the declaration of war and includes fascinating account of life in a French concentration camp. It was also, incidentally, the first of his books to be written in English. These books wer followed by a volume of essays called *The Yogi an*

[1]"Perhaps deepest cause of Socialists' failure that they tried to conquer the world by reason." (Quoted from diary, *Scum of the Earth.*)

the Commissar (1945). Koestler is a master of literary imagery, which explains, among other things, why he was such a brilliant popularizer of often difficult and abstruse ideas. The Yogi and the Commissar represent for him the tug-of-war that lies beneath all human development—and also human retrogression. To take the Commissar first: he believes that the great problems facing humanity can be solved only by social action; he looks outward; his best exemplar is the Communist party. The Yogi believes that human advance can come only through the individual; he looks inward; his best exemplar is the Eastern mystic. These, according to Koestler, are the extremes of the human spectrum. Some people necessarily gravitate to one end or the other; most tend to cluster in the center but are constantly subject to urgent pulls from the opposed ends.

On the whole this volume is mainly concerned with the Commissar and is in fact a tremendous onslaught on the Soviet system, whose major mistake, Koestler felt, had been its failure to recognize the decisive importance of the spiritual factor—that is, the Yogi. "Based on the axiom that the end justified the means, quickly tired of the inertia and dumbness of the peasant masses, they treated the living people as raw material in a laboratory experiment," Koestler wrote in an essay entitled "Soviet Myth and Reality." And he ended the essay as follows:

> The Russian revolution has failed in its aim to create a new type of human society in a new moral climate. The ultimate reason for its failure was the arid nineteenth-century materialism of its doctrine. It had to fall back on the old opiates because it did not recognise man's need for spiritual nourishment.

He identified the "old opiates" as the inheritance of privilege (largely in the form of money and education), the tremendous range of income between richest and poorest (greater than in any Western bourgeois democracy), oppressive labor conditions and servile trade unions, all of which led to the establishment of a new ruling class.

In the original essay from which *The Yogi and the Commissar* takes its name (it appeared in the literary review *Horizon*) Koestler wrote: "I wish one could still write an honest infra-red novel without an ultra-violet ending." The colors, of course, represent the Commissar and the Yogi and their flatly opposed viewpoints. This is a perceptive statement, although it is not easy to understand why Koestler regretted it. He had already stated that no honest socialist could write a survey of the left's defeats without accounting for the irrational factor in mass psychology. When he more or less abandoned politics and turned to science, he asserted that no honest scientist could publish a book on physics without a metaphysical epilogue.

One aspect of Koestler's upbringing played an important part in his psychological development. He had been partly educated in Vienna, the city that gave birth to psychoanalysis. Many young writers between the wars took a keen interest in psychoanalysis and often tried to cast their fiction in categories that yielded to Freudian critical analysis. It is noticeable that when Koestler came to write about his political experiences he fell back again and again on psychoanalytical interpretations. The signs are meager in *The Gladiators* (1939) and *Darkness at Noon* (1941), but they become strong in *Arrival and Departure* (1943), and by the time of his last political novel, *The Age of Longing* (1951), they tend to disturb the balance.

When he complained that Marxists paid insufficient heed to psychological matters, Koestler had in mind a particular school of thought, the Freudian—although he was prepared to admit elements from the rival doxies of C. G. Jung and Alfred Adler. The aberration of the sexual drive, Koestler claimed, is paralleled by a corresponding type of disturbance of the political libido. (The use of the term "libido" in a political association is significant.) He gives examples. Sexual ambivalence occurs when one both loves and hates the same object. Is not the relationship between Britain and the U.S.A. an example of political ambivalence, he asks? Fetishism is illustrated through the prevailing adoration of flags and uniforms, the fervent singing of partisan songs, Hitler's forelock, Churchill's cigar. As for eternal adolescence, the examples are endless: he cites for one the enthusiastic Communist who founds a Trotskyite opposition group only to discover that half the members are deviationists, whereupon he starts an anti-capitalist, anti-Soviet, anti-pacifist "little mag."

It is time to consider his fiction. This is almost entirely political in content and reflects the personal history just recounted and discussed. One of his novels, however, *Thieves in the Night* (1946), is reserved for consideration in a later section, as it is set in a completely different area from the others. Whereas the others take place in Europe against a background of communism, fascism, and totalitarianism, *Thieves* is set in Palestine, where the protagonists are Zionists, Arabs, and British administrators.

THE EUROPEAN NOVELS

There are four European novels, ranging from *The Gladiators* to *The Age of Longing.* Koestler has said that the first of these constituted a trilogy along with *Darkness at Noon* and *Arrival and Departure. The Gladiators,* which is a fictional account of Spartacus and the Roman slave revolt, is concerned with the ethics of revolution, the problem of ends and means. *Darkness* restated the problem in a contemporary setting, and *Arrival* shifted it to the psychological level. It is doubtful that Koestler actually planned a trilogy. Writers often see the common strands that run through their work after its completion and tend to make groupings that are adventitious. But no harm is done, no dishonesty has been committed, and a case can easily be made for attaching each of Koestler's works, up to his final break with active politics, to one dominant theme. Words like "trilogy" are, however, misleading in such a context.[2]

Some critics have hailed *The Gladiators* as Koestler's best novel. It is a judgment on form, based on the traditional treatment of the material. Koestler himself thought it was "because the passions and angers which contemporary events aroused in me were here projected on a screen remote in space and time, and purified from the topical dross which tends to clutter up my other books." The novel starts in Capua and ends there. In *The Age of Longing* Capua represented the decadent West, a sanctuary for those who could not bear "social reality." Before 73 B.C. Capua was apparently stable; the slaves were rebellious but could be flogged into submission. People still paid to watch gladiators kill each other. Sulla, great Sulla, was five years dead. After sacking three cities the slaves returned to Capua, which resisted them. "Great depression haunted the horde; here they had rain, dripping tents, annoyance and disappointment; over there was the town, dry and warm, filled with the smells of cookshops and the spices of the markets, Italy's most luscious city after Rome." The implication is obvious: why not go back to enjoy the security of slavery?

This novel is Koestler's *Animal Farm,*[3] but without the latter's simple force. One could not deduce a political ideology from *Gladiators,* only a political critique. As in *Darkness,* the message is ambivalent. (This will be elaborated later.) The horde feels betrayed, a new tyranny has arisen, yet Spartacus is presented sympathetically. The philosopher Zozimos stands for despair and frustration:

> "Can't you see how you've been betrayed? Woe, for a new tyrant has emerged from the bleeding womb of revolution; woe unto us who assisted at his birth! From the broken chains we ourselves forged new chains; the burnt crosses sprouted up again. A new world we were going to erect, and what happened? Spartacus negotiates alliances with the lords."
>
> (ch. 11)

But if not Spartacus, then who? "Crixus was the man for them. He talked little. He decreed no laws. He was the man to lead them." Yet Crixus was a boor who thought solely of his own creature comforts. He was a man of blood. He was Stalin.

Orwell simply said that the Russian way was wrong, but a better way was possible. Koestler was defeatist because he was convinced that revolutions always ate their young; this, he felt, will never change. The novel ends as it begins, with Quintus Apronius, First Scribe of the Market Court, making his daily visit to the Dolphins. "He has learnt his lesson and knows that politics are nothing but the sinister conspiracy of invisible powers with the aim of robbing the little man and making his life a misery." Although Spartacus is the apparent hero, it is really Zozimos, a minor figure, around whom the novel revolves. He had preached revolution and had joined the rebels, believing they would welcome his views, but was rejected by them and found his ideals frustrated

[2]Koestler was a scheme addict. When his last and much later novel, *The Call-Girls* (1972), went into the collected (Danube) edition with two other short pieces, he wrote in an introduction that they were "intended" as "variations on a single theme." One wonders.

[3]George Orwell, author of *Animal Farm,* and Koestler became friends and political allies. Both of these books attack Russian communism through symbolism, one in the form of a fable, the other through a historical parallel.

The rebels had merely exchanged hunger for discipline. Life in the Sun City was as jaded and narrow as it had been before—the Imperator met councillors and diplomats and entertained them richly, despite the shortages the rest of the people underwent. One is reminded of the animals in Orwell's *Animal Farm* looking through the window at the pigs feasting with the neighboring farmer and his men. Fiction is usually more revealing than nonfiction. The latter is frequently a complex exercise in concealment; fiction reveals. Koestler never said he had lost political hope, but his political novels are doom-laden.

If Koestler had not written *Darkness at Noon* there might be no need to write this essay. Without questioning the merit of his other works, many of which are both highly original and models of clarity, one is compelled to accept the primacy of this novel. It is one of the great literary works of our time. It spoke *for* a whole generation, and it spoke *to* a generation, which is a different matter. It tackles one of the great political mysteries of the twentieth century: how unquestionably sincere revolutionaries had been persuaded to confess to crimes against the revolution they had helped to create. The Moscow Show Trials were part of a huge campaign to retain the allegiance of thousands to a tyranny; *Darkness at Noon* explains how this was done. Incidentally, there is a temptation to regard this novel proudly as a landmark in English literature, especially after Koestler settled into being an Englishman, but this view cannot be substantiated. The English translation by Daphne Hardy, a very good one, was made from the original German manuscript, which was lost, and the later German publication was a translation back from the English translation.[4]

The hero and victim of *Darkness* is N. S. Rubashov, one of the original leaders in the 1917 revolution. In *The Invisible Writing* Koestler states that he incorporated characteristics of both Karl Radek and Nikolai Bukharin in Rubashov. Although he met them each only once, in rather formal circumstances, he was deeply impressed by them. Rubashov is not presented as a faultless personality; like everyone else he has made mistakes. (One of the major strengths of this novel is its presentation of rounded characters, quite apart from Koestler's personal feelings about their views and ideologies.) In his cell Rubashov thinks of those he has betrayed for the party:

> The movement was without scruples; she rolled towards her goal unconcernedly and deposed the corpses of the drowned in the windings of her course. Her course had many twists and windings;[5] such was the law of her being. And whosoever could not follow her crooked course was washed on to the bank, for such was her law.
>
> ("The First Hearing," ch. 13)

The individual and his conscience was of no concern to her. Ivanov, the interrogator, is scornful of Rubashov's misgivings. "He has discovered a conscience and a conscience renders one as unfit for the revolution as a double chin. Conscience eats through the brain like a cancer, until the whole grey matter is devoured." Then follows this important declaration of the Stalinist approach to revolution:

> One may not regard the world as a sort of metaphysical brothel for emotions. This is the first commandment for us. Sympathy, conscience, disgust, despair, repentance and atonement are for us a repellent debauchery. . . . Most great revolutionaries fell before this temptation, from Spartacus to Danton and Dostoievsky; they are the classical form of betrayal of the cause. The temptations of God were always more dangerous for mankind than those of Satan. As long as chaos dominates the world, God is an anachronism; and every compromise with one's own conscience is perfidy. When the accursed inner voice speaks to you, hold your hands over your ears.
>
> ("The Second Hearing," ch. 7)

And Ivanov puts the seal on this approach by stating that to sell oneself for thirty pieces of silver is an honest transaction but to sell oneself to one's own conscience is to abandon mankind. History is a priori amoral and has no conscience. Wanting to conduct history according to the maxims of Sunday school means to leave everything as it is, which is another way of saying that to take no interest in politics means to vote Conservative.

The root of the argument lies in the familiar ends-and-means controversy. For Ivanov the principle that the end justifies the means remains the

[4] As a matter of literary curiosity, exactly the same thing happened to *Vathek,* an eighteenth-century fantasy by William Beckford.

[5] Exactly the same point had been made about Spartacus' policy. In *The Gladiators* it is referred to as the Law of Detours.

only rule of political ethics, and therefore it is necessary to sacrifice the comparatively guiltless Rubashov. He declares that there are only two conceptions of human ethics, and they are at opposite poles. The Christian and humane ethic declares the individual to be sacrosanct and asserts that the rules of arithmetic are not to be applied to human units. The opposing ethic holds that all other interests are subordinate to the collective. Thus, according to this ethic, which Ivanov upholds, the individual should always be sacrificed to the community whenever the two come into opposition. Experimental rabbit, sacrificial lamb—no matter how one views it, Rubashov's execution is a revolutionary necessity.

Rubashov keeps a diary. In it he states his belief that there is a pendular movement in history: it swings from absolutism to democracy and from democracy back to absolute dictatorship. Sometimes the lines appear to be crossed, as when a tyranny declares its belief in democracy. (It was in describing this kind of sinister paradox that Orwell did much of his best work.) According to Rubashov, every technical advance creates a new complication in the economic apparatus. Intellectual development tends to be left a step behind. When the level of mass consciousness catches up, some form of democracy is possible. Then comes another jump in technical civilization; once again the intellectual aspect lags behind and there is another recourse to absolute leadership.

> This process might be compared to the lifting of a ship through a lock with several chambers. When it first enters a lock chamber, the ship is on a low level relative to the capacity of the chamber; it is slowly lifted up until the water-level reaches its highest point. But this grandeur is illusory, the next lock chamber is higher still, the levelling process has to start again. The walls of the lock chamber represent the objective state of control of natural forces of the technical civilisation; the water level in the lock chamber represents the political maturity of the masses. It would be meaningless to measure the latter as an absolute height above sea-level; what counts is the relative height of the level in the lock chamber.
>
> ("The Third Hearing," ch. 1)

This passage is an example of Koestler's skill in presenting a point of view through vivid imagery expressed in lucid language. It was always one of his major strengths and served him well in his second phase, where his main concern was scientific and metaphysical theory.

The ideological aspect of *Darkness at Noon* is its raison d'être; without it the novel would be a run-of-the-mill political thriller. But the story is a human one. If it had been mere ideology and nothing else, it would have been forgotten by now. As it is, the story contains convincing portraits of utterly committed commissars and others of varying faiths, tragic victims and innocents who have been unfortunate enough to lie in the path of the Stalinist steamroller. Naturally, the comrades were infuriated by the book. A Marxist member of the French National Assembly named Roger Garaudy ridiculed Koestler for the statement in *Darkness* that a leading agriculturist had been shot with thirty collaborators for maintaining that nitrate artificial manure was superior to potash. No. 1 (Stalin, though not named) was all for potash. Yet a few years later scientists and agriculturists were persecuted, if not shot, for adopting a Mendelian approach to genetics. They were opposed by Lysenko, who adapted his genetic policy to Marxism. Later Lysenko was refuted and disciplined.

The French Communist party actually helped *Darkness at Noon* become a bestseller by instructing local party branches all over the country to buy up copies and destroy them. Within a few weeks of publication 200,000 copies had been sold. One could hardly wish for a better example of Communist obscurantism or for a stronger testimonial to the power of the novel.

Arrival and Departure marks the merging of politics and psychology in Koestler's creative method. It is to some extent a dramatization of conditioned response. It is also a reply to Marxism that uses Marxism's methods, but instead of finding the dominant force in human economic affairs, it discovers it in psychology. "What, after all, was courage?" asks one character. "A matter of glands, nerves, patterns of reaction conditioned by heredity and early experiences. A drop of iodine less in the thyroid, a sadistic governess or over-affectionate aunt, a slight variation in the electric resistance of the medullary ganglions, and the hero became a coward, the patriot a traitor." Koestler's growing interest in psychoanalysis tends at times to reduce this novel to the status of a case history determined to make a point. The characters talk like psychoanalysts and editorial writers, at times like minor poets.

Underneath the novel's action one can sense Koestler's nagging fear that he has been disloyal. Although he knew he had excellent reasons fo leaving the Communist party he could not dismiss the idea that he had betrayed it. Betrayal is the focal point of the novel. Peter Slavek, its hero, has to explain away his past. He does so by deciding he has always had a craving for martyrdom, resulting from certain events in his childhood. In Koestler's view it was not significant whether a man was a hero of the proletariat or a martyr of the Catholic Church: "the real clue was this suspect craving for martyrdom." Thus causes do not create heroes. The cause is private guilt atoned for by public suffering. The novel is the product of anguish, and it shows Koestler at the crossroads of his political career.

How does an apparently solid party man become an apostate? Peter Slavek had become a hero to his generation because he had not talked under fascist torture. "What the revolution needs is not heroes but iron civil servants," retorts a party member. But for Peter this new attitude spells the end of the movement for him. "The idea behind it, the one great vision of the age, was dead, strangled in the noose of their sound reasons; and there was nothing to replace it." The great vision had burned itself out. The old two-front war (capitalism versus labor, socialism versus fascism) was finished. There were now three sides to the struggle, and Koestler illustrates his skill in the use of his new language by identifying them as follows: "one side was utopia betrayed; the second, tradition decayed; the third, destruction arrayed." The first two are indisputable; the third is presumably his description of fascism. One had to fight against it, there was no other choice: "but it was a duty, not a mission—and for dead illusions there was no resurrection."

The Age of Longing lay in the shadow of the Third World War. Koestler's wife, Cynthia, typed the final pages as the Korean War started, and Koestler had left for Berlin to speak at the Congress for Cultural Freedom, which was a desperate counteroffensive against the rising tide of totalitarianism. Cynthia Koestler was filled with melancholy. It is clear from *Arrow in the Blue* that Koestler thought Europe was doomed. The advance of communism, the disarray of the opposition, the conviction of the one and the demoralization of the other, seemed to him irreversible. The latter part of the novel is set in the immediate future, but it is a future that has already become past, and the disaster has so far been avoided. The Soviet Union has renamed itself the Commonwealth of Freedomloving People and is referred to as the Free Commonwealth. Orwell's doublespeak is given official recognition. Terms such as "right" and "left" have become meaningless, the point that Koestler hammered home at the congress.

The Age of Longing is a preach-novel. Koestler was not a born novelist in the way that Charles Dickens, D. H. Lawrence, and Christopher Isherwood were. He was closer to Aldous Huxley, putting ideas into fictional form instead of deriving ideas from preconceived fiction. Writers of this type occasionally produce a good novel (as Koestler did) by sheer power of conviction, but with the passage of time the critical apparatus overwhelms the creative. In *The Age of Longing* totalitarians of various hue are ranged against helpless liberals, decent but ineffective people in the political world. Hydie is a Catholic totalitarian and is thrown into conflict (love modulating into hate in the approved psychoanalytic style) with the Marxist totalitarian Nikotin. An insane God is contrasted with an insane Stalin, who (as in all Koestler's novels) is never mentioned by name. Other characters, such as Anatole, whom the author appears to admire (the model was probably André Malraux), are merely rhetorical. But it is not surprising that Anatole should appeal to Koestler, who very easily slipped into the stream of rhetoric himself.

The novel should be read in conjunction with the latter part of *Arrow in the Blue,* where Koestler describes his own conversion to communism and then analyzes, with the aid of hindsight, the forces that made him a Marxist. One of the Marxist beliefs is that social development is historically determined. Nothing can change the course of this development. Marxists like to use a capital H for history, making it a kind of substitute for God. One of the more interesting figures in this novel is Vardi, who is a sort of there-but-for-the-grace-of-God-go-I Koestler. He is a renegade Marxist, but he has decided, unlike Koestler, to return to the flock. He is compelled to admit that he is one of history's puppets. He exasperates the French poet Julien Delattre by opting for "that side which the logic of History indicates." What oracle has revealed this? asks Julien. Vardi evades an answer by resorting to jargon: "I have never departed from that solid dialectical foundation which alone enables one to see order in apparent chaos." Julien points out that leading scholastics in the past gave their blessing to the crusades and heresy hunts. Vardi regards them as "necessarily painful spasms" that usher in a new age. It is all part of the logic of History.

Koestler projected his own problem in writing fiction onto Julien, who says in effect that the only subject he considers worth taking up in a novel is the advance of communism, which would mean preaching a sermon—"and when a writer becomes a preacher, he is finished." Koestler had enough sense to take his own advice, although the statement would be more accurate if he had used the word "novelist" instead of "writer." A writer can preach, and preach very effectively, as Koestler continued to do for the rest of his life. It is fiction that must resemble the street rather than the lecture hall.

When, twenty-one years later, Koestler produced another novel *(The Call-Girls),* he abandoned politics as a subject. The call-girls are members of a cultural congress held to discuss not the advance of totalitarianism but man's approaches to survival. God has died some time ago; materialism has now followed Him. Mankind is at the crossroads, but the real danger comes from the division between those who care and those who don't. Those who care must care enough to be firm and unsentimental. Finally, the only member who we feel does care states that he no longer cares. This is the impasse we have arrived at. And so, although Koestler changed his field of action, his mood remained very much the same.

In recounting Koestler's personal history I stopped arbitrarily in 1940 with his escape from France to Britain. I have necessarily overstepped this borderline in discussing his fiction, because there is naturally a time lag between the event and its literary reflection. Taking up the story where I left off, in 1944 Koestler met Mamaine Paget. At the time he was married to but separated from his first wife, Dorothy, the sister-in-law of Peter Maros, a fellow member of the Communist party in Berlin. After their divorce in 1950 he married Mamaine at the British Consulate in Paris. It was a stormy partnership and they eventually separated, though they remained friends. Mamaine died of asthma in 1954. In 1965 Koestler married his secretary, Cynthia (*née* Jefferies), who had been married and divorced and who changed her name to Koestler by deed poll before her marriage to Koestler. After some hesitation, Koestler decided to settle in the United Kingdom and bought an old farmhouse in North Wales.

During 1944–1945 Koestler returned to Palestine on a tour of observation and went there again in 1948 with Mamaine. In the meantime Palestine had become Israel. In the postwar period Koestler traveled widely; he made a successful American lecture tour in 1948. He became a naturalized British subject on 7 January 1949. In 1950 he made a great impression at the Berlin congress. In 1954 he was one of the leaders in the National Campaign for the Abolition of Capital Punishment, and the success of that movement probably owed more to him than anyone else. In 1955 he announced a "vocational change," which virtually meant a retreat from politics, celebrated in a book of essays entitled *The Trail of the Dinosaur.* His prison experiences remained vivid in his memory, and in 1960 he instituted the Arthur Koestler Award for creative work by prisoners. On 3 March 1983, in great pain from Parkinson's disease, he committed suicide with Cynthia, who preferred not to live without him. A gypsy had once predicted that he would die suddenly and violently.

A JEW IN THE TWENTIETH CENTURY

In *The Invisible Writing* Koestler had said that he set out for Palestine as "a romantic young fool" to work in a collective settlement. He had believed that the Jewish question, like the Negro question and the Armenian question—in fact, all the world's questions—would be solved by socialist revolution. By the time he came to write his Jewish novel, *Thieves in the Night,* he had gone beyond this kind of naiveté. It is a patchwork novel, less satisfactory than the others. It has three elements: narrative, which is good; reports of current events, in the John Dos Passos style; and extracts from the chronicle of Joseph, one of the settlers in a commune. The latter element is artificial because Koestler transfers his job to one of his characters in a very unconvincing way. Joseph's entries are in fact incredible chunks of fictional reportage. The device works in *Darkness at Noon* because there, in the circumscribed area of a prison, it is completely credible and natural.

Joseph comes to the conclusion that the Jews of Palestine must resort to terrorism. Although we may assume that Koestler held similar views, he was nevertheless scrupulously fair in putting forward the official British viewpoint. The Assistan

Chief Commissioner defends the appeasement policy, as it applied to both Hitler in Europe and the Arabs in Palestine, as carefully and plausibly as Stalin's policy is defended in *Darkness at Noon.* (One young sabra once told Koestler that after reading *Darkness* he felt greater sympathy for communism.) It was Koestler's strength that, as a novelist, he was capable of looking at, explaining, and defending both sides of a problem. But a politician who is involved practically must not do this. "Go to hell," says Bauman, who has joined the Stern group, "you've got that intellectual squint which makes you see both sides of the medal at the same time."

Koestler regarded the Jews as representing an extreme condition of the human race, and he expressed this view in both this novel and *Promise and Fulfilment* (1949), which he wrote after the establishment of the State of Israel. After an attack on the commune has been beaten off, Joseph wonders about life on other planets such as Jupiter: "I wonder whether Jupiter too has its Jews. . . . No doubt it has; no species would be complete without its Jews; they are the exposed nerve, an extreme condition of life." Both Joseph and Koestler maintained that the Jew is the product of continuous segregation. If you keep slinging mud at people, he said, they will smell. Persecution has been going on for twenty centuries; there is no reason to expect it to end now. Jewry is a sick race: "its disease is homelessness and can only be cured by abolishing its homelessness."

Koestler did not believe in national characteristics. He maintained that whenever a race appears to bear distinctive features, these are the product of treatment, conditioning, and environment. Thus convicts, monks, and actors, to name only three groups, develop similar characteristics. In 1976 Koestler upset many people by declaring that the modern Jew has very little blood relationship with the Jews of the Old Testament. In a book published that year, *The Thirteenth Tribe,* he asserts that the great majority of European Jews, mainly those of Poland and Eastern Europe, came from the old Khazar state that lay between the Caspian and the Black seas, and not from Germany or the West. In other words, they were not descendants of Jews of the diaspora, as had always been supposed, but of Khazarian converts. (The Khazar king had indulged in one of those mass religious conversions of his people that were so popular with monarchs of the Dark Ages.) There was no genetic connection with the Jews of Palestine; and yet there was the Jewish type. This, Koestler argued, was simply because these Khazarian "Jews," like mainstream Jews, had been shut up in ghettos and deprived of the freedom and flexibility enjoyed by other peoples. "Their way of life affects not only their facial expression but also their physical features, thus giving the mistaken impression that these traits are of hereditary or 'racial' origin." Koestler called this the most cruel hoax that history had ever perpetrated.

Koestler had paid a visit to modern Palestine in 1937 as correspondent for the *News Chronicle,* but his most crucial experience came in 1948, when he went there with Mamaine and kept a journal that he incorporated in *Promise and Fulfilment.* Palestine had become the sovereign State of Israel. Uppermost in Koestler's mind was the necessity for every Jew, wherever he was, to make a decision on his identity: was he first and foremost a Jew, or was he a citizen of the state in which he lived? Koestler himself had no doubts. He chose Europe for its history and tradition, vital realities to him. He rejected the Zionist state with its missing two thousand years of national history. International Jewry had done what it could to supply a haven for the homeless:

> Now that the State of Israel is firmly established, they are at least free to do what they could not do before: to wish it good luck and go their own way, with an occasional friendly glance back and a helpful gesture. But, nevertheless, to go their own way, with the nation whose life and culture they share, without reservations or split loyalties.
>
> (epilogue)

The mission of the Wandering Jew is over, Koestler said. It would be quite hypocritical of the Jew in future to toast "next year in Jerusalem"; there was nothing to stop his going there.

Koestler was expert at incurring odium. When he left the Communist party the comrades fell all over each other showering abuse and insults on their former colleague. Now it was the turn of the Jewish community, especially the Zionists. Their attacks stimulated a reply that he called "Judah at the Crossroads," which was published in *The Trail of the Dinosaur* (1955). He repeated the argument he had elaborated in *Promise and Fulfilment,* that a Jew should either go to Israel or be assimilated into his host nation. He also quoted an interview with the *Jewish*

Chronicle from May 1950. When asked if he still considered himself a Jew he replied: "I regard myself first as a member of the European community, secondly as a naturalised British citizen of uncertain and mixed racial origin, who accepts the ethical values and rejects the dogmas of our Helleno-Judaeo-Christian tradition. Into what pigeon-hole others put me is their affair." Perhaps at the back of his mind lay the suspicion that he was a Khazar.

Koestler had the habit of using each of his books to illustrate an abstract idea. (We have already seen him deploying the Law of Detours and the Logic of History.) *Promise and Fulfilment* became the vehicle for an idea that colored his thinking in the philosophical, psychological, and metaphysical books that were to follow. This was his conception of life as lived on two planes, which he called the tragic and the trivial. According to this notion most of us for most of the time live on the trivial plane, but every now and again we are lifted onto the tragic. Koestler's book on Israel provides many examples. When Yehuda Sprung, a thin, timid little man who looks like a tailor, sees a real tank in action for the first time in his life, he does not run away but throws a bottle at it from ten yards, "and thus, in a half-dazed state, crossed the equinoxial line which divides the trivial from the historic plane." Koestler recalls other instances from history and folklore: David and Goliath, Stendhal's Fabrice wandering across the vast muddle he later learned to call the battle of Waterloo. What marks this aspect of human existence is the contrast between the tiny scale of events and their global resonance. The transition is rarely the result of any human striving. The petrifaction of schoolboys playing with marbles in Pompeii, entirely fortuitous, is given as another example.

At times the notion of life lived on two planes seems too vague to be taken seriously, but later Koestler applied it to careers that some might term heroic, such as that of Richard Hillary, an airman who almost nonchalantly defied death and mutilation. When Koestler turned to his later studies of creativity he found the trivial/tragic dualism exactly what he wanted as a key to understanding. Great art and the insights of science occur when trivial human concern is crossed by or raised briefly to the level of something beyond normal mundane understanding. The hours by the window were to bear unexpected fruit.

THE NEW ENGLISHMAN

By the war's end Koestler found himself without a country. A return to Hungary under Communist rule was out of the question. Out of loyalty to Zionism he acquired Palestinian nationality but never felt happy about it. There was something arid and unsatisfying about the new state, probably the "missing" years, the years when Jewish culture stood still. He realized that he was a European in every inch of his being and that he would find it impossible to renounce European culture. In *Arrow in the Blue* he wrote that he had had his fill of the East—"both of Arab romantics and Jewish *mystique.* My mind and spirit were longing for Europe, thirsting for Europe, pining for Europe."

But Koestler had been knocked about rather a lot in Europe. Sometimes he had felt he wanted to get away, and so his thoughts turned to that country established by and for people disenchanted with their homelands: the United States of America. He went there and, after overcoming a high degree of official suspicion because he had once been a Communist, he obtained a residence permit. But he did not stay. (When this author asked him why, he simply answered, "I am a European.") In an essay entitled "Reflections on a Peninsula" in *Drinkers of Infinity* (1968) he refers to Europe as a historic persona with a distinct individual profile. It emerged at the same time as others did in China and India, through the agencies of Confucius, Lao Tse, and Buddha:

> A March breeze seemed to blow across this planet, from China to the Aegean, stirring men into awareness like the breath in Adam's nostrils. But at the same time, there was also a parting of the ways between the Asian and European philosophy of life, of their attitudes to the basic problems of existence.[6]

But where to live in Europe? At first sight, for someone as imbued with European culture as

[6]Koestler had, as is clear from his writings, acquainted himself with oriental philosophy, but in 1958 he decided to undertake a more personal study by visiting the Far East. The result was *The Lotus and the Robot* (1961), which contains typically Koestlerian accounts of both Yoga and Zen. These had their attractions, but they needed to be filtered through the apparatus of Western criticism rather than being swallowed whole. "Yoga and Zen, *as practised today,* are spurious and degenerate," he wrote in "Between the Lotus and the Robot" *(Drinkers of Infinity).* The italics are his.

Koestler, it had to be the fountainhead, France. He considered this possibility but finally rejected it. It was the glory and tragedy of the French genius to serve as "a burning lens of Western civilisation." The glory attracted, the tragedy repelled. Immediately after the war he felt the French had got themselves into a mess by their own efforts and, one might say inevitably, Europe had followed suit. Koestler's view of France was not that of the expatriate who arrives wishing to be dazzled. He had first gone to Paris as an Ullstein correspondent in 1929. He stressed that he went there to work and not to frequent bars or to join literary movements: "I had settled down to married life with Paris in shirt sleeves and slippers on the first day of our acquaintance; the courtship and the falling in love came long afterward. Thus from the start I became immune against future disenchantments." The French he found extremely individualistic, but theirs was a resigned and defensive individualism, quite unlike the youthfully aggressive American type. The French were obsessed with *securité;* they took their ease behind the Maginot Line. Koestler came to know the French bourgeoisie rather than the intellectuals; he even grew to like them, though he did not respect them. This was a new experience for a green romantic such as he was in those days.

The Age of Longing is set in Paris, and nothing illustrates more strongly Koestler's ambivalence toward the French. He felt that Paris was a delicate balance between Nordic industry and the relaxed hedonism of the South. The French had perfected the art of living, but the balance required as much skill as tightrope-walking; by the 1950's their famed skill was in decay. On the strength of this novel one feels Koestler had come to dislike Paris. (One major cause was that he disapproved of what he saw as the dishonesty of Parisian intellectuals such as Jean-Paul Sartre, who Koestler felt cheerfully shut his eyes to abuses when they emanated from the Soviet Union while decrying those nearer home.)

The attitude toward France and the French that eventually became uppermost in Koestler's mind was expressed in an early article bearing the evocative title "The French Flu." This article first appeared in *Tribune,* a London left-wing weekly, and was included in *The Yogi and the Commissar.* Koestler referred to the malady as a recurrent epidemic that afflicted the French to a greater extent than other, possibly more stolid, races.

> Its symptoms are that the patient, ordinarily a balanced, cautious, sceptical man, is lured into unconditional surrender of his critical faculties when a line of French poetry or prose falls under his eyes. . . . If an English poet dares to use words like "my fatherland," "my soul," "my heart," etc., he is done for; if a French one dispenses musical platitudes about *la Patrie, la France, mon coeur,* and *mon âme,* the patient begins to quiver with admiration.

The occasion of this attack was a review of three works that had recently come out of France and were treated as literary revelations. Koestler exposed their commonplace character and pointed out that if they had originated in English, no one would have taken them seriously. He spoke of a French predilection for "melodious bombast."

It was this attitude of Koestler's more than anything else that finally caused him to opt for England as his new home. He could be irritated by the English, especially the dullness of much of English life, but he respected England's solidity. In his usual fashion he managed to identify the English character with a striking piece of imagery, which in fact became the title of a publication, *The Lion and the Ostrich* (1973): the courageous fighter who buries his head in the sand when faced by difficulties that require thought to solve rather than action.

Koestler never became completely assimilated—and why should he have? Mary Warnock, reviewing *Janus* (1978), remarked on how "extremely un-English" it was. (This is perhaps part of the fascination his work has for us.) Apart from Samuel Coleridge, English writers and thinkers have avoided comprehensive systems that purport to explain everything. This is a continental characteristic—vice, many English people would call it—and even if the English cannot always fully accept it, it provides a breath of fresh philosophical air to their literary environment. Mary Warnock called it a "spectator sport." Ian Hamilton, Koestler's biographer, has said that Koestler admired the cool Anglican voice walking the *via media,* which Koestler respected but could never follow for long. At times it exasperated him. Koestler's choice of England represented the attraction of opposites. Nevertheless, despite his heavy accent (of which he was keenly aware), his assimilation into English society was astonishing. The fact that he was awarded the C.B.E. in 1972 and the much more prestigious Companionship of Literature in 1974 speaks for itself. But most remarkable of all was his mastery of the English language. It is true that minor errors could have been corrected by an editor, but no editor could have injected into his writing references that, for most English people, belong to childhood. It is not an easy task for a foreigner to conscript into service the essentially English Alice of Looking Glass fame or the Grand Old Duke of York, who spent his time marching soldiers up and down a hill—or to quote "I do not love thee, Dr Fell" convincingly—but Koestler managed it in one book as gracefully and easily as a native scholar.

In the collection entitled *The Heel of Achilles* (1974) there is an essay, "Solitary Confinement," which is in fact a discussion with Anthony Grey, who, like Koestler, had been a political prisoner—in Grey's case, of the Chinese. The two men obviously had the experience of imprisonment in common, including the mysterious "hours by the window" that Koestler had described in *The Invisible Writing.* Grey makes this significant observation:

> You said that England with its muddled ways lives closer to the text of the invisible writing than any other country. You said that the English people are suspicious of causes, contemptuous of systems and bored by ideologies and sceptical about Utopias. It's a country of potterers in the garden and stickers in the mud. This is why you chose to live here. Do you still feel this is true today?

Koestler replies: "Yes. There are certain inroads, disquieting inroads. But on the whole I think it is so."

In 1976, on his seventieth birthday, a celebratory volume entitled *Astride the Two Cultures* was presented to him. It was made the occasion for a *Times* profile written by Norman Moss, who was mainly concerned with the reasons for Koestler's switch from politics to psychology and metaphysics. In the course of the interview Koestler stated his belief that England was still a more civilized country than most. It is apparent that by the term "civilization" he understood the qualities of tolerance—not getting unduly worked up about things that irritate or annoy you, not imagining that a few axioms or dicta will contain the secrets of either society or the universe, the decision to get along without killing each other, as Orwell noted. It was the murderous positiveness of the totalitarians that had finally revolutionized Koestler's own thinking. But there was also a warning. He went on to say, "The things that made it more civilised are going, but they're going more slowly than in other countries. I find living here a lesser evil, the least evil." Linking this with the "disquieting inroads" he mentioned to Grey, one realizes that he believed the values he stood for were still under pressure.

Probably Koestler's most remarkable achievement as an "Englishman" was his part in the campaign for the abolition of capital punishment. To promote the cause he produced two books: *Reflections on Hanging* (1956, later bound up with the uniform Danube edition of *The Trail of the Dinosaur*) and *Hanged by the Neck* (1961), which he wrote in collaboration with C. H. Rolph and which incorporates material from the earlier book. Koestler was a superb polemicist, and John Grigg called *Reflections* "a polemic of extraordinary power." (It is in fact a bonus for democracy that the totalitarian camp had no one who could touch him in this art.)

The first reference to capital punishment in Koestler's work appears in *Arrow in the Blue* when he states that the liberal, decent Ullsteins were opposed to it. But, as with so much Weimar decency, this evaporated in face of the Nazi threat: "We capitulated before the rapidly increasing brutalisation of the masses." The Ullsteins sacrificed their principle that the function of justice was not punishment but the protection of society. This shocked Koestler more than a direct political betrayal. During his political period Koestler learned one lesson that he was never to forget, and that he applied to every new situation as it arose: appeasement never pays. Appeasing Hitler led to the invasion of Poland; appeasing the Soviet government led to Czechoslovakia; just as certainly, appeasing the hanging judges (that is, accepting their prejudices disguised as arguments) led to the defeat of justice. His main objection to hanging was its irrevocability and the inevitability of mistaken judgments. *Reflections* is slightly more academic and therefore more muted in tone than *Hanged by the Neck.* In the latter he concentrates on the absolute obscenity of hanging. He ends one chapter with these words:

> The gallows is not only a machine of death, it is a symbol. It is the symbol of terror, cruelty and irreverence for life; the common denominator of primitive savagery, medieval fanaticism, and modern totalitarianism. It stands for everything that mankind must reject, if mankind is to survive its present crisis.

It is ironical that the country that Koestler chose to live in for its decent and kindly ways possessed what he deemed a horrific legal system. But it is symbolic that he, more than anyone else, was responsible for the changing of this system, and the abolition of hanging.

THE REVOLUTION IN SCIENCE

The Trail of the Dinosaur marks the turning point in Koestler's work. He acknowledged it freely. In the preface to *Bricks to Babel* (1980), a comprehensive selection from his work, he says it was necessary to divide the volume into two distinct parts: book 1, "In Search of Utopia," which is an account of his political career, and book 2, "In Search of a Synthesis," which is devoted to science and philosophy, hence ultimately metaphysics and the paranormal.

In *The Invisible Writing* Koestler described how he had come to the conclusion that there were three orders of being. The first is the narrow world of sensory perception, the basis for the materialist philosophy that his early training as an engineer and his later Marxist studies had led him to hold. This world is enveloped by the second order of being, the conceptual world that is not directly perceivable; it includes such forces as gravitation, electromagnetic fields, and curved space. The third order envelops, interpenetrates, and gives meaning to the second. It contains occult phenomena that cannot be apprehended or explained on either the sensory or conceptual level, but which occasionally invade them "like spiritual meteors piercing the primitive's vaulted sky."

But scientific orthodoxy does not accept even the existence of the occult. It maintains that all phenomena of the type commonly called paranormal can be explained by the scientific laws established by Newton and his successors; if they cannot, it is simply because the information has been misread. The scientific discoveries of the twentieth century challenge this view. Each scientific revolution in turn becomes an orthodoxy and then a closed system. Medieval philosophy collapsed not because of Galileo, but because of its own absurdity. Something similar seems to be happening today, says Koestler. Scientific thinking is based on faulty axioms: that biological evolution is the outcome of random mutations preserved by natural selection; that mental evolution is the outcome of random tries preserved by "reinforcements"; and that man is a self-regulating, passive automaton reacting to stimuli in the environment. New research batters, at first helplessly, against the old ideas—and then the citadel falls. Science thus advances in a discontinuous, unpredictable way, with rapid changes of tempo. Koestler maintains that exactly the same kind of spasmodic movement can be noticed in the history of art, where periodic upheavals alternate with long periods of assimilation. The understanding of art and science as two aspects of one activity rather than two separate and distinct activities was an important part of Koestler's thinking.

The first of his works of scientific inquiry was *Insight and Outlook* (1949), subtitled *An Enquiry into the Common Foundations of Science, Art and Social Ethics.* Hamilton called it the "seminal work of synthesis from which Koestler's later scientific writings were to flow," but Koestler himself said it was marred by "academic pedantry." It introduced his concept of "bisociation," by which he meant "any mental occurrence simultaneously associated with two habitually incompatible contexts," and what he called the "integrative tendency" in the evolutionary process, concerning the relationship of the part to the whole. He returned to these ideas with much greater clarity in *Janus: A Summing Up* (1978), which also incorporated his trivial/tragic view of life.

Koestler had intended to follow this up with a study of Kepler, which in fact turned into *The Sleepwalkers* (1959). (The title refers to the manner in which some of the most important scientific discoveries remind one more of a sleepwalker's performance than a rational or logical advance.) This book, which is subtitled *A History of Man's Changing Vision of the Universe,* forms with *The Act of Creation* (1964) and *The Ghost in the Machine* (1967) a remarkable trilogy that constitutes the center of Koestler's work and thought in this period. It explores various scientific themes and led to a highly technical volume called *Beyond Reductionism: New Perspectives in the Life Sciences* (1969), which Koestler edited with J. R. Smythies. This book is a transcript of an interdisciplinary symposium held at Alpbach and organized by Koestler himself.

In *The Sleepwalkers* Koestler claims that the modern enemy is "the cocksure, arrogant and intolerant 'scientism' of the nineteenth century still surviving in the rationalistic-mechanistic philosophies of the twentieth; in neo-Darwinian orthodoxy, in behaviorism and reductionism transformed from useful methodologies into dogma." Professor Victor E. Frankl, the neurologist, called this tendency "the nihilism of today." Materialism had become dominant, and there was an absence of philosophy or moral direction. Instead there was scientism or nihilistic determinism.

This sort of theorizing, especially its constipated language, seems far removed from the elegance of the autobiographies. But Koestler was now aiming at a different audience. On 19 September 1965 the *Sunday Times* published a transcript of a conversation between Koestler and Cyril Connolly in which Koestler said:

> *The Sleepwalkers* is not popular science, it is a reinterpretation of the history of the philosophy of science written with as little jargon as possible, and as little technicality as possible. And *The Act of Creation* is, on the one hand, a frontal attack on that school of psychology and philosophy which dehumanises man's behaviour and on the other on logical positivism. But on the positive side it is, for better or worse, an original theory.

The Act of Creation puts forward a theory of scientific discovery and artistic creation. The key concept is "bisociation." *The Ghost in the Machine* is a splendid Koestlerian title for an attack on behaviorism, in which a "ratomorphic" view of life has replaced the anthropomorphic. It proposes a cosmic hierarchy in which everything is both a whole composed of constituent wholes composed of . . . and so "downward" and "inward" ad infinitum; and a mere part of a whole which is a mere . . . and so "upward" and "outward" ad infinitum. *Beyond Reductionism* is an attack on what Koestler called "the pillars of unwisdom," which are the doctrines of scientism, materialism, and logical positivism.

Janus is an excellent summing up of Koestler's critical approach to scientific orthodoxy. In an author's note he calls it a continuation of works published since he turned from writing about politics to books about the evolution, creativity, and pathology of the human mind. It is his final rejection of materialism as a reliable guide to our knowledge of the universe. There are signs, however, that his political experiences have played their part in his new orientation. He illustrates one aspect of the mind's activity by a reference to party loyalties and he ends the book with a quotation from *The Invisible Writing.*

He stresses the hierarchical principle in nature, where holons display two faces (Janus)—one integrative and reaching upward and the other self-assertive, pointing downward. Applying this scheme to human affairs, he claims that the danger for mankind lies in the vagaries of the integrative tendency. This idea sounds extremely remote from our daily concerns, until Koestler tells us that it is simply a new term for an old concept, the idealistic craving that so often leads to totalitarian submission. He thus sees the sacrifice of the critical faculty in a new, metaphysical light. Here lies the link between the two phases of Koestler's career. He quotes Stanley Milgram, who wrote in his *Obedience to Authority:* "The disappearance of a sense of responsibility is the most far-reaching consequence of submission to authority." We are back in the world of *The Yogi and the Commissar.*

Koestler's challenge to the long-accepted laws of nature naturally brought him into contact and sympathy with what is sometimes called fringe science. He noted with satisfaction that Einstein and his followers have accustomed us to the idea of particles with no weight, no mass, and no precise location. Dr. J. B. Rhine, head of the Parapsychology Laboratory at Duke University, Durham, N.C., and his followers accepted the existence of extrasensory perception and telekinesis. Koestler himself was fascinated by the occurrence of coincidences, which he called confluential events, and this led him to the possibility of synchronicity, as investigated by Jung and Paul Kammerer, about whom he wrote in *The Case of the Midwife Toad* (1971).

Orthodox science had for Koestler become to divorced from the normal experiences of ordinar men and women. It seems at times that everyon believes in the existence of, say, telepathy excep a few academics. Koestler was something mor than a scientist: he was a political journalist turne scientist, and this involved an orientation denied t the university research worker. Koestler argu that for the first time in its history *homo sapiens* is danger of destroying itself as a race. The mea might be scientific, but the destructive decisic would be political. Unlike most people who a appalled by contemporary violence, he believ that the real danger lies not in the self-asserti tendency but in the integrative one—that is, t idealistic craving to serve a cause or a leader. Ultimately the problem is biological, and there is a cure. Humans need something that will reduce their idealistic urge to proportions where it will not dominate their entire being. This something can only be a drug. And here Koestler realizes he is on very treacherous ground:

> I have learned from painful experience that any proposal which involves "tampering with human nature" is bound to provoke strong emotional resistances. These are partly based on ignorance and prejudice, but partly on a justified revulsion against further intrusions into the privacy and sanctity of the individual by social engineering, character engineering, various forms of brain-washing, and other threatening aspects of overt or covert totalitarianism. It hardly needs saying that I share this loathing for a nightmare in whose shadow most of my life was spent.
>
> (ch. 5, "An Alternative to Despair")

There is no doubt that whereas most of us would reject any suggestion of "mind control" made by a communist or fascist, when it comes from someone with a personal history like Koestler's, we are tempted to listen and at least consider. Koestler felt the situation was so dangerous that the resources of science, especially biology and psychology, must be used to evolve order out of disorder.

Here and there readers might feel, in the course of this most impressive book, that they are being conned. Koestler's literary virtues, his fluency and vivid imagery, tend at times to be counterproductive; at times they seem to degenerate into glibness. In places there is voluminous discussion of, for example, the cooperative and competitive faculties, with new terminology. Something that has been said before (and often by Koestler himself) is being said again but in a new way. This can arguably be justified because so many people remained unmoved by his earlier efforts at persuasion. It is also noticeable how the earlier fascination with Freud has been diluted; Koestler still pays homage to Freud's pioneering work, but in *Janus* he questions much of the teaching. When, for instance, Freud first claimed that wars were caused by pent-up aggressive instincts in search of an outlet, readers tended to believe him because it made them feel guilty, although he did not produce a shred of historical or psychological evidence. Again, Freud postulated two basic drives, Eros and Thanatos, which were conceived as mutually antagonistic universal tendencies inherent in all living matter. In fact, both these drives are regressive, as they both aim at the restoration of a past primeval condition. It was not a bad thing for Koestler to get Freud out of his system. His autobiographies are excellent, but they are occasionally marred by his practice of finding a new complex for every situation he describes.

A careful reader of Koestler's earlier work would not have been surprised when Koestler turned his attention to the paranormal, despite having been a "prim little materialist" in his youth. His first encounter with the supernatural (or inexplicable) occurred while he was staying with Maria Kloepfer on the shores of Lake Lugano. He had always been a skeptic; Maria, on the other hand, possessed what are sometimes called psychic powers. A picture suddenly fell off the wall. The wire was unbroken and the hooks were still firmly embedded in the wall. Koestler's doubts were diminished by his "hours by the window" and his growing belief that much of life is "a text written in invisible ink." ESP, or extrasensory perception, excited him. A scientific friend of his admitted that, if ESP existed, "the whole edifice of materialist philosophy crumbles." One of his later books, *Roots of Coincidence* (1972), consists mainly of researches into the psi-factor, the name given to unexplained psychological forces. From here it was only a short route to mysticism. According to Mamaine, this became his abiding interest.

Koestler also believed in miracles. A psychologist who was also a specialist in the study of miracles said that there was no logical reason not to believe in them, and Koestler accepted this. In her notebook Cynthia Koestler said that her husband was once shocked by a distinguished Catholic priest who argued that mystical experiences were meaningless. Koestler made the significant comment that the Catholic establishment regarded mysticism with as much distrust as the Comintern leadership regarded genuine communism.

Having seen capital punishment abolished, Koestler turned his attention to euthanasia and wrote a preface for a pamphlet produced by the Voluntary Euthanasia Society, later renamed EXIT: The Society for the Right to Die with Dignity. It is a technical guide for those determined to end an intolerable existence, as he himself did when the pain of his illness became unbearable. In his will he left a sum of money for the endowment of a chair in Paranormal Psychology, which was eventually taken up by Edinburgh University. Even more significant is the fact that he contributed an essay, along with Arnold Toynbee and several others, to a volume entitled *Life After Death.* His essay "Whereof One Cannot Speak . . . ?" was the final one and was a kind of summation. In it Koestler stresses the demise of the strictly deterministic, mechanistic world view, which has become a Victorian anachronism. "The nineteenth century model of the universe as a mechanical clockwork is a shambles; and since, with the advent of relativity and quantum theory, the concept of matter itself has been de-materialised, materialism can no longer claim to be a scientific philosophy," he states. It seems reasonable to assume, he goes on, that some of the basic insights gained by modern physics are applicable to the psychic field, which is complementary to it as mind is to body and corpuscle to wave: "Perhaps the most profound of these insights is the re-discovery, on a higher turn of the spiral, of the Pythagorean (and Vedantic) concept of cosmic unity, where 'everything hangs together.' "

It was an amazing path that Arthur Koestler followed, from the engineering school in Vienna through the maze of the Marxist dialectic to a position where death meant a "merging into the cosmic consciousness—the island vanishing below the surface to join the sunken continent—or Athman joining Brahman—whichever image you prefer." The ordinary person, especially the ordinary Westerner, finds such a view difficult to grasp, let alone accept. But when it is the final resting place of a mind as sensitive and active as Koestler's, of a mind that had been exposed to most of the major currents of twentieth-century existence, one is obliged to pause and consider—and tolerate—his new ideas; and finally perhaps to revise those certainties which previously guided one's life.

SELECTED BIBLIOGRAPHY

I. SEPARATE WORKS. *Von weissen Nachten und roten Tagen* (White Nights and Red Days) (London, 1933), propaganda work written for the Soviet government, truncated version in German issued by the Ukrainian State Publishers for National Minorities; *Menschenopfer Unerhört* (Unprecedented Human Sacrifice) (London, 1937), trans. in French as *L'Espagne ensanglantée,* in English as *Spanish Testament,* containing *Dialogue with Death,* the latter alone surviving as part of accepted Koestler canon and published separately (London, 1941); *The Gladiators* (London, 1939), novel, trans. from German by E. Simon; *Darkness at Noon* (London, 1941), novel, trans. from German by D. Hardy, a special ed. distributed by Heron Books and undated but appearing in 1970 in the series "Books That Have Changed Men's Thinking"; *Scum of the Earth* (London, 1941), personal experience, first work written in English; *Arrival and Departure* (London, 1943), novel; *The Yogi and the Commissar* (London, 1945), essays; *Twilight Bar: An Escapade in Four Acts* (London, 1945), play; *Thieves in the Night* (London, 1946), novel; *Insight and Outlook: An Enquiry into the Common Foundations of Science, Art and Social Ethics* (London, 1949); *Promise and Fulfilment* (London, 1949), Palestine 1917–1949; *The Age of Longing* (London, 1951), novel; *Arrow in the Blue* (London, 1952), autobiography; *The Invisible Writing* (London, 1954), autobiography; *The Trail of the Dinosaur* (London, 1955), essays; *Reflections on Hanging* (London, 1956), capital punishment; *The Sleepwalkers: A History of Man's Changing Vision of the Universe* (London, 1959), intro. by H. Butterfield; *The Watershed* (London, 1961), biography of Johannes Kepler, an extract from *The Sleepwalkers; The Lotus and the Robot* (London, 1961), travels in the Far East with reflections on Yoga and Zen; *Hanged by the Neck: An Exposure of Capital Punishment in England,* with C. H. Rolph, incorporates material from *Reflections on Hanging; The Act of Creation* (London, 1964); *The Ghost in the Machine* (London, 1967); *Drinkers of Infinity* (London, 1968), essays, 1955–1967; *The Case of the Midwife Toad* (London, 1971); *The Roots of Coincidence* (London, 1972); *The Call-Girls* (London, 1972), novel; *The Lion and the Ostrich* (London, 1973); *The Heel of Achilles* (London, 1974), essays, 1968–1973; *The Thirteenth Tribe* (London, 1976), the origins of modern Jewry; *Janus: A Summing Up* (London, 1978); *Bricks to Babel: Selected Writings with Comments b[y] the Author* (London, 1980); *Kaleidoscope* (London, 1981), essays from *Drinkers of Infinity* and *The Heel of Achilles,* wit[h] later pieces and stories.

II. BOOKS PARTLY BY OR EDITED BY KOESTLER. Drs. Nor[-] man Haire, A. Willy, L. Vander, O. Fischer, R. Lothar, e[t] al., *The Encyclopaedia of Sex Practice* (London, 1938), "Dr. A[.] Costler" (Arthur Koestler) contributed book 5: *Man an[d] Woman in Their Everyday Relations;* M. Foot and R. Cross[-] man, *A Palestine Munich* (London, 1946), according to Hamilton largely by Koestler; R. Crossman, ed., *The G[od] That Failed: Six Studies in Communism* (London, 1950), essay[s] by Koestler, I. Silone, R. Wright, A. Gide, L. Fischer, Spender; *Suicide of a Nation: An Enquiry into the State of Brita[in] Today* (London, 1963), ed. by Koestler; *Beyond Reductionis[m:] New Perspectives in the Life Sciences: The Alpbach Symposi[um]* (London, 1969), ed. by Koestler with J. R. Smythies; *T[he] Ethics of Change* (Ontario, 1969), with N. Frye and othe[rs]

The Challenge of Chance (London, 1973), with Sir A. Hardy and R. Harvie; A. Toynbee, ed., *Life After Death* (London, 1976), essays by Koestler and others; H. Harris, ed., *Stranger on the Square* (London, 1984), by Arthur and Cynthia Koestler, autobiography.

III. Uncollected Essays. Article on Johannes Kepler in *The Encyclopaedia of Philosophy* (New York, 1967); article on humor and wit in the 15th ed. of the *Encyclopaedia Britannica.*

IV. Biographical and Critical Studies. Sir P. Chalmers-Mitchell, *My House in Malaga* (London, 1938), the author met Koestler in Spain just before the latter's arrest; L. Hughes, *I Wonder as I Wander* (New York, 1944), the author met Koestler during his period in the Soviet Union; J. Lewis and R. Bishop, *The Philosophy of Betrayal* (London, 1945), an analysis of the anti-Soviet propaganda of Koestler and others; G. Orwell, *Critical Essays* (London, 1946), contains a friendly appreciation; R. Mortimer, "Arthur Koestler," in the *Cornhill,* no. 969 (1946), an unfriendly criticism from the non-Marxist fellow-traveling camp; R. Garaudy et al., *Literature of the Graveyard* (New York, 1948), a Marxist broadside; J. Atkins, *Arthur Koestler* (London, 1956); P. A. Huber, *Arthur Koestler: Das literarische Werk* (Zurich, 1962); J. Calder, *Chronicles of Conscience* (London, 1968), a study of Orwell and Koestler; W. Mays, *Arthur Koestler* (London, 1973); H. Harris, ed., *Astride the Two Cultures: Arthur Koestler at 70* (London, 1976), festschrift; I. Hamilton, *Koestler* (London, 1982), biography; C. Goodman, ed., *Living with Koestler* (London, 1985), Mamaine Koestler's letters.

SAMUEL BECKETT

(1906–   )

Jean-Jacques Mayoux

I

SAMUEL BECKETT was born at Foxrock, south of Dublin, of thriving Protestant stock, on Friday, 13 April 1906: a Good Friday. Beckett, like Herman Melville, felt predestined. Nosy critics have discovered that he must have been in love with his nurse: a wise and not unusual beginning if one gets over it; if one does not, some trauma must result. A few memories of childhood seem to have been recorded, untransformed, in the works: for example, a rather terrifying close-up of an oversize ornate mother's face bent over his babyhood *(How It Is);* and since Beckett was obviously, unlike Marcel Proust, a father's child, it was the father who soothed his anguish every night with some story such as "Joe Breem" or "Breen." He was, he tells us, born grave, as others are born syphilitic; he must have been a bright student, however, for Trinity College sent no others as *lecteurs* to the École Normale Supérieure in Paris, where we find him in 1928. A very brilliant young Irishman, arriving in Paris, had, of course, to sit at James Joyce's feet and to write for *transition;*[1] Joyce perceived his worth, and it is not only alphabetically that Beckett is the first of the twelve apostles employed to make *Our Exagmination,*[2] nor has he lost his admiration and reverence for the elder genius. They shared Dante, they did not share Vico. Neither did they share René Descartes, on whom Beckett was working—though, he insists, he is no philosopher—when in the autumn of 1929 he had a visitor who mentioned a prize offered by Nancy Cunard and The Hours Press for the best poem on Time. It happened to be the closing day for entries, but he was sufficiently stirred to set to work and, in the small hours, to deliver the 98-line poem, *Whoroscope,* on Descartes and time. The reasons for the attraction of Descartes for Beckett can be inferred from the next thirty years: Descartes's dualism separated mind from body, and the true life was in the mind. The body to which the mind was tied was, like all animals, a machine. Now Henri Bergson had shown that all machines are comic. Beckett decided to make perfect buffoons, or rather buffooning imperfects, of his men-machines or body-machines.

Descartes may have been the strongest of any influences on his mind. Descartes, entrenched in the cell-like solitude of his German *Stube,*[3] where he composed the *Discours de la méthode,* might be taken for a living metaphor of the condition of the mind. We are all the fools of time; Beckett in the poem enjoyed turning the time connection into images. Once he had decided (since, as his biographer Adrien Baillet tells us, Descartes "liked his omelette made of eggs hatched from eight to ten days") that "the shuttle of a ripening egg combs the warp of his days," the egg must recur, so as to mark the progress of his time symbolically, from

> What's that?
> An egg?
> (1–2)

to

> Are you ripe at last?
> (84)

[1]*transition* was an avant-garde international quarterly published successively in Paris, The Hague, and New York from 1927 to 1938. It was the first journal to publish extracts from Joyce's *Work in Progress* (later *Finnegans Wake*).

[2]Beckett contributed to a collection of essays on Joyce: the volume was entitled *Our Exagmination Round His Factification for Incamination of Work in Progress,* Paris, 1929.

[3]Descartes relates that the idea from which the *Discours* originated came to him in Germany in 1619. It was elaborated in the years that followed, and the *Discours* was published in 1636.

Larger tensions, other than this food-fad, must span this philosophical existence, culminating in the anguished desire to preserve from the fatefulness of (w)horoscopes

> my second
> starless inscrutable hour
> (98)

Descartes's *cogito, ergo sum* had provided thus early a formula attuned to Beckett's conviction that all existence was in the head and all "external" contact was an illusion. The young poet in the first piece of *Echo's Bones* (1935) could conjure "The Vulture"

> dragging his hunger *through the sky*
> *of my skull shell of sky and earth*
> (emphasis added)

Soon his prose was to graduate from Descartes to his northern disciples and to play with Leibniz's preestablished harmony, or with Geulincx's[4] astonishing occasionalism, according to which mind and body, although completely separate, are fortunately synchronized, like a film and its sound track. But all philosophy, as Beckett absorbed it, turned to images; so he wrote poetry, drawn like an ellipse round the two poles of culture and selfhood. Dante, the Provençal troubadours, the German *Minnesinger* are heard behind such titles as "Enueg," "Alba," "Serena," "Da Tagte es." But it is Ovid, the poet's poet, who brings the myth that will be with Beckett as long as he lives. Echo's Bones, all that is left of Echo, are turned to stone, but the voice remains. It might serve as the general title of his opus, not of a group of poems only. Echo entails Narcissus, and a dark narcissism is obvious in the circumstantially autobiographical poems as it later runs through the prose. A bicycle ride, a walk, a night in Dortmund, an episode in a Paris brothel; these are the bare subjects, which are decked out in fantastic images, set to a strange poignant music—for this is a musical mind—and which foreshadow many of the later themes:

> ah to be back in the caul now with no trusts
> no fingers no spoilt love
> ("Sanies 1")

The "ruined feet" of "Enueg 1" already suggest the theme of the hated body turned to disgusting object. Yet a love poem has escaped the disarray, the beautiful "Cascando" (1936), which achieves a purity of lyrical statement and a grave, anguished simplicity:

> if you do not love me I shall not be loved
> if I do not love you I shall not love
> . . .
> terrified again
> of not loving
> of loving and not you
> of being loved and not by you
> of knowing not knowing pretending
> pretending

From 1937 onward the French poems, with their astonishing directness and quasi-native ease of language, are the work of a truly international poet who could bind, in a sort of French haiku,[5] the emotion of a moment with a memory of Friedrich Hölderlin.

II

In 1929 Beckett wrote about Joyce, as if to please Joyce, in an objective spirit. In 1931 he wrote about Proust, when he was starting on the quest of himself, as if in the hope of advancing this quest. The influence of Proust succeeded that of Descartes and took its effect from the creative angle: it taugh[t] Beckett that the alien world begins with one's body, so that the conscious personality is necessar[-] ily split; Proust taught him that "one lies all one's life . . . above all to that stranger whose contemp[t] would cause one most pain: oneself" (*Proust,* p. 47[)]. Since Proust's quest turned on a criticism of self[-] identity, it must seek satisfactory conditions fo[r] its experiment: the chance comes, Beckett write[s], "when we escape into the spacious annexe of men[-] tal alienation, in sleep, or the rare dispensation o[f] waking madness" (p. 19). Sleep and madness a[re] thus seen as similar kinds of privileged stat[es] purified from illusory external connections. We a[re] then back in "the only world that has reality an[d]

[4]Arnold Geulincx (1624–1669), Belgian philosopher, was a disciple of Descartes and one of the leading exponents of the speculative doctrine known as "occasionalism."

[5]A Japanese poetic form consisting of seventeen syllables a[r]ranged 5–7–5; it was popular from the seventeenth centu[ry] onward.

significance, the world of our own latent consciousness." That is, then, what we must call to life. To this end "the only fertile research is excavatory, immersive, a contraction of the spirit, a descent. From this deep source Proust hoisted his world" (p. 48). It is significant that Beckett should have stressed in these terms Proust's perception that man's only conquest of reality depends upon his use of the involuntary memory. We see in the passage here quoted a metaphor building itself up that could describe Beckett's whole effort as well as Proust's, and that we shall find enacted in terms of conflict in *The Unnamable.* Beckett quotes Proust himself to support his view of our doom of solitude: "Man is the creature that cannot come forth from himself, who knows others only in himself, and who, if he asserts the contrary, lies" (p. 49). This "impenetrability of all that is not *cosa mentale*" means that the artist's truth is to be found nowhere else. Thus in 1931 Beckett the critic gives us a clearer indication of what his art is going to be than he shows as yet in his achievement. For although from his earliest prose Beckett gives himself a persona, a personal representative whom he can know and probe as *cosa mentale,* yet he presents him at first as engaged in the nonexistent external world, and his resource must then be to show the connection as grotesque, so that the character alternately attempts it and withdraws from it, in burlesque indecision: this is what we may call the Belacqua phase of Beckett.

More Pricks than Kicks (1934) is (as might be guessed from its obscene though unassuming title) marked and annulled by the author's frantic self-consciousness. In these short stories Beckett is never done with torturing the language, which constantly approximates to fine writing and is constantly brought back to the level of jest or parody. The persona here is Belacqua, a character taken straight from canto 4 of the *Purgatorio,* where Dante sees him as "more idle than if laziness itself were his sister." In Dante's poem Belacqua is found among those souls who out of sheer sloth have always postponed repentance in their moral life, and who are condemned to wait for their admission to Purgatory for a period equivalent to that of their stay on earth. Here we may have a foretaste of *Waiting for Godot.* But it is worth noting that while for Dante's Belacqua "waiting" is a period of expectancy and looking forward, for Beckett's it is a completely negative experience. At any rate, in this character Beckett incarnates for the first time his wish for the physical, emotional, and mental immobility that should lead to a near-mystic quiet: such a state is in conflict with the pull of the world, represented by the obstinacy of desire, essentially sexual, and by the insistence of women. Since Belacqua is clearly a whipping-boy set up by the author, he suffers for him in his grotesque body ("his spavined gait," "his feet were in ruins") and his burlesque, buffoon-like behavior, to which are added, remembering perhaps Stephen Dedalus, dirt and impetigo. His unsavoriness remains unperceived by other characters and he is assailed—assaulted—by half-a-dozen randy women, whom he exhorts in vain to find elsewhere the proper sort of male. For these stories the Joyce of *Dubliners* (1916) has been not a model but a memory: "The Dead" and its landscape of universal snow seems to be recalled in the universal rain at the end of "A Wet Night"; it may also have inspired the wedding speech in "What a Misfortune."

There is a first unpublished draft of *More Pricks* entitled "A Dream of Fair to Middling Women" in which (perhaps through beginner's naiveté) the hero had come closer to Beckett's ideal: here Belacqua's mind, "at last its own asylum," ceases to be "an annexe of the restless body." "The glare of understanding being switched off, the lids of the hard aching mind closed, there is suddenly gloom . . . a waking ultra-cerebral obscurity . . . when the mind went wombtomb." This precious passage presents us with some of the keys to the writing of the next thirty years, which was to be essentially of the nature of an extensive metaphor or metonymy of body for soul. The passage holds many key words, starting with "asylum" and ending with "wombtomb." From these early years, Beckett sees the withdrawal of the mind into itself ("making himself a captive," he has said) as the nearest approach to the peace of the fetus in the womb: "I want . . . to be back in the caul on my back in the dark for ever" ("Fingal" in *More Pricks than Kicks*). "Asylum" stands for the symbolic refuges of various kinds to which the wanderings of the Beckettian hero will ever tend, as well as for the lunatic asylums where he will find the truly wise who have also withdrawn from the restlessness and the absurdity of life.

The "glare of understanding" is seen here as switched off. For "glare" we shall find everywhere in Beckett's works "light," which is meant to suggest full consciousness related to the external world. "Desert. Dazzling light": such are the first words of *Act Without Words I.* "Expanse of scorched grass . . . Blazing light" is the stage direction to *Happy Days;* "Table and immediately adjacent area in strong white light," that to *Krapp's Last Tape;* "This mime should be played at back of stage violently lit in its entire length," to *Act Without Words II.* And it is the obstinate light of consciousness that seems in *Play* to persist compellingly after death.

Opposed to light will be the dearly sought "gloom in the mind," a "waking ultra-cerebral obscurity." Murphy will be addicted to the dark, and his mental chamber will "picture itself as a sphere full of light fading into dark" (p. 78). It is important to emphasize how early the foundation of Beckett's imaginative system was laid. It is accompanied by an early criticism and reversal of vital values: Beckett could have made, perhaps fifteen years earlier, Malone's confession: "I began again [to live]. But little by little with a different aim. No longer in order to succeed but in order to fail."

"We were Pylades and Orestes for a period. . . . But I gave him up in the end because he was not serious." Such is Beckett's verdict—justified—on Belacqua. *Murphy* (1938) is indeed much more serious, a better means of self-investigation. The hero is a Dubliner living in London, and he conceives his mind to be "a large hollow sphere hermetically closed to the universe without." He wishes, so far as is possible, to exclude the world because the chaos that he sees there makes him deprecate any prospect of coming to terms with it. His mind is his refuge. And his method of withdrawing into it is to strap himself into a rocking chair and then to rock and rock until he "comes alive in his mind." Sitting up straight as Memnon in his chair, his hands tied to its arms, his eyes open in the dark, he is a "seedy solipsist" more convincingly than Belacqua was "a dud mystic." Denying the concrete world of the senses, Murphy, like Watt, or Molloy playing with his sixteen stones, abstracts himself in games that exhaust numerical relations or serial combinations, such as his predictable 120 permutations of the five assorted biscuits of his lunch—until a dog comes and gobbles them up. He is too contemplative to do his share of social work, until he joins the staff of a lunatic asylum. The inmates, having opted out of a "colossal fiasco," are seen as the nearest to sanity of all human beings, and the padded cells are worthy of them: "the three dimensions, slightly concave, were so exquisitely proportioned that the absence of the fourth was scarcely felt. . . . The compartment was *windowless, like a monad*" (emphasis added). These hints, and the color scheme—the tender luminous gray—set us in Beckett's little world of the human head (p. 125). The indispensable chair is transferred to Murphy's garret, which is perfect, since it is so small that he can hardly squeeze himself in: it is almost as good as Descarte's "hot cupboard." Moreover, Murphy finds a natural affinity in the person of Mr. Endon, the schizophrenic, whose case presented "a psychosis so limpid and imperturbable that Murphy felt drawn to it as Narcissus to his fountain."

Even if Murphy and Endon are two, and not simply Form (μορφή) and Inside (ἔνδον), the relation of the first to the second does partake of narcissism and culminates in an uncomfortable scene, where Murphy treats Endon's eyes like a reflecting water and plunges to meet him (in order to meet himself) brow to brow, face to face, in a sinister quasi-erotic contact (p. 190). As Beckett's metaphor-bearing visions are of precise significance, we shall find that they recur, and this relation will be echoed in *Watt* by the Sam–Watt connection.

In order to stress the pattern of the quest (fo Beckett sees himself in Murphy as Murphy does i Endon), a rescue party is sent from Dublin to fin the hero in London. But in the meantime, Murph has accidentally been burned to death while in on of his self-induced trances in his rocking chair. Th rescuers arrive in time to discover his burnt bod and a will desiring that his ashes should be dis posed of in the W.C. of the Abbey Theatre. The end on a pub floor, "swept away with the sand, th beer, the butts, the glass, the matches, the spit, th vomit."

"All these characters," Beckett tells us, "are pup pets, all except Murphy, who is not a puppet. There will be a Murphy in every work. Murphy Beckett's delegate or rather avatar, and the puppe are in his service. The book emanates from him. S when he is disposed of by death, the others on t same occasion are released from the various infli tions and penances that are meant as significa symbols. Thus Cooper, "one-eyed, triorchous could neither take his hat off nor sit down, a went about with "the hunted gait of a diabe pauper in a strange town," but as soon as Murp has gone, Cooper takes off his hat and firmly sits on it.

Murphy's mind is elaborately described in chapter 4 as made up of three zones, one of conflict in relation to the external world, one of autonomy and compensation, turning kick to caress, one of a dark flux of forms. It is in the dark zone that he loves himself (*Amor intellectualis quo Murphy se ipsum amat,* so runs the epigraph), with the love that Spinoza's God bears himself. It is in the lighter zone that, in spite of himself, he loves Celia, the tender-hearted prostitute from whom he runs away to preserve his integrity; in spite of which she is the only female creature who seems to have melted Beckett's heart. She has not only grace but dignity, which she shows in the speech beginning, 'I am a prostitute." This first novel being also the only one where he still lets himself express a sensi-:ive perception of externals, some lovely passages are given to her, as if her due.

> There was not much light, the room devoured it, but she kept her face turned to what there was. The small single window condensed its changes, as half-closed eyes see the finer values of tones, so that it was never quiet in the room, but brightening and darkening in a slow ample flicker that went on all day, brightening against the darkening that was its end. A peristalsis of light, worming its way into the dark.
>
> (ch. 5)

We leave her at the end looking up at the London sky "simply to have that unction of soft sunless light on her eyes that was all she remembered of Ireland."

The sky will never be so present again: Beckett at thirty is taking leave of girls and childhood, with tender regret for one joy at least, that of kite flying. It is transferred to that unworthy old man, Celia's grandfather; but at least she *looks:* "the rack broke behind them as she watched, for a moment they stood out, in a glade of limpid viridescent sky."

III

BECKETT was by now settled in Paris. Then it was war and occupation. In this preestablished chaos, Beckett, in spite of Proust, remembered friendship and, in spite of Geulincx, action. When his friend Alfred Péron, whom he had helped in the Resistance, was arrested, he had to flee to the south and become, as Vladimir and Estragon have been, an agricultural laborer in the Vaucluse. It was in the bitter solitude of his unpleasant refuge that he wrote *Watt* (circa 1943–1944, published 1953), allegedly to keep in practice.

If the book is probably to some extent an exercise, it is a fascinating one. Watt is, after Murphy, the next avatar, again the means of a mental experiment. When the book opens, we are in the world, with the prurient Mr. Hackett and the gross Nixons. We watch an object, a thing, which is identified in time as a subhuman type, Watt, a complex combination of the grotesque and the odd. At the end, in a small railway station, we shall again with common humanity be watching that same miserable misfit. In the meantime, in a kind of *Alice in Wonderland* journey, or first stage of an initiation novel, by train and by foot, Watt, whose walk, after a half-page description, can be described as that "of a headlong tardigrade," reaches Mr. Knott's, the goal of his quest. Unlike Kafka's hero, he has no difficulty in entering this castle: preestablished harmony has seen to it that the door should be open, that he should be expected. Soon after his arrival he is greeted by a loquacious character named Arsene, apparently a retainer in Mr. Knott's house. But the sum of things being constant, when Watt arrives, Arsene must go. As in a dream or in *Finnegans Wake,* characters that appear to be separate merge in time and reveal that they are one and the same. Slips of Arsene's tongue identify Watt's behavior and evolution with his own. Substituted for Arsene in whatever fashion, Watt is going to repeat him, to go like him into the service of Mr. Knott, through it and out of it—to go, as well, through the same moods. Existence, or whatever we call it, at Mr. Knott's, is termed "existence off the ladder" (p. 44), anticipating *The Lost Ones* and their mournful climbing by some twenty-five years. The ladder, here, since it is unlikely (but nothing is impossible) to refer to Jacob's, probably embodies the grotesque up-and-down scurry from which each one hopes to benefit. Knott, no character but a mere hypothesis, is an extremely ambiguous creation; a negation, not or nought, a knot, a Gott perhaps and a predecessor of Godot.

The experience is of what? It would seem, of withdrawal from the external world in order that the truth of the relation to it should be judged in a philosophical and critical spirit. "Something has happened today," we say in current speech. Can we state as a fact that, for instance, two men, father and son, have come to tune the piano? What is the reality of the phenomenon? What have we experienced? What remains in what we term our memory? "A mere example of light connecting bodies, . . . incidents of great formal brilliance and indeterminable purport." Watt now sets about trying names on things and on himself "almost as a woman does hats." But can anything in a world of fluid contingencies be identified? "Looking at a pot, . . . it was in vain that Watt said Pot, pot. . . . For it was not a pot, the more he looked at it. . . . It resembled a pot, it was almost a pot." So things have already become unnamable. Who is there in any case that could do the naming? Shall we suggest that the fault lies in the characters being ineffectual projections? The author would retort that he does not feel more "real" than he makes them. There are phases, moments, aspects, in a confused process of existence, Arsene's or Watt's.

> One fleeing, fleeing to rest,
> One resting on the flight.
> (*Watt,* sec. 1)

"He," "I" makes no difference; there are no characters or, at most, Beckett would see his characters as players of parts, as if he foresaw the plays. Arsene utters his "short statement" (twenty-four brilliant pages) with the modest doubts that will be echoed by Pozzo and Hamm: "haw! I began a little low perhaps."

Let us make a proposition: that the subject of each of Beckett's novels is exactly and entirely in its title, and that each represents an avatar of Beckett, who knows that he exists and signifies only to himself. We shall then admit that everything in *Watt* deals with aspects of Watt, including Mr. Knott. A god-image, yes, of course: Knot, nought, Gott. But he "of himself knew nothing. And so he needed to be witnessed. Not that he might know, no, but that he might not cease" (p. 203): this is clear.

Murphy had impudently appropriated the intellectual love that Spinoza meant for God. Mr. Knott's "tireless servants" are all of two kinds, either lanky or pot-bellied, as Mercier and Camier are soon going to be: Beckett's tireless servants. The oddity, in every sense of the word, of Mr. Knott's footwear—"on the one [foot] a sock and on the other a stocking"—has been Watt's and shall be Estragon's. If we accept that Beckett intends every word he writes, these hints should not be thrown away.

As Beckett sets his figures before us, whether Watt or Knott, a certain quite deliberate element of freedom and gratuitousness goes to their ornament and gives them a presence. But the author never intends it to be an identity. We read "this refusal by Knott, I beg your pardon, by Watt, to assist at the eating, by the dogs" (p. 115). Watt is a feeler sent by Beckett toward the religious vision, and the stay at Mr. Knott's has been no feast of egotism but, rather, complete self-forgetfulness, as Watt will state later (I turn back to front his inverted paragraph):

> Abandoned my little to find him. My little to learn him forgot. My little rejected to have him. To love him my little reviled. This body homeless. This mind ignoring. These emptied hands. This emptied heart. To him I brought. To the temple. To the teacher. To the source of nought.

Watt, like *Murphy,* leans heavily on a philosophical system that it half follows, half mocks an parodies, that of Leibniz. Mr. Knott as keystone o a Leibnizian world may represent, in opposition t the single actuality effectively retained, the infinit number of possibles held in reserve: this is an ide on which the whole book thrives, since it contain page after page of enumerations arranged with incredible care and precision, of exhaustive and some readers will say, exhausting series, makin (see for instance the croak of the three frogs, pp 137–138) a prose of numbers constructed like silen music.

The phrase "the little world of Mr Knott's establishment"—it has three levels like Murphy' mind—reminds us that, to use Beckett's phras "we are in a head." Confirmations are not lackin We read (p. 131) that "nothing could be added t Mr Knott's establishment and from it nothin taken away." We had read of Murphy's little wor the same tale of complete virtualities. Of Mr. Kno we read, "In empty hush, in airless gloom, M Knott abode" (p. 200). Fifty pages earlier we ha read, "to us in our windowlessness, in our bloc heat, in our hush, to us who could not hear th wind, nor see the sun what call could come . . . ea in his separate soundless unlit warmth" (p. 152

Obviously both "states," as William Blake might say—Watt and Knott—are one and the same, tried at two levels; substantially the same state will serve for Malone. It is a state of contraction, rid of time, space, and contingency, in which all necessities of material existence are replaced by tokens and symbols, the totality of food and drink for instance being jumbled together in a single, weekly, most unsavory mess. Similarly, since no life-pattern subsists except a rhythm of alternation we may have in a matter of minutes, in *Endgame* (1957), Hamm's "getting up" and his "going to bed"; it will be represented by the putting on and the taking off of a sheet.

Having gone through the Knott state, Watt re-joins Sam, the author as narrator, in some other "spacious annexe," where they compose a fantastic narcissist act, on the model of Murphy and Endon but infinitely more elaborate. "We began to draw ourselves forward . . . until our heads, our noble bulging brows, met, and touched." Thus starts a complicated ballet that the two figures dance together. "I felt," Sam declares, "as though I were standing before a great mirror"; and soon mirror speech comes, the inversions becoming more and more intricate and difficult. Ethical inversion follows. There is great slaughter of trustful robins, and for the rats, the delicate attention of feeding the young to their mothers. "It was on these occasions, we agreed . . . that we came nearest to God." Watt appears by degrees, with his "little red sudarium"[6] "to staunch eventual blood," a Christ figure, a Christ outraged, stoned, revived at the end by a pail of dirty water flung in his face. A self-image, he appears to Sam in this guise: "his face was bloody, his hands also, and thorns were in his scalp." No work of Beckett's declares his frustration more bitterly than this:

> Of his anxiety to improve, of his anxiety to understand, of his anxiety to get well, what remained? Nothing.
>
> But was not that something? . . .
> So sick, so alone.
> And now.
> Sicker, aloner.
> Was not that something?
>
> (sec. 2)

[6] napkin for wiping sweat from the face. It is used to refer to the cloth with which, according to legend, Saint Veronica wiped the face of Christ, and upon which his features remain impressed.

We have tried to pick the philosophical bones of this difficult book clean of flesh. It should be said now that it is very funny. The endlessly contrived succession, first of the dogs that appear in order to eat the remains of Mr. Knott's food, then of the attendants on the dogs and of their families with their fantastic accumulation of disgusting diseases and mutilations, should not be skipped, but, as François Rabelais's are, enjoyed. Disgust becomes gusto and some of the scenes, including the opening one, show enormous verve. Dean Swift is not so remote an ancestor.

Side by side with the solemn parodist we see also the suppressed poet, suddenly taken advantage of by insidious solicitations that come straight from childhood. The language feels the enchantment: "In his skull the voices whispering their canon were like a patter of mice, a flurry of little grey paws in the dust." Yet the power of Beckett's English prose style is not in such rare faintly nostalgic musics but in the gift, which after all has made *Watt,* of seeing the abstract not only as concrete but as concrete intensities. When Watt leaves Mr. Knott's establishment, when in other words he undergoes one of his mutations, we find round him "the grey air aswirl with vain entelechies." The power is there.

IV

Watt is still baroque and wit-ridden. Beckett may have thought that he would never be able to tear the leafy scrolls from his thyrsus until he as a writer changed his skin. In any case he saw all language as "external." While he turned with increasing resentment against its externalities, they had better be shown up by an external language. The French poems written since 1937 had shown the way to detached utterance: the *Nouvelles* or stories of 1945 took it. He never wrote better.

Two of the three *Nouvelles* (1955) have such a similar start as shows an obsessive resentment against birth: the experience is presented not as entering life but as leaving the womb. In "The Expelled" the door opens and the narrator is thrust violently down the steps onto the pavement; then his hat is flung after him. The hat has been a constant symbol, from Murphy's Cooper onward, of an inflicted doom. Here the father is recalled saying, "Come, my son, we are going to buy your hat, *as if it pre-existed from all eternity*" (emphasis added): in other words, the hat is psychologically the father-directed superego, metaphysically the God-ordained predestination. In "The End," the victim is as decisively sent away from the hospital. Expelled, he has to look for a refuge, some kind of substitute for the womb or at least for the "hot cupboard" of Descartes. In the first case, it is, briefly, a cab. In "The End," which becomes much more of a dramatic vision, it is a boat, which he turns into a bed, home, and coffin all in one, and which he finally scuttles into nothingness, rather in the manner that Malone's visions will also vanish with him.

From now on our author refuses to play the silly game of literary verisimilitude. He has "made" a cab, made a horse, as a child might: what of it? "I had enough of that horse." And as suddenly as Alice would the guinea pigs, he suppresses him. In "The End" it is the "creation" that we witness, as he makes for his boat a lid of stray boards: "it's incredible the number of boards I've come across in my lifetime, I never needed a board but there it was." Elsewhere he notes that if he needs a hunchback, here comes the hunchback at once with his goodly hump, glad to be of use. In *Watt,* the piano tuners, even if they were a phenomenon of light, had still appeared to be external. By now Beckett is before us making up a story, never quite letting it appear as made but rather unmaking it at some point of the process. In "The Calmative," after exclaiming in disgust against the "nightmare thingness" ("cette horreur chosesque" is more expressive) into which he has strayed, he asks us not to mind, "for we are, needless to say, in a skull." The conventional writer of fiction proceeds after choice and rejection so as to let us see only a smooth surface of narrative. If an absurdity or even a merely clumsy phrase comes into his head, he is careful not to let us know; he has probably suppressed it midway to clear consciousness. Beckett is careful to utter it and to add, "no wrong" ("The End"). Similarly, Malone will tell us:

> Sapo had no friends—no, that won't do. Sapo was on good terms with his little friends.
>
> (*Malone Dies,* p. 190)[7]

[7]All references to quotations from the "trilogy" are to the one-volume edition of the three novels, London, 1959.

This, as Gertrude Stein would say, is "arrangement," a better arrangement. But the imaginings in their immediacy are of the nature of dreamcraft: the creative writer, or perhaps anybody, possesses this gift to conjure images or simply to let them come and to organize them as they come—to "play with them"—as he says. An element of freedom is thus inserted in the dire compulsion or quasi-metaphysical predestination of the writer held to his task by invisible judges, a doom that becomes an obsessive part of his personal mythology.

The only subject of the writing is Beckett at work. Nothing in the told is antecedent to the telling, nothing preexists to the word uttered as part of a sequence of words: the past tense is a silly pretense. "What I tell this evening is passing this evening at this passing hour" ("The Calmative").

"And now here, what now here," he will ask ir "Text for Nothing II." "One enormous second as ir Paradise," such is the inner life, with the "past" floating in it, at most hypothetical, and the "now" no true present, but a thick stagnant limbo. Doe the narrator thus situated really exist? Is the con fused dream that goes on in his head any proof The question is put in "The Calmative" (p. 39) "But then, the sweet?" If a little boy has given hir a sweet, he must exist.

"I am I," Gertrude Stein says, "because my littl dog knows me." The *Nouvelles* are the earliest pros writings in the first person. The reason is simpl the narrator has to say "I" if he is to questio efficiently the validity of the I, of the personalit They are also the beginning of a long interior mor ologue that covers the French novel trilogy and *Ho It Is.*

V

QUEST, refuge; motion, motionlessness. What else there? Watt moves in quest, finds refuge, has leave it. Mercier and Camier, in the first, sho French novel of that name, go on a journey fro town and inevitably back to town: since *Finnega Wake* all moves thus round and back. A pair agai like Watt and Sam, they decline to be taken f Narcissus and image, being differentiated like t two types of Mr. Knott's servants, one tall a lanky, one short and pot-bellied. Insofar as th are two, they must necessarily come to the hor of being two. There are omens: when they come together to arrange their journey, they are confronted by two dogs who after mating try very hard to separate.

Their journey is no formal quest; but like Watt's, or Moran's in *Molloy,* it brings initiation into awareness of the nullity of all, hence refusal. The going out of town, without any explicitness, must be interpreted as going out of life-routine. Bicycle or umbrella disintegrate and Camier destroys and throws away his memoranda, as Hamm in *Endgame,* to make an end, discards his possessions, or Buster Keaton in *Film* tears his photographs.

In spite of the constant blind alleys of travel and of argument, *Mercier and Camier* is more constantly comic than anything since *Murphy,* because it is mostly dialogue, and Beckett has the gift of comic, or rather humorous, dialogue. The book is a prolonged act or number, the two protagonists are clowns, as Vladimir and Estragon are, and what it promises on top of what it achieves as a novel is the clowning theater of *Waiting for Godot* and *Endgame.* After *Watt,* before the "trilogy," *Mercier and Camier* s what we may term an open tale, never separated rom the author, so that the characters are animated forms commanded by his purpose. For the irst time, being "in a head," "characters"—Mercier nd Camier—are confronted by one whom they do ot know but who knows them from the cradle: heir predecessor, Watt. This is in a playful mood. n *Texts for Nothing, Malone Dies,* and *The Unnamable,* ve shall see the creative mind become a haunted lace where Molloy, Malone, and all these others o round and round in a sinister little gray hell.

VI

My name is Molloy": thus he finally tells the poce in the book that bears his name (1951). Characristically it costs him considerable effort to reember that: "even my sense of identity was rapped in a namelessness often hard to peneate." "There could be no things but nameless ings, no names but thingless names." Here the ndition of the lost self is linked with a lost perption of reality, which I suggest is its conseence, although Beckett's "even" seems to put the neral loss first. It seems obvious that we cannot ild our world otherwise than by starting from our personal center. A criticism of experience is based on this finding. Perceptions become phantasmic. Will Molloy recognize A and C if he sees them again? "What do I mean by seeing and seeing again?" A sort of dim cinema, all fade-ins, fade-outs, follows in dreamy travelings these faint and evanescent silhouettes. There are references everywhere to a lost reality, similar to Proust's: "my region," "my town," never left but carried along by the alienated mind. There has been a secession from the world of the so-called living. Molloy, after Murphy, after Watt, has reached a refuge, which in his case may be final, and which is termed his mother's room (wombtomb?).

In relation to *Watt, Molloy* shows many changes, the decisive one being that here structural form dominates, and organizes substance. Molloy goes on a vague quest marked by growing physical difficulties in getting about, the symbol of growing spiritual difficulties. He has passed through a forest where he has disposed of an intruder and, judging from the glee of the episode, worked off the author's capricious aggressiveness. And now, renewing the quest motive, Beckett gives full power to the mirror pattern used briefly in *Murphy* or *Watt,* and which confirms, by repeating it, the fatality of the process of deprivation and decline. Moran is sent explicitly in quest of Molloy, as Molloy, like Murphy, had been sent implicitly in quest of Beckett. A machinery of secret orders from a mysterious hierarchy briefly echoes Franz Kafka. In the end Moran feels dispossessed: he has become Molloy; the grading from comfort to discomfort, from conformism to nihilism, has been a significant experience. We must understand that Beckett's findings about himself are doomed to remain the same.

"I was already settling into my raglimp stasis." The sentence cannot properly be attributed to Molloy. It is obviously Beckett who is using him as his own raglimp stasis; of his personae this is one of the most systematically repulsive to see or smell, and scatological to hear, a creation reminiscent of Swift: a crippled Yahoo, one-eyed and, even before his final decrepitude, with never more than one leg in use. Beckett, who shares with Alfred Jarry an obsessive interest in cycling, goes to great pains to make Molloy invent a way of passing from crutches to bike. Since such characters remain dependent projections on whom the author in self-punishment has inflicted what he terms "his dream infirmities," from time to time the persona forgets and acts as if he were whole. Beckett is ever playing with his incarnation, making him remark: "You don't remember immediately who you are, when you wake."

From novel to play this sado-masochistic dream, punishment, diminution, mutilation, proceeds until it inurns Mahood's trunk in *The Unnamable,* and legless Nagg and Nell in *Endgame,* where the substitution of dustbins for jars adds the connotation of refuse. Symbols are more complex than metaphors and carry a sort of genetic memory, so we should remember that in *Molloy* (p. 49), the sealed jar means enclosure: it betokens the separate, autonomous little world, opening out in ecstatic self-forgetfulness; "yet mostly I stayed in my jar which knew neither seasons nor gardens": this is the smallest model of Mr. Knott's private world and the forerunner of Malone's bed where, having passed outside time, he is "never hot, never cold."

"Up there," where there are seasons and gardens, solitude is unbearable, so that relations are invented, friendship, sex, anything to be two, or to pretend. Watt makes shift with Mrs. Gorman's one breast (castration again)—in any case, "he does not have the strength, and she does not have the time"; Molloy is seduced by Lousse but will never know clearly whether he has dealt with man or woman. The loves of Macmann and Moll in *Malone Dies* are cruelly grotesque. If such insubstantial human substance be denied, only abstract formalities remain to fill the mind. "I saw the world," Molloy states, "in an excessively formal manner." Sixteen sucking-stones to be distributed among four pockets so that the whole series has been sucked before the same stone recurs: here is a problem, and a tense situation. It all amounts to a process of annulment, life values being destroyed by a constant injection of absurdity. Gradually, until we get to the pure formalism of *Lessness,* materiality will count less and less, organization more and more. We shall have in the end the nearest approach to abstract expressionism in literature.

VII

Malone Dies (1951) has for its subject a mental, not a physical, process. Malone is in appearance a bedridden moribund receiving from invisible hands his daily necessities of food and chamber pot. He is once more, in truth, man withdrawn from the external categories of time or space into his own private world. His stick, which blind Hamm of *Endgame* inherits as his gaff, is of apparent use to pull the daily tray to his bed, but essentially it is the metaphorical tool of the quest and is so used in *The Unnamable* to grope for the creatures lost in the gray depths of the microcosmic pit. This active tool of man is replaced by the passive burden of the sack or bag in *How It Is* and *Happy Days.*

Malone (Me alone) plans a time schedule of mental activity designed to last precisely as long as his pseudo-existence. He must make first of all an inventory of "his possessions," useless or rejected waifs, a pipe bowl, a horse chestnut, that have made an appeal to his solitude because they too were broken and derelict (p. 248) and have elicited the same kind of childish tenderness as the lanterns of the cab do in "The Expelled." Then he must tell himself a story, the almost Zolaesque one of Sapo whom he loses, and has to seek again, by Proustian "excavation." "I have taken a long time to find him again, but I have found him" (p. 226). In that ingeniously grotesque Beckettian garb which he wears always minutely described in shopkeeper style, i[t] must be he. "I slip into him, I suppose, in the hope of learning something." Macmann, for Sapo ha[s] reappeared under the new name, does indeed provide him with the usual vision, in a blend of masochism and suffering: "he began to wish that th[e] rain would never cease, nor consequently his sufferings or pain" (p. 243).

Malone Dies is beautifully true to its plan: it ha[s] the most perfect ending. Malone and the story, th[e] teller and the telling, fade together into nothingness, as time passes into eternity on the flanks [of] the Grecian urn:

> Lemuel is in charge, he raises his hatchet on which t[he] blood will never dry, but not to hit anyone, he w[ill] . . . not hit anyone anymore, he will not touch anyo[ne] anymore, either with it or with it or with it or with
>
> or with it or with his hammer or with his stick or wi[th] his fist or in thought in dream I mean never he will ne[ver]
>
> or with his pencil or with his stick or
>
> or light light I mean
>
> never there he will never
>
> never anything
>
> there
>
> any more

VIII

Malone Dies gives the first formal picture of the microcosmic landscape, the haunted limbo where Beckett's creatures await their call or their doom, alternately stiff as Memnon, like Murphy, like Macmann, like the later Hamm of *Endgame,* or "rag-limp" like Molloy, and variously grotesque. There they are in "this foul little den all dirty, white and vaulted, as though hollowed out of ivory": a dishonored picture of a human head, yet by virtue of the usual paradox that equates microcosm to universe, this one is well furnished "with my little suns and moons that I hang aloft." "Up there" the so-called living move and jostle, while down in the gray the strange shadowplay goes on that will be so powerfully exteriorized in *Endgame.*

Texts for Nothing, written about 1950, and *The Un-namable* (1953), even though this last work is in-cluded by Beckett himself in a trilogy with *Molloy* and *Malone,* seem to me to mark a decisive and dramatic break, a progress in the disruption of the world image, in the separation of the subject from it, as well as in the heroic effort to discard all vital illusions and to reach at all costs the truth of personality. It is by leaning on external reality and building connections that we establish our sense of personal identity. How then could any secure identity outlast this cutting adrift? The query of the ost, "Where would I go if I could go, who would be, if I could be, what would I say, if I had a oice?" ("Text IV") passes into the last denial, who says this saying it's me?" The identity of the elf is now shattered, and what has threatened om the earliest utterance has come to pass: the oice, the language are unrecognized and unac-nowledged by the innermost personality. "Je est n autre," as with Rimbaud, an alien speaks; yet a rther dimension of self-mockery sees through is crazy construction: "here is a fine trio, to think at all that makes only one and that one makes othing" ("Text XII"). Remember the three zones Murphy's mind. The Beckettian personality lits, generally, into three—the outer one is amed Basil in *The Unnamable:* a man of time, space, d words—the words of the tribe. In *Words and usic* Croak, Bob, and Joe (Milord, Music, and ords) constitute the same sort of "trio."

To the alienness of language corresponds the ali-ness of all reality, which no language can cope th, being a powerless middle term between two educible forms, the mind and the rest. "What is it, this unnamable thing, that I name and name?" ("Text VI"). Watt had already echoed, before his pot, the scholastic despair before the unreality of denomination.

The inner man hearing the outer speak "the words of others" has a sense as if of demonic possession: these "others" then become the agents of an invisible court, responsible for his doom, to utter more words, to write more "pensums." This is less a theme than an obsession, which reaches its peak in *The Unnamable.* The feeling that one serves a sentence entails the hope of release, the possibility that this is the right and so the last "pensum." However, the dwindling length of Beckett's writings in the course of years is connected not so much with this hope as with the conflict and resistance of which *Texts for Nothing* give the first impressive witness. Such a conflict is apparent in the vehement, panting utterance, the short hurried sentences, the inchoate, self-checked progression of the language. We find it again in a context that is strongly suggestive of emotional disturbance, that is, in *The Unnamable.*

The Murphys, Watts, Molloys, Malones are "inside"—all that Beckett has left of them; but now their castigator, who had great hopes of them, knows that he has fostered dangerous traitors, who lure him from his dark refuge, back and up among the "living," since they must pretend to be living. Hence there is a more savage retraction than ever before from these auxiliary selves, as well as fiercer self-punishment. Mahood, or Mahood's invention, in *The Unnamable* is deprived of all four limbs, stuck in a jar, and made to serve as the sign for a restaurant near the shambles, his excreta being taken from under him once a week to manure the garden. This cruel fantasy, upheld heroically for many pages, represents a symbolical equivalent of utter mental solitude, humiliation, and misery; and the narrator sufficiently traces its creation from a growing alienation and denial of the body: "I know I am seated, my hands on my knees. Were it not for the distant testimony of my palms, my soles . . . I would gladly give myself the shape . . . of an egg." What we witness is willful self-mutilation, carried to a frantic extreme. Kafka, in similar mood as the father-despised object, turned his Gregor into a bug in *The Metamorphosis* (1937). Beckett echoes him: "my monster's carapace will rot off me" (p. 327). The obsessive shapes of the ball, the sphere, the cylinder should be noticed as enclosed shapes. The two creatures of *Imagination Dead Imagine,* then the many "lost ones," will be thus enclosed.

The technique has become a violent and fantastic expressionism: the book, starting from worse than a hermit's solitude, reads like a Bosch *Temptation of Saint Anthony*—we also read of "my tempters." The imaginative movement becomes a whirl. The narrator of *The Unnamable,* haunted like a phenakistoscope[7] by revolving figures, may feel at first that he has always been sitting "there," but he is caught in his turn in an imaginary spiral race toward a center where all the grotesque seductions of home life await him but are, just in time, gleefully annihilated. Later on he changes parts: instead of his telling the story of the persona, the persona tells his. So it is as the creature of Mahood that he is stuck in the jar, until they merge, as indeed all identities here tend more and more to merge. Worm is their final reduction to a kind of debased Knott-state, without any kind of self-knowledge. He must first be hoisted out of the sinister equivalent of the Proustian limbo, out of the gray, "with a long pole perhaps, with a hook at the end . . . that tiny blur in the depths of the pit, is he" (p. 361). A new development of the Beckettian vision presents a fierce struggle between the powers that want Worm to be quite born and brought "up there," and the narrator's resistance: "Mahood won't get me out, nor Worm either—they set great store on Worm, to coax me out." But Worm remains fragmentary like Hamm's three-legged dog: "Let's leave him his eye too, it's to see with, this great wild black and white eye." "Feeling nothing, knowing nothing, he exists nevertheless, but not for himself, for others, others conceive him and say, Worm is, since we conceive him" (p. 349). This reminds us of the formulae used for Knott. We have moved from Descartes and Leibniz to Bishop Berkeley—even if an inverted Berkeley: from God to Worm, *esse est percipi.* Beckett's images are significantly persistent: "Worm will see the light in a desert, the light of day, the desert day" (p. 369). This is the light of consciousness, the desert of conscious life, in which Winnie, the heroine of *Happy Days,* will be stuck, but which we detected as "glare" in the early "Dream." The book is a long fight for impossible integrity or unity, against dispersal into time, space, and accident, and the diverting attraction of those tricky puppets, among whom Worm will not be allowed finally to take his place. The obsessive alienation into language remains a leitmotif: "I'm in words, made of words, others' words" (p. 390).

[7]A disk with figures on it arranged radially, representing a moving object in successive positions.

The metaphysical judges have been a diversion, an unavailing means of forgetting loneliness and dereliction. The inner conflicts have never been so fierce. The despair has never been so total. The heroic persistence remains. The last sentence reads: "I can't go on, I'll go on."

IX

Obviously this is a breaking point, and *How It Is* (1961) is a novel to deny the novel and its puppet-play. Since any novel traces a pattern of human relations, this one will reassert that all such patterns boil down to solitude ("travel"), pretended relation, and redoubled solitude; in other words, "before Pim, with Pim, after Pim." All relations are shown in rough expressionist terms, as brutal intrusions. Molloy "communicated" with his mother by a code of knocks on the head. Pim is dealt with by a system of jabs of a tin-opener in the buttocks supplemented again by knocks on the head, which in time, through suffering, as one drills rats, will bring out the social qualities of understanding and awareness. The narrator persecutes Pim, is later persecuted by Bom: it is all chance, as Pozzo will say. And all relations are narcissistic, all sadism is auto-sadism: "I too am called Pim," the narrator says. Seeing, even more than his predecessors, language as a compulsion, the narrator *hears* voices on all sides: they do the telling. A determined poetic symbolism has swept away all remnants of realism: the book is a sort of narrative poem, a staccato succession of verselike units, each flashing its image in an aggressively curtailed, quasi-telegraphese form of words recording an endless interior monologue. The slowly diminishing quota of unchanging necessities carried through life according to the stoic vision *(omnia mecum porto)* is here symbolized by the sack with its content of tins. Remembering Giacomo Leopardi's "the world is mud" ("fango è il mondo"), Beckett makes mud the ubiquitous environment of life and even vision: "another image so soon again a woman looks up it wasn't a dream . . . nor a memory . . . it was an image the kind I see sometimes . . . in the mud."

Besides the purely graphic writing, which is

triumph over given speech, the great novelty here is to see literature not as transmitting the substance of anything else but as offering a self-sufficient arrangement of words, in part a multiple rearrangement of the same words:

this voice these voices no knowing not meaning a choir no no only one but quaqua meaning on all sides megaphones *possibly technique* . . . unless recordings on ebonite or suchlike a whole life generations on ebonite one can imagine it nothing to prevent one . . . *mix it all up change the natural order play about with that* [author's italics].
(p. 115)

"Technique," "recordings on ebonite or suchlike," mean the distancing of the dreaded usurping personality, but at the same time the renewed immediacy of the past, the endless possibility of significant repetition, the dramatization, by contrasted presence, of the shifts in selfhood. In this way *Krapp's Last Tape* is almost described in *How It Is,* where in the meantime the final "arrangement" takes the form of a complicated arithmetical pattern setting forth "an endless procession" of such unequal couples, a million strong, in a spatial structure that in 1961 foresees that of *The Lost Ones* ten years later.

X

BECKETT's art had become in time more and more of a projection of images generated by his inner pressures; in other words it had become more and more expressionist because more and more oneiric, and because, in its externalizations, it ignored the external world. Intenseness, aggressiveness, violence, as they are the motive force of the artist, will remain part of the art, leading to the distortion of whatever shapes it borrows, and to vehement incoherence in their disposition. Such an art is ever strongly dramatic: the dialectic of conflict and the clash of assertion and denial in *The Unnamable* are strikingly so. Beckett has already turned to the stage.

What stage? As we watch *Waiting for Godot* (1952) we know at once that this play, in its time avant-garde, is closely related to the popular vision of the old music hall or circus, or the early comic cinema of Mack Sennett. The potent attraction of the piece comes from the association of this comic vision, medium, technique, and the bitterness of the message: persistence, knowing itself hopeless; resistance to disintegration, aware of its absurdity. The art to convey this could be termed philosophical clowning. But is not clowning the philosophical essence of parody? Beckett assumes the whole tradition of such art from Shakespeare on. In it the clown debunks, demolishes his "betters," and destroys all values because all values, once fixed, are false. The clown ridicules "status": see the stiff shirt front that is but a clumsy piece of celluloid (Murphy had worn it already), and the bowler hat, and the morning coat, the tails of which flap over baggy trousers. The grotesque remains of the pompous clothes of the Establishment that he wears are meant not to fit, and to be revealed as a disguise. While making the serious members of society conscious as of a distorting mirror, they leave the wearer as free as the man of stoic vision before the gods have cast him for a part. The clown will never be cast. He ridicules action, patiently going about it with minute care, contriving his failures and tumbles until he reaches ultimate success as an anticlimax. *Act Without Words I* (1957) and *II* (1959) are perfect clowning: in the second, the two clowns come out of their sacks, go through the day's work and back into the sacks, in possibly ten minutes. One is brisk and active and does a lot of things in quick time. The other is sluggish, uninterested, indolent as Belacqua himself, and achieves very little. But when they are back in their sacks, after killing exactly as much time, the way they killed it makes no difference.

Vladimir and Estragon in *Waiting for Godot* seem to be outside any definition of clowning; perhaps we should be content with calling them clownish actors, but they do an act rather than play a part. In fact, Beckett has been careful to insert enough farce to discourage pathos in spite of the pathetic elements in the text. Thus the pulling off of a stubborn boot, the horse-play with Lucky, and the kicks and howls and the tumbling of all the characters in a heap, and the juggling interlude (with a probably unconscious Laurel and Hardy origin) involving two heads and three hats, are carefully inserted with a dual purpose: such amusements that pass the time must be felt as representing the inanity of all active "diversions," truly so called, so felt, ever since Murphy tried to reach mystic unity. Moreover, aesthetically speaking, clownish clothes and clownish acting are part of the rejection of all realism. A realistic setting would spoil everything. We do not mean only scenery but, even if marked in the most sketchy and symbolic manner, a precise and external localization of the setting. In *Waiting for Godot,* the stage ("a country road, a tree") is in fact all the world and a stage, of which the players show their awareness in their mocking dialogue: encouraging Estragon's flight toward the auditorium, Vladimir exclaims, "Not a soul in sight!" And Pozzo thinks the place must be "The Board."

Vladimir and Estragon are waiting for Godot. Each one of us, as long as he has something to expect, can insert Godot as the unknown factor or providential visitor. But Godot is he who never comes, a Kafkaesque vision again. He has sent a "messenger" (in Greek, ἄγγελος), only to say that he won't come that day but the next; on the second day, the message is to the same effect, but the Messenger destroys all hope of a real connection by asserting that he has never come before. Vladimir and Estragon are not *known,* nor ever will be. *Esse est percipi,* and Beckett's characters will feel more and more inexistent because unperceived.

Godot of the divine undertones does not come, but in a Manichean world, Pozzo does: a mean man-devil, with his slave and carrier, Lucky, whom he drives like an animal, by rope and whip. Lucky and Pozzo, abject slave and cruel bully, seem almost to sum up human relations, as *How It Is* will again set them forth. Yet Vladimir and Estragon show, with attraction and repulsion significantly alternating, a more equal relation between two desperate solitudes, with a note of elder brother protection on one side (Vladimir) and sullen rebelliousness on the other (Estragon). The games of friendship help pass the time like other vital illusions, such as the leafless tree being found in sudden leaf.

"Waiting," the seemingly endless, fruitless, meaningless waiting, points to the heavy anguish of time that dominates the play as an image of life. Pozzo himself, the tyrant gone helplessly blind on the second day, sums up the nullity of time and of life-in-time: ". . . one day we were born, one day we shall die, the same day, the same second. . . . They give birth astride of a grave, the light gleams an instant, then it's night once more." Blind Pozzo now jerks Lucky's rope: "On!"—surely, thus situated, the most dramatic word in the play, and which sums up the heroic absurdity of mankind.

Much has been said of the theological implications of the play, which are almost too obvious. Their purport is another matter. There is nothing here except the author's images, *cosa mentale.* So we can only speak of theological images, and pass on from one more "mythology."

XI

Endgame (1957), more definitely even than *Godot,* is "in a head," and the brain-gray bare room with its two high windows is evidently a gloomy inner aspect of the microcosm. "Reality" is here twice removed: it is not Beckett's but Hamm's vision, sick, subjective, severely coherent as such, yet again slyly bursting those bounds; and double-leveled since Hamm pointedly is an actor playing Hamm:

CLOV: What is there to keep me here?
HAMM: The dialogue.

And again:

HAMM: I'm warming up for my last soliloquy.

The four characters who must be seen as inter-dependent fantasies are thus in every sense "in th room": Hamm, blind, paralyzed, what can hardly b called his life bleeding away, as the tyrannic cente of personality; Clov ("stiff, staggering walk"), sort of adopted son; Nagg and Nell, Hamm's legles parents, set in two dustbins like Mahood's person in his jar in *The Unnamable,* and as Winnie, up to he bust, will be in the mound of *Happy Days.*

Just as Malone had contrived for his end a time accompaniment of words and tales, so with Hamr comes the end of Hamm's world, which is all w see, for his surroundings have been brought int being by his creative act—everything has been prc jected from him. Yet all the news of the process h initiated must now be brought back to him; n more bicycle wheels, no more pap, no more natu (significantly there is an addition: "in the vici ity"), no more tides, no more coffins. Hamm hi self enlightens us as to the nonobjective charact of the vision that is the play: "I once knew a ma man who thought the end of the world had cor . . . I'd take him by the hand and drag him to t window. Look! There! All that rising corn! And there! Look! The sails of the herring fleet! All that loveliness. . . . All he had seen was ashes."

It is all the reflection of a mental act, but whose? Ultimately, perhaps, that of the sado-masochistic creator, who once more makes use of his creatures to carry out an experiment of decay. It is in fact a rite that we see performed before us with cruel precision. The realistic data have been suppressed, including objective time references; they are now merely symbolical. Hamm sits as Malone lay through un-days and un-seasons, playing with the signs of getting up and going to bed and taking his medicines.

Hamm stands in the center not of the room only, but of Beckett's imaginings, and all relations connect with him. He exerts the gloomily cruel authority of the father-figure over his own father and mother. His relation to Clov, like that of Pozzo to Lucky in act 2 of *Waiting for Godot,* depends on acceptance; it is accepted because suffering and making someone else suffer seem to be a need for both parties in a human partnership. The model in this case might be August Strindberg's expressionist play, *The Dance of Death,* where the Captain, Alice's hated and hating husband, throws out of the window cards, whiskey, cigars, glasses, and on the floor torn photographs of his wife, as Hamm here discards gaff, toy dog, whistle. There is a striking likeness in the bitter mood, in the dialogue, in the weary fatality of hate.

Hamm is as deadly and cruel as Hamlet, because he is as completely desperate. The apparent paradox is that this sadist sees himself as a Christ figure and victim; but so does Estragon, and so had Watt appeared to Sam; every human being is a Christ. Hamm retains his bloody *sudarium,* with which he covers himself as the curtain falls. He has speculated, almost in the Teilhard vein of seeing God as terminal evolution, as to whether out of the absurd our heroism might not create some sort of meaning.

XII

Happy Days (1961) is not an easy play to interpret. The dazzling desert light that Winnie shares with *Act Without Words I* and *II,* in contrast to the gray endocephalic light of *Endgame,* should mean that we are "up there," in a desert which is both that, external, of life, and that, nearest to external, of full consciousness; yet the position of the heroine and her gradual reduction to a head emerging out of the mound are purely symbolical. Willie explains Winnie: living "on the other side," again in a sort of Kafkaesque burrow, browsing over old newspaper items and filthy postcards, he declines almost until the very end to become aware of her, and embodies her doom not to communicate. The suppression of Winnie's body means that it has ceased to be acknowledged and thus to be significant. *Esse est percipi;* Beckett again plays variations on the formula of Berkeley's idealism. Winnie feels a desperate metaphysical need thus to be perceived: "Strange feeling that someone is looking at me. I am clear, then dim, then gone, then dim again, then clear again . . . in and out of someone's eye."

What are we to think of her "happiness"? Is it merely silly, is it on her part consciously ironical, does the irony stand somewhere between author and protagonist? It is part of the attraction of the play that we do not quite know what to make of it, of those snatches of sentimental songs, those tags and clichés of banal poems with which she enlivens—stoic, or deluded fool—the emptiness of her days. In either respect, or both, for they need not be exclusive, we should see her not as a particular "character" but as a symbol and reflection of our own condition. Of the last "visitors" she has had, the man gaping at her wondered what she meant, and his wife turned fiercely on him, asking him what he thought *he* meant. If her absurdity is thus shown as ours, her happiness is indeed a reflection of whatever we may feel in that line "Blind next—ah well—seen enough"; her making the best of it is only an exaggeration of our current attitudes. "A bell rings piercingly": that is how the play opens. Winnie is, as we all are, conditioned to go through her days.

The two players in *Act Without Words II* are prodded into the actions of the day, similarly, by a goad.

XIII

For Samuel Beckett 1956 was the year of a decisive and unexpected turning. Since to him language was the symbol of all impositions of the social over the individual, the most social form of language, that of the newspaper, of advertising, of the media, was held in special horror. Yet when he was asked to write a radio play for the BBC he realized that he was entering a world of singular power, the world of sounds, which he could adapt to his expressive ends by practicing a preliminary dissociation of the senses. *All That Fall* (1957) brings to us this language and renders, through it, in a vein of broad Joycean humor, the animation of an Irish road and a small Irish station. Sounds create visual images, while the visual image would not expand into sound. The enormous bulk of Mrs. Rooney is conveyed by the "sound of efforts" when she is pushed into the car better than it could be by any padded actress. Moreover, language as language is given its chance by being presented strongly to the ear as a significant fabric of words. This covers, perhaps to some extent hides, the power of the play, which is tied to the character of blind Mr. Rooney. While listening to the play we are functionally blind; but his blindness, which ours seems to parallel, is in fact in strong contrast: sinister negation, madness, and crime perhaps; it becomes our mystery. The absurd death of a child connects, again audibly, with a sermon on God's support for all that fall, and with Schubert's music, "Death and the Maiden."

All That Fall provides lively, ambiguous, suggestive prose. *Embers* (1959), by contrast, is a somber poem of an old man haunted by what he wants to hear and what he has to hear of his past, obsessive moments connected with his child or his wife, memories of his drowned father brought by the noise of the sea, alternating with a story that, like almost every protagonist of Beckett's, he is telling himself. Whatever has happened in *All That Fall,* the dialogue in itself is not dramatic. Henry's monologue in *Embers* is fantastically so: its inner tensions are revealed in true expressionist style by the hallucinations that they bring before us, as the inner and external worlds intermingle. The ghostly sounds of hooves or of a piano lesson (connected with the miseries of his little daughter's education and ultimately of Beckett's own), which his miserable witchcraft has summoned to his ear, and which come vividly to ours from the dimension of nightmares, blend with the voice of his wife, who of course might be present, but who is probably part of the past, for only his feet audibly disturb the shingle. This is a rare and moving masterpiece.

XIV

Krapp's Last Tape (1958) is a short stage play. Yet it connects with the radio and television plays, while it fulfills the idea put forward in *How It Is* of disposing the sequences of a piece not chronologically but according to the most expressive arrangement. Krapp is the last of Beckett's clowns, and since Beckett's particular mode of distancing insists on the character being a clown playing a part, it is a pity that some recent productions have ignored the white face and red nose, the "rusty black narrow trousers, too short," the "surprising pair of dirty white boots, size 10 at least, very narrow and pointed," with the grotesque near-sighted peerings to match, and the ways of a habitual drunkard. This singular object will, by his own seeking, be confronted by mirror-images of his past self made present: fragments of his own tape-recordings. He can listen to himself again—"again" is a druglike word for him—living through some capital scenes, the death of his mother, and a love scene, the unhappy issue of which must have been the beginning of his self-destruction. He measures the change from the lower depth of his present decay, appreciates with bitter chuckles the absurdity of his Belacqua past, of his grotesque attempts to live and love; yet the attraction of that external memory is such that he has to come back again to the failed love affair, the girl, the boat on the sedgy lake. The mood, sarcastic, contemptuous, fascinated, and the process, are obviously to be set beside *Embers.*

XV

THE misery of consciousness could outlast death and be hell: the futilities of which human life is made may not be laid to rest even after burial (urn-burial for Beckett's purpose) has taken place. This is the fundamental meaning of *Play* (1964). The title is telling. Like Gustave Flaubert or Joyce Beckett is inventing a literature of the human sum free from particular contingencies. *Play* is as universal as *Everyman,* to which end it must be utterly insignificant (as the critics have severely—but obtusely—noticed).

A man, M, and two women, W1, W2: such is th

material. Man, wife, mistress. Petty jealousies, petty resentment, petty lies are the grotesque and repetitive stuff of the triangular relation. Their little hell, or at least purgatory, is the doom, once they have gone through their complaints, accusations, threats, vociferations, of having to start all over again. In *Waiting for Godot,* the repetition, between first and second act, went with substantial variation; here it is formal and constitutes a prose *da capo.* But *Play* is essentially distinguished by the mode used to bring those three to vocal self-expression, while, seen with their heads sticking out of the three large urns, they seem so far gone and eaten up by death. As Joe, in *Eh Joe,* is the victim of the cruel insistence of the camera, timed like an Edgar Allan Poe death-machine, stalking him inch by inch, so each of the three is held by a particular spotlight, which is switched on and off in alternate intervals measured in seconds, and compels speech because it restores a sort of galvanic consciousness. The spotlight is both external stimulus and the symbol of consciousness itself. Can the penance ever end? Beckett seems to leave the three a loophole: there seems to be a slight opening of their imaginations as the ordeal goes on. Each of course, immured in the solitude of death, which is even more absolute than that of life, is unable to have any present awareness of the others, yet seems to have some sort of anxiety about them, so that the tortured desire for total oblivion, "as if it had never been," may be fulfilled after all. There is even a hint of moral sanction: "Is it that I do not tell the truth, is that it, that some day somehow I may tell the truth at last and then no more light at last."

Yet human torment is two-faced in monstrous contradiction, and means, now ever to be held to account, now never to be recognized as existent. M has the last words of *Play:* "Am I as much as . . . being seen?" Perhaps the solution of the contradiction is to be sought in Clov's last speech: "Clov, you must be there better than that if you want them to let you go—one day."

XVI

THE *percipi* series after *Play* gives us the extraordinary *Film* (1969), in which the actor (Buster Keaton by Beckett's choice) is in near-secure flight from unidentified persecution when the angle of pursuit is 45 degrees or less, while he is in a panic when the angle becomes 46 degrees or more, that is, when his "percipience" begins. What pursues him—dubbed O for Object—is E or Eye. The eye in pursuit is a camera. It is presented here as a primary symbol of perception itself—of sight—and as a secondary symbol of self-perception. What the victim does not know is that while he is inhabited by a living consciousness, it is vain to contrive means of escaping observation. His flight has brought O to the usual "refuge" of a room where he makes his last stand, desperately suppressing all that might function as Eye: window, to be masked by curtain; mirror, to be covered (in "The Calmative," twenty years before, the only wish had been that all mirrors might be destroyed); dog and cat to be thrown out (a superb clowning act, as cat will come back when the door is opened to eject dog, etc.); print of God the Father with severe look, to be torn up; goldfish bowl or parrot cage—so many eyes—to be veiled; lastly the photos, including his own, in a folder, as eyes from the past (a brief equivalent to Krapp's tapes), to be torn to pieces. Finally, as he thinks he may go to sleep in the peace of impercipience, he will wake up again, facing for the first time the camera, which is consciousness and on which he has so far constantly turned his back, to find attentive eyes, his own, looking at his face, from his face.

The film, which lasts twenty-two minutes, is very impressive. It has, first of all, the association with the clown of clowns, Buster Keaton, which Beckett sought in order to dispel, as in all his dramatic pieces, any implications of realism by the unreality of the acting, as of every other visible element—a mite of a dog, a giant of a cat. Beckett took an enthusiastic share in the direction of the film in New York in 1964. It brought a revelation to his imagination and a possibility to his fantastic art: the camera was alive, without needing to be visible, in its action, in the terror it brought, in what was perceived as its malevolence. But in a film the relation between camera and object suffers from distance. Its proximity in television must have come to his mind with appreciation of its possibilities as a hunter.

Eh Joe (1966) brings before us a guilty soul hunted down, detected and tormented by light and sound.

A voice, which would seem to be external although it belongs to no visible body, a woman's voice mercilessly recalls his miserable meanness, and how it brought a girl, almost a child, to kill herself. As the voice in bouts carries on its task, the camera takes it up in relays, advancing methodically on its helpless victim. Beckett, whose imagination is passionately technical, adjusts seconds to inches in this alternate association of movement and sound, with the fiendish precision of a thriller. There were a few hints in *Happy Days* of Winnie's need to be perceived. The *esse est percipi* theme had become for Beckett more and more engrossing; from *Play* marginally, from *Film,* and from *Eh Joe* fully, it will be obvious that to be an object of perception is alternatively desirable (Mahood's man in the jar thought that if he was noticed by some passerby it would prove that he had lived) and also the crowning horror.

XVII

WITH that group of dramatic pieces, which we may call the *percipi* group, we find alternatively the split-mind group. It had been forecast in the furious tussles of *Texts for Nothing* and *The Unnamable.* It comes out, brought to perfection, in *Words and Music* (1962) and *Cascando* (1963), two radio plays, the first in English, the second in French. Both have an important demonstration value. They compel us to remember that the Beckettian character, at least since *Watt* and thus for about twenty years, had been not a body but an embodiment; and since Beckett had made it clear that our utter solitude prevented access to anything but our own immediate consciousness, it could only set forth aspects of that unique querying and queried personality. In *Words and Music,* Words is the discursive mind. The critics who have gravely analyzed the nonsense discourse that Lucky produces when he is ordered to "think," in order to extract from this decoded rigmarole Beckett's Weltanschauung, do not seem to me to take into account his most determined intention, which is to hold up the automatism of thinking, giving the haphazard touch to the regurgitation of all the notional "words" that have been crammed into the unhappy individual. But we shall be told that Lucky's words are all the more significant because they have come to Beckett and from Beckett haphazardly. Of course.

Words, like Lucky, speaks as might a computer badly programmed and suddenly gone wrong, ignoring the useful element of appropriation of word to thing. Hence the piece of rhetoric first called forth by the "theme" of sloth, which has quickly passed from emptiness to nonsense, will be applied to love without a change; until, shaken into a more attentive state, or perhaps because at last instead of "passions" he has to deal with a reality, Words deals more sensibly with old age.

Words would carry on lonely and unaware, while Music, his detested partner in the community of the self, will try to arrange into song whatever he presents. There is between them alternate conflict and effort to come together, with the weary encouragement of Milord, significantly nicknamed Croak, and obviously the central principle of personality. The humor of mocking pseudo-realism that mixes so wonderfully with Beckett's deepest gloom appears in the gift of material existence that those "characters" receive: as Milord approaches we hear a shuffling of slippers that begins to bring him alive. It will be realized that they can exist only as invisibles: proper radio creatures.

To *Film,* to *Eh Joe,* in order to ensure the clockwork precision of acting and production which it is part of Beckett's dramatic genius to conceive and to exact, are annexed pages of fascinating diagrams, marking the vivid interest that he takes in the slightest space-time relations involved. A very short piece like the lovely and moving *Come and Go* (1967) is accompanied by this same ruthless pattern of directions. On closer examination the play is actually shaped by them, as if the human plight were precisely to be controlled by this clockwork of invisibilities. Even *Breath* (1971)—a dramatization of Pozzo's famous tirade on the simultaneity of birth and death, all contracted to the one inhaling and exhaling—if it is almost denied time is yet granted literary and even dramatic expansion by the same exacting tenseness and challenging abstract power of the directions.

Not I (1973), a playlet in size, is large and impressive as an expression of human sympathy—a gesture of compassionate arms facing human distress. The only articulate character is quite simply a woman's mouth. The essential element, unchanged since *Echo's Bones* fifty years previously, is the voice the difference is that here it does not persist, but comes last, at last, from just a mouth, as a comment on the emptiness of a life, on its total solitude, on the impossibility that it has experienced of constituting a self. In this way the title indicates the terrible detachment of the third person, of the she.

The staging, long since a paramount interest of Beckett's, and a primary element in the working of his dramatic creation, has constantly produced new inventions. Here, the vivid lighting concentrated on the mouth ("microphone invisible") turns a monologue to haunted dramatic presence.

The voice, frequently plural, as detached from a split personality, comes back to it combined in various ways with the visible. In *That Time* (1976) a subtle, quasi-musical arrangement brings the same voice alternately from three distinct sources, conveying from the one personal past three distinct memories (frustrated attempt to return to childhood, dereliction, hopeless love). A variation, by new means, on *Krapp's Last Tape.*

Similar is, in *Footfalls* (1975), the interplay of two voices, one of them ghostly, with the over-audible footfalls, which scan and encompass in the width of the stage and the length of the speech the nightmare of a haunted life—Beckett's source being the cruel memory of his neurotic mother's night walking through the house.

Rockaby (1981), coupled with *Ohio Impromptu* and a third piece as "occasional pieces," is beautiful to watch and moving to hear. To the double scanning of the chair that alternately rocks and stops and the on-voice of the seated woman calling for her own voice off to carry on, it desists finally to a "rock-off."

XVIII

BECKETT'S evolution—instead of literary evolution one is tempted to say evolution from literature—has been heroic and exemplary. The author of *More Pricks than Kicks* and even perhaps of *Murphy,* with his great gifts of wit, verbal invention, and brilliant narrative, his buffooning, his mixture of aggressive satire and sensitive poetic perceptiveness, might have developed into, let us say, an Anthony Burgess—if we must have a name in the Joycean affiliation—had he been at all pleased with himself. But in his imagination a somber demand that absolute truth (which I will not call metaphysical if I can help it) must prevail over aesthetic requirements made him dissatisfied with all contingencies. Moreover, the fact of being cornered into life, as his Protestant vision saw it, became, since he was a writer, being cornered into writing. The impulse to write, which had to be writing of something, and referred to the external world, was promoted to a form of doom and became for a while the center of a mythology of damning judges. When they were gone, they left the emptiness of utter solitude, and he felt that all his writing should be of his own personal condition, turned into symbolical expressionist constructions. If writing was not an end, there should be an end of writing as soon as its work was done. Hence the dissatisfaction and the abrupt turnings. Hence after 1965, instead of novels or stories, for some years superb, recondite, difficult poetic texts in French, a few pages long, that we may distinguish, from the prevailing mood, as visions and fables. Perhaps only lack of perception in this reader prevents the visions from being seen also as fables.

The most impressive of the visions may be *Sans* or *Lessness* (1969). An unguided reading is enough to convince the reader of the strange, subdued, lyrical beauty of this journey to more than one refuge, all of them now ruins, an inner landscape of compelling grandeur. But a French critic in the author's confidence has shown how the sixty sentences, of which the twenty-four verselike units are made up, are rigorously structured word by word and very literally combined and composed, as is music of its notes and phrases. Again it might be said that words and word-groups are put down like touches of pure color, the "meaning" being the weave of their relations.

Most of these texts deal with shapes—rotunda, cylinder—enclosing two bodies (*Imagination Dead Imagine,* 1965) or many (*The Lost Ones,* 1970). But is body the right word for these ghostly presences? The light—white, gray, yellow, sourceless, shadowless—is obviously not of this world. The faint cagelike structures in which Francis Bacon often encases his awesome creatures gives a visible parallel to those strange scenes. In *Imagination Dead Imagine* two creatures in fetal position subsist back-to-back in the death-in-life of a lethargic limbo. *The Lost Ones* is of the fable type, a fable of a sinister micro-

Hades, a last circle, gloomier than Dante's, in which creatures of apparently human build, yet dry as insects, mechanical in their motivations, antlike in their scurrying, climb or do not climb up ladders into niches, and in occupying the ground or ladders must conform to an obscure set of rules and prescriptions of arbitrary or meaningless purport, but not perhaps more so than those which govern our societies.

What is it a fable of? Generally, without a doubt, of the futility of life, of social organizations and institutions, of individual yearning. Various critics have decided to connect these ladders more specifically with Ludwig Wittgenstein's and with the problems of true thinking. Whoever reads *The Lost Ones* honestly will realize how little specific likeness there is: the climbers are seekers, but they have long ago forgotten what they sought. Once again, it is the terrific potency of the vision that counts in this fantastic, multitudinous "act without words III."

Two important pieces, *Company* (1980), in English, and *Mal vu mal dit* (1981), in French, might show Beckett's determination not to be labeled an English or a French writer, leaving us free to term him one of the first great international writers. In *Company* the familiar self-figure, lying down on his back in the dark, in his utter loneliness looks for company—apart from sundry little games that are literally pastimes—to memories of childhood, early signs of self-sought solitude, of tender trust in father's love, of cruel conflict with mother, of well-meant action resulting in disaster and inducing guilt, self-distrust, and withdrawal—making all in all a significant self-portrait.

Conversely, contrasting yet in a sort of diptych with this self-centered piece, in *Mal vu mal dit* the creator, instead of being central, is marginal, is "off." He seems to have received from his fund of obsessive memories the intense figure of an old woman clad in jet-black, possibly a somber, distorted mother image, with whom he plays a gloomy game, giving her a tentative, inchoative setting, shifting her about, finding her in turns vividly present and precise, or evanescent, or totally vanished. Through these variations the constant vivid definition and beauty of the rendering belies the "ill seen ill said" of the title and denies in advance Beckett's perverse determination to go *"Worstward Ho,"* the title of his very negative latest utterance (1981).

XIX

At some time or other every Beckettian narrator states that *he is not there, that he has never been there.* The existentialist *Dasein,* if it has ever touched him, must date back to the illusions of childhood. *Murphy,* it is true, exceptional in many ways, does acknowledge some recognizable externalities, such as Kensington Gardens and the Round Pond. Otherwise Molloy's statement must be held as valid for his creator: "my native town was the only one I knew, never having set foot in any other." It will be pennies, (not many) that the characters of his French novels have in their pockets. Insofar as any setting is external, it will be Irish: shrillness of seagulls and curlews, black peat, spongy bogs underfoot. No trees will signify, except the larches with the first green of which he was born. An "accurst country" perhaps, but Molloy still hears "the awful cries of the corncrakes that run in the corn, in the meadows, all the short summer night long, dinning their rattles." Who could deny that there is happiness in the irrepressible zest with which Beckett created Irish road and station in *All That Fall?* Where the literary landscape is austere, who could fail to perceive as dominant in it the zest of Dean Swift's irony and Laurence Sterne's humor?

Beckett, it must be stressed again, has never claimed objective validity for his vision. We have quoted Hamm from *Endgame,* although himself engaged in a process of abolition of the universe, contrasting his madman's vision of ashes with the living variety of things. Hamm's final remark, however, must not be left out: "It appears the case is . . . was not so . . . so unusual."

"The case": a sickness, yet "not so unusual." In an age of tragic uncertainties Beckett has brought together in a solid mass all uncertainties and has made a black world of powerful symbols out of them. He is contemporary with existential pessimism, and he has turned into a coherent system of images a sense of dereliction that is very widespread. His way of dealing with it is unorthodox: instead of creating order out of disorder, form out of the formless, as Joyce did to T. S. Eliot's satisfaction in *Ulysses,* he has created an exploded form to reflect an exploded world. When nothing was left, he stood facing his own visions; by a curious and perhaps significant coincidence, to a world that was ceasing to be interested in anything but pattern and structure, he offered compact gems of pattern and structure, words used as pure tones in abstract arrangements.

"The Aegean, thirsting for heat and light, him I killed, he killed himself, early on, in me." So says Beckett's persona Molloy. His efforts to suppress in himself the will-to-art with the will-to-joy were very conscious and only moderately successful: he had been born a poet, a man of images and of song, and one could cull out of his writing, almost to the last, snatches of brilliantly worded imaginings. They were largely suppressed; but, where extant, they hint at desperate sympathies for whatever is small, frail, forsaken, suffering; and they might some day be constructed into self-pity. The keen ear goes on listening in spite of all to the little music of life, and echoing it. There is a long, tender elegy dispersed under the crude, fierce, gross surface. There is also, as if we had a parallel here to Arthur Rimbaud's dual mood of near ecstasy and savage rejection, a power of heroic vision that can join in spans of fantastic imagery the individual coenesthesia to the universe. Of prose writers in our time only William Golding, I think, gives some approximation to such power of language. The miracle is that Beckett can do it in two languages, and, I think, with more musical subtlety in the French. Compare a phrase from *Malone Meurt,* ". . . vers la noire joie de passer seul et vide ne rien pouvant, ne rien voulant, à travers le savior, le beauté, les amours," with his own rendering, ". . . the black joy of the solitary way in helplessness and will-lessness through all the beauty the knowing and the loving." The magic has gone: Beckett, like all poets, cannot be translated, even by himself.

SELECTED BIBLIOGRAPHY

I. Bibliography. R. Federman and J. Fletcher, *Samuel Beckett, His Works and His Critics: An Essay in Bibliography* (Berkeley, Calif., 1970).

II. Collected and Selected Works. *Endgame: A Play in One Act, Followed by Act Without Words: A Mime for One Player* (New York and London, 1958), contains *Fin de partie* and *Acte sans paroles,* translated by the author; *Molloy, Malone Dies, The Unnamable: A Trilogy* (London and Paris, 1959); *Poems in English* (London, 1961); *Samuel Beckett: Proust: Three Dialogues* (London, 1965), with G. Duthuit; *Comédie et actes divers* (Paris, 1966), includes *Va et vient, Cascando, Paroles et musique, Dis Joe, Acte sans paroles II; Eh Joe, Act Without Words II, Film* (London, 1967); *No's Knife: Collected Shorter Prose, 1945–1966* (London, 1967); *Tetes-mortes* (Paris, 1967), contains *D'un ouvrage abandonné, Assez, Imagination morte imaginez, Bing; A Samuel Beckett Reader* (London, 1967), ed. by J. Calder; Selected Bilingual Edition (Paris, 1972), ed. by J.-J. Mayoux, contains *Words and Music, Play, Eh Joe; Tetes-mortes augmenté* (Paris, 1972), includes *Bing* and *Sans; Pour finir encore et autres foirades* (Paris, 1976); *That Time* (London, 1977); *Ends and Odds* (London, 1977); *Pas, suivi de quelques esquisses* (Paris, 1978); *Poèmes, suivi de mirlitonnades* (Paris, 1978); *Rockaby, and Other Short Pieces* (New York, 1981); *Catastrophe* (Paris, 1982); *Three Occasional Pieces* (London, 1982).

III. Separate Works. "Assumption," in *transition,* 16–17 (June 1929), short story; "Dante, Bruno, Vico, Joyce," in *Our Exagmination Round His Factification for Incamination of Work in Progress* (Paris, 1929), by S. Beckett and others; *Whoroscope* (Paris, 1930), poem; *Proust* (London, 1931), criticism; "Sedendo et quiescendo," in *transition,* 21 (March 1932), short story, from unpublished "Dream of Fair to Middling Women"; "Dante and the Lobster," in *This Quarter* (December 1932), short story; *More Pricks than Kicks* (London, 1934), short stories, includes rev. version of "Dante and the Lobster"; "A Case in a Thousand," in the *Bookman,* 86 (1934), short story; *Echo's Bones, and Other Precipitates* (Paris, 1935), poems; *Murphy* (London, 1938), novel, French version by the author (Paris, 1947); "La peinture des van Velde, ou, Le monde et le pantalon," in *Cahiers d'art* (1945–1946), criticism; "Poèms 38–39," in *Temps modernes,* 14 (November 1946); "L'Expulsé," in *Fontaine,* 10 (December 1946–January 1947), short story; "Three Poems," in *transition,* 48 (June 1948), French and English; "Peintres de l'empêchement," in *Derrière le miroir,* 11–12 (June 1948), criticism; "Three Dialogues," in *transition,* 49 (December 1949), criticism.

Molloy (Paris, 1951), novel, translated into English by P. Bowles and S. Beckett (Paris, 1955); *Malone meurt* (Paris, 1951), novel, translated into English by the author as *Malone Dies* (New York, 1956); *En attendant Godot* (Paris, 1952), translated into English by the author as *Waiting for Godot* (New York, 1954); *L'Innommable* (Paris, 1953), novel, translated into English by the author as *The Unnamable* (New York, 1958); *Watt* (Paris, 1953), novel, translated into French by L. and A. Janvier, with S. Beckett (Paris, 1968); *Nouvelles et textes pour rien* (Paris, 1955), includes rev. versions of "La fin" and "L'Expulsé," translated into English as *Stories and Texts for Nothing* (New York, 1967); "Trois poèmes," in *Cahiers des saisons,* 2 (October 1955); *Fin de partie, suivi de Acte sans paroles* (Paris, 1957), play and mime, translated into English by the author as *Endgame: A Play in One Act, Followed by Act Without Words: A Mime for One Player* (New York and London, 1958); *All That Fall: A Play for Radio* (London, 1957), translated into French by R.

Pinget and S. Beckett as *Tous ceux qui tombent* (Paris, 1957); "From an Abandoned Work," in *Evergreen Review,* 1 (1957), separately published (London, 1958); *Krapp's Last Tape and Embers* (London, 1955), plays, *Krapp's Last Tape* first pub. in *Evergreen Review,* 2 (1958), translated into French by P. Leyris and S. Beckett as *La dernière bande* (Paris, 1960), *Embers,* a play for radio, first pub. in *Evergreen Review,* 3 (1959), translation by R. Pinget and S. Beckett as *Cendres,* first pub. in one vol. with *La dernière bande; Comment c'est* (Paris, 1961), novel, translated into English by the author as *How It Is* (New York and London, 1964); *Happy Days: A Play in Two Acts* (London, 1961), translated into French by the author as *Oh, les beaux jours* (Paris, 1963); *Words and Music,* in *Evergreen Review,* 6 (1962), radio play; *Cascando,* in *Evergreen Review,* 7 (1963), radio play, in French; *Play, and Two Short Pieces for Radio* (London, 1964), translated into French by the author as *Comédie,* pub. in *Les lettres nouvelles,* n.s. 12 (June–August 1964); *Imagination morte imaginez* (Paris, 1965), translated into English by the author as *Imagination Dead Imagine* (London, 1965); *Assez* (Paris, 1966); *Bing* (Paris, 1966), translated into English by the author as *Ping* and pub. in *No's Knife* (London, 1967); *Eh Joe* (London, 1967); "Dans le cylindre," in *Biblio,* 35 (1967); *Come and Go: A Dramaticule* (London, 1967), translated by the author as *Va et vient* and included in *Comédie et actes divers* (London, 1966); *Poèmes* (Paris, 1968); *Sans* (Paris, 1969), translated into English as *Lessness; Film* (New York, 1969), Beckett's scenario with A. Schneider's exposition; *Premier amour* (Paris, 1970), fiction, translated into English by the author as *First Love* (London, 1973); *Mercier et Camier* (Paris, 1970), novel; *Le depeupleur* (Paris, 1970), fiction, translated into English as *The Lost Ones* (London, 1972); *Breath, and Other Shorts* (London, 1971), play; *Not I* (London, 1973), play; *Footfalls* (London, 1975), play; *That Time* (London, 1976), play; *Pas* (Paris, 1978), play; *Company* (London, 1980), fiction; *Mal vu mal dit* (Paris, 1981), fiction; *Worstward Ho* (New York, 1981).

IV. Biographical and Critical Studies. H. Kenner, *Samuel Beckett: A Critical Study* (New York, 1961; London, 1962); R. Cohn, *Samuel Beckett: The Comic Gamut* (New Brunswick, N. J., 1962); F. J. Hoffman, *Samuel Beckett: The Language of Self* (Carbondale, Ill., 1962); R. Coe, *Beckett* (London, 1964); J. Fletcher, *The Novels of Samuel Beckett* (London, 1964); M. J. Friedman, ed., *Configuration Critique de Samuel Beckett: Textes réunis* (Paris, 1964); W. Y. Tindall, *Samuel Beckett* (New York, 1964); M. Esslin, ed., *Samuel Beckett: A Collection of Critical Essays* (Englewood Cliffs, N. J., 1965); R. Federman, *Journey to Chaos: Samuel Beckett's Early Fiction* (Berkeley and Los Angeles, 1965); A. S. Nathan, *Samuel Beckett* (London, 1965); L. Janvier, *Pour Samuel Beckett* (Paris, 1966); J. -J. Mayoux, *Uber Beckett* (Frankfurt, 1966); J. Fletcher, *Samuel Beckett's Art* (London, 1967); M. J. Friedman, *Samuel Beckett's Art* (London, 1967); A. Reid, *All I Can Manage, More than I Could: An Approach to the Plays of Samuel Beckett* (Dublin, 1968); H. Kenner, *Samuel Beckett: A Critical Study* (Berkeley, Calif., 1968); O. Bernal, *Langage et fiction dans le roman de Beckett* (Paris, 1969); L. Janvier, *Samuel Beckett par lui-même* (Paris, 1969); L. E. Harvey, *Samuel Beckett, Poet and Critic* (Princeton, N. J., 1970); F. Doherty, *Samuel Beckett* (London, 1971); D. Nores, ed., *Les critiques de notre temps et Beckett* (Paris, 1971); J. Fletcher and J. Spurling, *Beckett: A Study of His Plays* (London, 1972); A. Alvarez, *Samuel Beckett* (New York, 1973); H. P. Abbot, *The Fiction of Samuel Beckett* (New York, 1973); H. Mayer and U. Johnson, *Das Werk von Samuel Beckett, Berliner Colloquium* (Frankfurt, 1975); J. Pilling, *Samuel Beckett* (London, 1976); *Samuel Beckett, Cahier de l'Herne* (Paris, 1976); V. Mercier, *Beckett/Beckett* (New York, 1977); D. Bain, *Samuel Beckett: A Biography* (New York, 1978); F. Busi, *The Transformations of Godot* (Lexington, Ky., 1980).

WILLIAM GOLDING

(1911–)

Stephen Medcalf

I

WILLIAM GOLDING was born in Cornwall on 19 September 1911 into a world "of sanity and logic and fascination." "My life is passed in a condition of ravished astonishment!," the exclamation he gives to the experimental scientist in his play *The Brass Butterfly,* might have been, and perhaps was, spoken by his father, Alec Golding. But the first memory that he has given us of his childhood, in the autobiographical fragment "The Ladder and the Tree," is of terror and darkness: darkness and indescribable terror made objective in the flint-walled cellars of their fourteenth-century house in Marlborough, and in the graveyard by which it stood.

He offers a social cause for this contact with darkness:

> Had my mother perhaps feared this shadowy house and its graveyard neighbour when she went there with me as a baby? She was Cornish and the Cornish do not live next to a graveyard from choice. But we had very little choice. My father was a master at the local grammar school, so that we were all the poorer for our respectability.
>
> (*The Hot Gates,* p. 167)

But clearly this matter of class is not a cause but only part of the conditions for a personal plight. It seems less important, so to speak, to Golding that Marlborough was an inward-looking, snobbish, provincial town than that it is at the edge of the "prehistoric metropolis [whose cathedral] was Stonehenge. . . . To spend your life here in Wessex, as I have done, is to live where archaeology is as natural, or at least as usual, as gardening," he says in "Digging for Pictures": and the archaeologist, the explorer of the darkness under the earth, has, he suggested in a review of Grahame Clarke's *World Prehistory* (1961), replaced as culture-hero the "wise men, at once distinguished and responsible, who emerge from the Admiralty or Government background of Buchan's novels."

The key event that marked loss of faith in the wise men he dates in the same review to the time when he was an infant. "I remember my mother once confiding to me that her awareness of the world as an exhilarating but risky place dated from the day on which she heard that the *Titanic* had sunk. She could not say why. She only knew that the years before that had been sunny and placid, while the years that came after seemed by nature full of storm": that is, after mid-April, 1912.

By the time Golding was seven he had begun to connect the darkness, although not the storm, with the ancient Egyptians. From them he learned, or onto them he projected, mystery and symbolism, a habit of mingling life and death, and an attitude of mind skeptical of the scientific method that descends from the Greeks. Already as a child, he says in "Egypt from My Inside":

> I know about symbols without knowing what I know. I understand that neither their meaning nor their effect can be described, since a symbol is that which has an indescribable effect and meaning. I have never heard of levels of meaning, but I experience them. In my notebook, the scarab, the ankh, the steps, the ladder, the *thet,* are drawn with a care that goes near to love.
>
> (*The Hot Gates,* p. 74)

He tried to find a focus to stare into the eyes of a carved face on a sarcophagus, "the face prepared to go down and through, in darkness." And therefore,

> though I admire the Greeks, I am not one of them. . . . I am, in fact, an Ancient Egyptian, with all their unreason, spiritual pragmatism and capacity for ambiguous belief. And if you protest on the evidence of statistical enquiry they were not like that, I can only answer in the jargon of my generation, that for me they have projected that image.
>
> (pp. 81–82)

In all this, if not necessarily cause, there is at any rate a picture of Golding's present genius—of a way of writing existing at the edge between an acutely skeptical and organizing consciousness and a powerful awareness of the darkness beneath consciousness. It is proper too that he lives near Stonehenge, the temple of astronomy almost Greek in its entasis[1] and proportion, whose effect, he once pointed out in conversation, partly lies in the way that weathering, lichens, and the channels worn by rain have made it seem like something emerging from unhuman nature.

His first book, the *Poems* (1934), published when he was twenty-two, reveals something of this only to hindsight and meditation. He has called the poems "poor, thin things," but curiosity about them is immediately aroused by his remark: "The novelist is a displaced person, torn between two ways of expression. . . . You might say I write prose because I can't write poetry."

In fact, they are not so bad. They deal with emotions—as they come out in the poems, rather easy emotions—of loss and grief, reflected in nature and the seasons. The beauty of the world, in several not unmemorable pieces, suggests loss. There is satire, some cheap and some good. The rhythms are traditional, on the whole conventional. The book is, by and large, very Georgian, echoing Edward Thomas, Walter de la Mare, A. E. Housman, and Siegfried Sassoon.

But when it is put in a Georgian context, a kind of crack appears, letting in something visionary, something Blakean although not derived from Blake:

> The phoenix rose again and flew
> With crest and plume and pinion
> In splendour from grey ashes flashing
> Like a jewel turned beneath the sun.
>
> In cities and in palaces,
> Or toiling through the hot dumb sand
> Bare-footed in the barren hills,
> Men saw—and would not understand.
>
> But some there were among the fields
> That let the swerving plough jolt on
> And stood and gazed against the light
> Through wide eyes filled with tears as bright,
> Until the burning bird was gone.
>
> Oh Phoenix! did they hear as I
> The agony, the lonely cry
> Of mateless, mateless, mateless Beauty
> Echoing in the desert sky?
> ("The Phoenix Rose Again")

In general the poems—another example is "Isobel"

> The worm that the scythe bites,
> The flower in the grass,
> Shadows and sunlight that
> Flutter and pass,
>
> Thunder that mutters,
> Brooklets that murmur,
> Are words that she utters,
> And runes to confirm her.

—suggest an attempt to do what de la Mare did, but missing de la Mare's supreme mastery of the auditory imagination.

Between the *Poems* and *Lord of the Flies* (1954), Golding experienced two things that he counts the greatest influences on his writing—first, the war and his service in the navy, and second, in the same years, his learning ancient Greek. The former confirmed for him the process, begun with the sinking of the *Titanic,* of shattering the liberal and optimistic image of man. The latter perhaps had large effects on his style. There is something dynamic, concrete, and living about Greek to which one may guess he responded. It is (as Owen Barfield has observed[2]) a language in which we find ourselves not so much conscious of having long hair as "conscious *in* the growing of our hair, [feeling] it as *movement* in something the same way that we still feel our breathing as movement"; in which we do not say "So and so—is—young," but "So and so blossoms" or "blooms" without any necessary consciousness of metaphor; and in which even abstractions acquire a concrete and substantial quality. The war and Greek literature together perhaps confirmed the dissociation from current and ephemeral affairs which makes Golding say that if the novelist "has a serious, an Aeschylean, preoccupation with the human tragedy . . . he is committed to looking for the root of the disease instead of describing the symptoms" ("The Writer in His Age").

It is illuminating to approach his prose by con-

[1]An almost imperceptible swelling of the shaft of a column, used in ancient Greek architecture to counter the effect of optical distortion.

[2]*Romanticism Comes of Age,* London, 1944.

sidering what he does *not* do in his poems. Clearly it is not by mastery of elusive and delicate effects of tune and sound in their relation to meaning that he moves us in his poems. Yet he is a master of words; and he says that from childhood he has had the poet's "passion for words in themselves, and collected them like stamps or bird's eggs" ("Billy the Kid"). It is perhaps permissible to guess that his feeling for words has something synaesthetic, something visual rather than auditory about it. That is, the words stand out in his prose much as one would expect if he sometimes feels as his Jocelin does in *The Spire*:

> "When you hear things, do you see them?"
>
> He lay in his nowhere, turning his headache from side to side as though he could shake it off. Footsteps walked past the window, and the looped line of cheerful whistling. Drearily in his head, he watched the whistling disappear round a corner.
>
> (*The Spire,* p. 195)

The description of the same feeling in *Pincher Martin* sounds very like a metaphorical account of the style: "Words and sounds were sometimes visible as shapes. . . . They did not vibrate and disappear. When they were created they remained as hard enduring things like the pebbles."

This synaesthetic faculty would perhaps accompany, as it does for Jocelin, Martin, and Lok in *The Inheritors,* the intense visual imagination that Golding recounts from his childhood: "I had no doubt that if one frowned long enough at the page it would brighten and come alive. Indeed, it did. The words and paper vanished. The picture emerged. Details were there to be heard, seen, touched."

Elusive effects of words become subsidiary to vivid, dynamic, and detailed imagination. This does not apply only to sound. Golding's words tend not to have meanings of the incantatory kind that exploit the whole spider's web of developed connotation and association, as they would have to do if he were to be a poet of the kind of de la Mare or T. S. Eliot. Instead he tends to use words in unexpected disjunctive combinations, which allow only the single meaning he wants. Perhaps this is part of the reason for his love not only for ancient Greek but also for Old English—the fact that in both the words are relatively clean of association, hard and sharp.

This kind of attitude toward meaning rests in its turn on the whole approach of his books to experience. His genius seems to lie in pushing already formed and distinct conceptualization back to the point where it is just experience: on the largest scale, some of his books, for all their originality, began as parodies, as *Lord of the Flies* is a parody of *The Coral Island.* This again might disqualify him for the elusive de la Mare kind of poetry that he attempted, a poetry in which all depends on catching the experience before any distinct conceptualization has taken place.

Golding might have learned some of this pushing of concept back to percept from the concreteness of ancient Greek. But he has given his own image for the mental process involved, in "Fable":

> I remember, many years ago, trying to bore a hole with a drilling machine through armour plate. . . . In my extreme ignorance, I put the drill in the chuck, held by half an inch of its extreme end. I seized the handle and brought the revolving drill down on the armour. It wobbled for a second; then there was a sharp explosion, the drill departed in every direction. . . . Wiser now, I held the next drill deep in the chuck so that only the point protruded, held it mercilessly in those steel jaws and brought it down on the armour with the power behind it of many hundred horses. This operation was successful. I made a small red-hot hole in the armour, though of course I ruined the drill. If this small anecdote seems fatuous, I assure you that it is the best image I know for one sort of imaginative process. There is the same merciless concentration, the same will, the same apparently impenetrable target, the same pressure applied steadily to one small point.
>
> (*The Hot Gates,* p. 97)

He has also given a word for it when he asks what future, if the sense of value is impaired, there can be "for the novel which tries to look at life anew, . . . for intransigence."

II

GOLDING'S novels therefore move at the level of phenomena, of things happening in the physical or spiritual worlds, and develop their own forms for experience. One consequence of this is that, perhaps more than with any other novelist, the process of reading a Golding novel is overwhelmingly important. You ought not to be the same person at the end of one of them as at the beginning; and the book itself therefore ought not to be the same. Golding's usual way of achieving this effect involves a process of reinterpretation which begins approximately as soon as the first picture of what is happening has been established—let us say after the first chapter. At some point the reader finds himself so involved in the principal character's perceptions that his own judgment of what is happening is swallowed up. The second interpretation forces itself more and more upon the first, grows more and more toward covering all the phenomena; when this is complete, the book moves suddenly into a more normal world, and ends. Golding once rashly used the word "gimmick" for this way of ending, and readers who feel resentfully that they have been fooled have used it against him. But the whole structure of the book depends on the process of reinterpretation, and the shift to normality is needed to drive it home.

But although the change in the ending is not a mere gimmick, the effect of a Golding novel is marred if one knows how it is reinterpreted before the first reading: by existing over and above the text, the reader misses an involvement that affects his subsequent readings also. It is especially unwise, therefore, to read about one of these novels before reading it.

At the beginning of *Lord of the Flies,* the reader has two forms of reality offered him, one in the text, the other in the title. The text begins with a well-known sort of story: boys making their own lives on an island, apart from adults. The immediate model is made clear enough: Robert Michael Ballantyne's *The Coral Island* (1858), in which three adolescents, Ralph, Jack, and Peterkin, create a happy simple life on a Pacific island. But one can feel many others of the genre hovering about the story, notably Arthur Ransome's *Swallows and Amazons* and even more his *Secret Water,* in which a naval officer's children play at explorers in the marshy islands behind Walton-on-the-Naze in Essex until confronted by local children whose game is to be a savage tribe with corroboree, ritual dance, and mock human sacrifice. But the children are all very nice and responsible children, and everything remains at the level of game.

Ballantyne's names, Ralph and Jack, are those of the two principals in Golding's book; and the first chapter differs from Ballantyne's and Ransome's shape for the world only in Golding's peculiar, detailed, almost hallucinatory awareness of physical reality. But for a year before the war and from its end until 1961 he was a schoolmaster, and he draws on this experience both to enlarge (the behavior and language of the boys is accurate enough) and to alter this shape. Another schoolmaster, F. McEachran, has said, "If you want to understand the spirit of Nazism, make a class of adolescents, with teeth clenched, bellow out Hitler's sentence 'Niemand hat je gesagt, ich wäre feig gewesen' (No one has ever said I was a coward)."[3] The first real intimation of change in *Lord of the Flies* comes at the end of the first chapter when—trying to repel his own horrified inhibition against cutting into living flesh, even a pig's—Jack responds like one of McEachran's boys. He "snatched his knife out of the sheath and slammed it into a tree trunk. Next time there would be no mercy. He looked round fiercely, daring them to contradict" (p. 41).

But instead of disappearing, the timidity that has to be rebutted actually grows. The smaller boys are frightened of their own nightmares of the island, and presently Jack admits that "in the forest . . . when you're on your own . . . you can feel as if you're not hunting but being hunted; as if something's behind you all the time in the jungle" (p. 67). Fear denied, blood lust let loose, and projection of both these spread among nearly all the boys until at the end they are at the point of sacrificing Ralph to the Beast that for them haunts the island.

From the beginning, the title of the book suggested a world in which something like this would happen. For a reader who does not know its hidden reference, the name *Lord of the Flies* provides a haunting, an unease that comes to light when the head of the first pig killed, spiked on a stick and offered to the Beast, speaks to the visionary boy Simon. The flies that swarm around it "were black and iridescent green and without number; and in front of Simon, the Lord of the Flies hung on his stick and grinned" (p. 171). Simon's sense of "mankind's essential illness" speaks through it: "I'm part of you? Close, close, close! I'm the reason why it's no go?"

Concept is now reduced to sheer experience. The concept so treated, Golding declares in "Fable," may "seem trite, obvious and familiar in theological terms. Man is a fallen being. He is gripped by original sin. . . . I accept the theology and admit the triteness; but what is trite is true." But the book

[3] *Spells,* Oxford, 1954, p. 41.

presents sheer religious experience, sheer phenomenon as close to unmediated experience as the descriptions of the island are to unconstructed physical sensation; so much so that we may even venture to disagree with this reformulation of it.

If the book were about original sin—about a state of alienation from good by which all mankind is equally gripped from birth—there would be no propriety in the boys' apparent innocence at the beginning, in the evident continuing innocence of Simon and the commonsensical Piggy, nor in the resistance to evil put up by Ralph. These things may be factually compatible with believing that the three also are alienated at heart, but they are not shown to be so in the novel. Again, original sin might lead one to expect some dealing with the mysterious ways out from it that are offered under names like grace and redemption. (In fact, Golding eschews these in his first three books; there are hints of them in *Free Fall* and *The Spire,* but they are not dealt with centrally until *Darkness Visible* and *The Paper Men.*) The sense in *Lord of the Flies* of struggle with something itself wholeheartedly corrupt suggests something different. Matthew Arnold (when he suggested in *Literature and Dogma* that the Bible should be regarded as written in an experiential and unconceptualized way, such as Golding's essentially is) used for the word and concept "God" the empirical sensation of the "power not ourselves making for righteousness." What speaks through the pig's head sounds analogous to that—namely a power not ourselves, but in ourselves, making for corruption. As the title suggests, then, the book is about the experience behind the biblical name for God's adversary, Beelzebub, which does indeed mean "Lord of the Flies." It is proper enough that the boys who are killed in sacrifice to him should be the innocents, and the one about to be sacrificed at the end, the resister. Golding gives the passage in which the Lord of the Flies speaks to Simon as his example of what happens when imagination concentrates like the drill on armorplate. "The point of the fable under imaginative consideration does not become more real than the real world, it shoves the real world on one side. The author becomes a spectator, appalled or delighted, but a spectator." It is at this point that for the reader also the book re-forms. For a while we forget that we are reading about boys and identify ourselves with the mere human being in his predicament: the human being faced with that which it is a mistake to name—because we then commit the boys' own error of projection—but a greater mistake not to recognize, the error of Piggy, the one boy who remains true to what he understands of liberalism.

Simon commits neither error. There is something sitting on the mountain in the middle of the island which the boys believe to be the Beast. Simon insists on climbing the mountain to find out what it is. Against the boys' derision he says, and against the warning of the Lord of the Flies he repeats, "What else is there to do?" His intransigence in climbing the mountain, his insistence on understanding, is a metaphor for what the book itself does.

In the new world of the Lord of the Flies, Simon is no longer only a helpful boy who likes praying in the forest where Jack finds only terror, no longer even what the connection of his name with Peterkin, the third of Ballantyne's heroes, would suggest, Simon called Peter, "the Rock." A Christ figure, he has Christ's reward. Going down the mountain to tell the rest that the thing on it is the fallen corpse of an airman, he is killed by them because they think he is the Beast.

In the world where they are humanity confronted by evil, the boys behave with as much fitness as they do if they are considered only as silly little boys. I have heard two young Germans arguing whether corruption spreads from Jack or is latent in all the boys, and they knew that they were arguing about Hitler, *Führerprinzip,* and the German nation. The book's realism allows both explanations.

It even allows that the corruption need not absolutely have taken place. The rule of the Lord of the Flies is not total. There are two points in the book, both associated with the swell of the ocean, that pierce beyond him. In one, when Ralph, on the other side of the island, where there are no "filmy enchantments of mirage," feels clamped down before the ocean, Simon suddenly, inexplicably, and rightly says, "You'll get back to where you came from." In the second, Simon's broken body is described in a passage of deliberate beauty as moving out in obedience to the pull of the tide toward the open sea, "a silver shape beneath the steadfast constellations." It is a kind of resurrection. Some kind of factuality in the world is other and greater than evil.

Within the ordinary human and diabolic world, the book moves toward its climax, the second point where the reader totally identifies with one of the characters; this is where we see Ralph, hiding in the forest from the rest,

> looking straight into the savage's eyes.
> Don't scream.
>
> (p. 245)

Simon's words, the assurance from beyond the world in which he is trapped, suddenly well up, like a spring so deeply buried that it is almost not seen: "You'll get back." Then Ralph bursts out, "hopeless fear on flying feet, rushing through the forest . . . rolling over and over in the warm sand, crouching with arm up to ward off, trying to cry for mercy."

At once he dwindles back into little boy. A naval officer looks down on him. In one way this is rescue, properly and ironically accounted for; the boys had tried earlier and unsuccessfully to attract ships with the smoke of a bonfire, and now, by setting fire to the whole island in the attempt to smoke out Ralph, they have succeeded. But in another way, the naval officer and his cruiser remind us at the end of the book (like the crash landing of the boys at the beginning and the fall of the airman in the middle) that the boys are themselves escaping from a world war. The shift of viewpoint from child to man only drives home what we learned among the children, the things Ralph weeps for, "the end of innocence" and "the darkness of man's heart."

The end of innocence, a fall of man, does take place after the first chapter of *Lord of the Flies.* To begin with, the boys are afraid of shedding blood, but they are at home in the forest. Presently, they create rituals and an embryonic society that centers on hunting and killing, but they project their own fears and bloodlust onto a presence in the woods. It is partly from this contrast that the *The Inheritors* (1955) develops. In it, Golding's prose reaches perhaps its highest achievement in expressing the consciousness of primitive man, of a man who conceptualizes very little and knows little of chains of reasoning, only that some imaginative pictures help in forming others—the consciousness of a man as he feels in words such as he could never have imagined. The book is consequently in a way the finest of the novels (in fact Golding's own favorite), but also the hardest to read. Unless one's visualization is constant and intense, one is apt to miss what is going on.

The people not only do not conceptualize, they know nothing of art; their religion is devoid of ritual, although they pray and make offering before Oa, who brought forth the earth from her belly and is present where Awe is. Since art and ritual are, like conceptualization, a kind of shaping of experience, and a projection and division of the self, it is understandable that they should go together. But the people have other qualities, which seem obscurely connected with these first three. They are like the boys at the beginning of *Lord of the Flies,* innocent, usually mutually affectionate, excited by their world; they are at home in their forest; and, although they are omnivorous, they will not eat meat unless something else has killed it and sucked the blood. Even then they feel guilty about it and make excuses ("The meat is for Mal who is sick") to cover their guilt. Yet perhaps if they feel guilt, it is wrong to call them "unfallen." They live on the edge of the Fall—just as in physical actuality they live on a ledge above a fall of water. Their evil is perhaps latent, and held in check by their innocent lack of consciousness.

Although they are conceived in sharp reaction to the nastier fancies of some believers in survival of the fittest—of aggressive, contentious, competitive weapon-users—one is apt to think that they must be our early ancestors. The epigraph from the most brilliant of monuments to the belief in progress, H. G. Wells's *The Outline of History* (1919–1920), warns us that the subject of the book will be the encounter between *Homo sapiens* and Neanderthal man with a quotation from Sir Harry Johnston: "The dim racial remembrance of such gorilla-like monsters, with cunning brains, shambling gait, hairy bodies, strong teeth, and possibly cannibalistic tendencies, may be the germ of the ogre in folklore."

Nevertheless, it is a long time before one is finally convinced that the people through whom we see are Neanderthal men, and the "other," by whom they are at first attracted and eventually destroyed, our own forerunners. Neanderthal man has something in common with our unfallen ancestors, as mythically imagined in a reaction against Wells and rationalism similar to Golding's by C. S. Lewis in *The Problem of Pain* (1940), a book Golding was moved by when it came out during the war:

> All that experience and practice can teach he had still to learn: if he chipped flints, he doubtless chipped them clumsily enough. He may have been utterly incapable of

> expressing in conceptual form his paradisal experience. . . . If the Paradisal man could now appear among us, we should regard him as an utter savage, a creature to be exploited, or, at best, patronized. Only one or two, and those the holiest among us, would glance a second time at the naked, shaggy-bearded, slow-spoken creature: but they, after a few minutes, would fall at his feet.
>
> (ch. 5)

But in form Lewis's description is really closer to Wells's, a fable. And although both Golding himself and his critics have applied the word "fable" to his novels, they really are not that. Lewis and Wells begin with a concept of primitive man viewed from outside in terms of their respective value systems —Lewis's belief in the Fall, Wells's in survival; and their concepts, however much they flesh them out, remain externally drawn shapes. In all Golding's novels valuing is essential, is part of the "intransigence" he demands; but he begins his imagining from the inside out. He has criticized Stevenson's *Treasure Island,* saying "the island as it stuck out of the sea, the reason for it being there, and the relationship between the parts, escapes me even when I used the overrated chart. An island must be built, and have an organic structure like a tooth." This may not be quite fair to Stevenson, but it is good analysis of Golding. The island of *Lord of the Flies* and the way in which the minds of Lok and Fa are drawn in *The Inheritors* have mythic purposes, their final shape is strongly value-laden; but they are built up from inside with an organic structure, like a tooth. We live in Lok's mind, Lok exists to that extent, as Wells's and Lewis's men do not.

This unity of some of the qualities of fable with the method of inner exploration is the special quality of a Golding novel. In *The Inheritors,* as in *Lord of the Flies,* part of the way it is achieved is the shift at the end, once the reader is completely involved in a new world, to a more normal one: the naval officer's grown-up view in one, and in the other the viewpoint of the Inheritors, Homo sapiens, our own ancestors. And they, we realize, are unquestionably fallen. Like the boys at the end of *Lord of the Flies* they kill freely, have hunting rituals, and project their own evil onto the forest. "They are frightened of the air where there is nothing," says the Neanderthal woman Fa.

Above all, they project their own evil onto the Neanderthalers. When Tuami, the artist among the new men, draws pictures of the first men at the bidding of the witch doctor Marlan, it is Marlan at his most evil they resemble. "The hair stood out round the head as though the figure were in the act of some frantic cruelty . . . as the hair of the old man had stood out when he was enraged or frightened." Indeed Marlan becomes more like his own projected evil side; when we see him through Tuami's eyes, he has acquired the Neanderthaler's red hair and the tense posture and blind eyes of the pictures: "The sun was blazing on the red sail and Marlan was red. His arms and legs were contracted, his hair stood out and his beard, his teeth were wolf's teeth and his eyes like blind stones"; and later, in a moment of terror, "his eyes were glaring like stones"—Golding's use of repetition at its most intense and obsessive.

H. G. Wells's view of the Neanderthalers is that of the new men: the vision of our own projected evil selves. So far as that view contains facts, it is true, even to the cannibalism. The Neanderthalers' old leader, Mal, asks as he dies, "Do not open my head and my bones. You would only taste weakness." It is evidently nothing sinister, but a posthumous act of love. But the new men eat a Neanderthal girl, Liku, because they are hungry and do not care to eat the fungi and other things the Neanderthalers eat. Golding makes use of a further detail that Wells mentions, which points the other way from the contrast of ogrelike Neanderthaler and amiable Homo sapiens. The Neanderthaler's "canine teeth were *less* marked, *less* like dog-teeth, than ours," says Wells—our "teeth that remembered wolf," as Golding's Neanderthalers see them; Marlin's "wolf's teeth," as Tuami sees them.

But to Wells and to the new men, the Neanderthalers are devils who live in the darkness under the trees. In between the world as seen by the Neanderthalers and the world of the new men, Golding sets a passage in detached authorial style, visual, avoiding words of value or emotion. In context, because we know the "red creature" it describes is Lok, and see his discovery of the death of Liku, his tears, and presently his own death, the detached style makes it one of the most poignant passages in Golding's works; and the projection of evil onto Lok is the more pathetic and appalling. In Golding's first draft, this was the last chapter, and by itself corresponded to the shift of consciousness at the end of *Lord of the Flies.* But in the published version he doubled the shift. We now learn about the projection of evil through the mind of Tuami, the artist, and find it bound up with the capacity of the new men to conceptualize and to perform developed magical rituals that center on art, the painting of the stag they would kill and of the Neanderthaler they fear. The new men can distance themselves from themselves and can therefore live in self-deception. Their power of conceptualization is, in short, bound up with their fallenness. In this, Golding is closer than C. S. Lewis to the biblical myth. For Lewis, the Fall can only have been men's wish to exist independently of God, "to be on their own, to take care for their own future, to plan for pleasure and for security, to have a *meum* . . . which . . . was theirs not His."

Golding pushes fallenness back to the division in the self, the awareness of oneself over against everything else, which is the precondition of Lewis's fallen wishes. Fa has dim pictures—that shoots might grow nearer the shelter and water be carried in shells—which approach Lewis's notion, but she has not enough detachment from her pictures to see how to do it; and the Old Woman of her people warns her off even from these as if from poison. And we do not even see that the people prepare flint tools for future use (as the Neanderthalers known to archaeology did), although they use the stones they find. They seem therefore to be unaware even of the means "to be on their own." Lewis has the classicist's notion that in paradisal man there was already a division between will and appetites, although the appetites obeyed the will; Golding, the romantic's idea of a man in whom will and appetite are innocent and undivided. His Neanderthalers are not divided even from one another. "One of the deep silences fell on them, that seemed so much more natural than speech, a timeless silence in which there were at first many minds in the overhang; and then perhaps no mind at all." The new men only get drunk together and make savage love. They have done what the Bible perhaps expresses in the eating of the fruit of the tree of *knowledge* of good and evil, when Adam and Eve first knew that they were naked.

It is possible, though, that after all the fall is not complete. The first people may be among our ancestors. For the new men carry a stolen Neanderthal baby with them as they flee from their own fears. Moreover, Golding's fall has something of the paradoxical idea of the Fortunate Fall. Golding's first draft of *The Inheritors* had no place for the physical symbol of the fall, the fall of water. It came to him as a symbol of the law of entropy, the dissipation of energy in the physical universe against which Life, concentrating and organizing energy, must move. It sweeps away the innocent: but the new people, the Inheritors, are "people of the fall." They struggle against entropy, and although in so doing they fall morally, they do make headway against it. They move upstream. At the end of the book, when in Golding's second ending we are given access to Tuami's mind, it is not the Neanderthalers with whom we would prefer to be, but Tuami, with the conceptualization and art that Lok thought was "like Oa." Tuami is making an ivory knife to murder Marlan. But as he sees the rump of the Neanderthal baby devil against the head of the spoiled, lustful woman Vivani, he forgets the knife's use. "The rump and the head fitted each other and made a shape you could feel with your hands. They were waiting in the rough ivory of the knife-hilt that was so much more important than the blade. They were an answer, the frightened, angry love of the woman, and the ridiculous, intimidating rump." Tuami's art is honest, strips projection off, is inclusive and looks toward something new. In all this it is an image of the novel itself. We turn away from the Neanderthalers, whose happiest thought is "Today is like yesterday and tomorrow," to peer forward with Tuami, even though it is into an image of darkness like that at the end of *Lord of the Flies,* "to see what lay at the other end of the lake, but it was so long, and there was such a flashing from the water that he could not see if the line of darkness had an ending."

Pincher Martin (1956) also has a root in *Lord of the Flies,* as can be seen in the moment when Ralph stands on the other side of the island and, in contrast to the mirages, the hopes of rescue, and the defending shield of the lagoon by which the boys usually stay, finds that "faced by the brute obtuseness of the ocean, the miles of division, one was clamped down, one was helpless, one was condemned, one was—." Martin, lost at sea in the war and struggling to survive on the island he believes to be Rockall, shares both the fact of isolation and the mirages of rescue and defense. The identification of reader with character is overwhelmingly important in this book. It is made very easy for us, with the strong sensuous impact of the sea and (once again built up organically like a tooth) the island, its rocks, waters, and sea vegetation.

We are given a strong sense of what it is like to

be *in* Martin's body, feeling his specific pains and looking out through the orbs of his eyes. It is made easy, too, by the familiarity and detail of the reminiscence, to live Martin's memories of his earlier life through. Golding gave to Martin more of the external conditions of his own life than to any other of his characters, from Oxford (so far as can be made out, Golding's own college of Brasenose) through a period of acting and theater life to a commission in the wartime navy. And behind all this is the emotional pressure of many myths of man suffering, building his fate, defying the elements. Martin himself invokes Atlas, Ajax, Lear, Prometheus; and others are present: the sailors cast up on Prospero's island, Milton's Lycidas whelmed beyond the Hebrides, and, above all, Robinson Crusoe. We cannot but share in the desperate ingenuity of Martin's work to survive, to which Golding gives all his own love of technical device. We applaud, as we share in, his will to conquer, to continue his life; so much so that we excuse, and even identify ourselves with, the gradually apparent fact that he is an unusually evil man.

Of the three parts we know of his life, it is the acting that is strongest in Martin: with all his will to conquer, he is a hollow person, with few characteristics other than that will. He is a series of masks. He contrasts with his own manipulation of his face people whose expressions rise "spontaneously from the conjectural centre behind the face," people like his friend Nathaniel Lovell, who *is* what he offers, who has a character without division, a face that immediately incarnates his spirit. Pincher, divided between will and attitudes, the true survivor, is also at the opposite extreme from the Neanderthalers. In his memory the cheats, seductions, and thefts involved in his conquering—which end with murder—so pile up that at some point the whole thing begins to reverse. In place of excusing his selfish will by the good use he makes of it to survive, we begin to feel that the appetite for survival, one of H. G. Wells's prime values, is itself evil. The whole ethic of Robinson Crusoe, the ethic of the entrepreneur and possessive individualist, begins to reverse itself—to reverse itself exactly, since there are traces in Defoe's *Robinson Crusoe* of an ethic that condemns Crusoe for his willful discontent and makes his adventures a punishment for his contempt for the life he has deserted like the prodigal son. But Defoe was carried away by his hero's patience, courage, and enterprise, and the suggestion of allegorical condemnation that is implied in the prodigal son image tends to be swallowed up in what Crusoe actually did.

One might say that the epoch of mercantile capitalism in life and realism in literature that *Crusoe* heralded is given its discharge in *Pincher Martin.* But this would not go nearly deep enough. It is not man of any particular epoch who is being criticized, but man himself. Crusoe was not the world's first sailor, wanderer, possessive individualist—all of which are only images for man as survivor. Martin's first ancestor in literature seems to be Odysseus. One might trace his appearance, cast up on his rock, with "the bleached wrinkles" of his hand and the "corrugations at the finger tips" to one of Golding's childhood visual imaginings:

> When he was washed up in Phaeacia his hands were white and corrugated and his nails bled—not because of the rocks but because he bit them . . . I saw him . . . while he peered at the dark, phantom dangers. . . . The wily, the great-hearted, the traveller, the nail-biter.
>
> (*The Hot Gates,* p. 172)

But although Martin is related to Homer's Odysseus, he seems to be Dante's even more—the wicked counsellor of the twenty-sixth canto of the *Inferno* who, abandoning the loves he owed his son, father, and wife, told his crew that it is man's business to break all horizons, and took them with him into the Atlantic, until they went down before the rock of Purgatory, "as pleased Another."

It becomes increasingly clear that it is something like this rock that Martin is on, and that he is in conflict with the same Other—God. The laudatory images of man building his fate that come into Pincher's mind are classical or Renaissance, but in the general pattern of what happens to him they are dominated by medieval and condemnatory images—not only of Ulysses but also of Judas Iscariot, whom in Irish legend Saint Brendan saw reprieved from Hell on an Atlantic rock. Pincher's fellow actors, moreover, in a morality play find for him the part of Greed. Yet in his conflict with God, evil as he is, he is also Everyman. Golding has given him something more out of his own autobiography, his childhood fear of the darkness of the cellar and the coffin ends crushed in the walls from the graveyard outside. The darkness universalizes him. It becomes increasingly but always properly laden with symbolism: the darkness of the thing that cannot examine itself, the observing ego; the darkness of the unconscious; the darkness of sleep, of death, and beyond death, heaven. "Take us as we are now," his friend Nathaniel told Martin at Oxford, "and heaven would be sheer negation. Without form and void. You see? A sort of black lightning destroying everything that we call life."

But heaven is also God, and Martin, as he is forced to face that Other, hears "the cellar door swinging to behind a small child who must go down, down in his sleep to meet the thing he turned from when he was created." Golding made these symbols explicit in a letter to John Peter, in which he says that the cellar suggests "that God is the thing we turn away from into life, and therefore we hate and fear him and make a darkness there. . . . Pincher is running away all the time, always was running, from the moment he had a *persona* and could say 'I.' " But it is clear enough in the book, when the imagery and events are put together. The fourteenth-century mystic Walter Hilton has the same philosophy in his *Ladder of Perfection:* if you abstract your mind from all images of physical sensation and look within, he says, you will find nothing. "This 'nothing' is none else than darkness of mind. . . . Were the roots of sin greatly reduced and dried up in you, then if you looked into your heart you would not find nothing. You would find Jesus."[4]

Martin sees God in his own body, with a bloodshot eye, in seaman's clothes. He says to it:

> "You are a projection of my mind. But you are a point of attention for me. Stay there."
>
> . . .
>
> "Have you had enough, Christopher?"
>
> . . .
>
> "I could never have invented that."
>
> (p. 194)

Perhaps Golding has taken a hint here from a passage he admires in C. S. Lewis's science-fiction novel *Perelandra,* where a man—a philologist—faced with the necessity to do something he cannot bear to do argues with a presence in the darkness that surrounds him until it says:

> "It is not for nothing that you are named Ransom."
>
> And he knew that this was no fancy of his own. He knew it for a very curious reason—because he had known for many years that his surname was derived not from *Ransom* but from *Ranolf's son.* It would never have occurred to him thus to associate the two words. To connect the name Ransom with the act of ransoming would have been for him a mere pun.
>
> (p. 168)

There is a similar pun in the way Martin is addressed—Christopher, "the Christ bearer." But Pincher Martin will not recognize it; it is not this that makes him recognize that he is speaking to God, but the questioning of the prime urge of his being:

> "Enough of what?"
>
> "Surviving. Hanging on."
>
> . . .
>
> "I hadn't considered."
>
> "Consider now."
>
> . . .
>
> "I will not consider! I have created you and I can create my own heaven."
>
> "You have created it."
>
> (pp. 195–196)

He has created it. The fear of facing the darkness within himself, where his self comes to an end in God, made him once take refuge in aggression: "I climbed away from the cellar over the bodies of used and defeated people, broke them to make steps on the road away from you." Now, he has taken refuge in solipsism. The rock, the whole business of survival, is nothing but his own mirage, blotting out God. (In *Perelandra* the waves of the sea suggest self-abandonment to divine providence,[5] and the rock the desire "to make sure—to be able on one day to command, where I should be the next and what should happen to me." This idea seems closer in *Pincher Martin* than in *The Inheritors.*) Before the presence of God everything surrounding Martin vanishes, and he himself is left nothing but a center of consciousness and a pair of claws against which the black lightning of heaven plays, "prying for a weakness, wearing them away in a compassion that was timeless and without mercy."

[4]Walter Hilton, *The Ladder of Perfection* 1.53, L. Sherley-Price, trans., London, 1957.

[5]The title of a book by J. P. de Caussade, 1861.

This terrific epiphany is not the end. In *Pincher Martin,* as in the first two books, we shift from this wholly remade world into a more ordinary consciousness. On the Hebrides, a Mr. Campbell asks a naval officer come to examine Martin's corpse if there is any survival. The officer, not comprehending that this is a question about personal immortality, responds, "Don't worry about him. You saw the body. He didn't even have time to kick off his seaboots."

But this was the first thing Martin did: we saw him do it on the fourth page of the first chapter. Not a part, but the whole of his effort to survive was hallucination, indeed deliberate self-deception. When one rereads the book one realizes that from very early on Martin was fighting against a series of realizations, among them that the rock and the other rocks breaking the impact of the waves on it are nothing but his own teeth, a barrier against the outside world, the "wall of the teeth" of which Homer speaks. The whole story took place either in the moment of death, or after death in eternity—the latter, it would seem, for there is no break as Martin's imaginings surrender to the compassion that is timeless.

No doubt some readers pick up the hallucinatory nature of Martin's experiences relatively soon. I can only record that at first reading the last sentence left me trembling.

The novella "Envoy Extraordinary" (1956) was published along with stories by John Wyndham and Mervyn Peake, all three sharing the theme of someone disruptive coming on a static or dying society. It reveals in Golding a skeptical and ironic commentator on the themes of his own novels, one who treats the same ideas as the darkly mystical, Ancient Egyptian Golding, lightheartedly, satirically, and externally, with little question of identification with any of the characters. The intellect, imagination, and drive toward conquest of the universe that Tuami and Pincher Martin had, together with the confident enlightenment of Piggy, are given to the charming Phanocles, whose ecstatic proclamation of absorption in science is quoted at the beginning of this essay. He produces in the late Roman Empire a confusion with his invention of the steamship that is only put right, disastrously, by his second invention of high explosives. Before the third, the printing press, can take effect, the emperor packs him off as ambassador to China. For he comes up against men with other ruling passions—Postumus, heir to the empire, whom we have met before as Jack, with the lust for power; the emperor, whose passion is memory, to recover the intense enjoyments of youth, and who welcomes steam only for the sake of the recovery of flavor in the pressure cooker—but whose headmasterly wisdom points out a certain selfishness in Phanocles' irresponsible urges; and Mamillius, who being still young has no ruling passion until he falls in love with Phanocles' sister Euphrosune. She is silent, perhaps the only unselfish person in the story, since she has no ruling passion; she is also perhaps the most intelligent, since she saves the situation that the others have made for themselves. In the excellent witty play, *The Brass Butterfly* (1958), made from the story, she is given her own ruling passion, a youthfully ecstatic Christianity. I think this an improvement. The play remains Shavianly ironic: Golding's preface describes the ruling passions as Sacred Cows or Unexamined Beliefs.

Free Fall (1959) returns from ironic and skeptical comment—what Golding in an essay on "Thinking as a Hobby" called Grade Two Thinking—to Grade One Thinking, the passionate enquiry after truth. It attempts both a new structure and a new style in obedience to a question left hanging in *Lord of the Flies:* whether the end was necessitated by the beginning, the savage tribe already potential in the schoolboys, the moment when Roger kills Piggy latent in the moment when Ralph pretended to machine-gun him. In spite of the implicit presence of the Fall in *The Inheritors* and *Pincher Martin,* no transition was shown. If we reject the idea of states of being that either do not change, or develop inevitably one from another, if we believe with the Jews and Christians that there are times of total free will, how do we express this in a novel? How indeed do we recognize such a moment in our own lives?

This is not a question for the first reading of a Golding novel of the classic shape. Such a novel, moreover, cannot take the question-begging way out, of simply portraying one state as suddenly existing where there was another a paragraph before; this must not happen except at the point where our self-identification with the text is to be disturbed. Sammy Mountjoy, the autobiographer of *Free Fall,* questions his memory like a critic reading a classic Golding novel for the second time, going back to see where one interpretation superimposed itself on another, one self on another, the end of the process on the beginning. He circles about his life until he finds the very moment of fall; and he returns to the present to find, in a passage like the final twist of the earlier novels, what the consequences of his fall were. But self-consciousness is an endlessly involuting thing, and Sammy finds himself rather like T. S. Eliot in the *Four Quartets,* especially "Burnt Norton," looking for an answer to the problem of freedom, not in the loss of freedom but in the moment when he found himself detached enough from time and process to look at them from outside. So reading *Free Fall* is not only like rereading *Pincher Martin* with an eye to Martin's memories. In a sense a structure of the classic Golding two-worlds kind is superimposed on the structure that Sammy Mountjoy at first creates as he explores his past experience. But a reinterpreting of the questioning itself occupies the place of the taking over of one world view by another. So that now we must ask how the questioning itself changed; and that means one more shift of viewpoint in the final paragraph.

In fact, reading the book is not as complicated as that, because like the paths in *Alice in Wonderland* the questioning shakes itself and becomes one question. At the beginning Sammy finds himself living in two worlds, the mystical and moral world of the spirit and the world of sense and matter. To the end, he is looking for a bridge between them. Since we can speak of responsibility and freedom there must be such a bridge; but can it be expressed in the language of either world?

This problem is that which Dante wrote the *Divine Comedy* to solve. Dante, like Sammy, came to himself in the middle of his life, in a dark wood, unable to remember how he came there, "so full of sleep are we in the instant at which we leave the right way." His only way out is to see the world whole and himself in its light. Hell, purgatory, and heaven are revealed to him directly, himself and this world of sense in glimpses from the standpoint of divine justice and eternity. Golding took something like this course in *Pincher Martin;* in *Free Fall* his intent is to show this world directly, the other in hints and guesses. He is involved therefore in showing directly the moment of fall at which Dante only hints. He has a hero without reference points, who therefore lives in the vertigo of free fall, reproachful of an age in which those who have a morality or a system softly refuse to insist on them; a hero for whom no system he has will do, but who is looking for his own unity in the world —and that, the real world, is "like nothing, because it is everything." Golding, however, has the advantage of being able to bring Dante's world in by allusion; and he does so with a Paradise Hill on which a Beatrice is met.

Dante's style is answerable to his vision: pure, but capable of moving from high to low in a moment. Sammy begins his book in a divided style that harshly yokes the two worlds in the uncertain glory of "I have walked by stalls in the market place where books, dog-eared and faded from their purple, have burst with a white hosanna." He feels himself too divided to effect a union; fallen, like Pincher Martin, split between a too undetermined inner self—"the unnameable, unfathomable and invisible darkness . . . at the centre . . . always different from what you believe it to be"—and a self wholly determined, unfree.

When he goes on to tell about his childhood, he and his style are assured enough, as certain that he was free then as Dr. Johnson with his massive probity ever was; he almost echoes Johnson's "Sir, we *know* our wills are free, and *there's* an end on't." He looks for no excuses there for his later life, in his fatherless life in a rural slum or the overwhelming personalities of his mother and of his friend Evie, and the queer longing he receives from them to be a girl. His style moves easily in an undivided world from his mother on the bog to the Traherneian picture of a tree in moonlight in the general's garden on Paradise Hill. "There was one tree between me and the lawns, the stillest tree that ever grew, a tree that grew when no one was looking . . . Later, I should have called the tree a cedar and passed on, but then, it was an apocalypse." He was tough enough and a bully, but his actions were innocent because unreflective, and set up no permanent division, no habit of fallenness.

From the last moment when he knows this wa true, at the end of childhood and his mother' death, he overleaps the doubtful time of transition to the first moment when he knows he was unfree He is in love with Beatrice, he has already interpreted this love as a need to possess and subdue, h possesses, subdues, deserts her. She is like the mai object of Pincher Martin's jealousy, Mary Love who married Nathaniel; but he is too possesse with the wish to break out of his ego to be a

Pincher Martin to her. His childhood wish to be a girl transforms itself into the wish to know what it is like to be Beatrice. She is innocent and possesses a unity, a transparency of matter to spirit like Nat's or Mary Lovell's. But although she is in this sense a symbol, she has no words to explain what it is like to be a symbol. Further, Sammy says, "I was not wise enough to know that a sexual sharing was no way of bringing us together. . . . We had had our revelation of each other." He goes to queer byways of sadism to find her out, but in a way he knows her all the time. "After the last and particularly degrading step of her degradation," he paints her; and his imagination is a real artist's, not like Martin's, the means of his self-deception. He is not Martin but Tuami. He can still make the truth he cannot recognize. In his painting, Beatrice lies in gold "scattered from the window . . . looking out of the window as though she had been blessed."

In a German prison camp, the psychologist Dr. Halde singles Sammy out as someone weak enough to tell the Gestapo what he is sensitive enough to know, which of his fellow prisoners has the temperament for trying to escape. Halde puts him blindfolded into a dark cupboard to be left for torture to his imagination.

The narrative moves back to the end of childhood to find that Sammy began to be afraid of the dark when he lost the "way of seeing, which was a part of innocence"; when transferred from his slum to a lonely rectory he felt the "certain want and horror . . . beyond imagination" that Thomas Traherne also describes as happening at the end of childhood's vision.[6] Golding has endowed Sammy, like Martin, with his own childhood terror of the dark. But what Martin resisted, Sammy surrenders to: his imagination drives him onward toward every torture the Gestapo may have in store for him, and he screams for help. The recognition of the need for help changes him: "The thing that screamed left all living behind and came to the entry where death is close as darkness against eyeballs. And burst that door."

He does not say on what the door opened—perhaps on God. But he comes out of the cupboard reduced to a child again: silly and blessed; dead and resurrected. He finds the world transfigured. He draws his fellow prisoners in the image of cigarette cards he collected as a boy, "the haggard unshaven kings of Egypt in their glory." He knows as ego what he always knew as artist, that the substance of the world is love. Pincher Martin's cosmos is turned inside out. In the light of the transfigured world Sammy sees his "center" free, defying the determinist's "law of the conservation of energy," creative of endless shapes of evil.

Like Dante in the dark wood, he rediscovers the memory of Beatrice and sees her transfigured, in her "clear absence of being," a fullness that had "once shone out of her face." He goes back now to the transition period, the bridge between childhood and guilt; remembers himself at school, dominated by two teachers, Miss Pringle in whose room he was told that "as a sign to Moses that the Lord was present, the bush burned with fire but was not consumed away," and Mr. Shales next door, who says, "Matter can neither be destroyed nor created." He is offered a bridge between them when Beatrice sits for the class as a model and Sammy in the act of drawing her is born as an artist. "I saw there . . . a metaphorical light that none the less seemed to me to be an objective phenomenon." But he has already chosen Mr. Shales's universe because Mr. Shales is a good man, a saintly Phanocles, although that universe provides no context for his saintliness. The light then can only be reduced to the brute fact of sex. Sammy discovers, looking back, the day on which his headmaster told him that there is such a thing as the ruling passion; and he chose for his ruling passion his lust for Beatrice, changed into the need for her abjection if she denied him total possession of her. He has found the moment of fall at last.

Returned from his vision in Germany, he meets Beatrice again on Paradise Hill, an idiot in a lunatic asylum, sent there by his treatment of her, although quite possibly her cool, dumb self-possessedness would have issued in idiocy anyway. Once again he can see no bridge; the book almost ends in the statement of his belief in two separate worlds. But the last paragraph returns to a German Commandant letting him out of the darkness. It functions partly as a shower of cold normal consciousness on Sammy's transports, since the darkness is only a cupboard; partly, like others of Golding's endings, to stress the reality of the now distanced abnormal consciousness. Yet in both worlds a door has opened. Golding himself has

[6] Thomas Traherne, *Centuries of Meditations* 3.23.

remarked that the opening of the cell door is like the "handprint on the canvas that changes the whole thing," and that when he saw that, it became "the first genuine passion I felt about the book."[7] But this is not convincingly conveyed, if only because Sammy has already told us that the "Commandant came late and as a second string." Nevertheless, Sammy clings as to a bridge between the two worlds to the Commandant's saying, "The Herr Doctor does not know about peoples." Whatever realization happened in the cupboard—and that is still only obliquely known—finds some response in this, perhaps because it declares that the way of putting nature to the test by torment and questions, the way the psychologist took with him and he with Beatrice, is not the way to knowing what is there. But the resolution remains thick and uncertain; and, perhaps because Sammy has already tried to do it for us, the second reading of the book provides nothing new. Alone among Golding's novels, *Free Fall* is more of a puzzle fragmentarily solved than a mystery to be known, although it has long, illuminated stretches.

In the same year as *Free Fall,* Golding also published a short story, "The Anglo-Saxon," which deserves resuscitation from its back number of *The Queen.* A story trying to express the world of a downland drover who has a language of 650 words hung in the "dark, angry cupboard" of his head, who is confronted with a world of laws, new men, and new exigencies that he does not understand, it goes closely with *The Inheritors* and might be bound up with it in case anyone takes from the novel the notion that inarticulateness necessarily means unfallenness.

Golding's two short stories are like the later ones of Rudyard Kipling, in that by omission and obliquity they try to convey in a very short length the emotional intensity of a novel. His other one, "Miss Pulkinhorn," written in 1951, was not published until 1960, after appearing as one of his two radio plays in the same year. The radio plays, in contrast, having in regard the difficulty of a form only heard and not to be reread, are explicit in their buildup. "Miss Pulkinhorn" is one of the rare pieces in which one feels Golding at his full intensity while dealing with a situation neither of the past nor on a distant island, but in twentieth-century England. Both the setting, a cathedral and its close, and the peculiar emotions involved are eccentric to the age, however, although the ultimate theme—the uncompromising strangeness of the religious passion—is universal. That passion takes the form of the dependency of an Anglo-Catholic (that is, a strongly sacramental Anglican) on the reserved sacrament of Christ's body, the consecrated bread kept for the communion of the sick and adored by some, and the violent hatred that this adoration can arouse. Anglo-Catholicism is a peculiarly experiential religion; its adherents, who have, unlike traditional Roman Catholics, little repose on the authority of the Church, find their repose instead in the Holy Communion; and some will center so intensely on the experience that it is a common Anglo-Catholic claim that there is a recognizable difference between a church that has the presence of the reserved sacrament and one that has not. Golding, who once observed that hearing a great line of Shakespeare is a moment "no more to be defined than taking a Sacrament, or bearing a child, or falling in love," is well fitted to present this kind of perceptual and experiential religion; indeed we have seen similar things in *Lord of the Flies* and elsewhere.

In the radio play the emotion is presented at length. It is first prepared for in the awe of the cathedral, then in the devotion of an old, crazy, holy man and emphasized by the intense repugnance of Miss Pulkinhorn; and given a ground of more widely shared emotion in the repetition in cathedral services of Christ's words, "Take, eat This is my Body which is given for you"; and one more widely shared still in Gustav von Holst's setting of the carol in which Christ says:

> Sing O my love, O my love, O my love, my love
> This have I done for my true love.

This in its turn has a context in human falling in love, as a boy repeats it to his girlfriend. The words however, also suggest that religious feeling in the man and in Miss Pulkinhorn may not be free of unconscious sexuality. We are well prepared when the man says, "They'll light the light, just as though I needed a light to tell me He's there . . . I'll see Him . . . and He'll see me—and I shall whisper 'Hosannah' just as we did in Jerusalem"; and, when on an evening when the Sacrament has been

[7] V. Tiger, *William Golding: The Dark Fields of Discovery,* p. 160.

removed to communicate a dying person, Miss Pulkinhorn relights the light that is the sign of the presence of Christ's body, we can fully comprehend the enormous violation done to the man as, while he adores something that is not there, the verger puts out the light. We can believe both in his subsequent death and the breaking down of Miss Pulkinhorn by her realization of what she has done, until she kneels before the light herself; and feel the force of her still declaring, "My conscience is perfectly clear."

In the story the buildup is absent; the old man does not speak and remains ambiguous. The emotions are seen to happen; but unless one knows them at first hand, they remain, as it were, in a foreign language. Tauter and finer than the play, intensely moving to those who know its emotions, the story remains relatively inaccessible, the purest example of the merits and defects of Golding's intransigence. It sets in fact a problem of exposition that he solves in *The Spire,* to which "Miss Pulkinhorn" is related as "The Anglo-Saxon" is to *The Inheritors.* The emotion and ambiguity of "This have I done for my true love" in the play; and the old man's assertion, using Christ's justification for his shout of Hosanna, "If these held their peace, the very stones would cry out," again in the play; and in the story the assertion that the old man has the posture of Abraham in one of the cathedral windows—images of the strangeness of the religious passion—all find their place in the novel.

The second radio play, "Break My Heart" (1966), is very pure radio drama. It is essentially a quasi-documentary of a day in the life of a country school in the late 1950's. But the welter of voices gradually centers on the problem of Malcolm Smith, until this term an unexceptionable and happy boy, now apparently stupid and "against everybody." At the very end of the play, we find, in between two attempts to teach him one of Hamlet's soliloquies, that he is in Hamlet's situation, his mother committing adultery with his father's brother. When *Break My Heart* is read in script, something of a conflict appears between the themes of the opacity of man's heart and the incomprehension of society. Smith's situation as presented seems even too explicable, the masters' incomprehension a matter largely of overwork. The strong stresses needed for radio are apparent here: the play is said to make excellent listening.

In *The Spire* (1964) the interest is all in the opacity of the man and in a further exploration of man's all-sacrificing will. Jocelin, dean of a cathedral about 1330, is first seen with the light exploding in his face through a window that pictures Abraham sacrificing Isaac. In theme and intensity the book is one to put alongside Søren Kierkegaard's treatment of Abraham in *Fear and Trembling* (1843). Jocelin says, listing Noah, Job, Hosea, and Abraham among the God-possessed figures of the Old Testament:

> "Even in the old days God never asked men to do what was reasonable. Men can do that for themselves. They can buy and sell, heal and govern. But then out of some deep place comes the command to do what makes no sense at all—to build a ship on dry land; to sit among the dunghills; to marry a whore; to set their son on the altar of sacrifice. Then, if men have faith, a new thing comes."
> (p. 121)

Genesis takes the reality of the command from God as an assumption. Kierkegaard thought that the ruling passion is self-justifying, if it is the thing inexplicable to anyone else that every man has as the heart of his individuality, his unique relation to God. It may be possible to make a mistake, but a man who makes a mistake in this is a monster. Even so, no one can know enough to judge such a man except himself and God.

It is the possibility of mistake, and the dubiety of the whole concept of self that follows, which Golding explores. He returns to the classic Golding shape to do so. The first chapter, however, differs from this shape in that while we are not told as in *Free Fall* that the innocent world presented is less than the whole story, still the noises of warning are louder than in the three earliest novels. Jocelin is to give his cathedral a new spire. The life of the cathedral is serene and ordered. It is the day of the new beginning. He is full of joy, looks with love on everyone, very gently rebukes two young men for talking uncharitably, feels a warmth at his back as he prays. And if there is doubt about the strength of the cathedral's foundations, faith answers that God will provide.

This may be well enough. But the reader picks up the suggestions that it is not only the physical foundations that are at fault, but the foundations of Jocelin's personality. Jocelin is blameably ignorant in having no notion that the young men may be talking about him; that his affection for his daughter in God, the wife of Pangall the sexton, may be not quite unmixed; that Pangall is bitterly unhappy because he is impotent and the workmen mock him for it; that his unassertive chaplain Father Adam (being under obedience) will stand indefinitely if not countermanded; and that the money to build the spire which comes from his aunt, the late king's mistress, is not only tainted but unpaid for: for she wants in return a tomb in the cathedral, which he will not give her.

It is hard therefore for the reader to identify himself with Jocelin. What we do identify ourselves with is the work. Jocelin's Abrahamic single will is not imposing itself on something that, like Pincher Martin's imagination, it can only falsify. Form is being imposed on matter, matter that resists, but that also is the potential substance of what is to be made. All Golding's delight in technical contrivance is brought into play in the shifts of Roger the mason in his impossible task; all his brilliance of sensuous imagination in rendering the resistance opposed to it—a resistance which does not seem to be that of dead matter, but of life being tamed. Under the strain imposed on them, the pillars sing and pebbles move on the earth like "some form of life: that which ought not to be seen or touched, the darkness under the earth, turning, seething, coming to the boil."

Simon's climbing the mountain, Tuami's carving the knife, Sammy's drawing Beatrice, were images within each book of the whole of each book. Pincher Martin's falsifying imagination was an image of half the book—the book at first reading, so to speak. But the whole of *The Spire* is an image of the writing of it: the reader shares in the drill biting into the armor plate, the intransigence.

The book's tendency therefore is to abandon the original sense that it is about the religious will for the sense that it is about art. That it never finally does so is due, first, to the fact that Jocelin and Roger Mason both remain in our eye, both necessary to each other. Jocelin has not only the will but the idea of what Roger does, so much so that Roger falls in love with Pangall's wife; and Jocelin assents in him to a passion he does not even recognize in himself because it will keep Roger at the work. Roger in turn—and therefore Jocelin—is involved in the actions of his men: what he thinks is what they do. They murder Pangall and put his body under the spire as a good luck offering. But because it is Jocelin's consciousness that we inhabit, a consciousness now (like Martin's) cut off from reality, except for his dependence on Roger Mason who must keep in touch with reality, we learn about Pangall's death only as it forces itself on Jocelin's mind, after he has seen, from the spire, fires of pagan offering on Midsummer Eve in the valley of the Hanging Stones: Stonehenge. Spire and Stonehenge recognize each other as places of sacrifice.

The other reason why religion and art, idea and means, are never separated, Golding partly owes to the fourteenth century. A cathedral is itself symbolic, is worship, and may be, as it is in Golding's hands, the whole of a man. Jocelin lays hands on himself when he lays hands on the cathedral, and in stirring up the darkness under the earth, begins to see the darkness within himself.

It seems to be all one process, therefore, that as Jocelin pushes the spire up by Roger's means he realizes that his urgency to build the spire is connected with his love for Pangall's wife—even obscurely that the spire is phallic, a club brandished in the sky toward the constellation called Berenice's hair; and that the warmth of the angel at his back is tuberculosis—that the vision in which he felt his body as the cathedral with the spire growing from it was deception. From it follow debts, the church deserted, discord, the murder of Pangall, the death of Pangall's wife bearing Roger's stillborn child, the despair and destruction of Roger and Jocelin themselves, and an "ungainly crumbling" spire. "This have I done for my true love" means only that visionary religion is repressed sexuality, and God exists if anywhere "lying between people and to be found there."

Thus Golding succeeds in bringing a philosophy of 1964 into the language of 1330: fittingly, since the century of Walter Hilton, already quoted, and of William Langland and the author of *The Cloud of Unknowing,* understood better than any other the ambiguity of religious vision. And ambiguity remains: there are two interpretations still to come. In "Miss Pulkinhorn," the narrator observes that his visionary was not a saint. "Read about the saints, even the least spectacular among them, and somewhere in their characters you'll come across steel, sheer adamant, something that can't be driven." This is realized in *The Spire* in a sudden revelation of the character of the least spectacular of its people, Father Adam. It is he who explains to Jocelin that his vision is a result of the capacity for visualizing that goes along with seeing sounds when one hears them—and with a beautiful unshakeability consoles Jocelin as one who was never taught to pray, since it is part of the science of prayer that such visions as his are encouragements only "just above vocal prayer." "Your prayer was a good prayer certainly: but not very."

But something so dry and undramatic finds little comprehension in Jocelin. His vision must be either all, his spire pierce all the stages of prayer, or nothing. He has a momentary comfort seeing an appletree—like the terrible tree that is his image for all the consequences of his will, like the Tree of Knowledge, but with more than one branch and a real tree. "It was there beyond the wall, bursting up with cloud and scatter, laying hold of the earth and the air, a fountain, a marvel, an appletree"; and near it "all the blue of the sky" is condensed into the flash of a kingfisher. But he only reacts into a depressed version of Father Adam's comment: "I make too much fuss among the appletrees and the kingfishers."

Only, as he dies, he sees his spire, dividing "the blue of the sky." It is beautiful, it astonishes, it glitters "like an upward waterfall" defying entropy, and his work culminates in it: "The substance was one thing that broke all the way to infinity in cascades of exultation that nothing could trammel." After all, we are doing something in building and praying. Whatever the cause (Jocelin thinks with a text from Christ's entry into Jerusalem, Luke 19:40), "our very stones cry out." And Jocelin dies, crying out at the very limits of language: *"It's like the appletree!"*

This is *The Spire*'s utmost reach into what cannot be expressed and Golding's most aspiring raid so far on poetry. In 1977 he was to refer to the final image in conversation as a symbol for a novel that succeeds. "It's a single activity, it's a beautiful thing, it's like the appletree growing out of a seed." Most certainly this is true of *The Spire;* and novel, spire, and appletree, if they are like the Tree of Knowledge, are like it as the tree of the Fortunate Fall. What Jocelin's cry does lack is the steel of the vision of God in *Pincher Martin.* And that is supplied in the last sentence:"Father Adam, leaning down, could hear nothing. But he saw a tremor of the lips that might be interpreted as a cry of: *God! God! God!* So of the charity to which he had access, he laid the Host on the dead man's tongue."

"It's like the appletree!" "God! God! God!"—alternative expressions; charity and the action of giving the Sacrament; and a silence between Jocelin's cry of *"the appletree"* and Father Adam's response, which may be like the shifts of consciousness in the earlier novels but can be felt as holding the mysterious fullness intended by the opening of the door at the end of *Free Fall.* Golding achieves something like the silences in Eliot's *Four Quartets,* revelatory silences, bridges into another world.

But he did not raid further into poetry for fifteen years, except in the articles and autobiographical fragments, some of which are assembled in *The Hot Gates* (1965), which we have already sampled. They make one wish for more autobiography. *The Pyramid* (1967) was, indeed, at first reading a disappointment to anyone who had acquired the taste for strong Golding. But no more than the others is it the same book at the end as at the beginning. At the beginning it seems to be a mixture of *Bildungsroman* and class novel. The title suggests the "social pyramid," a phrase out of *Free Fall;* the epigraph, also Egyptian—"If thou be among people make for thyself love, the beginning and end of the heart"—seems to refer to the emotional education of Oliver growing up between the wars in Stilbourne (more or less Marlborough). The episodes give his contact with three twisted lives—Evie Babbacombe, lower class, sexy, and exploitable, particularly as relief from Oliver's dreamlike infatuation for the middle-class Imogen; Mr. Evelyn de Tracy, a homosexual whom Oliver fails to understand, but who gives him his release from Imogen; and Bounce Dawlish, his music teacher, in frustrated love with Henry Williams, who introduced cars and garages to Stilbourne, and going mad. At this stage the book seems pleasantly written, but in low key. It seems only a defect in its fulfilling of its aims that there is no special subtlety in observing the marks of social differentiation, and that after all the social structure has little to do even with the fate of Evie—would she, or Oliver's feelings for her, have been strikingly different if she too had been a dispenser's child?—and nothing at all with those of Mr. de Tracy or Miss Dawlish. And the one flash of strong Golding at the end seems only an anomaly, as Oliver stands by the tomb of Clara Cecilia

Dawlish, 1890–1960, with the inscription "Heaven is Music":

> It was here, close and real, two yards away as ever, that pathetic, horrible, unused body, with the stained frills and Chinese face. This was a kind of psychic ear test before which nothing survived but revulsion and horror, childishness and atavism, as if unnameable things were rising round me and blackening the sun.
>
> (p. 213)

But then the whole book moves into a new key as Oliver realizes for the first time: "I was afraid of you, and so I hated you. It is as simple as that. When I heard you were dead I was glad." Finally he finds burned and smashed in Miss Dawlish's garden all her music books and papers, her father's metronome, a bust of Beethoven, and her father's photograph. The only person who could have done this was Bounce herself: in rebellion against her father and his phrase "Heaven is Music." Paying Henry Williams for petrol, Oliver sees Williams and himself as people who will pay a reasonable price to help others; but never more than a reasonable price.

After all, the book is not a picture of Oliver's emotional development; at most, a development to the point where he realizes our failure in emotion, the difficulty of making for ourselves love. In fact, in its original context in *The Maxims of Ptah-hotep,* "make for thyself love" is likely to have the merely prudential sense "make yourself liked": and that becomes likely too to be its sense for Oliver's life. As for *The Pyramid,* it seems that a better title might have been that originally given to the story of Bounce—*Inside a Pyramid:* her body in the image of Marlborough graveyard, in the darkness where Golding's childhood imagination began.

When the first meaning of pyramid becomes tomb, a chill is sent back through the whole book. Bounce was entombed all her life long—except for some years in which she was relaxed, smiling, and actually mad. And though the idea of social ascent is still present, it is penetrated by the coldness of the little town, the shut-inness of every house surrounding the square, the deathliness.

We know now too that the horrible pathos of Bounce's life issued from the beatings and discipline given her by her thwarted father; and this reflects back violently onto Evie's life, a girl brought up to masochism from a guessed-at early relationship with her father. And the general theme of the pathos of music, the reflection of a harmony that no one achieves, takes up even the partly comic episode of *The King of Hearts* as produced by the Stilbourne Operatic Society under Evelyn de Tracy. Not Evie's singing voice, nor the opera, nor Oliver's practice, nor the Savoy Orpheans (a radio orchestra) to whom Oliver compares Evie, nor any relationship described in the book offer what Sir Thomas Browne talked of:

> Even that vulgar and Tavern-Musick, which makes one man merry, another mad, strikes in me a deep fit of Devotion . . . it is . . . such a melody to the Ear as the whole world well understood would afford the understanding . . . a sensible fit of that harmony which intellectually sounds in the Ears of God.[8]

Music serves as a metaphor once again for the achievement of the novel: but the harmony of art is in the end a chilly thing beside love.

The Pyramid has the obliquity of Golding's short stories—it is not explicit that it was Bounce who destroyed her music, and Evie's sexual relationships are also not made plain. In *The Scorpion God* (1971), he returned to the more relaxed satiric novella. It seems to be built around the previously published "Envoy Extraordinary": in place of the original stories by Peake and Wyndham, Golding puts two of his own, making a trio concerned with what one might call the beginning of history. "The Scorpion God" itself presents the beginning of political history as we understand it, for the first historic Pharaoh of united Egypt was called "The Scorpion." The culture of predynastic Egypt and the hot, bright country itself are re-created with an odd, vivid mixture of satire and love. The opening description of the Heb-Sed race (by which the Pharaohs proved their strength and consequent capacity to rule) reads like historical clairvoyance. And simultaneously the first page majestically echoes the sculptural world of the older gods at the opening of Keats's *Hyperion*—the numinous stillness that Keats embodied in light seeds on feathered grass, a leaf that falls and does not stir, the voiceless river, the Naiad among her reeds and Saturn in his fall, is marvelously, and detail for detail, paralleled. But gradually the story shifts key, following a suggestion out of Herodotus that the Egyptians do every

[8]*Religio Medici,* II§9.

thing the opposite way from other nations, to become a clever satire, not unlike Wells's *Mr Blettsworthy on Rampole Island,* on the modern age. The Scorpion, a comic version or parody of Pincher Martin, in Egypt, which believes that to die is to begin to live, refuses to join the Pharaoh in "life," indeed kills a number of people to avoid it, and at the end is clearly about to destroy the traditional assumptions of Egypt—he seems to be a Greek—by marrying the dead Pharaoh's wife, Pretty Flower, and becoming Pharaoh. The chief minister, a physician of the soul who works on opposite principles from those of our psychoanalysts, says of him, "He has a death wish." Myth has been transformed into history. "Clonk Clonk," set long before the beginning of history, presents the advantages of being a misfit in traditional society once again: a man whose weak ankle goes "clonk," giving him something of the disadvantages of a woman who cannot hunt, and a woman whose mind (she says) goes "clonk," giving her the forebodings and tendency to poetry proper only to men. They marry, to each other's great advantage, and happily nothing further happens, the woman's forebodings being unfulfilled. In this context, "Envoy Extraordinary" joins with the other two stories in presenting the silliness and comfort of the three disturbed societies and a vivid, sensuous recreation of heat which makes the excessive activity of the three heroes particularly obnoxious.

The skeptical, rationalistic Greeks of "Egypt from My Inside" seemed to have defeated the imaginative, spiritually pragmatic Egyptians in Golding's work: the relatively detached satiric style of *The Scorpion God* fits its skeptical heroes. And he published no more imaginative writing until 1979.

III

FROM the eight years' silence, it was Egypt that called Golding back. When in 1976 he went for the first time in geographical reality to Egypt, his imagination was caught by the Colossi of Memnon—the pair of giant statues of Amenophis III whose faces, he said in a lecture a few months later,

> have been struck away as if blasted by some fierce heat and explosion. All that is visible there is shadow. Their heads preserve nothing but a sense of gaze, their bodies nothing but the rubble of posture on a royal throne. Here might be an image of a humanity indomitable but contrite because history has broken its heart . . . of a creature maimed yet engaged to time and our world and enduring it with a purpose no man knows and an effect that no man can guess.
>
> (*A Moving Target,* p. 168)

What he describes bears more than a little resemblance to the broken body with "the ruin of a face" of the airman in *Lord of the Flies,* which became the Beast; to his exegesis of it in *Fable* as suggesting the inescapableness of human history; to the "terrible knees and feet of black stone" of the gods in the cellar in *Pincher Martin;* and to "the haggard unshaven Kings of Egypt in their glory" in *Free Fall.* The stone Pharaohs embody history, and the destructiveness of history, and some purpose more than human in history. But this description adds new elements: contrition (in significant contrast with Simon's idea of the Beast "a human at once heroic and sick," there is "humanity indomitable but contrite") and fire.

It is fairly clear that this perception became the nucleus of what is perhaps the most remarkable single passage in Golding's works, the opening eight pages of *Darkness Visible.* It is a passage that works like the overture of an opera, announcing themes and images in what amounts to a symbol of great intensity and complexity, and in so doing finds a way of developing the raid on poetry of the kind that happened at the end of *The Spire.*

The Egyptian statues merge with the archetype of the burning babe, which one can find as a picture of Christ in Thomas Campion's poem on Christmas day; which smites itself into the host in Thomas Malory's description of the mass of the Grail at Carbonek; which is implicit in the three children in the fiery furnace in the book of Daniel; and which is seen as it were in manhood at the beginning of the Apocalypse, the Son of Man with eyes and feet like fire, a face like the sun, and a two-edged sword coming from his mouth.

With this weight of meaning behind him, but himself speechless, Matty walks, a child maimed and with his face blasted by heat and fire, out of the blitz on London on a night of full moon when the water mains broke. What he comes out of has many more significances: the tower of Babel struck down by fire from heaven when the languages of mankind were divided; the burning bush; the infernal city; the ruins of Pompeii; the pillars of smoke and fire that went before the Israelites at the Exodus, but here are seen as sacred to the moon. The scene is also a vivid and concrete evocation of a night in the blitz. The final note is perfectly built up to—the grief of the captain of firemen who sees Matty's appearance, "not for the maimed child but for himself, a maimed creature whose mind had touched for once on the nature of things."

The work of *Darkness Visible* is to fit the mythic and symbolic figure of Matty into a realistic novel. As regards Matty himself, it perfectly succeeds. Matty comes out of mystery and fire, and goes back into mystery and fire at the end, when he is for a second time in contact with an exploding bomb and comes burning from it—to rescue another small boy, a figure like himself of destiny, from probable murder. The book is haunted by the sense that he is a visitant from the other side of things; a little before his death he comes to that sense of himself. But for most of the book he is what was adumbrated in the Lovells in *Pincher Martin* and in Beatrice Ifor in *Free Fall,* the literal side only of a symbol that stretches into mystery. He is in fact a pathologically literal person, whether he is reading the Bible with a reverence that includes the verse numbers or responding to other people's ironic remarks; and he is besides driven by compulsions, which a psychiatrist might class as neurotic but which he identifies, like Jocelin in *The Spire,* with the compulsive symbolic actions of the possessed men and prophets of the Bible. Left maimed in mind and body by the fire, in his isolation he asks first "Who am I?" then "What am I?" and finally "What am I for?," wandering like the biblical Abraham in search of an answer to the other side of the world. In 1965, however, he begins to have visions and to record them in a journal, in which we follow him between then and 1978, growing up to them so that, for example, the "spirits," one of whom is "in red with a hat on," while the other "in blue had a hat too but not as expensive," become "red and blue elders" who "took off their crowns and threw them down 'before' the white spirit with the circle of the sun round his head."

Matty throughout is both scapegoat and visionary, like Simon and like Nathaniel Lovell. He is shown "the seamy side where the connections are," and through him it is shown to others. Here again is something that his visit to Egypt seems to have enlarged in Golding's attention. He says in the superb essay he wrote in 1977 as a twin for "Egypt from My Inside," "Egypt from My Outside," that the mythology of ancient Egypt, the "beautiful, wise, malevolent and insane language of the wall-paintings," possessed his mind in a way that brought a verse of the psalms with it: "Day unto day uttereth speech and night unto night sheweth knowledge" (19:2). For, he adds, "I believe that life is central to the cosmos and that there are some times for some people when the deeps of that cosmos like the deeps of our minds open out."

For Matty, day does utter speech to day. His visions are of light and of things that are not within himself—a glass ball filled with sunlight on a dull day, Orion seen in Australia "with his dagger bursting fiery up," even the elders who—as the change in their description shows—are as objective as a pure vision can be. The one vision that someone has as a result of meeting him that is described in detail is of the palm of his own hand "made of light."

Matty is a saint translated into a language that is plausible for a late-twentieth-century realistic novel. "The knowledge that night shews to night" is given to the other principal character of the book, Sophy, who is in the same kind of translation a diabolist, a witch. She is as pretty and clever as Matty is ugly and half-witted; she has the same capacity for vision of the other side of things, and perhaps—though this is never quite unambiguously said of either—shares with him a capacity for miracles. Both Matty and the elders recognize her as the same kind of being as himself. Early in their lives, both have done something that they regard as a miracle—Matty cursed a boy who seemed to threaten his teacher, Mr. Pedigree, and the boy died. Sophy threw a stone at a dabchick and hit it. Pedigree is blamed for the boy's death and tells Matty, "It's all your fault": Matty accepts Mr. Pedigree's guilt as well as his own, and spends the rest of his life in contrition. Sophy, moved partly by an intense, in the end incestuous, jealousy over her father, thinks she has learned that she must follow the rhythms behind the universe, and in the end identifies those rhythms with entropy, the unraveling of the world into black nothing, symbolized in *The Inheritors* by falling water, and now by fire which it is her nature to urge on by outrage. Matty, who comes out of the burning bush, a symbol her as in *Free Fall* of what burns and is not consumed, and therefore of what is not subject to entropy, sees that behind himself and behind every human being is "a spirit like the rising of the sun." Sophy knows that there is blackness in her, at the mouth of which she lies, and chooses to identify herself with that blackness.

The book is at once prolific of patterns and bursting with untidy life. The only passage that matches Matty's first epiphany in its intensity is that in which Sophy deliriously abandons herself, as a final outrage, to an imagination of knifing the boy whom in fact Matty has already saved from her by the burnt offering of his death. But that passage also drives home the parallel between her and Pedigree, who like her obeys an entropic rhythm, the rhythm of his pederasty, but in the end dies resisting it when he feels it driving him to the point where he will find himself murdering a boy. And the passage describing Pedigree's death is the closing movement of the book, which partly answers to the overture: it is Matty who brings Pedigree both the help, which is death, and the love that he needs. Matty is transfigured in ways that again draw on Egypt—Pedigree's dying vision of him begins with the sun with many golden hands, like the sundisc that the Pharaoh Akhnaton worshiped, and Matty himself is seen transformed to burning gold with the face—though this not made explicit—of a Pharaonic coffin. The epilogue has neither the intensity nor the complex overtones of the overture, and the reader is not lost in it; we do not forget it is a vision given only to Pedigree, are indeed continually reminded of this in the narration.

This is characteristic of the novel. The practice of the earlier novels of identifying the reader with a consciousness within the novel is, except in Sophy's horrid fantasy of murder, subjected to a distancing. We do indeed see the inwardness of Matty, Sophy, Pedigree, and a little of a fourth narrative eye, Sim Goodchild, an old bookseller who begins, in a kind of further parallel to Pedigree, with a muted passion for Sophy as a child, but ends as Matty's disciple; but we see this inwardness at the same kind of distance as in reading someone's journal, as in literal truth we do Matty's. This fits one of the minor themes of the novel, the partitions between people, and Matty's power momentarily to break them down. There is an almost Dickensian frequency of minor characters of whose inwardness we see nothing—most tantalizingly in the case of Antonia, Sophy's twin, who may well be a closer parallel than Sophy is to Matty, since she is capable of commitment: once, like Matty, to Jesus; later to a destructive political terrorism. Almost certainly she is a much more interesting person than Sophy, but Sophy naturally does not think so, and we see her only through Sophy's eyes. All the other characters—the twins' father, Sophy's men, Matty's employers, the inhabitants of the town where most of the story happens—serve severally to define the four whose inwardness we see, and collectively to give a satiric and somewhat hyperbolic account of England's and civilization's development in Matty's and Sophy's lifetimes.

The novel's fertility in characters adds a sense of compulsive growth to its compulsive parallelisms, which matches the compulsions of Pedigree, Sophy, and Matty. This compulsiveness is suggested by the novel's epigraph, which is from Virgil's invocation at the beginning of his description of the underworld, in the sixth book of the *Aeneid,* "Sit mihi fas audita loqui" (May it be lawful for me to say what I have heard), as if the book is the author's record of visions like Matty's visions. Something of the same meaning is given to the title by Sophy's reflecting on her "desire for the impossibilities of the darkness and the bringing of them into being to disrupt the placid normalities of the daylight world."

But this, the knowledge that night gives to night, is only half the book. C. G. Jung remarked that "one does not become enlightened by imagining figures of light, but by making the darkness conscious." This would be a suitable description of what Golding seems to be doing in all his earlier novels, and in Sophy's side of *Darkness Visible.* But it is Matty's side, the knowledge that day gives to day, which is victorious in the total story. In the set of lectures that includes "Egypt from My Outside," Golding tentatively suggests that novelists may have "a tincture" of the inexplicable perception of character possessed by some saints, notably —although he was "near enough a half-wit"—by the curé d'Ars. Matty, less consciously intelligent still, has that power. And Golding, as it were mimicking the character whom he created, is compelled to try to see the central characters of the book and to break down the partitions between them as Matty does. Thus the image that, like others of Golding's novels, it carries of itself within itself is not Sophy's witchcraft but the principal symbol that Matty brings from the other side of things, his legacy to Sim Goodchild, his journal.

Thus *Darkness Visible,* like Matty's journal within it, might be said to be a prophetic symbol. If so, what it prophetically warns of is the final decay of Western civilization. The title, from *Paradise Lost,* and the epigraph from the *Aeneid* are balanced at the end by a tag from their common predecessor, Homer's *Iliad.* Sebastian Pedigree's outwardly squalid pederasty is compassionated and dignified by the words τηλίκου ὥς περ ἐγών (old, as I am), which compare his longings to Priam's when he begs Achilles to give him the corpse of his son Hector. This quotation in the general narration perhaps justifies Pedigree's own more terrible and pitiful appropriation, in the Greek of the Bible, of Christ's cry on the cross, "Διψῶ Διψάω" (I thirst). Cumulatively, the four quotations in the—now less and less understood—original languages, from the Bible and the three great epics, claim for *Darkness Visible* in the whole great tradition of Western literature a place they may be at once a consummation and—so far as Sophy's experience, the knowledge that night gives to night, goes—a degradation. The sword that proceeds from the mouth of the Word in both the Apocalypse and the novel, and that gives Matty the message of his death, is also promised to Matty himself by the elders. But his mouth is "not intended for speaking," and part of his message is against "reproduced words." He knows that words other than prophetic words distort experience. *Darkness Visible* embodies a crisis of faith in language and literature familiar in modernism and deals with it in a way that continually brings to mind Eliot's *Little Gidding,* looking like that poem for a new birth, out of pentecostal fire, of a spiritual language.

Within a year of *Darkness Visible* Golding published a novel, *Rites of Passage,* that in relation to it is like the other half of a diptych. It is mirrorlike on the one hand in having set within it the journal of a visionary, a scapegoat, and a wanderer, driven by unknown compulsions and undergoing a terrible rite of passage—the name anthropologists give to rituals that mark out and declare the meaning of a passage from one state of life, one identity, to another—on his way to the other side of the world. But on the other hand it is contrasted in being classic and formally composed, whereas *Darkness Visible* is romantic and riotous in growth; a historical novel set in about 1813–1814, whereas *Darkness Visible* ends in 1978, about a year before the date of publication; having its mythic qualities concealed in overtones and its social satire in the foreground, whereas *Darkness Visible* scarcely keeps its myth in bounds and its social satire is only scene setting; set in water whereas *Darkness Visible* is set in fire.

The nucleus of *Rites of Passage* is an anecdote—told by Elizabeth Longford in her biography of the Duke of Wellington, out of William Hickey's *Memoirs.*[9] A young "member of the 'higher classes' " called Blunt, a clergyman whom Hickey in 1797 persuaded Wellington—then named Colonel Wellesley—to take as chaplain on an expedition from Bengal against the Philippines, "got abominably drunk" and rushed naked from his cabin among the crew, talking and singing obscenities. Thereafter, shutting himself in his cabin in shame, he refused to eat. Colonel Wellesley himself rowed across to Blunt's ship. "He told him," says Hickey, "that what had passed was not of the least consequence, as no one would think the worse of him for the little irregularities committed in a moment of forgetfulness. . . . In short Colonel Wellesley laboured to reconcile Mr Blunt to himself, treating the circumstances as by no means calling for the deep contrition expressed and felt by him." But Blunt's contrition killed him in ten days.

This extraordinary confrontation between the code of a broadminded man of the world and violent religious emotion remains the essence of *Rites of Passage.* But Golding has made three conspicuous alterations. First, he has made the chaplain a peasant, with the look of a medieval peasant from the border of a psalter, risen from the laboring classes. This is part of the general structure of the book, which clearly intends to make the ship in which the Reverend Mr. Colley dies a microcosm of English society. The microcosm is drawn with elegance and wit; and yet, as in *The Pyramid,* one wonders if the concern with class does not distract from the real issue. It is not unfair to refer back to the actual incident, which confirms that Colley might have behaved in the same way even had he not

[9] *Wellington: The Years of the Sword* (London, 1969), p. 51.

been persistently humiliated for his plebeian unease in society. And a chance was rejected for a different and perhaps profounder comment on class, for the Reverend Mr. Blunt was of the same family that in Wilfred Scawen Blunt during the nineteenth century, and Anthony Blunt during the twentieth, produced two further examples of reacting against one's society from, even because of, a situation of ease and privilege within it.

The dramatic advantage of the change is that Blunt was not, but Colley is, isolated from the beginning. And this fits into a context with the second change, the small but important shift in date that brings the events into the hightide of the romantic age. Colley, although a religious man, is not like Matty a prophetic and mystical visionary and solitary, but rather a romantic one, whose romanticism is a compound of ecstasy in nature and evangelicalism. He dies as a kind of scapegoat, like Matty, and that too is drawn into the romantic age by being related to Samuel Taylor Coleridge's great myth of the fall in the killing of the albatross by the Ancient Mariner. And Colley's journal contrasts with the general narration of the book, which is also a journal, not like Matty's as mystical to secular, but as romantic and evangelical to Whiggish, classic, and of the Enlightenment. The keeper of this outer, covering journal is of the historical Mr. Blunt's social status, but not of his temperament, a young gentleman named Talbot under the patronage of a noble and influential godfather, for whom indeed the journal is kept. It is Talbot, naturally, who tried as long as possible to reduce the reasons for Colley's ruin to class and society; who, while Colley is in the process of shaming himself and the sailors are mocking him, reflects that "the civilized world has had cause to lament the results of indiscipline among the Gallic Race."

Third, there is a geographic change that subtly enhances the mythic element in the story. This is not any voyage, but the great voyage like the Ancient Mariner's across the equator to the other side of the world. As they cross the equator, Colley, at the edge of his humiliation in a mock rite of passage that itself prepares for his final shame and crisis, sees, with the eye of romantic religion, the sun and moon hanging level like the scales of God's justice. Talbot whimsically notes that the captain (who plays a large part in Colley's humiliations, but whose own birth in England was humiliating) has, when he turns away from the gardening of plants in his cabin that provides his only release for affection, "the stony or sullen face . . . of the expelled Adam." In the destinies of both Colley and the captain, there is as it were a myth of an English fall at the beginning of the history of modern Australia.

Yet the book is a little hopeful. There is in it the rarest of creations by any novelist, a convincing and likeable good man, Lieutenant Summers, who tells Talbot that either Colley's "wits are gone or he knows nothing of his own religion . . . a Christian *cannot* despair!" Hopeful in itself, this remark casts a doubt on Colley's earlier romantic piety. And yet again, at the end, Talbot—who at the moment of crossing the equator was farcically seducing an actress, and one of whose irresponsible words was probably the cause of the death of his servant—has by reading Colley's journal had his own rite of passage: he has grown up a little. It is only a very little; two pages from the end he makes the telltale mistake that Jocelin makes in the first chapter of *The Spire:* hearing two people talk unkindly about himself, he reflects on their uncharity but assumes it is directed against someone else. But two shifts in his consciousness happen in those last two pages. First, he realizes that Colley had actually done something to make him die of shame, and what it was; and with the realization comes further recognition and shame at his own implication in Colley's ruin. Second, having with a touch still of his Whiggish orotundity written that "men can die of shame," he shows in his final sentence how deeply he has been affected by reading Colley's vision of the sun and moon as the scales of God, how much his sense of both the human and the natural world has been enlarged: "With lack of sleep and too much understanding, I grow a little crazy, I think, like all men at sea who live too close to each other and too close thereby to all that is monstrous under the sun and moon."

Here, as throughout the book, sea, sun, and moon seem ambiguously to increase the claustrophobia of human society and to suggest that outside it there is something better—the sense provided by the steadfast constellations and the tide for Simon's transformed body in *Lord of the Flies.* They reinforce too the haunting presence of Coleridge; perhaps the changes of light suggest something like Coleridge's comparison of the power of poetry to "the sudden charm . . . which moon-light or sunset diffused over a known and familiar landscape."[9] At any rate, some of these ideas were brought together in the magnificent and rather Coleridgean lecture "Belief and Creativity," which Golding delivered about the time of the completion of *Rites of Passage* and published in *A Moving Target:*

> It may be—I hope it is—redemption to guess and perhaps perceive that the universe, the hell which we see, for all its beauty, vastness, majesty is only a part of a whole which is quite unimaginable. . . . The act of human creativity, a newness starting into life at the heart of confusion and turmoil . . . I guess . . . is a signature scribbled in the human soul, sign that beyond the transient horrors and beauties of our hell there is a Good which is ultimate and absolute.
>
> ("Belief and Creativity")

At the beginning of "Belief and Creativity," however, Golding sets a contrasting picture of himself as novelist peering out of the wrappings that have been tightened on him by the reading public in "a process of literary mummification." In his next novel, *The Paper Men,* he explores how far literary mummification and the power of words to displace experience can go. Here the journal form pushes out the external narrative of *Darkness Visible* and the observing exterior journal of *Rites of Passage.* In *The Paper Men* we have only the journal written and observe the world seen by a successful but deeply self-indulgent novelist, whose books have titles—*Coldharbour, All We like Sheep, The Birds of Prey, The Endless Plain, Horses at the Spring*—that recall not William Golding but Malcolm Lowry's *Hear Us O Lord from Heaven Thy Dwelling Place* or *The Forest Path to the Spring.* The theme of wandering becomes that of mere flight, of the novelist—Wilfred Barclay—from his critic, Rick L. Tucker; the rite of passage becomes the humiliation of Tucker, which Barclay performs as a seal to what he dramatizes as his own moral ruin. The visionary side of the journal remains, but has severe doubt cast on it by the hysterical and suggestible side of Barclay's imagination. Almost as soon as we encounter Barclay, he tells us that on him a placebo has all the power of an aphrodisiac: seeing Padre Pio's stigmata he thinks they are something of the sort, and by the end of the book he has pains in his own hands and feet which he interprets as his own stigmata. The deliberate diminishing of reality, not sublime like that in *Pincher Martin* but nevertheless telling, reaches its term when we discover that the journal was written by one kind of paper man, the novelist Barclay, for the other, the critic Tucker; and that we, the readers, are taking Tucker's part. As in Golding's previous experiments in the journal form, we remain a little distanced from Barclay, and we are only diminished in humanity and reality by acting like Tucker.

What strikes one as real, what momentarily identifies the reader's consciousness with Barclay's, is his suffering. When that appears, his style, which is normally choked with allusion and quotation, simplifies and intensifies. His memories are "like worms eating into the flesh, Rick pursuing, worms eating"—"the red hot worms under my carapace"—heat and a strain in his chest building up until the moment on an island off Sicily when he sees a silver statue of Christ "striding forward like an archaic Greek statue. It was crowned and its eyes were rubies or garnets or carbuncles or plain red glass that flared like the heat in my chest." He falls down with a stroke in front of it and wakes to know himself "created by that ghastly intolerance in its own image," one of the predestinate damned. He hints of it to Rick, tells him it was real and a rite of passage just before he pettily humiliates him as a further rite.

Thereafter he has a continual dream of walking across hot sand, and of protecting his burning feet by digging holes so deep and black that they are "sickening, like a hole in the universe." The digging is also "writing a strange language or making pictures." His novel-writing he now calls "hippityhop"—part of the grotesque attempt to escape the hot sand. He writes novels for the same reason he drinks, to find oblivion. But in the first chapter and again in the fifth he has used what the reader took then as an easy cliché, "footpaths in the sands of time," to describe all his writings, literary or otherwise, the biographical evidence mixed up with his sense of guilt, which Tucker wants to explore. Now the cliché has turned real for him, with the implication that in digging his holes he is only increasing his involvement with his guilt and the hot sand. And this is perhaps grotesquely confirmed by the next step in the dream logic—his hands and feet begin to hurt even when he is awake, the sensation he takes to be equivalent to having the stigmata.

[9]S. T. Coleridge, *Biographia Literaria,* 1817, ch. 19.

All this comes to the reader with the force of reality. Barclay's next vision is of an atonement, of being led down steps to a dark, calm sea—"since I have nothing to speak with but metaphor. Also there were creatures in the sea that sang. For the singing and the song I have no words at all." To Barclay this means that the boil of his strain and suffering has burst; the pain in his hands and feet is still there but feels "as if a doctor had put some sort of salve on them that hurt because it would heal." He goes home to try to make some reconciliation with his wife, his daughter, and even Rick L. Tucker.

But the most powerful of the strokes with which external reality breaks in on his monologue is to come. His wife dies, and when at the funeral he tells the local vicar he has the stigmata, the vicar "with a grin of quite unclerical teeth" says, "After all. There were three crosses." Barclay takes this as the gift of the peace "of knowing myself a thief," of no longer having to compare himself to Christ. The reader may be reminded of the remark Samuel Beckett attributed to Saint Augustine (it is actually bleaker and more arbitrary than anything Augustine says): "Do not despair: one of the thieves was saved. Do not presume: one of the thieves was damned." And with that remark one may find a parallel for *The Paper Men*—for Barclay's imagery of clowning, his dreams of the desert, and the novel's total ambiguity of hope and despair—in the play Beckett said was related to that epigram, *Waiting for Godot.*

The end of the book is, at least, peaceful. Barclay wonders why, if he has the wounds in the hands and feet, or the sensation of them, he has not the wound in the side that is peculiar to Christ and certified him dead. While Barclay wonders if the intolerance, which an orthodox theologian might call the justice, of God has let go of him, and records his intention to show his own kind of mercy to Tucker by giving him the journal, he receives the last wound, the death, which like Mr. Pedigree he wants.

The book is a successfully comic treatment of the themes of the traditional doctrine of the atonement. Guilt is done away with by suffering imaged in the crucifixion. And when death breaks in on Barclay's solipsistic discourse and the reader returns to ordinary reality by finishing the story, one might recognize a sad and ironic version of the psalm that traditionally is held to proclaim the atonement: "Mercy and truth are met together: righteousness and peace have kissed each other" (85:10). Golding once remarked that "any novelist is forgiving his own sins. If he has luck, he forgives other people's too." Perhaps Barclay succeeds in this, if not as novelist, at any rate as journal-writer.

It is as if in *Rites of Passage* and *The Paper Men* Golding were gnawing at the question left unanswered by Plato at the end of the *Symposium:* whether the master artist of tragedy, which Golding has certainly shown himself to be, is also the master artist of comedy. The comedy, although funny and at times farcical, remains sad. Afterward, however, Golding paid a second visit to Egypt and wrote a fourth journal of wandering, which brings gentleness, self-mockery, nonsense, an enjoyment of the process of things, and events that come to unassuming happy endings successfully together in a happier humor.

An Egyptian Journal is straightforwardly autobiographical; or rather Golding, having transformed himself for the length of *The Paper Men* into the sadly comic unreality of Wilfred Barclay, seems now determined on another comic quest for reality in the country that had already provided much of the stuff of his imagination. The conditions for reality are set oddly high, as when he says of the tombs of Beni Hassan:

> Unless you are a professional archaeologist there is more interest to be found in an illustrated book of a tomb than in the comfortless, rock-hewn thing itself. There is a primary degree of experience which lies in a touch of the hand on rock, as with the pyramids for example, and the realisation that *I am here!* After that, what is most of interest is the unexpected, and all the unforeseen surroundings of an unexpected event.
>
> (pp. 56–57)

Context at least is more important than the first part of this passage suggests, as indeed the latter part goes far toward saying. And the contrast between the two essays "Egypt from My Inside" and "Egypt from My Outside," together with the very existence of *Darkness Visible,* tells the opposite story about the impact of the monuments of Egypt on Golding at his other visit.

The result of this peculiar dislocation of and quest for reality is that *An Egyptian Journal* remarkably fills the gap left for comedy in Golding's oeuvre. It would be less surprising under the name of Eric Newby or Evelyn Waugh; it belongs in their tradition, the tradition of the English author as incompetent traveler, conveying obliquely even though his own miscomprehensions a good deal of truth and vivid reality. There is of course much of the earlier Golding of vivid dreams (Memphis on All Souls Night) and just sensuous description (Dawn on the Nile): but perhaps the real triumphs are in the farce (the unspeakable lavatory that is rendered sweet only by the failure of the steering) and in the slightly, but how memorably, drawn crew—above all the deeply touching Said, who, having worked in the Suez area forty years earlier, hates the English and begins by making Golding feel hated. After much shared struggle against "the unexpected," and attempts to establish communication which culminate in Golding's success in obtaining honey by sticking his thumbs in his ears and waggling his fingers, "meanwhile making a buzzing noise," Said says goodbye in the words: "English troubles all long time away." I should not enjoy *An Egyptian Journal* if I were a humorless Egyptian incapable of understanding the role given to the narrator, but Egyptians with a sense of humor must enjoy the indirect compliment to their country immensely. The narrator's archetype is Chaucer on the road to Canterbury.

These last four books with their repeated concern for the state of England, like Golding's first response to the news of receiving the Nobel prize, that he saw it as an honor for England, make apparent what was implicit in the earlier novels, that he is English of the English: the reading apparent in his books is that of the intelligent nonintellectual Englishman—apart from Anglo-Saxon, Greek, Egyptology, and Dante, it is Arthur Mee's *Children's Encyclopaedia,* childhood stories from the *Odyssey,* the *Aeneid* and medieval romance, H. G. Wells, Jules Verne, Arthur Ransome, R. M. Ballantyne, Stevenson, Defoe, C. S. Lewis, John Buchan, the Bible, Keats, Coleridge, Milton, Shakespeare, and Edgar Allan Poe. Yet his work is rootedly European. He claims the Greek tragedians as the greatest influence after Homer on his work; and Nietzsche's judgment in *The Birth of Tragedy* on them fits him: here the form-giver, Apollo, works in perfect balance with the urge out of darkness, Dionysus, unless the ironic intellect, Socrates, interposes. But in Golding the moral passion of the Hebrews is at least equally present, united with their awareness of the transcendent God. Naturally these urges center on a continual attempt in his books to describe something more specifically Christian, a symbol, an incarnation, a figure in human form who embodies the transcendent.

Perhaps this Graeco-Hebraic and Christian union of forces is why, if one wants to place him in English literature, the nearest writers are those of post-Puritan New England, Herman Melville and Nathaniel Hawthorne; perhaps one might think of Charles Williams also, or the Conrad of *Heart of Darkness.* But really his books relate primarily to themselves. The intransigence, the concern for truth, the fitting together of image and image into patterns of great constancy, the reduction of concept to experience, and the re-creation of language make something as new in English literature as there has ever been. One might well hope that he will be the father of a recovered freshness in the English language and its literature, and of something like his own intransigence in our approach to religion and human nature.

SELECTED BIBLIOGRAPHY

I. Bibliography. V. Tiger, *William Golding: The Dark Fields of Discovery* (London, 1974), contains bibliography of works by and on Golding, including essays, reviews, and chapters in general studies, up to 1972.

II. Separate Works. *Poems* (London, 1934); *Lord of the Flies: A Novel* (London, 1954); *The Inheritors* (London, 1955), novel; *Pincher Martin* (London, 1956), novel, reiss. in America as *The Two Deaths of Christopher Martin* (New York, 1957); *Sometime, Never: Three Tales of Imagination* (London, 1956), contains "Envoy Extraordinary," by Golding, "Consider Her Ways," by J. Wyndham, and "Boy in Darkness," by M. Peake; *The Brass Butterfly: A Play in Three Acts* (London, 1958), dramatized version of "Envoy Extraordinary"; *Free Fall* (London, 1959), novel; "The Anglo-Saxon," in the *Queen* (22 December 1959), short story; "Miss Pulkinhorn," in *Encounter* (August 1960), short story, repr. in C. Bradby and A. Ridler, eds., *Best Stories of Church and Clergy* (London, 1966) and presented as a radio play on BBC radio (20 April 1960); "Before the Beginning," in the *Spectator* (26 May 1961), review of G. Clark's *World Prehistory* (London, 1961); "Party of One Thinking as a Hobby," in *Holiday* (Philadelphia), 30 (August 1961); *The Spire* (London, 1964), novel; *The Hot Gates and Other Occasional Pieces* (London, 1965), reviews and articles, includes "The Ladder and the Tree," "Digging for Pictures," "Egypt from My Inside," "Fable," "Billy the Kid," and other autobiographical pieces; "Break M

Heart," unpub. radio play from 1966 available at Broadcasting House, London, in typescript; *The Pyramid* (London, 1967), novel; *The Scorpion God: Three Short Novels* (London, 1971), includes "The Scorpion God," "Clonk Clonk," and "Envoy Extraordinary"; "Survival," in the *Guardian* (9 May 1974), review of P. P. Read, *Alive* (London, 1974); *Darkness Visible* (London, 1979), novel; *Rites of Passage* (London, 1980), novel; *A Moving Target* (London, 1982), reviews and articles, includes "Egypt from My Outside"; *The Paper Men* (London, 1984), novel; *An Egyptian Journal* (London, 1985).

III. INTERVIEWS. O. Webster, "Living with Chaos," in *Books and Art* (March 1958); F. Kermode, "The Meaning of It All," in *Books and Bookmen,* 5 (October 1959); J. W. Aldridge, "William Golding," in the *New York Times Book Review* (10 December 1961); D. M. Davis, "Conversation with Golding," in the *New Republic* (4 May 1963); B. F. Dick, "The Novelist Is a Displaced Person," in *College English,* 26 (March 1965); J. I. Biles, *Talk: Conversations with William Golding* (New York, 1970); *William Golding Talks to Stephen Medcalf* (London, 1977), British Council recording and pamphlet.

IV. CRITICAL STUDIES. F. Kermode, *Puzzles and Epiphanies: Essays and Reviews, 1958–1961* (London, 1962), includes ch. on Golding; W. Nelson, *William Golding's "Lord of the Flies": A Source Book* (New York, 1963), contains most of the good articles on Golding's work up to 1963; C. B. Cox, *The Free Spirit* (London, 1963), pp. 172–184; S. Hynes, *William Golding* (New York, 1964; 2nd ed., 1968), Columbia Essays on Modern Writers, excellent short study of the six novels; J. R. Baker, *William Golding: A Critical Study* (New York, 1965), argues that Golding is more a classical than a Christian moralist; B. S. Oldsey and S. Weintraub, *The Art of William Golding* (New York, 1965), reads Golding in the light of his sources and analogues; H. Talon, *Le mal dans l'oeuvre de William Golding* (Paris, 1966); I. Gregor and M. Kinkead-Weekes, *William Golding: A Critical Study* (London, 1967; rev. ed., 1984), excellent study of the first five novels in relation to the nature of fiction; P. Elmen, *William Golding: A Critical Essay* (Grand Rapids, Michigan, 1967), short critique in the Contemporary Writers in Christian Perspective series; B. F. Dick, *William Golding* (New York, 1967), surveys all Golding's writing up to *The Pyramid;* L. Hodson, *William Golding* (Edinburgh, 1970), a biographical and critical study; J. S. Whitley, *Golding: "Lord of the Flies"* (London, 1970), in the Studies in English Literature series; G. Josipovici, *The World and the Book: A Study of Modern Fiction* (London, 1971), see ch. 10, "Golding: The Hidden Source"; E. Smith, *Some Versions of the Fall* (London, 1973), see pt. 3, "The Way of the Personal Myth"; V. Tiger, *William Golding: The Dark Fields of Discovery* (London, 1974), discusses all Golding's fiction as the creation in the reader of a confrontation with the spiritual world; J. I. Biles and R. O. Evans, eds., *William Golding: Some Critical Considerations* (Lexington, Ky., 1978); D. Crompton and J. Briggs, *A View from the Spire: William Golding's Later Novels* (Oxford, 1985); N. Page, ed., *William Golding: Novels, 1954–67* (London, 1985); J. Carey, ed., *William Golding: The Man and His Books* (London, 1986).

LAWRENCE DURRELL
(1912–)

*Keith Brown and Martin Dodsworth**

FORMATIVE INFLUENCES

LAWRENCE DURRELL was born in Darjeeling, India, on 27 February 1912, both his parents being members of British families that had for generations made careers in the Indian empire. Only the first decade of his own life was spent in India, however, as Mr. Durrell senior wished his sons—Lawrence's brother, Gerald, is a well-known zoological writer—to acquire the "hallmark," as he put it, of an English public school education. Nevertheless, Lawrence Durrell's early Anglo-Indian background, of which he remained very conscious, has in varying ways perceptibly marked his entire career as a novelist. His poetry, for whatever reason, does not seem to have been similarly influenced.

The pattern was early set. Brought back to England, the young Durrell was first sent temporarily to a central London grammar school, to equip him better to face the entrance examination for the boarding school of his parents' choice. Thus the London of the early 1920's—that same London which Virginia Woolf would be depicting a year or two later in *Mrs. Dalloway*—provided the setting for Durrell's first real meeting with English life; not surprisingly, the meeting was not a success, and echoes of the child's startled revulsion still stir in his voice when he describes it. In the city where Woolf could find light, beauty, dignity, and the vitality of the human comedy, a lonely small boy in dreary lodgings, torn from his childhood surroundings and the father he was never to see again (Durrell senior died in India a few years later), received largely an appalling impression of *blackness*—a blackness no less literal than spiritual. This was London before the Smoke Abatement Acts: the air grimed from hundreds of thousands of coal fires, public buildings draped in soot, and much of the population dressed to match. A child's eyes, still lit by memories of the color and sunlight of India, took in the avalanches of hurried black- or charcoal-overcoated commuters, each with black umbrella and hideous black bowler hat, and those other armies of respectable middle-aged working women, again more often than not in decent shabby black. Blackness, too, made mourning visible: many sleeves of other colors still carried a black ribbon or other mark in memory of some relation lost either in the war or in the great influenza epidemic that was its aftermath, or in some more recent bereavement. And it was natural for an uncomfortable child, inevitably interpreting the formal reserve of English post-Victorian manners as disapproval of himself, to see London's sable garb as the outward badge of an inner joylessness: a continuous puritan disapproval of every warm and natural human response. It is no accident that the adult Durrell first found his true voice as a writer in a scathing portrayal of "the English death" entitled *The Black Book,* and mainly set in London.

Eventually the unhappy schoolboy found an odd form of comfort. In Southwark Cathedral he discovered a group of fine Jacobean tombs and grave monuments, freshly recolored and gilded. In form, proportion, heaviness of decoration, and unapologetic brightness of color—particularly in color—they at once brought India to his mind: indeed they did more, seeming to him a kind of token or talisman; a guarantee of the continued existence of a world he had lost. He began to play truant from school, lingering around the tombs when he should have been in class. His English master discovered what was happening, and, mercifully, had imagi-

*In this essay Keith Brown wrote the sections on Durrell's life and prose writings; Martin Dodsworth wrote on Durrell's poetry and plays.

native sympathy enough to try to help rather than to punish. If the young Durrell so much liked the things that the Elizabethans and Jacobeans had *made,* he suggested, then perhaps he would like the things that they had *written,* too. The suggestion took root, the truant ending by becoming as obsessed with "collecting" Elizabethan literature as his classmates could be with collecting stamps or autographs. By the time he was seventeen, Durrell has been heard to claim, he had read every line of Elizabethan literature that still survives in print: doubtless a mistaken claim, but proof enough of the strength of the obsession.

This early period of intense reading, uncritical yet given coherence by the focus of so much of it on the work of a single period, essentially made Durrell as a writer; though the lessons planted so deeply and so early in his subconsciousness took time to surface. It was of course the *flavor* of Elizabethan writing that attracted so young a reader; from a strict critical or scholarly point of view, he must often have had little real comprehension of the text before him. But the verve and gusto of Elizabethan writing, that geniality that can somehow persist even in the most violent abuse, that relish for fully exploiting the resources of one's vocabulary, the unembarrassment about emotion, the richness of decoration, the pleasure in the eccentric, all these were qualities that a homesick schoolboy could savor; and in *The Black Book* and the *Alexandria Quartet* the mature Durrell was to make them distinctively his own. (His knack of allowing the last enchantments of the world of courtly love to sound hauntingly over sets of sexual musical chairs worthy of Iris Murdoch's *A Severed Head* is one the Elizabethans discreetly showed him, too.)

Unawares, however, he was also intuitively absorbing other literary values: a sense for the vital rhythmic and architectonic aspects of composition; and, gradually, some sort of notion—however unfocused—of the way a latent scheme of large ideas about the cosmos can often underlie the seemingly casual surface play of a Renaissance text. From such early intuitions emerged Durrell's own distinctive sense of what literature should be: one for which in his mind the Elizabethans have always remained the touchstone. In his novels this helps to account both for the investment of his fictions with a sort of lightly heraldic quality, and for that deliberately playful seriousness about ideas that has sometimes deceived reviewers into seeing him as a more trivial writer than he is. It is typical, too, that in an interview he accounted for the shift of emphasis in his career from poetry to novel writing by explaining that he had found it hard in poetry to approach "the rambunctiousness of Nashe"; while his response to another interviewer's query, about the gangsters' party at the end of *Livia,* was a surprised inquiry as to whether the questioner could have forgotten that Elizabethan tragedies ended with a jig. Yet others might surely have found parallels nearer home for the characteristic *festivitas* of a Durrell novel (as for other aspects of his work too) in the novels of Charles Dickens.

For Dickens is also a writer who early impressed himself on Durrell's consciousness, his influence perhaps helping to open the way for that of the Elizabethans. Already in India, around the age of eight, Durrell had startled his unbookish family by announcing that he intended to become an author, and had been promptly rewarded by a gift from his father of Dickens' *Collected Works.* Undistracted by television or by the mass of lightweight reading material so readily available to the normal modern English child, the grateful son, a little awed by the magnificence of the gesture he had provoked, at once started in on *Sketches by Boz* and kept going, thus laying the foundations, perhaps, for that negative Dickensian image of twentieth-century London he formed on arrival there. But a book-hungry child left alone with Dickens learns other lessons, too: not least, the tolerant patience to trudge trustingly on through slacker passages (such as the sentimentality wreathed around Esther Summerson in *Bleak House*) confident that soon the Pied Piper will again restore the magic to his narrative. In Durrell this lesson sank deep: his choice of comparison is hardly accidental when sixty years later he is to be heard commenting wryly that modern British critics work to double standards—praising the great names of the past, yet giving short shrift to any modern British author "who, like Dickens, needs to be allowed room to write badly in order to write well." (The comment bears reflection, for surely Durrell is right. One could not, for example, generate a greater novel from *Bleak House* merely by editorial deletion: somehow, the greatness of the work is the sum of all its parts, even the soggy bits. Of course it does not necessarily follow from this that, for instance, the first third of Durrell's own *Nunquam* would not have benefited by compression; but that is the risk the instinctual writer has to take. It remains a legitimate tradition, although nowadays the British seem only to permit new American members to share in it.)

THE MOVE TO THE MEDITERRANEAN

DURRELL emerged from his boarding school an omnivorous reader and a rebel, the two things being of course interconnected: in the climate of a minor English public school at that date, to take any interest in, say, Freudian psychology or D. H. Lawrence was itself an act of intellectual rebellion. Like many a sensitive public schoolboy before and since, he appears to have regarded his schooling as a kind of slowgoing spiritual rape. When he came to record the experience, in the heavily autobiographical middle section of his first novel (*Pied Piper of Lovers,* published in 1935 when he was twenty-three), the embarrassingly raw adolescent resentment flooding off his pages wrecks the book, although its well-written opening Indian scenes equal anything in the commercial best-seller fiction of the interwar years, with which he had plainly set out to compete. At school, the same helpless rage blocked him from doing himself justice in the (at that time very undemanding) admission examination to Cambridge University, which it seems he more than once failed.

Failure of this sort, however, was less a defeat than a step in a familiar ritual. For at least half a century, both London and popular fiction had been liberally stocked with rebel public schoolboys with artistic proclivities who spurned conventional careers and moved to the capital to live the *vie bohémienne* (on tiny incomes from their families) while becoming a Writer, or an Artist. Durrell, after first embarrassing the family by hopeless attempts to live such a life in bourgeois Bournemouth, was firmly packed off by his mother to London to do the same. The final section of the *Pied Piper of Lovers* is the fictionalized record of this period. From a literary point of view it is spoiled by the immature emotional heroics that carry over from the previous part of the book, although it is interesting as a social document of its period and for the light it throws on Durrell. (It also supplies rather necessary information about some of the characters in his next novel, *Panic Spring,* where they are transferred to a Mediterranean setting.)

Up to a point, Durrell enjoyed London's bohemia, although that point was relatively soon reached. The freedom, the conscious flouting of conventionality, the talk of the arts, the cameraderie, the small adventures—working for a time as a jazz pianist, escaping in the nick of time from a police raid on a club—all this had its obvious attraction. It was at this time too that Durrell met his first wife, Nancy, an art student at the Slade School.

Yet something in Durrell has remained unshakably the child of the empire: in one Mediterranean home after another, he has more or less deliberately sought—without the compensating benefits of an army of native servants—the rather spartan simplicities of his own parents' life in the Himalayan foothills. And equally unshakable in his mind, it is clear from many of his books, is the association of that preferred life style with the sense of a firm—if idiosyncratic and not always articulable—moral code: a kind of fusion of the nobler aspects of peasant mores with the generosity of the pioneering colonist at his best, plus a fundamentally religious respect for the physical dimension of life, underlying an apparent libertarianism. Despite the various individual friendships and admirations Durrell formed while on its territory, London's bohemia in general was obviously ill-equipped to match this code, and the close of his first novel documents its failure in the young man's eyes. As so often with Durrell, too, the youthful experience had crystallized a judgment that was never really to change. Although various friends and hallowed names (most notably T. S. Eliot) escape the anathema, Durrell, like his fellow "colonial" the poet Roy Campbell, always tended to find the London literary world a suffocatingly small-souled place. Politically, too, to the extent that he has concerned himself with politics at all, he has always been much closer to Eliot's Tory outlook than to that wobbly mixture of playboy communism and Fabian socialism more typical of young English middle-class writers of his own generation.

Retreat from London, then, became inevitable: at first only to a Sussex cottage shared with another couple, but soon further afield to a Greek island, Corfu. Already—he was in his early twenties—Durrell's only extended period of residence in Great Britain, some nine years, was over. The move to the Mediterranean, crucial to his subsequent career as a prose writer, was not, however, quite the shaking-of-the-dust-of-England-forever-from-one's-feet that it is easy in retrospect to make it seem. Certainly, there is some characteristically exuberant rhetoric in some of Durrell's letters; and in *The Colossus of Maroussi* Henry Miller—describing his visit to the Durrells in Greece—shows just how violently Durrell's countrymen could grate upon the latter's nerves before World War II a little emended his opinion of them. Nonetheless, the primary attraction of Corfu was that of a place where it would be easier for the Durrell family to manage on their limited incomes (as devotees of Gerald Durrell's books will know, the whole clan moved to the island, although he has rather ungallantly deleted Lawrence's first wife from the picture), and where, as a bonus, something of the sunlit and uncluttered quality of life in their lost Indian home could perhaps be recovered. But as far as publishing was concerned, Durrell continued to think of himself as a Britain-based writer, making enough return visits to keep in touch with English life. Some years after the war, indeed, he attempted to settle again in England, taking a cottage in Dorset; but as it turned out, his Mediterranean-born third wife's difficulties with the English climate were to drive him south again.

From the point of view of Durrell's own literary development, the years on Corfu were a great success. Despite the failure of *Pied Piper of Lovers, Panic Spring,* his second novel, was accepted in 1937 by Faber and also purchased for American publication (although Faber must have badly confused anyone who noticed the clear links between the two novels by its attempt to dissociate the second from the failure of the first, publishing it under the nom de plume "Charles Norden").

Panic Spring, though without the same autobiographical interest, is a marked improvement on its predecessor. It is a mildly philosophical comedy in a Greek island setting: a pleasant enough read for a wet afternoon, although defaced at one point by the unthinking cliché anti-Semitism of pre-1939 commercial fiction, and at times showing, too, that the emotional heroics of the *Pied Piper* had not yet quite worked their way out of the author's system. But such apprentice labors, as he rapidly realized, were a dead end for Durrell as a writer. More important, it was in the Corfu years that the miraculous explosion of *The Black Book* occurred, his poetry began to find an audience, and the notes were made for *Prospero's Cell*—the first of the three incomparable "island" books that have done nearly as much as the *Alexandria Quartet* to bring him international celebrity.

This was a noble harvest, yet one for which he perhaps paid a certain price. Among reviewers there has always been a tendency, usually muted but sometimes quite brutally expressed, to see Durrell's novels as gorgeous, shimmering, rainbow-colored bubbles, a delight and refreshment to the eye as they rise above the drab everyday life around us—but then (it is suggested) losing interest, except for purely escapist readers, precisely because they *are* so perfectly encapsulated, so without root in any feeling or concern for the texture of that humdrum day-to-day world in which ordinary people struggle with their problems and their quiet desperations. If one gets into a certain mood —and perhaps even his warmest devotees might admit they have experienced such moods momentarily—all the post-Corfu novels can indeed sometimes bore in much the way that very rich people tend to be boring: pleasant and exciting enough company at first, yet ultimately too bland to be really interesting, cushioned as they are against those small daily pressures that develop the grain and flavor in most people's characters. In such a mood there can be times, as one follows Durrell's comfortably situated protagonists vaticinating spaciously about their loves and hollow high designs through the streets of Athens/Alexandria/Avignon, when mutinous recollections stir of that sardonic man in Kingsley Amis' famous poem, inviting Our Lord to come down off the altar and "get some service in" before trying to tell *us* about life. But then—just as when we similarly begin to lose patience with Dickens' sentimentality—some marvelous piece of writing jolts the kaleidoscope, and our picture changes again.

Durrell is of course aware of such criticisms. His reply, backed by a natural consciousness of the almost worldwide recognition his books have brought him, is very simple; that the literature of social conscience has given us some very great works, he gladly acknowledges, but he himself merely happens to be a writer of another sort: surely that is his privilege, if he so chooses. It is a reasonable retort—after all, most of the great names of English literature by far predate the emergence of the literature of social conscience—yet somehow not altogether satisfactory. Behind the romance, the brilliant sensuous description, the high jinks and knockabout intellectual byplay, Durrell is a man excited by ideas and seriously engaged with them: a certain missionary vein, a drive to instruct, is inherent in all his serious novels. Yet those works are not short, tight parables; they are extended multivolume fictions, each creating a whole world. That Durrell does not intend these vast constructs to be facsimiles of quotidian reality is, up to a point, acceptable enough; it merely means that his books are to be seen (like Nathaniel Hawthorne's or Iris Murdoch's) as contributions rather to the tradition of the "romance" than of the "pure" novel. But if he intends, as it seems he does, that as we learn to find our way around these roomy, complex, free-floating structures we are *also* to be learning by analogue more about the labyrinth of our own reality, then we need a greater sense of recognition, a solider bridge, than he provides. Beneath the surface of his fictions, we need to sense the presence, however miraculously transposed, of the bread-and-butter patterns of everyday existence. And it has to be asked not only whether this is something that Durrell's post-Corfu fiction affords us, but also whether this is something that it is even *possible* for a chronic expatriate to provide, particularly when most of his limited time in his own country was spent cloistered in the very artificial environment of a public school.

A renewed comparison with Dickens may make the point. The image of London that builds up in the mind of a reader making his way through Dickens' novels is at least as profoundly mythopoeic as the image of Alexandria that Durrell builds up for us through the successive novels of the *Quartet.* The characters can be as fantastic, their names as bizarre; there is the same taste for a tincture of the melodramatic and the grotesque. But (leaving aside his awkwardness with aristocracy) we never doubt that Dickens really knows the kind of real people who lie behind his gallery of heightened, slanted, colored, selective, adrenalized portraits; that he not only has a feeling for the way they are interwoven in the fabric of society, but that he can, as it were, hear in his head—all the time, unhesitatingly—the way that they talk when they are alone together. Hence that sudden joyous feeling he can at times give us—our common humanity with people with whom we would have in fact found nothing whatsoever in common had we met them in the flesh—because he is himself part of the people of whom he writes, however unlike their individual circumstances may be to his own.

The roots of a similar gift are in Durrell; and in *The Black Book* (particularly in the moving figure of Gracie, the little cockney wife) one can see those roots beginning to flower. But *The Black Book* was written while Durrell's brief engagement with English society was still fresh in his mind; thereafter, the roots wither from lack of nourishment. In the *Quartet* only one character gives us the same mysterious Dickensian sense of comedy, pathos, and autonomous vitality—and that, significantly, is Scobie, a figure who is the very essence of the uprooted. Life on Corfu was not, in the long run, quite as inexpensive as the young Durrell supposed. And yet perhaps the price was worth it, when the unfulfillment of one of Durrell's talents made room for the flowering of so many others.

THE BLACK BOOK

The Black Book (1938) is a profoundly original work: a testimony as much to its author's poetic gifts as to his prose talents, and surely Durrell's most lasting achievement. Of course his reputation generally is high; yet the romance novel as a genre may eventually lose its hold on readers, as other forms of fiction have done in the past, while travel writing even at its most polished—as Durrell himself acknowledges—is still a secondary literary form. But *The Black Book* is *sui generis,* immune to fashions in genre. As long as literate English is enjoyed at all, new readers will discover with the same shock of excitement its exultantly articulate prose, as powerful as a waterfall hurtling into a hydroelectric turbine—and re-readers will discover that its effects are not diminished when come upon for the second or third time. Already, as time performs its familiar task of easing our assimilation of the author's ideas, this book seems less overloaded —"a faster read," though not in any dismissive sense—than its earliest admirers found it.

The catalyst that unleashed the torrent of *The Black Book* (the original typescript is said to have been four times the length of the published version) was Durrell's reading of Miller's *Tropic of Cancer* at a time when he was already realizing that success as a conventional commercial novelist—his original goal—was not going to satisfy him, even if such success could be had. *Tropic* helped break this mental impasse. In the first place, its determination to present its author directly, without the least literary gloss, awoke Durrell to the unconscious taint of derivative "literariness" in so much use of language, not least his own. Second, he was exhilarated—understanding the necessity for it—by Miller's majestic indifference to normal socio-sexual taboos, wherever these would have got in the way of total presentation not only of himself but also of the psychically troubled Parisian milieu in which he had found himself.

Miller's startling account of his early days in Paris thus broke over Durrell with the force of near-revelation, as his published correspondence with Miller shows: ". . . of course language is my problem. . . . I set out on a voyage to find myself —and find language. A vicious thing good writing is. I wish I wrote worse—in the good sense." *The Black Book* repeats the thought with greater desperation: "to try to escape from the chaste seminary of literature in which I have been imprisoned too long" (p. 66).[1]

But to what task should one's new freedom be devoted, could that escape only be achieved? Like most young writers, one of Durrell's greatest needs at this time was to find his own way forward out of the shadow of those older, established, contemporary authors by whom he had been most impressed. Miller ("a copybook for my generation") was indirectly showing him the way. Durrell's eager interest in Sigmund Freud, for instance, coupled with his unhappiness with what he felt to be the small-souled, emotionally constrained quality of contemporary English society, made him particularly responsive to the work of Lawrence: both the latter's knack of satirical social analysis and his gospel of sexual-instinctual liberation touched a ready chord in the younger man. Similarly, Durrell's own discontents, combined with the natural attentiveness of any ambitious 1930's poet to Eliot's ideas, also left him particularly open to *The Waste Land*'s wider image of the whole Western world as sick-souled and dangerously divorced from any real respect for the "fertilizing" sacramental aspect of life.

In both cases, however, his admiration was streaked with a certain impatience. A virile man, clearly more cheerfully experienced in sexual matters by his mid twenties than Lawrence would ever be, Durrell at his best shows in his writing a blessed capacity to take the natural experiences of life much as he might approach a fine meal: with thoughtful respect, no doubt, but with a distaste for any attempts to wrap the moment in agonized intellection. This, indeed, is the very lesson that Darley in the *Alexandria Quartet* will take over three volumes to learn; and in Durrell himself it generated a gently amused feeling that the Lawrencian gospel, for all its importance, was somehow slightly out of focus. Here Miller's serenely total outspokenness, free alike of Lawrence's tendency toward a certain shrillness and his residual streak of puritan prudery, seemed to suggest how the Lawrencian legacy might be moved to firmer ground. And in the process, the legacy of *The Waste Land* is picked up and remodeled too. For *Tropic of Cancer,* of course, can be read as a kind of Parisian documentation of everything Eliot's poem seems to say about the general spiritual sickness of the modern world; and *The Black Book*'s portrayal of the etiolated inmates of the shabby Regina Hotel fits equally well with Eliot's dreary image of modern London: thus far, the parallel between the two novels is obvious. But a difference comes with the divergence of styles: it is plain-spokenness that Durrell has learned from Miller, not stylistic plainness. On the contrary, the paradoxically exuberant fertility dance that his prose performs around the macabre negative central figures of Tarquin and Death Gregory, both spiritually buried alive by their incapacity to love, is clearly advocating something very like Lawrencian mystical values. "Art," the *Black Book*'s penultimate paragraph tells us, "must no longer exist to depict man, but to invoke God."

Yes, but what God? Certainly not Eliot's: Durrell's early taste of Jesuit schooling in India had left him with a distaste for Christianity that the pious hypocrisies, as he saw it, of English life only reinforced. Nor could Eliot's heavy stress on the vital importance of tradition, ecclesiastical and otherwise, seem to him anything but suffocating, almost a Freudian retreat-to-the-womb. It was a natural disagreement. Eliot, after all, was an American seeking assimilation into English life, hence into its traditions; Durrell was moving the other way, and finding it all the harder to do so because his own aesthetic sense left him as open as anyone to the seductions of "traditional" England. But his in-

[1]References in this essay for *The Black Book* are to the Faber paperback edition (1977).

stinctive fear of the dangerous English tendency to escape the realities of the present by taking refuge in the more picturesque legacies of the national past was sound enough. The letter to "Alan" that interrupts the flow of *The Black Book* puts things clearly enough:

> [You offer me] the whole of England . . . a medieval death in which I could live forever, stifled in the pollen of breviaries, noctuaries, bestiaries: split silk and tumbrils, aesthetic horses and ruined abbeys. . . . That is an England I am going to kill.
>
> (p. 136)

What is, then, the God that art must invoke? It is "life in her wholeness" (p. 234) accepted honestly and wholeheartedly, without any veil of rhetoric or screen of insulating theory, and absolutely without any form of mental retreat—whether from the physical inelegancies of existence or from the vital need always "to attempt" (pp. 238–239).

A main proof that this religious acceptance of life has been achieved is the capacity for experiencing genuine love, erotic but not solely sensual, free of any distortion or morbidity. (This belief was to remain fundamental to all Durrell's major fiction.) Yet how is an experience, which is so much more than merely verbal, to be presented without falsification in mere words-on-paper? "It is not words which grow in me when I see the tendrils of muscle climbing your trunk; . . . Not words, but a vocabulary which goes through us both like the sea" (p. 244). It is a theological truism that we can come to an understanding of God by contemplating that shape which is left when we have finished defining all the things that God is *not.* Durrell in *The Black Book* follows much the same strategy, with an intellectual deftness and subtlety for which he has never really received full credit.

The Black Book shows us the spiritually moribund inmates of the Regina Hotel, in a London whose occasional Whistlerian beauty is phantasmagoric and whose sordidness is all too real. Our sense of the unnaturalness both of their existence and of their surroundings is sharpened by intermittently contrasting glimpses of the pastoral English countryside and of the Levantine island to which the narrator has escaped; the work has in fact, as one of its early images indicates, a rather fugue-like form. The Reginans exhibit—at times to a level of near-obscenity—a wide range of complexes and inhibitions, all resulting in the same loveless misery; it is this, by implicit contrast, that can be taken as an oblique recommendation of a kind of Lady Chatterleyan sexual ideal. The lyrical celebration of the love-making of the narrator and his beloved, happy on their island, reinforces the impression, as does the treatment of the few working-class figures among the book's major characters. Morgan the hotel caretaker, for example, lit by honest wondering delight at his "sordid" coupling with a grubby kitchen maid, with his stripped torso lit, too, by the flames of the furnace that serves the hotel's heating system, is one figure of particularly obvious Lawrencian symbolism—a pointed antithesis to the sick society of his betters.

But *The Black Book* does far more than just explore such simple contrasts. It is no mere allegory; behind the ribaldry, the seriousness of its search for God brings all Durrell's poetic talent into play. Its ambiguities are the necessary ambiguities of art—not the incoherences of youth and inexperience, as readers, conscious that it was his first "real" book, can too easily assume. This may be seen, for instance, even in the case of a relatively clear-cut minor figure such as Chamberlain, who talks like a Lawrence but lives a life of essential sterility. Is this just because he is a petit-bourgeois whose Lawrencian stance is mere posturing affectation; or is he, rather, a bad case of (Lawrencian) sex-in-the-head? And if so, does that hint at an implicit judgment not merely on Chamberlain but on Lawrence too? For that matter, what is to be made of the fact that it is the genteely inhibited, mother-complexed Death Gregory, poor little Gracie's husband, who inscribes on his manuscript the Lawrencian emblem of the Phoenix: "a raving piece of heraldry to insist on the eternal desire in me to confess and be assoiled"? Given such a context, too, the extended surrealistic image (pp. 173–177) of the large-bodied Hilda (alias Frieda, perhaps?) as a great whale voyaging the oceans of the world with the narrator riding Jonah-like in her womb should also perhaps a little trouble those who prefer to see no more than the simpler Lawrencian pieties in *The Black Book.* Yet none of this can be dismissed as just that familiar sort of authorial spite that mars so much of literary history; for Durrell is essentially writing for himself—a young writer trying to find his own position by clawing his way toward it from that of the older man who has come closer than anyone else he knows. And the effort proved justified: not only is *The Black Book,* for all its outrageousness, in some respects a wiser work than anything Lawrence ever wrote,[2] it was also the first (as the author's preface to the 1960 edition notes) in which Durrell had the astonishment and delight of hearing his own real voice as an artist. Thanks to Miller, who promptly arranged for publication of the unexpurgated text in Paris (Faber was prepared only to print a bowdlerized version), a wider audience was given a chance to hear it.

When the book appeared, more than one leading figure in the English literary establishment pronounced it to be badly written—despite the praise of Eliot himself, who might perhaps be thought a competent judge of style. This initiated a certain vein of skepticism about Durrell's work that has tinged the attitudes of the English literary world ever since. Up to a point, reservations are understandable when facing the sort of generous-spirited writer who, if he crashes, inevitably crashes harder than other people. But perhaps it is also true that conscious stylists will always tend to dismiss as "bad writing" any style that differs from their own, when they have not sufficiently considered the job that it is doing. The complaint most frequently made against Durrell's prose is that it is slightly self-regarding, too knowingly "fine writing"; and anyone can find paragraphs in his works to document that charge, if ripped out of context—and sometimes, alas, even if they are not. But there is a considerable difference between the self-consciously achieved high gloss and decorative preciosity of ordinary belle-lettristic prose, and the unselfconscious eagerness with which Durrell more normally draws upon the full resources of his unusually rich vocabulary, wholly intent on delivering a scene or an image into his reader's brain with all the intense vividness with which it has impinged on his own—as Eliot, at least, seems to have recognized.

THE AUTHOR OF THE QUARTET

World War II ended the Corfu years. Soon Durrell was in Egypt, waiting to be drafted for military service. Instead, he was eventually assigned to the local British administration as a press and information officer, serving in both Cairo and Alexandria. His marriage broke up during the war years, like so many others, and he was later to marry Eve Cohen, a girl from a Jewish family settled in Alexandria. The family were devout, and they and their community seem bitterly to have opposed the match. A slow resentment at this attitude has perhaps colored some passages in the Avignon quintet.

Meanwhile his literary career continued. His poems continued to appear during the war years, along with some translations of Greek poetry, a jointly edited literary magazine, and other work. But he was still far from being able to support himself and a wife and family by his pen alone; and so continued in official service for a further eight years after the war ended: first as director of public relations with the interim British military administration on Rhodes, then a one-year stint as director of a British Institute in Argentina, and last about three years as press attaché at the British embassy in Belgrade. Dignified posts, not ill-paid, and congenial enough to that streak of Kiplingesque patriotism natural in a son of the Raj; but a bizarre setting for the author of *The Black Book* and a harassing waste of time for a dedicated artist, conscious that he had yet to consolidate his early achievement. His wife, Eve, became ill, too, and required lengthy absences for treatment in England.

The outcome was that in 1953, having (as he supposed) broken decisively with official life, Durrell found himself to all intents alone on Cyprus with the young daughter of his second marriage, hoping that his savings would suffice to allow him to concentrate on completing the first of the major novels that were to become the *Alexandria Quartet* (1957–1960). Not that his pen had previously been idle. Since the war, in addition to his poetry and other appearances in print, he had published three books and completed at least one more (the pleasantly John Buchanish *White Eagles over Serbia* [1957], written for the teenage market purely to raise funds, but showing his usual talent for evoking landscape). The first of the published volumes had been his radiant memoir of life on Corfu, *Prospero's Cell* (1945), then had come a novel, *Cefalû* (1947)—republished some years later as *The Dark Labyrinth*—and finally his British Council lectures from Argentina, *Key to Modern Poetry* (1952). The latter work does not altogether live up to the promise of its title, although it is a useful partial key to Durrell's

[2] An achievement, one may guess, owing something to Rémy de Gourmont. In the 1930's *The Natural Philosophy of Love,* in Ezra Pound's translation, was one of Durrell's valued possessions. Devotees of Durrell will find it thought-provoking reading in relation to his works other than *The Black Book.*

own poetry and a better one to some of the ideas that he would subsequently draw upon in writing the *Quartet*. *Cefalû* was described by Durrell as a morality play disguised as a thriller, and it fits that description. As in a real morality play, nearly all its characters are essentially stereotypes, drawn in this case—as Durrell's friend G. S. Fraser has noted—from the typical lending-library fiction of the interwar years. The sort of book that gets described as "a good read," it follows the various fortunes of a group of English cruise tourists trapped in a labyrinth of Cretan caves; the fate of each seems, in a sense, to be one that they were already bearing with them when they left the sunlight. It is enjoyably told, but is not one of the dozen works of fiction by which Durrell has said his reputation as a novelist must stand or fall; that is, *The Black Book, The Alexandria Quartet, Tunc* and *Nunquam,* and the five Avignon books. Of these, it is of course the *Quartet* that has so far attracted the most attention, both from the international reading public and from literary critics and scholars.

Much of the flood of critical commentary that the *Quartet* elicited, however, is less helpful than it might be. Critics have sometimes better understood what was being said in these novels than the way it was being said; yet that, too, is part of the meaning. The problem is in a sense a social one and has confronted every interviewer who has tried to hold Durrell to an extended discussion of his work, quite as much as it confronts readers of the *Quartet*. Perhaps, then, a look at Durrell himself, or at the selves he has chosen to make public, offers as good an approach as any to the mysteries of the *Quartet*.

Durrell, as many of his contemporaries have attested, has always had the knack of sociability, never having to exert himself very much before people around him found that they were having fun. As a novelist, he takes a similar pride in being an artist-craftsman whose first duty is to entertain. His hope that readers of the *Quartet* would find it immediately enjoyable as "a good yarn," no matter what further depths they might go on to perceive in it, was not just a wish for good sales. Conscious of the crucial roles that myth and the public storyteller have always had in human society, he genuinely saw the pleasure that he hoped his public would find in his tale as being quite as important to them as any idea perceivable at some "deeper" level in the *Quartet*. This outlook shows up very clearly at the close of the final volume, when the writer, Darley, having at last learned to take life simply, one day finds himself "writing down with trembling fingers the four words which presage the old story of an artist coming of age. I wrote: 'Once upon a time. . . .' And I felt as if the whole universe had given me a nudge!" Such an attitude throws some light on the striking memorableness of so many of the *Quartet*'s stagey and far-fetched yet magnificent episodes: for instance, the scene in which Justine transfixes the wretched flock of child prostitutes by her superb recital of a traditional Arab tale. Such moments, lightly stirring the vibrations of myth, are microcosms of the whole work, itself a vast, sumptuous once-upon-a-time for a prostituted world. Realizing this, one can take more lightly those anxious discussions of Einsteinian Space-Time into which the *Quartet* gently inveigles its more earnest readers. (For once-upon-a-time is no time, and no-where, at all.)

For Durrell does gently tease his interlocutors, in person no less than on paper; he really has no choice but to do so. Partly it is a matter of temperament, of an inner detachment watching, coolly, the warmth he is generating around him. "People with Durrell's peculiar gift of creating instant sociability are often very lonely people in, and by, themselves," G. S. Fraser remarks; but in the *Quartet* the novelist Pursewarden—another partial representative of the author—had already said much the same. (Occasionally, this coldness scars the writing. There are moments when it is impossible not to feel that if the author really had any full sense of the horror of the facts he is creating, as he tells of the disappearance of Justine's little daughter, for example, then both he and his heroine would be responding differently. The same trait sometimes shows sharply if briefly in the central volumes of the Avignon quintet.)

But to a greater degree, the games Durrell plays with us simply reflect the contradictory logic of his situation and of his beliefs. It is part of the general professionalism of his approach to the business of being a writer, to accept that it *is* precisely that: a business, with the usual need for packaging, marketing, publicity, and information—yet to do so without in the least lowering his artistic standards or ambitions. In place of our foolishly snobbish, Bloomsbury-descended, modern English distinction between "literature" and "commercial fiction," he operates with something more like a tacit mental division of his work into major and minor craftsmanship (on this, one might compare his contemporary Graham Greene's division of his own work into novels and "entertainments"). An early letter to Miller speaks of soothing the nerves by "literary gardening" in the intervals between trying to "compose for full orchestra." But the end product is always coded clearly enough to leave the reader in no doubt as to which is meant to be which. Some years ago, for instance, the serious English weekly reviewers tended to be somewhat scornful of Durrell's *Sicilian Carousel* (1977), the result of a publisher's request to him for a "travel book" about Sicily. Durrell had simply booked a seat on a bus tour of the island and written up a fictionalized account of his trip. There seemed to be a feeling that he had thus demeaned himself (wouldn't it have been more dignified for a major writer to apply for some sort of grant if caught short financially?) or that he had been guilty, in effect, of swindling his public by a cynically lazy exploitation of the name he had made by his three more serious Mediterranean island books. Reactions to *The Greek Islands* (1978) (another publisher's chore, in which the text, though speckled with instructive scraps of autobiography, does little more than space out a splendid collection of pictures) were much the same.

In fact such reactions, the fruit of our modern museum-and-conservatory culture, seem absurd. In the first place, the reading public is being neither cheated nor misled: the near-coffee-table format of *The Greek Islands* is an adequate warning to readers in itself, and *Sicilian Carousel* scrupulously makes clear in its first paragraph that Sicily is not one of those Mediterranean places to which Durrell brings the perceptiveness that comes from lengthy residence. That said, it then goes on to be a highly accomplished performance, even if its skills are those of distinguished journalism rather than high art. A thread of narrative holds the reader adequately amused through a steady flow of information and reflection, interspersed with touches of unashamed sentimentality, lightly caricatured characterization, and cheerful pastiches of the Durrell ambience. It is hard to dislike the author's businesslike assumption that there is no shame in undertaking this kind of honest craftsmanship, in between his assaults on the heights.

And so he accepts too that business requires one to talk to the customers. His publisher's files of cuttings bulge with countless interviews, the best of them (Marc Alyn's *The Big Supposer* [1973]) actually running to book length and published in two languages. His correspondence, also, has been upon a Herculean scale. But to forage among this mass of material is to realize how much hinders this author, talking so willingly and entertainingly with his many interrogators, from actually communicating with them. He does, for one thing, carry the "hallmark" his father sought: under the warmth and seeming openness is all the classic public schoolboy's determination "to stay buttoned up" and not betray deeper private emotions. (Only a cryptic dedication to one novel and a troubling paragraph in one pamphlet,[3] for instance, directly hint at what the unexpected early death of his third wife, Claude, must have meant to him, although it was in the years with her that his life and his career stabilized.) But that is a relatively minor barrier: a greater is that—like most authors of any significance—Durrell has read so much more than any professor floundering in his wake. A hungry writer moves through the world of books like a child loose in a supermarket, rapidly sipping or swallowing, and hurrying away in any direction, as impulse serves; academic critics, slowed by the formal requirements of scholarship, never have the least chance of keeping up. Moreover, half of Durrell's personal supermarket is French: he has lived for decades in Provence, knew the international literary community in Paris well in the 1930's, and is at home in French as in contemporary English letters. How many critics, academic or otherwise, can follow him there? A religious sensibility that can do nothing with Christianity but can find satisfaction in Buddhism, Taoism, or gnosticism is a little opaque to most Western readers, too.

Durrell, in short, is no less an intellectual than he is an artist, genuinely excited by theory, and with a reflective, analytic streak that is oddly in tension with his lyrical romanticism. This is perhaps partly the outcome of the lifelong intensity of his literary vocation, driving him to reflect unceasingly on the nature of literature and every aspect of the writer's business; enough of this side of him can intermittently be glimpsed to suggest that it is a minor tragedy that the fruits of those essentially philosophical reflections must now, as it seems, be largely lost. (To give a random illustration, he has

[3] *A Smile in the Mind's Eye* (1980), a charming "plug" for the work of a Chinese friend, and for a Tibetan monastery newly established in France. It is also the clearest statement of what Taoism and the *Tao Te Ching* have meant to Durrell.

been known to hold forth at some length, extremely instructively and with much interest, on the question of rhythm in the novel—a far from trivial consideration that conventional novel criticism largely ignores. That his own novels can nevertheless stumble at times in this respect—as in the rather static, "preachy" passages that most readers seem to feel clog parts of *Clea* and the first half of *Nunquam*—in no way discredits this Aristotelian dimension of his gifts.)

All of which is as much as to say that—no doubt like most artists, but to a quite unusual degree—in any discussion of his work Durrell is in about the same situation as an inhabitant of some ancient city, trying to discuss it with a stranger who knows the place only from postcards. Bored and mildly mischievous, therefore, he is apt to resort to a gently defensive romancing, something of which it pays to be aware when exploring the secondary literature that has grown up around his work. Inquirers are always liable to be gravely handed, interlaced with perfectly accurate information, a few elegantly sculptured alternatives to fact; as witness his success in blandly putting about the notion that he is somehow an Irish writer. It is a harmless way of sowing a minefield around his privacy while yet maintaining that style of openness necessary to *festivitas.*

Penetrate the minefield, however, and further complications lie in wait. Durrell has been described above as a natural intellectual; yet he is widely thought of (and this, as already suggested, is perhaps why so many of his interviews have been so thin and disappointing) as a mere dilettante of ideas, whose interest in them is only on the level of smart cocktail-party conversation. This is because one of the ideas about which he is most serious is that we should never—outside the confines of specific disciplines and technologies—be too serious about ideas. That is to say, he believes profoundly in the artist (but "the artist" is an intensification of something in all of us) as *Homo ludens:* humankind creatively, vitally at play. No set of ideas can wholly tell the truth about the reality from which we extrapolate it; if, therefore, we accept any such set of ideas too rigidly, too wholeheartedly, it becomes a set of prison bars, obscuring and distorting the world that we try to see through its grid. Play with it more lightly, however, perhaps try it out in seemingly absurd or unexpected contexts, and it may prove an unexpectedly useful tool, helping us toward a truer, if unformulable, nondiscursive sense of *real* reality: that timeless "heraldic universe" of which Durrell's writings so often speak and of which he feels that art, when it attains the mythopoeic, can give us a kind of glimpse. Those who would hear in this echoes both of Carl Jung and of the mysticism of Asian religions are not mistaken.

Squaring with all this is Durrell's separate belief —not, of course, unique to him—that the wellsprings of art do not lie in the conscious, rational mind and can indeed easily be dried up by overmuch contact with it. Twice during the lively conversation that followed the account of novel-rhythm referred to above, he broke off with a look almost of alarm and issued the apologetic explanation that the matter in question was something he could not afford to let himself think about, much less analyze, as he was at present at work on a novel and "afraid of destroying [his] own creativity." The response is a too familiar one to suspect a leg-pull. Yet at the same time he certainly considers that a novel requires idea-content, and conscious attention to form and proportion. There is no way to resolve this collision of the rational and the irrational at the core of art and creativity. A work of art must have pattern, form; yet a literary work of art must nevertheless capture at least something of the quality of an ultimate reality that is *not* thus patterned. (What is alarming, Pursewarden tells Darley in part 2 of *Justine,* is not the realization that God does not care, "but that he does not care *one way or the other.*") Equally, the rational intellect, though its contribution to the form of the work of art is a necessary one, must somehow do its job without suffocating or contaminating that spontaneous intuitive flow in which the true life of the work inheres. At the heart of a work of art, or of the concept of art, we thus meet again something very like the concept of God: definable only as the shape left when we have said all the things that it is not—a powerful mystery that holds its own universe together, like the Black Hole at the center of our galaxy. Grant this view, and there is ample evidence that it is Durrell's, and the essence of any true work of art becomes something that can only at best be glimpsed momentarily out of the corner of the eye, even by the artist himself. Clearly, this does not simplify for him the task of explaining, even to himself, what it is that he has done in his major compositions.

All this finds its reflection in *The Alexandria Quartet.*

THE ALEXANDRIA QUARTET

DURRELL had already conceived the beginnings of what was to become the *Quartet* during the war years in Egypt, but it was not until his time on Cyprus that *Justine* (1957), the first novel of the sequence, took final form. Even on Cyprus he was not as free for undistracted composition as he had hoped: when the pre-independence struggle began, he felt it his duty to accept the local British administration's request that he yet again take up a post as director of public relations. But that is the story of *Bitter Lemons,* treated separately below.

The first three volumes of the *Quartet* all describe the actions of approximately the same group of people over approximately the same period of time. The fourth volume shows us the same persons at a later date. *Justine,* the opening volume, is Darley's first-person account of his memories of his life among the Alexandrians before World War II; the main focus, however, is on his physical and emotional obsession with Justine herself, the Jewish wife of a rich Coptic banker. Then in *Balthazar* (1958), the second volume to appear, Darley revises and expands the picture given in the previous volume, in the light of startling new information from Balthazar, one of his Alexandrian acquaintances. Then follows *Mountolive* (1958), a third-person narrative built around a British diplomat in Egypt, in which Darley himself appears in a minor background role. This may be read more or less independently of the two previous volumes, despite the links between them. *Clea* (1960) returns to Darley's first-person narration and spans most of the 1940's while also supplying much retrospective information, again often disillusioning.

In other words, *The Alexandria Quartet* can surely be described well enough as a fairly normal first-person three-decker novel, plus a companion volume. If we focus on the narrator himself, rather than on the period of his life to which his thoughts so constantly return, then the three "decks" are consecutive in time in the usual way for such novels; and the events presented finally bring Darley to a more mature view of life,—exactly as if he were Joseph Andrews, or Elizabeth Bennet, or Dr. Lydgate, or one of Dickens' young men. The specific lessons he learns are surely those taught by many other novels, too: that appearances can deceive, that the same facts can fit a variety of explanations, that truth may defeat any attempt at formulation, that the same individual can turn out to be more than one person, that erotic bewitchment can pass, and so on. (The objectively told *Mountolive* is technically necessary to convey without cumbersomeness the information we need to see the full depth of Darley's misunderstandings. If one worries about the breaking of the first-person illusion by this intrusive volume, it is quite possible to regard *Mountolive* simply as a book that was written much later by Darley in Paris after he and the diplomat had met again there, and improved on the intimacy that is clearly dawning between them in *Clea.*) It is only the distractingly exotic setting, the emphasis on the personality of the City, and the accompanying near-total dissociation of all moral judgments from any libido-driven action, plus the "burying" of the hero behind the vivid foreground personalities of Justine and her associates, that impedes our recognition of these familiar literary forms.

What, then, is to be made of the notorious note prefacing *Balthazar,* which offers a very different picture of an apparently much less conventional work?

> *I . . . am trying to complete a four-decker novel . . . based on the relativity proposition.*
>
> *Three sides of space and one of time constitute the soup-mix recipe of a continuum. The four novels follow this pattern.*
>
> *The first three parts . . . are not linked in a serial form. They interlap, interweave, in a purely spatial relation. Time is stayed. The fourth part alone will represent time and be a true sequel. . . .*
>
> *This is not Proustian or Joycean method—for they illustrate Bergsonian "duration" in my opinion, not "Space-Time." . . .*
>
> *These considerations sound perhaps somewhat immodest or even pompous. But it would be worth trying to see if we cannot discover a morphological form one might appropriately call "classical"—for our time.*

Considered strictly as physics, these Einsteinian propositions are gibberish. But letters and interviews make clear that Durrell is perfectly aware of that. The implied claim to literary originality seems overstated, too: both Robert Browning in *The Ring and the Book* and George Meredith in *Modern Love* had attempted to "refract" an idea or situation somewhat in Durrell's way. But that again he knows;

there is a smile behind the note's further grand announcement that "the central topic of the book is an investigation of modern love."

Nonetheless the invocation of Einstein is not simply to be shrugged aside. What we are offered in the *Balthazar* note is the approximate equivalent to a conceit in a metaphysical poem: something for the reader to explore and savor just so far as it continues to amuse him and to sharpen, by its perversely unexpected relevance, his sense of the object it is describing. In short, we again face here Durrell's belief in the artist as *Homo ludens,* a man at play with ideas but seriously so, to create in us all, by a kind of inspired inadvertence, a truer feel for the way things are. "Poets," says Pursewarden early in part 2 of *Balthazar,* "are not really serious about ideas or people. They regard them much as a Pasha regards the members of an extensive *harim.* They are pretty, yes. They are for use. But there is no question of their being true or false, or having souls."

"They are for use." Usefulness presupposes relevance. The allusion to the idea of relativity is relevant to the *Quartet* in several different ways and on several different levels, not all of which are equally open to being grasped by the average book buyer, and seem worth reviewing here.

In the first place, the allusion to relativity does tend to force the reader to try to think about the interrelationships of the *Quartet*'s four volumes—to try to comprehend it as something other than the mere sum of its four parts. Similarly, it also helps to settle the reader's gaze firmly on the secondary narrative level of the work; that is to say, on the Alexandrian world that Darley evokes, rather than on Darley himself alone on his island with Melissa's child, remembering the City.

Moreover, when our vision is focused in this way, it is even possible to find a kind of rococo accuracy in the notion that the first three books of the *Quartet* correspond to the three dimensions of space. The narrative line of *Justine* is crossed by that of *Balthazar,* with *Mountolive* undeniably standing at an angle to both of them: Justine is first presented as in love with Darley, then this is represented as her way of hiding her real love for Pursewarden, then we find her ultimate motives were political.

In contrast, the note's claim that "time is stayed" in the *Quartet* until the appearance of the final volume does seem wishful thinking. The earlier volumes hark back to *Moeurs,* the book that Justine's first husband, Arnauti, had written about her, in just the way that *Clea* harks back to them. *Mountolive,* too, is saturated with the sense of time passing (not just Bergsonian duration), tracing as it does the near-lifelong effect on a British diplomat of an early love affair.

On the level we have so far considered, then, the relativity analogy, though it may help prod the reader's attention in the right directions, does not really seem quite close enough to the *Quartet* to warrant the prominence Durrell has given it, except perhaps as bait for new readers. There are, however, at least two other ways to view the *Balthazar* note's invocation of Einstein, and these, since they also seem to illuminate various rather gnomic pronouncements in the novels themselves, perhaps bring us closer to the essence of Durrell's thought here. Relativity physics has deconstructed our world's traditional conception of physical matter. It also, among much else, raises unusual doubts about the possibility of arriving at objective truth in many scientific contexts, not least where it can be shown that the very presence of the observer affects the results of the experiment he is observing. Darley similarly sets out to write a kind of explanatory report on the Alexandrians, only to discover that his presence among them had been corrupting *his* findings. And in the process he realizes too—though less forcibly than his creator—that the traditional notion of personality has been shown to be as illusory as the pre-Einsteinian notion of matter or substance. In "The Kneller Tape" (reprinted in Harry T. Moore's *The World of Lawrence Durrell*), Durrell is quite explicit: "Human character? A sort of rainbow I should say, which includes the whole range of the spectrum. I imagine that what we call personality may be an illusion, and in thinking of it as a stable thing we may be trying to put a lid on a box with no sides." One can see how in the author's mind the Einsteinian reference could become a kind of metaphor or shorthand for this whole complex of ideas.

The four dimensions of space-time have clearly also chimed together in Durrell's mind with other sets of four. Durrell has always been fascinated by what nowadays might be termed the interface of Eastern and Western thought—a natural response to his own family history. Part of the attraction he has always felt for the Greeks is related to his awareness that in ancient times Greece was, as it were, the membrane through which the ideas of the East were filtered and transmogrified to found the intellectual traditions of our own civilization. This, of course, also accounts for much of the excitement that inheres for him in the very idea of Alexandria, whose culture in the days of its greatness so comfortably merged the mysticism of the East and the ordering rationalism of the West, and whose very location and setting still seem to emblematize its antique role; in the *Quartet* Alexandria, with its characters and grotesques, is not just another Dickensian London washed in sunlight. It is also the logical stage, since Plotinus was the greatest of its philosophers, for the dance of Plotinian ideas that the *Quartet* sets in motion.

Reference has already been made to Durrell's frequent allusions to "the heraldic universe," by which he seems to mean a total and immediate, nondiscursive, nonanalytic apprehension of the world. (At the end of the Avignon quintet and at the beginning of *A Smile in the Mind's Eye,* he speaks rather of "reality prime"; but the thought is the same.) This apprehension of reality is for Durrell the *sine qua non* of great art, and can indeed scarcely be communicated to the world at large by any other means. "As for the analytical faculty," he says in "The Kneller Tape," "wasn't it given us to help us inch up on the illumination?" It is a way of thinking that in him seems inborn, but it has been pointed out that it also coheres remarkably well with Plotinian concepts. What for Durrell (and his character Pursewarden) is heraldic reality is for Plotinus knowledge of self: a spiritual pinnacle that both great love and a sudden access of "cosmic consciousness" may help one to scale. It is to these heights that the artists, Clea and Darley, have attained by the end of *Clea;* what is striking, therefore, is the fact that the three previous volumes seem to correspond equally well to the three lower faculties of the mind through which, Plotinus holds, one can rise to this higher level of illumination.

First comes the faculty of sensation: *Justine,* centering on Darley's sensuous obsession with the financier Nessim's wife, to which the innocent Melissa is blindly sacrificed, is a self-evident correlate to this. Next comes imagination: *Balthazar,* much concerned with stories of variations upon the basic sexual act (for instance, Justine and Clea's lesbian affair) that often require disguises and dressing-up (Scobie, Pombal, Toto de Brunel)—and revealing too the extent to which Darley had been imagining the situation he had described in *Justine*—again fits the Plotinian scheme very well. So too does *Mountolive,* since the third Plotinian faculty is that of reason or rational ordering: hence *Mountolive*'s objective third-person narrative and tidy traditional form. The odd rational coolness of the diplomat's love affair with Nessim's mother and the book's preoccupation with politically motivated action are also consistent with this stage in the Plotinian scheme—and *Clea* we have already considered.

More remarkable still from a constructional point of view, although there is no room to go into detail here, is the way in which the same four-part Plotinian scheme is again reflected *within* the four-part internal structure of *Justine* (and therefore also paralleled in *Balthazar,* a commentary on the manuscript of the earlier work.) The same rhythm continues into *Mountolive,* whose sixteen sections deal with four main topics: Mountolive's history until his return to Egypt, Pursewarden's entrapment into suicide, political intrigues, and the destruction of Narouz. The Plotinian "trellis" of the *Quartet* (to borrow a term from James Joyce's account of the rather similar use he had made of Giambattista Vico) seems, in short, firmly enough constructed. It also makes good the claim of the *Balthazar* note that the *Quartet* will offer an "investigation" of modern love—to be viewed, as we can now recognize, in its sensuous, imaginative, conspiratorial, and creative aspects, with conventional morality always *hors concours.*

But within this foursquare frame, in a favorite Durrellian (and Pythagorean) conjunction, there is also the circle: the cycle of life, hence of love, whether "modern" or eternal. Duplications of incident and situation are plentiful in the *Quartet,* both within the individual volumes and among them. In his relations with Clea, Darley experiences again—sometimes with and sometimes without significant variation—moments from his previous relationships with both Melissa and Justine. Both Pombal and Scobie amuse him by the absurdity of the female headgear in which they dress up. Both Justine and Clea are envisaged bending over a dirty sink with a human fetus in it. The setting of a scene in a house of child prostitutes recurs in different contexts, and so on. These repetitions have a threefold purpose. They contribute to Durrell's effort to "stay time" in his first three volumes by keeping it circling back upon itself. They mate with the frequent mentions of mirrors in the story, to underline

Durrell's loss of belief in the old idea of a stable monolithic personality (for when we successively see two people in essentially the same scene, our sense of their unique personal identity is a little undermined, just as much as when five mirrors around Justine all show a different image even while reflecting the same person.) But most of all, they serve a quasi-musical function, to which we must return in a moment when considering the *Quartet* in its more vital aspect as the living plant growing up and around this fixed trellis-work of ideas.

But first the ideas of the *Quartet* must be pursued a little further. In all his more serious work, whether prose or verse, Durrell remains fundamentally a poet, if in his novels an unusually philosophically minded one; and it has been one of the curiosities of twentieth-century literary history that, whatever else poetry in the English language has been about, it has remarkably often also simultaneously been about the business of being a poet, or the nature of poetry; the trait is so marked as to amount virtually to a tic in the nervous system of British intellectual life. This self-reflexive quality is equally present in the *Quartet,* a work that its author has been known to categorize as an "allegory," a description that is doubly true. The *Quartet*'s story does not merely offer a kind of allegory of those quasi-Plotinian/Taoist/gnostic/Pythagorean perceptions that have been at the core of Durrell's deepest beliefs for most of his working life; it is also a species of allegory or complex emblem of the very business of being an artist committed to the novel form, as Durrell personally experiences it. While we follow Darley, slowly learning the difficulties of relating appearance to reality, or of capturing either by verbal description or theory, we follow also a mostly one-sided debate about their art between Darley and the wiser Pursewarden, largely conducted inside the latter's head. And behind this again may be dimly discerned the figure of the author himself, *in propria persona,* quietly having the same kind of thoughtfully experimental fun with the critical dogmas of his own day that Shakespeare had with the doctrine of the unities when he wrote *The Tempest.* The sheer cheek, not to say courage, that Durrell showed in this respect was comparable to Samuel Beckett's famous complaint at the dress rehearsal of the first English production of *Waiting for Godot,* that it was "not boring the audience enough!" To this day, critical persons can be found who abandoned the *Quartet* some way through their reading of the first volume because they found *Justine* embarrassingly reminiscent of the emotionally overblown, romantic hothouse atmosphere of Daphne du Maurier's *Rebecca.* Were they to read on, they would of course discover in *Balthazar* that the author himself was fully aware of this weakness from the start, that by now the narrator had also become aware of it, and that it formed a necessary and justifiable part of the overall scheme of the *Quartet:* in short, that a neat practical joke—of which Durrell, with his interest in the theory of his trade, cannot have been wholly unaware—had effectively been played upon the New Critics, with their stress upon autonomy of the text and disregard of authorial intention. For a writer in the 1950's, hungry for recognition, such jokes required a certain nerve. Other critical banana-skins appear to have been half-absentmindedly dropped here and there throughout the rest of the work, not only for the benefit of New Critics: Pursewarden's scathing reference (in *Clea,* ch. 3) to "our older universities where they are still painfully trying to extract from art some shadow of justification for their way of life. Surely there must be a grain of hope . . . for decent honest Christian folk in all this [literature] which is poured out from generation to generation" seems to glance squarely at the great Cambridge moralistic critic F. R. Leavis and his disciples, to whom the climate of Durrell's Alexandria cannot have been wholly congenial. In fact, Leavis had already attacked Durrell.

Darley and Pursewarden are generally described by critics as Durrell's personifications of two opposing sides of his own nature as a writer; and there is much truth in this, although the reality is more complicated. Reactions to Pursewarden vary with the degree of seriousness with which one takes the things he is given to say. To the present writer he seems a moving, troubling, and impressive figure, the only convincing depiction of a major artist in the history of English literature, despite the slightly chocolate-boxy contexts (such as the early history of his relationship with his blind sister) in which he is at times presented. The achievement is the more impressive precisely because Pursewarden is not a purely autobiographical creation. His diplomatic posts, and other details of his life, do match Durrell's own experience, and he is made a mouthpiece for many of Durrell's most cherished beliefs—as well as offering chilling momentary glimpses of the detached intelligence that sits behind the genial Durrellian facade. "I suppose I do arse around rather a lot," said Durrell in a sober moment in an interview with the present author, "but you know, all the time I have a feeling that there is this great bird that sits upon my shoulder, and watches all I do, and is never fooled." Pursewarden is as near as he has ever come to a depiction of that bird, and it sits unblinking upon Darley's shoulder until its vision becomes Darley's own. But he is also an impressive person in his own right, with a style that is by no means that of his creator. Unforced intellectual authority, and that bleak gaiety to be found in those isolated by their very clarity of vision, have never been better presented. Nor have the limitations to this superiority, which holds only within the confines of Pursewarden's own domain of letters, and even there allows an admixture of inconsistency. Thus he mocks Darley for his excitement about art and eager interest in literary-critical discussion ("for the artist . . . no such thing as art exists; it only exists for critics and those who live in the forebrain" [*Mountolive,* sec. V]), yet himself offers pronouncements about art incessantly. And the advice he offers his ambassador proves to be completely misjudged: again the element of allegory in the action of the book is here clear. Thus, though for much of the *Quartet* Darley may roughly be said to embody the Aristotelian and Pursewarden the creative strains that Durrell recognizes in his own nature, their inseparableness for him is accurately reflected too.

This then, at least in broad outline, is the structure of ideas on which *The Alexandria Quartet* appears to be based. It should not, however, be mistaken for the structure of the work itself, which it only partially expresses. It was noted earlier that a main force in shaping Durrell as a writer was his youthful obsession with Elizabethan literature; and one of the fruits of that interest, as it matured, was an increasing conviction that the sense of vitality that the best works of this period gave him was not due only to their imaginative and verbal energy. It depended at least as much, he eventually concluded, upon a successful balance within the work between a static and a dynamic patterning or structure. Where one of these was absent or overdominant, the work in question dwindled into a museum piece. He puts the point in conversation in terms of the familiar idea of a wave moving through the legs of Brighton pier, to break upon the beach as it reaches the pier's end: the architectural frame—the regular, or at least regularly proportioned, spacing of the legs of the pier—sharpens by contrast our perception of the vitally asymmetric form and rhythm of the wave moving through it. This principle consciously underlies Durrell's own compositions, including the *Quartet;* and so far, of course, we have for the most part been considering the legs of his pier.

When we turn to consider the wave, however, we begin to move beyond the province of analysis, just as with music. (Measuring durations and so forth can reduce a piece of music to a set of statistics, but no one can show from such figures that we *must* find greatness in that particular composition while another statistically similar one strikes us as uninteresting.) Admittedly, up to a certain point dynamic form in literature can be just as rationally planned or analyzed as any more static "architectural" ordering of the text. Thus the pace of a narrative, for instance, can be deliberately varied—virtually halted for one of Durrell's famous set-piece descriptions, such as the fish-drive at the beginning of *Mountolive,* or speeded up, as in its final chapter, sweeping Narouz ruthlessly into death and the rites that lie beyond it. And any such set-piece description, too, though static in relation to the overall movement of the story, can further be given its own interior dynamic; so that, for example, the opening account of the fish-drive in *Mountolive* is written in prose that gives us just the same sense of slow but relentless acceleration from a leisured start also generated by the closing chapter, despite their different status vis-à-vis the general structure of the narrative. Or the various parts of a literary work may stand in a quasi-musical relation to each other, which can also be deliberately planned. If, for instance, *The Alexandria Quartet* is an exploration of the uncertainty of human identity set in a mythopoeic city, so too, it might be said, is W. B. Yeats's famous poem "Easter 1916," the third of whose four parts has a lyrical quality that relates to the heavier tones of the other sections in much the way that the parts of a sonata interrelate. And at one stage further removed from aural effects, the same is true of the third section of the *Quartet* itself, with its unexpected shift to a less emotional third-person narration and its pleasant real-life fairy tale of a nice man rising deservedly to the splendor and charming absurdities of ambassadorship. Of this, Durrell himself was naturally aware. Sending a copy of *Mountolive* to Miller, he explicitly warned him that the book was not to be judged in its own right but as one movement of a kind of symphony.

This musical analogy should be taken quite as seriously as Durrell's alternative description of the *Quartet* as a species of allegory. For his name was first made as a poet, and he remains a poet—first cousin to a musician—even when composing his novels. And poet and composer alike need an "inner ear," an intuitive feel for timing, placing, and variation, far beyond the scope of the kinds of calculable design touched upon in the last paragraph. In the *Quartet* as in *Tunc* and *Nunquam,* in fact, the rather heavy "architectural" top-loading of Plotinian-Pythagorean ideas seems partly a device to keep Durrell busy enough to leave his creative subconscious free—to say or do what is required, unmolested.

To say or do: there is a difference. To a considerable extent, the creative imagination seems to make shapes for their own sake; to bring out, or complete, or set reverberating the patterns, rhythms, parallels, contrasts, already emergent in any uncompleted work. But inevitably such shapes implicitly carry half-accidental meanings, often elusive, paradoxical, and unexpected, that can interplay oddly with the overt meaning of the piece in which they appear. Yet conversely, the imagination often seems also to be deliberately articulating, via something like the language of dreams, particular perceptions just too elusive or multifarious to be captured any other way; even a name ("David Mountolive," for example) can thus be lit with an eloquence more easily felt than explicated.

If this doubtless holds for almost any piece of nontechnical writing, it is particularly valid for a work such as the *Quartet.* Many tens of thousands of readers have been well content to enjoy *The Alexandria Quartet* at what might irreverently be called the chocolate-box level, as a marvelously articulate set of descriptions of vividly colored, exotic scenes and characters. A doubtless smaller but still large number have engaged themselves at least to some extent with the minuet of ideas that it presents. But it is unclear (partly, of course, because it is so difficult a thing to write about) how many readers really fully enjoy what the *Quartet* has to offer on every interpenetrating level. So approached, it is a demanding "read," because it makes such unexpectedly contrary calls upon us—reflecting, as I have suggested, the division in its author's own mental makeup. But the demands, if met honestly, are repaid. What is asked of us, as it were, is that we both watch *and* listen. We watch Durrell's rich, almost Spenserian tapestry unfolding; and we watch as the narrative falls tidily into shape around the underlying structure of ideas—again in a somewhat Spenserian way. But if we are not listening too, then the books will still go wrong for us. The deliberate repetitions and duplications in the *Quartet,* already noted above, are the simplest illustration of this. To straightforward seekers of escapist entertainment, these are momentary failures of invention, to be shrugged forgivingly aside because the author is offering such a marvelous time in so many other respects. To those who suppose the *Quartet* to be wholly reducible to allegory, gift-wrapped in tinsel and travel writing, its echo-effects can seem both overschematic and untidily placed. But to anyone willing to approach the *Quartet* less strenuously, yet with a wider range of attention than this, the repetitions are part of the fluid, shifting pulse of something alive within the work, wreathing and coiling back upon itself in the manner of music or of poetry; and what it is attending to is not the dry warfare of philosophers' ideas.

This is not to pretend that the *Quartet* is unflawed. Nearly all readers find a certain woodenness, a feeling of something imperfectly realized, in the figure of Clea; and large tracts of the first third of the novel called after her are generally felt to be equally wooden, too. The mystery that is made of Justine's psychological hang-ups in the first two volumes tends to be more tedious than intriguing. But anyone who supposes that it is on such grounds alone that the future will determine whether *The Alexandria Quartet* is eventually to live or die knows nothing of literary history and has never read Dickens, or sat through the dire debate between Macduff and Malcolm in *Macbeth.* At least as important is Durrell's possession—although sadly he often neglects or abuses his gift—of the authentic *hwyl*[4] of the born mythmaker. "Hear," he

[4]A Welsh word denoting the high-pitched rhetoric used by Welsh preachers and orators.

cries, "the names of the Alexandrians"; and even if the absurd list were but chanted by an old blind crowder—

> Tony Umbada, Baldassaro Trivizani, Claude Amaril, Paul Capodistria, Dmitri Randidi, Onouphrios Papas, Count Banabula, Jacques de Guéry, Athena Trasha, Delphine de Francueil, Djamboulat Bey, General Cervoni, Ahmed Hassan Pacha, Pozzo di Borgo, Pierre Balbz, Gaston Phipps . . .

—one may suspect that, within the context of the novels, the hearts of most auditors would still be moved as much as with a trumpet.

THE ISLAND BOOKS

THE inner rhythms or music of *The Alexandria Quartet* can be difficult to apprehend until a second or third reading, partly because of the sheer size of the work and the distracting effect of the division into four volumes, and partly because there are patches (such as the long letter that closes *Balthazar*) where the poetic life of the books temporarily fades. As one gets to know the work better, one finds that its inner life is quite strong enough to carry these passages; but on a first reading they do tend to dull one's ear for the movement of the *Quartet,* even if they do not spoil it as entertainment.

One simple and delightful way to help tune oneself in to the rhythms and movement of the *Quartet,* however, is to read *Prospero's Cell* (1945), written and published during the years when the *Quartet* was germinating in Durrell's mind. Despite the difference in subject and genre, the mental continuity between the two works is clear—as witness, for instance, Durrell's comment on Count D., "the possessor of a literary mind completely uncontaminated by the struggle to achieve a technique; he lacks the artifice of presentation, the corrupting demon of *form.*" It is the voice of Pursewarden.

Prospero's Cell is a book written from notes taken by Durrell during the last two years of his life on Corfu before the outbreak of World War II. By this time he had learned Greek and made friends among his country neighbors, as well as among the island's modest cosmopolitan intellectual community. He had an enchanting home and an enchanting wife, the makings of a literary reputation, and friendly correspondents in the intellectual worlds both of London and of Paris—and he was also in love with Corfu itself: its landscapes, legends, traditions, and ways. He had, in short, all the requisites for a life of perfect happiness—or as close to it as a man may come in this imperfect world, with his present sense of enjoyment of his bright sunlit life increasingly sharpened, as time slipped by, by awareness of the coming inevitability of war. All this *Prospero's Cell* captures to perfection from the first exultant sentence: "Somewhere between Calabria and Corfu the blue really begins." The work it perhaps comes closest to in feeling is *Love's Labour's Lost;* and the Shakespearean allusion in the title (Count D. has a theory that Shakespeare had Corfu partly in mind when he wrote *The Tempest*) makes one wonder quite how conscious Durrell himself was of this. Count D. and his little court of friends —though real people for whom Durrell clearly feels the same kind of affection and respect that he does for his peasant acquaintances (no patronized yokels here)—are presented with the gaiety, innocent bookishness, and faint comicality that invests Shakespeare's King of Navarre and his circle. Like the king, the count bans women from the endless discussions that he conducts with his friends on his arcadian estate; but he is very conscious of the Roman nymph in the rotonda in his garden, and his friends' wives will be invited again for the vintage. Meanwhile his American guest, Caroline, while pretending indifference, drifts as irrevocably into love with Durrell's friend Nimiec as any heroine of Shakespearean comedy. The young country folk in their bright costumes at the local festivals dance and court each other; and though there is here no Entertainment of the Nine Worthies, as in *Love's Labour's Lost,* we do watch the delighted Corfiote crowd at a shadow-play of their beloved folk-hero Karaghiosis and his familiar friends. If one speaks of Hector, in Shakespeare's play, Don Armado will reply: "The sweet war-man is dead and rotten; sweet chucks, beat not the bones of the buried: when he lived, he was a man." When the demon woman rises from the Corfu seas to put her question, one must reply (lest in rage and grief she overset one's boat), "Alexander lives, and reigns": a different hero and a different context, but the irrational-historical-nostalgical tug at the heartstrings is the same. So too Durrell receives a letter from Zarian's wife, as overwritten as anything from the hand of Armado; and, although we are not shown another Nathaniel and Holofernes rejoicing in their rustic latinity, we are offered a much superior equivalent in the affectionate vignette of the Durrells' neighbor Anastasius excitedly discovering the story of the Odyssey for the first time, in his little daughter's school primer:

—I don't understand . . . then is the story true?
—Quite true. . . . Don't you know that it was here that Nausicaa lived, that the palace of the King was in Corcyra?
—Before God?
—Before God.

And as Mercade brings the tidings of the death of the princess's father to cloud the scene and scatter the revelers at the end of Shakespeare's comedy, so the shadows of coming war darken the ending and dispersal of Durrell's own perfectly poised pastoral: "Zarian is bound for Geneva next week. Nimiec for Poland. . . . Tomorrow we are separating." ("You that way, we this way.") It is all perfectly achieved: the feeling of a continuing, almost dreamlike happiness—yet with brain and senses fully engaged—has never been better caught on paper. And there is a further magic in the fact that one is licensed to think as one reads, "But this is all true, it happened"; although that is a truth with modifications, for Durrell's facts have been so narrowly focused and selected as to be in practice translated into art. It is a distinct shock to discover from reference books that the smallish Eden-like island that his book and its pretty map seem to portray is actually forty miles long, that its inhabitants number over 25,000, and that its products include sulphur and coal. But that is no criticism of *Prospero's Cell,* which never sets out to do more than recapture a feeling forever linked in the writer's mind to a particular time and place.

The technical skill with which this is done is considerable. As a great number and variety of facts have to be presented, Durrell adopts a mosaic technique, with much of the book consisting of shortish passages from his notebook or diary. The contents of these passages display a timeless world; but their consecutive dating, moving steadily nearer to September 1939, has the effect of a quietly but ominously ticking clock. To avoid monotony, an initial pattern is established by which "mosaic" chapters are alternated with chapters of continuous prose; then monotony is further avoided by an increasing loosening-up and variation upon this pattern, although the feel of it is never quite lost. The result is a book that is unusually "light on its feet," with a clear lyrical quality unsubdued by the jumble of anecdote and fact.

The same light grace is not apparent in *Reflections on a Marine Venus* (1953) and would in any case have been inappropriate to a picture of a country that had suffered as the Greeks had during the war. It is a longer, heavier book, wrestled into shape from an even greater mass of material with the help of Eliot's secretary, the poet Anne Ridler, recording the very happy two years that Durrell had spent working in the temporary British administration on Rhodes after the German surrender. Rhodes is an island richer both in history and historical remains than Corfu, and with a dramatic beauty enhanced in unusual ways by the often beneficent fruits of the long years of Italian administration. For many this is their favorite Durrell book, for it is filled with fascinating information about a fascinating place, with descriptions as dazzling as the best colored photographs in their depth and clarity. Durrell's friends among the British administration, too, including the cheerfully eccentric Gideon, are perhaps easier for most readers to relate to than the unfamiliarly named quartet—Theodore Stephanides, Zarian, Max Nimiec, and Count D.—with whom he had drunk and debated on Corfu. Nonetheless, *Reflections on a Marine Venus* cannot really be said to be more than a distinguished addition to two minor literary genres, the personal memoir and the travel book. But *Prospero's Cell* is something more. It carries, unmistakably, the stamp of the poet.

Bitter Lemons (1957), as its very title indicates, is different again: another record of at any rate intermittent island happiness; but with sadness this time supervening, not with the ultimate departure but much earlier in the book, with the beginning of the pressures that will ultimately enforce that departure. As noted earlier, Durrell had moved to Cyprus in hopes that his savings would enable him to survive there as a full-time writer at least until he had completed the first volume of the *Quartet.* With his mind filled with happy recollections of Corfu and Rhodes, he found himself yet another delightful house in a Greek village, and again made friends among the local population. The financial burden on him was however greater than he had originally hoped, so that he was also compelled to take a teaching post in a city grammar school—which in turn brought him into contact with yet another facet of Greek life. All this is well and vividly recorded in the book, along with the progressive clouding of the scene by the increasing violence of the Greek Cypriot independence movement. This left Durrell emotionally trapped between his hereditary imperial loyalties and his love and admiration for the Greeks, with his feelings still more exacerbated by his impatience with what he saw as the insensitivity and unimaginativeness of the British response to the situation. The pressure on him was further increased when he was put in charge of British public relations and information services on the island. In the end, his village friends had to warn him that his life was no longer safe in their community, and a Greek friend was assassinated perhaps just because of his liking for Durrell's company. Meanwhile, his own response to the situation had become doubly paralyzed. It had been natural for him to hope, when he accepted employment with the Cyprus administration, that his special knowledge of the Greek community would enable him to serve as a bridge-builder between ruler and ruled. Instead, he had the bitterness of discovering that it had merely led him into seriously underrating the extent to which the terrorist organization had spread its roots within a society of which he himself yearned to think nothing but good; the analogy with Pursewarden's wrong advice to Mountolive is exact. Moreover, although the British had at last awoken properly to the realities of the situation, they had done so too late. Durrell himself could see that they now had no option but to pursue a military response to the crisis, even though this would in the long run be politically disastrous. Heartsore, despairing, he did not renew his initial contract of employment but left Cyprus. It was his last island, and his last period of residence within the embraces of the British establishment. For some three decades his home has been Provence, on which he is now writing what he says will be his last book.

When it appeared, *Bitter Lemons* was an immediate success. Written and published at great speed, partly because Durrell was in urgent need of funds, and partly so as not to lose its topical news value, it made Cyprus a real place for its readers and clarified a confusing conflict. It also, in the tale of Durrell's purchase of his village house, offers one of the most splendid comic episodes in English literature. Nonetheless the book has been the main target of a scathing attack on Durrell and all his works by Martin Green, an avowed adherent of the critical values of the great F. R. Leavis.

This attack on Durrell and *Bitter Lemons* should be read (it is conveniently reprinted in Harry T. Moore's *The World of Lawrence Durrell*), although its opening disparagement of the *Quartet* shows greater blindnesses in the critic than in the work he attacks. It also indulges in the unattractive Leavisian smear by association, pointing out Durrell's patent affinities with the rather soft-centered cult of the warmly-pagan-South school of writing epitomized by Norman Douglas, prominent in British writing earlier this century. The observation, so far as it goes, is valid; what is less valid is the trick of presenting it in such a way as to create the impression that it automatically discredits Durrell himself, despite Green's own admission that the *Quartet* "cannot be explained away so easily." But that said, it has to be admitted that nearly all Green's comments on *Bitter Lemons* itself do seem to land squarely on target, and a fair-minded reader must at least ask himself to what extent his general perception of Durrell's other work is modified as a result. The book, says Green, shows a man incapable of taking anything in life more seriously than he takes a historical novel; a man blinkered by romanticism, looking only for "the picturesque, the noncontemporary, the nonserious," able to move so comfortably between Greek village and Govern ment House only because he is insufficiently skep tical about his own selective, glamorizing picture of both. This is a man who has to explain to himself quite as much as to his readers, why Cypriot might prefer to be governed by their own kind; and to whom a friend's comment that the blessings of three-quarters of a century of British rule have left Nicosia still without even a bookshop or a theate much less a university, "came to me with the forc of a revelation." The embarrassing strain of adul tion in the references to Government House figure and the unresolved contradictions—and worse—i some of the book's comments ("wobbling electo ates at home unable to stand bloodshed and te rified of force")—all are ruthlessly spotlighted b Green, although he does allow, too, the real po gnancy of the tragedy of personal feeling in whi it is obvious that Durrell was sincerely involve

All Green's charges can be substantiated if o takes the text of *Bitter Lemons* as it stands; but it patently unjust to do so. In the first place, the studied glamorization of various British officials in the book verges upon caricature, and one has only to look at the parallel passages in *Mountolive,* so much better phrased, to realize that it is impossible that so conscious a stylist as Durrell should not have been aware of how gross he was being. The clue is surely given in *Bitter Lemons* itself, when Durrell explains his care to ensure that his resignation would not unfairly embarrass his colleagues, already struggling with a hopeless situation. Given that honorable attitude, then in a work that his already established reputation as an author of "island" books would guarantee a worldwide circulation he clearly had to be even more careful—especially as he had severely critical comments to offer on the colonial office, the crown agents, the British community on Cyprus, and the record of the island's administration. The most tactful way to do this was to stress that he had himself been at least as naive as anyone else despite his special knowledge of the Greeks, while cushioning the import of what he had to say by a few stylized bursts of patriotic trumpet music. The strategy must be admitted to have worked: tens of thousands read his criticisms, with a quiet defense of Archbishop Makarios slipped in for good measure, yet he was even offered (but refused) the Order of the British Empire. And his novels surely survive Green's strictures virtually unscathed, except to the degree that they are seen as travel writing.

The decade (1957–1967) following the close of Durrell's career in officialdom saw the publication of his very popular series of brief satiric skits on diplomatic life, collected as *Esprit de Corps, Stiff Upper Lip,* and *Sauve Qui Peut.* These anecdotes, unashamedly embarked upon as a simple fund-raising project, are very slight and not always in themselves particularly funny; but they do convey a sense of fun, especially through their lively pastiche in the P. G. Wodehouse manner.

TUNC *AND* NUNQUAM (THE REVOLT OF APHRODITE)

The collective title for this double novel seems unhelpful and will not be used here. Durrell told the present writer that it was chosen only after the original publication (1968–1970), at the request of an American publisher. That he does not really feel it to be his seems attested to by his long continued habit of referring to the work in letters by such abbreviations as TN, TuncNunc, and so on. (Readers who embark on any detailed study of the organization of Durrell's books will at times find discrepancies between British and American editions. Where this occurs, A. G. Thomas, the acknowledged bibliographical authority on Durrell's work, considers that the British text is normally to be followed.)

Tunc–Nunquam (Latin for "Then–Never") is by far Durrell's greatest intellectual achievement—a work, from this point of view, for which the more popular *Alexandria Quartet* is hardly more than a mere set of apprentice exercises. That, of course, is not any necessary guarantee of its literary quality; but in an age of increasingly short-winded readers, anyone inclined to speak dismissively of this double novel should at least first ask himself whether he has ever had the stamina for more than a couple of books of *Paradise Lost* or a couple of cantos of *The Faerie Queene*—though the Milton is the better test, for it is the latent architectonic power that marks this last of Durrell's major works.

On the surface *Tunc–Nunquam* is a brightly colored modern version of the familiar Gothic romance, with all the approved ingredients: flat characters, a Keatsian belle dame sans merci, crumblingly picturesque Mediterranean settings, the Alps, a mysterious great English country house, madness and suicides, enigmatic and sinister goings-on only explained many chapters later, and a naive central character coming unscathed through it all (though of course only after a serious illness). The usual Victorian extras are also stirred into the mix—a pinch of J. K. Huysmans, the faintest scintilla of erotic sadism, a touch of horror story, a *Boys' Own Paper* glimpse of the British Army, a good deal of pastiched scientific and philosophical discussion, and a dose of post-Frankensteinian science fiction. Less usual is the steady flicker of humor, with several characters exhibiting a kind of Dickensian vitality and their own versions of Scobie's wry exuberance of speech in the *Quartet.* It is all great fun, if not taken too seriously, especially if you skip when the characters begin speechifying.

The main story line is quite simple. Merlin's, a multinational conglomerate whose tentacles extend worldwide, discovers a brilliant young inventor called Felix Charlock, detaches him from his delightful Greek mistress Iolanthe, and secures a monopoly on his talents by maneuvering him into marrying Benedicta, the heiress to the firm. Benedicta is deeply disturbed psychologically, thanks to the hold on her of her demonic brother Julian, so that the marriage does not go well, while Felix simultaneously comes to feel more and more imprisoned within the grasp of the firm. At the end of *Tunc* he tries to escape by faking suicide but is recovered by the firm's organization and awakes with a head injury in a Swiss mental hospital. From the beginning of *Nunquam* all starts to go well for him. Julian has meanwhile been humanized by his obsessive love for the now dead Iolanthe. He persuades Felix to help him create a robot facsimile of her and eventually, trying to escape from them, the robot drags Julian to his death as it falls spectacularly from the Whispering Gallery, high inside the dome of St. Paul's Cathedral. A cluster of histories of secondary characters, tracing their fates within the framework of a society where Merlin's influence is everywhere, surrounds this main narrative. Finally, Felix burns all the contracts and records on which the firm's structure and power is built, thus in a sense freeing the world. But for what? In any case the title suggests that this will never happen.

Taken on this level, the real tour de force in this tale is the story, in the second half of the second volume, of the creation and ultimate self-destruction of the "dummy" Iolanthe. Durrell shows great skill in giving the idea of the manufacture of the new Iolanthe imaginative credibility. (It was, for instance, a brilliant idea to preface the peak of the performance by a demonstration-lecture by the embalmer Goytz, effectively shifting our normal perception of the human body.) In unobtrusive ways, too, wholly unlike the nauseous rhapsodizing and "poeticizing" of much modern science fiction, Durrell's poetic skills are fully deployed to help us feel the magicality and the eeriness of such a technological feat, while further reverberations are set off by the fact that what is being created is a person we already know. The "dummy" does not merely possess the real Iolanthe's voice, mannerisms, and appearance: programmed into her are all Iolanthe's memories too, as far as they can be recovered. Thus when she "awakes," she believes herself to *be* the real Iolanthe; cannot indeed cease to "be" Iolanthe in her thinking even when, loose in southern England, she discovers that she is entirely a human construct. With great tact, Durrell sketches in this last phase of the history of Iolanthe only by glimpses and indirect evidence, and it is the more convincing as a result. We realize that the consciousness of Iolanthe, reassembled by no wish of its own within this machine, cannot but feel, unbearably, that it has undergone an intrusion a thousand times worse than any normal rape; and that the natural and logical result is to generate in the machine of which she has become a part a frantic desire for freedom from the very organization on whose technology it is, in fact, pathetically dependent. Again the title *Nunquam* takes on a grimmer resonance than we expected. The oscillation in our minds as we follow this person/thing pleading desperately, through the mechanical faults already audible in her voice-box, "O please God don't let them get me . . . I'll do anything, anything"—and then leaping frantically to destruction as the hunt closes in—can generate in the reader a degree of distress that, one realizes with surprise, very little in modern fiction outside the pages of Beckett can match. And the reason, of course, is partly that we recognize in the facsimile Iolanthe an accurate emblem of all too many uncomfortably suppressed truths about the nature of our own existence. Durrell has never better vindicated his contention that accumulation of naturalistic detail is not the path that will lead the novelist closest to "reality prime."

Even so, a great deal is lost if *Tunc–Nunquam* is merely taken for a two-decker romance enshrining a parable about freedom. It is better to follow Durrell's own clear hints (in the source of his title, and in the concluding letter to his dead wife Claude) that this work is further meant to be seen in the tradition of Petronius' *Satyricon:* that is as belonging to the genre that the critic Northrop Frye has taught us to think of as the "anatomy," or "Menippean" satire. To list the characteristics of Menippean satire is in fact virtually to define *Tunc–Nunquam:* the seeming looseness of the form often leads to its being confused with the romance. Thus Menippean fiction is often erudite in its use of allusion and parody, exploits the fantastic and the grotesque (as in Durrell's account of the Merlin family's home life), and draws upon the tradition of philosophical debate (as in Caradoc's Acropolis speech in *Tunc* and Julian's corresponding disquisition on the Constaffel mountain in *Nunquam,* and a many other points as well). Its view of society skeptical and ironic, it is less interested in people than in mental attitudes, it interweaves a variety of styles and contrasting effects, and its technique is apt to be contrapuntal—all of which is as much as to say that the Menippean mode encapsulates about half of those qualities that had early attracted the young Durrell in his reading of Elizabethan literature.

What is remarkable about *Tunc–Nunquam,* however, is the seemingly effortless way in which it also assimilates and redeploys the other half of the Elizabethan legacy as well: that steady drive—coming to its most conscious flowering in the Stuart court masques—to turn art into a form of sympathetic magic, to match the order of God's cosmos with the order of a work of art in hopes that the healing and harmonizing force immanent in the cosmos might thereby be drawn down upon one's own community. Ultimately it is this, however dimly felt, that underlies the constant tendency in Elizabethan writing to echo, and tacitly celebrate, the Pythagorean-influenced configurations of "the Elizabethan world picture." And within the context of a different age, *Tunc–Nunquam* is doing the same. It does have the usual Durrellian "pier-and-wave" structure, although it is most marked in *Tunc,* where the pulse of emotional high points comes with steadily increasing frequency through an almost rigidly symmetrical layout of events (thus Felix meets the head of the eastern branch of Merlin's one-third of the way through the book, has his marriage into the firm arranged at the book's midpoint, and sees the head of the western branch two-thirds of the way through the story. The actual marriage occurs at the middle of the middle section of the middle chapter.) But beneath this is another underlying form in the work, which in a sense *is* its meaning: the two books jointly enact what they are talking about.

What they are talking about is the rescue or resurrection of a world that all can now see to be expiring within its own death grip upon itself: hence the ending of the work, with Felix and Benedicta at last dancing happily together, an age-old symbol of cosmic harmony. This harmony, however, needs to be achieved at every level: through psychic integration within the individual (in one interview Durrell happily admitted having "buried" the psychologists) as well as in personal relationships (the couple, the postface to *Nunquam* tells us, reflects the basic duality out of which every aspect of culture is constructed), and through a recovery of a better balance within our civilization. The action of *Tunc–Nunquam,* down to quite small details, can be followed through equally well in terms of any of these lines of thought—which is in itself a kind of quasi-verification of Durrell's conviction that they are manifestly related. Thus the mystery of what is going on between Felix, Benedicta, and Julian, for instance, evaporates if one sees them as the Jungian libido, anima, and shadow, and their story as an enactment of the Jungian theory of psychic integration; whereas other characters such as Vibart also fall into place within the same psychic drama (sometimes as embodiments of other facets of Felix's nature left in mere potentiality by the actual course of his life). On the larger social scale, Durrell's postface to *Nunquam* gives clear enough notice of what is afoot: "a sort of novel-libretto based on the preface to *The Decline of the West.*" But it is Freud, whom the postface also insists is "very much there," who seems at bottom responsible for the division into two volumes, which reflects the Freudian view of the duality of human nature, ruled by both Eros and Thanatos (life force and death wish). Thus *Tunc*—Then—is for the most part told by Felix to a recording machine, substituting, as it were, for a note-taking psychiatrist. The chronological confusion of the narrative combines with the nature of many of the scenes depicted to give a curious dreamlike feel to the whole, which is also heavily death-oriented, ending with a suicide, an attempted murder, and a faked death.

In short, the obvious function of *Tunc,* seen in this Freudian perspective, is to free the narrator from the nightmare burden of his Thanatos-ruled past in order to help clear the way for his return to full psychic health, along with his love, Benedicta, who is similarly healed. *Nunquam,* which then tells this happier story, is therefore chronologically much clearer: the drive of the life force expels the disorder of death. It is also appropriately more "organic": the heavily constructed symmetries of *Tunc* are not repeated; although this is not to say that the book's shape is merely left to chance (we still, for instance, start with the Paulhaus, a mental hospital, and end, for all practical purposes, with St. Paul's Cathedral).

Durrell's reference to Oswald Spengler *(The Decline of the West)* perhaps needs amplification, however. Spengler was interested in trying to trace the contours of the three eras or cultures of which our present civilization is the heir: the classical or "Apollinian" (Greek and early Roman), the aborted "Magian" culture (late Roman and pre-medieval), and our own "Faustian" world. The Faustian world, as the very choice of name implies, is doomed, and can lead us only back to barbarism. Its linear, dynamic view of life, its will to power and lust for absolute knowledge, drive it helplessly forward into conflict with the limitations imposed by nature; and nature, being the stronger, must inevitably win in the end, even if the world's interior conflicts do not break it first. The healthier "Apollinian" outlook, as Spengler saw it, was more wisely static, thinking of history more in cyclic terms, concerned not to lose touch in its culture with human scale and proportions. This Faust-Apollo antithesis of course chimes with the Freudian Thanatos-Eros antithesis in *Tunc–Nunquam,* with the firm of Merlin standing for both Thanatos and the Faustian. But a wider symbolism, that of Circle and Square, subsumes all this and much besides, literally shaping the work to a remarkable degree.

The Circle traditionally stands for unity, harmony, wholeness, permanence, life—hence for the natural and organic. (In terms of Socrates' charming fantasy, even true lovers, in their urge to embrace, are behaving as the severed halves of a once perfect spherical being.) In the present context it is therefore natural to associate the Circle with the healthy, balanced Apollinian outlook, which desires nothing in excess. The Square, standing for the manmade, the constructed, is the logical Faustian counterpart, though it indeed has positive connotations within the ancient traditions of our culture. Four, the first "square" number, is the Pythagorean symbol for the material world. Within the sacred *tetraktys,* taught the Pythagoreans, all things were contained; and in time an entire culture came to know that this included four elements, four qualities, four humors or temperaments, and so on. And the idea of a progression through the four elements (from earth to water to air to fire) also became intrinsic to alchemical thinking, in which both Jung and Durrell interested themselves.

Most of Durrell's mental life has in fact been spent on the intellectual Grand Trunk Road that leads from the Elizabethans on to Jung, and back through the classical world to the ancient Asian origins of Pythagorean concepts. The kind of information sketched in the last paragraph is part of the furniture of Durrell's mind—in much richer detail than it is possible to indicate here. Yet he is also a poet of the age of New Criticism, capable of writing the kind of "crystalline" poems that his age admired, so intricately interlaced semantically as to be susceptible to extraordinarily complex networks of analysis. What then seems to have happened in *Tunc–Nunquam* is that this mass of reading and idea-historical meditation fused together to produce a double novel with the same density of multifarious, coherently complex allusion and cross-reference that we might more normally expect to look for in a short, tight modern poem. It is not a question of his ploddingly planning a complicated allegory; so much is going on in this text—especially in view of the speed with which Durrell is known to compose—that a great deal of it can have been happening only at the subconscious level, as in poetic composition. More fully even than his other major novels, *Tunc–Nunquam* is essentially a long poem.

Demonstration of such an assertion within the confines of an essay of this kind is of course impossible. (Skeptics must turn to the last item in the bibliography if they wish more fully to satisfy themselves on this question.) But a few glimpses can be given here. Thus it has been shown, for instance, that there is a clear alchemical progression through the four elements (and their associated colors and qualities) in the two volumes, from the underground cellar (earth) in which *Tunc* opens, to the projected destruction of the firm's contracts (fire) with which *Nunquam* ends. This can govern even quite small details of personality or appearance, such as the lugubriousness of the architect Caradoc's assistant. Or again, the three cities among which Felix moves—Athens, Constantinople, and London—clearly stand for the three Spenglerian cultural epochs (Classical, Magian, and Faustian), with the fourth age waiting to reveal itself after the destruction of the contracts: Will it be barbarism or the world dictatorship that Spengler fears, or is it possible for us, by some Charlock-like move, to recover the Classical Apollinian mode again?

The same idea of a three-part sequence, with a fourth term waiting for us to discover or create echoes again in *Tunc–Nunquam*'s use of visual markers. There appear to be three of these, spaced out through the two volumes: a talisman consisting of a Latin palindromic square (*Tunc,* ch. 3, first section); a sketch of Caradoc's Pacific island home (*Tunc,* toward the end of the penultimate section of ch. 5); and another talisman consisting of a word-square around a stylized sketch of the female sexual organs (*Nunquam,* ch. 2, second section). Each of these markers precedes a major new stage in Felix's spiritual odyssey: first his commitment of himself to Merlin's, second his initial attempt at asserting his independence from the firm, and last his commitment to the building of a replica-Iolanthe. The three markers (Durrell has confirmed that they were intended to be so interpreted) logically break up the work into four sections; but when considered in that light something seems to be wrong, for the final section is out of proportion to the others in its length—and in any case, surely there ought logically also to be a fourth and final marker to preface the final stage in Felix's odyssey, when he conceives the ambition of freeing not just himself but the whole world from the grip of the firm.

And the marker is in fact there and even visually reminiscent, as Felix himself notes, of the earlier talisman in the same volume; it is manifestly the written prophecy (*Nunquam,* final section of ch. 5) of the placing of the guests at dinner on the night when Felix is to destroy Merlin's contracts. The only difference is that this time no visual reproduction of the marker has been inserted into the text; the reader has to hunt for it himself once he has grasped the underlying scheme of the work—just as Felix has to find out, once he has grasped the problem, what to do in a world dominated by Merlin's. The book, in short, is built over a structure that itself enacts a kind of surrogate for the very thing it is talking about.

Nor is that all, for *Tunc–Nunquam* "enacts" itself structurally in other ways, too. Most notably, and most appropriately, it "squares the circle." If we are to escape the coming age of barbarism that Spengler fears, then according to his scheme of ideas, which Durrell *(Homo ludens)* is here accepting, our Faustian civilization must be refounded into something closer to classical or Apollinian concepts. In terms of the dominant imagery of Durrell's two-decker, that is equivalent to saying that the square must be accommodated to the Circle—and that is precisely what this work does. Admittedly it is only a private joke (or "mason's mark") of the author's that he has let his work fall into 44 sections and 7 + 7 chapters ($\frac{11 \times 4}{7+7} = \frac{22}{7} = \pi$), but the joke is significant even so. *Tunc–Nunquam* is not only full of shadowings of quaternary schemes, it is full of every kind of circle, too. The symmetries of *Tunc*—which are a kind of circularity—have already been glanced at. The story of Felix in the same volume begins and ends in Athens. In the central section of this symmetrical book, the hero not only in effect inherits the globe by marrying Benedicta, but also travels right around the world; and there are other circular journeys. In the beginning of *Nunquam,* Felix's head is "a cosmic egg." There are repeated references to domed or circular architectural structures—the domed library of Benedicta's country house, Stonehenge and Woodhenge, the circular threshing-floor on which Jocas wishes to build his mausoleum, and finally St. Paul's Cathedral (where the proportions of the domed central space, in the center of which Julian and the false Iolanthe end their existences, were in fact laid off by the architect from the rotation of a double square). The catalog could be extended.

All this is but the beginning of an analysis; but it doubtless will suffice to give readers unsympathetic to Durrell the feeling that he has here somehow confused literature with crossword puzzle-making. It is an understandable response but would be unjust, because it is a response not to the work itself but to the analysis. There is not the least evidence that Durrell expected his readers generally to be able to undertake the kind of exhaustive decoding sketched above, or that he would even have been entirely conscious of many of its details himself in the heat of intuitive composition. The ancient cosmological idea-schemes are subtle, complex, have wide reference, and hold many poetic antinomies comfortably. They have afforded Durrell the images for what he wished to express in *Tunc–Nunquam,* and also a frame of reference that has helped him not to lose his way in the composition of the work. In essentials, that is all. (The novelist Muriel Spark has used the doctrines of the Catholic church in much the same way.) When we admire some splendid healthy animal, we know that what we see is dependent on the presence within it of an equally healthy but rather differently shaped skeleton. But it is at the animal itself that we look, even if our gaze may be usefully sharpened by some grasp of the articulation of the underlying skeleton.

There are in *Tunc–Nunquam,* partly set as it is in Constantinople, just a few references to "thick-skulled" Turkish servants and the like—just as there are elsewhere in Durrell's work a few passing expressions of revulsion at some aspects of Mohammedanism as practiced in some non-Western parts of the world, and at some of the human debris of Egypt. To this may be added a few denigrating references to African blacks and some uncomfortable-sounding remarks about Jews. On a shrinking globe, where it becomes increasingly essential for all races to learn to live together, we are learning new taboos and revised conventions of speech that make it dishonest not to face this squarely. Some new readers may be provoked into turning away from Durrell's work merely because he does not always follow our new conventions, even when this does not in fact mean what we nowadays too automatically tend to suppose.

It is true that by suppressing contexts and counterbalancing remarks, it is possible to collect a tiny anthology of Durrell quotes that could make him sound distinctly racist; perhaps this is even the solution to the mystery of why his country has never offered this world-famous author any public honor for his services to literature, for there must surely be some reason for so bizarre a slight. But the answer is simply that Durrell is a romance writer: a writer of serious, philosophical romances, meant to modify our perception of reality but only, as it were, at one remove, by analogue. His secondary characters are as deliberately stylized and simplified as secondary characters in an opera, and for the same reason. He certainly expects his readers to command sufficient sophistication to appreciate this. The Turkey where his Merlin family have their home, for example, is a fantastic dream world that bears approximately the same relation to the real Turkey as a seraglio in an eighteenth-century opera. When it comes to transcribing actuality, as in *Bitter Lemons,* of course Durrell does not need telling that Turks are not to be dismissed as thick-skulled—the very friend who brilliantly blocks the maneuvers of an entire Greek village when Durrell buys a house is a Turk. Were such worries to be put to Durrell himself, one may guess that he would point out with some amusement that sooner or later he has been rude about everybody except Tibetans and Chinese, and most continuously rude about his own countrymen and their official faith. There is nothing in Durrell's comments on Christianity, either, to match the haunting beauty and meaningfulness with which the cry of the *muezzin* is invested in the *Quartet:* nor can a lifelong expatriate who in many ways feels most at home with Himalayan Buddhists be said to be showing much faith in Western cultural superiority. The only passages that stir real discomfort are references to Jewishness in the middle stretches of the Avignon quintet; it is possible to understand what has happened there, but upon rereading, the discomfort does not go away, although the failure is rather in the apparent strategy of the work than in Durrell's normal good will. (As for the black Miss Smith in *The Black Book,* it is worth looking at some of the poems of the great Nigerian poet Gabriel Okara before taking mechanical offense at Durrell's account: there are some noticeable similarities of ideas.)

THE AVIGNON QUINTET (MONSIEUR, LIVIA, CONSTANCE, SEBASTIAN, QUINX)

Tunc–Nunquam was described at the beginning of the previous section as the last so far of Durrell's major works. That does appear to be the case, although the reservation must be made that the Avignon quintet (or "quincunx") has only very recently been completed, and it has in the past taken a little time before new Durrell novels have come into proper focus. Nonetheless, these five novels—perhaps more realistically described as "four and a tailpiece"—will be only fairly briefly considered here, although Durrell himself reckons them to be among the dozen by which his reputation must stand or fall. And certainly the ambitions of the project are not in a minor key.

A little anxiously, Durrell repeatedly signals in the Avignon quintet (1974–1985) what is going on. The very term "quincunx," which he seems to prefer in correspondence, gives the first clue: a *quincunx* is a group of five points or objects arranged in the form of an X—a square with a midpoint. One thing that this means is that Durrell is again trying to break with the normal "linear" tradition of fiction. These novels interrelate but form a group, not a straightforward consecutive sequence: "five panels, for which your creaky old *Monsieur* would simply provide a cluster of themes" (*Livia,* p. 11). This suggests a larger *Alexandria Quartet* with Avignon replacing Alexandria; but that cannot be, for Durrell has by now come to hold that "from the absolute point of view all persons are the same person . . . obstinately I dream of such a book, full of not completely discrete characters . . . could such people walk in and out of each other's lives without damaging the quiddity of each other? Hum" (*Constance,* p. 123). For Durrell, that quiddity or "eidolon" (*Monsieur,* p. 119) is knowable only to intuition. To the rational mind, people have become for him even more radically unknowable than he had earlier supposed: mere clusters of psychic particles endlessly throwing off differently patterned refractions of themselves. Yet life requires us to act on the premise that we do know, however incompletely, who (and what) other people are; so that we substitute for the real person synthetic portraits assembled from our private library of stereotypes: there is no other choice. "The human psyche is almost infinitely various. . . . How poor is the pathetic little typology of our modern psychology. That is why our novels, yours and mine Robin, are so poor" (*Livia,* p. 37). For we cannot even fully know ourselves.

What then are poor novelists to do? Before exploring Durrell's answer to that question it is worth noting what he himself is actually doing, in one completely different sense, in this particular novel cluster. It will not have escaped the reader's notice that Durrell's invocation of the idea of the "quincunx" potentially brings us back into the world of Pythagorean numbers again. Within that frame of reference, it is relevant to note that if one raises the central point of a quincunx to a higher plane, one generates a pyramid, with all its time-defying and funerary connotations. Durrell is an "X" to himself, a mystery—but a mystery that an artistic quincunx, with its crowd of interpenetrating characters, all expressing aspects of their creator, may perhaps help both to clarify and preserve against the flux of time. Aware from the outset that this would have to be his last major project, he is almost literally erecting his own pyramid on the foundation of his own mystery, decorating its secret passages and chambers as vividly as he possibly can, and encapsulating as much as possible of his own multifarious self within it.

A great deal of what is said and shown within the five volumes seems to be guided by this implicit underlying metaphor. There are constant reminders of Egypt, and Egypt is in turn associated both with the thought of royalty (the Prince) and death. The lost Templar treasure has to be tracked down through mysterious quarried galleries, and we are reminded (*Quinx,* p. 190) of Egyptian folk tales of serpents left to guard hidden treasure just before we seem about to reach that of the Templars, with their links with gnosticism and thus with the ancient lore of Egypt. Even back in *Livia* (p. 12) the novelist Blanford, perhaps the most evident Durrell substitute in the books, having outlined the quincunx-novel idea only half a page earlier, is described as "trying to sum it all up—from the point of view of death." And it has to be admitted that a pyramid of half-a-million words, enriched with ancient lore, constitutes an imposing funerary monument.

But still the question remains: if we reject that materialistic, hard-edged, ego-centered metaphysic of which the traditional novel is perhaps our clearest literary reflection (and it is this that follows from the abandonment of any normal belief in the idea of "personality"), what happens to narrative fiction?

At first sight nothing very much seems to have happened: the "quincunx" novels are set in the late 1930's and the following decade, and present a rather classy set of young professional people—doctor, diplomat, don, novelist, psychoanalyst, and so forth, all sexually entangled—and their shadow-doubles. Full supporting cast includes Catholic Nazi general, Egyptian prince, Jewish plutocrat peer, and (in *Quinx*) hundreds of gypsies. *Constance,* the numerically central volume, makes a rather worrying effort to fit the moral and psychological facts of the Nazi horror into our picture of the era, but also depicts a triumphant love affair between the psychoanalyst Constance and Affad, an Egyptian Gnostic. Affad's fusion of sexual gifts with mystical insight, fertilizing Constance's own Freudian training, carries her far beyond Freud to a deeper, half-intuitive insight into what genuinely healthy human relationships, overtly sexual or not, should really be. This vision, essentially identical with the sex-mysticism associated with more than one Asian faith (and not always too happily expounded in these works), is the only therapy that Durrell can prescribe for that sickness of the soul of our civilization of which atom bombs and Nazi atrocities are merely the most dramatic symptoms. In short, his aim at one level is that which G. K. Chesterton credited to Dickens: to change the world by changing the expression on the face of mankind, although he is not naive about the obscurity, difficulty, and remoteness of that hope.

Nonetheless, it works for Constance, who, at

first shattered by Affad's death (in *Sebastian*), eventually consummates her early love for Blanford *(Quinx),* and the couple move—as we are told rather than shown—toward "dealing seriously *at last* with human love, which is a yogic thought-form, the rudder of the human ship of fools." (*Quinx* is rather oversupplied with Blanford's *obiter dicta.*) Then the remainder of the work moves into the leisurely preparations for the uncovering of the treasure referred to above, with which all five volumes have been intermittently concerned along with much else. It is pleasant, though, that it should be the artist Blanford, not Affad the mystic, who gets the psychiatrist pregnant, even if it seems that she may die in childbirth—although surely *Livia* implies that she didn't.

And there's the rub. To continue this kind of conventional résumé of the Avignon quintet/quincunx would in fact be absurd: the work is a critic's minefield, deliberately sown. None of the temptingly handy miniature self-reviews that litter *Quinx,* for instance, is really safe to use. Vast tracts of narrative are curiously flattened in pace and tone. Levels of reality are mixed until it is logically impossible to disentangle them and too tedious to try, with the author blandly indicating that he is fully aware of this. Normal novel-reading expectations are repeatedly aroused, only to be led gently into a morass. It is typical, for instance, that the teasing climax of *Quinx* does not actually bring us to the Templar treasure, which in any case now seems to represent something else. None of this is incompetence (although Durrell was reportedly very ill at one stage during the composition of the series, and the "quincunx" does seem to the present writer to have somewhat lost its balance, sense of direction, and even, for a while, humor, after that). Rather, Durrell is deliberately breaking down our normal novel-reading expectations, but gently, in order to open our minds to the possibility of a new, more fluid, open-ended, "Tibetan" kind of fiction. In this he may be said to have succeeded, though it is unclear quite how the new form would differ from a mistier version of the usual anti-novel, or attempts to bring fiction closer to the condition of music. The only trouble is that he hasn't really made his new vision very interesting, to judge from published reactions so far.

This is not to say that the books themselves are without interest. On the contrary, there has been wide agreement among reviewers that the Avignon quintet contains some of the most brilliant set-piece descriptions—an account of being bombarded by mortar shells, an Egyptian courtship, river journeys, evocations of Avignon—that Durrell has ever written, and there is a good deal else to enjoy, fitfully perhaps, as well—a mood deftly captured, or a person or an event deftly imagined, such as the lunatics from the bombed asylum passing through the town. But it is an intermittent brilliance that shines among a good deal of duller and some distinctly unlikable material. The latter patches generally seem to come where a kind of *festivitas* or extra vitality is being willed into the narrative without being felt. The elaborate scene in *Sebastian* of the Jewish Lord Galen in a brothel is perhaps a case in point—equally unfunny, in its uncomfortable sense of a real animosity below the smiling account of what is in effect a ritual humiliation, both on first and second reading. But is that animosity real? There is a trick often played by Durrell in his novels that has its risky side, and of which every reader of Durrell needs to be aware. This is the device of trying to make an ultimate moral point by first using the full authority of the narrator to seduce the reader into partaking of an attitude that is bad—even evil—in order that he may subsequently feel upon his own pulses the world's corruption when he realizes the error. This can be very easily demonstrated in *Tunc–Nunquam,* for example, where the first volume is studded with pronouncements (clearly meant to tempt every male reader) expressing a jovially brutal attitude to relations with women, which at the time one is given the tacit impression that the author at least to some degree shares. It is only when we come to *Nunquam* that we realize that everything said in its predecessor came out of the Thanatos-poisoned brain of a Felix in the grip of Merlin's, and that to the extent we agreed with him we were Thanatos-poisoned, too. Since Durrell saw Nazi-anti-Semitism in Gnostic terms, not as a self-contained phenomenon but as a symptom of the general grip of evil on the world, it is natural to assume that he is using the same kind of tactic in the *Sebastian* passage—but that he as it were lost his way, as he seems to do in other respects as well in *Constance* and *Sebastian.*

That, however, is too negative and niggling a point with which to conclude this journey through the writings of an author of Durrell's stature. Let us rather, with a rustle of anticipation, turn to await the book on Provence.

POETRY

DURRELL's reputation as a poet was at its highest in the early 1950's. But then the great success of *The Alexandria Quartet* overshadowed the achievement of the poetry, in any case associated with the 1940's, a decade rapidly going out of fashion. Durrell's fourth book of poems, *The Tree of Idleness,* appeared in the same year as Philip Larkin's *The Less Deceived* (1955). There is some symbolism in this; Larkin's poetic fortunes thereafter rose, as did those of other members of the movement whose manifesto-anthology was Robert Conquest's *New Lines* (1957). Durrell, however, became less prolific as a poet—there was an eleven-year gap before his next book of verse, *The Ikons,* came out in 1966—and suffered a noticeable loss of warmth in the reviews he then received. In *The Big Supposer* (1973), the book of interviews that Marc Alyn conducted with him in 1970 and 1971, he speaks with a not altogether convincing resignation about the change in his public status as a poet:

> Before the novels, I had an excellent reputation as a poet. No one pretended I was a genius, but I was among the six or seven good poets whose names would invariably be cited after the greats, Eliot, Auden, Dylan Thomas. I would often be somewhere in the next five. Two of my poems were included in the *Faber Book of Modern Verse* for twenty years. And then recently the anthology needed some new blood: five of us were shifted out to make room for five younger poets. So there you are. That's the position at the moment.
>
> (p. 120)

But Durrell speaks of his poems in these interviews with unnecessary despondency, the product of his own high valuation of poetry: "I would so much like to be a poet . . . and I'm not sure that I'm up to it. Perhaps two or three of my poems will be bull's-eyes, but as far as consistency goes, I've failed, missed the boat" (p. 93).

The remarkable thing about Durrell's poetry is, in fact, the consistency with which it holds to his own distinctively modern concept of what being a poet entails. As a poet he plays for high stakes; his own estimate would be that nothing less than greatness in poetry will do. In his remarkable *Key to Modern Poetry,* Durrell says that "in the last analysis great poetry reflects an unknown in the interpretation and understanding of which all knowledge is refunded into ignorance. It points towards a Something which itself subsists without distinction" (p. 90). Throughout the book Durrell discusses poetry in terms of its reflection of the "unknown." Poetry is *essentially* a matter of intuiting a spiritual reality that lies far beyond appearance. Durrell's view in this aspect derives ultimately from the French symbolists; he would agree with Stéphane Mallarmé's account of the "magic charm of art" in "Crise de Vers," though his interpretation of Mallarmé's last clause would be unorthodox. Mallarmé says that "beyond the confines of a fistful of dust or of all other reality, beyond the book itself, beyond the very text, it delivers up that volatile scattering which we call the Spirit, Who cares for nothing save universal musicality." If not to be a great poet is not to have access to the reality in which something like Mallarmé's "Spirit" is to be found, then it is not to be a poet at all, so decisive is Durrell's emphasis on the poet's function as a prophet and seer.

Durrell is fascinated by Einstein's theory of relativity and the idea of the space-time continuum, because in his view they confirm the truth of the poet's intuitive vision, which is a denial of "logic." Neither reason—"only a trusted middleman in the commerce between logic and illumination" (*Key to Modern Poetry,* p. 3)—nor logic has much part to play in the work of the poet. At best they may play some secondary role: "The artist . . . does not exactly think while he works. He uses the ratiocinative side of himself only when he comes to arrange and edit what he has written or painted" (p. 6).

But Durrell does not have much to say about this secondary role; his *Key* offers a sketch of modern intellectual history in which poetry and science are coming closer and closer together, united by a common interest in what lies beyond reasoning. "If reality is somehow extracausal, then a whole new vista of ideas is opened up—a territory hitherto only colonized by intuition" (p. 30)—the intuition, that is, of the artist. Durrell's grasp of Einstein's theories is questionable, to say the least, but given the value he puts on intuition, that cannot matter to him. The artist's goal, one might say, is illumination; art itself is merely incidental. Illumination is reached through nonattachment to the self, and as he speaks of it Durrell's tone becomes almost apocalyptic:

> But if the artist today is concerned with the transcending of personality—if his confessed motives are a desire to reach desirelessness and a desire to grow beyond the ego—what is to happen to art? Is it to become pure metaphysics—or is it to die out gradually? At any rate some new transformation is foreshadowed in the new mystical departures.
>
> (p. 162)

The context of ideas for Durrell's poetry is not to be seized sympathetically in an age that pits pragmatism against other more radically committed ideologies, an age that, in the West, has turned its back on the kind of religious and spiritual thinking that the last two paragraphs have exemplified. These ideas, however, are ideas well established in poetry as a whole. In Mallarmé and in Eliot, whose concept of poetry reflected French symbolism, they are compatible with work of profound beauty. Durrell proclaims himself a romantic rather than a classical author; the English romantic poets were also poets of vision, and their achievement is not negligible. Indeed, the emphasis on questioning the quotidian action of reality may even now be held to have its value. These are considerations that must be borne in mind if we hope to gain anything from a reading of Durrell's poetry.

It is not altogether surprising, in view of what has already been said, that he does not recognize a meaningful distinction between poetry and prose. In the *Key,* he discusses Joyce and Marcel Proust alongside Eliot and Yeats without apology. If there is a distinction, then it lies in the greater density of poetry. Poetry compresses feeling; prose is more relaxed. But its subject matter is not necessarily different. In fact, much of Durrell's prose is like his poetry in that it describes the path to illumination; it is about being or becoming an artist. One possible way of describing *The Alexandria Quartet* is to say that it is about Darley's winning through to the true vision of the artist, to claim for himself a place "in the kingdom which Pursewarden calls the 'heraldic universe.' " By way of reinforcing this aspect of its subject matter, the *Quartet* reflects and refashions aspects of the archetypal modern poem in English, Eliot's *The Waste Land.* Within a couple of years of the publication of the *Quartet*'s last volume, an American critic, Eleanor N. Hutchens, remarked that Darley's rescue of the drowning Clea and her return to life represented a rehandling in positive spirit of the "Death by Water" section in Eliot's poem, the most striking of a series of parallels and allusion to his work throughout the four parts of Durrell's major achievement as a novelist. Similarly, Durrell's first "serious" prose work, *The Black Book,* makes creative use of Eliot's "Gerontion" to clarify its meanings, and once again, these meanings cluster around the process of becoming an artist.

In the *Key to Modern Poetry* Durrell takes "Gerontion" as the very type of the modern poem in its presentation of a character in despair, living in the shadow of myths that have died and unable to affirm positive values. *The Black Book* alludes by its title to one of the many books written to warn the guileless reader of Elizabethan or Jacobean times about the underworld of criminality in country and city, as though to emphasize Durrell's exposure of the squalor of London in the 1930's through the involuntary memories of his narrator. But Durrell's use of "Gerontion" is not primarily intended to associate his despair with that of *The Black Book*'s narrator. His allusions are intended to establish a radical difference between his book and Eliot's poem, a difference indicated in the original subtitle, "an agon"—a struggle. The struggle is one with the despair represented by Eliot's figure, a struggle for life of which Gerontion is incapable; the struggle, that is, between the narrator apparently removed to safety on his Greek island from the horrors of life in the Regina Hotel in London, and the memories of those horrors that threaten to overtake his psyche altogether. "It puts the case for the difficulty of self-liberation," Durrell told Marc Alyn, emphasizing the book's failure to confirm the liberation so much talked about within its pages ("God save the mark, it is I who am chosen to interpret these frantic syllables which rise up between us, apocalyptic, dazzling, clarion" [*Black Book,* p. 241]). The book ends in ambiguous contradiction, its penultimate sentence a vision of new life: "the breathing yolk, the durable, the forever, the enormous Now," its last sentence a denial of that life: "This is how it ends."

The allusions to Eliot's poem are what enable us

to read the unresolved conflict of these last two sentences in a positive spirit. Eliot's narrator is an old man, Durrell's is a young man "born old. Not dead but old" (p. 241). Eliot's narrator inhabits "a draughty house / Under a windy knob"; Durrell's island home is *on* the "knob"—a "tough black button of rock" (p. 20), and it is at the center of a storm. The dryness of Gerontion's house symbolizes barrenness, but Durrell's narrator lives within "the four damp walls of a damp house, under an enormous wind" (p. 21), the dampness connoting either decay or the possibility of growth. Gerontion's memories of Mr. Silvero, Hakagawa, and the others are like the memories in *The Black Book*—in the *Key to Modern Poetry* Durrell describes them as "a gallery of *personae* such as one might only see in some small Florentine pension, or perhaps in a Bloomsbury boarding-house for foreign students" (p. 12)—but Durrell's narrator is able to hold apart from them enough to pronounce a valediction, and by love to make his salutation to life itself: "I cover you with my body and whole universes open silently, like a door into a sudden garden" (p. 240)—the allusion here being to Eliot's "Burnt Norton" and its "door we never opened / Into the rose-garden."

"The whole thing is a poem, a colossal poem": Miller's dazzled exclamation identifies correctly the arena in which *The Black Book,* excessive, prolific of words, vulnerably impassioned, makes its challenge. He then goes on to raise a question that might well have occurred to many readers since: "Why you should ever want to write little finished poems I don't know. Anything you write as a poem can only be a whiff after this. *This is the poem*" (*Lawrence Durrell–Henry Miller: A Private Correspondence,* p. 72).

An answer to this question would be that whereas *The Black Book* was a poem about the struggle to become a poet, "little finished poems" were required as testimony that the author had come through, achieved his epiphany or his series of epiphanies—that, in short, he was a poet, not merely someone struggling to be one. *The Black Book* is described by its narrator as "the projection of my battle with the dragon who disputed my entry into the heraldic baronies" (p. 219). The "little finished poems" would proclaim that Durrell himself possessed a "new barony whose language I am taking at dictation." The "barony" denotes the status of the "seer" in the natural hierarchy whose outline Durrell probably owes to Lawrence. The poems are short poems because they stand for moments of illumination, when the seer has access to what Durrell calls the "heraldic universe." The phrase recurs throughout his work—we have already seen it in *Clea,* and he has described it in this fashion:

> It is not a "state of mind" but a continuous self-subsisting plane of reality towards which the spiritual self of man is trying to reach out through various media: artists like antennae boring into the unknown through music or print or words, suddenly strike this Universe where for every object in the known world there exists an ideogram.
>
> (*Personal Landscape,* I, 4 [1942], p. 8)

Durrell writes "little" poems not because he has a lyric gift but because he conceives of the work of art as something static: an ideogram, a single signifier. This idea underlies one of his first and best poems, perhaps written even before *The Black Book* was completed, "Carol on Corfu":

> I, per se I, I sing on.
> Let flesh falter or let bone break
> Break, yet the salt of a poem holds on,
> Even in empty weather
> When beak and feather have done.

The subject of this "carol" is the poem itself, conceived as a vitalizing insight into reality: "I quicken, / Leaven and liven body's prime carbon. . . ." Its role is curative: "This is my medicine: trees speak and doves / Talk, woods walk . . ." (Durrell wrote to Miller in April 1937, "I believe in artists as healers"). And because its origin is in the "extracausal" reality where all time and space are one, it transcends death, the artist's death and the fact of death itself:

> O per se O, I sing on.
> Never tongue falters or love lessens,
> Lessens. The self of the poem lives on
> Like this carol of empty weather
> Now feather and beak have gone.

"O" replaces "I"; someone becomes no one, but the poem affirms its own truth to survive such changes.

This poem is unembarrassed by the debts it proclaims to other poets, most notably Gerard Manley Hopkins and Dylan Thomas (a great influence, especially in other poems of the first regular collection, *A Private Country* [1943]). It has no reason to be embarrassed. The poem's "I" is the poem itself, speaking *through* the poet; he therefore takes no credit and is unconcerned about originality insofar as that implies a valuing of one's own thoughts above those of others. "I read not only for pleasure, but as a journeyman, and where I see a good effect I study it, and try to reproduce it" (*Writers at Work 2,* 1963, p. 274). In rhythm and alliteration "Carol on Corfu" owes much to Hopkins, but the overall effect of the poem is quite different, combining response to the *élan vital* with a kind of impersonality unknown to the earlier poet, whose "effects" are here simply put to use in the cause of celebration.

There are a number of poems, some of Durrell's best, that are celebratory like "Carol on Corfu." The dislocations of war and the tumult of personal life reduced their number, perhaps, but they are fundamental to his poetry. An example might be the beautiful poem "Politics" (*Collected Poems,* p. 191), dedicated to his friend George Seferis and praising the diplomat's art of bringing together:

> As the writer unites dissimilars
> Or the doctor with his womb-bag joins
> The cumbersome ends of broken bones in
> A simple perishable function,
> To exhale like a smoke ring the O: Joy.

"O per se O": it is a cry, it is the sign of nothing, it is a symbol of perfection, and it is unseizable; it cannot stand still but is exhaled "like a smoke-ring." The idea is given more complete expression in one of the poems called "The Anecdotes." In the contents for *On Seeming to Presume* (1948), this sequence figures as "Journals of Progress," although the more familiar title appears in the text. The failure of the earlier title to stick is significant, suggesting the extent of Durrell's commitment to the idea of experience as a series of momentary encounters with "extracausal" reality and his skepticism about the nature of "progress":

> If space curves how much the more thought,
> Returning after every conjugation
> To the young point of rest it started in?
> The fulness of being is not in refinement,
> By the delimitation of the object, but
> In roundness, the embosoming of the Real.
> (*Collected Poems,* p. 204)

However, this poetry does more than celebrate the mysterious quality of life itself, the quality that exceeds the grasp of rational mind, because that

> arranges,
> Explains, but can never sufficiently include:
> Punishes, exclaims, but never completes its arc
> To enter the Round.
> (*Collected Poems,* p. 213)

It is concerned with particular aspects of experience also. The "heraldic universe" is a kind of "ocean where each kind / Does straight its own resemblance find"; it comprises types that may be seized in the act of poetic intuition. The sequence "Eternal Contemporaries" (in *On Seeming to Presume*) is a kind of typology of the male Greek island character, ending with the "Rhodian Captain":

> while we thought him voyaging through life
> He was really here, in truth, outside the doorpost,
> In the shade of the eternal vine, his wife,
> With the same tin plate of olives on his lap.
> (*Collected Poems,* p. 180)

Poems such as this fit perfectly the usual description of Durrell as a poet of place, and especially of the Mediterranean lands. But the clarity and particularity of "Eternal Contemporaries" is exceptional. Durrell describes himself as suffering from "the defect of vision . . . I can't remember any of the wild flowers I write about so ecstatically in the Greek islands" (*Writers at Work 2,* p. 272). Place-names are prominent in all his books of poems, but the places they belong to are rarely described. A few details evoke atmosphere, and very speedily the poet is off on some untopographical voyage. Sometimes not even details are given:

> At Corinth one has forgiven
> The recording travellers in the same past
> Who first entered this land of doors,
> Hunting a precise emotion by clues,
> Haunting a river, or a place in a book.
> (*Collected Poems,* p. 86)

Durrell is not, in his poetry, deeply interested in the *look* of things but in their relation to his metaphysical "reality." Places matter for their influence upon spirit, for their power in the shaping of culture: "so long as people keep getting born Greek or French or Italian, their culture-productions will bear the unmistakable signature of the place" (*Spirit of Place* [1969], p. 156). Alexandria is Durrell's *Waste Land* long before the *Quartet* comes to be written, because it is by nature a Waste Land:

> Ash-heap of four cultures,
> Bounded by Mareotis, a salt lake,
> On which the winter rain rings and whitens,
> In the waters, stiffens like eyes.
> (*Collected Poems,* p. 127)

As for the Greek islands, the fact that they are scattered in the sea is what holds Durrell to them. They are the very types of those intuitive moments that are visionary poetry:

> On charts they fall like lace,
> Islands consuming in a sea
> Born dense with its own blue. . . .
> (*Collected Poems,* p. 132)

> . . . the islands will never grow old.
> Nor like Atlantis on a Monday tumble,
> Struck like soft gongs in the amazing blue.
> (*Collected Poems,* p. 66)

This, too, is the secret of their appeal for the English reader. In Durrell's poems of the Mediterranean the *voyage à Cythère,* that is, to the true island of true love, is always ready to begin, a journey into the moment itself, the traveler borne in boats that have

> The pathetic faculty of girls
> To register and utter a desire
> In the arms of men upon the new-mown waters. . . .
> (*Collected Poems,* p. 133)

Love, for Durrell, is a voyage of discovery, just as sailing is a matter of love for the sea. One of the most successful of his love poems is "Chanel":

> Scent like a river-pilot led me there:
> Bedroom darkness spreading like a moss,
> The polished wells of floor in blackness
> Gave no reflection of the personage
> Or the half-open door, but whispered on. . . .
> (*Collected Poems,* p. 220)

Durrell follows Robert Graves in the old-fashioned belief that "man does, woman is"; this is doubtless part of what he means when he calls himself a romantic ("all poets and most writers, including those who seem to be 'classical,' are romantics" [*The Big Supposer,* p. 86].) His poetry endows women with little personality or individuality; they have the good or bad fortune to represent for him the "mystery" he feels to underlie existence itself, a mystery well evoked in the multiplying images of the passage quoted above, allied to the teasing syntax of a sentence that unfolds with an effect of continuous surprise. Durrell very early on perfected the ability to manage syntax in this ambiguous and tentative manner; it is one of the lessons he may have learned from the later Eliot, but it connects also with his admiration for Thomas. His most obscure poems are too heavily committed to the convolutions of Thomas' poetic style ("The Sonnet of Hamlet," for example, in *A Private Country*), but in poems such as "Chanel" he achieves a symbolist confusion of the senses with an impressive economy of means.

The rapid succession of images is a basic element of Durrell's style. In the beautiful poem "Patmos" (*Collected Poems,* pp. 197–198), it is once again linked to a deliberate exploitation of syntax; the first stanza is one sentence, a single main clause ending in a full stop, and the second and last stanza can be "discovered" only by reading through to its end:

> When from the Grecian meadows
> Responsive rose the larks,
> Stiffly as if on strings,
> Ebbing, drew thin as tops
> While each in rising squeezed
> His spire of singing drops
> On that renewed landscape
> Like semen from the grape.

Strings, tops, spire, and semen—the sequence is disorientating, as is the discovery that to make sense this clause has to be latched on to all that precedes it. In the *Key to Modern Poetry* Durrell quotes with approval Rainer Maria Rilke's description of poems that "state lyric totals, instead of lining up the stages necessary to the result" (p. 37). The deliberate confusions of imagery and syntax in "Patmos" (allied with a musical and orderly use of rhyme) are an attempt to state a "lyric total," the sum of a moment of vision.

In his poetry of place and in his love poems, Durrell is faithful to the idea of the poet's privileged insight into a metaphysical and "extracausal" reality. This consistency of view may to some extent redeem even those poems, to be found especially in *Cities, Plains and People* (1946), in which the idiom is almost exclusively that of W. H. Auden. Poems such as "La Rochefoucauld," "On First Looking into Loeb's Horace," and "Poggio," for all that they echo another poet almost uncannily, are thoroughly Durrellian in their subject matter (the consequence of subjecting intuitive power to reason) and in their indifference to personal voice. When Durrell uses a basic Auden word such as "lucky," the effect is quite different because the context of belief is different: *"Partings like these are lucky. At least they wound"* (*Collected Poems,* p. 129). Durrell's revulsion from "the English death," which is a death of feeling, is emphatically not Auden's sense of happiness as purely gratuitous: "Lucky to love the new pansy railway" (*The English Auden* [1978], p. 152).

Durrell's ideas have their root in Eliot, symbolism, and English romanticism (he is anticipated, for example, by Samuel Coleridge in "The Eolian Harp": "O! The one Life within us and abroad, / Which meets all motion and becomes its soul . . .") but also in his reading of prophets and seers as widely distinguished as Freud, Lawrence, and Lao Tze. Among these an important place is occupied by the psychoanalytic healer Georg Groddeck, about whom Durrell writes at length in the *Key to Modern Poetry.* He reveres this unorthodox thinker because for him "the Whole was an unknown, a forever unknowable entity whose shadows and functions we are" (p. 75). More particularly, Groddeck thought of human beings as the means by which the unknown entity, the It, realized itself: "for Groddeck the whole psyche with its inevitable dualisms seemed merely a function of something else—an unknown quantity—which he chose to discuss under the name of the 'It' " (*Horizon,* 17 [1948], p. 385). It is as though Groddeck were describing the point of contact between "extracausal" reality and the world as ordinarily experienced. The full meaning of "Carol on Corfu" must include an allusion to this idea of a vital force that expresses itself equally in life and death, which is an unfolding of energy from a realm beyond reason.

Groddeck's teachings emphasize the incompleteness of the ego-consciousness and the coexistence of opposites within the It. The latter idea is of special importance to Durrell not only because of his belief in an "extracausal" reality where the mind has to "accept two contradictory ideas," but also, I think, because he thinks of himself as of divided inheritance, born of an Irish mother and an English father: "From my mother I inherited the Irish side of my character: laziness and bohemianism. From my father I acquired two qualities, quite foreign to the Irish: a love of order and a sense of responsibility. I am a mixture of all that" (*The Big Supposer,* p. 24).

PLAYS

THE divided or dual self—and it is significant that one cannot use only one of these terms—recurs throughout Durrell's work, in "Je est un autre," "Byron," "Self to Not-self," and other poems, but most clearly in his verse plays. In *Sappho* (1950) there are the twins, Pittakos and Phaon, man of action and man of contemplation; there are the two towns of Eresos, the old town sunk beneath the water in an earthquake and the new; and there are the two voices of Minos, one questioning the other —not to mention Sappho's own voice, which gives way in her to the voice of the oracle. In *Acte* (1964), apart from Fabius, "a Roman soldier who loves Scythia" and so betrays his Roman-ness, there is Nero, the mad poet (and enemy of "reason") who "wears a mask pushed on to the back of his head which, when he turns, gives the illusion of a second face which is exactly like his. . . ." In *An Irish Faustus* (1963), Mephisto is "almost the double" of Faust, a fact given much emphasis.

Durrell's interest in a self that is divided between ego and all that the ego suppresses and is not, would seem to promise distinguished dramatic writing; he is naturally drawn to the oppositions that are the stuff of good theater. But his plays have not become part of the modern repertoire. There are good reasons for this: *Sappho* is far too wordy, and even in the two later plays where the action develops at a better pace, difficulty arises with stilted dialogue.

Sappho is the story of a poet who is untrue to her inspiration when she falsifies the oracle; the consequence is political and personal disaster. Though the true poet Phaon rehearses Durrell's view of their kind—"For whom there are no single images / But a continual marriage of attributes" (p. 83) —his own style in this play and the others is full of single images, perhaps in consideration of the audience, that they may understand. The result is too often banal, as in Sappho's words to her daughter at the play's end:

> Weep, little Kleis. You shall weep for both of us,
> For the whole world if you have tears enough,
> And for yourself long after you imagine
> There are no tears left in the world to weep with.
> (p. 186)

The large gesture ("the whole world") is too much entangled with poeticality ("tears enough," "no tears left") to create the sense of personal and immediate utterance. *Sappho,* though it is an important repository for Durrell's philosophy, does not work.

Acte, like *Sappho,* is about art and life: Nero, the inferior artist, is outmaneuvered by Petronius Arbiter, who knows that "Yes, it *is* possible to become an adept of reality" (p. 75), and does so by not merely dying his death but "achieving" it. The trouble with this play is that the expository passages are solemn but unconvincing, and the emotions expressed are stagey rather than dramatic ("Who invented us? / Why are we here? Whither shall we vanish?" [p. 67]).

This makes the success of *An Irish Faustus* all the more remarkable. Faustus is not a poet, but he is a seer, much the same thing in Durrell. In the implausible Ireland of the play (mountains that are impassable six months of the year), he comes to terms with his own weakness, lives through his own despair, and emerges into a state of nonattached illumination where he can swap reminiscences with the master who has preceded him, Matthew the Hermit. When he asks what it is he has to do, Matthew replies:

> Hm. . . . If duty is what you cannot help,
> then I have none;
> For I am helping everything by doing
> nothing. I see you smile.
> I help the moon rise, the sun to set. I eat and
> drink.
> (pp. 87–88)

"I see you smile"—the ludicrous is everywhere in this play, with its mad queen, vampire king, and ring of alchemical gold, but the Eliotian dramatic style allows weight to none of this. The ironic structure of the drama in which Faustus rids himself of his demon is what is complemented by this deadpan style:

> when nothing begins to happen at long last
> Everything
> Begins to cohere, the dance of the pure forms
> begins.
> (p. 85)

This uses Eliot and parodies him too, and recalls that odd remark in the *Key to Modern Poetry:* "one should never forget that poetry, like life, is altogether too serious not to be taken lightly" (p. 90). *An Irish Faustus* is not the philosophical statement that it seems to be, but rather an act of provocation, and what is ludicrous in it is, more pointedly, also absurd in the modern sense, deliberately withholding its values from the audience.

CONCLUSION

THIS play sums up Durrell's poetic and dramatic work, which has the weaknesses and strengths of the ideas that underlie it. Though he is far from unintelligent about literature, as the *Key to Modern Poetry* often shows, he believes that intelligence has little to do with art of any kind. Art is *healing;* what it says is of secondary importance: "in understanding poetry it is always the words which get in the way. It is a great pity that we cannot inhale poems like scents" (p. 84). Such a view is very flattering to all that is extravagant and also to all that is slapdash and silly in Durrell's art; it accords with his ability to rate the later work of Edith Sitwell alongside that of Eliot and with much else of doubtful value in his critical work. It explains the relative infrequency of fully achieved poems in his oeuvre and the difficulty they present to us in perceiving them. At the same time Durrell exemplifies a late flowering of symbolist theory (the scents in the last quotation surely come from Huysmans' *À Rebours*) under the influence especially of Eliot and Thomas; his successful poems are success enough, a powerful rebuke to that form of rationalism which is also imaginative confinement. Above all, Durrell's work as a poet emphasizes the role of feeling and intuition in human experience. Though complicated by the poet's own doubts and hesitations about the role he has to play, a reflection of that dual inheritance which, in the promotion of his "Irishness," Durrell has attempted to forget, his achievement is a real one, significant in the history of English poetry, rich in personal significance, and challenging to every preconception we may have as to the place and function of poetry in society.

SELECTED BIBLIOGRAPHY

I. BIBLIOGRAPHY. A. G. Thomas and J. A. Brigham, *Lawrence Durrell: An Illustrated Checklist* (Carbondale, Ill., 1983), the indispensable guide for any student of Durrell, covers not only Durrell's own work in English but also translations, magazine articles, prefaces to the works of others, recordings, musical settings, radio, television and film, memoirs, and critical works by others.

II. COLLECTED WORKS. J. A. Brigham, ed., *Collected Poems 1931–74,* supersedes *Collected Poems* of 1960 (enl. 1968); *The Alexandria Quartet: Justine, Balthazar, Mountolive, Clea* (London, 1962), contains the four novels in one vol. with revised text and new preface; *Spirit of Place: Letters and Essays on Travel* (London, 1969), gathers essays and travel pieces together with letters and extracts from *Pied Piper of Lovers* and *Panic Spring,* two earlier novels.

III. SEPARATE WORKS. *Quaint Fragment* (London, 1931), poems; *Ten Poems* (London, 1932), poems; *Ballade of Slow Decay* (Bournemouth, 1932), poem; *Transition* (London, 1932), poems; *Pied Piper of Lovers* (London, 1935), novel; *Panic Spring* (London, 1937), novel, pub. under name Charles Norden; *The Black Book* (Paris, 1938; repub. London, 1973), fiction; *A Private Country* (London, 1943), poems; *Prospero's Cell: A Guide to the Landscape and Manners of the Island of Corcyra* (London, 1945), travel; *Zero, and Asylum in the Snow: Two Excursion into Reality* (Rhodes, 1946), included in *Spirit of Place; Cities, Plains and People* (London, 1946), poems; *Cefalû* (London, 1947), fiction, repr. with minor revisions as *The Dark Labyrinth* (1958); *On Seeming to Presume* (London, 1948), poems.

Sappho (London, 1950), play in verse; *Deus Loci: A Poem* (Ischia, 1950); *Key to Modern Poetry* (London, 1952), criticism, pub. in U.S. as *A Key to Modern British Poetry; Reflections on a Marine Venus: A Companion to the Landscape of Rhodes* (London, 1953); *The Tree of Idleness* (London, 1955), poems; *Private Drafts* (Nicosia, 1955), poems; *Bitter Lemons* (London, 1957), travel; *Esprit de Corps: Sketches from Diplomatic Life* (London, 1957), short stories; *Justine* (London, 1957), novel; *White Eagles over Serbia* (London, 1957), fiction; *Balthazar* (London, 1958), novel; *Stiff Upper Lip: Life Among the Diplomats* (London, 1958), short stories; *Mountolive* (London, 1958), novel; *Clea* (London, 1960), novel; *Beccafico* (Montpellier, 1963), essay; *An Irish Faustus: A Morality in Nine Scenes* (London, 1963), verse play; *Acte* (London, 1964), verse play; *Selected Poems, 1935–63* (London, 1964); *Sauve Qui Peut* (London, 1966), short stories; *The Ikons* (London, 1966), poems; *Tunc* (London, 1968), novel.

Nunquam (London, 1970), novel, sequel to *Tunc; The Red Limbo Lingo* (London, 1971), poems and prose fragments; *On the Suchness of the Old Boy* (London, 1972), poem; *Vega and Other Poems* (London, 1973); *The Plant-Magic Man* (Santa Barbara, Calif., 1973), prose; *The Best of Antrobus* (London, 1974), selected short stories; *Monsieur, or the Prince of Darkness* (London, 1974), novel; *Blue Thirst* (Santa Barbara, Calif., 1975), lectures; *Sicilian Carousel* (London, 1977), travel; *The Greek Islands* (London, 1978), travel; *Livia, or Buried Alive* (London, 1978), novel; *A Smile in the Mind's Eye* (St. Alban's, Hertfordshire, 1980), philosophical memoir; *Constance, or Solitary Practices* (London, 1982), novel; *Sebastian, or Ruling Passions* (London, 1983), novel; *Quinx, or the Ripper's Tale* (London, 1985), novel, completes the Avignon quintet, which begins with *Monsieur.*

IV. LETTERS AND INTERVIEWS. *Art and Outrage,* correspondence about H. Miller between A. Perlès and L. Durrell, with intermission by Miller (London, 1959); G. Wickes, ed., *Lawrence Durrell–Henry Miller: A Private Correspondence* (London, 1963); F. Barker, trans., *The Big Supposer: A Dialogue with Marc Alyn* (London, 1973); I. MacNiven and H. T. Moore, eds., *Literary Lifelines: The Richard Aldington–Lawrence Durrell Correspondence* (London, 1981).

V. BIOGRAPHICAL AND CRITICAL STUDIES. D. Stanford, *The Freedom of Poetry: Studies in Contemporary Verse* (London, 1947), contains critical essay on Durrell; G. Durrell, *My Family and Other Animals* (London, 1956), contains warm sketches by his brother of Durrell as a young man; *Two Cities,* I (15 April 1959), special issue on Durrell with contributions by H. Miller, A. Perlès, R. Aldington; G. Durrell, "Lawrence Durrell by His Brother Gerald," in *The Evening Standard* (5 Oct. 1961); A. Perlès, *My Friend Lawrence Durrell* (London, 1961); F. Kermode, "Durrell and Others," in *Puzzles and Epiphanies: Essays and Reviews 1958–61* (London, 1962); H. T. Moore, ed., *The World of Lawrence Durrell* (Carbondale, Ill., 1962); J. Unterecker, *Lawrence Durrell* (London, 1964); J. A. Weigel, *Lawrence Durrell* (London, 1965); A. Nin, *The Diary of Anais Nin 1934–39* (New York, 1967), and further diaries *1955–66* and *1966–74* (New York, 1976, 1980); *Modern Fiction Studies,* XIII, 3 (1967), special issue on Durrell; G. S. Fraser, *Lawrence Durrell: A Study* (London, 1968; rev. ed. 1973), contains bibliography and A. G. Thomas, "Recollections of a Durrell Collector."

A. W. Friedman, *Lawrence Durrell and the Alexandria Quartet* (Norman, Okla., 1970); *Entretiens, XXXII: Lawrence Durrell* (1973), contains contributions by H. Miller, D. Menuhin, A. Perlès, C. Logue; *Deus Loci: The Lawrence Durrell Newsletter,* I (1977–), contains memoirs, critical articles; *Labrys,* 5 (1979), special Durrell issue, contains reminiscences by J. Fanchette, D. Gascoyne, G. Durrell, and noteworthy article by T. Rugset on *Tunc–Nunquam;* L. E. Cawley, "Chaos to Cosmos: Form as Meaning in *Tunc* and *Nunquam,*" Oslo University doctoral dissertation (1984; unpublished), indispensable reading for those seeking detailed discussion of double novel.

PATRICK WHITE

(1912–   )

R. F. Brissenden

INTRODUCTION

AMONG Australian writers the one who is best known outside his own country is unquestionably Patrick White. His being awarded the Nobel Prize in 1973 naturally had something to do with this. But he had enjoyed an international reputation since the publication of *The Tree of Man* in 1955. Enthusiastic reviewers of this, his fourth novel, set him in the company of most of the great novelists of the last hundred years. From that time on his work has been translated into several languages. The prize, moreover, came not at the end of his career but when he was at the height of his abilities. The works he has produced since then include some of his most powerful and substantial novels, a number of plays, a volume of short stories (his second), and an autobiography, *Flaws in the Glass.*

To see White primarily as an Australian writer is in some ways to do him an injustice. Although with one exception—*The Living and the Dead*—his novels are set predominantly in Australia or have Australian characters, they do not belong to what has generally been regarded as the Australian literary tradition, a tradition summed up best, perhaps, in Joseph Furphy's laconic comment on his own novel *Such Is Life*: "temper, democratic, bias, offensively Australian"; and most clearly exemplified in Henry Lawson's naturalistic and beautifully understated stories of bush life. White in most of his work writes as if Furphy and Lawson had never existed. This is not surprising: he received his education in England and spent much of his early life away from Australia. Yet he does not clearly fit into the normal English literary patterns either. During his formative years the writers who influenced him most profoundly were French and German. Since he read modern languages at Cambridge and spent a considerable amount of time on the continent, it is perhaps understandable that, when he began to write, he should have been more familiar with the work of Heinrich von Kleist and Georg Büchner, of Honoré de Balzac, Marcel Proust and the symbolists, than with the novels of Samuel Richardson, George Eliot, or Henry James. Yet he was in no way insulated from contemporary English writing: his first novels were produced in an atmosphere conditioned and in part created by the achievements of James Joyce, D. H. Lawrence, and Virginia Woolf, and they bear the evidence of this.

The tradition to which his fiction belongs is in the broadest sense European—but only in the broadest sense. Although he may seem atypical, White is inescapably Australian. Indeed it was not until he returned, both in fact and in imagination, to his own country that he began to produce work of any real authority and distinction. His talents are such that he would almost certainly have become an unusually good novelist no matter where he chose to write. But Australia has clearly presented him with just that challenge and that stimulus which were necessary to develop his powers to the full. If he did not in some sense belong to Australia he could not feel such an urgent necessity to come to terms with it. He brings to the encounter, however, a sensibility at once more complex and more cosmopolitan than that possessed by most Australian writers.

Everything White has produced bears the impress of an authentically creative imagination; and nowhere is this creative power more apparent than in his treatment of the Australian scene. Indeed it could be argued that Australia has supplied him with the only medium, the only terminology, through which he could make fully meaningful his intensely personal view of the world. As a result he has achieved in his later novels and plays a vision of life that is both distinctively individual and generally relevant, a vision that illuminates in a fresh, sometimes strange, but always revealing manner the familiar universe, and that at the same time adds a quickening and transforming element to our experience of it. What White offers us, of course, is not the "real" Australia (whatever that may be) but a world of his own making. Like Feodor Dostoevsky's Russia or William Faulkner's Yoknapatawpha County, White's Australia reflects and incorporates its nonfictional counterpart, and it has grown out of the author's struggle to render reality in terms of art. But the world he has brought into existence is animated by its own inner vitality. The name of Voss can be found nowhere in the history of Australian exploration, nor can the suburb of Sarsaparilla be discovered on any map of Sydney, but their existence is undeniable. "Knowledge was never a matter of geography," says Laura Trevelyan in *Voss.* "Quite the reverse, it overflows all maps that exist. Perhaps true knowledge only comes of death by torture in the country of the mind." It is a mark of White's quality that he is one of those few writers who have created their own recognizable countries of the mind.

LIFE AND PUBLICATIONS

PATRICK WHITE belongs to a relatively old and well-established Australian family. Paradoxically enough, this explains why he should have been born and educated in England. His parents had sufficient means to travel fairly extensively, and it was during one of their visits to Europe that Patrick Victor Martindale White was born, in Knightsbridge, London, on 28 May 1912. Six months later the family was back in Australia, where Patrick was to remain until he was thirteen.

The money that enabled his father to lead the life of a gentleman of leisure came mainly from the land. In the 1820's Mr. White's grandfather had settled in the Hunter River Valley, near Muswellbrook; and today several of his descendants are "on the land" in New South Wales. By the time Patrick was born the family was thoroughly Australian. England, however, was still regarded as "home," and it was almost inevitable that he should be sent to the Old Country for his schooling. At the age of thirteen he was duly enrolled at Cheltenham College, where he "loathed every minute" of the four and a half years he spent there.

When he came back to Australia, he followed another familiar pattern by putting in a couple of years jackerooing, or working as an apprentice hand on sheep and cattle ranches, or "stations." He lived on stations in the Monaro, the high foothills of the Snowy Mountains, and later at Walgett. But station life was boring to a young man who had already decided that he was going to be a writer. He produced novels in his spare time, which nobody would publish, and prepared for the entrance examinations for King's College, Cambridge.

In 1932 he returned to England and spent the next three years reading modern languages at King's. During the long vacations he wandered about Germany; and, of course, he kept on writing. Two plays (now lost) that he wrote at this time were staged briefly at Bryant's Playhouse, a little theater in Sydney; and when he came down from Cambridge in 1936 he was as interested in writing drama as he was in writing fiction.

For the next three years he lived in London. His friends were mainly artists, like the Australian painter Roy le Maistre, and theater people. He wrote sketches for revues at the Little Theatre and the Gate Theatre; published in 1935 the usual slim volume, *The Ploughman, and Other Poems;* had some short stories accepted by *The London Mercury;* and in 1939 he brought out his first novel, *Happy Valley.*

His second book, *The Living and the Dead,* appeared in 1941. By this time, however, the young novelist had been caught up, like everyone else, in the war. For the next four years he was in the Intelligence branch of the RAF, stationed mainly in the Middle East: Palestine, Egypt, and, in the concluding phases of the war, Greece. In Alexandria he had met a Greek officer, Manoly Lascaris, who was to become his friend and lifetime companion. The Lascaris family had fled from Smyrna during the war with Turkey. Many of them now lived in Athens, and White, who was stationed there during the last twelve months of the war, saw a great deal of them.

Throughout these years his memory and imagination had been haunted increasingly by visions of the Australian landscape. London, when he was demobilized there, seemed to him an intellectual and artistic graveyard; and, although ideas for new work were crowding in upon his mind, he realized that he would have to get away from the place if he were to survive as a writer. And so, in 1946, he returned to Australia. Except for occasional trips abroad—including a return to Greece described vividly in *Flaws in the Glass*—he has lived there ever since.

PATRICK WHITE

Before leaving England White wrote two plays, *Return to Abyssinia* and *The Ham Funeral. Return to Abyssina* (now lost) was produced for a short season at the Boltons Theatre in London; *The Ham Funeral,* a tragi-farce in two acts, had to wait thirteen years before it was finally staged in Adelaide in 1961. The production was an unqualified success, and something of an embarrassment to the Adelaide Festival Committee members, who had refused to accept the play because they considered it too daring and controversial. While in London White also commenced a novel, *The Aunt's Story.* When this appeared in 1948 it received favorable reviews in both Britain and the United States, and the author justifiably felt that it marked a clear and exciting stage in his development as a writer. *The Aunt's Story* is an assured and subtle study of loneliness; and in this novel, as in his play *The Ham Funeral,* White achieves for the first time his own distinctive style: nobody else could have written these works. In subject, treatment, and in the attitudes they embody, they are strikingly individual.

White may have needed Australia, but Australia, apparently, did not need him: *The Aunt's Story* raised only the faintest ripple of interest among his fellow countrymen, and no Australian theater was willing to risk attempting *The Ham Funeral.* Driven in upon himself by the blank indifference with which his work was received, he found that he was no longer able to write. He found, too, that he was having to rediscover the country he had left fifteen years before: "I had to re-learn the Australian language."

With Manoly Lascaris, who had now joined him in Australia, he bought Dogwoods, an old house standing on six acres of ground at Castle Hill, then a scattered rural suburb on the edge of Sydney, where the bush mingles with the bedraggled outskirts of the city. They grew flowers and vegetables (for sale), bred goats and dogs, and sold milk and cream. And the novelist looked at his new neighbors, the people among whom he had chosen to live, wondered about them, and eventually began to write about them. The result was *The Tree of Man,* a novel in which White has said he "wanted to try to suggest . . . every possible aspect of life, through the lives of an ordinary man and woman . . . to discover the extraordinary behind the ordinary, the mystery and poetry which could alone make bearable the lives of such people" ("The Prodigal Son," *Australian Letters* I, 3 [1958]).

The Tree of Man was published first in the United States in 1955, and then in Great Britain the following year. It had the reception every author dreams about: reviewers hailed it as a great novel and White was acclaimed as a major writer. In Australia, however, the response to begin with was tepid and confused, although not so deliberately hostile as the author's understandably bitter comment—"here . . . the dingoes are howling unmercifully"—may suggest. The initial coolness gave way almost immediately to a wide acknowledgment of his outstanding talent.

The Tree of Man was followed in 1957 by *Voss,* an almost hallucinatory study of an attempt to cross the Australian continent from east to west, and in 1961 by *Riders in the Chariot,* an apocalyptic, allegorical, visionary novel, set mainly in Sarsaparilla, White's imaginary outer-Sydney suburb. Sarsaparilla is also the setting for *The Solid Mandala* (1966) and for several of the short stories in *The Burnt Ones,* a collection published in 1964.

After the successful production of *The Ham Funeral,* White turned again to the drama and wrote three more plays, *The Season at Sarsaparilla, A Cheery Soul,* and *Night on Bald Mountain.* These were all successfully produced and were collected and published under the title *Four Plays* in 1965. In 1977 a fifth play, *Big Toys,* was produced. It was published in the following year. Since then *The Night the Prowler* (1978), originally a short story, *Netherwood* (1983), and *Signal Driver* (1983) have been staged; but these last three plays have not yet appeared in print.

When White wrote *The Tree of Man* he called the district in which his ordinary man and woman, Stan and Amy Parker, lived, Durilgai, "which means 'fruitful.' " At that time Castle Hill, where he lived himself, was still almost a country town. But Showground Road, on which Dogwoods once stood in relative quietness, was eventually to become a roaring thoroughfare. "The spoilers . . . moved in," the surrounding paddocks were subdivided, and the fibro homes and the brick boxes began to go up. The high hedges around Dogwoods, and the books and paintings—mostly by contemporary Australian artists—that lined its walls were for a while sufficient bulwark against the gray encroaching tide of development. But in 1963 White and his friend decided to give up the battle and retreat to the city.

But the writer was to have his revenge—and also to pay nostalgic homage to the place where he had lived for sixteen years—in the creation of Sarsaparilla. This is the suburb that forms the setting for many of the novels, stories, and plays that he wrote in the 1960's—and whatever Sarsaparilla may mean it is certainly not "fruitful."[1]

> When Xanadu had been shaved right down to a bald, red, rudimentary hill, they began to erect the fibro homes. Two or three days, or so it seemed, and there were the combs of homes clinging to the bare earth. The rotary clotheslines had risen, together with the Iceland poppies, and after them the glads. The privies were never so private that it was not possible to listen to the drone of someone else's blowflies. The wafer-walls of the new homes would rub together at night, and sleepers might have been encouraged to enter one another's dreams, if these had not been similar. Sometimes the rats of anxiety could be heard gnawing already at bakelite, or plastic, or recalcitrant maidenhead. So that, in the circumstances, it was not unusual for people to run outside and jump into their cars. All of Sunday they would visit, or be visited, though sometimes they would cross one another, midway, while remaining unaware of it. Then, on finding nothing at the end, they would drive around, or around. They would drive and look for something to look at.
>
> (*Riders in the Chariot,* ch. 17)

Sarsaparilla, like Queequeg's island in *Moby Dick,* "is not down on any map." But then, as Melville says, "true places never are."

White's next two novels, *The Vivisector* (1970), the story of an Australian painter, and *The Eye of the Storm* (1973), a study of old age, death, and spirituality, are set mainly in Sydney. These were followed by *A Fringe of Leaves* (1976), the central character of which is based on Mrs. Eliza Frazer, a woman who survived a shipwreck on the Queensland coast in 1836 and six weeks of life among hostile aborigines; and by *The Twyborn Affair* (1979). This, his last novel, is a long, complex, and engrossing study of ambivalent sexuality. It contains some of White's most lyrical and powerful writing. This was followed two years later by his autobiography, *Flaws in the Glass.*

White's other publications include another volume of short stories, *The Cockatoos* (1974), and a number of plays. A film, *The Night the Prowler,* has been made, based on his short story of the same name; and in 1986 the opera, *Voss,* with libretto by David Malouf and music by Richard Meale, had its premiere at the Adelaide Festival.

[1]It is the name of a not very pleasant drink made from the root of *Smilax officinalis.* In Australia, a small native creeper with purple flowers, *Hardenbergia violecea,* is also called sarsaparilla.

HAPPY VALLEY

THE bleak but savagely comic vision of suburban hell that dominates the concluding scenes of *Riders in the Chariot* doubtless found its immediate inspiration in White's experience of life in the outer environs of modern Sydney. But emptiness, sterility, and rootlessness seem always to have struck him as dominant elements in Australian life. Or it may be more accurate to say that these—together with the isolation of the individual—are aspects of human life in general by which he has always been haunted and obsessed, and for which the Australian milieu, from the beginning, has seemed to offer him a peculiarly fitting symbol.

In *Happy Valley,* his first novel, the symbolic implications of the Australian scene are explored awkwardly and tentatively, but with an imaginative power and insight that, though uneven, are undeniably impressive. Happy Valley itself, the township that ironically (and not untypically) gives its name to the novel, is an isolated settlement in the foothills of the Snowy Mountains—snowbound in winter, drought-stricken in summer. White's descriptions of it finely evoke that air of impermanence which characterizes so many outback towns: collections of tin-roofed buildings that seem haphazardly set down, superimposed on the landscape rather than organically related to it. And the brooding (but relatively unfocused) sense of moral disquiet that permeates his presentation of the township and its people prophetically foreshadows the mood of *Riders in the Chariot:*

> Happy Valley became that peculiarly tenacious scab on the body of the brown earth. You waited for it to come away leaving a patch of pinkness beneath. You waited and it did not happen, and because of this you felt that there was something in its nature peculiarly perverse. . . . It seemed to have no design. . . . You anticipated a moral doomsday, but it did not come.
>
> (ch. 11)

The moral doomsday eventually descends on Sarsaparilla, when the perversity that lies beneath the emptiness of suburbia expresses itself in the mock crucifixion of Himmelfarb, the Jew. There is even, in *Happy Valley,* as Vincent Buckley has noted, a possible anticipation of the incident itself, in the passing reference to the drover who "ran amuck and crucified a roadman on a dead tree. . . . It was like a scarecrow . . . only it didn't scare."

The novel opens in midwinter on a note of sterility: Dr. Halliday, exhausted after an all-night struggle to deliver a stillborn child, skis back down the valley and observes a hawk hovering in the chill, morning air. "All its life it would probably know no pain," he thinks,

> not like Mrs. Chalker writhing about on the bed at Kambala. The hawk was absolved from this, absorbed as an agent into the whole of this frozen landscape, into the mountains that emanated in their silence a dull, frozen pain while remaining exempt from it. There was a kind of universal cleavage between these, the agents, and their objects: the woman at the hotel forcing the dead child out of her womb, or the township of Happy Valley with its slow festering sore of painfully little intrigue.

Despite the force with which the feeling of profound alienation is conveyed, the language here is tortuous and fumbling (what exactly do the words "agent" and "objects" mean, for instance?) and the symbolism rather obvious. It would be easy to dismiss the passage as a clumsy example of the pathetic fallacy: mountains do not, as a matter of fact, emanate pain or any other human feeling. But the notion of pathetic fallacy is itself perhaps misleading: the relation of the individual to his material environment is a two-way affair—while each of us invests the world about us with his own moods and emotions, these in turn are modified and partly brought into being by our surroundings. White's awareness of the complexity of this relation, and his ability to suggest the uniqueness of each individual's vision of the world, are among his most distinctive talents. If the attempts at impressionism in *Happy Valley* are sometimes more deliberate than successful, they look forward to the brilliant and subtle writing of the later novels, where the way in which characters such as Theodora Goodman, Voss, or Miss Hare experience their worlds is used to suggest the essential singularity of each person.

No one character is strong enough to dominate *Happy Valley,* however: the point of view is located somewhat unsatisfactorily in a disembodied narrator, and the action is resolved in a disconcertingly melodramatic manner. Again one is reminded of one of the author's later novels, *Riders in the Chariot,* where the lives of several people in a small community are shown developing in relative isolation from each other, but along paths that inexorably converge. In *Riders in the Chariot* this final confluence is made meaningful (perhaps not altogether successfully) in terms of myth and allegory. In *Happy Valley* the contrivance is embarrassingly apparent. Nonetheless, White does succeed in this first novel in establishing his highly idiosyncratic sense of the community as a social group, in which the lives of its individual members do not so much interact as impinge, strike against each other tangentially and almost at random, with results that are often grotesquely disproportionate to the slightness of the initial glancing contact. In *Happy Valley* the beating of a child by an overwrought teacher leads eventually to murder, death, and the frustration of plans in the lives of people only remotely connected with the initial incident.

Life, of course, is like that: the universe seems at times to strike people down with blind malignance. But White obviously wants to say something more than this. As an epigraph to the novel he quotes some words of Mahatma Gandhi: "It is impossible to do away with the law of suffering which is the one indispensable condition of our being. Progress is to be measured by the amount of suffering undergone . . . the purer the suffering the greater is the progress."

The characters in *Happy Valley* suffer, but they do not in any clear sense progress; mainly because the pain they endure is brought about not so much by their own actions as by the random cruelty of life. When Dr. Halliday tries to leave his wife and family and run away with Alys Browne, it is sheer bad luck (or the author's manipulation) that destroys their chance of happiness. When the headlights of his car show up a dead body on the road, Halliday is faced with a responsibility that, as a physician, he cannot evade. The implications are clear enough, but the total impact of the novel blurs them. The reader is left not so much with the impression that these people have learned something valuable through suffering as with the feeling that the anguish of living for most of us is futile and meaningless.

PATRICK WHITE

THE LIVING AND THE DEAD

IN technique his second book, *The Living and the Dead,* shows a remarkable advance on *Happy Valley.* White handles a large and varied group of characters and a complicated series of events with skill and assurance; and the tone of the novel is firmly controlled, although it is not yet completely his own. It is in no clear sense derivative, but there is an air of Virginia Woolf, Aldous Huxley, and T. S. Eliot of *The Waste Land* pervading its pages. It is very much of its period.

Set in London, mainly in the 1930's, it is concerned for the most part with three characters and their response to life: Elyot Standish, his sister, Eden, and their mother. Mrs. Standish, aging, delicately sensual, charming, and faintly ridiculous, is a finely observed and beautifully sustained piece of characterization. She is, however, clearly not intended to occupy the center of the stage. The main emphasis falls on her two children: Elyot, a donnish, reserved, and detached young man who holds himself aloof from life, participating in it and observing it without ever committing himself to it; and Eden, who throws herself impulsively and unselfconsciously into experience. Eden falls in love with Joe Barnett, a working man, the cousin of the family servant and a socialist. Joe goes to Spain and is killed; and Eden decides to follow him. Her decision is not basically political, however: "I'm sick to death of politics. . . . The political lie," she tells Joe.

> Oh, I can believe, as sure as I can breathe, feel, in the necessity for change. But it's a change from wrong to right, which is nothing to do with category. . . . We were not born to indifference. Indifference denies all the evidence of life. This is what I want to believe. I want to unite all those who have the capacity for living. . . . I want to oppose them to the destroyers, to the dealers in words, to the diseased, to the most fatally diseased—the indifferent.
>
> (ch. 8)

Elyot, only superficially indifferent, is shocked into a sense of purpose—his own purpose—by Eden's departure, and also by his failure to stop a drunk from falling under a bus (one is reminded of the corpse in the roadway in *Happy Valley,* of the old man that Stan Parker sees in the floods in *The Tree of Man,* and of Himmelfarb's failure to be with his wife on the night the Jews are arrested in Holunderthal). As the novel closes, Elyot, like the young man in *The Ham Funeral,* leaves the house in Ebury Street in which he has existed for so long and walks out, not merely into the London night, but into life. He has no apparent goal, but he is at least liberated from his family and the past:

> A bus received Elyot Standish. It was any bus. He was bound nowhere in particular. There were no reservations of time or place, no longer even the tyranny of a personal routine. . . . He yawned. He felt like someone who had been asleep, and had only just woken.

There is much to admire in this novel, but the reader can be forgiven for feeling a certain disappointment when he reaches the end. Despite the brilliance of certain passages it has a curiously muffled air: the image of London shrouded in fog appears (rather unfairly) to dominate it. And ultimately there seems to be no striking difference between the living who know themselves and have learned to live with the knowledge, and the dead who know nothing.

THE AUNT'S STORY

THE awakening of Elyot Standish may form an anticlimactic conclusion to *The Living and the Dead,* but there can be no question of its importance in White's development. The successful completion of this novel marks the end of his apprenticeship; and his next work, *The Aunt's Story,* signalizes just as unmistakably his full discovery of himself as a writer. In some ways he has never produced anything finer than this somewhat slight but beautifully wrought and finished book. In the central character and the situation in which she is placed White found, for the first time, something wholly congenial to his particular talent and cast of mind; and what he then discovered has remained with him as a continuing source of inspiration. The human problems that he explores in this novel are obviously, for him at least, fundamental and abiding ones: they are, basically, the questions with which he is preoccupied in all the major work he has since produced.

On the title page to part one of *The Aunt's Story* the author has placed a quotation from Olive Schreiner:

> She thought of the narrowness of the limits within which a human soul may speak and be understood by its nearest of mental kin, and of how soon it reaches that solitary land of the individual experience, in which no fellow footfall is ever heard.

It is a passage that could serve as an epigraph to almost everything he has written. Indeed it seems at times that White is moved most deeply not by specific emotions, incidents, or characters, but by the general condition of solitariness from which none of us can ever escape completely. His work is haunted by the sense that some element in all experiences—perhaps the most important—must remain private, personal, and incommunicable. And some of his most distinctive and successful achievements as a novelist have resulted from his attempt to convey the uniqueness of personality, the special qualities that distinguish one person's vision of the world from another's.

It is this which makes *The Aunt's Story* such an impressive piece of fiction: we are made to see the world through the eyes of the central character, Theodora Goodman, but at the same time we are never allowed to forget that most people look at things in a very different way, and that Theodora herself must appear to them as rather strange and puzzling, a person at once comic and pathetic, and always faintly disturbing.

Awkward, shy, proud, and physically not very attractive, Theodora is one of those who can never deceive herself into forgetting that "there is no lifeline to other lives." The basic source of her isolation, however, is a peculiar honesty and intensity of vision. She observes herself and others with a naked, innocent, and painfully uncompromising eye: it is this which cuts her off from her fellows, and which finally drives her into the comfortable refuge of insanity. "You'll see a lot of funny things, Theodora Goodman," the Man who was Given his Dinner prophetically tells her. "You'll see them because you've eyes to see. And they'll break you." And Miss Spofforth, her teacher (herself a lonely old maid), recognizes that Theodora is one of those who will "see clearly, beyond the bone," but who will suffer because, although honest, she is barren; lacking "the artist's vanity, which is moved finally to express itself in objects," she will be rewarded only by "moments of passing affection, through which the opaque world will become transparent."

Theodora is the first of White's *illuminati,* the forerunner of Laura Trevelyan and Voss, of mad Miss Hare and Himmelfarb, of Miss Quodling, the old goat woman of his last play, *Night on Bald Mountain,* indeed of all those who have been at once blessed and cursed with the ability to see with unusual clarity; and who have as well, perhaps, a sense of perfection, an awareness, as William Blake put it, of "the infinite in everything," an intuition that behind or immanent in the world of ordinary, imperfect experience, there is another world of timeless order and beauty. As her name implies, Theodora Goodman has a special virtue, and it is the gift of God.

For Theodora this sense of otherness is awakened first by her vision of Meroë. The first Meroë was the ancient capital of Ethiopia, ruled by a dynasty of queens. Meroë is also the name of the homestead on which Theodora Goodman spends the first twenty-odd years of her life. Why this substantial but otherwise rather ordinary Australian country house should have been given such an exotic name no one knows. And when her father tells her that "there is another Meroë . . . a dead place in the black country of Ethiopia," Theodora is unaccountably troubled:

> . . . she could not, she did not wish to, believe in the second Meroë. She could not set down on the black grass of the country that was called Ethiopia their own yellow stone. . . .
>
> . . . she wanted to escape from this dead place with the suffocating cinder breath. She looked with caution at the yellow face of the house, at the white shells in its placid, pocked stone. Even in sunlight the hills surrounding Meroë were black. Her own shadow was rather a suspicious rag. So that from what she saw and sensed, the legendary landscape became a fact, and she could not break loose from an expanding terror.
>
> Only in time the second Meroë became a dim and accepted apprehension lying quietly at the back of the mind. She was free to love the first. It was something to touch. She rubbed her cheek against the golden stone. . . . It was Our Place. Possession was a peaceful mystery.
> (ch. 2)

As a child Theodora may be able to accept the realities of ordinary life, the certainties of yellow stone, peacefully and unquestioningly, but as a woman she finds them increasingly difficult. Living in the world of normality becomes in the end an unbearable torture, far more terrifying than the legendary landscape of Meroë; and as she begins to lose her hold on sanity the image of Ethiopia, black and burning, increasingly dominates her imagination. "I have seen and done," she writes to her sister, "and the time has come at last to return to Abyssinia." She is in fact returning to Australia from a world tour; but in the middle of America she leaves the train that has been moving across the endless summer plains of yellow corn and wanders off into her own black Abyssinian inner world. The counterpoint of black and yellow, one of the most subtle and beautiful features of the novel, is resolved in the concluding paragraph as Theodora puts on her hat with its black rose: "Her face was long and yellow under the great black hat. The hat sat straight, but the doubtful rose trembled and glittered, leading a life of its own."

Meroë has triumphed: she has indeed returned "to Abyssinia." But Abyssinia means much more than madness: Abyssinia is the dream of perfection, the dream that in Theodora's case has led to madness because she "cannot reconcile joy and sorrow . . . or flesh and marble, or illusion and reality, or life and death."

The phrase "return to Abyssinia," as Manfred Mackenzie and Ian Donaldson have pointed out, has implications that extend beyond this particular novel. For one thing it forms the title of White's play, now lost, which was produced in London shortly before he wrote *The Aunt's Story.* The phrase is taken from Samuel Johnson's *Rasselas,* in fact from the ironic concluding sentence: "They deliberated a while what was to be done, and resolved, when the inundation should cease, to return to Abyssinia." It is no more possible for Rasselas and his companions to return to the valley of perfection than it is for mankind to go back to its state of antediluvian happiness.

But the Abyssinian motif appears to have been present in his work from the beginning: the title of his first novel, *Happy Valley,* by a fortunate accident also occurs in Rasselas, although when he wrote *Happy Valley* White had not yet read Johnson's Abyssinian tale. The title of his first collection of short stories, however, *The Burnt Ones,* seems to me to have a clear (though again perhaps not deliberate) Abyssinian ambience. (It is initially the literal translation of a modern Greek phrase, *Oi Kaymenoi,* which has the colloquial significance of "the poor unfortunates.") According to one derivation of the word, "Ethiopian" means "one who is burnt" (by the sun, presumably), and the ancients thought of Ethiopia as the land of fire and monsters. Pliny in his *Natural History* remarks, "It is by no means surprising that the outermost districts of this region produce animal and human monstrosities, considering the capacity of the mobile element of fire to mould their bodies and carve their outlines."

White's "burnt ones," of whom Theodora is the first clear example, have all been molded, at times distorted, by the fires of life—but many of them have also been involved at some climactic moment in their lives in actual conflagrations. Theodora is struck by lightning, and the final stage of her madness is precipitated by the burning down of the Hôtel du Midi. The bushfire in *The Tree of Man* not only destroys Glastonbury, the pseudo-baronial mansion of Mr. Armstrong the butcher, but it also burns off the beautiful Madelaine's hair, thus shattering Amy Parker's Bovaryesque dreams, and it gives Stan Parker a sudden blinding vision of life outside his own small world. In *Voss* the last ordeal of self-discovery through which the explorers pass takes place in a fiery, waterless desert, and it is paralleled by Laura Trevelyan's burning fever. Voss had indeed already foretold their fate to one of his party, Frank Le Mesurier: "In this disturbing country . . . you will be burnt up most likely, you will have the flesh torn from your bones, you will be tortured most probably in many horrible and primitive ways, but you will realize that genius of which you sometimes suspect you are possessed." And as the expedition enters its last desert, Le Mesurier remarks: "Dying is creation. . . . In the process of burning it is the black that gives up the gold." The Chariot in *Riders in the Chariot* is, of course, a chariot of fire; and Miss Hare, alone in Xanadu, can even perhaps be seen as the Abyssinian maid of Coleridge's poem; she has certainly, like the other three *illuminati,* "drunk the milk of paradise." One of them, Himmelfarb, also suffers ordeal by fire several times: in the Holunderthal purge, in the destruction of the camp at Friedensdorf, and finally in the burning down of his house in Sarsaparilla. And the play *Night on Bald Mountain* concludes with a vision of the holocaust of atomic war, seen with faint hope as a purifying fire from which a world "fit for goats and men" may emerge.

The universal vision that White attempts to summon up on the heights of Bald Mountain may seem far removed from the world of Theodora Goodman. But, like so many other things, it is implicit in *The Aunt's Story,* which as well as being an excellent novel in itself forms a most illuminating introduction to White's work as a whole.

PATRICK WHITE

THE TREE OF MAN

The Tree of Man, which first brought White to general attention, remains in some ways his most impressive achievement. It is not difficult to see why people should have responded so enthusiastically to this massive novel. It is a positive, poetic, affirmative work in which the writer dares to suggest that the lives of even the most ordinary people can have some significant shape, structure, and value. Moreover, he attempts to do this in the large, old-fashioned, conventional manner by telling us the life story of his characters. In theory nothing looks simpler; in practice nothing is more difficult. The secondhand bookstores are littered with hundreds of family sagas that no one will ever read again. White's successful handling of such a traditional form clearly invites the comparisons that have been made with D. H. Lawrence and Leo Tolstoy.

In outline the novel is uncomplicated and direct. It opens with a man alone, except for his horse and dog, in the virgin bush. He stops and makes his camp between "two big stringybarks . . . rising above the involved scrub with the simplicity of true grandeur." He establishes a farm, marries, has children and grandchildren and dies. By the time of his death his farm has been reduced to a pocket of land surrounded by the enveloping flood of suburbia, the respectable brick houses, "deep purple, clinker blue, ox blood and public lavatory." But "in the end there are the trees. These still stand in the gully behind the house, on a piece of poor land that nobody wants to use." And through them, as the book closes, walks the dead man's grandson, "with his head drooping as he increased in stature. Putting out shoots of green thought. So that, in the end, there was no end."

White's main intention, clearly, is to give a comprehensive picture of the life of a man and his family, a group who can be taken as representative of common humanity, but whose lives, like the two towering stringybarks, stand out with a distinct shape of their own against the involved and meaningless tangle of society. In general he succeeds remarkably well: Stan and Amy Parker, as he presents them, assume a genuinely grand simplicity. Among the weaknesses already hinted at is, most noticeably, a striving for effect that leads occasionally to heavy-handed attempts at symbolism (as in the bush-fire sequence) or to a stylistic deliberateness that is mannerist if not precious. But the underlying structure of the novel—which is organic rather than obviously artificial—is vital enough to make such flaws seem unimportant. The whole book is pervaded by a sense of the larger rhythms of life, the endless cycles of birth, growth, reproduction, decay, and death to which we will contribute and by which we are all subsumed.

The pattern of the novel is symphonic: the four parts, with their unobtrusive symbolic coloring, develop within themselves and are related to each other like four movements in a piece of music. In part one the time is usually morning, the season spring, and the imagery is all of young, fresh, growing things—like the young cabbages:

> In the clear morning of those early years the cabbages stood out for the woman more distinctly than other things, when they were not melting, in a tenderness of light.
>
> The young cabbages, that were soon a prospect of veined leaves, melted in the mornings of thawing frost. Their blue and purple flesh ran together with the silver of water, the jewels of light, in the smell of warming earth.
>
> (ch. 4)

In part four, in the fading winter of her days, Amy Parker's memory of the cabbages comes back like a *leitmotif,* a musical phrase:

> One day as Amy Parker was walking between the cabbages, as was her custom now, she was trying to remember something. Some restlessness had begun to possess her, of association. Then it was her youth that began to come back in the world of cabbages. She heard the dray come up with the mound of blue cabbages, and the snap of straps in the frost, as putting her shoulders through the window she spoke to her husband. She was remembering all mornings. And the little ears of cabbage seedlings that he stuck into the earth, into the holes that he had made with a shovel handle. She remembered the arms of her husband as they worked in the sunlight, the little hairs on the forearms and the veins at the wrists. It seemed to her suddenly as if she would not see him again.
>
> (ch. 21)

Later still, when she is older, they remain for her a symbol of happiness, even though by now she has forgotten what it was about them that gave her such delight. "She would come to him often amongst the cabbages. They were happy then, warming themselves on flat words and their nearness to each other."

As Vincent Buckley has amply demonstrated in

his excellent essay on *The Tree of Man,* its manifold and beautifully organized structure is one of its most impressive features. Nonetheless, it tends at times to dwarf the people, just as the style does when it assumes Lawrencian and biblical overtones, and Stan and Amy are described with elemental simplicity as "the man" and "the woman." Stan Parker, in particular, seems to become only intermittently the character the author wants him to be. He is convincing as an old man and he is convincing as a young man; but somewhere in between there is a gap: one cannot quite understand how old Mr. Parker, with his fragmentary revelations of the immanence of God, has developed out of young Stan, who gave no obvious sign to the casual speculator that "his soul . . . might not harden in the end into the neat self-contained shape it is desirable souls should take."

There are times when Stan is somehow not sufficiently interesting to bear the symbolic weight the author wants him to carry. The characterization of Amy Parker, however, is difficult to fault: she is a triumph of observation and creative imagination. There is no break in the growth and development of her character; it seems to broaden and mature as steadily and inevitably as her thickening body, or as her wilderness of a garden that eventually almost envelops the house. The picture the author gives of her gradual but inevitable decline into old age is remarkably convincing and moving. It is compassionate without being sentimental, tender without being condescending and, despite the pathos and terror of old age, often surprisingly humorous. There is much in White's work—especially his later work—that is harsh, angry, and even slightly repellent: but the spirit that animates his presentation of Amy Parker and her husband is one of love and sympathy.

Yet the most memorable aspect of his rendering of the marriage of these two people is the way in which he suggests the waxing and waning not so much of their *love* for each other and for their children, as of their *understanding.* Love is there: it is what each seeks in the other and it is what grows between them. But they are driven by an even deeper hunger to communicate, a hunger that is satisfied rarely and imperfectly, and that, especially for the woman, remains a source of continual frustration. They never attain the rapport they long for with their children: and, as the years pass, Stan and Amy, though still loving and needing each other, become locked more and more securely within the circles of their own souls:

> Stan Parker would sometimes fail to recognise his wife. He would see her for the first time. He would look at her and feel, this is a different one, as if she had been several . . .
>
> Or again, they would look at each other in the course of some silence, and she would wonder, she would wonder what she had been giving away. But he accepted and respected her mysteries, as she could never his . . .
>
> . . . the eyes of her husband . . . were at best kind, at worst cold, but always closed to her. If she could have held his head in her hands and looked into the skull at his secret life, whatever it was, then, she felt, she might have been placated.
>
> (ch. 11)

Ironically, both find some of the easy understanding they desire in relations with their shy, quiet, self-contained grandson. The reason is clearly suggested: "Amy Parker had not attempted to possess this remote child, with the consequence that he had come closer than her own."

And so, although *The Tree of Man* is a "family" novel in which the writer is concerned as much with the human community as with individuals, it leaves us, as do all White's stories and plays, with an overpowering sense of solitariness. It opens and closes with a vision of man alone: Stan contemplating the empty landscape in which he will set his home and family; his grandson wandering by himself through the trees. The climax of the novel—if it can be said to have one—comes with the illumination that is granted to Stan Parker as an old man in the moments before his death. "A great tenderness of understanding rose in his chest. . . . It was clear that One, and no other figure, is the answer to all sums." But this revelation is incommunicable: it dies with him, and his wife is left alone, dimly comprehending that she has lost her husband without ever really understanding or sharing in the most secret and vital elements of his life.

VOSS

Voss is both a remarkably complex and an unusually coherent and unified work of fiction. It is a historical novel; it is an attempt to investigate the psychological motivations of exploration; and it is a many-leveled allegory, a parable in which White tries to illuminate, in religious terms, the struggle in man's heart between pride and humility, faith in oneself and faith in God, and in which he tries also to analyze and lay bare the nature of Australian life, to cut through to the spiritual center of Australian society just as Voss, his hero, struggles toward the geographical center of the continent.

What is most remarkable, perhaps, is the extent to which the manifold purposes of the novel are successfully accomplished. Like *The Aunt's Story,* it is a book in which the author's idiosyncrasies of style and his particular preoccupations all seem to work together to produce a richly harmonious and satisfying effect. *Voss* is a luminous work, in which the allegorical implications shimmer perpetually through a surface of detailed and careful realism. The meaning, in short, even when most baldly stated, never seems arbitrarily imposed upon the narrative.

One of the main reasons for this is that the central characters, Voss and Laura Trevelyan, and the most important members of Voss's party, are aware from the beginning of the significance of their actions. They participate naturally in the allegory because for them the enterprise in which they are involved has not only great personal meaning, but also an obvious historical and metaphysical importance.

This is why the book is so effective as a historical novel. The period in which it is set—the mid-nineteenth century—appears to us now as one in which men, particularly artists, intellectuals, or explorers (and Voss is all three), seem, more often than not, to have seen their actions either in a religious light or in a light conditioned by the absence of religion. For Voss it would not have been enough to say (like the twentieth-century conqueror of Mount Everest) that he had to cross the center of Australia "because it was there." Nor would it have been enough for most explorers of his age.

Voss, indeed, is a very credible explorer. Despite his painful eccentricities and idiosyncrasies he is similar in many ways to the men who, in the nineteenth century, explored the Australian continent. In outline his story resembles, of course, that of Ludwig Leichhardt, whose company disappeared without trace on his attempt, in 1848, to cross Australia from east to west. And Voss's character, as White presents it, suggests at least some answers to the fascinating questions that are raised by exploring as a human activity. One reason for becoming an explorer, of course, is simply curiosity—the desire to know what lies over the horizon. But when the country to be explored is as lonely, arid, and inhospitable as much of Australia is, one is prompted to seek for a less obvious answer. In the journals of the Australian explorers such an answer is suggested, if not always explicitly stated; as Kathleen Fitzpatrick has said (in her preface to *Australian Explorers,* a collection of extracts from their writings), "one feels that either they did not know or were not willing or able to tell the whole truth about their motives." Beneath their professions of a simple desire for fame, or a wish to serve the public good, it is, however, possible to detect a more fundamental urge: the obsessive craving to place themselves in situations that they know beforehand will test them to the utmost. Like the mountain climber, the racing driver, or the test pilot, the explorer seems to be driven constantly to arouse, confront, and defeat the image of his own death. Such a contest can create an intoxicating exhilaration. Leichhardt (to whom Voss bears a certain resemblance) was always so overcome by the terrors and joys to which he submitted himself that he found them "indescribable," a word that occurs often in his journals. Edward John Eyre, Charles Sturt, Captain James Cook, and others achieved an exaltation that, despite the conventional phrases in which it is often described, was genuinely religious. To glance through the journals of these men after reading *Voss* can arouse nothing but admiration for the way in which White has entered into and re-created the imaginative world of the explorer. Compare, for instance, with the admittedly more tortured musings of Voss, a typical piece from Eyre's account of his expedition from Adelaide to King George's Sound, a passage that evokes the miseries, terrors, excitements, and spiritual consolations of exploration:

> A few hours before hope itself seemed to be extinguished, and those only who have been subject to a similar extremity of distress can have any just idea of the relief we experienced. The mind seemed to have been weighed down by intense anxiety and over-wrought feelings. At first the gloomy restlessness of disappointment or the feverish impatience of hope had operated upon our minds alternately, but these had long since given way to the calm settled determination of purpose,

and cool steady vigour of action which desperate circumstances can alone inspire. . . . It is in circumstances only such as we had lately been placed that the utter hopelessness of all human efforts is truly felt, and it is when relieved from such a situation that the hand of a directing and beneficient Being appears most plainly discernible.

(*Journals of Expeditions of Discovery into Central Australia*, entry for 30 March 1841)

Voss, also, sees his whole expedition in religious—or antireligious—terms. He is, indeed, a typical nineteenth-century romantic *Übermensch* (though perhaps a little before his time): "You have contempt for God," he is told by a kindly old Moravian brother, "because he is not in your own image." At the same time he has contempt for simple atheism: "Atheists are atheists usually for mean reasons," he tells Laura Trevelyan. "The meanest of these is that they themselves are so lacking in magnificence they cannot conceive the idea of a Divine Power." Voss is not without magnificence: his most obvious quality is a sublime arrogance, and his ideal is a godlike self-sufficiency. As Clemens Brentano put it:

. . . ohne Sinne, dem Gott gleich
Sich selbst nur wissend und dichtend
Schaft er die Welt die er selbst ist. . . .

. . . without senses, like God
Knowing and singing only himself
He creates the world which he himself is. . . .
("Nachklange Beethovenscher Musik, 3")

And in his contempt for the petty and trivial, Voss anticipates Friedrich Nietzsche: it could well have been Voss to whom Zarathustra eventually delivered his message:

Flee, my friend, into your loneliness, see, you are bitten by poisonous flies. Flee hence to where the wind is rough and strong.

Flee into your loneliness. You live too close to the petty and miserable. . . .

As Laura tells Voss, his expedition is "pure will," a process of self-exploration and self-assertion:

You are so isolated. That is why you are fascinated by the prospect of desert places, in which you will find your own situation taken for granted, or more than that, exalted. You sometimes scatter kind words or bits of poetry to people, who soon realise the extent of their illusion. Everything is for yourself. Human emotions, when you have them, are quite flattering to you. If those emotions strike sparks from others, that also is flattering. But most flattering, I think, when you experience it, is the hatred, or even the mere irritation of weaker characters.

(ch. 4)

What saves Voss is his apprehension that self-realization must involve self-denial. "To make yourself it is also necessary to destroy yourself," he tells Le Mesurier, echoing Goethe's *"Stirb, und werde!"*—"Die and become!" But at the beginning of his journey he does not wholly grasp what this means: this, after all, is why he is making the journey. What he discovers at its agonizing conclusion, as he suffers death by torture in the desert (which is also the country of his mind), is that man is not and never can be self-sufficient. He who in his arrogance has rejected all affection and sentiment and human sympathy as weakness is forced to learn that it is only through complete humility that man can triumph: "When man is truly humbled, when he has learnt that he is not God, then is he nearest to becoming so. In the end, he may ascend." Since Voss has previously set himself so deliberately in the role of Anti-Christ it does not seem improper that the ritual of his death should assume some of the dimensions of crucifixion. He is not that symbolic cliché of so much contemporary fiction, a "Christ-figure"; but the outlines of the Christian legend run like a luminous thread through the major incidents in his story. Because it is not overstressed it genuinely illuminates: *Voss* always remains a novel, that is, a convincing fictional representation of credible human beings, and it never hardens into the abstract oversimplifications of pure allegory.

And the implications of his story are very specific as well as general. In *Voss* White is trying to say something about the human condition as a whole but he is also very much concerned with the particular problems of his own country. His picture of colonial society in nineteenth-century Sydney is affectionate and at times nostalgic: the Bonners provincial elegance and the simple but consciously intelligent goodness of the Sandersons' life at Rhine Towers are a far cry from the stifling sterility of Sarsaparilla. But it is a limited society in which most of the "gentry, or what passes for it, hav eaten themselves into a stupor of mutton," whose future we are made to feel may lie in the hands of people like the squatter Brendan Boyle, who tears the covers off Homer to prop up the leg of his table, because he belongs to "that order of males who will destroy any distinction with which they have been born, because it accuses them, they feel, and they cannot bear the shame of it." The great peril of a society such as this is what one of its members specifies as its inherent "mediocrity." It is this quality which Voss, with his Nietzschean faith in human potential, his belief that "Man is something . . . to be surpassed," sharply and often comically exposes. His arrogance and Laura's humility are clearly intended to demonstrate a greatness of spirit that is lacking in a society where the premium is on the safe, decent, respectable virtues; a greatness of spirit without which any culture is doomed.

RIDERS IN THE CHARIOT *AND* THE BURNT ONES

DOOM is the note that sounds most strongly through White's next novel, *Riders in the Chariot.* In the opening scenes our attention is focused on Mary Hare, an old maid uglier and stranger than Theodora Goodman, retreating like a cornered animal into the tangled gardens and crumbling ruins of Xanadu, the extravagantly beautiful house that her eccentric wealthy father had built toward the end of the previous century. Eyebrows, of course, had been raised when Norbert Hare had built his Pleasure Dome: *"Pleasure* is a shocking word in societies where the most luxurious aspirations are disguised as moral ones." Its erection, however, was evidence of the possibilities for the spontaneous flowering of beauty and elegance in the sort of life that is affectionately recalled in *Voss.* It is a decadent and fruitless gesture, however: Norbert Hare kills himself—or drowns accidentally—before the eyes of his useless daughter; and in the closing episodes of the novel Miss Hare dies, and the brick and fibro boxes of Sarsaparilla, The Friendly Suburb, spread over the site of Xanadu, now "shaved right down to a bald, red, rudimentary hill," by the bulldozers of progress.

But *Riders in the Chariot* has for its subject something more vast and terrible than the triumph of suburbia. It is, in fact, an exceptionally ambitious novel, and if, like Xanadu, it must be judged to some extent a failure, it should be similarly admired for the daring and magnitude of its conception. Its subject, though complex, is basically twofold: it is first of all sanctity—White is concerned more directly in this novel with the nature of that spiritual illumination with which he assumes the saint, the artist, the natural mystic, and the naturally good person to be fired; second, it is the nature of evil and its perpetual warfare with good, in particular the way in which the gray, conformist forces within society perpetually seek to crucify the individual—or the group—who dares to be different, or who cannot disguise his or its essential singularity. The destruction of Xanadu and the general slovenly intolerance of Australian society are set in savage juxtaposition to the attempt by the Nazis to eliminate the Jews; and the climactic scene in the novel is the pseudo-crucifixion of Himmelfarb, the old Jewish refugee, by his workmates at Rosetree's Brighta Bicycle Lamps factory.

Riders in the Chariot takes its title from the passage in which Ezekiel describes his vision of the four living creatures, with wings but in the likeness of men, riding in the fiery whirlwind. White's "Riders" are the four main characters in the novel: Miss Hare, Mordecai Himmelfarb, Alf Dubbo, an aborigine who paints, and Mrs. Godbold, the mother of a large family who has a drunken husband and takes in washing. They are all isolates, Mrs. Godbold less so than the others and not so obviously. Miss Hare and Alf Dubbo, however, are almost utterly alone; until they meet the other two *illuminati* they have never suspected that there is anyone else in the world with whom they have anything fundamentally in common. What they share is their awareness of the "infinite in everything," and also the vision in which the awareness manifests itself in its most intense form: the vision of the fiery chariot.

There are many splendid things in this novel. The characters themselves—especially Miss Hare, Himmelfarb, and Alf Dubbo—are further evidence of White's remarkable ability to get inside the skin, as it were, of the odd and the unusual person. His rendering of Miss Hare's animal-like experience of the world is extraordinarily convincing, as is his re-creation of Himmelfarb's middle-class academic

German-Jewish milieu, or the utterly different vagabond existence of Alf Dubbo among the tin humpies[2] of country towns and the slums of Sydney. The sheer versatility displayed first in imagining these people and then in bringing them together and setting them dramatically against a conventional suburban background is very great.

The Himmelfarb section is the most forceful and at the same time the most carefully restrained and muted piece of writing White has yet produced. As a realistic account of Jewish life in Germany it may be inaccurate in detail, but the total effect is utterly convincing. The evocation of the nightmarish final days, and in particular of the train journey to the death camp at Friedensdorf, is Kafka-like in its intensity; and all the more horrifying because of the quiet, almost detached manner in which it is presented. What the reader is forced, almost against his will, to accept is the appalling fact that for the majority of its members the society that destroyed six million Jews was a *normal* society.

It is patently White's intention to suggest, through Himmelfarb's "crucifixion," that within an ordinary Australian suburb the same evil forces that animated Nazi Germany exist, at least potentially. The intention, unfortunately, is not completely realized. One reason may be that societies just do differ qualitatively: the hell of Auschwitz and Buchenwald is not the hell of Australian suburbia, and to equate them must inevitably seem grotesquely disproportionate. Ordinary people may behave monstrously, but only under extraordinary pressures, and these do not at present appear to operate in Australia. Such communal cruelty as does occur is usually the cruelty of neglect, ignorance, or an amused and shallow contempt.

There is nothing incredible about a mob of hooligans in a Sydney factory bashing up an old Jew just for the fun of it. That they should *crucify* him, however, seems at once too deliberate and too imaginative. Ritual and allegory are acceptable in *Voss* because these are the terms in which the central character normally sees his life. It is much more difficult to believe that Blue and his beer-sodden mates would have not only enough inventive malice to pin Himmelfarb to a tree on Good Friday, but also enough religious sensibility to appreciate the significance of what they are doing. Also, in a dramatic and psychological sense, the incident is insufficiently and unconvincingly motivated. Mrs. Flack who, from the background, instigates the whole affair, is too much of a caricature (brilliantly comic though the caricature may be) to be really terrifying.

The difficulty with *Riders in the Chariot* is that the reader is asked to accept too much. It is hard enough after all to believe that people see visions, without having to believe in addition that four people so different as Miss Hare, Alf Dubbo, Himmelfarb, and Mrs. Godbold should sense what is basically the same vision. Even more damaging is White's failure to substantiate his sweeping indictment of Australian society. As the novel moves to its climax, the demands imposed by his allegorical intentions force him to present things in terms that are increasingly bald and simple—and unrealistic. "Sodom," he tells us, "had not been softer, silkier at night, than the sea gardens of Sydney. The streets of Nineveh had not clanged with such metal. The waters of Babylon had not sounded sadder than the sea, ending on a crumpled beach, in a scum of French-letters." This is empty rhetoric, and it forms the conclusion of a passage that is clearly intended as a passionate denunciation, but comes dangerously close to hysterical petulance.

"The voice of honest indignation is the voice of God," says William Blake in a passage that White quotes at the beginning of *Riders in the Chariot.* One can sympathize with White's indignation; and the brilliance with which he renders the chrome and plastic glitter of the supermarket society in which we live convinces us that there is something to be indignant about. But he cannot convince us that the people who live in Sarsaparilla are so thoroughly and inhumanly evil as to deserve the unmitigated anger and disgust with which he finally presents them. A major reason for this failure, I suspect, is that he is not himself convinced of this to start with.

Riders in the Chariot is a challenging book, but a very imperfect one. Its allegorical design gives it a certain unity, but it is not a unity grounded on the logic of character and event. It is rather a spatial, almost a pictorial coherence: the book impresses one finally, perhaps, as a vast canvas on which, against a contemporary background depicted with minutely detailed realism, the rather bemused inhabitants of Sarsaparilla find themselves enacting the major incidents in the Christian legend; rather in fact, as if Stanley Spencer, the twentieth-cen

[2]Primitive huts.

tury British naif religious painter, had been let loose in the outer suburbs of Sydney.

But the virtues of painting are not necessarily those of fiction. In the end, it seems to me, White's allegorical intentions and his more obvious fictive ones operate against each other to distort and shatter the work as a whole. Moreover, the structure of the novel permits the uninhibited expression of some of the writer's strongest and least fully explored emotions: his ambivalent and conflicting response to the society with which he has immediate and continuing daily contact. The most debilitating element in the novel is the air of exasperation and sheer irritability that keeps breaking through. Flawed and imperfect though it is, *Riders in the Chariot* nonetheless remains, in Manfred Mackenzie's phrase, "a wonderful thing," wonderful both for the authenticity with which the individual segments in its fantastic structure are rendered, and for the splendor and originality of its basic design.

Several of the short stories in *The Burnt Ones* are also set in Sarsaparilla. Two of these, "A Cheery Soul" and "Down at the Dump," are among the finest things White has written. Freed from the necessity of accommodating his picture of ordinary life to the demands of an all-embracing allegorical plan, he achieves in these stories a vision of suburbia at once more convincing and more compassionate than anything in *Riders in the Chariot.* Miss Docker, the "cheery soul," is a vigorous old maid in whom the desire to do good is a disease. She is cast in the same mold as Mesdames Jolly and Flack, but she is a much more complex and powerful piece of characterization. In her voice, flat, humorous, apparently good-natured, but fundamentally selfish and brutally insensitive, White has caught the essence of suburban vulgarity. At the same time, in forcing both himself and the reader to consider Miss Docker, he grapples head-on with things we often find it convenient to ignore: the sordid loneliness and terror of old age, the tiny hypocrisies and cruelties we practice on each other, the little kindnesses that eventually kill their victim, the frailty of good intentions. "A Cheery Soul" is a richly ambiguous work, a darkly comic exposure of the contradictions that lie at the heart of life.

In "Down at the Dump," the final and in some ways the most impressive story in the collection, White at last seems to come to terms with Sarsaparilla and all it stands for. Here in one densely packed but lucid vision he raises and exorcises those elements in life, particularly Australian life, by which he is obsessed: the loneliness of the individual, the impersonal cruelty of society, the necessity for love and, paradoxically, the indestructibility of humankind.

The Tree of Man concludes with the boy, whose grandfather has just died, alone among the trees, "putting out shoots of green thought," ready to contribute with his own life to the general cycle of existence. "Down at the Dump" presents us with a similar confrontation of death and adolescence, but the situation is imaged in harsher and crueler terms. When Lum Whalley wanders off on his own he moves across the wasteland of the local garbage dump:

> . . . Pitfalls abounded: then rusty traps of open tins lay in wait for guiltless ankles, the necks of broken bottles might have been prepared to gash a face. So he went thoughtfully, his feet scuffing the leaves of stained asbestos, crunching the torso of a celluloid doll. Here and there it appeared as though trash might win. The onslaught of metal was pushing the scrub into the gully. But in many secret, steamy pockets, a rout was in progress: seeds had been sown in the lumps of grey, disintegrating kapok and the laps of bursting chairs, the coils of springs, locked in the spirals of wirier vines, had surrendered to superior resilience.

The struggle for survival clearly presents itself in more desperate terms to White now than when he wrote *The Tree of Man.* But about the final outcome of the contest he has no doubts: the resilience of the green vine is superior to the dead blight of industrial, urban rubbish. "Down at the Dump" concludes on an unmistakable note of hope: "The warm core of certainty settled stiller as driving faster the wind payed out the telephone wires the fences the flattened heads of grey grass always raising themselves again again again."

THE SOLID MANDALA

WHITE's next novel, *The Solid Mandala,* also concludes on a note of hope and affirmation, but it is nonetheless a very strange and disturbing book. The setting, Sarsaparilla, is familiar enough; and the account of life in "the friendly suburb" that he presents is, at one level, as sharply realistic as ever.

At another level, however, it is even more bizarre and fantastic than the apocalyptic vision he offers us in *Riders in the Chariot.*

The main characters are twin brothers, Arthur and Waldo Brown. We see them first as old men: two eccentric, untidy, and certainly smelly old men, accompanied by two aged and even smellier dogs, wandering hand in hand along the road from Sarsaparilla to Barranugli. They live in a weatherboard cottage in Terminus Road—a hot, brown box that had been built for their father when he came out from England about the turn of the century with his wife and two young children. The Browns' weatherboard box is distinguished from its fellows only by its peaked verandah roof—a "classical pediment"—which Mr. Brown had specifically requested from the builder, and which gives the house "the appearance of a little, apologetic, not quite proportionate temple."

Our first sight of Arthur and Waldo is through the windows of the Sarsaparilla–Barranugli bus; we see them, indeed, very much as they appear to their neighbors. Mrs. Poulter, who lives opposite them, and is as old as they are, clearly likes them and finds them interesting. She seems in a strange way almost to be proud of them, though she fails to convince her new friend, Mrs. Dun, that they are in any way admirable. Most of Sarsaparilla, we are left feeling, would share Mr. Poulter's view of what he calls the Brothers Bloody Brown: "That pair of poofteroos. . . . A couple of no-hopers with ideas above 'emselves."

After this brief introductory glimpse of the twins we are given, in the two main sections of the novel, an account of life in the Brown family, first as it appears to Waldo, then as it appears to Arthur. The novel closes with an epilogue, "Mrs. Poulter and the Zeitgeist," in which we are brought back to the ordinary world of Sarsaparilla.

White's management of this apparently simple structure is technically brilliant. In the two long central sections he ranges freely backward and forward in time without ever losing the threads of continuity or development. In a remarkable way he succeeds in suggesting both the immediacy of a particular event as it happens and the significance it will later assume in the memory.

Waldo it seems is the more intelligent of the twins. He has intellectual and literary aspirations, but he never becomes a writer. He works as a librarian at the Sydney Municipal Library and the public library, never marries, never leaves Sarsaparilla, never really gives himself to anyone or anything. "Waldo hated what he could never in any way take part in," and as he grows older his hatred —which is really a hatred and denial of life— gets steadily deeper and more self-destructive. It focuses itself more and more on Arthur, his awkward and apparently simple-minded twin, whose childish behavior has always profoundly embarrassed him.

Waldo's world is one of thwarted aspiration and cold disgust. It is filled with the smell of excrement and old age: fluff and guilty secrets lurk in its dark corners and the washing up is never done: "All this while the mutton fat was curdling round them in skeins, clogging corners, filling bowls with verdigris tints and soft white to greyish fur. You couldn't be bothered to empty the mutton fat out. Like a family it was with you always. Set."

The "family" is Arthur, the twin and opposite from whom he can never escape, whom he never allows himself to love, and whom he never understands. Just how completely Waldo misunderstands his twin is revealed when we are allowed to see their life together as it has appeared to Arthur. Arthur's world is one of warmth, sunshine, and easy love. He bumbles about happily and innocently, a holy hermaphrodite who, because he finds it impossible to disguise his own feelings, has the knack of making most people feel honest with themselves (their capacity to accept this experience, of course, is a mark of quality of their characters; Waldo, "truly tortured by . . . innocence in others," cannot bear it).

Arthur's spontaneous love of and reverence for life naturally assumes a protective form. Although he has no religion (the Brown parents are earnestly agnostic) he is innately religious. Leafing through a book one day he comes on a passage that strikes him with the force of a revelation: "The Mandala is a symbol of totality. It is believed to be the 'dwelling of the god.' Its protective circle is a pattern of order superimposed on psychic chaos. Sometimes its geometric form is seen as a vision (either waking or in a dream) or danced."

Arthur finds the tangible form of the mandala in the glass marbles he has cherished since boyhood and which he still carries in his pocket. But these are not so important as the mandala he tries to create around the people he loves—Waldo, Mrs. Poulter, the Feinsteins; or the mandalas he perceives to exist in the lives of some other people; or the one he dances for Mrs. Poulter.

Waldo finally dies (under circumstances of peculiar horridness), and Arthur is placed in the local asylum. Before he leaves, however, he is comforted by Mrs. Poulter, who then declares her faith in him to the bewildered policeman whose duty it is to take him away: "This is a good man, Sergeant. . . . This man would be my saint, if we could still believe in saints. Nowadays we've only men to believe in. I believe in this man."

Mrs. Poulter may believe in Arthur Brown, but there are many readers, I suspect, who may find it difficult to do so. The trouble with the brothers Brown is that they have been too obviously designed to illustrate a thesis. There is, especially in the opening passages of the novel, an air of deliberate artifice and contrivance about the narrative, which I find irritating and distracting. The symbolic framework of the action seems superimposed on the suburban realities of Sarsaparilla; it sits there as awkwardly and obviously as does Mr. Brown's classical pediment on the front of his weatherboard cottage.

This is not to say that the symbolic pattern of the novel is not developed with great skill and subtlety (an article will one day be written on the significance of glass, mirrors, and windows in *The Solid Mandala*); nor that it does not refer to profoundly important issues: the duality of man, the validity of the spontaneously religious gesture, the value of reverence and affirmation—these are matters of central human significance. It must be acknowledged, also, that in certain episodes, Waldo and Arthur do assume a genuine life of their own. This is so especially in their relationship to a Jewish family, the Feinsteins. White's account of the first meeting between Waldo and Dulcie Feinstein, or the visits of the brothers to the Feinstein house, is effortlessly convincing: with wonderful economy, firmness, and sympathy he manages to suggest a social situation of considerable complexity. Mrs. Poulter, too, like the Feinsteins, has an air of solid reality about her (she seems much more convincing than Mrs. Godbold, a very similar character, in *Riders in the Chariot*). And her final encounter with Arthur is unexpectedly moving: the grotesque world of the brothers and the world of normal, fallible, but often compassionate humanity are brought together in a way that is at once convincing and illuminating.

Indeed there are many moments of sudden illumination in this extraordinary book—moments when the familiar everyday world is surprisingly revealed to be strangely beautiful or sinister. But *The Solid Mandala* remains for me a somewhat unsatisfactory novel, in the way that *Riders in the Chariot* is unsatisfactory. White seems still to be struggling to impose his own "pattern of order . . . on psychic chaos." He is attempting to do so in one of the most difficult of modes, the symbolic novel. It is perhaps not to be wondered at that he is not always completely successful. In making the attempt, however, he produces fiction of a remarkably high order. *The Solid Mandala* may be in some ways unsatisfactory, but it is also an undeniably exciting, beautiful, and important book.

THE VIVISECTOR

WHITE has remarked more than once that he wishes he were a painter or a composer rather than a writer: he finds the medium of language in itself restricting and less attractive than he imagines paint or music to be. So it is not surprising that after developing so successfully the character of Alf Dubbo in *Riders in the Chariot* he should turn his attention even more closely to the painter as an example of *illuminatus* and creative genius. In *The Vivisector* he offers us the life story of such a person: Hurtle Duffield, a wholly imaginary great Australian artist.

White's primary concern in the novel is with Duffield himself; and he proves to be one of his most substantial and interesting characters. But in *The Vivisector* White is also concerned with a number of general issues: the nature of art as a way of knowing; the relation of art and the artist to society; the moral question of the relation between high art and wealth; and the characteristics of the artistic personality, in particular the immediate social conditions under which such a personality can emerge, be fostered, and develop.

The title of the novel and the name of its hero are suggestive: "Hurtle" can be abbreviated to "Hurt"; and the vivisector, in his search for knowledge, has to hurt, to inflict pain on, living beings. Art may be a joyful celebration of the nature of things—of "the truth"—but in his search for truth the artist, like the vivisector, must inflict suffering on his fellows and on himself: suffering indeed is essential to the accomplishment of his vocation. And this, as much as its celebratory nature, can be seen as a mark of the sacred character of art.

In one of the epigraphs to the novel the painter Ben Nicholson is quoted as saying: "Painting and religious experience are the same thing"; and on the wall of his sunlit dunny,[3] Duffield, meditating over his morning motion, writes:

> *God the Vivisector*
> *God the Artist*
> *God*
> (ch. 6)

The suffering of the world is part of the divine purpose—and God, like the artist, is necessarily involved in the suffering.

Although naturalistic in tone and manner, *The Vivisector* is allegorical in structure. Duffield's life follows a pattern as emblematic as that of a medieval saint. He is born into a poor family with a legendary aristocratic connection; his genius manifests itself "miraculously" at an early age (he teaches himself to read, his text being the Bible); he is sold by his natural parents to a wealthy and cultured couple who long for a son; the changeling now finds his "true" home: his adoptive parents give him the education his talent needs and deserves, bring him up in the expectation of inheriting their wealth, and then are almost magically removed from the scene, leaving him penniless; he is loved and supported by a prostitute and is inadvertently the cause of her death—a death that, nonetheless, in a sacrificial manner ensures the flowering of his talent; at crucial points in his career he is supported by a mysterious patron who acts, dressed in sacerdotal white, as a fairy godmother; and his death is brought on by a stroke that occurs when, in old age, he breaks the taboo by making, for the first time since his childhood, physical contact with his natural family.

But although this structure is demonstrably there, it is not obtrusive. Duffield himself is a credible, substantial, and always interesting character, and the world through which he moves—predominantly that of Sydney—is rendered convincingly with a wealth of concrete physical and social detail. One never has the feeling in this novel that the form has been imposed on the material: it is a remarkably unified and coherent work, and the structure serves always to illuminate the theme. Duffield emerges as a man who fulfills his destiny as an artist, not merely because he is at once alienated from and nourished and supported by his society, but because the relation is dynamic and fruitful: he both incorporates his world and is detached from it—when he performs his role as vivisector he must cut as deeply into himself as into his community.

The Vivisector is a rich, satisfying work, intellectually challenging, emotionally engaging, and engrossing as a narrative. It has all the virtues of the traditional nineteenth-century novel while at the same time being thoroughly contemporary in feeling.

THE EYE OF THE STORM *AND* THE COCKATOOS

PUBLISHED in 1973, *The Eye of the Storm,* like *The Vivisector,* is a large, assured work, though perhaps dense and more complex in texture. There are associations and similarities with the earlier book, however, that make *The Eye of the Storm* seem in som ways its natural sequel. The atmosphere of bot novels shimmers with light and color; the mai setting, the eastern suburbs of Sydney, is the same and in each book White explores the problem raised by the apparently unavoidable nexus be tween art and wealth, and the question of how sensitivity to and apprehension of either natural c manmade beauty can provide a medium, a way c understanding, between humankind and God.

It is easier, we are told, for a camel to pa through the eye of a needle than for a rich man t enter the Kingdom of Heaven. Elizabeth Hunter rich. She is also old, bedridden, half-blind, an preparing for death as the novel opens. She h been beautiful, she is still proud, and in some way despite her charm and beauty, she is—or has be —a decidedly unpleasant woman. The gates of t Kingdom, one would assume, are shut to her. Y she is ruthlessly honest with herself; and she has

[3] A toilet, usually outside and separate from the house.

authenticity and has attained a spiritual humility that affect and impress those about her who have the capacity to respond to such things.

The most significant occasions in her life on which she has been offered the possibility of being still, of accepting an awareness of transcendence, have occurred during the terminal illness of her husband, and in a tropical cyclone on an island off the Queensland coast. There, in the strange calm at the eye of the storm, she experiences a moment in and out of time—to use T. S. Eliot's phrase—a vision of "glistening peace" in which she, like "a flaw at the centre of this jewel of light," is allowed to see herself as part of a cosmic unity.

The radiance of this vision pervades the novel—it is full of images of light that give it both a symphonic and a visual coherence. *The Eye of the Storm* is the sort of book that Henry James could have envisaged—although had he gone on to write it, no doubt it would have been a very different work.

Elizabeth Hunter is the focus of attention; and her character, as it is revealed to us through her memories and through the recounting of earlier episodes in her life, is a complex and fascinating one. But the dramatic tension in the novel comes mainly from her relations with the people around her, and in particular from the varying ways in which they respond to her unique and paradoxical blend of arrogance and humility and eventually to her death. Lotte Lippmann, her cook, a one-time Berlin cabaret artiste; her two nurses, appropriately named Sister de Santis and Sister Manhood; her lawyer Arnold Wyburd; and her two middle-aged children, Dorothy, now Princess de Lascabanes by marriage, and Basil, now Sir Basil Hunter, a fading West End Shakespearean actor, provide a set of sharply differentiated and vividly realized dramatis personae.

The term is apposite: *The Eye of the Storm* is remarkable both for the dramatic tightness of its action and for the glittering and at times tawdry theatricality of many of its scenes. The dying woman's bedroom becomes a stage on which she reenacts her past, is dressed and bejeweled and made up not for a ball but for her daily session on the throne (her commode), and watches tottering old Lotte sing and dance. The ecstatic serenity of much of the action is balanced by a lively element of vulgar and vigorous Dickensian comedy.

It is an assured and classic work; and within the canon of White's own writing it is remarkable for the ease and effortlessness with which he attains effects that in earlier novels he sometimes seems to strain for and stumble after. It is entirely appropriate that this novel should have provided the occasion for the award of the Nobel Prize.

The following year saw the publication of White's second collection of shorter fiction, *The Cockatoos.* The six works it contains are novellas rather than short stories, and most of them are concerned with what happens to human relationships—marriages, friendships, enmities—as people enter middle and old age. They are subtle, beautifully controlled stories that throw an oblique and revealing light on the strange, the grotesque, and the unexpected aspects that are to be discovered in what seem to be the most ordinary and humdrum lives. *The Cockatoos* also contains the story "The Night the Prowler," which has been made into a play and a film.

A FRINGE OF LEAVES

The place where Elizabeth Hunter is granted her vision of peace is Fraser Island, the colored sands of which make it an area of unique and fragile beauty. The island is named after Mrs. Eliza Fraser—and perhaps her husband, Captain James Fraser.

Captain Fraser's brig, *The Stirling Castle,* was wrecked off the Queensland coast on 22 May 1836. After several days at sea in open boats—in the course of which Mrs. Fraser produced a stillborn child—the survivors reached land. Then their troubles really began. The aboriginal people they encountered treated them harshly. Mrs. Fraser saw her husband speared to death. Another man was burned alive. Eventually a handful of survivors was rescued by convicts and soldiers from the Moreton Bay penal settlement. One convict played a particularly gallant role in snatching Mrs. Fraser, naked but for a fringe of leaves, from the tribe with whom she was living.

It is a haunting, savage, strangely beautiful story. It captured the imagination of people in Australia and Great Britain at the time, and in recent years has inspired a number of books, a film, and a series of paintings by Sydney Nolan. White's novel *A Fringe of Leaves* is based on the incident; and one of Nolan's paintings is used as an illustration on the dust jacket.

But Ellen Roxburgh, White's heroine, is not Eliza Fraser; and her story differs significantly from its original. White's novel is a work of the imagination; it is not a "historical" novel in the documentary sense. In other ways, however, it is very much a historical exercise. It is a work that, like *Voss,* invites its readers—particularly its Australian readers—to examine their history as a white society, and to think particularly about their origins. As White himself has said, "perhaps . . . they [can] sense in its images and narrative the reasons why we have become what we are today."

But *A Fringe of Leaves* is only incidentally about society. Like all White's fiction it is concerned primarily with individual human beings and with their essentially private problems. Ellen Roxburgh, like many of White's characters, is a combination of the normal and ordinary with the highly distinctive and unusual. Above all she is a survivor: a tough, pragmatic, unsentimental human animal. But she is also one of those who are set aside from the mass of humanity through a capacity to see things from time to time with almost supernatural clarity and in a different light. She is not bizarre or eccentric like Theodora Goodman or Miss Hare—her intimations of immortality are subtly hinted at rather than presented directly—but she is, nonetheless, one of White's *illuminati.*

She is also, like Hurtle Duffield, dispossessed and alienated. Her marriage transcends the barriers of class, her experiences with the aborigines and her trek naked through the bush with her convict rescuer reduce her to the fundamental core of her identity. White has never written anything more simple, more honest, or more moving than the passages in which he presents the flowering and consummation in the wilderness of the love between Jack Chance, the convict, and Ellen Roxburgh in her fringe of leaves.

A Fringe of Leaves is slight by comparison with most of White's novels. But it has a narrative power, a poetic intensity, and a thematic and formal coherence that combine to make it one of his most successful—and accessible—works.

THE TWYBORN AFFAIR

WHITE has said that among his novels the three he likes most are *The Aunt's Story, The Solid Mandala,* and *The Twyborn Affair.* They are certainly among his most idiosyncratic and original works: one cannot imagine their having been written by anybody else. And *The Twyborn Affair* in particular displays a quite extraordinary range of sympathy in characterization and brilliance in invention. If it is indeed the last novel White will write—as he sometimes hints it may be—it will provide a fitting conclusion to a remarkable body of fiction.

Looked at in one way *The Twyborn Affair* is little more than an outrageous high camp romp. The plot is as extravagantly artificial and improbable as the plot of *The Magic Flute.* The hero/heroine, Eddie/Eadith Twyborn, scion of a respectable Sydney legal family, is introduced to the reader first as the transvestite companion of a wealthy Greek on the Riviera, arousing unrequited passions in the hearts of a masturbatory French shopkeeper and a sentimental Australian matron on the grand tour. Next he/she is shown returning to Australia after World War I as a dashing young naval lieutenant with a DSO. Lieutenant Eddie effects a partial reconciliation with his parents and goes off jackerooing on a sheep station in the Monaro high country. There, despite his best intentions, he simultaneously charms the pants off the boss's lush wife—surprisingly called Lushington—and his thoroughly ocker[4] station-manager, Don Prowse. Part three of the novel gives us our protagonist as Mrs. Eadith Trist, madam of a high-class Chelsea brothel. At the height of the blitz she makes contact once more with her mother, who is in London. Walking through the streets toward a final reunion, and having reverted to the role of Eddie Twyborn, he is killed in an air-raid.

Stated baldly like this, it seems a preposterous and incredible story. As we read the novel, however, the wildly disparate episodes are rendered with such effortless authority, and the individual characters are imagined and presented with such sympathy and conviction, that the artificialities of the plot and the sleight of hand of the narrator cease to bother us: all that matters is that the situations their contrivance makes possible should work effectively.

The paradoxical relation between artifice and authenticity is one of the themes of *The Twyborn Affair* it forces us to acknowledge that no matter how naturalistic, how "true," a fiction may be, it remains a fiction, a contrivance. And what holds tru

[4]Typical of the Australian working man: uncultivated, chauvinistic, but good-humored, resourceful.

for art also holds true, at least to some degree, for life: we speak most truly when we wear a mask; the greatest freedom is ensured through the proper definition of limits.

A parallel concern in the novel is the relation between sexuality, in all its physical variety, and love. Twyborn's last lover is Lord Gravenor, under whose patronage her brothel flourishes. Their love is never physically consummated; but paradoxically this authenticates it—and points to the existence of another and greater love that is all-pervasive and transcendent. A letter Eadith receives from Gravenor affords Eddie a final revelation before his death: " 'Love' is an exhausted word, and God has been expelled by those that know better, but I offer you one as proof that the other still exists."

FLAWS IN THE GLASS

In 1981 White published *Flaws in the Glass: A Self-Portrait.* It is an impressionistic essay rather than a full-scale autobiography, but it gives a compelling account of the development of a writer. It also casts a revealing light on White's novels and plays, and on the themes and subjects with which he is overridingly concerned.

It is a remarkable book in many ways. Two things in particular distinguish it. The first is the affection and generosity with which White pays tribute in it to the man who has shared his life, Manoly Lascaris. The second is the frankness with which he acknowledges his homosexuality—or, rather, his "ambivalence"—and the claims he makes for it. "Ambivalence," he asserts, "has given me insights into human nature, denied, I believe, to those who are unequivocally male or female . . . I would not trade my halfway house, frail though it be, for any of the entrenchments of those who like to think themselves unequivocal."

THE PLAYS

It remains to say something about White's achievements as a dramatist, although in the space at my disposal it is not possible to give his plays more than a cursory appraisal. (I have discussed the earlier plays in some detail in an article, "The Plays of Patrick White.") His work for the theater, like his fiction, is inventive and unmistakably his own. Although no single play (with the possible exception of *The Ham Funeral*) can be judged a complete success, taken together the four pieces he published in 1965 constitute a body of work more substantial and more promising than had been achieved by any other Australian dramatist at that time. He played a significant and catalytic role in the evolution of the new Australian drama.

In his plays, as in his fiction, White is fascinated by the problem of isolation and communication, and in particular by the problem of how to participate in the normal process of living without sacrificing one's identity. "My dilemma in the play," says the Young Man in *The Ham Funeral,* "is how to take part in the conflict of eels and survive at the same time." But the "conflict of eels" goes on and involves us in it whether we like it or not: the cycles of "birth, copulation, and death" work themselves out through the life-patterns of the individual members of the species with quite impersonal inevitability. In *The Ham Funeral* the Landlord dies, and the Landlady, moved by forces beyond her control, seeks a new lover (indeed, she and the Young Man, merely by the generation of their mutual but as yet unacknowledged passion, have unwittingly helped to bring about his death). In *The Season at Sarsaparilla,* the residents of that respectable suburb cannot shut their ears to the frenzied yelping of the dogs as they mill around the bitch in heat; and Nola Boyle is as incapable as the bitch of saying "no" to the male who really desires her. "Everything begins," says the Landlady " . . . over and over again." "Over, and over, and over," repeats Pippy, the pubescent girl, beating time remorselessly, "for ever, and ever, and ever. That's nature." As Denis Craig, the young academic, remarks rather ironically, in *Night on Bald Mountain,* "continuity is reassuring." But it can also be terrifying. Moreover, it can assume different forms, the forms of life or the forms of death: the rhythmic mating ritual through which the Landlady leads the Young Man, or the stereotyped emptiness with which the Relatives, the embodiment of suburban morality, echo each other's gestures; the cycle of desire and love, of passion and its fruition, in which the Boyles, Pippy Pogson, the Knotts, and the furious dogs are caught up in Sarsaparilla, or the razzle-dazzle of time, the sterile pattern of urban living, to which the Pogsons have succumbed, and which destroys poor Julia Sheen and her unborn child; the unselfconscious sexuality of the goats on Bald Mountain, or the self-defeating maze of pride, frustration, and death into which Professor Hugo Sword forces all those who fall within his orbit.

At the risk of gross oversimplification one can, I think, isolate these two centers of interest in White's plays: on the one hand the individual, struggling to come to terms with himself and with the universe in which he lives—a universe in which inanimate objects and the world of nature can be as important as other human beings; and on the other, the cyclic processes of living, impersonal, inscrutable, and inescapable. Dramatic tensions and interests are generated in his work not only out of the relations of the characters with each other (as is the case of most plays) but also out of their involvement with these larger biological and physical forces.

These preoccupations are reflected in the structure and style of his plays. *The Ham Funeral* is frankly expressionist and symbolical: as the Young Man (whose name we never know) remarks, "The time doesn't matter. The same applies to my origins. It could be that I was born in Birmingham . . . or Brooklyn . . . or Murwillumbah." And although White's later plays are cast in more obviously naturalistic terms, they all have unmistakably symbolic overtones.

Expressionism, as a dramatic form, can be depressingly sterile and empty beneath the immediate theatrical brilliance of its techniques. What saves White is his uncannily accurate ear for language and his ability to create character. Despite the structural weaknesses of his plays, they live because of the credibility and distinctiveness of the people in them, and the vitality with which they speak. Language is the heart of all great drama, and it is through language as much as situation that the action of a White play grows and moves forward, through language that his characters live most vividly. Thus, *A Cheery Soul,* which is, I think, an unsuccessful attempt to translate one of his finest short stories into theatrical terms, compels our attention through the vividness with which Miss Docker, that self-tormented Fury from the hell of suburban morality, is brought to life on the stage. And she lives through her voice: the vulgar, humorous, unquenchable voice of the Australian suburbs, a voice that rattles in our ears long after the curtain has fallen.

To have created this voice is evidence not only of White's extraordinarily accurate ear but also of the transforming power of his imagination. For in Miss Docker's voice the Australian vernacular is not just reproduced, it is concentrated and fused into a darkly comic poetry. The process is carried on even further in *Night on Bald Mountain*: Miss Quodling, the sibylline old goat woman, speaks with a quintessentially Australian accent: her idiom is tough, slangy, humorous, sardonically realistic, and amazingly fluent and flexible. It is the range that surprises and delights: in her speeches White has enlarged the dimensions of the Australian language in a unique and creative way, revealing unsuspected potentialities for poetry and eloquence. There has never been anything in the Australian theater quite like Miss Quodling's hymn of praise with which *Night on Bald Mountain* begins. Like that great speech in which Volpone hails his gold and the sun, it establishes powerfully and firmly the dominant mood of the play. Some notion of its quality may be gained from the concluding passage:

(She flings open back gate of yard, and stands holding it, as invisible goats pour down the mountainside.)
(An urgent pattering music to accompany the following speech.)
(shouting) There, now! Run! Jump! My little beauties! My little darluns! What would a woman do without her goats? Scamper, kids! Listen to the pellets patter on the rocks! Oh yes mornun is wonderfullest when the goats burst out of the yard. I lay all last night with that nag nag nag in me off-side shoulder, but mornuns . . . you forget the nights.
(pause)
(admonishing) Dolores? Don't you dare! Do you hear me, Dolores? You've got the world, but want to butt the hell out of that poor Jessica's full belly. I never saw anything like goats. . . .
(She turns, comes down and leans on front fence of yard. The risen sun hits her and her first hymn should be accompanied by a music, at first prickly, icy, then dissolving, as the mists disperse, and objects take on complete shape.)
Mornun . . . I love it even when it skins yer! Oh, yes, it can hurt! . . . When the ice crackles underfoot . . . and the scrub tears the scabs off yer knuckles . . . and the spiders' webs are spun again . . . first of all . . . out of dew . . . it's to remind that life begins at dawn. Bald Mountain! I wasn't born here. Oh, no! But know it, how I know it! I've learnt to understand the silence of rocks. Only the barren can understand the barren. I tasted the little runty apples . . . and sour apricots . . . that somebody

planted before they died. On Bald Mountain, nobody else has survived. Nobody else. I've lived here so long, I've forgotten now. (pause) I don't go down . . . (pointing behind her) . . . not down there . . . though I watch the lights . . . at night . . . that glitter too much to be trusted. In the end, you can't trust anythun but goats and silence. Oh, yes, I know now! I've seen the mountains from a distance, too . . . moisture glist'nun on its bald patch . . . on bare rock. Sun on rock . . . that's the kiss that never betrays . . . because it doesn't promise nothun. . . .

Night on Bald Mountain can be regarded as only partially successful. But to have brought eloquence and poetry such as this into the theater is evidence that White possesses dramatic talents of a high order.

Big Toys is a more naturalistic and in some ways less ambitious play. Its subject is corruption and materialism: the big toys of the title are the physical objects and devices we strive and struggle for, the things with which we divert ourselves and with which we attempt to impress others. The action takes place in a luxurious penthouse overlooking Sydney Harbour. The three characters are a successful barrister, Ritchie Bosanquet, his fashionable wife, Mag, and Terry Legge, an Irish-Australian union leader. Legge is the first "toy." He is played with in various ways—sexual and social—by the Bosanquets; he is tempted with a toy—a Ferrari—with which Ritchie tries to bribe him; and over the whole play hangs the threat of the ultimate nuclear explosion, the biggest and most dangerous toy of all.

It is a competent and timely piece of theater and probably more fully integrated than any of the earlier plays; but it lacks the drive and originality that distinguishes them.

In 1983 White published two more plays, *Signal Driver* and *Netherwood.* Both pick up and echo themes and situations that have been dealt with in earlier works of drama and fiction. *Signal Driver* in particular, with its chorus of two filthy but angelic down-and-out deros (derelicts), recalls White's first published play, *The Ham Funeral.* It is a slight piece, but achieves real power in its presentation of the two main characters, a suburban husband and wife, in their old age.

Netherwood is a much more substantial and more fully realized play, and may well be judged eventually as one of White's most successful works for the theater. "Netherwood" is a large, decaying country house in the mountains not far from Sydney. Its occupants are a group of social and psychological misfits—"burnt ones"—attempting to come to terms with themselves through a sort of communal group therapy. Fantasies of sexual identity, of domination and dependence, of power and submission, are worked out through a series of confrontations and encounters. These scenes are by turns funny, pathetic, and moving—and always compelling and interesting.

Netherwood, though obviously contrived, is never labored or heavy-handed. It is theatrically brilliant and entertaining, even at the gory and melodramatic finale in which the forces of rural respectability, sanity, and law and order burst in with guns blazing and make the world safe once more for decent, normal people.

Should *Netherwood* turn out to be White's last play, his career as a dramatist will have ended not with a whimper but with a very lively bang.

CONCLUSION

When attempting to sum up White's achievement at an early stage in his career—it was shortly after the publication of *Voss*—I suggested that the image of humankind presented in his novels, though "delineated with a brilliant, an almost neurotic clarity," was possibly "distorted and even sinister." The passage of time and the full flowering of his talent have shown just how limited that assessment was: "sinister," in particular, strikes me as a remarkably inappropriate term to apply to the achievement of a writer whose vision is fundamentally so humane. White, of course, is preoccupied with humans' capacity for evil—and this is unquestionably a sinister thing. But it is the reverse of sinister to reveal this for what it is: to set Golgotha, Friedensdorf, and Sarsaparilla next to each other may be shocking, but the shock is of the sort that illuminates: it leaves us with a new and disturbing vision of humanity.

But despite his very great virtues as a novelist and playwright it must be confessed that White suffers from certain limitations. These limitations strike us the more strongly perhaps because of the very richness, versatility, and originality of his talent. As Margaret Walters, in an astringently commonsensical review of his work, has pointed out, the very brilliance of his manner can be deceptive.

Miss Walters misses a great deal, I think, especially in her treatment of *Voss,* but one must admit that White does have a tendency to "make elaborate gestures at a significance which dissolves under closer scrutiny." There is, especially in *Riders in the Chariot* and *The Solid Mandala,* a deal of rhetorical "sleight of hand" that under the guise of pointing to a genuine mystery, often appears to be used to draw our attention away from problems the author has not fully investigated. For a novelist of such stature, too, White's range of characterization seems unduly restricted. The odd, the abnormal, the eccentric dominate his fictive world; and although his "burnt ones" effectively throw light on the conditions of normal life, they could scarcely be described as a generally representative group of characters. Solitariness may be fundamental to human existence, but few of us are so painfully and continuously aware of our isolation. Even Stan Parker, that "ordinary" man, is unusually self-absorbed: he has acquaintances but no friends, and the life of the Parkers is remarkable for its lack of social warmth.

One may acknowledge these limitations, however, and still recognize that White is an author of quite unusual power, individuality, and integrity. It is impossible not to feel, after reading his fiction or seeing his plays, that he belongs to that small group of writers who really make you look at the world—at yourself and other people—in a new way. And while this is generally true, it has particular relevance for Australians: White has compelled his fellow countrymen, as no other writer has done, to see themselves in a fresh and often painfully revealing light. As Laura Trevelyan says of Voss, the country "is his by right of vision."

SELECTED BIBLIOGRAPHY

I. Bibliography. A. Lawson, *Patrick White,* in *Australian Bibliographies* (Melbourne, 1974); G. Dutton, ed., *The Literature of Australia* (Ringwood, Victoria, 1976); L. Kramer, ed., *The Oxford History of Australian Literature* (Melbourne, 1981); W. H. Wilde, ed., *The Oxford Companion to Australian Literature* (Melbourne, 1985).

II. Separate Works. *The Ploughman, and Other Poems* (Sydney, 1935), verse; *Happy Valley* (London, 1939), novel; *The Living and the Dead* (London, 1941), novel; *The Aunt's Story* (London, 1948), novel; *The Tree of Man* (New York, 1955; London, 1956), novel; *Voss* (London, 1957), novel; *Riders in the Chariot* (London, 1961), novel; *The Burnt Ones* (London, 1964), short stories; *Four Plays* (London, 1965), contains *The Ham Funeral, The Season at Sarsaparilla, A Cheery Soul,* and *Night on Bald Mountain; The Solid Mandala* (London, 1966), novel; *The Vivisector* (London, 1970), novel; *The Eye of the Storm* (London, 1973), novel; *The Cockatoos* (London, 1974), novellas and short stories; *A Fringe of Leaves* (London, 1976), novel; *Big Toys* (Sydney, 1978), play; *The Twyborn Affair* (London, 1979), novel; *Flaws in the Glass* (London, 1981), autobiography; *Signal Driver: A Morality Play for the Times* (Sydney, 1983); *Netherwood* (Sydney, 1983), play.

III. Articles and Interviews. "The Prodigal Son," in *Australian Letters,* I, 3 (1958), repr. in G. Dutton and M. Harris, eds.; R. F. Brissenden, "The Plays of Patrick White," in *Meanjin,* XXIII, 3 (1964); *The Vital Decade* (Melbourne, 1968), an autobiographical piece; "Patrick White," in C. McGregor, ed., *In the Making* (Melbourne, 1969), interview; T. Herring and G. A. Wilkes, "A Conversation with Patrick White," in *Southerly,* XXXIII (1973), interview.

IV. Biographical and Critical Studies. G. Dutton, *Patrick White* (Melbourne, 1961; 4th ed. rev. and enl., 1971); *Southerly,* XXV, 1 (1965), a Patrick White issue; B. Argyle, *Patrick White* (Edinburgh and London, 1967); F. W. Dillistone, *Patrick White's "Riders in the Chariot"* (New York, 1967); G. A. Wilkes, ed., *Ten Essays on Patrick White, Selected from "Southerly" (1964–67)* (Sydney, 1970); B. Hickey, *Aspects of Alienation in James Joyce and Patrick White* (Rome, 1971); P. Morley, *The Mystery of Unity: Theme and Technique in the Novels of Patrick White* (Montreal and St. Lucia, Queensland, 1972); I. Bjorksten, *Patrick White: A General Introduction* (Vanersborg, 1973), tr. by S. Gerson (St. Lucia, Queensland, 1976); J. R. Dyce, *Patrick White as Playwright* (St. Lucia, Queensland, 1974); P. Beatson, *The Eye in the Mandala* (London, 1976); W. Walsh, *Patrick White: "Voss"* (London, 1976); W. Walsh, *Patrick White's Fiction* (Hornsby, New South Wales, 1977); R. Shepherd and K. Singh, *Patrick White: A Critical Symposium* (Adelaide, 1978); D. Myers, *The Peacocks and the Bourgeoisie: Patrick White's Shorter Fiction* (Adelaide, 1978); B. Kiernan, *Patrick White* (London, 1980); A. M. McCulloch, *A Tragic Vision: The Novels of Patrick White* (St. Lucia, Queensland, 1983); K. Hansson, *The Warped Universe: A Study of Imagery and Structure in Seven Novels by Patrick White* (Lund, 1984), contains an excellent selected bibliography.

ANGUS WILSON

(1913–)

K. W. Gransden

I

ANGUS WILSON was born at Bexhill, Sussex, on 11 August 1913 and educated at Westminster School and Merton College, Oxford. He served during World War II in the Foreign Office (his work in a code-breaking station is the setting of the early story "Christmas Day in the Workhouse"). Both before and after the war he was on the staff of the British Museum, where he worked in the British Library (then the museum's Department of Printed Books), and he served as Deputy Superintendent of the Reading Room from 1949 to 1955. The success of his first stories led to his resignation from the museum so that he could concentrate on writing, although from 1966 to 1978 Wilson also held a Chair of English at the University of East Anglia. He was knighted in 1980.

Wilson has provided some fascinating information about his life in relation to his early fiction in *The Wild Garden, or Speaking of Writing,* originally a series of lectures given in California in 1960 and first published in 1963, fourteen years after the appearance of his first book of stories, *The Wrong Set* (1949). *The Wild Garden* also corrects a misconception—the South African childhood referred to in the Penguin editions of his books. Although his mother was South African, Wilson did not visit that country until he was nine; his childhood was largely passed in hotels in the south of England and at a London public school. Only one of his early stories, "Union Reunion," has a South African setting.

Childhood and the family forms the deepest autobiographical layer in Wilson's fiction. It is also perhaps the most English of all literary subjects: Wilson writes here in the tradition of E. M. Forster and Christopher Isherwood. The mother in his devastating attack on the family, "Mother's Sense of Fun," is akin to Mrs. Lindsay in Isherwood's *All the Conspirators.* A disgusted view of family life is seen in "Union Reunion." The lonely, sensitive child is the subject of the story "Necessity's Child" (in the second book of stories, *Such Darling Dodos,* 1950). Rodney, neglected by his smart-shallow parents, escapes into fantasy like the boy in Forster's story "The Celestial Omnibus," though the form taken by the fantasy is significantly different. The hearty clergyman in Wilson's story resembles Mr. Bons in "The Celestial Omnibus" and Mr. Pembroke in Forster's novel of sensitive childhood, *The Longest Journey.* Wilson's Rodney tries to make himself interesting to adults by romancing: first he pretends that his mother is ill, then that a kindly old couple he met on the "front" (the story is set in an English seaside town) have shown him obscene pictures. In his final fantasy he imagines his parents are drowned, with confused memories drawn from his reading—the sinking of the *Titanic* in 1912 and of the *Pequod* in *Moby Dick.* A more violent version of this fantasy occurs in "Mummy to the Rescue," while another story, "Mother's Sense of Fun," also ends with a nightmare in which Donald (whose mother, like Rickie's in *The Longest Journey,* has really died) realizes that "she had tied him to her and now she had left him for ever."

But whereas in Forster's "Celestial Omnibus" the boy's fantasy about the bus that goes to heaven is "truer" and more beautiful than the prosaic "reality" of the adult world, in "Necessity's Child" this idealistic resolution is characteristically rejected. Forster's concept of salvation through innocence becomes in Wilson a matter of makeshift, of "getting by" in the corrupt adult world by using its own language of disgust. The irony of the story lies in the fact that the timid Rodney gains through his lies a false reputation for being "a very brave boy." The pressures of adult selfishness on the child's mind produce in him the sort of revenge-fantasy from memories of which, years later, Wilson himself was to start writing. In his earliest story, "Raspberry Jam," the obscene reminiscence of two crazy, drunken old women "was largely meaningless to the boy, though he remembered it in later years."

Wilson wrote "Raspberry Jam," probably the most horrific of his stories, in 1946, when he was thirty-three, at a time of personal crisis and conflict. He was then an assistant keeper in the Department of Printed Books at the British Museum. Several of his early stories can be seen as attempts to come to terms with the past, in order to shape the future into something new. This pattern in his own life is reflected in the lives of the central characters of several of his novels, for example, Gerald Middleton in *Anglo-Saxon Attitudes.*

II

THE museum is both a great center of scholarship and a department of the civil service, and is unofficially linked in a nexus of influence to the world of the universities, the art galleries, and the BBC. Wilson's work there gave him an understanding of the management of English high culture, which forms the second important layer in his work. He used his experience of this world in several stories, in the first two novels, and later in *The Old Men at the Zoo* (1961), where the zoo stands in a kind of transposition for the museum (or any other great institution), and the "old men" are the traditional administrators who belong to the Athenaeum Club, cover up their errors, and conceal their private inadequacies behind the image of the system.

The museum also stands in Bloomsbury, the quarter of London associated earlier in this century with an influential intellectual coterie that included Forster, Leonard and Virginia Woolf, Lord Keynes, and Lytton Strachey. Of this liberal-humanist tradition Wilson is both the spiritual heir and the satirical critic.

The cultural establishment is also the milieu of Wilson's only play, *The Mulberry Bush* (1956), which deals with one of his central themes: the dilemma of intellectual idealists in post–1945 England. The play opens with the retirement from a college headship of Professor Padley, a high-minded member of a famous liberal family. He says of his successor, a new-style bureaucrat (the situation resembles that in an earlier story, "Realpolitik"): "I've no doubt that his great business acumen will be of inestimable service to the college in these days of high-powered administration." The irony here is directed not just against the bureaucrat, unlikable though he is clearly meant to be: it is also directed against Padley himself, who uses the hallowed language of reasonableness yet cannot face the fact that society has rejected his ideals and values. The decline of the liberal tradition forms the theme of the first two novels and also of the story "Such Darling Dodos," in which opposition to the Oxford radical humanism of Robin and Priscilla (the Dodos of the title) comes from an ironically handled, intellectually meaningless alliance between the younger generation (for whom the 1930's is almost a dirty word for the failure to make ideals work) and Cousin Tony, an elderly Catholic aesthete: when Tony is told by the students that his cousins are living in the past, "he hadn't felt so modern since the first production of *L'Après-midi.*"[1]

Most of Wilson's middle-aged liberals are nagged by feelings of self-doubt, failure, or guilt, yet they continue to accept the Victorian ideals of progress and enlightenment with which they were brought up. The phrase "all the things there are to do" in *The Mulberry Bush* is almost an echo of Alfred Tennyson's "so much to do, so little done."

The weakness of liberal humanism in post-1945 England is demonstrated in much of Wilson's work by weakness on the part of its adherents in the one field they traditionally most respected—that of personal relations. They fail because they cannot practice what they preach. Some of them are so obsessed with scruples about their own motives that they cannot act at all; they are moral paralytics. In *The Wild Garden* Wilson speaks of the "tragic paradox" that "the self-knowledge necessary to bridge the chasm" between liberal intentions in personal relations and actual failure becomes "itself the agent of the stultified will."

The most positive character in *The Mulberry Bush* is Professor Padley's protégé, Peter, who gives up historical research (which equals "truth") for administration ("power") rather than accompany the professor on yet another "do-gooding" mission.

[1]A famous landmark in twentieth-century art—the production by Serge Diaghilev of the ballet *L'Après-midi d'un faune* (music by Claude Debussy) in Paris, 1912.

(The play is contemporary with the novel *Anglo-Saxon Attitudes,* which also explores the relation between historical research and "getting things done.") Peter is accused of abandoning ideals, but for him his choice represents the saving of all the Padleys stood for, without the patronage and self-satisfaction, the helping hand extended so readily to criminals and misfits. This charge of self-indulgence is also brought by implication against Bernard in *Hemlock and After* (1952). Similarly, in *Anglo-Saxon Attitudes* Mrs. Middleton's left-wing idealism is shown up as the sentimental stupidity of a rich woman when she takes into her house a charming Irish boy who is in fact a homosexual layabout and a thief, and who later nearly destroys her son, John. (One thinks here also of Ernest's attempts to reform prostitutes in Samuel Butler's *The Way of All Flesh.*)

In *The Mulberry Bush* Peter says, "Just because the Padleys have gone dead, it doesn't mean it can't be done: it can, but not here, not in their way. I have the sense to face reality." This—facing up to reality—is the challenge that faces all Wilson's liberal humanists: sometimes it defeats them. Bernard in *Hemlock and After* has won support for a country home for writers, but in his speech at the opening of the house he throws his victory away: "he seemed quite unable to leave the subject of motivation, so that the more inattentive of his audience got the impression that they were involved in a discussion of some mysterious crime." What they are involved in is the liberal-humanist death wish: the failure of will, the fatal self-consciousness, the too-scrupulous conscience that also bedevils Gerald in *Anglo-Saxon Attitudes.*

Wilson's work is valuable as social documentary. He records with great accuracy the changing idiom, habits, and fashions of English society in his lifetime: references like the one in "A Bit Off the Map" to Carroll Levis' *Discoveries,* a now defunct radio program, will furnish material for future research students. But the primary aim of his early stories is satirical, not sociological. In story after story he ruthlessly exposes the naked truth, the secret motives and humiliations, behind the public mask of pomposity and self-congratulation. Many of the early stories contain passages of violent physical disgust. In "Union Reunion," set back in 1924 (the year of the Great Empire Exhibition at Wembley, referred to in the story), South Africa is seen through the eyes of Laura, a middle-aged woman revisiting her relatives after many years in England. She is struck by their grossness and vulgarity: they have been coarsened by years of cheap food, cheap servants, and cheap cars. The cosy family dinner party is described in language that is deliberately orgiastic:

> Stanley himself had seen to the menu and had ordered a massacre in the poultry-yard that would have challenged Herod—a goose, a turkey, two ducks and two fowls had all shed their blood that Laura might feel welcome and Aunt Liz's eighty-eighth birthday not pass unhonoured.

The biblical allusion turns what is already gross into something cruel and evil. Eating habits are frequently treated with disgust, as in the sickening description of Mrs. Wrigley's meal of sardines and stewed tea in her paraffin-heated cottage (in *Hemlock and After*), or the description, in the story "Higher Standards" (included in the third and last collection of stories, *A Bit Off the Map,* 1957), of a "grunter," a baked suet roll filled with unappetizing leftovers: "Mrs Corfe retained the humour of the tradition by inserting two burnt currants for the pig's eyes and a sprig of parsley for its tail." Wilson frequently uses animal imagery to give a disgusted view of humanity. Brian Capper's smile in "Totentanz" is "equine with gum-recession"; Gwen in "Rex Imperator" "had retained her peroxide shingle and the rolls of blue stubbled fat at the back of her neck added to the bull-dog illusion."

Wilson is both fascinated and disgusted by characters like Mrs. Wrigley, or Mrs. Salad, the Dickensianly named ex-lavatory attendant in *Anglo-Saxon Attitudes.* He combines satire and social documentary in his descriptions of such characters, who form a kind of subworld in his early work. These characters live on the very edge of respectability, or beyond it. Some are stupid (like Mrs. Wrigley); others, like Ron Wrigley or Mrs. Salad's grandson Vin, are on the make, usually by exploiting themselves sexually. A few are wholly evil, notably Mrs. Curry in *Hemlock and After,* almost a monstrous Dickensian caricature. Wilson draws a sharp moral distinction between those who exploit themselves and those—like Mrs. Curry—who exploit others. It is indeed Ron Wrigley who finally helps to expose Mrs. Curry, who conceals her "business" of procuring a thirteen-year-old girl for a "respectable" architect under the catchphrase "We can do with a bit of love in this crazy old world, can't we?" Her definition of love is contrasted in the novel with the romantic, guilt-ridden pederasty of the hero, Bernard Sands.

The characters in Wilson's underworld often form parasitic relationships with the respectable. This is particularly true of his homosexual or "camp" characters (the word occurs in the punning title of one of the chapters of *Hemlock and After*). This world of waiters, designers, interior decorators, theater types, and so on, is almost a subculture. Typical Wilson camp characters are Guy in "Totentanz," with his "great flair for pastiche" and his "flat cockney whine," and Sherman in *Hemlock,* who also affects this cockney voice. The peculiar brittle, "bitchy" tone of camp conversation is brilliantly caught in the scene in *Hemlock* in the theater bar during the interval of Ibsen's *Ghosts* (the choice of this play, with its obsession with family guilt, is significant for the whole novel). Here is Sherman talking to Bernard:

> "Terence," he said, "is battling at the bar. It suits him to the ground. Pure Barkers' sales. Bless his little Kensington heart. Bernard, my dear, you look tired. Oh, I know, bitching me! Tired equals old. You must make him rest, dear," he said to Eric. "You know, feet up and forty winks. Not that I should think you'd be much good at making people rest," he stared Eric up and down. "You look a proper little fidget to me."
>
> (ch. 5)

Wilson makes these venal and often sad relationships satirically explicit, repudiating the "gentleman's agreement" by which they used to be regarded as unmentionable or disgusting or embarrassing (compare the reactions of two respectable characters, Gerald in *Anglo-Saxon Attitudes* and Harold in *Late Call,* to the discovery that their sons are homosexual). Christopher Isherwood has described interclass homosexual relationships through characters like Otto, the beautiful working-class Berlin boy in *Goodbye to Berlin,* but has generally shown them in cosmopolitan settings. Wilson does not show his camp characters as exotics, nor are they seen as if by a tourist slumming with a camera. They are shown as part of the very fabric of English society. Ron's attempt to pick up Eric, Sands's boyfriend, in *Hemlock and After* takes place in the shadow of St. Albans Cathedral. Like Dickens, Wilson shows the private links, the secret interdependence, between different worlds.

III

THE success of Wilson's early stories lies in their sharp, vivid, satirical analyses of people's vulnerability, failure, and self-deception. His technique is to show a character as he wishes to appear to others and as he has succeeded in appearing to himself, and to interpose ironic deflationary comments that reveal the resentments and true motives hidden behind the veneer. Here is the master of a Scottish university in "Totentanz": a colleague has just received a legacy and a London professorship:

> "How typical of women," he said in the unctuous but incisive voice that convinced so many businessmen and baillies that they were dealing with a scholar whose head was screwed on the right way. "How typical of women to consider only the legacy. Very nice, of course, a great help in their new sphere." There was a trace of bitterness, for his own wife's fortune, so important when they started, had vanished through his unfortunate investments. "But Capper's London Chair is the important thing. A new Chair, too, Professor of the History of Technics and Art. Here, of course, we've come to accept so many of Capper's ideas . . . " He paused, staring eaglelike beneath his bushy white eyebrows, the scholar who was judge of men—"that we forget how revolutionary some of them are." He had, indeed, the vaguest conception of anything that his subordinates thought, an administrator has to keep above detail.

A character frequently satirized in this way is the ex-officer, the gentleman down on his luck, the professional cadger with his sentimental reminiscences of better days. He recurs with minor variations throughout Wilson's work and may be compared with the portrait of the author's father in *The Wild Garden.* He appears as old Mr. Nicholson in "Rex Imperator": he refers to his successful son-in-law, on whom he is sponging, as "young master Rex," the patronizing tone being a pathetic attempt to cover his resentment and humiliation (Captain Calvert in *Late Call* similarly refers to *his* successful son as "young master Harold"). When Mr. Nicholson "risked what little cash he still had from Rex's last loan" on a horse, and won, "like the brave old sportsman he was," the last phrase is the author's satirical comment but is also the character's view of himself ("with all my vices I can safely say I've never been mean").

A more fully realized version of this type is Maurice Legge in the story "What Do Hippos Eat?"

(set, like a later novel, in the London zoo). Maurice is "worn out with schemes and lies and phoney deals." His self-deception is ruthlessly emphasized: "he had told so many stories for so many years, truth and falsehood were so inextricably mixed, that to check a new falsehood by a poorly remembered old one made him feel that in some way truth must be involved somewhere." Maurice is in fact no better at facing reality than are privileged idealists like Padley. He thinks he has at last found a girl who will support him, but Greta, for all her "childlike" manner, and though she admires his old-fashioned style and worldly experience, is not taken in by him: "Greta's realism had begun at sixteen as a waitress, Maurice's had never really got going: it was hardly an even match."

The climax of this story, and the point of its title, comes when Maurice, in order to impress Greta, persuades the keeper of the hippos to take them behind the scenes. But Maurice, who is tired, nearly falls into the pool, and his suit is splashed with mud. The young keeper apologizes but exchanges "an amused smile" with Greta, who says, "It's a terrible old thing anyway. I'm going to get him a new one tomorrow." Enraged at this snub to his manhood, Maurice puts his hands on Greta and is about to push her into the pool when he is checked by his ignorance of hippos' diet: were they carnivores, "or would they turn away from the floating Greta in disgust, in which case he would simply have mucked up all his schemes"? So he lets his hands drop, and Greta, who has misinterpreted his gesture as one of affection, puts on her "wide-eyed" act, turns to him, and asks, "What *do* hippos eat, darling?"

Many of the early stories revolve round similar snubs or humiliations. In "Realpolitik" the pushing, newly appointed administrator-head of an art gallery snubs his staff; only his admiring secretary remains loyal, but even she punctures his self-esteem, and his final thought is "perhaps a graduate secretary would really be more suitable now." Other stories that end with a snub are "Learning's Little Tribute," "Et Dona Ferentes," and "Christmas Day in the Workhouse."

Many of the stories begin on a quite realistic note and are then pushed deliberately over the edge of realism into a climax of farce, hysteria, or violence: the author contrives a situation in which the characters lose control. Thus, after the orgiastic dinner in "Union Reunion," one of the characters accuses another of letting Laura's young son, many years previously, die through neglect. The most violent climax is the famous ending of "Raspberry Jam" in which two crazy, drunken old women tear a live bird to pieces in front of a child. Violence is blended with farce in the climax of "A Bit Off the Map," in which a psychotic "Teddy boy" assaults a mad colonel, and in the macabre party that ends "Totentanz":

> Only the moon lit the vast spaces of Brompton Cemetery, showing up here a tomb and there a yew tree. Professor Cadaver's eyes were wild and his hands shook as he glided down the central pathway. His head still whirled with the fumes of the party and a thousand beautiful corpses danced before his eyes. . . . At last he reached his objective—a freshly dug grave on which wooden planks and dying wreaths were piled. The Professor began feverishly to tear these away, but he was getting old, and neither his sight nor his step was as sure as it had been; he caught his foot in a rope and fell nine or ten feet into the tomb. When they found him in the morning his neck was broken. The papers hushed up the affair, and a Sunday newspaper in an article entitled "Has Science the Right?" only confused the matter by describing him as a professor of anatomy and talking obscurely of Burke and Hare.[2]

Farce and hysteria are extravagantly blended in the tragicomic scene, in *Hemlock and After,* of the opening of Vardon Hall as a home for writers; the guests get out of control and indulge in camp orgies after a speech by Bernard in which he too loses his "civilized" self-control and betrays his fears and guilt in a series of "unfortunate" Freudian slips. In such scenes Wilson offers an almost surrealist distortion of reality.

Wilson uses nuances of speech not only to place his characters socially and psychologically but also with satiric intent, to invoke a reaction in the "knowing" and discriminating reader—usually a kind of wincing distaste. Thus Arthur in "A Visit in Bad Taste" refers to port as "very fruity, very tasty" and speaks of "Nature's call." (Stanley in "Union Reunion" refers similarly to "where you can't go for me.") Maurice Legge calls his heart "the old ticker" "even to himself." Mrs. Carrington's verbal mannerisms in "Mother's Sense of Fun" are mercilessly listed in her son's mind:

[2]Burke and Hare, notorious body snatchers in Edinburgh in the 1820's, provided corpses for surgeons by robbing graves and also by murder.

He had often thought that to find his mother's phrases one would have to go to English translations of opera or the French and German prose books that he had used at school. It always "rained cats and dogs," that is if the rain did not "look like holding off"; Alice Stockfield was "a bit down in the mouth" but then she "let things get on top of her"; Roger Grant was "certainly no Adonis" but she had "an awfully soft spot in her heart for him."

Wilson's early stories were first published in *Horizon,* the leading avant-garde literary magazine of the 1940's (it is caricatured as *Survival* by Evelyn Waugh in *Unconditional Surrender*). Yet although the appeal of these early stories is to make the reader feel both clever and fastidious, the style in which they are written shows little regard for elegance, since it consists frequently of breathless, underpunctuated sentences that reflect the sudden release of a long-suppressed creative urge:

Claire was standing by a pot of hydrangeas, the return of physical desire had animated her features as he had not seen them since the early years of their marriage. "Hullo, Pookie," he said, "care for a dance?" The use of her pet name after so many years came strangely to Claire, she knew quite well that his sudden interest was only an interval in the usual routine of their lives, she knew that there was no reciprocal feeling in herself, that she would regret the loss of her new hunger for Tom, but habit was very strong and it shut down upon her emotions, she could not resist an opportunity to strengthen the frayed marital tie.

("Saturnalia," *The Wrong Set*)

It is as if, one feels, Claire's thoughts must be recorded quickly, before they can be arranged and (therefore) falsified.

It is as if, too, while offering his first stories to a coterie of the discriminating, Wilson were already probing toward a larger public primarily interested in matter rather than manner, in life rather than art. And in the novels that follow *Anglo-Saxon Attitudes* Wilson seems deliberately to widen his subject matter, moving away from both the liberal dilemma and from the "raffish flotsam" (his own phrase in *The Wild Garden*) of his hotel childhood into characters and milieux with which the middle-class novel reader can identify. And, even in the first two novels, the cleverness and the externalization of the early satirical stories are deepened by the sympathy and understanding with which the central characters are developed.

IV

WILSON's first novel, *Hemlock and After* (1952), remains arguably his best because it is the most passionately written. Its theme is Forsterian: the relation between the inner life and the outer, and the question of the effectiveness of liberal humanism in our time. Bernard Sands, a successful novelist, is Socratic (hence the book's title) because he ironically and high-mindedly questions accepted values and also because he can be accused of "corrupting youth"; though married, he has become a practicing homosexual. The story moves from victory to disaster—or, looked at in another way, from self-deception to self-knowledge. It starts with Sands triumphant: he has secured Vardon Hall, a local country house, as a home for writers. Because of his personal standing, he has even won government support for his liberal belief that the house should be run without state interference. In a sense, he vouches for an entire moral structure: as soon as he loses confidence in his motives, his whole world, including Vardon Hall, collapses into chaos. Wilson argues that liberal humanists tend to fight their battles inside their own consciences rather than against the real evil in the outer world. This evil is portrayed in the book in Mrs. Curry, the procuress. She too wanted the Hall; Bernard says, "It would have been interesting to see what she would have made of it." But this scrupulous and high-minded fairness is at once discredited by the author's comment that Bernard in fact knew very well what she would have made of it: "a second-rate profiteering road-house," or, as a retired admiral more bluntly puts it, "a high-class knocking-shop." The dishonesty of liberalism is already apparent.

Sands is forced to face the problem of moral evil not only through Mrs. Curry's activities, about which he learns from his camp connections, but also through his homosexuality. One night in Leicester Square he sees a man arrested for importuning, and, though he is not himself involved and refuses to give the police any evidence, he realizes that the incident has given him a *frisson.* This incident makes him reexamine the predicament of the individualist in an authoritarian society: "a humanist, it would seem, was more at home with the wielders of the knout and the rubber truncheon." A civil service friend, Charles Murley, says to Sands, "You people want the pleasures of authority without any of its penalties." Sands realizes that the liberal humanist's greatest weakness is that which is also his most precious moral and intellectual luxury: his ambivalence, his freedom to move between two worlds, the world of the Athenaeum and the college high tables, and the world of the Leicester Square bars: the quality that a camp acquaintance refers to less flatteringly as "versatility."

By the time of the opening of Vardon Hall, Bernard has lost faith in the scheme and in his own authority. Instead of the "clear, humorous, high-minded speech" everyone had expected him to make, he makes a long, confused, and "disastrous" confession of guilt, dwelling on evil and defeat. Afterwards he says, "I see Nothing behind nothing," echoing the anti-vision of the Marabar caves in Forster's *A Passage to India.* He has now made his choice and has puzzled both his respectable and his camp friends. "I must stand with the unfortunate," he writes in his last letter, just before he dies.

Because of what Murley refers to as "his mood of exaggerated conscience" Bernard cannot bring himself to denounce Mrs. Curry publicly. This is done by his wife, Ella, after his death. During his earlier period of triumph Ella had been in a state of neurotic withdrawal from the world, and this is structurally related to Bernard's withdrawal into sickness and despair in the second half of the book. When he dies, Ella comes back to life. At the end of the book their daughter says to Ella: "It seems strange that his books will have such influence when in his life he got so little done. I suppose it's because you were always the doer." "My dear," Ella replies, "doing doesn't last, even if one knows what one's doing, which one usually doesn't."

The point that "doing doesn't last" is neatly illustrated when we learn that Mrs. Curry used her time in prison, from which she is released after two years as a result of good behavior, to form "a most useful group of loving dutiful girls through whom she could bring snugness and cosiness to respectable gentlemen." Bernard's failure in the world of action is further illustrated by another irony: after his death, Vardon Hall is to be run by a public relations man, "quite young and very pushing," clearly a similar type to the administrators in "Realpolitik" and *The Mulberry Bush.* Bernard deliberately destroys his own charisma; yet he dies content, retaining a kind of innocence. Ella sees him as a small boy. Like many of Wilson's characters, he never grows up. Even the self-knowledge he attains is masochistic. Murley's loyalty to him seems exaggeratedly deferential, though this is perhaps necessary to balance the dislike felt for him by Mrs. Curry and Eric's mother. Wilson's treatment of him is more romantic than anything in the later novels.

The humanist crisis of conscience is more objectively examined in the next novel, *Anglo-Saxon Attitudes* (1956), the best plotted of all Wilson's novels. The title, taken from Lewis Carroll's *Through the Looking-Glass,* exemplifies the author's addiction at this time to jokes, puns, and clichés in his titles and chapter headings: it refers not only to the Anglo-Saxon period (the novel is about medieval historians) but also to that elusive complex of attitudes and prejudices that make up the English temperament during the present time, in which the action of the book is set.

In 1912, before the action proper begins, a pagan idol was discovered in the tomb of a seventh-century bishop excavated at Melpham in East Anglia by the late Professor Stokesay, a medievalist who in his last years discredited his profession by becoming a political journalist and pro-Nazi. (The find is elaborately documented by Wilson in a spoof appendix.) The discovery has led some medievalists to construct theories about the survival of paganism in early Christian England. The plot turns on the probability that the idol was planted in the tomb by Stokesay's son, Gilbert, a neurotic poet killed in World War I. Such a joke, perpetrated out of revenge against a too-famous father and out of a youthful iconoclast's desire to show up the vanity and lack of imagination of scholars, might be hard to explain outside England (the England that produced Butler's *The Way of All Flesh* and Edmund Gosse's *Father and Son*), and this is part of the point of the novel. It may seem a rather technical theme for a long book, but the result is a fascinating detective story as well as an exploration of the character of English intellectuals during the forty years between World War I and the 1950's.

The forty years cover the adult life of Gerald Middleton, the novel's hero, a retired professor of medieval history. In a long reverie that forms most of the first half of the novel, he relives many of the earlier events of his life. Despite—or because of—his charm and distinction, he feels he has failed both in his personal life and in his professional career. He has failed as a husband (he lives apart from his wife), as a father (his children ignore him), and as a lover (his ex-mistress, Dollie, Gilbert

Stokesay's widow, has become a dipsomaniac). He also doubts the value of historical studies. His failure to face up to the truth is symbolized by his failure to voice his suspicions (based on a clearly remembered conversation with Gilbert when the latter was drunk) that the Melpham idol is a hoax. Thus the central theme of the novel continues the inner debate begun in *Hemlock and After;* but while Bernard dies, Gerald at last succeeds in confessing his suspicions about Melpham and resumes his long neglected historical work.

Like Sands, Gerald has an "exaggerated conscience." His friend and mentor, Sir Edgar Iffley, doyen of English medievalists, finds Gerald's handling of the Melpham affair "finicking and highstrung," "typical of these rich tradespeople" (the Middletons run a family business from which Gerald, though taking no part, draws large dividends), "more like a Dissenter than a gentleman." Once again, Wilson is analyzing the nonconformist conscience as seen in a certain type of cultivated English intellectual.

At the very end of the book, Sir Edgar is seeing Gerald off at London airport on a trip to Mexico. They run into Clarissa Crane, a second-rate novelist whom we met in the opening chapter, when she attended a meeting of medievalists (this meeting is perhaps the most brilliantly observed scene in all Wilson's writing) in search of copy. Sir Edgar had then taken a dislike to Miss Crane, putting her down as a time-waster. Now she criticizes Middleton to him for not having done much with his life (the same criticism as that made of Sands at the end of the previous novel). Sir Edgar answers, "I can imagine someone who hardly knew him at all thinking so," and departs, thinking (and these are the last words of the book), "God knows who the woman was—never seen her face or heard her name before. One thing was perfectly clear to him, however: she was a time-waster."

Once again, Wilson's own sympathies toward an ambivalent central character are clear. It is significant that Gilbert, who perpetrated the Melpham fraud, is a disciple of T. E. Hulme and Wyndham Lewis, who opposed the Bloomsbury liberal tradition. Wilson maintains that this tradition, for all its vulnerability and self-doubt, remains more attractive and also more valuable than anything else in English intellectual and moral life. In satirical contrast to Middleton stands Professor Clun, unattractive, efficient in research, a man who could never suffer a psychological block or a crisis of conscience. The judgment that it is better to fail with Middleton than succeed with Clun is characteristic of Bloomsbury.

Besides its main theme, *Anglo-Saxon Attitudes* (the most spacious and Dickensian of Wilson's novels) contains several subplots, built around members of Middleton's family, his fellow historians (there are a number of delightful satirical portraits for those who know this world), and the survivors of Melpham; some of these subplots also take us into the camp world.

Meg, the heroine of Wilson's next novel, *The Middle Age of Mrs Eliot* (1958), is a female version of Gerald Middleton. She too is rich, charming, attractive, sensual, a dilettante by temperament (both collect works of art): she even "drawls" like Middleton. Her husband, Bill—a successful though rather neurotic barrister—dies suddenly early in the book, in Forsterian style, and the novel is the story of how Meg rebuilds her life. The book is, however, less interesting than its two predecessors. Meg tends to collapse into a set of rather tiresome mannerisms (such as her habit of saying "Dear God"). Her perceptions are treated more schematically, more externally, than Bernard's or Gerald's. One is perhaps reminded of Forster's treatment of Helen Schlegel in *Howards End.* Yet Wilson has said in *The Wild Garden* that he consciously identified himself with Meg rather than with her two predecessors, and that he sought to relate her dilemma —a crisis of despair followed by a new self-knowledge—to his own. We are told in the novel that Meg was "made to judge," which puts her with Bernard and Gerald: like them, too, she looks ironically on her own conclusions yet is also (in a curious way typical of the liberal sensibility) satisfied with them: so that her final self-assessment—"I'm quite a silly person really"—does not emerge as a criticism.

The book's other main character is Meg's brother, David, who has abandoned the academic world to keep a market garden in Sussex with Gordon, a homosexual friend. In *The Wild Garden* Wilson stresses the importance of gardening in his work and in his life since he left the museum and made his home in a cottage in East Anglia. But I do not think he makes this subject interesting. Perhaps it is something one has to do, not write about. David's house, with its Saxon name (Andredaswood), is perhaps a symbol of English life in retreat: indeed, the novel has echoes, both in this symbolic house and in the heroine's name, of *Howards End.* But David's life seems sterile, like his relationship with Gordon. After Gordon's death David toys with the idea of going back to research. Just before Meg leaves Andredaswood, where she has been recuperating, there is a brief nursery idyll in which she helps her brother to rearrange his notes on eighteenth-century fiction. But David's eremitical detachment is alien to Meg's worldly energy.

Meg's rehabilitation is depicted rather on the level of an article on a superior "woman's page": as a lesson in "pluck," in "managing"—the kind of attitude the earlier Wilson might have satirized. Perhaps because one is antagonized by Meg's "enviable" coolness and "exotic" glitter at the beginning of the book, one feels little sympathy for her later vulnerability. Meg has virtues, notably adaptability, courage, and independence, and for these one may admire her; but she remains somehow hard to like, while the other characters never really come to life.

The Old Men at the Zoo (1961) is an ambitious attempt to break new ground. Set in the 1970's, it is about who shall run England, a moral fable on the theme that power corrupts. The London Zoo is not only, in the novel, the famous national institution; it also becomes, like England itself, a battleground of conflicting values and interests; its various administrators are the traditional bureaucracy, whose failure is shown as both disastrous and degrading. After a brief and rather unconvincing war, England emerges committed to "Pan-Europeanism," which is revealed as even more unsavory than the ancien régime. When the zoo reopens, its new director, a Central European scholar ironically named Englander, allows it to be used for unscholarly and disgusting propaganda. Thus "an old mangy Siberian bear" is exhibited with one leg tethered and the label "The Russian Bear in Difficulties." Later, one of the "new men"—the kind of men, it is suggested, whom violence brings to power—wants to stage public fights in the zoo between animals and political prisoners. Englander is sent to prison for acquiescing in this suggestion, and the last of the "old men" has gone. At the end of the book there is a characteristically Wilsonian episode in which Simon Carter, the book's narrator, secretary of the Zoo and now a candidate for the directorship, faces the vice-president, Professor Hales, an unsympathetic figure, rather like Clun in *Anglo-Saxon Attitudes.* Hales refers to the past as "a very bad period" (and as with Clun, the judgment is correct—it is the tone, the lack of insight, that is criticized). He asks Carter how he feels about "the new world before us." Carter's answer is that of the unrepentant humanist: "It excites me enormously, especially because I shall always be involved with the old."

Carter is torn—in a typically Wilsonian dilemma—between administration and scholarship. When he has to act in a crisis, he says, "I needed all my irony to protect myself from the absurd pretension of the action," and this need for irony is characteristic. The question is, can a man keep his integrity in a world of power? As in *Hemlock and After,* personal vulnerability affects public decisions. Earlier in the book, a plan to start a nature reserve in the country is defeated by the forces of reaction (who want to keep the zoo as a popular London spectacle) and by a scandal involving the nymphomaniac daughter of the then director.

The zoo animals are shown as the victims of human violence and stupidity. At the beginning of the book a giraffe, most harmless of large animals, accidently kills a keeper; then an Alsatian dog is shot because of human concupiscence; in the war, Carter kills and eats a badger—another large, harmless animal on which he is an amateur authority.

For all its detail and its intelligence, and despite some very powerful scenes, especially in the second half, this novel does not succeed in holding the reader's unflagging attention throughout its great length in the way *Anglo-Saxon Attitudes* does. This may be partly due to the use of first-person narration. It is not a technique that suits this author: the other example of it, the first half of the story "A Bit Off the Map," is also unsuccessful (the second half, when the device is abandoned, is far better). We are obliged to take Carter at his rather dull face value, and he tends to blur and confuse some of the events.

With *Late Call* (1964) Wilson returns to the high comedy of his earlier manner yet also offers, in Sylvia Calvert, one of his most sympathetic central figures. This is perhaps the most enjoyable of the later novels. After a poor country childhood (described in a curious and touching prologue that is almost a Lawrentian short story) Sylvia marries; but her husband, Arthur, "the Captain," has never got over World War I and has ever since led a disreputable yet somehow defiant saloon-bar existence. Sylvia has therefore had to work all her life, as a hotel manageress. When the novel proper opens, the couple are coming to live with their son, Harold, in Carshall New Town. Harold, a widower with teenage children, is a successful schoolmaster with an extrovert, hearty, patronizing manner and a tiresome sense of humor that prevents self-criticism. His "new-style" progressivism is well-intentioned but spiritually blinkered. He lacks the saving Wilsonian irony and is consequently fair game for ironic treatment. The family setup is splendidly satirized. When Sylvia, unused to central heating, dares to adjust the thermostat, Harold, highly offended, issues a "rota" of household duties that ends "Temperature Control: Harold." He has a boyish enthusiasm for his "ranch-type" house and for the expensive gadgets that his extra income from writing textbooks has brought him. His demonstration to his mother of his electric cooker—with its "autotimer" fitted with a specially muted "pinger"—is brilliantly held on the very edge of caricature:

> "Now take this meal we're cooking this evening. Of course, it's not a normal meal. I've specially designed it to illustrate all the equipment," he smoothed his moustache with a certain pride. "The goulash in your top oven. And just for this evening—an example of conspicuous waste—an apfelstrudel in your lower oven. Of course, that's really reserved for the big fellows, turkeys and such and for any fiestas. We'll bake there for this little party we're giving for you before Christmas. Then, on the drop-in hob—soup for Dad on the simmerstat, and on the two hob points two veg, also for my conservative-minded parents"—he winked at her—"and then a special treat for Dad whose true blue palate can't take goulash—a half chicken for the grill. Frankly I shouldn't have pandered to him like this if it hadn't been a very useful way of demonstrating the roto-roaster."
>
> (ch. 2)

Like Meg Eliot, like nearly all Wilson's heroes and heroines, Sylvia has to come to terms with a new life. And this involves, as so often, a judgment between two ways. Despite Harold's patronage Sylvia manages to assert her independence. She refuses to be put out to grass in the humanely heartless modern way. Her furniture is shabby and doesn't fit in, but though itself valueless, it somehow manages to question the value of Harold's status symbols. And her natural East Anglian good sense and dignity—even though somewhat overlaid by simple clichés from lowbrow fiction and television—contain more wisdom than the committees and communal schemes over which Harold wears himself out.

At the end of the book there is a family crisis in which Harold discovers that one of his sons is homosexual. He reacts, not like Gerald (who faces the same problem with detachment in *Anglo-Saxon Attitudes*), but with conventional anger, and throws himself with fresh gusto into work. His mother decides to set up on her own (Arthur has now died). She has made an independent friendship with an American family through whom she relives a little of her own past. She realizes that her son does not need her: they operate in different worlds. If we care more about her than we do about Meg Eliot, this is perhaps both because she is a nicer person and because she has been provided with a more interesting fictional context.

No Laughing Matter (1967) is the most complex and ambitious novel Wilson has yet written. It has no proper plot, but is a series of episodes or "takes" that follow, as in a movie, the fortunes of the Matthews family through the changing social and political scene of the last half-century. (Like *Anglo-Saxon Attitudes,* it goes back to 1912; there are other resemblances also, though the Matthewses are more theatrical and highly colored than the Middletons.) The narrative is interspersed with playlets that parody various contemporary dramatic styles, and in which members of the family play all the parts, as in charades. In some of the sketches, the identities of the various members of the family merge into one another: Wilson here uses a technique rather like that of James Joyce in the "Nighttown" fantasy in *Ulysses.*

The father, "Billy Pop," who has the same Christian name as the author's own father, is a familiar Wilson type: a self-pitying failed writer. The mother, "the Countess," has vitality and lovers. The cockney servant, Regan, is like Mrs. Salad in *Anglo-Saxon Attitudes.* Most of the children become successful—Rupert as an actor, Quentin as a womanizing political journalist and, in his later years, a television pundit (like John Middleton), Marcus as a homosexual art dealer, Margaret as a novelist. Wilson seems to identify more closely with Margaret than with any of his previous characters: her literary career is a paradigm of his own, and through her self-criticisms he explores some of his own problems as a creative writer. Her early stories are "wonderfully nasty": "You catch them without their bathing-trunks, don't you?" says someone.

Her first subject is her own family (disguised as the Carmichaels), and at one point a parallel is suggested with Margaret Kennedy's famous best-seller about a bohemian family, *The Constant Nymph.* Margaret repudiates the parallel, but it is clearly intended to enter the reader's mind as a possible "treatment."

This question of treatment is important in the book, which explores technical problems about the relation between "art" and "reality," between texture and theme: a kind of experimental documentary. Wilson seems to be reassessing the panorama of English family life as a literary mode. Can the saga still come off? Must it involve parody? Can it be aesthetic as well as social? A character makes this point about John Galsworthy—again, Margaret dismisses him, but that is in 1937: by 1967, when the novel appeared, Galsworthy had become popular again—largely because of the BBC's television version of *The Forsyte Saga,* which is mentioned in the last chapter of the novel. Thus, *No Laughing Matter* offers in its very title an ambivalent attitude to its subject. The questions it raises are important to Wilson, who has here tried to reflect an even larger area of English life than in his previous books. The fact that English families have so often been treated cosily and sentimentally (as in radio and television sagas, or in Noël Coward's famous period-piece *This Happy Breed*) is also relevant. "The family" so often has a Peter Pan quality. The Matthewses grow older in each "take," yet somehow never grow up: and the author's awareness of this is part of the irony.

This dense, allusive novel confirms Wilson's preoccupation with the family as a not-so-dear octopus (to borrow the title of a famous period-piece by Dodie Smith) and with the past, of which the family is a living embodiment, a *tableau vivant* of all those memories we try to escape but cannot. In Wilson's fiction the weak succumb to the past, the strong make use of it. In his earlier family stories he savagely caricatures and condemns the past; here it is re-created in detailed, Proustian researches. The Matthewses in their posturing theatricality represent, perhaps, those "Anglo-Saxon attitudes" of the years between the wars in which the self-indulgence and taste for the ironies of life of the British became both their undermining weakness as a nation and, in another sense, their strength to survive and adapt themselves to change. In this book, the weak characters are recurrent aspects of this self-indulgence, especially the paterfamilias who has failed to satisfy his wife sexually and thereby bequeaths problems to his children (the sins of the fathers). Margaret surmounts her heritage through her creative abilities; Marcus is drawn through his Jewish lover into the political and social conflicts of the 1930's, having metamorphosed from a self-conscious schoolboy flirting with his sexuality into a gilded butterfly of the 1920's and thence into a successful art expert and a man to be reckoned with.

The weakness of this novel lies paradoxically in the very variety of its technique. Not only is the chronological narrative itself only intermittently engaging (the caperings and self-dramatizings of the family are often wearisome until we reach a point where the author can provide an interesting social-documentary texture out of his own experience); but the book, for all its considerable length, is without a single example of those serio-comic *tours de force* (the meeting of the Historical Association in *Anglo-Saxon Attitudes,* the arrival of Arthur and Sylvia in the new town in *Late Call*) that had become almost a hallmark of Wilson's work. In addition, the playlets in which the Matthewses act out their family relationships pose a further problem. The excerpts from Margaret's "Carmichael" stories are justified and, as it were, guaranteed by the main story of which they represent further fictional removes. But the playlets turn the characters (on whose realism the texture of the main narrative insists) into marionettes manipulated by Wilson himself. How much are they really telling us and how much is a protective screen? For the first time in Wilson's fiction the reader is conscious of a confusing imbalance of manner over matter. This in a writer so keenly self-aware may be intentional. The playlets in the manner of Anton Chekhov and others may denote a criticism of England between the wars, a failure of creative nerve that the times could not redeem, a tendency to lapse into imitation and parody, to settle for the second-hand. Coward's *This Happy Breed* was held together by a conventional patriotism that nevertheless struck a response even from intellectuals in the year of the overthrow of fascism (1945). In *No Laughing Matter* we may see a self-doubting and self-analyzing version of the English panorama in which, as the title itself proclaims, we can no longer feel any confidence in "seeing the funny side."

As If By Magic (1973) in some respects offers a return to Wilson's earlier manner. The style is less overtly experimental, and there is a clearer narrative theme. Again, the family appear, though the emphasis now is less on the group than on two members of it, neither of whom really belong; both are outsiders. The book is written not in short "takes" but in long, carefully constructed set pieces, each having its own pace and climax (or anticlimax), a technique that Wilson used successfully in his earlier novels.

The two main characters, Hamo Langmuir and his goddaughter, Alexandra Grant, are seen together only at the beginning and near the end of the book. Langmuir is an internationally distinguished biologist who has invented a new strain of rice hybrid called Magic (this far from exhausts the meanings of the book's title). He is sexually frustrated, though in a different way from Gerald Middleton or Bernard Sands, with whom he shares the exemplary professional standards of his class. He is obsessed with young men, and his attempts, of which we learn in flashback, to raise the age of the objects of his desire by injections and hypnosis, offer another ironic comment on "magic" (science does not have all the answers) and emphasize the power of sex to destroy those who cannot control it acceptably. The ironic question "Is this magician as fertile as his magic?" is finally answered when Langmuir dies on a world tour of the Asian rice fields while trying to explain the failure of his rice in the poorest areas. If the magic fails, it is the god himself who has failed.

The other main character, Alexandra, daughter of a former "angry young" novelist who makes a belated comeback with a best seller, goes off to live in a hippie commune in India. It is thus that her path crosses Hamo's. Before they both leave London, she gives him a pair of binoculars; these "magic glasses" are given by Hamo to a native boy, who uses them to spy on the naked hippies. The horror and violence of the boy's death at the hands of some self-appointed vigilantes while he is in a state of extreme sexual excitement form the first of the book's climaxes, leaving little to the imagination and leading directly to the no less violent account of Hamo's own death in a peasant riot. Even more extraordinary is the scene, which no other novelist could have written, in which a group of elderly and distinguished European homosexuals give a party for some native boys at which the chief "uncle," a Dutch Jonkheer, inaugurates the proceedings by letting off a cannonade of farts like a ceremonial salute. The comment of the French uncle is a brilliant throwback to Wilson's special comic-pedantic vein (the trick is to treat a piece of grotesque vulgarity with monumental seriousness):

> The French uncle, Armand Leroux, apprehensive no doubt of English concern for the social aspect of events, said to Hamo: "No. But really. This is quite extraordinary. One so easily forgets the deeply traditional quality of the Dutch noblesse. The cheap *Paris-Match* image of the house of Orange has obscured it. Something of this kind must have been the customary honouring of a favourite page by the Jonkheer's ancestors of the fifteenth or even, one may venture, of the fourteenth century. We have nothing here to do with the vulgarities of Frans Hals' burghers of the dyke lands. No, this is the *petite noblesse* of Louvain and Brabant at its best—what in France we called the *hobereaux.* An aristocratic *franchise* that found an easy response in the *moeurs* of its own peasantry, in those broad-cheeked arses of the merry-eyed skaters and drinkers of Breughel or Jan Steen. No! No, really—such a lack of bourgeois *pudeur* is completely delightful."
>
> (bk. 2)

In this scene Hamo's puritan aloofness and the sexual tastes that had so troubled his scrupulous nature while in England are critically juxtaposed with the rampant and complacent pederasty of the "uncles": this treatment recalls the ending of *Hemlock and After* in which Eric, former lover of the late novelist Sands, is picked up by a clergyman whose crude technique is contrasted with Sands's personal distinction and refined self-searchings.

> Looking about him, Hamo was conscious of real dislike, almost hostility in the eyes of his hosts; and, indeed, they practised their own precepts, for in their worship of the *truly* boyish they had rid themselves of every conceivable trace of vestigial youth—skins were leathery, necks bulging, stomachs vast, everything aimed towards a geriatric magnificence; even Mr. Derek Lacey's thirty-five-year-old face and body were disguised under layers and layers of carefully acquired corpulence. Hamo was aware that his disciplined, lean figure was an ephebic insult.
>
> (bk. 2)

It is characteristic of Wilson to direct our sympathies both through his principal character's values and by taking the "uncles" to the very verge of caricature. They live in a Peter Pan world of the prep school and the adventure yarn, while Hamo emerges as more heroic, more serious, dedicated to the alleviation of human suffering, not by largesse dispensed in a homosexual brothel disguised as a club, but by scientific work. Yet one sometimes feels uneasily that an intellectual—even an aesthetic—point is masquerading as a moral one. In the tradition of Forsterian liberalism, Wilson is saying that Hamo, like Sands or Gerald Middleton, for all their apparent failure, is a finer being who deserves our sympathy; but this point of view remains an unrepentantly elitist one, belonging to the cultural tradition of Bloomsbury.

As If By Magic has a stronger moral and didactic pattern than *No Laughing Matter.* Its concern for truth recalls both *Hemlock and After* and *Anglo-Saxon Attitudes,* though this concern is less clearly articulated and is often lost sight of during long stretches of travelogue (the Singhalese and Indian settings are brilliantly described). The book's moral proposition, perhaps too schematically insisted on in the symbolism of the title, is that magic of whatever kind—sexual, social, scientific—cannot solve all life's problems. This is stated by Alexandra in a final soliloquy that has overtones of Virginia Woolf. The result is a powerful but uneven book in which passages of static and desultory narrative are heightened with scenes of extreme technical and psychological brilliance.

Wilson's most recent novel to date, *Setting the World on Fire* (1980), is the story of Tothill House, described by the author in one of his characteristic pseudo-historical forewords as "the only great house in London with large formal gardens and a park remaining in private hands . . . situated just behind Westminster Abbey." It is also another "family" novel: the Mossons, who own Tothill, and their various in-laws and hangers-on have the same kind of larger-than-life theatricality as the Matthewses. The chief characters are the two brothers Piers and Tom, who continually address each other by the nicknames Pratt and Van (Vanbrugh), after the two architects who contributed to Tothill—a somewhat tiresome whimsicality of the author's that hardly seems justified by the over-insisted-on distinction between the Palladian and baroque aspects of the house. Vanbrugh's baroque Great Hall becomes the setting of the opera *Phaethon* (music by Lully) and later of a projected play; the producer is Piers, a Westminster schoolboy when the novel begins, a famous producer when it ends, although the novel's time span of twenty years is presented as a series of separate set-pieces rather than as a developing narrative of character. Indeed, the preparation for and performance of the opera takes up most of the book. The two brothers head a fairly typical Wilsonian family cast, including rakish and impoverished uncles of the Edwardian variety, and there is the usual washing of dirty linen in public, though the set-piece of the family luncheon lacks the fizz and excitement of Wilson's earlier work (the debacle at Vardon Hall in *Hemlock and After,* for instance).

Indeed, compared to almost any of the earlier fictions, this one seems lacking in conviction and pace. The theme of the opera does not really engage the reader, and indeed the topic of the private theatrical performance was more interestingly dealt with in A. S. Byatt's novel *The Virgin in the Garden* (1978). Here the author's mannerisms seem to be more in evidence than his skills: in particular, the conversation of the Italian Marina Luzzi is tediously represented, as is her frankness at the expense of her fiancé's sexual inadequacies:

> "So you wanted a little shepherd boy's doodle to play with, Mama, eh? 'Cos I am taking your 'Ubert away from you. Rub my doodly, Marina, 'e says—is that 'ow you told 'im to say it?"
>
> Hubert rose from his chair; his floppy cheeked face was scarlet. Piers thought he was going to hit Marina and she must have thought so too, for she dodged away. Then Hubert drew back and in a tight controlled voice said:
>
> "Marina, I will not have you . . ."
>
> "No, you won't 'ave me and I won't 'ave you. Do you think I want to see your white bottom any more—'Make it red, Marina.' Get *'er* to do it. Go back to your prostitutes."
>
> (pt. 2, ch. 6)

At the end of the novel reality breaks in: there is a terrorist attack and Tom is killed. Before he dies, Piers promises him to "do his own thing" and not to let "these terrorists turn art and shape into any fucking happening." One cannot fail to sympathize with this cry for traditional order and beauty (of which Tothill is of course the symbol) and with Piers's determination to "do his own thing," though the book's last sentence sets up an ominous parallel: "Go up, Master Builder, go up! Now. Lest delaying, you lose the power to ascend the towers of imagination." The architectural metaphor is appropriate to a book dominated by descriptions of the baroque, but the Ibsenite allusion casts a shadow over the efforts and aspirations of the creative will. Moreover, all the artistic creativity that we see in the book is lavished on the revival of a work from the remote and privileged past, an aristocratic court entertainment. Perhaps it is here that we are supposed to detect an authorial irony: that in our time, taste is merely the adding together of money, chic, and flair—but if so, it emerges as a rather flat and negative thesis. Wilson does not seem to have broken any fresh ground here, but is perhaps marking time nostalgically in an Edwardian sunset London centered around the Westminster school of his boyhood. The novel reads at times like a *catalogue raisonnée* of the civilized arts—music, architecture, landscape gardening—while its characters seem cosily wedded to the kind of chi-chi, upper-middle-class museum culture its author once so brilliantly satirized.

V

Setting the World on Fire is Wilson's eighth full-length novel, and by now it is becoming possible to chart his strengths and weaknesses, although we ought not to suppose that a writer of such fecundity and vitality will as yet have given us all he has to give. He has clearly set out his claim to be both a satirist and a chronicler in the great Anglo-European bourgeois tradition, focusing his eye and his imagination not only on the moral and psychological problems of the individual but on the wider spectrum of the family and the social fabric of our times. His novels are written with such an acutely accurate eye and ear that future students will be able to determine precise sociological "layers," like geologists or archaeologists: after only a few years one can study in *As If By Magic* the lost generation of peace-loving hippies who drifted out East, as though one were turning over the records of a recently unearthed culture. The dense and detailed texture of Wilson's prose enables him to project the immanence of reality with enormous, documentary conviction, albeit a reality sometimes distorted or caricatured when the satirist takes over from the social realist. It is perhaps this sense of immanent reality, and of the novelist's preeminent responsibility to portray it, that has led him to write full-length studies of two English novelists who themselves possessed in full measure this quality: Dickens and Kipling. (Wilson published an earlier study of Émile Zola in 1952.)

The last pages of *The World of Charles Dickens* (1970), an illustrated critical biography, contains some powerfully relevant insights into the ways in which, in the last analysis, a novelist engages with the life of his time: "The joy in watching human behaviour is the key to his greatness, and perhaps also a measure of his limitation." He sees Dickens as dedicated to, and limited by, human predictability, by which he means "the power to predict the goodness, the wickedness and the absurdity of his own characters." But, as he goes on to admit, all but a very few of the greatest novelists share this "limitation": to transcend it is to create *War and Peace,* in which the only limits are those of life itself (to which one might add, not just the life of individual characters but the life of nations, human history). "For the rest," Wilson maintains, "the apparent unexpectedness of some fictional life [is] no more than a brilliant technical trick."

Wilson also understands, from his own background and early literary career, Dickens' technique of heightening and dramatizing family life, and the kinds of pressure that motivated it. The histrionic tone of so much of Dickens' fiction finds an echo in some of his own sensationally "heightened" treatment of the family, whether in the early stories or in the scenes depicting the Middletons and Matthewses "at home." He is also acutely perceptive on *Our Mutual Friend,* Dickens' last completed novel, which he rates less highly than some modern critics yet perceives to be unique in its anticipation of, and prophetic insights into, the modern world, the world of Oscar Wilde and Henry James. Discussing the style of this last period, Wilson argues that Dickens evolved "a new and brilliant shorthand" to attack a rotten society. Himself a restless experimenter in styles, no longer wholly satisfied with traditional bourgeois chronicle-narrative, Wilson understands Dickens' sense of dissatisfaction that his "old ironic style" had been taken over by journalists and public speakers; yet he also believes that this new style, a mixture of fresh insights and successes repeated from earlier books, represents a "triumph that doesn't come off." Again, Wilson himself has been much concerned with the problems of depicting a society with increasingly fewer taboos while remaining broadly committed to the moral traditions hitherto inseparable from social-realist narrative.

Like Robert Browning's Bishop Blougram, Wilson's interest lies "on the dangerous edge of things," and for his third major critical study he again selected a novelist whose special power lies in the intensity with which he controls experience and its fictional treatment on the very edge of dramatic hysteria. As with Dickens his method in *The Strange Ride of Rudyard Kipling* (1977) is to fuse the life with the work, in the belief that with certain kinds of imaginative writers something subsists over and above the sum of their individual works, a kind of "imaginative system" that he likens to planets revolving round their creator. As with Zola and Dickens, what attracts him is an affinity—here with what he calls Kipling's "rarely combined gifts —delicacy of craft and violence of feeling, exactitude and wild impressionism." This precisely places the technique in those scenes of Wilson's own fiction in which things start in controlled sobriety and are allowed, indeed encouraged, to get out of hand, to reach the frontier between the verifiable and the fantastic.

Wilson is also interested in Kipling as the poet of that lost imperial dream that lingered round his own childhood from his mother's South African roots (the country that gave Kipling some of the landscapes of the *Just So Stories*). But of course, Kipling is primarily India, and the most sustained piece of criticism in a book that is on the whole deficient in sustained criticism, placing as it does more emphasis on biography than did its predecessor, is that devoted to *Kim,* Kipling's masterpiece. It is to India that Wilson himself has gone for some of the landscapes of *As If By Magic.*

Kipling also shares with Dickens a savage sense of comedy and a fascination with crime, violence, and low life. All these are to be found also in Wilson. Perhaps in one quality he excels them both—self-knowledge. In our post-Freudian age obsessions that earlier writers would have censored are now allowed free rein, though this does not automatically mean an artistic gain (most critics would rank Forster's "censored" *The Longest Journey* higher than the "uncensored" *Maurice*). Repression, taboo, buried symbolism work powerfully in Dickens as in Kipling. The sense of mystery and strangeness that informs so much of their work is perhaps absent from Wilson's, upon which, it seems, the light of modern psychosocial analysis beats down without mercy like the noonday sun.

Wilson has now a substantial set of large-scale fictions to his credit, and it is perhaps appropriate at this stage of his career to turn back to an essay he published in 1958 on British fiction since 1945. He suggested that a renewed interest in the socially rooted, serious adult novel on a broad canvas, of which *Middlemarch* remains the exemplary archetype, may in part have been a reaction against the frivolous experiments of the Bloomsbury novels of personal relations, in which emotions were often isolated in a social vacuum. Yet he also saw the drawbacks inherent in neo-social fiction: "we are on the threshold of a psychology for which the older novel forms do not provide." He proposed Dostoevsky rather than George Eliot as the nineteenth-century writer who came nearest to expressing these newly discovered depths while retaining a broad social and narrative sweep. He concluded his article with two observations that were to bear fruit in the four novels of the next twenty years:

> To combine depth with breadth seems to me the principal problem that must preoccupy the contemporary English novelist. . . . Two things, I believe, demand the novelist's strict attention: the viewpoint of narration and a re-examination of the interior monologue form to see how its artificiality can be more happily combined with the direct effects of dialogue and action.
>
> ("Diversity and Depth")

SELECTED BIBLIOGRAPHY

I. Separate Works. *The Wrong Set* (London, 1949), stories; *Such Darling Dodos* (London, 1950), stories; *Émile Zola* (London, 1952), critical study; *Hemlock and After* (London, 1952), novel; *For Whom the Cloche Tolls: A Scrapbook of the Twenties* (London, 1953), with P. Jullian; *The Mulberry Bush* (London, 1956), play; *Anglo-Saxon Attitudes* (London, 1956), novel; *A Bit Off the Map* (London, 1957), stories; *The Middle Age of Mrs Eliot* (London, 1958), novel; *The Old Men at the Zoo* (London, 1961), novel; *The Wild Garden, or Speaking of Writing* (London, 1963), a series of lectures given at U.C.L.A. in 1960; *Late Call* (London, 1964), novel; *No Laughing Matter* (London, 1967), novel; *The World of Charles Dickens* (London, 1970), critical biography; *As If By Magic* (London, 1973), novel; *The Strange Ride of Rudyard Kipling* (London, 1977), critical biography; *Setting the World on Fire* (London, 1980), novel.

II. Articles and Interviews. "Diversity and Depth," in the *Times Literary Supplement* (15 August 1958), article on the English novel after World War II; "Evil in the English Novel," in the *Listener* (27 December, 1962; 3, 10, 17 January 1963), based on the Northcliffe Lectures, 1961; M. Cowley, ed., *Writers at Work* (London, 1958), contains an interview of A. Wilson by M. Millgate.

III. BIOGRAPHICAL AND CRITICAL STUDIES. A. O. J. Cockshut, "Favored Sons: The Moral World of Angus Wilson," in *Essays in Criticism,* 9 (1959); I. Scott-Kilvert, "Angus Wilson," in *A Review of English Literature,* 1 (1960); J. Gindin, *Post-War British Fiction* (Los Angeles, 1962); C. B. Cox, *The Free Spirit* (London, 1963); J. L. Halio, *Angus Wilson* (London, 1964), Writers and Critics series, contains a bibliography of Wilson's literary journalism; R. Rabinovits, *The Reaction Against Experiment in the English Novel, 1950–1960* (New York, 1967); B. Bergonzi, *The Situation of the Novel* (London, 1969); M. Bradbury, "The Fiction of Pastiche: The Comic Mode of Angus Wilson," in *Possibilities* (London, 1973); D. Escudie, "Deux aspects de l'alienation dans le roman anglais contemporain de 1945–50: Angus Wilson et William Golding," in *Études anglaises,* 58 (Paris, 1975); M. Bradbury and D. Palmer, eds., *The Contemporary English Novel* (London, 1979), Stratford-upon-Avon Studies; P. Faulkner, *Angus Wilson, Mimic and Moralist* (London, 1980); N. McEwan, *The Survival of the Novel* (London, 1981), contains an essay on *No Laughing Matter;* K. McSweeney, *Four Contemporary Novelists: Angus Wilson, Brian Moore, John Fowles, and V. S. Naipaul* (Kingston, Ontario, 1983).

DYLAN THOMAS

(1914–1953)

Leslie Norris

DYLAN THOMAS was born in Swansea, Wales, on 27 October 1914. No examination of his work can ignore the importance of his birthplace. Even his death in New York in 1953 is less a simple fact than an allegory of how far from home the poet had traveled. From this distance in time it is very easy to see that all his work is based on an assumption that Swansea and its surrounding green county is the center of the world, that all the poet saw and said resulted from the relation of his experience to the small miles of Wales in which he grew up.

No poet of our time lived more in the eye of the world than Thomas. His early recognition—he was famous in the little community of modern poets when he was nineteen—the accounts of his bohemian life-style, the impact of his work on critics and on other poets, all made him a public figure. At the time it seemed that readers waited for the small collections he published every few years as if starved of poetry. As his fame spread, Thomas was regarded as the very type of the romantic poet, wild, dissolute, inspired. This was not the complete truth, but when he died in 1953, tragically and sensationally after a bout of drinking, it was as if Dionysus had died again.

That was a long time ago. We ought to be able to look more objectively at the verse, to see it as it is presented to us in the *Collected Poems* (1952), to realize that it is the whole life's work. It should be possible to decide how much of Thomas' poetry has stood up against insidious time and against changing fashion in verse. We should, moreover, realize that the man's prose has grown in importance since his death, that it is easier to see him as a more interesting figure, more complex and complete, developing marvelous gifts of narrative and humor, than as a poet dead before his time. It has long been acknowledged that Thomas was a conscious artist, well aware of what he was doing, industrious, serious, and dedicated. His letters to his friend Vernon Watkins, particularly the earlier ones, are clear proof of how seriously he took his craft. To read through the *Collected Poems* is to experience a continuous development and refining of Thomas' technical skills, from the rather heavy iambic early verse through the conscious experiments of his middle period to the extraordinary mastery of his late poems. The truth is that Thomas was always an artist, not only aware of what he was doing but delighting in it. He would have agreed with William Butler Yeats that there is no art without toil.

He realized early that he could write, and he was serious about the possession of such a gift. His father, David John Thomas, was an English master at the local grammar school, a man of taste and intelligence, widely read. Although he came from a Welsh-speaking background, he made his home one in which English was the sole language and its literature valued above all others. A fine reader, he introduced his son to the great poets at an early age. His example, together with the splendid voice he passed on to Dylan, was to result in the extraordinary public readings that made Thomas' work familiar to many people who would normally not have been interested in poetry. D. J. Thomas came of a family famous in South Wales. His uncle, William Thomas, had been a prime mover in the Unitarian movement in western Wales and had been politically active in the unrest between landlords and tenants in the years after 1867. He was, moreover, a good poet in the Welsh language, using the bardic title of Gwilym Marles.

It was a proud inheritance, and D. J. Thomas paid tribute to Gwilym Marles when he gave his son the middle name of Marlais. Yet he tried to ensure that any trace of Welsh language influence was erased when he insisted his two children have elocution lessons. Thomas grew up without the distinctive

Swansea accent. He spoke an English untouched by any regional tinge.

Similarly, he remained unaware of much of what was happening to his country outside his immediate experience. It was a bad time for Wales, and other young poets—a little older than Thomas, it is true—were aware of the despair of the miners, of ruinous unemployment, and wrote about these subjects. He seemed sublimely uninterested in politics. If he knew no Welsh, he had a traditional Welsh attitude toward poetry. It must be rich in sound, it must be beautifully crafted, it must be glorious and as far as possible immortal. He prepared himself to write such poetry. His verse had been influenced, too, by the great English poets, particularly the romantics. The modern poets he read were those whose work his father possessed, Walter de la Mare, John Masefield, the Georgians. From his wide reading he had already mastered a formidable technique, but it was a technique quite unlike that of his contemporaries. David Daiches, in his essay on Thomas in *Dylan Thomas: A Collection of Critical Essays,* writes: "No modern poet in English has had a keener sense of form or has handled stanza and verse-paragraphs—whether traditional or original—with more deliberate cunning." This is an indication of the individuality of Thomas' voice and his technique. Of all the poets of his generation, he alone seemed to have been uninfluenced by the work of T. S. Eliot, then preeminent in English poetry. For Thomas it was as if Eliot had never written. We know from his letters, however, that the younger poet was very well aware of Eliot's work, and it is possible that he wrote differently because he knew his own gifts well, realized that he would travel in other directions.

The unusual thing is that Thomas came to this knowledge while still very young. The *Collected Poems* of 1952, prepared by Thomas himself, contains a total of ninety poems. When the poet's friend Dr. Daniel Jones published his edition of *The Poems* in 1971, he included many more poems; even so, he was at pains to state that this was still a selection. Most of these additional poems were written while Thomas was yet a schoolboy, but so were many of the poems Thomas selected for the collection he chose himself.

Between the years 1930 and 1934, that is, between the ages of fifteen and nineteen, Thomas wrote "at least four times more poetry than in the remaining nineteen years of his life" (*The Poems,* introduction, p. xvi), according to Dr. Jones. Thomas' published *Notebooks* offer convincing evidence of his astonishing early industry, as well as showing how this wealth of early work was revised, sometimes only very slightly revised, to become the poems from which the poet formed his successive books. Although he did write new poems for each new book, a surprising number were rescued from the poems of his adolescence.

It is obvious, then, that the majority of the poems remain the work of a very young man, a provincial young man untouched by London literary society or the discipline of a university. In a sense, despite the influence of his father, Thomas was an autodidact, unaware of the very latest in poetical fashions. He had trained himself in the orthodox metrical forms of English verse and was far away from the current new poets, W. H. Auden, Stephen Spender, and C. Day-Lewis. Working almost alone in Swansea—for he did not meet Watkins, perhaps the most helpful of his friends, until after the publication of *Eighteen Poems* in 1934—his most interesting subject matter was himself. So that when he began to publish, both his matter and his manner, traditional though they were, seemed astonishingly new and very exciting.

Certainly *Eighteen Poems* was received with unusual attention. "I was in London with him," wrote Glyn Jones in *The Dragon Has Two Tongues* (p. 183), "soon after his book appeared . . . and it was a delight to me to witness the excitement with which the book, and its author, were received." Jones had very early recognized the unique quality of the poetry and remains one of the most acute and objective of Thomas' admirers.

It is as well to consider here, since we have stressed that much of Thomas' verse is orthodox and traditional, just what was unique in the work of the new arrival. First there is the important influence of Thomas' environment. Hard though D. J. Thomas fought to give his son the sense of an English language culture, the boy was exposed every day of his formative years to an atmosphere very largely based on Welsh values and mores. He would have heard the language even, since it was more commonly spoken in Swansea during his boyhood than it is today, and in the country districts to the west of the town it was very largely the first language. This means that the English Thomas heard in the streets and classrooms, even that he would use when with his friends, was in a sense a transitional language, its syntax and its rhythms very slightly askew when compared to the language of Englishmen. The poet's usage thus acquires a kind of exotic strangeness and power, adding to his awareness of language—in Thomas' case, an obsession with language that might have been the most obvious facet of his poetry. "I wanted to write poetry in the beginning," wrote Thomas in 1951, in reply to a student's questions, "because I had fallen in love with words" (*Modern Poets on Modern Poetry*, p. 195). He was never to fall out of love with them.

And if his language was exotically rich and musical when we think of the thin, political poetry popular at the time, then its form too was unusual, again for what we might think of as Welsh reasons. Welsh poetry is complex and difficult in form, its poets skilled in the craft to a high degree, the traditional meters demanding long training. I do not suggest that Thomas knew very much about the forms of Welsh language poetry, despite efforts by a few critics to show a deliberate use of some of the constructions, but he grew up in a community in which formal poetry—the belief that poems must be well made—was universal. This is a not an unusual circumstance among poets from Celtic countries. "Irish poets, learn your trade, / Sing whatever is well made" ("Under Ben Bulben," V), admonished Yeats. Certainly Scottish, Irish, and Welsh poets seem for these reasons to use poetic form and language sufficiently unlike that of their English contemporaries to make their work recognizably Celtic. It is not entirely fanciful to suggest that Thomas' mastery of intricate forms had something to do with his nationality and his background.

So his work was significantly novel in both word and form. It is true that there were poets writing at that time who were influenced by the current interest in surrealism; despite superficial similarities—the use of striking imagery is an example—Thomas' extreme control is enough to show that he has no place in such a group. Nor was his adolescent interest in himself, and in particular in his own sexuality, a common subject for verse in 1934. This was a period in which many young writers were greatly concerned with social and political themes. In prose and verse many of them were trying to analyze the causes of great political upheaval in Europe, and to warn about the war that they saw as inevitable. Thomas seemed untouched by this concern, just as he was not influenced by savage unemployment and poverty in his own country. And if these young people, some of whom were to go on to fight in the Spanish Civil War in a few years time, seemed to represent that call for individual and political freedom which had been so potent a charge in the early nineteenth century to poets like William Blake and William Wordsworth, to Percy Shelley and Lord Byron, then Thomas perhaps represented the viewpoint of even younger poets, who had not outgrown the natural interest in self, shown not only in budding lyrical poets but in all normal adolescents. We have to remember just how young Thomas was at this time, and to recall, moreover, just how much younger he had been when he had written the work in *Eighteen Poems.* Whatever the reasons, young poets found his work exciting and in a sense liberating. His work influenced that of poets in England and America to an extraordinary extent, as a reading of almost any anthology of poetry of the time will show. In retrospect it seems that he changed the direction of contemporary English poetry with his first book, although its real virtues were not always recognized.

In addition to all these factors, Thomas came of families long settled in the Swansea and Carmarthenshire areas. He had a familiar, age-old environment of sea and shore and surrounding hills in which to place his work. His very provincialism, far from being a handicap, gave him safety and strength. His is a recognizable country. His advantages were formidable.

All this is more easily seen from a reading of *The Collected Poems* than from a study of the work in his first book alone. The poems in *Eighteen Poems,* though, are still exciting enough to help us understand some of the furor they caused in the small world of poets, and a few of them remain among the best that Thomas ever wrote.

An old poet has told me how, when he was an undergraduate, he and his friends would walk the streets chanting the poems of Algernon Charles Swinburne, and a similar, almost mesmeric, incantatory quality is felt when one reads these early poems of Thomas. I, as a boy of thirteen, read "The force that through the green fuse drives the flower" in an anthology, and could not believe that it was a poem. It seemed like something alive and physical, too vital for the page to contain. It could well be that such an immediate effect, a feeling that the words contained something beyond meaning and appealing with enormous power to the senses, is not only the first quality of Thomas' early verse, but its most permanent quality, still to be felt. Yet there was, too, a certain confidence in the statement of the poetry, something in addition to the music and the mystery, which persuaded many of us that Thomas was saying something important. How strong some of the opening lines still seem: "I see the boys of summer in their ruin"; "A process in the weather of the heart / Turns damp to dry"; "Where once the waters of your face / Spun to my screws." The poetry was obscure, but with a peculiar kind of obscurity. John Bayley has pointed out ("Chains and the Poet," *New Critical Essays,* p. 57) that we were hearing once again "the Bard's voice" and that even if the words seem obscure, the message is very simple. "Thomas," wrote Bayley, "was the first great and evident talent of the modern movement . . . to concentrate on what it felt like to be himself, to make his poetry the feeling of his being."

But no poet can be entirely absorbed in self. We know from the evidence of his friends in the Swansea of his youth that Thomas was observant, fond of company, funny. His later stories and broadcasts demonstrate very clearly that little went by his keen and tolerant eye, so it is fair to assume that his adolescent concern with himself was abnormal only in that it formed the matter for much of his poetry, that he was very much aware of the external world and his place in it. Like other intelligent young people he was concerned with the great imponderables, time, sex, life, religion. His poetry could be said to attempt to balance such forces within himself and in the world in which he lived.

That effort is serious and arduous. Early critics who felt that Thomas worked thoughtlessly and without effort saw neither the skill, for so young a man, nor the struggle throughout poem after poem to find a conclusion that satisfied his doubts. He certainly knew what he was doing. In many of his poems he uses man as a microcosm and himself as a mirror of the huge and inexplicable world in order to assert some order over chaos. It is not mere rhetoric that he intends (nor, it seems to me, did he ever intend mere rhetoric) when he ends a superbly serious poem, "If I were tickled by the rub of love," with a simple declaration—"Man be my metaphor." It is a truth he remained loyal to throughout his career. If we remember this, some of the difficulties of the work in *Eighteen Poems* seem less perplexing when we read:

> Light breaks where no sun shines;
> Where no sea runs, the waters of the heart
> Push in their tides;
>
> ("Light breaks where no sun shines")

or, even more illuminating, these lines from the same poem:

> Dawn breaks behind the eyes;
> From poles of skull and toe the windy blood
> Slides like a sea.
>
> (13–15)

It is not, however, simply that Thomas saw himself as the world or the world as himself; he saw himself as being subject to the same forces as the world, and his effort is to understand those forces and to see how they affect him. Much of his poetry, then, is a journey in self-discovery. Those strong, confident lines are also paths of doubt and uncertainty, and the poem was successful only when he had successfully negotiated a way to a conclusion the poem had found for him. Much of the supposed obscurity of the early poetry is the result of the division between the confidence of the technique and the uncertainty—more correctly, the innocence—of the thought. But we can certainly understand more readily now just why these poems use so many images of blood and body. They are not merely images, they form the subject matter of Thomas' first public utterances.

And when the poem works, it is very successful. Such an example would be "The force that through the green fuse drives the flower," in which everything combines to produce a remarkable unity. Here Thomas makes his complete identification with the natural world even more apparent than in other poems. It is not merely an identification with the external world that Thomas understands; it is an interrelationship so firm that its very statement is the poem. The poem opens with something that is almost a definition of the life force, in that the poet shows us how it affects both the flower, representative of external life, and himself:

> The force that through the green fuse drives the
> flower
> Drives my green age; that blasts the roots of trees
> Is my destroyer.

He shows us, then, his place in the natural world. It is precisely that of every other living thing, subject to growth and decay. He links his youth to that of the flower by his use of the common adjective "green"; he anticipates the hardening of age by aligning himself with "the roots of trees." But he does not understand the force he is considering; in fact, he is unable to explain to the rose marred by winter that he is subject to the same fate:

> And I am dumb to tell the crooked rose
> My youth is bent by the same wintry fever.
> (4–5)

The next two stanzas follow a repetitive pattern, insisting not only on the poet's relationship with the natural world and its laws—

> The force that drives the water through the rocks
> Drives my red blood;

but on his inability to explain the nature of relentless time, of inevitable decay. He is "dumb" for these purposes; not only is he unable to explain to the dying rose the reason for its death, he is identically powerless to explain it to himself:

> And I am dumb to mouth unto my veins
> How at the mountain spring the same mouth sucks.
> (9–10)

Water and blood, the springing liquids of external and internal worlds, both are ruled by the same inexplicable forces.

Paradoxically, it is the realization of his inability to do more than recognize the intricate relations of natural things ruled by time, to be unable to explain any more than this, which gives power and assurance to the poem, qualities reinforced by the relentless drive of the rhythm, by the repetition of the formal pattern, and by the separated couplet with which he ends the poem. This last piece of virtuosity also brings out clearly the hidden pun the poet intends when he uses "dumb" to describe his helplessness. In it he ironically accuses himself of being stupid when he fails to persuade the dead lover of the universality of death:

> And I am dumb to tell the lover's tomb
> How at my sheet goes the same crooked worm.
> (21–22)

All in all, this is a most subtle and engaging poem, well worth lengthy study. Even in small matters, as in the manner the poem is rounded off by the final image of the "crooked" worm echoing that of the "crooked" rose—and both, possibly, reminding us of William Blake's "sick rose"—the poem is the work of a young man of great ability, writing at the top of his form.

It is this topic of death and decay that is most frequently examined in the first poems, and the universality of the subject in some measure helps to disguise the extreme introspection of much of the work. Yet it is clear that in all these poems, Thomas is firmly at the center of his world, relying almost entirely on his own sense perceptions. He is hardly ever objective in the ordinary meaning of the word, his thought and his emotion seeming to be an amalgam of these qualities, almost a new and highly individual power. His poems arise, as he tells us, straight out of his senses—"I see the boys of summer"—and we are tempted to think that without that first sight the boys would not have existed at all, nor the poem either. As it is, they can go on living in thoughtless and careless folly, blind to their certain ruin:

> I see the boys of summer in their ruin
> Lay the gold tithings barren,
> Setting no store by harvest, freeze the soils;
> There in their heat the winter floods
> Of frozen loves they fetch their girls,
> And drown the cargoed apples in their tides.

But not all the first poems can be so classified. "Especially when the October wind" is made more recognizably from the visible world in and about Swansea (and is probably the first of several poems written in succeeding October months when the poet celebrated his birthday) and, by some process of relation, from the act of writing poems. "Where once the waters of your face" also seems a more direct and external poem than most. What difficulties exist in the reading of this poem ease when it is realized that we are listening to a boat (or perhaps the owner of a boat) speaking to the ghost of a water that has dried up.

> Where once the waters of your face
> Spun to my screws, your dry ghost blows,
> The dead turns up its eye;

Here, too, we are given such a wealth of sea and tidal images that we are reminded that Thomas lived most of his life by the sea, was increasingly influenced by seascape in his work. It is in this poem that we find the poet perhaps for the first time offering some measure of protection against time and dissolution, even if it is to a dry pool:

> There shall be corals in your beds,
> There shall be serpents in your tides,
> Till all our sea-faiths die.
> (22–24)

I have suggested that despite the energy and strength of the rhythms of these poems, they are sometimes less than sensitive, sometimes monotonous and heavy, and I believe this to be true. Yet the best, and the best made (for these are nearly always identical with Thomas), are free of this charge, and an examination of his rhymes would show how cleverly he avoids any suggestion of monotony here. His use of half-rhyme and false rhyme, easily to be seen in the lines already quoted, will show how successful he was. Admirable, too, is his strict search for accuracy; one can only be delighted by the combination of "dry" and "ghost," for instance, in "Where once the waters of your face."

All this meant that Thomas had established at once an easily recognized style and a highly individual voice, strange, exciting, and genuinely poetic. The poems to be found in *Twenty-five Poems* (1936) support and confirm the nature of his gifts, although there are some that seem simpler and more direct and a few that suggest a sadder and less convinced poet. Examples of the first kind are "This bread I break," "Ears in the turrets hear," "The hand that signed the paper," "Should lanterns shine," "I have longed to move away," and "And death shall have no dominion." They form no small proportion of the work, and while a few of them are new, some are poems that Thomas had rejected for his first collection and revised for this later publication. The poems of melancholy can be represented by the beautiful "Out of the sighs," with its wavering cadences, its slow melody:

> Out of the sighs a little comes,
> But not of grief, for I have knocked down that
> Before the agony; the spirit grows,
> Forgets, and cries;
> A little comes, is tasted and found good;
> All could not disappoint;
> There must, be praised, some certainty,
> If not of loving well, then not,
> And that is true after perpetual defeat.

Perhaps not sufficient attention has been paid to this poem, one of the few pieces that contains none of the famous Thomas images, indeed hardly any images at all, yet no other poet could have written it.

There are more typical poems, some of them going over old ground, looking once again at the apparent division of flesh and soul, exhibiting the presence of death in the newborn:

> I, in my intricate image, stride on two levels,
> Forged in man's minerals, the brassy orator
> Laying my ghost in metal,
> The scales of this twin world tread on the double,
> My half ghost in armour hold hard in death's
> corridor,
> To my man-iron sidle.
>
> Beginning with doom in the bulb, the spring
> unravels. . . .
> ("I, in my intricate image")

And there are a few poems so frankly obscure ("Now," "How soon the servant sun,") that they are almost jokes. I do not pretend to understand them at all.

But the most important and substantial work of this period are the ten religious stanzas called "Altarwise by owl-light." Written between December 1935 and the summer of 1936, these poems, or rather this poem (since I agree with Dr. Jones that this is a single poem with ten sonnet-like stanzas [*The Poems,* p. 262]), is something of a watershed in Thomas' work. It is his longest piece up to this time, and also the most compressed and the most highly metaphorical. It has been the subject of controversy and explication since it first appeared as a whole in 1936, and opinion has ranged from outright dismissal to prolonged and complex analysis such as that by Elder Olson (*The Poetry of Dylan Thomas,* pp. 63–87). Experts are even divided about how it should be read, some of them (for example, Marshall W. Stearns, "Unsex the Skeleton," *Transformation* 3, 1946) convinced that it is a series of separate sonnets despite Thomas' own statement that "this poem is a particular incident in a particular adventure" (*Sunday Times,* September 1936). Obscure it certainly is, compressed it certainly is. Afterwards, as if he had gone as far as he wished in those directions, Thomas' verse became more free, its music more varied and lyrical.

"We were both religious poets," wrote Watkins (*Letters to Vernon Watkins,* p. 17), and there is enough proof of this statement throughout the work of both poets to sustain this assertion. In Thomas' case we have the example of his early poem, "Before I knocked," in which he speaks for the Christ-child even before His birth:

> Before I knocked and flesh let enter,
> With liquid hands tapped on the womb,
> I who was shapeless as the water
> That shaped the Jordan near my home
> Was brother to Mnetha's daughter
> And sister to the fathering worm.

And there are references to his continued absorption with religion right up to the final statement of his prefatory note to *The Collected Poems.* "These poems, with all their crudities, doubts, and confusions, are written for the love of Man and in praise of God."

Thomas was twenty-one when he wrote "Altarwise by owl-light." It represents a remarkably sustained and unified effort by the young poet. The poem came quickly to him, when one considers its density and complexity, but it is in no way an easy poem and remains one of the most challenging for the reader. Dr. Jones suggests that we should think of it as "absolute" poetry, and that "comprehension is irrelevant" (*The Poems,* p. 263). Its difficulty he considers akin to that of a Bach fugue, and certainly the intricate weaving of images and the stern control of the sonnet form give this opinion some credence. But the poem is also made of words and possesses the properties of meaning.

What seems evident is that Thomas has taken for his subject the biblical themes of divine redemption and the reality of human sacrifice in an attempt to reconcile them. He has not confined his resources, his imagery, his information, to the material of the Old and New Testaments; the poem is made of all his concerns, and part of its difficulty is the wide range of Thomas' curious and personal learning and our difficulty in relating its disparate elements.

Each of the fourteen-line stanzas is organized into an octet and a sestet, the rhymes regular in pattern but not in sound, Thomas using the half-rhymes common with him:

> Altarwise by owl-light in the half-way house
> The gentleman lay graveward with his furies;
> Abaddon in the hangnail cracked from Adam,
> And, from his fork, a dog among the fairies,
> The atlas-eater with a jaw for news,
> Bit out the mandrake with to-morrow's scream.

This is Thomas' version of the Nativity. It is no traditional Christmas scene, full of radiance and the light of promise. Christ's mortality is recognized as early as line 2. He is not surrounded by angels, but by furies. He is descended from Adam, so already aware of sin. Abaddon is an unlikely figure here; he is the Angel of the Bottomless Pit, so the Christ-child, born at dusk, or owl-light, is in dangerous and cast-out company from the time of his birth. His half-way house is already one of dreadful omen.

The second stanza continues the story, so it is possible to see that Thomas, wrestling with words and meaning, was on a journey of understanding as profound as any he had yet made. The child whose birth we attended in the first stanza is growing up:

> Death is all metaphors, shape in one history;
> The child that sucketh long is shooting up

—but we are told again of death toward the end of this stanza:

> Hairs of your head, then said the hollow agent,
> Are but the roots of nettles and of feathers

It is, too, a precise and horrible prophecy that Death ("the hollow agent," a skull) gives, since we are reminded that Christ will wear on his head a crown of thorns, or nettles.

I cannot pretend that it is other than very difficult to trace Thomas' thought through these extraordinarily powerful stanzas, but some of them treat the theme more directly than others. One such is the eighth stanza, which states its message with urgency:

> This was the crucifixion on the mountain,
> Time's nerve in vinegar, the gallow grave
> As tarred with blood as the bright thorns I wept;
> The world's my wound, God's Mary in her grief,
> Bent like three trees and bird-papped through her
> shift,
> With pins for teardrops is the long wound's woman.

There is little of the extreme difficulty here of some of the other stanzas, since Thomas has followed closely the Gospel accounts of the Crucifixion. The images are those we would expect and at the same time reinforce and interrelate with each other: for example, Christ's tears are as savage as the thorns he wears, Mary's are as sharp and hard as pins. In her grief, Mary is bowed with that invisible weight exactly as the three trees are bent with the weight of three men. The stanza ends with Christ's statement that he is there to heal the world:

> I, by the tree of thieves, all glory's sawbones,
> Unsex the skeleton this mountain minute,
> And by this blowclock witness of the sun
> Suffer the heaven's children through my heartbeat.

He first unsexes "the skeleton" of Death, and then, as the blowclock witness (which I take to be a seeding dandelion, something to be found everywhere, and whose seeds are carried everywhere by the wind, a symbol of delicate and silent power), measures that eclipse of the sun which accompanied the execution; Christ suffers "the heaven's children" through his "heartbeat." This is quite explicit. His suffering allows us into heaven; as his heart stops, we, "the heaven's children," are promised immortality.

This stanza is for me, perhaps because it is the easiest to read, the high point of the poem. Stanza nine is extremely difficult and does not seem to continue, as the first eight do, a retelling and examination of events. But the final stanza, puzzling as it is in its confused syntax and images, ends on a note of hope, a prayer almost, in which Thomas asks that the garden, essentially the garden of Eden, which he has imagined sunken beneath the sea, shall rise again and, holding Adam's tree and Christ's tree, allow the serpent to build "a nest of mercies" in "the rude, red tree," the bloodstained tree upon which Christ died.

This was the last poem in *Twenty-five Poems.* After this, Thomas was never again as fertile a poet. He was at this time living in dire poverty, newly married—he married Caitlin MacNamara in October 1937—and despite the marvelous reception given to *Twenty-five Poems,* the book made little money. He began to work on the autobiographical stories later collected in *The Portrait of the Artist as a Young Dog* (1940), in the hope that these would be more successful financially; but first he put together a volume of seven stories and sixteen new poems, called *The Map of Love.* This was a beautiful book, the stories a selection from Thomas' early prose and the poems including some most exciting work, all proving an even greater technical virtuosity, a number—for example, "After the funeral"—destined to be among his most famous. But ill-luck of the most unhappy kind attended the appearance of this book. Coming out at the end of August 1939, it was overwhelmed by the outbreak of World War II. Neither this nor *The World I Breathe,* a sizable collection of his poetry and prose that appeared in December of the same year and was his first American volume, did very much to relieve his financial straits.

The poems in *The Map of Love* do, however, mark a departure. Much more varied in theme and in style, they form a most interesting group. Still completely personal, they demonstrate a much greater interest in the external world. There are still poems that aroused the conservative critics to anger—particularly the opening poem, "Because the pleasure-bird whistles"—and there are fine poems of the sort we have met before, like the splendid sonnet "When all my five and country senses see," but through them all there runs like a slender narrative thread a suggestion that the poet is no longer alone. "We lying by seasand" begins a poem of recognition that the poet cannot disturb the ravages of time, but it is also a poem of tender resignation, allowing that "wishes breed not" and that the poet and his companion should watch "yellow until the golden weather / Breaks." We are in fact being given a map of love. "If my head hurt a hair's foot" is a poem in which his unborn child speaks to its mother, and the mother responds. "Twenty-four years"—another of the poems for his own birthday—is a celebration of his journey toward death ("sewing a shroud for a journey") and of his responsibilities as husband and father:

> Dressed to die, the sensual strut begun,
> With my red veins full of money,
> In the final direction of the elementary town
> I advance for as long as forever is.
>
> (6–9)

It seems that the poet has new directions to explore as well as a new viewpoint for his perennial themes. His love, too, extends outside his immediate concerns. The aunt with whom he had spent much time when a child, on the farm he was to immortalize in "Fern Hill," had died, and he made for her the passionate elegy, "After the funeral."

The original version of this poem was written on 10 February 1933, a few days after his aunt's death. Five years were to pass before Thomas went back to the poem and transformed it into the deeply felt elegy we now have. He is bitter and angry at what he feels to be an insufficient sorrow among the mourners, calling their conventional sadness

> . . . mule praises, brays,
> Windshake of sailshaped ears, muffle-toed tap
> Tap happily of one peg in the thick
> Grave's foot, blinds down the lids . . .
>
> (1–4)

But he moves through his memories of the living Ann Jones into a noble eloquence, assuming for her a position as "Ann's bard on a raised hearth," calling all

> The seas to service that her wood-tongued virtue
> Babble like a bellbuoy over the hymning heads,
> Bow down the walls of the ferned and foxy woods
> That her love sing and swing through a brown chapel.
>
> (22–25)

And he offers her his continual service of love and eloquence until the dead return to life:

> . . . until
> The stuffed lung of the fox twitch and cry Love
> And the strutting fern lay seeds on the black sill.
>
> (38–40)

It is in these poems that we see for the first time a poet who is part of the outside world, offering as a partial solution to all the puzzles of life his personal love. In "After the funeral," for instance, we are shown a most careful ordering of the imagery, all the properties being those in and about the farm, the "stale fern," "the stuffed fox," the woods behind the house. Dr. Jones has told us that Thomas was not a ready observer of the world of nature, but that "if observation was directly relevant to his central interests, and only in that case, he could observe, and where the relevance was great, his observation could be keen" (*My Friend Dylan Thomas,* p. 56). The force of this remark can be appreciated when we remember that the flower in "The force that through the green fuse" remains an unnamed flower, but that in "After the funeral" a wealth of observed images are identified and ordered into powerful use. This ability was to be used more and more often, reinforcing Thomas' great auditory gifts. Thomas' changed status as a husband gave to him a wider range of subject and a greater involvement with other people.

This was part of a process that led to the comparative clarity and luminosity of the later poems. For a variety of reasons, possibly related to Thomas' work as a film-script writer and to the lack, until he removed to the Boathouse, Laugharne, in 1949, of a settled home, fewer poems were written. These years saw the growth of his reputation as a reader of poetry, not only his own. In February 1946 he published *Deaths and Entrances,* a tiny volume in size but great in achievement and influence. Here were such anthology pieces as "The Hunchback in the Park," which drew on his childhood memories of Cwmdonkin Park; the few war poems included in his work; two long narrative poems, "A Winter's Tale" and "Ballad of the Long-legged Bait"; poems of superb virtuosity like "There was a Saviour," in which a complex rhyme scheme is incredibly maintained; and, amid a whole galaxy of wonderful things, "Poem in October" and "Fern Hill."

It has been fashionable to think that Thomas' early work is superior to these later poems. That must be mistaken opinion. That they are different in many respects, while retaining Thomas' highly individual style, is fairly obvious. The main reason for this difference is one that the poems in *Deaths and Entrances* reflects. Previous to these poems, Thomas had been busily adapting the work contained in his early notebooks, that series of exercise books now in the Lockwood Memorial Library in Buffalo. For seven years these books had held the material for his poetry, but in the spring of 1941 he sold them to a London dealer in rare books and manuscripts. "It would be hard," wrote Constantine FitzGibbon, "to imagine a more significant gesture on Dylan's part, a greater renunciation of his past, than this. Those notebooks were his youth, those notebooks were his poems, those notebooks were Dylan the young poet. . . . The boy-poet, the Rimbaud of Cwmdonkin Drive, had ceased to exist (*The Life of Dylan Thomas,* p. 247)." What we have from this time on are the poems of the mature poet. They demonstrate his presence in wartime London, prey to "many married London's estranging grief," and his growing concern with other sufferers ("The conversation of prayer," "A refusal to mourn," "Ceremony after a fire raid"). Among such resonant elegies, the most personal is probably the best known, the touching poem to his father, "Do not go gentle into that good night." For many of his admirers, the new clarity of these poems, the recognizable scenes of his meditations, were increasing virtues.

By almost any standards the poems in *Deaths and Entrances* are remarkable. They display technical virtuosity of dazzling proportions, ranging from the strict villanelle in which Thomas contained his love for his father in "Do not go gentle," through the ode-like forms of "Into her Lying Down Head" and "Unluckily for a Death"; the revived medieval patterns of "Vision and Prayer"; the invented stanza of "A Winter's Tale"; and the relatively simple shapes of "The Hunchback in the Park" and "In my Craft or Sullen Art." As a demonstration of the poet's craft they are almost unique, and Thomas himself suggests the importance of his skill when he places "craft" before "art":

> In my craft or sullen art
> Exercised in the still night
> When only the moon rages
> And the lovers lie abed
> With all their griefs in their arms,
> I labour by singing light
> Not for ambition or bread
> Or the strut and trade of charms
> On the ivory stages
> But for the common wages
> Of their most secret heart.

And surely there cannot be a more complete statement of the poet's calling than that, nor a more complete refutation of any possibility of Thomas' lack of utter seriousness as an artist. Here he even tells us that he writes now for an audience, even though such people may not be aware of his existence. The young poet who sang himself only is certainly gone.

There are, however, two poems that are personal, not from the absorbed, fascinated examination of self that had characterized the young poet, but poems filled with a piercing melancholy because time has taken away the innocence of childhood. They are "Poem in October" and "Fern Hill."

These famous poems have much in common. Their structure is similar; the verse stanza in each is complex, formal, and invented by Thomas. The difficulty of such forms must have been most challenging, yet Thomas succeeded in making them lyrical, musical, their intricacy and complexity never obtrusive but necessary to the unity of the poetry. To read them aloud is almost to have to sing them. "Poem in October" has seven stanzas, each of ten lines. The lines are syllabic; that is, Thomas, as he had been doing for some time, did not write them in regular rhythmic patterns but adopted the method of counting the syllables, so that the first line in every stanza has nine syllables, the second line twelve syllables, the third nine, the fourth three, and so on. The rhyme scheme is both unusual and far from obvious. Thomas is using a convention that can be seen in other poems of this period, in "There was a Saviour," for example. He rhymes the vowels only—in our example he rhymes "saviour" with "radium." In "Poem in October" the rhymes are not quite as easily recognized, yet they are there and tactfully hold together the verse stanzas despite the variety of line lengths and the strength and dance of the rhythms. We can see that "heaven" in line 1 rhymes with "heron" in line three, "beckon" in line 5, and "second" in line 9. Similarly, "wood," "rook," and "foot" share the same quality of vowel sound, as do "shore" and "forth." One can easily identify this technique in the other stanzas.

The poem is one of that series of October poems in which Thomas celebrates his birthday; others have already been noted. Here he is not so much celebratory as apprehensive, looking back from the anniversary of his "thirtieth year to heaven" to earlier birthdays, those of his innocence, when he

> . . . saw in the turning so clearly a child's
> Forgotten mornings when he walked with his mother
> Through the parables
> Of sun light
> And the legends of the green chapels
>
> (46–50)

What he sees is "the true joy of the long dead child" who was himself. His final lines express the hope that his "heart's truth" may "Still be sung / On this high hill / In a year's turning."

The poem is unashamedly nostalgic, something that has caused some critics to minimize its importance; yet it is also beautiful and perfectly written. It is possible that Thomas idealizes the innocence of childhood, creating a brief moment of visionary happiness in which "a boy . . . whispered the truth of his joy / To the trees and the stones and the fish in the tide." But this is a startling achievement, and he has offered us the vision in highly sophisticated verse, from an adult point of view, and in the hope that he can retain such perfection of truth in the future. Imperfect though his life may have been, his aim is both the perfection of his art and, through it, a vision of perfection.

"Fern Hill" seems to me an even better poem. "Poem in October" includes merely a glimpse of the child's heaven; here he makes heaven as the boy knew it palpable and visible for us. Like the children in Blake's *Songs of Innocence,* the child Dylan on his aunt's farm, in a country world flawless and shining and without enemies, plays in ignorance that he is a prisoner of time:

> . . nothing I cared, at my sky blue trades, that time allows
> In all his tuneful turning, so few and such morning songs,
> Before the children, green and golden
> Follow him out of grace
>
> (42–45)

The poem is much more than a paean of regret for times past and lost. Sensuous, opulent in language, rich in imagery and music, it paradoxically mourns the passing of an innocent vision that has made a heaven from a poor hill farm in rough country, something possible only for a child who loves the place, and even while mourning its passing re-creates that very heaven, its brilliance of color, the music of its smoke, its magical horses and foxes. Thomas knows that he has made Eden once again: "So it must have been after the birth of the simple light / In the first spinning place." To lose such a condition, and to know one has lost it, is an appalling plight. It was Thomas' strength and his fate that he never lost such knowledge, that he kept the child's vision and the man's knowledge. His poem possesses both. He has made both his innocence and his sense of loss clear for all of us as long as his language remains.

There are not many poems after this. Whatever the reasons, Thomas wrote few poems in the last years of his life. He includes in his *Collected Poems* only six more poems, if we count the prologue written specially for that volume. Among them are two that few of his admirers would wish to be without, "Poem on His Birthday" and "Over Sir John's Hill." Both reflect the landscape about his house on the shore—"his house on stilts"—at Laugharne; both are calmer, more resigned. It is tempting to see in them some foreknowledge of the poet's death:

> And freely he goes lost
> In the unknown, famous light of great
> And fabulous, dear God.
> ("Poem on His Birthday," 46–48)

and to suggest that his frequent references to God mean that he has made his peace and no longer fears time, that he possesses some consolation. But it seems to me that these are probably the more mature manifestations of his old obsessions: death, religion, the inevitability of time. If he had some peace, it was, as he says in his "Author's Prologue," a poor peace.

> In my seashaken house
> On a breakneck of rocks . . .
> At poor peace I sing
> To you strangers. . . .
> (4–5; 23–24)

His "true joy" remains what it always was, that his "ark sings in the sun."

Although poems were few in his later years, he was not idle. Apart from his reading tours and his broadcasts, he continued to write prose, and he was a superb prose writer. His letters are joyous documents, his telegrams even. Having left his shirts in Dr. Jones's house, he sent his friend a wire that read, "For Pete's sake send my shirts, Love Pete" (*My Friend Dylan Thomas,* p. 114). Prose was the medium in which he found an outlet for his narrative skill, for his humor, for all the sides of his life for which poetry—and it will be remembered that for him poetry was used only for the most serious and profound and mysterious work—was not possible. He had a great deal to offer. He was a born teller of tales.

From the very beginning of his career he knew this. He thought of himself as a writer of poems and stories. This is how he describes himself in a letter, written when he was nineteen, to Glyn Jones: "You ask me to tell you about myself, but my life is so uneventful it is not worth recording. I am a writer of poems and stories" (*The Dragon Has Two Tongues,* p. 172). His life did not remain uneventful, but he was to remain a writer of poems and stories. He had contributed stories as well as poems to *The Swansea Grammar School Magazine.* In an appendix to *The Collected Stories* (1984), the editor, Walford Davies, includes three of these schoolboy pieces, the earliest having appeared in the school magazine in April 1931. There is plenty of evidence that Thomas considered poems and stories equal products of his talent, drawing no distinctions between them, knowing they came from the same source. The magazine he hoped to found and edit, on which he spent some time in the effort to promote it, was to be called *Prose and Verse.* It never appeared, but it is noteworthy that he allows prose to appear first in its title. And Glyn Jones and other friends have told us that when they visited him at his parents' house he was as eager to read his stories to them as he was his poems. They were, indeed, very like his poems.

If we read "The Tree," or any of the stories that eventually appeared in *The Map of Love,* it is evident that they possess the same obsessive imagery, are written in the same heightened rhythms, deal very largely with the same interior world as the poems of that period. It is true that, since they are narratives, Thomas had to pay more attention to the observable world; but it remains largely a place of dreams, the details not very clearly the result of observation; nor do the events of the story necessarily proceed from each other with the force of the inevitable. But they have the same sensuous power as the poems, and their very texture is exciting to discover.

> Rising from the house that faced the Jarvis hills in the long distance, there was a tower for the day-birds to build in and for the owls to fly around at night. From the village the light in the tower window shone like a glow-worm through the panes; but the room under the sparrows' nests were rarely lit.
>
> ("The Tree," *Collected Stories,* p. 5)

When Thomas first went to London in November 1934, he had already published stories in the magazines. Arriving in Soho, he found his poetry and prose equally admired. In "Where Tawe Flows," one of the autobiographical stories yet to be written and which would be included in *Portrait of the Artist as a Young Dog,* Thomas remembers this period: "Young Mr Thomas was at the moment without employment, but it was understood that he would soon be leaving for London to make a career in Chelsea as a free-lance journalist; he was penniless and hoped, in a vague way, to live on women."

But all this was in the future. And if the appearance of his first book of poems in December 1934 meant there was to be a comparative neglect of his prose, Thomas was not aware of it. He continued to write his stories, to send them to editors. From the room off the Fulham Road he shared with his Swansea friend Fred Janes, and where "for yards around" there was "nothing but poems, poems, poems, butter, eggs, mashed potatoes, mashed among my stories and Janes's canvases," he wrote with pride of the stories that had been accepted by various periodicals. He was a teller of stories all his life.

They were not, however, collected into a vol ume as the poems were, and when *Eighteen Poem* was followed by *Twenty-five Poems,* Thomas wa firmly established as a poet, not a prose writer. H tried to persuade Richard Church, his editor a Dent's, to publish a collection of stories, bu Church refused, judging the work obscene. Thi opinion was shared by the printers, who refuse to set the stories for another publisher a littl later. It was not until 1939 that a representativ sample of Thomas' stories appeared in book forn when seven were included with the poems of *T Map of Love.* In December of the same year *T World I Breathe,* a collection of the poems of th first three books and three stories in addition those in *The Map of Love,* was published in Ame ica. At last the early prose, or those stories which were considered suitable, had found a home.

Thomas, too, had found a home. He and Caitlin had moved into a small house in Laugharne, the little seaside town in Carmarthenshire that was to be his home for much of the rest of his life. They were very poor, and Thomas set about earning money by writing a different kind of story altogether. Glyn Jones recalls that in the summer of 1938 he mentioned to Caitlin Thomas that he was engaged on a volume of stories about childhood: "She seemed very surprised and told me that Dylan had already started doing the same thing. His were the autobiographical stories which in 1940 appeared as *Portrait of the Artist as a Young Dog*" (*The Dragon Has Two Tongues,* p. 191). The new stories were direct, uncomplicated evocations of the Swansea in which Thomas had grown up. They were not at all dreamlike; instead they revealed a most observant eye for the oddities of behavior, and an ear for the eccentricities within patterns of ordinary speech, that allowed Thomas to create credible and individual characters for the men, women, and children who people his stories. And while Thomas had written these stories—there were ten of them—at great speed and in the hope that they would be more commercial than his previous narratives, they also proved that this was the medium he could use for all his skills as a commentator on the world in which he lived, for his sense of fun, for his understanding of the small inevitable tragedies that fill ordinary lives.

Just as he had learned his trade as a poet from his reading of the great poets, particularly those of the nineteenth century, so he had served his willing time with the short-story writers. Among other authors, he knew the work of D. H. Lawrence, H. E. Bates, and Liam O'Flaherty; he had read James Joyce's *Dubliners;* he was an admiring student of Charles Dickens. Among Welsh writers he had a particular interest in the work of Caradoc Evans, whose stories had already used a Welsh background with success. With Glyn Jones he had visited the older man in 1936. They had driven north to Aberystwyth, the two young men wearing each other's hats, to speak to "the great Caradoc Evans," as Thomas called him in a story included in *The Portrait of the Artist as a Young Dog.* There is no direct influence of the Cardiganshire writer's work on Thomas, but he is probably important as someone whose example may have inspired the poet to write about Swansea and its people.

Again, Thomas had been living unprotected in the world for a number of years, his eye and his wits sharpened, his naturally alert senses alive to what was about him. He had already abandoned in many ways the interior universe of his early work and, as we have seen in his poems, was ready to create a world more related to that in which he lived. Above all, he had become a great storyteller, famous (as he almost said himself) about the bars. He realized that there were great areas of his ability and his personality that he would never use for lyric poetry, but he could use them in his stories. From this time on, the difference between his poetry and prose was marked.

Thomas believed that poetry is a solemn art, and he was a serious poet, dedicating his life to the service of his muse, restricting his themes to a few great and inevitable subjects. There is a great deal of word-play in his verse, of ecstatic delight in the combination of opulent sounds and highly exact, unusual meaning, in the presence in his lines of serious puns, but there is no room for laughter. Yet he was also a brilliantly funny man, and it is in the ten stories we are considering that a comic Thomas made his appearance. The stories, united in that they have as a central character "young Mr Thomas," move from the innocence of the first three stories ("The Peaches," "A Visit to Grandpa's," "Patricia, Edith, and Arnold"), through two splendid stories of his school days (in one of which, "The Fight," we meet Dr. Daniel Jones as a boy), to a more complex and jaunty person, Thomas as a cub reporter, his cigarette worn in admiring imitation of the old reporter he accompanies through the public houses of the town ("Old Garbo"). We see him as a haunter of deserted winter beaches, as a young man about to leave the town for London. It is with this portrait of himself that Thomas takes as decisive a leave of his younger self as he did with his sale of his notebooks.

The stories are full of wonderful talk, something in which Thomas himself excelled. We hear and recognize the characters as they preach from the back of a cart:

> I sat on the hay and stared at Gwilym preaching, and heard his voice rise and crack and sink to a whisper and

break into singing and Welsh and ring triumphantly and be wild and meek. The sun through a hole shone on his praying shoulders, and he said: "O God, Thou art everywhere all the time, in the dew of the morning, in the frost of the evening, in the field and the town, in the preacher and the sinner, in the sparrow and the big buzzard."

("The Peaches," *Collected Stories,* p. 128)

They are irreverent to school teachers, joke and wisecrack their way to the shore, stare in sadness and despair at the sea. A great mimic, Thomas realized his exceptional narrative skills in these stories: his sense of place, his fine ear for speech, and his love, appreciative and unjudging, for the people he creates. These are the qualities that make him a fine writer as distinct from a fine poet, and they are the qualities that helped to make him generally popular. Had he not written his stories he would have been a lesser, and a less interesting, figure.

Portrait of the Artist as a Young Dog is a title that pays clear tribute to Joyce, but it is not Joyce's *Portrait of the Artist as a Young Man* that one is reminded of when reading Thomas' book. Rather, the stories are clearly of the same type as those in Joyce's *Dubliners,* and Thomas is surely telling us this. Both books are set in provincial cities, both relate the important small events in unimportant lives and make them important. Stylistically, however, they are very different. Thomas himself denied that there was any Joycean influence on his work:

I cannot say that I have been "influenced" by Joyce, whom I enormously admire, and whose "Ulysses," and earlier stories, I have read a great deal. . . . As you know, the name given to innumerable portrait paintings by their artists is, "Portrait of the Artist as a Young Man." . . . I myself made a bit of doggish fun of the painting title and intended no possible reference to Joyce.

("Notes on the Art of Poetry,"
Texas Quarterly, Winter 1961)

Be that as it may, it is certain that "the bit of doggish fun" is his own. Although Thomas' title is said to have been the suggestion of Richard Hughes, the distinguished author of *A High Wind in Jamaica* and other fine work, Thomas had almost used it years before when he wrote, in 1933, to his friend Trevor Hughes. In that letter Dylan had advised his friend to "dive into the sea of yourself like a young dog." In his own stories, Thomas had taken his own advice and dived into the sea of his childhood and youth.

Portrait was published in 1940, the last of Thomas' books to appear until the war was over. He was—after a short period in which things looked very uncertain—working fairly regularly as a writer of film scripts and a broadcaster, his own writing pushed aside somewhat. He was, however, working intermittently on a novel, and was sending parts of it to London publishers, without success. This was the comic novel, just as autobiographical as his stories, eventually called *Adventures in the Skin Trade.* It was never completed and was published posthumously in 1955.

Despite its late public appearance—an extract had been published in *Folios of New Writing* in 1941 —most of it seems to have been written in the summer of 1941. Its hero, Samuel Bennet, seems to be none other than the young Mr. Thomas of the *Portrait,* and he continues where that young man left off, departing from Swansea by the very train that Thomas himself left home in "to make a career in Chelsea as a free-lance journalist." Vernon Watkins, who wrote an interesting foreword to the novel when it eventually appeared, thought that it remained unfinished because of the impact of the war, particularly of the air raids on London, on what he called Thomas' "essentially tragic vision," but he also thought that Thomas mistrusted his own facility. Certainly Thomas was able to write this sort of prose very quickly, but I feel that there may well have been other reasons for the failure to continue the adventures of Samuel Bennet. The novel is loosely structured as picaresque and moves forward in an arbitrary and rather casual manner. Thomas, that deliberate artist, must have felt very dubious about it; it is impossible to see, for example, any serious reason for it to end anywhere, or indeed to continue. It is funny and inventive, with passages of brilliant slapstick, but Thomas may simply have come to the end of what he had to say. He was, moreover, not a natural novelist; he was a natural short-story writer; the novel was too long for him. The very nature of his talent, selective concentrated, meant that he was not at home with the novel, a form into which one can pack almost anything. And while Thomas recognized his kin ship with Dickens when he called *Adventures in the Skin Trade* "a mixture of Oliver Twist, Little Dorrit Kafka, Beachcomber, and 3-adjectives-a-penny belly-churning Thomas," it was Dickens' energy and humor that he was acknowledging, the furious poetry. Thomas never actually put his novel awa entirely. As late as 1953, the year of his death, he was still suggesting that he might continue it.

For all practical purposes the novel was abandoned when Thomas went to London to work, and the demands on his time from then on resulted in there remaining only seven short narratives from this last period of his life, and six of the seven were written for broadcasting. It is ironic that his great popular reputation may rest on one or two of these and on *Under Milk Wood,* his "play for voices." It is also understandable, for they are entirely memorable pieces, bringing us the whole man, his warmth, the wide range of his humor, his pathos, his brilliant images, his incredible memory for the days and places of his childhood, his moving sadness for what had gone forever, and even enough magic to remind us that he was a great poet.

The first of these late pieces, "Quite Early One Morning," reads like a first draft of *Under Milk Wood,* for it deals with the dreams of a small sleeping town in the early morning, where Captain Tiny Evans, a trial Captain Cat, sleeps and dreams of "a rainbow of flying fishes." But it is "A Child's Christmas in Wales" that everyone knows. All over the world, in the days immediately before Christmas, we can hear from schools and houses the poet's voice rebuilding for us an impossible and utterly satisfying Christmas. Compounded of two similar stories, "Memories of Christmas" and "Conversation about Christmas," this was first published in *Harper's Bazaar* as "A Child's Memories of Christmas in Wales" in December 1950. It is a rich confection, as rich with gifts as any Christmas can hope to be, its snow untouched, its parties warm and musical, packed as a pudding with fruit and brandy. Dickens is not far away, but there are unforgettable Thomas moments too, like that when "with dog-disturbing whistle and sugar fags, I would scour the swatched town for the news of the little world, and find always a dead bird by the white Post Office or the deserted swings; perhaps a robin, all but one of his fires out" (*The Collected Stories,* p. 300).

"The Followers" is a ghost story of the most cunning and surprising sort. On a wet night, so beautifully realized that we must believe it, two bored young men, almost penniless but bravely keeping up appearances, one with a gallant cap, the other with a rolled umbrella and an attempted mustache, follow an ordinary girl home through the soaked, domestic streets. In such a world, so solid and convincing, ghosts should not happen, and it is all the more credible and terrifying when they do—and also funny. Thomas has learned how to select and create his detail; he has looked hard and lovingly at his world.

"The Followers" is the only one of these late narratives not written for broadcasting, and perhaps the only one that does not have the sound of Thomas' unique voice in it as a result. Certainly the uproarious events of "A Story" were made for him alone to tell, and the very structure of the sentences as they lie on the page seems to carry with them the man's own telling:

> But there he was, always, a steaming hulk of an uncle, his braces straining like hawsers. . . . As he ate, the house grew smaller; he billowed out over the furniture, the loud check meadow of his waistcoat littered, as though after a picnic, with cigarette ends, peelings, cabbage stalks, birds' bones, gravy.
>
> (*The Collected Stories,* p. 337)

Reading again these short narratives, as personal as any he wrote as a young man, it is impossible not to regret the loss of the work he might have written, and to wonder in what direction Thomas might have moved. We have not considered yet *Under Milk Wood,* the play for radio that was successively broadcast, adapted for the stage, and filmed. This might suggest that Thomas would have turned more and more to the stage for his work. His death put an end to the projected opera libretto he was to write for Igor Stravinsky, but we know he was enormously excited by the prospect. *Under Milk Wood* was first performed, in almost its final form, in New York only weeks before Thomas died there. He was working on it even during its performance, sending altered and additional lines to the actors as they read, and Thomas continued to tinker with it almost to his death.

Yet it is astonishly complete and unified, its cast of daft characters amiably dependent one on the other, the laws of its self-contained community thoroughly justifiable in the terms of that community. It cannot be said to have a plot. Its events are those of a single day in a small sea town in South Wales, Laugharne maybe, with echoes of New Quay, in Dyfed, where Thomas also lived. Raymond Williams has distinguished "three kinds of writing" in the play, "narrative, dialogue, song," an observation that helps to define the simplicity of its structure and to point the subtlety of the writing. The unity of the play, its corresponding and related oppositions, of darkness to light, of public chorus to individual musing, of song to prose, of innocence to innocent guilt—these make it remarkable. In it, suggests Williams, "Thomas wrote his adequate epilogue, his uproarious and singing lament" ("Dylan Thomas's Play for Voices," in *Dylan Thomas,* C. B. Cox, ed., p. 98).

There are always difficulties in measuring the stature of a poet. It seems to me that Thomas wrote enough remarkable poetry to justify our calling him great. There are poems that have enriched our literature, and his work has influenced a whole generation of poets. He changed the direction of English language poetry, his example being just as powerful in America as in Britain; nor were they always poets younger than himself who followed his lead. His life may well seem chaotic and without direction, yet it was purposeful and direct when we think of his one aim, to wait for his poems and to write them to the very best of his ability. All his working life he "laboured by singing light" to refine and perfect his skill; he was a great craftsman. For nearly a year he worked on the "Author's Prologue" to his *Collected Poems,* refusing to allow the book to go forward until he had completed to his satisfaction the almost impossibly difficult task of writing a poem of one hundred and two lines, in which line 102 rhymes with line 1, line 101 with line 2, and so on, until they meet in a couplet at the heart of the poem. My belief is that the poetry is as remarkable as the technical ability. And there may be another test of greatness, perhaps one that is more important than the opinion of any critic. On 1 March 1982, when the ceremony for the dedication of the poet's memorial stone took place in Westminster Abbey, the great hall was full. People stood in the aisles, at the pediments of pillars, wherever there was a foot of room. Hundreds stood outside in the rain, unable to hear a word of the proceedings. Ordinary people as well as the great and famous had come to pay their respects, many years after his death, to the poet. "He was loyal to the poem," said Theodore Roethke (*Encounter,* January 1954, p. 11), "he was one of the great ones." And the people had come to agree with that judgment, to affirm that poetry was necessary for the language and to honor the man who had proved it for them. That may well be greatness.

SELECTED BIBLIOGRAPHY

I. Separate Works. *Eighteen Poems* (London, 1934); *Twenty-five Poems* (London, 1936); *The Map of Love* (London, 1939); *The World I Breathe* (Norfolk, Conn., 1939); *Portrait of the Artist as a Young Dog* (Norfolk, Conn., and London, 1940); *New Poems* (Norfolk, Conn., 1943); *Deaths and Entrances* (London, 1946); *Selected Writings of Dylan Thomas* (New York, 1946); *In Country Sleep and Other Poems* (New York, 1952); *Collected Poems 1934–1952* (London, 1952); *Under Milk Wood* (London, 1954); *Quite Early One Morning* (London, 1954); *A Prospect of the Sea* (London, 1955); *Letters to Vernon Watkins* (London, 1957); "Notes on the Art of Poetry," in *Texas Quarterly* (Winter 1961); *The Notebooks of Dylan Thomas* (New York, 1967), ed. by R. Maud, also pub. as *Poet in the Making* (London, 1968); *The Poems* (London, 1971), ed. by D. Jones; *The Death of the King's Canary* (London, 1976), with J. Davenport; *The Collected Stories* (London, 1984), ed. by W. Davies.

II. Biographical and Critical Works. H. Treece, *Dylan Thomas, "Dog Among the Fairies"* (London, 1949); E. Olsen, *The Poetry of Dylan Thomas* (Chicago, 1954); J. M. Brinnin, *Dylan Thomas in America* (Boston, 1955); C. Thomas, *Leftover Life to Kill* (Boston and London, 1957); E. W. Tedlock, ed., *Dylan Thomas: The Legend and the Poet* (London, 1960); H. H. Kleinmann, *The Religious Sonnets of Dylan Thomas* (Berkley, Calif., 1963; New York, 1979); C. FitzGibbon, *The Life of Dylan Thomas* (Boston and London, 1965); C. B. Cox, ed., *Dylan Thomas: A Collection of Critical Essays* (New York, 1966), includes essay by D. Daiches; J. Scully, ed., *Modern Poets on Modern Poetry* (London, 1966); G. Jones, *The Dragon Has Two Tongues* (London, 1968); R. Maud, *Dylan Thomas in Print* (Pittsburgh, Pa., 1970); W. Davies, *Dylan Thomas* (Cardiff, 1972); W. Davies, ed., *Dylan Thomas: New Critical Essays* (London, 1972); R. M. Kidder, *Dylan Thomas: The Country of the Spirit* (Princeton, N. J., 1973); R. B. Kirshner, Jr., *Dylan Thomas, The Poet and His Critics* (Chicago, 1976); D. Jones, *My Friend Dylan Thomas* (London, 1977); P. Ferris, *The Life of Dylan Thomas* (London, 1977); J. Ackerman, *Welsh Dylan* (Cardiff, 1979); C. Thomas, *Caitlin* (London, 1986), with G. Tremlett.

ANTHONY BURGESS

(1917–)

Carol Dix

LIFE

JOHN ANTHONY BURGESS WILSON drops the ends of his name, or rather, as he describes it, pulls the cracker of his name to reveal the pseudonym; a name to him is like a toy or paper hat. Reading the wealth of his novels, criticisms, essays, reviews, and journalism, one can similarly peel off layer upon layer of his life. He hides nothing. His own experience is the touchstone or the setting for novels that comment on contemporary life, on racial harmonies in British colonies, on modern suburban England, on human nature and the cyclic patterns of history, on the role of the artist and his relation to society, even on the very nature of artistic inspiration, whom it attacks and why.

He began writing novels seriously in his early forties after service in the army and a career as a teacher both in England and abroad with the colonial civil service. It is almost as if everything before then in his life had been an accumulation of experience and material for his novels. Autobiographical facts leap from the pages. Born on 25 February 1917, in Manchester, the son of a pianist father and music-hall mother, beautiful Belle Burgess, who died when he was a baby, he was brought up under the influence of a stepmother who reappears as a grotesque figure in *Inside Mr Enderby.* The other dominant influence in his life both at home and at school was the Roman Catholic Church, which is described in many of his novels. In the early chapters of *Tremor of Intent,* for example, he uses his childhood memories of the Xaverian College, Manchester, to paint a delightful portrait of growing schoolboys' minds as they face the deadening impenetrability of Catholic doctrines. Burgess has a remarkable ability and facility with languages of all kinds and with words in general. He wrote poetry as a boy (F. X. Enderby's poetry is, of course, his own), but he originally intended to be a musician. A failed physics matriculation exam kept him out of the music course at Manchester University, so he studied English language and literature and has been fascinated by the close relation of words and music, in a Joycean way, ever since.

His first novel (written in 1949 and published in 1965 under the pseudonym Joseph Kell) concerns the life of a failed musician. Richards Ennis, in *A Vision of Battlements,* is the first of Burgess' anti-heroes who is in the cruel process of learning about his failures, and not only in music either. The novel is significantly set in Gibraltar, in the postwar period when the soldiers are waiting around to be given something to do. The setting is real. Burgess wanted to write about the conflict of feelings, of lives and ideas, he experienced in Gibraltar; about the experience of leaving England, its moderate climate and tepid passions; about arriving in continental lands where there may be more sin, more violence, and more evil, but to him, a Catholic, also a deeper reality. The novel was not published for many years because it dissatisfied both him and his publisher. In between he wrote and published the Malayan trilogy, inspired by his teaching in Malaya and Borneo, where he found, in the conflict of races and tensions between the colonizing British and the independent-minded Malays, a "confluence of cultures," the subject matter of many of his novels.

But Burgess' vision of the anti-hero is barbed with humor. He writes in a style of comic satire, similar to Evelyn Waugh's, which again can be seen to derive from his own experience of life. In 1959 he was invalided home from Malaya and his work with the colonial civil service, with a suspected brain tumor. In an interview with Samuel Coale, published in *Modern Fiction Studies,* which devoted a special volume to Burgess (Autumn 1981), the author explains something behind the myth that he began writing with the "year-to-live" gun to his head. It was the colonial experience itself that started him writing: for the first time he had some extra money, and, with the help of servants, time, so that writing was affordable. The dramatic return to England destroyed his conditions of luxury, leaving the myth-seeking Burgess with an emptiness in his life he did not know how to fill. Writing became the justification for his life, and five novels in one year, for the prolific writer, was, he claims, no problem. He and his wife rented a flat in Sussex and, by doggedly writing every day, he was able to complete five novels without great difficulty. He has never lost that ability to pour words onto paper. Some twenty years later he has published his twenty-eighth novel, *The Kingdom of the Wicked* (1985), reportedly writing seven days a week for a good eight hours a day. Those novels include *The Doctor Is Sick* (1960), drawing on his own near-tragic situation, and also *Inside Mr Enderby* (1963), *The Worm and the Ring* (1961), *The Wanting Seed* (1962), and *One Hand Clapping* (1961). For two of these novels he used the pseudonym Joseph Kell, as publishers and critics had begun to frown on so much productivity.

Burgess, who is now approaching seventy, continues to dabble in various forms of literature. But the critical essays, biographies, learned discourses on the language and art of Joyce, newspaper and magazine articles, television and film screenplays, television tie-in novelizations, and mountains of book reviews have led to an equivocal position in the halls of literary fame. One critic said recently: "In my opinion Burgess is, with the possible exception of Graham Greene, the finest living writer in the English language . . . challenging yet approachable" (A. A. De Vitis, *Modern Fiction Studies,* Autumn 1981); yet another critic points out that in recent years "his last four or five books have received scant attention . . . have met with either contempt or patronage" (Professor John Stinson).

Stinson (also in *Modern Fiction Studies,* Autumn 1981) cites the main reasons given for Burgess' insecure position: he writes too fast; he is a prodigious, gifted hack who writes for money; he lacks respect for serious readers and should discipline himself better; his ideas are half-baked; his themes are confusing because he is not certain what he is really saying. Stinson, however, goes on to refute those charges, believing that Burgess holds a unique place in the history of contemporary British fiction writing.

Other parts of Burgess' life story have appeared as flamboyant and arresting as the stuff of his novels. Married to a Welsh student whom he met at university, Burgess became free to marry the woman who three years earlier had borne him a son when his first wife died of cyrrhosis of the liver. He has said that his first wife was a highly sensitive and neurotic woman whose excessive drinking brought the couple into disfavor in their years in Borneo. His marriage to Liana Macellari caused quite a scandal; it took place only months after he had become a widower, their affair having become all too evident with the birth of their child. It is hardly surprising, then, that they have lived abroad most of their married life (although tax liabilities for the writer beginning to be successful probably provided the more pressing reason). They settled in recent years in Monaco, taking occasional trips to America on the lecture circuit. Burgess' popularity as a writer has become more firmly established in America than it ever was in Britain.

It seems to be a life story of its own large proportions, yet Burgess claims that he lives a very quiet life, preferring to read and listen to (or play) music rather than to suffer the society of other people. The facts are there in his writings; his essays collected in *Urgent Copy* (1968) reveal even more of the life story. He does not write out of any great didactic vocation to preach or to teach. His early novels are funny: witty, imaginative, very clever, informed, and above all, entertaining. We learn certain things about the man- -that he is an intensely active thinker whose philosophies stem from an Augustinian Catholic upbringing; that his approach to writing is through the sound of the word and that he loves to play linguistic games, enjoys punning and theorizing on the meaning of words and language; that the only writers he envies or emulates are Shakespeare, James Joyce, and Vladimir Nabokov. He sees himself, the artist, as an objective animal, withdrawn and contemplative, uninvolved and uncommitted; humanity, on the other hand, he sees as doomed to ironic comedy. Its aims, its loves, its ideals are pathetic. He prefers to live in the past, in exile, or in a rarified world of literature and music. His writing cannot really be categorized, but for convenience I have split my discussion of the novels into three sections. The first deals with novels of social realism and satire;

the second with the more philosophical novels; and the last with the novels that display his interest in language and the art of creation from words.

COMEDY

BURGESS is a contemporary of such English writers as Kingsley Amis and Angus Wilson, and he shares with them in his early novels certain traits such as a decided traditionalism and a preference for provincial or local subject matter. It has been said of today's English writers that they are too concerned with England's past. Burgess, however, brings new light to old themes, writing as an exile, with an objective eye cast both on the colonies and on England. Much good literary work is concerned with watersheds in time, the changes of values involved in some process of history. In his earlier novels—*Time for a Tiger* (1956), *The Enemy in the Blanket* (1958), and *Beds in the East* (1959) (Malayan trilogy); *Devil of a State* (1961); and *A Vision of Battlements* (1965)—Burgess sees the colonies (and also England in *The Right to an Answer* [1960] and *The Worm and the Ring* [1961]) as passing through phases of transition.

His views of both types of environment share that wry tone which when dramatized becomes comic irony. In Malaya, for example, there is a melting-pot of races: Malays, Chinese, Tamils, Sikhs, Eurasians, and British, each openly contemptuous of the other. Here is no liberal humanism of the school of Angus Wilson: Burgess is a social realist, or perhaps pessimist, and he drops no hints of a better, more united future. Yet he believes in imperialism, seeing the conflicts it creates as good for society (or for novelists at least). His view of England is of a contemporary society anaesthetized by television, supermarkets, pop singers, and strikes. The conflict is there, too, in his love for the England of the past and his alienation from its present.

In an essay in *Urgent Copy,* writing about his introduction to the novelist's trade in Gibraltar, Burgess expresses surprise that his novels turned out to be comic. He sees himself as a man of gloom and sobriety, and his comedy has to be seen in this light—not through the eyes of a man taking a gentle laugh at the world; it is rather the humor of one who finds a profound lack of things to believe in, and who consequently finds little that is real to him. His comedy is keyed in the pessimistic tone of Shakespeare's "As flies to wanton boys are we to the gods, they kill us for their sport" or the profound Augustinian despair of Graham Greene's *The Comedians.*

But Burgess' underlying despair is effectively offset by the vividness of the characters he creates. The central character of the Malayan trilogy (in American publications *The Long Day Wanes*) is Victor Crabbe, a man who has come to teach in Malaya out of a fervent belief that this is what he was meant to do. No other colonialist, however, allows him to rest for long in this belief. The cynics soon make it clear that he came because there was no other job for him at the time. The Malays and the Chinese don't want him; they want independence. The novels pinpoint the lazy, decadent, but essentially kind and liberal English characters, and the very different Malays and Tamils, including the delightful and colorful Alladad Khan (who courteously woos Crabbe's wife, Fenella) and the homosexual Ibrahim. The trilogy contrasts ancient Asian traditions in the Moslem world with crumbling British traditions.

The Crabbes' marriage, for instance, is shown in two stages. In *Time for a Tiger* Fenella is horrified by Victor's affair with the Malay girl Rahimah; in *The Enemy in the Blanket,* Victor is flirting dangerously, in such a narrow community, with Ann, another British exile's wife, and Fenella realizes that it is up to her to leave him. Crabbe is suffering from the loss of a first wife whom he can never stop loving. He is fond of Fenella but feels guilty for what he is not capable of giving her. He hesitates and is indecisive. The conflicts in their marriage are set against a background of terrible heat and forest skirmishes as the Communists try to take over the Malaysian province. Some of the best scenes weld all these elements, such as the trip with Alladad Khan and Nabby Adams to the north of the country to see an encampment of primitive people. Nabby Adams is a wonderful picture of decadent Britishdom, a warm-hearted, gregarious alcoholic who leans on the crumbling Crabbes for his only security.

Their little trip is doomed. They end up being ambushed in a skirmish, and as usual nothing is resolved. The delay brings another theme in the story to a climax. Victor has constant trouble at the school, where his white imperialist presence is not wanted. At the previous school the authorities discovered a Communist past; now again they are busy accusing him of Communist infiltration and influence on the boys. The day he is late is the day of the school sports. The boys have ganged up together, as schoolboys will, but with Communist help (not Crabbe's), and bring the sports day to a silent halt. No one will take part in any event. The school sports day is a perfect example of English manners transposed straight and unmodified into a different society, and the scene a brilliant illustration of the farcical elements of these societies clashing and not mixing.

The Worm and the Ring and *The Right to an Answer* are both about Burgess' feelings toward England. Once more they offer objective portraits of a country in transition, but the views are more personally slanted, for they involve Burgess' Catholic background and his contempt for a civilization of suburban streets, television antennae, and lack of moral and ethical standards, be it the low pay and status awarded to teachers, "indigent as medieval clerks," or the suburban wife-swapping in a Midlands town. The narrator, Denham, is surprised to find that this practice causes chaos, for, he says, "I thought the idea was to swap partners at weekends. An innocent suburban game like tennis."

The Worm and the Ring is the more sympathetic novel, although it wanders greatly in the gloom of despair. Christopher Howarth is the epitome of Burgess' sometimes self-indulgent intellectual despair. A grammar-school teacher, he reads Rilke—"Who, if he were to cry, would hear him among the angelic order?"—and can feel only pity, not love, for his son, Peter, who will have to go through the same life. He, his wife, Veronica, and Peter share no joy, no generosity or enthusiasm for life. Their humdrum existence is Burgess' view of English life, which offers unrewarding teaching followed by halves of cider in the local pub. Similar feelings are expressed in *The Right to an Answer,* more cuttingly through Denham, who describes Sunday visits to his sister's house for lunch, traveling by bus, as a "gape of Sunday ennui. So we Sundayed along, rattling and creaking in Sunday hollowness."

Howarth begins to be involved in life when he meets Hilda Connor, another teacher. She reawakens his sexuality and introduces some vitality into his life. The novel is firmly based on Burgess' own teaching experience while in England at a grammar school in Banbury. Unfortunately, one of his characters was too lifelike, and although the book was originally published in 1961, few copies were available until revisions were made and it was reissued in 1970.

The narrative involves a secret diary kept by one of the schoolgirls that is exploited by an up-and-coming young teacher, Gardiner, in his play for the headship of the whole complex of local comprehensive schools. Burgess sees Gardiner as a specimen of the new breed of Englishmen. While this new England is growing out of the old, he sees no place for those still living in the past. The end of the novel trails off rather weakly with Howarth suddenly acquiring both money and a sense of purpose: he will emigrate to Italy. "They were going to seek the other half of themselves in an exile which was not wholly exile, for England had not been completely a home for them and their kind for nearly four centuries." Fortunately Burgess does not oversimplify to the extent of wrapping Veronica and Peter neatly up in this parcel. They are allowed their regrets, but also feel that to be in England is to compromise.

In *The Right to an Answer,* the narrator, Denham, gives the novel a similarly weak ending by executing a sudden volte-face and changing the views he has stood by so strongly throughout the novel. The novel's great strength is the exile's loveless, objective view of England. It carries Burgess' form of social humor to its furthest extent, creating what today would be called "black comedy," as the social satire goes on to include murder upon murder.

Denham is a voluntary exile home on brief leave (as was Burgess). He stays with his father in a small Midlands industrial town, where he becomes involved with the small-minded community, entangled in their attempts at adultery and escape, and is horrified by their insensitive destruction of what he sees as the principal asset of their life, stability. But the Midlands town also becomes inadvertently involved in another form of destruction, through Mr. Raj, a friendly, garrulous Singhalese sociologist who at first seems only too willing to be accepted into the community, for what we later find are insidious reasons.

Raj and his ancestors have been ruled by the paternalistic British for so long that he wants to get some revenge, and the way to do this is to become the father himself. He kills old Mr. Denham by suffocating him paternalistically (and farcically) with curry. The blackness of the comedy only really becomes apparent as Raj shoots his beloved Alice's wayward husband and then himself, the two dying together on a bed beneath a painting of *The Last Watch of Hero.* Denham's contempt and sympathy for their pathetic lives is vividly dramatized in this tale of a feeble suburban passion, which is diluted even further by television. The police laugh at the report of such murders: go home and watch television, they say. Burgess laughs too at "Hero Alice," who is waiting for "her weekly lover Leander-Jack Brownlow, perhaps to swim the stormy straits for a night of Pimms No. 1 and love."

But in spite of his attacks upon England, some of Burgess' strongest writing, his most characteristically witty and imaginative language, is found in these two novels, where words are used for aural effect as much as for visual image and literary connotation. The best writing is found perhaps in the descriptions of the England he loves to remember. In *The Worm and the Ring,* he describes a small English town on its market day in language reminiscent of either Shakespeare, Hopkins, or Dylan Thomas: "A bleating sale of grazing legs, ewes and couples was on. The town was rich today in the blessed beasthood of the older gods, brown and red and golden through the drizzle."

These browns and reds and golds are symbolic of life more vibrant, more exotic, more sinful, more primitive than Burgess finds in contemporary England. This is an important theme in his writing, the search for the past, almost for a Golden Age. It is something he found (or so he tells us in the last essay of *Urgent Copy*) on arriving as a soldier in Gibraltar, where he felt inspired by the European environment to write. Brought up as a Catholic, he identifies with the Mediterranean society and has said that if it had not been for the Reformation, England would have been a better place—not the country of television, the Beatles, and strikes that it seems to him.

What he perceives in England is an Eliot-like "spiritual death," such as is evoked in *The Waste Land,* with Prufrock-like characters wandering around in an atmosphere of hesitation and inertia. This theme is skillfully embodied in the withdrawn, passive, or despairing figures, often his anti-heroes, that people most of his books. It is important to notice the different methods that he uses to portray them; he uses intellectual, sexual, and creative sterility to embody this theme. Victor Crabbe, in the Malayan trilogy, is the impassive or, more subtly, impotent central character, unable to give anything to Fenella. Similar anti-heroes are Denham, Howarth, and Richard Ennis (in *A Vision of Battlements*). Denham is left deliberately cool and uninvolved to narrate the events and make objective comments. Howarth, Crabbe, and Ennis, however, are asexual, and their lives are sterile.

Burgess develops this type in Edwin Spindrift in *The Doctor Is Sick* (1960). Spindrift, a linguist, is a man more at home with words than life, who really cannot cope with a world "where words are attached to things"; and F. X. Enderby, of the group of novels *Inside Mr Enderby, Enderby Outside* (1968), *The Clockwork Testament, or Enderby's End* (1974), *Enderby's Dark Lady, or No End to Enderby* (1984), is a similar creation, although here the image takes us into a cognate theme concerning energy and the nature of creativity, which is discussed in the last section of this essay. Enderby is a poet, but his lack of involvement leaves him a minor poet and is itself a symbol of sterility. His asexuality becomes the center of many comic scenes, and Burgess puts it to his usual clever and imaginative uses. For Enderby indulges in Portnoy-like masturbation (as in Philip Roth's *Portnoy's Complaint*) and even leaves a female predator in "mid-orgasm" as he rushes to attend to the whims of his Muse.

This theme of inertia has been treated by many contemporary authors, including the American writer John Barth, who in his character Jacob Horner in *The End of the Road* describes the sensation as one inspired by Laocoon. In the legend, Laocoon, through his inertia fails to prevent his sons from being killed. In an early critical work, *English Literature: A Survey for Students* (1958), Burgess widens its associations with a reference to Robert Burton's *Anatomy of Melancholy,* a sixteenth-century work that he sees as a treatise on the mental ailment from which Hamlet suffers. He describes this as "an inability to make up one's mind, to perform necessary actions, or to get any pleasure out of life."

This "spiritual death" is symptomatic of contemporary English society. In these novels Burgess is exploring his attitude toward the concept of stability by drawing a picture of contemporary life against a vision of the past. With reference to his novels of colonial life, he describes the conflict as a "confluence of cultures"; the same holds true of his novels of English life, only the cultures are of the past and the present. Bernard Bergonzi, in *The Situation of the Novel* (1970), describes this as a trend among contemporary English writers, to wander between nostalgia and nightmare. The nightmare is what Burgess wants to portray. Later he develops more sophisticated methods.

PHILOSOPHY

IN *The Reaction of Experimentation in the English Novel, 1950–60* (1967), Rubin Rabinovitz makes a criticism similar to that expressed by Bergonzi, to the effect that English novelists are too content to live in the past—although he does admit that Anthony Burgess has, in *A Clockwork Orange* (1962), tried some successful experimentation. Rabinovitz fails to discuss the novel, and indeed it received surprisingly little attention from critics in either England or America until the release of the film, directed by Stanley Kubrick, that suddenly catapulted Burgess' name into the public consciousness and made of him a highly celebrated prophet of modern times. This is a role that Burgess has since decried. He does not believe *A Clockwork Orange* is his best work or even a very significant literary work, calling it "tricky and gimmicky." But of course he has to agree that, almost like a parody of his own concerns, it achieved a mythical impact. *A Clockwork Orange* and its counterpart, *The Wanting Seed* (1962), have come to represent two of the more important avant-garde creations of the 1960's.

A Clockwork Orange was not written in the year of the first five novels, but it was published only a year later. Yet it is the kind of book that one might well expect to hear required a lifetime of work from its author—not just another novel quickly written, to be followed by another in the same year. For Burgess' imaginative scope here not only encompasses a whole vision of society in the future but is even stretched to the formation of a language or vernacular, and neatly gives that society an identity, a history, and a reality. The language experiment, called "nadsat," is the derivative vernacular of Alex and his gang of "droogs" and is derived in turn from Burgess' own interest in linguistics and the history of language (see his work published in 1964, *Language Made Plain*). The vernacular is cleverly based on odd bits of rhyming slang; it includes a little gypsy talk and its basic roots are Russian. It is not impossible to understand; after a few pages, context and meaning make the language perfectly comprehensible. For example, "We gave this devotchka a tolchock on the litso and the krovvy came out of her mouth" roughly translated means, "We gave this girl a blow on the face and blood came out of her mouth."

Nothing is told about the history or whereabouts of this strange futuristic society, but deductions can be made from the language. The society obviously has been subject to both American and Russian intervention if not invasion. The derivative language, spoken by the young, probably indicates the effects of propaganda through subliminal penetration. This is not a difficult situation to imagine, and one not too far removed from the present. The English language today bears the traces of numerous invasions and the resulting influence on the English people, most notably that of the Scandinavians, the Romans, and the Normans. Alex and his gang are simply the products of an England that Burgess showed us in *The Right to an Answer,* pushed to its logical extreme. There he feared for England's sanity (under America's influence). The bourgeois middle class in the novel have become so quiet and so passive that the young who have succeeded them have chosen evil as their way of life, as an assertion of the will.

They beat up old men, rape girls, and kill, with no qualms. They are cheerful and spirited in their criminality, and Alex, despite his violence, will not listen to pop but only to classical music. For the violence is not thoroughly bad. It may be evil, but in terms of humanity it is better than inertia. Burgess' romantic view of violence in this light is that of an old-fashioned traditionalist who can see no good in a leveled-out contemporary society that leads to gray totalitarianism. These romantic views again stem from his Catholic upbringing of a strict Jansenist kind. He calls himself a sort of Catholic Jacobite and hates England's present-day pragmatic socialism because, as he explains in *Urgent Copy,* "any political ideology that rejects original sin and believes in moral progress ought strictly to be viewed with suspicion by Catholics."

It is this suspicion of our contemporary liberal humanism, of our willingness to reform rather than to punish, to educate rather than to discipline, that is seen in *A Clockwork Orange* as a traditionalist's fear of the future. Alex is eventually caught by the police and punished for his crimes by being sentenced to be "cured." He is given electric shock treatment and is told, "You have no power of any choice any longer. You are committed to socially acceptable acts, a little machine capable only of doing good." Burgess feels that there is potentially more good in a man who deliberately choses evil than in one who is forced to be good. Men are what they are and should not be coerced by any social conditioning or pressures. Alex ends up as a free individual with all his criminal impulses and, incidentally, his love of music, restored. He is considerably matured and ends optimistically, saying: "Tomorrow is all like sweet flowers and turning vonny earth and the stars and the old luna up there and your old droog Alex *all* on his oddy knocky seeking like a mate." But then Alex has never been unlikable. Even at his most violent he is charming and witty as narrator-hero, comparable perhaps to *King Lear*'s Edmund, who has all the forces of nature and the audience on his side. Alex symbolizes violence as an act of assertion, as a positive force.

Burgess' fear, then, is of passivity. In its human form it leads to the dulling of the spirit, as happened to Denham, Crabbe Ennis, or Howarth. But the "spiritual death" can also be seen in the wider context of a political or philosophical sterility that afflicts whole countries given over to a totalitarian view of life. Later—if we can use the critic's license and jump now to a work published in 1966—Burgess wrote *Tremor of Intent* with a theme similar to that of *A Clockwork Orange;* it may not succeed like the latter as a novel, yet as a vehicle for expressing Burgess' philosophical theories it is an important work.

In his journalism, Burgess has made it clear that he was not impressed by what he calls Wilsonian pragmatism ("Letter from England," *Hudson Review,* Autumn 1966), which is his definition of Harold Wilson's form of socialism under the Labour government of England from 1964 to 1970. He hates the state and any way of life that is dominated by it. One would not expect him, therefore, to be a great adherent to Communist principles. In 1961 Burgess visited Leningrad to gather material for a novel, *Honey for the Bears* (1963), from which he invented a story of imaginative social satire on the mixed-up values of and hostilities between East and West, commenting on the eagerness with which the Bears (Russians) lap up the honey (American materialism). It is a novel containing Burgess' usual mix of strange adventures, witty dialogue, and critical commentary on people's lives, but one that remains minor. Yet that same topic was to provide material for a far more ambitious novel, in which he tries to embody his quasi-theological concept of the world in the form of a contemporary spy narrative, *Tremor of Intent.*

Burgess uses the cold war between the East and the West, and the spying game, a very contemporary activity that plants the book firmly in the present, as a metaphor for a life of indeterminate acts. What he wants life to be is a reflection of ultimate reality, of a duality based on good and evil, God and the devil. The danger lies in "neutrality," or what I have previously called "passivity" or "inertia," for the duality of existence can be truly seen only when man is positive. He must be totally violent, totally sexual, totally gluttonous. The novel is called an "eschatological spy novel" because it deals in the flesh (hence the spirit) through gross eating, carnal lusts, and horrifying murder. Unfortunately it contains too many elements, too many characters symbolizing separate strands of the theory, so that one cannot help but be confused. Yet the story can be read purely as a James Bond-type thriller. It has a totally involved hero, Dennis Hillier, and it has Goldfinger-type manipulators, such as Theodorescu and his beautiful accomplice, Miss Devi. It has spy and counterspy, plot and twist and counterplot. It has sex, violence, and lots of action.

The novel changes its tracks halfway through. It begins with the tale of Roper, Hillier's boyhood friend, who defected to the Russians because he lost his faith in Catholicism and then in patriotism. He tried to renew both these convictions first through Brigitte, his German (and also Nazi) wife, who lets him down by turning prostitute; and then through communism, which also lets him down in the end. But the novel soon proves to have little more than a functional narrative interest in Roper, and follows Hillier instead. In Hillier, Burgess has found a character very similar to Norman Mailer's Stephen Rojack in *An American Dream.* Indeed, Burgess shares with Mailer a hatred of totalitarianism, a fear that this is where today's passivity will lead, and a belief in the romantic nature of violence, on the grounds that it is symbolic of commitment and assertion.

Hillier needs to act. He rapes Brigitte after he has discovered her prostitution. He seduces Clara, a young girl who is like a daughter to him. Embarking on a gastronomic cruise, he is drawn with Theodorescu into a grotesque orgy of overeating. Burgess plies the reader with an orgy of murders at the end of the novel, as plot and counterplot unfold before our bewildered eyes. Murder becomes, not the ultimate evil, but the ultimate response to reality—it is interesting to see that again there is a parallel treatment in Mailer's writings: "Hillier's eyes were drawn to the weapon; if he were to engage in the ultimate intimacy, he had at least to know its name. It was a Pollock 45, beautifully looked after." Any description of the narrative is bound to confuse, as too much happens to too many disparate characters. The novel begins on a realistic level with Roper and Hillier at school together, facing the problems of Catholic dogma as it presents itself to bright, youthful minds. The development of Hillier's spying on Roper marks a neat twist in their friendship. But, as the novel continues, the characters become "enciphered," and it is the reader who is then involved in decoding the hidden messages.

It is not until the last few pages, when we discover that Hillier the spy has become Hillier the priest, that the novel's philosophical meaning is made apparent. Hillier the spy-priest says:

> "We're too insignificant to be attacked by either the forces of light or the forces of darkness. And yet, playing the game, we occasionally let evil in. Evil tumbles in, unaware. But there is no good to fight the evil with. That's when one grows sick of the game and wants to resign from it."

Hillier, an Irish priest, directs the reader into the knowledge that the whole grotesque story has been a discussion, in quasi-theological terms, based on Manichaeism. This religion, which originated in the third century A.D. and combined Gnostic, Christian, and pagan elements, was based on a dualistic theology of light and darkness, good and evil, God and Satan, the soul and the body: it envisages a perpetual conflict between the demons and the angels for the possession of mankind. Hillier reveals that everything is a great counterfeit of the real war that goes on in heaven. Just as East and West fight it out in our world, with spies intermingling for possession of the "body politic," so is the great heavenly war taking place, with priests as the subversive elements.

It is the duality that keeps life going, the tension of opposites. This is a difficult thesis, but it relates again to Burgess' despair at "spiritual death," because it is neutrality and inertia that stultify this tension or duality. He sees that what we need are "new terms. God and Notgod. Salvation and damnation of equal dignity, the two sides of the coin of ultimate reality." It is as if he were saying he had lost the religion that was a part of his upbringing, and what *he* needs, too, is a renewed faith in something.

The renewal of religious fervor, or of vitality in life, is also dramatized in *The Wanting Seed,* along with a discussion of his metaphysical theories, followed through several generations of a nation's life. The vision of a cyclic pattern of history that takes nations from socialism to authoritarianism and back is again an expression of Burgess' intellectual despair. *The Wanting Seed* is a picaresque tale of the adventures of Tristram and Beatrice Foxe in a land in the future. The story moves between different locations and different times. Its form necessarily leads to an episodic structure that does not hang very closely together.

In fact, *The Wanting Seed*'s significance is to be found as much in its ideas as in imagination and black humor. The philosophical theory of the novel is put into the mouth of Tristram, a history teacher. Tristram believes that history follows three phases. First comes the Pelagian phase or "Pelphase" (named after a British monk who believed in human perfectibility). In this era, the forces of liberal humanism are at work. Everyone expects the best, people believe in man's innate goodness. Overpopulation is treated by contraception and/or homosexuality; reformation subsumes punishment. There is no discipline. This is followed by the Interphase of transition, and then we go into the Augustinian phase or "Gusphase," which is one of strict discipline, with the stress on human depravity. Discipline and punishment return along with heterosexuality and fertility. Wars are organized and arranged for keeping the population down ("extermination sessions"). Then the more liberal attitudes creep back, and the cycle begins again.

The narrative contains some of Burgess' most imaginative writing. It involves a vision of an England in the future (owing something to both Aldous Huxley and George Orwell) and an England whose urban sprawl has enveloped London, Lowestoft, Brighton, and Birmingham. In the Pelphase, childbirth is frowned upon and homosexuality is condoned. Beatrice Foxe, Tristram's wife, becomes pregnant by her brother-in-law, Derek, who has been pretending homosexual status in order to get on in their world. Beatrice runs away to the North, which is relatively uncivilized, to a State Farm, where her sister Mavis is married to the natural, unaffected Shonny, and where children and nature are not frowned upon. The tale becomes truly horrific with the account of her struggle to have the baby and of Tristram's macabre adventures. He is thrown into prison, to be released only as the Gusphase takes over from the Pelphase. As the new order takes over, the people, who are starved of food and human contact, suddenly find new life and sexuality: "The crop had failed and a faithful sow was dying but a new life was preparing to thumb its nose at the forces of sterility." The novel ends with Tristram wandering the country, where he discovers with amazement a pagan renewal of life that involves cannibalism, and acceptance of the flesh and the spirit. It is a sort of neo-Catholicism in which human flesh is consecrated instead of the host.

In his later novels, Burgess has continued to explore his Manichean theme: the world as a twofold creation, an unresolved conflict between good and evil. In the novel *1985* (published in 1978), he paints another of his rather bleak futuristic portraits: the England of 1985, owing much to Orwell's 1984, is a country of all-pervasive dullness, where there has been a leveling of intelligence, taste, and knowledge. *The Man of Nazareth* (1977), Burgess' ambitious retelling of the Gospels (written in conjunction with a long television series on that theme), uses the Bible as the perfect starting point for that particular world view.

Earthly Powers (1980) has proved to be Burgess' best-received novel of later years, but in some ways it is also his most controversial, and here his philosophies finally came under scrutiny. Are his ideas, as Burgess has been accused of, half-baked, those of a man gone beyond his prime, left ranting and debating his own themes with no one other than himself? Burgess took the controversial position of using as narrator of *Earthly Powers* Kenneth Marchal Toomey, an eminent novelist and unsympathetic homosexual who has outlived his contemporaries to survive into honored, bitter, luxurious old age—a character reportedly modeled on W. Somerset Maugham. But Burgess' obvious anger at homosexuality, his often crude and unflattering portrait of the homosexual in today's society, was not well accepted in a liberal, tolerant world where a large proportion of his readers may well be homosexual. In Toomey's homosexuality, are we meant to see the Burgessian concept of universal sterility, of a world gone wrong? This massive and ambitious novel, which deals with most of twentieth-century history in its 600 pages—encompassing, often comically, descriptions of concentration camps, mass suicides, the making of a pope and a saint, the exorcism of an evil spirit and much more—offers a jaded view of the world.

Unfortunately for Burgess' admirers, the novels that have followed *Earthly Powers* tend to confirm the vision of Burgess as one aspect of Toomey (a man who has lived beyond his time). His latest, again very long novel, *The Kingdom of the Wicked* (1985), takes on early Christianity's rise during the Roman Empire, beginning with the Crucifixion, exploring the corrupt reigns of Caligula, Claudius, Nero, and Domitian, and ending with the eruption of Vesuvius. An apparently easy vehicle for his basic theme—man's freedom to choose between good and evil—the novel unfortunately lacks a real point of view and in it, as one critic comments, Burgess appears to have nothing illuminating to say. The vision of good and evil is too simplistic. The novel uses old historical novel-writing devices, such as bringing in pivotal characters to explain what is happening and giving famous people scenes in which they act out what we all know they are supposed to have done; Burgess seems to be rehashing old material, shoe-horning it into yet another written work. Burgess' critics are all too aware that *The Kingdom of the Wicked* was written to tie in with a television series, and it is not hard to fault him for careless, rushed work. To some readers, it appears unashamedly like a soap opera of the first century A.D., with the court of imperial Rome juxtaposed against the more peasantlike world of the Apostles.

Advocates of Burgess' fine writing, his vigorous prose style and marvelously inventive imagination, often wish he would write less, or perhaps now in his maturity concentrate on smaller, more finely honed books. Bernard Bergonzi commented recently that Burgess' later novels "show [his] ceaseless ingenuity and inventiveness, but they provide few of the ordinary satisfactions of fiction. He remains a uniquely clever and energetic novelist, but recent development is not encouraging."

LANGUAGE

On the narrative level, Burgess' novels may be said to be based on societies in transition: within the resulting social flux Burgess perceives much that forms the basis of human nature and its failures. On the intellectual level, they are novels concerned with the author's own transition from a Catholic upbringing to some new belief. Novels are not only an art form based on social and intellectual perceptions, but also artifacts created with words, and Burgess is one of the few authors writing today in English who makes the fullest use of the raw materials of writing, the words themselves. His linguistic explorations or experiments make him one of England's most adventurous writers; they also make him a difficult writer, for the experiments are often esoteric and academic, and cut him off from the ordinary reader. One has always to remember that Burgess is not only a skillful craftsman in the construction of plots and creation of characters, but an extremely clever and agile-minded man who draws upon all the resources of his knowledge in his writing. Some of his novels could perhaps benefit by a glossary.

At least a third of his total output is critical work. This fact should not be forgotten in a study of his fiction, if only for the clues that it provides to his fictional imagination and the theories behind the writing. From such works as *Here Comes Everybody: An Introduction to James Joyce for the Ordinary Reader* (1965), *The Novel Now* (1967), and *Urgent Copy,* we have learned his artistic theories and views on creativity. Words are his trade. He sees himself as a professional, who on the one hand has to come to terms with publishers' deadlines and the need to earn a living, and who on the other hand has to serve not only his readers but also the world of literature. An accomplished musician as well as writer, he finds that his approach to the written word is highly aural, and the only writers for whom he admits any respect are those similarly inspired.

Burgess has suffered to an unjustified degree from critics who have mocked him for his "productivity," and there are times when his treatises on the novel are barbed with self-defense. In *The Novel Now* he justifies his part in helping to overpopulate the world of books by explaining that as an author he has half-invented people and half-conceived actions that need completion and release. He says he is not romantic in his view of art but rather coldbloodedly professional. If the critics and commentators find anything of any worth in what he writes, then obviously he is pleased. But he himself can see only good in fecundity, because of his need to earn and his fears of untimely death.

Perhaps it was the serious threat of a suspected brain tumor, but Burgess has a desire to cheat death. And there are times when his energy, both physical and imaginative, is overpowering. As one critic of his survey of contemporary literature, *The Novel Now,* deduced from its bibliography, it seemed as if Burgess had been reading one contemporary novel a day, Sundays off, for the then six years of his active writing career. His reading and his general and specific knowledge cannot pass unpraised.

His theories of the writer of course find expression in his novels too, especially in the Enderby series and in the fictional re-creation of Shakespeare's life, *Nothing Like the Sun* (1964). Enderby is one of Burgess' most sympathetic characters. A minor poet, he voluntarily withdraws from a world of sharks, fools, exploiters, and shady little people. Enderby would rather be involved in no action and with no people. Yet he is dragged into more than his fair share.

Enderby offers one of the best examples of Burgess' humor. The comic satire of the novels is based on Enderby himself, who is partly mocked and partly respected. Burgess has described how Enderby came to life. In Malaya, after a party where he had drunk too much, he staggered into the bathroom and felt he saw a man sitting there writing poetry. Of course there was no such person, but the image sprang to life and has emerged as one of Burgess' most popular characters. The first of the series, *Inside Mr Enderby,* was written in the first year of great productivity and rushed to the publishers; and the series was continued five years later with the companion *Enderby Outside* (1968). The first novel is not crammed with characters. Enderby meets Vesta Bainbridge, a glamorous widow from the pop world and employee of *Fem* girls' magazine, who lures him into marriage. He is alarmed by the high level of sexuality and intimacy the relationship requires of him and eventually escapes. The other major character is Rawcliffe, a decadent and deceitful poet who has achieved a little more worldly success than Enderby through expediency. Rawcliffe significantly steals one of Enderby's ideas and gains money and fame by turning it into a film. Depressed by the disappearance of his Muse after these adventures, Enderby attempts suicide and is discovered, cured, and delivered to Wapenshaw, a behavioral psychiatrist who robs him of his poetic gift and makes him "normal." Enderby becomes Hogg, a bartender, and we leave him thus transmogrified.

Enderby Outside begins with Enderby-Hogg just beginning to relocate his poetic gift. He visits Wapenshaw to tell him the good news, but in an admirable satire of modern psychiatric methods, the doctor is furious, as Hogg had taken pride of place in a new book of case histories. The reversal quite destroys the case. Enderby's adventures become more picaresque now. Vesta has married again, into the pop world, to the singer Yod Crewsey, whose fame is beginning to border on idolatry thanks to his poems. Enderby recognizes the poems as his own, stolen by Vesta, and when Crewsey is murdered, he is unjustly accused of the crime. He escapes the country—the theme of the traveler without suitcase is popular with Burgess (witness *The Doctor Is Sick* and *The Right to an Answer,* where both Spindrift and Denham find themselves in such a dilemma), and it may be that the fear of being unidentifiable as a traveler is symptomatic of modern confusion, chaos, and nightmare—but again he falls prey to Woman, this time a selenographer, Miranda Boland. He arrives in Tangier, where he meets a group of weird poets spawned by the psychedelic revolution (Burgess' own friend, the writer William Burroughs, lived at one time in Tangier). He again encounters Rawcliffe, who reminds him of his mortality, and also meets a strange young girl who seems to be the representative of his own Muse and has a thing or two to tell him about his art: "Poetry isn't a silly little hobby to be practised in the smallest room of the house."

In these two novels, there are several different types of people in the service of art. There are pop singers and drug addicts who, to the accomplished musician and literarily educated Burgess, mock both music and words; and various women, Vesta, Miranda, and the girl/Muse, who all try to reawaken Enderby, through sex, to his artistic failings. But failure or not, Enderby at least retains his integrity. He may be funny, he may be pathetic, but he is still their superior. His poetry is traditional and craftsmanlike. He is perhaps the equivalent to Burgess the novelist, not writing out of any great commitment to art and the Muse, but writing because he feels a love of words and the need to write.

Perhaps Enderby's poetry is part of Burgess' general view of a cosmic joke and the irony of life, namely that those who feel the inspiration to write are not necessarily going to be great. But at least they achieve more than those who exploit art. As a traditionalist who has said that he sees himself not quite in the potboiler category but not in the avant-garde either ("Letter from England," *Hudson Review,* Autumn 1966), Burgess identifies with Enderby, whose Muse figure admonishes him: "You lack courage. You've been softened by somebody or something. You're frightened of the young and the experimental and the way-out and the black dog."

Enderby, like Edwin Spindrift the linguist, is happiest in the world of words, unrelated to life. Out of this idea comes one very important theme: the conflict within Burgess himself about the nature of creativity. An accomplished linguist and musician, Burgess finds the idea of the ivory towers of academe a pleasant refuge for the sensitive artist, for whom society and involvement are too demanding. Burgess, who choses to live in exile, has been quoted often on his dislike of life, in the sense that its only interest consists in being able to withdraw and to produce bizarre characters from his imagination or observation. Yet this hermitlike existence conflicts with his predominant feeling that creativity comes from the expenditure of energy and that it entails total involvement. The embodiment of creativity and energy is Shakespeare, whom he characterizes in *Nothing Like the Sun;* but before discussing that novel, I would like to consider certain implications of Burgess' first novel, *A Vision of Battlements,* which cast some light on these ideas.

In his last essay in *Urgent Copy,* Burgess records that he first felt inspired to write when he arrived in Gibraltar, where he sensed the presence both of European civilizations and of a Catholic environment. In *A Vision of Battlements* Richard Ennis, a failed musician waiting in Gibraltar for the chance to return to England now that the war is over, suffers the same kind of sexual alienation experienced by Enderby, Crabbe, Howarth, and Denham. He wants to compose music but lacks the energy or the drive. He then meets Lavinia, a sort of goddess who writes poetry, but he finds her manner overforceful and uninspiring and wishes "he were back in the billet with Julian, in the calm epicene atmosphere, where lust could be transmuted into creative energy." Ennis has been sharing a billet with Julian, a homosexual. There is no strong implication that he is homosexual himself, just that he enjoys the calm, cool, unimpassioned atmosphere in which he feels he would be able to compose (or write).

In the same novel, Lavinia quotes these lines from a Shakespeare sonnet:

> The expense of spirit in a waste of shame
> Is lust in action, and till action, lust
> Is perjured, murderous, bloody, full of blame.

They neatly sum up Burgess' conflict: a desire for the epicene coolness of noninvolvement (with a hint of homosexuality) contrasted with the belief that in order for creative energy to be released, one has to give way to all one's lusts and be totally involved in life.

Of the title *Nothing Like the Sun,* Burgess has said that it emphasizes the impossibility for us of conveying the authentic effulgence (the sun). WS (Burgess' fictional Shakespeare) may not be able to emulate the energy of the sun, but he certainly throws himself into life, finding himself the mere plaything of the gods' will. His lusts take him away from those he really loves, destroying all his better purposes and eventually his health. Behind this tale of WS's adventures we hear Ted Arden's (from *The Right to an Answer*) voice moralizing on his ancestor's ways: "Will really is a terrible example for everybody, showing what happens when you leave the wife of your bosom and go off whoring after other women." The cruelty of life's irony is perceived by no one more piquantly than WS. In London, away from his family, he receives the message that his son, Hamnet, is dying. WS says grimly, "We are all caught, are we not, between two worlds? Our sin and our sickness is not to choose one and turn our backs on the other, but to hanker after both!" And in Lear-like despair he dreams of what he might have hankered after, given another life, through his vision of the life Hamnet might have had. For his son he desires not this lusting after the flesh and writing plays by the dozen, but a life of sterility: that intellectual world of literature and learning mentioned by Richard Ennis.

In these thoughts Burgess makes WS admit to a confusion in his ideas. He thinks of Hamnet, "He could not act, but he had no need to act: no violent assumption of commitment could ever come to disturb his sad calm." Burgess' WS dreams secretly of that stoic calm, yet knows that literature comes from the other way of life; that the force of literature is a copy of the force of life: "Let us have no nonsensical talk about merging and melting souls, though binary suns, two spheres in a single orbit. There is the flesh and the flesh makes all. Literature is an epiphenomenon of the action of the flesh." Next to God, Burgess has said, Shakespeare created most.

Nothing Like the Sun was his tribute to the great master for the quatercentenary year (1964). It was also an opportunity for Burgess to match his skills against Shakespeare's. In filling in the blanks of his life, he was able to furnish the character of WS with his own image, but above all he was able to emulate Shakespeare's mastery of the language. So, young WS is seen talking, thinking, and daydreaming in language that leads on to his playwriting without any real break. The passage that follows illustrates Burgess' thorough understanding of Shakespeare's words and imagery:

> Goat. Willow. Widow. Tarquin, superb sun-black southern king, all awry, twisted snakewise, had goatlike gone to it. So *tragos,* a tragedy. Razor and whetstone. But that was the other Tarquin. . . . But a willow was right for death.
>
> (ch. 1)

The language of the entire novel is a remarkable achievement of taut, packed sentences and Elizabethan phraseology, with the invention of a new vernacular to fit the society in question (as in *A Clockwork Orange*). Shakespeare has remained a preoccupation with Burgess over the years, and he later completed a more factual account of his life and works in the large illustrated volume entitled *Shakespeare* (1970). Shakespeare is Burgess' type of the writer; he wrote, it could be maintained, not out of any great love for art, but for money and status. He was also a writer very much aware of the musical qualities of language and very much in love with the sound of words. But Shakespeare's love for words is superseded for Burgess by James Joyce's, to whom he has devoted a lot of time and energy in the preparation of *Here Comes Everybody*

(1965) and *A Shorter Finnegans Wake* (1966) (in which he has cut the text down for the more bewildered reader).

Joyce is, to Burgess, the supreme example of the proper difference between literature and the popular novel. Joyce uses his knowledge of languages (both he and Burgess mastered at least six or seven) and his knowledge of literature throughout his writing. Burgess' admiration for Joyce's work is important to notice with regard to *MF* (1971), in which he employs all his knowledge of linguistics, literary and mythical allusions, even fashionable intellectual theories. Reading his essay and reviews in *Urgent Copy* can again help, for there, Burgess explains the source of the Algonquin legend upon which he based this novel. It is a tale he derived from an essay by Claude Lévi-Strauss, "The Scope of Anthropology," which deals with Lévi-Strauss's views on myths and riddles. It is a complicated story of Oedipus-like origins that involves incest, which Burgess relates to that other family—of languages.

The narrative in *MF* is an odd mixture of grotesque nightmare and fairy tale. Not particularly successful as a novel by conventional standards, it is more a work of the comprehensive literariness that Burgess has always admired and understood in Joyce. The guiding idea is that literature, as language, should affect the reader as total experience, or synthesis; analysis of its parts is a contemporary and sophisticated practice. In *Language Made Plain* (1964), Burgess' book on linguistics, he explains that primitive people did not speak in pidgin English; rather, they spoke in synthetic terms that encompassed a total experience. Joyce writes in the same way, in what we refer to as "epiphanies," or moments of revelation. And Burgess has attempted that style here.

MF is an erudite, sophisticated novel that could benefit from a glossary, although Burgess would be the first to refute this. Unfortunately, if the ordinary reader's knowledge is not on a par with the author's, this resetting of the ancient myth of the Iroquois Indians may not have any special appeal. However, when *Finnegans Wake* was criticized for being too erudite and beyond the normal reader, Burgess defended it by saying we must become as erudite as Joyce. He felt reviewers who criticized the wealth of Joyce's mind, were saying that Joyce's great crime was to know too much. Indeed, how can it be a crime to write a truly literary novel, fulfilling, as Burgess describes it in *Here Comes Everybody,* "the author's egotistical desire not merely to add to English Literature but to enclose what is already there"? Yet in concentrating on the erudite, on the literary, Burgess may be letting down, as Bergonzi has charged him, his ordinary reader, no longer making those witty and comic comments on our society that make his body of writing such a gift to contemporary English literature.

Indeed, *MF* is the first of his later works that embodies an obsession with literary craftiness at the expense of readability. These works very often appear to be nothing more than literary quizzes, aimed at graduate students on campuses throughout the Western world who enjoy pitting their wits against a master of erudition—to translate the novels for everyman or woman. They give some grounds for the suspicion that Burgess, who became a sort of cult figure for American youth in the early 1970's, may have willingly played into the hands of such students, providing them the sort of material they crave for interpretative papers. Or, from another angle, maybe Burgess finally discovered the sort of reading audience he had in turn always craved—those prepared to be as erudite as he is himself.

Burgess scatters his later novels with signposts and landmarks such as the subtle use of myth, legends, manipulative games, word games, snatches of film dialogue, poems, set pieces from television talk shows, Hebrew, Latin, and Greek names, historical references; and just as an Eliot or a Greene, he expects to be interpreted. If he has to describe a room, Burgess may turn to a page in the dictionary, any page, and see if he can describe the room making use only of words on that page. In *MF,* Burgess has explained, there is a description of a hotel vestibule derived from page 167 of the Malay-English dictionary.

On another level, though, Burgess' fascination with language and the use of language is to be taken very seriously. He writes, "When I am criticized that I write English clumsily . . . I take this as a compliment, because once you start writing clearly contained . . . periodic sentences, you're not being true to the subject matter . . . to the flow" (*Modern Fiction Studies,* Autumn 1981). His own criticism against much contemporary English writing is that it is too clean, too neat and precise, and the energy, the vitality of life, goes missing. "Language is extremely dangerous," says Burgess. "Language probably bears no relation to ultimate reality. It's a ritual making device. It's a ritual making process." And, he implies, behind those rituals, we all hide and to some degree die a small death.

Burgess' intellect, his extremely agile and inventive mind, may yet lead to a secure place in English letters and history. More like an American than a typically British writer, he shows the power and the vision of a man not prepared to narrow his sights or his creative scope—and for that we should be grateful.

SELECTED BIBLIOGRAPHY

I. Separate Works. *Time for a Tiger* (London, 1956), novel; *The Enemy in the Blanket* (London, 1958), novel; *English Literature: A Survey for Students* (London, 1958), criticism; *Beds in the East* (London, 1959), novel; *The Right to an Answer* (London, 1960), novel, rev. (London, 1970); *The Doctor Is Sick* (London, 1960), novel; *Devil of a State* (London, 1961), novel; *One Hand Clapping* (London, 1961), novel, pub. under the pseudonym Joseph Kell; *The Worm and the Ring* (London, 1961), novel; *The Wanting Seed* (London, 1962), novel; *A Clockwork Orange* (London, 1962), novel; *Honey for the Bears* (London, 1963), novel; *Inside Mr Enderby* (London, 1963), novel, first pub. under the pseudonym Joseph Kell and reiss. under his own name (London, 1966); *The Novel Today* (London, 1963), criticism; *Nothing Like the Sun* (London, 1964), fictional biography; *The Eve of St Venus* (London, 1964), novel; *Language Made Plain* (London, 1964), linguistics; *Here Comes Everybody* (London, 1965), criticism; *A Vision of Battlements* (London, 1965), novel, pub. under the pseudonym Joseph Kell; *Tremor of Intent* (London, 1966), novel; *A Shorter Finnegans Wake* (London, 1966), a shortened version of Joyce's novel; *The Novel Now* (London, 1967), criticism; *Urgent Copy* (London, 1968), critical essays; *Enderby Outside* (London, 1968), novel; *Enderby* (New York, 1968), novel; *Shakespeare* (London, 1970), criticism; *MF* (London, 1971), novel; *Cyrano de Bergerac* (New York, 1971), translation of play by Edmond Rostand; *Joysprick* (London, 1973), an intro. to the language of Joyce; *Napoleon Symphony* (London, 1974), novel; *The Clockwork Testament, or Enderby's End* (London, 1974), novel; *Beard's Roman Women* (New York, 1976), novel; *Moses* (London, 1976), narrative verse; *New York* (Amsterdam, 1976), nonfiction; *A Long Trip to Teatime* (New York, 1976), essay; *ABBA ABBA* (London, 1977), novel; *Man of Nazareth* (London, 1977), novel; *1985* (Boston, 1978), novel; *Ernest Hemingway and His World* (London, 1978), biography; *Earthly Powers* (New York–London, 1980), novel; *On Going to Bed* (New York–London, 1982), nonfiction; *This Man and Music* (London, 1982), nonfiction; *The End of the World News* (London, 1982), novel; *Enderby's Dark Lady, or No End to Enderby* (New York–London, 1984), novel; *The Kingdom of the Wicked* (New York–London, 1985), novel; *Homage to QWERTYUIOP* (London, 1986), essays and reviews.

II. Critical Studies. J. Mitchell, ed., *The God I Want* (London, 1967); R. Rabinovitz, *The Reaction of Experimentation in the English Novel, 1950–60* (London, 1967); G. Aggeler, "Mr Enderby and Mr Burgess," *Malahat Review,* 10 (April 1969); G. Aggeler, "The Comic Art of Anthony Burgess," *Arizona Quarterly,* 25 (Autumn 1969); B. Bergonzi, *The Situation of the Novel* (London, 1970); F. McDowell, "Recent British Fiction: Some Established Writers," *Contemporary Literature* (Summer 1970); W. Sullivan, "Death Without Tears: Anthony Burgess's Dissolution of the West," *Hollins Critic,* 7, 2; G. Aggeler, *Anthony Burgess, Artist as Novelist* (University, Alabama, 1979); "Unearthly Powers of Anthony Burgess," *Saturday Review,* 7 (December 1980); J. Brewer, *Anthony Burgess: A Bibliography* (New York and London, 1980); S. Coale, "Interview with Anthony Burgess," *Modern Fiction Studies,* 27 (Autumn 1981), a special issue on Burgess.

MURIEL SPARK

(1918–)

Ruth Whittaker

I

MURIEL SPARK was born Muriel Camberg in Edinburgh 1 February 1918. Her father was Jewish, but she was educated in the Presbyterian atmosphere of James Gillespie's girls' school. There she learned Latin and Greek and was "the school's Poet and Dreamer, with appropriate perquisites and concessions" ("What Images Return"), and she gained prizes for her school by winning essay and poetry competitions. Her formal education was abruptly ended when she went straight from school to Central Africa at the age of eighteen. Here she married and had a son, Robin. Her marriage broke up, and in 1944 she returned to England and worked in a branch of the intelligence service for the remainder of the war.

The years between the end of the war and the publication of her first novel in 1957 were difficult for Muriel Spark. She did a variety of jobs based in London, including writing for a trade journal and working as an editor. She had continued to write poetry, though, and in 1947 became secretary of the Poetry Society, a national organization for the encouragement of the art. From 1948 to 1949 she was editor of the society's magazine, *Poetry Review,* for which she wrote lively editorials, and to which she encouraged new, young poets to submit their work. In 1949 she began a magazine of her own called *Forum,* which ceased publication after two issues for lack of financial backing.

In the early 1950's Spark began editorial collaboration on a number of critical works, and wrote books on Mary Wollstonecraft Shelley and John Masefield. Her first published fiction appeared in 1951, when she won the *Observer* short story competition with a strikingly original story called "The Seraph and the Zambesi." In 1952 her first collection of poems was published.

In 1954 Spark was received into the Roman Catholic Church, having been greatly influenced by the writings of Cardinal Newman. During the period leading up to her conversion she had become ill, partly through malnutrition. She was trying to write a commentary on the Book of Job, and like Job was suffering from a variety of afflictions. At this time she received financial help from various people, including Graham Greene, and through an advance for a novel from Alan Maclean of the publishers Macmillan. She completed her first novel, which was published as *The Comforters,* in 1957. To date she has published seventeen novels. In 1962 Spark moved to New York while still maintaining a base in London. In 1966 she moved to Italy to live, first in Rome, then in Tuscany. She has never remarried.

This brief outline of Muriel Spark's life reflects the economy that is the central principle of her fiction. Each part of her life has been transformed through the alchemy of her art into her novels, but her thrifty viewpoint extends beyond the utilization of her own experience and affects her whole perception. Her fiction is dominated by her Roman Catholic perspective and by her keen and interrelated exploration of the novel form. It is significant that Spark resisted writing a novel until after her conversion, an event that gave her a sense of unity: "from that time I began to see life as a whole rather than as a series of disconnected happenings" ("How I Became a Novelist"). This is also the viewpoint of the novelist: every event has its purpose in the narration, nothing is wasted. Thus, throughout her work Spark economically exploits the connection she sees between God and the novelist, both omniscient authors, creators of worlds in which everything, however contingent and trivial, is shown finally to be causal and significant.

Spark sees the everyday world as sacramental. In an article on Proust she says, "the visible world is an active economy of outward signs embodying each an inward grace." This belief strongly affects the structure and style of her novels. She is not a writer in the English realist tradition, because for her the reality she seeks to convey is not of this world but the next. She does not strive for mimesis since her real concern is with the inimitable. Therefore, whenever our attention is drawn to the familiar or commonplace within her novels, it is, paradoxically, to alert us to the extraordinary potential of everyday events. Her novels are usually short and allegoric; realism is merely a vehicle for a supernatural or divine revelation. For example, in *The Girls of Slender Means* World War II is used as a backdrop to the main event of the novel, which is the revelation of grace to the agnostic hero. *The Abbess of Crewe,* although inspired by the Watergate scandal in the United States, transcends the realistic comparison and becomes a timeless parable about corruption wrought by power.

Spark's religious viewpoint also affects her attitude toward the concept of time. She sees the world *sub specie aeternitatis*—under the aspect of eternity—and this means that the straightforward sequential treatment of events is jettisoned in her fiction. "Let us not strain after vulgar chronology," says Lister in *Not to Disturb,* and the more perceptive of her characters realize the everlasting status (in religious terms) of momentary actions. In *The Comforters* Caroline says, "The next few eternal minutes are important." And unlike a realist novelist, Spark frequently gives away the ending of her novels early on, so that the reader's interest is redirected from simple linear suspense to the more interesting speculations of how and why.

A further deviation from the English realist tradition is Spark's treatment of character. In the nineteenth-century novel particularly, the realist emphasis is on the freedom and independence of a novel's characters; their careful, loving depiction ensures identification and sympathy. This is alien to Spark. Her view of character is of a being bound, willingly or unwillingly, by the ordinances of God and, by analogy, to the restrictions imposed by the novelist. As readers we are denied a sense of the unrestricted individuality of her people, since we are made constantly aware that their choices and actions function within both a divine and a novelistic plot. Sometimes, as in *The Comforters,* the protagonist fights back, resisting awareness of authorial omniscience. Or, as in the *The Driver's Seat* and *Not to Disturb,* the protagonists cooperate with the fictive process and collude with the events necessary for the conclusion of the novel. But because their roles are predetermined, it is part of Spark's economy not to give an interior psychological view of her characters or to reveal their thoughts and motives. This is particularly true of her five middle novellas, from *The Public Image* (1968) to *The Abbess of Crewe* (1974), where she seldom gives us sufficient information about her characters for us to feel an easy sympathy with them. Very few of them have families or a sense of belonging somewhere, and there is no sense of experiential growth, as there would be in a nineteenth-century realist novel; at best her people fulfill what is shown to be their already latent potential (for good or evil) through circumstances beyond their control. It is as if this social and emotional isolation enables Spark to get down to essentials; the impression given is that the careful nurturing of sympathy for the foibles and nuances of personality is an unnecessary distraction when the state of the soul is what needs to be considered.

This detachment can be attributed in part to Spark's religious perspective, which is clearly illustrated in a short story called "The Portobello Road." In it she describes the brutal murder of a young girl and then the reaction of one of the victim's close friends: "Kathleen, speaking from that Catholic point of view which takes some getting used to, said, 'She was at Confession only the day before she died—wasn't she lucky?' " That is a shocking sentence, hardly softened by Spark's unusually generous admission that this angle of vision "takes some getting used to." But it is a viewpoint that sees potential in all things. Indeed, in *The Bachelors* Ronald Bridges says, "The Christian economy seems to me to be so ordered that original sin is necessary to salvation." In her novels Spark delights in providing examples of divine irony, where pious characters are abandoned while those who sin sometimes receive unexpected and unlooked-for grace. In *The Prime of Miss Jean Brodie* Sandy sleeps with Teddy Lloyd, who is married and a Roman Catholic. Sandy incidentally becomes interested in Catholicism: "Her mind was as full of his religion as a night sky is full of things visible and invisible. She left the man and took his religion and became a nun in the course of time." Frederick's histrionic suicide in *The Public Image,* designed to shatter his wife's career, does just that, the irony being Annabel's profound sense of liberation as she is released from the bonds of her image. Above all, these stories illustrate a divine plan superimposed on worldly events. Nothing is gratuitous, and what may have seemed to the readers (and to the characters) appalling or unnecessary evil during the course of the narrative is revealed at the end as necessary and redemptive.

Nevertheless, Spark's novels consistently abound in blackmail, manipulation, deception, terrorism, violence, and sudden death. We may begin to wonder if she believes that the end justifies the means, a doctrine condemned by several popes. Her insistence that there is "another world than this" *(The Ballad of Peckham Rye)* is meant to direct our attention to the realm of God. But, goaded by the sameness, the blackness, and the brisk cynicism of her fiction's universe, one may protest that there is indeed "another world than this," where in reality people occasionally behave with love and altruism.

Many of Spark's novels are reflexive, examining their own form within the texts. When the narrator points out in her first novel that "the characters in this novel are all fictitious," we are jolted from our "suspension of disbelief" and forced to reconsider the novel as something other than an attempt to lull us into its (albeit temporary) veracity. We are reminded, in other words, that for Spark reality lies not in the novel or in the everyday world, but in the realm of God. By sabotaging her own creation of an autonomous, fictional world she disclaims her own powers and endorses her view of God as omniscient author, and if the reader employs the tangible world as a source of reference, it is shown to be an insufficient source of verification.

This perhaps makes Spark's fiction sound more solemn than it is. Released from the conventions of realism, she mocks them with exuberance. Her plots deliberately echo fictive stereotypes such as the thriller, the detective novel, the desert-island castaway tale, schoolgirl stories, ballads, fairy tales, and the Gothic novel. *The Comforters,* for example, is almost a parody of the thriller-cum-detective story; *Robinson* clearly draws on the reader's preconceptions about castaways from *Robinson Crusoe* and *The Swiss Family Robinson;* the tone and theme of *The Prime of Miss Jean Brodie* parody the conventional schoolgirl stories of Angela Brazil and Enid Blyton. *The Ballad of Peckham Rye* is offered with a deceptive lightness and succinctness influenced by the Scottish border ballads. The events of this novel are given a distance, a fictionality, by passages at the beginning and the end that firmly place its episodes in a distant realm of hearsay and fable. Near the beginning we are told, "The affair is a legend referred to from time to time in the pubs when the conversation takes a matrimonial turn." And, at the end, "Much could be told of Dougal's subsequent life . . . for economy's sake, he gathered together the scrap ends of his profligate experience —for he was a frugal man at heart—and turned them into a lot of cockeyed books" (ch. 10). The mock deprecation at the end of this quote conveys Spark's awareness of its superficial untruthfulness.

A similar distancing process takes place in *Not to Disturb,* which frequently reminds us of its debt to Jacobean tragedy and the Gothic novel. Wind howls round the shutters, lightning flashes, and a "zestful cretin" raves in a locked attic. This mixture of Mrs. Radcliffe and the Brontë sisters, and the frequent dramatic and poetic allusions (which also occur in *The Abbess of Crewe*), confirm the novel as part of an established literary tradition. Spark does not seek to escape the connotations of such a tradition in order to claim originality. Rather she makes use of its implications to emphasize an inevitable relationship with former works of literature, and the acknowledgment of this debt further undermines the realism of a novel such as *Not to Disturb,* which reflects not real life but methods of fictionalizing it.

II

SPARK'S first novel, *The Comforters* (1957), has a conspicuously overdramatic and complex plot involving a diamond-smuggling gang, bigamy, blackmail, diabolism, and death. It satirizes our expectations of a realist novel while simultaneously fulfilling them by exploiting such novelistic devices as coincidence and happy endings. What this novel does most economically is to explore two kinds of conversion: the religious conversion of the heroine and the artistic conversion of reality into art. In other words, it is an intense combination of Spark's principal fictive interests, religion and the novel form.

The heroine, Caroline Rose, has just become a Roman Catholic and struggles with the problem of exercising free will in a universe that she is now aware is divinely controlled. Her role as a Roman

Catholic has frequent parallels with her role as a character in a novel. A hallucinatory, authorial voice, accompanied by the tapping of a typewriter, exercises its omniscience over Caroline's actions, and she has to come to terms with both the voice and the dictates of her new faith. She says, "The fact of the author and the facts of the Faith . . . are all painful to me in different ways." Caroline herself is writing a book called "Form in the Modern Novel" and is "having difficulty with the chapter on realism." She knows the passive role that she as a fictional character is expected to take, but she fights back. She tries to assert her independence by attempting to outwit the plans of the authorial voice: "I intend to stand aside and see if the novel has any real form apart from this artificial plot. I happen to be a Christian." She uses the fact of her Christianity—that is to say, her knowledge of her participation in a greater plot—to give her the confidence to stand aside from the ostensible plot and to test its validity. She comes to realize that she has to reconcile her everyday life (the "artificial plot" of the novel) with her new life as a Roman Catholic:

Her sense of being written into the novel was painful. Of her constant influence on its course she remained unaware and now she was impatient for the story to come to an end, knowing that the narrative could never become coherent to her until she was at last outside it, and at the same time consummately inside it.

(ch. 8)

Thus Spark links the role of a character in a novel with the role of a person in real life, both subject to a plot that is imperfectly understood at the time. Only at the end of a novel or a life do events and people become finally significant, since a plot has emerged from their interaction.

The Comforters is a novel about fiction making, and Spark therefore feels free to demonstrate the fictiveness of one of her characters in a peculiarly surrealistic way. A particularly repulsive woman called Mrs. Hogg is made to disappear—that is, attention is drawn to her disappearance—whenever she is not currently involved in the plot: "as soon as Mrs. Hogg stepped into her room, she disappeared, she simply disappeared. She had no private life whatsoever." Another character says that Mrs. Hogg "is not all there" and "hasn't any life of her own." These clichés are recycled by Spark as a joke about the fictive conventions taken for granted and used so conveniently by the realist novelist. Having been introduced to characters in a novel, one usually assumes their quiescent fictional existence somewhere in the background, even when they are not specifically mentioned. Spark demonstrates with Mrs. Hogg that fictional characters, constructs of the novelist, "exist" only at the precise invocation of their creator.

In this novel, written soon after she became a Roman Catholic, Spark writes unsentimentally about her new religion and satirizes its adherents. Caroline Rose epitomizes what one comes to recognize as a typical Sparkian heroine: a sharp, intelligent, independent thinker, not given to displays of emotion, and, if a Catholic, reluctantly so, with an abhorrence of Catholic cliques and prejudices. "Caroline was an odd sort of Catholic, very little heart for it, all mind." Mrs. Hogg shows herself adept at needling Caroline:

"Mm . . . I know your type," Mrs. Hogg said, "I got your type the first evening you came. There's a lot of the Protestant about you still. You'll have to get rid of it. You're the sort that doesn't mix. Catholics are very good mixers. Why won't you talk about your conversion? Conversion's a wonderful thing. It's not *Catholic* not to talk about it."

(ch. 2)

A further satiric target in *The Comforters* is the semiliterary, self-consciously "bohemian" world of London poets and booksellers, a world Spark knew intimately in the 1940's and 1950's. She is very interested in close, hermetic communities, which emerge time and again as fruitful territory to explore in subsequent novels. They are shown to have specific locations, obsessions, rules (written or unwritten), even a language and traditions of their own. On her temporary return to the London she had left, Caroline sees clearly the shallowness of her former associates: "In the second pub . . . a fair fat poet said to Caroline, 'Tell me *all* about your visions, my dear'; . . . and another sort of writer, a man of over fifty, asked Caroline who was her psycho-analyst, and told her who was his."

The Comforters acts as a showcase for Spark's literary preoccupations, although she never again uses such a wide variety of characters and subplots in one novel. Subsequent works are more elegant, less raffish. She is much more discriminating with her material, which is used with great refinement.

Robinson (1958), her second novel, is a tightly

constructed Freudian allegory in the guise of a violent castaway tale. It is perhaps Spark's weakest novel. It has irritating hints of autobiography couched in metaphoric terms, and it succeeds neither as allegory nor as realism.

With *Robinson* Spark ends the relative introspection of her first two books. In her next novel, *Memento Mori* (1959), there is no character obviously resembling the author; it is as if she has become comfortable with her faith and can now apply her new-found convictions to the world around her. *Memento Mori,* of all Spark's novels, is the most lyrical and the most religiously assured. Several elderly people are telephoned by an anonymous caller who says, "Remember you must die." Throughout the novel the reader's interest is focused on the wide variety of responses to this message, which range from hysteria to calm acceptance, according to the moral bearing of the recipient.

The characters in this novel are highly credible, and Spark gives them the obsessions and eccentricities of the very old, with humor but also with sympathy. And, as in *The Comforters,* her style conveys more than is actually said. In *Memento Mori* the last rites are described, and the prose becomes slower in pace and reiterative, the process of thought expressed becoming almost a meditation in itself:

> Miss Valvona's tears dropped into her supper. She was thinking of her father's Last Sacrament, after which he had recovered to live a further six months. The priest behind the screen would be committing Granny Barnacle to the sweet Lord, he would be anointing Granny Barnacle's eyes, ears, nose, mouth, hands and feet, asking pardon for the sins she had committed by sight, by hearing, smell, taste and speech, by the touch of her hands, and by her very footsteps.
>
> The priest left. A few of the patients finished their supper. Those who did not were coaxed with Ovaltine. At seven the sister took a last look behind the screen before going off to the dining room.
>
> "How is she now?" said a Granny.
>
> "Sleeping nicely."
>
> (ch. 9)

The contrast is self-evident. The affirmative prose leaves with the priest, as it were, and the ordinary world reasserts itself. The point of the novel is that the awareness of the inevitability of death should imbue everyday actions with significance: those with faith are reminded that they will be accountable to God; those without faith need to live fully and well in order to redeem their existence from nullity.

The argument of *Memento Mori* is primarily for a religious appreciation of life, and within it references to religious beliefs are made in the lucid, utterly authoritative tone usually reserved for indisputable fact. For example: "In the course of the night Granny Trotsky died as the result of the bursting of a small blood-vessel in her brain, and her spirit returned to God who gave it." Each fact, the name of the patient, her death and its cause, and the return of her spirit to God, is given the same narrative weight, having the status of truth rather than of pious hope or personal opinion.

The *memento mori* tradition is not popular in the twentieth century; our scientific postponement of death seems to make contemplation of it less relevant than in previous centuries. *Memento Mori* is striking not only because it is a twentieth century novel about death but also because it does not euphemize the mental distress and physical degeneration involved in the process of dying. It is not a morbid or a gratuitously shocking book, although a certain macabre humor threads its way through the novel. Death is put in perspective for the reader through the absurdity of the characters who panic at the thought of it and the good sense of those who accept it as the culmination of a natural cycle. "Remember you must die" is reiterated throughout the novel, and for once readers cannot dissociate themselves by the consoling thought that it is only a fiction. In this way the fantasy device, the warning voice, paradoxically becomes the most realistic aspect of the novel, because it applies not only to the fictional characters but to ourselves. Thus *Memento Mori* is a work of meditation and an aid to meditation. It is a *memento mori* in itself.

Spark's next two novels, *The Ballad of Peckham Rye* and *The Bachelors,* were published in the same year, 1960, and both deal with small sections of London-based communities. In *The Ballad of Peckham Rye* the protagonist, Dougal Douglas, is an ambiguous creature, half-angel, half-demon. Like the mysterious phone calls in *Memento Mori,* he acts as a catalyst for the local inhabitants, disturbing the spiritual torpor of Peckham and in some cases making people miserably aware of the narrowness of their lives. Their lethargy erupts under Douglas' influence into violence, breakdown, and murder. This novel shows clearly Spark's skill in fitting her narrative tone to her theme. One of the funniest (and saddest) scenes in the novel is an account of two lovers spending Midsummer's evening together. Instead of the magical romance this suggests, the affair is a wasteland of stale and unloving habit. Here is Spark's description of Merle and Mr. Druce waiting for their meal to finish cooking:

> "The brussels are not quite ready," she said, and she sat in her chair and took up her knitting. He perched on the arm. She pushed him with her elbow in the same movement as she was using for her knitting. He tickled the back of her neck, which she put up with for a while."
>
> (ch. 4)

When she wrote *The Ballad of Peckham Rye* Spark was living near this part of London, and it reveals her acutely accurate ear for dialogue. In a later novel, *Loitering with Intent* (1981), the narrator says, "My ears have a good memory. If I recall certain encounters of the past at all, or am reminded perhaps by old letters that they happened, back come flooding the aural images first and the visual second."

Jargon and clichés have always been Spark's satiric targets, and in this novel they are recorded sharply:

> "One of Richard's great mistakes—I'm speaking to you quite frankly," she said, "was insisting on our *living* in Peckham. Well, the house is all right—but I mean, the environment. There are simply no people in the place. Our friends always get lost finding the way here; they drive round for hours. And there are blacks at the other end of the Avenue, you know. I mean, it's so silly."
>
> (ch. 8)

The words "ignorant" and "immoral" permeate the novel; used indiscriminately by the characters about each other to describe a range of activities from incorrect grammar to adultery, they are shown also to be an accurate description of Peckham life. And yet, even in this, one of her most pessimistic novels, Spark shows the dreariness and immorality of Peckham to be transcended. In a description of the Rye, or common land, we are told that one of the characters "saw the children playing there and the women coming home from work with their shopping bags, the Rye for an instant looking like a cloud of green and gold, and people seeming to ride upon it, as you might say there was another world than this." This is a view of Peckham that is not shown in the course of the novel, but Spark insists that what we have seen is not the total sum of man's human condition; this brief and poetic statement is pointedly made the final sentence of the novel.

The Bachelors is also concerned with demonology, in the person of Patrick Seton, a medium who uses his powers for evil ends. He is counterbalanced by Ronald Bridges, who suffers from epilepsy, an illness associated in the past with demonic possession. Patrick is a dualist whose contempt for the material enables him to contemplate murdering his mistress, Alice, as if he were doing her a favor: "I will release her spirit from this gross body." Spark insists on respect for the material as significant and sacramental, and Ronald Bridges' epilepsy is seen within the control of God. After a particularly bad night involving demonic thoughts and culminating in a seizure, Ronald decides to go to confession the next morning, "to receive, in absolution, a friendly gesture of recognition from the maker of heaven and earth, vigilant manipulator of the Falling Sickness."

Nowhere else in her work does the author so clearly convey the frustrations of a person in whom an awareness of God coexists with such soul-sickening depression. The murky atmosphere of *The Bachelors* is of deception, emotional and moral expediency, of people battening on one another with leechlike tenacity. *The Bachelors,* unlike *The Comforters,* does not end with a climax of evil overcome. Patrick is put in prison and Alice is married to someone else, but Ronald's struggle goes on. His triumph is not in defeating his demons in favor of God, but in accepting the fact that throughout his life they will coexist and then, with faith, getting on with life as best he can.

III

THE publication of *The Prime of Miss Jean Brodie* (1961) brings a change of manner and emphasis in Spark's work. This novel and its successor, *The Girls of Slender Means* (1963), are works of great assurance and authority. Supernatural events no longer occur, and Spark concentrates on portraying evil as manifest through the actions of an individual or through the godlessness of contemporary society, leaving it to the reader to postulate a moral system thus violated. We are given hints that Roman Catholicism provides such a system, but it is no longer shown explicitly to be an enabling factor or a saving grace.

The Prime of Miss Jean Brodie is perhaps Spark's most famous novel. It has been adapted as a stage play, a film, and a television series, but none of the adaptations completely captures its flavor and tone. Written in eight weeks, it was first published in its entirety in *The New Yorker,* an appropriately urbane showcase for this brilliantly polished work.

Spark's novels are highly concerned with plot and counterplot. They show her shrewdness about worldly methods of manipulation and her moral ambiguity toward her characters, who are themselves plotters and schemers. *The Prime of Miss Jean Brodie* shows an individual planning other people's lives, and Jean Brodie is Spark's arch-manipulator. Her motivating image is the beneficial effect of her "prime," and she is intoxicated by the power of her own personality. As a teacher, she offers her own fictions for her pupils' guidance. She quotes to them from the Bible—"where there is no vision the people perish"—but makes sure that the vision they see is of her own ordering, which means that it is not, in her case, divinely inspired. She is nothing so crude, though, as an unbeliever. She goes to different denominations in rota every Sunday, excluding the Roman Catholic Church—"only people who did not want to think for themselves were Roman Catholics"—and "she was not in any doubt, she let everyone know she was in no doubt, that God was on her side whatever her course." Spark has doubts, nonetheless, and the theme of *The Prime of Miss Jean Brodie* is the true faith versus Miss Brodie's fictions.

Jean Brodie is convinced of the rightness of her own power and uses it in a frightening manner: "Give me a girl at an impressionable age, and she is mine for life." This is Miss Brodie's adaptation of the Jesuit formula, but whereas the Jesuits claim the child for God, she molds the child for her own ends and plans its destiny: "You are mine," she says, "of my stamp and cut."

Sandy Stranger is Miss Brodie's principal confidante, and it is she who realizes the extent of her teacher's megalomania: "She thinks she is the God of Calvin, she sees the beginning and the end." When Sandy discovers that Jean Brodie has precipitated the death of a girl by encouraging her to fight in the Spanish Civil War, she realizes that she will stop at nothing to fulfill her own desire for power. She informs the headmistress that Miss Brodie is a "born Fascist." Although this, as Sandy says later, was "only a side line . . . it served as an excuse." Sandy's abhorrence of Miss Brodie is not simply for her sexual or political intrigues, but for what they represent: her usurpation of God's power in the world and her arrangement of other peoples' destinies.

Nevertheless, Sandy's betrayal of her teacher is complicated by the ambiguity of her motives, which are not necessarily as disinterested as they appear. Sandy herself is a plotter and is fascinated by Miss Brodie's "method of making patterns with facts." It is through Sandy's sharp little eyes that the reader observes most of the action of the novel. In particular, it is Sandy's view of Miss Brodie that predominates and in her eyes that Miss Brodie finally stands condemned. But there is no authorial endorsement of Sandy's condemnation, and we are left uneasy. Sandy sleeps with Teddy Lloyd not so much of her own volition but to thwart Miss Brodie, who had planned such a liaison for another of her pupils. There is a hint that Sandy is jealous of Teddy's obsession with Jean Brodie; although he sleeps with Sandy, his portraits of her turn out to look like her teacher. Our suspicions of Sandy's motives are reinforced by the strange description of her as a nun, later in life. She is not serene and composed, as after a right and justifiable action: "She clutched the bars of the grille as if she wanted to escape from the dim parlour beyond, for she was not composed like the other nuns." At the end of the novel this is repeated more emphatically: "Sandy clutched the bars of her grille more desperately than ever."

Spark has said of her writing, "I am intent on getting a tone of writing suitable for a theme—this means that I (very personally) have to get into an actual frame of mind which corresponds to the theme" (interview with E. J. Howard). *The Prime of Miss Jean Brodie* is remarkable for its consistency of tone. The narrative voice is precise and authoritative and faintly pedantic, exactly right for a story about an Edinburgh schoolmistress in the 1930's. In addition, the narrator is given other registers when appropriate: biblical language is used to imply and alert us to religious parallels; schoolgirl jargon abounds, not simply in the mouths of the girls themselves but as part of the narration. For example, we are told at the beginning of the novel that the girls in Miss Brodie's set are each "famous" for something—sex appeal, mathematics, gymnastics —the tone being one of breathless schoolgirlish enthusiasm reminiscent of Angela Brazil. When Sandy has tea with the Lloyds the narrator says factually, "The Lloyds were Catholics and so were made to have a lot of children by force." This is obviously Sandy's viewpoint, but the statement is made without being attributed to her and without quotation marks. A similar technique is used to convey the puritan attitudes of Edinburgh. We are told that "Sandy's mother had a flashy winter coat trimmed with fluffy fox fur like the Duchess of York's, while the other mothers wore tweed or, at the most, musquash that would do them all their days." "Flashy" and "fluffy" are, in this context, clearly condemnatory, representing the Edinburgh view of such fashions, whereas the monosyllabic, functional description of musquash echoes precisely the puritanism it describes. Such details, unobtrusive and often unremarked, recur in Spark's fiction and illustrate her unerring skills in fitting form to theme.

In 1963 Spark had a play produced in London at the New Arts Theatre Club called *Doctors of Philosophy.* This is a sharp and funny look at women academics and the conflicts between academe and domesticity. In 1963 she also published *The Girls of Slender Means,* a novel set in a girls' hostel in London in 1945. The title has a triple meaning, referring not only to the financial and moral poverty of the girls but also to their "vital statistics," aspects that are all skillfully woven into the plot. The moral polarities of the novel are symbolized by Selina, who is beautiful and evil, and Joanne, who is wholesome and good. Attracted in different ways to each of them is a young man called Nicholas Farringdon, a bisexual anarchist of great charm who makes love to Selina on warm summer nights on the flat roof of the hostel.

Because clothing is rationed after the war, the girls share their clothes. One girl has a Schiaparelli evening dress, which is much sought after and lent out to slim people in return for other scarce commodities, such as soap or candy coupons. The climax of the novel comes when a bomb explodes in the garden of the hostel and the girls are trapped. Selina, being slim, manages to escape easily through a small lavatory window. While the others are desperately waiting for firemen to rescue them, Selina goes back into the hostel through the window. Nicholas, to his horror, sees her coolly returning through the window a second time, holding the Schiaparelli dress like a limp body in her arms. As she sees Nicholas she says, "Is it safe out here?" and he replies, "Nowhere's safe," realizing the extent and tenacity of evil. He crosses himself involuntarily as protection against Selina and the diabolical element she embodies, and also as an assertion of an alternative reality to the one she represents. Joanna, bearing witness to that alternative, recites the evening psalm of the day while the girls wait in terror. She is last up the fireman's ladder to freedom, and the building collapses, killing her. Nicholas commits himself to Christianity and thence to martyrdom in Haiti.

The Girls of Slender Means illustrates Spark's sense of the paradox that she has called "that deep irony in which we are presented with the most unlikely people, places and things as repositories of invisible grace" (essay on Proust). In this novel we keep our spiritual expectations on pure Joanna, the vicar's daughter, and our secular expectations on the sexy Selina. But ultimately it is the recognition of evil in Selina that is to Nicholas a means of grace, since he is aware that "a vision of evil may be as effective to conversion as a vision of good." Nevertheless, by this time Spark's religious emphasis has shifted. Joanna is of course a Christian, but she is not a Sparkian Christian, beset with skepticism and apt to ask awkward questions. And this, oddly, makes her less convincing. She is meek, accepting and entirely unselfish, and obliquely Spark suggests that through an endless capacity for self-sacrifice she is emotionally destroyed long before the fire kills her. Nor can Nicholas be taken to exemplify Christian or Catholic values. The narrative concentrates almost entirely on his life before his conversion, and in fact we are told nothing about his life as a missionary brother. The chronicle of events in *The Girls of Slender Means* becomes significant only by an awareness that it is unified by faith. Hints are given towards this end, particularly by the relevant juxtaposition of Joanna's biblical and literary quotations with the novel's action, but God and religion are displaced as central narrative concerns.

In her next novel, *The Mandelbaum Gate* (1965), Spark reverts to her earlier examination of God as crucial to the life of her protagonist. Her treatment of Catholicism is, however, different. By the time she came to write *The Mandelbaum Gate,* Spark had been a Catholic for over ten years, and the novel is not merely a reaffirmation of her faith but a reexamination of it.

Her heroine, Barbara Vaughan, is a half-Jewish Catholic convert who falls in love with an archaeologist called Harry Clegg. Her Jewishness (which she associates with her sexuality) enhances her love life, but her Catholicism causes a conflict between her desires and those sanctioned by her church. Her lover is a non-Catholic, and she is forbidden to marry him unless he is able to have his former marriage annulled. This crisis between two aspects of her personality, symbolized by her Jewishness and her Catholicism, causes Barbara to travel to the Holy Land to reestablish her identity. While she is there she discovers that her Jewish blood prevents her from legitimately making a pilgrimage to the shrines in Jordan. For Barbara, an avid pilgrim, this is a genuine deprivation, just as the celibacy imposed by her religion is a deprivation of a different kind. The theme of *The Mandelbaum Gate,* as personified by Barbara and epitomized by the city of Jerusalem, is division and the means of unity. But this novel does not offer the Roman Catholic faith as a painful but unqualified solution. Other factors force themselves into consideration, such as Jewish heredity and culture, the demands of sexual love and marriage, and the need for Barbara to integrate both inherited and adopted faiths. *The Mandelbaum Gate*'s exceptional theme stresses its departure from the norms previously established in Spark's work. The earlier novels, for all their soul-searching, are demonstrations of faith with an implied QED at the end of each one. In *The Mandelbaum Gate* the heroine not only finds the practice of her religion almost intolerable, as did Caroline Rose and Ronald Bridges, but actually doubts its truth and relevance to her own life.

This is shown in the description of Barbara's love affair. Having broken the rules and slept with Harry, Barbara is obliged to confess and repent in order to be reconciled with her church. This she cannot do: "It is impossible to repent of love. The sin of love does not exist." This is a feeble excuse in the eyes of the church, and it is also an unfamiliar statement coming from Spark. The claims of human love are given precedence (albeit temporarily) over the claims of religion, and this is a reversal of her former priorities. Barbara is tormented by the alternatives of marrying outside the church or of giving up Harry altogether. While in Jerusalem, she ponders on this dilemma and also on whether to take the risk of visiting Jordan to see the Holy Places. This would be extremely dangerous because of her Jewish blood, and she is persuaded not to go. In Spark's novels, though, unexpected incidents change the course of events. Barbara attends one day of the Eichmann trial and is appalled by the discrepancy between the reality of the past massacre and the cool legal discourse in which it is now being expressed. Having heard the testimony of Eichmann, the distancing of the horror by the impersonal language, Barbara decides, almost unconsciously, to go to Jordan regardless. That evening she tells Harry that she will marry him anyway, with or without the blessing of the church. We are not told precisely how the Eichmann trial changed Barbara's mind about these two vital decisions; indeed Spark makes clear that it was not a precise process. But we are shown that what horrifies her is Eichmann's pose as an unthinking automaton obeying bureaucratic instructions: "The man was plainly not testifying for himself, but for his pre-written destiny. He was not answering for himself or his own life at all, but for an imperative deity named Bureau 1V-B-4, of whom he was the High Priest."

Earlier in the novel we learn that Barbara, a mixture of Jew, Gentile, and Catholic, seeks to define her identity to herself. As the clues accumulate we realize that for Barbara the Eichmann trial has presented in an acute form the dangers of shifting one's own responsibilities and decisions onto an impersonal force, whether it be the church or a political party or a national movement. The trial reveals an abyss that she herself has to confront. Eichmann's mindless obedience makes it imperative for her to exercise her own moral judgment, in the hope that God will ratify her decision. But the crucial point of *The Mandelbaum Gate* is that Barbara makes up her own mind prior to the church's opinion, believing this process to be essential for her to establish her own identity. She feels the need to acknowledge the Jewish part of herself before acknowledging the Catholic, and then to try to unite the two. During a conversation with a Jewish archaeologist "she . . . remarked, without relevance, that the Scriptures were specially important to the half-Jew turned Catholic. The Old Testament and the New, she said, were to her—as near as she could apply to her own experience the phrase of Dante's vision—'bound by love into one volume.' " Nothing is irrelevant in Spark's novels, and the analogy of the Bible, incorporating both Jewish and Christian doctrine, one prefiguring the other, represents for Barbara the unity she is trying to achieve.

The Mandelbaum Gate is the last novel in which Spark makes the serious treatment of Roman Catholicism her central theme. In her later work the material world becomes much more dominant, its atmosphere caught by using a salient aspect of it, such as the *dolce vita,* inflation, or terrorism, as emblematic of people's moods or behavior. The former all-encompassing divine power becomes the *deus absconditus* manifest in the harsh milieus of most of her subsequent novels. One of the ways in which Spark makes this increasingly secular statement is by transferring her attention from God's patterning in the world to people's designs for one another. As an analogy, she concentrates reflexively on the formal design that constitutes a novel, her protagonists being aware of their roles as manipulators of characters and events, the narrator commenting on the novel's structure.

In *The Public Image* (1968) the theme of plots or counterplots is dominant. Here we are shown image making on both a professional and a private scale: the manufacture of a film star, Annabel, by the publicity industry, and the subsequent fictions invented by her and her husband, Frederick. The novel is set in Italy, and Spark capitalizes on the Italian love of drama and Italy's sensational journalism.

Annabel and Frederick are portrayed as an ideally happy couple with a baby, sophisticated and formal by day, their phlegmatic English appearance concealing a life of passionate sexuality by night:

> It was somehow felt that the typical Englishman, such as Frederick Christopher was, had always really concealed a foundry of smouldering sex beneath all that expressionless reserve. . . . Later, even some English came to believe it, and certain English wives began to romp in bed far beyond the call of their husbands, or the capacities of their years, or any of the realities of the situation.
> (ch. 2)

In order to distinguish for the reader the realities of the situation concerning Annabel, the narrator reveals them in statements prefaced by the words "in fact," or they are given veracity by the use of the words "real" or "reality." Annabel says, in contradiction of her public image as a sex symbol, "But in fact, in fact, I don't like tiger-sex. I like to have my sexual life under the bedclothes, in the dark, on a Saturday night. With my nightdress on." And we are told, in the authoritative prose Spark uses to convey certainties, that "the baby Carl was the only reality of her life. His existence gave her a sense of being permanently secured to the world which she had not experienced since her own childhood had passed."

Frederick is jealous of the baby and of Annabel's successful career. He formulates a real-life plot to rival that of the film industry and designed to smash Annabel's career. He commits suicide, having first arranged a disreputable party at his wife's flat to coincide with the time of his death. He leaves dramatic farewell notes (including one to his long-dead mother) inventing and condemning Annabel's appalling unfaithfulness and destroying her public image of grace and virtue. Annabel retaliates by a skillful performance as a grief-stricken widow. But she is blackmailed by threats of publication of Frederick's suicide notes, and when it comes to the point she has a change of heart. She produces the letters herself, destroying her public image for good. Afterwards, her lawyer asks why she did it and she replies, "I want to be free like my baby." She flies unnoticed to Greece, taking the baby with her.

This is one of Spark's most lyrical books. The scenes of Annabel looking after the baby are tender and practical, and depict one of the few genuinely loving relationships in Spark's work. It is as if Annabel's salvation, her outlet for true feeling, is, temporarily, her author's also; the baby enables the expression of warmth that Spark is unable to give to adult relationships in her novels. The film industry, Frederick, Annabel, and her blackmailer all invent their separate plots in this novel; finally none of them persists. What predominates is Annabel's reliance on her feelings for her baby. She is not aware of making a moral decision, but an instinctive decision, which in the context of the novel is shown to be morally right. The spare, cool tone of *The Public Image,* and its total lack of sentimentality, disguise the fact that it is unique among Spark's novels in its strong endorsement of instinctive action not finally contained within a religious framework. And it is typical of Spark's reticence that she does not state outright the momentous nature of Annabel's decision. Instead, she ends *The Public Image* with a beautiful and moving passage, emphasizing the resonance of Annabel's inner wealth:

> She felt as if she was still, curiously, pregnant with the baby, but not pregnant in fact. She was pale as a shell. She did not wear her dark glasses. Nobody recognized her as she stood, having moved the baby to rest on her hip, conscious also of the baby in a sense weightlessly and perpetually within her, as an empty shell contains, by its very structure, the echo and harking image of former and former seas.
>
> (ch. 8)

In all her novels Spark uses the theme of the plotter and fiction maker to point out the prevalence of deception and the danger when these people extend their fictions into real life. But almost invariably she introduces into the narrative a sudden, unexpected action or revelation. Then, what has previously seemed a predictable narrative sequence is revealed as being also a divine or moral plot that has been immanent, although hidden, from the beginning. In her early novels the intervention is in the form of the supernatural; later plots are disturbed by moral action effected through an individual's insight or decision, God's power at one remove. What the novels have in common, up to *The Driver's Seat,* is that the surface narrative set up at the beginning is never allowed to run its course. But in *The Driver's Seat* and in the later novels there is a further change in technique: the plotters are allowed to achieve their own ends. The characters cooperate with their author, and the formal qualities of the novel are foregrounded.

The Driver's Seat (1970) is a remarkable novel about how a novel is written. It is used in some university courses to teach the theory of fiction, but it works simultaneously on two levels, the realistic and theoretic.

The heroine, Lise, tries to control the plot, to manipulate her own destiny. Recognizing the formal potential of the novel, she plans to cooperate with it, arranging events so that her death, her end, coincides with the ending of the novel. She gradually takes over the driver's seat figuratively by assuming control of the novel, and realistically in that she drives herself to her final destination, where she plans to be killed. The vehicle for Lise's aspirations, the narrative, is simple. She flies from a northern European country to a southern European city to begin a holiday. She is seeking a man to murder her. She is a determined victim, a potential murderee with an obsessive quest. She finds her man and achieves her end.

The realistic world of this novel is depressing and nasty. We are shown arid aspects of twentieth-century life: a riot, traffic jams, airline food, a dirty hotel room, a deposed Middle Eastern ruler. These scenes and incidents are given sparely, without narrative comment or evaluation. Lise's obsession with finding her murderer enforces a detached view of all other events, and in this novel her insane perspective dominates. She refuses all distractions as irrelevant to her death, and the novel similarly refuses the reader any deviation from the dynamic of the end-directed plot.

In *The Driver's Seat* Spark tells us the ending early on. This enables her readers to see clearly that what might appear to be arbitrary detail is in fact significant. So, as one reads the novel, what is offered is both a narrative and a demonstration of how a narrative is constructed. As soon as the reader learns that Lise is to be murdered, random events become full of meaning. For example, Lise buys a dress for her holiday, then angrily refuses it when the salesgirl points out that it is made of stain-proof material. Discussing this with a holiday acquaintance later in the novel, Lise says, "As if I would want a dress that doesn't show the stains!" What stains? Why does she buy such unforgettably vivid clothes? Why does she destroy evidence of her identity but make such a conspicuous scene at the airport? The narrator soon tells us, in a series of flash-forwards. We are told how, in the determined future tense, "She will be found tomorrow morning dead from multiple stab-wounds . . . in a park of the foreign city to which she is travelling." So, because she is intent on being a murder victim, she buys a dress that will show bloodstains. Lise is cooperating with her author; in novels murder victims have bloodstained clothing. Thus, seemingly innocent episodes in the novel become ironic according to the reader's knowledge of their relevance to the ending. In another example, Lise meets a woman who talks about her nephew, imagining a romance between them: "You and my nephew are meant for each other," she says. And indeed they are, since the nephew is chosen to be Lise's murderer.

The impetus of the plot seldom allows any emotion to be expressed. It is only at the end of the novel that the reader is reminded that actions, events, plots, however clear-cut, cannot finally be separated from the imprecision of feeling. After murdering Lise, her killer "sees already the gleaming buttons of the policemen's uniforms, hears the cold and confiding, the hot and barking voices, sees already the holsters and epaulettes and all those trappings designed to protect them from the indecent exposure of fear and pity, pity and fear." The Aristotelian formula reminds us, if we need reminding, that the novel is a tragedy of a young woman who dies a violent death. Lise, without any relationship or purpose to live for, is reduced to making drama out of the most elemental plot of all, the knowledge that her life will end. But it is only with the final lines of *The Driver's Seat* when "pity and fear" are finally emphasized, that we realize their absolute relevance and their nagging omission from the story.

Not to Disturb (1971) continues the theme of fiction making. In this novel Spark scarcely sustains a balance between realism and the revelation of fictive theory, and the techniques of realistic narration are treated with some contempt. The author and the characters conspire to sabotage the story's credibility by constantly referring the reader to the methods of its construction.

The novel is set in a large lakeside house in Switzerland. The servants, headed by the butler, Lister, discuss the forthcoming deaths of their employers, the Baron and Baroness Klopstock, and their male secretary. The couple, the reader is given to understand, are notorious, and the servants have sold their "exclusive" stories to *Paris Match* and *Stern* magazines. They are also negotiating interviews and film contracts. Like Lise, Lister takes over the organization of the plot, marshaling messy human events into clean patterns. Lister is highly concerned with form: "To put it squarely, as I say in my memoir, the eternal triangle has come full circle." Throughout the novel, he is on guard against contingencies that might spoil his plot. He says, "There is a vast difference between events that arise from and those that merely follow after each other. Those that arise are preferable." Lister's "characters," like a novelist's characters, are allowed no freedom of action. Anything or anyone who cannot be accommodated in his plot is eliminated from the story. When two visitors make themselves a nuisance by refusing to leave the estate (and the narrative), the narrator helps Lister by getting rid of them in a subordinate clause: "Meanwhile the lightning, which strikes the clump of elms so that the two friends huddled there are killed instantly without pain, zig-zags across the lawns, illuminating the lily pond and the sunken rose garden."

This callousness is, of course, a literary joke about the process of selection and rejection entailed in writing a novel, but it is callous nonetheless. It reduces people to mere fictional components, artificial little constructs of words. Inevitably all authors do this, but it is the gratuitous display of power that is so disagreeable.

Indeed, artifice and indifference are the keynotes of this novel, and what is happening here is the overt dominance of formal plot over character. If Lister and the servants tacitly allow their "characters" to die, Spark is also involved in their quiescence, since there is little shift in viewpoint between narrator and protagonist. Indeed, almost the only ironic distancing from the narration is the title, *Not to Disturb.* It *is* a disturbing book, and a sardonic admission from Spark that worldly plots do indeed take precedence over God's divine plans. In her early novels this was cause for more explicit regret. Here it is stated, unembellished, merely as a matter of fact.

Spark's next novel, *The Hothouse by the East River* (1973), again has death as its central theme. In the course of the novel the reader realizes that the characters are all, in fact, dead, having been killed in London by a bomb in 1944. It is in many ways an unsatisfactory novel; the analogy of life in New York with that in purgatory is made the basis of puns and double-entendres but is patchy and unsustained.

It was followed by a dazzling novel called *The Abbess of Crewe* (1974). This is based on the Watergate scandal surrounding Richard Nixon's second term of office as president of the United States. Whereas some contemporary novelists have confessed to feeling imaginatively overtaken by the absurdity of present social realities, Spark evidently has felt no such difficulty. Indeed, she viewed Watergate with delighted recognition since the manufacture of worldly fictions has always been the subject of her novels. She said in an interview that "it had seemed to her that Nixon has been carrying on according to the old Benedictine rule, whereby what the superior has said is the justification for everything" (interview with I. Hamilton). Spark transforms Watergate into a fiction both satirical and speculative about power and its purposes and justifications. But Alexandra, the abbess, outclasses Nixon at every point and makes him look, in comparison, not evil but merely inept.

Scandalous goings-on at a convent are revealed by a nun, Sister Felicity, who claims that the convent is "bugged" with electronic devices and that the abbess Alexandra is corrupt. The novel shows how Alexandra turns all these rumors to her advantage, making out of them a plot and openly rejoicing in her powers. She distorts facts to fit in with her "scenarios" and prevails upon her nuns to do the same: "What are scenarios?" says Winifrede. "They are an art-form," says the Abbess of Crewe, "based on facts. . . . They need not be plausible, only hypnotic, like all good art."

The difficulty in accepting this novel as totally satirical lies in Spark's love for the abbess, Alexandra. There is no doubt that the abbess, for all her megalomania, is, and is meant to be, far more attractive than Felicity, against whom she is morally aligned. Felicity would seem to represent the radical element in the Christian church, which seeks a more practical approach to twentieth-century problems such as poverty and overpopulation. Alexandra, though, refuses to implement the reforms of the Second Vatican Council and says pityingly, "Felicity will never see the point of faith unless it visibly benefits mankind." Poor Felicity, who merely commits sins of the flesh, is far outclassed by the abbess and her fellow conspirators. "The nasty little bitch can't stand our gentleness," they exult, and it is Felicity who, having escaped the convent, is excommunicated and, vulgarly suffering from guilt, ends up in the hands of a psychiatrist.

Spark continues her interest in contemporary themes in her next two novels, *The Takeover* (1976) and *Territorial Rights* (1979). Attitudes toward such topics as ownership, affluence, inflation, and terrorism are described with casual, worldly authority. These events are on a global scale, and the narrative stress is no longer on the moral stupidity of an individual (although this is still evident) but on the larger absurdities of the 1970's. These novels are a satiric inquiry into the nature of wealth and ownership. In a world without religious faith as a source of security, material goods may seem a measure of stability; Spark gleefully shows that they are not. Faith in the material world is shown to be misplaced, and possession itself a farce. Territorial claims, whether related to real estate or sexual monopoly, are dramatically undermined. Both these novels are set in Italy, where the impression is given that the twentieth-century decline and fall is speeded up and intensified. And this acts as emblematic of Spark's view of the world at large.

In *The Takeover* Spark lays unusual stress on the pressure of political and economic transition that takes her characters unawares:

> It was not in their minds at the time that this last quarter of the year they had entered, that of 1973, was in fact the beginning of something new in their world; a change in the meaning of property and money. . . . Such a mutation that what were assets were to be liabilities and no armed guards could be found and fed sufficient to guard those armed guards who failed to protect the properties they guarded.
>
> (ch. 9)

She proceeds to show that the apparent solidarity of things is illusory, in a way that illustrates the nature of wealth in a time of inflation. Burglars install burglar alarms, or, posing as art historians, are courteously given guided tours of the house they intend to burgle. The heroine, Maggie, is one of the world's richest women, but her checks bounce as her fortune decreases through fraud and swindle. Even bricks and mortar are not as solid as they would appear: Maggie's new house at Nemi turns out to be *abusivo,* that is, built on land fraudulently acquired and thus deemed not to exist. We learn that the property laws are very complex, very Italian. A claim to Maggie's *abusivo* house "depends . . . on whether the land they own is only the top-soil. In Italy, sometimes the sub-soil belongs to somebody else; it could belong to the Church or the State."

This novel mocks a pagan cult founded by one of the characters, and this is a typical target of Spark's. In these later novels, secular forces often include what could be called religion substitutes—philosophic movements, psychoanalysts, dietary cults. In satirizing them she draws attention not only to their futility in comparison with Christianity, but also to the irony that it is mankind's recognition of spiritual need that gives rise to a series of secular cults to fulfill it. But this moralizing is implicit; the events of *The Takeover* are given no clear evaluation. Paradoxically, this omission makes a moral point by giving the affairs of the world far less importance than is commonly attributed to them. If *The Takeover* is chronicling the decline of Western civilization, it does so with a relaxed zest that at first seems inappropriate, then exhilarating. It suggests that nothing on earth is as important as we think, and, having freed our minds from the fears of this world, Spark sets us at liberty, if we so choose, to focus on the next.

Territorial Rights continues Spark's mocking scrutiny of contemporary problems such as terrorism and political defection. Set in Venice, the plot involves spies, adultery, murder, blackmail, betrayal, kidnapping, and terrorism. The complexity of the plot is reminiscent of the density of *The Comforters* and is a long way from the uncluttered story line of Spark's elegant novellas. The fictive-sounding plot, with all its clichés, is established as realism by Spark, who accepts and capitalizes on its unrealistic aspects and its absurdities.

A slice of dialogue from *Territorial Rights* confirms this impression:

> "It all sounds very far-fetched," said Anthea.
>
> "It may seem far-fetched to you, Anthea, but here everything is stark realism. This is Italy."
>
> (ch. 12)

No longer is the difference between appearance and reality made a moral issue as in *The Public Image.* It is as if Spark, after living for years in Italy, has abandoned her belief in any such difference. *Territorial Rights,* in common with *The Takeover,* has an exuberant air of deliberate superficiality, a refusal, almost, to engage profoundly in moral issues when survival without hypocrisy is about the most one can hope to achieve.

After the diffuse impersonal quality of *The Takeover* and *Territorial Rights,* Spark's next novel took many people by surprise. *Loitering with Intent* (1981) is a novel about a young woman writer living in London in the 1940's. It is tempting to consider its autobiographical qualities, and there is little doubt that Spark has some resemblance to the heroine, Fleur Talbot. What comes over most strongly is her conviction in her vocation as a writer: "How wonderful it feels to be an artist and a woman in the twentieth century," says Fleur. Success or failure are byproducts only. The mature novelist as narrator looks back at her youthful enthusiasm without the slightest trace of amusement or condescension, since it is clear that her attitude toward her vocation is still that of eagerness and wonder.

Throughout *Loitering with Intent* Muriel Spark capitalizes on the idea of the veracity of fiction and its peculiar capacity sometimes to preempt fact. Fleur is writing a novel that is not a retrospective but a prophetic account of events. Spark demonstrates that a novelist's intuitive perception of people can ensure a reasonably accurate prediction of their future actions. Thus Fleur seems doubly creative, almost as if by her fiction she is manipulating characters in real life.

This novel's play with the relation between the real and the fictional does not make arid reading. It is exceptional in Spark's canon for her loving depiction of character. Unlike most Sparkian heroines, Fleur is allowed to exercise her ability both to construct a plot and to express emotion. This capacity gives Fleur a dignity and humanity lacking in many of Spark's earlier characters, who are equally skilled at plot making. Fleur constructs plots, but she lives first. As her plots in turn come alive, it is an indication of the vitality with which she has endowed them, and not an abnegation of life itself. This is one of Spark's finest novels, in which she combines both warmth and wit without the slightest trace of sentimentality.

Spark's most recent novel is *The Only Problem* (1984). In it she reverts to a theme of recurrent interest to her, the plight of Job and the problem of suffering, which was also the motivation for her first novel, *The Comforters.* The central character, Harvey, is writing a monograph on the Book of Job to try to understand why a benevolent God allows the innocent to suffer. Harvey himself undergoes misery of a very Sparkian, very twentieth-century kind. His wife, Effie, becomes a terrorist and has a baby by another man. Harvey is taken over by her less attractive sister, Ruth, who becomes pregnant by him. Harvey is visited by a series of well-meaning friends, but like Job's comforters they do not help him. Harvey contemplates the pain in his own life:

> Is it only by recognizing how flat would be the world without the sufferings of others that we know how desperately becalmed our own lives would be without suffering? Do I suffer on Effie's account? Yes, and perhaps I can live by that experience. We all need something to

suffer about. But *Job,* my work on *Job,* all interrupted and neglected, probed into and interfered with: that is experience, too; real experience, not vicarious, as is often assumed. To study, to think, is to live and suffer painfully.

(ch. 9)

This is the message of the book, and it is offered without the entertainment or the lavish intricacy of *The Comforters. The Only Problem* is a philosophical novel, and the tone is cool and detached. Spark is not a comforter, and her fiction is less and less a diversion or a consolation. In its way *The Only Problem* is as much an invitation to meditation on unpleasant truths as *Memento Mori.*

IV

It is difficult to draw a firm conclusion about an author who is still writing and whose work is still surprising. After Spark's readers had become used to her sharp, succinct novels, her eighth book, *The Mandelbaum Gate,* was detailed and elaborate in setting, plot, and characterization. Then, after five highly formal and cool novellas, she published *Loitering with Intent,* which is much warmer and more personal in tone. *The Only Problem* reverts to her spare, detached style, and it is impossible to prophesy her next move. Nevertheless, there are two consistent and related aspects of her work to date: one is its symbolic nature and the other is the distance at which Spark remains from her material.

In an interview Spark said: "As a novelist I think I approach things from a poetic point of view. . . . I see things in a . . . symbolic way" (unpublished interview with H. Davis). This means that her novels are to be taken as parables, where the realism is consistently metaphoric. (This is true even of her one children's book, *The Very Fine Clock* [1969], which is about a clock called Ticky who refuses the offer of a professorship in case he should lose all his friends.) For Spark the everyday world is sacramental. In *The Mandelbaum Gate* a priest says, "There is a supernatural process going on under the surface and within the substance of all things." This makes her demonstrate in her novels the immense potential of apparently mundane actions or events; for example, Selina rescuing the Schiaparelli dress and incidentally converting Nicholas; Sandy becoming a Catholic through sleeping with Teddy Lloyd; Annabel's refusal to be blackmailed and her subsequent freedom. The means of grace are everywhere in her fiction, disguised until the narrator chooses to reveal them. The form of the novel itself acts as a metaphor for a divinely ordered world and also of the godlike powers of the novelist. The economy of this structure appeals to her, and throughout her career she has exploited it to the full. Even the shortest Spark novel can be read on two levels; like shot-silk, the realistic narration becomes, from another perspective, something else: a theological argument or a demonstration of literary aesthetics.

Spark's work is noticeably cool and unemotional, even in the novels where she has clearly drawn on her own experiences, such as *The Comforters, The Mandelbaum Gate,* and *Loitering with Intent.* It would be a mistake to say that these novels are autobiographical, although there are, for example, incidents similar to those described in *The Mandelbaum Gate* in her personal letters written during a visit to Israel. But she is intensely an artist, and events, even if they actually happened, are assigned to her imagination and emerge transformed for the purposes of her fiction. Spark the author is always removed from the varying tones she adopts for the narration of each novel. This lack of involvement can be chilling and occasionally diminishes the force of her work. Her novels are always dazzlingly well written, but sometimes the narrative callousness is inappropriate.

Nevertheless, there is no doubt that Spark is one of the most original novelists alive today. Unlike many of her contemporaries she does not agonize over the state of the world. Rather, she records it dispassionately, as if judgment were irrelevant or a divine prerogative. She is no longer a religious writer in the same sense as she was at the beginning of her career. But she still writes *sub specie aeternitatis,* a viewpoint that accounts for the patient irony with which she chronicles the follies and allegiances of the temporal world.

SELECTED BIBLIOGRAPHY

I. Separate Works. *Child of Light: A Reassessment of Mary Wollstonecraft Shelley* (Hadleigh, Essex, 1951; repr., London, 1963); *The Fanfarlo and Other Verse* (Aldington, Kent, 1952);

John Masefield (London, 1953; repr., London, 1962; New York, 1966); *The Comforters* (Philadelphia and London, 1957); *The Go-Away Bird and Other Stories* (London, 1958; Philadelphia, 1960); *Robinson* (Philadelphia and London, 1958); *Memento Mori* (Philadelphia and London, 1959); *The Ballad of Peckham Rye* (Philadelphia and London, 1960); *The Bachelors* (London, 1960; Philadelphia, 1961); *Voices at Play: Stories and Ear-pieces* (London, 1961; Philadelphia, 1962); *The Prime of Miss Jean Brodie* (London, 1961; Philadelphia, 1962), first published in the *New Yorker; Doctors of Philosophy* (London, 1963; New York, 1966), play; *The Girls of Slender Means* (New York and London, 1963); *The Mandelbaum Gate* (New York and London, 1965); *Collected Poems* (London, 1967; New York, 1968); *Collected Stories I* (London, 1967; New York, 1968); *The Public Image* (New York and London, 1968); *The Very Fine Clock* (New York, 1968; London, 1969), children's book; *The Driver's Seat* (New York and London, 1970); *Not to Disturb* (London, 1971; New York, 1972); *The Hothouse by the East River* (New York and London, 1973); *The Abbess of Crewe* (New York and London, 1974); *The Takeover* (New York and London, 1976); *Territorial Rights* (New York and London, 1979); *Loitering with Intent* (New York and London, 1981); *The Only Problem* (New York and London, 1984).

II. BOOKS EDITED BY MURIEL SPARK. *Tribute to Wordsworth: A Miscellany of Opinion for the Centenary of the Poet's Death* (London, 1950), with D. Stanford; *A Selection of Poems by Emily Brontë* (London, 1952), with an intro.; *The Brontë Letters* (London, 1953; Norman, Okla., 1954; repr., London, 1966); *Emily Brontë: Her Life and Work* (London, 1953), with D. Stanford; *My Best Mary: Selected Letters of Mary Shelley* (London, 1953), with D. Standford; J. H. Newman, *Letters* (London, 1957), with D. Stanford.

III. ESSAYS, ARTICLES, ADDRESSES. "The Religion of an Agnostic: A Sacramental View of the World in the Writings of Proust," in the *Church of England Newspaper* (27 November 1953); "The Mystery of Job's Suffering," in the *Church of England Newspaper* (15 April 1955); "How I Became a Novelist," in *John O'London's Weekly*, 3 (1 December 1960); "My Conversion," in *Twentieth Century*, 170 (Autumn 1961); Foreword to *Realizations: Newman's Selection of His Parochial and Plain Sermons* (London, 1964), intro. by V. F. Blehl, S.J.; "The Poet's House," in *Encounter*, 30 (5 May 1968); "What Images Return," in K. Miller, ed., *Memoirs of a Modern Scotland* (London, 1970); "The Desegregation of Art," in the *Proceedings of the American Academy of Arts and Letters*, 1971, the Blashfield Foundation Address.

IV. LETTERS. Muriel Spark Collection, Washington University Libraries, St. Louis, Missouri, unpublished correspondence.

V. BIOGRAPHICAL AND CRITICAL STUDIES. E. Waugh, "Something Fresh," in the *Spectator* (22 February 1957); J. Updike, "Creatures of the Air," in the *New Yorker* (30 September 1961); D. Stanford, *Muriel Spark: A Biographical and Critical Study* (London, 1963); C. Ricks, "Extreme Instances," in the *New York Review of Books* (19 December 1968); K. Malkoff, *Muriel Spark* (New York and London, 1968), Columbia Essays on Modern Writers, no. 36; F. Kermode, "Muriel Spark," in *Modern Essays* (London, 1971); D. Lodge, "The Uses and Abuses of Omniscience: Method and Meaning in Muriel Spark's *The Prime of Miss Jean Brodie*," in *The Novelist at the Crossroads and Other Essays on Fiction and Criticism* (London, 1971); D. Reed, "Taking Cocktails with Life," in *Books and Bookmen*, 18 (11 August 1971); P. Stubbs, *Muriel Spark* (Harlow, Essex, 1973), Writers and Their Work, no. 229; M. Bradbury, "Muriel Spark's Fingernails," in *Possibilities: Essays on the State of the Novel* (London, 1973); L. Sage, "Bugging the Nunnery," in the *Observer* (10 November 1974); P. Kemp, *Muriel Spark* (London, 1974); B. Harrison, "Muriel Spark and Jane Austen," in G. Josipovici, ed., *The Modern English Novel: The Reader, the Writer and the Work* (London, 1976); D. Stanford, *Inside the Forties: Literary Memoirs 1937–1957* (London, 1977); A. Massie, *Muriel Spark* (Edinburgh, 1979); A. N. Wilson, "Cause for Rejoicing," in the *Spectator* (23 May 1981); R. Whittaker, *The Faith and Fiction of Muriel Spark* (London, 1982); P. Parrinder, "Muriel Spark and Her Critics," in the *Critical Quarterly*, 25 (Summer 1983); G. Josipovici, "On the Side of Job," in the *Times Literary Supplement* (7 September 1984); A. Bold, ed., *Muriel Spark: An Odd Capacity for Vision* (London, 1984).

IRIS MURDOCH

(1919–)

A. S. Byatt

I

IRIS MURDOCH'S achievement as a novelist has frequently seemed problematic to critics, reviewers, and even readers, though her books have always sold extremely well, both in Britain and in other countries. When her first novels appeared in the mid-1950's, she was immediately classed with the "Angry Young Men," for reasons now hard to discern, since she was certainly not angry and was interested much more in philosophical games and in the nature of fiction itself than in social protest (although she had been a Marxist, and had worked with the war refugees in camps for displaced persons). What she had then in common with writers like Kingsley Amis and John Wain was an interest in rapid comedy, and the long English tradition of the farcical episodic novel, though in fact, even then, her work was much more closely related to that of Samuel Beckett and the French existentialists and surrealists than to the eighteenth-century comic novels that Amis and Wain admired. Later, while she herself was claiming that she was "a realist," and a novelist in the English realist tradition as exemplified by Jane Austen, George Eliot, and E. M. Forster, academic critics were, with some justification, elucidating her novels as elaborate reconstructions of Celtic fertility myths *(A Severed Head)* or Freudian kingship *(The Unicorn).*

Iris Murdoch was born in Dublin on 15 July 1919. She was educated at Badminton School, Bristol, and Somerville College, Oxford, where she took her B.A. in 1942. She then worked for two years as an assistant principal at the Treasury, and next as an administrative officer with UNRRA in London, Belgium, and Austria from 1944 until 1946. In the following year she was elected Sarah Smithson Student in Philosophy at Newnham College, Cambridge. From 1948 to 1963 she was a fellow and a university lecturer in philosophy at the University of Oxford, and since 1963 has been an honorary fellow at St. Anne's College, Oxford. In 1956 she married the writer John Bayley, who is now Wharton Professor of English at the University of Oxford. From 1963 to 1967 she was a lecturer at the Royal College of Art, London. In 1970 she was elected a member of the Irish Academy; in 1975 an honorary member of the American Academy of Arts and Letters and in 1982 of the American Academy of Arts and Sciences; in 1986 she was elected an honorary fellow of Newnham College, Cambridge.

There is a large and flourishing academic community of Murdoch students, and there are a large number of suspicious reviewers and readers who find the elaborate, in some ways intensely artificial, world of her novels difficult to take. She is accused at once of being mandarin and sensational. She is described as the heir to the liberal humanism and technical subtlety of E. M. Forster, and at the same time compared, with some justice, to best-selling writers of melodrama (Daphne du Maurier) or of detective stories enjoyed by dons. (There is certainly something recognizably akin to the Murdoch world in the fantastic, busy, contrived, yet emotionally pleasing world of Margery Allingham's detective stories.) There is a perpetual debate about the probability, or improbability, of Murdoch's plots, centering largely on her characters' sexual behavior. Her characters fall in love, fall in and out of bed, across barriers of age and sex normally assumed to be impassable, even break the incest taboo, with a kind of dancelike formalized frequency that some critics find fascinating, and indeed lifelike, some irritating, and some to have deep cultural or ritual symbolic meaning. (All three responses may, and do, occur at once in some readers.) I hope, at least, in what follows to elucidate some of the ideas, about life and about fiction, behind the construction of this world, and then to return to the question of its success.

II

Iris Murdoch is a philosopher as well as a novelist. Her philosophical work deals largely with the relations between art and morals, both of which she sees as, at their best, sustained attempts to distinguish truth from fantasy, particularly in the presentation of a sufficiently complex image of the human personality, and to find out what we mean by, what we really hold to be, "Good." It seems to me that the relations between the kind of conceptual thought and the kind of fiction she writes have been unusually fruitful, very much part of the same search for ways of understanding, both historically and practically, how human beings work. It seems, therefore, a good way to begin a discussion of her novels by mapping out some of her ideas.

Perhaps her best-known piece of conceptual writing is "Against Dryness," published in 1961 in *Encounter,* in which she argues that one of the major problems of the modern novel is that after two wars and the philosophical debates of the Enlightenment, romanticism, and the liberal tradition, "we have been left with far too shallow and flimsy a view of human personality." Briefly, she distinguishes between two archetypal modern ideas of man. Ordinary Language Man, as exemplified in the works of modern English linguistic philosophers,[1] characteristically sees himself as

> rational and totally free except in so far as—in the most ordinary law-court and commonsensical sense—his degree of self-awareness may vary. He is morally speaking monarch of all he surveys and totally responsible for his actions. Nothing transcends him. His moral language is a practical pointer, the instrument of his choices, the indication of his preferences. . . . His moral arguments are references to empirical facts backed up by decisions. The only moral word he requires is "good" (or "right"), the word which expresses decision. . . . The virtue which is fundamental to him is sincerity.

The alternative image of human nature is Totalitarian Man, particularly exemplified in the works of Jean-Paul Sartre and the French existentialists. This Man feels anguish, or *Angst,* in the face of an absurd or hostile universe. His highest value is his own will, his assertion of his solitary self, against a society suffering from an absence of God and its own hypocrisy and pointlessness. Again, Totalitarian Man's major virtue is sincerity, that is, a scrupulous attention to presenting himself as he sees himself. Miss Murdoch feels that both these images of the human self are profoundly inadequate, partly because they are egoistic, partly because they do not allow for the *variety* of experience, of men, of language, that human beings in practice encounter. She attempts to reassert the implicit and explicit values of the great nineteenth-century novelists who (partly because nineteenth-century society was dynamic and interesting) were more interested in the precise details of life, and the relation to these of complexities of thought. She writes, in "Against Dryness," in prose of true eloquence:

> What have we lost here? And what have we perhaps never had? We have suffered a general loss of concepts, the loss of a moral and political vocabulary. We no longer use a spread-out substantial picture of the manifold virtues of man and society. We no longer see man against a background of values, of realities, which transcend him. We picture man as a brave naked will surrounded by an easily comprehended empirical world. For the hard idea of truth we have substituted a facile idea of sincerity. What we have never had, of course, is a satisfactory Liberal theory of personality, a theory of man as free and separate and related to a rich and complicated world from which, as a moral being, he has much to learn.

In other philosophical essays, particularly "The Sublime and the Beautiful Revisited" and "The Sublime and the Good" (both 1959), Murdoch attempts to be more precise about the processes by which we, historically and personally, arrive at experiences of freedom, or virtue, or beauty. She wrote in 1970:

> When I was young I thought, as all young people do, that freedom was the thing. Later on I felt that virtue was the

[1] I take these to be the philosophers who have learned from Ludwig Wittgenstein, such as Gilbert Ryle, and the Logical Positivists, such as A. J. Ayer. The particular example Murdoch offers in "Against Dryness" is drawn from Stuart Hampshire's *Thought and Action.*

thing. Now I begin to suspect that freedom and virtue are concepts which ought to be pinned into place by some more fundamental thinking about a proper quality of human life, which *begins* at the food and shelter level.
("Existentialists and Mystics," p. 179)

In her book on Sartre she is much concerned with limiting and defining his notions of freedom, both in art and in politics. In "The Sublime and the Beautiful Revisited" she comes to define freedom and virtue as in some ways identical—and they are related to beauty, too, because they are related to the kind of *formal* truth-seeking of the artist:

Virtue is not essentially or immediately concerned with choosing between actions or rules or reasons, nor with stripping the personality for a leap. It is concerned with really apprehending that other people exist. This too is what freedom really is; and it is impossible not to feel the creation of a work of art as a struggle for freedom. Freedom is not choosing; that is merely the move that we make when all is already lost. Freedom is knowing and understanding and respecting things quite other than ourselves. Virtue is in this sense to be construed as knowledge and connects us so with reality.

One of the moral and aesthetic terms to which Murdoch most frequently returns is "attention." Attention is a word used by Simone Weil to describe the constantly renewed attempt to see things, objects, people, moral situations truly as they are, uncolored by our personal fantasies or needs for consolation. Attention is in this sense a willed, thoughtful, selfless contemplation: Simone Weil remarks that those who *attend* properly to life make their moral decisions in terms of what their attention has made of them. They are not free to make random leaps of faith or violence; the freedom was in the choice of attending in the first place. In Murdoch's thought, such attention is connected to Immanuel Kant's concept of *Achtung* (attention) or respect for the moral law, which is "a kind of suffering pride which accompanies, though it does not motivate, the recognition of duty. It is an actual experience of freedom (akin to the existentialist *Angst*), the realization that although swayed by passions we are also capable of rational conduct." It is such attention that causes Murdoch in "On 'God' and 'Good' " (1969) to be able to write that "freedom is not strictly the exercise of the will, but rather the experience of accurate vision which, when this becomes appropriate, occasions action."

The concept of attention in Murdoch's terms is closely related to the concept of good, or goodness. Throughout her philosophical writings she returns to the question of perfection, of the nature of truth, of whether there can be said or seen to be any transcendent good outside human imperfections and vanities, in some way beyond the operations of time, chance, and necessity, which can be a meaningful object of contemplation. In "The Idea of Perfection" (1964) she criticizes the critics of G. E. Moore. Moore believed that "good was a supersensible reality, that it was a mysterious quality . . . that it was an object of knowledge and (implicitly) that to be able to see it was in some sense to have it. He thought of the good upon the analogy of the beautiful." Moore's critics (especially Ordinary Language Man) thought "good" was a subjective value-judgment, "a movable label affixed to the world," not "an object of insight or knowledge but a function of the will." Murdoch said she agrees almost entirely with Moore, and not with his critics.

Murdoch's own discussions of the process of attention to moral (and aesthetic) goodness are conducted with the assumption that such attention will bring with it a sense of where goodness and truth and reality *are,* that they are neither subjective nor arbitrarily open to the election of the will. Her most powerful discussions of the term "attention" use in primary moral ways words that have become part of the technical language of literary criticism: realism, fantasy, naturalism. For instance:

I would suggest that the authority of the Good seems to us something necessary because the realism (ability to perceive reality) required for goodness is a kind of intellectual ability to perceive what is true, which is automatically at the same time a suppression of self. *The necessity of the good is then an aspect of the kind of necessity involved in any technique for exhibiting fact.*
("On 'God' and 'Good,' " in *The Sovereignty of Good,* p. 66)

Or, from the same essay, a little earlier:

One might start from the assertion that morality, goodness, is a form of realism. The idea of a really good man living in a private dream world seems unacceptable. Of course a good man may be infinitely eccentric, but he must know certain things about his surroundings, most obviously the existence of other people and their claims.

The chief enemy of excellence in morality (and also in art) is personal fantasy: the tissue of self-aggrandizing and consoling wishes and dreams which prevents one from seeing what is there outside one. Rilke said of Cézanne that he did not paint "I like it," he painted "There it is." This is not easy, and requires, in art or morals, a discipline. One might say here that art is an excellent analogy of morals, or indeed that it is in this respect a case of morals. We cease to be in order to attend to the existence of something else, a natural object, a person in need. We can see in mediocre art, where perhaps it is even more clearly seen than in mediocre conduct, the intrusion of fantasy, the assertion of self, the dimming of any reflection of the real world.

(p. 59)

In terms of the relations between aesthetics and morals, Murdoch's descriptions of the objects of fictional attention are instructive. She claims that true "goodness," almost impossible to be clear about in life, can be discerned in art, that we can build an aesthetic, and a moral vision, from attempting to understand the precise nature of the excellence of Leo Tolstoy, or, above all, William Shakespeare. To these great writers she ascribes a quality that she initially names "tolerance" or "agnosticism"—related both to Simone Weil's impersonal "attention" and to John Keats's "negative capability."[2] To this quality she later gives the name love. She writes:

Art and morals are, with certain provisos . . . one. Their essence is the same. The essence of both of them is love. Love is the perception of individuals. Love is the extremely difficult realisation that something other than oneself is real. Love, and so art and morals, is the discovery of reality. What stuns us into a realisation of our supersensible destiny is not, as Kant imagined, the formlessness of nature but rather its unutterable particularity; and most particular and individual of all natural things is the mind of man.

("The Sublime and the Good")

The unutterable particularity, of experience in general and of individual human beings in particular, is something to which, both as philosopher and novelist, she returns again and again. "Against Dryness" ends with a plea to modern novelists, and modern liberals of all kinds, to avoid simplified theories, Marxist or existentialist, that assume that "reality is a given whole," that there can be a theory that immutably describes our world. We must, she says, respect contingency and learn a new respect for the particularity of "the now so unfashionable naturalistic idea of character." "Contingency" is a crucial and recurring word in Murdoch's philosophical writings, and indeed in her novels also. It is used to describe what is random, accidental, simply factual, about things and people—what is both immediate, and not part of any formal plan or pattern:

Real people are destructive of myth, contingency is destructive of fantasy and opens the way for imagination. Think of the Russians, those great masters of the contingent. Too much contingency of course may turn art into journalism. But since reality is incomplete, art must not be too much afraid of incompleteness. Literature must always represent a battle between real people and images; and what it requires now is a much stronger and more complex conception of the former.

There is a great deal of tough thought behind these generalizations, these definitions of concepts. The same qualities of moral toughness and intellectual decisiveness have led Murdoch to be able to make some precise and imaginative generalizations about the state of modern fiction and its relation to the fiction of earlier times. It should by now be clear that Murdoch prefers the major nineteenth-century novels, on grounds both moral and aesthetic, to twentieth-century ones. In "Against Dryness" she offers a brilliant description of the modern novel as either "crystalline" or "journalistic." The crystalline novel is "a small quasi-allegorical object portraying the human condition and not containing 'characters' in the nineteenth-century sense."[3] It is related to symbolism and symbolic form; it sees a novel as an *object.* The journalistic work is a "large shapeless quasi-documentary object, the degenerate descendant of the 19th-century novel." Both of these relate to the

[2]"Negative capability" is a phrase used by Keats in a letter to describe the particular quality of Shakespeare's imagination—the capacity not to formulate ideas or patterns but to be "capable of being in uncertainties, mysteries, doubts, without any irritable reaching after fact and reason."

[3]Examples of the crystalline novel might be French philosophical myths like Sartre's *La nausée* or Albert Camus's *La chute (The Fall);* or in English some of the elegant, beautifully shaped late fables of Muriel Spark—*The Driver's Seat, The Public Image;* or William Golding's *Pincher Martin,* an allegorized vision of a man coming to grips with his death. Much good recent American fiction, such as that of Thomas Pynchon, is also "crystalline" in form.

impoverished images of human nature I described earlier. Totalitarian Man is interested in the Human Condition, not the messy particular individual. His art is the crystalline work, with himself a symbolic representative of mankind. Ordinary Language Man produces documents, concerned with social facts of behavior, eschewing metaphysical depths.

In a later essay, "Existentialists and Mystics" (1970), Murdoch creates another dichotomy, between the existential novel and the mystical novel. The existential novel derives like Totalitarian Man from romanticism: it believes in the individual will and vision, in a society where there are no longer political or religious certainties to give automatic depth to a picture. It is "the story of the lonely brave man, defiant without optimism, proud without pretension, always an exposer of shams, whose mode of being is a deep criticism of society. He is an adventurer. He is godless. He does not suffer from guilt. He thinks of himself as free" (D. H. Lawrence, Ernest Hemingway, Camus, Sartre). The mystical novel tries to return to the concept of God, or good, or virtue, and has to invent its own religious images in an empty situation (Graham Greene, Patrick White, Saul Bellow, Spark, Golding). Murdoch claims that the new generation, concerned with human needs, now always present to our consciousness, for food, shelter, survival, is in fact utilitarian in that it works, morally and spiritually, up and out from biological survival. And this utilitarianism is a form of *naturalism,* she says, and implies that this naturalism could possibly create an aesthetic of its own, with stories in which goodness will be seen to be empirically necessary, particular, subject to chance and necessity, but valuable. The particularity of this new naturalism could not be the particularity of Tolstoy or George Eliot, because they were working and observing human beings in a world where there was a strong consensus about the nature of religion, society, politics, duty, whether one chose to elaborate or contradict this consensus. But, Murdoch claims, art has always presented recognizable images of human value or virtue that survive social and metaphysical upheavals (the kindness of Patroclus or Alyosha, the truthfulness of Cordelia and Mr. Knightley).[4]

[4]Patroclus in Homer's *Iliad;* Alyosha in Feodor Dostoevsky's *The Brothers Karamazov;* Cordelia in Shakespeare's *King Lear;* Mr. Knightley in Jane Austen's *Emma.*

One last word about Murdoch's general ideas about art and life, before I proceed to a particular discussion of her fiction. She is a writer with a powerful sense of the difficulties entailed by any process of formulation in our attempts to attend to reality. She opens the essay "Existentialists and Mystics" with a remark on this subject: "Art represents a sort of paradox in human communication. In order to tell the truth, especially about anything complicated, we need a conceptual apparatus which partly has the effect of concealing what it attempts to reveal." In "Against Dryness" she was pleading both for "more concepts in terms of which to picture the substance of our being" and for a suspicion of the forms we *do* use to think, to perceive with. This sense runs through all her works, of a contrary tug of value between attempts at form and attempts to live with the knowledge that "what *does* exist is brute and nameless, it escapes from the scheme of relations in which we imagine it to be rigidly enclosed, it escapes from language and science, it is more and other than our descriptions of it" (*Sartre, Romantic Rationalist,* ch. 1).

Her aesthetic remarks about this subject are, I think, both unusually clear and unusually subtle. She has, in her book *Sartre, Romantic Rationalist,* an excellent passage on the problems created by our modern attitude to language. This is impossible, in its admirable suggestiveness and precision, to summarize, but it is concerned with the effect on literature of our *self-consciousness* (historically exacerbated by the advent of scientific method, scientific symbolic languages), about the relationship of words and things. We know our language, both descriptive and emotive, creates the way we see things and also can be changed, is relative, if we use other concepts, other languages. So we think *about* words, as well as thinking *with* words. We are, says Murdoch, "like people who for a long time looked out of a window without noticing the glass—and then one day began to notice this too." We began to question the *nature* of referential language, which produced phenomena like Sartre's hero's nausea at the fact that the word *tree* bore no relation to the thing he saw, or, alternatively, Stéphane Mallarmé's attempts to make language self-referring, abstract, like paint, like music. As Murdoch says, the novel is naturally "referential" because it tells a story, and "the telling of a story seems to demand a discursive referential use of language to describe one event after another. The novelist seemed to be, by profession, more deeply rooted in the ordinary world where things were still things and words were still their names." But the novel, too, has become (in ways she defines in *Sartre*) linguistically self-conscious.

Murdoch's call for more and better-defined moral concepts, on the one hand, and her passionate belief in the importance of *stories,* of primitive human recounting of events, on the other, seem to me to be important ways of dealing with this problem. In "The Idea of Perfection" she tells the story of the moral process whereby a mother-in-law comes to attend to the reality of a daughter-in-law she doesn't like, realizing that she is not "vulgar" but "refreshingly simple" and so on. This story is a novel in little: it also requires that reader and character *use* the conceptual words involved. Murdoch says of this example:

> I drew attention to the important part played by the normative-descriptive words, the specialised or secondary value words (such as "vulgar," "spontaneous," etc.). By means of these words there takes place what we might call "the siege of the individual by concepts." Uses of such words are both instruments and symptoms of learning.

In an article on T. S. Eliot as moralist, Iris Murdoch praises Eliot both for asserting the impersonality of the artist and for "a continual concern, in the midst of difficulties, for the referential character of words." Eliot has never "made war upon language," and this is good.

Shifting language, shifting concepts, never adequate, continually to be reestablished and modified. Murdoch makes Lawrentian claims for the importance of the novelist. "The writer has always been important, and is now *essential,* as a truth-teller and as a defender of words. (There is only one culture and words are its basis.)" She sees the primitive force of stories as a way of preserving, against our self-questioning, our culture and our language:

> The story is almost as fundamental a human concept as the thing, and however much novelists may try, for reasons of fashion or art, to stop telling stories, the story is always likely to break out again in a new form. Everything else may be done by pictures or computers, but stories about human beings are best told in words, and that "best" is a matter of a response to a deep and ordinary human need.
>
> ("Existentialists and Mystics")

Truth, the preservation of language, stories. But although *"the novelist is potentially the greatest truth-teller of them all,* he is also an expert fantasy-monger." Throughout Murdoch's work runs a warning against the consolations of form:

> Tragedy in art is the attempt to overcome the defeat which human beings suffer in the practical world. It is, as Kant nearly said, as he ought to have said, the human spirit mourning and yet exulting in its strength. In the practical world there may be only mourning and the final acceptance of the incomplete. Form is the great consolation of love, but it is also its great temptation.
>
> ("The Sublime and the Good")

III

IRIS MURDOCH is now the author of seventeen novels. It is clearly not possible to discuss all of them in detail. What I propose to attempt is to group the novels in terms of the technical and philosophical preoccupations that seem to have been paramount in the writing of them.

The first two novels, *Under the Net* (1954) and *The Flight from the Enchanter* (1956), differ from all the later ones in various obvious ways. Formally, they could both be classified as "fantasy-myth" in Murdoch's own terms, and are akin to Beckett's *Murphy* and still more, Raymond Queneau's *Pierrot mon ami,* a gentle surrealist picaresque fantasy. (Both *Murphy* and *Pierrot* are in Jake's library in *Under the Net,* which is dedicated to Queneau.) Both are philosophical fables, using a proliferation of characters and dramatic incidents, farcical or tragic, to illustrate a central theme. In *Under the Net* that theme is the one to which I have just referred, the necessity and danger of concepts, forms, in thought and action, in the worlds of art, of politics, of work, of morals and of love. In *The Flight from the Enchanter* the theme is social, and concerns the proper and improper uses of power, personal and public, playing comic and bitter games with various forms of enslavement and emancipation, sexual, financial, bureaucratic, military. Both novels are close to Murdoch's work on Sartre, in the sense that, lightly but profoundly, they take up the Sartrean issues, the relations of the individual, and of art, to political structures and ideals, the nature of freedom, the nature of language. The central figures of both works, Jake Donaghue and Rosa Keepe, are Sartrean in the sense that they

> move through a society which [Sartre's man] finds unreal and alien but without the consolation of a rational universe. His action seems not to lie *in* this social world; his freedom is a mysterious point which he is never sure of having reached. His virtue lies in understanding his own contingency in order to assume it, not the contingency of the world in order to alter it. It seems as if what "justifies" him is just this precarious honesty, haunted as it is by a sense of the absolute.

Sartre's heroes, Murdoch says, are "anti-totalitarian and anti-bourgeois." Jake is certainly both—he won't write socialist propaganda for Lefty Todd, he won't, equally, attach himself more than peripherally to the capitalist world of bookmakers, filmmakers, and moneymakers whom he occasionally cynically exploits. Rosa, aware of the faults of the welfare state diagnosed in "Against Dryness," aware that modern liberalism is not enough, although descended from a family of battling reformers and suffragettes, has retreated into a kind of stultified identification with the oppressed and is operating a machine in a factory. She is floating and unrelated. "She had ceased to imagine that her life would ever consist of anything but a series of interludes." "Where beauty and goodness were concerned, Rosa had, of course, no particular expectations from her new life."

I want to leave consideration of *Under the Net* for later, but it might at this point be worth going in further detail into the relation between thought and form in *The Flight from the Enchanter.* This novel puzzled reviewers and irritated critics, who tended pompously to castigate it for failures in realism of a kind it was not attempting, or, like F. R. Karl, for "creating characters who are suitable only for the comic situations but for little else" (*The Contemporary English Novel,* London, 1979). In fact the power of this novel lies in the intricate patterning of its variations on a theme that, however comically treated, is shown to the *mind* to have tragic implications.

It is a novel about the rootlessness caused by World War II, and is full of refugees and persons without political identity—from Nina, the dressmaker, the archetypal victim first of violence, then of bureaucracy, finally of Rosa's obsession with her own fantasies of enchantment, to Annette, who is rich, young, emotional, and in a sense untouchable. Murdoch, besides her interest in the fate of liberalism, is an admirer of Simone Weil, whose studies of "affliction," in communities or individuals, contributed much to the depth of this book. Simone Weil was interested in the mechanical way in which suffering is transferred from person to person, a blow is passed on, the damaged attract violence and in their turn inflict damage. Uprooted Central European refugees, the Lusiewicz brothers, Mischa Fox provide the daemonic forces of enslavement, loose unconnected power, both in the fairy tale, in the sexual, and in the social areas of this work. The novel is pervaded by images of traps and hunts, machines that savage their slaves (Nina's sewing machine, Calvin Blick's camera), fish and underwater guns. Sexuality is seen largely in terms of enchantment, pursuit of a free creature, enslavement of a free creature. (Rainborough has fantasies of Annette as a smooth little fish, "graceful, mysterious, desirable and free—and the next moment there is only struggling and blood and confusion. If only, he thought, it were possible to combine the joys of contemplation and possession.")

Mischa Fox, at a much more extreme point, is caught in the same paradox. Obsessed by suffering, caught in its machinery, he sees power as protection, and protection paradoxically leads to destruction; he is compelled to destroy what he protects, from chickens to "slaves" to women. His battle to gain possession of the suffragette periodical, *The Artemis* (named after the virgin huntress, edited by Rosa's brother, Hunter Keepe, his name the paradox of pursuit and possession in little), typifies both political and sexual themes. A central moment of the novel is the wildly funny scene in which the elderly suffragettes frustrate the bid to assimilate the paper to Fox's empire. An old lady says:

> "Why the very fact that 'female emancipation' still has meaning for us proves that it has not yet been achieved."
>
> Calvin . . . said suddenly, "Would you agree, Madam, that the fact that the phrase "emancipation of the serfs" is significant, proves that the serfs are not yet emancipated?"
>
> (p. 187)

This book is precisely light testimony to Murdoch's knowledge that *neither* is emancipated—and that our own society does not have the will and the means to see or deal with this.

If these early novels ask Sartrean questions, they do not offer Sartrean answers. Sarte's heroes agonize and contemplate in a lucidly tortured solitude. Murdoch points out that Sartre claimed that "the mode of self-awareness of the modern novelist is the internal monologue," which is not primarily concerned with "character" and "individuality" in either the narrating consciousness or the other people reflected through it. She criticizes his novels, further, for not presenting individuals in the world of action:

> Sartre's individual is neither the socially integrated hero of Marxism nor the full-blooded romantic hero who believes in the reality and importance of his personal struggle. For Sartre the "I" is always unreal. The real individual is Ivich [the silent sister in *Les chemins de la liberté*], opaque, sinister, unintelligible and irreducibly other; seen always from outside. . . . Sartre, like Freud, sees life as an egocentric drama.
>
> (*Sartre, Romantic Rationalist,* ch. 7, 8)

There is a sense in which the comic and densely populated worlds of Murdoch's first two fantasies are a kind of meaningful game with the Sartrean universe. Jake tries an internal monologue, but discovers that the world is full of other people whose views he has misinterpreted but *can learn.* Rosa fails to observe properly the individual life and needs of Nina—but they are there *to be observed,* and Rosa can learn. No single view of the world, no one vision, is shown to be adequate, in a form of novel where everyone is always offering epigrammatic views on the nature of society or reality or suffering. No one is right, but everyone—Dave Gellman, the linguistic philosopher; Lefty Todd, the socialist; Rainborough, the mediocre modern elite bureaucrat—is there, and reader and other characters must take them into account. I have described elsewhere how I think the last scene of *Under the Net* is a comic parody of the end of *La nausée.*[5] Both Jake and Roquentin are saved from a sense of futility and drudgery by a vision of their future induced by hearing a song. But Roquentin turns *from* the nauseating horrors of the world and society to the pure necessity of art. Jake finds a way into curiosity about, and delight in, the endless differences of people and proliferation of things. It is the villain of *The Flight from the Enchanter,* Calvin Blick, who offers the solipsistic view, to Rosa, that "you will never know the truth and you will read the signs in accordance with your own deepest wishes. That is what we human beings always have to do. Reality is a cipher with many solutions, all of them right ones."

This is not so: no solution is complete, but some are wrong, and freedom consists in *not* reading the signs according to personal fantasy or desire. And this can be done. The sense that the characters in these books have reached new insights and new beginnings is worked for, and valuable.

Murdoch also wrote of Sartre that he had "an impatience, which is fatal to a novelist proper, with the *stuff* of human life." He has an interest in the details of contemporary living, and a passionate desire to analyze and "build intellectually pleasing schemes and patterns. But the feature which might enable these two talents to fuse into the work of a great novelist is absent, namely an apprehension of the absurd irreducible uniqueness of people and of their relations with each other" (*Sartre, Romantic Rationalist,* ch. 10). Her next book, *The Sandcastle* (1957), is dedicated to her husband, John Bayley, and her work from *The Sandcastle* onward shows an increasing concern with the moral and critical principles explored in his book *The Characters of Love,* and later in *Tolstoy and the Novel.* John Bayley argues that the contemporary impatience with the idea of "character" as an attempt to create a unique individual is a sign of both a literary and of a moral failing. Both he and Murdoch quote with approval Henry James on Honoré de Balzac's characters—"it was by loving them that he knew them, not by knowing them that he loved." Both see it as a function of the English novel at its greatest that the writers, and thus the readers, *loved* the characters and felt them to be free agents, in some sense. Both are troubled at the erosion of the sense of reality of characters created by insistent aesthetic symbolism in novels, or by the attempt to write allegories of the Human Condition. Murdoch's technical interest in nineteenth-century "realism" is an interest in the re-creation of a fictional world in which separate individuals meet, change, communicate. A good novel is "a house fit for free characters to live in." Before *The Sandcastle* Miss Murdoch's models were French, or Irish; now she makes a sustained effort, in *The Sandcastle, The Bell* (1958), *An Unofficial Rose* (1962), to learn from Jane Austen, George Eliot, Henry James.

[5]See A. S. Byatt, *Degrees of Freedom* (London, 1965).

The Sandcastle is a not entirely successful attempt at a description of a "normal" but difficult moral problem—the attempt by Mor, a middle-aged schoolmaster, to break out of a largely dead marriage when he falls in love with a young woman painter, Rain Carter. It contains a character—Bledyard, the art master—who combines T. S. Eliot's view of the impersonality of the artist with John Bayley's sense that the individual human being is a mystery, a compelling moral object, incredibly difficult to comprehend. Bledyard argues that the true artist "is humble enough in the presence of the object to attempt *merely* to show what the object is like. But this *merely,* in painting, is everything." And he asks, "Who can look reverently enough upon another human face?" Bledyard argues further that Mor, planning a violent bid for freedom, is indulging in fantasy. "You do not truly apprehend the distinct being of either your wife or Miss Carter."

In *The Bell* and in *An Unofficial Rose* Murdoch makes much more successful and sustained attempts at showing efforts, failures, and partial failures to apprehend the distinct being of other people. Both novels are concerned with the relationship of freedom and virtue, and also of beauty and truth. Both could be described, as *Howards End* or *A Passage to India* could be described, as English symbolic novels, in which a powerful formal element is provided by the relationship of plot and characters to certain symbolic objects.

In *The Bell* the central episodes of the plot concern the substitution of the medieval bell (legendarily supposed to have flown from the abbey belfry into the lake when a nun had a lover) for the new bell, decked to enter the abbey as a bride or postulant, and to open a new kind of speech between the enclosed, silent religious order and the outside world. The bell represents art: it is engraved with characters from the life of Christ, who are Murdoch's real other people—"squat figures—solid, simple, beautiful, absurd, full to the brim with something which was to the artist not an object of speculation or imagination." As art, it is related to all the other music in the novel, jazz records (primitive sexual urgency), Bach, the "hideous purity" of the nuns' plainsong, birdsong that to Kant was the only pure because the only free music, natural without concepts. It is also related to the other works of art seen by Dora in a vision in the National Gallery, a moment of truth where Gainsborough's portrait of his children is an image of Murdoch's idea of the recognizable authority of the Good.

The central symbols in *An Unofficial Rose* are analogous. They are, first, the Tintoretto portrait of Susannah, golden, serene, authoritative, a source of power and value, both moral, aesthetic, and social (it is sold, for a large sum, to purchase a fantasy of freedom for Randall, rose-grower and errant husband, a freedom in itself an enslavement to a factitious beauty). And second, the rose itself, like the birdsong a *natural* beauty, with a *natural* form, also, on a rose farm, a source of value, vision, or even money. Both novels are about intermittent human attempts to reach perfection, vision, a life that shall seem to have a sense of form or destiny. Both describe a large number of patterned, related, individual successes and failures. Both, also, like *Under the Net* and some later books, are about the pull between silence as purity, and the use of language as a necessary means to discovery of truth and complexity. What is most impressive about both is the degree to which Murdoch succeeds in her aim of creating free and individual characters, whose experience is diverse and not to be summed up.

In "The Sublime and the Beautiful Revisited" Murdoch makes a very useful distinction between what she calls "convention" and "neurosis," which are, she explains, "the two enemies of understanding, one might say the enemies of love; and how difficult it is in the modern world to escape from one without invoking the help of the other." "Convention" is the force that drives Ordinary Language Man, who believes that moral issues are simple—there are rules and choices, and an existing decorum made by a civilized society. "Neurosis" drives Totalitarian Man, who sees the world and his life as a dramatic myth, who requires his life to have an absolute form and purpose. In the delicate and detailed descriptions of the moral decisions of the principal characters in *The Bell* and *An Unofficial Rose* we can see the effort, reasoned or instinctive, to understand and love falling away constantly into one or the other. Neurosis drives Randall, who leaves his wife to suffer enslavement at the hands of Lindsay Rimmer; while Lindsay herself, an earthly Venus, not a heavenly one, is the slave of Emma Sands, who writes detective stories with structured plots and whom Randall's father, Hugh, rejected, for no clear reason, in order to stay with his wife. Randall leaves the natural roses to be "a writer"—for form—and ends up living off his father's sale of the Tintoretto in an empty freedom designed, he suspects, as part of Emma's vengeance. Convention drives his father, Hugh, who could not leave his wife. It drives, supremely, Randall's wife, Ann, the "unofficial rose" of the title, who is in love with Felix, a soldier and a gentleman, also held by convention, and who is unable to distress her daughter or abandon the faithless Randall, to choose happiness against duty.

In *The Bell* it is Michael Meade, homosexual schoolmaster, who—with his sense of destiny in his call to the priesthood, his sense of patterns and portents in his life, his imaginative vision of moral situations when he falls in love with Nick as a boy, or impulsively kisses Toby—is tempted toward a neurotic vision (although he ironically fails Nick by a contrary recoil into self-protective convention). Convention is represented by James Tayper Pace, who finds it easy to say that some things are *simply* forbidden, and to close a moral argument. There is not space here to describe the patience with which Murdoch explores the fluctuations between vision, convention, neurosis, and fantasy in these characters. But it is worth remarking that the fates of the most important—Hugh and Ann in *An Unofficial Rose,* Michael and Dora in *The Bell*—are unpredictable precisely because several outcomes are possible to their dilemmas; they are, in other words, "free" characters. And this is no mean achievement.

In *The Characters of Love* John Bayley, analyzing James's *The Golden Bowl,* describes Maggie's love of the Prince as a saving use of convention—she avoids drama, avoids knowledge even, she "finds in the refuge of convention and deliberate 'ignorance' salvation both for herself and for the others." I have always felt that Ann in *An Unofficial Rose,* whom Randall hates for "living by rules," who seems to attract suffering, who feels herself "shapeless and awkward," is related to Maggie, who is mysterious in the way in which "to be human is to be virtually unknown" and of whom it might be said "the conventional and the mysterious are closely allied, are indeed one and the same thing."[6] She is also related to Lionel Trilling's description of Fanny Price in *Mansfield Park* as one who is "poor in spirit" and thus blessed.[7] One feels, with these early "realistic" novels of Murdoch's, that much of her hope of combining a well-formed novel with a sense of the mystery and formlessness of people's lives has been fulfilled. And it has partly been fulfilled by a profoundly intelligent use of concepts such as convention and neurosis, not as total patterning devices, but as instruments for exploration of character and motive.

Malcolm Bradbury, one of Murdoch's most intelligent critics, has argued that her practice as a novelist in many ways runs counter to her theoretical beliefs. She claims, he says, that life has finally no pattern, no meaning, that we are ruled by necessity and chance, yet one of the strengths of both her plotting and her symbolism is that it explores fully the sense in which we feel that our lives *are* gripped by formative forces that function below our conscious knowledge or choice. She describes those aspects of sexual and social behavior in which men are remarkably similar to each other, and meaningful patterns and generalizations can be drawn whose power can be felt. I refer particularly to the ideas of psychoanalysts and of students of myth, where they are interested not in the individual whole person, but in the machinery of behavior.

Murdoch frequently uses the word "machinery" to describe recognizable patterns of human behavior. In *A Severed Head* (1961), Palmer Anderson, the psychoanalyst, claims that "the psyche . . . has its own mysterious methods of restoring a balance. It automatically seeks its advantage, its consolation. It is almost entirely a matter of mechanics, and mechanical models are the best to understand it with" (ch. 5). I used to think that this was simply an indication that Palmer was a totalitarian man, unaware of the irreducibly unique individual. I now see that his remark is a statement of a partial truth that interests Murdoch very much. Only unremitting attention to what lies outside the mechanism can save human beings from being entirely controlled by this psychic machinery. Thus Michael Meade is caught in the (excellently described) *machinery* of guilt and repentance. The title of *The Sacred and Profane Love Machine* (1974) itself indicates the strength of that novel, which is its exploration of the automatic elements involved in most love, most efforts at virtue, that, imperfectly understood, can grip and destroy. In "On 'God' and 'Good'" Murdoch claims that Freud made an important discovery about the human mind that

[6]John Bayley, *The Characters of Love: A Study in the Literature of Personality,* London, 1960, ch. 5.

[7]Lionel Trilling, "Mansfield Park," in *The Opposing Self,* New York, 1955.

"might be called a doctrine of original sin." This doctrine she describes in this way:

> Freud takes a thoroughly pessimistic view of human nature. He sees the psyche as an egocentric system of quasi-mechanical energy, largely determined by its own individual history, whose natural attachments are sexual, ambiguous, and hard for the subject to understand or control. Introspection reveals only the deep tissue of ambivalent motive, and fantasy is a stronger force than reason. Objectivity and unselfishness are not natural to human beings.
>
> (*The Sovereignty of Good,* p. 51)

Later in the same essay she specifically describes a psychic mechanism that has certainly affected her own understanding of behavior, and played a major part in the plots of her novels:

> A chief enemy to such clarity of vision, whether in art or morals, is the system to which the technical name of sado-masochism has been given. It is the peculiar subtlety of this system that, while constantly leading attention and energy back into the self, it can produce, almost all the way as it were to the summit, plausible imitations of what is good. Refined sado-masochism can ruin art which is too good to be ruined by the cruder vulgarities of self-indulgence. . . . Fascinating too is the alleged relation of master to slave, of the good self to the bad self.
>
> (p. 68)

There are several novels that one could call "mythical" novels in which Murdoch's interest in these mechanisms, in parodies of good, in patterning, leads to the structure seeming to hold more aesthetic power than the individual characters—even though the morality of these novels continues to assert the paramount imperative of observing the free individual. Such novels include *A Severed Head, The Unicorn* (1963), and *The Time of the Angels* (1966).

The first of these is slightly different from the others, in that it is not concerned with overall metaphysics, but with patterns of social and sexual behavior. Its cool elegance, its "dream-like facility," to quote Murdoch on crystalline fantasy-myth, has a bite that comes from observing human helplessness before human incomprehension of the machinery. The central image—the severed head, image of the petrifying Medusa, the dark (female) Celtic gods, the soothsaying Orpheus—has a poetic force that the delicate imagery of Venus and Mars in *Under the Net,* for instance, is not required to carry. Alexander, the sculptor of that novel, making a portrait head swathed in bandages, like a death's-head, talks, as Bledyard in *The Sandcastle* talks, of the use of portraiture as a means to truth. But the associations are those of magic, myth, and ritual. At the same time, Murdoch's technical, cool interest in the sadomasochism of a man who tries to love his wife's lover is reinforced by her use of the contrasting Freudian and Sartrean concepts of what the ancient image of the severed head, the Medusa, meant. Freud saw the head as a symbol of male fear of castration, "the female genitals, feared not desired." Sartre saw it as an image of the basic fear of being observed. Murdoch plays one off against the other. In this novel it is woolly, greedy, selfish Antonia who holds a watered-down version of the Bloomsbury ethic of loving individuals, which is crushed by the powers of sexual violence as easily as Martin's assumed "tolerance" of her behavior. Castration, the voyeuristic witnessing of secret sex, including incest, underlie the plot of this drawing-room comedy and contribute to its ambiguous elegance. The sexual shifts, the changes of partners that annoy many of Murdoch's readers, are here part of a stylized fictional representation of the ways in which we are all puppets of blind and incomprehensible forces.

The Unicorn and *The Time of the Angels* are both, as is made explicit in *The Unicorn* itself, "fantasies of the spiritual life." The good man, the saint or artist, "nothing himself, lets all things be through him." Hannah Crean-Smith, the guilty, enclosed "princess" of *The Unicorn,* attempts a kind of renunciation of the ego—and ends, maybe, with a monstrous sadomasochistic parody of such a renunciation. Carel, the priest of no god in *The Time of the Angels,* sets out to destroy the fantasies of religion that persist from the days when Christianity was alive: he tries to be "good for nothing," which not only he but Murdoch, in "On 'God' and 'Good,'" claim is all that is morally possible in a world where God is dead and Good an undefinable sense of direction only. He is aware, like his creator, that at the human level life is random and horrible, subject to chance and necessity, without form, without consolation. He therefore creates for himself the Nietzschean drama, a high version of the existentialist drama of the lonely, defiant hero. He commits incest with his daughter out of a compulsion that might be part of a Gothic novel or might be related to Nietzsche's description of Oedipus as the man who has seen the secret of life, "the horror of nature,"[8] the reality of death and the meaninglessness of existence, and who thus knows that all is permitted because all is equally valuable and valueless. In any case, his behavior, in his attempt to annihilate his ego, is a reinforcement of the sadomasochistic mechanism again.

Murdoch is concerned with religious terrors. She is aware, in a way I think no other English novelist is aware, of the importance for our cultural life of the decay of believed Christianity, the loss of a sense of central authority, believed in or opposed. She is aware of the importance of spiritual experience. Various of her characters make sustained attempts at the spiritual life, which, with its selflessness, as she says both in *The Bell* and in *The Unicorn,* is not dramatic and has no story. People have moments of true vision—Effingham, on the point of death in *The Unicorn,* sees that love and death are the same, sees the universe flooded with light and meaning because he himself has for a moment been expunged. Carel in *The Time of the Angels* offers the contrary vision, in fact the same, of the true Chaos and Old Night, the vision of the Book of Job that "there is only power and the marvel of power, there is only chance and the terror of chance." But neither they nor the other characters can live by these visions, and the moment story, drama, action are resumed, so are the psychic mechanisms that pattern them. It is not possible not to have a story.

Sigmund Freud says in *Totem and Taboo:* "It might be maintained that a case of hysteria is a caricature of a work of art, that an obsessional neurosis is a caricature of a religion, and that a paranoiac delusion is a caricature of a philosophical system." Hannah Crean-Smith's "religious" behavior in *The Unicorn* is profoundly ambiguous, but it bears a close resemblance to Freud's description of obsessional neurosis, as the behavior of her dependents and retainers bears a close resemblance to Freud's quotations in *Totem and Taboo* from Sir James Frazer about the treatment of kings as gods in primitive communities. The novel is a poetic image, an intellectual game, expressing general truths about human habits and fantasies. (The elements of high Gothic[9] in both these novels are part of the same human interest in primitive forces and the forms in which they can be described.)

It might, in this context, also be worth quoting a remark that Murdoch made about the relations of life and myth in a review of Elias Canetti's *Crowds and Power.* "Canetti has . . . shown, in ways which seem to me entirely fresh, the interaction of the 'mythical' with the ordinary stuff of human life. The mythical is not something 'extra'; we live in myth and symbol all the time" (*The Spectator,* 7 September 1962).

Literature, Murdoch has said, is "a battle between real people and images." In an interview with Frank Kermode she remarked that she felt her novels "oscillate rather between attempts to portray a lot of people and giving in to a powerful plot or story." In those of her later novels where she is attempting psychological realism, free characters, the portraiture of "a lot of people," she has come to be able to make a very sophisticated use of Shakespeare, both as matter for allusion and as a source of reference, depth, a real myth of our culture. The plots of *The Nice and the Good* (1968), *A Fairly Honourable Defeat* (1970), *The Black Prince* (1973), among others, owe much to Shakespeare, and what they owe is fascinating and valuable.

There are two excellent reasons for Murdoch's interest in Shakespearean plotting. The first is that she seems to understand, instinctively or as a matter of intellectual decision, that it is a way out of the rather arid English debate about the preservation of the values of nineteenth-century realism against the need to be modern, flexible, innovating, not to say experimental. Nathalie Sarraute once remarked that what crushes modern writers is less the sense that their society and situation is incomprehensible than the sense of the weight of their predecessors' achievement, the *use* and exhaustion of the art form by the great writers of the distant and the immediate past. In a sense Shakespeare, an eternal part of our culture and mythology and yet

[8]See Friedrich Nietzsche, *The Birth of Tragedy,* which is very illuminating in the context of *The Time of the Angels.*

[9]High Gothic is a literary mode, originally very popular in the eighteenth century, that relies on some, or all, of the following constituents: a reference to medieval times, an element of the supernatural, horror, mystery, ruins, and haunted castles. It was satirized by Jane Austen in *Northanger Abbey* but has been used, especially by American writers, as a framework for metaphysical speculation and spiritual explanation.

a great technician, is available to learn from in a way that neither George Eliot nor Forster is. Reading him can be formally exhilarating. The second reason is an intrinsic part of Murdoch's aesthetic: Shakespeare is the Good, and contemplation of the best is always to be desired.

What Murdoch seems to me to have learned technically from Shakespeare is, again, two things. The first is, as a matter of plotting, that you can have intense realism of character portrayal without having to suppose that this entails *average probability* as part of your structure. Real people may—do—dance in the formal figures of a Shakespearean plot (or indeed, a grotesque Dickensian one) without the sanction of the sense that one is studying a *probable* developing person in a *probable* developing society, which is so necessary to the scientific and sociological beliefs of a George Eliot.

The second is that a very large cast, including a number of peripheral people who are felt to have a life outside the plot, makes for the desiderated "spread-out substantial picture of the manifold virtues of man and society." In two radio interviews I have had with Murdoch, she returned to Shakespeare's comic people, to Shallow and Silence and the *particularity* of their lives, as an example of a moral and aesthetic achievement beyond most of us. In the 1930's and 1940's novelists such as Elizabeth Bowen were placing immense stress on "relevance"—to plot, to novel-as-a-whole—as a criterion for inclusion in a story. Murdoch has rediscovered the richness of adding apparently gratuitously interesting people and events. These indicate worlds outside the book they are in. (A good example is the strange letters from nonparticipating people that chatteringly punctuate *An Accidental Man,* offering passion, tragedy, comedy, somewhere between Evelyn Waugh, Shakespeare, and Charles Dickens; these letters are outside the central plot but enrich our vision of it.)

In these Shakespearean novels with their huge casts, the central enchanter figures, representing metaphysical powers or truths, are less powerful. Radeechy, whose death and courting of evil in *The Nice and the Good* is a little thing beside the Shakespearean dance of paired lovers, moral mistakes and discoveries, is a poor relation of Carel in *The Time of the Angels.* Julius King, the enchanter, the Prospero, the master of ceremonies in *A Fairly Honourable Defeat,* enchants and manipulates both more or less, depending on the moral powers of the people whose lives he touches. He is related to Mischa Fox in that his rootless violence (he is a germ-war scientist) has its roots in his experiences in Dachau; but his power is less than Mischa's, and the people he meets are denser. He is, like Carel, Nietzschean in his compelling vision of life as a formless joke. Indeed, his relationship with his victim, Rupert, is very like that of Carel with his brother Marcus. Both Rupert and Marcus are writing ethical treatises on Good, on morality in a godless world. Both are unaware of their true dependence on the power of the vanished religion to sustain their hierarchies of value and discrimination. Both are vulnerable to the ruthlessness and violence that mock their morality. But Julius, unlike Carel, does not behave like a Frazerian mythical god-man. He copies the plot of *Much Ado About Nothing,* and like a naturalistic Mephistopheles uses Rupert's own moral blindness and secret complacency to destroy him.

This novel is in many ways my favorite of Murdoch's later works because in it both reader and characters are drawn through the experience of *attention* to the being of others that Miss Murdoch sees as the heart of morality. Julius destroys Rupert. He does not destroy the homosexual marriage of Simon and Axel because, as we are shown, as we experience, they know each other too well. They love each other, talk to each other, consider each other, and reach a breaking point when they automatically discuss Julius' lies and manipulations for what they are. Just as, in the scene where the black man is being beaten in the restaurant, the characters react typically, morally, entirely convincingly —one is amused (Julius), one intervenes incompetently (Simon), one makes a moral generalization (Axel), and Tallis, who represents Murdoch's new vision of starting from real human needs, as well as the self-denying gentleness that can seem repellent or abstract—Tallis knocks the thugs down. This is a novel in which a patterned plot, the thoughts of the characters, the multiplicity of people, the events, add up to a moral and aesthetic experience both unexpected, delightful, and distressing.

At this point it might be worth returning to the critical doubts and debates I discussed briefly in my opening paragraphs. As I hope I have to some extent shown, much of the trouble readers and critics have in responding to and evaluating Murdoch's novels is a result of a tension between "realism" and other, more deliberately artificial, even "experimental," ways of writing in her work. Robert

Scholes, in his book *The Fabulators,* includes *The Unicorn* as an example of a new kind of narrative art that returns to older forms of "fable" rather than following the realist tradition of the novel proper. His other examples are mostly American, and critics who admire the work of such modern American fantasists or parable writers as Kurt Vonnegut, John Hawkes, and Pynchon have found Murdoch timid or old-fashioned by comparison. Such critics tend to see *Under the Net* as her most successful work, as well as her most original, and her painstaking efforts at creating a fuller and more realistic world in her later books as an aberration or a retreat into English bourgeois complacencies. Political criticisms have been leveled at her for the increasingly narrow scope of her social world—criticisms that on moral grounds she herself does not feel to be valid. If you are interested in unique individuals, she argues, they can as well be located in the English *haute bourgeoisie* as anywhere.

I would agree, in many ways, that *Under the Net* is aesthetically Murdoch's most satisfying novel: the balance of lucid philosophical debate, lightly but subtly handled emotional pace, and surrealist fantastic action is new in the English novel and beautifully controlled. *A Severed Head* has the same qualities of delicate control and fusion of several styles and subject matters; drawing-room comedy shading into French bedroom farce, combined with Jungian psychoanalytic myth and cool philosophical wit. At the other end of the scale, *The Bell* seems to me arguably Murdoch's most successful attempt at realism, emotional and social—the tones of voice of the members of the religious community are beautifully caught; the sexual, aesthetic, and religious passions and confusions of the three main characters, Dora, Michael, and, to a lesser extent, Toby, are delicately analyzed with the combination of intellectual grasp and sensuous immediacy of George Eliot.

It is, as I have tried to suggest, with those novels in which Murdoch has tried to combine widely differing techniques and narrative methods that confusions arise, sometimes because readers are insufficiently alert and flexible, and sometimes because the writer herself creates jarring effects or difficulties for them. I have suggested, for instance, that *The Time of the Angels* is best read as a mannered philosophical myth, or fantasy, playing games with Nietzsche's *The Birth of Tragedy* and the new school of "Death of God" theology. The introductory description of the character of Pattie O'Rourke, half-black, half-Irish, however, is written with a clarity, sympathy, density, and lack of irony that involve the reader in a way that suggests that the rest of the story will have the emotional immediacy of *The Bell.* Pattie's actions are in fact almost entirely part of Carel's religio-sexual myth (she has to be the Black Madonna to balance the White Virgin Princess, his incestuously seduced daughter Elizabeth). The reader who responds to that initial description has a right to feel that the author has promised something she has not performed, whatever the illumination provided by the myth.

In general, Murdoch's careful introductions and histories of her characters are among her best passages of prose, thoughtful, clear, compact—I think of Michael and Dora again, in *The Bell,* of Simon and Axel in *A Fairly Honourable Defeat,* of Hilary Burde in *A Word Child* (1975). Hilary Burde, like Pattie, is a case of a character where a change in both prose style and plotting jars a reader prepared for emotional density and realism. He is, as initially seen, a character created by education, a man made civilized by learning grammar and language to a level of high proficiency, a man of clear mind on a limited front, and violent and ill-comprehended passions. His story, though dramatic and cleverly related to the story of *Peter Pan* (a recurrent preoccupation of Murdoch's), is not the story of the man we first meet. It is an adventure story, with two accidental deaths and very contrived repeated relationships; it is a Freudian game with incest, with the compulsion to repeat the actions that trap and terrify us. It is rapid, perplexing, funny, and terrible. It does not satisfy the realistic expectations aroused by the patient and delicate introductory analysis of the main character.

There is also a problem with Murdoch's use of symbolism, which she herself mocks in *The Black Prince.* This problem arises more with the carefully "realist" novels than with the more contrived ones: the recurrent images of severed heads, sculpted, dreamed, analyzed, in *A Severed Head* work as both joke and myth. The bell itself, in *The Bell,* seems to me the weakest part of a fine novel, because it is so much more patently contrived as a narrative device than either the severed heads or the use of the house, abbey, and lake in *The Bell* itself to suggest the divisions between conscious and unconscious, secular and spiritual worlds. The bell is an emblem, used as such in the sermons of Michael and James;

it is also a crucial actor in the narrative; and, as I have suggested elsewhere *(Degrees of Freedom)*, its moment of action, when Dora rings it, is a substitute for a real action in the real world inhabited by the characters. Dora beats it to "tell the truth"—but the truth she has to tell has nothing really to do with the bell. The connection is the novelist's.

The English have arguably never handled the symbolic novel as well as the French, Germans, or Americans—Marcel Proust's symbols, Thomas Mann's symbols, are woven into the very texture of their prose in a way that neither Lawrence's, Forster's, nor Murdoch's exactly are. In *A Passage to India* Forster made his landscape symbolic and real together; Murdoch attempts such a fusion in *The Bell,* with wood, water, and abbey. In *Howards End* and *The Longest Journey* Forster's symbols are rather too deliberately pointed at as symbols of England or social truths (including Howards End itself). I would argue that this is the case with the roses and painting in that nevertheless excellent novel, *An Unofficial Rose.*

The critic approaching Murdoch's later novels for the first time needs to do so in the awareness that many serious English novelists are technically moving away from simple realism, from social analysis and precise delineation of the motives and emotions of individuals to forms much more overtly and deliberately "unreal." Not only Murdoch but Angus Wilson and others are taking an interest in the fairy stories buried in Dickens' plots, in the grotesque caricatures, so like fairy-tale characters, who move among Dickens' more "real" characters. If *The Black Prince* is overtly artificial, drawing attention to its own fictive nature and to other works of literature in a parodic manner, so are Wilson's novels *No Laughing Matter* and *As If By Magic.* So, also, are the excellent series of brief novels by Muriel Spark, which call constant attention to the fact that they are just "stories," fictions, and that that is what is interesting about them. Both Wilson and Murdoch have deep roots in, and strong moral attachments to, the English realist tradition. Both are writing novels that combine old realist morals and old realist techniques with a new kind of literary playfulness of which the reader needs to be aware.

A comparison of Murdoch's first novel, *Under the Net,* published in 1954, and *The Black Prince,* published in 1973, shows a remarkable consistency of themes. These two novels are interesting because both are first-person accounts by men who want to be, or to see themselves as, serious artists, and who are, in this capacity and as lovers, bedeviled by the problems discussed earlier in this essay—the tension between the attempt to tell, or see, the truth, and the inevitability of fantasy; the need for concepts and form and the recognition that all speech is in a sense distortion, that novelists are fantasymongers, and that, as Hugo says in *Under the Net,* "the whole language is a machine for making falsehoods."

Jake in *Under the Net* has central conversations with Hugo, who holds the view that "all theorizing is flight. We must be ruled by the situation itself and this is unutterably particular. Indeed, it is something to which we can never get close enough, however hard we may try, as it were, to creep under the net." (The image of the net comes from Wittgenstein's *Tractatus Logico-Philosophicus* in which he likens our descriptive languages to a mesh put over reality, to map it, and continues that "laws, like the law of causation, etc., treat of the network and not what the network describes.")

In *The Black Prince,* Bradley Pearson, trying to write his magnum opus, the story of his love for the daughter of a rival novelist, despairs frequently in the manner of Bledyard in *The Sandcastle* about the impossibility of precise description:

> How can one describe a human being "justly"? How can one describe oneself? With what an air of false coy humility, with what an assumed confiding simplicity one sets about it! "I am a puritan" and so on. Faugh! How can these statements not be false? Even "I am tall" has a context. How the angels must laugh and sigh. Yet what can one do but try to lodge one's vision somehow inside this layered stuff of ironic sensibility, which, if I were a fictitious character, would be that much deeper and denser? How prejudiced is this image of Arnold, how superficial this picture of Priscilla! Emotions cloud the view, and so far from isolating the particular, draw generality and even theory in their train.
>
> (*The Black Prince,* pt. 1)

Jake has a high sense of difficulty: he has concluded that the present age is not one in which one can write an epic, stopping just short of concluding it is not one in which it is possible to write a novel. He remarks that "nothing is more paralyzing than a sense of historical perspective, especially in literary matters." He publishes a philosophical dialogue, as does Bradley, who also has a crippling sense of difficulty and the requirements of true excellence. "Art comes out of endless restraint and silence." Jake is an unconnected floater, Bradley an income tax inspector who lives austerely waiting for the work of art. But both are prepared to feel gripped and driven by a sense of destiny, of direction, of a source of power, ambivalent to the last, art, love, or fantasy.

Both are measured against prolific, apparently "bad" writers. Jake lives off translating the best-selling French novelist Jean-Pierre Breteuil, who suddenly turns out to be serious, wins the Prix Goncourt, and imposes on Jake a "vision of his own destiny" that entails trying to write, whatever the theoretic objections. Bradley has a conversation with his alter ego, Arnold Baffin, a prolific writer whose performance suggests a kind of parody of unflattering critical views of Murdoch. Baffin's work is "a congeries of amusing anecdotes loosely garbled into 'racy stories' with the help of half-baked, unmeditated symbolism . . . Arnold Baffin wrote too much, too fast."

In *Under the Net* it is Jake's experience of his misprision of people and situations, his undervaluing of their difference from himself and of their complexity, that makes him use concepts, makes him write. Bradley Pearson is invigorated by a contact with the Black Prince, Apollo Loxias, Hamlet, the Love that is the same as Death, the Nietzschean vision which insists that Apollo the Lord of the Muses and Dionysos the god of drunkenness, destruction, and chaos are both necessary to art. Bradley is wise and witty in a Murdochian manner about the sadomasochism involved in this vision of art, as he is about his own shortcomings. The fact that these narratives are first-person accounts by intelligent men makes the reading hard, since the narrators' illusions are refined illusions. In *The Black Prince,* Murdoch comically layers this difficulty with references to Bradley's own fictionality, to the idea that both he and Apollo might be "the invention of a minor novelist," and with other, partial, accounts of the plot by other characters. Yet Bradley says much that she has said herself on her own account, and he is clearly, among other things, an authorial joke about the relations of author and character. It is in this context that Bradley's description of Shakespeare's achievement in *Hamlet* becomes fascinating from the point of view of Murdoch's work. She believes, she has said, that the self of the artist should be expunged from his work, that Shakespeare's greatness is his anonymity. Yet she recognizes, in the Sonnets and in *Hamlet,* a kind of "self" that Bradley discusses in this speech. Shakespeare, he says,

> "is speaking as few artists can speak, in the first person and yet at the pinnacle of artifice. . . . Shakespeare here makes the crisis of his own identity into the very central stuff of his art. He transmutes his private obsessions into a rhetoric so public that it can be mumbled by any child. He enacts the purification of speech, and yet this is something comic, a sort of trick, like a huge pun, like a long almost pointless joke.
>
> "*Hamlet* is words, and so is Hamlet."
>
> (*The Black Prince,* pt. 1)

In a sense, here, we have another version of Murdoch's "Good," which is virtually impossible to attain—the complete creation of a character in *words,* using the writer but *for* the language. It is an extraordinary example of one of the high moments of art where there is no contradiction between words and things, between men and the images of men. But it is also, as Murdoch and *her* character point out, endlessly comic. And Murdoch's novel conducts a comic joke itself around the vision of *Hamlet.* "All novels" she has claimed, "are necessarily comic," just as her Apollo claims, in his epilogue, "all human beings are figures of fun. Art celebrates this. Art is adventure stories." Another thing for which one increasingly admires Murdoch is aesthetic courage: knowing, better than most writers, the historical difficulties of writing good novels now, the moral difficulties of writing good novels at all, she continues to produce comic metaphysical adventures of a high order. What Arnold Baffin did not say, but might have said, in his quarrel with Bradley Pearson about being an "artist" and being a "professional writer" is that Shakespeare was both of these, too.

POSTSCRIPT 1986

Since 1976, when this essay was first published, Murdoch has written four more novels and the important and beautiful essay *The Fire and the Sun: Why Plato Banished the Artists* (1977), which continues and extends her study of the conflict or tension between the artist and the saint. If there have been no violent changes in her preoccupations or forms, there are nevertheless various shifts in emphasis and changes in technique that can be remarked on.

The most striking formal change is an increase in length and in apparent looseness of structure, as though the novelist was exploring more seriously the nineteenth-century fictional model that Henry James called "loose, baggy monsters." Favorable reviewers of *The Good Apprentice* (1985) have remarked on a kind of deliberate roughness in her style, which more than one has connected to a fear of the seductions of art. Stephen Medcalf calls this "a deliberately throwaway style, a piling up of wanton expression, as if she fears the temptations and magic which a perfect style would offer." Her characters certainly communicate increasingly in long, rushing, self-revelatory outpourings of thought about themselves and the nature of things, with words heavily italicized for emphasis, concepts grasped at rather than thought through. In this they are reminiscent of Dostoevsky's endlessly fascinating, endlessly maddening self-revealed casuists and pleaders. In a communication at a conference in the University of Caen, Murdoch made a statement about her ideal novel that is illuminating both about the novel she had then just finished *(The Sea, The Sea),* and about the conjunction of moral and aesthetic principles that guide her later work:

> The advantages of writing in the first person are obvious. In a way they are enormous because you can then ramble around endlessly, you can address your reader, and you can produce a tremendous amount of verbiage which has got a sense in relation to the speaker. . . . On the other hand, the danger of this is that it's harder then to create other characters who can stand up to the narrator, because they're being seen through his eyes. And I think my ideal novel—I mean, the novel I would like to write and haven't yet written—would not be written in the first person, because I'd rather write a novel which is more scattered, with many different centres. I've often thought that the best way to write a novel would be to invent the story, and then to remove the hero and the heroine and write about the peripheral people—because one wants to extend one's sympathy and divide one's interests.
>
> ("Rencontres avec Iris Murdoch," 1978)

The witty and often startling use of the "peripheral people" in her later novels is worthy of comment. Many of them contain long passages of formalized social chatter, full of news and views, spoken by a kind of drawing-room chorus of minor characters, which have been excellently analyzed by Barbara Hardy in an essay in her book *Tellers and Listeners,* on the uses of talk in fiction.

An example I would offer here is the chorus of family and friends in *Nuns and Soldiers* (1980) who wait, in the early chapters, for Guy Openshaw to die, and whose discussions punctuate, half shape, and permeate his widow's subsequent remarriage to one of their number, the painter and hanger-on Tim Reede. Guy refers to them as "les cousins et les tantes": Murdoch takes pleasure in giving us glimpses into their private hells and passions, outside their public choric function. She even slips into the stream of talk (on p. 309) a few lines making it clear that one of their number, a scientist, has made a discovery that might indicate a "cosmic disaster" about to take place; but the rush of talk absorbs this information unthinkingly and moves on, to love and art and gossip. Two of this chorus, Manfred and Mrs. Mount (a kind of earthly Venus, with Tannhäuser associations), turn out in the penultimate chapter to have manipulated quite a lot of the plot of this novel, but are no hidden gods: a very minor character indeed then makes his only appearance, and, we are told, knows "more about them than they imagined."

Another example might be the density of Murdoch's creation of the small spa town of Ennistone in *The Philosopher's Pupil* (1983), with its streets, housing, old families, varying religions, and of course its network of talk and gossip, centering on the public baths, a most imposingly *concrete* imaginary structure and institution, a natural force, the hot spray, contained in buildings and decor, utility and frivolity, of various decades. Connected to this specificity is the strange and almost fanatical gourmet regime of Charles Arrowby, the highly unsuccessful Prospero of *The Sea, The Sea* with his kippers and Cox's Orange Pippins, a saving grace in his fantastic world. Murdoch's new, shifting, and leisurely pace means that her work can contain, without apparent furious shaping (which would be "magic"), a multiplicity of things and voices that embody the variety and strangeness of the known world. There are ways of looking *out* from all the private dramas of her protagonists and other vantage points from which to look in.

The idea of the danger and seduction of "magic" is not new in Murdoch, although she continues to explore both magic and magicians with subtlety and invention. In *The Fire and the Sun* she writes that Plato "always feared magic," and locates his disapproval of art in a fear of its unconscious sources and its indulgence of the human desire for power and fantasy. Plato's objections to theatrical illusion stand, lightly and comically, behind her choice of Charles Arrowby, a retired theater director, as the hero-narrator of *The Sea, The Sea,* who incarcerates his childhood beloved in order to *make* her accept freedom and love at his hands. Art, according to Plato, according to Murdoch,

> is dangerous chiefly because it apes the spiritual and subtly disguises and trivializes it. . . . Art delights in unsavoury trivia and in the endless proliferation of senseless images (television). Art is playful in a sinister sense, full of (φθόνος) a spiteful amused acceptance of evil, and through buffoonery and mockery weakens moral discrimination. The artist cannot represent or celebrate the good, but only what is daemonic and fantastic and extreme; whereas truth is quiet and sober and confined.

There are enchanter-artists in these later books, dangerous manipulators related to Mischa Fox and Julius King, but there is also an increased interest in a "natural magic," in forces in the earth not part of our moral system or urgently related to it. There is much good magic in *The Sea, The Sea,* partly connected with Charles's Buddhist and military cousin James, a self-disciplined saint who keeps demons in boxes and can descend into a churning sea-cave to rescue his cousin from death. There is a sea-serpent and there are seals, whose strangeness and yet human appeal has always seemed magical to us. In *The Good Apprentice* the prodigal son, Edward, who has killed his best friend by mistake, is sent by a Prospero figure, a lay analyst of unusual scrupulousness in Murdoch, in search of his natural father, Jesse Baltram, a painter who lives with his beautiful wife and two daughters in an enchanted castle, which is also an absurd ad hoc religious community called Seegard. Jesse's name suggests Frazer's dying gods: he is the progenitor, as Jesse at the foot of the Tree of Jesse in church windows led to Christ through David. Baltram suggests Beltane fires and religions of vegetation. He has a sickness like the Fisher King of the Grail legend, and is almost animal in his intense sexuality, in his hairy body and huge eyes, in his mute dying. Animals in Murdoch are always innocent and alive, from spiders to the "papillon" dog whose consciousness she briefly inhabits in *The Philosopher's Pupil.* Edward's quest for his father brings him into contact with a mysterious natural world of women like withered golden apples and threatening "tree men," but I think we are not meant to read these events as a bad fantasy but as a healing brush with old myths. Murdoch has said that in writing of Jesse she was thinking of *Sir Gawaine and the Grene Knight,* of magical powers in the world that have nothing to do with Christianity and our system of ethics. Jesse has named his environment for sex and death: there is a "lingam stone" in a forest glade, and the dining room is not the refectory but the Interfectory (killing place).

This increase in magic connects with a considerably increased urgency in Murdoch's concern with Christianity, with what she sees as a contemporary need for a religion, albeit a religion without a God, for a new Christianity, centering on the acceptance of a mythical Christ who is Goodness, or the good man. In the colloquy at Caen she spoke of the difference between nineteenth- and twentieth-century novels in terms of religion. The nineteenth-century novel was, she said, "a major product of religion, and one could say that the most important change we have experienced during this century has been the disappearance of religion as something that goes without saying, in the sense in which all the great nineteenth-century writers were, to a remarkable degree, religious thinkers—however they defined themselves—for whom the religious background went without saying." She goes on to claim that in England the demythologizing of religion, the new consideration of dogmas as myths, could "bring religion back into the realm of the believable." Here art would be religious in the Tolstoyan sense, would *make* religion.

I believe this hope for a revitalized, demythologized religion is central in all these later novels. It takes a Buddhist form in *The Sea, The Sea,* inventing supernatural events to endorse the moral insight of the selfless James. In *The Good Apprentice* Edward the prodigal son is counterbalanced by his brother (by upbringing, not parentage), Stuart, who apprentices himself to Good and has the lack of charm often associated with good people in Murdoch's work—for example, Ann, in *An Unofficial Rose,* or Tallis, in *A Fairly Honourable Defeat,* an explicit Christ-figure. Stuart practices celibacy, meditation, and a kind of disciplined annihilation of the ego. (He is interesting because his ego is powerful and determined.) He is perceived by others as a "white maggot" and by Jesse, when they encounter each other, as death itself. He makes innocent and purposeful interventions in the complicated lives of others, resembling in this Dostoevsky's innocent, occasionally disastrous, not quite human Prince Myshkin, the Idiot who imitates Christ and shares Christ's apparent ignorance of sexual life. Some of Stuart's acts produce good, some are more doubtful, but the *ideal* of virtue is credible and attractive (if that is not a dangerous word). Edward has too much myth, Stuart none. He is explicitly *not* the Sorcerer's Apprentice, but the elder brother in the parable of the Prodigal Son, who, Murdoch feels, has had a rough deal, morally.

If Stuart represents a possible and credible modern religious stance, both *The Philosopher's Pupil* and *Nuns and Soldiers* offer us moments of myth, or art, where Christ is present. In *The Philosopher's Pupil* it is a whole scene, a beach picnic, where the innocent young man, Tom, is overcome by his discovery of Christ's legendary visit to Britain with Joseph of Arimathea; and where the daemonic George braves the Murdochian rite of passage of near drowning to rescue the papillon dog, which is subsequently nestled between his sister-in-law's breasts, watched by his nephew, Adam, who loves the dog. The papillon is, in its way, the soul (papillon = butterfly in French = Psyche, in Greek). George harrows hell to fetch it back to Adam, who has named it Zed, because he and it are Alpha and Omega, the beginning and the end. In this scene, which I can only adumbrate and took several readings to understand, *everyone* is Christ, contributes to Christ as part of the community, even George, and despite the usual Murdochian tensions, bickering, life of chatter and triviality, power struggles and pain. In this novel, too, is Father Bernard, a successor to Carel in *Time of the Angels,* a priest of no God, who celebrates masses and prays to a Christ he knows to be dead and not risen. "And it is essential that he did not rise. If he be risen, then is our faith vain." At the end of this book, which opens with a near-murder and is in many ways blacker in its vision of human nature than many of Murdoch's novels, Father Bernard defines religion:

> "Metaphysics and the human sciences are made impossible by the *penetration of morality into the moment-by-moment conduct of ordinary life:* the understanding of this fact *is religion. . . .*
>
> "There is no beyond, there is only here, the infinitely small, infinitely great and utterly demanding present. This too I tell my flock, demolishing their dreams of a supernatural elsewhere. So you see, I have abandoned every kind of magic and preach a charmless holiness. This and only this can be the religion of the future, this and only this can save the planet."

In *Nuns and Soldiers* Anne Cavidge, who has given up being a nun because she has lost her faith in God, has the most direct and startling experience of Christ, when she is visited by him in her kitchen and told "almost carelessly" that there is salvation, but "you must do it all yourself, you know." Also: "I am not a magician, I never was. You know what to do. Do right, refrain from wrong." This Christ is very real and somewhat inconsequential; interestingly, he shares with all Murdoch's "good" people a blanched look: "He had a strangely elongated head and a strange pallor, a pallor of something which had long been deprived of light, a shadowed leaf, a deep sea fish, a grub inside a fruit."

It is Anne, another of the community of religious godless, who says something that connects this religious morality to the form of Murdoch's novels:

> "Your life doesn't belong to you," said Anne. "Who can tell where his life ends? Our being spreads far out beyond us and mingles with the being of others. We live in other people's thoughts, in their plans, in their dreams. This is as if there were God. We have an infinite responsibility."
>
> (ch. 8)

For this reason the peripheral characters spin their half-glimpsed stories. Edward, at the end of *The Good Apprentice,* has a familiar vision of life as both particular and accidental and intensely ordered, like art:

> "In a way it's all a muddle starting off with an accident: my breakdown, drugs, telepathy, my father's illness, cloistered neurotic women, people arriving unexpectedly, all sorts of things which happen by pure chance. . . . In another way it's a whole complex thing, internally connected, like a dark globe, a dark world, as if we were all parts of a simple drama, living inside a work of art. Perhaps important things are always like that, so that you can think of them both ways."

IRIS MURDOCH

Murdoch's novels think of life in both ways, accidentally and as a complex order. If the drive to represent particularity, the accidental, the unknown, the unfinished is at present even more powerful, the artist has found new ways of dealing with, representing, and ordering that drive. There is no other English novelist whose understanding of the patterns and lapses in our thought and attention is so careful and so morally exacting.

SELECTED BIBLIOGRAPHY

I. BIBLIOGRAPHY. R. L. Widmann, "An Iris Murdoch Checklist," in *Critique: Studies in Modern Fiction,* 10 (1967), pp. 17–29; A. Culley and J. Feaster, "Criticism of Iris Murdoch: A Selected Checklist," in *Modern Fiction Studies,* 15 (Autumn 1969), pp. 449–457, Iris Murdoch special number, lists works by and about Murdoch, including selected reviews of the novels.

Note: Forthcoming is J. Fletcher, *Iris Murdoch: Her Work and Her Readers, 1933–1983* (New York), which will be the standard work of reference.

II. SEPARATE WORKS. *Sartre, Romantic Rationalist* (London, 1953), philosophy and literary criticism; *Under the Net* (London, 1954), fiction; *The Flight from the Enchanter* (London, 1956), fiction; *The Sandcastle* (London, 1957), fiction; *The Bell* (London, 1958), fiction; *A Severed Head* (London, 1961), fiction; *An Unofficial Rose* (London, 1962), fiction; *The Unicorn* (London, 1963), fiction; *The Italian Girl* (London, 1964), fiction; *The Red and The Green* (London, 1965), historical fiction; *The Time of the Angels* (London, 1966), fiction; *The Nice and the Good* (London, 1968), fiction; *Bruno's Dream* (London, 1969), fiction; *The Sovereignty of Good* (London, 1970), philosophy, contains three previously pub. philosophical papers: "The Idea of Perfection," in the *Yale Review* (Spring 1964), "The Sovereignty of Good over Other Concepts," Leslie Stephen Lecture (in 1967), "On 'God' and 'Good,'" in *The Anatomy of Knowledge* (New York, 1969); *A Fairly Honourable Defeat* (London, 1970), fiction; *An Accidental Man* (London, 1971), fiction; *The Black Prince* (London, 1973), fiction; *Three Arrows and the Servants in the Snow* (London, 1973), plays; *The Sacred and Profane Love Machine* (London, 1974), fiction; *A Word Child* (London, 1975), fiction; *Henry and Cato* (London, 1976), fiction; *The Fire and the Sun: Why Plato Banished the Artists* (London, 1977), based on the Romanes Lecture (1976), philosophy; *A Year of Birds* (Wiltshire, 1978; rev. ed. London, 1984), poems with engravings by R. Stone; *The Sea, The Sea* (London, 1978), fiction; *Nuns and Soldiers* (London, 1980), fiction; *The Philosopher's Pupil* (London, 1983), fiction; *The Good Apprentice* (London, 1985), fiction.

III. ARTICLES. "Rebirth of Christianity," in *Adelphi* (July–September 1943); "Worship and Common Life," in *Adelphi* (July–September 1944); "The Novelist as Metaphysician," in the *Listener* (16 March 1950); "The Existentialist Hero," in the *Listener* (23 March 1950); "The Existentialist Political Myth," in *Socratic,* 5 (1952); "Nostalgia for the Particular," in Proceedings of the Aristotelian Society, supp. vol. 30, *Dreams and Self-Knowledge* (London, 1956); "Knowing the Void," in the *Spectator* (2 November 1956); "Important Things," in the *Sunday Times* (17 February 1957), review of S. de Beauvoir, *The Mandarins,* repr. in *Encore: A Sunday Times Anthology* (London, 1963); "Metaphysics and Ethics," in D. F. Pears, *The Nature of Metaphysics* (London, 1957); "Hegel in Modern Dress," in the *New Statesman* (25 May 1957); "Existentialist Bite," in the *Spectator* (12 July 1957); "T. S. Eliot as a Moralist," in N. Braybrooke, ed., *T. S. Eliot: A Symposium for His Seventieth Birthday* (London, 1958); "A House of Theory," in N. Mackenzie, ed., *Conviction* (London, 1958), repr. in *Partisan Review,* 26 (1959); "The Sublime and the Beautiful Revisited," in *Yale Review,* 49 (1959); "The Sublime and the Good," in *Chicago Review,* 13 (Autumn 1959); "Negative Capability," in *Adam,* 284–286 (1960); "Against Dryness," in *Encounter,* 16 (January 1961); "Mass, Might and Myth," in the *Spectator* (7 September 1962); "Speaking of Writing," in the *Times* (13 February 1964); "The Darkness of Practical Reason," in *Encounter,* 27 (July 1966); "Existentialists and Mystics," in W. W. Robson, ed., *Essays and Poems Presented to Lord David Cecil* (London, 1970); "Salvation by Words," in the *New York Review of Books* (15 June 1972); "Socialism and Selection," in C. B. Cox and R. Boyson, *Black Paper* (London, 1975), 3rd ed.; "Epistolary Dialogues," in *Soviet Literature* (London, 1977), pt. 2, with V. Ivasheva; "Art Is the Imitation of Nature," in *Cahiers du Centre de recherches sur les pays du nord et du nord-ouest,* no. 1 (Caen, 1978).

IV. INTERVIEWS. F. Kermode, "House of Fiction: Interviews with Seven English Novelists," in *Partisan Review,* 30 (1963); P. Orr, interview recorded 27 May 1965, the British Council, London: F. Dillistone, "Christ and Myth," in *Frontier* (Autumn 1965); S. Nettell, "An Exclusive Interview," in *Books and Bookmen,* 11 (September 1966); W. K. Rose, "An Interview with Iris Murdoch," in *London Magazine,* 8 (June 1968), also in *Shenandoah,* 19 (Winter 1968); R. Bryden and A. S. Byatt, interview recorded March 1968, partly reproduced in the *Listener* (4 April 1968); A. S. Byatt, "Talking to Iris Murdoch," forty-minute interview recorded 26 October 1971, BBC Archives; "Iris Murdoch in Conversation with Malcolm Bradbury," recorded 27 February 1976, British Council tape no. RS 2001; M. Jarrett-Kerr, "Good, Evil and Morality," in *CR Quarterly Review of the Community of the Resurrection,* no. 266 (Michaelmas 1969); J.-L. Chevalier, ed.,

"Rencontres avec Iris Murdoch," Centre de recherches de littérature et linguistique des pays de langue anglaise, Université de Caen (Caen, 1978); B. Magee, *Men of Ideas: Some Creators of Contemporary Philosophy* (London, 1978); H. Ziegler and C. W. E. Bigsby, eds., *The Radical Imagination and the Liberal Tradition: Interviews with English and American Novelists* (London, 1982); J. Haffenden, "John Haffenden Talks to Iris Murdoch," in the *Literary Review,* 48 (April 1983).

V. Critical Studies. K. Allsopp, *The Angry Decade: A Survey of the Cultural Revolt of the Nineteen-Fifties* (London, 1958); G. S. Fraser, "Iris Murdoch: The Solidity of the Normal," in J. Wain, ed., *International Literary Annual II* (1959); G. Pearson, "Iris Murdoch and the Romantic Novel," in *New Left Review,* 13–14 (January–April 1962); M. Bradbury, "Iris Murdoch's *Under the Net,*" in *Critical Quarterly,* no. 4 (Spring 1962); J. Souvage, "Symbol as Narrative Device," in *English Studies* (2 April 1962); W. Van O'Connor, *The New University Wits and the End of Modernism* (London, 1963), contains an essay on "Iris Murdoch: The Formal and the Contingent"; G. Martin, "Iris Murdoch and the Symbolist Novel," in *British Journal of Aesthetics,* 5 (July 1965); A. S. Byatt, *Degrees of Freedom* (London, 1965); P. Wolfe, *The Disciplined Heart* (London, 1966), contains useful information but some very odd interpretations of the moral structure of the novels; R. Scholes, *The Fabulators* (London, 1967), contains an essay on *The Unicorn* as fable; R. Rabinovitz, *Iris Murdoch* (New York, 1968), Columbia Essays on Modern Writers, no. 34; J. Bayley, *The Characters of Love: A Study in the Literature of Personality* (London, 1968); H. German, "Allusions in the Early Novels of Iris Murdoch," in *Modern Fiction Studies,* 15 (Autumn 1969), special issue on Iris Murdoch; P. Kemp, "The Fight Against Fantasy: Iris Murdoch's *The Red and the Green,*" in *Modern Fiction Studies,* 15 (Autumn 1969); A. P. Kenney, "The Mythic History of *A Severed Head,*" in *Modern Fiction Studies,* 15 (Autumn 1969); H. German, "The Range of Allusion in the Novels of Iris Murdoch," in *Journal of Modern Literature* (1971); F. Kermode, *Modern Essays* (London, 1971); R. Hoskins, "Iris Murdoch's Midsummer Nightmare," in *Twentieth Century Literature,* 19 (January–October 1972); R. Haskins, "Shakespearean Allusions in *A Fairly Honourable Defeat,*" in *Twentieth Century Literature,* 19 (January–October 1971); M. Bradbury, *Possibilities: Essays on the State of the Novel* (London, 1973), a very illuminating essay, extending his earlier work on *Under the Net;* P. Swinden, *Unofficial Selves* (London, 1973), pursuing Murdoch's ideas about character, esp. good on *A Fairly Honourable Defeat;* B. Hardy, *Tellers and Listeners* (London, 1975); L. Sage, "No Trespassers," in the *New Review* (September 1977); L. Sage, "The Pursuit of Imperfection," in *Critical Quarterly,* 19 (Summer 1977); M. Scanlan, "The Machinery of Pain: Romantic Suffering in Three Works of Iris Murdoch's," in *Renascence,* 29 (Winter 1977); Z. T. Sullivan, "The Contracting Universe of Iris Murdoch's Gothic Novels," in *Modern Fiction Studies,* 23 (Winter 1977–1978); Z. T. Sullivan, "Iris Murdoch's Self-Conscious Gothicism: *The Time of the Angels,*" in *Arizona Quarterly* (1977); R. Scholes, *Fabulation and Metafiction* (Urbana, Ill., and London, 1978); M. Bradbury and D. Palmer, eds., *The Contemporary English Novel* (London, 1979), contains L. Sage, "Female Fictions" and A. S. Byatt, "People in Paper Houses: Attitudes to 'Realism' and Experiment in English Postwar Fiction"; R. Todd, *Iris Murdoch, The Shakespearean Interest* (New York, 1979); M. Weldhem, "Morality and the Metaphor," in *New Universities Quarterly* (Spring 1980); P. J. Conradi, "The Metaphysical Hostess," in *English Library History,* 48 (Summer 1981); P. J. Conradi, "Useful Fictions," in *Critical Quarterly,* 23 (Autumn 1981); N. Vance, "Iris Murdoch's Serious Fun," in *Theology* (November 1981); E. Dipple, *Iris Murdoch: Work for the Spirit* (London, 1982); A. MacIntyre, "Good for Nothing," in the *London Review of Books* (3–16 June 1982); R. Todd, *Iris Murdoch* (New York and London, 1984); S. Medcalf, "Towards Respect for Reality," in the *Times Literary Supplement* (27 September 1985); P. J. Conradi, *Iris Murdoch: The Saint and the Artist* (London, 1986).

Note: The author wishes to thank Peter Conradi for help in the preparation of this bibliography.

DORIS LESSING

(1919–)

Michael Thorpe

LIFE AND ATTITUDES

DORIS LESSING was born of British parents in Kermanshah, Persia, on 22 October 1919. Her father was then managing a bank for the Imperial Bank of Persia; in 1924, disillusioned with business life, he made the romantic retreat to a farm on the high veld in Rhodesia, now Zimbabwe. From Lessing's autobiographical and fictional writings it is clear that, while the farm turned out to be no happy haven for her parents, it became their imaginative daughter's lucky spiritual home. A "neurotic" child, she wasted no more time than she could help in the classroom, at a convent school in Salisbury. She left school at fourteen and became a nursemaid for a time before returning to the farm. Like Olive Schreiner, her nineteenth-century forerunner as novelist of Southern Africa and of an isolated, aspiring girl's life—and her fictional heroine Martha Quest—she was formed on the one hand by her intense response to the living body of Africa, on the other by independent reading and reflection.

A deeply felt recollection of that early life occurs in the second chapter of *Going Home* (1957), an account of her last visit to Rhodesia, in 1956 (after which the Rhodesian government did her the honor of declaring her a prohibited immigrant). There she comments: "The fact is, I don't live anywhere; I never have since I left that first home on the kopje. I suspect more people are in this predicament than they know." It was a house literally made of the earth to which it had long since returned; in her loving, detailed description of it the reader who may have begun with the later Lessing, whose characters insecurely inhabit an urban wilderness—"I have lived in over sixty different houses, flats and rented rooms during the last twenty years and not in one of them have I felt at home"—may be surprised in working back to discover her afresh as one of the major artists of the African landscape and seasons.

Having written two bad novels on the farm and destroyed them, she returned to Salisbury in the guise of a telephone operator. Her life sharply changed direction, turning outward into the flux of the brashly provincial settlers' capital. She immersed herself, she says, in "the kind of compulsive good time described in *Martha Quest.*" This led to marriage with a civil servant and the birth of a son and a daughter. When this marriage broke up, she had to leave the children. She remarried, to a German exile named Lessing, who was an active Communist in Rhodesia during the war. When this marriage also failed, she brought out of it with her to England a second son and retained her husband's name.

Establishing herself in London was a struggle at first. In those drab postwar years it was "a nightmare city," but so it might have seemed anyway to one who had known nothing during her first thirty years but bright light, sun, and clean air. Still, it was "the old country": her mother was a Londoner; her father, an Essex man, had talked nostalgically of the tamed, eternally green countryside. In any case, London was the inevitable launching point for an African writer at that time. In an autobiographical sketch opening her contribution to *Declaration* (1957), a symposium of authors' "positions," Lessing notes that she had already written and destroyed six novels, but the one she brought with her, *The Grass Is Singing,* was accepted at once and acclaimed as one of the outstanding novels by a postwar English writer. It was reprinted seven times within five months, and by 1971 the Penguin edition alone had sold 70,000 copies. Her early experiences in London were saved for semiautobiographical treatment until *In Pursuit of the English* appeared in 1960. In tone it is the lightest of her books. By the time it appeared it could already be considered "dated," but it remains a convincing impression of London working-class life in those gray years of postwar austerity and well illustrates the author's insight into people's ordinary lives. The sympathetic outsider's bias is less marked than in the documentaries of George Orwell, but it is there, and mention of it points to some preliminary consideration of her political and social concerns.

Like Martha Quest, the heroine of her *Children of Violence* novels, Lessing had been involved in leftist politics in Rhodesia as a Marxist but not as a card-carrying Communist. Three years after coming to England she joined the Communist Party, but although she left the party in 1956, it was not, she has informed me, simply because of the Soviet invasion of Hungary—"I didn't leave in the sense of some dramatic event, I simply let the thing fade away . . . there were many reasons." In 1954 her first novel dealing explicitly with Martha's political involvement, *A Proper Marriage,* had come out. Her previous books about Africa had, however, all implied a strong concern, humanitarian rather than political, to expose the sterility of white "civilization" in Rhodesia and its unjust dealings with the Africans.

It must be admitted that the English reader who comes to her writing about politics with a knowledge of the literature of the 1930's and 1940's, which reflects a similar swing from optimistic commitment to utter disillusion, will often have a sense of déjà vu. But it is the themes and attitudes that will seem overfamiliar, not the mode of presentation. What Lessing set herself to do, she tells us in her preface to a new edition (1972) of *The Golden Notebook*—and the statement applies equally well to the *Children of Violence* novels—was "to give the ideological 'feel' of our mid-century," and it is hard to think of any other English novelist who has matched her achievement in this respect. Dated such work must be, as her preface concedes, for "'Marxism' and its various offshoots have fermented ideas everywhere, and so fast and energetically that, once 'way out,' it has already been absorbed, has become part of ordinary thinking." Later in the preface she makes the point that takes us to the heart of her political concern: "I think it is possible that Marxism was the first attempt, for our time, outside formal religions, at a world-mind, a world ethic." This was its appeal to her, as it was to the six famous contributors to *The God That Failed,*[1] and to millions without a name.

Her search for "a world ethic" did not end with the recognition that the Marxist dream had turned into a nightmare; unlike many disenchanted writers, at no time had she compromised her artistic integrity in the service of a narrow creed. In her contribution to *Declaration,* "The Small Personal Voice," she justly attacked critics for failing to see that the theme of *Children of Violence* was "a study of the individual conscience in its relations with the collective." The Marxist word "collective" should not mislead: the unity she seeks is older than any political dogma and is the goal of the questing artist, not the politician. She looks back in *Declaration* to the great realists, praising their "humanity" and "love of people"—Leo Tolstoy, Honoré de Balzac, Feodor Dostoevsky, Stendhal—and names Thomas Mann as the last of those whose work was capable of "strengthening a vision of a good which may defeat the evil" (today she would surely add Alexander Solzhenitsyn). It may be noted that these names are all European; there is, partially excepting D. H. Lawrence, little precedent in English fiction for the kind of visionary sweep over society, evoked in numerous individual lives, that she aims at. Comparing the English novelists of the 1950's, she criticizes their parochialism; the anti-heroes of John Wain and John Braine are "petty" (her own heroine, Martha, feels alienation but fights it). She accuses the more seriously influential work of Albert Camus, Jean-Paul Sartre, Jean Genet, and Samuel Beckett of a "tired pity," "emotional anarchy," and indulgence in "the pleasurable luxury of despair." Her positive claim for the novelist, on the face of it modest, in fact asks as much of him as can be hoped: "In an age of committee art, public art, people may begin to feel again a need for the small personal voice; and this will feed confidence into writers and, with confidence because of the knowledge of being needed, the warmth and humanity and love of people which is essential for a great age of literature." More recent developments beyond this humanistic attitude will be discussed in the latter parts of this essay, but it remains central to her view of the writer's value, as is shown

[1] *The God That Failed: Six Studies in Communism,* by Arthur Koestler, Ignazio Silone, André Gide, Richard Wright, Louis Fischer, and Stephen Spender, edited by Richard Crossman, 1950.

in her lectures of thirty years later, *Prisons We Choose to Live Inside* (1986).

THE GRASS IS SINGING *AND OTHER AFRICAN STORIES*

WHEN it appeared in 1950, *The Grass Is Singing* at once joined the company of *Heart of Darkness, Mister Johnson,* and *Cry, the Beloved Country* as one of the few profound explorations of the tragedy of the white man's presence in Africa. Lessing's characteristic strength was already refined and matured. Though the subject cries out for the liberal's moral indignation, her narrative is controlled throughout. There is commentary, but we are so completely immersed in the inward study of a claustrophobic "double solitude" ("The world was small, shut in a room of heat and haze and light") that it never obtrudes. It is restricted to the barest details, and seldom does Lessing even allow herself irony; the story could speak for itself.

The epigraphs from *The Waste Land* and the "Author Unknown" point at the novel's double purpose: to show the true nature of "white civilization" in settled Africa and to write a parable of the coming overthrow of white oppression by black force. To achieve these aims Lessing took the clichés of white supremacy, especially that of white infallibility, and exposed them to the implicit judgment of fallible lives. The whites can survive only so long as the fiction of infallibility sustains them, as Charlie Slatter and the Police Sergeant realize when they seek to cover up the Turners' weakness.

The Turners, neither pioneers nor Boer trekkers, represent the commonplace middle of any class or color; lacking "guts," they find no prop in belonging to a superior race, but above all they are cursed with fatal weaknesses of temperament. This stems from lives that have taught them a fear of insecurity and a hopeless dependence; they are temperamentally unsuited to either enter the settlers' enclave or relieve each other's loneliness. Yet they must make a pretense of strength—Mary in her fatalistic "struggle" with her servants, Dick in imposing his will on both native and fickle land. Their shared tragedy shows them all too human: Dick lacks the absoluteness of a Charlie Slatter, who "like the natives he despised" recklessly rapes the land, bullies his "niggers," and passes on, seeing in Africa no abiding home. Mary and Dick, though conditioned to acceptance of their white role, are nevertheless sensitives, dreamers whom the system cannot afford. In portraying them Lessing evokes a sympathy with which we can see them beyond the stereotype of oppressors as victims themselves—pitiably failing to live up to the inhuman image their race has created. We pity Dick, nursing his grove of young gum trees, his tribute to the land, or clutching a handful of the soil he must forsake. Mary, too, is pitiable; for her hot Africa has been the perpetual antagonist, yet the same country can offer every cool June, as it does on her last morning, a glimpse of delusory peace, even a transcendent vision: "as if she were holding that immensely pitiful thing, the farm with its inhabitants, in the hollow of her hand."

The Grass Is Singing, tracing every stumbling step of this couple's fated life together, builds up an almost intolerable tension like their own. We inhabit with them the heat-choked house, watch Moses, the epitome of black force, loom through Mary's eyes, feel how the bush bars escape and only waits to complete the final violation, when bush and native merge in her "last thought." Mary's obsession with Moses, which lesser novelists would have vulgarized, develops as in a dream; she herself never understands it. Ironically, it is with an inferior native that Mary is forced for the first time in her life—with white or black—into "the personal relation." "It was like a nightmare where one is powerless against horror: the touch of this black man's hand on her shoulder filled her with nausea; she had never, not once in her whole life, touched the flesh of a native." What does Moses feel? Jealousy, clearly, of the new white assistant who stands between him and Mary, but at the end Lessing retires, like Joseph Conrad in his Malayan stories—though without Conrad's rhetoric—from the incomprehensible: "what thoughts of regret, or pity, or perhaps even wounded human affection were compounded with the satisfaction of his completed revenge, it is impossible to say."

The Grass Is Singing was soon followed by Lessing's first collection of short stories with an African setting, *This Was the Old Chief's Country* (1951), *Martha Quest* (1952), and *Five* (1953)—five novellas, of which four are set in Africa. (*Martha Quest,* the first volume of *Children of Violence,* will be discussed later.) The early African stories and novellas were in 1964 combined with other stories published or written up until 1963 to form a collection of thirty pieces entitled *African Stories* (reprinted in two volumes in 1973).

In a preface to *African Stories* Doris Lessing recalls that her first two books "were described by reviewers as about the colour problem . . . which is not how I see, or saw, them." The reviewers' bias was, of course, symptomatic of what was in the early 1950's an awakening interest in the problem. Her deeper concern, already evident in the compassionate handling of her first novel, was with the *human* problem: "colour prejudice is not our original fault, but only one aspect of the atrophy of the imagination that prevents us from seeing ourselves in every creature that breathes under the sun." This perception is reinforced by her vision of "Africa which gives you the knowledge that man is a small creature, among other creatures, in a large landscape." This attitude infused her work from the beginning; only once does a narrow didacticism limit her achievement, in the long story from *Five* entitled "Hunger," a failure, as she recognizes in the preface, because she deliberately set out to write a story of social purpose. Although she is convincing in her attempt to bring us close to Jabavu's experience from primitive hut to city shebeen, the story as a whole conforms to the "Joe comes to Jo'burg" morality tale, of the native "child's" corruption by the evil white city. Ironically, perhaps because of its very predictability, "Hunger" has been, she thinks, "the most liked."

Another reason why "Hunger" may seem to fail is the reader's inevitable doubt about the authenticity of the white writer's adoption of the African's viewpoint. Nowhere else, if one excepts so universally intelligible a story of sexual jealousy as "The Pig," does Lessing attempt this. As with Moses in *The Grass Is Singing,* she confines herself to what she has observed and, within plausible limits, imagined. Her main business is with the white settlers she knows best; in portraying their lives she inevitably includes, but does not concentrate upon, racial problems.

In fact two-thirds of the African stories are about the personal lives of the white settlers, with the natives in the background. Lessing refuses to limit herself to the doctrinaire viewpoint that because the monstrous shadow of the racial conflict blots out the African sun, it is impossible to write on any other topic or to treat the white oppressor as an ordinary human being. In Africa, as elsewhere, ordinary people are preoccupied with their own loves, ambitions, and dreams: great sensitivity in these areas may lie side by side with an indifference, conditioned from infancy, to the quality of the lives of those considered "inferior." (Consider the irrelevance of the relatively modern concept of "social conscience" to our response to the novels of Jane Austen and much of the work of Henry James and even George Eliot.) Few can become heroes or self-sacrificing martyrs in any condition of life—and few indeed can be masters of their own lives. The pathetic, sometimes moving, ordinariness of the supreme race is one of the abiding impressions these stories leave; in their fears and insufficiency they are simply and vulnerably human. This is brought out in a wide range of subtle studies: "Eldorado," where the possessed dreamer represents those hundreds who fail for every one who succeeds in converting the far country into the material stuff of dreams; "Old John's Place" and "Getting Off the Altitude," in which the child's unblinking eye searches out the shabbiness of adult lives behind the prosperous, full-living face; "Lucy Grange" and "Winter in July," taut studies of the emotional cost to those numerous lonely women sacrificed to the obsessed settlers' lust for the land; and, at a lower social level, we meet in "A Road to the Big City" the white counterparts of Jabavu, no less than he prey to a cruelly deceptive dream.

That loose political category, "white," is broken down under the novelist's eye into a spectrum of shades of opposition and difference. Two of her most complex renderings of this awareness are "The Second Hut" and "The De Wets Come to Kloof Grange." We find in these not only the traditional antagonism between Englishman and Afrikaner but a deep exploration of the pathetic inner lives of people struggling, as all do, to build themselves a secure world to live in. There are no simple contrasts. In "The Second Hut" the English pair and the Afrikaners alike are struggling to cling to the last shreds of dignity and what they call life in an Africa—natural as well as human—bent on expelling them. Although the Van Heerdens, living "native," obviously have the greater capacity for survival, for both pairs of white intruders the country offers only an ironic promise and fertility and a passage to a further "grey country of poverty." In both this story and "The De Wets Come to Kloof Grange," as in so much of the African writing, the isolated women attract strongest feeling. Major Carruthers' wife takes to her bed, while Major Gale's has built a more soothing, but nonetheless fragile, retreat in her eighteenth-century English room and tamed two acres of garden—"she had learned to love her isolation." Upon this intrudes the unwanted presence of the new Afrikaner overseer's young wife, Betty, bringing with her the passion and disquiet Mrs. Gale has long since shed. She brings, too, a disturbing affinity for the Africa beyond the English garden, for the river in the "green-crowded gully," with its "intoxicating heady smell": this Mrs. Gale has learned to ignore, raising her gaze to "*her* hills," but to the brash girl it is "a lovely smell" and she walks alone through the bush to seek it rather than Mrs. Gale's reluctant companionship. Just as Van Heerden's wife in "The Second Hut" finds content in her droves of children: it is they who collaborate, however crudely, with "Africa," while the finer whites pale behind their gentlemanly ideal. Mrs. Gale glimpses this truth when, after Betty has pretended to run away, she "hated her garden, that highly-cultivated patch of luxuriant growth, stuck in the middle of a country that could do this sort of thing to you so suddenly"; but when she learns the girl's flight was faked, a provoking demand for her husband's love, she rejects her insight and labels it "savage." In such stories Lessing is as powerful as Lawrence, blending revelation of her characters' inner lives with an intense evocation of setting and atmosphere to expose simultaneously the flaws in both character and society.

Where Lessing does write explicitly of the "color problem," what interests her most is not the crass exercise of white power, but the complex predicament of the "good" white. Excellent examples are "Little Tembi," "No Witchcraft for Sale," and the ironic novella from *Five,* "A Home for the Highland Cattle." "Little Tembi" explores the pathetic outcome of a well-intentioned white mistress' nursing of a sick African boy, who later develops so jealous a dependence upon her affection that he turns into a petty criminal, stealing to gain attention. It brings out with moving irony the risk involved in the stock attitude the Jane McClusters adopt when they approach the native sympathetically—"They are just like children, and appreciate what you do for them." In "No Witchcraft for Sale," as in "Little Tembi," the good mistress' humane treatment of her cook is at bottom dangerously self-gratifying—"she was fond of the old cook because of his love for her child." The cook, a "mission boy," collaborates in his mistress' comfortable view of the white-black relation as "God's will." When a tree-snake spits in the little baas's eye, Gideon heals it with a mysterious root from the bush, but afterward, when the whites want him to lead them to where it can be found, he hoodwinks them. It remains Gideon's secret, "the black man's heritage," which lies deep below the white man's shallow possession of the land. Gideon has the last, unconsciously ironic word: "Ah, Little Yellow Head, how you have grown! Soon you will be grown up with a farm of your own."

Lessing's most sustained ironic treatment of the dilemma of the newer-minted white liberal is "A Home for the Highland Cattle." Marina Giles

> was that liberally-minded person produced so plentifully in England during the thirties . . . somewhere in the back of Marina's mind had been a vision of herself and Philip living in a group of amiable people, pleasantly interested in the arts, who read the *New Statesman* week by week, and hold that discreditable phenomena like the colour-bar and the black-white struggle could be solved by sufficient goodwill . . . a delightful picture.

It all comes down to something more basic—the servant problem, dear to our Victorian forebears, but which nowadays one goes abroad to encounter. While Philip, her agriculturist husband, pursues the African's well-being in his practical, worthwhile way, Marina struggles in their semidetached box at 138 Cecil Rhodes Vista (wicked name) to practice human equality upon her "boy," Charlie. From the beginning Charlie is groping to comprehend this new variety of "madam," and clearly it will not be long before he takes advantage of her weakness.

As a central serio-comic symbol, Lessing has chosen one of those Victorian pictures of highland cattle ("Really, why bother to emigrate?"), left in Marina's keeping by Mrs. Skinner, her landlady. Marina, naturally, abhors it, but Charlie seems to admire it—an admiration dimly connected, she supposes, with the part played by cattle in tribal life "that could only be described as religious." This part is the use of cattle as *lobola,* or bride-price, now as shown in this story in a pathetic state of decay. Gradually, Marina works herself into a false position: her attempts to treat Charlie more humanely "spoil" him; she becomes so embroiled in his personal life that she lands in the ancient role of white paternalist, with the African as foolish child. Her attempt to get him married to Theresa, his pregnant girlfriend, brings the picture into play. Thinking it valuable, Charlie has the bright idea of presenting it to Theresa's father in lieu of *lobola;* and Marina, betraying her white integrity, agrees to give it to him. She and Philip drive the pair and the picture out to the wretched location where the father lives, only to receive from the broken-down old man a nostalgic homily on the degeneration of the old ritual and courtesies. Nevertheless, he accepts the picture. Philip and Marina drive back, grim but little wiser, leaving the couple unbeknown to them to celebrate in an illicit liquor den.

The sequel is no less sordid. When Mrs. Skinner gets an inkling on her return what those "white kaffirs" have done with her precious picture, she has no difficulty in getting Charlie arrested for stealing a few worthless objects, including a "wooden door-knocker that said *Welcome Friend.*" Later Marina, by now a truly colonial madam in a smarter suburb, passes a file of handcuffed prisoners in a street "in this city of what used to be known as the Dark Continent," thinks she recognizes Charlie among them but, intent on discovering that "ideal table" at once, dismisses the thought. Her well-intentioned but amateurish meddling has caused both his misfortune (although he accepts it with easy philosophy) and her tired indifference. In this story, exercising a light but firm ironic control comparable to E. M. Forster's in *A Passage to India,* Lessing has, like that earlier analyst of the inner contradictions of imperialism, subtly exposed the perils of liberal efforts at "connection," if unsupported by extraordinary character and intelligence.

Marina is a "liberal" outsider; if she utterly fails, what more can be expected of those who grow up conditioned to acceptance of the system? We glimpse in "No Witchcraft for Sale" how the white child is formed to rule; he is unlikely ever to begin to imagine affinity with the native. More deeply, "The Old Chief Mshlanga" exposes through the eyes of a sensitive, solitary girl, who has herself never known any home but Africa, the ignorant assumptions that perpetuate master racism. It is an intense moment of wakening for her to realize that "this was the Old Chief's Country" and a painful stage in her maturing to recognize her inherited guilt for dispossessing him. The child's-eye view provides a naive naturalness of response and a strong focus of values; its advantages are most fully explored in "The Antheap," from *Five.* At its center is a sensitive white child, Tommy Clarke, who questions the double standard he is expected to live by as he grows older; forbidden to play with "a lot of dirty kaffirs . . . now you're a big boy," he feels something vital is lost and "wept bitterly, for he was alone." While his father's boss, Macintosh, grubs a fortune from the antheap, Tommy forms substitute playmates from clay and gives them names—a striking contrast in the exploitation of the African earth. One figure Tommy names Dirk —after a "kaffir" boy whose lighter color intrigues him. It is fitting that Dirk should be one of Macintosh's half-caste children: as the illicit bond between these boys strengthens, through their hard-won friendship Lessing is naming the price that the Macintoshes of Africa should be made to pay for their reckless abuse of the land and its people. The forced union between the two worlds has produced that most tragic being, the "colored," accepted by neither; he is in the flesh inextinguishable witness to the whites' double standard. In tracing the boys' love-hate relationship through the years and the baffled response of old Macintosh, Lessing concentrates on the play of emotion among groping, passionate people, letting our sense of the "problem" emerge without insistence. The boys' "victory" is equivocal: "now they had to begin again, in the long and difficult struggle to understand what they had won and how they would use it."

"The Antheap" is the one story in which connection is really achieved, and then it is between white and colored, not white and black—in the circumstances the only probable connection. Elsewhere, the most that can be hoped for is a fair give-and-take in the master-servant relationship, such as exists in " 'Leopard' George" until the white master blunders ignorantly through his favorite African's sensibilities. And, ultimately, through his own: for that "undeveloped heart" (E. M. Forster's phrase) is tragically immature, slow to grasp connections, not nonexistent. In a story similar in theme to " 'Leopard' George" but more strongly dramatized, "The Black Madonna," Lessing uses in a way reminiscent of Forster the Italian artist Michele to point to the want of "heart" in "a tough, sunburnt, virile, positive country contemptuous of subtleties and sensibility." In her portrayal of the Captain we see how the double standard divides mind and heart against each other: "You can't have a black Madonna," the Captain protests, seeing no contradiction in his assumption that you *can* have a black mistress, his "bushwife" Nadya. "Black peasant Madonna for black country," answers Michele simply. Under the skin the Captain senses the true meaning of this—in human as in spiritual love—but fears to let it out. So it remains at the end; Michele, like Forster's Italians, is potentially a liberating agent, but the offer is declined. The Captain, when Michele visits him in hospital, refuses to accept the picture of the black girl, but, when the white-haired Italian leaves, turns his face to the wall and silently weeps. After an acid beginning, "The Black Madonna" develops into one of Lessing's most compassionate portrayals of the white man's tragedy. The necessity to maintain an impregnable front before "the lesser breeds," the male drive needed to "tame" the land, must warp the personal life at its deepest levels.

Together, *The Grass Is Singing* and *African Stories* provide a complex inner portrait of an anachronistic society, which has failed to adjust to the pace of change; they make us see and feel that it consists of people little different from ourselves, who demand understanding, even sympathy, as well as judgment. This can surely be more deeply felt by English readers today in what has itself become, since Lessing's African writing first appeared, a multiracial society.

CHILDREN OF VIOLENCE

THE *Children of Violence* quintet (1952–1969) takes us from an African experience as remote and closed as that of Schreiner's *The Story of an African Farm* through layer upon layer of Anglo-colonial society, out of Africa altogether to London, where Lessing's heroine's life closes in again, a life of rooms, flats, decaying claustrophobic houses, in each phase deepening the study of "the individual conscience in its relation with the collective." Lessing's narrative owes nothing to structural experimentation and supplies little debatable symbolism. As her heroine's Bunyanesque name, Martha Quest, and the title of the series suggest, she does not mask her intentions. Several modern novelists, following Marcel Proust, have used the novel sequence, centering upon one character's experience but giving a detailed impression of movement through time. In English we think of Ford Madox Ford, Evelyn Waugh, Joyce Cary, Anthony Powell, Lawrence Durrell, C. P. Snow; and the form continues in Edward Upward's political trilogy and the work of younger novelists such as Frederic Raphael. How can we distinguish Doris Lessing's series from these? Most obviously, for its African subject matter, as a narrative of the never-to-be-repeated experience of growing up in an isolated white settlers' enclave and striving, like Schreiner's Lyndall in the nineteenth century, to move outward into a world of fuller experience and wider values. Second, in centering upon a woman's experience, to a degree unmatched in intensity since Virginia Woolf. Further, while "feminist" would be a less dubious label to attach to Lessing than Woolf, her fiction stands in a *critical* relation to the question of the position of women and is no mere instrument of it. The sequence is also (like Cary's and Upward's) one of those rare works that treat politics seriously, without reducing the characters to puppets.

All these aspects except the political (initially relatively slight) combine in the strong first volume, *Martha Quest* (1952), which covers the period from Martha's critical awakening in adolescence to her first marriage. The opening pages indicate the major themes and sketch Martha's heavy consciousness of herself—derived from books—in relation to them and the spirit of her time:

> She was adolescent, and therefore bound to be unhappy; British, and therefore uneasy and defensive; in the fourth decade of the twentieth century, and therefore inescapably beset with problems of race and class; female, and obliged to repudiate the shackled women of the past.

We watch her seeking to thrust outward away from her parents' "ironic mutual pity" and her father's "dream-locked" existence, but see that she is —as so many of Lessing's protagonists will be—a dreamer too, and will have a hard journey toward her "noble city" where there is "no hatred or violence"; the traditional symbol of the ideal city lives in Martha's imagination until her death, and provides the binding symbol of the series (discussed at length in this author's "Martha's Utopian Quest," *Commonwealth,* 1972). While lucidly defining Martha's typical dilemma, Lessing nevertheless gives us a complex awareness of the "many selves" Martha must choose from in her individual effort to take "the responsibility of being one person, alone," together with a sympathetic insight into the baffled lives of those who surround her. Although she sees the colony as in "a sickness of dissolution," Martha, a child of her time and place, is infected herself. One self is drawn to the false unity, the "system of shared emotion," of the Club—this is the modern girl who "knew everything was allowable"; another, deeper self responds to individuals whom she sees as trying like herself to forget a painful separateness. Hence the shameful affair with the despised Jew, Adolph King, and her marriage out of tenderness and a willed conviction of a shared aspiration to freedom to Douglas Knowell. Yet beneath all is a deeper self:

> the gift of her solitary childhood on the veld; that knowledge of something painful and ecstatic, something central and fixed, but flowing . . . a sense of movement, of separate things interacting and finally becoming one, but greater—it was this which was her lodestone, even her conscience.
>
> (pt. 4, ch. 1)

This description of Martha's "individual conscience" is reinforced more strongly in this than in the later books by Lessing's passionate recollection of the body of Africa; it links her heroine with the romantic impulse of aspiration toward a cosmic unity beyond the reach of any political or social idea—a link we may lose sight of as the series progresses but which the final novel confirms and carries forward.

Of the first four novels, *Martha Quest* leaves the most rounded impression: we see Martha's restless development against the permanent reality of her spiritual Africa; African setting and atmosphere are dense, suggesting a true point of departure and potential return. The next three novels trace her erratic movement through flawed relationships in the makeshift colonial capital toward the desired but distant establishment of herself as a "free spirit"—in which attempt, despite her modern advantages, she is hardly less hampered by convention and conformity than are George Eliot's Dorothea or James's Isabel Archer. Disenchantment with the suburban "bourgeois" marriage, which threatens to reduce her to wifely dependence, has become a stock theme now, but it was not so in the 1950's. *A Proper Marriage* (1954) remains distinguished for its calm characterization and objective analysis of a subject too often treated by later writers with feminist indignation; we see that Douglas, no less than Martha, is the victim in this dishonest marriage, and both are guilty. (Lessing is no bigoted feminist in her portrayals of men: see in *The Habit of Loving* [1957] "The Witness" and "He," and in *A Man and Two Women* [1963] the title story, and even "One Off the Short List" with its distasteful compulsive seducer.)

At the end of the second novel Martha has shed husband and daughter and temporarily, at least, substitutes for the failed personal relationship attachment to the "collective," influenced by the young Communists in the Royal Air Force, a new and utterly alien element in Zambesia. Although she has a brief, happy affair with one of them, *A Ripple from the Storm* (1958) mainly explores the ramifications of love for "the people," which for Martha may also be seen as an outlet for her romantic "passion for the absolute" (to quote the novel's epigraph from Louis Aragon). As such, it is destined for disillusion. Unlike mid-1930's Europe, the colony offers the tiny Communist group no footing in the "mass"; it is cut off from its natural base among the Africans by their ignorance and suspicion. Repeating recent European history, the group forms a reluctant alliance with the Social Democrats and becomes fragmented, but it is the flaws of its members that Lessing brings out so shrewdly. She shows how political purism may betray individual weakness and, in practice, destroy the individual it pretends to serve. Even Anton Hesse, who may be termed Martha's ideological second husband, a German who has suffered for his Marxist beliefs, becomes insidiously seduced by bourgeois "furniture." Only Athen, the doomed Greek, who is presented sympathetically but unsentimentally, possesses a felt, unselfish Communism. Futility is the mood of *A Ripple from the Storm,* and it will repel readers who crave romance with their politics (which would have been a fictional combination indeed for that place and time); but since neo-Marxist revolutionism continues to sacrifice the individua to a "collective" absolutism, it remains a valuable cautionary tale.

While the political theme continues in *Landlocked* (1965), which covers the late 1940's, it is felt increasingly as mere background to Martha's revitalized emotional life. This novel is the least satisfying of the series, largely because of its very success in reflecting through a fragmented narrative the tedium and frustration, the truly "landlocked" condition of the reactionary colonial backwater. The old political scene is dissolving and new African radicals and white extremists are taking over, but Martha has discovered love and "from this centre she now lived." Her love for Thomas Stern, the Polish Jewish peasant, snatched at intervals in the loft at the foot of his brother's garden, is insulated from the world of argument at first and reaches a lyrical intensity; it is the most obviously "Lawrentian" episode in her work. It cannot last: Thomas, a child of violence, goes to Israel to fight for the Promised Land and when he returns is utterly changed. After his death, of blackwater fever, caught in an equivocal Kurtz-like involvement with tribal Africans, Martha has no reason to remain; her father dies too, so ending a chapter in the "quicksand" of Martha's irritable, compassionate embroilment with her parents, which is tenderly drawn throughout the series. Martha now yearns toward the liberating sea, and beyond it England—the traditional bourne of the "free spirit." Africa has shrunk to a backdrop of arid immensity; Zambesia is abandoned to the "enemy," the racist settler Sergeant Tressell.

The title of *The Four-Gated City* (1969), the final volume in the series, harks back to Martha's youthful vision of a utopian city upon the veld (suggestive in shape of Campanella's fifteenth-century utopian republic, City of the Sun—though this was unknown to Lessing), but, though Africa reappears in the prophetic appendix as a refuge from nuclear holocaust, London is the novel's city.

At first it is shabby postwar London, physically and psychically desolate. There, inevitably, Martha seeks the working class, the mythical "proletariat" Africa denied; she finds them warm but depressing, no ideal beings (a realization *In Pursuit of the English* had already expressed, more lightly, in 1960). Martha's renewed quest is neither political nor sexual in emphasis: neither can "create" her now; more active and independent than before, she embarks on inward self-exploration, now clearly her chief concern. Yet at the same time her life at the center of the distraught, liberal Coldridge household is a focus of widening responsibility toward and understanding of others, not an engrossment with self. There are no absolutes now, individually or collectively. The novel's great length is justified by its intensive exploration of the most complex and vital experience. Particularly impressive are the portrayals of "this remarkable traffic between parents and children," in both Martha's last painful confrontation with her mother and the conflict between the adults and the questioning youth of the 1960's, and the tracing of Martha's anguished inner probing whose pace is set for her by Mark Coldridge's "mad" wife, Lynda. Not since Virginia Woolf has an English novelist explored so thoroughly the labyrinth of the strained sensitive mind, or pleaded so strongly for a more enlightened science of the mind than a dogmatic psychiatry provides. In this area Martha's individual conscience reaches out toward a deeper connection with the needs of the "collective" than any abstract cause could offer, probing "this strange disease of modern life" (Matthew Arnold's phrase) at its root. We may be unable to share Martha's newfound hope in extrasensory powers or Lessing's prophetic vision of the survival, after atomic devastation, of a scattering of "new children" with an inborn telepathic capacity to "see" and "hear" more finely: "grown up . . . mentally and emotionally . . . they are beings who include that history [of this century] in themselves and who have transcended it." To them the dying Martha consigns the guardianship of the "four-gated city" some future race will build. The climax offers as the only hope a faith in evolutionism derived, in Lessing's version, not from positive Darwinism but (as several of the novel's epigraphs indicate) from her study of Sufism[2] in the writings of Idries Shah. However skeptically one views this "solution"—Shah too closely resembles the Shaw of *Back to Methusaleh*—*The Four-Gated City* is an admirable attempt to "strengthen a vision of a good," to make us see and feel how we do and should live now and here. When it appeared, it seemed likely to become her most influential work, but fascination with break-

[2]Sufism is an Islamic form of mystical monism; in recent years it has had, like Hindu mysticism, a growing appeal in the West. See A. J. Arberry, *Sufism,* 1950, and Idries Shah, *The Way of the Sufi,* 1968.

down as "higher sanity" has cooled: it seems more likely that *The Golden Notebook* will stand as her major novel.

THE GOLDEN NOTEBOOK

UNTIL *The Four-Gated City* appeared, *The Golden Notebook* (1962) had stood for several years as Lessing's most ambitious work. It may remain her best known; the interest it has aroused as one of *the* novels of our time was marked by its reissue in a hardback edition with a lengthy author's preface in 1972.

In this preface she states that her intention was to follow the great European—not English—novelists of the last century in producing a comprehensive work "describing the intellectual and moral climate" of her time, not to produce (as weekly critics eagerly assumed) a feminist broadside. She had already demanded in her *Declaration* essay, "*Why* should the sex war be offered as a serious substitute for social struggle?" She aspired instead to meet the need for the more varied view of the human condition such as a Tolstoy or a Stendhal could provide. *The Golden Notebook,* with a writer now as protagonist, is about this need and how hard it is in our time for the novelist to meet it. The action is a purgative process that may—or may not —fit Anna to convey "a vision of a good."

Being a "free woman" is certainly a strong twin theme—and the more general one; it is "the disease of women in our time," especially for those who like Anna attempt to "live the kind of life women never lived before." But this is inseparable from the universal theme of the individual's isolation: in a world that supplies no dependable values, Anna, like Martha Quest, must make her life as she goes along, or be torn and fragmented by it. Like many people, she knows "I'm scared of being alone in what I feel" and fears emotion in a hostile world, but as an artist, "driven to experience as many different things as possible," she has to face the question of responsibility. If literature is concerned with the self, it is also concerned with self-control: in the beginning Anna cannot write because she fears spreading her feelings of "disgust and futility" (contrast the contemporary anti-hero's indulged alienation); by the end she has learned to "live through" her divided selves, "naming" the horrors. This, for a writer, is also her duty. We do not see Anna's predicament as separate from her society, its ideals and failures; she does reflect these, the frustration and sterility of "living like this" without "a central philosophy," but, forced like Martha to accept the fading of the Marxist dream, she seeks a new center.

Her search is reflected in the book's unusual structure, which despite its bulk is no Victorian "baggy monster" or rag-bag of writer's scraps. There is ample precedent for dislocated narrative in such modern novelists as André Gide (*Les Faux-Monnayeurs* also includes a novelist as a character writing a novel about his experience within the novel), Woolf, James Joyce, Aldous Huxley and, more recently, in the *nouveau roman.* In *The Golden Notebook* the discontinuity reflects not only the novelist's viewpoint but the lack of unity in Anna's life and life as she sees it: hence her writer's block. By means of the Notebooks Anna "divided herself into four" to avoid facing up to the chaos; in one, the Blue, she tries to be honest, and this especially is in the end superseded by the Golden, *all of me in one book.*

The Notebooks punctuate installments of a conventional novel entitled "Free Women," in which Anna herself is a character, using experience in the Notebooks selectively. If "literature is analysis after the event," the Notebooks represent event, "Free Women" the literature or fiction. If we read the Notebooks, then the novel, in that order, we would see how Anna, the unblocked writer of "Free Women," is using her fragmented experience recorded in the Notebooks, compelling it into a *positive* whole, with control, not raw subjectivity. The African material of the Black Notebook that she cannot "use," though it describes some of her most deeply felt experience, disappears. At the center of "Free Women" is the Richard-Tommy-Marion triangle, from which, in the Notebooks, Anna appears excessively detached. The Notebooks are used in Anna's novel as a crucial factor behind Tommy's suicide attempt—absent from the "real," but central in the fiction: thus Tommy becomes Anna's surrogate, he goes through the experience she evaded. After his blinding, Molly comments with tragic irony, "he's all in one piece for the first time in his life." The suicide motif had already been approached by Ella in the Yellow Notebook "novel," but as a fictional projection of her own despair; in placing the Notebooks as a power for evil in "Free Women," Anna is accepting moral responsibility for them.

Previously in the Yellow Notebook we have seen Anna trying to fictionalize her experience, making Ella a simplified, more coherent version of herself. Ella is "not interested in politics"—all the Red material, Anna's albatross, is cast off. In this Notebook occur anticipations of themes that will be converted to positive use in the more integrated Golden Notebook: for example, Paul's image denoting his split attitude to his profession when he tells Ella, "We are the boulder-pushers . . . we are the failures" recurs in an almost identical passage in which Anna envisions Paul and Michael merged in a single heroic figure who reassures her, "But my dear Anna, we are *not* the failures we think we are"—the boulder-pushers are needed by the prophets at the summit; finally, Anna can tell Saul that they are both boulder-pushers, and in doing so implicitly accepts for herself the attitude of Mathlong, the African nationalist, described in the Blue Notebook: "He was the man who performed actions, played roles, that he believed to be necessary for the good of others, even while he preserved an ironic doubt about the results of his actions . . . this particular kind of detachment was something we needed very badly at this time."

Anna has been blocked as a writer because excessive self-concern has distorted her vision. Parallel with this theme is her struggle toward a fulfilled love, to achieve which she must recognize, as in the artistic sphere, that she cannot "force patterns of happiness or simple life." In the Yellow Notebook the story Ella must write, of "a man and a woman . . . at the end of their tether . . . cracking up because of a deliberate attempt to transcend their own limits," yet winning "a new kind of strength," foreshadows the "acceptance" born of Anna and Saul's stormy relationship, the subject of the unified Golden Notebook. Although the devils that dominate the first page of the Black Notebook are exorcized on the first of the Golden, this is almost the latter's solitary indication of "happiness." This, Anna notes, is left out, and we are caught up in the violently fluctuating emotions of two people seeking transcendence, breaking each other down, yet building out of mutual self-recognition a new acceptance and control. This is reflected in the reduction of ninety emotional pages of the Golden Notebook to barely ten in the Milt episode of "Free Women": the Anna there, like Ella, is more "intelligent"; Milt, like Saul, can "name" her and she him. They part to write the works they inscribe to each other, to push their boulders as best they can; Anna (with some irony?) also to take up marriage welfare work.

If we see "Free Women," as these comments suggest, as representing Anna's positive reshaping of her experience, we are bound to ask how good a novel it is. Could it stand alone? It is doubtful whether this is a very useful question: we do not read it alone, but as a skeletal piece of fiction whose flesh in "life" the Notebooks provide. They flesh in the depth and complexity of Anna's experience—most strongly evoked in many passages, especially the African Mashopi episodes, which the selective, conventionally shaped novel omits. *The Golden Notebook* must be judged as a whole, whose aim is to explore the plight of the socially responsive and responsible writer in the phase of disorientation and alienation in which we live. The fact that it also explores in depth the dilemma of the "free women," woman's most intimate experience (as in the clinically faithful description of Anna's day, 17 September 1954), is incidental though indispensable to this theme. Lessing's "free spirits," no less than those of the Brontës or George Eliot, have to love and be loved: this need creates the muddle that makes them human—and humanity, no single segment abstracted from it, is the novelist's business. The fact that many readers eagerly abstracted from *The Golden Notebook* ammunition to fight their own local battles is symptomatic of the author's succeeding in what she set out to do. Her protagonist as artist is no remote being, but one who has an uncommon responsiveness to common experience; this is recorded with such fidelity that some readers have overlooked Anna Wulf's primary significance *as artist*—if this is lost sight of, it is impossible to respond adequately to the novel's larger meaning.

JOURNEYS WITHIN: BRIEFING FOR A DESCENT INTO HELL; THE SUMMER BEFORE THE DARK; THE MEMOIRS OF A SURVIVOR

The Golden Notebook could be done only once. Having made a statement that throws serious doubt on the value of art, the artist might be expected to fall silent. Nevertheless, Lessing, like her fictional "creature," has continued boulder-pushing. We have already considered *Landlocked* and *The Four-Gated City,* the novels that followed *The Golden Notebook* in the 1960's. In these we can trace an intensifying concern with exploring the mind's frontiers: relatively limited in *Landlocked,* in the episode of Thomas Stern's paranoia and breakdown before death, this becomes central in the inner Golden Notebook, where Anna and Saul break down into each other and form new self-knowing personalities, and in the characterization of Lynda and of Martha's arduous struggle to achieve self-transcendence in *The Four-Gated City.* Looking further back, we can see early indications of this development in the portrayal of the unbalanced Mary in *The Grass Is Singing* and in the fluid presentation of Martha's many selves in the earlier novels of the series. (Outside the novels it is at the heart of the African stories about lonely women and is strongly sustained in later "English" stories such as "To Room Nineteen" in *A Man and Two Women.*) It is not, therefore, surprising that this novelist so often loosely associated with such rationalist obsessions as Marxism and feminism should in 1971 publish *Briefing for a Descent into Hell,* a concentrated study of a middle-aged man's mental breakdown and, reflecting her interest in the ego-extinguishing inward vision of Sufism, his confrontation with the God within.

The descent motif, symbolizing man's perilous exploration of inner space in his search for truth, is, of course, as old as literature. The novel's title points back to the heroic journeys to the Underworld of classical literature; in modern times, the fictional prototype is Dostoevsky's *Notes from the Underground* (1864), followed by variations in Joseph Conrad, Franz Kafka, Samuel Beckett, Albert Camus, and many more. Today, under the ever-increasing evidence of civilized man's tragic self-division, few themes are more compelling for the responsible novelist than the dubious meanings of "sanity" and "normality"; he is strongly supported in this by the work of humanist psychologists such as C. G. Jung and, more recently, Michel Foucault and R. D. Laing.

In *Briefing for a Descent into Hell* Lessing cast as protagonist an outwardly successful and established professor of classics, Charles Watkins. We meet him confined to an observation ward, suffering from amnesia. Under sedation, cut off from the social world that gave him identity, he undergoes an inner voyage of great imaginative richness, exploring both the horrors of his journey and its risks of transcendental illumination. In these dreams the perfect city is threatened (as was Martha's) by Yahoo-like creatures that inherit and—like us—degrade it. From above, borne by a blessed White Bird, he looks down upon a warring Earth exposed beneath the Moon's full light, then undergoes a descent into corruption and possible forgetfulness. Interspersed with these inner searchings are the disconsolate voices of Doctors X and Y, who label his dreams religious paranoia and labor to restore his sense of "reality": their role, like Mother Sugar's in *The Golden Notebook,* is treated critically as undermining in its attempt to explain away individual pain by means of a witchcraft of rationality. To Watkins his dreams form a vision of "Knowing. Harmony. God's law," but he cannot cling to the fable. His doctors probe after his outer identity, recruiting through letters the witness of wife, colleagues, friends. These demonstrate both how little he had liked or communicated with others and throw ironic light upon the idea of "personality." The most significant letter, in Watkins' pocket when he is found, is from Rosemary Baines, a woman who had seen him only once, lecturing in a humdrum local hall, but who was moved by some submerged quality in him. It is this quality, unexplored by his outer self, that his "schizophrenia" offers him a chance to approach—but the ego has its defense. Self-deceivingly, Watkins submits to shock treatment, hoping to "remember properly," but as another intuitive observer, the patient Violet Stoke, fears, it turns out "just that—you are Professor Watkins." "Sanity" triumphs and Watkins, "in possession of his faculties again," writes letters in his turn, disengages himself from Rosemary Baines, and returns to the insincerities of his outer life.

Briefing for a Descent into Hell is no mere casebook (it may be contrasted in this respect with the fragmentary account of the "ten-day voyage" of Jesse Watkins in R. D. Laing's *The Politics of Experience* [1967]). The fabular night journey within is a vividly imagined divided universe in which anarchy and harmony blend, dissolve, and confront each other in dynamic tension. Counterpointed against this are the studied rationalizations of the doctors and the self-entangled prejudices of the "normal." If, compared to previous novels, it seems under-dramatized, this serves the purpose of deepening its protagonist's isolation. It is a novel strong and forceful in both theme and structure, as economical and self-contained as *The Grass Is Singing.* [3]

The Summer Before the Dark (1973) continues the search for the undivided self through a more realistic narrative reminiscent of the early Quest novels, into which is woven an inner motif of dream-discovery. The narrator, who continually interprets the narrative and the protagonist's representative significance, introduces Kate Brown in mid-life, "queen termite" to a family who now need her decreasingly. Confronting "this truth, that the faces and movements of most middle-aged women are those of prisoners or slaves," she senses she must change to meet the cold wind blowing from the future, but—a less individual figure than Martha Quest—she is less apt to choose for herself. During her husband's lengthy absence abroad, she accepts the chance to put her translating ability to work for Global Food, only to become there, as in her family, "tribal mother," a valued organizer of others' lives. She travels to Turkey, then Spain, having drifted involuntarily into an affair with Jeffrey, a thirtyish drop-out who "did not know how he wanted to live." The affair almost comically fails to answer her need: Jeffrey is fretful, restless, yearning after his slipping youth; he falls ill and Kate becomes again the maternal slave. After much patient waiting, she too falls ill, but wills herself back to London and retreat into one of those solitary rooms where Lessing's women confront themselves. Her prolonged illness involves shedding the superficial images of self: "she, Kate Brown, Michael's wife, had allowed herself to be a roundly slim red-head with sympathetic eyes for thirty years." Wasted and unkempt, she achieves, moving into the north-facing room of a basement flat shared with Maureen (another dropout), a potent nullity, free of the sex-shaped cocoon of "other people's recognition of what she had chosen to present." What she is emerging from is pointed at by the dilemma of Maureen's ineffectual escapism, fluctuating between infantile regression, her desire to be herself, or many selves, and a compulsive attraction to rival males in Philip and William, each of whom would impose a "male" order upon her life. Whatever Maureen's choice—if she can choose—it remains uncertain at the novel's close, and Kate scarcely influences it.

The real action of the summer, for Kate, has been her "serial dream" of a stranded seal she must drag through the Arctic waste to the life-restoring sea: "What I think has really been going on," she tells Maureen, "is my dream. It hasn't been all the other things, at all." She feels when her journey is complete in a sun that "seemed to sing" in front of, not behind, her that she has accomplished an act for others, not just herself (the seal she has felt symbolizes her life), but Maureen cannot profit by it: "cages and being shut in are much more my style" (women's lot?). Kate herself can return, strengthened by discovering "the self behind," the capacity to struggle toward self-recognition and survive—to a home that will no longer cage her because she can say, "No: no, no, no, NO—a statement which would be concentrated in her hair." That, untinted now, will image her true stage of life and acceptance of "the dark": aging and death.

The narrative of *The Summer Before the Dark* is tightly controlled, its psychological and psychic meanings constantly pointed: character and action in the literal world are subordinated to the novel's purposeful exploration of midlife crisis. The control excludes the potent threat of schizophrenia in *Briefing,* making a novel that can reach readers at a level closer to the "normal." Kate Brown's apprehension of impending cataclysm at the opening of *The Summer* remains undeveloped but is experienced by her successor (or, more aptly, Martha's), the narrator of *The Memoirs of a Survivor* (1974), a woman living alone who is, significantly, nameless, almost impersonal. Her significance is concentrated not in her "real" life or in the concretely realized action, but in her psychic receptivity and growth.

Marooned in her rooms in a decaying apartment block, in a London through which Kate Brown's cold future wind is blowing, the narrator is witness and interpreter of that breakdown of urban order envisioned in *The Four-Gated City* and *Briefing.* Disorder is no longer elsewhere, "out there": it is in the gangs and migrating bands of the homeless, the slackening powers of government and police, the disintegration of family loyalties and the ethical norms of community. The narrator lives this experience by proxy in the forced growing up of the adolescent Emily, whom a stranger mysteriously leaves with her—together with Hugo, the cat/dog,

[3]This discussion of *Briefing for a Descent into Hell* repeats parts of this author's two reviews of the novel in *Encounter* (September 1971) and *The Journal of Commonwealth Literature* (June 1972).

embodiment of fidelity and fearful intuition, whose fate is at risk throughout. The external action focuses upon Emily; with Gerald, her hero of the pavement life, she struggles to build a center of order, to provide a caring center for the outcast children who are slipping into unrestrained savagery. Like Martha in the Coldridge house, the narrator observes the trials of youth with mingled emotions, an anxious compassion for their efforts pitted against her conviction of their futility against "it"—"above all a consciousness of something ending," beyond human control.

The bizarre internal action is the narrator's: more comprehensively than the serial dream of *The Summer,* it is another world of consciousness she can enter, through and beyond her flat's limiting wall. An extension of the complex self, it is inevitably no ideal world, is like the outer world subject to chaos and destruction; its scenes centering upon the young Emily, loveless and oppressed, image the perverted relations that have always obstructed possibilities of wholeness. Yet it also offers a sustaining vision of plenitude: "Gardens beneath gardens," and a personal "presence . . . as pervasive as the rose scent." As the outer action approaches utter breakdown, Emily, who at fourteen has the disenchanted understanding of a Kate Brown, "the jaded woman of our dead civilization," realizes she can "give" no more. A few survivors huddle in the stricken, almost airless room, then the walls dissolve and the worlds converge: "one person I had been looking for . . . was there," "that One who went ahead showing them the way out of this collapsed little world into another order of world altogether." Clearly, this ending is not realistic: the narrator's history, which records the absorption into the transcendent world of the diverse figures foremost in her consciousness throughout, suggests that the whole narrative—"an attempt at autobiography," according to Lessing's words quoted on the dust-jacket—may be read as occurring within a mind struggling to achieve "integration." One uses a Jungian term, but Lessing's acknowledged bent is toward Sufism, which "says that you cannot approach [it] unless you are able to think that a person quite ordinary in appearance and in life can experience higher states of mind. . . . 'Be in the world, not of it,' is the aim" (*Encounter* [August 1972], p. 62). The narrator and her experience accord with this description; mystical vision is indeed scarcely communicable, but it has one striking element: the maternal or Earth Motherly aspect of the "One" renders as beneficent an image that, in human terms, Lessing's fiction has devalued.

"SPACE FICTION": THE CANOPUS IN ARGOS, ARCHIVES

LESSING prefaces *The Sirian Experiments,* the third volume of the *Archives,* with comments on her intentions and expectations in making her contribution to "this genre of space fiction."[4] Her central concern is shared with that novel's protagonist: "ideas must flow through humanity like tides. Where do they come from?" Her wish, as an imaginative writer, is that "reviewers and readers could see this series . . . as a framework that enables me to tell (I hope) a beguiling tale or two; to put questions, both to myself and to others; to explore ideas and sociological possibilities." As in the Sufi tradition, she (a living "sage") seeks to enlighten by means of teaching-stories whose inner meaning transcends the literal interpretations to which familiar elements may tempt the reader.

The first archive, *Shikasta* (1979), like so much of her earlier work, is a comprehensive diagnosis of our world's condition, but new in its thirty-thousand-year span of vision and the antidote prescribed. Shikasta, "the hurt, the wounded one," put in its humble place in the universal scheme as a colony of Canopus, is viewed compassionately through the eyes of Johor, the Canopean visitor and secret healer. Such, we infer, must be the visionary writer's role—within, yet not of, her human community. Like Johor in the novel, Lessing sees our Earth as in its Last Days, closing a century of destruction; her mission, like his, is to alert a saving remnant who will ensure the continuity and regeneration of life after the apocalypse. The latter part of *Shikasta* enlarges upon and refines the message of the brief appendix to *The Four-Gated City.* It finally banishes her ideal urban vision and points in Old Testament fashion the way back to renewal in desert places.

Those who may have expected Lessing, the Sufi

[4]Not her first: the story "Report on a Threatened City" adopts the viewpoint from outer space, chronicling through progress reports by invisible visitors from another planet our insouciant acceptance of inevitable annihilation (in *The Story of a Non-Marrying Man,* 1972).

convert, to have turned aside from our political and social realities, of which she does despair, will find in the Canopean history of Shikasta an authoritative analysis of modern world history. This stresses exploitation of the globe by "the narrow fringes of the north-west" and the iniquitous class system of the dominant nation, the breaking of its power in the World Wars, to be succeeded by "The Age of Ideology." As in *The Golden Notebook* we find vivid symptomatic histories of individuals (thwarted idealists, oppressed women, perverted terrorists) and an exposition of the significance of the generation gap, updated from *The Four-Gated City.* The indictment of *Shikasta* in the book's mock trial of the offending White Races is historically even-handed: while the "shadow city" of *The Four-Gated City* has now engulfed the Western metropolis, Third World resentments are not flattered. Their skeletons—the homemade slave-trade, or entrenched Indian injustice to untouchables—rattle loudly too.

However, the sweep of vision and the ideas are more telling than the fictional effects. The central figure, Johor, in his guise of George Sherban, the inspiring youth leader, is a kind of holy man, whose influence is in inverse proportion to a capacity for persuasive talking, which the reader must take almost wholly on trust. His goodness and the Sufi mystical sense of oneness beyond our straitened reality—reflected in the SOWF (Substance-of-we-feeling) that has drained away from erring Shikasta—remain incommunicable articles of faith, lacking fictive realization. Goodness, like evil, is not readily communicable: evil is an almost melodramatically present malign force whose agents, the Empire Puttiora and its rogue planet Shammat, so far answer all too readily the stereotypes of conventional science fiction.

The Marriages Between Zones Three, Four and Five (1980) has little or nothing to do with *Shikasta* and is in no way a sequel; this is typical of the series as a whole. In *Shikasta* the three Zones are mentioned in passing by Johor as "lively and for the most part agreeable places, since their inhabitants are those who have worked their way out of and well past the Shikastan drag and pull." What this means is unclear. The Zones are governed, respectively, by a pacific matriarchy (Three), a militaristic, male-dominated hierarchy (Four), and a combative Amazonian queen (Five). The leaders and the ways of life they nurture correspond to certain stereotypes of human personality. The subject matter is ahistorical: government, war, racism, power struggles, and areas of influence are not particularized. Male and female qualities, struggle and compromise, monopolize action.

More than *Shikasta* the narrative "beguiles," with the qualities of fable, legend, and myth. "Anon" might have written it, though with a clearly personal tone that is serene, humorous, tolerant of man's (and woman's) posturings in the search for love and dominance. The central episode, and the main subject of the Zone Three chroniclers' narrative, is the account of the marriage ordained by "The Providers" between Al-Ith, the queen of their Zone—peaceable, paradisiac (man the animals' friend, understanding their language), artistic, and intuitive—and the warrior king, Ben Ata, of Zone Four. Al-Ith, the unifying feminine, labors to soften her boorish husband, who slowly responds to his utmost; their son will rule Zone Three and perhaps combine his parents' best qualities. Ben Ata must subsequently obey a new ordinance to marry the wild and willful queen of Zone Five, where anarchy rules; he eases this difficult union with the deeper understanding Al-Ith has nurtured—while she, believing "we must find out what we are for," withdraws, finally to disappear into Zone Two, the country of higher consciousness few dare explore.

The familiar quest is not this novel's focus: its main action is animated by Lessing's warm and tolerant reexploration of pleasures, pains, and errors by a man and a woman seeking a balanced, understanding union. Masculine and feminine dissolve into a complex, volatile striving; the "sting of otherness" allows no relaxed consummation. The *Marriages* can be relished with the free commitment proper to myth and fable, beyond the pressures of contemporary sexual politics. It is both new and familiar, a distillation of the stuff of myth filtered through a ripened imagination. The Providers, like the traditional gods, impose harsh demands upon or succor their chosen ones; a warrior people chafe restlessly against an inner sense of deprivation, while their hedonistic and sensitive opposites grow "fat and mindless." Both share an unwillingness to attempt the mountains of longing and aspiration; their leaders must undergo the agonies of ascent and descent. Interwoven into this traditional scheme are numerous minor classical echoes, as when a faithful intuitive horse awaits his mistress' return before giving up the ghost. The narrative flows, sweetened with Lessing's mature spirit of concern for human complexities.

The third archive, *The Sirian Experiments: The Report by Ambien II, of the Five* (1981) is an illustrative memoir, composed in exile by Ambien II, a disgraced high colonial administrator and social scientist of the Empire Sirius (an anagram for U.S.S.R.?). She finds herself writing, uncharacteristically, "a history of the heart, rather than of events"—in effect, a narrative of the soul's search for perfection. She shows how her colonial work of social engineering, controlling and conditioning the satellites of the Sirian Empire, had turned under the mysterious compulsion of her encounters with representatives of a higher system, Canopus, into a quest for the ultimate meaning and source of what Sirius "compassionately," yet mechanically, does. Ambien II is well equipped as omniscient narrator to embody Lessing's aims. She is virtually immortal: "We of the superior Sirian mother-stock . . . do not expect to die except from accident or a rare disease." Through Ambien's timeless perception, as both actor and observer, Lessing allows herself the utmost freedom to pursue her manifold quest.

Lessing's quasi-allegorical fictive cosmology embraces legendary, pre-, or factual world history; myths and beliefs about good and evil; an eclectic range of social and political ideas. The action centers again upon Shikasta (in Sirian, Rohanda) and leads up to that of the first archive, Shikasta's Last Days. "Good" (Canopus) and "evil" (Puttiora/ Shammat) come more fully into focus now, yet constantly, tantalizingly beyond their struggle for ascendancy in Shikasta lies the Canopean recognition of the hidden Necessity (a Sufi concept) that governs all. Earth-visiting gods, immaculate conceptions, UFOs, talismanic magic, Wellsian echoes combine with freely shuffled episodes from our world's history—Aztecs and conquistadores, Mongol invasions, the modern global wars—to form an imagined whole whose metaphysical direction remains open, and intriguing, to the end. However, meaning and message, as in *Shikasta,* tend to smother fictional effect; one is seldom taught by indirection.

The Making of the Representative for Planet 8 (1982) is told again by a single, involved narrator, and the narrative is the most firmly integrated and the most compelling of the first five archives. The doom The Ice threatens is evident from the outset in the narrator's use of the past tense and in the prospect held out by the Canopean agent, Johor again, of transferring the threatened population of the planet to Rohanda, "a beautiful plane"; readers of *Shikasta* already know the news Johor will later break to Doeg, the narrator: "Rohanda is . . . Shikasta, the broken one, the afflicted." The narrative, then, is of hope and despair, and beyond, of seeking to understand and accept an inevitable fate. Canopus is not omnipotent; yet salvation is not where Doeg and the other Representatives expect it: it is not in life, but through death. Those who are fitted to learn this, who are attuned to "a general and shared consciousness" beyond the solipsistic "I" (one recalls the SOWF of *Shikasta*), are led by Johor's questioning and the struggle to the end he shares with them to "earn" their return to an original world, inwardly apprehended: "A world of dazzling light, all a shimmering marvel—where the colours you yearn to see are shining—from whence you came." (One recalls the luminous imagery of Henry Vaughan, a seventeenth-century devotional poet). They become, finally, one Representative, a mystical "new being" in a transcendent otherness. The action, the struggles against The Ice, the contrivances of survival, the wrestling with bodily and spiritual limitation are all concretely rendered. In her afterword Lessing reveals that her imagination was deeply imbued with the accounts of Robert Scott's expeditions to the Antarctic, in writing both this novel and *The Sirian Experiments.* She quotes from Apsley Cherry-Garrard's *The Worst Journey in the World* (1922) and George Seaver's biography *Wilson of the Antarctic* (1933)—Wilson died with Scott. The lesson of their example is less, for her, in their sense of duty (unfashionable today) than in their obeying the "need to break out of our ordinary possibilities. . . . This need may well be the deepest one we have." In Wilson she finds united a noble selflessness with an urge to use his life to the utmost in the pursuit of knowledge. Thus, the legendary Antarctic expedition of 1910–1913 inspired in *The Making* a myth of endurance and faith, of simplicities by no means modern.

The fifth archive, *Documents Relating to the Sentimental Agents in the Volyen Empire* (1983), is not among the more "beguiling" tales. The narrative mode, Klorathy's reports to Johor in Canopus on the events surrounding the collapses of the Volyen Empire, distances the reader; the opening sections, clotted with reference to persons, place, and events, handicaps initial response. As in *Shikasta* the play of ideas and political allegory, rather than of character or character conflict, is dominant. The motif of the sentimental agents, Canopeans not fully tempered by experience of inferior worlds, focuses upon the errors of Incent (the Innocent) in a vein of obvious comedy that palls in the telling. The School of Rhetoric and the Hospital for Rhetorical Diseases, alias the Institute for Historical Studies, and the therapeutic technique of Total Immersion are, however, worthy of the Third Book of *Gulliver's Travels.* The revolutionary is the ultimate sentimentalist. As in the first archive, in Volyen's history and politics we recognize much of our world: the relations between developed and underdeveloped countries, imperial mission and its decline, accompanied by an influx of unwanted immigrants; in the role of Sirius, Soviet Russia and the link between revolution and empire. Volyen, treated more sympathetically than Shikasta, suffers from markedly English afflictions: though comparatively pleasant, its idealistic youth agitate to undermine it; Sirian agents are (like the Cambridge Communists of the 1930's) members of Volyen's privileged classes. As with the trial that closes *Shikasta,* the Indictment of Volyen's vulnerably open society produces an acute and stimulating conflict of ideas and attitudes. Behind all, gifted with foresight, though aware that solutions are bound by Necessity, hovers Canopus. It is the arbiter of ultimate value—what our world lacks, certainly—and the source of choice (free will); Klorathy, on duty in a Volyen afflicted, like Shikasta, with "self-destructive dementia," sometimes pines for its unnameable quality. While it is perhaps essential that Lessing should preserve Canopus as a vague principle of justice, it threatens to become a fine-spun abstraction, a romantic figment closer in spirit to Shelley's *Prometheus Unbound* than to those eighteenth-century rationalists her political satire recalls.

THE DIARIES OF JANE SOMERS

"SINCE writing *The Golden Notebook* I've become less personal. I've floated away from the personal. I've stopped saying, 'This is *mine,* this is my experience. . . . I don't believe any more that I have a thought. There is a thought around" ("Doris Lessing at Stony Brook" [1970], reprinted in *A Small Personal Voice* [1974]). Her ensuing work has been faithful to this piece of self-analysis until the surprising news, broken in 1984, that parallel with her writing the *Canopus* series Lessing had published two linked novels in her earlier "realistic" style under the pseudonym of Jane Somers. In 1984 these were reprinted as her work in one volume, with a tart preface where Lessing explains that she had made the experiment to combat publishers' and reviewers' entrenched prejudices in favor of established and against unknown writers. *The Diary of a Good Neighbour* (1983) and *If the Old Could . . .* (1984) were both written in the most personal of forms, the diary, self-preoccupied and self-revealing. Yet this is only technically a return to the personal mode: the preoccupation is not with a thinly disguised authorial self, but with crises of experience and understanding readily apprehensible, one supposes, to middle-aged women like Janna Somers, established in her career but emotionally unfulfilled. Janna is again that familiar, pre-Canopean heroine, a representative figure akin to such as Kate Brown who in *The Summer Before the Dark,* facing the "cold wind" of solitude, age, and irrelevance, had found the resources within herself to live beyond the roles she had outgrown.

If in their pseudonymous guise these novels were not detected as Lessing's this may partly be due to her protagonist's unlikely identity and striking authenticity as a women's magazine editor and romantic novelist. Yet Janna Somers' pattern of life and anxiety for change will be familiar: she preserves a careful face in her public world, but while apparently self-contained and successful, is conscious, like all Lessing's heroines, of her incompleteness. Having failed both husband and mother as they neared death, she resolves "to learn something else," to change. The opportunity comes from an unexpected quarter—the very old Maudie, one of the unnoticed, unnoticeable old women who merely survive in the crannies of the metropolis, a London that belongs to the young, the healthy life-forcers. Realizing "how afraid we are of age," instinctively Janna allows herself to be drawn into this subterranean world, where she falls in love with Maudie's indomitable spirit. The theme is not entirely new: one recalls the story "An Old Woman and Her Cat" in *The Story of a Non-Marrying Man* (1972), a deeply felt but unsentimental sketch of a homeless old woman's dogged evasion of society's efforts to put her and her pet to sleep. The emotional intensity this story shares with Lessing's treatment of the Janna-Maudie relationship does stem, one may infer, from the personal attachment she mentions in the afterword to *The Making of the Representative for Planet 8,* a book finished the day "after the death of someone I had known a long time. . . . It took her a long cold time to die, and she was hungry too, for she was refusing to eat and drink, so as to hurry things along. She was ninety-two, and it seemed to her sensible."

The faithfulness to every detail of Maudie's struggling, squalid existence, the close delineation of Janna's ambivalent responses, and the broad insight into the nature of this contemporary London Underworld are all conveyed in a brisk, concrete style, alive with Janna's shrewd commentary upon her fluctuating feelings—an index of ours—reminiscent of such earlier journal-novels as *The Golden Notebook* and *The Memoirs of a Survivor* (1974). However remote from the Lessing of Canopus, it now seems odd that her hand escaped detection (the novels escaped this writer altogether on first publication). In both novels another familiar element is the scrupulous, even dogged fidelity with which the close relations between women are captured.

In *If the Old Could . . . ,* Maudie's death having closed The Diary, Janna the romantic novelist becomes caught up in a middle-aged romance that reality—Richard's duty to wife and family, Janna's chastened sense of the claims of self—denies. In the margin Annie, Maudie's less appealing aged counterpart, persists as a reminder of "a world . . . few of us, ever, want to think about until we have to." This novel is weighted with Janna's burden of obligation to young and old alike; the negative emotions of guilt and self-doubt vitiate self-realization and the urge to self-gratification in both Janna and Richard. Personal relations are stifled by the moral imperatives and uncertainties of familial ties. Some relief is felt in the harmonious colleagueship of Janna's editorial office, or in her delight with Richard in discovering the pleasures of London and its "salty and original" people, recapturing at times the exuberant flavor of the early *In Pursuit of the English.* These novels often refreshingly revisit ordinary life with gusto, curiosity, and engaged social concern: their strength, in relationship, is in that between Janna and Maudie; if one feels as a weakness in the second book a diminution of interest in a character who is acted upon rather than embodying a positive force, this is nevertheless symptomatic of Lessing's fidelity to Janna's unslaked search for satisfaction and her own refusal to impose a neat romantic resolution.

While Lessing may value *The Diaries* below her *Canopus* series, their appearance arrested a growing perception that a preoccupation with the figment of a transcendent absolute had led to the shedding of common reality. Yet even in that series of generally less admired works, at their best one is engaged and moved by Lessing's consistent twin concern with the individual in himself and in relation to society; while in her best work, she achieves insight simultaneously into the private life and the "wider public life" by which, George Eliot commented in *Felix Holt,* the private is determined. *The Golden Notebook* is the modern counterpart to *Middlemarch.* Like Eliot, Doris Lessing does not shrink from earnestness and unblushing didacticism, and although (especially in her "English" short stories) she more often lightens her narrative with a teasing humor, she frequently employs a similarly authoritative, astringent irony, the "dryness" she aptly notes in her preface to *The Diaries.* Like Eliot, too, she insists on keeping absolute values before us. So serious and prolific a writer, always responsive to the pressure of the time, is likely to be uneven. I have not stressed the lapses, even in her best work, into protracted documentary or circumstantial narrative and slack, unrevised prose. Ultimately, these defects matter little, because of the power of the mind that creates. Lessing is worthy to be spoken of in the company of those great novelists before her who used the novel not to divert with a sensational or aesthetic experience, but to change us —Eliot, Hardy, Conrad, Lawrence. If she shares with them also—as with her nearest comparable contemporary, Patrick White—the unevenness of writers who reach for the utmost inclusiveness, this is redeemed by the unteachable quality of keeping the reader morally alive. No English novelist today is more responsibly concerned with keeping literature critically in touch with life, as it is and as it should be.

Literature and history, these two great branches of human learning, records of human behaviour, human thought, are less and less valued by the young, and by educators, too. Yet from them one may learn how to be a citizen and a human being. We may learn how to look at ourselves and at the society we live in, in that calm, cool, critical and sceptical way which is the only possible stance for a civilized human being, or so have said all the philosophers and the sages.

(*Prisons We Choose to Live Inside,* 1986)

POSTSCRIPT: THE GOOD TERRORIST

THE unattributed epigraph to her first novel, *The Grass Is Singing,* would stand aptly at the beginning of *The Good Terrorist* (1985): "It is by the failures and misfits of a civilization that one can best judge its weaknesses." Another could be Hannah Arendt's dictum on the sources of the kind of situation the novel attempts to capture: "loneliness and the logical-ideological deducing the worst that comes from it represent an anti-social situation and harbour a principle destructive for all human living-together" (*The Origins of Totalitarianism,* New York, 1973, p. 478).

Lessing's new "children of violence," founders of the C.C.P. (a would-be independent Communist Center Party), are emotional amateurs, not ideologues, stemming from several varieties of alienation in contemporary England—unemployment, miseducation, child abuse, family breakdown, color prejudice; they are gays, lesbians, narcissists, idlers, and one fiercely righteous bomb maker, who find an uneasy unity in their disaffection, however deviously it is reached. Their conspiracy to overthrow a "stinking" society is mostly a tragicomedy of errors, which escalates almost involuntarily into a tragedy in earnest (reminiscent of the Oxford Street bombings in 1977) for which none is quite prepared, least of all Alice, Lessing's protagonist: "Had she not believed the bombing was serious, then? No, not really; she had gone along with it, while feeling it was not right—and behind that was the thought that *serious* work (whatever that might turn out to be) would come later." The millenium is never today. Alice is the only "revolutionary" whose mind and past life we enter, yet she is probably the least typical. She is neither merely sentimental nor fanatical, but "good" in a Lessing succession we recognize; closest to her among "caring" heroines is the Martha of *The Four-Gated City*—and indeed she might have borne the same name, as one "cumbered about much serving . . . careful and troubled about many things" (Luke 10:40–41).

Until near the end, revolutionary acts are peripheral to Lessing's detailed exploration of the personal and political relations among the young people, at whose center the frenetic Alice works (and steals, from her "fascist" parents: thus, no guilt) to convert their condemned North London Victorian house, or "squat," into a decent habitation for the "family" she would have them become. In this apparently contradictory "bourgeois" behavior her "Comrades" both deride and depend upon, she sublimates the split between her parallel lives, the yearning for order and calm beneath the outbursts of hatred and anger the once good girl, good daughter, had suppressed. Behind her stand Dorothy, her mother, and her friend Zoë, hangovers from the fruitless demonstrations of the 1960's, from whose now merely intellectual concern the book-hating activist Alice early learned to block herself off—as also from sex, which means chaos and violation of the self. A professional Comrade (a Russian agent) distinguishes her from Lenin's "useful idiots" (her fellow revolutionaries) as a "pure good woman," by which perhaps he cynically means both credulous and susceptible, a vessel of pure faith, while the reader sees in her a naive, warped compassion for the marginal people whom life defeats. She drifts, with deadly innocence, into connivance with Lenin's cynical dictum, "Morality has to be subdued to the needs of Revolution." Too late she foresees the consequences but never reaches understanding.

The intense focus upon Alice allows little scope for broader vision. From her perspective society is bureaucratic, arbitrary, bullying; she has learned, using her intuitive, girlish self, to manipulate its softer-hearted functionaries, but her encounters with the police and members of the tired or simply uncomprehending older generation yield no hint of more fruitful possibilities beyond her grasp. The only somewhat constructive figures in this negative portrayal of disaffected youth, who join safe Greenpeace "demos" and plan their partnership in a flat for two, are ironically treated. The concentration upon Alice, who is no typical revolutionary, is difficult to explain: in symbolic terms she embodies a universal conflict between the desire to conserve and the impulse, springing from twisted and thwarted idealism, to destroy; more realistically, through her concentration on one who poignantly expresses wasted human quality in a "lost" generation, Lessing could sympathize rather than condemn. One is reminded of Conrad's problems, frankly expressed in his preface to *The Secret Agent:* his choosing the "ironic method" to enable him to speak "in scorn as well as in pity," and his focus upon Winnie Verloc, who tragically suspects that "life doesn't stand much looking into." But while *The Good Terrorist* lacks the control and concentration of Conrad's novel and of Lessing's earlier work, it reestablishes her challenging role as, to quote from *The Golden Notebook,* "a central point of awareness."

SELECTED BIBLIOGRAPHY

I. BIBLIOGRAPHY. C. Ipp, comp., *Doris Lessing: A Bibliography* (Johannesburg, 1967); S. R. Burkom, ed., "A Doris Lessing Checklist," in *Critique,* 11 (1968), includes a guide to reviews; A. N. Krouse, "A Doris Lessing Checklist," in *Contemporary Literature,* 14 (1973).

II. COLLECTED AND SELECTED WORKS. *African Stories* (London, 1964), contains the short stories in *This Was The Old Chief's Country,* reprinted together with the African stories from *The Habit of Loving* and *A Man and Two Women* and the four novellas from *Five* with an African setting ("The Other Woman" omitted), also "Traitors," first printed in *Argosy* (May 1954), "The Black Madonna," from *Winter's Tales* (London, 1957), and two early stories, "The Trinket Box" and "The Pig," printed for the first time; *Martha Quest and A Proper Marriage* (London, 1965); *Children of Violence* (London, 1966–); *Nine African Stories* (London, 1968), selected by M. Morland from *African Stories,* with intro. by the author written in 1967; *Collected African Stories* (London, 1973), vol. I: *This Was the Old Chief's Country,* vol. II: *The Sun Between Their Feet; Collected Stories,* vol. I: *To Room Nineteen* (London, 1978), vol. II: *The Temptation of Jack Orkney* (London, 1979).

III. SEPARATE WORKS. *The Grass Is Singing* (London, 1950), fiction; *This Was the Old Chief's Country* (London, 1951), short stories; *Martha Quest* (London, 1952), vol. I of *Children of Violence; Five* (London, 1953), short novels, includes "A Home for the Highland Cattle," "The Other Woman," "Eldorado," "The Antheap," "Hunger"; *A Proper Marriage* (London, 1954), vol. II of *Children of Violence; Retreat to Innocence* (London, 1956), fiction; "Myself as Sportsman," in the *New Yorker,* 31 (January 1956), personal narrative; *The Habit of Loving* (London, 1957), short stories; *Going Home* (London, 1957; rev. ed., 1968), personal narrative; "A Small Personal Voice," in T. Maschler, ed., *Declaration* (London, 1957), gives her writer's "position"; *A Ripple from the Storm* (London, 1958), vol. III of *Children of Violence; Each His Own Wilderness* (London, 1959), play, pub. in *New English Dramatists,* three plays introd. and ed. by E. M. Browne; *Fourteen Poems* (Northwood, 1959); *In Pursuit of the English: A Documentary* (London, 1960), personal narrative; *The Golden Notebook* (London, 1962), fiction (new ed. with author's preface, 1972); *Play with a Tiger: A Play in Three Acts* (London, 1962); *A Man and Two Women* (London, 1963), short stories; "What Really Matters," in the *Twentieth Century,* 172 (Autumn 1963); *Landlocked* (London, 1965), fiction, vol. IV of *Children of Violence; Particularly Cats* (London, 1967), personal narrative; "Afterword," in O. Schreiner, *The Story of an African Farm* (New York, 1968); *The Four-Gated City* (London, 1969), vol. V of *Children of Violence.*

Briefing for a Descent into Hell (London, 1971), fiction; "In the World, Not of It," in *Encounter,* 39 (August 1972), an article on Sufism; *The Story of a Non-Marrying Man* (London, 1972), short stories; "What Looks Like an Egg and Is an Egg?" in the *New York Times Book Review* (7 May 1972); "An Ancient Way to a New Freedom," in L. Lewin, ed., *The Elephant in the Dark* (London, 1972); *The Summer Before the Dark* (London, 1973), fiction; *The Memoirs of a Survivor* (London, 1974), fiction: *A Small Personal Voice: Essays, Reviews, Interviews* (New York, 1974), ed. by P. Schlueter; "If You Knew Sufi," in the *Guardian* (8 January 1975); "A Revolution," in the *New York Times* (22 August 1975); "The Ones Who Know," in the *Times Literary Supplement* (30 August 1976); *Re: Colonised Planet 5, Shikasta* (London, 1979), vol. I of *Canopus in Argos, Archives;* "My First Book," in *Author,* 91 (Spring 1980); *The Marriages Between Zones Three, Four and Five* (London, 1980), vol. II of *Canopus . . . ; The Sirian Experiments: The Report by Ambien II, of the Five* (London, 1981), vol. III of *Canopus . . . ; The Making of the Representative for Planet 8* (London, 1982), vol. IV of *Canopus . . . ;* "Our Minds Have Become Set in the Apocalyptic Mode," in the *Guardian* (14 June 1982); *Documents Relating to the Sentimental Agents in the Volyen Empire* (London, 1983), vol. V of *Canopus . . . ; The Diaries of Jane Somers* (London, 1984), fiction, with a preface by Lessing, previously pub. under the pseudonym Jane Somers as *The Diary of a Good Neighbour* (London, 1983) and *If the Old Could . . .* (London, 1984); *The Good Terrorist* (London, 1985); "Impertinent Daughters," in *Granta,* 14 (1985); "Autobiography (Pt. II): My Mother's Life," in *Granta,* 17 (1985); *Prisons We Choose to Live Inside,* CBC Massey Lectures (Toronto, 1986); *The Wind Blows Away Our Worlds* (London, 1987), personal narrative on Afghanistan.

IV. INTERVIEWS. R. Rubens, "Footnote to *The Golden Notebook,*" in the *Queen* (21 August 1962); R. Newquist, in R. Newgrist, ed., *Counterpoint* (Chicago, 1964); F. Howe, "Talk with Doris Lessing," in the *Nation* (6 March 1967); J. Raskin, "Doris Lessing at Stony Brook," in the *New American Review,* 8 (1970); L. Langley, "Scenarios of Hell," in the *Guardian Weekly* (24 April 1971); F. Howe, "A Conversation with Doris Lessing (1966)," in *Contemporary Literature,* 14 (1973); "The Doors of Perception," in the *Sunday*

Times (18 November 1979); M. Thorpe, "Interview," taped, for The British Council (London, 1980).

V. Biographical and Critical Studies. J. Gindin, *Postwar British Fiction: New Accents and Attitudes* (London, 1962), contains a chapter, "Doris Lessing's Intense Commitment"; D. Brewster, *Doris Lessing* (New York, 1965); M. Tucker, *Africa in Modern Literature* (New York, 1967); S. R. Burkom, " 'Only Connect': Form and Content in the Works of Doris Lessing," in *Critique,* 11 (1968); M. Thorpe, "Martha's Utopian Quest: Doris Lessing's *Children of Violence* Quintet," in A. Rutherford, ed., *Commonwealth* (Aarhus, 1972); P. Schlueter, *The Novels of Doris Lessing* (Carbondale, Ill., 1973); C. J. Driver, "Profile of Doris Lessing," in the *New Review,* 1 (1974); A. Pratt and L. S. Dembo, eds., *Doris Lessing: Critical Essays* (London, 1974); E. Showalter, *A Literature of Their Own: British Women Novelists from Brontë to Lessing* (Princeton, N.J., 1977); Mary Ann Singleton, *The City and the Veld: The Fiction of Doris Lessing* (Lewisburg, Pa., 1977); M. Thorpe, *Doris Lessing's Africa* (London, 1978); R. Rubinstein, *The Novelistic Vision of Doris Lessing* (Urbana, Ill., 1979); I. Holmquist, *From Society to Nature: A Study of Doris Lessing's "Children of Violence"* (Gothenburg, 1980); L. Sage, *Doris Lessing* (London, 1982); M. Green, *The English Novel in the Twentieth Century: The Doom of Empire* (London, 1984), contains a chapter, "Doris Lessing: The Return from Empire"; J. Taylor, ed., *Notebooks, Memoirs, Archives: Re-reading Doris Lessing* (London, 1982); C. Tomalin, "Mischief: Why a Famous Novelist Played a Trick on the Literary World," in the *Sunday Times* (23 September 1984); P. Harrison, "Seeking Mrs. Lessing," in the *Bookseller* (24 September 1984); A. Beck, "Doris Lessing and the Colonial Experience," in the *Journal of Commonwealth Literature,* 19 (November 1984).

N.B.: A *Doris Lessing Newsletter,* ed. by D. Seligman, at 35 Prospect St., Sherborn, Mass., 01770, is put out occasionally and contains research notes, essays, and reviews.

PAUL SCOTT
(1920–1978)

Patrick Swinden

I

Paul Scott was born on 25 March 1920 in Palmer's Green, North London, the second son of a family of commercial artists. His father does not appear to have been very successful in his profession, and Scott's origins are therefore only humbly professional middle class. He was educated at Winchmore Hill Collegiate and later, at his father's insistence, began training as an accountant, until he was called up in 1940 to begin his national service. He was a noncommissioned officer in Intelligence, in the United Kingdom, for three years. His commission in the Indian Army came with his arrival in India in 1943. He was posted to a supply unit that took him to Burma and Malaya as well as India—an experience he was to make much use of in his first novel, *Johnnie Sahib* (1952). But a year after his war service was completed, in 1946, he was demobilized and returned to England. There he was appointed secretary to the Falcon and Grey Walls Press, a publishing company run by a Labour Member of Parliament, Peter Baker. He left Baker's company in 1950 to become a literary agent with David Higham Associates. For ten years he was a director of the company, and produced four novels, from *Johnnie Sahib* to *The Mark of the Warrior.* Then he resigned his position (in 1960) to become a freelance writer and a regular reviewer for *Country Life* and the *Times.* He did not attract a large following as a novelist until the *Raj Quartet* was well under way, in the early 1970's; and real popularity came only with the publication of *Staying On,* which won the Booker Prize in 1977. He died on 1 March 1978.

Scott appears to have been a very private man. There are no tantalizing snippets of information about him in the literary magazines. Indeed there is little about his books either, in spite of the wide readership they came to attract. Apparently he loved music and the cinema as much as he loved literature. He married, in 1941, Nancy Edith Avery, with whom he had two daughters.

These are mere fragments of information, but they do emphasize the slightness of Scott's contact with India—three years between 1943 and 1946. One is led to inquire about the position of India as a country and an idea in the mind of a man who, on the surface, had so little to do with it. What it meant to him we can surmise from the way he writes about it. What it means to his characters is, I think, an altogether different thing.

The illusory nature of the world so many of Scott's characters inhabit clearly has much to do with their author's fascination with India. His fiction needs to be sustained by events in the Indian subcontinent between 1942 and 1947. This is the span of time that is traversed gradually, shiftingly, with many halts and retrospects, in *The Raj Quartet* (1966–1975). It is also the place and the period in which the events of all Scott's other successful novels take place. Even where the setting is a tiny island in the East Indies and the time long after the end of the war in the East *(The Birds of Paradise),* the real impetus of the novel springs from the India of between the wars and its transformation into a postwar independent state. The fighting in Malaya that provides the background of *The Chinese Love Pavilion* is a consequence of the defense of India against Japanese invasion. Even in Scott's one successful and important novel that deals with events outside India and the war altogether *(The Corrida of San Feliu),* 1964 events in India play a significant part in the construction of the plot.

For Scott India was the supreme illusion. Here, for many of his characters, is a setting for their lives that they feel can be replaced by nothing else. They have defined themselves, their duties, their professions, their moral values, their habits of social behavior and personal assessment, in relation to India. Scott shows that for the British who lived there, India was an all-embracing experience. Their minds admitted only dim recollections of "home" in England. The houses and gardens of the Home Counties to which they were sent away to be educated, and from which they returned to take up positions as soldiers and administrators, had to be transplanted to a different climate and a more spacious geography.

Sarah Layton explains the Anglo-Indian response to England in the second volume of the *Quartet.* She is looking at England through the perspective of her Indian upbringing, though she is now walking with her aunt through an English meadow, walking in the direction of a brook—which reminds her of another brook back in India near her father's military cantonment:

> The brook babbling over the stones reminded her of Pankot in miniature. But then everything in England was on a miniature scale. She thought this had an effect on the people who lived there always. In comparison with her mother . . . Aunt Lydia [who returned to England permanently, unlike her sisters Fenny and Mildred] . . . seemed to Sarah to lack a dimension that the others didn't lack. Lacking this dimension was what Sarah supposed came of living on a tiny island.
>
> (*The Day of the Scorpion,* bk. I, pt. II, ch. 3)

People like Sarah Layton and her family have no option but to allow their vision and expectation to develop within the Indian dimension, to adjust themselves to a scale against which the landscapes of England appear as miniatures. Living in England will be as unnatural to Sarah Layton as she is later to suppose living in India, that is to say living in the new independent India, would be. In some ways more so, since the sense of physical scale and proportion has a great deal to do with the cultivation and assertion of a personal identity.

It is the triumph of the *Quartet* as a whole, and it is the triumph to a lesser extent of many of Scott's other novels, that he has fully understood, almost one might say shared, the illusion of India, the Englishman's India. He has given it a density, an animation, a capacity for movement and alteration, an ability to be looked at from many sides, to be experienced through a variety of points of view, which can be true only of something that possesses a certain reality. Indeed, reality of a kind must come into being when a landscape and a people are subjected to the creative pressure of so many minds, differing in any number of important ways, but ultimately controlled by an intangible idea of the rightness of their presence—more than that, their *superior presence*—in the place they now call home. But Scott has also understood the impermanence of this reality. And he has understood that when this impermanence is not recognized by those whose reality it is felt to be, then the reality, however substantial, however laden with the histories and emblems of those who have lived it, itself becomes an illusion.

In this respect one might see Scott as a latter-day E. M. Forster, making the same point in 1974 as Forster was making in 1924—about the folly of an alien rule in India and the illusions of grandeur and permanence it had created for itself. But Forster was deeply unsympathetic to those who "ran" the empire—perhaps in part because he never properly understood what qualities were required to "run" anything. He despised the individuals the raj comprised as much as he despised the raj itself. This is not so with Scott. On the contrary, he has an almost Kiplingesque admiration for some of the men who occupy positions of responsibility in India, whether in the civil administration or the army. All of his novels, not only the *Quartet,* contain examples of efficient and humane Anglo-Indians who could not have appeared in any novel Forster might conceivably have written about India. For one thing, Forster's Anglo-Indians do not seem to do any work. There is no hint in *A Passage to India* about how the empire was administered, policed, defended; whereas in Kipling, most of the things that happen, happen in a context of work. Whatever plot there is in a story by Kipling arises out of exigencies of a real situation based on work. Scott is like Kipling here. He has more of a "feel" for India than Forster had, and he knows how much of the Anglo-Indian's life in India revolved around work and responsibility, not merely some fake patriotic imperial sentiment. This makes it possible for him to look at the Anglo-Indian community much more dispassionately than Forster ever did.

It also helps Scott to identify aspects of Anglo-Indian life that, while growing out of the situation in which the British lived in India, more nearly approximate the lives of people wherever they live. I am referring to his preoccupation with his characters' ambitions—ambitions that are often impossible to realize because they have arisen not out of a real situation, which can be dealt with effectively one way or another, but out of a totally artificial situation. This is a situation that in his case India has seemed to stand for, but that has no more relation to the real India than the regimental trophies and the mock Tudor cottages have to the parts of India—Pankot, Ranpur, Mayapore—that Scott invented to stand for the whole.

Scott tried to create characters who feel that this India is real, and he sought to bring them to terms with the fact that it is not. He tried to make them recognize the illusory nature of the ambitions that drive them and the desires that perplex them. This preoccupation with what men most want for themselves, what they want to believe in, or, more subtly, what they want to suppose they *have* believed in, makes Scott a difficult writer; difficult because of the often complex states of mind that many of his characters possess, and difficult because of the way those states of mind shift and change under the pressure of what are often extraordinary experiences. In the novels we discover people engaged in a struggle with circumstances they will usually fail to understand, and instead reconstruct in the image of their ambitions and desires. That is why the stage of his fiction is so often populated by the obsessed, the deranged, the hypocritical, and the intensely self-deceived.

The men and women Scott was interested in are of two opposite kinds; those who foster the illusion of permanence most strenuously, and those who are beginning to recognize the illusion for what it really is. He was most interested in the second kind, because to feel as they do is to lose a part, perhaps a very large part, of their own reality—which has been over so many years dependent upon their connection with India. How is a man to hold on to a sense of personal reality when he can feel the external props that have sustained it for so long, at first gently and then violently being pulled away? This is the dominant theme of Scott's fiction.

The Raj Quartet represents Scott's most complete and profound history of this process. Here, the demise of British India is traced through the fortunes of an enormous cast of characters who respond to these problems of personal identity in a variety of ways. But from his earliest work, Scott sought to expose the characters in his fiction to the collapse of their illusions and the consequent threat administered to their sense of personal identity.

II

SCOTT's first work of fiction, *Johnnie Sahib,* is a story about a company of soldiers involved in ground-and-air operations in the jungles of Burma in 1942. It is a fine novel, particularly good at describing the frustrations and ambitions of men at work. But it does not in any significant way touch on what is to become Scott's major preoccupation: relations between men and women (and to a lesser extent between men and men) of different races. Later, in *The Raj Quartet* in particular, the coming together of white and colored in love, hate, and (more rarely) indifference will constitute the *raison d'être* of the fiction. There the base on which the edifice of politics, personal relationships, war, and family tradition stands is the birth of a Eurasian child to an English girl who has been raped by a gang of Indian youths.

In Scott's second novel, *The Alien Sky* (1953), the Eurasian subject is of fundamental importance. The plot hangs on the fact that the principal female character, Dorothy Gower, is a Eurasian, or "chi chi," although we don't discover this until halfway through the book. No one else, not even (especially) her husband, knows it until an American visitor to Marapore inadvertently discovers her secret. But the fact of Dorothy's mixed parentage has, in all but the literal sense (she is white), colored her whole life. Especially it has destroyed her relationship with her husband, forcing her to use him as a channel through which she can release her hatred of all that is unmixed, white or brown. The strain involved in her pretensions to English birth and upbringing, the maneuvers she has to invent to stay away from the country she has never seen and could never feel at home in, and the hatred of her Indian homeland that has forced upon her these subterfuges are all fully illuminated when MacKendrick, the American, discovers from a childhood friend of Dorothy's the fact of her Eurasian birth.

MacKendrick has come to Marapore to lay to rest a private ghost. He feels he has to make good certain deficiencies in his character that have been created by a bullying and sadistic brother. This brother, Dwight, has recently died in the war in the Pacific, and MacKendrick discovers that he has left a pile of letters from Dorothy, pleading with him not to abandon her to her unsatisfactory marriage with Tom Gower. He has also left a letter of his own, written to Dorothy, that he never sent to her. It contains the puzzling confession that "what you told me that time *would* make a difference." Before Judith Anderson's explanation of their childhood in Assam, MacKendrick has assumed that Dorothy meant that she couldn't have children (which in a sense is true, because they might have been brown). But now that MacKendrick has discovered the real reason, his attitude to the woman he had intended to take in order to score off his dead brother becomes more complicated. So does his relationship with the husband. Gower's suffering at Dorothy's hands is seen to be a hideously unjust retribution on the whole white male sex, of which he, with his unpopular liberal attitudes, is such an unrepresentative example.

Certainly the most powerfully moving scenes in this novel have to do with the treatment of Eurasians by members of the white community. The first of these describes a party at which Judith's pretensions to having been brought up in Brighton are cruelly exposed by an embittered English war widow—an event which is responsible for her confession about Dorothy to MacKendrick. The second is at the end of the book when MacKendrick, about to make love to Dorothy, accuses her of deceiving Gower for inadequate and totally sadistic reasons:

"You could have told him what you were long ago, couldn't you? You've deliberately not told him because all you wanted him to feel was how much you hated him. . . . What happens now? How long do you intend to hate me? That's how it's going to be, isn't it? Having your own back on me because of Dwight. Having your own back on Tom because you were forced to marry him. They're both the same. What happens when you've got nobody left to get your own back on? What happens when you've got nobody left to hate?"

(*The Alien Sky,* pt. III, ch. 2)

The predictable answer is returned:

"There'll be myself, won't there? That's what you want me to say! That there'll be myself!"

The scene is not melodramatic because it issues out of a fatally plausible conjunction of two people at a stage in their lives when they feel driven to hurt and be revenged on a world that has humiliated them. So when MacKendrick enters Dorothy, she makes an animal response. He is driven to impotence and she closes with him in scorn. He claims she was thinking of Dwight. She attributes her refusal to be possessed to her habit of withholding herself. And it is a fact that she withholds the truth about herself from Tom Gower on a physical level, as well as on the level of her "genetic" identity: " 'There's always been part of me he hasn't knowingly possessed. . . . If he knew what I was I'd have nothing left to withhold.' "

The episode is a very painful dramatization of the connection in Dorothy's mind between her racial secret, her social frigidity, and her manipulation of her sex to humiliate others. The fact that MacKendrick is the victim on whom she inflicts this humiliation is suffused with a most brutal irony. After all, his original attitude toward her was also based on a need to punish others and satisfy his injured pride. But now that he has discovered Dorothy's secret, both she and her husband have ceased to be mere "images." They are " 'people who exist outside you and in spite of you. You may know the image backwards but you don't know what's behind it or within it. You don't know *her* in the way you knew Dwight. You've set an image against a man and you've judged.' " Now that kind of judgment is turned against him as Dorothy fails to see in him also anything more than "an image." At the moment he tries to get beyond his previous role as Dwight's substitute, Dorothy sees him and Dwight and Tom as indistinguishable representatives of the despised white male sex, and herself as the white girl who won't play "chi chi." She withholds herself at the point where her sex and her mixed blood run together and stagnate.

Tom Gower has to be understood throughout as the unknowing victim of Dorothy's Eurasian conscience. Her frigidity, her infidelity, her mysterious changes of mind about whether she will go to England or whether she will go to one of the Princely States are all entangled with Gower's eviction from his farm and removal from his position on the newspaper he edits. Unlike MacKendrick or Dorothy, Gower feels that he is bound to an India that seems no longer to want him. On the one hand he has to accept that he has fifteen years of self-deception standing between himself and reality; on the other, that deception or otherwise, this is his world, "and a man and his world are inseparable." Tragically, on a merely physical level, the reality of his connection with India is in Dorothy. Her mixed blood is the physical equivalent of his mixed relationship with the world from which he cannot separate himself. But history and social attitudes and Dorothy's own attitude to these things, as well as her physical dislike, have removed this consolation from him. The book ends with his unsuccessful attempt at suicide and Dorothy's unloving return to their house; " 'I've come back here,' she said at last. 'And Tom will come back too, I suppose.' "

Two novels, *A Male Child* (1956) and *The Mark of the Warrior* (1958), complete Scott's apprenticeship, developing his interest in obsessional family relationships and the mystique of leadership. In the novels that follow (*The Chinese Love Pavilion, The Birds of Paradise,* and *The Corrida at San Felíu*), he evolved a much more complex narrative technique than the one he used in the earlier work. There he had relied on the direct representation of events in temporal sequence, incorporating the occasional flashback or abrupt change of scene. But he had done little to extend these techniques to produce a multilayered effect by superimposing narrative on narrative, cutting episode into episode, and tentatively organizing the whole around what is gradually discovered to be the central pivot of the novel's structure. In other words he had learned little from what had been such an important strategy in the novels of Conrad—whose example, I would suggest, had a great deal to do with Scott's preoccupations as well as his techniques as a writer.

After *The Mark of the Warrior,* a transformation of narrative into something densely suggestive of the mysteries and uncertainties attending the fates of men becomes more prominent. Scott begins to exercise control over the plots of his novels by arranging them in poetic rather than in merely sequential patterns. The narrative sequence does not break down altogether, but it tends to be dissolved and reorganized by a mind intent on reminiscence, or exploration, or even creative fabrication deriving from the "real" events that lie, inert and futile, behind the complex pattern of the novel.

Scott's first attempt to extend the implications of his narrative by allowing parts of it to move forward in the traditional manner while other parts of it stay still, or carry the reader back into a mysterious and uncertain past, is *The Chinese Love Pavilion* (1960). There have been strong hints of this in *A Male Child* and *The Mark of the Warrior,* in each of which the events preceding the action we witness become clearer, the closer the present action moves to its crisis. But most of the early novels use a particular landscape or a particular building, like the pavilion here, as a symbolic location, a place in which what has happened in the past has mysterious power to affect what is happening in the present—and which signalizes that this is so by its physical character as well as by the position it occupies and the use to which it is put. Aylward, in *A Male Child,* is the closest we have come to this so far. But compared with the pavilion, or the cage at Jundapur in *The Birds of Paradise,* or the Spanish locations in *The Corrida at San Felíu,* or the MacGregor House and the Bibighar Gardens in the *Quartet,* Mrs. Hurst's old house is only sketchily presented. Unfortunately, although the pavilion is a much more suggestively mysterious place, after the haunting prologue in which it is first described, too much of *The Chinese Love Pavilion* reads like a metaphysical version of *The Mark of the Warrior.* It is fundamentally the same kind of narrative, and the position of the pavilion within it is not so essential to whatever it contains that rises above the level of mere plot.

The Birds of Paradise (1962) is almost certainly Scott's finest pre-*Raj* achievement. Here the narrative is simple; the pattern of prospect and retrospect unforced and necessary; and the central image of the birds of paradise is tightly woven into the structure of the narrative and beautifully appropriate to the states of mind the novel explores. The exposition of a series of related themes through the slow unfolding of several narratives seems to be the ideal medium for Scott's mature art. It requires the play of memory, the act of the mind looking back into the past and separating deception from truth, teasing out the different forms of truth from the illusions that may have housed them. This recognition of how the truth of the past fades and reshapes itself in the interests of the present is at the heart of Scott's novel. Also at the heart of it is the fact that what a man might suppose is the essential nature of his present may be as illusory as the idealized past it has been built on; and that to see the past differently, from the perspective of a new experience, might be a powerful means of redirecting and reshaping his present. A man can live too much and too little in the past. Certainly he can become too absorbed in paradisiacal illusions out of which, in some cases, his past has been fabricated.

We first meet William Conway, the hero of *The*

Birds of Paradise, on Manoba, a volcanic island situated off the coast of New Guinea. It soon becomes obvious to us that there are two Manobas: the Manoba of the coastline and trading station with the S.I.A.T. (Straits Islands and Archipelago Trading Company) plantations in the background, and hutments and makeshift docks on the edge of the water; and the Manoba of the interior, which is a land of rumor and mystery, "a dark forgotten island whose warriors challenge your approach, make magic out of tins and mysteries out of birds." Conway lives near the plantation, having taken a year's sabbatical leave from his job in London in order to visit friends and acquaintances in India and the Far East whom he knew as a child and, later, as a P.O.W. in a Japanese camp. One of his fellow prisoners, Cranston, has settled another ex-P.O.W., Daintree, on the island, and certain of the details of Daintree's history have brought Conway there to meet him. Together they set off on expeditions to view the birds of paradise, which are supposed to inhabit the center of the island. But it may be that they are among the birds out of which the natives have made mysteries. By the end of the novel Conway has not found them.

One bird in the novel that is very definitely alive and, in its way, impressive, is a parrot called Melba. The story begins with an anecdote about this bird:

> If Melba interrupts her South American love song, and squawks, "Wurrah Yadoor-a!" I take no notice . . . but if the squawk is followed by the tinny sound she makes with her beak and claws when she tangles with the wire netting of her cage I leave the hut and go into the clearing to calm her down by tickling her stomach and ruffling the top of her head.
>
> (bk. I, ch. 1)

So far as the story is concerned, Melba is both a consolation and an embarrassment to Conway. She has been given to him as a present by two childhood friends, Dora Salford and Krishanramarao, after his return to Jundapur—one of the Indian Princely States he knew well in his boyhood. The parrot had got used to imitating his name, and "Krishi" had said that he couldn't bear the thought of her going through life shouting "William Conway" unless she had William Conway close at hand to hear. " 'Love's path never ran smoothly,' he said, but there were limits to the obstacles that should be put in its way." So Melba becomes Conway's personal gift, in a way his lover. He says that "the parrot would be my personal bird of paradise" and later (to Cranston), that she is a "mock bird of paradise, the only bird that could easily be obtained living, unless you visited islands like Manoba." Clearly Melba's presence is of considerable emblematic significance. By looking into the circumstances of Conway's reception of her, and therefore of her connection with other, more authentic birds of paradise, we might be able to clarify Scott's attitudes to romance, illusion, and the quest for reality, which lie at the heart of the novel.

William Conway had first known Krishi and Dora in Jundapur back in the 1920's and 1930's, when he was the son of the British political agent at the palace of the maharajah of Tradura, and Dora was the daughter of a major stationed in a town just outside the agency territories. Krishi was the eldest son of the maharajah of Jundapur. William had known Dora in Tradura, and had conducted a juvenile love affair with her in the grounds of the palace. They had both met Krishi at Kinwar in the winter of 1928–1929, shortly before William's departure for England—from which, it developed, he was not to return until now. The short period of the Kinwar tiger hunt and William's stay at the palace at Jundapur with Krishi and Dora during the spring of 1929 compose the thematic center of the novel. Out of this experience Conway forged the terms of his entry into the adult world. He imprinted on his spirit a picture of what the world was like, or might be like, or might, in the future, seem to have been like, which was to shake down into the basic elements of his adult personality.

It is not surprising that later in his life Conway should continue to nurture an ambition to test the illusion that the inheritance he had received from his father had built around him, and that his experience with Dora and Krishi at Jundapur had seemed to invest with a poetic, even mythical substance. At first he applies the test to Cranston, the Quaker doctor he knew in the prison camp at Pig Eye; then to Daintree, Cranston's friend and mentor, now working for S.I.A.T. on Manoba. But in each of these cases the work that was their life is no longer available or no longer satisfies: "The illusion of my life had been that a man should love his job, be dedicated to it, born to it." This was what he thought he had found, in reality, in Cranston's medical work at Pig Eye; and what Cranston thought he had found in Daintree's struggle to eradicate yaws from the Malayan jungle tribes. But it was an illusion, nevertheless. After 1945, Cranston's work was over. When penicillin was discovered, Daintree's struggle became futile. So Conway has to move further into the past, into his own past, into the heart of the illusion where, strangely, it may be that what is most real to him, his own reality, might be found:

> I hadn't killed the past by going back to Jundapur. I hadn't buried my dead. The dead weren't dead. Everything had grown directly out of the past, undeviatingly; you could squint from the rather blowsy flower down the stem and see the living root; a root which had shaped me.
>
> (bk. IV, ch. 3)

This takes him back again to the palace at Jundapur, to Dora and Krishi, and to the birds of paradise.

The birds perched on branches of trees and shrubs in a spacious hexagonal cage constructed in the middle of an island on the rajah of Jundapur's estate. Though the roof was hollow, looking up at it Krishi, Dora, and William had been able to see the *paradisaeidae* suspended there, or swooping, hovering, and soaring above the leaves and branches of their natural forest. Beneath them, in a glass-topped cabinet, was a set of colored drawings of the birds, with an account of their habits and the curious legends that surrounded them.

But the birds were dead, stuffed, brought to the island stuffed and dead years before by the rajah's father:

> Periodically a Muslim servant called Akbar Ali, using a tall stepladder which could be unclasped from the walls of the cage, climbed up and unscrewed the birds from their rods one by one, and brought them down to inspect the wire frames. In the leather bag he brought there were coils of wire, pliers, a pot of Vaseline jelly and little bottles of fluid which he applied to the body feathers.
>
> (bk. I, ch. 7)

The jellies and lotions that Ali applied to the birds, imparting to them their magnificent gloss and splendor, betrays a hint of tawdriness, of artifice at the heart of experience. It is a more successful bringing together of the significant and the absurd, the urgent and the theatrically cosmetic, than was represented by the Chinese pavilion in the earlier novel. More successful because the subtle blend of nostalgia, romance, and inner, emotional reality that the birds represent is so satisfyingly produced in the behavior of the three characters to one another both then, in the past, and now, during Conway's period of return—when Dora is still, surprisingly, a guest at Jundapur, and the birds of paradise remain undisturbed in their gorgeous but stilted postures.

William and Dora row to the island one afternoon and reenter the cage. Though Ali has been dead for two years, from the ground there is no sign of decay. By now there has been an explicit identification of the birds as symbols of the raj, and later of the Princely States during the British occupation of India. But it has become clear that they mean very much more than that, on a personal level, to William and Dora, though what they mean is intimately tied up with William's and Dora's Indian history and background. What they most profoundly represent is brought out by a picture of one of the birds, an engraving in the old cabinet entitled "Natives of Aru Shooting the Great Bird of Paradise." Here the first victim lies on the ground stunned by the blunt tip of an arrow, waiting to be killed in a way that won't damage its plumage or reduce the market value of its skin. Looking at the engraving, Conway's mind slips back thirty years to the moment when he first saw it. Those thirty years are "sucked back into the vacuum their going had created," and he is back as a young boy by the side of Dora as a young girl. All the illusions of imperial glory, the dreams of a past in India that might have been—even in a simulated form in the Princely States with their ossified and irrelevant splendors—drain away from the memory and the fantasy of those thirty years. But they have helped to bring back the truth of William's feeling for Dora, disentangled from the fantasy that will always be incomplete, because involved with so much that was real and lasting: "The . . . lines at the corners of her eyes . . . , the husky memsahib voice became, briefly, focuses for my tenderness, and acquired beauty as did all the traces left on her by her years, for her years were her life, and I had loved her as a child."

The myths and legends of the birds go much further to complicate our feeling for what Conway has lost and the illumination he has now, fleetingly, achieved. No one can say how seriously their mythical powers were taken by the natives who hunted them and sold them, or how far they cultivated their air of mystery as a merely commercial asset. The belief that they were footless ("Apoda") emphasized their ethereal, immaterial potentialities. Or the suspicion that their feet were cut off by native traders merely emphasized the brutal retribution men exact from whatever is beautiful and strange. The power of the birds, even when their dead forms are capable of giving wing only to fantasy and dreams in the hearts of mortal men, is demonstrated in the strangely isolated moments William, Dora, and Krishi remember having experienced in the cage. One of them was always absent, and in the minds of the two who were there, there was always a difference of opinion about what had happened between them.

Conway's return to Jundapur and his journey to Manoba are stages in a search for what might lie behind the *maya* (illusion) he suspects his father thought was all, finally, life had to offer. At first he looks for the importance a man might possess in his own eyes, then in the histories of others: in Cranston, and, on Manoba, in Daintree. But the most substantial object of his quest remains, in a sense, the most fanciful: the birds of paradise that, if they existed and were found, would make the illusory splendors of his past take wing. And if they do not exist, and are only the fabrications of Daintree's good humor and the vocal tricks of native boys, there is still Melba, the mock bird of paradise, singing of the hills, valleys, and forests of her youth. She "sings as though she sees them through her wrinkled, lidded eyes, which she half closes. There is contentment in her singing, happiness in recollection and a mature acceptance that so much of her youth was *maya,* so much of it illusion."

The Corrida at San Felíu (1964) provides the most extreme example of the temporal dislocation of the narrative that had already been used so successfully in *The Birds of Paradise.* At first glance this is Scott's most puzzling book. In fact it is not so much (apparently) one book as a collection of papers, short stories, and an unfinished novel called *The Plaza de Toros.* These are the creations of a novelist called Edward Thornhill, whose journey from nervous collapse to despair and suicide is charted by the way the editor of these manuscripts had contrived to assemble the psychological dynamics in the life of the man who created them. The core of Thornhill's personality, and the deep reasons for his tragedy, emerge from a complete appraisal of his own behavior and its relation to the behavior of his fictional characters. Since these characters tend to change, in situation and personality, from draft to draft, and since we are able to apply things that we know about Thornhill (and his wife) sometimes in advance, sometimes with hindsight, to his present situation, *Corrida* is a strenuous novel to read. In the end, it may be that it is defeated by its own cleverness. Nevertheless it is a very powerful book, and the quality of the writing in it—often rhetorical, but sometimes spare and unfussily accurate about the most interesting and complex states of mind—prepares the reader much better than its lightheartedly picaresque sequel (*The Bender,* 1963) for the *Quartet* that follows.

III

THE events of *The Raj Quartet* extend over a period of five years, from the "Quit India" motion of the All India Congress Committee in August 1942 to the preparations for partition that followed the British retreat in August 1947. The first volume, *The Jewel in the Crown* (1966), traces some of the causes and consequences of two events that occur during the riots that followed the Congress vote. The first of these is the assault on Miss Edwina Crane, a supervisor of Protestant schools, and the murder of her colleague, Mr. Chaudhuri. The second, more lengthily developed event is the rape of Miss Daphne Manners—the niece of Lady Manners, widow of an ex-governor of Ranpur—by a gang of Indian youths.

In the first part we are offered a history of Edwina Crane's career in the Indian Education Service. In parts 2, 3, and 6 several characters meditate on her experience and offer opinions about the sort of woman she was. In the course of these meditations we learn that she killed herself by dressing in Indian clothes and immolating herself in something like the traditional manner of *suttee.*

The rest of the novel is devoted to the story of Daphne Manners. After her parents' death she has been brought up by Sir Henry and Lady Manners, and is now staying in Mayapore, at the house of an old friend of her aunt called Lili Chatterjee. During this time she enters into two emotional commitments. One of them, with the district superintendent of police, Ronald Merrick, is not at all of her choosing, and she eventually refuses an offer of marriage from him. The other, with a young Indian called Hari Kumar, who has been brought up in England and educated at one of its most prestigious public schools, develops into a serious relationship that transports them both across the racial barrier. It is after consummating their love in the Bibighar Gardens that they are set on by a gang of Indians who beat up Kumar and rape Daphne. Merrick tries to pin the crime on Kumar and five of his associates, but certain technical details and, most damagingly, Daphne's refusal to give evidence that would implicate him make it impossible to charge him with the offense. Nevertheless, he is detained in prison under the Emergency regulations, being "suspected" by Merrick of subversive activities against the British during the riots.

The Day of the Scorpion (1968) touches on the relationship between Daphne and Hari only in passing. We are reminded that Daphne died in childbirth and that Hari remained in prison. The baby is christened "Parvati" by its godmother, Lady Manners, and accompanies her on her travels through northern India. The only extensive development of the Bibighar affair is an examination of Kumar by a Captain Nigel Rowan, which produces an exhaustive account of the details of Kumar's arrest, detention, and treatment at the hands of Ronald Merrick. This treatment, according to Kumar and a fellow detainee, was brutally sadistic, indicating strong homosexual tendencies in Merrick, which are at variance with the public image he presents to the world at all other times.

The main narrative of the second volume, however, has to do with the Laytons, an Anglo-Indian military family who do not appear in *The Jewel in the Crown.* Their long-standing involvement with India is documented with profuse details from their family tree and the social-regimental connections they enjoy. Before their removal from Ranpur to Pankot, in the hills, the youngest daughter, Susan, is to marry a captain in the Indian army called Teddie Bingham. The wedding takes place in the Princely state of Mirat, where the nawab, a pro-British progressive who has allowed himself to be guided toward a liberal and democratic constitution by a White Russian *émigré* called Count Bronowsky, has offered the Laytons the hospitality of his guest house. The only embarrassment occurs when a stone is thrown into the limousine in which Teddie Bingham and his best man are traveling to the service. This best man is Ronald Merrick, now a captain in Military Intelligence. The incident of the stone is followed by a distressing scene on the station platform, where Merrick is approached by an Indian woman in a white sari who pleads with him, falls on her knees, and places her forehead on the ground before his feet. These are the first signs that Merrick's treatment of Kumar and the other boys has not been forgotten. Further details of the hounding of Merrick by Indian fanatics, intent on making political capital out of the Kumar case, are given in the second part of *The Towers of Silence.*

Before the wedding, when the Laytons were spending the summer in Kashmir, the elder Layton sister, Sarah (who now emerges as one of the most important characters in the *Quartet*), secretly visits Lady Manners on her houseboat and sees the baby, Parvati. After the wedding she discusses the Kumar case with Merrick. Though she dislikes him, she begins to form a relationship with him that is further developed as a result of events that occur shortly after the wedding. After getting Susan pregnant during their honeymoon at Nanoora, Teddie goes off with his regiment on active service and is killed on reconnoiter. Merrick, who is with him at the time, tries to save him, but is badly burned and mutilated.

While at Mirat, Sarah has formed a friendly, though distant, relationship with the count's *protégé,* Ahmed Kasim, the second son of a prominent Congress (though Muslim) politician now incarcerated by the British. His arrest, his interview with the British authorities, and his dealings with Congress and the members of his family constitute the first part of *The Day of the Scorpion.* His history and that of his two sons are taken up again in the last volume of the *Quartet,* where the Muslim dilemma over partition or absorption into the new independent state of India is dealt with at great length.

Very little new information about the main characters is provided by *The Towers of Silence* (1971). The presiding genius of the book is Barbie Batchelor, an old acquaintance of Edwina Crane. She has been accepted by Mabel Layton, Sarah and Susan's great-aunt, as a paying guest at her home in Pankot. Barbie's loyalty to Mabel, and her evident unselfishness and good nature, serve as an admirable touchstone against which to measure the behavior of the rest of the English community in Pankot. Also, Barbie's association with Miss Crane, developing into a morbid obsession as her health deteriorates and the news of her old colleague becomes more and more disturbing, eventually turns into an intermittent self-identification with the dead woman. In this way we are provided with yet another example of the disintegration of character brought about by the manner in which a personality in many ways distinguished, and certainly distinctive, is affected by the Indian experience.

The fourth novel, *A Division of the Spoils* (1975), carries the story forward to the British retreat in 1947. A new character, Guy Perron, is introduced. He is a sergeant in Field Security and acts as a medium through which many of the reflections on the historical significance of what is happening are communicated. Perron is also an interesting character in his own right, and he is brought into contact with Ronald Merrick and Sarah Layton in ways that tell us a great deal more about both of these familiar landmarks of the *Quartet.* Also, Nigel Rowan's contribution to the story becomes more important. He is now the political aide to the governor. As such he becomes involved in the neutralization of Mohammed Kasim's political ambitions and Bronowsky's efforts to persuade the nawab of Mirat to have his territories included in the new independent Indian state. He also has to deal with the backwash of the Kumar case as it affects Ronald Merrick and, through him, large numbers of less important characters who are to a greater or lesser extent subject to Merrick's authority. Eventually Merrick, who has married Susan Layton only a year before, is killed by certain anonymous young men who have attached themselves to him at Pankot. He is strangled and then hacked to pieces with an ax.

A great many other things happen in this long novel: Colonel Layton returns to Pankot; an attachment develops between Sarah Layton and Guy Perron; Perron is involved in several adventures in Bombay and Pankot under the watchful eye of Merrick and his Pathan servant (comically described as the Red Shadow—indeed there is a great deal more comedy in this book than there is in the other volumes of the *Quartet*); Bronowsky plans to create a new political order in Mirat by marrying Shiraz, the nawab's only daughter, to his *protégé,* Ahmed (who is, after all, a member of the illustrious Kasim family); and there is the final, awful debacle on the train from Mirat to Ranpur in which the struggle between Muslim and Hindu gets out of control, and Ahmed is killed by a marauding band of Hindu thugs.

The *Quartet* ends, in human terms, where it began: with a dead Indian on the road, being tended by representatives of the English ruling class who are powerless to help him. In the first instance there was a single victim, the nominally Christian Mr. Chaudhuri; in the last, the Muslim victims spread out into the distance on either side of the arrested train. It is an imbalance that gives some indication of the solemnity and often depressive quality of Scott's vision of life. But it also conforms with strict accuracy to the movement of events between August 1942 and the other August of five years later.

In several of the novels Scott was writing shortly before the *Raj Quartet,* relationships among people are mirrored in relations among the places in which they met. This is true, for example, of the cage, the island, and the encircling estate at Jundapur, with its legend of Krishna's encounter with a prince and a princess, which appear in the central scenes of *The Birds of Paradise.* Here again, at the beginning of the *Quartet,* the event on which so much of the plot depends—the rape of Daphne Manners—occurs in and near places that have a symbolic relation to each other, and whose symbolic ambience is brought out by the author in a vivid description of their histories.

"Next, there is the image of a garden: not the Bibighar Garden but the garden of the MacGregor House." So, at the opening of Daphne's story, the two most important places that belong to it are linked in the same sentence. Like the Bibighar, the garden here at the MacGregor House is steeped in the green shadows of a rank and overgrown vegetation. In the shadows "there are dark blue veils, the indigo dreams of plants fallen asleep, and odours of sweet and necessary decay, numerous places layered with the cast-off fruit of other years softened into compost, feeding the living roots that lie under the garden massively, in hungry immobility." The passing of the years has done nothing to obscure the essential history and character of the place. Quite the contrary: the years seem to have nourished what has happened in the past and brought it alive into the present scene.

The history, which is explained to us in great detail, suggests that the MacGregor House and the Bibighar Gardens are closely connected by the passions of those who have inhabited them in the past. But it also suggests that the connection has always issued in violence, and, finally, separation—especially when lovers have tried to cross the seemingly impregnable barrier of race. An invisible river runs between the two places. "No bridge was ever thrown across it. To get from one to the other you could not cross by a bridge but had to take your courage in your hands and enter the flood and let yourself be taken with it, lead where it may." Through the mouth of one of his characters Scott is commending Daphne's decision to immerse herself in what Conrad called "the destructive element." That is what the history of the two houses, and her own sense of duty, impel her to do.

The rape in the Bibighar Gardens destroys whatever might have evolved out of the consummation of Daphne's love for Hari Kumar. Daphne cannot provide Hari with an impeccable alibi for the time at which the assault took place, because Hari was there and had been making love with her immediately before the Indians arrived. No British court of law could have been expected to believe that the penetration of a white woman by a colored man was anything other than rape. But because Daphne finds other ways of protecting Hari from the accusation of rape, Merrick has to separate him from her by bringing forward the charge of "association" with known political radicals. Therefore Kumar languishes in jail during the first three volumes of the *Quartet,* remaining ignorant of the fact that Daphne has died giving birth to Parvati, who is probably his child.

The color issue is discussed by many of the characters, but clearly, in view of the role she plays, Daphne's opinions about it are of paramount importance. The first thing Daphne notices when she admits to herself that she is in love with Hari is how much larger the world has grown. In a way this is true in a literal sense, because it opens up areas of the city of Mayapore with which few other members of the white community are familiar. It is even more true in another sense, which one hesitates to call psychological or moral, but which contains elements of both of these qualities. The truth of it dawns on Daphne when she notices the characteristic expression on the faces of the English. It is one of strain—"the strain of pretending that the world was this small. Hateful. Ingrown. About to explode like powder compressed ready for firing." It is about to explode because of the disappearance of any sense of mission or service or identification with Indian purposes among the English during the present century. The relationship with India is now exposed as one based on "violations":

> Perhaps at one time there was a moral as well as a physical force at work. But the moral thing had gone sour. Has gone sour. Our faces reflect the sourness. The women look worse than the men because consciousness of physical superiority is unnatural to us. A white man in India can feel physically superior without unsexing himself. But what happens to a woman if she tells herself that 99 per cent of the men she sees are not men at all, but creatures of an inferior species whose colour is their main distinguishing mark? What happens when you unsex a nation, treat it like a nation of eunuchs? Because that's what we've done, isn't it?
>
> (*The Jewel in the Crown,* pt. VII)

This is an exemplification of a point made by many historians of the post–Mutiny phase of the raj, that the breakdown of trust between the two races was severely exacerbated by the conduct of the memsahibs. The result was that "there's dishonesty on both sides because the moral issue has gone sour on them as well as on us. . . . It's our fault it's dead because it was our responsibility to widen it, but we narrowed it down and narrowed it down by never suiting actions to words."

It is one of the ironies of the situation at the Bibighar that Daphne's behavior after the assault is entirely consistent with the point of view she adumbrates here about the superiority of white skin to brown. The attack on her exemplifies the point she had made about the primitive instinct to destroy or defile anything that is different; nothing could have been more obviously or superficially different than the color of Daphne's skin as compared with that of her Indian assailants. But what follows from the assault—Daphne's own insistence on taking control of the situation—is an even more convincing manifestation of the truth of what she has said. Even in her panic, she admits, "there was this assumption of superiority, of privilege, of believing I knew what was best for both of us, because the colour of my skin automatically put me on the side of those who never told a lie." Daphne's lie is intended to work to Hari, the Indian's, advantage. But it is only half successful because she has underestimated Merrick's hatred of Hari, his burning sense of having been humiliated by Daphne's preference for Hari over himself.

Daphne exposes the British idea of justice in India, the idea that still provides them with the illusion of moral superiority and therefore the dispensation to rule. She compares it with a robot. "We've created a blundering judicial robot," she says:

> We can't stop it working. It works for us even when we least want it to. We created it to prove how fair, how civilized we are. But it is a white robot and it can't distinguish between love and rape. It only understands physical connection and only understands it as a crime because it only exists to punish crime.
>
> (pt. 7)

When she goes on to wonder what would happen if someone came along and, by error or good judgment, fixed into the robot "a special circuit with the object of making it impartial and colour blind," she looks forward, without knowing it, to what she herself is to achieve during the inquiry that follows Hari's arrest. Then she is given the opportunity, through the questions Judge Menen puts to her, of creating that "special circuit." She is able to go to the heart of the judicial mechanism, to expose it for what it is, "by imposing an impossible task on it—the task of *understanding* the justice of what it was doing, and of proving that its own justice was the equal or the superior of mine." She is able to do this by making two claims: that the youths who raped her could have been white youths with blacked faces; and that one of them was circumcised and must therefore have been a Muslim, and not one of the five Hindu suspects who were arrested with Hari. These are "facts" the robot is not equipped to deal with. The customary assumptions about relations between black and white, which the Bibighar case seemed to exemplify so easily, are thrown into confusion as the racial identities of the parties concerned are shown to be ambiguous—resistant to categories of black and white on the basis of which the judicial machine is programmed to function.

No one inside the English community can bring himself to disbelieve in the judicial system entirely. That is why when Daphne's baby is born, she is given into the protection of Lady Manners, who exists now quite outside the English circle and the raj. When Lady Manners dies the child will be brought up by her Indian friend Lili Chatterjee. She will grow up among people who will have remained untouched by the racial bitterness that the British move toward independence and the Indian move toward partition are fomenting at the heart of the political system.

It is of great symbolic importance that Sarah Layton is the only English person in the *Quartet* to visit Lady Manners and see the baby. As Barbie Batchelor suggests to her, it is strange how closely involved Sarah has become, in a roundabout way, in the Bibighar affair—although it occurred more than two years before she arrived in Pankot, and most clearly concerned two people whom she had never met and would never meet. For not only has Sarah visited Lady Manners, she has also become closely involved with Ronald Merrick, the "third party" to the affair, whose relationship with her sister, Susan, involves Sarah closely in all that is most willfully destructive of the Anglo-Indian "embrace."

The way the plot keeps coming back to Bibighar, forcing the characters to discuss it and investigate it, and occasionally increase our knowledge of what happened in it, will need no emphasizing. The last volume ends with Guy Perron's unsuccessful attempt to find Hari in one of the poor quarters of Ranpur. Also, I have tried to show how the affair between Daphne Manners and Hari Kumar contains within itself all the essential properties of the Anglo-Indian situation. Others who are caught up in that situation, especially Sarah Layton and Ronald Merrick, are drawn to it through mixed motives of guilt, curiosity, necessity, the possibility of learning something. Merrick's career is interrupted again and again by reminders of Bibighar: painted signs, a woman in a sari, sinister and ubiquitous bicycles. They are visible symbols for him of all that Bibighar means, and that he carries inside himself.

The dense texture of the writing, with its rich and suggestively reiterated imagery, testifies to the feeling of sadness at what has been destroyed. In particular, the love affair between Hari and Daphne; in general, the rather different affair between the English and India, which was not altogether lacking in love. When he considers it appropriate, Scott is able to produce some of the sparest and tautest narrative prose of this century. At the beginning and the end of the *Quartet,* the descriptions of the assault on Edwina Crane and Mr. Chaudhuri, and the slaughter of the Muslims on the train to Ranpur, are startlingly vivid and succinct. But the variety of Scott's prose should be assessed by looking not only at these rapid accounts of violent ends but also at the comedy of Perron's dealings with the "Red Shadow"; the pathetic little episode of Pinkie and the psychiatric records at Pankot; the brutally honest description of Major Clarke's seduction of Sarah Layton in Calcutta; even the recording of historical events through the medium of invented cartoons at the beginning of the second book of *A Division of the Spoils.* The surfaces of the novels are more various than my account of them so far might have suggested. Nevertheless, it would be true to say, I think, that the staple of Scott's prose is a slow-moving, hesitant, grammatically complex and heavily loaded sentence structure, which gathers together fragments of what has already been, more than it propels forward events that are about to come into being. In this respect the writing is a perfect mirror of the formal stasis of the novel. It provides ample opportunity for the subtle deployment of Scott's symbolism as well as the expression of his essentially elegiac tone.

Some of the symbolism of the *Quartet*—like the painting of "The Jewel in the Crown," or the destruction of a scorpion in a ring of fire on the lawn of the Layton compound—is uncomplicated, though it is used over and over again to bring out unexpected areas of relevance. Events in the *Quartet* are often of this kind. Indeed the central event of the rape in the Bibighar Gardens is a symbolic occurrence that in a sense absorbs into itself everything else that happens. But the local symbolism is more likely than not to attach itself to an object that can be transferred from person to person, gathering into itself a richer and richer significance as it does so. One such object, which plays an especially important part in the narrative though it has little effect on the plot, is a volume of poems by the eighteenth-century Urdu poet Gaffur.

The poems of Gaffur first make their appearance when Sarah Layton is looking for a suitable gift to express the gratitude of the Layton family to the nawab of Mirat. Lady Manners tells her of the relationship between the eighteenth-century poet and the present-day nawab, both of whom are members of the Kasim family. The gift of the book by Sarah to the uncle and prospective father-in-law (if Bronowsky's plans succeed) of Ahmed Kasim, then, is the suggestion of Daphne's aunt and Parvati's godmother—a minor consequence, in other words, of the Bibighar affair. The nawab is not the only recipient of a volume of Gaffur's poems. Guy Perron receives a similar gift from Count Bronowsky, who has translated them. One way or another Gaffur's poems circulate among several of the characters. For example, Barbie knows several quotations from them by heart.

We are not offered any one complete poem by Gaffur until the very last page of the *Quartet,* when Guy Perron decides to examine his copy on the plane out of Ranpur. Earlier he had been writing to Sarah in the airport lounge, mentally incorporating in his letter a passage from an article by "Philoctetes" in the *Ranpur Gazette.* Guy has realized that "Philoctetes" is Hari Kumar. So when he slips the letter to Sarah between the pages of Gaffur's poems, a conjunction of sentiments of the most powerful kind provides Scott's novel with an exemplary epilogue. Kumar's prose recalls his life in England:

> I walk home [he writes], thinking of another place, of seemingly long endless summers and the shade of different kinds of trees; and then of winters when the branches of the trees were bare, so bare that, recalling them now, it seems inconceivable to me that I looked at them and did not think of the summer just gone, and the spring soon to come, as illusions, as dreams, never fulfilled, never to be fulfilled.
>
> (*A Division of the Spoils,* bk. II, ch. 4)

Gaffur's poem also emphasizes the inevitability of loss and the heartbreaking illusoriness of dreams: for Kumar, England; for the Laytons and the Muirs, India. But the poem also circles back on its own sentiments and gathers together the experiences that have been lost, in a formal structure that will not let them go—repeating them over and over again for as long as anyone is there to read the novel in which it is embedded:

> Fleeting moments: these are held a long time in the eye,
> The blind eye of the ageing poet,
> So that even you, Gaffur, can imagine
> In this darkening landscape
> The bowman lovingly choosing his arrow,
> The hawk outspacing the cheetah,
> (The fountain splashing lazily in the courtyard),
> The girl running with the deer.
>
> (bk. II, ch. 6—coda)

Bronowsky is clearly the Arthur Waley of the court of Mirat. But Scott has arranged that he shall be so, and has provided the original sentiments as well as their translated form. As the pages of Gaffur's poems fold over the reminiscences of Hari Kumar, and they in turn are entwined in Guy Perron's thoughts of Sarah Layton, the *Quartet* comes to rest with a characteristic superimposition of details.

IV

At a later date, Sarah Layton marries Guy Perron and goes back to England as his wife. Susan marries for a third time, a Scottish doctor with whom she appears to be happy and contented. Susan and Teddie Bingham's son has also become a doctor. These and other snippets of information do not appear, as they would in a Victorian or Edwardian novel, in a brief concluding chapter, tying up all the loose ends of the story. In fact they do not appear anywhere in the *Quartet.* Scott has circumvented the problem of letting his readers know "what happened" to his characters by incorporating their later histories, briefly and tantalizingly, in the odd corners and antechambers of another novel.

Two of the principal characters of *Staying On* (1976) are "Tusker" Smalley and his wife, Lucy, an army couple who play very small, almost walk-on parts in the *Quartet.* Their association with the Laytons is commemorated by a photograph of the family's farewell party in the garden of Commandant House in 1947. As well as the then Colonel Smalley and his wife, it is possible to pick out Sarah and Guy, who have returned from Delhi before flying home to his Aunt Charlotte in England. The Smalleys, however, do not go home. They "stay on" in India and retire to Pankot, where they become tenants at the lodge of Smith's hotel. It is there that we find them, twenty-five years after Independence, at the beginning of Scott's last, wonderfully comic and deeply moving novel.

Tusker and Lucy are old people in a foreign country (when the novel opens he is seventy, she is sixty-six). They cannot avoid leading lives that are trivial at best and irritable most of the time. Their lives revolve around arguments as to who should exercise the dog, Bloxsaw; how to deal with the weeds that are taking over the compound and choking the canna lilies; whom Lucy should invite to Tusker's birthday celebrations; and whether they can afford chicken pulao to be brought over from Smith's or should make do with a poached egg, cooked by themselves, for dinner. Events like these are punctuated by arguments with their Muslim servant, Ibrahim, arguments with the mali, arguments with their landlords, Mr. and Mrs. Bhoolaboy, and most often, arguments with each other. These last arguments are among the comic glories of the novel.

While *Staying On* is in much of its detail a very funny novel, its overall effect is one of profound sadness. With all its comic strengths and its sophisticated documentation of the new Indian class structure, this novel's main claim on our attention arises from the extent to which it makes us care about the fortunes of the people in it. These are Tusker and Lucy especially, but also a large cast of secondary (and tertiary) characters who include not merely Ibrahim and Mr. Bhoolaboy's accountant, but Coocoo Menektara, the senior regimental officer's wife.

"I have had rather a sad life. . . . Yes, from the beginning I had a sad life," Lucy says to herself as she seals her letter to Sarah Layton. "A life like a flower that has never bloomed, but how many do?" Certainly her own life cannot be said to have "bloomed." It had been given no romantic nourishment from Tusker after his premarital visits to the solicitors' office where she used to work in London. At that time he offered her the dreams a young inexperienced rector's daughter might long for in the person of a young officer, a stranger from the mysterious East. But her dreams withered with the clumsiness and infrequency of his sexual possession of her. Her dreamless days were stultified by the routine and hierarchy of Anglo-Indian military life, the weakness of her husband's ambition, and, finally, the uselessness of any ambition he might still have nurtured after 1947 and Independence. Having stayed on into the 1960's and early 1970's, she has had to make the sharp adjustment from being a colonel's wife in the British Army to being a person whose role is negligible or simply nonexistent.

The Anglo-Indian community that has deserted Pankot and Ranpur has been replaced by "a new race of sahibs and memsahibs of international status and connexion . . . and Lucy and Tusker had become for them almost as far down the social scale as the Eurasians were in the days of the raj." Now, in 1972, these are represented in the Smalleys' personal lives by members of the new Indian entrepreneurial class such as Mrs. Bhoolaboy and Mr. and Mrs. Desai, "the emerging Indian middle class of wheelers and dealers who with their chicanery, their corrupt practices, their black money, their use of political power for personal gain were ruining the country or if not ruining it making it safe chiefly for themselves." Their symbol is the Shiraz hotel, and their stranglehold over the old India is demonstrated in their conspiracy with Mrs. Bhoolaboy to take over Smith's in order to raze it to the ground and extend their own monstrous building. The Smalleys, Mr. Bhoolaboy, Ibrahim, and Joseph (the new mali) are simply nuisances who will have to be got out of the way.

The full impact of the change is felt by no one more than by the Smalleys. They have made different investments in India, or so they feel, but in each case the new India has let them down. In Lucy's case, though, the heights from which she has descended are largely fictional. It is true that, at the very end, later than she had ever hoped, she became a colonel's wife. But the years before were filled with disappointment and chagrin. Tusker's lack of ambition had ensured that even when he was promoted, to major and then to lieutenant-colonel, the wives of other majors and lieutenant-colonels would leave her in no doubt that she and her husband were the junior, because most recent, members of that particular "club." The pain this constant assumption of inferiority has caused her, and the bitterness toward Tusker it has left with her, are harshly illuminated by her behavior after his recovery from his first heart attack. She is terrified about what her financial position will be if he dies first. In a desperate attempt to get him to explain what provision, if any, he has made against such an eventuality, she lets fly at him all the resentment she feels about the way she has been treated.

This is the past of which she regrets the passing, just as it was the future into which she was proud and excited to enter, after her vicarage wedding and her humdrum life at the office. She imagined fellow officers "standing to make a little roof of crossed swords over our heads," and a maharajah as a guest, "with pearls looped round his neck and the Star of India on his turban." None of these things materialized. In fact, life in India was every bit as depressing and diminishing as life in England had been. The trouble was, " 'I've always had this tendency to imagine, to fantasize, to *project.*' " But there was nothing substantial to project her imagination onto, or, now, to reflect it back against—except a picture of army life in Pankot and elsewhere from which the petty humiliations and embarrassments have been removed, and the life of a typical pukka memsahib substituted for them. In her less self-deceiving moments she knows that the life she and Tusker led before 1947 was much like the life they are having to live after it. The deterioration in their finances makes a difference, though, and so does the fact that the people who look down on her and Tusker now are not white, but brown.

None of these things would have been significant if Lucy could have depended on Tusker. But the novel shows how during the period between his first and his fatal heart attack, Tusker persistently lets her down, and then behaves badly as a response to her behaving badly over being let down. Her efforts to provide a mali who will appear to be paid by Mrs. Bhoolaboy instead of by herself, so that in his own eyes Tusker will not have lost face, are greeted with a complete lack of response, an unwillingness even to notice that the mali is there. Having invited the new rector to dinner at the bungalow, he makes no attempt to help Lucy arrange for the visit. Instead he throws up difficulty after difficulty, as if he had no responsibility in the matter. His treatment of Ibrahim nearly loses them their only servant at a time when to possess at least one servant is crucial. But underneath his apparent boorishness and insensitivity to his wife, there festers a deep sense of guilt at the way she has been treated that he has never been able to confess to her, and that has exacerbated rather than softened his emotional brutality.

It is therefore of great importance to Lucy that her anxieties about her financial position at Tusker's death do at least elicit a letter from him that contains a statement of the appropriate details. What is important is not the information about the money (which does not give many grounds for optimism), but the fact that Tusker did write to her, and, from her point of view though perhaps not from ours, in astonishing terms. His explanation of what has happened to the money brings with it a much wider explanation of his failure to provide Lucy with what he knew she wanted, but which he knew it was not in him to achieve:

"I still think we were right to stay on, though I don't think of it any longer as staying on, but just as hanging on, which people of our age and upbringing and limited talents, people who have never been really poor but never had any real money, never inherited real money, never made real money, have to do, wherever they happen to be, when they can't work any more. I'm happier hanging on in India, not for India as India but because I can't just merely think of it as a place where I drew my pay for the first 25 years of my working life, which is a hell of a long time anyway, though by rights it should have been longer. But there you are. Suddenly the powers that be say, Right, Smalley, we're not wanted here any more, we've all got to bugger off, too bad you're not ten years younger or ten years older. I thought about this a lot at the time and it seemed to me I'd invested in India, not money which I've never had, not talent (Ha!) which I've only had a limited amount of, nothing India needed or needs or has been one jot the better for, but was all I had to invest in anything. *Me.* Where I went wrong was in thinking of it that way and expecting a return on the investment in the end, and anticipating the profits."

(*Staying On,* ch. 14)

Limited talent and meager finances discourage Tusker's ambition and produce a willingness in him to settle for mere security. But through all the humiliations and vexations Lucy and Tusker have grown together, as well as apart. The letter Tusker has written, blessedly, at the eleventh hour, make it clear to Lucy that this is how he sees it: "You've been a good woman to me Luce. Sorry I've not made it clear I think so." They are sentences that give Lucy something to hold on to, that show her, after he has died, that her life with Tusker has not been totally useless and empty. When she goes to sleep on the night before his death, "peace enveloped her. She turned on her side away from the light from the living-room and let her sleepy fingers find their way to the envelope that contained the only love letter she had had in all the years she had lived."

There is some consolation here. Even so, of all Scott's many images of spiritual desolation this one is among the bleakest. For Lucy, "staying on" has become an even more permanent and hopeless condition than it had seemed to be during those twenty-five years with Tusker. The comic mood has entirely disintegrated, leaving behind it the figure of a woman who is, for the first time in her life, alone. She is Scott's last survivor. The price she pays for that honor is, as we would have expected with the *Quartet* behind us, a cruelly high one.

SELECTED BIBLIOGRAPHY

I. Collected Works. *The Raj Quartet* (London, 1966–1975), includes The *Jewel in the Crown, The Day of the Scorpion, The Towers of Silence, A Division of the Spoils.*

II. Separate Works. *I, Gerontius: A Trilogy* (London, 1940), poems, "The Creation," "The Dream," "The Cross"; *Pillars of Salt* (London, 1948), drama, in H. F. Rubinstein, ed., *Four Jewish Plays; Johnnie Sahib* (London, 1952), novel; *The Alien Sky* (New York and London, 1953), novel; *A Male Child* (New York and London, 1956), novel; *The Mark of the Warrior* (New York and London, 1958), novel; *The Chinese Love Pavilion* (New York and London, 1960), novel; *The Birds of Paradise* (New York and London, 1962), novel; *The Bender* (New York and London, 1963), novel; *The Corrida at San Feliu* (New York and London, 1964), novel; *The Jewel in the Crown* (New York and London, 1966), novel; *The Day of the Scorpion* (New York and London, 1968), novel; *The Towers of Silence* (New York and London, 1971), novel; *A Division of the Spoils* (New York and London, 1975), novel; *Staying On* (New York and London, 1976), novel.

III. Biographical and Critical Studies. J. Mellors, "Raj Mahal: Paul Scott's Indian Quartet," in *London Magazine,* no. 15 (June–July 1975), pp. 62–67; C. Moorhead, "Getting Engrossed in the Death-Throes of the Raj," in the *Times* (20 October 1975), p. 7; B. Parry, "Paul Scott's Raj," in *South Asian Review,* no. 8 (July–October 1975); M. Beloff, "The End of the Raj: Paul Scott's Novels as History," in *Encounter,* no. 46 (May 1976), pp. 54–73; F. Giles, "Real Rubies of the Raj," in the *Sunday Times* (4 December 1977), p. 16; F. S. Weinbaum, "Aspiration and Betrayal in Paul Scott's *The Ra Quartet,*" in *Dissertation Abstract International* 37: 6481A (1977); F. S. Weinbaum, "Paul Scott's India: *The Ra Quartet,*" in *Critique,* no. 20 (1978), pp. 100–110; P. Ableman, "Paul Scott: A Cosmic Vision?," in *Books and Book men* (November 1978), pp. 47–49; R. R. James, "In th Steps of Paul Scott," in the *Listener,* no. 101 (8 Marc 1979), pp. 359–361; J. Banerjee, "A Living Legacy: A Indian View of Paul Scott's India," in *London Magazine* no. 20 (April–May 1980), pp. 97–104; K. Bhaskara Rac *Paul Scott* (Boston, 1980), Twayne's English Authors Series; P. Swinden, *Paul Scott: Images of India* (London, 1980 M. M. Mahood, "Paul Scott's Guardians," in the *Yearbook of English Studies,* 13 (1983), pp. 244–258; P. M. S Dawson, "Race, Sex and Class in Paul Scott's *Raj Quartet,*" in *Literature and Imperialism* (London, 1983), pp. 170–180.

PHILIP LARKIN

(1922–1985)

Alan Brownjohn

I

IN his very funny and self-revealing poem "I Remember, I Remember," from *The Less Deceived,* Philip Larkin dashes any supposition that he may have had an eventful, or romantic, or conventionally poetic early life. Sardonically, he denies, in turn, any childhood visionary experiences, any release into entertaining adventure from the routines of family living, any overwhelming first-love recollections—

> The bracken where I never trembling sat,
>
> Determined to go through with it; where she
> Lay back, and "all became a burning mist."

—any hint whatsoever of juvenile genius detected and nurtured by discerning elders. Larkin's down-to-earth contention is that his formative years were monumentally ordinary. There were so few excitements that he can, he feels, truthfully describe his childhood as "unspent," meaning that it scarcely happened at all.

The poem is partly a rejoinder to those fanciful, autobiographical excursions in which writers have traced in their childhood all the magical stirrings of their later talent. But it is also, underneath the humor, a considered personal statement about how Larkin saw both life and poetry. It was never a matter of blinding revelations, mystical insights, expectations glitteringly fulfilled. Life, for Larkin and, implicitly, for all of us, is something lived mundanely, with a gradually accumulating certainty that its golden prizes are sheer illusion, that second-best things will have to suffice.

As a poet he took as his themes such things as the gap between human hope and cold reality; the illusory nature of choice in life; frustration with one's lot in a present that is dismal, and in face of a future that brings only age and death. Against all this, on the positive side, he could set only images of a personal, or a national, past in which life was more ordered and attractive than it is now; a reverence for places and activities that contain and perpetuate the deepest and best human feelings; and certain indefinable images of purity and serenity, known mostly at solitary moments, that enabled him to rise above the soiled terrain of living. It may seem unlikely ground on which to build major poetry. But Larkin produced the most technically brilliant and resonantly beautiful, profoundly disturbing yet appealing and approachable body of verse of any English poet in the last forty years.

Larkin's "unspent" childhood was lived in Coventry, where he was born 9 August 1922 to parents in the professional middle class (his father was the city treasurer). It would indeed seem, if one puts together the details from the one or two autobiographical pieces he published, that Larkin's early years, like most people's, were typical rather than remarkable. There were no indications of the child prodigy, but plenty of the expected boyhood enthusiasms (playing with model trains, collecting cigarette cards, following cricket fanatically). One early ambition was to be a jazz drummer. He was educated in a very good, staid grammar school that uncovered no literary flair, though he contributed humorous prose monologues and poems to the magazine. In 1959, in the third number of *Umbrella,* a small literary magazine published in Coventry, Larkin wrote of reading at this period "at the rate of a book a day, even despite the tiresome interruptions of morning and afternoon school." Eventually he deserted his drumming ambitions "to settle upon a literary career. . . . I wrote ceaselessly . . . now verse, which I sewed up into little books, now prose, a thousand words a night after homework, resting my foolscap on Beethoven's Op. 132, the only classical album I possessed."

From school he went up to read English at St. John's College, Oxford, in 1940, a wartime undergraduate of eighteen who expected to be called into the armed forces before long. Larkin recalled the atmosphere of austerity and the unsophisticated boyishness of his undergraduate generation. But in terms of friendship and stimulation from his student peers, this wartime university education seems to have denied him little. Among his friends were the novelist Kingsley Amis, the detective-fiction writer Edmund Crispin (the late Bruce Montgomery), the poet Alan Ross, the politician Edward du Cann. Failing his army medical, he was able to complete his Oxford years without interruption, and took first-class honors in 1943.

Larkin's subsequent career was as outwardly uneventful as his early life: librarian's posts in a public library in Wellington, Shropshire, and then in academic libraries at the University of Leicester (then the University College) and Queen's University, Belfast. He became the librarian in the Brynmor Jones Library of the University of Hull in 1955, a post he occupied until his death. Deliberately, but fully in keeping with his temperament and inclination, Larkin resisted that element of public living which opens itself as an opportunity or a snare for many poets, as their talent and fame develops. He avoided the poetry-reading circuits completely, declaring shyly but emphatically, in 1973, when persuaded to read his celebrated poem "The Whitsun Weddings" before a studio audience for a radio broadcast, that "this is the first time I've ever read a poem in public, and if I have any say in the matter it'll be the last."

He wrote little about his own verse, though he prefaced his readings on the record made of the complete book *The Whitsun Weddings* with some fascinating comment, and some of his jazz reviews and occasional literary criticism throw light on both the writings and the personality. Awards (they include the Queen's Gold Medal for Poetry, several honorary degrees, and appointment as a Companion of Honour) came to this very private man without his striving after them, as did the esteem of the critics. All of it left him modestly surprised that such things should have happened to him at all.

II

THE poems in Larkin's first volume, *The North Ship* (1945), are indisputably those of a private, solitary person. Though full of interest, *The North Ship* is not a very good book, and comparison with the vigorous scene-setting and characterization of Larkin's first novel, *Jill,* published one year later, would have suggested at the time that his talent lay in fiction rather than poetry. At the same time, critical attempts to separate it entirely from the later Larkin, as something quite untypical as well as inferior, are mistaken.

Introducing the new edition of 1966 (with slyly amusing reference to the circumstances of its original publication), Larkin saw in the poems evidence of "not one abandoned self but several"—the ex-schoolboy for whom W. H. Auden was the modern master, the undergraduate looking to Dylan Thomas, and "the immediately post-Oxford self, isolated in Shropshire with a complete Yeats stolen from the local girls' school." But though there are certainly signs of all these poets (the first and third in style and content, the second in the realm of nature that the poems mostly inhabit), there is never any slavish imitation, conscious or unconscious. And already the voice has some characteristic Larkin tones that will be heard again in each of his later, mature volumes, especially at those crucial moments of removal from the real world into a purer because more lonely existence.

The North Ship has thirty-one poems. Of these twenty-three are simply and self-effacingly numbered, and of the remainder some have noncommittal titles such as "Dawn," "Winter," and "Night Music"—never a good tactic for leaving a clear impression on the reader's mind. In fact, the impression left by *The North Ship* is that of a poet struggling sensitively—with unambitious technical care rather than verbal energy or imaginative stamina—to pit some private experiences of exhilaration and release, or some recurrent images of purity and vitality in nature, against the dullness of ordinary, solitary existence and the prevailing sense of death; so the later Larkin *is* here, though writ very small. Poem I celebrates spring and renewal only to curtail its strenuous bursts of joy with a mildly forbidding Yeatsian refrain:

> Every one thing,
> Shape, colour and voice,
> Cries out, Rejoice!
> *A drum taps: a wintry drum.*

The earth, in III, contains nothing as pure as the simple light of the full moon, an idea to which Larkin will return much later; and the same earth is most "brilliant" (VII) when it is most "unearthly." In IX, a sonnet, Larkin submits himself exultantly to the music of nature, the wind and air in a high place, as a romantic poet might; but is carried back relentlessly to the harder human world:

> How to recall such music, when the street
> Darkens? Among the rain and stone places
> I find only an ancient sadness falling,
> Only hurrying and troubled faces,
> The walking of girls' vulnerable feet,
> The heart in its own endless silence kneeling.

The enjoyment of being solitary, the sad faces of the urban crowd, the abjectness of the heart expressed in the effective final line recur frequently in *The North Ship* and will all crop up again in the later Larkin, though not quite in the same form. The "Ugly Sister" of poem XIX (who is "not bewitched in adolescence / And brought to love") will, for example, return as the isolated figure in the later books who is constantly preferring the silences of nature to the conversation of people, his own company to that of others. The parting lovers in X, XXIV, XXV, and XXX will again be separated, by time, space, and the protagonist's sense of his own inability to love, in several more arresting poems in subsequent volumes.

There are other elements of continuity from the vein of *The North Ship* that are worth noting. The remarkable—remarkably optimistic—"Wedding Wind" in *The Less Deceived* reads like a full-bodied version of one of the brief, cryptic "situation" poems in the first book. And clear parallels in the nature of the imagery and its uses can be made with poems like "Dry Point" (sexual imagery opposed to a metaphor of light representing purity and freedom) and "Absences" (sea imagery providing a link between the strained celebration of natural forces in *The North Ship* and some powerful, intensely mysterious features of a poem like "Livings" [II] in *High Windows*).

But what will not be repeated is the clear debt to Auden in the untypical allegory employed in "Conscript" (X), or the Yeats-like cadences of XIII and XX. Larkin ascribed the weaknesses of *The North Ship* to the power of Yeats's influence ("pervasive as garlic") and any improvement at that time to his new-found admiration for the poetry of Thomas Hardy. But "Waiting for Breakfast," a further poem added at the end of the new edition of *The North Ship* (written a year after the others and showing "the Celtic fever abated and the patient sleeping soundly"), is a fully developed achievement of the mature Larkin, who is a very individual poet indeed. And the main difference between *The North Ship* and the books of poems that follow it (three only, brought out at ten-year intervals) is that the first volume, despite flashes of promise, contains scarcely anything that is more than fragmentary and tentative. The poems are mostly short, the full, authentic Larkin voice is heard only faintly (if still more distinctly than anyone else's), and the later themes are only hinted at. The abundant technical expertise has not yet come into operation. Above all, the typical Larkin protagonist —humorous, self-deprecatory, observant—seems shyly reluctant to show himself.

After *The North Ship* Larkin endeavored unsuccessfully, for a few years, to publish a second book of poems with the title *In the Grip of Light.* Finally, he sent out in 1951 a privately issued pamphlet, *XX Poems,* which attracted no public attention at all, even though several poems in it were to be praised when they were reissued in his hardback volume *The Less Deceived.* This book, a collection of twenty-nine poems, was venturesomely published by the little Marvell Press in Hull in 1955, when the poet was thirty-two, and the change and improvement since the early book is instantly apparent. One gains an immediate sense, from the first page, of growing technical command and range (in the highly wrought nine-line stanza of "Church Going" and the witty, terse quatrains of "Toads"); of greater substance, and of a careful, sensitive thoroughness in the working through of ideas (in work as different as the reflective, nostalgic love poem "Maiden Name" and "Poetry of Departures," with its mordant observations on freedom of action). There is now, for the first time, a thread of wry, decidedly disconcerting humor ("I Remember, I Remember"; and "If, My Darling," where he writes at once nakedly and bizarrely about private quirks and fears). There is some lovingly detailed observation of a real world ("At Grass" and "Church Going" again). But the largest difference is summed up in a new ability to convince and to move the reader through the confidence of a fully developed poetic personality; because Larkin had now discovered that it was perfectly valid, and indeed liberating, to be entirely himself, using his own language.

The poem of which the closing lines provide the

title of the book is called "Deceptions." It is concerned with the drugging and rape of a young girl in the London of the last century: Henry Mayhew's *London Labour and the London Poor* provides the epigraph. This choice of a very specific starting point, together with the direct manner of the poet's compassionate address to the girl, immediately distinguishes the poem from any in *The North Ship:*

Even so distant, I can taste the grief,
Bitter and sharp with stalks, he made you gulp.
The sun's occasional print, the brisk brief
Worry of wheels along the street outside
Where bridal London bows the other way,
And light, unanswerable and tall and wide,
Forbids the scar to heal . . .

The unobtusively adept play of rhyme and rhythm, the studied appropriateness of diction and imagery (the exact pathos of "Where bridal London bows the other way" and the characteristic Larkin light image) are the hallmarks of the poet's mature style. And the message the poem proceeds to offer is also characteristic:

What can be said,
Except that suffering is exact, but where
Desire takes charge, readings will grow erratic?
For you would hardly care
That you were less deceived, out on that bed,
Than he was, stumbling up the breathless stair
To burst into fulfilment's desolate attic.

Consolatory comment would be irrelevant, but one can at least be certain that the rapist would have known desolation more bitter after the fulfillment of his desires.

In varying forms, the idea here is a recurrent and important one in Larkin. The recognized rewards and goals in life are deceptions. This applies not only to crude sexual success or worldly fame, but to acknowledged ends such as happiness in marriage or among social groups. It is more sensible not to strive for such things. In *The Less Deceived,* "Places, Loved Ones" advises against hoping for the ideal circumstances of life to arrive:

wiser to keep away
From thinking you still might trace
Uncalled-for to this day
Your person, your place.

"Wires" tells of the young and hopeful cattle (but it is not only cattle) who, "scenting purer water," blunder up against electric fences that turn them into old cattle from that moment. And the marvelous and haunting "Next, Please" (the first of numerous ironically sinister Larkin titles) argues that life's "sparkling armada of promises" is an illusion in face of death:

Only one ship is seeking us, a black-
Sailed unfamiliar, towing at her back
A huge and birdless silence. In her wake
No waters breed or break.

There will often, however, be some degree of self-reproach and self-questioning at not somehow having managed to contrive a different kind of existence from the sober one he finds himself landed with. Being average, ordinary, even dull may be just what you would wish for a child (in "Born Yesterday"), if that brings more happiness that the possession of high talents or other "uncustomary" qualities. But Larkin acutely senses, at this stage in his writing, a dilemma of choice between a life of risk and adventure and the steady rituals of secure employment. In two entertaining and challenging pieces, "Toads" and "Poetry of Departures," he examines the possibility of getting away from the plodding, timid world of work and home:

Why should I let the toad *work*
  Squat on my life?
Can't I use my wit as a pitchfork
  And drive the brute off?

Six days of the week it soils
  With its sickening poison—
Just for paying a few bills!
  That's out of proportion.
("Toads")

* * *

We all hate home
And having to be there:
I detest my room,
Its specially-chosen junk,
The good books, the good bed,
And my life, in perfect order:
So to hear it said

He walked out on the whole crowd
Leaves me flushed and stirred,

> Like *Then she undid her dress*
> Or *Take that you bastard;*
> Surely I can, if he did?
> ("Poetry of Departures")

Larkin's vigorous colloquial mode here, blended subtly with serious, nicely paced argument, catches the momentary intensity of people's frustration with their routines. But in the end, in both poems, the speaker decides he cannot make the break. Something toadlike inside him prevents it, or else he analyzes (rationalizes?) this desire to get away from it all as "artificial." Nevertheless, the dilemma does not go away and is closely bound up with the virtual impossibility of sorting out matters such as time, freedom of will, the seizing of life's opportunities. In "Triple Time" the present moment, soured and uneventful as it is, was what one looked forward to in childhood as a time of "adult enterprise"; but in the future it will come to resemble

> A valley cropped by fat neglected chances
> That we insensately forbore to fleece.

All these are common attitudes, dilemmas, and conclusions, and much of the appeal of *The Less Deceived* lies in Larkin's ability to define them and enclose them in a poetry very much that of "a man speaking to men." The larger the questions about the nature and purpose of human existence become, the more impressive the poem: he rises more impressively to the large themes with each succeeding volume. The most important poem in *The Less Deceived* is certainly "Church Going," about visiting a church in an age when religion no longer seems valid. The separation of the words in the title is deliberate, since the poet, having stepped awkwardly into the building, looked vaguely around it, and donated (it is legal tender, but faintly disrespectful in what is probably an Ulster Protestant church) "an Irish sixpence," starts wondering

> When churches fall completely out of use
> What we shall turn them into, if we shall keep
> A few cathedrals chronically on show,
> Their parchment, plate and pyx in locked cases,
> And let the rest rent-free to rain and sheep.
> Shall we avoid them as unlucky places?

The poem moves through this from its deceptively casual and distantly ironical opening to a grave and beautiful conclusion. The church deserves reverence as a kind of repository of the profoundest human feelings, which *should* somehow be invested in one spot:

> it held unspilt
> So long and equably what since is found
> Only in separation—marriage, and birth,
> And death, and thoughts of these

It therefore has the feel of a symbol of an ordered and stable society (Larkin's small-"c" conservatism here makes its first showing in his verse); something lost in our own less innocent, more brash, more disorganized times:

> A serious house on serious earth it is,
> In whose blent air all our compulsions meet,
> Are recognized, and robed as destinies.
> And that much never can be obsolete,
> Since someone will forever be surprising
> A hunger in himself to be more serious,
> And gravitating with it to this ground,
> Which, he once heard, was proper to grow wise in,
> If only that so many dead lie round.

Much of Larkin's best poetry in his next two books caters for that "hunger to be serious."

III

THE reputation Larkin established with *The Less Deceived* was triumphantly confirmed by his next volume of poems. Although he rejected the idea of "development" as a necessity for a poet, *The Whitsun Weddings* (1964) conspicuously carries his own progress several stages further. The technical range and finesse is ever more apparent. The blend of instantly recognizable social reality and a strongly individual slant on life is given us in a collection of poems that are the most accessible Larkin produced; however, the full implications of a Larkin poem rarely yield themselves up at first reading, and there have been some notable misunderstandings of his intention where he adopted a persona.

The captivating accuracy with which he catches the physical feel of life in England in his time in *The Whitsun Weddings* (look at poems like "Here," or "The Large Cool Store," or "Essential Beauty") led to considerable praise for Larkin as a social observer. This was entirely merited. It also led to the bestowal of the label "social poet." This was unhelpful, since it suggested concerns Larkin did not have, and boundaries to poetry that was all the time expanding in scope.

In each of his three mature collections of verse Larkin gave us one longer poem that lays claim to major status. If in *The Less Deceived* it is "Church Going" (and later, in *High Windows,* it is "The Building"), the title poem itself occupies that place in *The Whitsun Weddings.* The social detail, the whole sense of people and landscape, is rendered infallibly. Yet this sort of observation is far from being the whole point of the poem. Larkin's own position is that of a different kind of observer, one standing a little distance away from the happiness of others, unable to feel affinity with them, yet cautiously assuming such joy as they may be able to find. Such a stance is one of the "positives" in Larkin's poetry, which we may balance against the powerful articulations of despair.

The other people here are newly married couples, joining the poet's train on the journey to London one hot Whit Saturday, and drawn to his attention by the noise of rowdy send-offs on station platforms:

> The fathers with broad belts under their suits
> And seamy foreheads; mothers loud and fat;
> An uncle shouting smut; and then the perms,
> The nylon gloves and jewellery-substitutes,
> The lemons, mauves and olive-ochres that
>
> Marked off the girls unreally from the rest.

Larkin sees it detachedly: first with amusement (though without superiority or priggishness), then with wryly penetrating comment on what the moment means to each participant ("children frowned / At something dull; fathers had never known / Success so huge and wholly farcical"). And lastly, as the train approaches London, he draws the poem to a climax with these solemnly beautiful thoughts on the married futures of the dozen or so couples traveling with him:

> it was nearly done, this frail
> Travelling coincidence; and what it held
> Stood ready to be loosed with all the power
> That being changed can give. We slowed again,
> And as the tightened brakes took hold, there swelled
> A sense of falling, like an arrow-shower
> Sent out of sight, somewhere becoming rain.

As in "Church Going" he has moved from the position of the slightly ironical witness to that of the thoroughly involved thinker, searching out the deeper meaning of what he has seen. And though that "sense of falling" is ambiguous (falling *is* an uncomfortable thing), the suggestion of the change wrought in human destinies by carrying through certain observances, the hint of fruition achieved *somewhere* (that "arrow-shower / Sent out of sight, somewhere becoming rain") pay the same sort of tentative yet real tribute to the validity of some human rituals. We shall see more of this.

For all that, and despite the kind of hesitant affirmation he makes at the end of a lovely and remarkable poem like "An Arundel Tomb," the prevailing air of *The Whitsun Weddings* as a collection is bleak. The good things (the innocence before the cataclysm of "MCMXIV," New Orleans jazz in "For Sidney Bechet") are almost always of the past, to be regarded with resigned nostalgia. The realities of the present are mainly dispiriting, and human hope is drained away by time. But hope does still exist, in one important sense, in Larkin: in the humane precision with which hope*less* things are observed. A poem like "Faith Healing" concentrates in itself Larkin's particular kind of *compassionate* despair at the human condition; and while we can all feel this, nothing in life need be despondently written off.

The extraordinarily succinct appropriateness with which Larkin's mature diction works is evident in the opening:

> Slowly the women file to where he stands
> Upright in rimless glasses, silver hair,
> Dark suit, white collar. Stewards tirelessly
> Persuade them onwards to his voice and hands,
> Within whose warm spring rain of loving care
> Each dwells some twenty seconds.

The words enact exactly the appearance and posture of the healer, ministering to the ceaseless throng of women who pass for "some twenty seconds" through his hands, telling him "What's wrong." Any harsher note of irony than the "twenty seconds" and the "warm spring rain" (infinitely gentle in its reproach) would mar the quality of sympathy and tip the poem over into anger or cynicism. The women move on in silence, weeping, reacting to the unfamiliar touch of kindness:

> Moustached in flowered frocks they shake:
> By now, all's wrong. In everyone there sleeps
> A sense of life lived according to love.
> To some it means the difference they could make
> By loving others, but across most it sweeps
> As all they might have done had they been loved.
> That nothing cures.

"Faith Healing" is plainly not about just one healing service, but generally, and movingly, about the whole role—the deep and terrible necessity—of love in life.

"All they might have done had they been loved." Larking is careful never to suggest that happiness may be somehow arranged if only the proper steps could be taken. In "Love Songs in Age" a widow is looking at the sheet music she has kept since she was young (conjured, in visual terms, with immense skill):

> Relearning how each frank submissive chord
> Had ushered in
> Word after sprawling hyphenated word,
> And the unfailing sense of being young
> Spread out like a spring-woken tree

But love had never solved, or satisfied, or set anything in her life "unchangeably in order," and the time for hoping that it might is now gone. Already, the young marrieds, in "Afternoons," sense something "pushing them / To the side of their own lives." The possibility of happiness in Larkin's poems about love finally seems something very meager and elusive indeed.

Several poems in *The Whitsun Weddings* resume the fundamental Larkin themes of choice and purpose in life from where he left off in *The Less Deceived,* saying it all again with increasing power. One of them, "Toads Revisited," is a sequel to "Toads" in the earlier book, and written in similar quatrains. But the nonworking alternative to the life of sober routine (that, at least, supports him on his way "down Cemetery Road") is now more scaring and less enterprising. It consists of

> Being one of the men
> You meet of an afternoon:
> Palsied old step-takers,
> Hare-eyed clerks with the jitters,
>
> Waxed-fleshed out-patients
> Still vague from accidents,
> And characters in long coats
> Deep in the litter-baskets

Yet the life of tidy habits was one that "Mr Bleaney" relished. Bleaney, former inhabitant of the wretched lodgings resignedly taken by the speaker in the poem of that title ("Bed, upright chair, sixty-watt bulb, no hook / Behind the door, no room for books or bags"), represents a form of mediocre living from which the poet is theoretically emancipated. Yet, in renting the dreadful room, the latter has found himself in Mr. Bleaney's position; it's no great consolation to *realize* this, either.

In "Self's the Man," Larkin offers one of his comic, cruel depictions of the "happy" family life he has gladly escaped. Arnold chose to marry, so nowadays

> when he finishes supper
> Planning to have a read at the evening paper
> It's *Put a screw in this wall*—
> He has no time at all,
>
> With the nippers to wheel round the houses
> And the hall to paint in his old trousers
> And that letter to her mother
> Saying *Won't you come for the summer.*

But Arnold's choice of marriage was deliberate, and the only difference between him and the poet is that the latter was more adept at avoiding what might drive him crazy. Or—and the hesitation carries a world of doubt and fear about his single existence—he *supposes* he was. This is Larkin amusingly yet scaringly pointing up the dilemmas again, pausing unnervingly at those moments of profound self-doubt (or more simply, sheer panic) that occasionally overtake most men—and exploring the terror. But if we are to believe one of his very best poems, "Dockery and Son," there is really no question of choice or freedom at all: we are all predestined to, controlled by, the kind of life we happen to be leading.

Against the refined pessimism of these poems any offer of something positive seems an inadequate counterbalance. And yet paradoxically, in his fourth and best book, *High Windows,* published in

1974, alongside poems of the most intense gloom and alarm, Larkin developed the affirmative features of his talent. The exquisiteness of creative solitude is sharpened; the value of certain sorts of ritual observance is more strongly stressed; and the sense of hope to be found *somewhere,* happiness to be available for *some* people, is increased.

In *High Windows,* once again, some of the moments of utmost seriousness are approached through comedy, even broad comedy. In "Posterity," Larkin sees the far future as holding nothing better than Jake Balokowsky, an American research student bored with having to write his biography. Larkin is tedious to Jake because the poet's problems and anxieties were not attributable to any colorful aberrations. He was merely

> One of those old-type *natural* fouled-up guys.

The poem is an oblique onslaught on sensation-seeking in the modern world; and, implicitly, a defense of a passing world in which it was possible and comprehensible to be "fouled-up" in the private self without recourse to, say, drugs or other external stimuli. And "Vers de Société" approaches the topic of solitariness and privacy versus sociability through a dilemma over a party invitation. Initially, in the poet's mind, the invitation (in italics) is awarded a brusque reply:

> *My wife and I have asked a crowd of craps*
> *To come and waste their time and ours: perhaps*
> *You'd care to join us?* In a pig's arse, friend.

Nothing would be worse than the misery of party small talk, and he resents the way in which it has been instilled that *"All solitude is selfish"* and *"Virtue is social"* (in "Sympathy in White Major" the hollow sociability of the selfless "good chap" is held up to ridicule). But he sees how being sociable could represent something intrinsically decent: an effort to behave well toward others. The trouble is that he has uneasy personal reasons for finally accepting the invitation: a genuine dread of loneliness, a feeling that solitude is most enjoyed in youth, and that "The time is shorter now for company."

But the themes of how to live, of loneliness, age, and death are also treated in *High Windows,* pregnantly and alarmingly, in poems that have no trace of humor at all. Larkin increasingly feels he can face these subjects directly in his most ambitious poems, without the hesitation, the slightly apologetic flavor, that humor suggests. In the three major poems of the collection, "Livings," "The Old Fools," and "The Building," absolute solemnity (in the last two, a terrible, appalled solemnity) is maintained from the beginning in the development of the central ideas. All three are worth a close look.

"Livings" is one of Larkin's most impressive and startling poems: three separate ways of living, in different circumstances and different periods, are placed together and contemplated as samples of imaginable human existence. For each, the poet chooses a character. In the first section it is a traveling dealer in agricultural goods, in the 1920's; in the third it is a don among his fellow clerks in late-seventeenth-century Oxford. In the second, an astonishing center-piece, Larkin is nearest to showing his own existence. The speaker is a lighthouse keeper, alone in the midst of "the salt / Unsown stirring fields" of water, the nearest human beings as remote as the "lit shelved liners" that "Grope like mad worlds westward." Few of his poems illustrate so finely the full range of Larkin's talent and the richness of his subject matter. The trappings of the hotel in 1 are done with entrancing authenticity, though it is 1929 and it will not last long. The invocation of the larger, colder world outside the secure scholars' den in 3 suggests the vulnerability of *that* living. And between them rears up the poet's precarious vantagepoint, which is paradoxically more secure: the lighthouse symbolizing both creativity and intense loneliness. No kind of life, or living in the sense of a job, is safe; but awareness of the situation *is* a kind of mysterious advantage.

"The Old Fools" could lay claim to being Larkin's most desolating poem, a literal account of senility as accurate in its perceptions as "Faith Healing," yet far more chilling and comfortless. It begins by looking disgustedly (but still not harshly) at the mere hopeless *un*awareness of the very old:

> What do they think has happened, the old fools,
> To make them like this? Do they somehow suppose
> It's more grown-up when your mouth hangs open and
> drools,
> And you keep on pissing yourself, and can't
> remember
> Who called this morning?

Age could well be a condition in which one imagines it is still possible to put back the clock, but how can the old ignore that approaching oblivion which is not (unlike that of the womb) a preliminary to birth:

a unique endeavour
To bring to bloom the million-petalled flower
Of being here.

(This magnificent image temporarily counters the repellent realism of the opening lines.) Or it may be that senility is a baffled mental alternation between vague pleasures of the past and the starkness of a present lived "below / Extinction's alp." Whatever it is, we shall all discover the truth in time. The poem is horrifyingly, levelly truthful and, this time, scarcely compassionate because that cannot be the point. What Larkin achieves in "The Old Fools" is an appraisal of extreme old age that makes most other attempts to represent it seem false and unsuitable, whether done through sentimentality, or contrived realism, or black comedy.

It is, however, "The Building" that qualifies as Larkin's finest poem of all in *High Windows,* and this is a masterpiece by any standards. Put simply, "The Building" is about a clean new hospital, its outpatient waiting rooms, its wards and corridors, the view of the outside from its windows. On this level it is a feat of harrowingly specific observation. But one cannot read the poem even once without knowing that much more than this is going on in it. "The Building" is about the whole state of human living seen as a hospital. The people in its waiting rooms are

Humans, caught
On ground curiously neutral, homes and names
Suddenly in abeyance: some are young,
Some old, but most at that vague age that claims
The end of choice, the last of hope;

Being in this building (being alive at all?) signifies the end of the false dreams the world offered, the start of the true sense of death. On a more literal, less allegorical level, the hospital must somehow fulfill the role the church has lost and *oppose* the sense of death:

That is what it means,
This clean-sliced cliff; a struggle to transcend
The thought of dying, for unless its powers
Outbuild cathedrals nothing contravenes
The coming dark

But the "unless" is important; it is by no means certain that the building can, in its secular role, do any better than the cathedrals in their lost, religious one.

Even if the articulation of pure despair has become more refined and bleak in *High Windows,* the interest in the value and significance of rituals and observances faithfully maintained has become more intent. This is something that Larkin increasingly uses as a method of affirming, a more indirect way of holding back "the coming dark." Thus, in "To the Sea" he is delighted and reassured to find remembered seaside customs of his childhood still enacted on the crowded beaches. If "Toads Revisited" paid grudging respect to work habits, "To the Sea" finds a more positive virtue in habits of play:

If the worst
Of flawless weather is our falling short,
It may be that through habit these do best,
Coming to water clumsily undressed
Yearly; teaching their children by a sort
Of clowning; helping the old, too, as they ought.

"Show Saturday" works toward a related kind of conclusion through a wonderful accumulation of concrete detail, the poet moving through the enclosures, the stalls, and the tents of the seething field, watching the people drift home, concluding that the Show is good and valuable because it is

something people do,
Not noticing how time's rolling smithy-smoke
Shadows much greater gestures; something they share
That breaks ancestrally each year into
Regenerate union. Let it always be there.

The regularity, the "ancestral" quality of these activities, is significant. Larkin's lack of hope or expectations for individual men is partly compensated for by the strength inherent in some communal rituals, performed regularly in the same places and perpetuated by the will of men in general (they can even be funeral customs, in "Dublinesque"). Working against all this, of course, is the mindless destruction of rural England deplored in "Going, Going" and the substitution of the worship of money for the duties of an imperial role in

"Homage to a Government" (where Larkin's conservatism, to the distaste of some readers, begins to take on a large "C").

And there is at least one other pair of balancing opposites in *High Windows.* On the one hand, Larkin is still unable to think that there may be any kind of sure path to felicity in life. In "This Be The Verse" he adopts a cynical persona for a poem that takes parenthood to be undesirable since, through it, "Man hands on misery to man." In "Annus Mirabilis" he celebrates the release of others from sexual restraint (probably after the arrival of the contraceptive pill) with manifest irony: the implication is that happiness does not really lie in *that.* In the memorable title poem, the current freedom of the young from fear in sex is compared with the new freedom from religious forebodings in his own youth; but both freedoms seem unimportant beside the contemplation of some serene, indefinable purity represented by (at the end of the poem)

> the thought of high windows:
> The sun-comprehending glass,
> And beyond it, the deep blue air, that shows
> Nothing, and is nowhere, and is endless.

Beyond the deep blue air itself might lie death; or life. The question stays unresolved.

Such poems all, in varying degrees, take a pessimistic view of human existence. Opposed to these thoughts, however, is the recurrent reflection that others, particularly the young, might still find happiness in expectation. For all its traps and disappointments this is still a world in which (in "The Trees," the last of several Larkin spring poems) branches can seem to say "Begin afresh, afresh, afresh." Looking at the moon (as so often) in "Sad Steps" he rejects pretentious, literary thoughts and sees how

> the plain
> Far-reaching singleness of that wide stare
>
> Is a reminder of the strength and pain
> Of being young; that it can't come again,
> But is for others undiminished somewhere.

And with "How Distant," while the experience of youth is now remote from him, as the title suggests, he can nevertheless affirm its powerful sense of hopefulness:

> This is being young,
> Assumption of the startled century
>
> Like new store clothes,
> The huge decisions printed out by feet
> Inventing where they tread,
> The random windows conjuring a street.

In one obvious sense *High Windows* is Larkin's finest collection because there are simply more excellent poems in it than in any previous volume. But another reason for such a judgment would lie in the way in which all the various Larkin themes and motifs have here been brought together in a beautifully and precisely adjusted balance, and shown to us in an ever more confident and resonant use both of verse forms and of that immensely varied and flexible language that he made his own.

Larkin published no more than half-a-dozen new poems after *High Windows:* it is greatly to be regretted that he did not produce more. Of these later poems, "Bridge for the Living," in the *Christmas 1981 Poetry Book Society Supplement* (London), was a piece written to be set to music by the composer Anthony Hedges in celebration of the opening of the Humber Bridge in 1981. It is a very good "occasional" poem, setting the "domes and cranes" of the city of Hull elegantly against the background of its "remote three-cornered hinterland," where

> Wind-muscled wheatfields wash round villages,
> Their churches half-submerged in leaf. They lie
> Drowned in high summer, cartways and cottages,
> The soft huge haze of ash-blue sea close by.

"The Life with a Hole in It," in the Christmas 1974 version of the same publication, is a bleakly entertaining account of the struggle in any life between will, environment, and time:

> Your wants, the world's for you and (worse)
> The unbeatable slow machine
> That brings what you'll get.

But the best is "Aubade," which is Larkin at his most grimly memorable; it first appeared in the *Times Literary Supplement* (23 December 1977). In it, he depicts himself waking at four in the morning "to soundless dark" and experiencing a chilling confrontation with the knowledge of death. He surveys the consolations offered by both religion and rationality, neither of which help:

> realisation of it rages out
> In furnace-fear when we are caught without
> People or drink. Courage is no good:
> It means not scaring others. Being brave
> Lets no one off the grave.
> Death is no different whined at than withstood.

At the end of the poem, as "slowly light strengthens" in his bedroom, Larkin returns to the idea that routines of work may stave off thoughts of mortality; and also hints fascinatingly that social contact (since this is what the postmen bring as a cure) may be—as in "Vers de Société"—a remedy for this fundamental dread:

> telephones crouch, getting ready to ring
> In locked-up offices, and all the uncaring
> Intricate rented world begins to rouse.
> The sky is white as clay, with no sun.
> Work has to be done.
> Postmen like doctors go from house to house.

Larkin's early association, in the mid-1950's, with the loose grouping of poets known as "the Movement"—Kingsley Amis, Robert Conquest, Donald Davie, D. J. Enright, Thom Gunn, John Holloway, Elizabeth Jennings, John Wain—placed him among writers who were almost unanimously concerned to have their poetry lucid, tidy, and technically smooth. In this company, his own distinctive technical skills, the special subtlety in his adaptation of a very personal colloquial mode to the demands of tight forms, were not immediately seen to be outstanding; but his strengths as a craftsman have increasingly come to be regarded as one of the hallmarks of his talent. Although one first observes the argument of the poetry, and the way in which imagery mostly derived from everyday living is ordered so as to express the deepest, sometimes the most alarming, feeling, close attention to Larkin's technical means shows how much a care for perfection within his chosen forms contributes to the total effect.

As early as the first poems in *The Less Deceived,* Larkin's technical ease and command is evident. "Lines on a Young Lady's Photograph Album" depends, for its half-humorous, half-serious, tone, on the skillful handling of a flexible decasyllabic line and precise rhyming. "Wedding Wind" uses longer lines of varying length for a more meditated lyrical effect, introducing a pattern of less regular rhymes that unobtrusively tighten and control the structure of the poem. In other places in the book, he uses free verse (for example, in a lyric like "Coming" and a disarming fantasy like "If, My Darling"), though free verse is rare in his work and is used in a restrained way. And in the ingenious structuring of poems like "No Road" and "Wires" (with its adroit "palindrome" of rhymes over the eight lines: adcd dcba) he displays an inventiveness with form that is somewhat reminiscent of his admired Hardy. But it is in the elaborate stanza of "Church Going" that the full sweep and range of Larkin's technical resourcefulness first become apparent.

The impressive, nine-line rhyming verses of "Church Going," enabling a powerful and moving argument to develop through an extended treatment of the theme that mounts in grandeur as the poem proceeds, point forward to the eight-, nine-, ten-, and twelve-line stanzas of "Here," "Faith Healing," "Dockery and Son," and the title poem in *The Whitsun Weddings,* and to poems like "To the Sea," "The Old Fools," and "Show Saturday" in *High Windows;* and are the vehicle of Larkin's major statements in poetry. Larkin did not write easily. He composed slowly, and felt lucky if he wrote more than one or two poems in a year. One would guess that the achievement of the large structures of these poems was very difficult for him. But any sense of effort or contrivance is utterly absent: the diction of the poems, the beautifully judged selection of imagery, fit into frameworks that support and enhance them with immense metrical skill. The short, four-syllable second line in each stanza of "The Whitsun Weddings" creates an emphatic pause of deliberation before the verse continues with its flood of detail and its meditations upon the detail. A short final line to every verse of "The Old Fools" provides a chilling question ("Why aren't they screaming?"), or a link with the succeeding verse, or—at the end—a coldly final climax.

Yet Larkin's shorter poems, less outwardly remarkable in technical terms, may be no less skillful in the means employed: rhythms, stanza-forms, and line lengths that enable him to achieve a comic or sardonic tone in "Sunny Prestatyn" (where the comedy turns suddenly to menace) or "Naturally the Foundation Will Bear Your Expenses"; or a memorable lyricism in the cadences of "Cut Grass" and "Trees"; or a triumphant surprise in "The Explosion." "The Explosion," which concludes *High Windows,* is written in a line that echoes Longfellow's *Hiawatha,* a rhythm that has been used by English poets almost exclusively for the purpose of parody. The subject is a mine accident; and at the point at which the disaster occurs, Larkin breaks the well-known, regular, marching rhythm with a masterly use of changed emphasis and of punctuation:

> Down the lane came men in pitboots
> Coughing oath-edged talk and pipe-smoke,
> Shouldering off the freshened silence.
>
> One chased after rabbits; lost them;
> Came back with a nest of lark's eggs;
> Showed them; lodged them in the grasses.
>
> So they passed in beards and moleskins,
> Fathers, brothers, nicknames, laughter,
> Through the tall gates standing open.
>
> At noon, there came a tremor; cows
> Stopped chewing for a second; sun,
> Scarfed as in a heat-haze, dimmed.

"The Explosion" is an extraordinary and compelling poem in many ways; but not the least of its qualities lies in Larkin's capacity to astonish by the magnificent judgment with which he brings off, so movingly and unexpectedly, this technical stroke.

IV

APART from his poetry, Philip Larkin published two novels, *Jill* and *A Girl in Winter,* both written in his early twenties; and assembled in *All What Jazz* seven years of the jazz reviews he contributed to the *Daily Telegraph.* He edited the new *Oxford Book of Twentieth-Century English Verse* (a volume that succeeded the one compiled by W. B. Yeats in 1936). And in 1983 he brought together a generous and valuable selection of his prose articles and reviews —"miscellaneous pieces"—under the title *Required Writing.*

The two novels date from the period immediately after *The North Ship;* eight years elapsed between the second of them and the publication of *The Less Deceived.* Although neither book is outstanding, they are both better than their author assumed them to be; and might have seemed, set alongside the first volume of poems, to point to a future for Larkin as an able and sensitive novelist rather than a major poet.

Jill (1946) is about the first, and disastrous, term spent by a working-class boy, John Kemp, at Oxford. The year is 1940, and the undergraduate life Larkin describes wavers between carrying on as if World War II did not exist and accepting that unpalatable fact. Oxford is thoroughly settled into the wartime atmosphere: food is getting scarcer, "black-outs" cover the windows, square brick air-raid shelters stand in the streets, alarming news arrives of devastating bombing attacks on distant cities. The author's principal concern, however, is with the personal fortunes of the humble John Kemp. John is the grammar-school son of an ex-policeman, and has been selected and crammed for his scholarship by a coldly efficient English master (a remarkable study in dedicated, calculating mediocrity).

Arriving at his Oxford college, John finds he has to share rooms with Christopher Warner, a "hearty" from a minor public school who has already gathered a small clique of rowdy companions. Their life is socially smarter and faster than John's; and the shy working-class boy, fascinated, is drawn incongruously and calamitously into it. Overhearing some wounding conversation about himself between Christopher and his girlfriend Elizabeth, John responds to the impact of their expansive middle-class living by inventing an imaginary sister at a boarding school: the Jill of the title. Jill is someone round whom he can weave a fantasy life to compete with the glamorous reality of Christopher, his friends, and his mother. But fantasy transmutes itself into fact, with an actual Jill turning up in the form of a young cousin of Elizabeth's. John's idealization and pursuit of the real girl—his "hallucination of innocence"—ends in disaster: a drunken attempt to kiss her, the pitiable humiliation of being thrown into a pool, the term seen out in the college sick bay.

Jill makes numerous points about the nastiness of the class system, the resorts of the lonely, and the hazards of fantasy living; and makes them in a perceptive and moving way. Larkin is indubitably talented, here, in most departments of the novelist's art. His narrative has pace and surprise, there is variety and depth in the characterization, his ear for dialogue is hardly less than perfect. He also introduces one especially attractive and startling invention: the affectionate pastiche of a girls' school story, which Larkin has John Kemp compose as part of his exploration of the imaginary Jill. Again, though the compass of the novel is narrow (neither the academic life of the university, nor the student life outside John's orbit, is given any development), *Jill* catches the feel of living in this period with more than credible accuracy. It is, in fact, one of the better novels written about England during World War II, not so much for any conscious documentary effort put into it as for Larkin's characteristic scrupulousness in getting all the background details right. But neither *Jill* nor its successor equal in achievement the best that was eventually to come in Larkin's mature verse, and there is not much in the second novel to suggest that his talent for fiction could have diversified in such remarkable ways as his talent for poetry.

A Girl in Winter (1947) again has a wartime setting, and again places the central character in a position of acute psychological isolation. But this time the author himself is inventing a girl character, and Katherine Lind is no fantasy, but a real young woman set in a depressingly real world of dingy, humiliating routines and unattractive colleagues. Katherine is a foreign girl who finds herself (the exact circumstances are left unclear) employed in a library in an English provincial city. Her life is a desperately lonely one. She does not feel she can really try to resume acquaintance with the well-to-do family who entertained her as their son's school pen-friend shortly before the war; yet she finally writes a letter making tentative contact with them when she fortuitously finds a reference to the daughter of the family in a newspaper.

This is the first third of the book. The middle third is an extended flashback to Katherine's prewar English visit. There is more than a hint of fantasy and idealization in the treatment of the Fennels' home and family life, and in the social ease and maturity of the sixteen-year-old Robin. Then, in the final section, the story returns to the present, and deals with the changed, grown-up Robin's arrival at Katherine's lodgings in response to her letter; a soldier wanting a bed, which she grants him with an implicit acceptance of the fact of the present as something closer and more relevant than any dream of the past.

A Girl in Winter is widely regarded as an advance on *Jill* in technique and in imaginative range. Certainly the creation of Katherine Lind is impressive, and the resolution of the novel is both more ambitious and more satisfying than the abruptly unpleasant termination of the earlier book. Yet something is lost in Larkin's slight shift from a world of concrete, experienced reality in the Oxford of *Jill* to the memories and speculations in the mind of Katherine, however convincing the drab wartime world from which she retreats into them. *A Girl in Winter* leaves a sense of things happening out of time, of actions performed by characters imagined rather than people seen and known. If the tangible Oxford setting of *Jill* anticipates the wide-ranging social observation that strengthens so many of the later poems, *A Girl in Winter* is in many respects suggestive of the atmosphere of *The North Ship,* with a similar vague seeking after lonely fulfillment and release: in this sense it takes a step back. The development of the full strength of the later poetry seems to follow more directly from the first novel, and we may not need to regret Larkin's failure, despite considerable effort, to complete a third work of fiction.

Larkin contributed reviews of new jazz records and books to the *Daily Telegraph* beginning in 1961, and *All What Jazz: A Record Diary, 1961–1968* (published in 1970) brings together his monthly articles from that period. Larkin's jazz journalism is just occasionally rather stiff and didactic, but more often relaxed, readable, and informative: the book is very valuable as a comprehensive chronicle of jazz activity in the 1960's. He is, as might be expected, conservative in his taste in jazz. The driving force of his enthusiasm is nostalgia for the departed jazz world of his own youth, which, he sadly acknowledges, has gradually yielded to the challenge of a new jazz that he cannot enjoy. The last paragraph of his introduction to *All What Jazz* defines his situation. It is poignantly, and darkly, devoted to portraying his readers, and has the tone and detail of some Larkin poems:

> My readers . . . Sometimes I imagine them, sullen fleshy inarticulate men, stockbrokers, sellers of goods, living in thirty-year-old detached houses among the golf courses of Outer London, husbands of ageing and bitter wives they first seduced to Artie Shaw's "Begin the Beguine" or "The Squadronaires," "The Nearness of You"; fathers of cold-eyed lascivious daughters on the pill, to whom Ramsay MacDonald is coeval with Rameses II, and cannabis-smoking jeans-and-bearded Stuart-haired sons whose oriental contempt for "bread" is equalled only by their insatiable demand for it . . . men whose first coro-

> nary is coming like Christmas; who drift, loaded helplessly with commitments and obligations and necessary observances, into the darkening avenues of age and incapacity, deserted by everything that once made life sweet. These I have tried to remind of the excitement of jazz, and tell where it may still be found.

Earlier in this introduction, Larkin has charted his early love of the old jazz, at school and Oxford, and the dismay with which he came to the experiments of Monk, Davis, Coltrane, The Jazz Messengers, above all Charlie Parker. He mentions how he tried, patiently, to like innovation in jazz, and failed, and for a time muted his distaste when it came to writing about the records. He could appreciate the social and musical reasons for change, but he rapidly began to suspect the vocabulary in which the new jazz was discussed: "there was something about the books I was now reading that seemed oddly familiar. This *development,* this *progress,* this *new language* that was more *difficult,* more *complex* . . . Of course! This was the language of criticism of modern painting, modern poetry, modern music." And the term "modern," he goes on to say, when applied to art, "denotes a quality of irresponsibility peculiar to this century, known sometimes as modernism." "Modernism" in all its forms, and the critical journalism that goes with it, receive a comprehensive denunciation: Picasso, Pound, and Parker, and for that matter, Henry Moore and James Joyce, are all dealing in

> irresponsible exploitations of technique in contradiction of human life as we know it . . . [modernism] helps us neither to enjoy nor endure. It will divert us as long as we are prepared to be mystified or outraged, but maintains its hold only by being more mystifying or more outrageous: it has no lasting power.

In this sustained attack on the modern we have a key to Larkin's whole aesthetic. His views on jazz are closely paralleled by his personal judgments on modern poets. In trying to mute and adapt those views, in order to be fair and representative, in compiling his *Oxford Book of Twentieth-Century English Verse,* he arrives at a most uneasy compromise. The book has all those who surely *must* be included; but the addition of a large number of others who have written single poems, sometimes odd poems, which Larkin happened to like, overbalances and weakens the anthology. It conveys a most misleading impression of the character and quality of English poetry in the first seventy years of the twentieth century. Larkin's principal and, of course, fruitful admirations in poetry were for writers who have either predated modernism or evaded it: Hardy, William Barnes, Wilfred Owen, Stevie Smith, John Betjeman. Hardy (a benign successor to Yeats as an influence on the young Larkin) receives the highest praise: Larkin said that he would not be without one poem of the Hardy *Collected Poems.* And Betjeman, often patronized by the sophisticated as a joke-figure for his love of the old and the once unfashionable (the art and architecture of the Victorians), becomes something very different in Larkin's notice of the *Collected Poems* in 1959—"one of the rare figures on whom the aesthetic appetites of an age pivot and swing round to face an entirely new direction."

Betjeman is not only admired for writing poetry that is socially exact, that accepts the life of his times, that honestly faces up to death, that is characterized by robustness and "vivacious precision" —descriptions that would mostly fit Larkin—but also praised because he rejects modernism and also appeals to a wide public. One of the cardinal sins of modernism for Larkin is its ostensible separation of artist from audience, and in an earlier piece, a sort of extended preface to one of his rare reviews of new poetry, Larkin declares the need for poetry to try to move toward the reader: "at bottom poetry, like all art, is inextricably bound up with giving pleasure, and if a poet loses his pleasure-seeking audience he has lost the only audience worth having."

Required Writing contains five "Recollections," including Larkin's introductions to the reissues of *Jill* and *The North Ship,* two interviews, some excerpts from *All What Jazz,* and groups of short items under the headings "Writing in General" and "Writing in Particular." He believes that there is little coherence in the volume; but this very readable—and often very amusing—book is given coherence by the stamp of Larkin's personality. He offers few startling discoveries, and does not usually set out to infect the reader with his enthusiasms. Yet his opinions and preferences in essays like "The Pleasure Principle" and "The World of Barbara Pym" are always unequivocally clear and always entertaining.

In the critical pieces, written for a variety of magazines, he shows himself to be a master of the magisterial nudge, edging the reader in a commonsense direction in, for example, his appraisals of Andrew Marvell, or Rupert Brooke, or Sylvia Plath. Naturally he is drawn to poets with whose subject matter and temperament he feels a special affinity, and to those who show a sense of rootedness (a quality he stresses in his own poems): Betjeman, rooted in a disappearing or even an imaginary England, is a good example, and Auden, who uprooted himself, emigrated to the United States, and declined as a poet (in Larkin's view), is a warning.

Larkin's observations on the composition of poetry are undramatic yet eminently worth attention:

> Poetry is not like surgery, a technique that can be copied: every operation the poet performs is unique, and need never be done again.
>
> A poet's choice of subjects should show an action rather than a reaction.
>
> Whatever makes a poem successful is not an act of the will.

Such statements break no new ground and offer no manifesto; but Larkin would not have claimed to be regarded as a theorist or philosopher for his comments on either the particular or the general in writing. He would probably have been happy to be regarded as a somewhat conservative critic: implied in *Required Writing,* in almost all that he had to say about poetry and fiction, is that decisive rejection of the modernist aesthetic which he explicitly enunciated in *All What Jazz.*

It is easy to imagine that Larkin saw his own poetry as deriving from, or at least consistent with, these points of view about the modern in art, and these admirations. It is indeed true that many of his readers find pleasure and interest in Larkin's poetry for its apparent accessibility and its cultivation of verse forms that seem reassuringly traditional rather than "modernist" in respect of rhyme and meter. But what happens in the personal practice of a poet is often a very different thing from what a poet formulates in the way of attitudes toward other people's poetry and his own. There is much more in Larkin's poetry than the ready appeal of its surfaces; and for that matter, much more that is "difficult" and "complex"—and profound—than might be expected after his statements on modernism. In something of the manner in which a dedicatedly experimental artist may be closer to the tradition than he imagines, an artist who avows traditionalism may be making it newer than he believes.

Posterity, which, simply because Larkin lived and wrote, may have rather more sense and sensitivity than he feared, will perhaps sort out the paradox: Larkin looked for his values to the past and the customs deriving from it, seeing in the present only the irreversible recession of all innocence, worth, and sweetness from human living, and in the future nothing more than a process of unbearable decline and death, to be faced and defined with unflinching precision. Yet he made out of this bitter, unalterable situation a poetry that is indisputably modern in its content and its cadences, and is wrought excitingly out of the English of our own time; a poetry that catches and makes beautiful the stuff of the experience of common men in the twentieth century.

SELECTED BIBLIOGRAPHY

I. SEPARATE WORKS. *The North Ship* (London, 1945), new ed. with intro. by the author (London, 1966), poems; *Jill* (London, 1946), new ed. with intro. by the author (London, 1946); novel; *A Girl in Winter* (London, 1947; new ed., 1956), novel; *XX Poems* (London, 1951), privately printed; *Fantasy Poets, No. 21* (Eynsham, Oxfordshire, 1954), poems; *The Less Deceived* (Hessle, Yorkshire, 1955; 3rd ed., London, 1956), poems; *The Whitsun Weddings* (London, 1964), poems; *All What Jazz: A Record Diary, 1961–1968* (London, 1970), jazz criticism; *High Windows* (London, 1974), poems; *Required Writing: Miscellaneous Pieces 1955–1982* (London, 1983).

II. WORKS EDITED BY LARKIN. *New Poems, 1958* (London, 1958), with L. MacNeice and B. Dobree, anthology; *The Oxford Book of Twentieth-Century Verse* (Oxford, 1973), anthology.

III. RECORDINGS. *Philip Larkin Reads "The Less Deceived"* (Hessle, Yorkshire, 1958); *Philip Larkin Reads and Comments on "The Whitsun Weddings"* (Hessle, Yorkshire, 1965); *Philip Larkin Reads "High Windows"* (London, 1975); *Martin Bell, Muriel Berry, Tony Curtis, Douglas Dunn, Philip Larkin on Record* (1977), issued by the Yorkshire Arts Assoc.

IV. CRITICAL AND OTHER STUDIES. F. W. Bateson, "Auden's (and Empson's) Heirs," in *Essays in Criticism* (Oxford, 1957); A. R. Jones, "The Poetry of Philip Larkin: A Note on Transatlantic Culture," in *Western Humanities Review,* 16 (Spring 1962); J. Press, *Rule and Energy: Trends in British Poetry Since the Second World War*

(London, 1963); W. V. O'Connor, *The New University Wits and the End of Modernism* (Carbondale, 1963); C. Tomlinson, "Poetry Today," in *The Pelican Guide to English Literature* (Harmondsworth, 1964), vol. 7, *The Modern Age;* D. J. Enright, *"Down Cemetery Road,"* in the *New Statesman* (28 February 1964); I. Hamilton, "The Whitsun Weddings," in *London Magazine* (May 1964); J. Wain, "Engagement, or Withdrawal? Some Notes on the Poetry of Philip Larkin," in *Critical Quarterly,* 6 (Summer 1964); I. Hamilton, "Four Conversations: Philip Larkin," in *London Magazine* (November 1964); C. Falck, "The Whitsun Weddings," in *The Review* (December 1964); F. Grubb, *A Vision of Reality: A Study of Liberalism in Twentieth-Century Verse* (London, 1965); C. Ricks, "A True Poet," in the *New York Review of Books* (28 January 1965); A. Alvarez, ed., *The New Poetry* (Harmondsworth, 1966), discusses Larkin's poetry in intro.; P. Gardner, "The Wintry Drum: The Poetry of Philip Larkin," in *Dalhousie Review,* 48 (Spring 1968).

A. Thwaite, "The Poetry of Philip Larkin," in M. Dodsworth, ed., *The Survival of Poetry: A Contemporary Survey* (London, 1970); A. K. Weatherhead, "Philip Larkin of England," in *Journal of English Literary History* (December 1971); D. Timms, *Philip Larkin* (Edinburg, 1973), a book-length critical study; A. Thwaite, *Poetry Today, 1960–1973* (Harlow, Essex, 1973), a British Council survey; *Philip Larkin* (Stockport, Cheshire, 1974), special issue of *Phoenix,* contains essays on Larkin by F. Grubb, G. Hartley, E. Longley, C. Ricks, A. Thwaite, D. Timms, et al.; C. James, "Wolves of Memory," in *Encounter* (June 1974); D. Jacobson, "Philip Larkin: A Profile," in the *New Review* (June 1974); R. Murphy, "The Art of Debunkery," in the *New York Review of Books* (15 May 1975); J. R. Watson, "The Other Larkin," in *Critical Quarterly,* 17, no. 4 (1975); E. Homberger, *The Art of the Real: Poetry in England and America Since 1939* (London, 1977); B. K. Martin, *Philip Larkin* (Boston, 1978); N. Powell, *Carpenters of Light: A Critical Study of Contemporary British Poetry* (Manchester, 1979); P. R. King, *Nine Contemporary Poets: A Critical Introduction* (London, 1979).

B. Everett, "Philip Larkin: After Symbolism," in *Essays in Criticism,* 30, no. 3 (1980); B. Morrison, *The Movement: English Poetry and Fiction of the 1950s* (London, 1980); J. Haffenden, ed., *Viewpoints: Poets in Conversation* (London, 1981); A. Thwaite, ed., *Larkin at Sixty* (London, 1982), contains contributions by K. Amis, R. Conquest, D. Dunn, A. Motion, A. Brownjohn, C. Ricks, et al.; A. Motion, *Philip Larkin* (London, 1982), a book-length interpretation of Larkin's themes and styles; David Holloway, "Philip Larkin, Craftsman Poet who Achieved Fame with Slender Output," in the *Daily Telegraph* (3 December 1985); Craig Raine, "Closing Lines on a Life," in *The Guardian* (3 December 1985); A. N. Wilson, "Philip Larkin," in the *Spectator* (7 December 1985); Alan Brownjohn, "Philip Larkin: Poet Who Reluctantly Came to the Point," in the *Listener* (13 February 1986).

JOHN FOWLES

(1926–   )

Michael Thorpe

LIFE AND THOUGHT

John Fowles is probably the most widely read of middle-generation postwar English novelists. Each novel has been a runaway bestseller; *The Magus* is among the handful of contemporary novels that seem to speak to readers so intimately that it has become the object of a cult. Yet Fowles's work has been savaged by critics, in his own country especially, where best-sellerdom is inevitably suspect; by contrast his American following often seems not critical enough. Fowles's very success may either disarm or exacerbate judgment: between these two extremes—the foolish face of praise or the jaundiced one of prejudice—balanced criticism must seek to steer.

Though doubtless Fowles stands behind the opinion of his character Nicholas Urfe that "writing [is] about books, not the trivia of private lives," he has been generous in several interviews with biographical details and insights into his intentions. He was born on 31 March 1926 into a middle-class family at Leigh-on-Sea,

> a town at the mouth of the Thames, a small town dominated by conformism—the pursuit of respectability. The rows of respectable little houses inhabited by respectable little people had an early depressive effect on me, and I believe that partly caused my intense and continuing dislike of mankind *en masse.*
>
> (*World Authors 1950–70,* p. 485)

During World War II he was evacuated to Devon, an experience recaptured in the first chapter of *Daniel Martin,* and developed a love of the West Country, where he has now made his home; he is, in fact, "a quarter Cornish," and a great-grandfather was a Yeovil blacksmith. He was educated at Bedford School, becoming head boy and captain of cricket —"playing the game" to an extent that must surprise readers who draw facile parallels between an author and his fictional heroes. He did his military service as a lieutenant in the Royal Marines, though he never saw action. At New College, Oxford, he read French and German, graduating B.A. (Honours) in 1950. In 1954 he married Elizabeth Whitton.

For some fifteen years, until the huge success of *The Collector* (translated into fourteen languages) enabled him to turn full-time writer, Fowles taught, first at the University of Poitiers in France, then at schools in Greece and England, finally becoming head of the English department at a London College, St. Godric's, Hampstead. His teaching career included eighteen months on the Aegean island of Spetsai, the "Phraxos" of *The Magus.* His first two novels were filmed—*The Collector* by Columbia Pictures in 1965, *The Magus,* with Fowles's own screenplay, by Twentieth Century–Fox in 1968—but these versions pleased neither novelist nor critics. Fowles told an interviewer that he refused to sell the rights for filming *The French Lieutenant's Woman* without having a veto on the choice of director. The film was directed by Karel Reisz in 1980 and released in 1981, with a screenplay by Harold Pinter: the result was a convincing reworking in cinematic terms, with the Victorian romance counterpointed against a contemporary love episode, Pinter's device of an on-location affair between the actors who play Charles and Sarah.

Since 1965 John Fowles has lived a retired life in a large Georgian house overlooking The Cobb at Lyme Regis, the small Dorset holiday resort. Part of Jane Austen's *Persuasion* is set there, as is Fowles's *The French Lieutenant's Woman:* this opens with a quotation from a poem by one of his favorite Victorian novelists, Thomas Hardy, in whose Wessex Lyme lies, and whose shadow the novel deliberately enters.

Biographical entries in reference books give as

Fowles's "avocational interests" "nature and isolation." This lover in literature of "secret places," whose god-playing Conchis in *The Magus* desires "a fixed domaine on which no other of my species may trespass," has two acres of garden whose flora and fauna he disturbs no more than he must. He describes himself as "a good field naturalist," which includes bird- and spider-watching and botanizing. His ecological interest takes a practical form in his support of the Kenneth Allsop Memorial Trust, of which he is chairman. His nonfictional publications include a contribution to *Steep Holm: A Case-History in the Study of Evolution* (1978), which he introduces as intended "to present a case for the conservation of an island wildlife sanctuary, in memory of the [Dorset] naturalist Kenneth Allsop. The result is all that is known about Steep Holm, a rocky fifty acres in the middle of the Bristol Channel." Steep Holm was purchased by the Trust in 1976, with funds raised by public appeal. Fowles's essay "The Man and the Island" concludes: "In these sad times a love of nature . . . is empty if it is not also a will to safeguard and protect it." He has further shown his active dedication to this cause by devoting to it his royalties from the text of *Shipwreck* (1974), which finely reproduces shipwreck photographs taken by three generations of the Gibson family of Scilly.

Solitude and isolation characterize the life and thought of this very popular novelist, whom an interviewer has dubbed "The Reluctant Guru." He has said that "novelists have to live in some sort of exile," but he has not chosen the literal exile of a D. H. Lawrence or a James Joyce, believing that he must remain physically attached to a country about whose society and culture he feels deeply ambivalent:

> For me, the best place to be in exile . . . is in a town like this [Lyme Regis] in England . . . [novelists] have to keep in touch with their native culture . . . linguistically, psychologically and in many other ways. . . . I've opted out of the one country I mustn't leave. I live in England, but partly in a way one might live abroad.
>
> ("A Sort of Exile in Lyme Regis")

Fowles's writing constantly returns to this theme of internal exile and attempts to link it with the independent character. In an early, not altogether lucidly argued essay, "On Being English but Not British," printed—surprisingly—in *The Texas Quarterly,* he attempts to define "The Great English Dilemma . . . the split in the English mind between the Green England and the Red-white-and-blue Britain." The "English" mind is characterized by a respect for justice, the "British" by "imperialistic and master-race ideals"; the English would be Robin Hoods, "Just Outlaws," the British are the Sheriff of Nottingham, "Establishment" England of "caste, cant and hypocrisy." The problem for the truly English is "How to judge . . . without actually inviting judgment in return. The problem is insoluble, of course; but its specific insolubility is perhaps the most characteristic tension at the heart of all our best art." A further tension arises from the fact that the "grey" British and the "green" English worlds are both opposing and complementary, *need* each other that each may thrive. (This reads like a Jungian prescription for healthy national character —as befits a Jungian novelist). The artist, who belongs by birth and upbringing to this contradictory world calling itself "British," reflects its contradictions both in himself and in his fiction, as Fowles's first published novel, *The Collector,* illustrates: Clegg, the insane clerk, is also "grey" Britain and, significantly, destroys in Miranda "The Green-Englishman," distinguished like her prototype in the essay "by emotional naivety and moral perceptiveness." The ideas broached in this early essay persist in the consciousness converted to social action of the titular hero of Fowles's novel *Daniel Martin* (1977).

The "English" theme also embraces Fowles's constant preoccupation with the nature and possibility of freedom, but this is cross-fertilized by the influences of the French tradition in which, he has said, he was "really brought up": the ironist Gustave Flaubert is his most admired novelist, while his thought owes much to French existentialism (Jean-Paul Sartre, Albert Camus). In his ambivalent view of the novelist's role, Fowles has followed the modern French lead, using the narrator's persona to explore the issue openly within his novels themselves. Outside his fiction he has both affirmed more than once the novelist's total command of his material—"you really are creating everything" (see the Campbell and Sage interviews)—but reserved faith in the mystery of imaginative creation, in promptings that outrun the author's conscious intention. "Follow the accident, not the fixed plan," he has written; his open or alternative endings, as with other modern novelists, shun the rounded conclusions that fiction cannot, any more than life, supply. Yet, as a practitioner in a "free form" he risks undermining the very essence of his existentialist advocacy by didactic insistence. While his "I teach better if I seduce" has been richly borne out by the response to his first three novels, his latest work has moved toward greater explicitness.

Fowles's fiction is more original in plot and subject matter than in style. Though a weaver of mysteries, he is essentially a realistic storyteller, not a suggestive or spare stylist (closer to Iris Murdoch than to William Golding, though with affinities to both). While his "experimental" novels perhaps owe some inspiration to modern French example (Sartre, André Gide), he has preferred not to follow the contemporary extreme of the "nonfiction novel," the *nouveau roman* of Alain Robbe-Grillet; and, though a metaphysical novelist himself, he dislikes Samuel Beckett's early French novels. In "On Writing a Novel," he objects to Robbe-Grillet's stress on the need to discover new forms of the novel: "the other purposes—to entertain, to satirize, to describe new sensibilities, to record life, to improve life . . . are clearly just as viable and important"—aims that would have fitted so traditional a novelist as Charles Dickens, whose *Great Expectations* he admires and recalls in each of his first three novels. While it is true that Fowles sees *The Magus* as almost "a reworking of [Alain-Fournier's] *Le Grand Meaulnes,*" the affinity is one of spirit rather than style, his own novel being ten times the length of the concentrated French novella. His most economical novel, *The Collector,* has been called "French," but in brevity and intensity it belongs equally to the suspense thriller (an inspiration for an increasing number of "serious" novelists); its plot and themes are strongly and explicitly influenced by the English tradition.

Appropriately, the most revealing statement of his aims as an English novelist who admires but would not wish to imitate French fictional modes is the "Lettre post-face" (1977), which he contributed as a response to a Caen University symposium on *The French Lieutenant's Woman.* He airs perennial contrasts between English and French literary styles that can be traced back to the eighteenth century: "If what underpins the French mind is logic and a sense of structure, I am afraid with the English it is largely instinct and hazard"; writing is "a mainly organic process"; "Pseudo-hermeticism seems to me the prime disease of the art and philosophy of this century. . . . I hope an Englishman will be forgiven for confessing that he finds proof of this in a number of recent French exponents of structuralism and semiology." Describing himself as "essentially . . . the traditional bourgeois novelist" (though also a "social realist"), he takes his stand on content and interpretative power rather than style: "However ossified the structure and techniques of the traditional novel, its content, life itself and human society, must change. I would not mind, even denying them all subsequent developments in technique and style, reading Balzac and Stendhal on the world of 1976." In his own work it is *Daniel Martin* that, so far, goes furthest to vindicate his desire to rank highly as a social novelist.

Fowles's most "French" work is *The Aristos: A Self-Portrait in Ideas* (1964), "the sort of book a French writer would publish naturally," a numbered collection of thoughts *(pensées)* in a bald, dogmatic style intended to provoke the reader's reaction, but which Fowles himself has variously denigrated as "undergraduate," "rebarbative," and "arrogant." He sees it, with *The Magus,* as true to his younger self in manner, embodying ideas on free will, faith, politics, sex, life, and death that he still holds, but hopes are more subtly conveyed in his fiction. The philosophy expressed in *The Aristos* owes much to both modern existentialism and the pre-Platonic Greek philosopher Heraclitus' division of mankind into the *aristoi,* "a moral and intellectual élite," and the *hoi polloi,* "the unthinking, conforming many." Fowles has felt bound to defend the division as "biological" (against shallow "liberal" accusations of "Fascist") and attempts, in a passage that leads us toward a consideration of *The Collector,* to clarify a viewpoint important to a broad understanding of his work:

> In every field of human endeavour it is obvious that most of the achievements, most of the great steps forward have come from individuals—whether they be scientific or artistic geniuses, saints, revolutionaries, what you will. And we do not need the evidence of intelligence testing to know that the vast mass of mankind are not highly intelligent—or highly moral, or highly gifted artistically, or indeed highly qualified to carry out any of the nobler human activities. Of course, to jump from that to the conclusion that mankind can be split into two clearly defined groups, a Few that is excellent and a Many that is despicable, is idiotic. The graduations are infinite . . . *the dividing line between the Few and the Many must run through each individual, not between individuals.* In short none of us is wholly perfect; and none wholly imperfect.

On the other hand, history—not least in the twentieth century—shows that society has persistently seen life in terms of a struggle between the Few and the Many, between "Them" and "Us." My purpose in *The Collector* was to attempt to analyse, through a parable, some of the results of this confrontation. Clegg, the kidnapper, committed the evil; but I tried to show that his evil was largely, perhaps wholly, the result of a bad education, a mean environment, being orphaned; all factors over which he had no control. In short, I tried to establish the virtual innocence of the Many. Miranda, the girl he imprisoned, had very little more control than Clegg over what she was: she had well-to-do parents, good educational opportunity, inherited aptitude and intelligence. That does not mean that she was perfect. Far from it—she was arrogant in her ideas, a prig, a liberal-humanist snob, like so many university students. Yet if she had not died she might have become something better, the kind of being humanity so desperately needs.

(Preface to *The Aristos,* 1968, pp. 9–10)

Here there is a striking parallelism between the idea of the interdependent Few and Many and the English/British relationship sketched earlier in this essay.

THE COLLECTOR

FOWLES's intentions in *The Collector* (1963) were not plain to its reviewers. It was treated either as a thriller or, more plausibly, a riposte to the new class-conscious writing of the 1950's by others of his generation, notably Alan Sillitoe, John Osborne, David Storey, and John Braine. Thus Clegg, the perverted, impotent kidnapper, may be seen as more truly representative of the Many than virile working-class anti-heroes such as Sillitoe's Arthur Seaton and Arthur Machin. Clegg's victim herself compares Sillitoe's anti-hero of *Saturday Night and Sunday Morning* with her captor, as typical of "the New People," anti-life, anti-art. However, Fowles's viewpoint is not hers nor that of her mentor, G.P. While Fowles does exploit a favorite situation of the period—the ill-starred involvement of a lower-class hero (or anti-hero) with a middle- or upper-middle-class woman—he takes it to an extreme dictated rather by his mental squint ("I've always been interested in the Bluebeard syndrome": Campbell interview) and by the views just quoted from *The Aristos* than by a desire to jump belatedly on the bandwagon of the working-class novel. In any case, he was ill-qualified for it by background and sympathy.

As is often to happen in his work, the web of literary echo and allusion excludes a crude, single interpretation such as "parable of class warfare." One effect is of a romance given a modern, ironic twist—the captive princess in the clutches of an evil courtly lover, a "respectful" worshiper—beyond hope of rescue by the shining knight. Another is that Frederick Clegg's romantically chosen alias, Ferdinand, makes possible a bizarre, ironic variation upon the theme in Shakespeare's *The Tempest* of a chance-found naive love between the marooned Miranda and the first young man she sees, the shipwrecked Prince Ferdinand. Frederick, the modern Miranda soon realizes, is closer to the play's man-monster Caliban, while we see that in our real world Caliban can win, manipulate the anti-romantic plot.

Other ironic literary parallels may be traced in Miranda's narrative: she compares Clegg's unhappy relationship with his aunt to that of Pip "brought up by hand" by Mrs. Gargery in *Great Expectations,* while Pip's yearning for the unattainable Estella parallels Clegg's aspiration to possess Miranda. She herself compares her unformed, "creative" personality with that of Jane Austen's fallible Emma, a bitter parallel for she is to enjoy no happy outcome as "love object." There is also an implicit link with one of the first great English novels, Samuel Richardson's *Clarissa,* in which the rake Lovelace imprisons the heroine, determined to overcome her virtue, and causes her death. The epistolary form of Richardson's novel allows contrasts between different versions of the same events similar to those achieved by the parallel narratives of Fowles's protagonists. The contrasting outcome of the two novels—Clegg gets away with murder and everything else—points the sharpest irony: Lovelace is unmasked and receives justice, but Clegg's impunity is more consonant with our sense of the rarity of poetic justice in our world.

The Collector is a painful confrontation between an emotionally cramped, puritanical life-fearer, whose meeting face to face with another threatens the anxiously guarded self, and a life-seeker caught, in the novel's leading image, butterflylike in potential freedom, hopelessly vulnerable in her openness and uncertainty. Her imprisonment is an education, forced but never brought to fruition. The young voice of her journal breathes a constant love of life and a desire, pardonably somewhat priggish, to live fully and worthily. She aspires to contrast not two classes but two kinds of being, of sensibility: "I don't think of good or bad. Just beautiful or ugly." The terms are aesthetic, the impulse moral, but she is poignantly denied scope to live through the contradictions of freedom and desire and achieve "an intelligent and enacted goodness" (*The Aristos,* 11:3).

In Miranda's narrative we find her struggling to cope not only with Clegg's dominance but with her susceptibility to G.P., her artist mentor. Obviously he has helped her to think, but Prospero-like (loosely, that is, furthering the parallels with *The Tempest*) has dominated her with his wisdom of experience; so she solemnly lists "the ways in which he has altered me," but her independent spirit will break out. She remembers in her October 22nd entry standing with G.P. before the Rembrandt at Kenwood:

> He told me all about the background to the picture, what Rembrandt probably felt at the time, what he was trying to say, how he said it, as if I knew nothing about art. As if he was trying to get rid of a whole cloud of false ideas I probably had about it.

When later he apologizes, with artful self-disparagement, for betraying her with a woman she despises, she rebukes him with words that fit both episodes: "I'm not able to put life in compartments yet." She senses, despite her susceptibility, with a sure instinct that G.P. is a "phoney" advertisement for his attitudes. Fowles's handling of G.P., "one of the few" who voices many of his own ideas, illustrates the breadth of his irony and his willingness to let character have its head.

Miranda plainly has her creator's sympathy, but what impresses most is the imaginative identification, the sheer reach of intuitive understanding displayed in tracing her fluctuating thought and emotions, her instinctive reactions (for example, her anxious self-scrutiny in the mirror, November 20th entry). Her suffering and forced self-communing bring poignant enlightenment and no less poignant despair (December 5th, 7th entries).

Miranda forgives her jailer; so must we. There is no question of moral responsibility—absurdity rules—therefore no blame. Clegg's impoverished spirit, for which he who cannot feel others' need comprehensively pities himself, is an incurable sickness, beside judgment.[1] The "causes"—childhood deprivation, victimization by the class system, unequal opportunity—are merely contingent, efforts to rationalize in his cliché-choked fashion; his conclusion, "it's in my character, it's how I was made," is true enough. A leading theme in Fowles, the collector's obsession, is here seen at its most extreme, in one person absolutely ruling another's existence: "This is true of all collecting," reflects Conchis in *The Magus.* "It extinguishes the moral instinct." Clegg's crime is rooted in the denial of every man's possibility of freedom, to break out of the fixed self—which, in a perverted way, he thinks he is doing: "In my opinion a lot of people . . . would do what I did or similar things if they had the money and time, I mean, to give way to what they pretend they shouldn't." True, so "evil be thou my good"; yet we miss the point if Clegg is comfortably categorized as insane—this photographer who "shoots" his captive to make "art photographs," the depersonalized pornographic treasure enjoyed without restraint by a mass voyeuristic society ("permissive," not free). Mechanically, this convincingly ordinary man obeys his worse and safer, not the glimmerings of better, instincts. Miranda must die because he cannot himself learn to live.

In her instinctive passion for straight thinking and true feeling Miranda is the first embodiment of what G.P. glimpses as "the great inner secret," which Fowles's heroines (the old-fashioned word fits) share. She is the first to carry Fowles's conviction of an integrity, impenetrable, scarcely definable, possessed by certain women. They are to be the center of moral and spiritual value in his fiction. Miranda remains the most simply conceived, a candid and aspiring, still immature heroine who confronts, in the pathological negative figure of Clegg, the full force of what Fowles calls "the nemo" (nobody, no one in Latin), in some degree present in us all: "man's sense of his own futility and ephemerality; of his relativity, his comparativeness; of his virtual nothingness" (*The Aristos,* 3:7). Miranda's successor in *The Magus* is a more mature, freer figure whose task it is again to combat what is presented as a peculiarly male denial of life and love; she

[1]Compare in *The Magus* the Nazi Colonel Wimmel: "he was mad, therefore innocent" (ch. 53).

must be sought through a labyrinthine plot, complicated with a more elaborate range of themes and ideas.

THE MAGUS

FEW can read *The Magus* (1966; revised version, 1977) without feeling the old-fashioned urge to learn what happens next, like its protagonist "making a detective story out of the summer's events" (even if, with him, one thinks the detective story "one of the least" of literary genres). Such a reader will implicitly identify with Nicholas, the narrator/initiate, wishing the masque to continue, paying tribute to the author's magian ingenuity. *The Magus* was really Fowles's first novel, begun in the 1950's; even after publication, he could not let it alone and published the revised version (to be referred to as necessary) eleven years later.

The Magus is a more complex "parable" than *The Collector.* It is Fowles's contribution to the art of "fabulation,"[2] a type of fictional narrative that has come into vogue in both England and America since the mid-1950s; outstanding among his English forerunners are William Golding and Iris Murdoch. He shares with them a desire to revitalize the realistic novel with injections of romance and allegory, but in its ambitious scope *The Magus* seems rather to invite comparison with the first great modern novel to recharge ancient myth, James Joyce's *Ulysses*— whose model is the first great "quest" story, Homer's *The Odyssey.* Other major sources in classical mythology that Fowles exploits are the legends of Theseus aided by Ariadne, and the Minotaur, and Orpheus and Eurydice (compare the hero's name Urfe and the French form Orphée with his ancestral name, d'Urfé, that of a seventeenth-century French writer of pastoral romance). *The Tempest* (which supplies ironic and tragic counterpoint in *The Waste Land*) is again, as a mystery play of treachery and atonement, an ideal analogue for Fowles's purpose. Now, on an idyllic Aegean island, a place of "mysteries," a magic-wielding, self-styled Prospero (Conchis) deals with a more sophisticated Ferdinand/Caliban and "collector" of women (Nicholas Urfe) than his predecessor in *The Collector,* aided by the wiles of not one knowing modern Miranda but two.

Fables demand of us, in Samuel Coleridge's phrase, "a willing suspension of disbelief," that we obey the "pretend to believe" of the novel's magus, Conchis, for the sake of eventual enlightenment, that we *enjoy* the quest for meaning, welcoming puzzlement and seeming contradiction, that we are open to moral influence if it is seductively applied. The fiction of Fowles and other fabulists seems either to create or answer an enduring thirst for imaginative stimulus and parable art, rejecting the nihilism that recognition of the absurd can lead to. Yet Fowles's message is existential, not dogmatic; Conchis' creed echoes *The Aristos:* "There is no plan. All is hazard. And the only thing that will save us is ourselves"; "[Man] needs the existence of mysteries. Not their solution" (ch. 20, ch. 36).

Freedom and mystery combine in working out the sexual theme that brings Nicholas Urfe to a clearer understanding of his own nature and of love's demands: "In our age it is not sex that raises its ugly head, but love" (ch. 4). With this dictum, whose sense is often reiterated, Nicholas foreshadows the aim of the ordeal he will recount—to understand and accept love, which necessarily involves self-understanding and self-acceptance, and an acceptance, perhaps without full understanding, of the other (the loved one). The "mystery" invoked is to dispel that false mystique which Nicholas thinks has done much to form the consciousness of his own generation, "a nostalgia for that extinct Lawrentian woman of the past, the woman inferior to man in everything but that one great power of female dark mystery and beauty" (ch. 37). This is the conditioned temptation Conchis offers him in Lily, that he may learn through a severe disintoxication process the more profound female mystery that Alison, Nicholas' rejected mistress, incarnates: "Men see objects, women see the relationship between objects. Whether the objects need each other, love each other, match each other" (ch. 52). (The language is Sartrean, but Fowles offers a more balanced version of sexual relationships than Sartre). As narrator Nicholas recounts, presumably from a vantage point above the events, "the long and deliberate stripping [he] undergoes" (Fowles's words on the hero of *The Odyssey,* in *Islands,* p. 74), until finally he becomes "elect," his own judge. Part 1 provides a retrospect, prior to

[2]See Robert Scholes, *The Fabulators* (1967); in the Halpern interview Fowles calls both *The Collector* and *The Magus* "a kind of fable."

Nicholas' abortive suicide attempt (ch. 8), revealing his sterility and despair, his ripeness for change before "the mysteries began." He is an ideal subject for Conchis' "godgame"—apt in more than Nicholas' resentful sense—whether we see Conchis as puppeteer, sadist, narcissist, Jungian analyst, "novelist *sans* novel" (Fowles's persona?), or what Fowles intended: "a series of masks representing human notions of God, from the supernatural to the jargon-ridden scientific" (preface to revised version).[3] There are clear parallels with the Fall (through lust), perverting his free will, under the eye of a god-figure who creates the conditions but allows his subject's own nature to determine his actions. Nicholas is an Everyman (Urfe: Earth) who becomes "elect" by chance, a god's arbitrary vehicle of privileged experience. He soon grasps that "I was not interesting in myself, but only as an example"—of skepticism ("Your first reaction is the characteristic one of your contra-suggestible century: to disbelieve, to disprove"), of crass sexual "freedom" ("you have paid a price: that of a world rich in mystery and delicate emotion"), of Englishness even ("born with masks and bred to lie"; "I stood for something passive, abdicating, English"). This last again illustrates one of Fowles's most ambivalently treated subjects. In his Nicholas the negative aspect is stressed, with an eye upon the "rebel-drone," alienated, without a cause, a stock anti-heroic figure in the 1950's; this aspect is further stressed in the revised version, where Nicholas reflects on "the striving for individuality that had obsessed all my generation after the limiting and conforming years of the war, our retreat from society, nation, into self" (ch. 54). Nicholas stands self-condemned as selfish sensualist in his self-serving reaction to Alison's falsely reported death, which he determines to exploit to gain Julie's sympathy—and favors (ch. 52). Having put the working-class anti-hero in his place in *The Collector,* Fowles now deals no less severely with his middle-class counterpart.

The "half being" that Nicholas is ("inauthentic" in existentialist terms[4]) is most convincingly complemented and completed by Alison, the Australian "colonial"—and heroine. From her first appearance she has warmth, wit, candor, generosity, and is throughout "reality," *outside* the masque; that she lends herself to Conchis' "godgame" is less an error of judgment than of love. As with any whole characterization, she is revealed as much by her actions as by what she says or what is said of her. One remembers her leaving the London flat, not looking back (Eurydice showing Orpheus how it should be done), her simple compassion for the peasant children on the road to Parnassus, and her generosity to the muleteer, in each case rejecting Nicholas' calculating reserve. Their relationship on Parnassus and in Athens conveys through numerous nuances and gestures her good faith in love (she can, if need be, play the "prostitute") and exposes Nicholas' bad faith in condemning her against an image of Lily that can exist only in a mind susceptible to the seductive fantasy of the masque. Alison's "nose for emotional blackmail" contrasts not only with his exploitation of "the solitary heart," but more vitally with his deliberate, almost aesthetic manipulation of emotion—notably his "agreeable feeling of emotional triumph" after their first parting (ch. 6), his display during their Greek reunion of a refined duplicity, a narcissistic reveling in his "complexity" (ch. 42), his portrayal of "a sort of ideal self" to Lily, a mixture of attractive raffishness and essential inner decency, and most tellingly his calculating reaction to Alison's "suicide," to which I have referred.

Pain, love, remorse, confession are words that Nicholas understands only in the abstract sense; an aesthete of the emotions, he knows but cannot experience the depths of feeling. This denotes an unawakened potentiality whose lack he can feel sharply, as in his reactions to Conchis' story of his own and Anton's part in the tragic episode during the German occupation of Greece, which culminates in the one titled chapter—*Eleutheria*—"freedom"; what this means to Nicholas and in the novel's larger scheme is underlined in the revised version by many changes, such as that from chapter 54 already quoted.

Conchis' role and purposes, as they affect Nicholas, seem manifest. His phased autobiographical narrative, both real (so far as Nicholas can verify it) and invented, is shaped to act as a series of parallels or mirrors, a "meta-theatre" where Nicholas sees reflections or distortions of self. Thus, his own Lily matches Alison in Nicholas' life, his tales of the two wars show the older Conchis redeeming the younger (Nicholas, too, is to have a second chance).

[3]Conchis also suggests "conscious" or "conscience" (that of Nicholas), while his masque, like Hamlet's play for Claudius, is designed to catch the conscience of his fascinated guest.

[4]Fowles called him "a typical inauthentic man of the 1945–1950 period" in an interview with J. Campbell, *Contemporary Literature,* 17:4 (1976), p. 466.

Beyond these converging elements, but in key with them, are the extreme experiences, vicarious insights into states of mind: de Deukans, the refined collector who lapses into a decadent hedonism, the "prophet" of Seidevarre's dialogue with God, the journey into cosmic consciousness vouchsafed to Nicholas under hypnosis. With these Conchis is suggesting what must be included in a whole vision of life; but to this Nicholas long remains blind, with eyes only for the Miranda he believes (more explicitly in the revised version) that the possessive Conchis/Prospero denies him.

Prospero has sometimes been seen as akin to the jealous god—and there is, quite apart from Fowles's own declarations, reason enough, conceded by Conchis' accomplices, to see the magus from a similar viewpoint. To Nicholas until the last he is the maniac playing god, rather than the sane psychiatric surgeon of Mrs. de Seitas' description. Conchis' experiences, as he describes them to Nicholas, have been steps in his own enlightenment also. He uses Henrik the Jansenist, for example, to portray both a deluded visionary who "believed in a divine cruelty" and "could not see the objective truth, that destiny is hazard" and one blessed with the priceless gift—alien to our Beckettian age—of "not waiting to meet God. He was meeting God." Whatever the truth, "God" remains the inscrutable mystery, together with notions of God's love, justice, and so on; therefore—"Learn to smile. . . . Learn to be cruel, learn to be dry, learn to survive."[5] This is Nicholas' hardest lesson, learned when pressed in the final act of "metatheatre," as Conchis had been by the Nazi Wimmel, beyond all reason—"all this," he reflects in the revised version, "after I had at last told them about Alison." There is still more to endure: he clings "to something in Alison . . . a tiny limpid crystal of eternal non-betrayal," undergoes the purgatory of trial and revulsion against the "inauthentic" self he had been, only to be faced with the revelation that the "dead" woman he now values has lent herself, like Lily, to the cruelties of the godgame: "A crystal lay shattered. And all betrayed" (ch. 66).

Now comes the test of Nicholas' new-won understanding. If the revised version strengthens the original, it is largely in the closing chapters: in addition to Nicholas' conversations with Mrs. de Seitas in the Victoria and Albert Museum, Alison's complicity is made less deliberate, the astringent testing of the godgame is justified, Nicholas' "election" is explained as "pure chance," and his forgiveness of Lily is commended.

The last chapter opens:

> The smallest hope, a bare continuing to exist, is enough for the anti-hero's future; leave him, says our age, leave him where mankind is in its history, at a crossroads, in a dilemma, with all to lose and only more of the same to win; let him survive, but give him no direction, no reward; because we too are waiting, in our solitary rooms where the telephone never rings, waiting for this girl, this truth, this crystal of humanity, this reality lost through imagination, to return; and to say she returns is a lie.

Though Fowles adds, "what happened in the following years is silence; is another mystery," he rejects the fashionable mode of ironic comedy for the possibility of a true, if painful, reconciliation for Nicholas and Alison—affirmed by the closing Latin quotation, supplied Conchis-like without translation: *cras amet qui nunquam amavit / qui que amavit cras amet* (Let him love tomorrow, who never loved before: / He who always loved, let him tomorrow love, *Pervigilium veneris* [*The Festival of Venus,* 3rd–4th century A.D.]). Readers must tease out this meaning, and Fowles wishes it had been better understood. Yet, typically, the ending tantalizes: does Nicholas walk off stage, now his own magus, or does he affirm Nicholas and Allison's shared chance of freedom? The revised version (whose different ending provides another parallel with *Great Expectations,* the main one being the Miss Havisham/Pip/Estella and Conchis/Nicholas/Lily triangles) seems more consonant with Nicholas' new self-understanding and hard-won insight into Alison's value. In chapter 17 he saw that "she had been, or could have been, [his] protector" and later Conchis tells him that a woman as "keel" is "what you need" (ch. 35). The revised version tones down Nicholas' resentment and violence in the closing Regent's Park scene (though he still strikes Alison, out of frustrated love, the nervous demand that she turn back to him, renounce the godgame); his final appeal, "You can't hate someone who's really on his knees, who'll never be more than half a human being without you," shows unambiguously that he has learned

[5]Compare "No god can have a serious face: / It is the Smile that is the word." "Tourists at the Erechthcion," *Poems,* p. 12.

his need and confessed his nature. The ending remains open, but is imbued with promise.

Readers have naturally been disturbed by the ambiguity or unreality of Conchis, by the severity of his "godgame," and by the final disappearance of him and his players. The parallels with *The Tempest,* which Fowles strengthens in the revised version, may help. Prospero, in the interests of justice, allows a father to believe in the death of a dear son until he deems him worthy of release; he tells that son, Ferdinand, accepting him as son-in-law, "Our revels now are ended. These our actors, / . . . were all spirits, and / Are melted into air, into thin air"; when at the dénouement he tells the bewildered Gonzalo, "You do yet taste / Some subtleties o' th' isle, that will not let you / Believe things certain," his words might answer Nicholas' difficulty in believing at the close, "They ['the controlling divinities'] had absconded."[6] As in *The Tempest* the collocation of "real" relationships and mysteriously directed events has allowed the author liberty to combine disparate themes and to create extreme situations that compel the deepest response in his "actors." *The Magus* aspires, stressing "limits," to be what Fowles himself finds *The Tempest:* "a parable about the human imagination, and thus finally about Shakespeare's view of his own imagination: its powers, its hopes, its limits—above all, its limits" (*Islands,* p. 84).

FURTHER NOTES ON THE REVISED VERSION

In his foreword to the revised version, Fowles calls it chiefly "a stylistic revision," intended largely to remove infelicities of expression that leaped from the page as soon as he opened the first bound copy; but also he wanted to enhance characterization and clarify motive. Two erotic scenes (chapters 47 and 59) are elaborated—"merely the correction of a past failure of nerve"—as is the devious role of June, the second sister.

Fowles also identifies his literary influences, especially *Le Grand Meaulnes* by Alain-Fournier, published in 1912, *Bevis* (1882), Richard Jefferies' boys' adventure story, which must have fed Fowles's love of nature lore, and—less apparent to him than to a student who wrote to him "years after publication"—*Great Expectations.* These diverse works share what Fowles calls "a characteristic longing of adolescence," "the quality . . . of projecting a very different world from the one that is." This he rephrases in patently romantic terms in his introduction to *After London* (also by Jefferies) as the desire to fantasize oneself out of the prison of the world that is. In retrospect, he understands his novel's romantic appeal for younger readers—and the distaste it aroused in some older ones who condemned it as self-indulgent, obsessively "mysterious": "I know the generation whose mind it most attracts and that it must substantially remain a novel of adolescence written by a retarded adolescent."

An English translator of *Le Grand Meaulnes,* Frank Davison, describes it as "a book which cast a spell over a whole generation of French readers" (Penguin, 1966). The narrator, François Seurel, tells of the enchantment of his friend Augustin Meaulnes by a remote, mysterious *domaine,* an old chateau he stumbled upon by chance. The adventure brings wonder, ecstatic love, loss, and betrayal in its wake. Fowles tacitly pays tribute to Alain-Fournier's story in his use throughout of the poetically mysterious word "domaine" for Bourani, where Conchis builds his baffling maze, and in a method that seeks to emulate the French author's: "I like the marvellous only inside the real" ("The Magus Revisited"). Many of the minor changes seem designed to strengthen "the real." A continuation of the dialogue ending chapter 19 and an insertion in chapter 23 enable Nicholas to recognize earlier that Conchis is involving him in a mutually acknowledged "pretence"; in chapter 28 alterations in Lily/Julie's reactions to Nicholas and Conchis strengthen the plausibility of her part in the deception; this is reinforced by the clearer analogies with *The Tempest,* with Lily as Miranda and Conchis the possessive Prospero (in the revised opening of chapters 33 and 46 Julie herself suggests the parallel).

There is no space here to compare the two versions in detail. Enthusiasts will read both; those new to Fowles will receive, as he intends, a more coherent and consistent impression from the revised version.

If one hesitates to link *The Magus* with *Le Grand Meaulnes* as "one of the *great* parables of that aspect of the European spirit that prefers the dream to the reality" (note to *The Aristos,* emphasis added), it is because of the greater explicitness

[6]Compare *The Aristos,* 1:29: "If there had been a creator, his second act would have been to disappear."

and elaboration of Fowles's novel, which seeks to stimulate the reader on so many fronts into exploring social, cultural, and philosophical issues. In treating one of Fowles's central themes arising from Conchis' testing of Nicholas, the relationship between man and whatever may be called God, Kafka's *The Trial* (1925) provides a measure of the intensity that Fowles's episodic, potentially unending novel lacks.

THE FRENCH LIEUTENANT'S WOMAN

The French Lieutenant's Woman (1969) is neither simply an imitation nor a pastiche of the Victorian novel. Though mid-Victorian in setting and subject matter, 1867 evidently being chosen as the year of the Second Reform Bill and of the first volume of *Das Kapital,* it is not a historical novel, and its formal resemblances to works of the great Victorian novelists (George Eliot, Dickens, Hardy) are contrived to achieve purely modern effects of irony and contrast. For such effects to succeed fully the ideal reader needs to be well versed in Victorian literature and manners; however, the novel's great popularity, especially in America, suggests that no special knowledge is needed to enjoy it as a Fowlesian piece of suspense fiction, as a "courtship" novel in which one looks forward to the eventual union of hero and heroine, this perennial attraction enhanced by the nostalgic appeal of the carefully evoked Victorian atmosphere. This nostalgia has contributed greatly to revived interest in Hardy, with whom Fowles has some kinship—as in his avoidance of neat romantic endings. Perhaps many Hardy and Fowles enthusiasts relish seductive surface effects, but neither novelist lets such readers off lightly.

Fowles has called himself "an amateur student for years" of the Victorian age; certainly, much of his pleasure in writing the novel and ours in reading it stems from the skillful mimicry of "the conventions of Victorian fiction" (ch. 56). These include the vivid evocation of setting to reflect character, mood, situation, or theme: for example, the depiction in chapter 10 of the Undercliff, where Charles is to "fall" for Sarah, as "an English Garden of Eden" (there are similar uses of setting in Eliot's *Adam Bede* and Hardy's *Tess*), "an unbounded pastoral domaine"; its significance deepens thematically by chapter 29, where on his life's crucial morning the anxious Darwinian Charles senses "Nature's profoundest secret: the universal parity of existence." In the several, determining instances of what Hardy called "casualty," and Fowles "hazard" (as in *The Magus*) are pointed—what also concerned serious Victorian writers—the potentiality and limitations of free will in a Darwinian universe. Thus, by a series of misjudgments, some perhaps unconsciously willed, Charles slips into embroilment with Sarah, the French lieutenant's woman, and deception with Ernestina, his fiancée, while coincidence and accident conspire to deepen the entanglement. Meanwhile, the persona of the author/narrator is constantly at hand, with his confiding "I think," "I am afraid," to lend the narrative in the Victorian manner an engaging intimacy. This is reinforced, as George Eliot especially favored, with carefully chosen quotations set as thought-provoking epigraphs to each chapter.

The protagonists themselves embody a selective "picture of the age," in the social, cultural, and literary terms that best fit Fowles's aims.[7] Sarah is both the friendless, vulnerable lady's companion or governess (like Becky Sharp and Jane Eyre) and the "outcast," the French lieutenant's "fallen woman," stereotypes of Victorian fiction. By the novel's close, "no longer a governess," she has become transformed into the New Woman, "an electric and bohemian apparition," thus in her contrived career passing through both early and late stages of Victorian female stereotype. Charles, similarly, is both what might be termed the Victorian New Man (religious skeptic, Darwinian, scientific inquirer) and —a limitation, as we have seen—collector, but in sexual conduct the vacillating, confused orthodox "gentleman." In portraying Charles's divided self, torn between personal desire and expected social conduct, Fowles takes a theme central to the novels of Hardy, Eliot, and Trollope but develops it in a way that owes much to recent researches—for example, Steven Marcus' *The Other Victorians,* 1966—into the "secret lives" these novelists did not fully reveal. The material of chapters 39 and 40, including Charles's visit to another Sarah, the wretched

[7]"I was writing a novel, not a historical study . . . a truly 'global' view of the mid-nineteenth century was not in this context possible. The requirements of the fiction meant that many other aspects of the age received scamped or no treatment at all." ("Lettre post-face," p. 52.)

London prostitute, could only be hinted at in the most outspoken Victorian fiction and was left to the pornographic underworld or the factual reporting of early "sociologists" such as Henry Mayhew. Fowles's treatment of this episode, like his handling of the theme of pornography in his two previous novels, brings such materials out of the darkness of subliterature into the humane light needed then—and, surely, needed still.

The ironic interplay of past and present attitudes and possibilities is most strongly illustrated by the author's handling of Sarah's role. At first we are induced, with Charles, to see her as a conventional "outcast" figure. Eventually we learn that it is a role she has chosen out of pride, spurning that of pathetic female victim. She lies about giving herself to the lieutenant, but not about her motive:

> I did it so that I should never be the same again. . . . What has kept me alive is my shame, my knowing that I am truly not like other women. . . . Sometimes I almost pity them. I think I have a freedom they cannot understand. No insult, no blame can touch me. I have set myself beyond the pale.
>
> (ch. 20)

No wonder Charles, the Victorian male, "understood very imperfectly" what this means. Sarah is, in spirit, beyond his time; she takes smug convention by the throat and forces it to don the mask of her passionate selfhood. In the process it is she, not Charles, who is the seducer: the "poor girl" here leads "the gentleman" astray. The significance of Sarah and Charles as embodiments of Fowles's ideas may be clearly seen in the following passage from *The Aristos,* whose Adam and Eve analogy is strongly reminiscent of Hardy's aim and method in *Tess of the D'Urbervilles:*

> Adam societies are ones in which the man and the father, male gods, exact strict obedience to established institutions and norms of behavior, as during a majority of the periods of history in our era. The Victorian is typical of such a period. Eve societies are those in which the woman and the mother, female gods, encourage innovation and experiment, and fresh definitions, aims, modes of feeling. The Renaissance and our own are typical such ages.
>
> (*The Aristos,* 1970, p. 166)

The portrayal of Sarah is the touchstone of Fowles's ironic method. He also intriguingly plays with the Victorian convention of the omniscient author. To a degree he plays it for what it is worth, as a holiday from the "absent author" convention that rules today. It allows him to intercede with pleas for a sympathetic understanding of Victorianism and of the blundering of so muddled a Victorian as Charles: "See him for what he is: a man struggling to overcome history" (ch. 39). At the beginning of chapter 13 he allows himself several paragraphs to discuss the ramifications of "a convention universally accepted at the time of my story: that the novelist stands next to God." He argues, in modern terms quite foreign to the convention: "there is only one good definition of God: the freedom that allows other freedoms to exist." The issue is taken further in chapter 55: the Victorian writer "puts the conflicting wants in the ring and then describes the fight—but in fact fixes the fight." However, since *this* writer has only pretended to slip back to 1867, "It is futile to show optimism or pessimism, or anything else about it, because we know what has happened since." What is shown, rather, is then seen through the spectacles of now, with the aid of an authorial judgment that rejects a limiting conclusion; hence (leaving aside the premature "Victorian" one of chapter 44) the alternative endings from which we may take our choice as freely as we can, while the bearded author himself melts into the distance along the Embankment as he earlier merged with the throng at Paddington Station.

Readers reminded of the two endings Dickens wrote for *Great Expectations* may contrast his case with Fowles's as a typically Victorian double-minded hesitation between romance and realism. However, Fowles has admitted to a similar dilemma to Dickens', though obviously understanding it with a self-analytical candor beyond that of any Victorian novelist (including Hardy, who is the main subject of the essay from which this piece of self-revelation comes):

> I wrote and printed two endings to *The French Lieutenant's Woman* entirely because from early in the first draft I was torn intolerably between wishing to reward the male protagonist (my surrogate) with the woman he loved and wishing to deprive him of her—that is, I wanted to pander to both the adult and the child in myself. I had experienced a very similar predicament in my two previous novels. Yet I am now very clear that I am happier, where I gave two, with the unhappy ending, and not in

any way for objective critical reasons, but simply because it has seemed more fertile and onward to my whole being as a writer.

("Hardy and the Hag," p. 35)[8]

Yet, to return to the more objective aspects of the novel, Fowles has his own "fight" to arrange. It is to give full play to the freedom that such Victorian forerunners of the moderns as Eliot and Hardy desired for man, but saw defeated by his own nature, society, or circumstance; also, they too were of their age and could not imagine the condition of existential freedom. It is not too paradoxical to say that Fowles does "fix" his novel's outcome in freedom's favor: even Charles achieves freedom, through deeper insight painfully learned, for future growth. The world he walks out into, alone, is ours, the iron city of T. S. Eliot's *The Waste Land,* darkest London of Joseph Conrad's *The Secret Agent;* finally we arrive, with him, at our own reality.

Fowles has told an interviewer that *The French Lieutenant's Woman* started "from an obsessive image of a woman with her back turned, looking out to sea." So, in a sense, Sarah remains to the end of the novel. More than once the narrator disclaims all intentions of finding out, at crucial points in the action, "what was going on in her mind." She is to remain a mystery to Charles, the reader, the author (who in her case abdicates his "omniscience")—and to herself. Halfway through Charles glimpses in her "a truth beyond his truths, an emotion beyond his emotions, a history beyond all his conceptions of history" (ch. 33). Sarah lives W. B. Yeats's dictum, "Man can embody truth: he cannot know it." She knows only, "I wish to be what I am," to save her own "integrity," and she knows marriage to the uncomprehending Charles, to whom "freedom" is "terrible," will only smother that; there is no pretense that she is "happy" or "right." Fowles concludes, in part:

. . . I have returned, albeit deviously, to my original principle: that there is no intervening god beyond whatever can be seen in that way, in the first epigraph to this chapter; thus only life as we have, within our hazard-given abilities, made it ourselves, life as Marx defined it—*the actions of men* (and of women) *in pursuit of their ends.* The fundamental principle that should guide these actions, that I believe myself always guided Sarah's, I have set as the second epigraph ["True piety is *acting what one knows,*" Matthew Arnold]. A modern existentialist would no doubt substitute "humanity" or "authenticity" for "piety"; but he would recognize Arnold's intent.

(ch. 61)

Free choice, dictated not by abstract morality but by an intuitive understanding—hard enough in our age to live by, virtually impossible for the Victorian woman. Aptly we leave her with the last ending, in the household of famous Victorian "outcasts," the family of D. G. Rossetti (whose ideal physical type she resembles); the un-English Rossettis tried to "be one-minded about both art and life"—unlike those greater Victorians, Alfred Lord Tennyson, Arthur Hugh Clough, Arnold, Hardy, in whom what they wished to believe and act upon was so often at war with their instinct and intuition. Fowles names this quartet and distributes among them two-thirds of the epigraphs; these include ten from Clough, the most "modern" of the great Victorians in his capacity to see through the double-think and wishful illusions of himself and his age.

Clough and Hardy, who also strove to present truth and reality, positively reinforce the critical "picture of the age"; but Tennyson and Arnold, recalled as troubled figures of anxiety and doubt, are as liable with other eminent Victorians to have their utterances turned to the purpose of ironic contrast (compare the epigraphs to chapters 40, 41, 48, and 53 with the content of those chapters). It is, however, Arnold's lyric poem "To Marguerite," fully quoted in chapter 58, that supplies the central metaphor of the islanded self surrounded by "The unplumb'd, salt, estranging sea." It is one that Charles's hard quest teaches him to value and perfectly matches Fowles's imaginative vision in this and his two previous novels: Miranda, castaway in Clegg's prison; Nicholas, compelled to explore the island of self, which is Phraxos in its metaphorical aspect.

I have stressed the contemporary perspective Fowles gives his Victorian novel rather than the elements of pastiche. The minor characters illustrate these most clearly. They are the stock figures of Victorian popular fiction, each exquisitely and humorously "done," yet with touches of individuality: Ernestina, the pampered pretty violet, her

[8]Fowles's speculations about Hardy in this essay are more convincing than the dogmatic use he makes in *The French Lieutenant's Woman* of the myth in vogue in the 1960's of an enduring, tragic love affair between Hardy and Tryphena Sparks (see R. Gittings, *The Young Thomas Hardy*).

only purpose to bloom for the marriage market (yet Charles underrates her intelligence and potential); Mrs. Poulteney, the "Christian" hypocrite; the bluff Dr. Grogan, Charles's confidante, the mouthpiece of pragmatic, unimaginative male sense; Sam Farrow, Charles's shrewd manservant, explicitly contrasted with Sam Weller (Dickens' sentimentalized Cockney in *The Pickwick Papers*), closer in spirit to Bernard Shaw's or H. G. Wells's working-class figures at the end of the period, conscious of their human rights and alive to the advent of the century of the common man. Sam and his girl, Mary, are portrayed, like Sarah, with a more realistic eye for their humanity than is usually found in the Victorian novel. The formal, stilted dialogue of the average Victorian novelist is faithfully imitated, though with free play given to the expression of genuine feeling, whose effect is sharpened by contrast.

THE EBONY TOWER

In a "personal note" to the second story, "Eliduc," Fowles tells us that the original title of the five stories collected in *The Ebony Tower* (1974) was *Variations,* that is, "on certain themes in previous books of mine and in methods of narrative presentation," but it was rejected because certain "professional readers" saw no point in it. This seems odd, for the stories are plainly variations on earlier themes and on some within the collection itself.

In setting, theme, and pattern of relationships the title story—in length, a novella—strongly recalls *The Magus,* so insistently that, in the thinner medium, Fowles's treatment seems relatively banal, the eroticism strained. David Williams, an abstract painter, plays the inauthentic man, hoarding what he has, his crime "to dodge, escape, avert" the challenge of "the passion to exist." A representative deficient man of our time, like Nicholas Urfe, he enters a Celtic French "domain," the Coët, like Greece a mirror for the self, ruled by the old painter, Henry Breasley, in whom he confronts a "secret" beyond his nature, "not letting anything stand between self and expression"—the nature of true artistic freedom. The clash is patently also between the values of realistic and abstract art, a point too heavily underlined by Williams' self-judgment at the story's close. Breasley, far less articulate than Conchis, is still like him aided in his task by two complementary girl acolytes, one of whom David admires, but in too calculating a manner to succeed: "He sinned out of need and instinct; David did not, out of fear." Here one remembers, too, the Charles of *The French Lieutenant's Woman* and his fatal hesitation, while the medieval romance's pattern of relationships, the Old King, the enchanted princess, and the questing knight, is again turned, as in *The Magus,* to ironic effect.

"Eliduc," the plain, colloquial rendering of one of Marie de France's *Lais de Bretagne,* is introduced with a reference to medieval courtly love as "a desperately needed attempt to bring more civilization (more female intelligence) into a brutal society": a reader of Fowles's earlier novels recognizes a constant concern, explicitly voiced and enforced by Conchis. The true heroine of "Eliduc" is, of course, the deserted wife, Guildelüec, whose acceptance of a situation no abstract law or right can resolve with a noble, reconciling self-abnegation is not a sacrifice. This contrasts ironically with the vacillations of the contemporary figures of the "Ebony Tower."[9]

The next two stories, "Poor Koko" and "The Enigma," are tantalizing mysteries, convincingly circumstantial, encouraging the pursuit of motive, yet finally enigmatic. Both, in the handling of the central figures, the author-victim of the first and the disappearing Tory M.P. of the second, are characteristic studies in limited perception. The author tyrannized by the burglar in "Poor Koko" is stamped for what he is, life-denying, withdrawn, self-loving, from the outset of his narrative of misfortune. It is an exquisite irony that he comes to convince himself that the burglar's burning of his Peacock manuscript denotes envy of what he is, the son's revolt against the denying father (a further, hidden irony is that Fowles makes him a devotee of one of his own favorite Victorian novelists). His conclusion, "My sin was . . . that I live by words," carries a self-damning irony unintended by this expert in verbal nuance, and the sin is akin to that of the title story's limited protagonist.

The central figure of "The Enigma" never appears, and it is left to a clear-sighted, imaginative girl, blessed with the distinctive "honesty" of Fowles's young heroines, to reconstruct event and

[9]Clearly Fowles has bent the original to his own purposes: for a negative view see Constance Hieatt (bibliography).

motive leading to the M.P.'s disappearance. As Isobel narrates her "plot," she herself becomes a more enticing enigma (the eternal feminine) to the intelligent police sergeant; their potential new life springs from the sterility of the old, which John Marcus Fielding, M.P., and his milieu represent. "Hazard" has brought them together in a way a Conchis might have contrived: she herself speaks of "God's trick," the *deus absconditus* that theologians never cease discussing—and it refers to more than Fielding's presumed motive. This is confirmed by the closing affirmation: "The tender pragmatisms of flesh have poetries no enigma, human or divine, can diminish or demean—indeed, it can only cause them, and then walk out." Thus Fowles wittily turns to advantage the dilemma Isobel imagines for the author of Fielding's story: "His main character has walked out on him . . . without a decent ending."

The final story, "The Cloud," is comparatively dense in atmosphere and suggestion. Fowles wrote this story to please himself and, perhaps, "a more select audience" than his novelistic mysteries had seduced (see "Lettre Post-Face"). He has also invoked in connection with it two of the modern masters of the short story, finding in it a feeling of Joyce's "The Dead" (which closes *Dubliners*), but stating that he wrote it as "a deliberate homage to Katherine Mansfield" (*Publishers Weekly* [25 November 1974])—who shares more than a name with the story's hypersensitive central figure. One is also reminded of Jean Rhys, particularly in the enigmatic ending of *Good Morning, Midnight.* As in "The Ebony Tower" paradisal "enclosure" effects the bringing together of a chance-met group under conditions that force sudden connections and heighten emotion. Catherine, though quietly on the fringe at first, desolated by lost love, mourns "the only one who understood," closer to death than life. An earthly paradise simply mocks her. Her sister and brother-in-law, Annabel and Paul Rogers, lucky owners of this paradise, are too engrossed in balancing their own existence to reach out to her. This task falls to two contrasting figures, Emma, Catherine's little niece, and Peter, the TV producer, outsider and pusher: "Smart little rhesus, his cage is time." To Emma, Catherine tells the tale (a "Celtic" touch) of the luckless princess, promising the happy ending she doesn't believe in; thus she receives the warmth of affection the child can give and quietly releases her self-pity, herself the beseeching, abandoned oriole calling for its mate. By contrast it is Peter, who has throughout the day been stamped on Catherine's mind as the very antithesis of the child's openness to life, one "to whom the real, the living, the unexplained is the outlaw; only safe when in the can"—in the most obvious aspect of the symbolism the snake in this paradise—whom Catherine allows to possess her body. What is the meaning of this act, to give herself to one who personifies all that is anti-life to her?

In her consciousness before Peter comes upon her in the "hidden place," Catherine has touched the extreme of self-hatred, rejection of life and love, of all potentiality; so a bitter "princess," she lives without hope of a saving prince, but the body has needs the mind will not acknowledge and the psyche cannot bear utter isolation, the islanded state: "her arm, almost with the rapidity of the snake," reaches out, she invites possession, yet only of the body. It becomes an act of hate, not love, yet perhaps in the acceptance of touch, renewed contact with her kind, is the germ of recovery or atonement: "I will not return," she had thought, "not as I am." We do not see her return. Instead, the cloud rises "feral and ominous," canceling the "peaceful and windless afternoon" with the reality of—hate, death? Beneath the cloud "the princess calls, but there is no-one, now, to hear her": has Catherine committed suicide, merged with her own fantasy, or have we seen her accept the present, while whether the future will answer her call lies beyond the bounds of the fiction? Fowles points, typically, toward no clear explanation, but either is consistent with the drift of the tale. It is, again, for the reader to choose.

DANIEL MARTIN

Daniel Martin (1977) is Fowles's "artist's novel," his inevitable contribution to an especially modern branch of the novel, including famous English works by D. H. Lawrence, Joyce, Aldous Huxley, Golding, and Doris Lessing. Like these novelists Fowles has not wished merely to entertain or even to offer his own vision to speak for itself, but has often voiced public concern about the writer's responsibility and his relationship to his reader. His earlier fiction reflects this less directly. Daniel Martin, called in deliberately traditional terms "our hero," is himself a writer faced with a crisis of conscience about his work and, in the course of the novel, undergoes a conversion. The agent of conversion is no Prospero figure, though a riddlemaker—a woman now, "capable of a tenacity of right-feeling . . . humanity's trap and its ultimate freedom." Thus, with his two protagonists Fowles centers his novel upon his major, crystallized preoccupations: the writer's responsibility, the redeeming power of the feminine, the nature and possibility of freedom.

This novelist who had in the modern manner constructed a fictive maze, intervened in his narratives to stress their unreality and the difficulty of approaching the real, who had done as much as any English novelist to promote the "open ending," has in *Daniel Martin* made his choice at the crossroads:[10] he has abandoned the problematic novel in favor of the realistic novel's character and relationship, its thematic concern with the problems of living. He has exercised deliberately—and, as he reveals in "Hardy and the Hag," against his deepest inclination—the godlike prerogative of a happy ending. He forsakes erotic parables of adolescent emotion for an ambitious plumbing of a mature love imagined by Miranda and only glimpsed by Nicholas Urfe and Charles Smithson. So described, it seems his most straightforward fiction, but is therefore his most hazardous; it has suffered heavy criticism, especially in England.

Like Nicholas Urfe, Daniel Martin is presented as a representative problematic figure, though publicly a successful one as dramatist and scriptwriter in the lucrative spheres of London and Los Angeles. He is in self-doubting middle age, as we learn in the second chapter, set—by contrast with the youth in the Devon flashback of the first—in the synthetic world of "Harold Robbinsland," a gray world that has expunged the green. He has long lost the virtue of the novelist's opening words, "whole sight," and regards only the self: "Narcissism: when one grows too old to believe in one's uniqueness, one falls in love with one's complexity —as if layers of lies could replace the green illusion; or the sophistries of failure, the stench of success." The technique of juxtaposition continues in the third chapter, "The Woman in the Reeds," bringing three women in Daniel's "real history" into focus: Jenny, the "naked film-star" of the present; Jane, the fellow Oxford undergraduate whom he loved but did not marry; and, forcing them into a shared knowledge of what lurks beneath reality, the prostitute, found foully dead in the water. The following three chapters treat, respectively, Jenny's fictional account of "Mr. Wolfe" (Daniel himself, and, as David Walker has noted, S. Wolfe is an anagram of Fowles) after his departure; the call from Daniel's ex-wife, Nell, asking him to return to England to the deathbed of his estranged Oxford friend Anthony (whom Jane had married) and his decision to go; and finally, in "Aftermath," the sequel to the first Oxford chapter—the lovemaking with Jane as an "acte gratuit" or exorcism of their love, denied because of prior commitments to others. From "Passage" onward, the vexed relationships now sketched, the main narrative moves forward in the present, punctuated by occasional flashbacks less abruptly juxtaposed than in the opening chapters.

As in *The Magus,* a fortuitous event—Anthony's request, a voice out of the past, that Daniel should come to his deathbed, and the demand then that he help "disinter" Jane from her wasted life—breaks the impasse in Dan's life, forces fresh links, revives neglected possibilities. With Anthony's death, Jane becomes "free," only of course in the shallower sense: as the girl undergraduate she had been skeptical of the Rabelaisian doctrine *Fais ce que voudras* (Do what you will), and, needing moral purpose, had preferred the path of duty to desire. When they meet again, it is for both a critical time of self-scrutiny: Jane, Dan soon recognizes, feels "largely misgrown and to be censored," while if she is a prisoner of restraint, we have followed his insight that his cage is "freedom," freedom without purpose. In a leap out of his present condition, exercising "free will," he seizes upon the never recurring chance to "tame" (as he thinks) the unresolved enigma that Jane embodies: "It may have been something in femininity, in femaleness, but she was both her own, in a way he had never quite managed, and not her own, where he only too lazily and complacently was."

Jane, then, becomes the risky—because she is human and has her own ends—means by which Daniel may reassure himself of his authenticity. Initially, this takes an oblique path; in their conver-

[10]Compare David Lodge, *The Novelist at the Crossroads* (1971), an excellent study of the modern novel's options.

sations she confronts him with a rare strain of moral seriousness, of earnest concern to use one's life well, that aggravates Dan's self-doubt. Her strange gods are two Communist thinkers famous, not for political conformity, but the purity of their example and dedication to Marxism. Antonio Gramsci (1891–1937), co-founder of the Italian Communist Party, whose *Prison Notebooks* Dan finds in Jane's Oxford home, provides the "morbid symptoms" epigraph to the novel. Clearly, Dan is brought (in his conversations with the German archaeologist in Egypt) to recognize in his own case a major symptom of sick egoism in this age of chaotic transition: "as belief in an after-life died away and people more and more turned to the arts for escape . . . a frantic entombing, mummifying, surrounding with personal achievement; a morbid need to pupate, to build a chrysalis before the grub was fully grown."

Already, in such chapters as "Returns" and "Crimes and Punishments," Dan had recognized his complicity "in some ultimate treachery of the clerks" for his participation in the mass-manipulative media, the commercial cinema, "TV and Fleet Street liberalism," the world of the angrily portrayed Barney Dillon—ironically his daughter's lover, a distasteful mirroring of his own relationship with Jenny; and finally he develops "a contempt for his own safe, aided, compromising and communal art." By contrast, Gramsci acted and died for his convictions (in Mussolini's Italy).

The more searching voice Jane makes Dan hear is that of the Hungarian Marxist critic Georg Lukács. He becomes the authoritative diagnostician of the disease of the self-betrayed, defeatist "bourgeois," wallowing in angst or sub-Beckettian nihilism, not only in England but the whole West —the Nile tourist boat in the latter part of the novel becomes a ship of fools on the river of time, Dan a passenger:

> . . . barred by his past and his present from feeling anything but eternally spoiled . . . excluded, castrated by both capitalism and socialism, forbidden to belong. Our hero, spurned by one side for not feeling happier, despised by the other for not feeling more despair; in neither a tragedy nor a comedy, but a bourgeois melodrama.
> ("North")

Here Fowles squarely faces a central problem, that the novelist's protagonist is simply not important, or definite enough, that—like Nicholas Urfe—he must be cut back to size before he can become worthy. If we judge his inchoate character and possibility by the demands with which Lukács challenges "the contemporary bourgeois writer" (quoted in "Nile")—that he act, however modestly, to ameliorate the human condition—then, Fowles suggests, there is hope.

The emotional agent of the conversation for which Dan's self-judgment has prepared him is Jane, and it is their remade love that seals it. Unfortunately, despite some striking gestures, utterances, and the finely imagined scenes at Palmyra, culminating in the "Bitch" chapter, where love rises out of a felt complex of mutual desolation, need, and the desire for affirmation, Jane remains yet another of Fowles's women whose significance is more stated than enacted. Partly this derives from her role as Dan's counterpart. The novel traces their convergence from Dan's viewpoint (he even interprets hers); it ends, as courtship novels since Jane Austen have done, on the brink of the marriage that we have no reason to suppose will dim Dan's realistic "prospect of an irreducible obstinacy, a permanent psychological awkwardness she would bring." (We can ourselves assess *his* limitations.) That we see this is a tribute to Fowles's dogged presentation of "the real"; the happy ending, though deliberate, is no merely wishful gesture.

Dan's revolt against his contemporaries' abdication of the artist's responsibility—"It had become offensive, in an intellectually privileged caste, to suggest publicly that anything might turn out well in this world"—echoes his creator's own. Fowles told an interviewer: "I'm suggesting that one may find a qualified happiness in love, that there is some value in self-doubt and self-examination, and some reward may come of it" ("The Reluctant Guru"). In the same interview he cites Lukács and deplores the enlistment of Beckettian technique in fashionable leftist rejection of Western culture and society, where for him free effort toward change remains possible. We may smile when we learn in the fiction that Dan and Jane have become Labour Party members: going into local politics will hardly change the world. The message is to work with good will and compassion, for a community's sake in a limited sphere. It is not a despicable one, and it has a respectable English tradition behind it: the criticism must be less of that than of the novel's failure, as a whole, to convey its messages in action and through implication. Didactic assertion and dialogue are too often shaped to further what are the author's evident views on the condition of England, the biological inequality of man, the arts, and the creative artist seeking constructive purpose. Dan's promised political activism seems evidence rather of the novelist's goodwill than of a likely or at least lasting resolve from one who has seemed more strongly drawn to the idea of the (also Fowles-like) artist's "permanent inner exile" from Europe's "endless historical error."

The frequent coincidence between Dan's attitudes and his creator's weakens the desirable distance between author and protagonist (contrast Doris Lessing's more successfully distanced *The Golden Notebook*). This is both stressed and confused by the technique, in Dan's narrative, of switching from the first to the third person; obviously, this is to achieve immediacy and to point Dan's effort toward self-investigation, but it can remind us sharply of how heavily Fowles himself is involved (for example, the opening pages of "Crimes and Punishments": of course this will be less apparent to a reader new to Fowles's work). A different, more damaging example is the oddly undigested witness of Jenny, Dan's mistress: she is more intimately known (much as Alison was, in *The Magus,* through action and personal revelation) than Jane, with a shrewd self-understanding and what might impress the reader as acute insight into Dan's shortcomings and evasions. But Fowles—intent upon the central development of his plot—intervenes in "A Second Contribution" to correct her analysis and urge a more indulgent view of his hero. As Jane is restored to the center of Dan's life, and his past retrieved, Jenny's "presentness" and the ambience of "artifice" she inhabits must be demoted. In the light of the earlier fiction we may discern a renunciation of a cherished theme—that *"nostalgie de la vierge"* (nostalgia for the girl) which Fowles identifies in *The Aristos* as a vicious aspect of modern sexual freedom. Dan's and Jane's inevitably imperfect, mature relationship is striking rather as symptomatic of this change, in favor of realism and responsibility, than wholly convincing in itself.

As Dan himself knows, the novel is "where you [the writer] have to be someone else"—again echoing his creator's "the one basic *donnée* the novelist has is the ability to think other" (*New Statesman* review, 1977). If *Daniel Martin* fails to live up to this dictum, it is partly due to our familiarity with the ideas of a much fêted, widely quoted novelist who, moreover, has been rash enough to issue a whole volume of them. The seasoned reader may be on his guard, alert to detect the riding of authorial hobbyhorses. While the memorable "islands" of his technique remain (see *Islands,* p. 30)—witness such chapters as "The Umbrella," the unpatronizing "Interlude" of the Cockney sisters (a sympathetic counterpart to the handling of Charles's visit to the prostitute in *The French Lieutenant's Woman*), "Tsankawi," "Phillida," the tense climax of the Palmyra chapters—the sea of duller passages that they relieve, of flat narrative, didactic repetition, and pedestrian dialogue, also unfortunately dull the attention.

The novel's close, in the Kenwood gallery scene, invokes the "late Rembrandt self-portrait" as worthy (does Fowles even suggest?) of a greater novel: "Dan felt dwarfed, in his century, his personal being, his own art . . . behind the sternness lay the declaration of the one true marriage in the mind mankind is allowed, the ultimate of humanism. No true compassion without will, no true will without compassion."

We have already stood before this portrait, with G.P. and Miranda in *The Collector:* it is an image that speaks of the cost of great and profound art, of its seriousness, and a faith in its ends. Rembrandt's, too, was a violent age, his life harsh, his art ill-understood. In our age the artist most likely to match such a figure will be a novelist; the task is great, perhaps impossible, but John Fowles has joined the few ambitious enough to attempt it and to risk the most exacting standards of comparative judgment. *Daniel Martin* opens a new phase in his work, evidently to fulfill the writer's primary task, as defined by his admired Lukács, of "living through and thinking out the great contemporary problems" (*Solzhenitsyn,* 1970). *Daniel Martin* reveals him as more seriously attached to the matter and manner of the great Victorian novelists than the ironic *The French Lieutenant's Woman* suggests: to entertain and instruct by means of realistic, elaborate storytelling with explicit moral pointing, to console (the defiant "happy ending," as also in the revised version of *The Magus*), to delineate the vital relations between public and private life. The balanced achievement of these ends will be hard in a society whose challenges are scarcely less formidable than those faced by a Solzhenitsyn, whose work Fowles thinks demonstrates "the prime function of the novel . . . the establishment of free views of society" (*Dorset* interview).

If it would be an exaggeration to describe *Daniel Martin* as forging a major new direction in Fowles's work, it does seem to mark an important transition. Until *Daniel Martin* appeared, both the popularity of his fiction and the hostile reactions it had provoked in some quarters stemmed from its being read as little more than ingenious fiction of erotic complications (though scarcely with the pornographic tinge one finds in other popular yet "serious" novelists). This aspect of his appeal, I have tried to suggest, has not always been put in critical perspective; at the same time, it has tended to mask his genuine social concerns, from *The Collector* on. His fictions of love and narcissism in the west show an acute diagnostic insight—behind which is a frank self-analysis, as his interviews and essays such as "Hardy and the Hag" reveal. Thus far, if we apply to him Lukács' comments on how the "bourgeois realist" writer may advance understanding of a particular historical phase, Fowles can be seen as one who "may grasp an authentic human problem (and thus the authentic social problem) of a particular phase in the historical process without consciously anticipating subsequent political and social developments"—though these "may confirm his portrait of the age" (*The Meaning of Contemporary Realism,* London, 1963). The question posed by *Daniel Martin,* where Lukács is invoked as sage and guide for the writer struggling to emerge from the bourgeois chrysalis (or internal emigration) is whether Fowles will attempt or can encompass a work in the "critical realist" mode, which Lukács distinguishes as demanding a comprehensive understanding of social and historical forces and the individual's relation to them. While *Daniel Martin* turns in this direction, it ends upon the brink of social action and reveals no large grasp of the complexities of English society and politics. If *Daniel Martin* portrays a "hero" turning toward society, this may be yet another "morbid" symptom, qualitatively no better than Nicholas Urfe's detachment, a liberal humanist's tenuously willed commitment born of the bad conscience engendered by belonging to a corrupt capitalist society—in Lukács' phrase, a "romantic anti-capitalism." One cannot imagine Fowles transforming himself into Lukács' ideal novelist, the ideologically committed "social realist." Nevertheless, he has shown a developing, still open sensitivity to "the impact of new values on old ones, of ineluctable social evolution on individual man."[11] Whether, under the pressure of such concerns, he will preserve in his work a sense of fictive freedom, *Daniel Martin* leaves an open question.

Mantissa (1982) offers no reassuring answer. Perhaps this *jeu d'esprit* is the *reductio ad absurdum* of the "domaine" motif, the controlled enclosed space in which the solipsistic self may have full sway. More plainly than in *Daniel Martin* the protagonist, Miles Green, a novelist contending with his muse in "a small grey room, a pale grey, the colour of a herring gull's wing"—his own brain—is Fowles's self-projection, scarcely veiled. Fowles's humorous intention may have been to allow the eternal feminine full scope for retaliation and manipulation—through the agency of Erato, the muse of love poetry: a riposte to complaints such as Constance Hieatt's that "Fowles is almost exclusively concerned with the problems of men, even when he devotes a major part of the narrative to looking at a woman's point of view."[12]

Green is manipulated, sexually and psychologically, while in an amnesiac state by the transparently named Dr. A. Delfi and a young West Indian nurse, Cory (Queen of Hades, the Dark Lady), both avatars of Erato. She becomes the abused muse of fiction or, more narrowly, of erotic fiction. At first she manifests herself as a foul-mouthed punk rocker who derides her patient/devotee's "deeper levels" of meaning—"all you ever wanted of me was a quick lay"—but turns for most of the text true Grecian, exchanging electric guitar for nine-stringed lyre. The dialogue between self and muse allows both sharp thrusts at "campus faculty factories" and self-mocking allusions to the writer's own fictional contortions; Erato laments that no more worthy artist had invented her. Miles Green in turn, informs her that the novel is now "a reflexive medium, not a reflective one"; "writing about fiction has become far more important than writing fiction itself," though the author himself has been dethroned by deconstructionists. In an implicit allusion to *The French Lieutenant's Woman,* he rebukes

[11]G. B. Edwards, introduction to *The Book of Ebenezer Le Page* (1981), pp. vii–xiv.

[12]"*Eliduc* Revisited: John Fowles and Marie de France."

her for demanding "novelettish" effects in the simplification of "that text where I had twelve different endings—it was perfect as it was, no one had ever done that before. Then you got at it, and I'm left with just three." At the end of part 2, Erato fells her garrulous devotee with a timely uppercut.

Part 3 overextends the exchanges, though they are occasionally sharpened with jibes at self through arch Freudian analysis, Erato doubling as psychiatrist and fearsome feminist, putting down the hubristic erotic novelist. Fowles plays a risky game with his detractors, merging utterly with his mask who, like him, the *Times Literary Supplement* has distinguished as "an affront to serious English fiction." Finally, Miles and Erato couple, while the walls grow transparent and reveal a voyeuristic audience—the novelist's readers? In part 4 the humor indulges in merely arch literary allusion and one impatiently counts pages. Close to the end Fowles forecloses on the reader's reaction by volunteering a footnoted definition of "mantissae," upon which Miles feels Erato tempts men to "waste their vital intellectual juices." Mantissa: "An addition of comparatively small importance, especially to literary effort or discourse." Inevitably, as Fowles surely anticipated, several reviewers found this hostage to fortune irresistible.

If it is no mere diversion, *Mantissa* is perhaps symptomatic of writer's block, or more seriously, as the characterization of Daniel Martin partly foreshadowed, of Fowles's utter descent into self-indulgence or bantering complicity with his most complaisant readers.

A MAGGOT

THE opening of *A Maggot* (1985) is reminiscent of the prelude to a Hardy novel. The "cavalcade of five," closely observed crossing West Country moorland in early spring and approaching "the small town of C———," promise to become the passionately entwined protagonists in a tragic drama of remote provincial life, or in a pastiche of one. However, in a prologue the author has already placed the action a century earlier than such fiction and has disclaimed having written a "historical novel." "It is maggot": a whim or quirk, or more precisely the result of an obsession, a desire to create a particular woman and her qualities. Historical distancing serves artistic detachment, though the novelist is warmly attached to his creature. Like Sarah Woodruff in *The French Lieutenant's Woman,* she was first envisioned, then in the writing made flesh.

The historical Rebecca Lee was the mother of Ann Lee, who formulated the doctrine of the mid-eighteenth-century Shaker sect, that the godhead is dual, masculine and feminine, and Christ's second coming will be in female form—Ann's. In creating the unknown mother, rather than the—as many might consider—deluded daughter, Fowles is free to deal with essence and insight rather than brittle dogma. He endows Rebecca with a life history, again akin to Sarah's, though her woman's fate, especially a fallen woman's, a century earlier is even more harshly constrained by male-forged social and religious imperatives. While Sarah could herself be an agent of liberating change, Rebecca needs for the awakening of her female potential (or "nemo": *The Aristos,* 3:46) the mysterious, inspired, or divine intervention of "His Lordship," himself both redeemed and redeemer. This recalls Mary Magdalene's restoration by Christ's compassionate recognition, though for Rebecca it is not to become his disciple, but further, though she shrinks from claiming it, mother to the "woman-Christ." The "Adam society" (*The Aristos,* 9:93), stubbornly represented and defended throughout by her inquisitor, the lawyer Ayscough, is challenged by her feminine ethic (in the epilogue, the "striking feminism" of Shakerism). That world is rigidly hierarchical, exalts order, and worships property; human life is cheap, justice savage retribution; ethical reason repels emotion, individuality, human equality. Fowles's occasional authorial reflections upon that world, though sometimes deepening understanding of his protagonists' thought and relationships, are almost redundant beside the facsimile reproductions of pages from the 1736 issues of *The Gentleman's Magazine;* while these were inserted to provide a sense of the English of the time, they also graphically illustrate its harsh and callous tenor.

Yet no more than in *The French Lieutenant's Woman* are the ironies slanted in favor of the modern. We, including the novelist, "baffled before the real now," need still, though no longer expecting it, the revivifying example of Rebecca's "left-handed kind" who "confuse . . . upset . . . disturb." Rebecca's Golden Age vision aboard the maggot in the cave of mysteries (the ancient device used also in *The Magus*) reshapes the Christian paradise in a Samuel Palmer-like vision: the Father offers Holy Mother Wisdom a sinless apple, and the Trinity includes her in a new Holy Family. This is allegorical, no attempt to refurbish the outworn stuff of delusive vision, for Fowles writes as a declared atheist, and Rebecca is also compelled to endure a negative vision of man's inhumanity. Like D. H. Lawrence (one remembers "The Man Who Died" and the woman-centered rebirth motif of *The Rainbow*), Fowles uses the language and symbolism of the "established religions" he believes the world must "jettison." In this novel's past, however, as *A Maggot* shows, the religious mode is a valid expression of the timeless need for "more love," the customary greeting of Ann's sect.

It is not Ann's obsolete belief but the feminine mode, still comparatively untried, seen at its strongest in Rebecca's passionate advocacy, that *A Maggot* defends. Fowles's conviction, fused with the integrity of his "Eve," has produced his most concentrated and passionate work since *The French Lieutenant's Woman.* The narrative mounts in intensity, for a mystery is tantalizingly explored and kept alive through a series of interrogations, dramatically pointed and ending with passionate conviction in Rebecca's deposition. Fowles's weakness for didactic digression is relatively controlled; while his longest authorial statement is appropriately deferred to an epilogue outside the novel proper, it might have been omitted altogether; as with comparable advocates (Lawrence or Shaw), the reader must himself try to hold enactment and argument apart.

Mantissa and the subjective characterization of Daniel Martin had threatened Fowles's utter descent into self-indulgence or bantering complicity with his more complaisant readers. *A Maggot* recaptures the more disciplined, authorially poised manner of his two earliest "fables" of the modern fear of love, *The Collector* and *The Magus,* and his masterpiece of contemporary style and sensibility, *The French Lieutenant's Woman.*

SELECTED BIBLIOGRAPHY

I. SEPARATE WORKS. *The Collector* (Boston and London, 1963), fiction; *The Aristos: A Self-Portrait in Ideas* (Boston, 1964; London, 1965; rev. ed., London, 1968; Boston, 1970), philosophy; *The Magus* (Boston, 1965; London, 1966), rev. ed. with foreword (London, 1977, Boston, 1978), fiction; *The French Lieutenant's Woman* (Boston and London, 1969), fiction; *Poems* (New York and Toronto, 1973); *The Ebony Tower* (Boston and London, 1974), short stories; *Shipwreck* (Boston and London, 1974), text by Fowles with photographs by the Gibsons of Scilly; *Daniel Martin* (Boston and London, 1977), fiction; *Islands* (London, 1978), text by Fowles with photographs by F. Godwin, history, personal narrative; *The Tree* (London, 1979; Boston, 1980), text by Fowles with photographs by F. Horvat, personal narrative; *The Enigma of Stonehenge* (London, 1980), text by Fowles with photographs by B. Brukoff, history; *Mantissa* (Boston and London, 1982), fiction; *A Maggot* (New York and London, 1985), fiction.

II. ARTICLES, REVIEWS, EDITIONS, AND TRANSLATIONS. "In Paradise," the *Transatlantic Review,* 14 (Autumn 1963); "On Being English but not British," the *Texas Quarterly* (Autumn 1964); "On Writing a Novel," *Harper's Magazine,* 237 (July 1968), as "Notes on Writing a Novel," the *Cornhill Magazine* (Summer 1969), repr. with additional final paragraph as "Notes on an Unfinished Novel," in T. McCormack, ed., *Afterwords* (New York, 1969), and M. Bradbury, ed., *The Novel Today* (London, 1977), on writing *The French Lieutenant's Woman;* Introduction, glossary, and appendix to S. Baring-Gould, *Mehalah: A Story of the Saltmarshes* ([1880] London, 1969); "My Recollections of Kafka," *Mosaic,* 4 (Summer 1970); "Is the Novel Dead?" *Books* (Autumn 1970); "Jacqueline Kennedy Onassis and Other First (and Last) Ladies," *Cosmopolitan* (October 1970); "Weeds, Bugs, Americans," *Sports Illustrated* (21 December 1970), ecological conservation begins in your own backyard; Afterword to Alain-Fournier, *The Wanderer* (New York, 1971), trans. by L. Bair; *Cinderella* (Boston and London, 1974), adapted and trans. from C. Perrault, *Cendrillon* (1967), illus. by S. Beckett; Foreword and afterword to Sir. A. C. Doyle, *The Hound of the Baskervilles* (London, 1974); Foreword to P. Brendon, *Hawker of Morwenstow: Portrait of a Victorian Eccentric* (London, 1975); "Lettre post-face de John Fowles," in *Études sur "The French Lieutenant's Woman" de John Fowles* (Caen, 1977), Fowles comments on French critiques of his novel and contrasts English and French approaches to fiction; Claire de Durfour, *Ourika* [1824] (Austin, Texas, 1977), trans. with intro. and epilogue "For the Dark," the *New Statesman* (18 February 1977) review of M. Fraser, *The Death of Narcissus;* "*The Magus* Revisited," the *Times* (28 May 1977), amplifies intro. to rev. version; "The Man and the Island," in *Steep Holm: A Case-History in the Study of Evolution* (Milbourne Port 1978); "Hardy and the Hag," in L. St.-J. Butler, ed. *Thomas Hardy After Fifty Years* (London, 1977), personal response to *The Well-Beloved,* analyzing sources of Hardy's and his own inspiration.

Introduction to R. Jefferies, *After London: or, Wild Englan*

(London, 1980); Excerpt from *The Tree, Vogue* (March 1980); Translation and adaptation of Molière's *Don Juan,* produced at Cottesloe Theatre (London, Spring 1981); Introduction to C.B. Edwards, *The Book of Ebenezer* (London, 1981); Introduction to H. Pinter, *The Film Script of "The French Lieutenant's Woman"* (London, 1981); Introduction and annotations to J. Aubrey, *Monuments Britannica* (London, 1982), with R. Clegg; "Simple Things, Splendid Forms, Peasant Pottery by the Talbots of Le Borne," the *Connoisseur,* 213 (November 1983); Introduction to *Thomas Hardy's England* (London, 1984), text by J. Draper, photographs by H. Lea; "Theatre of the Unexpressed," the *Times* (15 April 1985), on translating J.-J. Bernard's *Martine* for the National Theatre; Introduction to *Fay Godwin's Land* (London, 1985).

III. Interviews and Biographical Articles. R. Boston, "John Fowles, Alone but Not Lonely," in the *New York Times Book Review* (9 November 1969); "The French Lieutenant's Woman's Man," in *Life* (22 May 1970); "No PLR Candidate for St. Marylebone," in the *Bookseller,* no. 3382 (17 October 1970), unsigned; D. Halpern, "A Sort of Exile in Lyme Regis," in *London Magazine* (March 1971); R. Molony, "John Fowles the Magus," in *Dorset,* no. 30 (1973); J. F. Baker, "John Fowles," in *Publisher's Weekly,* no. 206 (November 1974); L. Sage, "Profile 7: John Fowles," in the *New Review,* no. 7 (October 1974); R. Robinson, "Giving the Reader a Choice—A Conversation with John Fowles," in the *Listener* (31 October 1974); "John Fowles," in J. Wakeman, ed., *World Authors* (New York, 1975), pp. 485–487; J. Campbell, "An Interview with John Fowles," in *Contemporary Literature,* 17 (Autumn 1976); R. Yallop, "The Reluctant Guru," in the *Guardian* (9 June 1977); M. Gussow, "Talk with John Fowles," in the *New York Times Book Review* (13 November 1977); D. North, "Interview with Author John Fowles," in *Maclean's Jo* (14 November 1977); Pendennis, "Moods in a Wood," in the *Observer* (14 October 1979).

IV. Critical Studies. J. Mortimer, "Contra Clegg," in the *New Statesman* (2 July 1965); T. Churchill, "Waterhouse, Storey and Fowles: Which Way Out of the Room?" in *Critique,* 10:3 (1968); I. Watt, "A Traditional Victorian Novel? Yes, and Yet . . . ," in the *New York Times Book Review* (9 November 1969); R. Scholes, "The Orgiastic Fiction of John Fowles," in *Hollins Critic,* 5 (December 1969); C. Ricks, "The Unignorable Real," in the *New York Review of Books* (12 February 1970); W. Allen, "The Achievement of John Fowles," in *Encounter,* 35 (1970); P. Evarts, Jr., "*The French Lieutenant's Woman* as Tragedy," in *Critique,* 13 (1972); R. M. Laughlin, "Faces of Power in the Novels of John Fowles," in *Critique,* 13 (1972); J. Rackham, "John Fowles: The Existential Labyrinth," in *Critique,* 13 (1972); R. Berets, "*The Magus:* A Study in the Creation of a Personal Myth," in *Twentieth Century Literature* (April 1973); R. Binns, "John Fowles: Radical Romancer," in the *Critical Quarterly,* 15 (Winter 1973); M. Bradbury, "John Fowles's *The Magus,*" in B. Weber, ed., *Sense and Sensibility in Twentieth Century Writing* (Carbondale, Ill., 1970), repr. as "The Novelist as Impresario: John Fowles and His Magus," in M. Bradbury, *Possibilities* (London, 1973); A. Kennedy, "John Fowles's Sense of an Ending," in *The Protean Self: Dramatic Action in Contemporary Fiction* (London, 1974); W. J. Palmer, *The Fiction of John Fowles: Tradition, Art and the Loneliness of Selfhood* (Columbia, Mo., 1974), especially useful as a guide to literary, artistic, and other allusions and the inner structure of the first three novels; A. A. De Vitis and W. J. Palmer, "A Pair of Blue Eyes Glances at *The French Lieutenant's Woman,*" in *Contemporary Literature,* 15 (Winter 1974), examines Hardy's early novel as a source for Fowles's work; J. Mellors, "Collectors and Creators: The Novels of John Fowles," in the *London Magazine* (February–March 1975); A. Fleishman, "The Magus or the Wizard of the West," in the *Journal of Modern Literature* (April 1976); P. Wolfe, *John Fowles, Magus and Moralist* (Lewisburg, Pa., and London, 1976); J. Gardner, "In Defense of the Real," in the *Saturday Review* (1 October 1977), on *Daniel Martin;* W. H. Pritchard, "An English Hero," in the *New York Times Book Review* (24 September 1977), on *Daniel Martin;* I. Trewin, "Falling into a Cultural Gap as Wide as the Atlantic," in the *Times Literary Supplement* (28 October 1977), an "advertisement" exposing the sharp contrast between American acclaim and English depreciation of *Daniel Martin;* C. Hieatt, "*Eliduc* Revisited: John Fowles and Marie de France," in *English Studies in Canada,* 3 (Fall 1977); K. McSweeney, "Withering into Truth: John Fowles and *Daniel Martin,*" in the *Critical Quarterly,* 20 (Winter 1978); B. M. Olshen, *John Fowles* (New York, 1978); R. Burden, "The Novel Interrogates Itself: Parody as Self-Consciousness in Contemporary English Fiction," in M. Bradbury and D. Palmer, eds., *The Contemporary English Novel* (London, 1979); D. Walker, "Subversion of Narrative in the Work of André Gide and John Fowles," in *Comparative Criticism:* vol. 2, *A Yearbook* (London, 1980); R. Huffacker, *John Fowles* (Boston, 1980); *Journal of Modern Literature,* 8 (1980–1981), special issue on Fowles; P. Conradi, *John Fowles* (London, 1982).

A note on the Rembrandt "Self-Portrait at Kenwood," referred to in *The Collector* and *Daniel Martin:* This late self-portrait (c. 1663) is the masterpiece of the Ivaegh Bequest Collection at Kenwood, London. In the *Catalogue of Paintings* Anthony Blunt writes: "It lacks the tortured expressiveness with which Rembrandt often paints himself in his old age, but its solemnity is incomparable, heightened by the mysterious simplicity of the background, which is decorated only with two incomplete oval panels."

PETER SHAFFER

(1926–)

John Russell Taylor

During the years of the so-called New Drama in Britain, critics became used, almost to the point of being blasé, to dramatists making sensational debuts. From John Osborne on, the norm was a public career starting with a bang, a flash, outrage or incomprehension, conspicuous originality of some kind, either in subject matter or technique, and then a gradual easing into orthodoxy, achieved as a rule more by a change in the public's expectations and received ideas about what drama should and should not be than through some compromise in the direction of conformity on the part of the writer himself. But this pattern in contemporary arts, though frequent, is not necessarily standard. Some are born original, some achieve originality, and some have originality thrust upon them. If we think of music, for example, we can find many cases, like those of Arnold Schoenberg and Alexander Scriabin, where the beginnings are thoroughly conventional and only by a slow process of trial and error, of deliberate stylistic experimentation, does the creative originality of the artist evolve and make itself evident.

So it is with Peter Shaffer. He began his public career with a major success: *Five Finger Exercise* (1958), one of the biggest critical and commercial successes of the New Drama in its early days. But so conservative did it seem in its dramaturgy, so familiar in its subject matter and background to an audience nurtured on Terence Rattigan, that there was serious, if rather pointless, argument about whether the play and its author could be considered really to belong to the New Drama at all, except by a chronological accident. At the time of the play's production, Peter Shaffer was thirty-two; he was born 15 May 1926, which places him about midway in the generation of playwrights coming forward at that time—three or four years older than John Osborne, Harold Pinter, and John Arden, two or three years younger than Robert Bolt, Brendan Behan, and John Mortimer.

As a person, Shaffer was and has remained one of the most mysterious of his generation. Many of his contemporaries had contrived, or just happened, to become public figures, their opinions canvassed on matters of general interest, their activities outside the theater chronicled; in apparent reaction, some had made a point of their own reclusiveness, their personal inaccessibility. Shaffer took neither colorful path: he kept himself to himself, not particularly secretive, but evidently taking the reasonable attitude that his plays were the thing, and any information about his intellectual history and private life that he might care to vouchsafe was strictly coincidental to judgment of the work, and anyway not particularly interesting in itself.

So we know something about his early life, but not very much. He is one of twin brothers (and his twin, Anthony Shaffer, has also become a successful playwright with his ingenious thriller *Sleuth,* but a playwright, evidently, of a very different kind), born in Liverpool. He took a degree at Cambridge and worked for a while in a New York library, then for a London music publisher (in 1961–1962 he worked as a music critic for *Time and Tide,* and music was, and evidently from the plays still is, a major interest of Shaffer's). He began writing at Cambridge, or shortly after; accounts differ as to whether he was writing and tearing up plays at that point, or writing and tearing up detective novels. Whichever it was, only three detective novels written with his brother (two of them under a pseudonym) seem to have seen the light of day until 1957, when he managed to get a play he had written for the stage produced on television. In the line, somewhat, of his detective stories, it was a thriller about spies and counterspies battling over an intercontinental ballistic missile, called *Balance of Terror.* It was capable, but not in any way remarkable. A little odder was his second produced play, also for television. *The Salt Lands* (1957) is an apparently realistic drama of life in modern Israel that covertly adapts the situations and structure of Greek tragedy to an epic tale of two immigrant brothers, one a prophet-visionary, the other an urban-minded opportunist, who come into murderous conflict on a kibbutz; though the superimposition of classical motifs is rather patchily worked out, the play has passages of serious and even impassioned writing that stay in the memory.

After this came, seemingly out of the blue, *Five Finger Exercise.* It is a family drama of some intensity, and the obvious (if ultimately unilluminating) question is, is it autobiographical? This is the first question Shaffer was asked in a *Transatlantic Review* interview of 1963. His answer is, as one might expect, yes and no:

> All art is autobiographical, inasmuch as it refers to personal experience. This is so in both the plays and in the Inca play I have been working on *(The Royal Hunt of the Sun).* . . . The torment of adolescence is in all the plays, as is the essential pessimism in the face of certain death. These tensions and obsessions are autobiographical. But of course they are dressed up as stories, myths. That is theater.

And it is as theater that *Five Finger Exercise* calls for judgment. A rather old-fashioned sort of theater in many ways: a drawing-room drama set among the haute bourgeoisie in a weekend cottage in Suffolk. But as Shaffer reasonably remarks in the same interview:

> There are many tunes yet to be written in C major. And there are many plays yet to be written in a living room. As far as the form being old-fashioned, I suppose it is. But *Look Back in Anger* is just as old-fashioned in form. Anyway, form is dictated by content.

(Oddly enough John Osborne himself described *Look Back in Anger* five years after writing it as a "formal, rather old-fashioned play.")

Certainly, directly autobiographical or not, *Five Finger Exercise* is the play of Shaffer's that, up until *Equus* (1973) at least, most clearly centers on "the torment of adolescence." Although interest (and sympathy) is distributed very evenly among the five characters, there seems to be little doubt that Clive, the nineteen-year-old son of the house, is the central character. He and his younger sister, Pamela, are the children of impossible parents. Not, perhaps, impossible individually, but together they have turned their children into the battleground on which are fought out the resentments and dissatisfactions of their ill-advised marriage. One can see very easily how they came to be married in the first place: Shaffer shows a great skill in creating the whole fabric of a life before our eyes without a lot of heavy exposition and explanation. Evidently at one point sexual attraction was reinforced by a balance of differing attributes that probably seemed to complement each other: Stanley was a handsome, hearty, aggressive, ambitious, very masculine man; Louise was daintily nurtured (if not quite in such a grand style as she would now like people to suppose), sensitive, cultured, artistic, very feminine. Now, some twenty years after, she regards him as a blundering oaf, he regards her as an affected bitch.

And the children have to live with this situation as best they may. In particular, they have to try to live their own lives, develop their own personalities, in spite of the constant interference of their parents and the way they are always likely to be used as weapons. Inevitably, there is some reversal of roles: Pamela is a tomboy, more like the sort of son her father might have wished for, while Clive is the sensitive, vulnerable, and (his father would say) effeminate, mother's boy. Both children painfully want the approval (which they take to equal love) of both their parents, and neither, obviously, is going to get it. This seems to disturb Clive a lot more than Pamela, and in his disturbance he becomes his own worst enemy—the more frantically he tries to communicate with his father, the more worried and frightened his father is by his emotionalism, and the less he is likely to approve or understand. Pamela is safer by taking refuge in a certain (possibly calculated) stolidity: she just goes her own way and as far as possible lets the tides of emotion wash over her. Of course, she is only fourteen, and no doubt her time of trial is yet to come.

Into this already explosive situation comes a catalyst, in the shape of Walter Langer, a mature-seeming German of twenty-two, who has been hired by Louise to tutor Pamela in French. He feels like one of the family (which he romanticizes furiously as an ideally happy, balanced English family); he is thoroughly encouraged to feel that way, most effusively and explicitly by Louise but to some extent by everybody. In this feeling he is cruelly deceived; like the central character in Angus Wilson's television play *The Stranger,* he is fated to discover that there can be an unbridgeable gap between being one of the family and being "just like" one of the family.

Naturally Walter, even if he has stepped into the lion's den, has not come from nowhere. He has, as we gradually discover, his own problems, his own neurotic reasons for his excessive, instant attachment to the Harrington family. It is not so difficult to guess what these reasons may be, given his absolute refusal to teach German, which seems to be the logical thing for him to do, and his evasive insistence that his parents are dead, his own family background nonexistent. Of course his parents are not dead, and of course his reasons for this wholesale rejection of his Germanness have something to do with what he is hiding: that his father was a Nazi who used to beat into him Nazi precepts of anti-Semitism, anti-liberalism, and anti-Catholicism with his mother's approval. So much he eventually admits to Clive, partly in self-explanation, partly in order to make him see that his family situation is really not so bad after all.

In his own terms he is probably right; but then, other people's family problems always seem far easier to deal with than one's own. And Walter hardly realizes that his prime function in the Harrington family is that of a new toy, and that when they play, they play rough. The first round of the game occurs before we meet Walter and Pam: it is Stanley baiting Clive because of his arty-tarty friends and airy-fairy ways, and Louise in retaliation baiting him about his coarseness and lack of culture. Round one to the gentle people: Stanley slams out of the house with his golf clubs. After time out for introductions, battle is joined again, again between Stanley and Clive, with Louise intervening and Walter as a partial spectator. This time it is Clive who slams out, leaving Louise to play a rather different game with Walter, a sort of mock-seduction. Clive's return breaks this game up, and next it is Clive attempting another sort of seduction, by tempting Walter to come away with him, to be his special friend. Walter backs, none too gracefully, out of this particular situation, and in consequence Clive brings down the first act curtain in rousing style by telling Stanley in a fit of jealousy, malice, and revenge that he caught Walter making love to Louise. Game and set, though not yet match, to Clive.

Act 2 shows a series of regroupings. Pam talks to Walter about marriage in general and (obviously) her parents' marriage in particular; she is giving him a warning that he does not heed. Clive talks to Walter, with a more direct warning, and in the process elicits the truth about his family situation. Pam also takes it on herself to act as an interpreter of Clive to their father, but without much success. And at this time Walter makes his biggest mistake: pushed by Louise into an avowal of his feelings for her, he blurts out that he regards her as the mother he has never really had. This, of course, is not at all what Louise wants. It is hard to say exactly what she does want: probably not an affair, but at least an impetuous declaration of passion, about which she can feel flattered and act wisely, older-womanly.

The end of this particular round of games is in sight, and it is clear who is going to be the victim. Walter is still blissfully unaware, however, still trying to do his bit by sorting out the problems that the Harringtons, deep down, do not really want sorted out. He offends Pam by treating her too much like a child, he offends Stanley by trying to explain his son to him, and is then totally shattered when Louise gets Stanley to dismiss him, on the flimsy excuse that he is having a bad effect on Pam, and Stanley (on the equally flimsy excuse, which he really does not believe himself, that Walter is having an affair with Louise) carries it a stage further by threatening to have him deported back to Germany. Who is to blame? Everyone, to some extent. And who has anything to gain? Everyone, if they can see the situation rightly. But no one does: the confrontation between Stanley and Louise that might save their marriage ends in an armed truce at best, and the possibility that Clive might be able to get away and stand on his own feet is grimly scotched by Louise, who tries to destroy him by suggesting to him that his denunciation of her and Walter came not from jealousy over her attentions, but from homosexual attraction to Walter. So the most anyone has learned from the whole interlude is Clive's dawning awareness that he too has claws, he too can hurt and destroy if he wants to.

So far, so good. What Shaffer has given us is, in outline, a thoroughly effective, theatrical, traditional, well-made play. *Five Finger Exercise* is plotted with all the aplomb of an Arthur Pinero, getting characters on and off stage with neatly disguised skill and efficiency, planting enough background information without ever bogging us down in wads of obvious exposition, and ending each of its four scenes with a resounding curtain line. Although it emerged in 1958, it is technically very much part of the mainstream tradition of British drama; it would have been written in much the same way if *Look Back in Anger* and its successors had never happened. And, indeed, it is not necessarily any the worse for that. Its subject matter, if not highly fashionable at the time, was certainly perfectly legitimate then or at any other time; and the form, as Shaffer remarked, is governed by the content (as well as, to an extent, vice versa).

If one could complain about it (or express doubt at all) it would be on two counts. The first is perhaps largely temporary: the language of the younger characters is full of period slang that has got far enough back to sound dated without as yet taking on a period charm; and worse, as the superficial expression of relationships, it has too much heavy whimsy for comfort (we recognize that the playful exchanges between Louise and "Jou-Jou"/ Clive are meant to be embarrassing, but it is hard to be sure about those between Pamela and Clive). The other cause for complaint may also be rather subjective: it is that, in a period of unmistakably individual, personal drama, Shaffer seems to be resolutely impersonal. By using, as he does, the language of the tribe, he may be taking refuge, avoiding the sort of personal commitment (however sublimated in art) from which great drama comes. But then *Five Finger Exercise* is a good, commercial, West End play; at this stage Shaffer is still perfecting his craft, and does not aim or claim to be doing anything more.

Within this definition, though, there is one noticeable oddity the play has, from which, if we observe it, we might wonder whether Shaffer is more than he first appears to be. That is the way that the play, while functioning (very well) within a tradition that sedulously avoided eloquence, that cultivated the understated, the matter-of-fact (or to put it in more acceptable terms, tended to depend rather heavily on Harold Pinter's second silence, when what is really happening between people is apparently unrelated or very slightly related to what they are actually saying), does suddenly burst out every so often into sizzling monologues in which the characters reveal themselves in quite a different way. And not, of course, necessarily any the less natural a way—in "real life" people often talk in monologue, whenever they are given half a chance (maybe because the other person is not listening anyway)—but certainly by the conventions of 1958 a far less naturalistic way.

The only character who is not given at least one such monologue is Pamela—significantly, her longest speech is to her father about her brother, specifically relating a dream of his, in which he dreams that Stanley is literally (and therefore no doubt metaphorically) stripping him naked. But all the rest get the stage to themselves sooner or later for detailed self-revelation. Near the beginning Louise bares all her rather silly, rather pathetic pretensions to Walter in a long description—romanticized, we later discover—of her Anglo-French family background and upbringing. In response Walter blurts out something of his (also rather romanticized, we may think) regard for England and the English. Next Clive reveals something of his own mocking, would-be disaffected personality in a further long speech setting the record straight on his mother for Walter's benefit; and shortly thereafter he makes his most desperate attempt to explain himself to his father, who of course understands nothing of what he is saying. In the second act Walter gets his chances, first to tell Clive about his true family background, and then, again to Clive, trying to help him by describing his own first sexual encounter. And between these two speeches Stanley gets his say in a furious diatribe about the deceptions and disappointments of having a family, addressed nominally to Walter, but really, as the stage direction notes, spoken more or less to himself.

All these big speeches have one thing in common: they tell us something about the great preoccupation of drama during the decade of theater of the absurd—communication, its possibilities and impossibilities. Sometimes the speakers want to communicate and fail; sometimes, as with Louise's monologue, what is said is a smoke screen. Rarely do two characters succeed in communicating (perhaps only Clive and Walter manage to get through at all to each other), but if this is so, it is not so much because, as it was fashionable to say at the time, communication is impossible, but (again as Harold Pinter has pointed out) because people who can and do communicate perfectly will often fear to communicate. Stanley could understand what Clive is saying to him—he is not essentially a stupid man—but he does not want to; he fears the challenge it may pose to everything he has built his life on. So he takes refuge in deliberate obtuseness. Walter does not want his illusions about his ideal English family shattered. Clive comes to the point of wanting to hurt other people before they can hurt him too much. The variety of patterns within a single play is astonishing and already shows a special quality in Shaffer's drama that is not at first glance apparent.

But still, the playwright does not seem to be personally involved in his play to any significant degree. Although his comment about the torment of adolescence might lead us to suppose that he identifies most closely with Clive in the play (which may indeed be the case), he does not slant the play at all in his direction. Depending on our mood or our preconceptions, we could find any of the characters the most sympathetic, the most put-upon (except perhaps the tiresome Louise, but even she emerges ultimately as the victim of her own fantasies). One can certainly understand and sympathize with Stanley's mystification at his own children; Clive's need for the reassurance that his father loves him as well as requiring to be loved; Pam's desire to be treated like the adult she nearly is and not to be constantly put down by her mother; Walter's hope that he will be totally accepted by these funny English, that he will understand one day what makes them tick. The balance of sympathy in a dramatist is of course admirable and makes for effective drama. But might one not be forgiven for wondering if a vital spark of passion is not missing?

If so, Shaffer's next appearance before the theater-going public did not answer the question one way or the other; rather, it delayed our giving it serious thought and coming to even a provisional conclusion. For although during the following years Shaffer was working away darkly on a major project, what meanwhile emerged was a double bill of almost defiantly lightweight one-act comedies, *The Public Eye* and *The Private Ear,* first produced in London in 1962. Obviously, a couple of distinct snobberies may be operative in our judgment of these plays: those according to which we automatically feel some kind of respect for sheer size in the theater ("Oh, it's only a one-act play") and by which we tend to downgrade comedy by comparison with "serious" drama. Now as it happens, one of Shaffer's masterpieces, *Black Comedy* (1967), is in fact a one-act comedy (if not, even less reputably, a farce). And in this context we should perhaps be ready to look rather more closely at these two plays than we otherwise might.

The general feeling seems to be that, of the two, *The Public Eye* is the more successful. Shaffer himself apparently regards *The Private Ear* as a piece that never worked out quite right: it was written in four days, originally as a television play, and rewritten for the American production, and he has never been happy with it. Also, it ran into some criticism of a different sort from people who felt that Shaffer was not quite at home with a cast of working-class characters (it is the only real attempt he made to deal with one), and that maybe he tends to patronize them slightly. There is, I think, some truth in the first part of the proposition, but none at all in the second. Indeed, though Shaffer seems not quite in his element in details of dialogue and expression, there are ways in which the play gives the impression of being one of his most deeply felt, and makes one wonder if it is not rather the direct depiction of humiliation and the defeat of a kind of idealism for which he feels considerable sympathy which ultimately make him uncomfortable.

Be that as it may, he certainly seems to identify more openly with the awkward, idealistic, unworldly Bob than with any of his other heroes. Bob's great passion in life is music, classical music. That, and keeping his gramophone (known affectionately as Behemoth) fed with records, are the only things that make his menial office job acceptable. In music he is secure, controlled and in control; elsewhere he is liable to look like a bumbling idiot. And never more so than when in the company of his very different friend, Ted. Ted is the assured, realistic one who knows all the angles, has a way with girls, accepts his life and himself for what they are with no regrets. As he puts it at one point, Bob is

> a good boy. He wouldn't hurt a fly—and that's not because he's a fly himself either. Because he isn't. He's got feelings inside him I wouldn't know anything about. . . . Real deep feelings. They're no use to him, of course. They're in his way. If you ask me, you're better off without all that dreamy bit.

The business of the evening around which the action of the play revolves is that Ted shall help Bob counteract that dreamy bit and aid him to make a good impression on a girl he has met at a concert and has decided is his destined soul mate. Everything is right, from her Botticelli neck to her interest in music. The only problem is, can she be persuaded to take a serious interest in him, over an intimate *diner à deux* he is staging in his flat, with Ted's assistance? The answer to that question is apparent almost as soon as Doreen arrives. She went to the concert, we soon gather, only because there was a free ticket and it offended her frugal nature to waste it; she knows nothing about music, is painfully out of her depth and rather frightened by Bob, whom she finds incomprehensible and unaccountable. Ted is much more her type anyway; they can communicate, they both like dancing, they have the same idea of fun. We can see this, Ted can see this, but of course poor Bob, lost in his dreams, cannot.

The inevitable happens. Even with Ted playing reasonably fair, or as fair as can be expected, Bob's gaucherie and failure to grasp the realities of the situation are bound to get him nowhere, and he will certainly be left alone at the end, a sadder if, we may suspect, scarcely wiser man. And so it happens. But along the way the play includes two of Shaffer's most striking scenes. One of them, which contains the germ of his brilliant talent for manipulating the physical possibilities of the theater (most apparent in *Black Comedy* and *Equus*), is the scene in which not a word is said for some six minutes while Bob and Doreen circle each other warily, come nearly to a meaningful contact and then sharply separate again, all while the music of the love duet from *Madame Butterfly* plays on the gramophone. The other, which almost immediately precedes it, is at the opposite extreme of highly verbal expression, one of Shaffer's most sustained and deeply felt monologues, in which Bob tries to convey to Doreen something of his feeling (which is no doubt not so different from Shaffer's own feelings) for and about life and music:

BOB. When dad died I came south. If I could start again, I'd make myself study.
DOREEN. Well, you could if you wanted. You're still young. You could go to night-school.
BOB. No.
DOREEN. Why not? Your friend does.
BOB. Well, of course, he's got drive. You lot go on about drive, but you can't have drive without enjoying your work. Now Ted does. When he leaves the office he's as fresh as a daisy, but when I come home I've hardly got the energy to grill a chop, let alone pick up a French book; and what have I done? Filled in about sixty invoices. What a way to spend your day, with all the possibilities in you. And some of those people have been doing it for thirty years. Taking endless dictation. Typing thousands of meaningless letters. 10th of the inst. 11th ultimo. CIF E & OE. Thanking you in anticipation. Your esteemed order. Are you going to spend the rest of your life typing nonsense, top copy and two carbons?
DOREEN. Well, like I say, we haven't got much choice, have we?
BOB. Yes, we have. We must have. We weren't born to do this. Eyes. Complicated things like eyes weren't made by God just to see columns of twopence halfpennies written up in a ledger. Tongues. Languages. Good grief, the woman next to me in the office even sounds like a typewriter. A thin, chipped old typewriter, always clattering on about what Miss Story said in accounts and what Burnham said back. It's wrong! Do you know how many thousands of years it took to make anything so beautiful, so feeling, as your hand? People say "I know something like the back of my hand," but they don't know their hands. They wouldn't recognize a photograph of them. Why? Because their hands are anonymous. They're just tools for filling invoices, turning lathes round. They cramp up from picking slag out of moving belts of coal. If that's not blasphemy, what is? . . . I'll tell you something really daft. Some nights when I come back, I give Behemoth a record for his supper. That's the way I look at him sometimes, feeding off discs, you know. And I conduct it. If it's a concerto, I play the solo part, running up and down the keyboard doing the expressive bits, everything. I imagine someone I love is sitting out in the audience watching; you know, someone I want to admire me . . . Anyway, it sort of frees things inside me. At great moments I feel shivery all over. It's marvellous to feel shivery like that. What I want to know is, why can't I feel that in my work? Why can't I—oh I don't know—feel bigger? There's something in me I know that's big. That can be excited, anyway. And that must mean that I can excite other people, if only I knew the way . . . I never met anyone to show me that way.

Compared with this outburst *The Public Eye,* though much more poised and obviously accomplished, is certainly much lighter. But by no means negligible. It is also a three-character piece, about a stuffy husband who has (somewhat against his better judgment) hired a private detective to spy on his wife and find out if there is, as he suspects, another man. But by this time there is, even though the relationship is unbelievably innocent and remote: the "other man" is the detective, whose presence has been observed by the wife (though not understood) and developed into a distant nonspeaking companionship between them, as they wander the streets of London, together if still apart. The showpiece of the play is the eccentric character of the detective, an elfin Greek with an uncontrollable sweet tooth that keeps him constantly nibbling out of paper bags—particularly when nervous.

What the play is really about is the breakdown of communication in a marriage. Belinda is upset by Charles's "iceberg voice. I can't bear it. 'One would hardly say,' 'I scarcely think,' 'One might hazard, my dear.' All that morning-suit language. It's only hiding." Why has the man she loved and married turned into a stuffed shirt? What happened to all the fun and surprise? Why does she have to feel, as Clive does in relation to his father in *Five Finger Exercise,* watched, guilty, responsible, examined? Naturally, Charles suggests it is not all his fault:

> Let me tell you something. Each man has all those things inside him: sex, jokes, jazz and many more important things than that. He's got the whole of human history in him, only in capsule. But it takes someone who loves him to make those capsules grow. If they don't grow, he's not loved enough. And that kind of love can only be given by an adult.

The solution to their problem, engineered by Cristoforou, a whimsical and capricious *deus ex machina,* is that he and Charles have to change places (rather like the husband and the outsider in Pinter's *A Slight Ache,* only here the exchange is explained and rationalized). Charles and Belinda must wander wordlessly round the streets of London, showing each other things and taking each other places, for a whole month. Charles kicks against it, but he accepts; by playing an unlikely role, perhaps he will make some unlikely capsules grow. Otherwise, like the Yaghan Indians Belinda speaks of earlier on, all he can expect to do is to be scrapped by nature, fail like the crops, and sit on green water, waiting to die.

Indians were evidently already in Shaffer's mind, with reason, since he had been working for some time on various drafts of the play that finally reached the stage in 1964 as *The Royal Hunt of the Sun.* Originally it was intended for the Royal Shakespeare Company, but they seem to have been daunted by the magnitude of the production and size of the cast, and after some further rewriting (each draft, it seems, gained in clarity and simplicity compared with its predecessor) it was taken on by the National Theatre, to become one of their most remarkable popular successes. It is at once a spectacular drama and a think-piece written in a rather elaborate literary language. As Shaffer himself summarized its theme in an interview shortly before it was produced, it is "a play about two men: one of them is an atheist, and the other is a god." The atheist is Pizarro, Spanish conqueror of Peru, and the god is the Inca Atahuallpa.

> The play is about the relationship, intense, involved and obscure, between these two men, one of whom is the other's prisoner: they are so different, and yet in many ways—they are both bastards, both usurpers, both unscrupulous men of action, both illiterate—they are mirror images of each other. And the theme which lies behind their relationship is the search for God—the search for a definition of the idea of God. In fact, the play is an attempt to define the concepts of God.
>
> (*Plays and Players,* April 1964)

In other terms, Shaffer has explained that the vital thought process behind the play was that he

> felt more and more inclined to draw the character Pizarro, who is a Catholic, as an atheist, or at least as a man who explores what and who he is. When the Church is revealed to him as being wicked and suspect, and loyalty, friendship, is revealed as being suspect and wicked, he has a feeling of meaninglessness of life. It is this: what can one ultimately find to give one strength and stability?

All of which makes the play sound rather heavy going, and certainly unlikely material to have the makings of a major London and Broadway success. That it nevertheless turned out to be just that probably has quite a lot to do with the spectacular element, itself welcome in a theater starved—the musical apart—of spectacle. But even more important, of course, is the way the spectacle was handled in John Dexter's brilliant production and Michael Annal's extraordinary setting, with its transformable sun-motif that could close into a great medallion with the emblem of the conquistadores incised on it. This was a central feature that contributed greatly to the realization on stage of Shaffer's original intention, "a kind of 'total' theatre, involving not only words but rites, mimes, masks and magics." It is, he modestly observes in his author's notes to the published text, "a director's piece, a pantomimist piece, a musician's piece, a designer's piece, and of course an actor's piece, almost as much as it is an author's."

Clearly Shaffer has progressed a long way in his dramatic thinking from the easy naturalism of *Five Finger Exercise. The Royal Hunt of the Sun* is a chronicle play covering a period of over four years and many thousand miles of journeying. It is, for all that, quite tightly organized, but evidently all the material could not be encompassed in a naturalistic drama; it can be done only by calling on all the resources of the theater, deriving techniques partly from Kabuki, partly from Shakespeare's way with history, partly from Brechtian epic theater. The central thread of the drama is the mental and spiritual development of Pizarro, culminating in his strange relationship with Atahuallpa, his mirror image, the god he has caught in his net. After these two characters, the most important is Martin, Pizarro's retainer, who as old Martin acts as narrator for us and as young Martin undergoes the torments of adolescence, the slow, ugly process of learning by disenchantment, reconciling one's ideals with the harsh realities of life.

Pizarro begins to teach him early, before the expedition has begun, when he has only just recruited his men:

PIZARRO. Listen to them. There's the world. The eagle rips the condor; the condor rips the crow. And the crow would blind all the eagles in the sky if once it had the beak to do it. The clothed hunt the naked; the legitimates hunt the bastards, and put down the word Gentlemen to blot up the blood. Your Chivalry laws don't govern me, Martin. They're for belonging birds—like them: legitimate birds with claws trim on the perch their fathers left to them. Make no error; if I could once peck them off it, I'd tear them into gobbets to feed cats. Don't ever trust me, boy.
YOUNG MARTIN. Sir? I'm your man.
PIZARRO. Don't ever trust me. . . . Or if you must, never say I deceived you. Know me.
YOUNG MARTIN. I do, sir. You are all I ever want to be.
PIZARRO. I am nothing you could ever want to be, or any man alive. Believe this: if the time ever came for you to harry me, I'd rip you too, easy as look at you. Because you belong too, Martin.
YOUNG MARTIN. I belong to you, sir!
PIZARRO. You belong to hope. To faith. To priests and pretences. To dipping flags and ducking heads; to laying hands and licking rings; to powers and parchments; and the whole vast stupid congregation of crowners and cross-kissers. You're a worshipper, Martin. A groveller. You were born with feet but you prefer your knees. It's you who make Bishops—Kings—Generals. You trust me, I'll hurt you past believing.

(1.5)

As will be observed, Shaffer's Pizzaro is a great talker (the style of these speeches, with their cunning repetitions and echoes, is a fair sample of the play's texture), one of the world's explorers, mental as well as physical. He has tried everything, thought about everything, been disgusted or disenchanted by everything. Here he is on death:

Fame is long. Death is longer . . . Does anyone ever die for anything? I thought so once. Life was fierce with feeling. It was all hope, like on that boy. Swords shone, and armour sang, and cheese bit you, and kissing burned and Death—ah, death was going to make an exception in my case. I couldn't believe I was ever going to die. But once you know it—really know it—it's all over. You know you've been cheated, and nothing's the same again.

(1.10)

And here on time:

Listen, listen! Everything we feel is made of Time. All the beauties of life are shaped by it. Imagine a fixed sunset: the last note of a song that hung an hour, or a kiss for half of it. Try and halt a moment in our lives and it becomes maggoty at once. Even the word "moment" is wrong, since that would mean a speck of time, something you could pick up on a rag and peer at . . . But that's the awful trap of life. You can't escape maggots unless you go with Time, and if you go, they wriggle in you anyway.

(1.10)

And yet, like Tennyson's Ulysses, he has never ceased from searching. For what? Most of all, perhaps, for something to believe in, something by which he can cheat time and overcome the only ultimate reality, death. It is a curious fate that brings him, nominally in search of gold, fame, and a place in history, across hundreds of miles of privation, to the land of the Inca Atahuallpa, who can claim: "Not a leaf stirs in my kingdom without my leave." For Atahuallpa might be the something he can believe in. "He has some meaning for me, this man-God." And, paradoxically, Pizarro might be something for Atahuallpa to believe in, the white god from the East who will inaugurate a new era. The core of the drama takes place in the tranced stillness when Pizarro has Atahuallpa a prisoner ("What do worshippers do when you snatch their god? They do nothing") and Atahuallpa has Pizarro enthralled by his own conviction that he cannot die, that he rules death and, at the reappearance of his father the sun, he too will rise again.

It is in this situation that Pizarro the man of action finds himself for once ineffectual and indecisive. He admires the Inca civilization, to a point that one of the accompanying priests, De Nizza, finds blasphemous.

DE NIZZA. Look hard, you *will* find Satan here, because here is a country which denies the right to hunger.
PIZARRO. You call hunger a right?
DE NIZZA. Of course, it gives life meaning. Look around you: happiness has no feel for men here since they are forbidden unhappiness. They have everything in common so they have nothing to give each other. They are part of the seasons, no more; as indistinguishable as mules, as predictable as trees. All men are born unequal: this is a divine gift. And want is their birthright. Where you deny this and there is no hope of any new love; where tomorrow is abolished, and no man ever thinks "I can change myself," there you have the rule of Anti-Christ.

(2.4)

But Pizarro is not convinced:

DE NIZZA. When I came here first I thought I had found Paradise. Now I know it is Hell. A country which castrates its people. What are your Inca's subjects? A population of eunuchs, living entirely without choice.
PIZARRO. And what are your Christians? Unhappy hating men. Look: I'm a peasant, I want value for money. If I go marketing for Gods, who do I buy? The God of Europe with all its death and blooding, or Atahuallpa of Peru? His spirit keeps an Empire sweet and still as corn in the field.
DE NIZZA. And you're content to be a stalk of corn?
PIZARRO. Yes, yes! They're no fools, these sun men. They know what cheats you sell on your barrow. Choice. Hunger. Tomorrow. They've looked at your wares and passed on. They live here as part of nature, no hope and no despair.
DE NIZZA. And no life. Why must you be so dishonest? You are not only part of nature, and you know it. There is something in you at war with nature; there is in all of us. Something that does not belong in you the animal. What do you think it is? What is this pain in you that month after month makes you hurl yourself against the cage of time? . . . This is God, driving you to accept divine eternity. Take it, General: not this pathetic copy of eternity the Incas have tried to make on earth. Peru is a sepulchre of the soul. For the sake of the free spirit in each of us it must be destroyed.

(2.10)

At the last, inevitably, Pizarro is cheated. The Inca does not rise again, his empire falls in ruins, and soon afterwards Pizarro, who himself unwillingly and incredulously brought this all about, falls too. The play makes its points eloquently, to the extent of being overtalkative, were Shaffer's words not complemented by something more, something in the physical staging that balances and enriches the verbal debate. Anyone who saw the original productions will remember the way they looked, the extraordinary impression they created of a meeting of two worlds in a dead, empty space brought to life by the magic of the theater, long after any argument about the philosophical profundity of the words (or their culpable lack of it) has been forgotten.

The Royal Hunt of the Sun was a tour de force, to be followed a year later on the same open stage at Chichester by the same National Theatre Company with another, in its own way perhaps even more extraordinary, *Black Comedy.* This is a piece of physical theater at its most exhilaratingly virtuoso, based on an idea of dazzling simplicity. From seeing a Chinese theater company in action, Shaffer had retained the image of actors creating the idea of darkness by miming it. And from this grew the idea of making a farce by simply reversing the normal light values. The play begins in, for the audience, complete darkness, but evidently by what we hear from the stage the characters of the play are happily able to see. After a few moments' conversation, though, all the lights go out for the characters, and all come on for us. From there on we, the audience, are able to watch what nobody within the play can see, until at the end light is restored to them and taken away from us in the final blackout.

What happens in this pool of light between the two darknesses is all very much in the familiar farcical tradition. Brindsley Miller, an impecunious artist, is out to impress the very correct military father of his new, rather grand fiancée, whom he is about to meet for the first time. For this purpose he has decked out his studio flat with antique furniture "borrowed" from an absent antique-dealer neighbor. Also, an eccentric millionaire collector is coming to see Brindsley's sculptures this same evening. At which point the lights fuse. The girl's father does arrive, and so eventually does the millionaire, but not before a philosophically inclined electrical repairman has been embarrassingly mistaken for him. There are also some unscheduled visitors, including the prim spinster from upstairs (with a secret taste for gin, more than adequately indulged during the blackout) and, much worse, Harold Gorringe, Brindsley's ladylike neighbor and owner of the furniture, which has therefore to be covertly removed, piece by piece, before the lights can go on again, and Clea, Brindsley's recently discarded girl friend, on mischief bent. The action requires split-second timing and steely nerves on the part of the actors not to flinch noticeably just before they fall downstairs or make painful contact with some, to them, invisible obstacle. As a piece of sheer theatrical machinery the play is impeccable, as brilliant as anything Shaffer has done. And almost indestructible: even in a far less than perfect production the structure carries the play.

It would be laboring a point about this sublimely easy-seeming piece to try to maintain that there is "something more" to it. But Shaffer is not the sort of writer who can leave his evident intelligence in the cloakroom along with his coat and hat. Inevitably there are points of connection with his other plays, ideas that carry over. The colonel in *Black Comedy* suggests a more comic reexamination of Stanley in *Five Finger Exercise.* And Bob's remarks in *The Private Ear* about the beauty of hands and people's inability to recognize even their own because they have never really looked at them are reflected vividly in the "kinky game" Clea devises of guess-the-hand in *Black Comedy,* which gives rise incidentally to a moment of strange resonance when Harold, of all people, proves instantly able to recognize Brindsley's hand in the dark (is it possible that this figure of fun is, under it all, the only character able to step far enough out of his farcical context to have some real, intense feeling about someone else?). Miss Furnival from upstairs is also given at one point a drunken monologue of splendid irrelevance to all that is going on around her, which in Shaffer's best manner captures and holds like a bee in amber her character and her class-situation in the smallest possible space:

> Prams! Prams! Prams—in the supermarket! . . . All those hideous wire prams full of babies and bottles—cornflakes over there, is all they say—and then they leave you to yourself. Biscuits over there—cat food over there—fishcakes over there—Airwick over there! Pink stamps, green stamps, free balloons—television dinners—pay as you go out—oh, Daddy, it's awful! And then the Godless ones, heathens in their leather jackets—laughing me to scorn! But, not for long. Oh, no! Who shall stand when He appeareth? He'll strike them from their motorcycles! He'll dash their helmets to the ground. Yea, verily, I say unto thee—there shall be an end to gasoline! An end to petroleum! An end to cigarette puffing and jostling with hips . . . Keep off . . . Keep off! Keep off!

In the room, Clea's "magic dark room, where everything happens the wrong way round," a surprising amount of light is after all shed on a surprising collection of characters.

Shaffer's next play generates more heat than light, and not really very much of either. It is published in two versions, *White Lies* (1967), as it was originally produced in New York in a double bill with *Black Comedy,* and *The White Liars,* the final version produced in England in 1968. Neither is very satisfactory: the most striking change between the two is the addition of the tape-recorded voice of the old seaside fortune-teller's long-lost Greek lover, which haunts her dreams. All the characters are telling lies, mostly to themselves. The fortune-teller is a Middle European Jew pretending to be a baroness and trying to force a similar fantasy (in tape-recorded flashback) on her lover. The first of two clients, a pop-star's manager, tells her a long spiel about how he has suffered from anticipation of his wife's infidelity with his charmingly ruthless charge, and persuades her to put the fear of God (or something) into the latter. The second client, the pop-star, at first reacts with all the required superstitious wonderment at how the baroness can know so much about his deprived childhood and then, in an ingenious *coup de théâtre,* turns the tables by bursting into helpless laughter and telling her the true story of his eminently respectable middle-class background and his imposture in order to get noticed in a world where only working-class glamour gets you places. (It is as though Clive from *Five Finger Exercise* has decided for career purposes to pass himself off as Ted from *The Private Ear.*) The speech in which Tom, the pop-star, lays his cards on the table is a great set-piece for an actor, but otherwise *The White Liars* is the feeblest piece by Shaffer to remain in circulation.

Though not, even so, a commercial failure. This fate—the first time it happened to Shaffer—was reserved for his next full-length play: *The Battle of Shrivings.* The text of this as originally performed has not been published, and Shaffer has subsequently reworked the play for his own satisfaction and a possible American production under the title of *Shrivings;* this as yet unperformed version was published in 1974. The original is admittedly unsatisfactory. The idea is again, as in *The Royal Hunt of the Sun,* a head-on confrontation between two different ways of life, two opposing approaches to the business of living. But on this occasion the matter is talked out rather than acted out, and consequently the play seems to be lacking a dimension. It is not necessary to consider *The Royal Hunt of the Sun* or *Equus,* the two full-length plays that flank *The Battle of Shrivings* in Shaffer's work, with too much emphasis on the value or profundity of their philosophical ideas as ideas, because what is most fascinating about them is their brilliant visualization of these ideas in terms of theatrical event. But *The Battle of Shrivings* is a talk- and think-piece very much as many of Shaw's later plays are; it forces us to consider the ideas as ideas, and as such they tend to seem shallow and superficial.

The two characters whose views of life conflict in the play are Sir Gideon, a sort of Bertrand Russell character who has lived out his life as a philosopher and pacifist, and is now universally revered as something of a secular saint, and Mark, his ex-pupil, now a showily bohemian, almost equally famous poet (as it might be, Robert Graves or Lawrence Durrell), who after a long period out of England, writing on Corfu, has come back to be received into the arms of the establishment with a prize from Oxford University and also, possibly, into the arms of Mother Church. The prim, chaste, humanistic philosophy of Sir Gideon is anathema to Mark, and he declares war upon it over a week-end spent in Sir Gideon's pacifist, vegetarian home; if Sir Gideon can keep his cool during that time, and consistently turn the other cheek, then Mark will reconvert to humanism.

The "battle" is therefore a baiting game. Mark savagely insults Sir Gideon's wife during a "death game" (with some apples) derived from R. D. Laing (an influence to assume even greater importance in *Equus*), seduces the girlfriend of his son, and publicly announces that the son is illegitimate. Gideon takes it all, and so seems to win the battle, but in the process loses a lot of his own faith, even to the extent of striking his own wife, so that by the end the antagonists have changed places. So far, so reasonably good. Unfortunately the play is far too heavily talky, and none of the characters really comes to life (except maybe the son, whose cool manner of dealing with his relations and relationships suggests a Clive from *Five Finger Exercise* who has surmounted the torments of adolescence and managed actually to grow up). Mark is little more than his cloak and his swagger; Gideon, prim, whimsical, and rather chilly, seems to have strayed out of one of C. P. Snow's civil service novels, and though we are often told that he is a world-famous philosopher, he never says anything (let alone does anything) to convince us that this might possibly be so.

In his rewriting of the play for the published text Shaffer has certainly made it more consistent, and intensified its overall gesture. Starting from the structure, he has decided that the character of Gideon's wife was insufficiently developed and perhaps essentially irrelevant, and so eliminated her: Gideon now becomes a divorcé, and the motives for his wife's leaving him are left in the air, one more topic on which Mark can torment him and the rest of the household. (Was it because Gideon's determination on chastity was too much for her? Was it because Gideon was really interested only in young Mediterranean boys?) The removal of the wife means that Gideon has to strike someone else at the end, and that someone else has to be savagely humiliated in the death game with the apples. And the obvious object is the eager young American girl disciple, who now takes on much more prominence and much more life in the play.

Recognizing perhaps that one of the play's major flaws was its uncertain hovering between naturalism and a more extravagant rhetorical style, Shaffer has chosen in the reworking to key it up rather than play it down. Gideon becomes less of the uninvolved sage, more believably a man who has fought and is still fighting a battle with emotions that he intellectually rejects. Even the already extravagant character of Mark has been keyed up somewhat, so that one senses his torment, from which his destructive urges arise, as more genuine; that he is in fact much less in control of what he says and does to prove his point than seemed to be the case in the first version. His son, David, remains rather a sympathetic cipher, but even he is less cool than he was, more emotional, to the point that one can believe that Mark's announcement that his mother was a whore and that David is not his son (a lie, of course, as David recognizes even at the time) could have a traumatic effect on him.

The effect of the play, here as elsewhere throughout, has been moved further from statement (David is upset because his father announces that he is a bastard) toward a different dimension of psychological truth (David is upset because of the complex motivation his father would have in inventing such a lie). It is hard to know how the new version would play on stage—it would need a very careful and precise choice of style for its production and playing—but at any rate to read and imagine on the stage of one's own mind it is far more satisfactory. And far more clearly in the line of Shaffer's development toward *Equus.*

In this connection, a significant aspect of even the first version of *Shrivings* is the appearance in it of ideas derived from the psychologist R. D. Laing. It would seem that in the later 1960's Shaffer was taking an increasing interest in psychology as an intellectual discipline with philosophical ramifications. In 1967 he wrote a full-length television play about a middle-aged professor of English undergoing a psychological crisis while experimenting with LSD in Greenwich Village; he described it as "a play in which life is seen through the eyes of the old." It was written in a "Joycean, stream-of-consciousness style" and, whether because it was considered too obscure, too controversial, or merely too expensive, it never reached production. In 1973 appeared another play based on psychological researches, *Equus,* but this time, though verbally it is in places highly developed and breaks out into real eloquence, it is a piece that fully exists only in the theater, in terms of the astonishing visual imaging of the action and the way the thought is precipitated into meaningful, unparaphrasable happening.

In this respect *Equus* remains, with, in its very different register, *Black Comedy,* Shaffer's most impressive achievement in the theater. Like *Black Comedy* and *The Royal Hunt of the Sun,* it was first directed by John Dexter at the National Theatre, and though no doubt there are in theory many ways of directing all three plays, for anyone who saw the first production the stage embodiment of Shaffer's text remains ineffaceable. The action of the play was inspired, Shaffer tells us in his note to the published text, by a real-life case of which he was once told the bare outlines—that a highly disturbed young man had inexplicably blinded a number of horses—and no more. This occurrence has been woven into a texture obviously suggested by (or at least heavily influenced by) R. D. Laing's idea that (to oversimplify drastically) conventional modern psychiatry has been unconsciously molded by the establishment into a tool for social manipulation, for preserving the "norm."

The two principal characters of the play are Dysart, a middle-aged psychiatrist, and Alan Strang, the disturbed youth who has committed the shocking and mysterious crime. The form in which the subject is treated is very free: evidently this is the complete confirmation of Shaffer's remarks in relation to *Five Finger Exercise* and the first double bill in the *Transatlantic Review* interview: "I'm very grateful for the training I've had with these two plays. I've learned how to tell a story, draw characters, devise plausible entrances and exits. I've acquired a technique to stand me in good stead for the greater and less charted seas of semi- and expressionistic theatre."

The action takes place on a bare, darkened stage with a few basic props that are grouped and regrouped in view of the audience. Dysart acts as a sort of narrator, stepping in and out of the action, which flows freely backward and forward in time. And, most important, there are the horses constantly present in sight and sound, invading the psyche of the characters and providing a sort of chorus of sounds: the "Equus noise," which consists of "humming, thumping and stamping—though never of neighing or whinnying." The horses are seen as conventionalized creatures of theatrical ritual: Shaffer's note on their treatment is revealing enough to deserve quotation in its entirety:

The actors wear track-suits of chestnut velvet. On their feet are light strutted hooves, about four inches high, set on metal horse-shoes. On their hands are gloves of the same colour. On their heads are tough masks made of alternating bands of silver wire and leather: their eyes are outlined by leather blinkers. The actors' own heads are seen beneath them: no attempt should be made to conceal them.

Any literalism which could suggest the cosy familiarity of a domestic animal—or worse, a pantomime horse—should be avoided. The actors should never crouch on all fours, or even bend forward. They must always—except on the one occasion where Nugget is ridden—stand upright, as if the body of the horse extended invisibly behind them. Animal effect must be created entirely mimetically, through the use of legs, knees, neck, face, and the turn of the head which can move the mask above it through all the gestures of equine wariness and pride. Great care must also be taken that the masks are put on before the audience with very precise timing—the actors watching each other, so that the masking has an exact and ceremonial effect.

And what Shaffer shows us with this machinery—*shows* us, not really tells us—is the process of Alan Strang's gradual deviation from the respectable norm into neurosis and a crime of cruelty to animals that is found universally shocking, inexplicable, and prima facie evidence for his insanity and desperate need for psychiatric treatment, which may be hoped to restore him to "normality." Linked with this in the play's loose-seeming yet taut and economical structure is a progressive demonstration of the hollowness and self-questioning of Dysart, the psychiatrist who is charged with this job of mental restoration. Shaffer does not make the elementary mistake, any more than R. D. Laing does, of romanticizing madness into a vision of the truth denied to the "sane," but he does show us Alan's particular brand of insanity as a legitimate and valuable response to experience that brings its own benefits and has to be emasculated by society in the cause of self-preservation: Dysart, with his arid, uncommunicative relations with his wife, his academic devotion to his pet dream-world of classical Greek antiquity, comes eventually to a recognition that at the very least "that boy has known a passion more ferocious than I have felt in any second of my life."

The passion is for the dark god of his own creation, Equus, an amalgam of his first traumatic experience of ecstasy when given a ride on a horse by a passing stranger, and his masochistic devotion to the suffering, humiliated image of Christ offered to him by his mother's morbid religiosity. In the battle of his family background between his mother's refined, long-suffering religious beliefs and his father's brusque, self-educated atheism, both parties have one thing in common: a repressive puritanism and a related inability to cope with expressions of emotion. His father, as Alan discovers shortly before he commits the crime, takes refuge in blue movies that he affects to regard with horror and disgust; his mother prays to a God made in her own image. Neither can understand their son's development toward his own private mythology of Equus and his servant horses, the god of fierceness and fire and beauty, the jealous god whose temple must not be sullied by human sexual contacts, whose watchers must be blinded lest they see too much.

At one level the blinding lends itself to pat Freudian formulations. Alan's parents have forced him to suppress and so divert his normal sexual drives, so when he finds himself sexually involved with a girl at the stables where he works, his build-up of guilt finds expression in destructive action against the horse-god as the embodiment of his own super-ego. The crime thus brings his secret world out into the open and puts him in direct conflict with society. At which point Dysart has to take action, to enact the sacrifice required of him by society to the great god Normal—"a murderous, non-existent phantom." And what exactly is he sacrificing?

DYSART: (quietly) Can you think of anything worse one can do to anybody than take away their worship?
HESTHER: Worship?
DYSART: Yes, that word again!
HESTHER: Aren't you being a little extreme?
DYSART: Extremity's the point.
HESTHER: Worship isn't destructive, Martin. I know that.
DYSART: I don't. I only know it's the core of his life. What else has he got? Think about him. He can hardly read. He knows no physics or engineering to make the world real for him. No paintings to show him how others have enjoyed it. No music except television jingles. No history except tales from a desperate mother. No friends. Not one kid to give him a joke, or make him know himself more moderately. He's a modern citizen for whom society doesn't exist. He lives *one hour* every three weeks—howling in a mist. And after the service kneels to a slave who stands over him obviously and unthrowa-

bly his master. With my body I thee worship! . . . Many men have less vital relationships with their wives.

(2.25)

And to what end?

My desire might be to make this boy an ardent husband —a caring citizen—a worshipper of abstract and unifying God. My achievement, however, is more likely to make a ghost! . . . . Let me tell you exactly what I'm going to do to him!

He steps out of the square and walks round the upstage end of it, storming at the audience.

I'll heal the rash on his body. I'll erase the welts cut into his mind by flying manes. When that's done, I'll put him on a metal scooter, and send him puttering off into the modern world, and he'll never touch hide again! I'll give him the modern, Normal world where animals are treated properly—tethered all their lives in dim light, for example, just to feed it. I'll take away his Field of Ha Ha, and give him Normal places for his ecstasy—six-lane motorways driven through the guts of cities, extinguishing Place altogether, *even the idea of Place!* I'll give him the nourishing, earthy, Normal world where land is cemented over from one sea to the next, and sea itself lies dead—all holy waters—Aegean, Ionian, Tyrrhenian waters—stinking dead under three inches of sun tan oil! . . . With any luck, his private parts will come to feel as plastic to him as the products of the factory to which he will almost certainly be sent. Who knows? He may even come to find sex funny. Smirky funny. Bit of grunt funny. Trampled, and furtive, and entirely in control. Hopefully, he'll feel nothing at his fork but Approved Flesh. *I doubt, however, with much passion! (Pause)* Passion, you see, can be destroyed by a doctor. It cannot be created.

He addresses Alan directly in farewell.

You won't gallop any more, Alan. Horses will be quite safe. You'll save your pennies every week, till you can change that scooter in for a car, and put the odd fifty P on the gee-gees, quite forgetting that they were ever anything more to you than bearers of little profits and little losses. You will, however, be without pain. More or less completely without pain.

(2.35)

Is this good enough? What are these truths against the truth of Alan's own strange experience? The questions continue to vibrate after the play is over. But the fact that they do so is not so much because of Shaffer's verbal formulations, eloquent though they be. It is because in the play we ourselves have lived through Alan's experience with him, we have experienced vicariously some of his ecstasy in naked, pulsing contact with his god, we have made our own oblation to the dark gods of his dreams. The theatrical experience the play offers is mind-enlarging because it gets at our minds through our emotions, our instincts. It does not expound Laing's theories, it inexorably shows them worked out in practice, and silences argument. Its theatrical logic and power are unarguable, and if something of our instinctive response seeps into our intellect subliminally, that is probably no bad thing. At any rate, Antonin Artaud, who in his formulation of a Theater of Cruelty imaged the drama as so many immolations with actors and audience signaling to each other through the flames, would have had every reason to be proud of Shaffer as, in this play, one of his most eloquent and effective disciples.

There were seven years of gestation between *Equus* and Shaffer's next play, *Amadeus* (1980); more, in a sense, as even after its first production at the National Theatre Shaffer kept tinkering with it, revising it significantly for its New York production and again, more marginally, when it came back to London's West End. Even then he was not done with it; his work on the adaptation for Milos Forman's film version not only constituted a structural reshaping but also in some respects marked a further stage in Shaffer's developing view of his subject. Evidently it must be a subject dear to Shaffer's heart, and so in fact it is, combining his playwright's skills with the matter of music that has been throughout his adult life almost equally obsessive. The play concerns Mozart and his relations with his great rival and self-accused poisoner, the composer Antonio Salieri. The legend, begun by Salieri himself in old age and picturesquely elaborated by subsequent writers, was that Salieri, madly jealous of this young upstart, poisoned him but then, tormented by conscience, had to admit his guilt at the last. Shaffer, predictably, is not very interested in the truth or untruth of this on a basic factual level: enough for him that Salieri believed himself to be in some way responsible for Mozart's death. Round the crazed but strangely canny reminiscences of the old man, which form a framework for the play and film alike, Shaffer weaves a rather different drama about two interlinked themes: Salieri's tragic/ironic awareness from the first that Mozart is a transcendent genius, and that he, the most offended (for why would God do this to him?), is the only person admitted to this understanding; and Mozart's social and general awfulness, which sorts so alarmingly with his divine talents that we are forced, like Salieri, to question God's curious sense of humor in arranging matters thus.

The play has the same skill as *Equus* in wrapping up sometimes rather difficult and obscure material in a form that enables a large popular audience to approach and enjoy it. Or, some would say, Shaffer has what D. J. Enright has called "the secret of popular success in writing—to blend stock situations and characters with little nuggets of recondite information and occasional ventures into what might be called . . . the mandarin style." But whether or not we think that Shaffer's plays are finally slightly less intelligent than they pretend to be and require slightly less intelligence from their audiences than those audiences congratulate themselves on showing, there is no denying their theatrical success. *Amadeus* again offers its actors two meaty roles: Salieri, with his virtuoso shifts between relative youth and extreme old age (perhaps rather overdone in the original production) and his plotting and disguises; Mozart, the foul-mouthed, feckless, tactless overgrown boy with his sublime nonverbal gift. (For the film version, both actors were nominated for Hollywood best-performance Oscars; the Salieri got it.) Perhaps the ready-made psychologizing about Mozart and his domineering father—Leopold Mozart reappearing as the stone guest in *Don Giovanni;* Salieri posing as Leopold to commission the Requiem and drive Mozart to despair—is flimsy, but *Amadeus,* after all, is a play, not a tract, and the number of musical historians and devout Mozartians who have taken the trouble to refute it must tell us something about its potency as a dramatic fiction.

For like *Equus* the play is of the theater, theatrical. Curiously enough, though, it has transferred to the cinema more happily than any other of Shaffer's filmed plays: most of them have been tried, no doubt on account of their great theatrical success, but *Five Finger Exercise, The Private Ear* (as *The Pad—And How to Use It*), and *The Public Eye* (as *Follow Me*) emerged with no great distinction, and *The Royal Hunt of the Sun* and *Equus,* deprived of the great central images that made them work in the theater, diminished to their realistic dimension alone, failed miserably. *Amadeus,* Shaffer tells us, was forced through by its director to a complete rethinking, and produces an extraordinary equivalence of effect: those who liked the play like the film, and those who didn't don't.

It is an extraordinary development, from the sober, old-fashioned, intelligent but scarcely profound formulations of *Five Finger Exercise* to the equally controlled yet in effect explosive expression of *Equus* and *Amadeus.* At the outset of Shaffer's theatrical career it was possible to admire his work, to qualify that admiration on account of his seeming lack of emotional commitment to what he was writing about, to pigeonhole him as a safely accomplished technical conservative and leave it at that. But his gradual, unsparing exploration of the expressive possibilities of his chosen form, in which technical experiment has been accompanied by (necessitated by, no doubt, since as Shaffer says, the content dictates the form) an uncompromising rethinking of the material proper for drama, his own as well as anyone else's, has little by little established him as a major figure in world drama, a theatrical thinker who triumphantly escapes all narrow definitions and ends up a unique phenomenon, like nobody but himself. After *Five Finger Exercise* we might have agreed that the play was "promising" and felt pretty certain that we knew exactly what it promised. After *Amadeus* there is just no guessing what he may do next, but it seems inevitable that it will be grand and glorious.

SELECTED BIBLIOGRAPHY

I. Collected Works. *The Private Ear and The Public Eye: Two One Act Plays* (London, 1962); *Black Comedy, Including White Lies: Two Plays* (New York, 1967), *White Lies,* first version of *The White Liars,* not elsewhere pub. in orig. form; *The White Liars. Black Comedy: Two Plays* (London, 1968); *Equus. Shrivers: Two Plays* (New York, 1974); Collected Plays of Peter Shaffer (New York, 1982).

II. Separate Works. *The Woman in the Wardrobe: A Lighthearted Detective Story* (London, 1951), novel, by Peter Antony [Anthony and Peter Shaffer], with drawings by Nicholas Bentley; *How Doth the Little Crocodile? A Mr Verity Detective Story,* (London, 1952), novel, by Peter Antony [Anthony and Peter Shaffer]; *Withered Murder* (London, 1955), novel, by Anthony and Peter Shaffer; *Five Finger Exercise: A Play in Two Acts and Four Scenes* (London, 1958), also pub. in *New English Dramatists,* 4 (1962); *The Private Ear: A Play in One Act* (London, 1962); *The Public Eye: A Play in One Act* (London, 1962); *The Royal Hunt of the Sun: A Play Concerning the Conquest of Peru* (London, 1964); *The White*

Liars: A Play (London, 1968), second version of *White Lies; Black Comedy: A Comedy* (London, 1968); *Equus: A Play* (London, 1973); *Shrivings: A Play* (London, 1974), rev. version of of the play orig. produced as "The Battle of Shrivings"; *Amadeus* (London, 1980).

III. INTERVIEWS. "Shaffer and the Incas," by J. R. Taylor, in *Plays and Players* (April 1964); J. F. McCrindle, ed., *Behind the Scenes: Theatre and Film Interviews from "The Transatlantic Review"* (London, 1971), records an interview by B. Pree (1963); "Philip Oakes Talks to Peter Shaffer," in the *Sunday Times* (29 July 1973); "High Horse," by C. Ford, T. Buckley, in the *Guardian* (6 August 1973); " 'Write Me' said the Play to Peter Shaffer," by T. Buckley, in the *New York Times Magazine* (13 April 1975).

IV. CRITICAL STUDIES. F. Lumley, *New Trends in 20th Century Drama: A Survey since Ibsen and Shaw* (London, 1967), includes a discussion of Shaffer's work; R. Brustein, *The Third Theatre* (London, 1969), includes a critique of *The Royal Hunt of the Sun;* J. R. Taylor, *Anger and After: A Guide to the New British Drama* (rev. ed., London, 1969), contains a ch. on Shaffer; R. Hayman, "Like a Woman They Keep Going Back To," in *Drama* (Autumn 1970); A. Lewis, *The Contemporary Theatre: The Significant Playwrights of Our Time* (rev. ed. New York, 1971); C. A. Pennell, "The Plays of Peter Shaffer: Experiment in Convention," in *Kansas Quarterly,* 3 (1971); J. Vinson, ed., *Contemporary Dramatists* (London, 1973), includes an article and a bibliography of Shaffer's works by J. Elsom; J. Simon, "Hippodrama at the Psychodrome," in *Hudson Review* (Spring 1975); D. A. Klein, *Peter Shaffer* (Boston, 1979).

JOHN OSBORNE

(1929–   )

Simon Trussler

I

MANY of those who were excited into a new awareness of theatrical possibilities by John Osborne's work in the late 1950's and the 1960's find it hard to disguise their disappointment at his subsequent development. He has, it seems, withdrawn from spokesmanship for his intellectual generation to become a sniper from the sidelines of disgruntled middle age. In retrospect it is possible to argue that this is only a sideways shift—from the sympathetic treatment of nostalgia that informed even his earliest work to an overt declaration of hatred for contemporary values in the later plays. After all, the work for which he is still best known had us *look back* in anger. Yet Osborne's thematic concerns always meshed somewhat erratically with his structural skills, and one problem with his more recent work is that the almost serendipitous fusion of form with content in his best writing now produces less happy accidents. Certainly, the imaginative impulse behind his plays has shifted—not so much from the radical to the reactionary as from the challenging to the commonplace.

John James Osborne was born in a suburb of London on 12 December 1929. He remained in his family's south-of-the-river home until the early years of the war, but was eventually sent to a "rather cheap boarding school in the west of England," where he has confessed to being "unhappy for most of the time." Leaving school at sixteen, he worked briefly as a journalist on trade papers, then drifted almost accidentally into a career on the stage. In those austere postwar years he was already a devotee of the dying music hall, and long afterwards he was to write a moving tribute to one of its last great stars, Max Miller. In his enthusiasm there was already an element of nostalgia—not so much for the lost realities of the past as for those mythical certainties with which a later age has endowed it. In fact, the "long days in the sun" of Edwardian England, so vividly conjured up by Jimmy Porter in *Look Back in Anger,* were fraught with fears of industrial unrest and even of revolution. But in retrospect the period did acquire a golden glow, especially for those, like Osborne, who felt that they lacked roots—even the roots of commitment to a particular class. This yearning for innately "civilized" values and for an unquestioning morality can induce a sense of alienation from one's own age: and from *Look Back in Anger* to *Time Present*—their very titles suffused with an awareness of passing years—many of the characters in Osborne's plays have been afflicted by this alienation. It has been one of the disappointments of his later work that an acute recognition of the dangers of such alienation has been replaced by their seemingly uncritical absorption.

Not surprisingly, in this light, the best work of Osborne's recent years has thus been in the autobiographical rather than the dramatic medium. The first volume of his memoirs, *A Better Class of Person* (1981), marvelously conveys not just the personal ambience but the whole social sensibility of a genteel-shabby upbringing, and of the small-town bohemianism of his theatrical apprenticeship. Osborne acted for the first time in Sheffield in 1948, and for the next few years he did the rounds of the provincial repertory theaters. This was long before the blossoming of England's civic play houses had begun, and the standards of repertory productions tended to be as mediocre as their bills of fare. The experience of those years, however humdrum, nevertheless gave Osborne his practical education in theater techniques and encouraged him to attempt a play or two of his own. Of these pieces, only *Epitaph for George Dillon* has ever been revised for the London stage. Indeed, when Osborne's very first play, written in collaboration with Stella Linden and produced at Huddersfield in 1950, was revived ten years later at Croydon in the aftermath of his success, its title was changed and its authorship made pseudonymous. And its three fellow products of the early 1950's—of which one, like *George Dillon,* was written jointly with Anthony Creighton—have neither been printed nor restaged. But they were, at least, evidence of a prolific talent, learning to temper itself in the school of experience to the practical demands of the stage.

Osborne first acted in London as a member of the same English Stage Company that premiered *Look Back in Anger* in 1956. He continued to accept occasional roles on stage and, more recently, on television, but unlike many of his fellow playwrights he has avoided cutting any sort of figure in public life. His few essays in critical or polemical prose have been unsuccessful, and although he has fired off occasional epistolary squibs no less furiously from his present right-wing position than in his more revolutionary days, he is temperamentally a shy person. He certainly never resembled the "angry young man" whom the press were at first so eager he should personify. Indeed, the moments of bluster tend to occur when the reluctant celebrity is prodded a bit too far out of his shell. His notorious declaration of hatred, *To My Fellow Countrymen,* in the form of a letter to the left-wing weekly *Tribune,* was thus penned at the near-flashpoint of the Berlin crisis in 1961; more recently, he has taken to addressing mellow, almost middle-aged letters to *The Times* from his sedate country home in Sussex, where he lives in jealously guarded privacy with his fifth wife, Helen Dawson. Having written twelve plays in as many years between *Look Back in Anger* in 1956 and *The Hotel in Amsterdam* in 1968, in his later career Osborne has been no less prolific, but much less certain of either his audience or his sense of direction. Perhaps significantly, at the same time (so far as may be judged from his rare interviews and public utterances) he seems to have found a new personal happiness and security, which no doubt makes of lesser moment his relative lack of theatrical success. Yet, as his own character Bill Maitland recognizes in *Inadmissible Evidence,* that "fibbing, mumping, pinched little worm of energy" which so often springs from personal unhappiness or isolation can also generate a curious and compelling creative force.

II

THE first night of *Look Back in Anger* was on 8 May 1956; the next morning the newspaper critics damned it with faint praise or outraged virtue. But it was not only Kenneth Tynan's counterblast in the following Sunday's *Observer* that turned the tide in the play's favor. Arguably, the theatrical tide was already on the turn—after years in which upper-class-oriented plays by technically proficient but thematically worked-out writers had dominated the West End stage, and in which the hoped-for renaissance of poetic drama had proved abortive. Joan Littlewood's Theatre Workshop, at that time largely ignored in England, had for some years been impressing continental audiences with revivified productions from the classical repertoire; and the unexpected success of the first London production of Samuel Beckett's *Waiting for Godot* suggested that a native audience for original, intelligent drama did exist. Then, at the Royal Court Theatre, the newly instituted English Stage Company, under the direction of George Devine, declared its intention not only of actively seeking new plays, but of giving pride of place to writers—instead of revamping their works into "star vehicles" or into some fashionable director's *jeu d'esprit.* In short, the moment had arrived when a John Osborne could hope to earn more than rejection slips; and sure enough, *Look Back in Anger* was accepted for production at the Court, where many of its author's later works were also to be premiered.

The early plays in the English Stage Company's opening season—notably those by established novelists, unhappy in a new medium—were more worthy than world-shaking. For young writers had got out of the habit of accepting the drama as an appropriate form for the expression of new ideas. Thus it was Osborne's great contribution to the development of the so-called new-wave drama in England—its momentum sustained by such writers as Arnold Wesker, John Arden, and Harold Pinter—that he proved it possible for the theater to communicate once more with the kind of audiences who had responded to the poets of the prewar years, and who had hoped for better things from the one-shot novelists of the early 1950's. Osborne's influence as a torchbearer for drama as a genre should therefore not be underestimated; but he should be given less credit or blame than has been customary as a technical innovator, and he was never among the "committed" playwrights who conceived drama partly as an instrument of social and political reform.

Look Back in Anger itself is a conventionally constructed play in three acts—respectively of exposition, development, and resolution—and it takes place in a single, naturalistic setting. What mattered was that this setting is a slovenly provincial garret, not a sunlit suburban drawing room, and that it is peopled by characters whose emotions are writ larger than the theater had come to think civilized. But the play isn't about the lack of "good, brave causes" for its hero, Jimmy Porter, to espouse. Jimmy is a rebel right enough, but he isn't a typical rebel. It just so happened that Osborne's dramatic diagnosis of his highly individual and probably incurable estrangement reached the stage at a time of shifting allegiances—hastened by the crises over Suez and Hungary—among those who not only sought but were soon to find new causes to champion.

If *Look Back in Anger* owed some of its notoriety to such chance circumstances, its lasting success—and a tenth-anniversary revival, though set in period, proved the play to be more than a period piece—has been due to its intrinsic merit, and to the erratic but almost tangible dramatic energy with which it bristles. Its scene-setting dialogue is often clumsy, and it is flawed by a characteristic reluctance on Osborne's part to delineate developing rather than fully formed relationships; but as a study of a lonely man who is corrosively articulate about everything but his love for his wife, and of the couple's eventual acceptance of a marriage that will always need make-believe to paper over its incompatibilities, it is a work of real psychological insight and unsentimentalized compassion. Its dramatic force derives in part from Osborne's refusal to ferret out a moral or to give a false sense of finality to his climax. For he does not apportion blame either to Jimmy Porter or his wife, Alison; instead, he probes causes, demonstrates the impossibility of the couple's severing their bonds of mutual dependence, and shows them preparing to make the best of the leftover residue of their lives.

As the play's title suggests, the roots of Jimmy's impotent anger lie in the past—in his father's premature, lingering death, over which he stood youthful witness; and in his need to expiate by means of a self-imposed proletarianism his mother's inadequate, middle-class compromises. Although university educated, Jimmy has thus chosen to make a meager living by running a sweet-stall in an anonymous provincial town; and his marriage to Alison is a symbolic defiance of her upper-class parents, whose sense of the stable values of an imperial past he at once despises and envies. He uses his facility with words to nurture an ebullient image that his disillusion is constantly threatening to deflate; and the hovering boredom of an English Sunday afternoon spurs him into his first-act orgy of wife-baiting. From this he is occasionally lured away, into verbal or physical rough-and-tumbles, by his fellow lodger, Cliff; and the act ends with the arrival of Alison's actress friend, Helena. It is Helena who disturbs the precarious status quo—persuading the recently pregnant Alison to leave her husband—and who unexpectedly falls into Jimmy's arms as the second-act curtain falls.

Helena's is a thankless role for any actress. Her attraction for Jimmy presumably lies in the conquest of a social opposite and a sexual puritan; but her own part in the play is never more than functional, and when Alison returns—ready to grovel for Jimmy's affection in the aftermath of a miscarriage—she retires as arbitrarily as she came. Cliff, against whose aptly named stolidity the more tempestuous waves of Jimmy's rhetoric buffet, is more happily conceived; and so, briefly and suggestively, is Alison's father, a surprisingly likable character who is as resigned to his loss of touch with the times as Jimmy is weighed down by it. But Jimmy and Alison are the two people who really matter; both have forgotten "what it was to feel young, really young," yet they cannot even communicate this shared dissociation to each another. And they touch, physically and spiritually, only in the bears-and-squirrels fantasy that gives a strange dignity and fragility to the sexual encounters in which they find temporary solace.

Of course *Look Back in Anger* has strong social undertones. Jimmy's malaise derives from his feeling of classlessness—and his desire to achieve a proletarian pedigree accounts for the affection with which he regards the offstage figure of an uneducated old woman, who has meant to Jimmy all that his mother never could. This relationship, which we see only at second hand, would, however, be a cheap device dramatically if it merely personified a sort of inverted class struggle; but Jimmy's wish to be a vicariously dignified laborer is also a symptom of the gnawing sentimentality to which he ironically confesses. He looks back in anger only because he looks back in nostalgia; and his compulsive verbosity is a protective device, an armory of words with which an easily wounded man defends himself against those who best recognize his vulnerability. Thus, society matters only insofar as its past is colored by Jimmy's rose-tinted vision and its present is made the target of his invective.

Paradoxically, then, it is truer to say that Jimmy Porter is hopelessly maladjusted to his age than that he speaks for it; but neither simplification is really adequate. Jimmy's anger-in-a-vacuum *is* representative; his own inability to fill the vacuum is not. At some quarter-century's distance during which fighting for good, brave causes has come in and out of fashion, it is easier to see that Jimmy Porter was never really a rebel in search of the Campaign for Nuclear Disarmament, but a peculiarly modern tragic hero, at unequal odds not with fate but with his own birthright. The mid-1950's minutiae of the play—the "posh" Sunday papers, the trousers with turn-ups, the ironing board over which Alison interminably slaves—matter, in retrospect, much less than the topical trappings in *The Entertainer,* a play specifically of its place and time. One textbook theatrical tradition to which *Look Back in Anger* belongs, after all, is that of the eternal triangle rounded off in a vicious circle; but no such geometrical figure suffices to measure the sympathy with which Osborne has drawn his two central characters, or the neurotic as fit hero for a problem play without a solution. To have made Jimmy Porter the subject of a dramatized psychological casebook, beneath which a neat line of finality might have been drawn, would have been truer to the theatrical tradition—but false to life.

In his next play, *The Entertainer* (1957), Osborne tried to widen his stylistic range by mounting a domestic drama about a small-time music-hall comedian as if it were itself a succession of scenes and interludes on a variety bill. The interludes—in which Archie Rice puts over his desperate, corny patter while his imaginary audience waits impatiently for the striptease—do capture a genuine music-hall idiom. But the lengthier scenes of domestic life with which Archie's theatrical turns alternate are, paradoxically, couched in a more naturalistic style of family cross-talk than anything in *Look Back in Anger.* For, back in his dingy seaside digs, Archie—though as mechanically self-assertive as his stage persona—is part of a shaky but recognizable family setup; whereas Jimmy Porter and Alison live more fully in loneliness than in sociability. And so, for all the music-hall business that Osborne wrote into the stage directions of his play—harsh, bang-on lighting, turn numbers on the proscenium arches—what he actually created was the most complex *grouping* of characters he was to achieve until *The Hotel in Amsterdam.*

The ostensible plot of *The Entertainer* is no more than a catalyst, which precipitates a succession of family reminiscences and squabbles, and which clarifies the motif of Archie's failure. His son Mick, doing national service in colonial Cyprus, is captured by freedom fighters. His release seems imminent—then, traumatically, comes the news of his murder, in reprisal for the shooting of a terrorist. And the play amounts to a sustained reaction to this developing tragedy offstage. A great deal of tongue-loosening gin is consumed. Archie's wife, Phoebe, reiterates her misfortunes for the thousandth time, and Archie himself tries to tangle with yet another local tart. Like Jimmy Porter, he is of a lost generation. Stripped even of the vestiges of professional dignity that his father, Billy, retains, and long past sharing the political faith with which his daughter, Jean, tries to make the future bearable, Archie is struggling to stem the tide that is sweeping the music halls away. It is to this lost cause that Billy—second in the line of Osborne's sympathetic Edwardians—is sacrificed in the last act, broken by his son's attempt to force him into a stage comeback. And finally even Archie's façade crumbles, and the comedian is hauled off into the wings to confront the symbolic income-tax man he has evaded for so long. This merging of Archie's theatrical and real identity doesn't really come off; dramatically, it makes an effective climax, but the effect is isolative, and it is a pity that the play's closing moments should also be its weakest.

If Jimmy Porter's was a tragedy of turned-in aspiration, Archie's is one of mediocrity. It, too, is in part due to a desire to perpetuate the past; but in *The Entertainer* the physical texture of the present is much more closely and purposefully defined. True, Archie's other son, the stay-at-home and vaguely pacifist Frank, plays only a shadowy, stillborn part in the action; and various supernumerary characters—notably Jean's boyfriend, the unspeakable Graham Dodd—are disastrously ill-drawn. But the desultory, often maudlin family conversations, which give the play its real substance, are finely observed studies of its four main participants and of their ingrained speech habits—which become at times a form of family shorthand, at times an accepted means of avoiding too close contact with the truth. The talk often drifts into a dramatic stream-of-consciousness—incidentally getting across all the necessary exposition without any of Osborne's occasional clumsiness of narration—and although Archie dominates it, there is nothing resembling Jimmy Porter's hogging of the best lines. *The Entertainer* is not really about the isolation of a man and a wife—for Archie and Phoebe are tacitly reconciled to their separation. Rather, it is about the barriers that separate generation from generation—and, in particular, about the estrangement of one whole generation at one moment in history.

That generation is, of course, Archie's. His estrangement is more representative than Jimmy Porter's, partly because of the context that the elderly stoicism of his father and the youthful assurance of his daughter give it, and partly because of the closeness of real, identifiable events to the surface of the play and to Archie's responses. Thus, for Billy music hall has been a way of life, for Jean it is an irrelevant anachronism; to Billy the Cypriots are simply wogs who must be taught a lesson, to Jean they are the victims of imperialism. Archie is caught between such crosscurrents of contemporary history. He cannot react simply, and yet he simplifies endlessly, reducing his life to a search for draught Bass and available barmaids. That one can discern his actual complexity in spite of his own simplifications is a mark of Osborne's success in *The Entertainer*—a success that, having worked out his immediate preoccupation with the nature of nostalgia, its individual effects and its social implications, he was not to repeat until several years and several plays later.

III

Osborne's third play to reach the stage, *Epitaph for George Dillon* (1958), was actually a worked-over version of one of the collaborations of his apprenticeship, and it bears the marks of such origins. Dillon is a failed writer who manages to worm his way first into the household and then into the affections of the Elliots, a lower-middle-class suburban family. He becomes an object for Mrs. Elliot's thwarted motherly feelings, a confidant of the soured and sophisticated Ruth, Mrs. Elliot's younger sister, and the casual seducer of her daughter, Josie. His "epitaph" mourns the sacrifice of such talent as he may possess to the philistine values of the Elliots. He marries Josie and achieves success of sorts by watering down his plays into hack road-shows; arguably he could have done no better, but he has denied himself the chance of finding out.

Such a bald summary makes *Epitaph for George Dillon* sound more like a cautionary tale than it is. Actually, the play's great strength is its refusal to pass a moral judgment on its hero; whether he has compromised his artistic integrity or simply accepted his limitations is left for the audience to assess—and if the evidence seems weighted, it is not because Dillon himself has too many blemishes, but because these are not given the necessarily complicating context of the social milieu in which he should demonstrably find himself. Much later, in *Inadmissible Evidence,* Osborne was to evolve a suitable stylistic means of subordinating a bevy of minor characters to a single flawed hero, without papering over those flaws in the process; but the cardboard Elliots are not cut out for the naturalistic problem-play in which they find themselves. And there are related structural defects: the play is full of inept exposition, clumsy dramatic irony, and worked-up climaxes. It is, in short, a typically too-well-made play of its period, its claims to originality lying in its use of a humdrum suburban setting rather than a tasteful drawing room in Mayfair, and in those occasional passages of rhetorical force that foreshadow *Look Back in Anger*—notably, the nerve-exposing middle-act dialogue between George and Ruth. But even Ruth is more of a conversational foil than a consistently rendered match for George; and the other characters are never more than the sum of their expected attributes.

The next few years were among the least fruitful of Osborne's early career. Harassed by the press and prematurely pigeonholed by the critics, he gave vent to his simmering frustration in *The World of Paul Slickey* (1959)—the only musical he ever attempted, and the only one of his plays he has directed himself. It's a complicated rather than a complex work, at moments seeming to parody the mannerisms of musical comedy, at others inappropriately dependent upon them. And thematically it never decides on which of two separate story lines to concentrate. The opening theme—the one pounced on by the play's contemporary critics—is a pastiche of gutter journalism and of the values of its practitioners; but this soon gets stifled by a rambling story about evasion of death duties, set in a stately home among a stately family who just happen to have the ruthless gossip columnist Paul Slickey as a son-in-law. Starting out as a vicious hack, in the end Slickey comes off rather well—for Osborne's fire gets deflected onto various other targets, which are given a straw-stuffed substance for no other reason than to be shot at, sometimes by Slickey himself. There's an inane pop star, for instance, and a bloodthirsty female supporter of the capital punishment lobby who happens to get the only two songs in the show that bite as they were intended. What is really wrong with *Slickey,* though, is that not a single one of its proliferating bright ideas gets elbowroom to develop. It's a muddled musical, but by no means as unrelievedly awful as those who proclaimed their vested disinterest at the time tried to make out. Osborne had simply chosen a medium that neither suited him temperamentally nor served his satiric purpose adequately. Since the show made no sustained attempt to parody its own conventions, it is not surprising that its subject matter should have seemed incongruous, and that, despite the specificity of some of the songs, its overall diffuseness enervated its satire.

Continuing, it seemed, to cast about for a fresh form, Osborne next tried his hand at a play for television. Called *A Subject of Scandal and Concern* (1961), it deals with the trial and imprisonment of George Holyoake, the last man in England to be convicted of blasphemy. The printed text—though separated out into acts as if for the stage—shows Osborne both exploiting and hemmed in by the task of writing for the small screen. A sequence of short takes—of Holyoake's relationship with his wife and family, and later of his life in prison—is broken up by lengthier trial scenes and by interpolations from a latter-day narrator whose chief function, apart from scene setting, is to point out (with undisguised contempt for those who might expect any such thing) that the play has no moral. This comes dangerously close to suggesting that it has no point either; and the aimlessness of the piece is a pity, because it marks not only Osborne's first experiment in reshaping historic material into dramatic form, but also his first serious attempt to state a public case rather than to explore a personal malaise. As it happens, the statement is in precise and legalistic terms; and this use of a courtroom formula, combined with the distancing effect of the narrator's appearances, more or less compels an audience to reach "judicial" conclusions of its own—so that the content of the play, as so often in Osborne's less successful work, goes against the grain of its form. Holyoake himself has interesting enough outlines to make one wish he had been more fully drawn: a mild-mannered reformer, fighting not only social injustice but his own slight speech impediment and the shyness it induces, his development is stunted by Osborne's over-rigid plot and vagueness of purpose. That the vagueness is deliberate doesn't make it any less irritating or unrewarding.

Osborne's next stage play, *Luther* (1961), was more ambitious. By means of a series of episodes that range widely in time and location, Osborne tried to build up a portrait of the self-doubting, anally obsessed Protestant leader; and in this sense he made a daring stylistic departure from the single settings and closely knit time structures of his first three plays. For all its epic trappings, however, *Luther* remains most successful as a psychoanalytical study of its eponymous hero; when it attempts to relate the man's inner struggles to his religious and political charisma, the play obscures instead of mutually illuminating these two aspects of a complex personality. Strangely, Osborne suggests that after the first of his three acts "the physical effect . . . should be more intricate, general, less personal . . . concerned with men in time rather than particular man in the unconscious . . . caricature not portraiture." But although a comic auction of indulgences immediately sets such a tone, there turns out to be no such radical change of mood as it anticipates. The first act certainly concentrates on "portraiture" to the extent that it explores Martin's character by opposing it to either the staid rituals of his monastic order or the earthy interventions and recriminations of his father. But in the remaining acts the emphasis shifts only erratically away from the sweat-soaked, epileptic priest as he is transformed, episode by episode, from a questioning Catholic to an active Protestant. The sense of cloistered isolation is scrapped, as Martin's rejection of it requires; but there is no broader social or political fabric on which the suggested caricature can take shape. And there are only intermittent attempts to explain the political implications of Martin's reforms—of which the most notable is a soldier's disillusioned soliloquy on the bloody aftermath of the Peasants' Revolt. But this scene is in part a narrative necessity—a gap of four years separating it from Martin's retraction at the Diet of Worms—and it is in this sense also an apology for Osborne's failure to show how Martin's own nagging energy, fueled from within by his physical suffering, has been transmitted into a force that can move the minds and faith of his fellow men.

Thus, it is not to any inherent weakness in Brechtian-style epic theater that the play's apparent divergence along parallel lines of development can be attributed. Rather, the fault lies in Osborne's failure to complement his portrayal of Luther as an individual by demonstrating that individual's power over others; so that many of the episodes, instead of being self-explanatory in proper epic fashion, become merely fragmentary. To aggravate this problem, the lengthy time span of the action makes one of Osborne's recurrent bad habits seem more blatant here than in his earlier work—the habit of delineating fully matured stages in the development of his characters, instead of tracing the working out of each successive change. *Luther* suffers more than most of his plays from such instant transitions, while the failure to realize Martin's society—and more particularly the causes and effects of his impact upon it—flaws the characterization further by blurring the sharp focus that might have made for a more incisive individual study. Later, in *A Patriot for Me,* the strongly drawn *fin-de-siècle* setting conversely overshadows the homosexual hero of the play, Alfred Redl; so if that setting in part redeems Redl's lack of substance, in *Luther* it is Martin's rhetoric that lives while the Reformation it helped to shape remains a shadowy background. There are many passages of compelling Freudian insight in which Martin shares his excremental nightmare, and Osborne has "allegorized going to the lavatory" with undeniable scatological force; but as Martin also comments, "allegories aren't much help . . . except to decorate a house that's been already built by argument." And the occasional passages of genuine dialectic—notably the argument between Luther and his Vicar General, Staupitz, in the second act—do no more than lay the foundations on which Martin himself, however much compassion he evokes as a victim of conscience and constipation, can build nothing nobler than a privy.

It must in fairness be added that a number of critics at the time of its opening held *Luther* in high esteem. Its appeal as a costume drama with intellectual pretensions ensured it a longish run, and it was to become Osborne's most respectable "set-text" play. It thus had the effect of restoring confidence in Osborne, and perhaps his confidence in himself, at what in retrospect still seems to have been an uneasy period in his career. The uneasiness culminated in *Plays for England* (1963), a pair of one-acters that return both to the present day and to Osborne's preoccupation with the press. Little need now be said about *The Blood of the Bambergs,* a skit on royalty worship, except to note that its single specimen of royalty commands the kind of grudging respect one came to accord Paul Slickey in Osborne's first experiment in satire. The guying of such attendant flummers as civil servants, television commentators, and (inevitably) journalists has its moments of deadly accuracy; but it seems disproportionate to the sins of its victims, and the whole play now strikes one as essentially an occasional piece.

Under Plain Cover is a more interesting work, which starts off as a delicately textured study of shared sexual fantasy and then veers disastrously into a tale of a big bad journalist. So long as the play remains a duologue between Tim and Jenny, whose wedded bliss is heightened by a common delight in dressing up, it is a largely successful reconstruction of the kind of make-believe that can not only save a marriage—as the bears and squirrels save Jimmy Porter's—but give it added savor and even stability. However, the heavy-footed intrusion of the press, which has somehow discovered that Tim and Jenny's marriage is incestuous, complicates the argument and the action alike. What began as an easily wrought two-hander, full of quick, naturally interlocking cross-talk, becomes a sort of reporter's rakish progress into deserved oblivion; and insofar as the original theme isn't abandoned altogether, it is so arbitrarily complicated by the incest issue as to hint at some obscure connection between an accidental marriage with one's sister and an obsession with underclothing. *A Bond Honoured* was later to see Osborne relating one perversion to another in a similarly obtuse and mutually unilluminating manner; that such a subplot doesn't set in until two-thirds of the way through *Under Plain Cover* makes the play's eventual failure more infuriating, albeit less full-blooded.

IV

OSBORNE'S next play, *Inadmissible Evidence* (1965), marked a sudden, sober maturity. The piece makes great physical demands on its leading actor, who is on stage continuously for over three hours and doing most of the talking. If that actor should be off his form, the coughing and shuffling in the audience rises appreciably; but a similar danger stalks many of the world's major dramatic roles, among which Bill Maitland's will come, I think, to be numbered. Maitland is a shady small-time solicitor —not averse to marginal adjustments of evidence in his client's favor, but a man who keeps up the criminal side of his practice, at the expense of the more lucrative and respectable civil cases, from compassion as well as from morbid fascination. Ultimately, he is afraid of finding himself in the dock, arraigned on some ill-defined, portmanteau charge —into which his professional misconduct, his casual promiscuity, and, as he admits, his personal mediocrity will at last be compounded against him. The action of *Inadmissible Evidence* opens in this courtroom of Maitland's mind, and with the defendant's tongue-tied, nightmare-numbed apology for his life. This dream sequence is unlike anything Osborne had previously attempted. But it effectively sets an impressionistic tone that the cold light of morning in the solicitor's office seems to dispel, and that slowly reasserts itself as the action proceeds toward the climax of Maitland's mental breakdown—or, less literal-mindedly, toward a total isolation and stagnation that stretches away into his timeless personal purgatory.

At last Osborne had found a viable method of conceiving a character writ large, without scaling down his attendant "normals" beyond recognition or plunging a whole family into a kind of contagious neurosis. In *Inadmissible Evidence* the peripheral characters—managing and junior clerks, pretty little typists, and mistresses—emerge as individuals only in Maitland's own moments of lucidity. As his sense of reality recedes, so they are transformed into threatening pawns—pawns in what I have elsewhere described as Maitland's personal endgame. By the second and final act, almost all have deserted him—both literally and symbolically, as if by some predestined rote—and a succession of clients, who may or may not have an objective existence, materialize in Maitland's mind only insofar as they mirror his own inadequacies. Even the telephone has a human shape: it becomes something to be "stalked, abused, taken for granted, feared," as it threatens to cut Maitland off from even such tenuous contact as it might help him to retain with the outside world.

It is difficult to outline the plot and structure of the play—and at last the two have merged into an organic whole—without making them appear overmanipulated, merely plotting a predictable course toward an abstract, almost mechanical kind of self-destruction. But the play is mechanical only in the sense that its movement is as inexorable as an infernal machine's; indeed, it becomes a bourgeois tragedy more traditional than, say, Willy Loman's in *Death of a Salesman,* in that Maitland is entirely aware of what is happening to him. And if his grinding down into oblivion does have a certain simplicity in the compressed present tense of its surface action, this is redeemed by the continuous sense of a causality that reaches far back into the past. Maitland reminisces no less compulsively but much more articulately than Phoebe Rice, and the sum of a lifetime's recollected experience shapes and is shaped by each utterance. Maitland even indulges in a sort of anticipatory nostalgia, relishing word-pictures of what his future might have held if only he had escaped his creeping estrangement. Jimmy Porter had forgotten what it was like to feel young, and Bill Maitland, on the verge of middle age, hates and envies youth for its assurance and coolness. But he also ridicules its lack of his own "fibbing, mumping, pinched little worm of energy"—which is eating him up, but which might just have been channeled into the creative force that his junior clerk and his teen-age daughter so demonstrably fail to command.

These two youngsters bear the brunt of Maitland's attacks on their tender but good-and-pushy years. Not that either character comes to real dramatic life, but because of the form of the play this doesn't matter. The insufferably "normal" Graham Dodd, Jean's boyfriend in *The Entertainer,* is far too anemic for his full-bloodedly naturalistic surroundings; but Bill Maitland's young victims are his own creations and thus conform to his own prejudices, which are at their most blistering in the long, last-act soliloquy addressed to his speechless daughter. Of course, that daughter, mute and almost motionless, is physically *there* on the stage of a theater all the same, and the solipsistic nature of her reality is not easy to predicate in production. This is just another of the ways in which *Inadmissible Evidence* is so tortuously difficult a play to stage, but no more than *King Lear* should its difficulty condemn it to the closet. Osborne the wordsmith here stitched together a verbal patchwork that demands a correlative pattern of visual imagery—a pattern that is at last organic rather than an attention-focusing adjunct to a rhetorical flow. Indeed, the most compelling moment in the play is perhaps the total silence that engulfs Maitland, just before the final curtain, as he sits and waits for his telephone to ring—without even a Beckettian optimism that this electronic Godot will one day offer redemption.

There could have been no completer contrast to *Inadmissible Evidence* than *A Patriot for Me* (1966), in which Osborne developed to different effect the style of historical epic he had used in *Luther*—although he again failed to reconcile character with context or to concentrate clear-sightedly on one or the other. But the failure of *A Patriot* is at once more demonstrable and more interesting. Here, for the first time, Osborne actually set a play in that twilit period before World War I which has cast its shadow over so much of his work. Not unexpectedly, he has depicted its outlines with a touch of nostalgia that tends to diminish its ostensible decadence; and this distances the already rather austere central character of Alfred Redl—along with Holyoake, the least rhetorically flamboyant of Osborne's heroes—still further from his conflict with his society. Such a conflict should have been generated between the military elite of the Austro-Hungarian Empire and the sexually ambivalent junior officer who is struggling against the odds of his inauspicious birth to join its select few. By dint of sheer hard work—which may or may not be sublimation of his sexual uncertainty—he succeeds. But, as in *Luther,* Osborne never satisfactorily relates the private and public levels of his hero's progress. For Redl is involved not only in an inner struggle to reconcile himself to his homosexuality, but in military espionage, which he undertakes under pressure of blackmail and which terminates his ascendant career in a suicide that is, in dramatic tone, incongruously "honorable."

The historically based action spans so many years that, again as in *Luther,* Osborne's instant transitions from one stage of character development to the next are all the more obtrusive. There is little sense of Redl's gradual progress toward self-realization; and, surprisingly, so fully is he caught up in the socially and politically oriented scenes that it becomes difficult to separate out his own sensitive reactions amid all the military cavorting and high life at the Hofburg. The drag-ball scene—which might have served to demonstrate Redl's isolation even among his sexual kind—is supremely theatrical, but also distractingly so. Osborne is inexplicably preoccupied with sexual suspense—demanding that an audience should be as slow as Redl to realize his homosexuality, and that it should at first be taken in by the transvestite party. This sort of suspense for its own sake would be well-suited to a whodunit, but not to a serious work, which should mature and yield new insights on a second visit or a retrospective reading. The promise of *A Patriot for Me* is that it shows Osborne fully capable of sketching a convincing social environment, but its weakness is that Redl, who begins as a sick character in search of authority, should be dwarfed into a linking-device in a period spy thriller.

Thus, yet again, Osborne—who has never struck one as a careful, forward-thinking draftsman—changed courses in mid-theme, as he had done before in *Slickey* and *Under Plain Cover,* and was to do once more in *A Bond Honoured* (1966). This last work is an adaptation in one act of Lope de Vega's Renaissance masterpiece—though not so regarded by Osborne—*La fianza satisfecha,* and it was specially commissioned by England's National Theatre Company. The end product demonstrates that Osborne was as uneasy working to order as he had earlier been in purging his own pettier annoyances into plays. There is a half-hearted attempt to transmute the motiveless malignity of Lope's vicious hero, Leonido, into a kind of adolescent existentialism; but the idea is not sustained, and Leonido emerges as a curious mixture of overweening Renaissance man—finding, like some sixteenth-century Saul of Tarsus, a tortuous path toward a traumatic redemption—and of some latter-day nihilist in an anachronistic setting, who pays his overdue debt to society but values loss of life "no more than fluff at the bottom of the pocket." It is Osborne's updated hero, however, who dies exulting in his crimes, the victim of Old Testament justice, while Lope's Leonido is transfigured by New Testament mercy. Osborne also conjures up a few extra crimes for Leonido to commit, so that the rota of his sexual relationships with his sister and his mother becomes so convoluted as to verge on the ludicrous—all this in a manner for which the stage directions require an impossibly formalized style of production. *A Bond Honoured* might just have worked if it had concentrated, as at first it seems to be doing, on the incestuous love of Leonido for his sister, for this is rendered with something close to tenderness. As it is, Marcela's complicity in her own seduction eventually leaves her at the loosest of the play's many loose ends; and one gets the impression of Osborne the adaptor steadily tiring of a task he had not chosen—his plotting getting more and more discursive, and its philosophical correlative, where it is distinguishable from Lope's, more and more cursory.

V

It has already become apparent that Osborne was never a disciplined writer, in the sense that his absorption in words often tends to blind him to the technical requirements of his craft—so that plays with perfectly viable themes are either slightly yet distractingly flawed, like *Look Back in Anger,* or thrown out of gear altogether, like *Luther* and *Time Present* (1968), by the dramatist's failure to stand back a pace and ponder not only what is happening but how he is letting it happen. *Time Present,* as its ironical title anticipates, is about the vicissitudes of adapting to an age from which one feels a spiritual outcast. The play's heroine, Pamela, is sister to Jimmy Porter in that she draws on the ever diminishing resources of the past—as personified in the life of her old-style actor father—and lets the relationships and requirements of the present crumble around her. She has, too, her affinities with Bill Maitland—her willful rejection of proffered assistance and her half-conscious acceptance of isolation at the end of a severed telephone line. She is not simply a patchwork version of these earlier characters, but because she has to fit into a naturalistic environment otherwise peopled by "normals," her eccentricity often seems more pettish than neurotic. Indeed, it is possible that this was Osborne's intention, for he introduces into his last act a sprightly younger actress called Abigail, who is the antithesis of everything Pamela believes in, and who begins to be a match for her. But Abigail's entrance is too late: she merely blunts the bludgeoning Pamela has got away with in her absence, and is given insufficient chance to oppose her own lifestyle to her antagonist's. For Pamela, it is, indeed, a particular kind of "style" that is as irrecoverably lost as Jimmy Porter's idealized proletarianism. Its last vestiges vanish with her father's death, midway through the play, and it only remains for the minor characters to live down to her estimate of them.

Pamela's vaguely lesbian flatmate, Constance, a pragmatic female politician, functions more as a stage feed than a friend, and her commonplace lines set up only a self-parodying alternative to Pamela's world of faded press cuttings and bad old plays. The opening scene of emphatic exposition gets the action off to a bad start, moreover, and Pamela's mother and step-sister, who shoulder the task of telling each other what they already know, never recover from it. It is, admittedly, interesting that the work should be so dominated by its female characters—the few attendant menfolk are no more than begetters of babies or carriers of bags. And Pamela at her cattiest compels attention. But *Time Present* is essentially a throwback of a play, working over territory Osborne had explored long before without scorching a new trail—on the contrary, slipping into some bad constructional sidetracks.

Fortunately, *The Hotel in Amsterdam* (1968) opened only a few weeks after *Time Present,* as if to demonstrate that for Osborne each play is a fresh start—and that although he finds it hard to learn from past mistakes, he is equally capable of striking off along new and unexpected courses. Here, he regained the delicate balance between compassion and scorn that *Time Present* had upset. And his realistic form fits his theme—of reciprocity in human relationships—whereas it had seemed oddly inappropriate to that whittling away of a single personality that should more aptly have given *Time Present* something like the solipsistic shape of *Inadmissible Evidence.* Finally, its close, almost circular time-structure lends it a coherence—and almost neoclassical regularity—that Osborne had never before attempted.

Yet even the originality of the piece throws into

perspective Osborne's characteristic strengths and weaknesses. He has never been at his happiest in describing the development either of actions or characters. His distinctive method is to define a given human situation, and to explore it not forward but backward in time, by means of characters who burrow obsessively into their own pasts, although they have been long set by habit and experience in the mold of a present from which they feel themselves estranged. But in *The Hotel in Amsterdam* the boundaries of isolation are broadened: three couples, each of whose lives is in some way dependent upon the whims of an unseen film magnate, escape from this predatory familiar for one weekend—a weekend in search, as it were, of a little "Dutch courage." The play is a conversation piece, during which patterns of mutual affection and dependence among the half-dozen characters gradually clarify. Its unstated moral question is whether their shared hatred of their employer has in fact become a negative binding force; and the climax, in which the group hears of the director's suicide, suggests that this issue is about to be put to the test. The sudden suicide is the only jarring note in the play: it overstates and simplifies a psychological problem that has previously been kept in the background, and yet it avoids suggesting the resolution it precipitates. One senses a similar uneasiness as Osborne feels his way toward the much less traumatic but similarly worked-up conclusion to his first act, so that the play is remarkable among Osborne's output in succeeding best when its temperature is nearest normal. It might more naturally have drifted into a dying fall, and a dying fall does not demand a death.

As in *The Entertainer,* one character dominates the flow of conversation by dint of personality rather than a predominating dramatic purpose. In the earlier play, Archie Rice defensively allows end-of-pier patter to infiltrate his everyday talk; here, the scriptwriter Laurie has a professional gift of the gab that inclines him to hog the conversation—but not, as in *Time Present,* at the expense of reducing the other characters to cardboard. Indeed, the six characters need their companionship in direct proportion to their need to communicate verbally, and to deduce from this that the least talkative couple is also the best adjusted is perhaps to labor the obvious. But at last the two "normals" live as fully as their "neurotic" friends, and even Laurie in full rhetorical flood is recognizably talking to and not just at his listeners. In one of the most delicate scenes Osborne has written, Laurie declares his love for his friend's wife, and she accepts and returns it—a conventional enough situation, but one which doesn't erupt into conventional emotional fireworks because, like so much of the play, it simply puts into words what the characters have sensed for a long time. Most of the "action" at this weekend resting-place takes place between people sprawling in armchairs, and yet this static environment becomes a microcosm, encapsulating the lives and the living together of its inhabitants.

Osborne had traveled a long way from the provincial garret where Jimmy Porter lived out his loneliness to this smart continental hotel for the comfortably off, in which a group of six friends talks and drinks its way along the ebullient and the melancholy axes of friendship—spanning, or so I suggested at the time, a spectrum of dramatic insights from the Strindbergian almost to the Chekhovian. Now, as then, it seems to me that when Osborne's style has "emerged naturally from his theme, as it has done in *The Entertainer, Inadmissible Evidence,* and *The Hotel in Amsterdam,* his work is as nearly flawless in its shape as it is in its rhetoric." But, I added, "when he imposes a form from the outside, or lets himself lapse into a lazily 'well-made' kind of playwriting, his theme almost invariably finds itself at odds with its medium of expression." My self-quotation is, confessedly, defensive, since I now feel I was mistaken in the upbeat conclusion to my original essay that *Hotel in Amsterdam* bore witness to "a writer at last as sure of his control over his craft as he is in his understanding of his human material." In any event, of Osborne's subsequent full-length work for the theater, *West of Suez* (1971) set old imperial values against new anarchic tendencies in the thinly evoked location suggested by its title, while *A Sense of Detachment* (1973) tore into all and sundry in a style halfway between Pirandello and the Living Theater, but carrying the conviction of neither. Since then he has written an assortment of pieces for television and some workmanlike adaptations for live theater, but his original work for the stage has been essentially occasional and seldom redeemed by the old rhetorical flair.

It is perhaps no coincidence that while Osborne's first play was produced in 1956, his last work of major significance was staged in 1968, for both those years were also postwar political and cultural watersheds, between which a whole generation in England had been forced to come to terms with the end of the lingering dream. Osborne's plays contributed some valuable if often tangential insights to that necessary process. But the generation that came of age in 1968 took all such angst about the past for granted, and instead demanded the future—on its own terms. Of course, neither the terms nor the future were as simple as they seemed, and many members of that generation now look back with a nostalgia of their own, to the lost innocence of being young in 1968, just as Osborne's looked back to Edwardian "certainties" that were no less illusory. It was Osborne's great achievement to have found all those voices in his earlier plays which express the resulting inarticulacy and sense of deprivation. There is no reason why he should not transform the more complex insights of maturity into compelling dramatic shape, could he but shake off the "sense of detachment" that now too often transmutes the gold of raw experience into a leaden cynicism and tiredness of dramatic life.

SELECTED BIBLIOGRAPHY

I. Bibliography. C. Northouse and T. P. Walsh, *John Osborne: A Reference Guide* (Boston, 1974).

II. Separate Works. *Look Back in Anger* (London, 1957), play, screenplay with N. Kneale (London, 1959); *The Entertainer* (London, 1957), play, screenplay with N. Kneale (London, 1960); *Epitaph for George Dillon* (London, 1958), play; *The World of Paul Slickey* (London, 1959), musical play; *A Subject of Scandal and Concern* (London, 1961), television play; *Luther* (London, 1961), play; *Plays for England* (London, 1963), two one-act plays, *The Blood of the Bambergs* and *Under Plain Cover; Tom Jones* (London, 1964), filmscript; *Inadmissible Evidence* (London, 1965), play; *A Patriot for Me* (London, 1966), play; *A Bond Honoured* (London, 1966), one-act play; *Time Present* and *The Hotel in Amsterdam* (London, 1968), plays; *The Right Prospectus* (London, 1970), television play; *Very Like a Whale* (London, 1971), television play; *West of Suez* (London, 1971), play; *A Sense of Detachment* (London, 1973), play; *A Place Calling Itself Rome* (London, 1973), adaptation of Shakespeare's *Coriolanus* for stage; *The Picture of Dorian Gray* (London, 1973), adaptation of Oscar Wilde's novel for stage; *Jill and Jack* and *the End of Me Old Cigar* (London, 1975), television play; *Watch It Come Down* (London, 1975), stage play; *You're Not Watching Me* and *Try a Little Tenderness* (London, 1978), television plays; *A Better Class of Person: An Autobiography, 1929–1956* (London, 1981).

III. Critical Studies. I. Scott-Kilvert, "The Hero in Search of a Dramatist: The Plays of John Osborne," in *Encounter* (December 1957); B. Denning, "John Osborne's War against the Philistines," in *Hudson Review,* 11 (1959); A. E. Dyson, "Look Back in Anger," in *Critical Quarterly,* 1 (1969); M. McCarthy, *Sights and Spectacles* (London, 1959), see "A New Word," pp. 184–196, repr. in *Look Back in Anger: A Casebook,* below, pp. 150–160; V. D. Denty, "The Psychology of Martin Luther," in *Catholic World,* 194 (1961); C. K. Hunter, "The World of John Osborne," in *Critical Quarterly,* 3 (1961); C. Marowitz, "The Ascension of John Osborne," in *Tulane Drama Review,* 6 (Winter 1962), repr. in *Casebook,* pp. 161–165; A. Nicoll, "Somewhat in a New Dimension," in J. R. Brown and B. Harris, eds., *Contemporary Theatre* (London, 1962), pp. 77–95; J. R. Taylor, *Anger and After* (London, 1962), includes an appreciation of Osborne, rev. ver. in *Casebook,* pp. 75–96; H. van de Perre, *John Osborne—Boze Jonge Man* (Tielt, Belgium, 1962); R. Huss, "John Osborne's Backward Half-Way Look," in *Modern Drama,* 6 (1963); K. J. Worth, "The Angry Young Man: John Osborne," in W. A. Armstrong, ed., *Experimental Drama* (London, 1963), repr. in *Casebook,* pp. 101–116; G. E. Wellwarth, *The Theatre of Protest and Paradox* (London, 1964), see "John Osborne: Angry Young Man"; A. Seymour, "Maturing Vision," in *London Magazine* (October 1966); E. Gordon Rupp, "Luther and Mr Osborne," in *Cambridge Quarterly,* 1 (1965–1966); J. Whiting, *On Theatre* (London, 1966), see "Luther"; J. Kershaw, *The Present Stage* (London, 1966), includes "John Osborne: A Modern Romantic" and "Look Back in Anger: Language and Character"; L. Kitchin, *Drama in the Sixties* (London, 1966), includes "Redbrick Luther" and "The Wages of Sex"; R. Hayman, *Contemporary Playwrights: John Osborne* (London, 1968); J. R. Taylor, ed., *Look Back in Anger: A Casebook* (London, 1968), contains a selection of Osborne's journalistic writing as well as reviews of the first production of *Look Back in Anger* and general critical articles; S. Trussler, *The Plays of John Osborne: An Assessment* (London, 1969); A. Carter, *John Osborne* (Edinburgh, 1969; New York, 1973); J. R. Brown, *Theatre Language: A Study of Osborne, Pinter and Wesker* (New York and London, 1972); H. Ferrar, *John Osborne* (New York, 1973); M. Anderson, *Anger and Detachment: A Study of Arden, Osborne and Pinter* (London, 1976).

TED HUGHES

(1930–)

Keith Sagar

I

EDWARD JAMES HUGHES was born in Mytholmroyd, west Yorkshire, on 17 August 1930 in an end terrace house backing onto the canal. Beyond the canal was the main trunk road connecting the Yorkshire woolen towns and the Lancashire cotton towns, with its constant rumble of heavy lorries. Beyond that the railway. Then, rising almost sheer from the valley and seeming to fill half the sky, Scout Rock:

> This was the *memento mundi* over my birth: my spiritual midwife at the time and my godfather ever since—or one of my godfathers. From my first day, it watched. If it couldn't see me direct, a towering gloom over my pram, it watched me through a species of periscope: that is, by infiltrating the very light of my room with its particular shadow.
>
> "The Rock"

It seemed to seal off everything to the south. Since to the north the land rose almost as steeply from immediately in front of the house up to the high bleak moors, "the narrow valley, with its flooring of cricket pitch, meadows, bowling greens, streets, railways and mills, seemed damp, dark and dissatisfied" and felt like a trap. Mount Zion chapel literally stooped over his cradle:

> Above the kitchen window, that uplifted mass
> was a deadfall—
> Darkening the sun of every day
> Right to the eleventh hour.

Later he was dragged there every Sunday in an atmosphere of terror:

> The convicting holy eyes, the convulsed Moses
> mouthings.
> Men in their prison-yard, at attention,
> Exercising their cowed, shaven souls
> Lips stretching saliva, eyes fixed like the eyes
> Of cockerels hung by legs,
> As the bottomless cry
> Beat itself numb again against Wesley's foundation
> stone.
>
> "Mount Zion"

The purpose of the place seemed to be simply to eradicate the joy of life, even if that meant eradicating life itself. Once the place was thrown into a state of battle-fury by a cricket singing from a crack in the wall:

> Long after I'd been smothered in bed
> I heard them
> Riving at the religious stonework
> With screwdrivers and chisels.

Now the cracks are widening and the only singing heard in many of the chapels is the singing of crickets.

What the boys preferred to do with their Sundays was to dig, Sunday after Sunday, with iron levers, even while the bells summoned them elsewhere, for the Ancient Briton, supposed, according to local folklore, to lie under a half-ton rock:

> We needed that waft from the cave
> The dawn dew-chilling of emergence,
> The hunting grounds untouched all around us.
>
> "The Ancient Briton Lay Under His Rock"

That rock could not be shifted, nor what it hid, the buried life of England, the repressed needs of the human psyche, eradicated.

In the short story "Sunday," the boy has to endure a stifling, scrubbed Sunday morning, the churchgoing slopes spotless and harmless, forbidden grass in the Memorial Gardens, even the pavements "untouchably proper." The men wear "tight blue pin-stripe suits" and the boy his "detestable blue blazer." Sitting in chapel, the situation of greatest constraint he knows, he lets his imagination be taken over by the image of a wolf that "urged itself with all its strength through a land empty of everything but trees and snow." This wolf, the ghost of the last wolf killed in Britain, appears again and again in Hughes:

> These feet, deprived,
> Disdaining all that are caged, or storied, or pictured,
> Through and throughout the true world search
> For their vanished head, for the world
>
> Vanished with the head, the teeth, the quick eyes.
> "February"

The wolf is that in the boy which refuses to be constrained, tamed, disciplined; like those Vikings ("the snow's stupefied anvils") who spent themselves in "beforehand revenge"

> For the grueling relapse and prolongueur of their blood
>
> Into the iron arteries of Calvin.
> "The Warriors of the North"

The boy lives for the afternoon, when his father has promised to take him to Top Wharf Pub to see for the first time Billy Red kill rats in his teeth like a terrier. The Cretans sacrificed a living bull to Dionysus by tearing it with their teeth. Billy Red degrades this archaic religious act, communion with the god by eating the god, to a Sunday afternoon secular entertainment for a bored denatured public in exchange for a free pint. But the boy is not yet denatured. The thought of that savagery, that unthinkable closeness of the human and the animal, reduces everything else in his consciousness to unreality. The story is autobiographical. There really was a Billy Red.

Animals were of tremendous importance to Hughes from the beginning, living representatives of another world, "the true world," "the world under the world." Yet the only relation that seemed possible between town boys and the surrounding wildlife was to catch and kill. The lesson was being driven home that animals were, by nature, victims. It was the natural order of things that any creature outside the ordered world of men should be killed. And if a human being chose to step outside that ordered world, he became fair game. The lesson was reinforced by a story his brother told him "of the tramp sleeping up there in the bracken, who stirred at an unlucky moment and was shot dead for a fox by an alert farmer and sent rolling down the slope" ("The Rock").

The life we have already killed off and got under, which now marauds destructively in the underworld of the unconscious, is the wolf. The life now making its last stand in remote fastnesses is adder and otter. The life we keep trying to kill, but which somehow survives, is stoat (see "Strawberry Hill") and fox. The landscape itself is a huge animal that seems to let itself be tamed. The network of walls is "harness on the long moors." But now these Pennine hills are breaking loose again, slowly shaking the mills, chapels, and houses to pieces as in a great sieve. That landscape was Hughes's inheritance. It gave him his earliest metaphors, which later gave him his distinctive way of looking at the world and of thinking about himself, and anchored his consciousness in the permanent realities. The geography of his childhood world became his map of heaven and hell; the interplay of the elements in that place gave him his sense of the creating and destroying powers of the world; the local animals became his theriomorphic archetypes. That landscape was imprinted on his soul and, in a sense, all his poems are about it—not only those poems like *Remains of Elmet,* where the magical transformation from description to metaphor to myth takes place before our eyes. Hughes ends that early essay "The Rock" (1963) with these words: "From there the return home was a descent into the pit, and after each visit I must have returned less and less of myself to the valley. This was where the division of body and soul, for me, began."

It was a great advantage to Hughes to have been born not in a city, where he might have allowed himself to be shut up in the little box of the exclusively human—

> The country, to townies,
> Is hardly more than nice,
> A window-box, pretty
> When the afternoon's empty;
> When a visitor waits,
> The window shuts.
> (Kingsley Amis, "Here Is Where")

—nor in the country, where he might have become just another "nature" poet, but on the very frontier where the two were engaged in a "fight to the death." He suffered in childhood the crisis of our civilization in a very pure form. The experience forced him into a fiercely dualistic attitude to life that released the amazing energies of his first three books: *The Hawk in the Rain*, *Lupercal*, and *Wodwo.* The subsequent books have been a gradual healing of that split. From that deep early dualism Hughes has moved painfully but surely toward "a proper knowledge of the sacred wholeness of Nature, and a proper alignment of our behaviour within her laws."

When Hughes was seven, the family moved to Mexborough in south Yorkshire, where, like D. H. Lawrence before him in a similar area, he was obliged to lead a double life, one with the town boys, sons of miners and railwaymen, the other in his bolt-holes—a nearby farm or a private estate with woods and lakes. Mexborough Grammar School fostered his interest in poetry, and he was already writing it at fifteen, his favorite topics Zulus and the Wild West. In 1948 he won an Open Exhibition in English to Pembroke College, Cambridge, but before taking it up he did two years of national service as a ground wireless mechanic in the R.A.F. on an isolated three-man radio station in east Yorkshire, where he had "nothing to do but read and re-read Shakespeare and watch the grass grow." Reading English at Cambridge proved sterile, and Hughes changed to anthropology and archaeology. Cambridge gave him time to read a great deal, especially the ballads and Old English, and to learn by heart the *Collected Poems* of W. B. Yeats.

After graduating in 1954, Hughes worked briefly as a rose gardener, night watchman in a steel factory, zoo attendant, schoolteacher, and reader for J. Arthur Rank. In June 1956 he married Sylvia Plath, whom he met at Cambridge. From the spring of 1957 until the end of 1959 they lived in the United States. In 1957 Hughes's first book of poems, *The Hawk in the Rain,* was published.

II

"THE HAWK IN THE RAIN" stands appropriately at the threshold of the book, for it announces the major themes—man in relation to the animals, the earth, the weather, time and mortality—and expresses them with characteristic energy and hyperbole. The narrator feels like a "last-moment counting morsel in the earth's mouth" as he fights against mud (which sucks "with the habit of the dogged grave") for survival and identity,

> . . . but the hawk
>
> Effortlessly at height hangs his still eye.
> His wings hold all creation in a weightless quiet
> Steady as a hallucination in the streaming air.

The sea-drowner, any man buffeted and dying, must fix his eyes upon something stable, some "master-fulcrum of violence"—polestar or hawk's eye. The hawk himself will, ultimately, fall and "mix his heart's blood with the mire of the land," but "in his own time," with acquiescence.

And is it possible for a man, without madness, to draw that stability, assurance, into himself; to come to terms with a world of horrors and miracles hardly to be told apart? When Charles Tomlinson reviewed an anthology of new verse, *New Lines,* in 1957, he said of the poets represented there: "They show a singular want of vital awareness of the continuum outside themselves, of the mystery embodied over against them in the created universe." That vital awareness is perhaps the outstanding characteristic of Hughes's work, which was not represented in *New Lines.*

The mystery takes many forms. There is no ignoring it when it takes the form of a gale:

> The tent of the hills drummed and strained its
>   guyrope,
>
> The fields quivering, the skyline a grimace,
> At any second to bang and vanish with a flap:
> The wind flung a magpie away and a black-
> Back gull bent like an iron bar slowly. The house
>
> Rang like some fine green goblet in the note
> That any second would shatter it. Now deep
> In chairs, in front of the great fire, we grip
> Our hearts and cannot entertain book, thought,
>
> Or each other. We watch the fire blazing,
> And feel the roots of the house move, but sit on,
> Seeing the window tremble to come in,
> Hearing the stones cry out under the horizons.
>
> "Wind"

The window is the delicate membrane that separates us from the "wandering elementals" outside and within. The breaking of that membrane would be the end of books, thought, civilized human relationships, would be madness or miracle. To be at one with these forces, to answer unto death or life their terrible imperatives, is to be madman or martyr or genius, more or less than human. For the rest of us there are "moments of purity and crisis" that call in question the reality of our more ordinary lives.

Most of the time we can ignore the inaudible battle-shouts and death cries that are everywhere around us. But horrors not only nudge the root of the water lily. The largest horror continually presses against us. For that horror is simply the truth that kills everybody:

> The truth of a man is the doomed man in him or his dead body. . . . The murderous skeleton in the body of a girl, the dead men being eaten by dogs on the moonlit desert, the dead man behind the mirror, these items of circumstantial evidence are steadily out-arguing all his high spirits and hopefulness.
> (Introduction to the *Selected Poems of Keith Douglas,* 1964)

In "Six Young Men" Hughes adds his own evidence, a photograph of six young men on a Sunday jaunt, each as alive as any man you can confront "and shake by the hand, see hale, hear speak loud." Yet they all died within six months and forty years ago. One's own vivid life, for all its bulk and weight, is equally flimsy. The poet is no more alive than they were, than, here in this photograph, they still are, as, by a bilberried bank, a thick tree, a black wall "which are there yet and not changed," they listen to the waterfall that roars yet in that valley.

Some of Hughes's earlier poems are marred by overstatement, a forcing of rhetoric and imagery. We hardly ever find, in contrast to most of his contemporaries, any deficiency of force and sinew. There are occasionally echoes of other poets: of Yeats and Lawrence; of Gerard Manley Hopkins—"freer, firmer world found"; of Dylan Thomas—"the sargasso of a single sandgrain"; of T. S. Eliot at his worst (as in the choruses of *Murder in the Cathedral*):

> . . . with eel and hyena and vulture,
> With creepy-crawly and the root,
> With the sea-worm, entering its birthright.
> "Mayday in Holderness"

Such echoes are striking precisely because of their rarity in relation to the occasions inviting them.

For the most part we find a language characterized by its faithfulness to the facts, the evidence of the senses, shaped by a strong inspiration into images that, like those of Henry Moore, seem to have been waiting for aeons within the living rock, the living language, and now, released, will stand for aeons and could not be otherwise. It is a language spiced with great relish for experience, even when that experience is unpleasant or horrifying. Most distinctively it is a language able to cope with the biggest things; it can generate energies equal to the great primary energies of the world. In "Pennines in April" it is the thrust of the Pennines rolling like a huge sea from Yorkshire into Lancashire:

> Those barrellings of strength are heaving slowly and
> heave
> To your feet and surf upwards
> In a still, fiery air, hauling the imagination,
> Carrying the larks upward

In "October Dawn" it is the irresistible coming of winter:

> First a skin, delicately here
> Restraining a ripple from the air;
>
> Soon plate and rivet on pond and brook;
> Then tons of chain and massive lock
>
> To hold rivers. Then, sound by sight
> Will Mammoth and Sabre-tooth celebrate
>
> Reunion while a fist of cold
> Squeezes the fire at the core of the world,
>
> Squeezes the fire at the core of the heart,
> And now it is about to start.

The power here does not reside in the Mammoths and Sabre-tooths so much as in that ruthless march of monosyllables, that relentless rhythm. Hughes's language at its best has the same qualities to which he has himself testified in "the true ballads," where we find "words that live in the same dimension as life at its most severe, words that cannot be outflanked by experience" (the *Guardian,* 14 May 1965).

To release such linguistic resources, Hughes had

to get out from under "the terrible, suffocating, maternal octopus of ancient English poetic tradition," which meant getting back beyond Chaucer. Every educated modern English poet finds his head swimming with iambic[1] rhythms. English prose is still predominantly trochaic, true to its Germanic origins, but in verse the courtly, alien iamb drove the trochee and spondee underground, after William Langland's last stand, into folk songs, ballads, nursery rhymes, and dialect verse. In Hughes the old rhythms surface again (twenty-seven of the twenty-eight two-syllable words in the "The Hawk in the Rain" are trochees), and we see what we had lost in weight, sinew, and urgency in all those centuries of artifice and gentility.

III

Lupercal followed in March 1960. In *The Hawk in the Rain* there had been a relatively simplistic dualism —vitality versus death, mind versus body, ancient versus modern, and so on. In *Lupercal* there is a much higher degree of artifice and complexity, with occasional lapses into versified opinions, as in Auden.

The speedy recognition of a great talent at work in *The Hawk in the Rain* and *Lupercal,* not only as promise but as achievement, was not an unmixed blessing. For Hughes was labeled Nature Poet or, more patronizingly, Animal Poet. The titles alone contained horses, hawks, crows, thrushes, doves, a jaguar, a macaw, a fox, a bull, a mouse, a pig, an otter, a bullfrog, and a pike. The poems featured many other animals, most of them predatory. "Hughes is very fine, but what will he do when he runs out of animals?" was a comment that did not look as silly at the time as it does now. If we look a little more closely at these volumes, we see that the majority of the poems are not about animals; that many of the references to animals are metaphorical; and that even those poems which are about animals are usually also about human experiences, for which the animals serve as analogues.

In nearly all his poems Hughes strives to find metaphors for his own nature. And his own nature is of peculiar general interest not because it is unusual, but because it embodies in an unusually intense, stark form the most typical stresses and contradictions of human nature and of nature itself, as Shakespeare's did. The poems are bulletins from the battleground within.

In the early poems the metaphors Hughes found were so often animals because animals live out in such naked extremity the primary struggles, particularly that between vitality and death. They roar or bellow the evidence that men wrap in sophistry or turn a blind eye to. Their reality seems less questionable than ours. The "attent sleek thrushes on the lawn" are terrifying not for their ravening of writhing things, but for the too streamlined efficiency with which they pursue their unwavering purpose—the efficiency of a bullet (whose one path is direct through the bones of the living). Hughes stands in awe of animals. Their efficiency is too horribly automatic, like the shark's mouth

> That hungers down the blood-smell even to a leak of
> its own
> Side and devouring of itself.
>
> "Thrushes"

What a man does neither defines nor deifies him, nor can he, unless he is that hardly human thing, a genius, crash straight through doubts, obstructions, temptations, sin, guilt, and despair:

> how loud and above what
> Furious spaces of fire do the distracting devils
> Orgy and hosannah, under what wilderness
> Of black silent waters weep.
>
> "Thrushes"

Beyond the little area lit by his consciousness, his desk lamp, is a vast darkness peopled by demons. The distracting devils that sin, praise, or despair are those suppressed powers within any man which will not let him be satisfied with the heroisms he invents at his desk, nor with any enclosed self-worshiping activity. A man totally given over to those powers, genius or hero, is a madman or an automaton. A man totally cut off from them denies, trivializes, or perverts the life that is in him, drops out of the divine circuit from which alone come the energies to destroy or create.

The gulf between man and animal is also the gulf between civilized man and his animal self, which

[1]The iamb is a two-syllable verse foot (short-long) (e.g., forget); the trochee, a two-syllable verse foot (long-short) (e.g., music).

is also his angelic or demonic self—the only self capable of recognizing a divinity in the darkness and being at one with it. It is the doom of all animals to live according to one categorical imperative. Man's doom is different: the doom of consciousness and choice, the burden precisely of not knowing what to do, of perpetually questioning a deaf-and-dumb world and peering into the darkness for a sign.

IV

AFTER *Lupercal* was published, Ted Hughes and his wife returned to England. Their children, Frieda and Nicholas, were born in 1960 and 1962. Hughes and Plath entered upon a phase of intensely productive creative partnership until their separation in 1962. At least a third of the poems in *Recklings* and in *Wodwo* were written then; so were the stories and the play in *Wodwo* and other stories and plays (the BBC broadcast "The House of Aries" in 1960, "Difficulties of a Bridegroom" in 1962, and "Dogs" in 1963), and it was at this time that Hughes began to write regularly for children and to review regularly in the *New Statesman* and the *Listener.*

Hughes's first three books of verse for children seem to me undistinguished (though he added some better poems to later editions of *Meet My Folks!*, 1961). *How the Whale Became* (1963), Hughes's first prose work for children, is another matter. The stories are, in a sense, very traditional, taking their place in the tradition that runs from Aesop's *Fables* to Rudyard Kipling's *Just So Stories.* But they are also thoroughly original and could only have been written by a poet. The prose is simple but distinguished. The stories are witty but grounded, despite the free inventiveness, in reality—this owl cleans the blood from his beak. Some of them are moving—this elephant saves all the creatures of the forest, then disappears quietly into the depths. "We would make him our king," they say, "if we could get him to wear a crown." And some are imagined at the same depth as the adult poems—this bee has been made out of diamond-dust moistened by a demon's tears: "The sadness of the demon's tears was always in him. It was part of him. It was what flowed in his veins." The bee must steep himself in beauty and gather all its sweetness until it oozes from him to counteract that paralyzing sadness.

The Iron Man (1968) is another fine story, or rather three stories. In the first, the iron man falls over a cliff and is smashed to pieces on the rocks below. The parts laboriously put themselves together again, and the iron man, lacking only an ear stolen by gulls, walks into the sea. The story is vivid and eerie. It has the absolute authenticity of the inexplicable. *The Return of the Iron Man* is more conventional and straightforward. People try to kill him because he is eating all their machines. He is unkillable. Then they realize that they can use him to get rid of all the scrap metal and old cars.

The third story has the iron man no longer a threat to the human world, but its champion in single combat against a terrible space-monster the size of Australia. (This is not bedtime reading.) The monster is a star-spirit drawn down by "the battling shouts and the war-cries of the earth" to join in. The iron man lies on a grid over a great fire until he becomes white hot, then challenges the monster to do the equivalent by lying on the sun. Twice they compete and suffer and survive. At the third challenge, the scorched monster gives in, flies back into space and sings "a strange soft music that seemed to fill the whole of space, a deep weird singing, like millions of voices singing together," and this music brings peace to the world. The theme has much in common with Hughes's latest work. The iron man is the hero of myth who voluntarily undergoes the most terrible trials, agonies, purification, and, having given everything, miraculously redeems the world.

Even finer than his stories are Hughes's verse plays, written for radio, but ideal for school and children's theater productions. They will soon become classics of the repertory. They are mainly reworkings of myths and folktales. In each of them Hughes has something urgent to say, and the verse, at its best, is as good as anything he has done for adults:

> Once more we grew blisters inside our boots,
> Stumbling over the wastelands of this world.
> We came to the mountains, the blue tepees of the
> gods.
> I am a simple man, I believe in gods.
> We climbed, where wild goats leaned out
> Over gulfs full of the whisper of torrents

And gunfire of landslides. We climbed
Where eagles slid from us and hung out
Over a five-mile drop into the forest.
We climbed. We climbed till our brains altered
And we could see mountains upside-down
On top of the mountains.

(The Tiger's Bones)

The Tiger's Bones is a satire on the modern scientific mentality. The Master can build a telescope to look death in the face, factories and mental hospitals and crematoria, but he cannot make the dead live or create grass. When he does at last learn to bring to life a dead tiger with a hypodermic, the tiger eats him. In *Beauty and the Beast,* another play in *The Coming of the Kings* (1971), Hughes brings out, with no heavy-handedness, the psychological implications already there in the original story.

But the best of these plays is not in *The Coming of the Kings.* It is a play called *Orpheus,* broadcast in January 1971. The music Orpheus plays, pop music, is an expression of his happiness in the love of Eurydice. He ignores the warning voice telling him that every song must be paid for. Eurydice dies and he can no longer play. He goes to the underworld after her and there begins to play another kind of music (Hughes suggests Handel, Bach, Vivaldi, or earlier composers) that expresses his love of life, but also his recognition of death. He returns with the soul of Eurydice and refuses to play ever again the music of life and happiness only, which accumulates so many debts to reality. As the play ends, he plays his new music:

The trees did not dance. But the trees listened.
The music was not the music of dancing
But of growing and withering
Of the root in the earth and the leaf in the light,
The music of birth and of death.
And the stones did not dance. But the stones listened.
The music was not the music of happiness
But of everlasting, and the wearing away of the hills,
The music of the stillness of stones,
Of stones under frost, and stones under rain, and
stones in the sun,
The music of the sea-bed drinking at the stones of
the hills.
The music of the floating weight of the earth.
And the bears in their forest-holes
Heard the music of bears in their forest-holes
The music of bones in the starlight
The music of many a valley trodden by bears,
The music of bears listening on the earth for bears.
And the deer on the high hills heard the crying of
wolves
And the salmon in the deep pools heard the whisper
of the snows
And the traveller on the road
Heard the music of love coming and love going
And love lost forever,
The music of birth and of death.
The music of the earth, swaddled in heaven, kissed
by its cloud and watched by its ray.
And the ears that heard it were also of leaf and of
stone.
The faces that listened were flesh of cliff and of river.
The hands that played it were fingers of snakes and a
tangle of flowers.

This is for children at an age when they need to know what maturity means and what tragedy means, and it is not only for children.

Season Songs (1975) has so much to offer to adult readers that I shall deal with it later as a book for all ages. *Poetry in the Making* (1967) is the best book I know about the writing (and reading) of poetry in schools. It is about poetry as a natural and common activity; about the fun, but also the seriousness, the centrality, of this activity: "not 'How to write' but 'How to try to say what you really mean'—which is part of the search for self-knowledge and perhaps, in one form or another, grace." Writing poetry is not merely self-expression. The poem has a life of its own and a wisdom of its own that we must learn. To write a poem is to capture a wild animal (as in Hughes's first animal poem, "The Thought-Fox"):

The special kind of excitement, the slightly mesmerized and quite involuntary concentration with which you make out the stirrings of a new poem in your mind, then the outline, the mass and colour and clean final form of it, the unique living reality of it in the midst of the general lifelessness, all that is too familiar to mistake. This is hunting and the poem is a new species of creature, a new specimen of the life outside your own.

The poem is also seen as a series of events, or a lens, or a raid on the inarticulate; and the best way to release the single spirit that must move through the parts is by "headlong, concentrated improvisation," "an all-out flowing exertion"—against the clock. One's only reservation is that Hughes has nothing whatever to say about technique; the poetry he wishes to encourage is purely inspirational. Perhaps it is not worth bothering with any other sort. But is there not something to be done with the inspired verse afterwards? We see the dangers in Hughes's own practice in *The Earth Owl* (1963). However, what was wanted was a book that would help teachers to present the imagination of a pupil with opportunities, not restraints, with confidence and a natural motive for writing, so that "something of our common genius will begin to put a word in." His brief was to aim at ten- to fourteen-year-olds. In fact the upper age limit could be extended indefinitely, at least to the undergraduate level, and the book constitutes an invaluable commentary on Hughes's own method.

V

WITH the separation from Sylvia Plath in 1962 and her suicide the following year, Ted Hughes seems to have entered a fallow, if not sterile, period of two or three years during which he published only a handful of poems. Then, in a rush, came *Recklings* and *The Burning of the Brothel* in 1966 and *Wodwo* and *Scapegoats and Rabies* in 1967.

A note at the beginning of *Wodwo* tells us that the poems, stories, and play are to be read as constituting "a single adventure." It is perhaps easier to recognize the unifying theme by looking first at the stories and the play.

The earliest story in *Wodwo,* "The Rain Horse," is an exercise in the Lawrence manner, taking the opening from "A Modern Lover" and the encounter with the horse from *The Rainbow.* Nevertheless it is distinctively Hughes and shares its structure with two of the other stories, "Sunday" and "The Harvesting." First there is the evocation of a highly realistic scene, vivid and immediate. Then, into this reality erupts another, the nightmare, the reality of the nonhuman world beyond houses and Sundays and pinstripe suits and consciousness and time, a reality of crisis and instinct and violence in which the human protagonist is diminished and defenseless. He panics as though the monstrous horned God had revealed himself. In "Sunday" the screeching of the rats has the same effect as in the poem "Song of the Rat," "supplanting every human brain inside its skull with a rat body that knots and unknots." In "The Harvesting" the human mind is supplanted by sunstroke and enters the mind of a hunted hare in extremity. In "The Wound," the mind of a soldier has been supplanted by a bullet. As he staggers nine miles through thick mud, nightmarish horrors enter the hole in his head. In "Snow" the protagonist's mind has been supplanted from all he is and knows by God-knows-what disaster. And in each case the horror is more vivid and more real that the reality it supplants.

The man in "The Rain Horse" insists on bringing his rational intelligence to bear, trying to account for the horse's malice, predict its movements and outwit it, while the horse obviously inhabits a reality not subject to such reasoning: "Its whinnying snort and the spattering whack of its hooves seemed to be actually inside his head." He is running from and fighting against something he carries within him, from which he can escape only by damaging his heart and cutting out an important part of his brain. In a sense he has already done that, and this is what provokes these powers to such malevolence against him. He is tame. He has taken it for granted that horses are tame, either working or making their contribution to the picturesque landscape. This landscape refuses to gratify him by being picturesque. It is a part of his own life that he has denied which rears against him.

In "Snow" we have an even clearer case of a man attempting to interpret rationally a world for which there can be no rational explanation. His thinking proceeds with rigorous logic grounded in the merest hypotheses. He is dead or mad, certainly doomed. He deduces his own existence from his consciousness. He thinks of himself as commendably openminded, but, with Cartesian failure of nerve, his doubts stop there, at an article of faith he can no more dispense with than he can dispense with his absurd chair. The rest of his universe is made up entirely of evidence to the contrary.

Most of the poems are also about the risk of exposure to the other. When a man takes that risk,

> A leaf's otherness,
> The whaled monstered sea-bottom, eagled peaks
> And stars that hang over hurtling endlessness,
> With manslaughtering shocks

Are let in on his sense:
So many a one has dared to be struck dead
Peeping through his fingers at the world's ends,
Or at an ant's head.

"Egg-Head"

The risk is of losing the unreal stability of prudence and complacency, of losing self-assurance and sanity under the shock, of yielding up one's humanity to the staring angels, the huge and beautiful powers of the world, who, at night, become giant ghost crabs:

All night, around us or through us,
They stalk each other, they fasten on to each other,
They mount each other, they tear each other to pieces,
They utterly exhaust each other.
They are the powers of this world. . . .
They are God's only toys.

"Ghost-Crabs"

And the man who takes these risks, what will he be like? What will he do? In earlier poems Hughes had offered us heroes who are "huge chested braggarts," "their chariot wheels tumbling the necks of screams," "restuffing their deaf fame with fresh sacks-full of heads." More often now the Hughes hero is the humble Man Seeking Experience, the poet who looks at the world without arrogance, recognizes it as neither bad variant nor tryout, but what we are stuck with, sees the absence of clear signs and certainties (except for the mass of evidence of his own fragility), sees dangers and horrors, beauties and miracles in the way (though not the difference between them), and then, alert in all his faculties, moves forward to confront the world.

In *Sir Gawain and the Green Knight,*[2] the hero in his journey through the Wirral fights with, among other creatures of that remote region, wodwos. Etymologically the word simply means "wood-dwellers." The notes to the poem give "trolls." The *Oxford English Dictionary* gives "wild men of the woods." This uncertainty of status—man or beast or monster or goblin—is precisely what attracted Hughes. In "Wodwo," the speaker is a wodwo finding himself at large in a world inhabited by other creatures whose relation to himself he does not in the least understand, without roots ("dropped out of nothing casually"), not knowing why his nose leads him to water or his hands pick bark off a rotten stump, not knowing who he is or what he is doing there, supposing himself to be the exact center of "all this" and seeking to discover the circumference of himself. "Very queer," he concludes, "but I'll go on looking."

[2]An anonymous fourteenth-century poem much admired by Hughes.

Hughes is a wodwo in all his poems, asking these same questions of the world in which he finds himself, looking at that world and its creatures to discover where he ends and the other begins, and what relation exists between "the endless without-world of the other" and the "other" within—"the pitch dark where the animal runs." If he can come to terms with the facts of life and the fact of death, he will become the still center within the violence. He can know "the redeemed life of joy" in normal daily experience, when, with an unspectacular access of grace, the elements of a scene (human, animal, domestic, rural, cosmic) suddenly cohere and reveal a plenitude. Hughes, with supreme delicacy of utterance, captures it:

A cool small evening shrunk to a dog bark and the clank of a bucket—
And you listening.
A spider's web, tense for the dew's touch.
A pail lifted, still and brimming—mirror
To tempt a first star to a tremor.

Cows are going home in the lane there, looping the hedges with their warm wreaths of breath—
A dark river of blood, many boulders,
Balancing unspilled milk.

"Moon!" You cry suddenly, "Moon! Moon!"

The moon has stepped back like an artist gazing amazed at a work
That points at him amazed.

"Full Moon and Little Frieda"

The fragility and transience of that moment celebrated in "Full Moon and Little Frieda" is more evident in the original version of the poem (published in the *Atlantic Monthly,* December 1963), which has several additional lines and ends:

Any minute a bat will fly out of a cat's ear.

The eeriness of that line calls in question the boulderlike solidity of the cows and the reality of the familiar sights and sounds—dog bark and clank of bucket. Nor is the poem at all typical of *Wodwo* as a whole.

It now seems in retrospect that it ought to have been possible, from *Wodwo,* to predict the way Hughes was going. There was the uncompromisingly bleak vision of poems like "Pibroch," the savage humor of "The Warriors of the North"; there were poems inhabiting the no-man's-land between the human and the animal ("Wodwo") and between the natural and the supernatural ("Ghost Crabs"). Hughes showed in *Wodwo* that he had learned from Wilfred Owen and Keith Douglas how to present the evidence, from Emily Dickinson how to lighten its oppressiveness with a gnomic wit, and from Vasco Popa, a Yugoslav poet, how to evade the limitations of realism by the creation of miniature myths out of (in Popa's case) two bones or a quartz pebble:

> It is in this favourite device of his, the little fable of visionary anecdote, that we see most clearly his shift from literary surrealism to the far older and deeper thing, the surrealism of folklore. . . . Folktale surrealism . . . is always urgently connected with the business of trying to manage practical difficulties so great that they have forced the sufferer temporarily out of the dimension of coherent reality into that depth of imagination where understanding has its roots and stores its X-rays.
>
> (Introduction to *Selected Poems* of Popa, 1969)

What he had learned from Sylvia Plath is material for an essay in itself, but certainly his ability to anatomize pain under a fierce white light. He taught her to open herself fully to whatever powers might choose to speak through her.

Several poems in *Wodwo* clearly announce the coming of Hughes's later archetypal figure, Crow. Wodwo asks:

> . . . Why do I find
> this frog so interesting as I inspect its most secret
> interior and make it my own?
>
> "Wodwo"

Crow

> . . . plucked grass-heads and gazed into them
> Waiting for first instructions.
> He studied a stone from the stream.
> He found a dead mole and slowly he took it apart
> Then stared at the gobbets, feeling helpless.
> He walked, he walked
> Letting the translucent starry spaces
> Blow in his ear cluelessly.
>
> "Crow Hears Fate Knock on the Door"

In "Logos," "Reveille," and "Theology" all the main characters of *Crow* (1970) except Crow himself are assembled: God, Adam, Eve, and the Serpent. And all the conditions for his annunciation, the conviction that this cannot be the world God sought to create, perhaps not even the world he did create ("this is the dark intestine"), that there must be something outside God, prior to him, unimpressionable, inimical to his purposes, perhaps itself the creator of God or a precondition of his existence, or his necessary incarnation:

> Creation convulses in nightmare. And awaking
> Suddenly tastes the nightmare moving
> Still in its mouth
> And spits it kicking out, with a swinish cry—
> which is God's first cry.
>
> . . .
>
> God is a good fellow, but His mother's against Him.
>
> "Logos"

The nightmare may be the mother of God. It is certainly the mother of Crow.

VI

IN 1957 Ted Hughes met the American sculptor, engraver, and publisher Leonard Baskin. Baskin is obsessed by crows, which he engraves with disturbingly anthropoid characteristics. A later invitation from Baskin to Hughes to write a few little poems to accompany his engravings was the cause of the first Crow poems. Up to 1963 Hughes had never written about crows, though he was familiar with the prominent and rather grim part they play in so much of the world's folklore.

Why did Hughes choose a crow as his protagonist? The prevalence of ravens and crows in folklore derives largely from the real bird's characteristics. The crow is the most intelligent of birds, the most widely distributed (being common on every continent), and the most omnivorous ("no carrion will kill a crow"). They are, of course, black all over, solitary, almost indestructible, and the largest and least musical of songbirds. It is to be expected that the songs of the crow will be harsh and grating. He kills a little himself, and, as carrion eater, is dependent on the killing of others and first on the scene at many disasters.

Eskimo legend tells that in the beginning the raven was the only creature and the world was, like him, black. Then came the owl, and the world became white like him, with the whiteness of unending snow. Hughes's mythology of Crow is deeply rooted in such legends. The whole myth is to be told as an epic folktale in prose, with songs by and about Crow interspersed.

God, having created the world, has a recurring nightmare. A huge hand comes from deep space, takes him by the throat, half-throttles him, drags him through space, ploughs the earth with him then throws him back into heaven in a cold sweat. Meanwhile man sits at the gates of heaven waiting for God to grant him an audience. He has come to ask God to take life back. God is furious and sends him packing. The nightmare appears to be independent of the creation, and God cannot understand it. The nightmare is full of mockery of the creation, especially of man. God challenges the nightmare to do better. This is just what the nightmare has been waiting for. It plunges down into matter and creates Crow. God tests Crow by putting him through a series of trials and ordeals which sometimes result in Crow being dismembered, transformed or obliterated, but Crow survives them all, little changed. Meanwhile Crow interferes in God's activities, sometimes trying to learn or help, sometimes in mischief, sometimes in open rebellion. It is, perhaps, his ambition to become a man, but he never quite makes it.

(K. Sagar, *The Art of Ted Hughes,* 1975, p. 106)

His efforts to understand the world in which he finds himself bring him into contact with the products of human culture, with religion and literature and science, all of which seem to him to have got it all wrong, according to what he has seen of the world, so he rearranges the traditional elements in a way which seems to him more in accordance with the facts, in "Apple Tragedy" and "Song for a Phallus," for example. Also he tries his hand at original composition with notes for some little plays, always with the same two characters.

He becomes curious about his own nature and purpose, and wonders who could have created him. He finds himself embarked on a quest for this creator. His adventures bring him into contact with various women and female monsters. Because they are ugly, often horrific, he fights them, or evades them, or in some way mismanages the situation, not realizing that each time he is meeting his own mother, his intended bride. He comes to a river. Beside it sits a gigantic horrible female, an ogress, who will not let him cross unless he carries her on his back. As they cross, she gets heavier and heavier, driving Crow into the river-bed until the water is up to his mouth. Then she asks him a question to which he must sing the right answer, quickly. The questions recapitulate the various mistaken encounters he has had with her in the past; that is, they are all, in some sense, questions about love. He knows little about it, and desperately tries the principle of permutation, singing every answer he can think of until one satisfies her, and her weight decreases again. This happens seven times before they reach the other side. "Lovesong" is one of Crow's answers to the question: "Who paid most, him or her?." "The Lovepet" is an answer to the question: "Was it an animal? Was it a bird? Was it an insect? Was it a fish?" The right answer to the question: "Who gives most, him or her?" is the lovely poem "Bride and groom lie hidden for three days," also in *Cave Birds.*

(K. Sagar, rev. ed., 1978, p. 235)

Much misinterpretation of *Crow* has resulted from the failure of critics to read the jacket note, which explains that *Crow* contains only a selection of poems from the earlier part of this epic, the part that deals largely with Crow's mistakes and failures and dismemberments; but he is on the way toward an eventual successful outcome of his quest—his reconstitution and marriage in the Happy Land.

What first strikes the reader of *Crow* is the sheer rhetorical force and vitality. There are many different kinds of poems here. The language and poetic technique are more varied than before. In the best poems there is no striving for local effects; they are direct and spare, colloquial. The verse is less regular, more mimetic. And there is much more use of the oldest poetic devices—repetitions and refrains, parallelism, catalogs and catechisms, incantations and invocations. These devices are so powerful in Hughes's hands that they have scared many reviewers into defensive postures. They accuse Hughes of using these facile devices as a substitute for a fully controlled, rational ordering. It is the rational ordering that would be facile in comparison with the discipline needed to free the imagination from its constraints. Hughes employs these devices precisely to avoid a fully controlled, rational ordering, to free his imagination, stimulate it to come up from the depths and yield its secrets. Some of the finest poems in *Crow* are inexplicable, visionary, magical, but carry their own unquestionable authenticity, like some of the inexplicable poems or passages in Yeats and Eliot; and like them they will take root in us and work upon us unseen.

Hughes's symbols have no allegorical meanings and are not literary. Insofar as they have antecedents, they are in totemism, folklore, and the archetypes of Jungian psychology. They do not "mean" anything; they embody something, and perhaps magically invoke the powers they make manifest. Although inexplicable, they are more objective and more potent than symbolism that is invented for the purpose or drawn from some literary tradition. Some of Hughes's images are invented, but without a knowledge of anthropology and folklore as extensive as his own, it is impossible to say which. They are all drawn from the same depths of consciousness and racial experience. The myth controls the energies they release.

Crow has something of the wodwo in him—an embryonic conscience. He asks bigger questions than the wodwo and has all the evidence spread before him. That evidence seems to demonstrate conclusively that the world is uninhabitable by humans, habitable by Crow only because he is less than human, without spiritual aspiration, without a sense of sin, and specialized for survival.

What Hughes is seeking to communicate, centrally, is a vision of the wrongness of things, of humanity seeking to survive and live meaningfully in conditions for which it is patently unfitted. The survival is of the fittest to survive, of those who are able and willing to accept these conditions, since they are permanent, ingrained, part of the very fiber of the material world. But is survival on these terms worth the price? And is the material world the only world? Is it even real? In one of the earliest poems, "A Kill," the birth of Crow (or every man) is described as a death, or at least a loss of consciousness, life as a "dream flash." The title of the previous poem, "Examination at the Womb Door," indicates that Hughes wanted to keep open in these poems the possibility that the Buddhists may be right in believing that life is an illusion and the only worthy purpose in it is to learn to recognize it as such, to make oneself spiritually independent of it and thereby acquire the discipline that, after death, will close the womb-door and avoid further incarnation in a world that belongs entirely to death.

In some of the poems Crow is simply a witness of "the hallucination of the horror":

> He saw this shoe, with no sole, rain-sodden,
> Lying on a moor.
> And there was this garbage can, bottom rusted away,
> A playing place for the wind, in a waste of puddles.
>
> There was this coat, in the dark cupboard, in the
> silent room, in the silent house.
> There was this face, smoking its cigarette between the
> dusk window and the fire's embers.
>
> Near the face, this hand, motionless.
>
> Near the hand, this cup.
>
> Crow blinked. He blinked. Nothing faded.
>
> He stared at the evidence.

I choose to quote this poem, "Crow Alights," rather than several others in which Crow also stares at evidence, as an example of what Hughes can do with understatement. Here is no blood, violence, melodrama. Yet the evidence is just as conclusive, and perhaps more moving in its simplicity.

Sometimes Crow experiences the first stirrings of compassion:

> He grasped he was on earth.
> He knew he grasped
> Something fleeting
> Of the sea's ogreish outcry and convulsion.
> He knew he was the wrong listener unwanted
> To understand or help—
>
> His utmost gaping of brain in his tiny skull
> Was just enough to wonder, about the sea,
>
> What could be hurting so much?
> "Crow on the Beach"

He finds himself an unwilling participant in the horror:

> Crow thought "Alas
> Alas ought I
> To stop eating
> And try to become the light?"
>
> But his eye saw a grub. And his head, trapsprung,
> stabbed.
> "Crow Tyrannosaurus"

Crow is Everyman who will not acknowledge that everything he most hates and fears—the Black

Beast—is within himself. Crow's world is unredeemable. God made the Redeemer as a defeatist act of submission to Crow:

> When God went off in despair
> Crow stropped his beak and started in on the two
> thieves.
>
> "Crow's Song of Himself"

Christianity, for Hughes, is "just another provisional myth of man's relationship with the creator." Its inadequacies, as such, give rise to much of the comedy of *Crow,* where the God of Genesis figures as something of a well-meaning booby. "Apple Tragedy," for example, is also apple farce. Hughes here interprets the connection between the apple and original sin as cider, invented by God, drunk by Adam, Eve, and the serpent, and responsible for all their subsequent transgression. In "A Childish Prank," God, having created Adam and Eve, is beaten by the problem of how to invest them with any kind of purpose or stimulate them to any activity. In a Talmudic version of the creation, God, having made man and woman of the clay of the earth, tries for hundreds of years to lure into these inert bodies the free souls that fly through space. But the souls value their liberty and will be neither cajoled nor tricked into bodies. Crow steps in and invents sexuality, which has kept the race in perpetual motion ever since. An even more serious intervention occurs in "Crow Blacker than Ever":

> When God, disgusted with man,
> Turned towards heaven,
> And man, disgusted with God,
> Turned towards Eve,
> Things looked like falling apart.
>
> But Crow   Crow
> Crow nailed them together,
> Nailing Heaven and earth together—
>
> So man cried, but with God's voice.
> And God bled, but with man's blood.
>
> Then heaven and earth creaked at the joint
> Which became gangrenous and stank—
> A horror beyond redemption.

Here is an example of the ease with which Hughes can move from comedy to deepest seriousness, of how Crow's wildly improbable escapades can dramatize the biggest theological issues. The incongruity is already there in the gap between the world as it is and the world as a loving God must have intended it. What has this earth to do with that heaven, that men must strain to become light and God be nailed to a cross in a vain attempt to teach man to pronounce the word "love"?

One of the earliest essays on Hughes was called "The Violence of Ted Hughes"; many subsequent ones would have used the same title had it not been preempted. It has become axiomatic that Hughes is violent, both in style and subject matter, that violence is his stock in trade, that he admires violence. If any critic had stopped to ask seriously *why* Hughes writes obsessively about violence, especially in *Crow,* he would have had to recognize that Hughes does so because he lacks the thick skin, the layer of insulation or complacency, which enables most of us to ignore it, just as we turn a blind eye to such other uncomfortable and not quite respectable (certainly uncivilized) realities as birth and death. Hughes does not *invent* the violence in his poems, any more than he invents the newspaper headlines that we try not to register as we search for the arts and sports pages. Crow registers everything, puts himself to school to reality. He sees that a "mishmash of scripture and physics" has resulted in recurring wars that have come to be accepted as inevitable, normal:

> And when the smoke cleared it became clear
> This had happened too often before
> And was going to happen too often in future
> And happened too easily
> Bones were too like lath and twigs
> Blood was too like water
> Cries were too like silence
> The most terrible grimaces too like footprints in mud
> And shooting somebody through the midriff
> Was too like striking a match
> Too like potting a snooker ball
> Too like tearing up a bill
> Blasting the whole world to bits
> Was too like slamming a door
> Too like dropping in a chair
> Exhausted with rage
> Too like being blown to bits yourself
> Which happened too easily
> With too like no consequences.
>
> "Crow's Account of the Battle"

The issue of *Newsweek* in which *Crow* was reviewed carried on the front cover a photograph of Lieutenant Calley and the bodies of a few of his victims. Inside, a Gallup poll showed that 50 percent of those questioned thought that such incidents were common. Seventy-nine percent disapproved of the verdict against Calley, 20 percent because they thought that what had happened at My Lai was not a crime. Even Crow, the hard-bitten trap-sprung survivor, cannot evade the response of outrage or compassion; he is not yet that civilized.

Ted Hughes, as a poet, is very like the man in "Criminal Ballad." He is automatically tuned in to the suffering to which the rest of us are automatically deafened and blinded, because it is happening somewhere else and to someone else:

> And when he walked in his garden and saw his
> children
> Bouncing among the dogs and balls
> He could not hear their silly songs and the barking
> For machine guns
> And a screaming and laughing in the cell
> Which had got tangled in the air with his hearing
> And he could not turn towards the house
> Because the woman of complete pain rolling in flame
> Was calling to him all the time
> From the empty goldfish pond

Not at all by choice, he comprehends all the suffering of the universe, animal and human, as his own. It is the burden of the tragic artist. Hughes is not open to the charge of morbidity, for there is always the desperate hope that "having come so far, and against such odds," something might yet be won from the struggle.

Hughes is interested in reform and palliation like any other thinking and feeling person, and this interest occasionally enters his poetry, but it is not at the heart of it. For Hughes cannot take quite seriously any attitude to experience that takes for granted the continuance of our civilization with very much its present structure and values, the continuance of the race, or even the reality of the physical universe. To assume these things is to ignore or willfully misread the evidence.

> Popa, and several other writers one can think of, have in a way cut their losses and cut the whole hopelessness of that civilization off, have somehow managed to invest their hopes in something deeper than what you lose if civilization disappears completely, and in a way it's obviously a pervasive and deep feeling that civilization has now disappeared completely. If it's still here, it's still here by grace of pure inertia and chance, and if the whole thing has essentially vanished, one had better have one's spirit invested in something that will not vanish. And this is a shifting of your foundation to completely new Holy Ground, a new divinity, one that won't be under the rubble when the churches collapse.
>
> (*London Magazine,* January 1971)

Crow is part of Hughes's heroic search, on behalf of us all, for that Holy Ground.

Hughes published *Crow* in this incomplete form because he could not finish his epic, could see no way forward for Crow. He thought he had perhaps exhausted the possibilities of Crow; but Crow kept popping up, and a few years later, Hughes was able to return to *Crow* and continue it. It still remains to be completed.

VII

In 1971 Hughes accompanied Peter Brook and his International Centre for Theater Research to Iran for the Fifth Shiraz Festival. There he wrote *Orghast,* which is the name both of the play and of the invented language in which it is written. *Orghast* was based on several myths and folk tales, but at the center was the story of Prometheus. At the same time Hughes wrote a sequence of little poems about Prometheus, in English, twenty-one of which were collected in *Prometheus on His Crag* (1973) and revised in *Moortown* (1979).

Prometheus is immortal but shares with man the ability to suffer pain. As punishment for stealing fire from heaven to give to men (thus launching them on the path toward a godless technological civilization), Zeus has Prometheus nailed to a rock at the world's edge. Every day a vulture comes out of the sun to feed on his liver, which grows again overnight. Most of the poems are internal monologues in which Prometheus tries to get beyond his pain and anger to an understanding of his situation, of the god who has condemned him to it, of the vulture, and of his fellow-sufferer Io, a maiden turned by Zeus into a heifer perpetually pursued by a hornet. Prometheus' punishment is that he cannot move; Io's that she cannot rest.

Prometheus is not like the Contender in *Crow,* rigidly committed to a senseless trial of strength he can never win. He retains through all his agony a faith that there is some key, some secret, which would enable him to understand the situation and thereby come to terms with it. This faith develops through daily refinements of suffering and is focused on the vulture:

> It knew what it was doing
>
> It went on doing it
> Swallowing not only his liver
> But managing also to digest its guilt
>
> And hang itself again just under the sun
> Like a heavenly weighing scales
> Balancing the gift of life
>
> And the cost of the gift
> Without a tremor—
> As if both were nothing.
>
> (poem 10)

Prometheus, the prototype of the human condition, also hangs weighing the cost, but for a long time he can find nothing to set against its weight, the weight of the whole earth, but a butterfly in a dream. The first real clue comes, in poem 18, from a lizard

> Listening near the ear of Prometheus,
> Whispering—at his each in-rip of breath,
> Even as the vulture buried its head—
>
> "Lucky, you are so lucky to be human!"

All Prometheus has that the lizard has not is consciousness, which gives him the possibility of understanding the situation, and thereby converting the pain into the payment, redeeming mankind not by mere cunning and prescience but by the deepest knowledge that can be won only from suffering. In poem 20 Hughes permutes all the possible meanings of the vulture:

> Prometheus on His Crag
>
> Pondered the vulture. Was this bird
> His unborn half-self, some hyena
> Afterbirth, some lump of his mother?
>
> Or was it his condemned human ballast—
> His dying and his death, torn daily
> From his immortality?
>
> Or his blowtorch godhead
> Puncturing those horrendous holes
> In his human limits?
>
> Was it his prophetic familiar?
> The Knowledge, pebble-eyed,
> Of the fates to be suffered in his image?
>
> Was it the flapping, tattered hole—
> The nothing door
> Of his entry, draughting through him?
>
> Or was it atomic law—
> Was Life his transgression?
> Was he the punished criminal aberration?
>
> Was it the fire he had stolen?
> Nowhere to go and now his pet,
> And only him to feed on?
>
> Or the supernatural spirit itself
> That he had stolen from,
> Now stealing from him the natural flesh?
>
> Or was it the earth's enlightenment—
> Was he an uninitiated infant
> Mutilated toward alignment?
>
> Or was it his anti-self—
> The him-shaped vacuum
> In unbeing, pulling to empty him?
>
> Or was it, after all, the Helper
> Coming again to pick at the crucial knot
> Of all his bonds . . . ?
>
> Image after image after image. As the vulture
> Circled
>
> Circled.

Pain, the midwife at his rebirth, breaks for him the hard shell of his ego:

> And the cloudy bird
> Tearing the shell
> Midwifes the upfalling crib of flames.
>
> And Prometheus eases free.
> He sways to his stature.
> And balances. And treads
>
> On the dusty peacock film where the world floats.

Hughes's version of the myth dramatizes the resolution in Prometheus of all the basic dualities of human nature—spirit and matter, male and female, beauty and horror. But it happens abruptly and mysteriously. There remain big gaps between the last four Prometheus poems which call for further examination, perhaps when Hughes himself is surer that he is out of the psychic limbo and the mouth-sealing numbness out of which these hard little poems had grown as pearls grow upon sand-grains in the flesh. That surer, fuller, and more distanced elaboration was to come in *Cave Birds.*

VIII

It was in 1974 that Hughes saw a set of twenty bird drawings by Baskin—marvelous vivid drawings of owls and eagles and many other birds, real and imaginary—that again fired his imagination. Interpreting them in his own way, he wove a story round them, cast them as characters in a sort of static mystery play. At first there was simply a poem for each drawing—poems unusually studied and formal for Hughes. Then he felt the need to add eight more poems, outside the bird drama but parallel to it, giving the same story in direct and human terms, and in a free and simple style. Baskin then did eight more drawings to go with these.

The protagonist is an innocent ("that is," says Hughes, "a guilty one"), an Everyman. He has certain features in common with Socrates, whom Hughes holds responsible for the disastrous course of Western civilization, the committer of the original sin: "The whole abstraction of Socrates' discourse must inevitably, given enough time and enough applied intelligence, result in machine guns."[3] But since he is also an ordinary man trying to live in the modern world, he appears simply normal, no more guilty than any of us. In the bird drama the protagonist is, at this stage, a cockerel—a subtler version of what would have been called, in a mystery play, Pride of Life. All is apparently well with him: at least he thinks so. Suddenly, without warning, he suffers a psychic split; his consciousness is invaded by spectral birds who are representatives of an otherworldly court where he is to be tried for some nameless but apparently capital crime. The action passes to the underworld, where the protagonist is tried and condemned to death. Swallowed by a raven, he emerges as a Crow, to a new adventure, new trials. He passes through various initiation ordeals, supervised by owls and eagles, culminating in a marriage (he is by now almost human) with an earthly woman, which is also his rebirth as a falcon. Several poems from *Cave Birds,* especially the latter part, will probably also find their way into the complete *Crow.*

It gradually emerges that the protagonist's crime has been to get into a wrong relationship with the female. They are lost, dead, to each other. And since the female is not only wife and mother but also nature and psychic demon, this failure is both murderous and suicidal. No real living is possible until this damage has been repaired, but the remaking cannot begin until the criminal has been scoured of his Socratic rationality and egocentricity. The birds work on him like a team of alchemists, refining and refining, breaking down and reconstituting, until finally both he and his victim are able to take over and reconstitute each other in marriage:

> So, gasping with joy, with cries of wonderment
> Like two gods of mud
> Sprawling in the dirt, but with infinite care
> They bring each other to perfection.
>
> "Bride and Groom"

Never before had Hughes worked so closely with Baskin or any artist. The two are obviously very close in spirit, but their imaginations are not identical. As an artist Baskin is necessarily concerned with forms and surfaces and textures and the grotesque distortions to which they lend themselves. Hughes can do the verbal equivalent, and in some poems it is an appropriate thing for him to do, but it is not the way to the heart of his vision. That vision is revelatory not by distortion and construction but by far-seeing clarity and bare sensitivity, the qualities we find in most of the poems in *Cave Birds* that are outside the bird drama. Of the poems written to preexisting Baskin drawings only two, "The Knight" and "The Loyal Mother," seem to me to approach the quality of the others.

The themes of psychic split, guilt, suffering, ego-death, and rebirth are so important and central for Hughes, and certain elements (such as the use of marriage as a primary image of rebirth) so new and crucial for his development that, given the initial stimulus of the drawings, Hughes then needed all the freedom possible for his imagination to find its own framework without such exigencies as the need to write a poem to fit every Baskin drawing. In attempting to organize the Baskin drawings into a bird-drama that would enable him to follow the stages in the destruction and renewal of an essentially human protagonist, Hughes was surely attempting the impossible—like going for a four-

[3]From a reading at Leeds University, 10 March 1979

minute mile in a three-legged race. It is amazing that he came so near to bringing it off. He has given us a dozen fine poems, two or three great ones, some of which will, I hope, reappear in a less constraining context. For all its unevenness, *Cave Birds* constitutes a stage Hughes had to go though to find a way forward for Crow (toward his marriage in the Happy Land on the other side of the river), and to be able to write the epilogue to *Gaudete.*

IX

Adam and the Sacred Nine (1979) is, in a sense, a sequel to *Cave Birds.* Adam lies inert in Eden. The other creatures expect great things of him, but he feels miserably helpless and exposed. His dreams—of technological achievements and immortality—are so madly incongruous with his bruised body "too little lifted from mud" that they merely bewilder him. He is visited by nine birds, each of which offers him an image of how to live. The Falcon could not be more different from his weeping and shivering self, with its unfaltering gunmetal feathers, mountain-diving and world-hurling wing-knuckles, bullet-brow, grasping talons, tooled bill. Then the Skylark, living and dying in the service of its crest, cresting the earth, trying to crest the sun, with bird-joy. Then the Wild Duck, getting up out of cold and dark and ooze, and spanking across water quacking Wake Wake to the world. Then comes the Swift, wholeheartedly hurling itself against and beyond the limits. Then the Wren, who lives only to be more and more Wren—Wren of Wrens! Then the Owl, who floats, the moving center of everything, holding the balance of life and death, heaven and earth. Then the Dove, the perpetual victim, but rainbow-breasted among thorns. Then the Crow comes to Adam and whispers in his ear a waking, reject-nothing truth. Finally comes the Phoenix, which offers itself up again and again and laughs in the blaze. Each bird has found what Adam lacks, its own distinctive mode of living fully within the given conditions. It is not for Adam to try to imitate any of them. He is defined precisely by his lack of wings. His business is with the earth. He stands, and it is the first meeting of the body of man with the body of the earth. The sole of Adam's foot is grateful to the rock, saying:

I am no wing
To tread emptiness.
I was made

For you.
"The sole of a foot"

X

The development of Hughes's vision from the crucified Prometheus to the resurrected Adam spanned the years 1971 (also the year of his marriage to Carol Orchard) to 1976. Other work being done simultaneously also contributed to the remarkable access of hopefulness and affirmation. In 1968 Hughes had written *Five Autumn Songs for Children's Voices* for the Little Missenden Harvest Festival. On his return from Iran he set himself to write five poems for each of the other seasons, and these were published in 1974 as *Spring, Summer, Autumn, Winter.* A dozen more poems were added for *Season Songs* in 1975. While writing these poems Hughes was spending most of his time farming—cows and sheep—in partnership with his father-in-law, Jack Orchard. He had little time for anything else, but kept a rough verse diary of the more memorable events of the farming year, intending later to work these entries into poems. Jack Orchard died in 1976, the Moortown farm livestock was sold, and Hughes returned to the farming diary. But he found that anything he could do to the entries lost more than it gained, so he left them as they were and published them as *Moortown* in 1979. As with *Season Songs* it was Hughes's intention initially that these would be upbeat poems for children, but as the poems engaged his deeper concerns, the age of the "children" rose until he was writing for adults, but trying to stay within hearing of children.

Perhaps Hughes embarked on these poems as an attempt to cheer himself up after the limbo of *Prometheus on His Crag.* In the event, the renewed contact with the natural world, its births and deaths and failures and harvests—simply looking at things and recording them—proved so revitalizing, so revelatory, that it was to help to transform Hughes's entire vision, even the world of Crow, which had been, up to then, a world of fallen vision.

All the poems are sacramental, some of them

visionary, but they remain rooted in common everyday realities. They are poems of observation, but such is Hughes's knowledge of and feel for natural processes that the observed details are selected and rendered effortlessly, in such a way that they reveal not appearances but inner workings and connections. After the isolation and paralysis of *Prometheus,* all is now color and variety, bustle and change, as the earth swings through its cycles on the poles of birth and death.

One would have thought that there was little new to say about the seasons. And indeed Hughes is only showing us what we see every year but take for granted. He writes like the only one of us who is really awake.

> The sun lies mild and still on the yard stones.
>
> The clue is a solitary daffodil—the first.
>
> And the whole air struggling in soft excitements
> Like a woman hurrying into her silks.
> Birds everywhere zipping and unzipping
> Changing their minds, in soft excitements,
> Warming their wings and trying their voices.
>
> The trees still spindle bare.
>
> Beyond them, from the warmed blue hills
> An exhilaration swirls upward, like a huge fish.
>
> As under a waterfall, in the bustling pool.
>
> Over the whole land
> Spring thunders down in brilliant silence.
> "Spring Nature Notes"

Every April is our real birthday, when the world bombards us with gifts:

> And the trees
> Stagger, they stronger
> Brace their boles and biceps under
> The load of gift. And the hills float
> Light as bubble-glass
> On the smoke-blue evening
> And rabbits are bobbing all over, and a thrush
> Rings coolly in a far corner. A shiver of green
> Strokes the darkening slope as the land
> Begins her labour.

Season Songs tells us, and what amazing news it is, what it is like to be alive in this world, with five senses and normal feelings. They embody what Lawrence called "a man in his wholeness wholly attending." Hughes's earlier books record the hard struggle toward this wholeness. When it is achieved, life's charge flows freely again and can be communicated to others through poems. The agony of Prometheus is behind the apparently spontaneous and joyful balance of these poems and the humility of their thanksgiving. Perhaps the harvest poems illustrate this most fully. Here is one written too late for inclusion in *Season Songs:*

BARLEY

> Barley grain is like seeds of gold.
> When you turn a heap with a shovel it flows
> With the heavy magic of wealth.
> Every grain is a sleeping princess—
> Her kingdom is still to come.
> She sleeps with sealed lips.
> Each grain is like a mouth sealed,
> Or an eye sealed.
> In each mouth the whole bible of barley.
> In each eye, the whole sun of barley.
> From each single grain, given time,
> You could feed the earth.
>
> You treat them rough, dump them into the drill,
> Church them up with a winter supply
> Of fertiliser, and steer out onto the tilth
> Trailing your wake of grains.
>
> When the field's finished, fresh-damp,
> Its stillness is no longer stillness.
> The coverlet has been drawn tight again
> But now over breathing and dreams.
> And water is already bustling to sponge the
> newcomers.
> And the soil, the ancient nurse,
> Is assembling everything they will need.
> And the angel of earth
> Is flying through the field, kissing each one awake.
> But it is a hard nursery.
> Night and day all through winter huddling naked
> They have to listen to the pitiless lessons
> Of the freezing constellations
> And the rain. If it were not for the sun
> Who visits them daily, briefly,
> To pray with them, they would lose hope
> And give up. With him
> They recite the Lord's prayer
> And sing a psalm. And sometimes at night
> When the moon haunts their field and stares down
> Into their beds
> They sing a psalm softly together
> To keep up their courage.

Once their first leaf shivers, they sing less.
And start working. They cannot miss a day.
They have to get the whole thing right.
Employed by the earth, employed by the sky,
Employed by barley, to be barley.
And now they begin to show their family beauty.
They come charging over the field, under the wind,
like warriors,
"Terrible as an army with banners"
Barbaric and tireless, a battalion of Amazons.

That is how they win their kingdom.
Then they put gold, for their coronation.
Each one barbed and feathered, a lithe weapon,
Puts on the crown of her kingdom.
Then the whole fieldful of queens
Swirls in a dance
With their invisible partner, the wind,
Like a single dancer.

That is how barley inherits the kingdom of barley.

Season Songs is not at all sentimental or escapist. Death is ever-present. A fledgling swift suffers "the inevitable balsa death." Foxes and stags are hunted to death. A pheasant hangs from a hook with its head in a bag. A cranefly is going through with its slow death—the poet a watching giant who "knows she cannot be helped in any way." But death, for all the deep compassion it evokes, does not cancel vitality.

Any honest record of farming, especially of livestock rearing, is bound to be a record largely of disasters, and the proportion of deaths in *Moortown* is even greater than in *Season Songs.* Some, such as "February 17th," where Hughes describes in detail his decapitation of a half-born dead lamb, are likely to sicken the sensitive. But if we do not exact a full look at the worst, we falsify the whole and devalue the best. When a three-year-old nephew persistently asks, of a lamb killed by ravens, "Did it cry?" Hughes answers at last, "Oh yes, it cried." Death must be confronted, taken seriously. A lamb suffering from a disgusting and incurable disease must be shot:

I shot the lamb.
I shot him while he was looking the other way.
I shot him between the ears.

He lay down.
His machinery adjusted itself
And his blood escaped, without loyalty.
But the lamb life in my care
Left him where he lay, and stood up in front of me

Asking to be banished,
Asking for permission to be extinct.
For permission to wait, at least,

Inside my head
In the radioactive space
From which the meteorite had removed his body.

"Orf"

Such endings make doubly precious the survivals:

. . . We leave her
To her ancestors, who should have prepared her

For worse than this. The smell of the mown hay
Mixed by moonlight with driftings of honeysuckle
And dog roses and foxgloves, and all
The warmed spices of earth
In the safe casket of stars and velvet

Did bring her to morning. And now she will live.

"Little Red Twin"

XI

WE have all seen the newspaper headlines: "VICAR'S SECRET HAREM." "ORGIES IN THE VESTRY." "HUSBANDS HOUND VICAR FROM VILLAGE." Something works beneath the surface of a typically genteel English village, with its retired army officers, commuting businessmen, squire, farmers, poachers, doctor, publican, and priest, which erupts in this sensational way surprisingly frequently, to the great joy of the journalists. In 1964 Ted Hughes wrote a film scenario on such a theme, never used. From his attempt to understand the psychology of minister, women, and husbands, he found himself with a potent myth on his hands, which he later developed in the form of a long narrative poem, *Gaudete.*

Gaudete (1977), an amazing and unique work, is in three parts. In the Prologue an Anglican minister, Nicholas Lumb, is abducted by the powers of the spirit world in order to carry out an act of healing there. This part of the story takes place in a nightmarish landscape where everything is savage, potent, and pregnant, but little is clear. Lumb's task seems to be to heal the terribly scarred face of the goddess of that world, an injury for which man is somehow responsible. It is the ravaged face of the earth itself, a patchwork of the remains of all the living creatures mangled by men, the torn hearts of all the women denied, bullied, and exploited by men. His task is also to help her with a difficult birth. She must be reborn of him before he can be reborn of her. It is his own rebirth at which he must play the roles of midwife and mother. Meanwhile, a duplicate of himself, painfully created out of a live oak and given his memory and sense of himself, is sent to replace him. But the changeling cannot escape his own essential nature as a fertility spirit, a wood-demon. He comes from a world where nature is all, into a world of cars, fashions, interior decoration, elaborate social codes, rigid unspoken rules, Women's Institute meetings with cucumber sandwiches, a world where the sterile bodies of the women are owned by husbands whose only interest in nature is that it provides them with something to kill. Here he is obliged to preach and practice a religion he has been inadequately briefed in and misinterprets, woodenly, by the values of the other world. His spiritual orientation lost, he looks vainly for something in this profane world he can recognize as sacred, from which he can take his bearings. He stares at an image of the goddess he serves, "an archaic stone carving," a Sheela-na-gig:[4]

> Her square-cut, primitive fingers, beneath her
> buttocks
> Are pulling herself wide open—
> An entrance, an exit.
>
> An arched target centre
> A mystery offering
> Into which Lumb is lowering his drowse.
> (105–110)

He sees all the women of his parish as incarnations of that goddess. At first his effort is probably to haul up through that opening other spirits to renew the race. This he easily translates into a Christian framework by claiming that he is to father a second savior. What woman is to him, his only perceived hope of getting back into a meaningful, that is sacred, world, he is to the women of his parish, whose lives have become so desacralized that they are all too receptive to the offer of sacred sex, and the promise that one of them is to be the mother of a god. Later, when he is doomed, he wants to get back through that trapdoor into his own underworld, or, as an oak makes most mast when it fears death (as during severe drought), tries to broadcast his seed before his inevitable cancellation. But he is only crucifying himself. His frantic priapic sexuality, far from healing or renewing, or even providing an escape route, simply draws him into a fatal tangle of destructive passions leading finally to two suicides, two murders, and a conflagration.

The long central narrative section of *Gaudete* is about this changeling's last day, when the powers who created him abandon him to the murderous husbands, who hunt him down, then burn him together with his high priestess and his intended bride, in a parody of a Beltane bonfire.

In the Epilogue the real Lumb returns to this world, in the west of Ireland, transformed by his traumatic experiences in the underworld. There is no narrative of those experiences (though a few of them leak through into the consciousness of the changeling). Instead we are given forty-five short, beautiful, eerie lyrics that Lumb has written during or shortly after his exile, many of them prayers to the unnamed goddess of both worlds.

Many readers will already find themselves inclined to sneer. Spirits? Men made of oaks? Goddesses? Even the religious among us are conditioned to respond to these things as belonging, in the contemporary world, only to the context of horror films. But myths that are ever true myths cannot die, for it is part of their definition that they exist outside time, making intelligible the permanent realities. They can, of course, become inoperative, not because they have died but because we have died to them, after thousands of years of denial of the basic realities in the name of all the isms—rationalism, idealism, puritanism, humanism, materialism, dualism, asceticism. We need the haruspex more than the Etruscans did, to look into the depths of nature, come to understand its innermost workings, and show us what the implications of these realities are for human life.

No one can really invent new myths. It is a matter of selecting and recombining under high imagi-

[4]For a description and illustration of the Sheela-na-gig, see John Sharkey, *Celtic Mysteries* (London, 1975).

native pressure from the mass of mythic material that we have forgotten, or relegated to ancient history at the conscious level, but which lies in suspended animation in the unconscious waiting to be reactivated. There are several shamanistic myths in which the shaman is called upon to exercise his powers of healing upon the goddess herself in the other world. In one the Lady of the Seals is infested about the head with parasites that represent all the aborted children and needlessly slaughtered animals on earth. There are all the Scottish and Irish folktales and ballads of men abducted to the fairy world to marry or heal the fairy queen, and of changelings; all the resurrection myths collected by J. G. Frazer, especially those of Attis, Adonis, and Actaeon; all the myths of the moon goddess of creation and destruction gathered by Robert Graves in *The White Goddess.* There are all the Herakles and Dionysus myths; the *Bacchae,* though there Euripides put his thumb in the balance in favor of Dionysus, by draining his rites of all phallic and orgiastic content (all that is merely in the diseased imagination of Pentheus); and all the Grail legends, especially *Parsifal.*

Hughes has read very widely and makes full use of his reading, but not, like Eliot in *The Waste Land,* in the form of quotations and allusions; everything has to be recycled through his imagination to emerge fused, charged, authenticated. Charged, that is, not with a few thousand volts of Hughes's patented "verbal energy," as though that were something that could be switched on at will, but with the deepest contemporary human relevance and a deep, all-embracing compassion. His myth in *Gaudete* has a quality distinctive of all genuine myths, that it can be interpreted equally well as applying to a supernatural cosmos of spirits and powers, for those who can believe literally in such things, to the natural world, or to the psychic world. It is at its richest if we can apprehend its relevance to all three at once; when it forces us to realize the crassness of such distinctions. And the power of Hughes's writing ensures that this is so. *Gaudete* is Hughes's most deeply and overtly religious book. What he is attempting, as a matter of the utmost and immediate practical necessity, as a matter of life and death, is the recovery of the lost sense of the sacredness of nature—not, of course, the sentimental nature of traditional English nature poetry, but the savage, elemental, demonic (as well as incredibly lovely and tender and fresh) nature all his books go to define. Sacredness has nothing to do with metaphysics. "Sacred" means simply "real." That is, to see something as real, in all its fullness of being, is to recognize it as a hierophany, a manifestation of the sacred.

Hughes's method, in *Gaudete,* is to take the sacred, in the form of the flora and fauna of the world and the elemental powers beneath it, and the profane, in the form of our normal surface life, and to jam them into each other. They are, of course, never separate. The underworld pushes up into this world with every grass blade, explodes into it with every hatched egg, licks and flickers like green fire everywhere round the sterile houses. Every window is also

> . . . a door on to the furnace of the bright world
>
> The chill bustle
> Of the blossom-rocking afternoon
>
> The gusty lights of purplish silver, brightenings,
> sudden darkenings
> Teeming with wings and cries
> Under toppling heaven.
>
> (103–108)

The fullness of being of everything in the natural world continually invades the human world as if it were a vacuum, so that the reality of one of the husbands is almost extinguished by the mere lilac scents that waft into his room:

> He leans at the door, emptied, merely his shape,
> Like a moth pinned to a board,
> While the nectars of the white lilac
> And the purple and dark magenta lilac
> Press through the rooms.
>
> (84–88)

Human life is largely a series of devices to keep nature at bay. Nature is farmed, gardened, photographed, looked at through binoculars or the telescopic sights of a high-velocity rifle. What undermines this safe coziness from within is sex. The girls and young women of the village are walking incitements to devilry. And the older women, with the changeling, are flung

With more life than they can contain
Like young dogs
Unable to squirm free from their torturing infinite
dogginess.

(91–93)

He is impregnating the women with a reality too immense for their girdled bodies and etiolated selves:

She is gripped by the weird pathos of biochemistry, the hot silken frailties, the giant, gristled power, the archaic sea-fruit inside her, which her girdle bites into, which begins to make her suit too tight. She feels the finality of it all, and the nearness and greatness of death. Sea-burned, sandy cartilage, draughty stars, gull-cries from beyond the world's edge.

The human world is a waste land, a world of "polished modernity, the positioned furniture, in ultra colour, . . . like the demortalised organs of a body"; of "stuffed wild life," cactus windowsills, hall chimes, souvenir ashtrays. It cannot possibly accommodate a fertility spirit. It cannot even accommodate its domestic animals (a faithful retriever savages its master, who is savaging his wife; a cat becomes a demon and seduces his mistress) or real art (a Beethoven sonata havocs the house like a vandalizing demon). The village is a trap for the wood-demon as well as for its inmates. His powers, compromised by the straitjacket of his temporary human identity, cannot prevent him from being profaned, reduced to the helpless plaything of frustrated and jealous women and the victim of perverted and jealous men.

Meanwhile, the real Lumb, jammed into the world of the dead and unborn, his mind assailed by nightmarish horrors, cannot cope with all that. But he can and does survive, and brings back with him a tentative raw wisdom. His poems are the songs of a man who has come through, but only just. *Gaudete* means Rejoice! It is the only word on a gravestone. The resurrected Lumb brings back with him the capacity to rejoice even in that which appalls him, and the capacity to perform small miracles, like drawing an otter from the loch by whistling on the back of his hand. The miracle of summoning the sacred, which the changeling Lumb had so laboriously failed to perform for his parishioners, is now effortlessly performed by the real Lumb and magically communicates itself, through the innocence of three small girls, to an ascetic priest, an anchorite who is fired by the thought of what God had whistled up out of the waters of chaos:

And as he spoke the priest was suddenly carried away by his words. His thoughts flew up into a great fiery space, and who knows what spark had jumped on to him from the flushed faces of the three girls? He seemed to be flying into an endless, blazing sunrise, and he described the first coming of Creation, as it rose from the abyss, an infinite creature of miracles, made of miracles and teeming miracles. And he went on, describing this creature, giving it more and more dazzlingly-shining eyes, and more and more glorious limbs, and heaping it with greater and more extraordinary beauties, till his heart was pounding and he was pacing the room talking about God himself, and the tears pouring from his eyes fell shattering and glittering down the front of his cassock.

(epilogue, 165–175)

The priest then copies out the poems from the notebook Lumb has left with the girls. Here one will have to stand for all:

The grass-blade is not without
The loyalty that never was beheld.

And the blackbird
Sleeking from common anything and worm-dirt
Balances a precarious banner
Gold on black, terror and exultation.

The grim badger with armorial mask
Biting spade-steel, teeth and jaw-strake shattered,
Draws that final shuddering battle cry
Out of its backbone.

Me too,
Let me be one of your warriors.

Let your home
Be my home. Your people
My people.

(epilogue, 176–190)

These are poems to be possessed by. Each is like a fine bloody thread being pulled through our hearts.

The main narrative of *Gaudete* is based on the image of the split—the split psyche, the split between man and woman, man and nature, the sacred and the profane. The epilogue poems strain for atonement; the mind and body of a man precariously balanced on a fine taut wire of images above the chasm. They are the furthest any modern writer has gone toward the recovery of the sane and the sacred without forfeiting the real.

XII

Hughes's progress from the 1950's to the 1980's can be described using William Blake's "fourfold vision" as a paradigm. *The Hawk in the Rain* is about man imprisoned in single, fallen vision as in his own body, looking out through the window of his eye at the surrounding energies, the "wandering elementals," making no effort to come to terms with them, as though that were inconceivable, but cowering, hiding, peeping through his fingers, gripping his own heart, running for dear life; or with ridiculous arrogance and complacency posturing as a god in a universe that dwarfs him. In *Lupercal* the energies are released and confronted, but they are seen as nightmarish and destructive, so that it seems only a saint or genius or madman can live with them. This stage, "twofold vision," the release of the energies and the search for strategies to control them, continues through *Wodwo* and *Crow.* What is enacted here is a "descent into destruction," an ego-death, a journey to the source and back, which is followed in *Prometheus on His Crag, Cave Birds, Gaudete,* and *Adam and the Sacred Nine* by the painful process of reintegration in terms of a recovered innocence ("threefold vision") on the far side of experience. This brings with it a cleansing of the doors of perception, so that what had formerly been seen as ugly or horrific in nature is now seen as beautiful and holy. This atonement is "fourfold vision." It is apparent everywhere in Hughes's most recent work, most notably in the salmon poems in *River* (1983).

As in the farming poems, Hughes never takes his eye from the object. Never for a moment does the salmon cease to be a real salmon and become a counter for something else. Yet Hughes's vision reveals, without ever saying so, that the salmon is our prototype, its life cycle a paradigm of nature's purposes and of the religious life.

In "Salmon Eggs" the mating salmon are "emptying themselves for each other." This selfless giving, generosity, openness is a form of dedication or worship, as is the acquiescence of the October salmon in his slow death:

> All this, too, is stitched into the torn richness,
> The epic poise
> That holds him so steady in his wounds, so loyal to
> his doom, so patient
> In the machinery of heaven.
>
> "October Salmon"

The dying salmon is the defeated, torn, and sacrificed hero, about to become a god.

Blake asks:

> How do you know but ev'ry Bird that cuts the airy
> way,
> Is an immense world of delight, clos'd by your senses
> five?
>
> *(The Marriage of Heaven and Hell)*

What Blake means, surely, is that everything contains within itself the clue to the mystery, the principle of the whole, and being continuous with the whole (which cannot be seen in its immensity) witnesses to the whole and makes it accessible to vision. The mystery is "the redeemed life of joy." It is a mystery because there is no mechanistic or rational explanation for the transformation of suffering (and everything that cries out for redemption) into joy. The language of poetry can reenact it. Joy, as Blake or Hughes understands it, has little to do with happiness—a relatively trivial, uncreative state, a distraction, temptation, backwater from the true way through tragic experience. It is the grace of atonement, the exaltation of being used by the goddess for her sacred purposes, "her insatiable quest."

The language of all these river poems is a rich weave of interrelationships. A poem may be ostensibly about a single creature, but that creature is defined by its relations with other creatures, with weather and season and landscape. Since "all things draw to the river," it is therefore the language of atonement. The life of the salmon is the life of the living waters, sea and river, which is the life of earth and sky, which is our only life. Each poem is a microcosm. The salmon is part of a flow that "will not let up for a minute." The river is itself an archetypal image for life in time, process, the one-way helpless journey toward death. But a river is by no means a one-way wastage:

> Something else is going on in the river
>
> More vital than death—death here seems a
> superficiality
> Of small scaly limbs, parasitical. More grave than life
> Whose reflex jaws and famished crystals
> Seem incidental
> To this telling—these toilings of plasm—
> The melt of mouthing silence, the charge of light
> Dumb with immensity.
> The river goes on
> Sliding through its place, undergoing itself
> In its wheel.
>
> "Salmon Eggs"

And here the poem approaches the mystery. For the wheel, karma, the "cycles of recurrence," had formerly been for Hughes, as for most religions, images of horror or absurdity, needing to be transcended. Now it seems that the horror was a product of defective vision, the split psyche, the spiritual blindness caused by dualism, the hubristic desire to improve on the given life, to redeem nature. In the words of Lawrence's risen Christ (in *The Escaped Cock*): "From what, and to what, could this infinite whirl be saved?"

Since logical analysis is the language of single vision, one would expect the language of fourfold vision to be paradoxical synthesis. The very title of Blake's finest work, *The Marriage of Heaven and Hell,* declares that this is so. "Salmon Eggs" moves through a series of oxymorons—"burst crypts," "time-riven altar," "harrowing, crowned," "raptures and rendings"; appropriating on the way all the claims of the Christian mystery of transcendence—"crypt," "altar," "liturgy," "tidings," "Sanctus," "mass," "font"; claiming them all for the wheel itself, "the round of unending water," and the salmon egg that is its "blessed issue," toward the river's simple annunciation: *"Only birth matters."*

For this poem to work as a spiritually fertilizing experience, it is necessary to believe that these words express a truth uttered by the river, and not a theory uttered by Hughes. And that is unlikely to happen unless we have accompanied him imaginatively through the four stages of his arduous quest, through all the horrors, sufferings, and deaths that his earlier poems enact.

What saved Hughes in those worst years in the 1960's from despair and world denial and a Beckettian absurdism was a Blake-like tenacity, against all the odds, in holding firm to the conviction that the human spirit, with its desire for existence, is "the only precious thing, and designed in accord with the whole universe. Designed, indeed, by the whole universe," and that the universe knows what it is about: "The infinite terrible circumstances that seem to destroy man's importance, appear as the very terms of his importance. Man is the face, arms, legs etc. grown over the infinite, terrible All." These words were written by Hughes in 1966 in his introduction to Popa's poems. When he came to rewrite this essay in 1977, he attributed to the Eastern European poets something of the vision to which he had himself come in the interim:

> At bottom, their vision, like Beckett's, is of the struggle of animal cells and of the torments of spirit in a world reduced to that vision, but theirs contains far more elements than his. It contains all the substance and feeling of ordinary life. And one can argue that it is a step or two beyond his in imaginative truth, in that whatever terrible things happen in their work happen within a containing passion—Job-like—for the elemental final beauty of the created world.

Hughes could not have written that final phrase in the 1960's. Then he would have regarded beauty with suspicion, as something likely to blind man to the essential elemental starkness and awesomeness of the world. As his vision matured, beauty forced its way in again, and to the center, not as something cozy and pretty and picturesque, but as a radiance testifying to miracle.

The poem in which Hughes most fully receives and expresses that radiance is the poem with which he has chosen to end his *Selected Poems* (1982), "That Morning." In 1980 Hughes and his son, Nicholas, spent some weeks salmon-fishing in Alaska. The place and its creatures demanded a sacramental response. The sheer profusion of salmon was like a sign and a blessing:

> Solemn to stand there in the pollen light
> Waist-deep in wild salmon swaying massed
> As from the hand of God. There the body
>
> Separated, golden and imperishable,
> From its doubting thought—the spirit-beacon
> Lit by the power of the salmon

> That came on, came on, and kept on coming
> . . .
> So we stood, alive in the river of light
> Among the creatures of light, creatures of light.

The conclusion of Hughes's *Selected Poems* is the same as the conclusion of *The Marriage of Heaven and Hell:* "For everything that lives is Holy."

In December 1984, Hughes was appointed Poet Laureate. He is the first great poet to fill the post this century. His first poem in office, "Rain Charm for the Duchy," is an affirmation of the potency and sacredness of rain. Both the appointment and the poem were received mockingly by the Philistine press and grudgingly by the critical establishment. The most generous tribute came from the Irish poet Seamus Heaney, who saw that in that poem Hughes was reaffirming "a sacerdotal function for the poet in the realm."

SELECTED BIBLIOGRAPHY

I. BIBLIOGRAPHY. K. Sagar and S. Tabor, *Ted Hughes: A Bibliography 1946–1980* (London, 1983).

II. SELECTED POEMS. Thom Gunn and Ted Hughes, *Selected Poems* (London, 1962); *Selected Poems, 1957–1967* (London, 1972; New York, 1973); *Selected Poems, 1957–1981* (London, 1982), pub. in U.S. as *New Selected Poems* (New York, 1982).

III. SEPARATE WORKS. *The Hawk in the Rain* (New York–London, 1957), verse; *Lupercal* (New York–London, 1960), verse; *Meet My Folks!* (London, 1961; New York, 1973), verse for children; *The Earth Owl and Other Moon People* (London, 1963), verse for children; *How the Whale Became* (London, 1963; New York, 1964), stories for children; *Nessie, the Mannerless Monster* (London, 1963), reiss. as *Nessie the Monster* (New York, 1974), story in verse for children; *The Burning of the Brothel* (London, 1966), verse, lim. ed.; *Recklings* (London, 1966), verse, lim. ed.; *Scapegoats and Rabies* (London, 1967), verse, lim. ed.; *Wodwo* (New York–London, 1967), verse, stories, and a play; *Poetry in the Making* (London, 1967), pub. in U.S. as *Poetry Is* (New York, 1970), radio talks for children; *The Iron Man* (London, 1968), pub. in U.S. as *The Iron Giant* (New York, 1968), story for children; *Seneca's Oedipus* (London, 1969; New York, 1972), play; *Crow* (London, 1970; New York, 1971), verse; *The Coming of the Kings* (London, 1971), plays for children; *Crow Wakes* (London, 1971), verse, lim. ed.; *Poems: Fainlight, Hughes, Sillitoe* (London, 1971), verse, lim. ed.; *Eat Crow* (London, 1971), play for radio, lim. ed.; *The Tiger's Bones* (New York, 1974), plays for children, contains *Orpheus* in addition to the plays in *The Coming of the Kings; Season Songs* (New York, 1975; London, 1976), verse, reiss. with several new poems (London, 1986); *Moon-Whales* (New York, 1976), verse for children; *Gaudete* (New York–London, 1977), verse; *Moon-Bells* (London, 1978), verse for children; *Orts* (London, 1978), verse, lim. ed.; *Cave Birds* (London, 1978; New York, 1979), verse; *Remains of Elmet* (New York–London, 1979), verse; *Moortown* (London, 1979; New York, 1980), verse; *Under the North Star* (New York–London, 1981), verse; *A Primer of Birds* (London, 1981), verse, lim. ed.; *River* (London, 1983; New York, 1984), verse; *What Is the Truth?* (New York–London, 1984), story with poems for children; *Ffangs the Vampire Bat and the Kiss of Truth* (London, 1986), story for children.

IV. INTRODUCTIONS. *Selected Poems of Keith Douglas* (London, 1964; New York, 1965); *A Choice of Emily Dickinson's Verse* (London, 1968); *Vasco Popa: Selected Poems* (London, 1969), rev. for *Collected Poems* (Manchester, 1978); *Children as Writers 2* (London, 1975); *Selected Poems of Janos Pilinszky* (Manchester, 1976); Yehuda Amichai, *Amen* (New York, 1977; Oxford, 1978); Keith Sagar, *The Reef* (Ilkley, England, 1980); A. Fern and J. O'Sullivan, eds., *The Complete Prints of Leonard Baskin* (New York, 1984).

V. ESSAYS. "The Genius of Isaac Bashevis Singer," in the *New York Review of Books* (22 April 1965); "The Environmental Revolution," in *Your Environment,* 3 (Summer 1970); "Myth and Education," in *Children's Literature in Education,* 1 (1970); "Myth and Education," in G. Fox et al., eds., *Writers, Critics and Children* (London, 1976), a completely different essay; "Sylvia Plath," in *Critical Quarterly* (Summer 1971); "Orghast: Talking Without Words," in *Vogue* (December 1971); "A Reply to My Critics," in *Books & Issues,* 1 (1981); "Sylvia Plath and Her Journals," in *Grand Street* (Spring 1982).

VI. INTERVIEWS AND AUTOBIOGRAPHICAL PIECES. "Context," in *London Magazine* (February 1962); "The Rock," in *Writers on Themselves* (London, 1964); "Desk Poet," in the *Guardian* (23 March 1965); "Ted Hughes' 'Crow,' " in the *Listener* (30 July 1970); "Ted Hughes and 'Crow,' " in *London Magazine* (January 1971); "Orghast," in the *Times Literary Supplement* (1 October 1971); "The Persepolis Follies of 1971," in *Performance* (December 1971).

VII. CRITICAL STUDIES. G. Thurley, *The Ironic Harvest* (London, 1974); K. Sagar, *The Art of Ted Hughes* (Cambridge, 1975; rev. and ext. 1978), contains a full bibliography; A. Bold, Thom Gunn and Ted Hughes (Edinburgh, 1976); M. D. Uroff, *Sylvia Plath and Ted Hughes* (Urbana, Ill., 1979); E. Faas, *Ted Hughes: The Unaccommodated Universe* (Santa Barbara, Calif., 1980), with selected critical writings by Hughes and two interviews; S. Hirschberg, *Myth in the Poetry of Ted Hughes* (Dublin, 1981); T. Gifford and N. Roberts, *Ted Hughes: A Critical Study* (London, 1981); K. Sagar, ed., *The Achievement of Ted Hughes*

(Manchester, 1983), a collection of sixteen critical essays, with thirty uncollected or unpublished poems by Hughes; T. West; *Ted Hughes* (London, 1985).

VIII. RECORDINGS. *The Poet Speaks 5* (Argo PLP 1085), Hughes reading nine poems from *Wodwo; Jupiter Anthology of 20th Century English Poetry 3* (JUR OOA8), Hughes reading "The Hawk in the Rain" and "Hawk Roosting"; *Listening and Writing* (BBC RESR 19M), Hughes reading two talks, "Capturing Animals" and "Learning to Think"; *Crow* (Claddagh CCT 9–10), Hughes reading all but three of his *Crow* poems; *The Poetry and Voice of Ted Hughes* (Caedmon TC 1535), Hughes reading "The Thought-Fox," "The Jaguar," "Wind," "Six Young Men," "Mayday on Holderness," "The Retired Colonel," "View of a Pig," "Sunstroke," "Pike," "An Otter," "Hawk Roosting," "Icecrust and Snowflake," "Sheep 1," "His Legs Ran About," "Bride and Groom," and twelve poems from the epilogue of *Gaudete; Ted Hughes and R. S. Thomas Read and Discuss Selections of Their Own Poems* (Norwich Tapes, 1978), Hughes reading and discussing six poems from *Moortown; Selections from "Crow" and "Wodwo" Read by the Poet Ted Hughes* (Caedmon TC 1628); *Ted Hughes and Paul Muldoon* (A Faber Poetry Cassette), Hughes reading and introducing "Whiteness," "Go Fishing," and "An October Salmon," from *River,* "Life Is Trying To Be Life," "Ravens," and "February 17th" from *Moortown,* "Bride and Groom" from *Cave Birds,* "Do Not Pick Up the Telephone" from *Selected Poems 1957–1981,* "Emily Bronte" and "When Men Got to the Summit" from *Remains of Elmet,* and "Apple Dumps" from *Season Songs.*

HAROLD PINTER

(1930–   )

John Russell Taylor

I

IN his published writings Harold Pinter contrives to tell us remarkably little about himself, his life, and his background. It is part of his method. As against dramatists like John Osborne or Arnold Wesker, who unashamedly write plays as a sort of spiritual autobiography, with characters often little more than mouthpieces for their author's ideas or slightly adapted self-portraits, Pinter believes in covering his tracks, writing plays that are completely separated from himself to stand as independent, self-sufficient works of art. Perhaps Pinter is his plays, but he is certainly not in any obvious sense in them, and any deductions one might make from them about him are in the realm of speculative psychology.

Of course, equipped with a basic chronology of his life one might make a few reasonable guesses. He was born in Hackney, East London, on 10 October 1930; his parents were Jewish (of remotely Portuguese origin) and he an only child. He was educated in Hackney, and his first theater-going experience was to see Sir Donald Wolfit in *King Lear.* Though he had seen very little theater, he had ambitions to become an actor and studied at the Royal Academy of Dramatic Arts. He also, in connection with his national service, stood two trials as a conscientious objector. When he was nineteen he began an eight-year career as a repertory actor, playing all over the country and spending eighteen months with Anew McMaster's touring company in Ireland, a period recalled in his affectionate reminiscence of McMaster, *Mac* (1968). Meanwhile, he began to write: poems, mainly, plus a few short unpublished prose pieces and a semi-autobiographical novel, "The Dwarfs," which he finally abandoned as unsatisfactory, though it contributed elements (not recognizably autobiographical) to his later radio play of the same title. In 1957 he had an idea for a one-act play, and when suddenly faced with a request from an old friend to write a play for student production, he wrote *The Room* in four days. The experience of writing it and seeing it produced was sufficiently stimulating to make him embark right away on a full-length play, and the result was *The Birthday Party.* This, on its first production in London (fairly disastrous in terms of audience and critical response), established him as someone to be reckoned with in the booming new English theater of the time. Two years and four plays later *The Caretaker* became one of the big successes, commercial as well as critical, of the new movement, and since then Pinter's life, so far as it is known by and concerns the public at large, has been simply the succession of his writings—for the stage, for radio and television, and latterly also for the cinema.

And behind them all the man himself remains enigmatic, largely, I suppose, because he considers that he is and ought to be irrelevant to the appreciation of his work. Naturally his dramatic material, the characters and situations, must come from somewhere. In an interview, for example, he has told us that *The Birthday Party* had its beginnings in a situation and an atmosphere he encountered in a lodging house where he stayed in his acting days. But to the further question of why, in developing this material, he did not include a character representing himself in the play, he answered: "I had—I have—nothing to say about myself, directly. I wouldn't know where to begin. Particularly since I often look at myself in the mirror and say 'Who the hell's that?' "

In the same way, on the level of "interpretation" Pinter has constantly insisted that he has nothing to say, that he is in no more privileged a position than anyone else to say what his plays are about. At most he will sometimes volunteer that he did not consciously intend some particularly weird interpretation, such as that which sees the three characters in *The Caretaker* as God the Father, God the Son, and God the Holy Ghost, and the shed that one of them intends to build as Christ's Church on Earth. But, he will probably add, conscious intentions may well have little to do with it. The play is there, independent of him, to work as it may on audiences. If it works it will need no interpretation. If it does not work, all the interpretation in the world will not improve it.

The urge to interpret is nevertheless inescapable. Pinter tells us that he wants to write plays that tell a story, chronicle a series of happenings, without the artificial becauses and therefores of drama, but simply in the basic childlike terms of "and then . . . and then . . . and then." But his plays, while doing this very effectively, always have the teasing air of meaning more than they say, having resonances that hang disturbingly on the air and vibrate in the memory long after the tale has been told. It would, admittedly, be absurd to look in Pinter's work for a philosophical system or for "ideas" that can be taken out of context and considered on their own independent merits—as, for instance, one may do with the plays of Arnold Wesker. Pinter's plays are not conceived that way. Rather, they must be studied with the same sort of techniques we would bring to bear on lyric poetry, or on music: they define their own terms of reference, working not by the elaboration of ideas but by the development and transformation of themes and images, which take their value and significance entirely from their context.

II

Of all the drama produced in Britain since the inauguration of the dramatic revival with John Osborne's *Look Back in Anger* in 1956, Pinter's is the most completely, obsessively about nothing but itself, self-defining. Like Lewis Carroll's *The Hunting of the Snark,* his plays tend toward a conclusion that is entirely satisfactory in terms of their own logic, their own internal structure: "For the Snark was a Boojum, you see." Related to any reality outside the reality of the theatrical experience, they may mean anything or nothing. And yet just to describe this process involves one in interpretation. In other words it is impossible to describe without ipso facto interpreting, whether we are dealing with John Keats's "Ode on a Grecian Urn" or Pinter's *Old Times.* In each case, any attempt to say what the work is about, however well worth making, will select and distort; it may even murder to dissect. Ultimately there is no substitute for the poem but the poem, the play but the play. The best the critic can hope to do is indicate certain lines of continuity, to lay bare to some extent the mechanics of the work and suggest why it affects us as it does, when there seems to be no reasonable reason why it should.

In Pinter's case the critic's task is made easier by the unswerving logic with which each play follows from the one before, taking up, elaborating, or modifying themes and images with such ruthless concentration and precision that it would probably be possible, knowing nothing of Pinter and confronted with his complete oeuvre all jumbled up, to rearrange it in chronological order on internal evidence alone. In broader outline one may trace a number of major themes and images that run through his work, now one, now another taking the most prominent place in the composition. The most obvious are the Room, Menace, Communications, the Family, the Woman, Personality, Perception, and Memory—in approximately that order. It is some measure of the coherence of Pinter's imaginative world that all of them are present, embryonically at least, in the first tiny piece of dramatic dialogue of his that we know, a short, elusive sketch called *Kullus,* which dates back as early as 1949. Hence the elements are of the simplest. The narrator lets an outsider, Kullus, into his room. Kullus at once starts to take over: he calls in a girl who is waiting outside and without more ado they climb into the narrator's bed. This new situation carries the seeds of its own dissolution; the narrator is now the outsider, the menace to the status quo, and before long the girl, seemingly passive yet actually the determining element in the situation, is inviting the narrator to reverse it. In the process the characters of Kullus and the narrator seem to blur, combine, and exchange places; memory is annihilated as the three characters co-exist in a mysterious, ambiguous present.

All of which is no doubt a lot to read into three small pages of dialogue and narration. And yet every element, here only lightly, indirectly suggested, comes up for development and elaboration in Pinter's later work, so that, seen in the perspective of his plays, every word is full of significance

HAROLD PINTER

To begin with, there is the classic situation of Pinter's early plays: the room, representing warmth in the cold, light in the darkness, a small safe area of the known, apparently secure, peaceful existence of those inside. These are the principal constituents of Pinter's "comedy of menace," a term coined just when, at the time of *A Slight Ache* (1959)[1], it was ceasing to have any central relevance to his writing. But even if it bedeviled for a while discussion of *The Caretaker* and later plays (it is still trotted out occasionally, as though it pigeonholes everything Pinter has done), it remains a very apt and exact description of *The Room, The Birthday Party, The Dumb Waiter,* and *A Slight Ache,* the group of plays Pinter wrote in rapid succession in 1957–1958.

All these plays are both frightening and funny, creating an atmosphere of nameless, undefined terror and at the same time shocking us into laughter, shocking us sometimes by the very amiability, jollity even, with which the most alarmingly destructive attacks on the human mind are launched, which creates something very like complicity between audience and menace, as well as imaginative identification between audience and menaced. In *The Room* (1960), which remains Pinter's least mature and satisfactorily shaped play, the room itself is inhabited by a married couple, the Hudds. The play opens with a long monologue by Mrs. Hudd, during which we learn that her husband is a lorry driver and is about to go out on the icy roads. They are visited by their landlord, who gives a deliberately confusing account of himself, his home, and his family. Mr. Hudd leaves shortly after the landlord, and almost immediately another couple arrive, the Sands. They are looking for a room and have been told, or so they say, by someone in the basement that this room is vacant. Next the landlord returns and says that the man in the basement is eager to see Mrs. Hudd while her husband is out. Finally she agrees, and the man arrives. He proves to be a "a blind Negro" named Riley, who claims to know Mrs. Hudd, despite her denials, and begs her to come home with him. At this point Mr. Hudd returns, and quite casually kicks and beats up Riley. Mrs. Hudd is struck blind, and the curtain falls.

The play is prodigal of incident and diffused in its effect, as Pinter's work will never be again. But certain things are already apparent in it. First, the image of security and the threat from outside: the room is the Hudds' guarantee of security, and any intrusion is potentially menacing. The landlord exerts some control over their tenancy of it and could perhaps put them out (when asked where his bedroom is now he answers evasively, "Me? I can take my pick"). The Sands are rivals for the room, and bring worrying word that elsewhere in the house it is already regarded as vacant. Riley, on the other hand, wants to lure Mrs. Hudd out of the room's warmth and security, calling on some undefined loyalty or obligation to persuade her (is he in fact meant to be, or suggesting that he is, her father?). And attack is not a completely reliable way of defending the room and the security it confers: even within the room Mrs. Hudd can be struck blind, taking on, as it were, the disadvantages of her least powerful-seeming adversary. The trouble with the play is that it seems too evidently teasing, too deliberately mysterious: we find ourselves forced to ask questions that are probably irrelevant, to suppose that the characters have some sort of quasi-allegorical significance we cannot quite fathom. Why, for instance, is the last intruder "a blind Negro"? If the play were completely self-defining we would not ask; we would instinctively accept Pinter's statement that he does not know himself: at that stage in writing the play a door opened and a blind black man walked in, almost in his creator's despite.

If *The Room* is regarded as a rough sketch, *The Birthday Party* (1957) is Pinter's first finished work of art. In it he concentrates his attention on the central image of the Room and explores it in detail. Here the principal character is Stanley, idle, spoiled, content to do nothing and be pampered and fussed after by Meg, his stupid, doting, suffocatingly motherly landlady, who irritates him but is still very useful in making his life as comfortable as possible. The location of this room is particularized, as it never is in *The Room*—a down-at-heel boarding house in a seaside town—and the daily routine of its inhabitants' lives are observed in minutely realistic detail. All the more frightening, then, when into this familiar, humdrum household come two mysterious creatures straight out of lurid fiction, hired killers, it seems, out to get Stanley. But what for, exactly? That we never know. Perhaps even Stanley never knows. We gather that he

[1] Dates in text refer to first stage production; dates in bibliography refer to publication date.

may have been a pianist sometime in his life, but otherwise his past is a mystery, and so are the motives of those who threaten him, Goldberg and McCann. Not because they refuse to explain themselves; on the contrary, they offer far too many irreconcilable explanations. McCann, Irish and brooding, refers always to politics and religion, heresy and treachery to "the organization." Goldberg, jolly and Jewish, one of nature's traveling salesmen, is preoccupied instead with sex and property, suggesting that Stanley embezzled, murdered his wife, abandoned his fiancée, and so on.

GOLDBERG:	What's your trade?
McCANN:	What about Ireland?
GOLDBERG:	What's your trade?
STANLEY:	I play the piano.
GOLDBERG:	How many fingers do you use?
STANLEY:	No hands!
GOLDBERG:	No society would touch you. Not even a building society.
McCANN:	You're a traitor to the cloth.
GOLDBERG:	What do you use for pyjamas?
STANLEY:	Nothing.
GOLDBERG:	You verminate the sheet of your birth.
McCANN:	What about the Albigensenist heresy?
GOLDBERG:	Who watered the wicket in Melbourne?
McCANN:	What about the blessed Oliver Plunkett?
GOLDBERG:	Speak up, Webber. Why did the chicken cross the road?

(Act II)

The total picture created from these individual details is as inscrutable as the menace with which Stanley teasingly torments Meg at the beginning of the play: the men with a van, and in it a wheelbarrow, and the "certain person" they're looking for.

The lesson is obvious. The more particularized a menace is, the more it is a particular response to a specific transgression, the less imaginative effect it is likely to have, the easier it is for each member of the audience to dissociate himself from it. But we all have, somewhere, a hidden fear, an undefined sense of guilt, a consciousness of original sin or a Big Brother superego watching over us, which can in the right circumstances be played upon. Whatever it is in Goldberg and McCann, or in his own mind, which breaks Stanley down, leads to his ritual humiliation at his own birthday party and his reduction to silent conformity as he is led away the next morning, we never know—and therefore we are left all the more disquietingly with the feeling that the same thing could well happen to us. What Pinter has done, technically, with his material is to write a complete well-made play, except that the exposition and the denouement are left out: we get process and conclusion without explanation or revelation. And not merely as a trick to mystify, but because precise explanations and credentials would be destructive of Pinter's whole dramatic purpose.

Do his characters have any credentials; could they explain themselves if they wanted to? Pinter would probably say no:

> The assumption that to verify what has happened and what is happening presents few problems I take to be inaccurate. A character on the stage who can present no convincing argument or information as to his past experiences, his present behavior, or his aspirations, nor give a comprehensive analysis of his motives, is as legitimate and as worthy of attention as one who, alarmingly, can do all these things.
>
> ("Writing for the Theatre," *Plays: One,* p. 11)

But before Pinter can go on to explore the furthe[r] implications of this by delving more deeply int[o] the nature and even the possibility of communication, let alone the definition of human personality in terms of human beings' relations with one another, he has just one loose end from *The Birthday Party* to tie up, and he does so in *The Dumb Waiter* (1960). *The Birthday Party* leaves us, perhaps, asking what exactly are Goldberg and McCann? Are they in fact beings from another world, one of highly colored sensational fiction, or perhaps largely figments of Stanley's overheated imagination? Th[e] latter in many respects they may be, but Pinte[r] suggests that their menacing aspects, as apart from Stanley's own personal reading of them, are supplied by their context rather than inherent; that is that they are menacing only in relation to Stanley' special situation. *The Dumb Waiter* shows a ver[y] similar couple off duty, nonmenacing, vulnerabl[e] When the dumbwaiter in their basement roo[m] starts relaying intricate and unreasonable orde[rs] for exotic foods from aloft, it is their turn to b[e] menaced, to placate the mysterious force above a[s] best they can. And even then they are not sa[fe] together in their room-womb. Finally the mena[ce] invades the sacred domain itself, when they a[re] ordered to kill each other, each thereby becomi[ng] in context the other's prime menace. And, [no] doubt, if we were ever to encounter whoever is the other end of the dumbwaiter, he too, according to context, could be menace or menaced, and so on in an infinite Kafkaesque chain.

But this leaves another aspect of the question to be explored. In any given situation there is the menace and there are those who let themselves be menaced. Why do they let themselves be menaced? Do they know? Need there be two sides to the situation, or is one side's readiness to be menaced, willingness if necessary to invent a menace for himself, enough? To such questions Pinter's next works, the play *A Slight Ache* and its companion piece, the story-monologue *The Examination* (1961), provide some hint of his answer. Both of them present a menace-situation that is in effect one-sided, a breakdown, such as Stanley's, that is now unmistakably self-induced. In *A Slight Ache* a married couple, Edward and Flora, become aware of a passive, mysterious presence outside their gate, a matchseller who never seems to move, day or night. Each of them reads his nature and purpose according to his or her own fears and desires. For Flora he is the husband she really wanted, the pet she can fuss over, the child she can mother. For Edward he is an impostor; he may be someone returned from the past; he is sly and cunning, and after something he will get if Edward makes one false move. The intruder (who was anyway freely invited in) never says anything, never does anything (indeed, in the play as originally written for radio, it was uncertain whether he was really there at all). And faced with this monumental, unresponding presence, Edward gradually breaks himself down, until at last he changes places with the matchseller, Flora calmly accepting and even in a measure directing the exchange (shades of Kullus, again).

The Examination shows us precisely the same process from the inside. The narrator is the examiner, examining a character called Kullus for some undisclosed purpose. And just as Edward in *A Slight Ache* gradually breaks down faced with the mere presence of the other man, so here "I" breaks himself down in the presence of Kullus, for all that Kullus seems to be in every way obedient and submissive to his orders and arrangement of procedure. At the beginning the examination is taking place in "my room"; by the end it has become unarguably "Kullus' room," as in the long-previous sketch called *Kullus,* and as in the later television play *The Basement,* which turns on exactly the same balance of emotional power exemplified by changing ownership of "the room."

With *The Examination* Pinter completed one cycle in his writing, having worked his way pertinaciously through a wide group of associated images in various aspects and combinations. Though the room and menace do not disappear completely from his later work, they will not from now on be dominant themes. If up to now his characters have been, as he put it, "at the extreme edge of their living, where they are living pretty much alone," from *The Examination* onward they come nearer in to the center; they engage, if guardedly, in social intercourse, and so the focus shifts from the naked conflict of wills, the battle, even, of one individual will to retain its integrity and identity, to wider issues: the means of communication between people (if communication is possible), the definition of character through interrelation, the viability of the very idea of personality as something definable, recognizable, consistent.

III

THE first play he wrote in the second cycle of his work (after a few brief sketches for popular West End revues) points to this change of emphasis by its very title: *A Night Out* (1960). This was written originally for radio and television, and while it seems unlikely that the fact that it was destined from the start for a mass medium made any essential difference to its style or content, it is no doubt significant that at this stage in his career Pinter felt ready to tackle a mass audience directly. In the play Pinter develops a number of his earlier images in new ways, and most immediately he breaks away from the formerly inescapable room-womb in which the action of his early plays takes place. Admittedly Albert, the protagonist, has some difficulty in breaking free for his "night out." To his possessive mother, a development of Meg in *The Birthday Party,* home represents safety, sanity, and clean living: if he wants to get out, even for one evening, it must be because he is leading an unclean life and "mucking about with girls." All the same, he insists on going to a party given by the firm he works for, and finds that everything goes wrong, since he is blamed, quite unjustly, for a "liberty" taken by someone else with one of the girls. Maddened by his mother's renewed reproaches he storms out and falls in with a genteel prostitute. Though he goes home with her, they never really connect, since she persists in weaving her own fantasies about her life, while he cannot dissociate her from his mother, so that she becomes the indirect victim of his impotent rage against his mother. When finally he returns, having worked off his aggressions on the prostitute, nothing has changed: his relationship with his mother stands just where it always was.

The difference of approach between *A Night Out* and the earlier plays is at once apparent. The effect of the story depends upon the interplay of characters. In a situation that is never really mysterious or designed to create menace we learn about the people by watching their attempts to communicate with one another, and sometimes their inability or refusal to be communicated with. Albert's mother is impervious to communication; she just will not listen to anything that does not fit in with her established idea of things. The prostitute does not want to communicate too much; all she wants is something to bolster up the precarious fantasies that make her life bearable. Albert wants to communicate, but is too tied up in his stifling relationship with his mother to get through, either to her or to anyone else. All this involves them in some intense situations, but the tone of the play is much lighter than before, and none of the characters is entirely enclosed in private desperation. Compared with what has gone before, *A Night Out* represents a much more relaxed Pinter developing his images in terms of a sort of psychological comedy-drama, humanized and demystified.

With this in mind it is easier to "read" his next play, *The Caretaker,* than it was at the time of its first appearance in 1960. We are seemingly back to the room, the occupant and the outsider who comes to menace the existing state of affairs. But it does not work like that. Now there are three characters, of about equal weight, and all are provided with quite suffering backgrounds. There is Aston, the occupier of the room, living a more or less vegetable existence since (as we eventually learn in the play) he underwent electric shock treatment to alleviate a mental disorder. There is Davies, the shifty, opportunistic tramp he brings back to share his home. And there is Mick, Aston's volatile brother, whose game is more elusive, and who eventually succeeds in turning Davies' wiles against himself, so that the long-suffering Aston is moved, of his own accord, to turn him out.

But the word "succeeds" already implies interpretation. More ink has probably been spilt about the "meaning" of *The Caretaker,* what interpretation we should put on it, than on all Pinter's other plays put together. And in fact it does occupy a strange middle position in Pinter's work, neither so gnomic nor (if one chooses to see it that way) so willfully mystifying as his "comedies of menace," nor so blandly self-contained, so coolly observant of its own curious rules, as his later drama. It leaves the sort of loose ends that it is inviting to unravel and then knit up again into some new explanatory pattern. And even if we are content, as seems reasonable, to take Pinter's word for it that he had no allegorical intentions, that it is just about "three men in a room," then we are still left with enough information and enough fair ground for surmise to start speculating on the play's meaning in the more elementary terms of character motivation, of objectives and intentions in the mind of each character.

It is, in fact, virtually impossible to describe the happenings of the play without the description taking on color from one hypothesis or another. To say that Mick "succeeds" in ousting Davies obviously implies the assumption that he intends to do this and works toward it. If we choose to see the relationship between the brothers in this play as the first clear inkling of Pinter's later interest in the dynamics of the family unit (most clearly expressed in *The Homecoming*), then we may see the line of continuity in Mick's behavior as concern for his brother's health and happiness, encouragement at Aston's relationship with Davies as a first sign of Aston's return to the world, and (justified) mistrust of Davies as a suitable friend and support for Aston. If he wants to retain the mental advance Aston has made, but at the same time dispose of Davies, the unconscious agent of that advance, then all his behavior falls understandably into place. And, provided this reading works, it does not really matter whether it is "true," what the author primarily had in mind, or the only possible reading. The play, after all, can sustain an infinite number of readings, all of them more or less consonant with what happens before our eyes.

This is perhaps both its strength and its weakness. "Chekhov himself could not have devised a more satisfying finale," said one reviewer. True, and yet in a way disappointing. *The Caretaker* is a far more conventional play than any of Pinter's others, more approachable by traditional paths, more anecdotal almost. The speech in which Aston tells us of his hospital treatment is a distinguished piece of writing in itself, but somehow too explicit, lacking the richness and indirection of Pinter's best work. And not just because Pinter ought to be "Pinteresque," that is, in popular critical parlance riddling and obscure, but because Pinter's plays, even at their most explicit—and in many respects they grow more and more direct and explicit as we go on—make their effect not by direct, immediately analyzable appeals to our minds or our emotions, but by much more intricate, insidious workings on our instinctive responses. They are essentially poetic drama, with all the subtlety and ambiguity that implies. *The Caretaker* is an admirable play in itself and represents a stage that Pinter no doubt had to pass through in the course of his artistic development. But on the whole its means are not the means of poetry, but the means of prose.

However, a return to poetry was already in preparation: Pinter's radio play *The Dwarfs,* which followed after only a few months, and the unimportant interlude of *Night School,* a very slight television play that really only rearranged the constituents of *A Night Out* rather less effectively. If *The Caretaker* is Pinter's easiest, most approachable play, *The Dwarfs* is in many ways his most obscure and yet haunting. It uses the medium of radio to the full to take us inside its characters' minds, or rather inside the mind of one of its characters, Len, who seems to be on the brink of a nervous breakdown. There are three characters in the play, Len, Pete, and Mark. (A fourth in the novel, a girl, has been eliminated.) Pete and Mark are friends of Len, and nominally of each other, except that each mistrusts the other and regards his influence on Len as bad. Pete is slightly suggestive of Mick in *The Caretaker,* quick-witted, hard, and unpredictable: Len's image for him is that of a seagull, cruel and predatory, digging under stones in the mud. Mark is smooth and complacent, roused only when his vanity is affronted by the news that Pete thinks him a fool: Len's image for him is that of a spider waiting in his web. In effect, we see Pete and Mark largely through Len's eyes, refracted through his consciousness. And he, whether because he is perhaps going mad, or whether because Pinter already wishes to suggest that this is the way things are, consistently denies the possibility of knowing anything for certain about either of them, or himself, or anyone else. In a great speech, one of the high points of Pinter's writing, Len sums up the theme of the play, and provides the keynote for Pinter's further explorations into the nature of personality in *The Collection, The Lover,* and *The Basement:*

> Occasionally I believe I perceive a little of what you are but that's pure accident. Pure accident on both our parts, the perceived and the perceiver. It's nothing like an accident, it's deliberate, it's a joint pretence. We depend on these accidents, on these contrived accidents, to continue. It's not important then that it's conspirary or hallucination. What you are, or appear to be to me, or appear to be to you, changes so quickly, so horrifyingly, I certainly can't keep up with it and I'm damn sure you can't either. But who you are I can't even begin to recognize, and sometimes I recognize it so wholly, so forcibly, I can't look, and how can I be certain of what I see? You have no number. Where am I to look, where am I to look, what is there to locate, so as to have some surety, to have some rest from the whole bloody racket? You're the sum of so many reflections. How many reflections? Whose reflections? Is that what you consist of? What scum does the tide leave? What happens to the scum? When does it happen? I've seen what happens. But I can't speak when I see it. I can only point a finger. I can't even do that. The scum is broken and sucked back. I don't see where it goes. I don't see when, what do I see, what have I seen? What have I seen, the scum or the essence?

This raises, as the entire play raises, a quite different question of character verification from that raised in *The Birthday Party* or from that raised in *The Caretaker.* In *The Birthday Party,* as a matter of fact, the question is not raised within the play itself, and perhaps only suggests itself on more abstract consideration afterward. Within the confines of the play we accept that Stanley has some reason to fear Goldberg and McCann, and that Goldberg and McCann have some reason to come after him. We accept, equally, that it is not the play's purpose that we should be told these reasons; the question of verification therefore never really comes up. In *The Caretaker* we are invited to find a more everyday explanation for the contradictions and evasions of Davies and Mick (Aston is always straightforward) in what they say about themselves. When Aston asks Davies if he is Welsh and he replies, after a pause, "Well I been around, you know," it is not necessarily because his antecedents and place of birth are unknown, let alone unknowable, but simply that he is by nature untruthful and evasive. Despite what Pinter has said about characters who cannot give a complete account of themselves, this seems to be a refusal to verify, which is in ordinary psychological terms perfectly believable. Len's questions (addressed to Mark) are something else again: what he is denying is the whole basis of our relations with each other, the existence of a consistent, coherent core of personality underlying all the various facets and reflections we offer different observers on different occasions of our life. This assumption is merely the "joint pretense" on which we depend to continue, or, as Pinter has elsewhere said: "There are no hard distinctions between what is real and what is unreal, nor between what is true and what is false. The thing is not necessarily either true or false; it can be both true and false" ("Writing for the Theatre," *Plays: One,* p. 11).

Such a view, if sternly applied to character in drama, would seem likely to make the dramatist's job very difficult. Nevertheless, having logically arrived at this position, Pinter could not do otherwise than follow his apprehension through, if necessary into silence. But if it was to be silence, that would not come yet awhile; and before a period of silence he wrote three of his most striking plays, all produced in the first instance on television: *The Collection* (1961), *The Lover* (1963), and *The Basement* (written in 1963 as a film script). The first is an elaborately worked-out social comedy, based on a mystery surrounding what exactly, if anything, actually did happen between fashion designers Bill and Stella during the presentation of a collection in Leeds. Stella has told her husband, James, that Bill slept with her. James sets out to terrorize Bill into admitting it (a faint echo of the old menace situation), and, after denying everything, Bill agrees and begins to elaborate. Meanwhile Harry, the older man with whom Bill lives, is persuading Stella to retract her story. This done, Bill breaks down and admits that nothing really happened, though it might have. But is even this true? James presses Stella for an answer, but she remains enigmatic. Perhaps it is true, perhaps it is not true, perhaps it is both true and untrue. The pattern of the play prevents Bill and Stella, who are the only ones who might know the truth, from coming together to reveal it, if there is any truth to be revealed. The business of verification, in fact, has been moved into the play itself, instead of remaining something that no one in the play worries about but that might perhaps worry an audience. It is all an elaborate game, with its own rules, through which the various people in the play try to trap each other into revealing the one coherent person beyond the confusing and contradictory reflections. It may be a game, but it is carried on for all the sophistication of the participants in deadly seriousness.

The Lover shows us the game a stage further on. A husband says a fond farewell to his wife and goes out, casually asking her if her lover is coming that afternoon. Once he has gone she changes her clothes and assumes a new, "mistress" personality, and prepares to greet her lover, who, when he appears, proves to be the husband, suitably transformed. It is all a game they play to keep their marriage happy and successful; or to put it another way, it is their realistic response to the observed fact that every individual is really a number of different, contradictory individuals, and that, once this is recognized, once the contrived accidents can no longer be sustained, the only thing to do is to accept and come to terms with life's contradiction. *The Basement* goes a step further still: using the basic plot of *Kullus,* it refines the play of conflicting realities even more by showing not only people changing alarmingly, unrecognizably from moment to moment, but also their physical surroundings, the coveted basement flat, following suit.

IV

AT this point one might fear that Pinter had worked himself, as a dramatist, into a logical and emotional impasse. And indeed, for a couple of years he devoted his energies primarily to film adaptations of other writers' work—two of them, *The Pumpkin Eater* and *The Quiller Memorandum,* essays in writing technique; the other two, *The Servant* (based on Robin Maugham's story) and *Accident* (from a novel by Nicholas Mosley), taking on the character of Pinter creations, especially in the gradual reversal of the master/servant relationship in the first and in the enigmatic, feline character of the girl in the second, a Pinter woman in the process of definition between *The Collection* and *The Homecoming.* Then in 1965 came another television play, *Tea Party,* in which Pinter actually dramatizes his escape from the impasse his exploration of the nature of personality had brought him to. The play shows us an initially ambiguous situation such as we have encountered in the last three plays: the businessman Disson feels that around him things remain unspoken. His new wife's relationship with her brother, for instance, seems strangely intimate. Is he in fact her brother, and, even if he is, does that mean their relationship is innocent? Other things, such as Disson's highly charged relationship with his secretary, are almost equally ambiguous, but as he becomes increasingly engrossed in his own particular problems of verification, we, as it were, pull away from him; we accept that he is unable to find a coherent, consistent pattern in things, not because no such pattern exists to be found, but because he is going mad. And so at the end of the play, when his irrevocably fractured view of the world about him has driven him to total withdrawal, in a catatonic trance, we are left outside, observing him from a world in which familiar appearances can, after all, be adequately trusted.

This play led the way to one of Pinter's finest works, his third full-length stage play, *The Homecoming* (1965). Technically it is the end product of all Pinter had learned in his writing career: tight, compact, stripped down to bare essentials, seeming to conceal nothing, hold nothing back, and yet remaining as mysterious in its nightmarish clarity as the densest and most obscure of his early plays. It is the perfect embodiment of Pinter's ideals, the story told quite directly, without explanation, in terms of "and then . . . and then . . . and then." The long-absent son of an East End family returns equipped, as he hopes, to impose his own idea of himself on his family at last with the evidences of his worldly success, and with his beautiful wife. But none of it is to any avail: they walk over him, as they have always done, and then his wife, cool, feline, imperturbably in control of the situation, proceeds to walk over them. The play's dramatic inevitability is not in question. It may haunt the spectator, or it may say nothing to him at all. It is, either way, impregnable in its monumental detachment from what the spectator thinks: a monolithic statement of its own right to exist.

In the process it refers, fleetingly, to such familiar Pinter images as the room (all that we see of the family home); menace (the homecomer Teddy as a possible menace to his family; them, individually and collectively, as a menace to his sanity and well-being); the problem of verification (how much of Teddy's glowing account of his successful life in America shall we believe; how much of what his father, Max, and brother, Lennie, tell us about their own appalling exploits?). It is also about six people in a room, just as Pinter has said *The Caretaker* is about three people in a room, except that there he could not prevent audiences from doubting his word, whereas there is no doubt of its literal truth. But, more important, it brings to the fore some new themes in Pinter's work, or themes at any rate that have not received anything like such elaborate treatment before. These are the family as a unit (a subject one might expect to have particular significance for a Jewish writer, already hinted at in *The Caretaker* and developed more fully in *Tea Party*), the role of the female in the power-game of life, and the significance of memory. The most prominent of these themes is that embodied in the character of Ruth, Teddy's wife and the only woman in the play. She is the synthesis of all Pinter's sexually attractive women: the prostitutes/hostesses of *A Night Out* and *Night School,* Stella in *The Collection,* Sarah in *The Lover*, Anna in *Accident.* They all seem to be passive, enigmatic, and yet all of them, except the first, get what they want, regulate the game they will play with the men around them, dominate by their speed of reaction. Men who act will always dominate men who stop to think; women think and act simultaneously, as though with some deep unquestioning instinct, and therefore dominate both. And perhaps, too, it helps that, like cats, they have no remembered loyalties, no encumbering ties with the past. Memory—which is just the problem of verification seen from another angle—is likely to be a liability, committing one always to live out and relive the past instead of living in and taking full advantage of the present. All the men in *The Homecoming*, even the stupidest, are in some way debilitated by memory; only Ruth is free.

V

MEMORY is the main theme of the three short plays Pinter wrote after *The Homecoming: Landscape* (1968), in which an old couple seem to exchange recollections but actually go on living in their independent worlds, sublimely unaware of each other; *Night* (1969), in which a married couple, recalling the occasions of their first meeting and early happiness, are obviously so far from connecting that they might be talking about entirely different people; and *Silence* (1969), in which three characters, two men and a young woman, muse, mostly in separation, about a mysterious triangular relationship they have, haunted by fleeting images of an almost forgotten past. In all three short pieces (*Night* is only a seven-minute sketch) the tone is quiet, meditative, of emotion recollected, if not in tranquillity, at least in a state where all passion is spent, and the characters seem to be perennially waiting.

They are still waiting in *Old Times* (1971), which stands in the same sort of relation to *Landscape* and *Silence* as did *The Homecoming* to the group of one-act plays that preceded it. But if *Landscape* and *Silence* are about the shackles of memory, *Old Times* is in a sense about triumph over memory. As Anna, the old friend refound, says: "There are some things one remembers even though they may never have happened. There are things I remember which may never have happened, but as I recall them so they take place." But if *Old Times* takes as its starting point the material of *Landscape* and *Silence,* it transforms it into something very much more dynamic; as a full-length play (even a very short full-length play), it cannot afford to be merely meditative.

The play starts with deceptive directness and simplicity (or perhaps not so deceptive; Pinter's plays are direct and simple, the responses they evoke complex). Kate and her husband, Deeley, talk about an expected guest, Anna, of whom we learn that Kate once shared rooms with her, that she was not only Kate's best but her only friend, and that on occasions she would steal Kate's underwear. To be precise, Deeley talks about her, eliciting brief, gnomic answers from Kate, whose role almost throughout the play is that of a dreamy, uncommunicative object off whom the others bounce thoughts and feelings. It sounds like a conventional piece of exposition, preparing us for a classic Pinter situation, in which the interloper arrives to disturb what we presume to be the settled peace of an existing domestic situation. Except that Anna is there already, a palpable presence in the background—as though she has always been there, always a psychological presence in the marriage, even before she walks forward as the lights come up to become a physical presence.

Once the three characters are in conversation together, the play quickly becomes an exchange, and then a battle, of memories. Anna chatters on about the past she shared with Kate, when both were young secretaries in the culture-filled London of twenty years ago, and already we begin to wonder how accurate her memories are: do we really believe that these two people ever sat up half the night reading Yeats? Deeley hits back with a long recollection of his first meeting with Kate, who he picked up at some deserted suburban fleapit where they were showing *Odd Man Out,* so that their relationship began, as it were, under the patronage of Robert Newton. Anna's immediate reaction to this is the mysterious statement about memory already quoted, and then a long story about the inexplicable appearance and disappearance of a man one night in their room, hers and Kate's. After which she drops in casually that she went with Kate that hot afternoon to see *Odd Man Out.*

And behind and beneath all this there seems to be something more: a battle over Kate, conflicting claims of ownership, conflicting definitions of her nature. Even something so apparently innocent as a medley of recollections from the good old songs they don't write any more becomes subtly a jockeying for position; it is fundamentally Anna's recollection, but Deeley keeps capping each quotation, taking it over and by implication making it his own. And meanwhile Kate remains more or less passive, withdrawn, the object. She even complains at one point that they both speak of her as though she were dead, so preoccupied are they with redefining their past, her past, to their own ends. And right at the end of the first act Anna seems to be winning the battle for Kate, by taking the conversation with a wrench back to the old times, speaking as though they are back in their flat together, telling Kate what to wear, suggesting one man or another to her attention. But Kate at the last makes her own move: she will run her bath herself. Anna and Deeley are left alone as the lights go down.

But if the first act seems to be mainly a battle between Deeley and Anna for power over Kate, there are also implications of something else, a growing interest felt by Deeley in Anna. In the second act this comes to the fore, with Deeley insisting that he knew Anna too, in the old times, even before he knew Kate, and that in his experience she was not at all the genteel, cultivated figure she now represents herself as being. Gradually more and more memories are brought out and exchanged, canceling one another out, or seeming to ("the thing is not necessarily either true or false; it can be both true and false"). Anna and Kate blur, change places, until there is no knowing what happened to and with which.

At the end, when Kate at last speaks out, it seems to be an assertion of her existence, independent of Anna, her own choice of Deeley in place of Anna: Anna, in Kate's recollections, is seen as dead, smeared with dirt; but then she remembers trying to smear Deeley's face (if it was Deeley in her room) with dirt also. Only he refused, and suggested a wedding instead, and a change of environment. But by now the three are locked into some sort of erotic unity that cannot be broken quite so easily. In the silence after the last word spoken (by Kate) Deeley reenacts the scene remembered (or imagined) by Anna in the first act, when she saw, or thought she saw, a man in their room, cradled by Kate. And at the end Anna is still there, as at the beginning—the three of them are there, separate but inescapably together. Has time been regained and conquered, or is it a trap human beings can never escape?

Pinter's next full-length play (after a brief, slight television piece for one actor, *Monologue,* 1973) seems to represent a moment of stasis in this particular argument. In *No Man's Land* (1975) one old man, seemingly prosperous and established, has got into conversation with another, ferrety and rather disreputable, on the heath and brought him home for a drink. The play consists mainly of the fencing between the two, each guarded, each trying in some way to get the better of the other, in this "no man's land" that is also a *temps mort.* The very last words of Spooner, the visitor, in the play are: "You are in no man's land. Which never moves, which never changes, which never grows older, but which remains for ever, icy and silent." If time must have a stop, evidently it stops here. This is Pinter's winter piece: much of the imagery is of cold and silence, and it portrays the winter of life, presenting incidentally a splendid occasion for two of the British theater's grand old men, John Gielgud and Ralph Richardson, to demonstrate yet again that the fires of life never completely die down. In most respects the play seems to be a taut and economical long one-actor about the two old men in a room, but there are also some interludes of "early Pinter" concerning the host Hirst's two vaguely menacing sidekicks, who sometimes act like his keepers, sometimes like his servants, and indulge in the barbed cross-talk Pinter has always done so well, though here they seem to be around more to make the play into a full evening's theater than as an integral part of the original concept. In this sense *No Man's Land* is formally the least satisfactory of Pinter's major plays, though in the main section of the piece his dramatic logic continues to explore obsessive themes with the same inexorable precision as before.

In his next play, *Betrayal* (1978), all is from the formal point of view highly *soigné,* and the subject is again, glancingly, time, as well as the tangle of human relations and reactions suggested by the title: it depicts the course of an affair that involves husband, wife, and husband's best friend and agent over a period of some ten years, and the twist to it is that the play's nine scenes move backward in time, so that we start with the latest meeting of wife and ex-lover, ex-lover and husband, and then little by little uncover how the final situation came about. In terms of the Pinter we have known there are remarkably few ambiguities or mysteries: everything that is revealed seems to be revealed pretty unequivocally, and though we discover that the people in the play have been keeping all sorts of secrets from one another, they do not appear finally to have many secrets left from the audience. Except, of course, the ultimate, unrevealable secret of human nature and why people do the things they do. But then those have been enough for playwrights to be going on with since the beginnings of theater as we know it, and *Betrayal* certainly showed no weakening in the spell Pinter has always been able to weave around his audiences, drawing them inexorably into his own world. That his world had grown a bit closer to that the rest of us think we live in did not betoken any perceptible falling off in interest, but the play certainly made one wonder if it heralded a new "classicism" in Pinter's work.

The answer to that, as one might expect with Pinter, was at once yes and no. In 1980 he finally let a play he had written back in 1958, right after *A Slight Ache,* and had at various times mentioned in interviews as unsatisfactory and shelved, be performed with minimal revisions. *The Hothouse*, which concerns a lot of somewhat sadomasochistic goings-on in a mental hospital, with the usual dramatic doubts about which are sane and which are mad, proved to be, as Pinter had judged it, inferior to the mainline works he had presented to the public at the time of composition; but at the same time it demonstrated conclusively that even second-rate Pinter is better than first-rate most-other-people, as well as being, naturally, a field day for students of Pinter anxious to fill in all the available pieces. To aid in this process—for thesis-writing about Pinter had by now become a major academic industry on both sides of the Atlantic—he published all his screenplay adaptations, filmed and unfilmed, of novels as improbably varied as John Fowles's *The French Lieutenant's Woman,* F. Scott Fitzgerald's unfinished *The Last Tycoon*, and *A la recherche du temps perdu*, for which, in *The Proust Screenplay,* he accomplished miraculously the inherently self-defeating task of boiling down all of Marcel Proust's major themes and incidents into one dramatic unit denied the essential dimension of sheer length of time passing.

But his original work is really the thing, and in the period from 1981 to 1984 he fulfilled all possible requirements with a series of four short plays produced either singly or, at different times, in two groups of three and one double bill. The two groups of three were both called *Other Places:* at the National Theatre *Other Places* consisted of *Family Voices, Victoria Station,* and *A Kind of Alaska;* in the West End *Family Voices* was replaced by *One for the Road,* previously seen in a lunchtime double bill with *Victoria Station.* Significantly enough, in consecutive years Pinter won the *Drama* award for the best new play with a one-acter, *A Kind of Alaska,* in 1984 and with *One for the Road* in 1985, which would seem conclusively to bear out the oft-repeated judgment that he is England's "best living playwright."

Family Voices is, in a familiar Pinter manner, two intercut monologues by a mother and absent son who claim to be very concerned with each other but never actually connect, with brief interventions from the dead father. *Victoria Station* is a radio conversation between a taxi driver apparently undergoing some kind of nervous breakdown and the man who directs him from back at base, trying to get some information, any information, out of him about where he is and what he is doing. But the most substantial of the four are *A Kind of Alaska* and *One for the Road.* The first was inspired by case-histories in Oliver Sacks's book *Awakening*, about the effects of the new drug L-DOPA in arousing patients who had been comatose with sleeping sickness for upwards of fifty years. Obviously Pinter, with his long-established obsessions with identity, communication, and the subjectivity or otherwise of time, would find the subject fascinating, and his imagined awakening is handled very straightforwardly but with amazing subtlety and tact, so that the woman patient's return to life becomes—a quality one has not particularly associated with Pinter before—intensely moving. *One for the Road* was widely touted as a document of another kind of awakening, Pinter's first explicitly political play. But if Pinter were in fact to write anything like a piece of agitprop, then surely the less Pinter he. And sure enough, though the play does concern an apparently political interrogation and the techniques of intellectual intimidation and brainwashing, it is really about just the same ways in which one human being may seek to dominate another as is, say, *The Birthday Party.* What has changed is mainly his technical skill and sense of dramatic economy: everything seems to be absolutely explicit, stated quite directly, and yet the mystery and the totally compulsive quality of the drama remain completely intact. As ever, we never know what Pinter is going to do until he does it, and once he has done it, it proves to have the sort of inevitability that half-convinces us that we must have known all the time.

VI

In discussing the thematic development of Pinter's work from play to play we have largely left his style aside from consideration. And yet that in many ways is the most remarkable thing about his writing. His methods are the methods of poetry: he never preaches, never argues, but makes the significance of what he does emerge from the totality of the work. And yet any notion that "poetic" in his work means vague, generalized, avoiding awkward particularities, would be impossibly wide of the mark. The extraordinary effect of his dialogue comes not from its obvious richness and elaboration, its removal from everyday norms of speech, but from the opposite, the skill with which he captures the rhythms of modern English as it is really spoken, the rigorous discipline with which he cuts everything down to its essential. He gives us, in effect, not an artificial pattern of speech, but everyday speech patterns put under the microscope, examined in such minute detail that they seem, after all, as weird and unfamiliar as the speech of another planet. He has observed, as no one else has, the constant tugs-of-war in normal speech, such as that between the quick-witted talker whose ideas race on ahead of what he is saying and the slower-witted who is still stumbling along a couple of steps behind; or that between the inquisitive inquirer who wants to find out as much as he can while giving nothing away and the wary victim of his interrogation, who cannot or will not bring the conversation to an end but is determined to show himself as little as possible in what he says. Witness the following passage of dialogue from *The Caretaker:*

MICK. . . . Look! I got a proposition to make to you. I'm thinking of taking over the running of this place, you see? I think it could be run a bit more efficiently. I got a lot of ideas, a lot of plans. *(He eyes DAVIES.)* How would you like to stay on here, as caretaker?
DAVIES. What?
MICK. I'll be quite open with you. I could rely on a man like you around the place, keeping an eye on things.
DAVIES. Well now . . . wait a minute . . . I . . . I ain't never done no caretaking before, you know. . . .
MICK. Doesn't matter about that. It's just that you look a capable sort of man to me.
DAVIES. I am a capable sort of man. I mean to say, I've had plenty offers in my time, you know, there's no getting away from that.
MICK. Well I could see before, when you took out that knife, that you wouldn't let anyone mess you about.
DAVIES. No one messes me about, man.
MICK. I mean, you've been in the services, haven't you?
DAVIES. The what?
MICK. You been in the services. You can tell by your stance.
DAVIES. Oh . . . yes. Spent half my life there, man. Overseas . . . like . . . serving . . . I was.
MICK. In the colonies, weren't you?
DAVIES. I was over there. I was one of the first over there.
MICK. That's it. You're just the man I been looking for.
DAVIES. What for?
MICK. Caretaker.
DAVIES. Yes, well . . . look . . . listen . . . who's the landlord here, him or you?
MICK. Me. I am. I got deeds to prove it.
DAVIES. Ah . . . *(Decisively).* Well, listen, I don't mind doing a bit of caretaking, I wouldn't mind looking after the place for you.
MICK. Of course, we'd come to a small financial agreement, mutually beneficial.
DAVIES. I leave you to reckon that out, like.
MICK. Thanks. There's only one thing.
DAVIES. What's that?
MICK. Can you give me any references?
DAVIES. Eh?
MICK. Just to satisfy my solicitor.
DAVIES. I got plenty of references. All I got to do is to go down to Sidcup tomorrow. I got all the references I want down there.
MICK. Where's that?
DAVIES. Sidcup. He ain't only got my references down there, he got all my papers down there. I know that place like the back of my hand. I'm going down there anyway, see what I mean, I got to get down there, or I'm done.
MICK. So we can always get hold of those references if we want them.
DAVIES. I'll be down there any day, I tell you. I was going down today, but I'm . . . I'm waiting for the weather to break.

(Act II)

The problem of communication, so much commented on in Pinter's plays, is after all seldom failure or inability to communicate so much as unwillingness: as Pinter himself has put it:

I think that we communicate only too well, in our silence, in what is unsaid, and that what takes place is continual evasion, desperate rearguard attempts to keep ourselves to ourselves. Communication is too alarming. To enter into someone else's life is too frightening. To disclose to others the poverty within us is too fearsome a possibility.

("Writing for the Theatre," *Plays: One,* p. 15)

And so, his plays work quite as much on what they do not say as on what they do. In this sense they are not primarily literary theater at all.

So often, below the words spoken, is the thing known and unspoken. . . . There are two silences. One when no word is spoken. The other when perhaps a torrent of language is being employed. This speech is speaking of a language locked beneath it. That is its continual reference. The speech we hear is an indication of that we don't hear . . . when true silence falls we are still left with echo, but are nearer nakedness.

(pp. 13–14)

Therefore, the relations between Pinter's characters are always more complex than the words in which they seem to be expressed. The purely literary level of the dialogue is only the surface beneath which move strange and unpredictable monsters of the deep. And this is where Pinter's extraordinary poet's instinct comes in. The job of the poet is as much as anything to direct and define his reader's sensibilities, to use the relevant associations and cut off the irrelevant. Pinter has few equals among dramatists in this subtle, almost imperceptible direction of his audience. In his plays we never know quite what is hitting us or why, but it hits us with full force nevertheless, and with no waste of energy either. The supreme example of this process is *The Homecoming*, where nothing is implied and yet everything is implied, everything is stated and yet nothing is stated.

LENNY. And now perhaps I'll relieve you of your glass.
RUTH. I haven't quite finished.
LENNY. You've consumed quite enough, in my opinion.
RUTH. No, I haven't.
LENNY. Quite sufficient, in my own opinion.
RUTH. Not in mine, Leonard.
Pause.
LENNY. Don't call me that, please.
RUTH. Why not?
LENNY. That's the name my mother gave me.
Pause.
Just give me the glass.
RUTH. No.
Pause.
LENNY. I'll take it, then.
RUTH. If you take the glass . . . I'll take you.
Pause.
LENNY. How about me taking the glass without you taking me?
RUTH. Why don't I just take you?
Pause.
LENNY. You're joking.
Pause.
You're in love, anyway, with another man. You've had a secret liaison with another man. His family didn't even know. Then you come here without a word of warning and start to make trouble.
She picks up the glass and lifts it towards him.
RUTH. Have a sip. Go on. Have a sip from my glass.
He is still.
Sit on my lap. Take a long cool sip.
She pats her lap. Pause.
She stands, moves to him with the glass.
Put your head back and open your mouth.
LENNY. Take that glass away from me.
RUTH. Lie on the floor. Go on. I'll pour it down your throat.
LENNY. What are you doing, making me some kind of proposal?
She laughs shortly, drains the glass.
RUTH. Oh, I was thirsty.
She smiles at him, puts the glass down, goes into the hall and up the stairs.
He follows into the hall and shouts up the stairs.
LENNY. What was that supposed to be? Some kind of proposal?
Silence.

(Act I)

VII

ALLIED with this minute concern for the texture of his drama is, naturally but not inevitably, a passionate care for the shaping and structure of the piece. Pinter is, we know, extremely careful and fastidious in the writing and rewriting of his plays, especially in constantly refining them down, removing superfluities until only the absolute essential is left. It has been claimed that he is therefore necessarily a miniaturist. But while his concern for the minutest detail of expression is as great in one of his full-length plays as in the briefest sketches such as *Last to Go* (1959) or *The Black and White* (it is recorded that when asked if the Broadway production of *The Homecoming* was much different from the London one he replied, "I think we changed one comma"), this does not necessarily imply that his technique is any less suited to the full-length play, or any less capable of meeting its special demands. On the contrary, *The Birthday Party, The Caretaker,* and *The Homecoming* all demonstrate him entirely capable of articulating with perfect skill and confidence a long and complex structure. All his plays, from the longest to the shortest, are, if not in the historical sense at least in the literal sense of the term, impeccably well made.

It is all too easy, discussing Pinter's work in terms either of its recurrent images or of its supreme technical awareness and conscious mastery, to leave out of consideration altogether its quite individual flavor. To begin with, Pinter, though deadly serious in his approach to his art, is anything but solemn. His "comedies of menace" are real comedies, in which the humor has to match the horror every step of the way: when this has been lost, as in the first production of *The Dumb Waiter* (which took place in Frankfurt, in German), the results are disastrous, for much of his effect comes from lightness and speed, underlining nothing. In this he is, surprisingly enough, a very English playwright: if some influence from Samuel Beckett can be observed in his early plays, it is balanced in the later by a real kinship with Noel Coward, a dramatist whom he also vocally admires. His relationship with the Theater of the Absurd, as represented especially by Beckett and Eugene Ionesco, was clear enough in his "comedies of menace," but since *A Slight Ache* has grown very tenuous: *The Caretaker* is hardly absurdist drama at all, either in its theme or in its technique, and the later plays, while recognizably post–, shall we say, *Waiting for Godot,* are totally personal in their language and structure, refusing any neat pigeonholing with this or that school.

For Pinter is, unmistakably now, sui generis. It is easy just to make approving (or maybe disapproving) noises about his work, far harder to place him in any dramatic hierarchy, in Britain or in the world at large. Debate as to whether he is a "major" dramatist, for example, seems not only premature —who can know until posterity has decided the matter?—but heavily dependent on the criteria brought to bear, some of which, central to you, may seem totally irrelevant to me, and vice versa. Is clear moral commitment a necessary ingredient of "major" drama? If so, Pinter's drama is not major, for whatever Pinter the man may care about and stand for in the world of everyday moral decision (we remember, inter alia, his two trials as a conscientious objector), his plays resolutely steer clear of taking up any position in such matters, or even of handling subjects that seem to require commitment of that sort (even *One for the Road* is at best a dubious exception to the rule). They avoid, that is, the recognized "big subject," and stick instead to the obsessive exploration of a private world, of individuals living very much on the edge of their being. In his concentration on human relations abstracted to an almost "pure" state, Pinter seems far closer to Jean Racine than to any of his expansive, voluble contemporaries, or even to the great compressionist of our own time, Samuel Beckett.

It would, I am sure, be misleading to suggest that this is part of any conscious program. If *The Homecoming* takes place in a world where the dead mother can be referred to from moment to moment as an angel or a whore, without any suggestion that the characters subscribe to a hierarchy in which an angel is superior to a whore or indeed noticably different, that is because that is the way that Pinter sees his world, not because that is intellectually the pattern he wishes to impose on it. Indeed, Harold Pinter, most intelligent of British dramatists, is just about the least intellectual. That is to say, all his conscious exercise of intelligence goes into the shaping of the material itself, or a cool inquiry into its sources and significance. Instinct clearly plays an enormous part in his work, and his refusal to provide explanations reflects a very real need to take his instinct on trust, rather than mere perversity on his part. Technically he has few peers: in that sense he knows absolutely what he is doing and what effect he wants to create as he writes. But in the realm of ideas he really does not have any special knowledge of his own meaning; he chooses not to have, for fear, perhaps, of killing the goose that lays the golden eggs.

VIII

So, Pinter's plays give the critic little foothold, few rough patches that can be neatened by applying a coat or two of his ideas or convenient rifts through which the critic can insert himself into the body of the work. And the further on in Pinter's career we get, the more complete and self-sustaining the plays are, the more sublimely careless of exegesis. The most, finally, that the critic can do is describe, retell the story in less effective terms, and hope thereby to convey something of its quality. In Pinter's work, uniquely in the modern theater, there is really no substitute for the poem but the poem, the play but the play. We can observe the paradoxes—that Pinter is at once the least realistic and the most minutely realistic of contemporary British dramatists; that his world seems the smallest and most private, and yet covers a wider range of English society, a greater variety of human emotions, than anyone else's—and still come back to an elementary take-it-or-leave-it judgment of the finished plays. After all the complexities, subtleties, and refinements have been pointed out, it is still open to the spectator to say "So what?" and if he does there is no meaningful way of arguing with him. But to others it is this very self-contained quality in Pinter's work, its steadfast refusal to be considered in anything less than its own integrity, which makes him not only the most inescapably haunting of our modern dramatists, but the most likely to survive as a permanent part of our dramatic literature.

SELECTED BIBLIOGRAPHY

I. Collected Works. *The Birthday Party and Other Plays* (London, 1960), includes *The Room* and *The Dumb Waiter; A Slight Ache and Other Plays* (London, 1961), includes *A Night Out, The Dwarfs,* and revue sketches; *The Collection and The Lover* (London, 1963), includes *The Examination; Tea Party and Other Plays* (London, 1967), includes *The Basement* and *Night School; Landscape and Silence* (London, 1969), includes *Night; Five Screenplays* (London, 1971), includes *The Servant, The Pumpkin Eater, The Quiller Memorandum, Accident,* and *The Go-Between; Plays: One* (London, 1976), includes *The Birthday Party, The Room, The Dumb Waiter, A Slight Ache, A Night Out, The Black and the White,* and *The Examination; Plays: Two* (London, 1977), includes *The Caretaker, The Dwarfs, The Collection, The Lover, Night School,* and five revue sketches; *Poems and Prose 1949–1977* (London, 1977); *Plays: Three* (London, 1977), includes *The Homecoming, Tea Party, The Basement, Landscape, Silence, Night,* and five sketches; *Plays: Four* (London, 1981), includes *Old Times, No Man's Land, Betrayal, Monologue,* and *Family Voices; Other Places* (London, 1982), includes *Family Voices, Victoria Station,* and *A Kind of Alaska.*

II. Separate Works. *The Birthday Party: A Play in Three Acts* (London, 1959; rev. ed. 1965); *The Caretaker: A Play* (London, 1960; 2nd ed. 1962); *The Dumb Waiter: A Play in One Act* (London, 1960); *A Night Out: A Play* (London, 1961); *A Slight Ache: A Play in One Act* (London, 1961); "Pinter Between the Lines," in the *Sunday Times* (4 March 1962), based on a lecture delivered in Bristol to the Seventh National Student Drama Festival; *The Collection: A Play in One Act* (London, 1963); *The Dwarfs, and Eight Revue Sketches* (New York, 1965); *The Homecoming* (London, 1965; rev. ed. 1968); *The Lover: A Short Play* (London, 1966); *Poems* (London, 1968), with *Kullus,* 2nd ed. with additional poems (London, 1971); *Landscape* (London, 1968); *Mac* (London, 1968); *Old Times* (London, 1971); *Monologue* (London, 1973); *No Man's Land* (London, 1975); *The Proust Screenplay* (London, 1976); *Betrayal* (London, 1978); *The Hothouse* (London, 1980); *Family Voices* (London, 1981).

III. Biographical and Critical Studies. M. Esslin, *The Theatre of the Absurd* (London, 1962; rev. ed. 1968); J. R. Taylor, *Anger and After* (London, 1962; rev. ed. 1969); C. Leech, "Two Romantics: Arnold Wesker and Harold Pinter," in *Contemporary Theatre, Stratford-on-Avon Studies,* no. 4 (1962); G. E. Wellwarth, *The Theatre of Paradox and Protest* (New York, 1964); A. H. Hinchcliffe, *Harold Pinter* (New York, 1967); "The Art of the Theatre, III," in the *Paris Review* (January 1967), interview by L. M. Bensky; W. Kerr, *Harold Pinter* (New York, 1967); R. Hayman, *Harold Pinter* (London, 1968); D. Salem, *Harold Pinter: Dramaturge de l'ambiguité* (Paris, 1968); J. R. Hollis, *Harold Pinter: The Poetics of Silence* (Carbondale, 1970); M. Esslin, *The Peopled Wound: The Plays of Harold Pinter* (London, 1970), rev. ed. under title *Pinter: A Study of His Plays* (London, 1973); L. G. Gordon, *Strategems to Uncover Nakedness: The Dramas of Harold Pinter* (Columbia, Mo., 1970); A. Sykes, *Harold Pinter* (Quebec, 1970); J. Lahr, ed., *A Casebook of Harold Pinter's "The Homecoming"* (New York, 1971); J. R. Brown, *Theatre Language: A Study of Arden, Osborne, Pinter and Wesker* (London, 1972); S. Trussler, *The Plays of Harold Pinter: An Assessment* (London, 1973); A. Ganz, ed., *Pinter: A Collection of Critical Essays* (Englewood Cliffs, N.J., 1973).

V. S. NAIPAUL

(1932–)

Michael Thorpe

LIFE AND ATTITUDES

SINCE World War II, literature has blossomed in the former British West Indies. The fiction especially of Roger Mais, Edgar Mittelholzer, V. S. Reid, George Lamming, John Hearne, Wilson Harris, Andrew Salkey, Samuel Selvon, V. S. Naipaul, and, recently, his late brother, Shiva, forms a body of work that can stand comparison with any representative group of postwar British or American novelists. The nature of the publishing world has, in fact, compelled the comparison, since all these writers have been obliged to seek the approval of the larger readerships of the English-speaking world outside the very small countries they write about. They have not all been equally successful. Lamming made a strong impact with his semi-autobiographical *In the Castle of My Skin* (1953)—possibly with Naipaul's *A House for Mr Biswas* one of the two most widely known books—but like several others he has found it hard to sustain his promise; Wilson Harris has a faithful but exclusive following for his metaphysical novels of Guyana, but none has approached the breadth of appeal of V. S. Naipaul. Over a period of fifteen years half his books have been awarded the most coveted prizes the English literary world offers: the John Llewellyn Rhys Memorial Prize (*The Mystic Masseur,* 1957), the Somerset Maugham Award (*Miguel Street,* 1959), the Hawthornden Prize (*Mr Stone and the Knights Companion,* 1963), a Phoenix Trust Award for *An Area of Darkness* (1964), the W. H. Smith Annual Literary Award (*The Mimic Men,* 1967), and the Booker Prize, the most lucrative, for *In a Free State* (1971). Although as a "colonial" Naipaul has often deplored his want of a true society, he has certainly not lacked readers or recognition in the unbounded world of literature.

The new Commonwealth writers, treating their societies and pasts afresh, brought at first a strong renewed contact between the novel and society, a traditional strength of the novel that had been diminishing in the work of the more accomplished British and American novelists. The latter have sometimes argued that their societies are exhausted as subject matter; by contrast most of the newly emerging Commonwealth countries had never had a literature of their own. Typically, as in Naipaul's Trinidad, English literature—and language—dominated: local life, settings, speech were felt to be inferior material, and there had been little educational stimulus. "You ever hear of Trinidad people writing novels?" demands the contemptuous printer in *The Mystic Masseur.* In "Jasmine" (the *Times Literary Supplement,* 4 June 1964) Naipaul reflected on the inhibitions he had felt, as one sensitive to his society's "poverty and haphazardness" and conscious of the achievements of the long English literary tradition:

> It seemed impossible that the life I knew in Trinidad could be turned into a book. . . . Until they have been written about, societies appear to be without shape and embarrassing. . . . To attempt, with a full consciousness of established authoritative mythologies, to give a quality of myth to what was agreed to be petty and ridiculous —Frederick Street in Port of Spain, Marine Square, the districts of Laventille and Barataria—to attempt to use these names required courage.

Many literary pioneers have known such fears and have overcome them by confidence in themselves and their message, and by faith in the universal value of their insight into that segment of humanity they know best. However, as we shall see, though Naipaul's career began with a courageous use of his firsthand material, he has shown diminishing concern with his native society. This is through a deliberate preference for what he sees as a wider, more complex world, which, while it has gained him a large readership elsewhere, has made him a controversial figure among his fellow West Indians.

Vidiadhar Surajprasad Naipaul was born into a Brahmin family in Chaguanas, Trinidad, on 17 August 1932; he sums up his background as "fairly simple, barbarous and limited." Some thirty years before, his maternal grandfather had come out from Uttar Pradesh in India as an indentured laborer on the sugar plantations; Indians had begun coming to Trinidad for this purpose as far back as 1845, to replace the labor lost by the abolition of the trade in black slaves. This immigration ceased in 1917. Today East Indians (a term that distinguishes them from people of black or white descent and embraces both Hindu and Muslim Indians) make up over one-third of Trinidad's population, those of African descent just under half. The racial composition of Naipaul's island does not seem to have impressed him strongly in his early years, so clannish was the sphere of his extended family, but there is an intense awareness of racial issues in his work. Naipaul's was a large family, and there were many offshoots of it at all social levels: he had a brother and five sisters and (he estimates) over fifty cousins; a great-uncle was a millionaire, but in Naipaul's branch the money was on his mother's side and his own family was relatively poor. His father, Seepersad Naipaul, was a journalist and a struggling writer. Naipaul felt very close to him, but he describes him as "a defeated man," who evidently —like Naipaul's Mr. Biswas—felt alienated from the hierarchy of the family and solaced himself with "easy contempt."[1] His son had a way out: through his education at the prestigious Queen's Royal College in Port of Spain, and a Trinidad government scholarship at eighteen to University College, Oxford, where he read English, he was able to break out of the constricting molds of both orthodox Hinduism and limited means and opportunities. But this meant being educated in the tongue and into the cultural context of the English imperialists; thus he grew up divided between two sharply opposed worlds and into a consciousness that he could belong fully to neither—both were imported, neither was native to Trinidad.

[1]"The Novelist Talks About His Childhood in Trinidad," the *Listener,* 7 September 1972; and "Prologue to an Autobiography" (*Finding the Centre,* 1984), where Naipaul discusses relations between his life and fiction and comments on his father's contribution to the character of Mr. Biswas.

While Naipaul was at Oxford his father died. After graduating in 1954, Naipaul married an Englishwoman and remained in England, or more precisely, London. At first, like several West Indian writers before him, he did part-time work for the BBC (on the Caribbean Service) and wrote a prodigious number of book reviews, largely for the *New Statesman.* He does not think very highly of these now—like most hasty periodical reviews, few of them wear well—and not surprisingly he reprinted none in his collection of articles *The Overcrowded Barracoon.* He has used London as a publishing base from which he has frequently traveled as author-journalist to the many parts of the fragmented world that he has made his subject matter. These excursions included a year in his ancestral land, India, in 1962, a journey in abortive pursuit of the sense of belonging that has always eluded him. For some years the Indian world fed his imagination with an attachment to his unknown origins: in *An Area of Darkness* he records how his painful experience of India killed it and obliged him to become "content to be a colonial, without a past, without ancestors." Neither could he, he realized, become "English" without indulging in the "mimicry" he derides in those colonials who can only ape their erstwhile masters, even after "independence." Without country, culture, even race (which Naipaul rejects as a limiting label), the "colonial" stands peculiarly alone and unfortunately, perhaps, "free." It is a situation many are conscious of in the wake of the old British Empire, and among such Naipaul must have found a part of his audience. At the same time his explorations of rootlessness and estrangement contribute to the widespread contemporary experience of "alienation" even among those who in the old world may have once felt inheritors of a tradition in the sense that T. S. Eliot defined it, "[involving] all those habitual actions, habits and customs, from the most significant religious rite to our conventional way of greeting a stranger, which represent the blood kinship of 'the same people living in the same place' " (*After Strange Gods,* 1934). The Christian renewal Eliot advocated to restore a sustaining tradition against totalitarianism has not come about, nor is it the kind of remedy Naipaul puts forward. It may seem, in fact, that his nonattachment—to belief, society, place, or race—is total, and would disable him as the kind of universal writer he aspires to be; yet he believes "it is impossible to think of a writer, a novelist, as being anything but attached" ("The Writer," *New Statesman,* 18 March 1966). The development of his work reveals a painful struggle to sustain this attachment to the artist's only nourishing subject matter, the human condition and the need of "a contract between man and man" *(India: A Wounded Civilization),* despite all evident threats of universal breakdown. This struggle has ensured his continuing vitality and appeal to those who might say: "Now, we are *all* 'colonials.' "

APPRENTICESHIP

NAIPAUL'S first three books are set in the period from the outbreak of World War II to about 1950, the years of his boyhood and youth. He called these the works of his "apprenticeship." This is not an unduly modest word, though his writing was at once much praised. The 'prentice work is evident, not so much in style, which is at once assured, but in the narrowness of the author's attitude to his subject matter. All three early works may be viewed together as comedies of Trinidadian manners. The comic aspects inherent in a country's confused transition from a colonial to an independent status, in multiracial misunderstandings and rivalries, and in the ironic contrasts thrown up by the abrupt introduction of democratic processes in a largely illiterate and amorphous society are all fully exploited. There appear to be no tragic possibilities, and there is little invitation to the reader to become deeply involved in the characters' fates, apart from an occasional touch of pathos, especially in some of the *Miguel Street* sketches. The comic ironist is in control, observing, placing, providing a clear looking glass for folly and absurdity. The Trinidad of these first three books is still the dependent, colonial island of little importance. The formidable politicians of the struggle for independence and the early period of nationhood wait in the future; with the follies of a "free" people they will help to feed the savage indignation that enters some of the later work.

His third published book, *Miguel Street* (1959), was the first Naipaul wrote, a beginning he later described in "Prologue to an Autobiography." This is not surprising: collections of short stories are no easier to sell than single stories, and Naipaul wisely held his back until his first novel, *The Mystic Masseur,* had launched him with a more solid success. In form *Miguel Street* is reminiscent of the beginnings of such novelists as Charles Dickens and William Makepeace Thackeray, whose *Sketches by "Boz"* and *The Book of Snobs* are essentially collections of "characters"; they show the multiplicity of the writer's observations and insights rather than an informing, single vision. The seventeen sketches about Street personalities are narrated from the viewpoint of one looking back on the community he has been educated away from, recalling his early experiences with a detachment that includes sympathy but not intense involvement. Already present is the concern with the plight of man as poverty uncovers it. Man's essential vulnerability is seen most starkly in tight-knit communities—Miguel Street, Fuente Grove, Elvira—where men act out their lives as marked, closely observed individuals. Such communities, like a tribal unit, make basic, traditional demands that push men into almost mythical roles: in *Miguel Street,* much comic and pathetic play is made with the desire "to be a man, among we men" (quite half the stories turn upon this theme), or with its counterpart, which may be the subject equally of respect or of ridicule, to achieve wisdom as poet, seer, pundit ("His Chosen Calling," "Man-Man"—"seeing God was quite common in Port of Spain"—"Titus Hoyt, I A," "The Mechanical Genius").

Throughout, the narrator gives the Street full rein to speak in its racy language for itself. At the same time, he supplies insights into those lives which touch responsive chords in him, those of the "poets," the "artists," the solitaries. This allows the reader a wide range of response: while the chimera of education, "litricher and poultry" is absurd in the story of Elias' failure ("His Chosen Calling"), its purer, spiritual strain in the tale of B. Wordsworth, who fails to forge a poetic life from the commonplace, combines gentle irony on romantic attitudes with intense sympathy and understanding: "I . . . ran home crying, like a poet, for everything I saw." But the prevailing mood is that of the ironist who points up the comedy, futility, and absurdity that fill the gap between aspiration and achievement, between the public image desired and the individual's inadequacies, to recognize which may be called the education of the narrator: "I had grown up and looked critically at the people around me. I no longer wanted to be like Eddoes. . . . Everything had changed." This education is completed, however, or just beginning, when, crossing the tarmac to his plane of escape to England, he sees his shadow as "a dancing dwarf" (for its autobiographical significance, see *Finding the Centre,* p. 46). The darker note, besides adding a touch of humility, is a portent of *The Mimic Men,* Naipaul's first full study in an educated "colonial's" experience, still some ten years off.[2]

The three novels that followed *Miguel Street* develop and almost exhaust the fictional possibilities of Naipaul's early experience and insights as a Trinidad East Indian. His first published work, *The Mystic Masseur* (1957), is the most purely comic of the three, in that it allows the reader a nearly complete amused detachment; with an "eccentric" at the center, it comes close to farce. *The Suffrage of Elvira* (1958), while still predominantly comic, sharpens our perceptions of the ignorance, futility, and sheer inhumanity beneath the surface of comic action. Yet the full impact of this society's cramping influence on the individual remains to be felt, through an exploration in depth of a single character's development in an amply evoked environment: this is what *A House for Mr Biswas* (1961) offers, and it has rightly come to be regarded as the major achievement among Naipaul's earlier works.

In tracing in *The Mystic Masseur* the rise of "the Indian from the country" from laughingstock to success, against the odds of birth, race, and class, Naipaul exploits a universal comic theme, a strategy reminiscent of such English humorists of the rise of the underdog as H. G. Wells and Arnold Bennett. However, Naipaul's handling of the theme is more detached and suggests no comparisons between author and subject. Like his narrator, an educated "I" carried over from the *Miguel Street* sketches, he is presenting this career of absurdities for our response, not enforcing his own. It is a comedy of episodes, such as the kedgeree-eating ceremony, the political games, the governor's dinner, which carry message enough within the laughter without overt comment. Near the beginning there are a few such comments—the prefatory note ("although its politicians have taken to calling it a country, Trinidad is a small island"), the narrator's belief that "the history of Ganesh is, in a way, the history of our times"—which set the tone for our reaction, and from time to time throughout, a dry reductive irony keeps us always aware that we are viewing a kind of comic puppetry. With such material, what need of sharper pointing? The comic effect is allowed to build up round a reiterated set of objects, situations, or slogans, quickly conditioning the reader's response in the inevitable manner of comedy (you know what will follow, but you still laugh as readily as before): Ramlogan's tin of salmon and glass case, his "ch'acter and sensa values," Ganesh's versatile language, his changes of clothing, the Great Belcher's distinctive burps, Basdeo's plumpening figure, Bissoon's fading three-piece suit. There is matter for tears here, too, and a language to express them in—hints enough that Trinidadian English is no mere clown's lingo, as when Leela feels for the mother of the boy under a cloud, "she face small with sadness"—and material for anger, as in the narrator's rare caustic remark on the miserable people of Fuente Grove celebrating "the bounty of God . . . like the gaiety of a starving child," but not enough of either to disturb the comic tone, only to insinuate a sense of unease and of the darker possibilities of the subject matter.

In the larger perspective not only of recent Trinidadian history but also of the typical evolution of "democracy" anywhere, the comic tone does not seem misplaced. The political games that close the novel and bring Ganesh's career to its climax, the "mystic" at last stepping into the most fitting, up-to-date clothes, are satirized without indignation—though in his later travelogue *The Middle Passage* (1962) Naipaul speaks roundly of "the squalor of the politics that came to Trinidad in 1946" (when adult suffrage came in). Already outdated when Naipaul wrote, the motley semiliterate politicians of the first elections were almost innocently mischievous; they were deceivers but not self-deceived in the monstrous way of the intellectual idealist who, glimpsed first in the defeated Oxonian Indarsingh, awaits full development in *The Mimic Men.* There, the comic epilogue of identity that crowns Ganesh's career (G. Ramsay Muir, Esq., M.B.E.) is turned to tragic effect in a more searching study of identity such as the more detached irony of the early novel precludes.

In the next novel, *The Suffrage of Elvira,* the political

[2]"The Enemy," a story printed in *A Flag on the Island* (1967), was, Naipaul comments in a prefatory note, "written as part" of *Miguel Street.* While it fits better into its original context, perhaps Naipaul omitted it as being the only one in which the narrator's father plays a part; also, it contains episodes he was to use in *A House for Mr Biswas.*

theme is for the first time dominant; the treatment is still sustained comedy but with darker undertones that sometimes threaten to turn the mood toward black farce. Although the novel was written after the major election victory of Dr. Eric Williams' People's National Movement in 1956, Naipaul went back to the second general election of 1950, which belonged to the old Trinidad still firmly under the British colonial thumb. The main actors are the opportunistic, semiliterate, or illiterate adventurers we saw Ganesh falling in with at the end of *The Mystic Masseur.* The comic play is clearly defined by the extreme that Elvira represents, in "the smallest, most isolated and most neglected of the nine counties of Trinidad"; it is (recalling Dickens' *Pickwick Papers*) to be an Eatanswill election, a ridiculous battleground of provincial rivalries, suspicions, and superstitions. As in Dickens' England, the fruits of infant democracy are haggled over by cheap charlatans mouthing hollow ideals; the electorate is already wearily knowing—"People learning. You have to spend on them"—all is set for pointing the glaring disparity between the ideal and the actual that is comedy's essential stuff. The sustained tone is mock epic; trivial, absurd objects and incidents are elevated to portentous significance—the falling breadfruit, the mangy dog Tiger, the slaughtered chicken of valued lineage ("Ramlogan say he did know the chicken from the time it hatch, and he did watch it grow up. He say it was like a child to him, and when it dead it was a pussonal loss").

Given the characters' lack of sophistication, especially their superstitious susceptibility and their straining after meanings beyond them, there is no need for authorial commentary. Their muddled way with words allows an unconscious self-irony that does Naipaul's work in dialogue, as in Foam's tribute to progress—"we is a creeping nation"—while in narrative his own ironic exactitude puts events in their true light with a contrasting precision (on bribing the returning officers: "a pertinacious but delicate generosity rendered these officials impartial"; on Harbans' strong-arm helpers: "men of tried criminality"; on the meaning of it all: "So democracy took root in Elvira"). The darker notes belong to death, disease, violence, principally in the fluctuating feelings aroused by Tiger's role, by turns pathetic, revolting, menacing, yet beneath meaningless, in the bizarre death and wake of Mr. Cuffy, in Harbans' ugly reception on his return to Elvira; they insinuate a restless note into the comedy and foreshadow the darker side of his next and best-known novel, *A House for Mr Biswas,* an element that will give an increasingly somber tone to his work from now on. His "apprenticeship" is over.

NOVELS OF TWO MISTERS

A House for Mr Biswas is a work of rare distinction; it is both Naipaul's most widely read, popular novel and, at the same time, a "novelist's novel," a model work. The two aspects are closely allied. The book's popularity must be largely due to its universality of subject and theme, the struggle of one ordinary man to climb—or cling on to—the ladder of life; the ordinariness lies in his ambitions for home, security, status, his desire to live through his son, yet he remains an individual. The novel's artistry stems from a scrupulous attention to this subject and theme, through a rich blend of psychological and social realism, reinforced by symbolic overtones. In *An Area of Darkness* Naipaul later comments (of Kipling's creation of Simla): "No city or landscape is truly real unless it has been given the quality of myth by writer, painter or by its association with great events." *A House for Mr Biswas* makes Naipaul's Trinidad "real" in this sense; such a work, issuing from their stored early experience, most novelists write only once, if at all.

At first sight *Mr Biswas* seems an abrupt departure from Naipaul's previous fiction: in its concentration upon the life history of a single character it goes far deeper than *The Mystic Masseur,* and the mood is predominantly "serious," the still-pervasive comedy being subordinated to that mood. Yet on further consideration we can see *Mr Biswas* as the natural and consummate development of themes that run through the first three books: the perplexing relation of the individual to society, his struggle to impress himself upon it through achievement—or defy its pressures with a transforming fantasy that puts a gloss upon life and extracts order from the rude chaos of everyday existence. In this respect the individual is his own artist, a bringer of order—Popo, "who called himself a carpenter," B. Wordsworth, "the greatest

[poet] in the world," Uncle Bhakcu "the mechanical genius" ("very nearly"), Ganesh the miracle-worker, Lorkhoor, who finds his métier at the end of *The Suffrage of Elvira* as a facile journalist, as Biswas does, pushing everyday experience to its sensational limits. But Lorkhoor has to be lucky, the novel's mood dictates it; for Biswas, the portents are darker, in tune always with discordant probability.

Although Naipaul's raw material is new, the plot structure of *Mr Biswas* has behind it a long British novelistic tradition, as English readers must quickly have recognized: the tracing of a common hero's fortunes from birth to death or some climactic event, that hero rising from low status or obscurity through many reverses to some degree of success, often moving in the social spectrum from the stagnant country to the city (symbolizing "life"), searching always for self-fulfillment, transcending social and material limitations. From Fielding, Dickens, and Thackeray on, through Hardy, Wells, and Bennett to D. H. Lawrence and many contemporary "regional" novelists, this has been a recurring, seemingly inexhaustible pattern. In the long course of English literature such patterns have built up a complex, many-sided series of impressions, moving with the times, of the individual's relation to society, of that connection between literature and life which in his essay "Jasmine" Naipaul states is vital to him. For West Indian literature *A House for Mr Biswas* forged this connection with unbreakable strength and set up a model for emulation that no other "Third World" literature in English has yet equaled.

Novels that achieve this kind of distinction are likely to arouse and embody a common need. Biswas' quest is no mythical quest such as many Western novelists, tiring of realism, have turned to, but is akin to every common man's in the everyday flow of things; yet, like Wells's Mr. Polly, Mr. Biswas is more interesting than the ordinary man, more quirkish, a curious seeking spirit, in his way an artist. If in Naipaul's previous novels such men are "characters" we see from the outside, their ambitions material for an amusing sketch or aside (compare the treatment of the house Ganesh builds), *A House for Mr Biswas* brings us close to a man we come to know in and for himself, not as a mere social animal, with a new exploration of feeling and emotion. Much of the narrative treats of Mr. Biswas' isolation, of the feelings of one caged, weak, powerless, and of the frail fantasies he constructs to cope with reality. Nothing in the previous novels approaches the dark intensity of a "mind in turmoil," the scenes in the room at Green Vale and in Mr. Biswas' first shaky house, scenes that reach—as if *King Lear* were wholly written around the minor, common hero—"unaccommodated man." This is no extravagant allusion; it is deliberately invoked by the authoritative authorial tone of the last sentence of the prologue, where Lear's "unnecessary and unaccommodated" complete the aura of respect that Naipaul's introduction of his hero arouses. We should not doubt that the narrative is to be heroic, the quest for the house —however flawed in its realization—a victory over the chaos and anonymity into which the hero was born. The novel is such a man's celebration, his witness, and answer to the dismal refrain, "There was nothing to speak of him."

I have said that Biswas is both ordinary and extraordinary—or he would not be interesting. Since we see the world continually through his eyes and receive his interpretations of it, it is vital that his should be a truly seeing eye, an eye that, critically, makes sense of what it sees, that in fact *creates* the world—or seeks to create it. For, while Biswas' seeing enables the author, who rarely intrudes upon the page, to convey through him a sensitive interpretation of that world, his character remains that of the "weak," who can never control it. He shares with the artist-novelist the need to transcend messy reality by reordering it in his imagination, but he remains himself in life, for he cannot live a fiction: "The world was too small, the Tulsi family too large. He felt trapped . . . how often did Mr Biswas regret his weakness, his inarticulateness, that evening! How often did he try to make events appear grander, more planned and less absurd than they were!" (pt. 1, ch. 3).

In that he fails, as in his search for final meaning. What saves him, unconsciously, is his intuitive insight into the stuff of existence, as in his glimpsed vision of the "boy leaning against an earth house that had no reason for being there, under the dark falling sky, a boy who didn't know where the road, and that bus went"—consciously, his persistent sense of self, shaken, humorously self-deprecating, even reduced to madness, but always tenaciously alive. It is a rich self, everyman and more, compassionate and selfish, comic and maudlin, crass and witty, never until those last days a nullity. Only then does the narrative contract, to a final twenty pages for "The House" into which he has poured his life; after his burial his family returns, fittingly, to "the empty house."

The wider context of the novel fills out a satisfying whole. The Tulsi family is a microcosm of relationships, the antagonist through which Biswas grapples with the world. The family's full power will be missed by the reader who does not realize how total Biswas' humiliation is: according to Hindu practice, the new bride should join her husband's family and accept her mother-in-law's dominance; Biswas accepts the role of the Hindu *wife* in the Tulsi household. As time wears on, Mr. Biswas regains a tenuous self-possession, Shama and their children gradually become his equivocal allies; the muddled pity and affection Anand feels is an alternative viewpoint that strengthens as Mr. Biswas withdraws into himself. The family, a whole way of life, dissolves and dies with Mr. Biswas, while new lives—Savi, Anand, Owad—grow out and beyond it. *A House for Mr Biswas* is a fictional slice of Trinidadian Indian social history, looked back upon as something that can be placed, its lines of decay traced, its transition to amorphous modernity becoming inevitable. This subject was a shapely gift for a novelist who could grasp it. Some readers have complained that the shape is somewhat artificial and have questioned Naipaul's confining himself, in a multiracial society, to the East Indian experience and ignoring the non-Indian. Later, in *An Area of Darkness,* Naipaul defends himself against such criticisms when he notes:

> To me the worlds were juxtaposed and mutually exclusive. One [the Tulsi world] gradually contracted. It had to; it fed only on memories and its completeness was only apparent. . . . I can speak only out of my own experience. The family life I have been describing began to dissolve when I was six or seven; when I was fourteen it had ceased to exist.
>
> (pt. 1, ch. 1)

That was in 1946, and the Tulsi family's dissolution in the novel occurs in the early 1940's. The survivors are left with a possibility of the freedom toward which Mr. Biswas, the fumbling creator, had spent his life groping. It is with such possibilities in a wider world of "independence" and its equivocal liberties that Naipaul has since chiefly concerned himself.

Before pursuing this chief concern, it seems best for the sake of following Naipaul's development as closely as possible to turn aside—as in a way he was doing when he wrote the book during his Indian year in 1962—to glance at *Mr Stone and the Knights Companion* (1963), his next novel after *Mr Biswas.*

At first thought, the only one of Naipaul's novels with a completely English scene and English characters seems something of a sport. In fact there is a clear continuity in both characterization and theme; the London setting and idiom are closely observed and faithfully rendered, but purely as a means of obtaining satirical effects or for the sake of grotesque exaggeration, in such elements as the part played by the next-door cat in Mr. Stone's fantasies of the hostility of his suburban environment. This is no inward study of uniquely English life. It is rather as if Naipaul were testing his capacity for the sheer expertise needed to graft some of his main concerns convincingly upon a new, alien context. Mr. Stone's solitary, eccentric obsessions, his fantasies of transcendence, his contempt and repulsion for the social conformists (the Monster, the Male) who hem him in, his desire to proclaim his existence before it is too late through some overmastering creative act are strongly reminiscent of Mr. Biswas. His brainchild, the Knights Companion (by analogy with orders like K.C.B., Knight Commander of the Bath), is a scheme whereby retired employees of his company, Excal (Excalibur), are organized into a chivalric band who revive the comradely spirit by seeking out their old fellow-workers and doing their bit to lighten the lot of those whom a materialistic society has discarded. This scheme is akin to Mr. Biswas' exploits as the Scarlet Pimpernel, another attempt to ameliorate the harshness of ordinary life by transforming it into the stuff of myth that softens reality or keeps it at bay. There is, however, an extra dimension in the degree to which the protagonist's critical consciousness is capable of coping with the reverses reality deals him; while Mr. Biswas must die, Mr. Stone becomes reconciled to his anti-vision that "all that was not flesh was of no importance to man. All that mattered was man's own frailty and corruptibility. The order of the universe, to which he had sought to ally himself, was not his order." While he sees creation as futile, destruction as the only way to self-assertion, Mr. Stone can turn away in resignation to accept his littleness finally—too much wisdom, too late. This somber comedy of English suburbia written, significantly, in far Srinagar is an impressionistic *tour de force,* so swift and clean in narration that we hardly miss the deeper social placing of these lives a comparable English novelist, such as Thomas Hinde, might have given. The novel's limits are carefully observed and work, positively, to paint the universal nature of the character and the mind portrayed.

BACKGROUNDS

[Travel] broadened my world view; it showed me a changing world and took me out of my colonial shell; it became the substitute for the mature social experience—the deepening knowledge of a society—which my background and the nature of my life denied me

(Foreword, *Finding the Centre*)

THE novels of two Misters were punctuated by Naipaul's first travelogue, *The Middle Passage* (1962), in which he looks critically at contemporary Trinidad and other small West Indian countries still colonized or newly independent. After *Mr Stone* there came in 1964 *An Area of Darkness,* Naipaul's controversial view of modern India and reflections upon the East Indian attachment to Mother India; it goes behind the romantic figment, on which such "exiles" as the Tulsis had leaned, to its source. In 1967 there followed, aptly, a novel of contemporary political history, *The Mimic Men,* in which Naipaul was at last able to express in fictional form his somber conviction of the tragic futility of the politics of independence. This conviction also gives a controlling viewpoint to *The Loss of El Dorado* (1969), subtitled "A History," which has in its depiction of character and action in the early colonization of Trinidad a novelistic intensity. I will make my comments on the three nonfictional works a form of preface to discussions of *The Mimic Men* and *In a Free State* (1971).

In his foreword to *The Middle Passage* Naipaul thanks the prime minister of newly independent Trinidad and Tobago, Dr. Eric Williams, for suggesting that he write "a non-fiction book about the Caribbean," and the government for contributing financially to his research for it. There is a piquant irony here: as Naipaul put it, the book "sells nothing." Quite the reverse: it is consistent throughout with its title and first part, which imply that the "Middle Passage"—the atrocious journey that brought millions of black slaves from Africa to the New World—has never ended. It continues in mass emigration to the Old World and in the irredeemably slavish mentality of the West Indian, "the traveller who never arrives." The peoples Naipaul observes enjoy only a false emancipation or independence; James Anthony Froude's summing up in 1887 (quoted as the epigraph) holds good today: "There are no people there in the true sense of the word, with a character and a purpose of their own." Since Froude was among those British historians whose poor opinion of the future of the West Indies Dr. Williams has devoted his life to proving mistaken, and since Naipaul, an Indian, is criticizing predominantly black societies, it is not surprising that *The Middle Passage* aroused intense dislike and opposition.

Among its critics was the Barbadian novelist George Lamming, who had enthusiastically welcomed Dr. Williams' P.N.M. majority government in 1956; he found that Naipaul failed to understand the attitudes of West Indian blacks. Naipaul may or may not have understood, but it is clear that he does not sympathize with either black or Indian attitudes. Searching for balance and "order," of which "racial coexistence" must be a part, he is repelled by divisive attitudes: these may be equally the widespread black "African personality" cult and the extremist Ras Tafarians of Jamaica, or the roundly condemned Trinidad Indian community, "peasant-minded, money-minded . . . spiritually static because cut off from its roots"; the Trinidad Indian is "the complete colonial, even more philistine than the white." If there is bias, it is of the "plague on both your houses" variety. Naipaul's distaste for the "immigrant-type West Indian" and their "jabbering" leader opens the narrative with a pungent distaste that suggests anti-black prejudice, but this is later set off by the satirical portraiture of Indians such as the Ramkerrysinghs. However, it remains odd that the reforming aims of Dr. Williams and his party receive no mention, and we can only speculate as to why: did Naipaul look less closely than he might have done at what had happened during the ten years since he left Trinidad because his negative estimate of its people's potentialities was fixed and unshakable?[3] How could he have looked with a fresh, clear eye at the place he had returned to, he says, with "fear"?

One could debate the "facts" endlessly and still reach no objective judgment; that Naipaul's criticisms are echoed by one of Dr. Williams' chief black opponents, C. L. R. James, proves that the side one takes is not determined simply by race. In this personal narrative, there is without doubt an occasional stridency of tone, a note of anger and disgust that Naipaul's fiction avoids. The traveler is immersed, willy-nilly, in the disorder of life, the crowded boat, the plane, the cramped hotel, the steel bands (black, unfortunately), the futile small talk. His own untidy emotions will out; he is less the cool ironist, more the impulsive man of feeling. The careful novelist would not have risked the offensive simile in this statement: "Like monkeys pleading for evolution, each claiming to be whiter than the other, Indians and Negroes appeal to the unacknowledged white audience." Pity and anger are the moods of *The Middle Passage,* and no one who has seen, for example, the "two worlds" of Jamaica, with its ostentatious North Shore tourist hotels and such monstrous anachronisms as Frenchman's Cove sealed off from the choking slums of Kingston, can feel that Naipaul voices a merely personal disgust. His art captures the blatant contrasts: the description of the Kingston slum settlements backed by the mocking green hills—"against such a view lay a dead mule, its teeth bared, its belly swollen and taut. It had been there for two days, a broomstick had been playfully stuck in its anus"—is set off sharply against the unreality of the "Finale at Frenchman's Cove." The somber truth beneath is caught in such vignettes as this final paragraph on the old Indian at Coronie:

> A derelict man in a derelict land; a man discovering himself, with surprise and resignation, lost in a landscape which had never ceased to be unreal because the scene of an enforced and always temporary residence; the slaves kidnapped from one continent and abandoned on the unprofitable plantations of another, from which there could never more be escape . . . it held the full desolation of those who have made the middle passage.

A sense of history blends here, as elsewhere in the book, with strong feeling for the plight of one caught up in the wasteful, untidy movement of history. No cosmetic myths or fantasies will gloss over this (Naipaul has, misleadingly, been compared to Lawrence as a travel writer, but Lawrence might have wished to find vitality in the primitive Amerindians; Naipaul finds only "defeat and purposelessness" in their passivity): without stability, continuity, and order, there can be no civilization, and *The Middle Passage* gives scant hope of these conditions evolving in the Caribbean. To keep a proper perspective, it should be remembered that "in 1960 [Naipaul] was a colonial, travelling to far-off places that were still colonies, in a world still more or less ruled by colonial ideas" (Foreword, *Finding the Centre*).

If Naipaul's "derelict man" ever felt tragically bereft of the old, rooted civilization of the India he had left, as Naipaul's maternal grandfather had done, to come as an indentured laborer to the West Indies, he might have been disillusioned by *An Area of Darkness* (1964), Naipaul's report on his unsentimental journey in 1962 to the land of his ancestors. The "derelict man" was a lifelong alien; so, too, were Naipaul's forefathers—sentimentally attached to the old world, incapable of forming a new—yet the new was forming in spite of their "world which had lengthened out, its energy of inertia steadily weakening, from the featureless area of darkness which was India." "Featureless" it remains on close inspection: a country that lies to itself, that denies its squalor and inhumanity, in life and in art; which, utmost disenchantment, not only lacks the whole identity the innocent imagination had conferred on it, but is no less than Trinidad distorted by the "alien presence" of the so

[3]Compare Eric Williams, *British Historians and the West Indies* (1964), and its expressed faith in the development of "a new sense of values" in the independent West Indies. Perhaps out of courtesy Naipaul refrained from explicit reference to the prime minister. However, in a much later interview he derides "the silliness of political life there. . . . People saw that primitive society as Athens" (*Times Literary Supplement,* 30 July 1971). It was Williams who introduced the Athenian parallel (see his account of his lectures to large crowds in what he dubs the "University of Woodford Square" in Port of Spain, "a centre of university education for the masses, of political analysis, and of training in self-government for parallels of which we must go back to the city state of ancient Athens" (*Inward Hunger: The Education of a Prime Minister,* 1969, p. 133). However, in his next book, Dr. Williams concedes: "V. S. Naipaul's description of West Indians as 'mimic men' is harsh but true" (*From Columbus to Castro,* 1970, p. 502).

recently dominant English into "mimicry." Naipaul's critique of this Indian falseness is confessedly personal, colored often by temperamental aversion. Before the grinding poverty he refuses to get away with easy "compassion and pity," but confesses rather to "fear"—or "perhaps in the end it was fatigue that overcame me." His "horror of the unclean" disturbed his response to a degree some readers—some Indians especially—find unbalanced, but "balance" is easily purchased through conditioning oneself not to see what E. M. Forster, an earlier anxious passenger to India, called "unthinkable." Yet Naipaul's position was, and is, equivocal: "I was not English or Indian; I was denied the victories of both." So, no "gentle satire" upon the manners of the Indian mimic men will serve to mask awareness of the faceless, struggling mass, nor will a vogueish escape into Indian "spirituality." At the very least—a revealing aside —"it [Indian spirituality] is not a good qualification for the writing or reading of novels."

Although Naipaul has said he began writing a novel of India but abandoned it, *An Area of Darkness* is in some respects novelistic. The author plays the engaged narrator, provides setting, commentary, and interpretation, but allows character and action sufficient play to permit a many-sided impression of his subject to emerge. There is his own attachment to some persons, from the pathetic, displaced Ramon to the portrait of Aziz that dominates the third of the book set in Kashmir—a portrait as puzzled a testimony to an elusive personality as Forster's of *his* Aziz (in *A Passage to India*). This is contrasted with Naipaul's detachment from others, which enables him to place them as characters in a complex mosaic—Ramnath "the steno," the empty, mimicking Mrs. Mahindra, Rafiq, and Laramie the Sikh. It is only in them that the abstraction "India" acquires life: "To know Indians was to take a delight in people as people; every encounter was an adventure. I did not want India to sink." Yet, there is a continual seesaw between emotion and idea, will and fact; the author's final act, on his ultimate pilgrimage to the village of his ancestors, is one of irritable, weary rejection. The Indian lesson of "acceptance" has not been learned when he leaves for the West, but there too is futility, "a culture whose point . . . appeared to be homemaking," padded emptiness. India is not the sole area of darkness: any reader who comes to that conclusion has missed the author's wider viewpoint. Its last pages point forward to *The Mimic Men,* its structure to *In a Free State.*

However, before we turn to those novels something (too little) should be said of Naipaul's third and major nonfiction work, *The Loss of El Dorado.* Written between 1966 and 1968, when it was published in 1969 it added a thoroughly researched exploration of two major episodes in the colonial beginnings of Trinidad, a dark ground-note to the more contemporary and personal observations of the two travelogues. While historically disciplined, its fictional effects—ironies of character and circumstance, cross motives, commonplace error, and dubious achievement—lend convincing humanity to Elizabethan buccaneers, Spanish conquistadores, eighteenth-century slavedrivers, and romantic revolutionaries. No reader coming to this from Naipaul's earlier works will be surprised that the legend of "the complete, unviolated world" of El Dorado, the mythical Golden City in Guyana, should have seized his imagination; but he brings a more skeptical mind to the myth than those earlier seekers after an earthly paradise, hardly expecting to find in it a trace of the wholeness and integrity our muddled lives seem to have lost. Thus, his study of Ralegh's motives and behavior explores the complex relationship of the dream and the act and turns, like the characterization of Singh in *The Mimic Men,* into an analysis of a man's unfitness for power. Two centuries later on the Spanish side Miranda offers an ideal counterpoint and historical continuity, if not purpose. It is such men as they, and Fullarton, the flawed humanitarian—rather than the more prosaic Pictons, the carriers of romantic delusions—who made the New World one of "blood, fraud, and make-believe." Their high-minded responsibility for the innumerable atrocities against the weaker aboriginal or slave peoples created a cast of minor villains, acting out of similar delusions, fear, or sheer selfishness. Naipaul's dispassionate narrative of the humdrum, daily atrocities committed by those in petty authority, sanctioned by travesties of Christian righteousness, is a masterpiece of restrained indignation. Nor is there any neat reaction from such things into a welcoming endorsement of the new nineteenth-century myths of freedom; of the breakup of "free" Venezuela into factions Naipaul notes that Spain, though weak, had provided "however remotely, a code and a reference that the colonial society by itself was incapable of generating. Without such a reference, obedience, the association of consent, was no longer possible." This severely qualified analysis goes far beyond reactionary conservatism or nostalgia for empire and suggests the controlling viewpoint behind the novels to come. The closing sentence of the book—"On both sides of the Gulf the Spanish Empire, after three hundred years, had inheritors"—points even further forward to present-day Venezuela, Argentina, or Uruguay, and the newly independent territories represented by the Isabella of *The Mimic Men.* The ironies preclude a harking back to old solutions: "In 1807 one of the objections from Trinidad to the abolition of the British slave trade was that it was unfair to the Africans, who would now not only be denied civilizing contacts but would also be transported in cruel conditions in foreign ships. The argument, with its remote reference to several ideals, is recognizably English" (pp. 316–317). *The Loss of El Dorado* is a serious retrieval of history for use. It does not merely provide fictional "color" for the period, but recreates it in such a way that it helps us to understand the present and to see why there is no smooth way forward. When all the "fairy tales" have dissolved, independence has still to be created.[4]

THE MIMIC MEN

We pretended to be real, to be learning, to be preparing ourselves for life, we mimic men of the New World, one unknown corner of it, with all its reminders of the corruption that came so quickly to the new.

(pt. 2, ch. 4)

EARLIER I referred to *The Mimic Men* (1967) as tragic. I have attempted to sketch the context that defines and limits the nature of its tragedy. It is one neither of great action nor of noble character, centered upon a great, flawed protagonist and his fall. (As Naipaul notes in *The Middle Passage,* "We lived in a society which denied itself heroes.") The downfall of "Ralph" Singh is, rather, an inverted tragedy, a case history with all the squalid littleness of the contemporary seen as it is. The protagonist's illusions remain illusions; there is no place for the Homeric or Sophoclean elevation of the hero by sheer force of mythical transformation (like the sensitive boy, Hok, escaping into Charles Kingsley's *The Heroes,* we should turn elsewhere for such effects). *The Mimic Men* grows naturally from numerous insights and suggestions that are scattered throughout the earlier writing. No more than the dreaming inhabitants of Miguel Street can the gifted individual lift himself by sheer intellect and application clear of a messy society into a controlling eminence. From the wholly comic depiction of the Oxonian Indarsingh in *The Mystic Masseur* these reservations darken through the serious, skeptical studies of actual political life in the Caribbean, past and present, and in the false freedom of India and Africa: in all these situations "mimicry" is a dominant characteristic. There is no true freedom of either self or society; "the inheritors" succeed to a vacuum from which power, and certain imperial modes, have been withdrawn as abruptly as they were imposed.

With *The Mimic Men* Naipaul turns to the confessional narrative method favored by so many modern writers; he continues its use in two parts of *In a Free State* and in *A Bend in the River.* Singh, the failed politician and visionary, is his protagonist so far best suited to this mode. Singh has a many-sided mind, a capacity for self-observation and self-judgment that far surpasses that of his forerunners in Naipaul's West Indian novels, and Singh is more solidly established as a "life" than Mr. Stone, who runs in some ways a similar course of disillusion. A clear pattern of ideas soon becomes apparent to the reader familiar with Naipaul's work, who sees that many of Singh's attitudes and perceptions parallel his creator's. They share a sense of the formlessness of their society, a deep skepticism about its capacity to found a vital culture, a desire for order and form; at many points Singh obviously speaks for the author as he has been quoted elsewhere in this essay: "the restlessness, the deep disorder, [brought on by] . . . the great explorations, the overthrow in three continents of established social organizations, the unnatural bringing together of peoples . . ."; "To be born on an island like Isabella, an obscure New World transplantation, second-hand and barbarous, was to be born to disorder"; the "whole new mythology, dark and alien [of Black Power]." Such analyses and reactions, Singh's repeated application of Naipaul's twin

[4]For a more hopeful view and alternative interpretation of the El Dorado motif by Wilson Harris, see Hena Maes-Jelinek's "The Myth of El Dorado in the Caribbean Novel" (see bibliography).

ideas of "self-cherishing" and "self-violation" to behavior—most blatantly, his expressed "wish to avoid satire; I will leave out the stories of illiteracy and social innocence" (as if *he* had already written *The Suffrage of Elvira*)—are symptomatic of the author's imaginative closeness to a character caught between the dream and the action.

Yet we do not and should not read the novel as if Ralph Singh were Naipaul's mouthpiece. From its intimate opening, with the revealing reflection on the narrator's affinity for the element of snow, the agile mind flitting back and forth between present and past, describing his fellow-actors in the life drama with a raconteur's relish, we are in the company of a complex and interesting mind seeking self-understanding. This does not come easily to one now surprisingly alone and obscure, whose life until his fall had followed the path of leadership, of mastery, as a blind obsession, as if he could live out his dream undefiled in the real world of action. We realize gradually, with him, that self and community collaborate in a manner hardly separable into distinct strands, to make up his involuntary tragedy. His self-analysis teases at the mystery of leadership: the leader feels a call, a sense of "being marked," tracked by a "celestial camera"; but most revealing in Singh's case is the recurrent dream image of himself as the Central Asian horseman on the snow-stark steppe. This image is linked with his growing social sense in childhood and youth of himself on the unimportant island of Isabella as "the picturesque Asiatic": it is both a romantic form of the exceptional individual's desire to soar above "ordinariness" and also akin to the East Indian's harking back to the unknown, idealized India of *An Area of Darkness.* Singh's observations of others, such as Cecil's petulant millionaire father, help to distill possibilities of action—even in Isabella—out of the dream: "A man was only what he saw of himself in others, and an intimation came to me of chieftainship in that island." This is the fatal step, from dream to delusion.

As Singh unravels the pattern, he gradually achieves insight; the final part begins, "I question now whether the personality is manufactured by the vision of others. The personality hangs together. It is one and indivisible." This realization strikingly echoes Sammy Mountjoy's conclusions in William Golding's *Free Fall* (1960), whose confessional mode and categorical self-analysis are much akin to Naipaul's. With this perception, dream and act can be viewed dispassionately, as with the artist's mastering eye: the incidents of violence in part three, foreshadowed by Singh's beating at the hands of Dalip and Cecil earlier, the encounters with the pitiable prostitute, and lastly the inevitable bloody riot on Isabella—history entering fiction as a re-creation of the Black Power riots in British Guiana in 1964—precipitate (far more sharply than Mr. Stone's similar vision) the lesson of acceptance of a corrupt world of "vulnerable flesh." Yet the vision, projected as the memory of a photograph of the passive suffering of the Australian soldier "about to be beheaded," may be "cruel or fraudulent" to the living that suffer. Sitting at the center of the closed circle his narrative has described, Singh has become akin to the artist whose "word" balances the antinomies of being in the realm of possibilities; he has become "real," thus far, but the "order" he has glimpsed can only be brought to birth, if at all, by those who can use his dear-bought wisdom. They must first have overcome, it seems, Conrad's nihilistic perception in *Nostromo* (1904), the pioneering novel of an incomplete society in the New World, that "something inherent in the necessities of successful action . . . carried with it the moral degradation of the idea."[5] Some such skeptical view, implicit throughout Naipaul's work, seems to have governed the conception of *The Mimic Men* and determined its static, airless quality—appropriate to a brooding personal narrative of failure, but at the same time suggesting that this novelist is developing a fiction of diminishing possibilities. The wearying "dialogue of the mind with itself," which Matthew Arnold diagnosed as peculiarly "modern," can stifle creation.

IN A FREE STATE

After *The Mimic Men,* Naipaul's novels have appeared at four-year intervals, whereas only four years were needed for the publication of his first four works of fiction. (*A Flag on the Island* does not really violate this pattern, since all but the title piece belong to the years before *Mr Stone.*) If Naipaul wrote fiction exclusively, we might conclude

[5] *Nostromo,* part 2, chapter 2, quoted by Naipaul in his sympathetic appraisal "Conrad's Darkness," *New York Review of Books,* 17 October 1974, reprinted in *The Return of Eva Perón* (1980).

that he is slowing down, as many writers do after they have used their store of early experience. While this seems partly true, what in fact has happened is that his developing political and social concerns have led to the diverse forms of writing discussed earlier, several longer pieces of reportage such as "The Election in Ajmer" (included in *The Overcrowded Barracoon*), and a decreasing use of purely fictional outlets. Yet without these broadening concerns his fiction of the past fifteen years (since 1971) could not have been written. *In a Free State* (1971) seems to mark the climax of one important stage in his fiction, and in fact shortly after its publication Naipaul described it, in "Without a Place," as "a rather final statement" of themes he had already touched upon often.

Some have described *In a Free State* as a novel, others as a collection of short stories bound by a common theme. Only in the loosest sense can it be termed a novel, in that the parts are evidently so disposed as to form a unity; in the more conventional sense, the title story is a novella with characters and action much more fully developed than in the shorter autobiographical narratives that accompany it. Together, enclosed by the author's prologue and epilogue (a pattern continued from the travel books), the whole forms a unity with a clear, informing design that few story collections have (James Joyce's *Dubliners,* with its intended exposure of Irish paralysis, is comparable). The title also covers the whole, with multiple meanings. Each protagonist, including the seeing and, in the epilogue, even acting witness of the writer-narrator, enjoys an ambiguous freedom—he is free in that he is unattached to country, culture, or society, yet this freedom seems his heaviest burden, and free acquires the senses of "loose," "lost," "drifting." Each protagonist lives or moves in a political entity that passes for a free state, yet whether it be London, Washington, or Cairo, it is a place where political and individual freedoms diverge. Further, while there are several protagonists with separate experiences, it is possible to see them all as one: a universal wanderer inhabiting differing shades of skin and caste, occurring here and there yet essentially identical. All, including the author, are embarked upon a "middle passage" without destination.

Looking back, we can see how the universal statement slowly grew out of Naipaul's increasing perceptions of the wider world behind Trinidad. Santosh ("One Out of Many") makes a contemporary form of "middle passage" and ends little better off (except materially) than the "derelict man" at Coronie. He finds himself adrift in Washington, seen as the capital of the world; to him it means nothing, connects with nothing: his narrow viewpoint is carefully preserved, he is a deprived man, however imperfect the culture he left. "One Out of Many" is a bleak confession of alienation from self and life, the roots that nourished him even in "an area of darkness." The second displaced Indian, from the West Indies ("Tell Me Who to Kill"), has innumerable forerunners in the emigrants to England of *The Middle Passage,* but he most strongly recalls the pathetic Ramon in part I of *An Area of Darkness;* yet his is a desperate, dangerous pathos that Naipaul leaves with supreme restraint to our imagination, on the brink of violence. The title story, "In a Free State," distills the ample East African material Hughes acquired during his year as writer-in-residence at Makerere University in Kampala, the capital of Uganda (1965–1966). The political parallels are very clear: the struggle between the followers of King and President, the moves against the Asian community. For the ill-matched pair in the story we need hardly search for analogues. Naipaul's portrayal of Sandra in *The Mimic Men* had revealed an acute insight into that peculiarly English blend of liberal openness and master racism. The disconcerting, insidious way in which such open and closed minds betray themselves is perfectly caught in the subtle interplay of opinions in the dialogue of Linda and Bobby; their tolerance and intolerance are alike empty, the mouthings of futile aliens—expatriate, white slaves to their own cupidity. They, who see themselves as having chosen freedom, nonattachment to their origins, find support only in shabby snobberies and prejudice: no less than the semiliterate Indian of "Tell Me Who to Kill," their lives "spoil" (are spoiled).

Without place, purpose, or belief, the characters of *In a Free State* agitate in a void. They are incapable of positive action. Violence might bring relief, probably will one day, to the West Indian. Violence is done to Bobby, but it is casual, almost absent-minded, no less meaningless than the baiting of the tramp in the prologue. The violence within and between him and Linda is the inner truth beneath their veneer of civilization, and far more significant. A pervasive violence, as a sinister undertone, seems to exert an almost bursting pressure against the surface of every episode: the city burns "for four days" in the background of Santosh's personal anguish; the London vandals feed the Indian's hatred in "Tell Me Who to Kill"; in "In a Free State" the violent incident is trivial compared to the immanent violence throughout. It is a violence that cannot, it seems, be resisted; it will out. In the epilogue, though the "I" seizes the camel-whip from the Egyptian's hand, it is a gesture that no one really understands; the children, the victims, "were puzzled . . . I felt exposed, futile." Yet it is something. The chastened truth of this ending, and the unusually restrained (for these days) treatment of violence compel respect.[6] This is indeed fiction that, in Conrad's words, is (as it should be) "human history." And we read it aware, in each case, of the contemporary history pressing upon these lives: the *hubshi* ("Abyssinian": black) riots in Washington, the whites baiting immigrants in London, the tribal conflicts in Uganda and, finally, the brief desert conflict in 1967 in which the miserable Egyptian soldiers were routed. This is the final note, canceling the writer's romantic desire, realistically checked with a stern sense of the present, for what he feels is not only lost but (like El Dorado) may never have been:

> Perhaps that had been the only pure time, at the beginning, when the ancient artist, knowing no other land, had learned to look at his own and had seen it as complete. But it was hard, travelling back to Cairo, looking with my stranger's eye at the fields and the people who worked in them, the dusty towns, the agitated peasant crowds at railway stations, it was hard to believe that there had been such innocence. Perhaps that vision of the land, in which the Nile was only water, a blue-green chevron, had always been a fabrication, a cause for yearning, something for the tomb.

GUERRILLAS

THE title of *Guerrillas* may arouse expectation that Naipaul attempted a fictional treatment of such South American guerrilla movements as those in Argentina or Uruguay, of which he has already given a journalist's account. In fact, he returns for setting to an (unnamed) Caribbean island resembling both Jamaica and Trinidad—post-colonial but economically dominated by the United States;[7] the title is a metaphor.

"When everybody wants to fight there's nothing to fight for. Everybody wants to fight his own little war, everybody is a guerrilla." These words, placed as epigraph to the novel, are spoken by "James Ahmed (Haji)," a *hakwai* Chinee named Jimmy Leung—half-black, half-Chinese—founder of a People's Commune set up to offer an alternative return to the land for the island's unwanted ones. Obviously Ahmed's assumed name and title ironically imitate the Black Muslims' mimicry, doubly so since, as a half-caste, he can claim no authentic identity. (It is clear from a reading of "Michael X and the Black Power Killings in Trinidad" in *The Return of Eva Perón* [1980], that Michael de Freitas, alias Michael X, the mulatto Caribbean Black Power leader who was hanged for murder in 1975, supplied Naipaul with a substantial prototype.) Ahmed's personal war is an attempt to become complete, a true hero, his army a handful of offscourings from the slums; while the ramshackle commune is a peaceful protest, it is an anachronism doomed from the outset to fall prey to unappeasable violence. Some see it as a cover for guerrilla activity. At first Jimmy Ahmed is aided by Peter Roche, a white South African who had come to the island via England after suffering imprisonment and torture for espionage against the apartheid regime; but Ahmed distrusts him because Roche works for one of the old imperialist firms that have hypocritically discovered that black is beautiful. The trio of central characters is completed by Jane, Roche's mistress, in Jimmy's eyes one of "those liberals who come flashing their milk white thighs and think they're contributing to the cause." Jimmy has fled from her kind in England, where (like Michael X) he had been involved in a rape case, but still they pursue him, fleeing from the disintegrating old country, seeking a new world. It is this search, or desperate throw, that gives this deeply distrustful and antagonistic trio a common motive.

Early in *Guerrillas,* Naipaul's relentless pen paints the desolation of the unrestful country in which his characters chase their chimera: the derelict, exhausted plantations where Jimmy sets up his com-

[6]Compare the "documentary" exploitation of violence in contemporary fiction and film, and Naipaul's comment on this in "Violence in Art," *Twentieth Century,* Winter 1964–1965.

[7]Represented by Amal: American Aluminium (compare Alcan, the Canadian company in Jamaica).

mune, the frenetic city, the bauxite loading station and burning rubbish dump with their pervasive haze; while above the plain lifts the Ridge, where Jane and Roche, part of a jittery, insecure elite, look out from the hollow paradise of their privileged suburbs. Although the island is, like the Trinidad of *The Middle Passage* and the Isabella of *The Mimic Men,* "a place that had produced no great men," there is neither contempt nor condescension in Naipaul's new portrayal of a volatile, inchoate Caribbean society: we are always mindful that the England fled from will not be saved by its past, and that no larger "world vision" will offer deliverance.

We fancy our simplifying visions can be incarnated in beings, "leaders" less vulnerable than ourselves: they appear independent, and we lean upon them while their strength lasts. Naipaul delineates a fine-drawn web of interdependence spun by collective, tremulous need. More complex and many-sided than the Linda of *In a Free State,* Jane plays a major part as vehicle and victim of this need. She, the "dragon-woman," carries a false self-possession of which she has failed to unburden herself upon many lovers, the latest being Roche the "doer" and sufferer, and she now seeks "reality" by giving herself to Jimmy Leung, alias James Ahmed, the seemingly true prophet. Yet Jimmy is also seeking himself; caught between fantasy and action, his bruises of race and color unsalved, he cannot even master the needs of his protégés from the slums.

Naipaul's narrative moves smoothly through the tense action of a few days of crisis in this island of crises and between the viewpoints and experiences of the three main characters, yielding a complex understanding of their failures to resolve the dichotomies of flesh and spirit in a world that renders private sanities, if not impossible, irrelevant. While Roche is not the author's mouthpiece, he seems close in his perceptions of the lesser participants in the action to Naipaul's profound awareness of human limitation and matured compassion for those who struggle to survive in the interstices of an amoral, acquisitive society; Roche reflects in terms echoed later by Naipaul's authorial voice: "Fragile, fragile, this world, requiring endless tolerance, endless forbearance." Yet compassion is an impotent virtue if divorced from action, a lesson forced at last upon Roche who—having previously suffered—has attempted to travel lightly. For him there is life left to mend, but for others their acts of self-violation have precipitated irremediable violence.

As in *In a Free State* the violent end seems to have been sought by those who have flirted riskily with "reality"; it is at once the human need and fear, the primordial curse and the spasmodic, necessary release. It is only incidental that black slays white, and a stale hatred is played out yet again, for "every country is that kind of country"; there today, anywhere tomorrow. As Jimmy Leung/Ahmed knows, in a disordered world, "everyone is a guerrilla."

Although *Guerrillas* develops already familiar themes, our apprehension of them is deepened by the multiplicity of viewpoints and lives presented. After the claustrophic and straitened characterization and atmosphere of *In a Free State,* we move into an amply peopled society masterfully evoked by one who commands it as his own. Readers who may have respected and applauded Naipaul's abstention from riding the popular bandwagon of sex and violence—in "London" (1958) he said, "I cannot write sex"—will find it hard to digest one of the harshest scenes of sexual violation in modern literature. However, it is not gratuitous, and elsewhere fleeting intimations of love starved of fruition lend an unaccustomed tenderness to Naipaul's writing. While he is Conrad's heir as a political novelist, in his treatment of personal relations such intimations touch the chastened note characteristic of Hardy, whose *The Woodlanders* Naipaul's doomed heroine takes to read in bed on the night before her murder. We do not know what it meant to her, but its presence further suggests Naipaul's felt kinship with one who never shirked the bleak truth that, much as we may desire otherwise, we either love too little or too much to make ourselves and the earth anew. Yet he does not carry us into Hardy's realm of individual tragedy, of "the worthy encompassed by the inevitable." In Naipaul's uncompromisingly dark fictional world, what there is of worth seems destined to throw only a feeble and doubtful light.

A BEND IN THE RIVER

WITH *A Bend in the River* Naipaul's fiction occupies one of "the Conradian dark places of the earth" (see "Conrad's Darkness" in *The Return of Eva Perón*). It was first published dust-jacketed with an illustration of a riverboat tracing its lonely course between banks of impenetrable darkness toward a smoldering sunset. At once one thinks of *The Heart of Darkness,* and in reading, numerous parallels suggest themselves. In both stories we are plunged into interior Africa, a region of physical and symbolic darkness, the river the only escape route to the whited sepulchers of the West (Conrad's Brussels or London: Naipaul's London); in both the narrator is an observing outsider, and though Naipaul's Salim is a displaced East African Indian, much unlike Conrad's cultured English sea captain, his narrative like Marlow's records the insufficiency of Western ideas and structures.

We know Conrad was exposing, without naming it, Leopold's Belgian Congo. Naipaul's unnamed setting is also Central African, with a Belgian colonial past, a town crowded close to a broad river, backed by "the undifferentiated bush" with its ancestral villages as remote as ever in distance and time. It is Zaire, and the novel incorporates numerous details and observations from Naipaul's 1975 essay, "A New King for the Congo: Mobutu and the Nihilism of Africa" (reprinted in *The Return of Eva Perón*). The Big Man—a typical African phrase for a political leader—an opportunistic Western-oriented despot, exploits his people's ignorance and superstition, crossing Catholic madonna worship with that of the African Earth Mother to found a cult whose central figure is his own mother. Behind such incongruously blended images and the Maoist maxims he prints for mass consumption, he is as remote and faceless as Orwell's Big Brother.

The narrator, Salim, comes to the town to begin a "new life"—or, as a trading Indian, renew an old one—anticipating the imminent collapse of his east-coast Indian community (this recalls Tanzania and Zanzibar). He opens his monologue, "The World is what it is; men who are nothing, who allow themselves to become nothing, have no place in it." Only those who can accommodate themselves to a world in flux can survive, as we later find Salim's transplanted uncle and mentor doing in London's Gloucester Road. Salim, too, will wash up there in the end, surviving. Meanwhile, he tells of his displacement, his futile and irrelevant new life in the Big Man's country; it is the Biswasian agony again, but worse: "I will inherit no house, and no house that I build will now pass to my children. That way of life has gone." Its universal, symptomatic significance is explained by his university-educated, cosmopolitan friend Indar:

> We have to learn to trample on the past. . . . It shouldn't be a cause for tears, because it isn't just true for you and me. There may be some parts of the world—dead countries, or secure and by-passed ones—where men can cherish the past and think of passing on furniture and china to their heirs. Men can do that perhaps in Sweden or Canada. Some peasant department of France full of half-wits in châteaux; some crumbling Indian palace-city, or some dead colonial town in a hopeless South American country. Everywhere else men are in movement, the world is in movement, and the past can only cause pain.
>
> (ch. 9)

This passage defines Naipaul's subject and world view in this and all his work since *The Mimic Men.* It reiterates the viewpoint of "Conrad's Darkness" and is there extended to encompass the Africans' dilemma, seeking in the aftermath of colonialism authenticity in ancestral history: "The past has vanished. Facts in a book cannot by themselves give people a sense of history."[8]

A potent interest stems from Naipaul's subtle characterization of the young Ferdinand, the "new man of Africa"; he is torn between his village and ancestral background, and Western notions of social order and justice his intensive lycée education has fed him beyond all assimilation or use in mimicry of a Western city that his own enraged, betrayed people will again, as after the colonizers' flight, tear down upon their heads. Naipaul portrays the traumatic disorder that rules many an African's life with a sympathy of which *In a Free State* gave little evidence. Although Ferdinand and his "bush" mother Zabeth are the vital achievements in characterization, they remain externally presented; they and what they mean are nevertheless a challenge to African novelists to come.

Salim himself is an unconvincing, fractured protagonist: though he is the eternal Indian shopkeeper (a type hardly loved in Africa), ill-educated, untraveled, almost a negative being, presented as consciously "less complicated" than the sophisticated Indar, he is influenced by the latter and attains a remarkable pitch of understanding. His growth in self-understanding can be defended, but his articulacy and range of insight into events, persons, and motives—into the "liberal" pretensions of today's expatriate civilizers or the complexities of the new multiracial London—constantly distract

[8]In *The Return of Eva Perón*; see also "The Crocodiles of Yamoussokro" in *Finding the Centre.*

with inflections of his creator's voice. Africa is foil to Salim's modest growth in selfhood, as it was for Marlow; yet he seems, beside the potentially vital action and motive, which is African, a tangential, willed creation, less authentic as both actor and interpreter of action than Singh in *The Mimic Men.* Naipaul's comment, in "Conrad's Darkness," on the artistic limitations of *The Heart of Darkness* can be applied to *A Bend in the River:* it "breaks into two. There is the reportage about the Congo. . . . And there is the fiction," in which "the idea, deliberately worked out, remains an applied idea."

FURTHER JOURNEYS

Of the pieces collected in *The Return of Eva Perón* Naipaul comments in an author's note: "They bridged a creative gap: from the end of 1970 to the end of 1973 no novel offered itself to me." I have already linked the three pieces other than the title essay with my discussions of *Guerrillas* and *A Bend in the River.* I shall consider here two journeys that have not given birth to new fiction, *India: A Wounded Civilization* (1977) and *Among the Believers* (1981).

In *An Area of Darkness* Naipaul was exploring his ancestral land; he lived there, in various places, for a year and, though he learned "to take a delight in people as people," left "content to be a colonial," repelled finally by the impenetrable—and impervious—darkness. Nevertheless, India revisited (in 1975) still matters to him, and on the last page of *India: A Wounded Civilization* he affirms "there is the possibility of a true new beginning, of an emergence in India of mind, after the long spiritual night." But the stress throughout has been upon the "night," the persisting darkness, nor is that attributed to Mrs. Gandhi's "Emergency" rule, which, though seen as a signal instance of "self-wounding," is a mere episode. The narrative mode of this second book is more analytical, less personal; much less space is devoted to the author's direct experience; there is nothing like the Customs House encounter that forms the prelude to *An Area of Darkness,* or the bittersweet "A Doll's House on the Dal Lake," or the pilgrimage to the Cave of Amarnath. His travels, though still recorded in vivid detail, are more purposeful now, and one feels his findings are predestined.

Many of the earlier themes are pursued, extended, and argued more dogmatically: Western mimicry, Indian defeat and withdrawal; the self-cherishing of absorption with inner spiritual life, Indians' self-defeating idealization of the past and the preindustrial world; the two sides of the *dharma* coin—"this ideal of truth to oneself, or living out the truth in oneself, can also be used to reconcile men to servitude and make them find in paralysing obedience the highest spiritual good" (p. 169, Deutsch edition). In Naipaul's India, despite instances of positive action, paralysis predominates. Central to his indictment is the failure of Hinduism (which N. C. Chaudhuri has in *Hinduism* [1979] called "the true nationalism of India"): "It has exposed us [a revealing word] to a thousand years of defeat and stagnation. It has given men no idea of a contract with other men, no idea of the state" (p. 53). The indictment is supported by many instances of political misleading or failure to lead. Much of the third and final part, "Not Ideas, But Obsessions," is devoted to demonstrating how "the many-sided Gandhi permeates" modern India: his emphasis upon India's superior spirituality, which worked so well in promoting "national self-assertion," is seen as having become its own end, a home-grown source of "mimicry," whose prime embodiment in Vinoba Bhave is "a kind of magic" without valuable or effective aim. The widespread respect accorded Bhave exemplifies a debilitating reverence for the past.

A more telling case is the bogus village "farmer" who, "in white Gandhian homespun," is rather the eternal landowner and opportunistic Congress politician. He is produced for the visitor who wishes to meet a real farmer, while "around us [were] the serfs, underfed, landless, nothing, less than people, dark wasted faces and dark rags fading into the dusk" (p. 147). "Serfs": one of several implicit reminders of Holy Mother Russia before the revolution. Yet whence the "less than" people's deliverance? The Naxalites ("somebody else's idea of revolution"), the probing press ("journalism in India is . . . a gracious form of clerkship"), Jaya Prakash Narayan preaching a return to a mythical Old India, Western technology—the "mimicry within mimicry" of the National Institute of Design at Ahmedabad?

In India, as on the plantations of Naipaul's native Trinidad, or in London, Washington, Montevideo—wherever a "civilization" tolerates, unredressed, a condition of society in which "not all the people are people"—Naipaul has criticized and offended. No hurt appeals to ancient Indian history and belief, protesting at Naipaul's lack of "inner" comprehension of them, can charm away the facts so many Indians accept unquestioningly:

> . . . the huts of the landless along the Poona-Bombay road, the child labourers of Bihar among the blond hanks of jute, the chawls and squatters' settlements in central Bombay, the starved squatters in bright cotton slipping in and out of the stone ruins of Vijayanagar, the famine-wasted bodies just outside Jaipur City. It was like a calamity that no one could come to terms with. I was without the Indian defences; which were also the attitudes that contributed to the calamity.
>
> (ch. 7)

He refuses to be pointed instead toward the frescoes of Ajanta, a splendid Madras temple, or the scenery of Kashmir: he will not be fobbed off.

As a creative no less than a "documentary" writer, Naipaul has refused to treat his subjects in a rarefied air unpolluted by the world's gross inequalities and cruelties: the novel also is "a form of social enquiry" (p. 18). Despite his admiration for R. K. Narayan's art, Naipaul uses his fiction (somewhat selectively: *Mr Sampath* and *The Vendor of Sweets*) to demonstrate an Indian writer's ability to abstract from the "cruel and overwhelming" reality, in Hindu fashion, social comedies of India for the West—not India. For contrast he devotes five pages to describing U. R. Anantamurti's novel *Samskara,* whose theme is "a brahmin's loss of identity"; he praises its critical penetration, for "knowingly or unknowingly, Anantamurti has portrayed a backward civilization, where the books, the laws, are buttressed by magic, and where a too elaborate social organization is unquickened by creativity or ideas of moral responsibility, except to the self in its climb to salvation" (pt. 3, ch. 5).

To use two key Naipaulian phrases, "self-cherishing" is "self-violation"—for "the contract between man and man" he evidently believes to be a universal need, however little scope man's belief systems may allow it.

Naipaul's is an impatient compassion, tormented by the darkness and an urgent desire to see pain relieved; thus he understates or undervalues those whose views and actions might temper his negatives. There is the selfless Bombay engineer, the Shiv Sena leaders in Bombay's slums, while "one of India's best journalists" is quoted only very near the end. What were the students saying, the younger writers and film-makers—and in the many languages other than English? Any view of India is vulnerable to such questions: if Naipaul's cautious hope of "a new beginning" is scarcely borne out by this angry book, the "wound" is the author's no less than his subject's.

Among the Believers: An Islamic Journey is a more expansive work, closer in form and spirit to *An Area of Darkness* than *India: A Wounded Civilization,* in that the "delight in people as people" is again felt and underscores the concern. This persists, in Naipaul's accounts of his personal relationships in the four countries caught up in the Islamic revolution he visits, despite his rational aversion from the deluded, contradictory, even fanatical elements in each individual's anxiety for certainty and security. The drama of the book is felt repeatedly in the pull between "the pure response of man to man" (p. 147, Penguin edition, 1982), which he feels with such as Ahmed and Nusrat in Pakistan or Shafi in Malaysia, and his seeing through the fantasy of perfection, the reiterated "complete way of life" of Islam that grips them, obstructing clear vision of themselves and of their relation to the larger world. The voices of those Naipaul encounters, through whom he seeks to understand their society, its sense of itself and its past and the meaning of Islamic "revolution," are given ample scope. As interlocutor and prompter he records and responds as a serious enquirer, not the opinionated or too obviously skeptical investigator. Occasionally, when he oversteps this role, there is confrontation, as with the Pakistani journalist, Nusrat, and this is regretted, for he "after all, knew only Pakistan" (p. 154). The same Nusrat, six months later, having meanwhile suffered extremist intolerance, will say, "You've altered my life" (p. 368). We see, both in the relationships and the events as they unfold, especially in Iran and Pakistan, new perspectives emerging: revolution as conservative regression is the harsh education of Behzad, but he too, nursing his thwarted socialist revolution, clings to an alternative deadly absolute. Naipaul sees and regrets this, but when the Revolutionary Guards attack the Communists, "I got worried about you." Understanding precludes condemnation: "[Behzad] had been fed by so many civilizations; so much had gone into making him what he was. But now, at what should have been the beginning of his intellectual life, he—like the Muslims to whom he was opposed—had cut himself off" (p. 391).

While, clearly, Naipaul does seek a pattern of significance, the reader feels that this emerges from manifold oral witness: it is not imposed. The purpose of his writings, Naipaul explains to the Malay Shafi, is "comprehension" (p. 244). He is well fitted to comprehend what he sees, aware of a larger pattern: the passion for authentic identity in these new-made, formerly colonized or still West-dominated countries feeds on a fantasy of Islamic purity (as absolute as the Victorians' imperial "mission"), a fantasy of the past, yet cannot disengage its action from dependence upon the developed world: "money only turned people into buyers of imported goods, fixed the country in a dependent relationship with the developed world, kept all men colonials" (p. 250). It was possible to understand the withdrawal of someone like Shafi; the rage of the idol-smashers; and the wish, among other Malays, to pretend that they were Arabs, living as purely as in the days of the prophet.

So mimicry returns in another guise, but it cannot be worn easily. It is liable to be rendered absurd when the higher "Islamic civilization" proclaimed by governments and their indoctrinated followers is seen to depend upon that civilization the Muslims traduce for its buildings, communications, weapons, even ideas: "The Islam of protest was a religion that had been brushed by the ideas of the late twentieth century" (p. 361). Of Khomeini he writes:

> Interpreter of God's will, leader of the faithful, he expressed all the confusion of his people and made it appear like glory, like the familiar faith: the confusion of a people of high medieval culture awakening to oil and money, a sense of power and violation, and a knowledge of a great new encircling civilization. That civilization couldn't be mastered. It was to be rejected; at the same time it was to be depended upon.
>
> (p. 80)

One is reminded, in *A Bend in the River,* of the Big Man's crippling dependence on alien technology and ideas. The consumer goods from the West flow from "the new universal bazaar, where goods were not associated with a particular kind of learning, effort, or civilization, but were just goods, part of the world's natural bounty" (p. 79). To exploit, yet believe one is not exploited by this, one invokes the faith. "I was interested," Naipaul comments with restrained irony, "in this idea of the developed world as something just existing, just being there: part of an almost pre-ordained division of men: creative, uncreative; faithless, believing" (p. 242; compare p. 158).

The idea opposed to the Islamic panacea is that glimpsed by the Pakistani Masood: "The idea of struggle and dedication and fulfilment, the idea of human quality, [which] belongs only to certain societies" (p. 183)—and not such as Trinidad, for in Masood's "panic" Naipaul reads his own thirty years before. If Naipaul aligns his values with "the West," it is not for ideological reasons, but for the broad "idea" of "the contract between man and man" *(India: A Wounded Civilization),* the preservation, however relative, of scope for individual freedom and justice: "It was the late twentieth century —and not the faith—that could supply the answers —in institutions, legislation, economic systems" (p. 399). In *Among the Believers* the absence of such basic possibilities is made felt by Naipaul's achieving a sympathetic nearness to the individual lives of "believers" of many shades, an object lesson in the tolerance he implicitly preaches (a quality that some of his critics, conceding too little to his indignation, deny him).

AN ASSESSMENT

In an important interview with V. S. Naipaul, printed in the *Listener* (22 March 1973), Ronald Bryden credits him with discovering "the novel of the new synthetic world." This is at least a substantial half-truth. It is impossible for any novelist who really looks at the contemporary world to see his subject matter in any corner of it as a complex, organic society comparable to those we find in the works of the great nineteenth-century writers. However, this is not new. It goes back to turn-of-the-century, politically aware writers such as Conrad, whose vision foreshadows Naipaul's at many points; to novels by such as Forster ("everything echoes now"), Ford Madox Ford, Lawrence, Aldous Huxley (whose acute awareness, to the point of repulsion and disgust, of the vulnerable, corruptible flesh Naipaul's work often recalls); to the last, bitter novel of Virginia Woolf; to poetry such as Eliot's fragmentary, universal *The Waste Land;* and, more recently, to the comfortless drama of the Theater of the Absurd. Naipaul's work does not stand alone; the other half of the truth lies in defining its contribution to this general tendency in modern literature.

While Naipaul is by no means alone in coming from a makeshift colonial society and using the "metropolitan" language with a native sureness, these origins have motivated him more than any of his contemporaries from the Commonwealth to develop an inclusive view of many facets of the larger world, a view focused by his intense sense of displacement from society, race, or creed. Neither Left nor Right, nor any shade of color, has determined the range of his fiction and journalism. He has gone beyond local conflicts, isolated instances of the colonial experience, to attempt a comprehensive "vision of the world's half-made societies" ("Conrad's Darkness"). Inevitably the range is more often wide than deep—the only society he could give us in depth remains Indian Trinidad—but his insights and his manner of conveying them carry a persuasive truth. In his reports from what he calls the "unimportant," neglected places such as Mauritius ("The Overcrowded Barracoon"), Anguilla, and an obscure Indian state, what people, brought convincingly alive, do and say gets full play; we do not feel imposed upon by the roving journalist's slanted impressions. His last such work, *Among the Believers,* maintains this quality. Naipaul is himself not deceived by anti-imperialist, nationalist, or racist postures (his emotional leanings are there, frankly admitted, not masked): he invokes, instead, the artist's traditional touchstones, a governing idea of order and a concern for clear perception. His work reflects (and this also concerned the writers in whose wake he writes) an artist's cutting sense of the absence or loss in our splintering world of what some of the major creators of the past have enjoyed—"to be in conversation with your society" would have been the greatest good. For many, not only artists, this "conversation" has surely been an essential need, now thwarted. The society need not be ideal, but it does need to be complex and flexible, with cultural depth and variety; however, in turning away from his society for its narrowness and sterility, Naipaul overstressed the singularity of the colonial's plight, forgetting such forerunners as Henry James, Joyce, and Lawrence and their reasons for choosing exile from more complex societies. Like them also he can be charged with impatiently spurning his evolving society. Perhaps the advancing creolization of the Trinidad Indian, leading to a more homogeneous society that will, in turn, develop its distinctive culture, does not seem positive to him; perhaps he remains too "Indian" at bottom. In any case, as an artist who needed—as did Eliot, James, and Ezra Pound when they left the United States—the ambience of an older, more established culture, he did not wait upon the stumbling process of change in Trinidad.

Nevertheless, his work offers perspectives far beyond his personal feeling of deprivation. While the bias of which some of his fellow West Indian and Indian readers of *An Area of Darkness,* resenting his negativism, have accused him—some even setting him down as an "Indo-Saxon" struggling as hard as the Creoles he satirizes to be taken for white—can be discerned in his earlier work, I have tried to bring out how, as his range widened, Naipaul has treated white norms also with an even-handed skepticism. Although preoccupied with order and tradition, he does not identify these with any existing social state. Mr. Stone, like Mr. Biswas, inhabits a disordered world; British racism and empty "tolerance" take their place in his later works beside Black Power and Indian "spirituality," as aberrations from clear thinking, complex self-analysis, and self-knowledge. Thus he tellingly quotes Michael X's note: "My inheritance is London—all of it." It must, however, be admitted that only the most widely ranging readers of Naipaul will recognize the force of such criticisms. Like Conrad, he has not struck squarely at the heart of whiteness; it remains a center of relative order, tenuously sustaining "the contract between man and man." At a time when half the world is painfully emerging from imperial or social oppressions centuries old and looking about for voices to articulate its dilemma, Naipaul has spoken from and to more points within that world than any English writer—but his is not a comforting or hopeful voice.

Against writers whose criticisms of our condition are as negative as Naipaul's, readers usually complain of the failure to offer "solutions." The most that Naipaul offers is the means of seeing what is, clearing the ground for action. Asked if he were an optimist he replied: "I'm not sure. I think I do look for the seeds of regeneration in a situation; I long to find what is good and hopeful, and really do hope that by the most brutal sort of analysis one is possibly opening up the situation to some sort of action; an action which is not based on self-deception."[9] This is the stringent formula of Hardy, himself plagued with accusations of pessimism: "If Way to a Better there be / It exacts a full look at the Worst" ("In Tenebris"). Also like Hardy, he supplies none of the props even realists let us lean upon in the end: there are no consolidations—no religious belief, no humanistic faith in man's future, not even the personal supports of friendship or love (though his characters marry and have a sex life, they cannot be described as falling in love). Confessedly without religious belief, such as centers the work of a cosmopolitan writer like Graham Greene, or such unorthodox forms of it as that of his fellow West Indian, Wilson Harris' mystical vitalism, or as yet any temptation to embrace, as so experienced a colonial as Doris Lessing has done, a faith in man's moral evolution—but unwilling to write merely what will sell (sex or violence)—Naipaul's is one of the bleakest visions any imaginative observer alive has given us. It is tempting to rebuke him for this, to link him with those defeatist Western writers whom Alexander Solzhenitsyn castigated in his Nobel lecture (1972) for "merely [letting] the world have [their] bitter observations, as of a bystander, about how hopelessly corrupted mankind is, how petty men have become, and how difficult it is for lovely, sensitive beautiful souls today." Yet Naipaul shows none of the smug self-satisfaction of such doomsters; he remains engaged, not aloof, as is most evident in his constant reference to the plight of the poor, the eternally disregarded "less than people"; he refuses to leap to positive attitudes he cannot justify.

Naipaul would be the last to claim for his work that it represents a final or adequate vision; it is the record of one man's impressions of the world, and it does not pretend to be the whole truth about it. In his essay on Conrad, from which I have already quoted, he concludes with this (Conradian) view of the novelist's role:

> The novelist, like the painter, no longer recognizes his interpretative function; he seeks to go beyond it; and his audience diminishes. And so the world we inhabit, which is always new, goes by unexamined, made ordinary by the camera, unmeditated on; and there is no one to awaken the sense of true wonder. That is perhaps a fair definition of the novelist's purpose, in all ages.
>
> ("Conrad's Darkness," *The Return of Eva Perón*)

This is a memorable credo, one which Naipaul's own work has done much to substantiate; but there is reason to question whether in his latest fiction, in his urgent anxiety to awaken response, the "interpretative function" has not become overtly dominant and whether the apprehension he voiced in the foreword to *The Middle Passage* about the consequences of journalism for his art has not proved too well founded: "I hesitated. The novelist works towards conclusions of which he is often unaware, and it is better that he should."

[9]Interview with Adrian Rowe-Evans, *Transition,* 40 (December 1971). The shift in this quotation from "I" to the false first-personal use of "one," frequent in Naipaul's personal statements, is a striking instance of his use in ordinary speech of a markedly English (Oxonian, "upper-class") turn of phrase, suggestive evidence that he is less the separate colonial than he feels.

SELECTED BIBLIOGRAPHY

I. SEPARATE WORKS. *The Mystic Masseur* (London, 1957), fiction; *The Suffrage of Elvira* (London, 1958), fiction; *Miguel Street* (London, 1959), short stories; *A House for Mr Biswas* (London, 1961), repr. with author's foreword (New York, 1983), fiction; *The Middle Passage: Impressions of Five Societies —British, French, and Dutch—in the West Indies and South America* (London, 1962), personal narrative; *Mr Stone and the Knights Companion* (London, 1963), fiction; *An Area of Darkness* (London, 1964), personal narrative; *The Mimic Men* (London, 1967), fiction; *A Flag on the Island* (London, 1967), short stories; *The Loss of El Dorado: A History* (London, 1969), history; *In a Free State* (London, 1971), fiction; *The Overcrowded Barracoon, and Other Articles* (London, 1972), personal and political articles; *Guerrillas* (London, 1975), fiction; *India: A Wounded Civilization* (London, 1977), personal narrative; *A Bend in the River* (London, 1979), fiction; *A Congo Diary* (Los Angeles, 1980), personal narrative; *The Return of Eva Perón* (London, 1980), personal and political articles; *Among the Believers: An Islamic Journey* (London, 1981), personal narrative; *Finding the Centre* (London, 1984), autobiography and personal narrative.

II. ARTICLES AND REVIEWS. (*Note:* Items marked with an asterisk have been collected in *The Overcrowded Barracoon;* with a dagger, in *Finding the Centre;* with a double dagger, in *The Return of Eva Perón.*) "Wonne with a Nut," the *New Statesman* (23 November 1957), review of J. Winny, ed., *The Descent of Euphues;* "Insider Out," the *New Statesman* (21 December 1957), review of H. Nicolson, *Journey to Java;* "Where the Rum Comes From," the *New Statesman* (4 January 1958), review of V. Mehta, *Face to Face;* "Flowers for the Frau," the *New Statesman* (17 May 1958); "A Letter to Maria," the *New Statesman* (5 July 1958); *"The Regional Barrier," the *Times Literary Supplement* (15 August 1958), repr. as "London"; "Death on the Telephone," the *New Statesman* (28 March 1959), review of M. Spark, *Memento Mori;* "Caribbean Medley," *Vogue* (15 November 1959).

"Enemy," *Vogue* (1 March 1961); "On St George's Hill," the *New Statesman* (12 May 1961); "Reliques," the *New Statesman* (9 June 1961); "Taluqdars," the *New Statesman* (7 July 1961); "Reading for Pleasure," the *Times* (13 July 1961); "Tricks and Secrets," the *New Statesman* (28 July 1961); "Dark Places," the *New Statesman* (18 August 1961), a review of H. Basso, *A Quota of Seaweed;* "Red Rat-Traps," the *New Statesman* (26 August 1961); "Living Like a Millionaire," *Vogue* (15 October 1961); "Vacancies," the *New Statesman* (22 December 1961); "When I Was a Kid," the *New Statesman* (22 December 1961); "Trollope in the West Indies," the *Listener* (15 March 1962); *"In the Middle of the Journey," the *Illustrated Weekly of India* (28 October 1962); *"Jamshed into Jimmy," the *New Statesman* (25 January 1963); "Castle of Fear," the *Spectator* (5 July 1963); *"Sporting Life," *Encounter* (September 1963); "Speaking of Writing," the *Times* (2 January 1964); "Sebastian Rides Again," the *Spectator* (24 April 1964); *"Words on Their Own," the *Times Literary Supplement* (4 June 1964); "Australia Deserta," the *Spectator* (16 October 1964), review of P. White, *The Burnt Ones;* "Violence in Art: The Documentary Heresy," the *Twentieth Century* (Winter 1964–1965).

"Indian Autobiographies," the *New Statesman* (29 January 1965); "They Are Staring at Me," the *Saturday Evening Post* (10 April 1965); *"East Indian, West Indian," the *Reporter* (17 June 1965); "Images: Commonwealth Literature," the *New Statesman* (24 September 1965); *"The Last of the Aryans," *Encounter* (January 1966); "The Writer," the *New Statesman* (18 March 1966), review of C. Isherwood, *Exhumations;* *"Theatrical Natives," the *New Statesman* (2 December 1966); "What's Wrong with Being a Snob?" the *Saturday Evening Post* (3 June 1967); *"Mr Matsuda's Million-Dollar Gamble," the *Daily Telegraph Magazine* (14 July 1967); *"Tragedy: The Missing Sense," the *Daily Telegraph Magazine* (11 August 1967); *"Magic and Dependence," the *Daily Telegraph Magazine* (18 August 1967); *"Columbus and Crusoe," the *Listener* (28 December 1967); *"Jacques Soustelle and the Decline of the West," the *Daily Telegraph Magazine* (26 January 1968); "Writing Is Magic," the *Sunday Times* (10 November 1968); *"Anguilla: The Shipwrecked 6000," the *New York Review of Books* (24 April 1969); *"St Kitts: Papa and the Power Set," the *New York Review of Books* (8 May 1969); *"The Ultimate Colony," the *Daily Telegraph Magazine* (4 July 1969); "Et in America ego!" the *Listener* (4 September 1969), interview of R. Lowell; *"New York with Norman Mailer," the *Daily Telegraph Magazine* (10 October 1969).

*"Power to the Caribbean People," the *New York Review of Books* (3 September 1970); *"Steinbeck in Monterey," the *Daily Telegraph Magazine* (3 April 1970); "One Out of Many," the *Atlantic* (April 1971); *"The Overcrowded Barracoon," the *Sunday Times Magazine* (16 July 1972); "Without a Dog's Chance," the *New York Review of Books* (18 May 1972), review of J. Rhys, *After Leaving Mr MacKenzie;* "It Is Not Easy to Be Famous in a Small Town," the *Daily Telegraph Magazine* (17 November 1972); "The King Over the Water: Juan Perón," the *Sunday Times* (6 August 1972), repr. as ‡"The Corpse at the Iron Gate," in the *New York Review of Books* (10 August 1972); "A Country Dying on Its Feet," the *Observer* (10 February 1974), repr. in the *New York Review of Books* (4 April 1974); ‡"Argentina: The Brothels Behind the Graveyard," the *New York Review of Books* (19 September 1974); ‡"Conrad's Darkness," the *New York Review of Books* (17 October 1974); ‡"A New King for the Congo," the *New York Review of Books* (26 June 1975), Zaire explored with Conrad's *Heart of Darkness* in mind; Foreword to Seepersad Naipaul, *The Adventures of Gurudeva and Other Stories* (London, 1976).

"It's Every Man for Himself," the *Listener* (27 October 1977); †"Bogart, Hat and Popo: Prologue to an Autobiography," the *Sunday Times* (8 May 1983); †"Prologue to an Autobiography: Family Secrets," the *Sunday Times* (15 May 1983); "A Perpetual Voyager," the *Listener* (23 June 1983); †"Prologue to an Autobiography," *Vanity Fair* (April 1983); "Writing *A House for Mr Biswas*," the *New York Review of Books* (24 November 1983); "An Island Betrayed," *Harper's* (March 1984); "Among the Republicans," the *New York Review of Books* (October 1984).

III. Interviews. Interview with D. Bates, the *Sunday Times Magazine* (26 May 1963); Interview with F. Wyndham, the *Sunday Times* (10 September 1968); I. Hamilton, "Without a Place" in the *Times Literary Supplement* (30 July 1971); I. Shenker, "V. S. Naipaul: Man Without a Society," in the *New York Times Book Review,* 76 (1971); A. Rowe-Evans, "V. S. Naipaul," in *Transition* 40 (1971); N. Bingham, "The Novelist Talks About His Childhood in Trinidad," in the *Listener* (7 September 1972); R. Bryden, "The Novelist Talks About His Work," in the *Listener* (22 March 1973); B. Mukherjee and R. Boyers, "A Conversation with V. S. Naipaul," in *Salmagundi,* 54 (1981), a special issue with essays by R. Boyers, E. Goodheart, B. Belitt, L. D. Nachman.

IV. Critical Studies. C. D. Narasimhaiah, "Somewhere Something Has Snapped," in the *Literary Criterion* (Mysore, Summer 1965); W. Harris, *Tradition, The Writer and Society: Critical Essays* (London, 1967); L. James, ed., *The Islands in Between* (London, 1968), includes an essay on Naipaul by G. Rohlehr, "The Ironic Approach"; A. C. Derrick, "Naipaul's Technique as a Novelist," in the *Journal of Commonwealth Literature* (July 1969); K. Ramchand, *The West Indian Novel and Its Background* (London, 1970); H.

V. S. NAIPAUL

H. A. Gowda, "Naipaul in India," in the *Literary Half-Yearly,* 11 (Mysore, July 1970), H. Maes-Jelinek, "The Myth of El Dorado in the Caribbean Novel," in the *Journal of Commonwealth Literature* (June 1971); P. Theroux, *V. S. Naipaul: An Introduction to His Work* (London, 1972); A. Rutherford, ed., *Common Wealth* (Aarhus, Denmark, 1972), includes Shiva Naipaul, "The Writer Without a Society," and V. Ramraj, "The All-Embracing Christlike Vision: Tone and Attitude in *The Mimic Men*"; J. Ngugi, *Homecoming: Essays on African and Caribbean Literature, Culture and Politics* (London, 1972), contains an essay on Naipaul, "A Kind of Homecoming"; W. Walsh, *V. S. Naipaul* (Edinburgh, 1973); R. Hamner, *V. S. Naipaul* (New York, 1973); L. White, *V. S. Naipaul: A Critical Introduction* (London, 1975); R. K. Morris, *Paradoxes of Order* (Columbia, Missouri, 1975); R. Hamner, ed., *Critical Perspectives on V. S. Naipaul* (Washington, D.C., 1977); H. H. A. Gowda, "India: A Wounded Civilization," in *Ariel,* 10 (January 1979); "A Symposium on V. S. Naipaul's *Guerrillas*," in the *Journal of Commonwealth Literature,* 14 (August 1979); A. Boxhill, *V. S. Naipaul's Fiction: In Quest of the Enemy* (Fredericton, New Brunswick, Canada, 1983); M. Thorpe, *A Critical View on V. S. Naipaul's "A House for Mr Biswas"* (London, 1985).

DAVID STOREY

(1933–)

John Russell Taylor

I

Reticence has long been a quality not only prized but regarded as virtually a *sine qua non* of English literature. All the notions associated with it—understatement, distancing irony, the stiff upper lip—automatically take on an aura of approval, as though violent passions are things that only foreigners experience, and as though dealing with emotions must inevitably mean suppressing them or laughing them off. Of course, reticence was not always a trait of the English character—after all, up to the eighteenth century European visitors describe the English more as we would think of characters from a Dostoevsky novel, with violent alternations of high spirits and melancholia, a lot of kissing and crying and carrying on of all kinds. The great British sangfroid, literary and domestic, would seem to be associated with the rise and heyday of British imperial power, with the consequent obligation to behave nationally like parents in front of children, teachers in front of pupils, officers in front of men. Reticence and gentility were not exactly the salient characteristics of Geoffrey Chaucer, nor of the Jacobean dramatists; Emily Brontë was probably rather crazed, and D. H. Lawrence was certainly, as we all know, not quite a gentleman.

But things have changed. Almost without our noticing it, the British empire has melted away, and suddenly a generation has arisen for whom Britain is only a tight little island, a second-rate power at best, and there is no need any more to keep up appearances. Britishers today, like Noël Coward's Uncle Harry, are giving way at practically every pore, and few see much point in building a temple to that goddess of finer sense, Silence's half-sister Reticence.

II

David Storey, the most notable of British novelists born in the 1930's, takes full advantage of this new emotional freedom. Storey is not, emphatically not, a gentlemanly writer—not only because he belongs to the new class of writers who come from a working-class background and feel no necessity to give themselves a respectable bourgeois protective coloring, but also because the very concept is outdated: the English gentleman, paralyzed by his stiff upper lip, is as much an anachronism as the nanny or *Bradshaw's Railway Almanack.* Emotion, once recollected in tranquillity, if admitted to at all, can be confronted directly in Storey's works, and expressed in literary terms without being defused first, robbed of its power before it can be turned to the purposes of art.

Considering that the basic materials of Storey's novels and plays are so patently, even obsessively, autobiographical, the facts of his life are remarkably unrevealing. We can readily discover from the dust jackets of his books that he was born in Wakefield on 13 July 1933, the third son of a mine worker; became a student at the Slade School of Art in London; and to finance his art education signed a contract with Leeds Rugby League Club as a professional footballer, staying with them for four seasons. It seems he was successful at both these contrasted activities, winning a number of prizes at Slade while commuting between London and Leeds for three years. He also worked in his early days as a teacher, a farm worker, an erector of showground tents, a bus conductor, and a postman. In 1956 he married a London University graduate from Yorkshire, and they have four children. His third novel, several times rewritten, *This Sporting Life,* was published to considerable acclaim in 1960 and was rapidly followed by two more. In 1967 his first play, *The Restoration of Arnold Middleton,* was produced, and was followed by six more in the next six years, all of them successful.

So far, so good. Virtually every stage of Storey's adult life has contributed material to his writings, and though as yet we have not had a drama of life on the buses or in the post office, it may well be only a matter of time. The mining background appears again and again, notably in *This Sporting Life, Flight into Camden, Pasmore,* and *In Celebration.* Football is the background of *This Sporting Life* and *The Changing Room.* Painting occurs, usually peripherally, in *Flight into Camden, Pasmore, A Temporary Life, In Celebration,* and centrally in Storey's play *Life Class;* teaching is the usually unsatisfying occupation of important characters in *The Restoration of Arnold Middleton, Flight into Camden, Pasmore, A Temporary Life,* and *In Celebration;* tent-raising comes up in *Radcliffe* and *The Contractor;* farm work in *The Farm;* the theater and working in it in *A Prodigal Child* and in *Present Times.* In addition to these there are two further recurrent themes—that of nervous breakdown and neurotic withdrawal, allied usually (in *Arnold Middleton, Flight into Camden, Pasmore, A Temporary Life,* and *Present Times*) to an attempted marriage breakup, though sometimes, as in *In Celebration* and *Home,* just by itself; and that of parents' greed for attention, duty, and obedience on the part of their children (almost everywhere, but most prominently in *Flight into Camden, Pasmore, In Celebration,* and *The Farm*).

All these experiences must be Storey's own, or at least those of people he has known in spheres of activity with which he is well acquainted. And yet, for all this apparent closeness of relation between the life and the work, the direct autobiographical significance of the works is minimal, and the necessity of knowing the autobiographical background in order to understand and judge the works is absolutely nil. We can map Storey's world and see how various elements of it recur in different contexts, pictured from different points of view. But we could still do that if all we had to go on was the novels and the plays themselves. The interest is always, as it should be, not in what has gone into them but in what comes out, not the raw material but the finished product. Storey has a unique capacity for turning reality into symbols, making something presented with meticulous realism stand also, quite independently, for something more than itself, a drama of souls as well as (or perhaps sometimes instead of) a drama of tangible physical entities in conflict. It is no doubt significant that the only statement Storey has made about the autobiographical significance of his writings is in this sense: of the time at which he wrote *This Sporting Life,* when he had come to the end of his period split between professional football and art school, he said in an interview in the *Times* (28 November 1963):

> I really set seriously about sorting myself out . . . I then conceived a sequence of four novels which would constitute a sort of campaign for reintegrating myself. In the first I tried to isolate and come to terms with the physical side in the footballer Machin. In *Flight into Camden* I isolated the other half, the spiritual, interior and—as I conceived it—feminine part of my nature by writing a first-person narrative in which the narrator is a woman. In *Radcliffe* I bring the two halves face to face embodied in two separate characters, and then in the fourth, the key work . . . I am trying to reconcile them into one person: the conflict moves inside, and is fought out in one man's brain.

One may wonder what the effect of Storey's work will be when, or if, the fourth novel, which is to reconcile the warring elements, and upon which he has been working on and off for some twenty years now, is carried to a successful conclusion. Two of the novels that have come out since *Radcliffe, Pasmore* and *A Temporary Life,* are both separated, shaped elements from the work-in-progress, and all the other writings can be seen as, in various ways, interim statements, reports from the field where the battle is still being fought. Maybe the battle is the essential of Storey's creativity—that and the need to keep it under control, to exorcize the demons by shaping them into art.

III

For there is certainly something demonic about much of Storey's writing. A rough outline of his qualities can already be discerned in his first novel, *This Sporting Life* (1960). It is, centrally, the story of an *amour fou,* if not quite in the sense the term is normally used: a violent, tortured, suppressed love between two very unlikely people, the footballer Arthur Machin (Frank in the film, no doubt to avoid the near coincidence with the name of the author Arthur Machen) and his middle-aged, widowed, not particularly attractive landlady, Mrs. Hammond. It is a classic encounter between the irresistible force and the immovable object. Machin, all strength and determination, does all he can to batter down her resistance, to force her to an avowal that she cares for him, loves him even. She, though she does, grudgingly, give herself to him physically, seems to take a sort of perverse delight in refusing to admit to any emotional involvement, insisting instead that all her emotions are bound up with the dead husband, whose boots still stand, symbolically shiny and ready for use, on the hearth.

This strange relationship is the mainspring of the book, affecting every part of it. Early on Machin reflects (for this is a first-person narrative), "Her aggressive sort of indifference roused in me a kind of anger, a savageness, that suited the game very well," and the connection between his emotional life and his professional life as a footballer is something we are always conscious of. Equally it seems that the situation, however she may choose to define it, plays a radical part in Mrs. Hammond's life. She clearly regards Machin as an enemy, a menace to her peace of mind and body—except that without this enemy at the gates she soon declines into the passiveness of a dead thing. When she has a stroke and dies, it is perhaps partly the last, most desperate means of escaping from Machin and his demands on her; but even more it is the result of low morale and loss of the will to live in the year since they have ceased to be together. Whether what binds her to him is love or hate, who can say—certainly not Machin, from whose point of view the story is told. But it does not matter very much—there is passion of some kind masked by her aggressive indifference, and without that passion she has nothing to live for.

Both participants are self-destructive, both live out their emotional responses to the extreme, without caution or reticence. We may accept as convenient shorthand Storey's own formulation that Machin represents the physical side of the author's own nature. But he is clearly not a man incapable of thought or self-analysis. His life is to some extent ruled by his body, but that is because his mind recognizes his physical experiences as the most vivid, the most satisfying. It is not so much a deficiency in intelligence or sensitivity that prevents him from being able to cope satisfactorily with Mrs. Hammond—she is rather the impossible object, and it seems to be her very impossibility (not only for him, for anyone) that excites his interest. She, on the other hand, might echo the words of John Arden's Mrs. Phineus in *The Happy Haven:*

> I want to sleep but not to dream
> I want to play and win every game
> To live with love but not to love
> The world to move but me not move . . .
> Leave me be, but don't leave me alone.
> That's what I want. I'm a big round stone
> Sitting in the middle of a thunderstorm . . .
> (III.i)

Her needs are as urgent as, if more paradoxical than, his: the two cannot live with each other, and cannot live without each other.

The texture of the writing is rougher, slighter than that of Storey's later work. There is a certain matter-of-factness about its tone that helps us to understand, if hardly to excuse, the way in which critics first received it as yet another, though distinguished, example of the down-to-earth, semi-documentary kind of fiction then nearing the end of its brief 1950's vogue. Read now, with hindsight, *This Sporting Life* seems no more documentary than *Wuthering Heights,* its characters typical of nothing but themselves. The sense of time and place is vividly, economically captured, particularly in those parts of the book concerned with Machin's day-to-day life as a footballer. But it is only the stage setting for the titanic battle of wills at the center of the book, the way in which the tortured passions of the principals can be given a local habitation and a name. Though we believe implicitly in Machin's career as a footballer, we can no more see the book as a documentary about Rugby-league football than we can see *Lady Chatterley's Lover* as a documentary about gamekeeping.

To hindsight, also, *This Sporting Life* presents in rudimentary form certain themes and situations that are to recur frequently in Storey's work. Though we do not see much of Machin's parents, they present the same personality profile as the parent figures in most of his later writings—captious, bitter, domineering, impossible to satisfy. Parents in Storey's work always seem to represent some sort of negation of individuality. They assume—the fathers particularly—that children owe them everything, that it is the absolute duty of the child to be the sort of person they would have him be, lead the sort of life they would have him lead. Mothers sometimes try to understand and sympathize with their children as independent individuals, but fathers are almost always openly scornful of their children's successes, merciless in their criticism of failure, and ready at the slightest provocation to indulge in the most bare-faced emotional blackmail—they can be "killed" by the marriage of a child to someone they do not approve of, or by an irregular relationship with anyone at all; they go on endlessly about what their children "owe" them; they cling unshakably to the narrowest puritanical prejudices of their earlier days, and seem to want to punish their children for the hardships they themselves have gone through. Most of them are perfectly capable of simultaneously pitying themselves for having slogged out their lives down the mines in order that their sons should not have to, and complaining bitterly because their efforts have been crowned with success and their sons are safely ensconced in some white-collar job, or at any rate some more easily profitable job, instead of doing as they did, scraping a living by "honest toil." No wonder the central character of *Flight into Camden* bursts out at one point, "I hated the greed of my parents."

There is an incidental but perceptible element of sexual ambiguity in two of the background characters of *This Sporting Life.* Up to the present time in Storey's work this has proved directly relevant only in *Radcliffe,* which turns almost exclusively on passionate relations among men. It is not too fanciful to see a connection between Weaver, the local prosperous businessman, who more or less owns the team Machin plays for and is "supposed to be a fairy," even if "he only got round to patting and arms-on-your-shoulder stuff," and Leonard's dandyish bachelor Uncle Austen in *Radcliffe,* who develops an unaccountable obsession with the broken-down pub entertainer, Blakeley. There is also something of Johnson, Machin's rather creepy, idolizing hanger-on, in Blakeley, and of his evident fascination with Machin in Blakeley's hopeless passion for Radcliffe, who himself seems to represent another, more overtly destructive side of Machin. And Mrs. Weaver, the sexually confident, aggressive, and presumably maritally dissatisfied woman, has obvious connections with Helen in *Pasmore* and Elizabeth in *A Temporary Life,* both of whom involve themselves with the books' respective heroes in the same sort of aggressively indifferent way (a touch of Mrs. Hammond here too) and see their husbands have their respective lovers beaten up for their pains. It would not be surprising to discover, in the context of the long-in-progress *magnum opus* from which both these latter books spring, that Helen's and Elizabeth's husbands, with their strong-arm henchmen (if they are not, as they may be, the same character), have the same sort of sexual ambiguity that Weaver has.

The other obsessive theme in Storey's work is mental and emotional breakdown. This is at least hinted at in *This Sporting Life,* where Mrs. Hammond exhibits most of the symptoms of marked withdrawal and emotional collapse. (It is no doubt significant also that her relationship with Machin comes in a *temps mort* in another relationship, though this time, uniquely, with a dead husband rather than a living spouse, from whom the subject of the breakdown is temporarily separated.) Usually in Storey's writings it is the man who suffers the nervous breakdown, the urge to contract out of his present life.

IV

THE first fully developed example of this theme appears in *Flight into Camden,* his second novel, published like *This Sporting Life* in 1960. It is a first-person narrative told by an unmarried secretary at the Coal Board, who meets, through her lecturer brother, a teacher at the local art school (married, as it transpires, though at first he denies it), and begins an affair with him. At first she shows signs of a Mrs. Hammond–like ungenerousness of response, but later agrees to run off with him to London, from where he will divorce his wife and they will begin a new life together.

It rapidly becomes evident, though, that Howard is not the balanced, decisive sort of character Margaret has first supposed. His flight is a neurotic one, a way of staving off breakdown for a while. He cannot separate himself from his former life, from his wife and children, and he cannot begin a new life. Very soon he has drifted back into the teaching he despises, but further down the scale: instead of lecturing on industrial design at an art college he is teaching English and history in a secondary modern school. The couple's companionship becomes for a while sexless; he lies and prevaricates about his divorce, his confidence seems sapped by the transplanting of his life to London, especially since Margaret is more immediately successful. And there are external as well as internal forces working against them—Howard's wife, who will not make things easy for him, and Margaret's father, who comes down to reason with her. Finally, and, more surprisingly, there is her brother, who comes with every intention of taking her back by force to placate their parents, to whom, he maintains, she owes it to do as they think right rather than as she does, on pain of their death. Little by little Margaret comes to face the fact, unwillingly, that this is "a temporary life," that Howard will sooner or later go back to his family, and very probably when he has she will go back to hers.

Here, in one book, Storey outlines the subject matter of a whole body of interconnected works—the novels *Pasmore* and *A Temporary Life,* the plays *The Restoration of Arnold Middleton, In Celebration,* and *The Farm.* These, while each has its own strong individuality, seem, when taken together, to be going over and over the same emotional territory in different directions, arranging and rearranging the various elements to illuminate now one facet, now another, worrying at them to achieve a deeper, richer, or simply more exact truth. The elements are teaching, marital breakup, mental breakdown, and the generation gap between limited, censorious parents and children determined in spite of everything to make their own lives according to their own standards.

V

INDEED, *Pasmore*—most of which was written around 1964 although it was not published until 1972, when Storey had temporarily given up hope of making structural sense of all the material for his fourth novel in one book—is virtually a rewrite of *Flight into Camden* from the other point of view, the man's. Colin Pasmore is a teacher in a college, married, with children, apparently settled, just like Howard, and he too makes a "flight into Camden" —though admittedly his move is only a short distance from somewhere in north London. He finds himself living in a small flat near a street market that sounds remarkably like the London refuge of Howard and Margaret.

In other respects the subjects diverge slightly. There is another woman, but she is not central to his flight; rather, she is a temporary fixture of his life away from home. She remains private, mysterious. Pasmore knows no more about her than we do. She is well off, taking evening classes at his college to pass the time; she is emotionally reticent while sexually available, like Mrs. Hammond, and Elizabeth in *A Temporary Life;* and she has a jealous or at any rate possessive husband, who has Pasmore beaten up for his pains, like Colin Freestone in *A Temporary Life.* But what is going on in Helen's mind is not really germane to the subject of *Pasmore,* which, though not this time a first-person narrative, is told entirely from Pasmore's point of view. One may suspect that if *Flight into Camden* were told from Howard's point of view instead of Margaret's, Margaret would seem almost as mysterious, as incidental in Howard's breakdown and retreat, as Helen does in Pasmore's. For what Pasmore is really undergoing, we know (in Howard's case we suspect it), is a sort of male-menopause nervous breakdown. Obscurely dissatisfied with his job, his settled married life, he gradually slips into a state of psychological retreat, unable to make love to his wife, unable to communicate with his children, unable to work, unable, finally, to do anything.

The process begins with obscure, terrifying dreams, and eventually the whole of Pasmore's life becomes an obscure, terrifying dream. No explanation is offered: Pasmore himself cannot explain what is happening to him. But there seems to be some residual guilt in his feelings toward his parents, whom, when nearing the depth of his withdrawal, he goes to visit. They are, as always in Storey's work, greedily demanding, unconsciously ruthless in their application of emotional blackmail. The father is a miner, deeply ingrained in his bitterness and narrow morality—or conventionality, rather: there does not seem to be anything as definable as a moral position behind his objections to the news that Pasmore's marriage is on the rocks; it is simply that this is not what Pasmore's parents expect of him, not what he *owes* them. By doing something they do not approve of, he is ruining his parents' life and invalidating all they have done in their lives—no question of what might be best for him, best for his wife, best for his three children. The tone and family setup are immediately familiar: the marital breakup is his, as it is Howard's in *Flight into Camden,* but the disapproving parents are now his too. When his father reflects finally, "I wish to God you'd never been born. I wish to God you hadn't," it could be Margaret's father speaking, or Arthur Machin's; pushed a little further, it could be Mr. Shaw in *In Celebration* or Mr. Slattery in *The Farm* if they had not given up, retreated into a sort of self-pitying enjoyment of their own incomprehension of and by their children. In the end, Pasmore goes back to his wife, like Howard. Is it a happy ending? Hard to say for certain. The final words of the book leave us undecided:

> In the winter he returned to teaching. Outwardly, despite the events of the preceding year, little had changed. He still had a regular job, a home, a wife and children; the apparatus of his life from his books to the commercial van was virtually the same. Even the despair, it seemed, persisted.
>
> Yet something had changed. It was hard to describe. He had been on a journey. At times it seemed scarcely credible he had survived. He still dreamed of the pit and the blackness. It existed all around him, an intensity, like a presentiment of love, or violence: he found it hard to tell.

The jacket note, talking of his "regeneration," implies that the ending is affirmative, if not actually happy. Storey himself says not: in the context of the whole long, uncompleted novel of which *Pasmore* originally formed an element (its central character, apparently, is the husband of Pasmore's elusive girlfriend, glimpsed in the published work in just one scene), Pasmore is seen as the dropout, the failure, the character who gives up in his attempt to escape and goes back weakly to the situation he needed so desperately to leave.

It is possible, though, that Storey himself reacts more ambiguously to this solution than he is willing to express. The plot in this respect offers close parallels with that of Storey's first play, *The Restoration of Arnold Middleton,* written in 1959 just before *Flight into Camden* and extensively revised in 1964, at about the time Storey was writing *Pasmore.*

VI

ARNOLD MIDDLETON is also a teacher, also discontented, also, like the teachers we meet in *A Temporary Life,* somewhat given to iconoclastic jokes and sniping at the educational establishment. What is not so immediately evident is that he is also, like the teachers in *Flight into Camden* and *Pasmore,* drifting deeper and deeper into mental illness. The attitude that he adopts, interlarded with schoolboyish japes, tall stories about his trying to sneak an oversized suit of armor into school under the headmaster's nose, little academic jokes with other members of the staff, might seem to be a sort of Lucky Jim brainless philistinism (the play was first called *To Die with the Philistines*), but it arises from a real anguish at the world around him. The obsessive barrage of music-hall comedy and nursery-rhyme nonsense he puts up is a disguise, behind which the man is disintegrating.

And as he disintegrates, so does his marriage, of course. His wife finally determines to hit back, while his mother-in-law takes refuge upstairs in a state of collapse. But at this moment, having reached the point of total disintegration, he passes his crisis and starts to return to normal. Significantly, the moment of crisis is signalized by a long, loosely versified monologue in which Arnold refers to his parents, quotes his mother, and seems to be expressing, somewhat obscurely and indirectly, some sense of guilt and insufficiency in his relations with his parents: he has (or has not) lived up to their hopes and expectations for him:

> When I was young, my mother said to me:
> "Never drown but in the sea—
> Rivers, streams and other dilatory courses
> Are not contingent with the elemental forces
> Which govern you and me—and occasionally your father—
> So remember, even if the means are insufficient, rather
> Than die in pieces subside by preference as a whole,
> For disintegration is inimical to the soul
> Which seeks the opportunity or the chances
> To die in the circumstances
> Of a prince, a saviour, or a messiah—
> Or something, perhaps, even a little higher—
> You and me and several of your aunties,
> On my side, though working class, have destinies
> Scarcely commensurate with our upbringing;
> I hope in you we are instilling
> This sense of secret dignities and rights
> —Not like your father's side, the lights
> Of which, I hope, we'll never see again,
> Who have, I'm afraid, wet blotting-paper for a brain."
> *(Pause.)*
> "Please, please my son,
> Don't fail me like your father done."
> (ARNIE *stands for a moment regarding the wall, expectantly,*

tensed. Then slowly he relaxes. His head sinks, his shoulders droop. His forehead leans against the wall.)
Oh. Oh. Oh.
When I was young, when I was young,
There were so many things I should have done.
(Fade.)

(III.i)

But Arnold Middleton is restored, he does come back. He gets rid of his mother-in-law, he patches things up with his wife. He can, he is sure, come out; "the assumption is merely based, you understand, on a generality of feeling." We might ask, as of Pasmore's return to a sort of sanity, if this is a happy ending. Storey himself seems to be in two minds about it. As he first wrote the play, Arnie kills himself at the end. In his rewrite, he made Arnie come out, come back to normal (and even emphasized this in the new title). Maybe, he thinks, he should have stuck with the original ending, as more logical and more honest. On the other hand, the new ending has its own sort of honesty, since insofar as the play is autobiographical, in feeling if not in factual detail, Storey did himself come out of his state of extreme depression when he was a frustrated teacher. So to make Arnie live on and be "restored" is also honest in its fidelity to Storey's own perhaps unreasonable, illogical, but nevertheless lived experience.

A similar two-edged attitude toward others who take refuge in flight may be sensed elsewhere in Storey. The very idea of flight, escape, has something faintly discreditable: there are always those ready on the sidelines to say that you can't run away from yourself, you have duties to others; as you make your bed, so shall you lie upon it. Thus, despite a certain degree of identification with his heroes, Storey also seems to agree with this censure of them: certainly his escapers never seem to be strong and decisive enough to take their fate into their own hands, for good or ill, or to make their decisions confidently and carry them through. Pasmore, Howard, and Arnold Middleton are clearly going through a neurotic retreat from life, rather than making a purposeful change; the flight is a symptom of their sickness. The withdrawal of Colin's wife in *A Temporary Life* is into complete and seemingly incurable insanity, and the four principal characters in *Home* are undoubtedly insane. Nor is there any apparent attempt on Storey's part to suggest that the insane, as the world judges them, have access to some kind of wisdom and illumination denied to the sane. Storey's lunatics are just mad, and where we are offered any sort of explanation of their madness, as with Yvonne in *A Temporary Life,* it is merely the burden of caring about everything, being too personally involved with "issues," and, incidentally, trying too hard to live up to parents' exaggerated expectations and requirements.

VII

STOREY indicates that he regards Pasmore as a failure, one who gives in and goes back instead of going on to something new. How then does he feel —and expect us to feel—about Andrew, in his next play, *In Celebration* (1969), who has recently given up his secure job as a solicitor (a respectable position of which his parents can feel proud) to become a painter? His mother, of course, is critical: how about his wife of seventeen years; what about the two children; what about his responsibilities? On the other hand, she knows exactly where she stands in regard to another son, Steven, who has decided not to finish a book about modern society he has been working on for years: "He's better off looking after his wife and family, not writing books." Andrew is of course right when he admits to wanting revenge on his parents, for "projecting him into a world they didn't understand. Educating him for a society which existed wholly in their imaginations . . . philistine, parasitic, opportunistic . . . bred in ignorance, fed in ignorance, dead—in ignorance" (I.ii).

But it would be difficult to maintain that Andrew is presented as in any way a sympathetic character. His role is entirely destructive, and as Steven remarks, while not denying the truth of anything his brother has said, "The most tedious thing about his social attitudes, his moral insights, is the perversity of their motives." Even if he is right, it is surely time to forgive, or at least forget; one cannot let one's whole life be stunted by experiences way back, beyond the possibility of change. What difference if Andrew has discovered the terrible truth that their oldest, now long-dead brother was conceived out of wedlock, and that he and they have in different ways been made to pay for it throughout their lives. Does it still matter?

Apparently it does. While Andrew, the iconoclast, is busily pulling the structure of his life apart—more, it seems, to spite his parents than to make it any more satisfactory for himself—Steven, the quiet conformist, the model son who has of his own accord given up all that book-writing nonsense his parents could not understand or approve of, also seems to be on the brink of breakdown: he has given up his writing much as Pasmore gives up his as his breakdown comes upon him; he is racked by obscure, terrible dreams just as Pasmore is. If Andrew is the open-eyed, cynical self-destroyer ("I'll go into the garden and eat worms, then they'll be sorry"), Steven it seems is being destroyed by forces working up from inside, forces he cannot control. Steven appears to be, potentially at least, the same character as Pasmore and Howard; Andrew is more like Colin Freestone in *A Temporary Life*—a black, anarchic nihilist who does what he does from a dislike of everyone and everything, not least himself. His rough, rather heartless sense of humor is like that of Freestone, the ex-prizefighter (read: footballer?) turned art-school teacher; one could imagine him without too much difficulty picking fights in the same way that Freestone does, or recklessly, willfully antagonizing people.

These two types of contracting-out recur. Arthur, the unsuccessful poet son in the play *The Farm* (1973), seems to be a Steven type, and so, perhaps, does Newsome in the novel *Pasmore,* a painter who has spent more and more time painting less and less, until he has come finally to spending months in his studio contemplating a painting with just one spot on it "like a drop of blood." Arthur Machin in *This Sporting Life* is potentially an Andrew type, before his total disillusionment; so, curiously enough, is Margaret's careerist brother Michael, with his cruel, destructive side, in *Flight into Camden*—and there is a clear connection between Michael and the even more demonic Tolson in *Radcliffe.* To all of these might be applied the judgment offered on Tolson by one of his victims, Blakeley:

> "It's the *spiritual* things Tolson seeks to possess most of all. Things he can't acquire through his own temperament. He's bound to attack, to *consume* people in whom he recognizes some sort of spiritual quality. And naturally, they're the ones most vulnerable to his physical sort of energy."

In other words, many more characters than we might at first suppose prove to fit into Storey's own suggested dichotomy in his work between soul and body, between the spiritual, interior, "feminine" and the physical, exterior, "masculine." Seen in this light the relations of the principal characters in several of Storey's works take some unexpected forms. In *Flight into Camden* Margaret's problem seems to be essentially that she represents the "soul" side and gets entangled with someone she wants to be the "body" but who turns out to be "soul" also. Arnold Middleton seems like a mixture of the two kinds at war with himself, behaving sometimes like Colin Freestone for Pasmore-like reasons. Pasmore seemingly drifts off into a world of soul, with his strangely passive wife, Kay, and his painter acquaintance, Newsome, who has come to feel, like Howard, that "There is *nothing* to paint now. Except paint itself"; the only real incursion of "body" is the brief visit of his occasional bedfellow's husband, with its violent aftermath. In *A Temporary Life* this character comes into sharper focus in the person of Newman, the possessive, vengeful husband of Elizabeth, with whom Freestone has become involved (if that is the word for such a chilly, casual affair) while his own wife is in a mental home, apparently incurable. Newman manifests himself as a somewhat demonic "body" figure, but we may guess at an interesting development, in that at least he seems to function in a practical world, whereas Freestone, a less evolved "body" figure, is obviously fated to drop out, to destroy himself, or at least aid those who seek to destroy him, because he does not care. He is animated, as far as we can tell (this is a first-person novel unfolded with a minimum of psychological explanation or overt consideration of motives), only by something akin to Andrew's ingrained perversity.

VIII

In *Pasmore* (1972) and *A Temporary Life* (1973), Storey seems to be developing a rather different kind of novel, technically if not thematically—one of bare, stripped happenings, with little or no editorial comment or guidance for the reader, who is left to make of them what he will. On their first appearance, a number of critics speculated that this might be the result of Storey's coming back to the novel after some years devoted exclusively to drama. This cannot be the case, since, though published some years later, the books were conceived and mostly written in 1964 and 1965, before Storey had written any plays except the still unproduced *Restoration of Arnold Middleton.* But clearly the feeling of dissatisfaction with what he was at that time doing led to this laconic style in novel writing, and brought him shortly afterward to spend more and more time writing for the theater. As Storey himself has explained, he was very unhappy about the way *This Sporting Life* and *Flight into Camden* were received, feeling that the critics' gratifying enthusiasm was beside the point of his real intentions, praising him for a sort of documentary realism he was far from aiming at. So when he was completing *Radcliffe* and revising *The Restoration of Arnold Middleton* in 1963, he determined that this time round he would direct his audience's attention very specifically toward what he wanted them to see. Of *Radcliffe* he says:

> I wrote the book starting from about chapter five, then went back and wrote the first chapters—which didn't fit the rest at all!—and put in linking passages to impose on it a sort of overall pattern of significance, the significance I then saw in what I had written, according to which the two principal characters are facets of the same thing, body and mind, outer and inner life, brought together. The result was that *Radcliffe* is scattered with great big notices saying "Pay attention now, this is important," and I think that spoils the book.
>
> (*Plays and Players,* June 1970)

IX

CERTAINLY there is an element of truth in this: *Radcliffe* is at points unnecessarily, weakeningly overt about its designs on the reader, and there are times when the editorial comment is one-sided or misleading—very much the significance Storey saw in his work rather than something intrinsic; so that one could reasonably argue with him and question whether he is necessarily better qualified than anyone else to tell us what the book is about. Indeed, Storey went on to say, in a passage that throws some useful light on his creative processes:

> It seems to me that if, on reading something through, I know completely what it is about, then it is dead. It is when I feel that I don't really know what it is about that it lives—it lives for me almost in the measure that it escapes and refuses definition.

Radcliffe is a powerful, disturbing book—many would say his most powerful and disturbing—but a lot of its power comes from the sense we have of not quite grasping what it is about, and our feeling that the author does not either: that it represents an almost uncontrollable boiling up of violent emotions that are shaped and forged—but only just—on the anvil of art.

In this light, the author's occasional too-emphatic attempts to make his meaning—or at least his method—clear to us can be ignored. Also, considering the subject matter of the book, a certain amount of trepidation on the author's part is understandable. For on the realistic level *Radcliffe* is a homosexual love story. And whatever symbolic significance it may have, the realistic level is still important, since if it does not work there, it will not work at all. Whether or not on some symbolic level Leonard Radcliffe and his dark angel Tolson are aspects of the same person (Leonard at one point theorizes, "Just think what if this *separate* thing [the soul] were in one man, and the body, the acting part, in another? What if these two qualities were typified ideally in two separate men? Then, just imagine . . . just imagine the unholy encounter of two such people!"), the fact remains that in the book they are two people, two men, passionately involved with each other. The theme is carried through other generations: Leonard's bachelor Uncle Austen is said to have once developed an obsessive fascination for a broken-down pub singer, and later on it proves that this same singer, Blakely, is hopelessly in love with Tolson, to the neglect of his family—his daughter and the children he himself has had by her. Everything ends in very palpable physical disaster—Leonard kills Tolson. Blakely confesses to the murder and kills himself and his whole family; Leonard goes mad and eventually dies of a brain hemorrhage in a mental institution.

Obviously, such a plot is not usual for an English novel, and the author might well fear misunderstanding. It is hardly surprising that he should wish to make clear, even too clear, the "serious" intentions of this apparently sensational narrative. Moreover, at that time homosexuality in the English novel still tended to occupy a little pigeonhole of its own; the "homosexual novel" was almost a genre by itself, and was likely (Angus Wilson's *Hemlock and After* notwithstanding) to be about a problem rather than about people. *Radcliffe* is emphatically not about a problem. It emphatically is about people, not abstractions. And it certainly does not fit easily into the class of the genteel "homosexual novel"—even less than into that of the contemporary British novel as a whole. For that matter, although one would never mistake it for the work of any other writer, *Radcliffe* is the work of Storey's that goes farthest afield for its material. True, there may be some faint suggestions of the minor characters Austen and Blakeley in *This Sporting Life,* and the possibility of lining up Tolson (the body) and Leonard (the soul) with other characters in Storey's writings. But the relationships are indirect and theoretical, and none of the situations in the book corresponds to situations elsewhere.

The central character, Leonard, does not belong to the working-class mining family background so often encountered in Storey's novels, but to a kind of decayed squirearchy. At the same time, the rambling, semiderelict old house in which they live (as caretakers rather than owners) has a symbolic significance of the right kind, which is inherent in the plot rather than artificially applied by the author's formulation. The house symbolizes the state of the family and its relation to the industrial town that is encroaching all round, the town that in the final page of the book takes over so completely that even the site where the house stood is obliterated. Nor does Tolson have the familiar background—indeed, we learn little about his family except that his father is dead. None of the other Storey situations occurs here either, except possibly the mental breakdown (Leonard's that is); but even that takes a very different form from the quiet subsidence of Howard or Pasmore, or even, we are given to suppose (it happens before the start of the book) that of Yvonne Freestone in *A Temporary Life.* Instead, everything in *Radcliffe* centers on this violent, passionate, tortured relationship of the two men, in which the physical attraction is felt on both sides. It is Tolson who, though married and perfectly capable of casually sleeping with a passing girl just on impulse, makes the first physical approach to Leonard; and the need to dominate is present almost equally in the demonic Tolson and the seemingly passive, withdrawn Leonard.

The situation is theorized about in the book: at one point Leonard, describing his relationship with Tolson, says, "The thing's very simple. Either to be loved or to be destroyed," and his father replies, "Or to be loved *and* destroyed"; elsewhere, as we have noted before, Blakeley says to Leonard: "It's the *spiritual* things Tolson seeks to possess most of all. Things he can't acquire through his own temperament. He's bound to attack, *consume* people in whom he recognizes some sort of spiritual quality." And Leonard is nothing if not spiritual: even though his sexual attraction to Tolson is physically expressed, we are told early in the book that "he scarcely saw people as people, but more simply and certainly as states of feeling and association." But the characters and their relations transcend such formulations. Tolson and Leonard are not merely body and soul, they are not even primarily that. They are titanic figures whose struggle for supremacy takes on almost cosmic proportions, but they are also men localized in time and space. Like dark gods pietistically rationalized, they wear their cloak of flesh convincingly, but the wilder, stranger, more unaccountable elements keep bursting through. No reticences here, but a passion and a torment that Emily Brontë would have understood and the D. H. Lawrence of *Women in Love* sympathized with.

The larger-than-life quality of *Radcliffe* is inescapable. But Storey's skill in particularizing and authenticating his battle of the titans must not be overlooked. What keeps the book in its precarious but working balance is Storey's intense feeling for landscape and the hard external world of physical labor and bodily response. One cannot forget that Storey has himself experienced kinds of life that are predominantly—and no doubt partly as a means of escape from intellectual exertion—physical in their emphasis: his periods as a tent-erector and a professional footballer have marked his work just as decisively as his periods as an art student and as a teacher. The professional life of Arthur Machin in *This Sporting Life,* the episode of *Radcliffe* in which Leonard and Tolson work in a tent-erecting crew, are evoked with hallucinatory intensity and precision—nothing vague or symbolic about them. These backgrounds come into view in his plays *The Changing Room* (1972) and *The Contractor*

(1970), where the finespun human drama is, if not subordinate to a documentary depiction of the milieu, at least inextricably entangled in it.

X

FREQUENTLY in plays or novels we are told what the principal characters do for a living, but this is left as a token gesture rather than apprehended as the fabric of their lives. In *The Changing Room,* a football team (plus Sunday reserves and committee members) gather in a changing room, go out to play a hard game, return in the interval, come back afterwards to change and disperse—three acts covering their total day's presence in the one room. In *The Contractor,* five workmen come to put up a tent for the wedding breakfast of their boss's daughter, erect it, take it down the next morning and leave. The football game is a football game, the tent is palpably a tent. But the people are just as palpably people, and the delicate web of relations among them, the subtle pattern of strengths and weaknesses, understanding and illusion, that gradually emerges from the seemingly desultory banter and backchat of the workmen as they work, the footballers on the margin of the field, is totally convincing as a naturalistic depiction of real people in real life. Because it is so convincing, because the plays are so completely, satisfyingly self-defining as dramatic actions, it is possible to theorize here too—to see *The Contractor,* for instance, as having some sort of allegorical intention as a reflection on the decline and fading away of capitalist society, or both plays as metaphors for the process of artistic creation, its labor and its doubtful usefulness. Possible, but not necessary—this is something the author himself might read into what he has written after the event of writing, but it is never overtly presented as an explanation or validation within the writing itself.

The same is true even more intensely of *Home* (1970), at once Storey's simplest and most obscure play. In it virtually nothing happens externally, and very little that is directly meaningful is said. Its four main characters are physically very static and constantly return to the same commonplaces, the same conversational formulas. By the end of the first act, at exactly the same point that the author gathered this while writing, we gather that they are all inmates of some kind of mental institution. During the second act both men and one of the women have bouts of weeping, but we learn little or nothing of why they are there, where they come from, or any of the other things we would normally expect to be told in progressive revelation. The play is as much a physical event as *The Contractor* or *The Changing Room*—a theatrical situation of people on a stage speaking and moving, and people in an audience watching and listening, and understanding more through their instincts than through their intelligence. Except that it is a physical event in which virtually nothing physical happens, an evocation of a fabric of life that is close to no-life, to nonexistence. Presumably the mental-home situation, which occurs also at the end of *Radcliffe* and in *A Temporary Life,* has a personal significance for Storey similar to that of football or tent-erecting, but if so he has not told us of what sort. And, triumphantly, he does not need to: cast loose from its motivation in the mind of the author, the work of art is vividly, incontestably there.

Like all autonomous works of art, *Home* can be seen in many possible lights. The foregoing account of the play probably makes it sound decidedly grim and gloomy, but in fact there is a lot of humor in it—humor of character clash and misunderstanding, even verbal humor, particularly in the bickerings of the two old ladies. And humor is an element that, though one could hardly claim that it is dominant in any of Storey's works except possibly his strange little story-with-pictures *Edward* (1973), about a bishop who finds a key but cannot discover to what (and here the humor is no doubt more in Donald Parker's drawings than in the very brief text), does crop up regularly and tellingly throughout his writing. There is much humor in *The Restoration of Arnold Middleton*—so much so that for most of its length the play could be mistaken for an anarchic comedy somewhat in the line of *Lucky Jim.* In the later books, the subplot of *A Temporary Life* concerning Colin Freestone's relations with the eccentric principal of the art school where he teaches is deliciously funny in a cool, straight-faced way. The all-too-frugal dinner Colin is offered on his visit to the cottage leads to a lively comedy of embarrassment intensified by Colin's ironical determination not to be embarrassed; the ultimate revelation of the principal's oddity, when his private closet is found to be full of things supposedly stolen from the school and innumerable bottles of urine religiously preserved, caps it in a climax that comes close to farce. But it never goes over the edge, thanks to the tight hold Storey always keeps here on physical reality, however near he strays toward the fantastic.

XI

INDEED, it is only when Storey seems temporarily to lose contact with physical realities, to drift off too far into the realm of intellectual formulation or philosophical speculation, as in a few incidental parts of *Radcliffe* and in his symbolic drama *Cromwell* (1973), that he seems to go astray. *Cromwell* is deliberately unlocalized in time or place (one may say that it is England during the Civil War, but only the title points to that conclusion, and Cromwell himself is never seen or directly referred to) and seems overloaded with cloudy significances which, boiled down, appear to amount to little more than that military power corrupts, that civilians always suffer most in war, and that no one can escape by running away or opting out. But why seek to boil it down in this way? Why not accept it viscerally as a dramatic action just as one does *The Changing Room* or *Home*? One can see connections with other works of Storey. Two incidental characters, Irish mercenaries who provide a mocking, disaffected commentary on the main action, seem to stem directly from the Irish double-act of the tent-erectors in *The Contractor.* The spiritual odyssey of Proctor, the central character, from soldier to farmer to visionary, suggests an abstracted version of the flight into a new dimension attempted by Howard and Pasmore and maybe achieved by Leonard Radcliffe, Yvonne Freestone, and the four principal characters in *Home* when they go mad. Certainly Proctor's self-transformation into a figure from the Apocalypse does not seem any more satisfactory or hopeful than the progression of any of the others; for surely the dark river he and his family cross at the end must be the river of death, and the Boatman cannot but suggest Charon. In any case, Proctor's moment of illumination has turned out to be nothing more than a bad dream, like Pasmore's premonitions: "I dreamed I took conviction down to hell . . . cleansed and bathed its empty shell . . . and when I drank I found its contents turned to blood."

The generalizing tendency of the action, placed as it is in an overtly symbolic no-man's-land, works against Storey's best and most individual gifts as a writer. In his best work, the general is always rooted in the particular, the mental landscape coincides with the physical. Cut loose from particularity, his writing loses its peculiar vividness and density. Like D. H. Lawrence he is a superb writer about places, but unlike Lawrence he manages always to keep the people who live in these places alive and distinct. In *A Temporary Life* the action is punctuated by passages of description that seem self-sufficient but yet reflect light on the observing intelligence, that of the narrator Colin Freestone:

> I've been conscious for some time of the strange, inferno-like presence of the hill above my head, of the bursting sunlit mass of trees, of the encroaching mass of shadow; then, suddenly, as if it might have sprung from the ground itself, I see immediately before me the flame-like structure of the town, the domes and steeples, the vast, brick-fronted towers, caught now by the last, horizontal rays, a glowing, reddened edifice shot here and there with sudden gleams and flashes and lit, along its crest, by a strip of golden light.
>
> Even as I watch the light begins to fade. The darkness creeps up the separate blocks and towers. I feel the dew against my face, and the sudden chilling of the air as the hill itself falls into shadow.
>
> Birds have settled in the trees. Odd shapes are flung up, briefly, against the silhouetted leaves and branches.
>
> I start off down the hill. It's as if an aperture has opened; odd sighs and groans come up from its furthest depths. Above, the last pinnacles of the town still catch the light, long, orange fissures let into the blueness overhead. As I reach the bottom of the hill they too begin to fade; new lights, with fresh shadows, spring up from the growing darkness. Soon only a faint glow, somewhere to the west, remains.
>
> (pt. 1, ch. 1)

We know the place, but we know the man too. No connections are stated, but they are all there. For all the occasional violence of his writing, Storey is an artist in full control of his material: nothing is wasted, everything counts. When he describes at the end of *Radcliffe* the fate of the house after the people in it have gone, the writing has the force of a moral judgment:

When the workmen came, tractors tore effortlessly at the old stonework. Steel hawsers were clamped round the walls and pillars, and within a few days the building that, in its older parts, had stood for nearly five hundred years was levelled to the ground.

The church too was demolished, its foundations pronounced to be dangerous from subsidence due to the mining beneath; the cost of renovation was too high. Its various treasures were distributed amongst local museums, though the sculptured effigies themselves were broken up. A more serviceable church of brick was constructed and, although equally deserted, it was larger, cleaner and uncluttered by decoration.

The housing estate that had previously enclosed the Place on all sides seized quickly on this last piece of ground; a crescent was laid out where it had stood, and council houses, erected on either side, finally linked the two avenues that had flanked it and its denuded grounds for two decades. All this happened within two years, so that now there is no evidence, except for a slight undulation of the ground, that the Place stood on this particular spot, or that a family, whose history extended over six centuries, had ever made its mark on this hard and indomitable landscape. Occasionally, as men dig in the gardens of the new houses, they unearth fragments of carved stone. These they stack to one side against the low fences, or use to decorate their rockeries.

(p. 376)

XII

HERE, with the detailed evocation of place, and very much the same place it would seem, is where *A Prodigal Child* (1980), Storey's next novel but one after *A Temporary Life,* begins. Or is it his next? It is difficult to tell, with Storey's habit of writing in bursts, putting aside, and then reevaluating sometimes years later. He tells us that *Saville* (1975), the novel published between *A Temporary Life* and *A Prodigal Child,* was written some time before publication, put aside, then substituted at the last minute for a novel already with his publishers—not altogether to their pleasure, although ironically it went on to win the Booker Prize for Storey. *Saville* and *A Prodigal Child* tell, in a sense, the same story from different angles, or in different conventions. *Saville* is a painstakingly realistic account of a boy's maturing in North Country working-class surroundings during the 1940's and 1950's, the same time that Storey himself was going through a similar process in similar circumstances, though as usual he shrugs off any directly autobiographical reading. Whereas *Saville* carefully gives dates and chapter and verse, almost to the point of being labored, *A Prodigal Child* progresses in an increasingly dreamlike fashion from the late 1920's, when the building over the site described at the end of *Radcliffe* is complete, to the end of World War II, but deliberately covers its tracks on exact dating; its central boy character, a sensitive child with a rough rival brother, grows up unbelievably quickly into the lover of his own foster mother (by the age of eight or nine, apparently) and a successful sculptor (by the age of seventeen). It is unbelievable, that is to say, if we insist on forcing the story to make sense in baldly realistic terms. But evidently that is not its intention, and in any case Storey says that as published it is only the first half of the original conception, with a brief epilogue tacked on, and that one day he may come back to map in detail the development of the relationship of the boy and the much older woman.

In its dreamlike aspect, hovering between reality and fantasy, *A Prodigal Child* is more like *Radcliffe* than any of Storey's other books, hence perhaps the explicit connection between the closing of one and the opening of the other. But on consideration one realizes that a certain dreamlike (or sometimes nightmarish) quality is present in many of Storey's works, which create, often, a world without a clear sense of time and progression within the heart of a "real" world delineated with a deceptive amount of naturalistic detail. The quality is present very strongly, as the title indicates, in *A Temporary Life,* and in its female counterpart *Flight into Camden;* it is there in the play *Early Days* (1980), which consists mainly of the drifting recollections and reflections of an old man in retirement; and it is certainly there again, though harder to recognize, in Storey's 1984 novel *Present Times,* which concerns the aftermath of a marital breakup and the sportswriter hero's unavailing attempts to communicate with his children and his neurotic wife when she decides to return. His life is undeniably a nightmare, redeemed only by his looming success as a playwright, though it is a nightmare with enough comic sidelights to brand the book as "unacceptable" in America, where apparently no publisher dare handle it because it presents an alleged feminist (the crazed wife) in a decidedly unsympathetic light.

Present Times shows Storey striking out in rather a new direction, though still recognizably dealing with aspects of the same central body of material: the situation of a largely self-taught working-class writer; the unsuccessful attempt at a marriage breakup (with the husband, like the hero of *A Temporary Life,* moving out and getting beaten up); the conflict between generations and the greed of parents for regard (seen from a different angle, as the central character is now parent instead of child). The wry comedy is new, and so is the direct confrontation with what has, after all, been Storey's principal preoccupation during most of his adult life—writing, and specifically writing for the theater. The theater also occurs prominently in his latest play to be staged at time of writing, *Phoenix* (though it was written in a characteristic burst of activity some years before). It is about an anarchic theater director entrenched in his closed theater, due for demolition if he does not blow it up first, and his relationships with his ex-wife and other associates. Comedy, less alloyed than in any of Storey's other work, crops up in *Mother's Day* (1978), an Ortonesque farce starting from the simple premise that it would be interesting to write a piece in which all the conventional values are reversed, and crime and sin in the suburbs are taken as splendidly positive by everyone concerned.

But comedy does not in Storey's work stand for escape, and the extension of his subject matter, forward to his own life as a professional writer, backward to early childhood, and sideways into fantasy and dream, does not mean dilution. He remains very much the writer he has always been. If in his lack of reticence, his acceptance of openly expressed violence and passion as part of life and therefore, without embarrassment, as part of literature, Storey seems like a maverick figure on the British literary scene, the impression is superficial. It is merely that in his writing, as in that of other writers of his generation, things that have been buried for centuries come out. He can be seen as our first truly modern novelist because for him the traditional obstacles thrown up by middle-class education and the gentlemanly tradition of understatement are not consciously overcome; they quite simply do not exist.

SELECTED BIBLIOGRAPHY

I. Collected Works. *In Celebration and The Contractor* (Harmondsworth, 1971); *Home, The Changing Room, and Mother's Day* (Harmondsworth, 1978); *Early Days, Sisters, Life Class* (Harmondsworth, 1980); *In Celebration and Other Plays* (Harmondsworth, 1982), contains *The Contractor, The Restoration of Arnold Middleton, The Farm.*

II. Separate Works. *This Sporting Life* (London, 1960), novel; *Flight into Camden* (London, 1960), novel; *Radcliffe: A Novel* (London, 1963); *The Restoration of Arnold Middleton: A Play in Three Acts* (London, 1967), also printed in *New English Dramatists, 14* (1970); *In Celebration: A Play in Two Acts* (London, 1969); *The Contractor* (London, 1970), play; *Home* (London, 1970), play; *The Changing Room* (London, 1972), play; *Pasmore* (London, 1972), novel; *Cromwell* (London, 1973), play; *The Farm* (London, 1973), play; *A Temporary Life* (London, 1973), novel; *Edward* (London, 1973), juvenile, with drawings by Donald Parker; *Life Class* (London, 1975), play; *Saville* (London, 1975), novel; *A Prodigal Child* (London, 1980), novel; *Present Times* (London, 1984), novel.

III. Critical Studies. David Storey, "Writers on Themselves: Journey Through a Tunnel," in the *Listener* 1 (August 1963); "Speaking of Writing, II: David Storey," in the *Times* (28 November 1963); F. McGuinness, "The Novels of David Storey," in *London Magazine,* 3 (March 1964); J. M. Newton, "Two Men Who Matter?" in the *Cambridge Quarterly,* 1 (Summer 1966), a review of *Radcliffe;* F. Cox, "Writing for the Stage," in *Plays and Players* (September 1967); J. R. Taylor, "British Dramatists: The New Arrivals III: David Storey: Novelist into Dramatist," in *Plays and Players* (June 1970); S. Shrapnel, "No Goodness and No Kings," in the *Cambridge Quarterly,* 5 (Autumn 1970); R. Hayman, "Conversation with David Storey," in *Drama,* 99 (Winter 1970); J. R. Taylor, *The Second Wave: British Drama for the Seventies* (London, 1971); M. Bygrave, "David Storey: Novelist or Playwright?" in *Theatre Quarterly,* 1 (April–June 1971); K. J. Worth, *Revolutions in Modern English Drama* (London, 1972), discusses Storey's plays in the chapter "Realism in New Directions"; R. Hayman, *Playback* (London, 1973), includes an interview with Storey; "The Theatre of Life: David Storey in Interview with P. Ansorge," in *Plays and Players* (September 1973); W. J. Free, "The Ironic Anger of David Storey," in *Modern Drama* (December 1973).

EDWARD BOND

(1934–)

Simon Trussler

I

EDWARD BOND does not write about violence; he writes about the effects upon the human spirit of a violent environment. Only very occasionally is effect out of proportion to cause, and even then the surgical precision of the scrutiny, visual and verbal, prevents the violence from titillating, however much it may shock. Bond's plays yearn to explore the gentleness and compassion of which humankind is capable, and many of his characters display natural goodness under acutely difficult circumstances. But he is too honest an artist and too scrupulous a craftsman to dwell upon the tranquil moments in his plays—although when they do occur they thus work to deeper and truer effect. He believes himself an optimist that they occur at all.

In truth, one should not write about violence and Bond in the same breath. Yet not to do so would be to ignore the climate of critical opinion in which his work is too often discussed—whereas that climate, if it is to be changed, must first be defined. Why has Bond's work prompted so willfully obtuse a response from otherwise intelligent critics? How does its "cruelty" differ from that advocated by the French visionary Antonin Artaud, whose latter-day apologists too often conceive violence as an end in itself? Bond has his own answers, and increasingly has felt it necessary to provide them by way of prefaces to his printed plays, although the answers have arguably become less persuasive as the prefaces have grown longer. And should the plays themselves not be less open to misunderstanding, so that such special authorial pleading becomes unnecessary?

It has to be remembered that when Bond began writing in the early 1960's, humanity was still wreaking havoc, unchecked and unthinking, upon the world's material resources. There was no "energy crisis," little recognition that raw materials were not inexhaustible, and no real understanding of the long-term effects of blind technological advance. Nor had these matters much preoccupied the generation of playwrights immediately preceding Bond's. John Arden, Arnold Wesker, and (at least in his early work) John Osborne were all socially conscious writers, but essentially in an older tradition, of commitment to political solutions. Bond's early plays were thus prophetic—indeed, they remain so, in that the problems of which he writes are very far from solved, although they are now more widely recognized. The Victorian condemnation of Henrik Ibsen's *Ghosts* as a play "about" venereal disease is closely analogous to the enduring misconception that Bond's *Saved* is "about" stoning a baby to death.

Bond's plays probe causes and display effects. Sometimes, in his more naturalistic pieces, he extends awareness by a direct representation of a perhaps unfamiliar way of life; more recently, he has tended to work by universalizing rather than particularizing the human condition. Always, it is that condition with which he is concerned—a condition that is desperate because of the damage humankind persists in inflicting upon itself. Despite his avowed atheism, from the first he has exhibited an unquenchable faith in humanity's divine spark and in the slender but real possibilities for redemption —as he has come to believe, through the creation of a socialist society, whose building requires the dramatist to write not only problem plays but what he now describes as "answer plays."

II

EDWARD BOND was born on 18 July 1934, the child of working-class parents in the amorphous North London suburb of Holloway. He might never have left its drab, slum-pocked streets had it not been for the war, but in the event he was twice evacuated to the countryside—first to Cornwall, immediately after the outbreak of war, and then, following the blitz, to his grandparents in the Fens, close to the East Anglian setting of his first play, *The Pope's Wedding.*

Bond does not talk readily or easily about his early life, and this matters little since he is in no sense an autobiographical dramatist. But he has described the childhood experience that perhaps first aroused the writing instinct in him, and the definition of that impulse implicit in his description is interesting. "If I had lived all my life in London," he has said in an interview in *Theatre Quarterly* (1972), "I would have sensed what to feel about certain things when they happened: one would have been taught the responses. Being put into a strange environment created a division between feeling and the experience of things. If there is any one reason, I dare say it's because of that that I'm a writer." The war itself exacerbated this sense of division—the bogey-figure of Hitler in particular creating "an image of total evil . . . which was very curious, because it wasn't explained by anything which one had experienced before. Who was the nearest Hitler to me? That was the sort of problem it posed." Whether or not a capacity to sense "a division between feeling and the experience of things" is essential to all creative writers, it is certainly true that much of Bond's own work seeks to make comprehensible (as distinct from condoning) that which is outside "normal" human experience, yet which is perpetrated by "normal" human beings.

Returning to his family after the war, Bond went to a secondary modern school in Holloway, but he received little in the way of formal education: "the problem was just to organize the children into some sort of passive obedience." But in the *Theatre Quarterly* interview he described vividly a school trip to see Donald Wolfit in *Macbeth,* at the long-since-demolished Bedford Theatre in Camden Town:

> What came across from Wolfit's performance was a sense of dignity about people. Now it's not true that God is concerned every time a sparrow falls to the ground, because he couldn't bear it, but it is true that Shakespeare cared—even about this man Macbeth, who perhaps was like Hitler. And so I got from that play a sense of human dignity—of the value of human beings. Also a certain feeling, afterwards, of real surprise—that other people had seen this, so how was it that their lives could just go on in the same way?

That theater visit Bond now regards as the sum total of his education. He left school as soon as he legally could and worked at anonymous jobs, interrupted only by two years of National Service in the army. He began writing "very bad verse" around the age of twenty-one—"and it *was* very bad." But a combination of influences—the memory of Wolfit's *Macbeth,* the sudden renaissance of British drama in the late 1950's, a mind that "thought in terms of confrontations and speeches" —soon set him writing plays. His early output, though prolific, was, as he now describes it, "well-meaning but incompetent." He made no attempt to get this apprentice work staged—"it was a personal thing"—and although he did submit the script of one play before *The Pope's Wedding* to the Royal Court Theatre, he now thinks "that was just a desire for contact with other writers, to see what on earth they thought about it." The Sunday evening "production without decor" of *The Pope's Wedding* at the Court in 1962 thus represented a personal as well as a professional breakthrough: "It somehow worked. I didn't mind it being produced."

The play attracted little critical attention at the time, but Bond became a member of the Writers' Group at the Court, and many of his subsequent full-length works received their first London productions there. His belief that he "couldn't have worked in any other theatre" is probably correct. Apart from the support of William Gaskill—both artistically, in his sympathetic direction of most of the plays, and administratively, in the battles he waged to beat the attempted censorship of *Saved* and *Early Morning*—no other theater could probably have afforded to keep faith with a writer who has remained so resolutely without honor in his own country. Some of his plays have achieved a *succès de scandale,* many a *succès d'estime;* but none has yet achieved the economic success of a transfer to a West End theater. The major institutional theaters, the National and the Royal Shakespeare Company, have, however, become the natural homes for his later work.

Bond's second play to reach the stage, *Saved* (1965), won him not so much fame as notoriety and was at the center of a brief but virulent controversy over allegedly "dirty plays." Bond shrank from the ill-focused spotlight, although he was now able to give himself full-time to writing; and his next play, *Early Morning* (1968), caused an even more virulent row, largely on account of its phantasmagoric portrayal of a lesbian relationship between Queen Victoria and Florence Nightingale. In spite of the attempt to beat the Lord Chamberlain's total ban on its production by turning the Royal Court into a club theater, the piece escaped closing for only two performances—which, of course, did little to dispel the happy ignorance on which most of the abuse of Bond was based. The lack of any conceivable cause for public outrage in his *Narrow Road to the Deep North,* presented at the Belgrade Theatre, Coventry, in 1968, conversely ensured that it was little noticed.

In 1969, however, the Royal Court celebrated the abolition of the Lord Chamberlain's role as stage censor by mounting a full-scale season of *Saved, Early Morning,* and *Narrow Road to the Deep North.* The season established Bond as probably the most important writer to have emerged in the British theater in the 1960's, bringing him to the notice of continental directors and at last giving his work full public exposure. Soon afterward he wrote two short pieces for political causes with which he was in sympathy: *Black Mass*, for an anti-apartheid commemoration of the Sharpeville massacre in 1970, and *Passion,* for a rally organized by the Campaign for Nuclear Disarmament in 1971. And later in that year *Lear*—which many critics consider his finest work to date—reached the stage of the Royal Court.

By this time Bond had moved to a country home in Suffolk and had married Elisabeth Pablé. His two following plays alike suggest the sort of transitional, contemplative mood that often follows the writing of such a major work as *Lear.* Indeed, several critics used the adjective "Chekhovian" to describe *The Sea* (1973), while *Bingo* (1974) explored certain of the themes of *Lear* in a calmer, more personal context; and in its exploration of the relationship of Shakespeare's art and his sense of personal responsibility, this play also anticipated *The Fool* (1975), which sets the life and work of the poet John Clare in a broader social perspective. Already, Bond had so far expanded the boundaries of his craft that his relatively small canon of work covered a broader formal spectrum than that of any longer established British playwright, with the possible exception of John Arden. More instinctively, he was developing a quite remarkable gift for riveting the sensibilities through the sudden rightness of an image.

His more recent plays have sustained both formal flexibility and poetic fluency, but as his political commitment has taken a more explicitly socialist direction, a diminution in dialectical complexity has on occasion been evident. It's true that in *The Woman* (1978) Bond successfully embraces some of the concerns of feminism within a revolutionary reworking of the Hecuba myth; but *The Bundle* (1978) makes his own *Narrow Road* less rather than more complex in its reworking of that earlier play along a more politicized seam. And *The Worlds* (1979), despite the universality claimed by its title, reduces its argument and its action to a rather simplistic struggle between boardroom politicking and political board-gaming.

Restoration (1981) and *Summer* (1982) are much more successful in fusing originality of form with the heightening of Bond's political awareness—just as their first productions justified his increasing determination wherever possible to direct his own plays. Yet in his most recent work at the time of writing, the trilogy *The War Plays* (1985), the clotted thinking and congested style that have come too often to disfigure his prefaces begin to infiltrate the perimeters of the plays themselves. His career thus seems tantalizingly poised between the worthy demands of propagandist art—demands that, simply, he does not seem very good at meeting—and his compelling but often disconcerting personal vision. For this writer he remains one of the most exciting and challenging writers of his generation when he rejects the temptation to offer prepackaged solutions to the complex problems with which his work is engaged. As he puts it in his preface to *Lear:* "If your plan of the future is too rigid, you start to coerce people to fit it. We do not need a plan of the future, we need a *method* of change."

III

WHAT is striking about Bond's first play to reach the stage, *The Pope's Wedding* (1962), is not so much its intrinsic quality—though it is by no reckoning an undistinguished work—as its instantly recognizable voice. If there is occasionally a hint of Harold Pinter about the more monosyllabic and deliberately disconnected dialogue, and of the eponymous character of Pinter's *Caretaker* in the prevaricating recluse Alen, this is no more than a recognition of areas—areas of the mind—opened up by one dramatist, and here explored in quite a different way. For where Pinter creates context through subjective response or reminiscence, and so in some measure distorts it, in Bond's work, even at its most non-naturalistic, there is almost always an objective correlative, a yardstick against which to measure normality or eccentricity.

The Pope's Wedding presents as fully persuasive a glimpse of rural life as *Saved* does of an urban environment. Although its characters are (with the exception of the hermit Alen) very young, their futures are all-too-predictably mapped out; even the promiscuous, free-wheeling Scopey of the early scenes casually commits himself to a married rut that might have lasted him out a humdrum lifetime but for the obsessive interest he develops in Alen's way of life. The occasional references to other elderly people—to the veteran village cricketer Bullright or to the illness of "owd Tanner Lob," who "won't be 'arvestin this year"—reinforce the impression of a whole pattern of life into which this younger generation fits and to which (all but Scopey) it is more or less cheerfully resigned.

Pat, the randy wench of the early scenes and Scopey's semidetached wife later in the play, has always coped with Alen's little chores: kept him minimally clean and done the shopping his agoraphobia forbids. Where another dramatist might have made the exploration of the cause of Pat's allegiance the core of the play, here it is simply one of the facts of the situation. Maybe the old man once had an affair with Pat's long-dead mother, maybe he is the girl's father, giving Scopey's obsession with him, and the eventual murder, an added oedipal twist. But the nature of Pat's allegiance doesn't matter: it is an unthinking kindness, to set against unthinking callousness, just as the casual violence of the young men is balanced by the occasional glimpses of their creative activity, at work on the land or playing cricket.

While Alen arouses the hostility usually accorded by the pack to an outsider, he is in no sense the mysterious character Scopey finds him. "I never stopped gooin' after people," he says. "They stopped gooin' after me." Scopey doesn't believe him, but Alen conceals no secret, and murdering him merely reduces Scopey to the shell that was Alen. When Bond was asked why he had called the play *The Pope's Wedding,* he replied that it was "an impossible ceremony—Scopey's asking for an invitation to something that isn't going to happen." His initial curiosity about Alen is thus perverted into futile aggression, and this response is different only in degree from that of his former friends, who have previously talked of going to "turn owd Alen's dump over" as no more than a spur-of-the-moment idea to alleviate boredom. On this occasion they don't act on the idea—and Bond's technique of distinguishing verbal intention from physical action is characteristic. But when, much later, they do gather outside Alen's hovel to jeer and taunt, a shower of stones thrown against the wall is the limit of their violence. By then, it is Scopey who is inside, listening and waiting. His curiosity goes deeper, but because it cannot be satisfied, so is his capacity for violence increased.

The way in which different kinds of action are keyed to shifting verbal moods in *The Pope's Wedding* is entirely persuasive. Motivation emerges forcefully from the interplay of these moods, although motivation is too cumbersome a description for those tenuous tripwires that almost accidentally inspire action, when action is little more than a desire for a change. As a character, Alen is incidental—a catalyst alike to Scopey's quest for salvation and to society's need for a scapegoat on whom violence can safely be inflicted. There is little formal structure to the play, but its shape effortlessly accommodates the episodic succession of incidents, and the barely perceptible handling of exposition is masterly. Bond's preference for seeking a sustained, logically developed insight rather than an arbitrary apportionment of worked-up climaxes anticipates the more formal sense of dialectic process in his following plays.

There are minor weaknesses, of course. The relationship of Pat and Scopey, both before and after their marriage, is somewhat schematically presented, and there is little sense of development in Scopey's increasing need for Alen as a prop for his own personality. But Alen himself is carefully, almost affectionately right—a figure who has withdrawn from the configuration of his past into the enigmatic emptiness of his present. No noble savage or possessor of secret spiritual insights, he is merely a lonely old man whose meaningless daily rituals preserve a semblance of sanity—and who prefers evaporated milk and food straight from tins to the real thing. All the more persuasive, because Bond makes no effort to underline it, is the total acceptance of Alen's eccentricity by all the characters other than Scopey, whether as the object of Pat's casual care or of the gang's half-hearted hatred. Things are as they are. Only Scopey, trying to probe deeper, and inexorably drawn to murder as if it will reveal all, gets hurt; and he is probing not cause, as he thinks, but effect.

The youths who smear the baby in its own excrement in *Saved* and then stone it to death are also seeking a response that the child is incapable of giving. Alen has no secret to hide; he has merely withdrawn from contact with humanity. The baby, drugged into passivity, is incapable even of its own infantile signals of response. It is the fault of society that Pam, the child's mother, has deprived it of the capacity to respond; it is the fault of society that Pam has become that kind of mother. But here the quest for response is much more complex than in *The Pope's Wedding.* "Scopey is obviously Len in *Saved*," Bond has said: But Scopey sits waiting for retribution at the end of the earlier play, whereas Len sits mending a chair at the end of *Saved.* The action is positive; the title is not intended to be ironical.

From one point of view, the story of *Saved* is simple and sordid; from another, it is archetypal and oedipal. Somewhere in the terraced maze of South London a girl, Pam, picks up a young man, Len, and casually sleeps with him. She soon battens onto a new partner, Fred, but Len takes obstinate root as a lodger in her parents' home, remaining in faithful attendance even after she has given birth to Fred's unwanted child. The atmosphere is one of perpetual hostility, which erupts in open bickering between Len and Pam, and simmers in the watchful silence that has long since separated Pam's father and mother. And it is at the climax of another row—between Pam and Fred—that the girl leaves her child in its father's untender but not at first malicious care. Fred, however, is dared by his mates to live up to previously empty boasts of callousness and trapped into a sequence of refusals to chicken out; and the resultant petty violence feeds upon itself, reaching its climax in the child's murder.

A fluent self-determination of scenic structure has from the first been a characteristic of Bond's plays, and it is thus significant that, although the stoning to death occurs rather more than halfway through the play, Bond interpolates a further scene before indicating the interval. Fred is in prison, clearly taking sole responsibility for the crime. He is visited by Pam, in whom he has long since lost interest, and by Len, who watched but did not participate in the murder, and who, unlike Pam, remembers that Fred is going to need a plentiful supply of cigarettes in his remand cell. The lowering of tension works both in terms of straightforward plot development—there is no titillating suspense over whether the murder is to be punished—and in the subtler emphasis it places not on the atrocity as such but on its consequences.

After serving his sentence, Fred is feted by his grateful accomplices and firmly rejects the still enamored Pam. Len becomes enmeshed in the quarrel between Pam's father and mother, Harry and Mary, arousing a sort of desultory jealousy in the old man that erupts into a full-scale family row. The violence here is ironically tinged with bathos: a knife hovers in the air between Len and Harry, but it is a bread knife, being used for its proper purpose, and the worst that Mary can do is crown her husband with a freshly brewed pot of tea. Len plans to leave; but in the penultimate scene he creates what Bond calls "the chance of a friendship with the father," when the old man, pathetic in his long white drawers, dissuades him from going. The last scene makes its silent affirmation of adjustment to this new status quo. In his prefatory note, Bond comments: "Most theatre critics would say that for the play to be optimistic, Len should have run away. Fifty years ago, when, the same critics would probably say, moral standards were higher, they would have praised him for the loyalty and devotion with which he stuck to his post."

In a play that traces a recurring pattern of rejected love—Len's for Pam, Pam's for Fred, an infant child's for its mother—it might at first sight seem curious that Bond's note mentions love not once, but speaks often of morals and morality. *Saved* is indeed a moral play, however low-keyed its poetic justice. Guilt is punished, not only in Fred's perfunctory prison sentence but in the assurance of Len's prediction that he'll finish up "like some ol' lag, or an ol' soak. Bound to. An' soon." And if what Bond calls Len's natural goodness is not rewarded, neither is it corrupted: "He lives with people at their worst and most hopeless . . . and does not turn away from them. I cannot imagine an optimism more tenacious, disciplined or honest than this."

In traditional terms, then, *Saved* is a comedy, and not only in its achievement of an ending as happy as circumstances permit. For the traditional pattern of oedipal tragedy is also inverted; instead of the younger man murdering the father-figure with that tantalizingly available bread knife, Len is concerned to help. "Yer'll 'ave t' wash that cut. It's got tealeaves in it," he tells Harry, who (a stage direction informs us) "dabs at it with the tail of his shirt." The bathos here—Len's matter-of-fact advice and Harry's ineffectual response to it—relieves tension with laughter at a highly appropriate juncture. And the play is full of excellent and fully integrated comic moments, from the broad ribaldry of the opening scene, in which Pam and Len taunt the evidently prowling Harry with sexual double entendres, to a tiny tragicomedy of noncommunication over Pam's missing *Radio Times.*

Even the urban jungle offers its idyllic moments: Pam and Len in a hired rowing boat, in the postcoital lassitude of the second scene; Len and Fred fishing together in the sixth, discussing the provenance of their next cigarette with the same even-tempered, casual fellowship as their comparison of Pam's qualities in bed—the bed from which Len has by now been displaced. The dialogue here, as in the swift repartee among the other youths—its changes of conversational direction marked mainly by opportunities seized for a meaningless insult or a sexual innuendo—is observed with an accuracy just one step away from realism. It is idiomatically right, but it is very slightly distanced (just as, incidentally, the South London setting slightly but surely distances the play from Bond's own home ground, north of the river). Perversely, reciprocity is at its readiest when communication is least complete and language is being used as a cover for superficiality of feeling and response. When Len tries to probe deeper, both Pam and Fred resent it. Things are as they are. Pam cannot understand why Len wants to know more about her parents' estrangement, any more than Fred can endure his attempts to talk about his own relationship with Pam. "I come out for the fishing," he rebukes him, "I don't wanna 'ear all your 'ol crap." And he adds, after a slight pause, " 'Onest, Len—yer d'narf go on."

Len *does* "go on," just as Pam "goes on" at Fred, when she has lost him. But if Len is Scopey in *The Pope's Wedding,* seeking a response that is perhaps not there to be given, Pam is more like Alen—somebody people stop going after. As the faithful Len asks her: " 'Oo else'll 'elp? If I go, will they come back? Will the baby come back? Will *'e* come back? I'm the only one that's stayed, an' yer wan 'a get rid a me!" Yet if *The Pope's Wedding* was indeed an impossible ceremony, Len's quest for response may not be entirely fruitless. Given the context of the play, Bond might well describe it as "almost irresponsibly optimistic."

IV

Early Morning takes place in what the British critic Katharine Worth has aptly described as "a world of Blake's crossed with Lewis Carroll's." It is a powerful, complex, bursting-at-the-seams nightmare of a play, and it creates severe problems for any director, who must make sure that its surrealistic world takes on a sort of normality on stage, the better to shift stylistic gear into the nightmare-within-the-nightmare of the last act. It contains the seeds of *Lear,* and seems less deeply pessimistic in the light of the fully developed vision of that later work.

The play is set in and around the court of Queen Victoria and in heaven. It is taken for granted that people eat people—and on earth the offense is still punishable, albeit understandable. In heaven, cannibalism becomes a way of life, and devoured flesh renews itself on abandoned bones, for it is impossible to die. The action overflows with the grotesque political intrigues of the power struggle between a confidently entrenched Victoria, an Albert of bovine cunning, a Gladstone transmuted into a barrack-room shop steward, and a Disraeli who, trying to preserve an appearance of constitutional continuity, prefers to eliminate his opponents by hanging rather than by the firing squad. As heirs to the throne, the Siamese twins Arthur and George find themselves manipulated by whichever party is momentarily ascendant; but after the death of George, the opposition forces regroup around Arthur, who arranges with his mother for matters to be finally settled by means of a tug-of-war on Beachy Head. As planned by Arthur, who has come to regard mass murder as an act of civilized charity, his own supporters fall backward over the cliff top when their opponents release the rope—

and the crumbling cliff plunges the gloating victors in their turn into the sea.

This cataclysm is not, however, the climax of the play's second act. The interval, Bond specifies, must not occur until Arthur has walked to the cliff bottom, where he meets Florence Nightingale, who has also stood back from the Gadarene stampede—because Queen Victoria (who has earlier seduced her into a lesbian relationship) was quick to join it. Arthur tries to commit suicide, but a line of ghosts "in black cowls . . . joined together like a row of paper cut-out men" rises up. George detaches himself from it and is beginning to fasten himself once again to the dying, despairing Arthur as the scene ends.

The final act in heaven can perhaps best be likened to that part of a dream when one suddenly recognizes it for what it is, yet still cannot wake up; for, with platonic aptness, this heaven is one degree more real than the reality its inhabitants have left behind. Arthur alone cannot accept that people no longer need to consume one another merely metaphorically; and because his half of the Siamese twin has the stomach, his resolute abstinence also reduces George to near-starvation. The family party therefore consumes Arthur entirely, thwarting Florence Nightingale's effort to have a last, lingering love affair with the severed head; and he is encased in a coffin secured with Victoria's own teeth. The Queen now pronounces herself satisfied that her life's work has borne fruit: "There's no dirt in heaven. There's only peace and happiness, law and order, consent and co-operation." But Florence is crying silently to herself and, unseen, Arthur ascends after all from his coffin and into the air, a living irritant to Victoria's cannibalistic propriety.

Why Victoria? Rather for the reason that the timeless imperialists of *Narrow Road to the Deep North* were to be instantly identifiable with her reign, and that *The Sea* was to be set in its immediate aftermath; for Bond conceives much of our present malaise as a result of the moral—or rather, immoral—equilibrium of that age. It was a period of certainty—or rather, it achieved the appearance of certainty. It was also a period of sublime absurdity. Bond in *Early Morning* fuses the two elements. Can it be *doubted* that Victoria had Siamese twins, he asks; and one knows that she did, with the same ulterior knowledge that forces the calm acceptance in a dream of an unknown landscape peopled with unknown friends as part of one's body of experience.

Bond claimed in the *Theatre Quarterly* interview that the three acts of his play trace a careful dialectical process:

> The difficulty for Arthur is that he is attached to the socialized version of himself. In the first act the various problems are set up and in the second he has the reactions of the normal good citizen, the conventional western attitudes. But then he has a revelation which gives him a humanized view. The third act goes through the events of the first act, but this time he sees them clearly, sees society as it really is, without subterfuge. And what he sees is cannibalism. In seeing, he becomes creative, nearer freedom.

In this sense, Bond regards *Early Morning* as more optimistic than *Saved,* because Arthur is able to survive an even bleaker confrontation with reality. The problem the play poses in production is, of course, one of persuading us that its allegorized "reality" is theatrically valid. Allegory is an honorable form, but it depends upon our ability to interpret it from a relatively fixed moral viewpoint; here, it is being used to *challenge* a moral viewpoint that, while it is certainly no longer fixed, is nevertheless still widely held. I don't think Bond has entirely resolved the formal problems this poses.

Partly, this is a result of the play's own richness. Allegory needs to pursue a fairly straight moral line, but Bond introduces all sorts of intriguing tangents. In his heaven, "nothing has any consequences"—an absolute divorcement of cause from effect that, of course, immediately makes the play different in kind from *The Pope's Wedding* and *Saved,* and, for that matter, *Lear.* In his preface to that later play, Bond asserts that it is because Arthur comes to believe that the human race has no moral justification for its existence that he tries to kill himself, and declares it "astonishing that many people who share his beliefs are not forced to draw his conclusions, but can still go about their daily business." Yet in the third act, where no justification is needed for existence because every action is inconsequential, the final tableau is of resurrection. It could be argued that the "optimism" here is that of pornography—particularly the pornography of sadism, in which it is of the essence that action has no effect beyond its immediate heightening of sensation.

Of course, this is not to imply that *Early Morning,* however sensational, is pornographic. Its sensationalism is off-putting, even repulsive—an inducement, if anything, to the vegetarianism Bond himself practices. Quite simply, it is difficult to reconcile the intended dialectics that Bond declares to be at work with what is actually happening on stage. The vision is in this sense *too* powerful—in becoming so entirely self-sufficient the play loses its moral coordinates. Arthur himself is in direct descent from Scopey, and from Len in *Saved;* indeed, one of the characters pronounces by way of epitaph that " 'E weren' a bad bloke. Juss couldn't keep 'is-self to 'is-self." Thus, where the other characters accept things as they are, Arthur tries to probe deeper. During the *Alice in Wonderland* trial of a couple charged with cannibalism outside the State Cinema, Kilburn High Street, Arthur is the only one who wants to know *why,* but his agonized questionings work against the grain of the physical action. One accepts entirely the anachronisms—the iced lollipops in a Victorian cinema, the dreamlike logic that transforms a picnic hamper into a walkie-talkie radio—as one also accepts the spiritual truth that Arthur must continue to bear the burden of his brother's skeleton; yet as a connecting link between that world and ours, Arthur lacks authority. In getting rid of George, his "socialized" self, he also comes too close to severing the umbilical cord that links him to the world of the play.

Early Morning is, then, an arresting Gothic vision; but it is the only one of Bond's plays in which the moral force of the vision is diffused by the overwhelming physicality of the experience. As a dramatization of the legacy of Victorian thought and feeling, the play is, paradoxically, less successful than *Narrow Road to the Deep North*—which is set in Japan "about the seventeenth, eighteenth or nineteenth centuries," and which is as austere and straightforward in narrative line as *Early Morning* is decorated and discursive. Basho, the historical Japanese poet who perfected the haiku form, is about to depart for the Deep North in search of enlightenment. On the way, he sees a child abandoned by its starving parents at the water's edge. He feeds it, but leaves it to its fate. On his return thirty years later—during which time he has discovered only that "you get enlightenment where you are"—the abandoned child has grown up into the tyrannical Shogo, who has overthrown the old emperor and built a great city on the river's bank. Shogo seeks Basho's help in secretly rearing the infant child of the old emperor, but Basho plots with the Prime Minister to overthrow the tyrant, with the aid of the British colonialists who already rule over the Deep North.

The city thus exchanges Shogo's tyranny over the flesh for the tyranny over the spirit imposed by Georgina, evangelical sister to the conquering British Commodore. Shogo arms tribesmen from the North and succeeds in briefly recapturing the city—slaughtering the children of the mission school, the old emperor's heir among them, before British reinforcements can be brought up to defeat and capture him. He is condemned and dismembered, and the play ends as Kiro, a would-be disciple of Basho who has become lieutenant to Shogo, commits hara-kiri on stage. As he does so, there are cries for help from a swimmer in difficulties; the swimmer succeeds in clambering ashore and berates the corpse of Kiro for failing to come to his aid.

The slaughter of the innocents, as of Shogo himself, takes place offstage, and Kiro's disembowelment is a ritualized act, cleanly and quietly executed. As Bond has said, *Narrow Road* is not even *about* violence: "it is about the kind of situation in which violence occurs." The play is, indeed, concerned less with effects than with causes, and so is about those who create the conditions in which men live, rather than those who suffer from those conditions. And where Bond's earlier work had pitted a single, naturally good man against society at its worst, here it is difficult to mark out any character as naturally good or, for that matter, as absolutely evil. Even the tyrant Shogo is capable of acting humanely: he shatters a priceless vase that the hapless Kiro has got firmly lodged on his head, while lesser men think of saving the relic rather than the slowly suffocating young man. And Georgina, who uses Christianity quite consciously as an instrument of repression, is driven mad with grief by the murder of her infant charges: she flits about the stage like a pathetic, middle-aged Ophelia as the action draws to its close. Kiro comes closest to the lineage of Scopey, Len, and Arthur: he follows his savior Shogo only because Basho has refused to assist him in his own search for enlightenment, and his suicide is clearly a final abandonment of that search.

By committing suicide, Kiro declines to help the swimmer who might have drowned—withholds a simple, human gesture on a level with Shogo's shattering of the vase. Similarly, Basho, in the complementary refusal of responsibility with which the play opens, seals by his inaction the fate of the city thirty years later. But how *should* Basho have acted? Should he have taken charge of the child and so abandoned the vain search for enlightenment—or, as he himself thinks, have recognized the devil in its eyes and held it under the water "with these poet's hands"? And if the implication is that one way or another those hands should indeed have been soiled, how is one to reconcile this with the calamitous results of Basho's actual dabbling in politics?

If there are no simple answers to these questions—and the ambiguity is, of course, intentional—neither is there a ready synthesis of the opposing visions of Shogo and Georgina. Shogo sees the purpose of his city as giving the people something to do: "Instead of arguing and rotting away in hovels, they work for the city, they live for it." He describes himself as "the lesser of two evils," for "people are born in a tiger's mouth. I snatch them out, and some of them get caught on the teeth." Georgina believes that Shogo's system did not work because

> ". . . it left people free to judge him. They said: he makes us suffer and that's wrong. He calls it law and order, but we say it's crime against us. . . . So instead of atrocity I use morality. I persuade people—in their hearts—that they are sin, and that they have evil thoughts, and that they're greedy and violent and destructive. . . . When they believe all that they do what they're told. They don't judge you—they feel guilty themselves and accept that you have the right to judge them."
>
> (pt. 2, sc.1)

In its vivid realization of these contrasting modes of oppression, the play also finds time to be very funny indeed, from Kiro's mishap with the vase to Georgina's tambourine-touting rhetoric, to Shogo's demonstration of firearms for the benefit of the wondering tribesmen. It is true that the humor has a way of turning black, and there is a tragic as well as a comic gulf in the response of oriental to occidental civilization, which is summed up in Basho's laconic running commentary on the nursery-school language in which the Commodore conducts his affairs. ("They talk like that to keep their spirits up," Basho solemnly informs the Prime Minister.) But the humor leavens the play in precisely the manner that it needs: not merely by the way of comic relief, but by further formalizing an action that has already been carefully distanced in time and place—as indeed were all Bond's early plays, with the exception of the two short "occasional" pieces that he wrote between *Narrow Road to the Deep North* and *Lear.*

The first of these, *Black Mass,* is actually part of the *Sharpeville Sequence,* which also includes a story and three poems—all of which were performed at a commemoration evening arranged by the Anti-Apartheid movement in 1970 to mark the tenth anniversary of the Sharpeville massacre. In *Black Mass,* the Prime Minister of South Africa takes Communion from a priest, while an Inspector brings back encouraging reports on the progress of the massacre outside—rather as if it were an elaborate albeit unequal athletics event between police and "kaffirs." While the Prime Minister briefly interrupts his devotions to congratulate the "winning" side, Christ comes down from his cross and poisons the Communion wine; but the Inspector is quick to spot him as the Prime Minister's murderer, and Christ is banished from the church, his place on the crucifix taken by policemen on a two-hour duty roster.

The piece serves its purpose effectively, not bothering to preach to the converted for whom it was intended, but bringing out warped human attitudes in the sharp relief of political caricature—a technique Bond employed again in *Passion,* which he wrote for the "Festival of Life" organized by the Campaign for Nuclear Disarmament on Easter Sunday 1971. Here, an Old Woman mourns over the body of her son, a soldier killed in the Queen's service; but she quickly determines on the more practical course of traveling to ask the Queen to restore him to life. Unfortunately, the Queen has already performed her quota of resurrections for the week, and her Magician is busy making better bombs, so she claims that she still needs the dead soldier, to turn him into a bronze memorial statue. The monument is sited on the launching pad of the Magician's latest missile, and the unveiling and firing buttons are set side by side; but the statue proves to be a pig crucified upon a cross, and the enemy responds to the missile with a bigger and better one of its own. Wandering in the wilderness thus created, the Queen and her party meet Christ, supported by Buddha, on his way to the cross. Christ sees the pig set in his place and despairs: he cannot be "crucified for men, because they've already crucified themselves." The playlet offers a more compelling vision than *Black Mass,* its poetic images incongruously yet successfully set within the confines of a theatrical comic strip. Neither work is ultimately of great importance, but both show a craftsman completely in control of what he has chosen (or, in these cases, been asked) to do. The "Dead Soldier's Thoughts" that conclude *Passion* mark an appropriate end of the long road to *Lear:*

> Madmen, peace!
> You who bend iron but are afraid of grass
> Peace!

V

IF Bond's work can be said to have moved from its early concern with present-day forms of aggression to an exploration of the historical roots of a violent society in *Early Morning* and *Narrow Road to the Deep North,* with *Lear* the time scale becomes universal, even mythic. The play had its origins in what Bond felt was wrong with Shakespeare's version of the story: a failure to recognize either the old king's responsibility for the nature of Goneril and Regan or the potentially disastrous consequences of a ruler of Cordelia's kind. But it is a measure of Bond's achievement that he has created a work that not only stands on its own but will, like its model, surely continue to carry resonances for future generations.

Lear is building a wall to keep out his enemies and so bring peace to his kingdom, but good land lies neglected because of the wall's insatiable demands for manpower. During a tour of inspection with his daughters, Bodice and Fontanelle, Lear orders that a worker who has accidentally killed a comrade face the firing squad as a saboteur. Bodice and Fontanelle, who are secretly planning to marry the dukes of Cornwall and North beyond the wall, countermand the order and so provoke a crisis that results in civil war between father and daughters—the latter with complaisant husbands soon in tow. Broken and defeated, Lear finds sanctuary in the cottage of the Gravedigger's Boy and his wife, Cordelia, who live simply and self-sufficiently from the land. Cordelia does not like Lear's presence, but before she can persuade her more compassionate husband to send the old man away, soldiers arrive, kill the Gravedigger's Boy, and rape his wife—only to be slaughtered by the Carpenter, Cordelia's lover from the village, whose retaliatory rifle fire closes the first act.

A new conflict breaks out between Lear's daughters—who have recaptured Lear and would have sentenced him to death but for their husbands' intervention—and rebel peasant forces, led by Cordelia and the Carpenter. Lear is comforted in his prison cell by the Ghost of the Gravedigger's Boy, but loses him during the flight from the city as the victorious insurgents advance. Power changes hands, but little else is altered; Bodice and Fontanelle, their husbands long since fled, are put to death, Lear's eyes are put out to render him politically impotent, and construction of the wall continues. The final act returns to the house of the Gravedigger's Boy, whose decaying Ghost has found its way once more to cling to Lear for both their comforts. Susan, John, and Thomas now work the land here and look after the blinded Lear, whose prophecies and parables begin to draw dangerously large crowds. Cordelia returns to her old home, to warn Lear that he must be put on trial; but she cannot see the Ghost of her former husband, now a walking skeleton, who is soon to die for a second time in Lear's arms. In the closing scene, Susan leads Lear to the wall; he casts down a few spadesful of earth from its summit, but is quickly seen and shot by a passing officer. His corpse falls from the wall and is left where it lies.

The explicitness of the violence here is of its essence. To tidy it off the stage would be to invite precisely the sort of Sophoclean resignation that neither Shakespeare nor Bond will admit, although the effect of blindness, which Bond has himself called a "dramatic metaphor for insight," works for this Lear as it did for Oedipus and Tiresias, as well as for Gloucester. But violence here is not cathartic; it is dehumanizing, the product of a dehumanizing social structure of which the wall remains mutely symbolic. Bond advocates no alternative structure—certainly not the pastoral alternative of a Cobbettian cottage economy, although structurally the intervals at the house of the Gravedigger's Boy do fulfill the function of refreshing an audience's sensibilities. But the Ghost of the Gravedigger's Boy must die a second time—for the kind of life he has led was once viable, and, as Bond has said, Lear can "only rid himself of it with a great deal of nostalgia." Because it did once create "beauty and happiness," it has given Lear "this vision of a golden age, which his activities have helped to destroy." But Bond warns that "he has also to realize that its loss is irrevocable. . . . There are great dangers in romanticizing and clinging to the impossible. Some things are dead—but they die with great difficulty."

And so the Ghost does die, with great difficulty —a friend to Lear, but potentially a dangerous one, tempting the old man toward an easeful rather than a useful death. Freed from his influence, Lear can aspire only to a feeble gesture of defiance, but it is one that carries with it, like Len's chair mending, a kind of affirmation. If Bond, as he admits, "has not answered many of the questions" he raises, at least in this play he reveals the greater complexity of the problems. "It is so easy to subordinate justice to power," he writes in the preface to the play, "but when this happens power takes on dynamics and dialectics of aggression, and then nothing is really changed. Marx did not know about this problem, and Lenin discovered it when it was too late." It is surely no accident that in the final act, when Lear confronts Cordelia, he closely resembles a Tolstoy who, had he survived, might have confronted the early Soviet leaders with the consequences of subordinating justice to power.

The resemblance between Cordelia's forces and a modern guerrilla movement of "freedom fighters" is strong and unequivocal; and the doctor advances aseptic, twentieth-century arguments for removing Lear's eyes in the interests of medical science—with a device "perfected on dogs." Such anachronistic elements are consciously stressed rather than muted—indeed, the play begins and ends with death from a rifle shot. The "contemporary" ingredients have the effect of lifting the action above the merely mythic—so that, where an Elizabethan dramatist imposed a Renaissance setting upon his material simply from a less hidebound sense of history, here the more conscious use of anachronism has the positive effect of refusing an audience the moral refuge of safe historical separation.

It is glib to assert, as the critic B. A. Young has done, that in this, "his most dramatically mature play, Bond has still nothing more concrete to say than that power, rather than the misuse of power, is wrong." Quite apart from the ease with which it is possible to reduce many great plays to the level of a semantic quibble (does *Othello* have anything more "concrete" to say than that jealousy is a bad thing?), it is precisely because Bond does not repeat the ready liberal commonplace that only the *misuse* of power is wrong, that the play challenges our assumptions at such a fundamental level. It examines the very nature of power—in part through Lear's gradual self-recognition, in part through its vivid realization of a society for whose nature Lear has to acknowledge a major share of responsibility.

That society is occasionally shown in its formal functioning—as in the opening scene or in Lear's trial—but more often through the kind of human relationships and attitudes it has produced. Most obviously, if Bodice is more calculating where Fontanelle is almost sensuous in her cruelty, and although the sisters are highly individualized even in confronting their own deaths, they are their father's daughters nevertheless, and daughters of the society he has created. Yet Bond, in one of the most evocative scenes of the play, also summons the "ghosts" of the children that Bodice and Fontanelle once were, counterpointing the genuine affection between father and daughters with their easy acceptance of the deaths of the soldiers receiving mass burials offstage.

Bond's ability to juxtapose the almost unbearably poignant with the matter-of-fact renders the play's mythic material human and immediate at many points—even Lear's eyes are "received into a soothing solution of formaldehyde." "Mother's dead. I must serve tea," says Bodice, as the ghosts of the daughters leave Lear's cell. The Ghost of the Gravedigger's Boy is a walking embodiment of a creature simultaneously repulsive and infinitely pathetic. And Cordelia's almost casual condemnation to death of a would-be recruit, because "we can't trust a man unless he hates," is balanced against the genuine idealism for her cause expressed by the Wounded Soldier in the same scene, as he is left by his own desire, to die under the stars. "When we have power, these things won't be necessary," says the departing Cordelia.

Aside from the "ten or so main characters," there are "about seventy other speaking parts," which are, says Bond, "in a sense . . . one role, showing the character of a society." Some are glimpsed in just a single scene; some—the prison orderly, the farmer's son who turns soldier and shoots Lear—get caught up in the specifics of the action. Many have a kind of humanity, often suppressed out of fear; more are reduced to a desperate calculation that affords them their only hope of survival. "If you threaten an animal so that it can't behave in a normal way," Bond has said in the play's preface, "it becomes violent. And if you threaten human beings all the while, they become violent. . . . The sort of political community we've got is based on utilizing this aggression."

And, in the play, this image of the threatened animal recurs to express humanity under stress—as Lear's face "behind the bars," glimpsed in a mirror, and as the creature whom Lear dedicates himself to setting free from its cage. His final parable concerns a man whose caged bird refused to sing, and who is eventually locked up for the rest of his life in a cage. Humanity is the caged animal, the competitive and aggressive technological society its cage. "Our lives are awkward and fragile," says Lear, "and we have only one thing to keep us sane: pity, and the man without pity is mad." Lear himself learns pity, and through it is restored to sanity.

VI

AT first acquaintance, the distance from *Lear* to Bond's next play, *The Sea,* seems to be that from Shakespearean tragedy to Chekhovian comedy. And if the Chekhovian analogy proves on investigation to be as inadequate as the Shakespearean, the surface resemblances are worth noting simply as indications of the enormous stylistic strides Bond is capable of making from one play to the next. Certainly, the period in which *The Sea* is set is almost Chekhovian—that mid-Edwardian twilight of imperial assurance, when the sun, retrospectively, always shone, but at the time tidings of war and industrial unrest disturbed all but the blandest of sensibilities.

The Sea is set by the sea—sometimes, as in the opening scene, actually on the beach. By night, a young man, Willy, stumbles out of the lashing waves and calls in vain for Colin, his fellow victim of the storm, and for help. Neither the drunken beachcomber Evens nor the coastguardsman Hatch comes to his aid, and he despairs of Colin's life. By day, Hatch is a draper in the small East Coast town in which the action takes place, and in the second scene is serving the aging Mrs. Rafi—who aptly describes herself as "an emphatic woman." Mrs. Rafi places a large order for curtain material in his shop before asking her companion, Mrs. Tilehouse, to rap on the window and attract the attention of the passing Willy. It appears that the drowned Colin was to have been married to Mrs. Rafi's niece, Rose. The old lady advises Willy to consult the "peculiar" Mr. Evens about where the body might be washed up and invites him to luncheon. After their departure, Hatch summons three associates—evidently his fellow coastguards—from the back of the shop. All are convinced that Willy is a manifestation from outer space whose own world is threatened by disaster, and who plans with fellow creatures by the million to "take our jobs and our homes." Since "all these ships in distress are really secret landings from space," Hatch issues orders that no more help is to be given to them and a close watch be kept on Willy.

The remaining six scenes interweave the reality of Colin's death and its impact upon the rituals and rivalries of small-town society with Hatch's fantasy-world of extraterrestrial plotting and counterplotting. The clear implication is that, a few decades later, Hatch would have turned his attention to racist rabble-rousing; but there is compassion here for his warped mind—and for the pressures of class that place him at the mercy of the whims of Mrs. Rafi. Hatch's frenzied cutting-up of the old lady's expensive curtain material—the order cancelled when she learns of his failure to help Willy on the beach—makes an oddly moving stage picture, the draper accompanying his desperate slashes with a stream-of-consciousness commentary on his craft and his lot: "That's the makings of the good draper: finesse, industry, and an understanding of the feminine temperament. They stamp on you but they wipe their little boots first."

The formidable Mrs. Rafi reigns over all—over the amateur dramatics in aid of the coastguard fund, over the funeral arrangements for Colin and the scattering of his ashes at the cliff-top, and, ultimately, over the lives of men like Hollarcut, Hatch's most devoted follower—who finally allows himself to be pressed back into a conformist mold, and is to expiate his sins by hard work in Mrs. Rafi's vegetable garden. ("I dig for her," he tells Willy in the final scene, laying "the side of his index finger against the side of his nose" and looking crafty, "but will anything grow?") Yet Mrs. Rafi, for all her imperious self-assurance—as amateur theater director, she "sympathizes with God when he struggled to breathe life into the intractable clay"—is well aware of what lies in store for her. Now, as Rose puts it, "the town is full of her cripples," but soon she, too, will be a cripple, entirely dependent upon others—as she says, "old, ugly, whimpering, dirty, pushed about on wheels and threatened. I can't love them. How could I? But that's a terrible state in which to move towards the end of your life: to have no love. . . . I've thrown my life away."

If this self-pity has not yet been transformed into Lear's true pity, at least it has been provoked by a wish to prevent Rose and Willy from repeating her own mistakes; and the young couple do eventually escape from the town together. Willy's farewell to Evens in the final scene thus elicits a highly complex response. The hermit's declaration of belief in "the wise rat catcher" is a haunting image of his muted despair—and maybe Hatch's fantasies were closer to the truth than he knew: "You see why the draper's afraid. Not of things from space, of us. We're becoming the strange visitors to this world." Evens himself, perhaps, is a ghost of the Ghost of the Gravedigger's Boy—his life as a recluse attractive but of no help to Willy or Rose who, unlike Lear, are young and have time on their side. "You must still change the world," is Evens' parting plea.

Curiously, the image from which Bond has said the play developed—that of the dead Colin, washed ashore with his hands still raised up in the effort of freeing himself from an enveloping pullover—proves only peripheral, an empty object for Hatch's hatred and a pathetic witness to the growing understanding between Rose and Willy. Hatch's fruitless attempts to "kill" the corpse, which spurts water instead of blood, is the only overtly violent incident in the play, and for once Bond's description of it as "a comedy" can scarcely be quibbled with. Social comedy proves, indeed, an entirely appropriate form to contain what *The Sea* has to say. If the mock rehearsal stretches the comedy a little thin, the bizarre cliff-top scene—an upright piano gaunt against the sky as Mrs. Tilehouse turns funeral hymns into self-advertisements for the art of descant, and the nearby coastal battery shatters the vicar's few "foolish words"—heightens the comic reality in a manner that is uniquely Bond's (though some of John Whiting's lighter textured work achieves a similar vein of stage poetry, as Martin Esslin has rightly described it). Thus, although Evens' predictions of what humanity will imminently do to itself are all too accurate, they serve strangely to affirm his own insistence on hope. For the beachcomber's "wise rat catcher . . . can bear to live in the minutes as well as the years, and he understands the voice of the thing he is going to kill. Suffering is a universal language and everything that has a voice is human."

If *The Sea* provides a lighter reinterpretation of the themes of *Lear* and finally offers a more hopeful vision, *Bingo*—although again less densely structured—is *Lear* unredeemed. The Shakespeare of *Bingo* is a man of finely honed sensibilities, tortured by the knowledge of the pleasure his own audiences derive from torturing animals for sport—yet, ultimately, he is incapable of responding humanely to his family or his community, or honestly to himself, except in his final gesture. He commits suicide, while his daughter Judith rummages among the blankets in search of a later will that might have been kept from her.

The substance of the play seems almost incidental here, in the sense that one feels that by this last year of his life, exiled by his own choice to Stratford and New Place, Bond's Shakespeare would have arrived at self-inflicted death in spite of, rather than because of, anything that happened to him. The Old Man who works in Shakespeare's garden—his mind that of a twelve-year-old, thanks to the wars, but his bodily needs those of an adult—seduces a passing vagrant girl, who is whipped by order of the local justice, William Combe, and later hanged for arson. The Old Woman cares both for her infantile husband and for Shakespeare—whose own daughter is more concerned with her mother, unseen in an upstairs room. And the Old Woman's son combines evangelical fervor with radical action against Combe's plans for enclosing common land. Shakespeare makes ineffectual gestures of goodwill toward the girl, compromises with Combe by not opposing the enclosures, and indulges in a final, drunken binge with a compulsively itinerant Ben Jonson—from whom Shakespeare obtains the poison that Jonson once acquired in adversity but would never himself have dared to use. Out on the hills where the Young Woman's garrotted body is displayed, the Old Man is accidentally shot by his son during an encounter between his own and Combe's men, and the Old Woman leads Shakespeare back to what proves to be his deathbed.

Bond's preface makes clear that "part of the play is about the relationship between any writer and his society." And on the snowy hills Shakespeare has pronounced bleakly on that relationship: "Every writer writes in other men's blood. The trivial, and the real. There's nothing else to write in. But only a god or a devil can write in other men's blood and not ask why they spilt it and what it cost." Bond sees Shakespeare's historical complicity in the Welcombe enclosures as a betrayal of his art, the plays revealing the "need for sanity and its political expression, justice," but the man's behavior as a property owner bringing him "closer to Goneril than Lear." It is scarcely relevant that the view of history here is an unfashionably "Whig" one, judging Shakespeare by the standards of our own times rather than his—because the play is for our own times rather than his, as Shakespeare's plays are for our own times too. And the temptations for the artist to compromise his art for the sake of position and prestige are, of course, even greater today.

Bond subtitles *Bingo* "scenes of money and death," because he is writing about a society with "no natural rights, only rights granted and protected by money." We still live in an age of alchemy, he claims, for now "we try to turn gold into human values." *The Fool* has its own subtitle, "scenes of bread and love," and this suggests aptly enough the shift in Bond's perspective upon an apparently similar subject—here, the life of the worker-poet John Clare, who also found the impinging of market forces upon his art an unbearable burden, from which he withdrew into madness. But here the full social context of a later age of rural enclosures, as of urban industrialization, is realized with consummate skill, and Bond strikes an intriguing balance of sympathies between his characters and the values they embody. The opening scene of the mumming-play; a prizefight in Hyde Park; the continuing conflict between the economic aggrandizement of Lord Milton and the radical beliefs of Clare's friend Darkie; the poet's fragile relationship with his wife, Patty; the scenes in prison and in Clare's asylum—all bear witness to Bond's vividly *theatrical* vision, and to his ability to thread such disparate elements together into a unified work of dramatic art.

Bond's subsequent work has seen a struggle between the craftsman with a sure feeling for the complex interplay of social and personal relationships, and the politician, rather too self-assured about his own solutions to engage his audience in the process of analysis. I write from a political standpoint largely sympathetic to Bond's own—and for that matter arrived at rather sooner than his—but also from a sense that theatrical art works at its best as a political instrument when, like Bertolt Brecht's, it sends its audiences away "distanced" by seeing the familiar in an unfamiliar light and so asking questions, rather than by offering take-it-or-leave-it parables that persuade only the converted. Bond's *The Worlds* seems to me to pursue the latter course in its presentation of political kidnappings within the contrasted "worlds" of "good company men," trade union activists, and terrorist revolutionaries. In *The Woman,* on the other hand, Bond takes the overfamiliar theme of the Trojan War and introduces new and changed elements that have precisely the Brechtian effect of "making strange"—an effect assisted by the contrast in tone between a first half of terror and bloodshed and a second of ironic political accommodation to the demands of an imposed "peace." The contrast—which also involves the constant adjustment of our perception of narrative method—is completely successful. And the character of Hecuba is in the recast mythic mold of Lear—another supposedly "heroic" figure who learns to reject the qualities of conventional heroism.

One might no less pertinently contrast Bond's most recent plays—a trilogy on a postnuclear theme performed collectively as *The War Plays,* which ground its audience's sensibilities to dust through the very insistence on its indisputable message—with the two full-length plays that preceded them. *Restoration* intriguingly utilizes the format of a Restoration comedy of manners, replete with a central, foppish aristocrat, to explore unexpected themes of privilege, wealth, and justice. The no-less-unexpected prominence of the servant class points the relevance of those themes all the more clearly for the sense of sustained irony with which the play seems to push against protesting generic frontiers. And *Summer* shows Bond employing the familiar frame of a self-enclosed dramatic world to break yet other formal boundaries. Here, a group of survivors from the German occupation of an unspecified Middle European country, together with their children, gather on the occasion of one of the old people's imminent death. The resulting tensions test the contrasting "realities" of past and present, life and death, with a clarity and poetic power that resounds powerfully against the fourth wall of the naturalistic environment, as the play returns, arguably, to that oldest convention of all, the triumph of youth over age.

VII

CRITICS are notorious for their regular failure to recognize the quality of a major writer's early work, only to turn and rend him, once he has become "established," for not living up to his early promise. As one who can claim to have recognized Bond's importance in print from the very first, I find Bond's stature more rather than less substantial for his proven ability to follow a piece of stridently propagandist theater, which nourishes only the egos of the elect, with plays that redeem one's faith in the power of the theater to illuminate experience and to create whole worlds in creative parallel with our own.

Each of his best plays thus offers far more than a "meaning" that can easily be spelled out, and in *Saved, Narrow Road to the Deep North, Lear, The Sea, The Fool, The Woman, Restoration,* and *Summer,* there are just such "stage worlds" to be explored by each director anew. The formal range of the work is extraordinary and seemingly inexhaustible—for if *The Pope's Wedding* is recognizably cast in a generic mold similar to that of *Saved,* almost every one of the later plays builds its own form with impressive fluency and seemingly from scratch. And one has come to take almost for granted Bond's ability to create characters with the first words they speak, and to sustain those characters consistently within any appropriate formal dimension. In all the best work, too, there is an assurance of scenic flow, which both carries forward the necessary narrative line with the force of the born storyteller and also reveals an instinctive feeling for the moment when a scene has fulfilled its purpose. For although Bond is occasionally insistent about where an interval should be placed, he is not a dramatist who thinks primarily in terms of act divisions. He is, rather, an "episodic" dramatist, in the best sense of that much abused adjective.

Bond writes about man in his environment—and man has made that environment an unnatural one, whether in the South London streets of *Saved* or the mythic kingdom of *Lear.* Bond chooses elemental subjects—violence, pity, aggression, love, greed, fear—but conceives them in minutely particular and human terms. Whether or not he is an "optimist" is an academic point, for neither optimism nor pessimism is a measure of truth. And although some find Bond's truths unpalatable, and many find them uncomfortable, increasingly society is being forced by events to heed his warnings. Since he began writing, "technological advance" has been transformed in most minds from an election-winning slogan to a contributory cause of world crisis, and "growth" is increasingly recognized as a polite euphemism for unchecked material greed and wastage of precious resources. If men do recognize their dangers in time, it will not be directly due to Bond or, for that matter, to any artist; but it will be partly due to the climate of opinion his work has helped to create. So far, the hopeful signs may be of little more account than Len's mending of a chair, Lear's few spadesful of earth, or the final meeting of Ann and David in *Summer.* But they are there, the straws at which humanity must clutch. Bond's is the solid dramatic brickwork miraculously built of such straws.

SELECTED BIBLIOGRAPHY

I. SEPARATE WORKS. *Saved* (London, 1966), first pub. in *Plays and Players* (January 1966) with an intro. by Sir L. Olivier; *Blow Up* (London, 1967), screenplay, with M. Antonioni and T. Guerra; *Early Morning* (London, 1968); *Narrow Road to the Deep North: A Comedy* (London, 1968); *Laughter in the Dark* (London, 1969), screenplay; *The Lady of Monza* (London, 1970), screenplay; *The Pope's Wedding* (London, 1971), also includes two short stories, *Mr. Dog* and *The King with Golden Eyes,* with *Sharpeville Sequence: A Scene (Black Mass), A Story and Three Poems; Passion,* in *Plays and Players* (June 1971); *Walkabout* (London, 1971), screenplay; *Lear* (London, 1972); *The Sea: A Comedy* (London, 1973); *Bingo: Scenes of Money and Death* (London, 1974); *The Fool: Scenes of Bread and Love* (London, 1975); *The Bundle, or The New Narrow Road to the Deep North* (London, 1978); *The Woman* (London, 1979); *The Worlds* (London, 1979); *Restoration* (London, 1981); *Summer* (London, 1981); *The War Plays* (London, 1985).

II. INTERVIEWS. R. Cushman, "Three at Court," in *Plays and Players* (November 1965); "When Violence is Meant to Shock," in the *Guardian* (12 November 1965), a letter from Bond on *Saved;* G. Gordon, interview in the *Transatlantic Review* (1966), repr. in J. F. McCrindle, ed., *Behind the Scenes: Theatre and Film Interviews from "The Transatlantic Re-*

view"; W. Gaskill, interview in *Gambit,* 17 (1970), a special Bond issue that also includes a discussion between Bond and H. Hobson, I. Wardle, J. Howell, and J. Calder and reprints the *Sharpeville Sequence;* J. Hall, interview in the *Guardian* (29 September 1971); "Drama and the Dialectics of Violence," in *Theatre Quarterly,* 2 (1972), interview with the eds. analyzing the writer's life, work, and times.

III. Critical Studies. W. A. Darlington, "Has Mr Bond Been Saved?" in the *Daily Telegraph* (15 April 1968); R. Bryden, "Society Makes Men Animals," in the *Observer* (9 February 1969); I. Wardle, "The Edward Bond View of Life," in the *Times* (15 March 1969); D. A. N. Jones, "A Unique Style of Theatre," in *Nova* (June–July 1969); J. R. Taylor, *Anger and After: A Guide to the New British Drama* (London, 1969), 2nd ed., discusses Bond pp. 108–111; R. Bryden, *The Unfinished Hero* (London, 1969), includes a chapter on Bond; U. H. Mehlin, "Die Behandlung von Liebe und Aggression in Shakespeare's *Romeo and Juliet* und in Edward Bond's *Saved,"* in *Jahrbuch der deutschen Shakespeare-Gesellschaft West* (London, 1970), pp. 132–159; M. Esslin, *Brief Chronicles: Essays on Modern Theatre* (London, 1970), contains an essay, "Edward Bond's Three Plays"; A. Baiwir, "Le théâtre d'Edward Bond," in *Revue de l'Université libre de Bruxelles,* 2–3 (1971); J. R. Taylor, *The Second Wave: British Drama for the Seventies* (London, 1971), contains a chapter on Bond; K. J. Worth, *Revolutions in Modern English Drama* (London, 1972), contains a chapter on Bond; J. De Decker, "La mise en abîme de *Saved,"* in *Clés pour le spectacle* (19 March 1972); A. Arnold, "Lines of Development in Bond's Plays," in *Theatre Quarterly,* (1972), assesses and compares the earlier plays, the April–June issue of this journal includes a letter from Bond disputing this analysis; G. Dark, "Edward Bond's *Lear* at the Royal Court: A Production Casebook," in *Theatre Quarterly,* 2 (1972), a rehearsal log of the play and an interview with Bond discussing the part played by aggression in his work; W. Babula, "Scene Thirteen of Bond's *Saved,"* in *Modern Drama,* 15 (September 1972); I. Wardle, "Le théâtre d'Edward Bond," in *Travail théâtral* (Autumn 1972); J. Vinson, ed., *Contemporary Dramatists* (London, 1973), includes an essay by R. Cohn; J. Weightman, "Chekhov and Chekhovian," in *Encounter,* 41 (August 1973); H. Herbert, feature on Bond in the *Guardian* (14 August 1974); J. Weightman, "Shakespeare in Bondage," in *Encounter,* 43 (November 1974); H. Oppel and S. Christenson, *Edward Bond's "Lear" and Shakespeare's "King Lear"* (Mainz, 1974); A. K. Barth, "The Aggressive 'Theatrum Mundi' of Edward Bond: *Narrow Road to the Deep North,"* in *Modern Drama,* 18 (June 1975); J. Peter, "Edward Bond, Violence and Poetry," in *Drama* (Autumn 1975); A. P. Hinchliffe, *British Theatre, 1950–70* (London, 1975), discusses Bond in a chapter, "Recent Dramatists"; S. Trussler, *Edward Bond* (London, 1976); R. Schavine, *The Plays of Edward Bond* (Lewisburg, Pa., 1976); T. Coult, *The Plays of Edward Bond* (London, 1977); M. Hay and P. Roberts, *Edward Bond: A Companion to the Plays* (London, 1978); M. Hay and P. Roberts, *Edward Bond: A Study of His Plays* (London, 1980).

TOM STOPPARD

(1937–)

C. W. E. Bigsby

I

> Don't you see that nowadays tragedy isn't possible any more? . . . Today farce is the only thing possible.
> (*Tango,* by Slawomir Mrozek, adapted by Tom Stoppard)

IN the early 1960's the English theater seemed suddenly to have found itself. It celebrated with naive enthusiasm its belated discovery of naturalism and its new-found social concern. For a brief period playwrights tended to regard themselves as the cutting edge of a social revolution in which they would articulate the frustration of a new generation growing up in a society that seemed not merely complacent to the point of inertia but dangerously blind to the vital forces that lay encysted within a decaying art. Despite the fact that this fervor gave birth to disturbing sentimentality rather than hard-edged social or political analysis, the energy that had been released so suddenly created a compelling paradigm for the new writer. As Tom Stoppard has said, "after 1956 everybody my age who wanted to write, wanted to write plays—after Osborne and the rest at the Court."

But if increased financial support for the arts, the creation of major subsidized companies, the expansion of television services, and the growth of regional drama encouraged many young writers to work for the stage, it did not create an avant-garde studiously dedicated to fracturing the mold of twentieth-century drama. The newly liberated imagination largely turned to familiar forms; the revolution, it seemed, had more to do with renewal than iconoclasm. Certainly, despite the much-publicized working-class and Jewish origins of some new writers, the public school and Oxford and Cambridge continued to provide the majority of British dramatists. What these new writers did offer, however, was a control of language that placed them in a recognizable English tradition that in the previous half-century had produced Oscar Wilde, George Bernard Shaw, and Noël Coward. Preeminent among these is Tom Stoppard, who combines considerable talents as a parodist and wit with a genuinely personal vision. Recognizably derivative in his early work, he has since emerged as a writer of genuine originality.

Stoppard was born on 3 July 1937 in Zlin, Czechoslovakia. His father worked for the internationally famous Bata shoe company, and when the Germans threatened invasion, the family was transferred to the Singapore branch. Three years later they were forced to move again when Japanese troops captured the city. Stoppard's father was killed; with his mother and brother he was evacuated to India. Here his mother remarried and the family name, Straussler, became Stoppard.

On their return to England in 1946, he attended a preparatory school in Nottinghamshire and a boarding grammar school in Yorkshire, and in 1954 he began his career as a journalist, working first for the *Western Daily Press* and subsequently for the *Bristol Evening World.* As a theater reviewer he became interested in writing for the stage: in 1960 he resigned from his job and in three months wrote *A Walk on the Water.* This was eventually bought by a commercial television company, and Stoppard's public career as a playwright began, in November 1963. After several rewrites and a brief production in Hamburg, the play was finally produced on the London stage in 1968, two years after the success of *Rosencrantz and Guildenstern Are Dead,* under a new title, *Enter a Free Man.*

II

STOPPARD is a self-confessed aesthetic reactionary. That is, at a time when the avant-garde in theatre is deemphasizing language, stressing performance over text, preferring group composition to the insights of the individual author, he believes in the primacy of words. At a time when committed artists are asserting that art necessarily derives from social commitment, he regards it at times as a formalist exercise and at others as a moral gesture. As he has explained, "I don't set out . . . to write a play that will demand a new kind of theatre or a new kind of audience. But my feeling still is that the theatre ought to start from writing, come what may, even though in my view it is a delusion that a play is the end product of an idea; in my experience the idea is the end product of the play." In an article in the *Sunday Times* (25 February 1968) entitled "Something to Declare," Stoppard confessed that he had "very few social pre-occupations," writing, instead, out of a love of language and an avowedly intellectual fascination with "things I find difficult to express." "Some writers," he continued, "write because they burn with a cause which they further by writing about it. I burn with no causes. I cannot say that I write with any social objective. One writes because one loves writing." When he adds that he is "hooked on style," however, he is not only describing his own concern as a writer but also identifying the desperate strategy of so many of his protagonists, who feel, in the words of a character from his only novel, *Lord Malquist and Mr Moon* (1966), that "since we cannot hope for order let us withdraw with style from chaos."

Lord Malquist and Mr Moon is an exuberant farce, an absurdist romp that displays Stoppard's considerable talent for parody. The opening chapter offers a collage of literary styles used to ironic effect. His methodology is reminiscent of Salvador Dali's insofar as he treats improbable situations in a realistic manner, bringing together radically dissimilar elements. He peoples his novel with a black Irish Jew, two cowboys who stage a shoot-out in Trafalgar Square, a man who regards himself as the Risen Christ, and a peer of the realm who insists on behaving as though he were living in the eighteenth century, while assiduously seducing the wife of his biographer, Mr. Moon, a historian turned anarchist. This latter has set himself the somewhat daunting task of writing a history of the world, in the conviction that with perseverance it will manifest a coherent order that he not unnaturally finds hard to distinguish in the chaotic events that buffet him daily. The first and only sentence he has thus far composed for his great work has unfortunately so unnerved him, however, that he is unable to get any further. Having written the confident words, "History is the progress of Man in the World, and the beginning of history is the beginning of Man," he can write only the word "Therefore" before the demonstrable absurdity of his premise overwhelms him.

Half-recognizing the fallacy implicit in his own capital letters, he wanders through London equipped with a homemade bomb, none too sure whether he wishes to precipitate the chaos he feels to be implicit in human affairs, or to rectify some mistake that has inadvertently caused an otherwise reliable system to malfunction. He finds himself "without possibility of reprieve or hope of explanation," bemused by the bewildering anarchy of existence, and uncertain whether life would be more absurd if it were random or simply the mechanical enactment of a determined scenario. It is thus entirely consistent that the novel should be full of characters more distinguished for their bizarre life styles than for their authentic humanity, for they, like Moon, appear to have grasped a truth that Stoppard himself adheres to with apparent conviction, until *Jumpers* and *Travesties* reveal the tentative humanism that had in fact always lurked beneath his absurdist stance: Stoppard's characters have understood, that is, that "substance is ephemeral but style is eternal"—an assumption that, although it "may not be a solution to the realities of life . . . is a workable alternative."

Stoppard seems to suggest with Wilde that life may best be regarded as an imitation of art, that in a situation where nothing can be taken seriously farce is both the true realism and, by a kind of homeopathic logic, the only valid strategy for artist and individual alike. Yet this conviction seems to battle with a more deep-seated humanism that leads him not only to reveal a compassionate concern for his characters but also to advocacy of such a concern within otherwise absurdist dramas. For, after all, as one of his characters observes in *Jumpers,* "the whole point of denying the Absolute was to reduce the scale, instantly, to the inconsequential behaviour of inconsequential animals." Yet this logic is too implacable for Stoppard. He creates a series of characters who, although ultimately defeated by social and metaphysical forces, provoke or themselves embrace a human compassion that transcends the relativistic ethics of an absurd universe.

III

In his early plays Stoppard presents a series of images of the individual trapped inside a mechanistic world, warped and destroyed by a logical system that fails to accommodate itself to human aspirations. *If You're Glad I'll Be Frank* (1969) details the ineffectual rebellion of the telephonist who works as the automatic time-giver. In the battle between her fragile individualism and the social and mechanical forces, there can be only one victor. Like her lover, whose protests have to be accommodated to the schedules of his regular bus route, the most she can do is stutter out her protest before retreating once more into her social role. In *Albert's Bridge* (1969) the same battle is repeated, except that Albert actually embraces his mechanical job as a release from the alarming disorder of his mundane existence. Albert takes great pleasure in his career as painter on the Clufton Bay Bridge, discovering poetry in the bridge's symmetry and meaning in its geometrical precision. His own life lacks this coherence; human relations stubbornly refuse to display the patterned grace and predictable order of the machine. He abandons his wife and withdraws into the reassuring world of the bridge, attracted by the fact that it is "separate—complete—removed, defined by principles of engineering which make it stop at a certain point, which compel a certain shape, certain joints—the whole thing utterly fixed by the rules that make it stay up . . . complete." But the same logical rules that enable the bridge to be built also lead to its collapse when an army of painters march across it without breaking step. In other words, the existence of order and system do not of themselves imply purpose and meaning. Albert discovers order in narcissism only to perish like Narcissus.

The note in these early plays is one of compassionate irony. Faced with a situation that seems to offer "nothing, absolutely nothing," in which "I give nothing, I gain nothing, it is nothing," George Riley's conviction in *Enter a Free Man* that "a man must resist. A man must stand apart, make a clear break on his own two feet," that "faith is the key —faith in oneself" becomes merely ironic. It is a faith that can be sustained only so long as he refuses to recognize his absolute dependence on those around him, on the absurd fictions that he chooses to embrace. Like Willy Loman, the leading character in Arthur Miller's *Death of a Salesman,* Riley seems to feel that the stars projected on the clouds from the rooftops are real stars. As with Willy Loman the consequence is a combination of pathos and a curious dignity. In such a world the only value is indeed compassion.

Stoppard has confessed that *A Walk on the Water* was in fact *Flowering Death of a Salesman* (a combination of Robert Bolt's *Flowering Cherry* with *Death of a Salesman*), admitting that "I don't think it's a very true play, in the sense that I feel no intimacy with the people I was writing about. It works pretty well as a play, but it's actually phony because it's a play written about other people's characters."[1] Certainly *Enter a Free Man,* the rewritten stage version eventually produced in 1968 following the success of *Rosencrantz and Guildenstern Are Dead,* is a curiously eclectic work. Indeed, a number of speeches could have come straight out of Miller, as, for example, when the play's protagonist, George Riley, laments that

> my life is piled up between me and the sun, as real and hopeless as a pile of broken furniture. Thirty years ago I was a young man ready to leave the ground and fly. Thirty years. . . . More, perhaps much more than the time I have left, and when a man's past outweighs his future, then he's a man standing in his own shadow.
>
> (Act I)

There is the same tension between father and child as in *Death of a Salesman,* the same desperate attachment to illusion sustained by a wife every bit as compassionate and understanding as Linda in Miller's play. Stoppard even retains the name Linda, transferring it to the daughter.

Yet, despite this, Stoppard's own voice is clear enough, and in the figure of George Riley he creates the first of many portraits of a modern hero. Riley is a man who has dedicated his life to perfecting such devices as a reusable envelope (with gum on both sides of the flap) and an elaborate system of pipes designed to utilize rainfall to water indoor plants. Unaware of the logical flaws that make his inventions useless, he nonetheless pits his "tattered dignity" against a world that seems designed merely to taunt him. Described in the stage directions as "a smallish untidy figure in a crumpled suit . . . certainly not mad but . . . definitely odd," he is, we are assured, "unsinkable, despite the slow

[1] "Ambushes for the Audience," *Theatre Quarterly,* May–July 1974.

leak." And this "tattered dignity" is what characterizes the Stoppard hero, for while it is clear that none of his characters control their own destiny, that neither logic nor faith can confer meaning on their lives, it is equally obvious that their unsinkable quality, their irrepressible vitality and eccentric persistence, constitute what Stoppard feels to be an authentic response to existence. They are marginal men, uncertain of their own role and unsure of the true nature of the mechanism in which they feel caught. Like Samuel Beckett's clowns, John Osborne's music-hall entertainer, Harold Pinter's caretaker, David Mercer's morally confused minister, and Joe Orton's faithful retainer, they are the pathetic but touching remnants of a broken system. Dislodged from history even in the act of recognizing their own insignificance, their own inability to control events, they nonetheless assert a vestigial identity that they hold up against the flux of events. Even if their identities are disintegrating or scarcely exist (as is clearly the case with Rosencrantz and Guildenstern), they still pit their wounded psyches against a world they despair of understanding. And because the world that exists indistinctly and threateningly just beyond the focus of their vision is a brutal and uncompassionate one, the remnants of individuality that they can scrape together from the detritus of their hopes and fears make them heroes—ironical and inadequate, but heroes nonetheless, in a world that is presented as systematic and logical but devoid of moral purpose.

Yet there is a problem here, since in his first play Stoppard is drawn to both comedy and farce, the one implying a world in which values exist, the other an antinomian world of ethical relativity. In the former world, heroes, even those who can deploy only a tattered dignity, may not only survive but in doing so imply the survival of certain moral principles; in the latter, the most they can do is inhabit an autonomous world of their own creation. In *Enter a Free Man* Stoppard tries to have it both ways. The title is of course ambiguous. By all external standards George Riley is not free. He survives on handouts from his daughter, and his self-confidence is a fragile product of his family's compassion. But in another sense he is free. His imagination and self-respect survive repeated blows. He resists social pressure. And yet, although Stoppard seems to be celebrating Riley's self-sufficiency and his oddball courage, he is shown as inhabiting a genuine social environment replete with real psychological problems. Where Willy Loman sustained his illusions precisely because of the social pressures to which he was submitted, George Riley recognizes no social obligations at all. He inhabits his own "definitely odd" world, and thus the psychological and social realism of other sections of the play seem not merely irrelevant but fragments of a different work. Willy Loman could arguably have been a different man in other circumstances. He, too, wanted to make things, but in his case this was to establish a real identity in a world that dealt only in images. If George Riley had been a different man, if he had moved back into the moral world, he would have disappeared. His illogic is his prime virtue; it is his defense against the world.

IV

STOPPARD began work on *Rosencrantz and Guildenstern Are Dead* in 1964. During a five-month stay in Berlin on a Ford Foundation grant he wrote a one-act Shakespearean pastiche in blank verse. On his return he rewrote it, abandoning verse for prose, and it was duly performed by the Oxford Theatre Group as a "fringe" production at the Edinburgh Festival in 1966. Following favorable reviews it was subsequently staged by the National Theatre Company in London.

Few writers can have been accorded such instant recognition. Harold Hobson, in the *Sunday Times*, described this play as "the most important event in the British professional theatre of the last nine years"—in other words, the most important event since Osborne's *Look Back in Anger* had supposedly changed the direction of British drama. *The Observer* endorsed this view, calling it "the most brilliant début of the sixties."

A play that seemed to combine the brittle wit of Wilde with the mordant humor of Beckett, *Rosencrantz and Guildenstern Are Dead* takes as its main characters two of literature's most marginal figures, attendant lords who, as several critics pointed out, are actually excluded from some productions of *Hamlet.* Stoppard himself has said that "the chief object and objective was to exploit a situation which seemed to me to have enormous dramatic and comic potential—of these two guys who in

Shakespeare's context don't really know what they are doing. The little they are told is mainly lies, and there's no reason to suppose that they ever find out why they are killed." As he points out, "probably more in the early 1960s than at any other time, that would strike a young playwright as being a perfectly good thing to explore."

These two "bewildered innocents" act out a scenario that they cannot understand, uncertain of their own roles and increasingly disturbed by the apparent meaninglessness of their lives. Although aware that "the only beginning is birth and the only end is death," they are forced to believe that there is some purpose in their existence or to capitulate to a growing sense of terror. Like the Players who are to perform before Hamlet, they act out their assigned roles with diminishing confidence as they begin to suspect that life lacks both a transcendent dimension and an enabling logic. As the Player says:

> We're actors. . . . We pledged our identities, secure in the conventions of our trade; that someone would be watching. And then, gradually, no one was. We were caught, high and dry. . . . Even then, habit and a stubborn trust that our audience spied upon us from behind the nearest bush, forced our bodies to blunder on long after they had emptied of meaning, until like runaway carts they dragged to a halt. No one came forward. No one shouted at us. The silence was unbreakable, it imposed itself upon us; it was obscene.
>
> (Act II)

The theatrical metaphor is the dominant one in the play. The pointless prospect of actors without an audience expands to incorporate mankind in general. This is not a disordered world to be restored to consonance by self-sacrifice and heroic action; it is an arbitrary existence in which resolute action decays into mere performance. As Guildenstern observes, "We don't question . . . we don't doubt . . . we perform." The chief problem becomes the need to survive from moment to moment without succumbing to panic.

The strategies that they adopt in the face of this situation are familiar enough, particularly to audiences familiar with Beckett's *Waiting for Godot.* They blot out their incipient terror by playing Wittgensteinian language games, flipping coins, conversing, reaching out to one another for momentary contact. They attempt to discover pattern and purpose in their existence by use of scientific logic. But all these defenses crumble. The language games lead them to real and disturbing questions about their own identity, the coins persistently and alarmingly come down heads every time in defiance of the laws of chance, and conversation drains away until Guildenstern shouts out in despair, "Do you think conversation is going to help us now?" Logic is similarly ineffectual, for although Guildenstern asserts that "the scientific approach to the examination of phenomena is a defense against the pure emotion of fear," the logical explanations he laboriously constructs collapse under their own weight.

They are caught, then, trapped inside a play they did not write and doomed to enact roles they can never understand, lacking as they do vital clues as to the meaning of the total drama. Yet even the autonomous identity of the supposed author of that play is cast in doubt when Rosencrantz anachronistically recalls the famous analogy for the law of probability whereby, given time, six monkeys typing at random could produce the entire works of Shakespeare. In other words, the entire scenario may be simply the consequence of chance and not the ordered product of an omniscient creator. The metaphysical implications are obvious.

Rosencrantz and Guildenstern are forced to conclude that the only freedom they possess is that of sailors on a ship, free to move around on the vessel but unable to influence the wind and current that draw them inexorably onward. Or, more bleakly, theirs is the freedom to exist in a coffin, aware that one day the lid will be screwed down but able in the meantime to breathe, converse, exist. As Rosencrantz suggests, "Life in a box is better than no life at all. I expect. You'd have a chance at least. You could lie there thinking—well, at least I'm not dead! In a minute someone's going to bang on the lid and tell me to come out." This is the last resort: illusion, willed self-deceit of the kind Edward Albee had indicted in *Tiny Alice.* But even this cannot be sustained. When Guildenstern tries to convince himself that "we are not restricted. No boundaries have been defined, no inhibitions imposed. . . . We can breathe. We can relax. We can do what we like or say what we like to whomever we like, without restriction," Rosencrantz adds the necessary and deflating proviso: "Within limits, of course."

And as confidence drains away, as the ship, literal and metaphoric, nears its destination, so the defensive illusions begin to disintegrate, flake by flake. Language itself begins to collapse. Sigmund Freud saw speech not as a path to truth, as a means of destroying barriers between individuals, but as a means of holding truth at bay, of evading the vulnerability that is a necessary corollary of communication. This, indeed, is how Rosencrantz and Guildenstern deploy it. But as the terror of their situation becomes more and more compelling, this membrane between themselves and truth becomes permeable. The tissue begins to dissolve, and their loss of control is mirrored in a fragmentation of their language:

ROS: I want to go home.
GUIL: Don't let them confuse you.
ROS: I'm out of my step here—
GUIL: We'll soon be home and high—dry and home—I'll—
ROS: It's all over my *depth*—
GUIL: —I'll hie you home and—
ROS: —out of my head—
GUIL: —dry you high and—
ROS: *(cracking, high)* —over my step over my head body!—I tell you it's all stopping to a death, it's boding to a depth, stepping to a head, it's all heading to a dead stop—
GUIL: *(the nursemaid)* There! . . . and we'll soon be home and dry . . . and *high* and dry . . .

(Act I)

It is essentially the same technique as that used by Pinter in *The Birthday Party,* although here the menace is not objectified; it remains vague, generalized.

The play is full of theatrical references. There are plays within plays within plays, a device that implicitly raises questions about the nature of truth. Apart from the obvious references to *Hamlet,* there are others to Albee ("good old east," derived from "good old north" in *The Zoo Story*) and Osborne ("Don't clap too hard. It's a very old world," derived from Archie Rice's rather less metaphysical comment in *The Entertainer:* "Don't clap. It's a very old building"). We are, indeed, constantly reminded of the unreality of what we are watching. Rosencrantz on several occasions shows awareness of the presence of the audience, and the conventions of the stage are repeatedly mocked. The consequence is that the audience is reminded that it too is playing a role, collaborating in the establishment of contingent truths. As the Player reminds us, "truth is only that which is taken to be true. It's the currency of living. There may be nothing behind it, but it doesn't make any difference so long as it is honoured. One acts on assumptions." It is, in fact, precisely the existence of a world in which the only fixed points are birth and death that creates the need for fictions, for self-sustaining pretense; precisely the need for an ordering of experience that sends people to art, whose hermetic structures imply both a sequential code and a sustainable set of values. The willing suspension of disbelief thus applies not only to the content of a work but also to the assumptions about form, causality, and moral progress that have been corollaries of liberal art. Absurdist drama is thus not merely a rejection of liberal convictions about society and the nature of man; it is an implicit critique of the role ascribed to the artist. For he is no less a clown than Vladimir and Estragon, the two central characters in Beckett's *Waiting for Godot;* his audience is, for the duration of the play, in a temporal void as real as that occupied by Rosencrantz and Guildenstern and as pathetically dedicated to "passing the time" while awaiting with absolute faith, like the absurdist characters they observe, for structure to cohere into meaning.

Nor can one feel that Rosencrantz and Guildenstern's fate derives from their unique position as marginal individuals. For, as we discover, marginality is a matter of focus. In this play Hamlet is marginal, and if the two attendant lords face imminent death, this is no less than Hamlet, Polonius, Gertrude, Ophelia, and Laertes face. Hamlet's observations while holding Yorick's skull contain the essence of Stoppard's play, for it is precisely the existence of the grave that retrospectively deprives life of meaning. As Hamlet observes, what is the meaning of a beauty that simply conceals the skull; what the purpose of humor if it merely cloaks the black comedy of death? Yet such questions pursued too far lead to genuine madness, and having mocked passion and justified inaction, Hamlet acts with vigor and by doing so not only restores a secular order but reanimates the concept of order itself. This is not true of the world that Rosencrantz and Guilderstern inhabit. Here there is no definable truth, no established pattern, no tradition of morality to be pursued. Their individual qualities are irrelevant to their plight. One is intellectual, incisive, disturbed; the other obtuse, contented, placid. One is a leader; the other is led. It makes no difference. Such characteristics cannot alter their plight. Consequently they display an alarming uncertainty as to their identities, and as the pressure on them increases, they exchange roles, thus emphasizing that these are indeed roles, assumed modes of action generated by the exigencies of situation rather than by the compulsions of authentic character.

Is Stoppard, then, an absurdist? Like most arbitrary categories this is frequently more misleading than helpful, as has proved to be the case with writers such as Pinter and Albee. Yet the iconography of *Rosencrantz and Guildenstern Are Dead* is familiar to audiences who cut their critical teeth on Beckett and Eugene Ionesco. The absurdists captured a deracinated world—a world in which the potential for action and communication has been irrevocably eroded. The setting is timeless, the landscape an expressionistic desert reminiscent of Dali's lapidary wilderness[2] or the claustrophobic living room of modern, uncommunal living. The capacity for action is minimal and ironic. Language itself is simply an elaborate papering over of cracks, which constantly threaten to open up beneath those who remain either blithely unaware of their plight or numbed with despair. That anguish obviously exists in Stoppard's play—a work in which two men are seen "passing the time in a place without any visible character," clinging fiercely to the conviction that they "have not been picked out . . . simply to be abandoned," that they are "entitled to some direction," only to confess at the end of their "play" that "it is not enough. To be told so little—to such an end—and still, finally, to be denied an explanation." The only resources available to these abandoned characters are the compassion with which they respond to one another and the humor they deploy as a means of neutralizing their fear. Reinhold Niebuhr's comment that laughter is a kind of no-man's-land between faith and despair is clearly applicable to *Rosencrantz and Guildenstern Are Dead.* For Rosencrantz and Guildenstern themselves, humor is a means of preserving sanity; for Stoppard it is a natural product of disjunction—of the gulf between cause and effect, aspiration and fulfillment, word and meaning, which is the root alike of pain, absurdity, and laughter, and a clue to the relativity of truth—itself a subject to which Stoppard has repeatedly returned.

Stoppard has said that

> what I try to do is to end up by contriving the perfect marriage between the play of ideas and farce or, perhaps, even high comedy . . . to that end I have been writing plays which are farcical and without an idea in their funny heads, and I have also written plays which are all mouth . . . and don't bring off the comedy. And occasionally, I think *Jumpers* would be an example, I've got fairly close to a play which works as a funny play and which makes coherent, in terms of theatre, a fairly complicated intellectual argument.
>
> ("Ambushes for the Audience," *Theatre Quarterly,* May–July 1974)

While it is true that the argument behind *Rosencrantz and Guildenstern Are Dead* is not complex, its strength lies precisely in the skill with which Stoppard blends humor with metaphysical inquiry, the success with which he makes the play's theatricality an essential element of its thematic concern. It is, indeed, a kind of *Waiting for Godot* in which Vladimir and Estragon become university wits.

V

YET, as Stoppard has indicated, not all his plays have such serious aspirations. He followed *Rosencrantz and Guildenstern Are Dead* and *Enter a Free Man* with two adroit and well-constructed works (*The Real Inspector Hound* and *After Magritte*), whose chief fascination resides in the skill with which he unravels his own aesthetic conundrums. As he has said, "*After Magritte* and *The Real Inspector Hound* are short plays and they really are an attempt to bring off a sort of comic coup in pure mechanistic terms. They were *conceived* as short plays."

The ostensible subject of *The Real Inspector Hound* (1968) is the rivalry of two drama critics who, somewhat bewilderingly, are drawn into the action of the play they are reviewing. But we have Stoppard's warning that "the one thing *The Real Inspector Hound* isn't about, as far as I am concerned, is theatre critics. . . . I just got into it, and I knew that I wanted it somehow to resolve itself in a breathtakingly neat, complex and utterly comprehensible way." He does, admittedly, give free rein to his

[2]The adjective refers to Dali's paintings, which often picture desolate landscapes dominated by rocks and stones.

considerable talents as a parodist, mocking both the conventions of antiquated drawing-room whodunits and the critical styles of drama reviewers (Birdboot works for a popular paper: "let us give thanks and double thanks for a good clean show without a trace of smut"; Moon writes for a rather more pretentious readership: *"Je suis,* it seems to be saying, *ergo sum* . . . and here one is irresistibly reminded of Voltaire's cry, *Voilá!"*). But once again he is concerned with raising more fundamental questions about the nature of truth and theatricality, although no longer with the same degree of seriousness that he had brought to his first successful play. Once again he creates a play within a play; the audience, by a trick of the eye, is projected into the play that it is watching, as the two critics themselves will be later in the work. The opening stage direction indicates that "the audience appear to be confronted by their own reflection in a huge mirror." In many ways the play is cast from the same die as *Rosencrantz and Guildenstern Are Dead.* Birdboot, like Rosencrantz, is a literal-minded man whose reach does not extend beyond his grasp. Metaphysics disturb him, and he retains his grip on reality by reducing all experience to banalities. Moon, on the other hand, is reminiscent of Guildenstern. He sees significance in everything and is dominated by a growing sense of his own insecurity. Yet, however they may differ, both find themselves occupying the same stage, desperately trying to understand what they are doing, cast suddenly and without appeal in a second-rate drama.

Critics have inevitably invoked the name of Luigi Pirandello in relation to Stoppard's work, and there is, indeed, considerable similarity in their concern with the nature of reality, the relativity of truth, and the fluid nature of identity. Both writers have repeatedly resorted to the theatrical metaphor in expressing the conviction that individual existence consists of a number of overlapping roles, that appearance and reality are inevitably and instructively divorced from one another, and that life is more usefully regarded as a series of improvisations than as the acting out of a prepared scenario. Nor is it without significance that the play Birdboot and Moon are reviewing is a whodunit, the supreme example of rational art that, particularly in the parody version Stoppard offers us, derives its whole effect from the conviction that individuals are justifiably identified with their roles (victim, murderer, detective)—indeed gain their meaning purely in terms of the part they play in a highly structured scenario. It is also a form that rests on the conviction that reality is susceptible to rational analysis, since it turns so clearly on causality. But, as a character in *Jumpers* remarks, "unlike mystery novels, life does not guarantee a denouement." Thus, when the prepared text is suddenly disturbed, when the hapless reviewers find themselves on stage, these conventions are threatened. Stoppard then offers his audience a difficult choice, in that in order to restore a sense of order, to maintain the conventions, to avoid the conviction that the action has become irrational, arbitrary, and improvised, the audience is forced to accept a number of wholly absurd assumptions. It is placed, in other words, in the position of Rosencrantz and Guildenstern, who are forced for their own peace of mind to presume the paradigmatic nature of theater, to accept the conviction that performance at all levels implies the existence of an audience.

The Real Inspector Hound is not a wholly satisfactory play. It is more adroit than convincing. The parody, although at times brilliant, is too often facile; the metaphysical dimension, deliberately underplayed, is nonetheless too often sacrificed to the witty remark. A confessedly lightweight comedy, the play finally stops annoyingly short of examining the implications of its central premise.

VI

It is not surprising to learn that René Magritte is Stoppard's favorite artist, for both men secure their particular effects by essentially the same method. The wrenching of object from setting, of event from context, results not merely in a revealing absurdity but also in a perception of the contingent nature of truth. Yet Stoppard is no surrealist. The tableau at the beginning of his one-act play *After Magritte* (1971) is not a surrealist image designed to liberate the imagination, to energize the subconscious, but a teasing problem in logic, a conundrum to be unraveled. Its metaphorical significance remains largely unexamined, but, as Stoppard himself commented, it is "not an intellectual play, it's a nuts-and-bolts comedy."

The play opens with an old woman lying prone on an ironing board with her foot resting against an iron and with a bowler hat on her stomach. Of the two other people in the room, one is dressed for ballroom dancing and the other, a man equipped with thigh-length waders, is apparently trying to blow out an electric light bulb. The remaining furniture is piled against the front door, and a policeman is staring through the window. The play itself consists of an elaborate explanation for this apparently absurd situation. It is an adroit demonstration of the fact that truth is a matter of perspective. As one of the characters observes, "there is obviously a perfectly logical explanation for everything." Yet although logic does indeed hold, as it does in the radio plays *Albert's Bridge* and *If You're Glad I'll Be Frank,* it has no connection with the inner life of the characters. As George remarks in *Jumpers,* "if rationality were the criterion for things being allowed to exist, the world would be one gigantic field of soya beans! . . . In a wholly rational society the moralist will be a variety of crank." As a consequence these shorter plays are little more than five-finger exercises, displays of virtuoso talent that hint at a metaphysical dimension that they forebear to examine. The same could not be said of Stoppard's more recent work.

Stoppard has said that *Jumpers* (1972) was the first play in which he specifically set out to "ask a question and try to answer it, or at any rate put the counter question." And although once again he chooses a comic framework, the question is a serious one, and one moreover that leads on to the more avowedly political questions of *Travesties.* It is a play about the growingly materialist base of modern society and the desperate attempt by its protagonist to establish the existence and reality of transcendent values.

His protagonist, another bewildered individual assailed by authority and threatened by the positivist assumptions of his society, struggles manfully to establish by logical means the existence of moral absolutes and the credibility of God. As a professor of moral philosophy, George Moore tries to oppose the rationalist assumptions of his age by deploying a blend of intuitionist philosophy, deductive reasoning, and empirical evidence. He does so, however, in the most unpromising circumstances. The radical liberal party has just won an election and has begun the process of rationalizing society by appointing a veterinary surgeon as archbishop of Canterbury. A British moon landing, itself a victory for technology, has ended in near disaster, the captain pragmatically abandoning his companion in order to return to the equally pragmatic earth. And George's wife, Dotty, a well-known singer, who may or may not have murdered the professor of logic, has retired from show business, her lyrical invocations to the moon effectively destroyed not merely by an antinomian science that daily appropriates further aspects of human experience, but by a perspective that suddenly reduces human significance. As she explains:

> . . . it's all over now. Not only are we no longer the still centre of God's universe, we're not even uniquely graced by his footprint in man's image. . . . Man is on the Moon, his feet on solid ground, and he has seen us whole . . . and all our absolutes . . . that seemed to be the very condition of our existence, how did *they* look to two moonmen? . . . Like the local customs of another place.
>
> (Act II)

All George's convictions seem to be invalidated by events. As he tries to construct his logical defense of illogic and substantiate his faith in a nonrelativistic ethic, a group of acrobatic philosophers are busily engaged in disposing of the corpse of one of their colleagues—a logician who has come to doubt the morality of his own denial of moral values. Even the language he uses subverts his intention, since it too is relativistic, a pragmatic approximation. He is, in other words, in an absurd situation building logical structures as flawed as those of the bewildered George Riley in *Enter a Free Man.* Yet he and Dotty remain dedicated to humane values as well as to preserving an element of mystery in a society that regards human experience as wholly classifiable in rational terms. As he confesses:

> When I push *my* convictions to absurdity, *I* arrive at God. . . . All I know is that I think that I know that I know that nothing can be created out of nothing, that my moral conscience is different from the rules of my tribe, and that there is more in me than meets the microscope —and because of *that* I'm lumbered with this incredible, indescribable and definitely shifty *God,* the trump card of atheism.
>
> (Act II)

The irony of George's situation, however, resides in the fact that while he elaborates his defense of values in the admittedly somewhat limited privacy of his own study, the world outside is renouncing all interest in the matter. Engaged only on a theoretical level, he implicitly compounds the forces that he deplores. Just as life inevitably evades his attempt to pin it down with words, his elaborate arguments sliding off into anecdote and parenthetical byways, so his grasp on the real world is seen to be tenuous at best. Obsessed with validating an abstraction, he fails to grasp the totalitarian nature of the forces that have just come to power, blinded, ironically, by their use of the word "liberal." The fact that George succeeds ironically in destroying his own overelaborate proofs (when he kills the rabbit and crushes the tortoise with which he had planned to clinch his rational justification of irrationality) is evidence of his own ironic contradictions. As Dotty suggests, he is "living in dreamland."

Indeed, the final scene of the play is presented in what Stoppard calls "bizarre dream form." It consists of the symposium for which George has been preparing himself throughout the rest of the play. Following a parodied and semi-coherent statement of a materialist view of man by the decidedly materialist and incidentally lecherous vice-chancellor, the new secular archbishop of Canterbury is summoned. Himself an atheist, he proceeds to imitate Thomas Becket and voices the opinion, heretical in a rational state, that "surely belief in man could find room for man's beliefs." When the archbishop is consequently murdered for this affront to rationality and political expediency, George fails to intervene, unwilling to make the necessary connection between theory and practice. He simply excuses his detachment by asserting that "that seems to be a political quarrel. . . . Surely only a proper respect for absolute values . . . universal truths . . . *philosophy*—." His desperate desire to get the conversation back onto an abstract plane is interrupted by a gun shot, as the archbishop is deftly removed from the human pyramid into which the gymnastic philosophers had carefully incorporated him. Unmoved, George launches into his prepared text on the existence of moral values only to be interrupted again—this time, finally, by the vice-chancellor. He in turn glibly outlines a pragmatic defense of a positivist stance that, in its justification for baseless optimism over the plight of modern man, ironically applies not only to the radical liberals intent on eradicating an inefficient individualism but also to George.

George is so caught up in his own confident assertions of moral values that he fails to see the collapse of everything that gives those values meaning. This society is nothing if not pragmatic. The police force seems likely to be "thinned out to a ceremonial front for the peace-keeping activities of the Army," and the Chair of Divinity at the university no longer invites applicants and can be offered as a bribe to an overinquisitive policeman or as a reward for a particularly diligent porter. Against such a situation George's confused liberalism seems no defense. His convictions paradoxically lead him to contradiction and equivocation. His respect for reason leads him to attempt a rational justification for faith, and his commitment to tolerance makes him endorse the very forces that threaten his philosophy most directly. "It would be presumptuous," he says, "to condemn radical ideas simply because they appear to me to be self-evidently stupid and criminal, if they do happen to be at the same time radical." His passion is deflected into his work, into finding the right word, the right image, into creating a convincing structure. In many ways his problem is that of the playwright himself, in love with words and ideas but detached from the real world by virtue of his craft, as is the philosopher by virtue of his need to deal in abstractions rather than concrete realities. (At any rate, this question becomes central to Stoppard's later work, *Travesties,* which attempts to examine the whole question of the role of the artist.)

George inevitably fails in his attempt to prove the existence of God, as he does in his effort to establish the absolute nature of moral values. His convictions remain nothing more than an expression of faith disguised as logical inferences. But, after all, as the wholly irrational relationship of George and Dotty would seem to suggest, "the irrational, the emotional, the whimsical . . . are the stamp of humanity which makes reason a civilizing force." The anarchic energy of this embattled couple, alarmed as they are by the threatened collapse of their world but resisting with sporadic displays of affection, humor, and faith, contrasts sharply with the crudely rational world that intrudes on the television screen and in the pointless precision with which the philosophical jumpers turn their literal and metaphorical somersaults. As George remarks, "now and again, not necessarily in the contemplation of polygons or new-born babes, nor in the extremities of pain or joy, but more probably in some quite trivial moment, it seems to me that life itself is the mundane figure which argues perfection at its limiting curve." And if perfection is in fact unreachable, the existence of such moments is enough to justify the faith and lyrical yearnings of George and his vulnerable wife.

The real advance in *Jumpers* is not merely that Stoppard succeeds in fusing a comic approach with metaphysics, but that he begins to control the resources of theater with greater confidence and skill than before. The philosophical acrobats, performing their various contortions and constructing human pyramids, constitute a perfect image of the intellectual processes they enact. The huge television screen that projects the external world into the frenetic private life of the Moores is both an assertion of that connection between public and private morality which Stoppard is anxious to establish, and itself evidence of an alienating technology. Even the word games, the ambiguities, the puns, which are all recognizable marks of Stoppard's work, are entirely functional in a play that is in large part concerned with the inadequacy of attempts to capture reality with words, the palpable absurdity of measuring with a rule whose length obstinately varies from moment to moment. The apparent absurdity of the opening scene—during which a stripper flies across the stage on a trapeze, Dotty flounders through a bewildering medley of "moon" songs, and the yellow-uniformed gymnasts perform their feats until the death of one of their number precipitates an abrupt end—resembles the bizarre opening of *After Magritte.* Indeed, as in that play, these impossibly incongruous elements are shown to be capable of a perfectly rational explanation; but whereas in the earlier work Stoppard was largely content with his display of ingenuity, here the unraveling of confusions is endemic to the style and purpose of the play's protagonist. And although once again it becomes apparent that events can be shown to sustain a logical explanation, the simple unraveling of that logic leaves a residual problem, since it can offer no explanation for the irrational yearnings that torture both Dotty and George but which, it is increasingly apparent, are seen by Stoppard as constituting the essence of human nature, the core of individual resistance to reification.

VII

THE moral dimension of Stoppard's work appears at times to suffer from his own commitment to farce. He seems afraid to take himself seriously, to allow his humor to become a consistent critique—hence his penchant for parody rather than satire, his technique of building scenes through contradiction. As he once remarked, "I write plays because dialogue is the most respectable way of contradicting myself."

It follows that he feels "committed art" to be "a kind of bogus exercise." As he has explained, "I get deeply embarrassed by the statements and postures of "committed" theatre. There is no such thing as "pure" art—art is a commentary on something else in life—it might be adultery in the suburbs, or the Vietnamese war. I think that art ought to involve itself in contemporary social and political history as much as anything else, but I find it deeply embarrassing when large claims are made for such an involvement: when, because art takes notice of something important, it's claimed that the art is important. It's not."

Travesties (1975) attempts to debate essentially this problem. As Stoppard has said, "it puts the question in a more extreme form. It asks whether an artist has to justify himself in political terms *at all,*" "whether the words 'revolutionary' and 'artist' are capable of being synonymous or whether they are mutually exclusive, or something in between." It is a play that brings together the opposite extremes of the debate in the persons of James Joyce (whom Stoppard elsewhere quotes as saying that the history of Ireland, troubles and all, is justified because it led to a book such as *Ulysses*) and Lenin, who felt that the only justification for art lies in its political utility. Mediating between the two is Tristan Tzara, drawn simultaneously in both directions—on the one hand spinning neologisms and cascades of words like Joyce, convinced that the artist constitutes the difference between brute existence and any sense of transcendence, and on the other hand seeing the writer as the conscience of the revolution and justifying the brutality of its servants. However, the question is effectively begged by the form in which Stoppard chooses to conduct the debate. For the most part we see the characters only as they are refracted through the febrile imagination of a minor British consular official, Henry Carr. Just as *Hamlet,* viewed through the eyes of Rosencrantz and Guildenstern, is drained of tragic meaning, so too this clash of ideas loses much of its urgency seen from the perspective of a deluded, prejudiced, and erratic minor functionary. In this context, perforce, they become mere performers in a Wildean comedy, which jolts along with all the manic energy and manifest dishonesty of a bogus memoir.

In "The Critic as Artist," Wilde remarks of memoirs that they are "generally written by people who have either entirely lost their memories, or have never done anything worth remembering." This proves all too accurate a description of Carr's memoirs, which tend to confuse his own fictions with those of *The Importance of Being Earnest,* in which he had once scored a minor success. Indeed, apart from appropriating dialogue and even two of his characters directly from Wilde's play, he even restructures history so that it conforms to the requirements of high comedy. The title is thus an appropriate one as Stoppard, through Carr, presents a travesty of both literary styles and historical events.

Carr erroneously remembers himself as having been British consul in Zurich during World War I, at a time when Lenin, Joyce, and Tzara were living out an expatriate existence, plotting their various revolutions in art and society. In juxtaposing these forces, Stoppard seems to be suggesting that history is no less a fiction than Joyce's parodic constructions; that it has no more logic than Tzara's poems, which are themselves the product of pure chance. But something about this equation of literary performance and bravura politics fails to convince. In picking Lenin as the embodiment of political fabulism, Stoppard engages not merely a historically bound figure who can be parodied as a none-too-competent role player, but also a palpable reality whose particular fictions have assumed an implacable form. There is a degree, therefore, to which Stoppard seems to have been unnerved by the ineluctable consequences of revolutionary conviction. We know, or think we know, that the opinions expressed by the various characters in the play are those which Carr constructs. The single exception is Lenin, who stands, perhaps, as a corrective to those fictions—massive, real. The grand claims of Tzara, the self-confident assertiveness of Joyce, real or illusory, can only inhabit a world defined by the prosaic realities identified by Lenin. The massive scale of his impact on history, an impact that transcends the banality of both his life style and his literary style, is a fact tucked away in the mind of the audience. Just as his presence seems to neutralize the play's anarchic humor, to inhibit the irresponsible contempt for social realities, so his presence in the real world does much the same. He is a materialist, and the material has no time for fantasy, as Dotty had realized in *Jumpers.* The details of Lenin's career, solemnly narrated by Nadya, his Russian secretary (a narration that Stoppard incautiously invites his directors to edit to taste), contrast markedly with the anarchic frivolity of those other revolutionaries who surround him in Zurich, and whose revolutions are contained by the boundaries of artistic concern.

From his initial description of the characters through to Lenin's departure for Russia, it is the political activist alone who for the most part escapes parody. Carr's imagination makes both Joyce and Tzara perform a series of bizarre antics. Indeed, they become the chief actors in a baroque farce, likely at any moment to lapse into song and dance. Lenin remains stolidly detached. His speeches are authentic, a point that Stoppard is at pains to stress. He is the only character, in other words, who is not controlled by Carr's distorting imagination, although according to the conventions of the play he too should be molded to fit the elderly diplomat's psychic needs. And although this is perhaps a conscious comment on the nature of the difference between the artist and the social revolutionary, a difference that makes the fusion of the two roles unlikely, it also has the effect of dislocating the play. The second act is not merely less funny than the first, containing a detailed documentary account of Lenin's career (accompanied by objectifying photographs) as well as a debate about the role of the artist between Carr on the one hand and Tzara and Cecily (a librarian) on the other; it is also less effective. The sources for the first act are Wilde's play *The Importance of Being Earnest,* James Joyce's *Ulysses,* and the documented excesses of Dada; the source for the second is Lenin's biography. The change in mood is inevitable. The result is a curiously reverential treatment of the political leader, an approach quite at odds with the tone of a play that seems to suggest his poverty of imagination, his disregard for moral values, and his misconceptions about the function of art and history. Farce drains away as Stoppard comes to the heart of his concern, and although he is careful to conceal his own commitments by refusing to resolve the contradictory views expressed by his characters, the stylistic dislocation exposes the seriousness of his concern, as the play becomes at moments a genuine debate about the importance of being earnest—of adopting a humorless dedication to social realities.

Stoppard has called his distinguishing mark an "absolute lack of certainty about almost anything." This detachment, unnerving in some respects, gives him the freedom most of the time to criticize the materialist inhumanity of Lenin, the spurious artistic arrogance of Joyce, the cavalier socialism of Tzara, and the aristocratic hauteur of Carr. All seem squarely rooted in self-concern. But Stoppard's detachment slips once or twice. Despite his failure to locate a satisfactory mode of parody with regard to Lenin, his distrust of ideologists surfaces at moments, cutting through the comic banter that otherwise for the most part defuses any attempt at moral seriousness. Carr's rebuttal of Marxist analysis and Cecily's disingenuous justification for Lenin's inhumanity are too studied to sustain a credible commitment to ethical distance. The assumptions of farce come up against the moral presumptions of comedy, and the resulting clash disturbs not merely stylistic unity but also the momentum of the humor.

In a conflict between a materialistic view of history and an approach that translates the substantial realities of human life into fictions, fantasies, and plots, there can be little doubt where Stoppard's sympathies will lie—nor, by the end, can we be in any doubt that these two views are so clearly antithetical that the notion of a revolutionary artist is a demonstrable contradiction in terms. Yet, in his own way, Carr is as dedicated to a simplistic view of reality as is Lenin. He wants to believe in a world in which he can play a central role. Language must provide a precise symbolism, the artist must be a beautifier of reality, a licensed hedonist. He resists reality with as much dedication as either Joyce or Tzara. He is, of course, in a real sense a playwright. He "creates" the drama in which he casts himself as the central character (as, essentially, does each individual). He claims the same right to refuse social liability as he believes the true artist must do. As he remarks, "to be an artist *at all* is like living in Switzerland during a world war."

In this respect, also, he is close kin to Rosencrantz and Guildenstern, to George Riley and Professor Moore. Like Stoppard himself, these characters choose to respond to the bewildering vagaries of existence by creating games, plays, by remaking the world until its absurdities dissolve in simple performance. Lenin, Joyce, Tzara, Carr, all are equally pathetic and heroic as they inhabit with such apparent conviction the fictions they choose to regard as reality. Role players all, they seek to construct plots that will make sense of their urge for personal, social, or metaphysical order. Art, politics, philosophy, logic are deployed with varying degrees of conviction. But behind it all there lurks the savage joke that is implicit in the figure of the aging Carr, who reconstructs his past out of the same compulsions that led Beckett's Krapp to turn the switch of his tape recorder to replay the hopes and aspirations of his youth. It is Carr's distinction that he glimpses this truth for a moment and is still able to justify his challenge to reality.

VIII

THE pressure of history and the coercive power of the public world are such that at times humor seems to find less and less room to operate. Ironies are too apparent, language too obviously corrupt and corrupting, public fictions too evidently paraded as verities to require the writer to underscore them. So it seemed, at any rate, in 1982, when Stoppard responded to a request to write a television film about the situation in Poland. Martial law had been in force for a month; Solidarity had shown its first real signs of vulnerability. The problem was to write a play that addressed this situation without seeming to create the impression of a documentary realism for which the film could claim no authority. The solution lay in the creation of a "fallible narrator," whose expressed opinions and confident possession of fact could be undermined by the flow of events. But at the same time there was no doubt as to Stoppard's own position. *Squaring the Circle* was based on the conviction that freedom as defined by Solidarity could no more be reconciled with state socialism than a circle can be turned into a square with the same area. There was also no doubt as to where his sympathy lay.

Defined thus, the play might seem to be little more than an exercise in propaganda, and there were indeed those on the left in British cultural life who had begun to expect little more from Stoppard, seeing a certain irony in the sight of a playwright who, like the British prime minister, seemed to defend the rights of trade unions abroad while attacking their privileges at home. It certainly came as little surprise when he urged voters to support Margaret Thatcher in the 1983 elections. But the play was never to be simply this. It was, at least in intent, a play as much about colliding languages as about a conflict of values; a play that concerned itself with the differing models of reality that are a product of point of view.

Stoppard has written amusingly of the difficulties attending the film's production—an Anglo-American enterprise that suffered most of the problems implicit in such ventures. And it is tempting to see in the circumstances of the film's production—which required Stoppard to make flying visits to conferences at the Beverly Hills Hotel and to tolerate alterations to his work—an irony as sharp as any within the play. For, plainly, while he chose to focus on the shortcomings of an East European system that finds the concept of personal freedom and individual vision difficult to understand, let alone tolerate, his own battles with production companies and commercial interests (not to mention ideological presumptions) showed that the West is hardly immune to a similar myopia. Certainly, in the introduction to a collection of his plays, a disproportionate amount of space is devoted to an account of negotiations over the status and content of a film that purports to dramatize negotiations between the creator of a union and those with the power to deny that union access to the media.

That aside, however, the play seeks to show the incompatibility of systems of thought that no more share a common language than they do a common conception of freedom, democracy, or meaning. Lech Walesa is presented as sincere if naive; as honest, confused, courageous, and occasionally arrogant. The various party functionaries and political figures are seen as baffled, wily, Machiavellian. They control the vocabulary of the state, hence its power. But where in *Every Good Boy Deserves Favour* that fact becomes the basis of both the play's humor and politics, little is made of it in *Squaring the Circle.* The play is not without its humor, but this seems somewhat desperately worked for in a series of artful but ultimately, I think, unconvincing scenes, which attempt to find images commensurate with the political processes that the play dramatizes. The material was there to create either a powerful drama of colliding moralities or a work that exposes the contingent nature of all value systems, the fictionality of ideological convictions and political faiths. It ends up by choosing neither option, or failing to examine either with real wit or conviction. In fact, the drama remains inert, the metaphysical implications of Stoppard's own dramatic strategy unexplored, the humor uninspired and in some senses the political analysis disabled, as the creators of Gulag become comic puppet masters, more amusing than threatening.

There is no doubting the strength of Stoppard's conviction or his grasp of the subtleties, no less than the crudities, of power. He has increasingly involved himself in the battle and has written powerfully of a society in which "control over information aspires to the absolute and where reality can be rewritten." Indeed, in calling for a boycott of the 1980 Moscow Olympics, he insisted that "we have the chance to let it be known throughout the Soviet Empire that, contrary to appearances, there is some bread we will not break with the saviours of Eastern Europe and Afghanistan, not to mention Greater Russia; that morality has not yet been stood on its head on planet earth . . . there is still a decent way to govern people and an indecent way, that the difference is not relative but absolute."[3] The sentiments are unexceptionable, but curiously the anger that generated them dissipates in the artifices of *Squaring the Circle.* To be sure, it was not written as protest drama. For all the distance Stoppard has come since *Rosencrantz and Guildenstern Are Dead,* when notions of absolute values, clear political allegiances, and an assumed system of morality would have seemed irrelevant if not wholly without meaning, he has not become a purely political writer. The Marxist playwright Edward Bond chooses to characterize him as a "Fascist" and a "clown in a charnel house," but this description is painfully wide of the mark and does little to elucidate the paradoxes of Stoppard's work. He is, indeed, right-wing—in the sense that an eighteenth-century liberal might be said to be. That is to say, he apotheosizes the individual, seemingly accepts the inequities generated by a society that relates political freedom to what passes, in twentieth-century terms, for laissez-faire economics, and implicitly asserts a moral function for art. He deplores the erosion of the concept of the self that he sees as a corollary of state socialism, and he distrusts definitions of the real offered by

[3]"Tom Stoppard on the KGB's Olympic Trials," the *Sunday Times,* 6 April 1980, p. 16.

those who equate truth with ideology. But for the most part his plays have set themselves the task of exploring the processes whereby we create the worlds we inhabit through the language with which we choose to describe them; the extent to which we invent the determinism to which we willfully submit ourselves; the degree to which we deceive ourselves into believing ourselves agents rather than principals; and above all—and not in contradistinction to his own political and moral values—that the real and the true are ultimately only fictions, albeit fictions whose superiority is instinctively felt. In other words, in some final sense, he deals in faith. It is that which lies at the heart of *Squaring the Circle,* as it does of *Professional Foul, Every Good Boy Deserves Favour,* and, in some senses, *Jumpers.* It is a faith that in another sense underlies his commitment to humor, which, after all, crucially depends upon the ambiguity rather than the total authority of language, and which frequently, in intent and effect, resists precisely that humorless commitment to a singular interpretation of the real, which he increasingly sees as a primary enemy.

IX

STOPPARD began his career with witty, absurdist dramas. His work was distinguished by its humor, by brilliance and originality of construction, and by intellectual fleetness of foot. Then, having in effect argued for the primacy of aesthetics over ethics, he began to wish to find a way in which his moral convictions could find space to operate. And this meant reinventing the values he had so carefully evacuated from *Rosencrantz and Guildenstern Are Dead, After Magritte,* and so on. It was a process that he began in *Jumpers,* which continued in the debate, explicit and implicit, between Lenin and Joyce in *Travesties,* and which then found a clear focus in *Professional Foul, Every Good Boy Deserves Favour,* and *Night and Day*—in every one of which, beyond the political questions posed, he considers the possibility that a mere facility with language may in some sense be at the heart of corruption. The linguistic philosophers of *Professional Foul* (1978), the KGB colonel who is also a professor of philology in *Every Good Boy Deserves Favour,* the journalists of *Night and Day* (1978) are all people who, like Stoppard himself, create their own worlds of meaning with words. These are, in effect, all plays that, beyond their immediate political frisson, at least simulate a debate about the nature of the real and the extent to which language can capture it. And that remains true in *The Real Thing* (1982), in which two playwrights—one supposedly a mere wordsmith, content to amuse with his wit and entertain with his intellectual sophistication, the other a committed writer, crude in his construction of character but supposedly sincere in his beliefs—are contrasted with one another.

The former, Henry, is married to Charlotte, an actress currently appearing with an actor called Max in one of her husband's plays. Indeed, *The Real Thing* actually begins with a scene from that play, a fact that is, of course, lost on the audience, which takes as real the scene played out in front of them. In that scene Charlotte plays a woman whose marriage is collapsing, a fact whose hidden ironies become apparent only later, when we learn that Henry is in love with Max's wife, an actress called Annie. She, in turn, is involved with another actor, Billy, who plays the role of a young soldier called Brodie in yet another play in which he appears with Annie. Brodie, however, is not merely a character in this play; he is also its author, having been moved to write it by his somewhat confused involvement in an antiwar protest.

The complexities of plot, which make this such a difficult play to describe, are deliberate in a play that seeks to problematize the notion of the real while apparently staging a debate about the nature and role of the writer. The claim now discussed is whether the urgency of the subject justifies the work it provokes—in this case Brodie's less than competent play about his own antiwar protest—or whether clever construction, humor, and the elaboration of private and inconsequential dilemmas have their own justification. The dice are loaded with respect to both options. Brodie writes in clichés; Henry creates brittle plays about adultery in which character is subordinated to wit; in other words, he writes plays not entirely remote from those which had characterized Stoppard's own early career. Thus, Annie accuses her husband of being "bigoted about what writing is supposed to be like. You judge everything as though everyone starts off from the same place, aiming at the same prize. . . . Brodie isn't writing to compete like you. He's writing to be heard.

. . . He's a prisoner shouting over the wall." Elsewhere she insists that he is

> jealous of the idea of the writer. You want to keep it sacred, special, not something anybody can do. . . . *You're* a writer. You write *because* you're a writer. Even when you write *about* something, you have to think up something to write about just so you can keep writing. More well chosen words nicely put together. . . . You teach a lot of people what to expect from good writing, and you end up with a lot of people saying you write well. Then somebody who isn't in on the game comes along . . . who really has something to write about, something real, and you can't get through it. Well, *he* couldn't get through *yours,* so where are you? To you, he can't write. To him, write is all you *can* do.
>
> (II.v)

Since this is essentially the accusation once leveled at Stoppard, it seems precisely set up to enable him to justify himself, the more especially since Annie incautiously compares him to a writer who has something "real" to write about in a play in which the substantiality of reality is in question, and Brodie's commitment is itself seen as unreal because unfelt and unmotivated. Henry's reply, however, at least initially, has little substance, as he insists that writing is indeed a craft and that sincerity of feeling does not justify misuse of language. His more significant response is that slogans have no human content and that the committed writer is liable to fail to inspect his own motives, position, and deceits. He insists, centrally, that a willful abuse of language is itself actually an assault on the very implied contract that links people together. Words exist, he insists, so that "you can build bridges across incomprehension and chaos." Such a respect for language becomes crucial because, as he says, "if you get the right ones in the right order, you can nudge the world a little or make a poem which children will speak for you when you're dead. . . . If you know this and proceed with humility, you may perhaps alter people's perceptions." In other words, he has adroitly usurped the position of the committed writer, simply asserting that values reside in the imagination and in a commitment to language and not the mere authenticity of emotions—that aesthetic values may be the root of ethical values.

The only problem with this is that, at the very moment of making this speech, Henry is actually engaged in writing a totally banal movie script for purely monetary motives. He is also fully aware that words are themselves plastic, dependent for their meaning on context, inflection, nuance, and that as his own adultery and his play about adultery make plain, language is frequently deployed to conceal as well as to reveal truth: it is often enrolled in the service of private and public betrayals. And if the state can be indicted for its abuse of language, for its propensity to create fictions within which the rest of us must live our lives, then so, too, can the writer. Indeed, in *The Real Thing* there seems to be no irreducible reality. If we seek it in personal relationships, in the moment when, apparently, masks are removed and there is a nakedness of souls no less than bodies, then this, too, can become simple deceit, mere role playing. It certainly proves to be so in a play in which personal betrayal is a norm. And that raises another question: in a world of unreality, of competing fictions in which from moment to moment we are unable to distinguish the real, how can morality exist or express itself? Stoppard's only answer elsewhere in his work had been to insist on the superior nature of certain fictions; but even this required some irreducible value by means of which such judgment could be made, and increasingly this seemed to amount to little more than a simple declaration of faith.

In *The Real Thing* there is no irreducible reality, and it follows that the debate it contains is itself factitious, and that not merely because he chooses to parody both his writers, who are, anyway, themselves simple fictions. But insofar as it becomes anything more than a witty, inconsequential play, of the kind it contains, this is because the destabilizing of the real may itself be a moral act. Realistic theater presumes the knowability of the self and the transparency of social process; it presumes, in particular, that the real offers itself readily to our understanding. As Jean-Paul Sartre once observed, "The error of realism has been to believe that the real reveals itself to our contemplation, and that consequently one could draw an impartial picture of it. How could that be possible, since the very perception is partial since by itself the meaning is already a modification of the object." That perception does not deny the substance of experience, nor, in Sartre's case, the necessity to reinject meaning into language ("If words are sick," he once remarked, "it is up to us to cure them"). Indeed, he distrusted the incommunicable, seeing it as the root of social despair, hence of violence. But Sartre's remarks do indicate his belief that the real is not immediately apparent and that art works by indirection. What Stoppard is doing is to insist that our map of the world is an invented one, that states are no less factitious than our own lives, no less theatrical constructions. That is not to say that they do not have observable results. Writers are arrested, as they are in *Professional Foul;* dissidents are imprisoned in mental hospitals, as they are in *Every Good Boy Deserves Favour.* Myths can kill. But if we recognize them for what they are, it becomes possible for us to acknowledge their sheer contingency: the debate between the Soviet state and the prisoner assigned to a mental hospital, because his vision of the real differs from that of the state, is in essence a debate about which fiction we should be permitted to live by. It begins with the assumption that the fictions of the state have no ultimate authority.

Stoppard is attacked by the left not for being a bad playwright but for choosing to disregard the seriousness of moral issues, for being either a mere entertainer or, worse, an entertainer whose moral seriousness is reserved for threats to freedom deriving from the left. But if he is undoubtedly conservative in his politics, there is a radicalism to his work that tends to be disregarded. For his assault on the real is in effect an implied critique of those for whom the real presents itself in simple terms, those for whom complexity is a mere mask and the role of the writer to expose that reality. It was Sartre who said that "the work of art does not have an end . . . it is an end"; and while he, like Theodore Adorno, was aware that "there is no material content, no formal category of artistic creation, however mysteriously transmitted and itself unaware of the process, which does not originate in the empirical reality from which it breaks free," it is clear that the question of language and the manner in which it constitutes the real remained a crucial concern for him as it does for Stoppard. Indeed, it was Adorno who insisted that the real revolutionaries were Beckett and Franz Kafka because they assaulted from within, destabilizing our sense of the real, what others attack only from without.

Less surprisingly, in 1957 Alain Robbe-Grillet insisted that "to believe that the novelist has 'something to say,' and that he then tries to discover how to say it, is the gravest misconception. For it is precisely this 'how,' this way of saying things, that constitutes the whole, obscure project of the writer, and that later becomes the dubious content of his book. And in the final analysis it may well be this dubious content of an obscure project that best serves the cause of freedom."[4] True commitment, he insists, is to be aware of the problems of language, to be resistant to "fixed and ready-made meanings"; true hope lies in man and "the forms he creates that give meaning to the world." It sounds like a defense of formalism, but that same essay, in which he argues for the contingency of meaning and insists that it is the ability of art to declare its freedom from other structures of meaning which constitutes its power as a paradigm, ends with a disturbing question: "But how long," he asks, "will we have to wait?"

The cogency of Robbe-Grillet's argument for the centrality of language and form, as well as for the significance of the fictionalizing process in the construction of what we take for reality, is balanced by an awareness of the urgency of certain social demands, of the justice of those who advance the need for a frontal, if crude, assault on a system of power no less dangerous for its contingency. And it is the pressure of that question that has increasingly made itself felt in Stoppard's work. To some degree Brodie and Henry now coexist in Stoppard's sensibility, as once they did not (if we mean by that not the crude aesthetic values and political bad faith with which he chooses to parody the left-wing writer, but an acknowledgment of the justice of both ethical and aesthetic claims on the writer). Stoppard also seems to accept, as once he did not, that the writer is complicit in that manipulation of freedom which has become a central theme in his recent work. But he tends to locate his moral concerns in fictions whose very inventiveness constitutes the basis of their moral claim. In that way he has sought to accommodate his patent and unrivaled skills as a writer of witty, articulate, and brilliantly constructed comedies to a moral and even a political commitment, with which such skills might seem to be incompatible.

SELECTED BIBLIOGRAPHY

I. SEPARATE WORKS. *Introduction 2: Stories by New Writers* (London, 1964), includes "Reunion," "Life, Times, Fragments," and "The Story"; *Lord Malquist and Mr Moon*

[4]Alain Robbe-Grillet, *Snapshots and Towards a New Novel,* trans. by B. Wright (London, 1965), p. 70.

(London, 1966), fiction; *Rosencrantz and Guildenstern Are Dead* (London, 1966), play; *Enter a Free Man* (London, 1968), play; *The Real Inspector Hound* (London, 1968), play; *Tango* (London, 1968), play by S. Mrozek, adapted by Stoppard from the trans. from Polish by N. Bethell; *Albert's Bridge* (London, 1969), radio play; *If You're Glad I'll Be Frank* (London, 1969), radio play; *A Separate Peace* (London, 1969), play; *After Magritte* (London, 1971), play; *Jumpers* (London, 1972), play; *Artist Descending a Staircase* (London, 1973), radio play; *Where Are They Now?* (London, 1973), radio play; *Travesties* (London, 1975), play; *Every Good Boy Deserves Favour* (London, 1978), play; *Professional Foul* (London, 1978), play; *Night and Day* (London, 1978), play; *Dogg's Our Pet* and *The (15-Minute) Dogg's Troupe Hamlet* (London, 1979), in *Ten of the Best British Short Plays; Dogg's Hamlet, Cahoot's Macbeth* (London, 1980), plays; *Undiscovered Country* (London, 1980), adaptation of play by A. Schnitzler; *On the Razzle* (London, 1981), adaptation of play by J. Nestroy; *The Real Thing* (London, 1982), play; *Squaring the Circle* (London, 1982), play; *The Dog It Was That Died and Other Plays* (London, 1983).

II. ARTICLES. "The Writer and the Theatre: The Definite Maybe," in *Author,* 78 (Spring 1967); "Something to Declare," in the *Sunday Times* (25 February 1968); "Doers and Thinkers; Playwrights and Professors," in the *Times Literary Supplement* (13 October 1972); "Dirty Linen in Prague," in the *New York Times* (11 February 1977); "Looking-Glass World," in the *New Statesman* (28 October 1977); "Tom Stoppard on the KGB's Olympic Trials," in the *Sunday Times* (6 April 1980).

III. CRITICAL STUDIES. J. R. Taylor, *Anger and After: A Guide to the New English Drama* (London, 1962), includes a chapter on Stoppard; J. Simon, "Theatre Chronicle," in the *Hudson Review,* 20 (Winter 1967–1968); K. Harper, "The Devious Route to Waterloo Road," in the *Guardian* (12 April 1967); J. Weightman, "Mini-Hamlets in Limbo," in *Encounter* (29 July 1967); I. Wardle, "A Grin Without a Cat," in the *Times* (22 June 1968), on *The Real Inspector Hound;* V. L. Cahn, *Beyond Absurdity: The Plays of Tom Stoppard* (London, 1969); J. F. Dean, *Tom Stoppard: Comedy as a Moral Matrix* (London, 1981); F. H. Londré, *Tom Stoppard* (London, 1981); T. R. Whitaker, *Tom Stoppard* (London, 1983); "Tom Stoppard Moves into Political Writing," in *Newsday* (7 October 1978); "Faith in Mr. Stoppard," in *Queens Quarterly,* 86 (1979); "The Real Stoppard," in *Encounter* (February 1983).

INDEX

INDEX

Extended treatment of a subject is indicated by **bold-face page numbers.**